DOCUMENTS ON THE LAW OF UN PEACE OPERATIONS

Documents on the Law of UN Peace Operations

SECOND EDITION

BRUCE OSWALD, HELEN DURHAM, AND ADRIAN BATES
SECOND EDITION REVISED AND UPDATED BY BRUCE OSWALD

OXFORD
UNIVERSITY PRESS

OXFORD
UNIVERSITY PRESS

Great Clarendon Street, Oxford, OX2 6DP,
United Kingdom

Oxford University Press is a department of the University of Oxford.
It furthers the University's objective of excellence in research, scholarship,
and education by publishing worldwide. Oxford is a registered trade mark of
Oxford University Press in the UK and in certain other countries

First Edition published in 2010
Second Edition published in 2019

Impression: 1

Published in the United States of America by Oxford University Press
198 Madison Avenue, New York, NY 10016, United States of America

British Library Cataloguing in Publication Data
Data available

Library of Congress Control Number: 2018951650

ISBN 978–0–19–875728–3

Printed and bound by
CPI Group (UK) Ltd, Croydon, CR0 4YY

Preface to the Second Edition

This extensively revised edition addresses key normative principles, rules, and standards in United Nations (UN) peacekeeping that have developed since 2010. For example, in operations such as those conducted in the Democratic Republic of the Congo, the Central African Republic, and South Sudan, UN peacekeepers are engaged in building peace by fighting non-State armed actors. Consequently, those planning, managing, and conducting UN peace operations have had to consider issues concerning the application of law and policy governing the use of armed force when fulfilling a Security Council mandate. In relation to protecting civilians, the UN has continued to express principles and standards on themes such as women, peace, and security, and children in armed conflict. The UN and its peacekeepers are also increasingly being held to higher standards of accountability to ensure that they do not sexually exploit or abuse the local population, and that their engagement with local forces meets normative requirements found in international humanitarian law (IHL) and international human rights law (IHRL). The Articles on the Responsibility of International Organizations are also a development which is important when considering the responsibility and accountability of the UN. Many of the legal and policy developments recorded in this edition have assisted in improving the planning and conduct of UN peace operations.

Considering the above developments, several new documents have been included in this edition. I have updated the chapter concerning detention and imprisonment by including the revised United Nations Standard Minimum Rules for the Treatment of Detained Prisoners (the Nelson Mandela Rules). I have also updated Part Two D which deals with landmark Security Council resolutions by including the most recent resolutions concerning women, peace, and security; children in armed conflict; and the protection of civilians in armed conflict. In relation to sexual exploitation and abuse, I have included Security Council resolution 2272. Part Three, which addresses responsibility in peace operations, has been updated to include extracts of the Articles on the Responsibility of International Organizations. I have also included three documents in Part Three E: Accountability for Conduct and Discipline in Field Missions; the Human Rights Due Diligence Policy on United Nations Support to Non-United Nations Security Forces; and the Guidelines on the Use of Force by Military Components in United Nations Peacekeeping Operations. These documents are primarily concerned with stating policy rather than expressing legal rules or obligations.

I have expanded the Introduction to this edition to include some of the content that was in Part Five of the first edition. The introductions to the parts and the sections have also been updated and expanded to reflect developments relevant to planning, managing, and conducting UN peace operations. I have added introductions for the section concerning thematic resolutions and Part Three dealing with responsibility and accountability in peace operations.

The prefatory notes which precede the documents that were reprinted in the first edition have been updated to reflect how the documents have influenced contemporary peace operations. Where appropriate, cross-references have been added to other documents such as regional treaties or policy documents of regional organisations. References have also been added to the Select Bibliography.

To keep this edition manageable some difficult decisions needed to be made concerning what should be amalgamated or omitted. For example, as already mentioned, the Introduction to this edition has been expanded by amalgamating relevant sections of Part Five from the first edition. I have revised Part Two A by deleting the chapter on the Universal Declaration of

Human Rights and creating a single chapter to deal with both the International Covenant on Economic, Social and Cultural Rights and the International Covenant on Civil and Political Rights (now chapter 6: The International Covenants on Human Rights). Key points that were made in the chapter on the Universal Declaration of Human Rights have been included in the new chapter 6. Combining the three IHL chapters in the first edition into one chapter in this edition is another example of amalgamation. I have not included the research chapter because much of what is covered in that chapter remains relevant and there was therefore little point to reprint the chapter again. I have also left out the chapter on the protection of cultural property in the event of armed conflict, and the chapter concerning the landmark Security Council resolution dealing with HIV/AIDS because their relevance to contemporary UN peace operations has not changed since the first edition was published. The chapter concerning the Memorandum of Understanding between the Office of the High Commissioner for Human Rights and the Department of Peacekeeping Operations has also been deleted. However, the key point from that chapter is now in the Introduction to the General Human Rights Instruments (Introduction to Part Two A). The first edition had separate chapters on refugees and internally displaced persons. I have combined those chapters into one for this edition. Part Two A has a new chapter concerning justice and remedies and a chapter on public safety and the use of force. The chapter on public safety and the use of force combines two chapters from the first edition: the chapter concerning the Code of Conduct for Law Enforcement Officials, and the chapter on Basic Principles on the Use of Force and Firearms by Law Enforcement Officials. The chapter concerning the Secretary-General's Bulletin on sexual harassment has been omitted in this edition.

I have decided to leave Part Four, which concerns the key International Court of Justice (ICJ) cases, in this edition. These cases remain relevant to contemporary peace operations as evidenced by the fact that I have cross-referenced them in several prefatory notes.

In keeping with the decision made in the first edition, I have decided to reprint in whole or in part documents that are readily available on the web. There are two reasons for this. First, it might be the case that Internet is not available. Such a situation might arise, for example, when serving on a peace operation. I have certainly faced that problem on a few occasions during my military service on operations and on military exercises. Second, it is useful to have one set of documents which can be annotated for ease of reference and research.

Again, in keeping with the approach taken in the first edition, this edition does not reprint documents that are relevant to non-UN peace operations such as those conducted by regional organisations. To include such documents would have made this book unwieldy. In any case, it is a fact that several documents used by regional organisations, such as the African Union (AU), are similar to those developed by the UN.

This edition could not have been written without the support of several people. Francesca Marotta once again provided me with broad guidance concerning the role of IHRL in UN peace operations, and substantive comments in relation to chapters 20, 30, and 32. Jonathan Horowitz reviewed chapters 12, 13, and 33. Ralph Mamiya commented on chapters 19 and 33. Carrie McDougal commented on chapters 7, 17, 23, and 24. Boris Kondoch looked at the Introduction, and chapters 1 and 2 for me. Ben Buckland reviewed chapter 8. Steve Mathias discussed several matters concerning the law and policy applicable to UN peace operations with me and provided me with wise counsel. Katarina Grenfell has spent a considerable amount of time over several years discussing aspects of UN peace operations law and policy with me. Her comments in relation to several chapters greatly assisted me on settling the final version of this edition. Each of these individuals is extremely busy yet they gave me their time and guidance willingly. Their commitment to the legal and policy frameworks governing UN peace operations always inspires me.

My thanks go to Raoul Renard and Sophie Parr for their research assistance when I started the journey of revising this edition. Adaena Sinclair-Blakemore assisted me with proofreading and updating footnotes of early versions of this manuscript. Luke Chircop, who took over the proofreading for the final drafts of this edition, gave up a part of his summer break for me. I am grateful to both Adaena and Luke. I will always be indebted to Sati Nagra and Henry (Harrie) Bantick for their attention to detail and their unrelenting work ethic in undertaking the copyediting of this manuscript. Louise Ellis also has my thanks for her assistance in examining the manuscript proofs. Robin Gardner of the Melbourne Law School Academic Research Service came to my rescue in my hour of need and I cannot thank her enough for her support.

Others who have guided my reflections concerning this edition include Bill Durch, David Marshall, Helen Mulvein, Joanne Neenan, Bill O'Neill, and Ashika Singh.

Lizzie, as always, provided me with unstinting support. My thanks also go to my Law School for continuing to provide me with the perfect environment to research and write.

I am grateful to Helen Durham and Adrian Bates for permitting me to revise and update the edition. Both have moved on to other roles and responsibilities since 2010 but encouraged me to undertake writing this edition. It has been a joy to refresh myself on the wide-ranging legal and policy issues that arise in UN peace operations.

Finally, I acknowledge the sacrifices that peacekeepers make to protect the victims of armed conflict, and to assist States and territories to move to sustainable peace. At the time of writing this preface, 8 December 2017, at least 14 peacekeepers serving with the United Nations Organization Stabilization Mission in the Democratic Republic of the Congo (MONUSCO) have been killed and many more injured in an attack carried out by rebels. A stark reminder, if one is required, that peacekeepers put their lives at risk to carry out their duty.

BRUCE OSWALD CSC

Melbourne Law School and Director of the Asia Pacific Centre for Military Law
University of Melbourne
ORCID: 0000-0003-3106-9062

Contents

List of Abbreviations

ACABQ	General Assembly's Advisory Committee on Administrative and Budgetary Questions
AMISOM	African Union Mission in Somalia
ARIO	Articles on the Responsibility of International Organizations
AU	African Union
ASEAN	Association of Southeast Asian Nations
C34	General Assembly's Special Committee on Peacekeeping Operations
CAR	Central African Republic
CARICOM	Caribbean Community and Common Market
CAT	Convention against Torture and Other Cruel, Inhuman or Degrading Treatment or Punishment
CCTARC	Civilian Casualty Tracking, Analysis, and Response Cell
CDU	Conduct and Discipline Unit
CEDAW	Convention on the Elimination of All Forms of Discrimination against Women
CELAC	Community of Latin America and Caribbean States
CESCR	Committee on Economic, Social, and Cultural Rights
COE	Contingent-Owned Equipment
CRC	Convention on the Rights of the Child
CSW	Commission on the Status of Women
DFS	Department of Field Support
DDR	Disarmament, Demobilization and Reintegration
DPA	Department of Political Affairs
DPKO	Department of Peacekeeping Operations
DSRSG/RC/HC	Deputy Special Representative of the Secretary-General/ Resident Coordinator/ Humanitarian Coordinator
DUF	Directive on the Use of Force
EAC	East African Community
ECCAS	Economic Community of Central African States
ECCC	Extraordinary Chambers in the Courts of Cambodia
ECHR	European Convention on Human Rights
ECOSOC	Economic and Social Council
ECOWAS	Economic Community of West African States
ECtHR	European Court of Human Rights
ESDP	European Security and Defence Policy
ESS	Emergency Special Session
EU	European Union
EUFOR RCA	European Union Force in the Central African Republic
EUFOR RD Congo	European Union Force in the Democratic Republic of the Congo
FAO	Food and Agriculture Organization of the United Nations
FARDC	Forces Armees de la Republique du Congo
FC	Force Commander
FIB	Force Intervention Brigade
FPU	Formed Police Unit
HIV/AIDS	Human Immunodeficiency Virus/Acquired Immunodeficiency Syndrome
HOM	Head of Mission
HRC	Human Rights Committee
HRDDP	Human Rights Due Diligence Policy on United Nations Support to Non-United Nations Security Forces
HRuP	Human Rights up Front
IBRD	International Bank for Reconstruction and Development
ICAO	International Civil Aviation Organization
ICC	International Criminal Court

ICCPR	International Covenant on Civil and Political Rights
ICESCR	International Covenant on Economic, Social and Cultural Rights
ICJ	International Court of Justice
ICL	International Criminal Law
ICRC	International Committee of the Red Cross
ICTR	International Criminal Tribunal for Rwanda
ICTY	International Criminal Tribunal for the former Yugoslavia
IDP	Internally Displaced Person
IFOR/SFOR	NATO-led Implementation Force/Stabilization Force in Bosnia and Herzegovina
IHL	International Humanitarian Law
IHRL	International Human Rights Law
ILC	International Law Commission
ILO	International Labour Organization
IMF	International Monetary Fund
INTERFET	Australian-led International Force in East Timor
IPTF	International Police Task Force
ITU	International Telecommunication Union
KFOR	International Security Force in Kosovo
LAS	League of Arab States
MFO	Multinational Force and Observers
MINURCA	United Nations Mission in the Central African Republic
MINURCAT	United Nations Mission in the Central African Republic and Chad
MINUSCA	United Nations Multidimensional Integrated Stabilization Mission in the Central African Republic
MINUSMA	United Nations Multidimensional Integrated Stabilization Mission in Mali
MINUSTAH	United Nations Stabilization Mission in Haiti
MISCA	Mission internationale de soutien à la Centrafrique sous conduite africaine
MONUC	United Nations Mission in the Democratic Republic of the Congo
MONUSCO	United Nations Organization Stabilization Mission in the Democratic Republic of the Congo
MOU	Memorandum of Understanding
NATO	North Atlantic Treaty Organization
NGO	Non-governmental Organization
OCHA	Office for the Coordination of Humanitarian Affairs
OAS	Organization of American States
OHCHR	Office of the United Nations High Commissioner for Human Rights
OIOS	Office of Internal Oversight Services
OLA	Office of Legal Affairs
ONUC	United Nations Operation in the Congo
ONUMOZ	United Nations Operation in Mozambique
OROLSI	Office of Rule of Law and Security Institutions
PBPS	Peacekeeping Best Practices Section, in the United Nations Department of Peacekeeping Operations
PC	Police Commissioner
POC	Protection of Civilians
PW	Prisoner of War
RAMSI	Regional Assistance Mission to the Solomon Islands
ROE	Rules of Engagement
SADC	Southern African Development Community
SCSL	Special Court for Sierra Leone
SEA	Sexual Exploitation and Abuse
SGB	Secretary-General Bulletin
SOFA	Status-of-Forces Agreement
SOMA	Status-of-Mission Agreement
SOP	Standard Operating Procedure
SRSG	Special Representative of the Secretary-General
TCC	Troop Contributing Country
UDHR	Universal Declaration of Human Rights

UMA	Arab Maghreb Union
UN	United Nations
UNAMID	African Union/United Nations Hybrid Operation in Darfur
UNAMIR	United Nations Assistance Mission for Rwanda
UNAMIR II	United Nations Mission for Rwanda II
UNAMSIL	United Nations Mission in Sierra Leone
UNASUR	Union of South American Nations
UNDP	United Nations Development Program
UNEF I	First United Nations Emergency Force in the Middle East
UNESCO	United Nations Educational, Scientific and Cultural Organization
UNFICYP	United Nations Peacekeeping Force in Cyprus
UNHCR	United Nations High Commission for Refugees
UNICEF	United Nations Children's Fund
UNIDO	United Nations Industrial Development Organization
UNIFL	United Nations Interim Force in Lebanon
UNISFA	United Nations Interim Security Force for Abyei
UNITAF	Unified Task Force
UNMIK	United Nations Mission in Kosovo
UNMIL	United Nations Mission in Liberia
UNMIS	United Nations Mission in Sudan
UNMISS	United Nations Mission in South Sudan
UNMIT	United Nations Integrated Mission in Timor-Leste
UNOCI	United Nations Operation in Côte d'Ivoire
UNOGIL	United Nations Observation Group in Lebanon
UNOSOM I	First United Nations Operation in Somalia
UNOSOM II	Second United Nations Operation in Somalia
UNPROFOR	United Nations Protection Force
UNSF	United Nations Security Force in West New Guinea
UNSOM	United Nations Assistance Mission in Somalia
UNTAC	United Nations Transitional Administration for Cambodia
UNTAE	United Nations Temporary Executive Authority
UNTAET	United Nations Transitional Administration in East Timor
UNTSO	United Nations Truce Supervision Organization
UNV	United Nations Volunteer
UPU	Universal Postal Union
WHO	World Health Organization
WPA	Women's Protection Adviser

Introduction

> *[I]f the rule of law means anything at all, it means that no one, including peacekeepers, is above the law.*[1]

In the current environment of complex and rapidly changing threats to international peace and security, United Nations (UN) peace operations have become increasingly multidimensional and complex.[2]

The term 'peace operations', as used in this book, refers to operations that have an international character and a primary purpose of maintaining international peace and security. As such peace operations cover a broad spectrum of activities including conflict prevention, efforts to establish sustainable peace with the agreement of the warring parties in the host country, coercive measures to stop armed conflict between warring factions, and rebuilding a State after conflict so as to reduce the likelihood of the State returning to armed conflict.[3] Such operations are led by the Department of Peacekeeping Operations (DPKO)[4] and are to be distinguished from political missions and good office engagements which are led by the UN Department of Political Affairs (DPA).[5] The term 'peacekeepers', as used in this book, refers to both armed and unarmed international military and police personnel, and the civilian components serving on peace operations. The focus of this book is on those operations that are led by DPKO.

Other terms that are also used to describe the types of operations dealt with by this book include 'peacekeeping', 'peace support operations', 'peace and stability operations', and 'multidimensional peace operations'. More recently, UN peacekeeping operations have been defined as actions 'undertaken to preserve peace, however fragile, where fighting has been halted and to assist in implementing agreements achieved by the peacemakers'.[6] The term 'multidimensional UN peacekeeping operations' refers to 'a mix of military, police, and civilian components working together to lay the foundations of a sustainable peace'[7] in the context of 'undertaking peacebuilding tasks and address[ing] root causes of conflict'.[8] These types of operations are also referred to in this book as peace operations.

Since this book focuses on the UN's involvement in peace operations it is important to note that the UN may:

- *establish* an operation where the UN exercises operational authority and control over the activities of the operation (hereafter referred to as 'UN peace operations'). An example of a UN peace operation is the United Nations Mission in South Sudan (UNMISS); or

---

1 'Report of the Secretary-General: The Rule of Law and Transitional Justice in Conflict and Post-Conflict Societies', UN Doc S/2004/616, 23 August 2004, [33].

2 For an overview of the complexity of contemporary peace operations, see 'Report of the High-level Panel on Peace Operations on Uniting our Strengths for Peace: Politics, Partnership and People' in the Secretary-General, Identical letters dated 17 June 2015 from the Secretary-General addressed to the President of the General Assembly and the President of the Security Council, UN Doc A/70/95–S/2015/466, 17 June 2015 (hereafter High Panel Report).

3 For more details on the spectrum of UN peace and security activities, see United Nations, 'United Nations Peacekeeping Operations: Principles and Guidelines', 2008, Annex 2 (hereafter UN Principles and Guidelines, but also known as the Capstone Doctrine), 17–18. <https://www.un.org/ruleoflaw/blog/document/united-nations-peacekeeping-operations-principles-and-guidelines-the-capstone-doctrine/> accessed 8 April 2019.

4 The DPKO is the UN department that plans, prepares, manages, and directs UN peace operations. In 2007, the DPKO was restructured and a new Department of Field Support (DFS) established to complement the DPKO by concentrating on providing support to UN field operations. Such support would include: logistics, communications, information technology, transportation, and field personnel. Full details on the role of the DPKO and DFS can be found on the UN Peacekeeping website <https://peacekeeping.un.org/en> accessed 8 April 2019. For a detailed understanding of the organisation of DPKO, see Secretary-General's Bulletin, 'Organisation of the Department of Peacekeeping Operations', UN Doc ST/SGB/2010/1, 5 February 2010. The UN has established 70 peace operations. For a list of all the UN peace operations established since 1948, see <https://peacekeeping.un.org/en/our-history> accessed 3 January 2018.

5 For a more detailed description of the work of the DPA see <http://www.un.org/undpa/en> accessed 1 November 2018.

6 UN Principles and Guidelines (n 3), Annex 2.

7 Ibid.

8 SC Res 2086 (2013) of 21 January 2013, Preamble.

- *authorise* another entity (a State or a regional arrangement or agency) to conduct the operation under that entity's command and control (hereafter referred to as 'UN-authorised peace operations'). Such operations are also sometimes referred to as 'UN authorised operations'. An example of a UN-authorised peace operation is the Australian-led International Force in East Timor (INTERFET).

In some circumstances, peace operations have been created without the express authorisation or endorsement of the UN. These operations are hereafter referred to as 'non-UN peace operations'. An example of a non-UN peace operation which was endorsed by the UN is the Regional Assistance Mission in the Solomon Islands (RAMSI) established pursuant to the Agreement between Solomon Islands, Australia, New Zealand, Fiji, Papua New Guinea, Samoa, and Tonga concerning the operations and status of the police and armed forces and other personnel deployed to the Solomon Islands to assist the restoration of law and order and security, which was signed on 24 July 2003.[9] An example of a non-UN peace operation which was not endorsed by the UN is the Multinational Force and Observers (MFO) established pursuant to the Protocol to the Treaty of Peace between Egypt and Israel, which was signed on 3 August 1981.[10] Generally, non-UN peace operations are created by a State, regional arrangement or agency, or by a coalition of States. In such cases the operation is established or conducted pursuant to an agreement with the host country. Furthermore, any non-UN peace operations cannot undertake enforcement actions without the authorisation of the Security Council.[11]

Whilst this book focuses upon UN peace operations, its contents are relevant to all peace operations as it deals not only with the applicable legal framework, but also with the guidelines that all operations are encouraged to follow. Similarly, this book provides those serving in peace operations, whether in military, police, or civilian components, with a better understanding of the legal framework and generally accepted practice to observe when fulfilling their mandates.

To better understand how the law addresses the legal and policy issues that arise during peace operations, particularly those established by the UN Security Council, this book reprints—in whole or in part—key international legal and UN policy documents that are relevant to establishing, managing, and conducting UN peace operations. Accompanying each document is a prefatory note which is intended to provide the reader with a deeper appreciation of the relevance of the document to UN peace operations.

In keeping with the focus on UN peace operations, this introduction is divided into the following sections:

1. Historical Development of UN Peace Operations
2. Establishment, Management, and Conduct of UN Peace Operations
3. Principles of UN Peace Operations
4. Sources of Law Applicable to UN Peace Operations
5. Application of Law
6. Principles of Selection of Documents
7. Arrangement, Title, and Texts of Documents
8. Prefatory Notes to Documents
9. Bibliography

---

9 See Security Council, Press Statement on Solomon Islands by Security Council President, UN Doc SC/7853, 26 August 2003 <http://www.un.org/press/en/2003/sc7853.doc.htm> accessed 1 November 2017.

10 Protocol to the Treaty of Peace between Egypt and Israel (signed 3 August 1981) UNTS 17813. The MFO was established pursuant to the Protocol and deployment commenced on 20 March 1982.

11 Charter of the United Nations (opened for signature 26 June 1945, entered into force 24 October 1945) 1 UNTS XVI (hereafter Charter), Art 53. See ch 1 below.

1. Historical Development of UN Peace Operations

With the establishment of the UN in 1945 peace operations have generally been established pursuant to the Charter[12] to maintain international peace and security.[13] The Charter, a multilateral treaty, recognises that a key purpose of the UN is the maintenance of international peace and security. While there is no express power or provision in the Charter for the UN to undertake peace operations it is accepted that pursuant to its implied powers[14] the UN may establish peace operations in furtherance of fulfilling its purposes.

The practice of the UN undertaking peace operations has evolved from deploying unarmed military observers to supervise ceasefires, to the use of armed military, police, and civilians to undertake a range of functions and tasks to address human rights and security concerns in the context of internal armed conflicts. The first peace operation was established by the UN in 1948 with the deployment of the United Nations Truce Supervision Organization (UNTSO). That operation was an unarmed operation mandated to supervise the truce created during the Arab–Israeli armed conflict in 1948.[15] The use of armed military peacekeepers did not commence until 1956 when the UN mandated the United Nations Emergency Force (UNEF I) to 'secure and supervise the cessation of hostilities'[16] which had commenced when Israel, Britain, and France attacked Egypt.[17] The first deployment of both military personnel and international police to a UN peace operation occurred in 1960 with the establishment of the United Nations Operation in the Congo (ONUC).[18] Today, the increasing use of peace operations to deal with restoring a State's ability to maintain security and public order, building political and legal institutions in disrupted States, and promoting a culture of law, democracy, and social and economic recovery has led to international military, police, and civilian personnel engaging in 'multidimensional peace operations'.

Two other developments have also occurred in the way in which the UN has undertaken peace operations. The first is 'transitional administrations'; and the second is the use of 'hybrid peace operations'. The term 'transitional administrations' refers to peace operations where the Security Council has mandated the operation to undertake functions usually performed by a government so as to 'assist a country during a government regime change or to pass into independence'.[19] Examples of such operations include the United Nations Mission in Kosovo (UNMIK)[20] and the United Nations Transitional Administration in East Timor (UNTAET).[21] The term 'hybrid peace operations' refers to 'the deployment of military, police, or civilian personnel from two or more entities under a single structure'.[22] A recent example of such an operation is the United Nations and African Union Hybrid Operation in Darfur (UNAMID) established in 2007.[23]

The functions and tasks undertaken by peace operations have included monitoring ceasefires, establishing and policing buffer zones, assisting with negotiating peace agreements, disarming warring factions, establishing safe areas, providing humanitarian assistance, monitoring respect for human rights and elections, administering territory, and protecting civilians under threat.

---

12 See ch 1 below.

13 For a historical overview of the development of peace operations since the 1800s, see Derek Bowett, *United Nations Forces: A Legal Study* (The Lawbook Exchange 1964) 4–11. For a historical overview of UN peace operations, see <https://peacekeeping.un.org/en/our-history> accessed 8 April 2019.

14 See *Reparations for Injuries Suffered in the Service of the United Nations* (Advisory Opinion) [1949] ICJ Rep 174.

15 For a more detailed history of this operation, see <http://untso.unmissions.org/> accessed 1 November 2017.

16 GA Res 1000 (ES-I) of 5 November 1956, Operative Part [1].

17 For a more detailed history of this operation, see <https://peacekeeping.un.org/sites/default/files/past/unefi.htm> accessed 8 April 2019.

18 For a more detailed history of this operation, see <http://www.un.org/Depts/DPKO/Missions/onuc.htm> accessed 1 November 2017.

19 See UN Principles and Guidelines (n 3), Annex 2.

20 For a more detailed history of this operation, see <http://www.unmikonline.org/> accessed 1 November 2017.

21 For a more detailed history of this operation, see https://www.un.org/en/peacekeeping/missions/past/etimor/etimor.htm> accessed 1 November 2017.

22 See UN Principles and Guidelines (n 3), Annex 2.

23 For a more detailed history of this operation, see <http://unamid.unmissions.org/> accessed 1 November 2017.

In keeping with the increasingly diversified nature of peace operations, the various actors engaged in managing and conducting such operations have also changed since UNTSO was established. Traditionally, peace operations were dominated by military personnel who were either serving as military observers (and therefore unarmed) or as part of an armed military component. However, since the first police contingent deployed in a UN peace operation—the United Nations Peacekeeping Force in Cyprus (UNFICYP) in 1964—there has been an increasing number of police deployments, as well as civilian staff serving in peace operations. Currently, international and national personnel are employed in a variety of occupations including in humanitarian affairs, information management, human rights, rule of law, social affairs, public information, civil affairs, and economic affairs.

Contemporary UN peace operations are viewed as a 'global partnership' in the sense that they bring together 'the General Assembly, the Security Council, the [UN] Secretariat, troop and police contributors ... the host government'[24] and regional organisations.

2. Establishment, Management, and Conduct of UN Peace Operations

In keeping with the focus of this book, this section details the ways in which peace operations may be established and explains some of the key UN documents that influence the establishment, management, and conduct of peace operations.

UN Peace Operations

UN peace operations are established by the Security Council pursuant to its functions and powers as provided for in the Charter. While the General Assembly has established peace operations on two occasions, the First United Nations Emergency Force (UNEF I) in 1956 and the United Nations Security Force in West New Guinea (UNSF) in 1962, the accepted practice since 1962 is for the Security Council alone to establish UN peace operations. However, the budget and resources allocated to the peace operation are approved by the General Assembly.

The Security Council and Its Resolutions

The Security Council is the organ with primary responsibility for the maintenance of international peace and security and can make decisions, which all Member States of the UN are required to accept and implement pursuant to Article 25 of the Charter. This obligation was confirmed by the ICJ in its advisory opinion on the *Legal Consequences for States of the Continued Presence of South Africa in Namibia (South West Africa) notwithstanding Security Council Resolution 276* (*Namibia Case*):[25]

> when the Security Council adopts a decision under Article 25 in accordance with the Charter, it is for member States to comply with that decision, including those members of the Security Council which voted against it and those Members of the United Nations who are not members of the Council. To hold otherwise would be to deprive this principal organ of its essential functions and powers under the Charter.[26]

When the Security Council establishes an operation, it does so by adopting a resolution often referred to as an 'enabling resolution'. When amending an existing operation's functions and tasks, the Council will do so by again adopting a resolution. Both the enabling resolution and the subsequent resolutions consider a variety of documents including other relevant Security Council resolutions, statements made by the President of the Security Council, reports by the Secretary-General, and relevant peace agreements. However, in many instances, the key document on

---

24 See <https://peacekeeping.un.org/en/what-is-peacekeeping> accessed 1 November 2017. See also High Panel Report (n 2), [53]; and Report of the Secretary-General, Partnering for Peace: Moving Towards Partnership Peacekeeping, S/2015/229, 1 April 2015.

25 *Legal Consequences for States of the Continued Presence of South Africa in Namibia (South West Africa) notwithstanding Security Council Resolution 276* (Advisory Opinion) [1971] ICJ Rep 16 (hereafter *Namibia Case*).

26 Ibid, 54.

which the resolution(s) is based is the Secretary-General's report relating to that operation. That report will, amongst other things, cover relevant political, policy, and military matters concerning the potential operation, and will recommend 'options for the possible establishment of ... [an operation], including its size and resources'.[27]

The Security Council's resolutions serve several purposes including establishing the key principles that will apply to settle the dispute that the peace operation is intended to deal with. The resolution also identifies the key aims of the operation, the functions, tasks, and powers of peacekeepers, and the obligations of the host country and Member States, as well as the role of relevant regional arrangements or agencies.

A Security Council resolution will usually contain two parts. The first part is the Preamble that establishes the general principles and factors that are to influence the way the peace operation is to be conducted. In most instances, the Preamble will begin with a reference to other Security Council resolutions and Secretary-General reports that are relevant to the situation in the host country. The Preamble will also identify fundamental principles applicable to settling the dispute such as respecting the host nation's sovereignty and supporting the political processes in that country. It is also likely to refer to fundamental norms such as those contained in landmark Security Council resolutions dealing with women, peace, and security,[28] children and armed conflict,[29] and the protection of civilians in armed conflict.[30] In some cases, the Preamble will note the requirement that warring factions adhere to principles of international human rights law (IHRL)[31] and international humanitarian law (IHL).[32] Where appropriate, the Preamble will also refer to relevant ongoing peace agreements and the work of other key organisations, such as regional organisations, in seeking to resolve the dispute which forms the subject of the resolution. The Preamble usually concludes by stating words to the effect that 'the Security Council determines that the situation in the [host country] is a threat to international peace and security'. Where such a conclusion is made, it is most often the case that the Security Council is exercising its enforcement powers pursuant to Chapter VII of the Charter.

The second part of the Security Council resolution contains what is often referred to as the 'operative paragraphs'. These paragraphs establish the mandate for the operation and provide further guidance to the host country and Member States, including those countries contributing troops or resources to the operation. The operative paragraphs usually begin with the Security Council deciding to establish the peace operation, or where the operation is already in existence, deciding to reaffirm, amend, or extend the operation's mandate. Recent Security Council resolutions dealing with complex threats to international peace and security in peace operations, such as those undertaken in the Central African Republic, have begun with references to the political process for ensuring peace and security and subsequently refer to the conduct of peace operations.[33] The final sentence of a resolution dealing with a peace operation (other than a resolution terminating an operation) will state that the Security Council '[*d*]*ecides* to remain seized of the matter'.[34] The purpose of this sentence is to ensure that the Security Council, pursuant to Rule 10 of its procedures, continues to consider matters relating to the operation without having to renew the debate as to whether the matter should be on the Security Council's agenda.[35]

27 UN Principles and Guidelines (n 3), 49.

28 See ch 17 below. The phrase 'landmark Security Council resolution' refers to the first resolution of the Council to deal with a thematic issue.

29 See ch 18 below.

30 See ch 19 below.

31 See chs 4–13 below.

32 See chs 15–16 below.

33 SC Res 2301 (2016) of 26 July 2016.

34 Ibid, Operative Part [59].

35 Rule 10 of the 'Provisional Rules of Procedure of the Security Council', UN Doc S/96/Rev.7, states:

> Any item of the agenda of a meeting of the Security Council, consideration of which has not been completed at that meeting, shall, unless the Security Council otherwise decides, automatically be included in the agenda of the next meeting.

The Rules are available at <http://www.un.org/en/sc/about/rules/> accessed 1 November 2017.

A significant component of the resolutions that govern the establishment and ongoing powers and functions of a peace operation is the mandate. The term 'mandate' refers to the functions and tasks that those involved with the peace operation are required by the Security Council to undertake. A mandate for an operation may deal with such matters as the extent to which peace operations may assist national authorities of the host country; the extent of the authorisation to use force to protect civilians, humanitarian personnel and UN personnel, and property; and the role peace operations have in relation to maintaining the territorial sovereignty of the host country. It may also cover the extent to which peacekeepers are to assist the host country in maintaining law and order, and other relevant organisations and stakeholders with whom peacekeepers are to strengthen national institutions. The mandate, put simply, establishes the functions and tasks of the peace operation and governs the parameters which the Security Council sets for the accomplishment of the mission.

Resolution 2086, adopted in 2013 by the Security Council, recognised that multidimensional peace operations could be mandated to undertake a range of functions and tasks such as providing support for basic safety and security in the host State, supporting and strengthening law and order institutions, helping to establish the necessary security conditions, contributing to the protection of human rights, protecting civilians, and supporting the participation of women in conflict prevention.[36] To that list other functions such as conducting offence operations against armed groups, and warfighting, may be added. Resolution 2098 authorising the United Nations Organization Stabilization Mission in the Democratic Republic of the Congo (MONUSCO) Force Intervention Brigade (FIB) to undertake offensive military operations against non-State armed actors in the Democratic Republic of the Congo is an example thereof as it authorises UN forces to use offensive force.[37] Examples of peace operations which extend a State's authority or maintains a State's authority include the United Nations Operations in Cote d'Ivoire (UNOCI),[38] the United Nations Assistance Mission in Somalia (UNSOM),[39] and the United Nations Multidimensional Integrated Stabilization Mission in the Central African Republic (MINUSCA).[40] These recent trends perhaps demonstrate a departure from the traditional UN approach to peace operations—maintenance of peace—to a more robust approach, making peace through the use of armed force even in situations where there is no peace to be kept.

A Security Council resolution, if issued as a decision of the Security Council, is considered binding on those to whom the resolution is directed.[41] A 'decision' of the Security Council is manifested by such words as 'must' or 'shall'. The Security Council's resolutions are also 'binding by implication'[42] on the organs of the UN, as appropriate. The binding nature of a resolution is important in determining the responsibility of the UN. As stated by the UN in its submissions to the International Law Commission (ILC) a 'binding resolution entails the responsibility of the organization at the time of its adoption'.[43]

It is also noteworthy that when interpreting Security Council resolutions, the European Court of Human Rights (ECtHR) has opined that there is a presumption that the Security

36 SC Res 2301 (2016) of 26 July 2016, Operative Part [8].

37 SC Res 2098 (2013) of 28 March 2013, Operative Part [12](b).

38 SC Res 1933 (2010) of 30 June 2010, Operative Part [16](a).

39 SC Res 2102 (2013) of 2 May 2013, Operative Part [2](b).

40 SC Res 2100 (2013) of 25 April 2013, Operative Part [16](a).

41 See Article 25 of the Charter which states: 'Members of the United Nations agree to accept and carry out the decisions of the Security Council in accordance with the present Charter.'

42 See 'Note to the Under-Secretary-General for Peacekeeping Operations relating to the Applicability of Security Council Decisions to the United Nations Organizations Operating in Afghanistan', signed 24 March 2006, [3], reproduced in the UN Juridical Yearbook 2006, 471–2.

43 International Law Commission, 'Responsibility of International Organizations: Comments and Observations received from International Organizations', UN Doc A/CN4/637/Add1, 17 February 2011, 21.

Council does not intend to impose obligations on States to breach fundamental provisions of human rights. As explained by the Court in the case of *Al-Jedda*:

> the Court must have regard to the purposes for which the United Nations was created. As well as the purpose of maintaining international peace and security, set out in the first sub-paragraph of Article 1 of the Charter of the United Nations, the third sub-paragraph provides that the United Nations was established to 'achieve international cooperation in ... promoting and encouraging respect for human rights and for fundamental freedoms'. Article 24 § 2 of the Charter requires the Security Council, in discharging its duties with respect to its primary responsibility for the maintenance of international peace and security, to 'act in accordance with the Purposes and Principles of the United Nations'. Against this background, the Court considers that, in interpreting its resolutions, there must be a presumption that the Security Council does not intend to impose any obligation on member States to breach fundamental principles of human rights. In the event of any ambiguity in the terms of a United Nations Security Council resolution, the Court must therefore choose the interpretation which is most in harmony with the requirements of the Convention and which avoids any conflict of obligations. In the light of the United Nations' important role in promoting and encouraging respect for human rights, it is to be expected that clear and explicit language would be used were the Security Council to intend States to take particular measures which would conflict with their obligations under international human rights law.[44]

The General Assembly

In relation to contemporary peace operations the General Assembly has two roles relating to peace operations: financing them, and dealing with general issues. It therefore does not engage in UN peace operations in the same way as the Security Council. Nonetheless, the General Assembly's influence in peace operations is considerable.

The General Assembly's role in financing peace operations is undertaken pursuant to Article 17 of the Charter. The General Assembly's principles relating to financing peace operations were outlined in its resolution 55/235 of January 2001.[45] The scale of funds required of UN Member States is based on a State's average per capita gross national product with the permanent members of the Security Council paying a premium.[46] A list of assigned levels for contributions can be found in Annex A to that resolution. The administrative and budget aspects of UN peace operations are dealt with by the Fifth Committee (Administrative and Budget). The Advisory Committee on Administrative and Budgetary Questions (ACABQ) deals with financial issues arising from the reports of the Secretary-General relating to peace operations.

The General Assembly also discusses issues relating to peace operations in the Fourth Committee (Special Political and Decolonization) and the Special Committee on Peacekeeping Operations (C34). The Fourth Committee undertakes a 'comprehensive review of the whole question of peacekeeping operations in all their aspects' and will consider such matters as the role of the African Union (AU) in peace operations and the AU's relationship to UN peace operations.[47] The C34 is mandated to conduct a comprehensive review of all issues relating to peacekeeping pursuant to General Assembly resolution 2006 (XIX) of 18 February 1965. The Committee in 2017, for example, dealt with matters such as guiding principles; definitions, and implementation of mandates; safety and security; conduct and discipline; and cooperation with regional arrangements; enhancement of African peacekeeping capacities, best practices and training, and financial issues.[48]

---

44 *Al-Jedda v United Kingdom*, App No 27021/08, 7 July 2011, [102].

45 GA Res 55/235 (2001) of 30 January 2001.

46 Ibid, [10].

47 See 'Report of the Special Political and Decolonization Committee (Fourth Committee)', UN Doc A/71/495, 28 October 2016 referring to the Identical letters dated 22 September 2016 from the Secretary-General addressed to the President of the General Assembly and the President of the Security Council, UN Doc A/61/410-S/2016/809, 28 September 2016.

48 Report of the Special Committee on Peacekeeping Operations, UN Doc A/71/19, 21 February–17 March 2017.

The deliberations of the various Committees of the General Assembly are usually reported to the General Assembly which may adopt resolutions based on those reports. The discussions in the Committees and in the General Assembly are also influenced by Security Council resolutions and reports of the Secretary-General. Having deliberated on a matter, the General Assembly might issue a resolution which is specifically directed to peace operations, thereby binding the actions of such operations. An example of such a resolution is resolution 52/247 of 26 June 1998 on third-party liability of UN peace operations.[49]

Secretary-General Reports

Once the Security Council establishes a peace operation it is the practice of the Security Council to delegate the management and conduct of that operation to the Secretary-General. In order to ensure that the peace operation is able to carry out its mandate, the Secretary-General is delegated with certain powers and functions. These include the capacity to enter into agreements with the host country, and to establish rules pursuant to which the operation is to be undertaken, and the authority to further delegate certain powers and functions.

A key means used by the UN to ensure that the Secretary-General is undertaking his delegated powers appropriately is the requirement for him to report to the Security Council and the General Assembly on matters relating to peace operations. Such reports might concern a particular threat to international peace and security and a recommendation as to how to deal with that threat. A Secretary-General's recommendation concerning a threat to international peace and security might deal with a range of matters including the political and security situation, options or recommendations for establishing a peace operation, the mandate to be given to the operation, strategic priorities for the mission, specific results the mission is seeking to achieve, and key timelines for achieving those results. Where an operation is already established, the Secretary-General will issue reports as required by the Security Council to update it on its work or by the exigencies of the situation. Such reports usually contain the Secretary-General's views concerning the security and political situation, the extent to which the mandate is being implemented, the role of the various components of the peace operation, and observations for the future of the operation. Reports by the Secretary-General might also cover broad matters relating to peace operations such as the role of women in international peace and security,[50] or dealing with allegations of sexual exploitation and sexual abuse by peacekeepers.[51]

Department of Peacekeeping Operations

Based on the resolution establishing an operation, the DPKO together with the Office of legal Affairs (OLA) negotiates an agreement between the UN and the host country that defines the legal status of both the peace operation and individuals serving with that operation. Such agreements are generally referred to as Status-of-Forces Agreements (SOFAs) or sometimes as Status-of-Mission Agreements (SOMAs). Generally, SOFAs are entered if the mission includes an armed military component.[52]

The DPKO also formally approaches Member States to seek contributions of resources for the operation. Member States may contribute resources in the form of military, police, or civilian personnel, or through logistical support. In some cases, Member States may also be approached by the UN to commit to a trust fund for the management or conduct of the operation. If a Member State agrees to contribute troops or a formed police unit (FPU) to the operation, a Memorandum of Understanding (MOU) between the UN and the Member State is entered into. If a State agrees to provide police or military observers, then the individual police or

49 See ch 22 below.

50 See, for example, 'Report of the Secretary-General: Women, Peace and Security', UN Doc S/2015/716, 16 September 2015.

51 See for example, 'Report of the Secretary General: Special Measures for Protection from Sexual Exploitation and Sexual Abuse', UN Doc A/70/729, 16 February 2017.

52 See ch 2 below.

military observers enter agreements with the UN, whereby the individual accepts an appointment to serve with the UN.

Consultations with countries likely to contribute personnel or resources will usually occur at the key stages of a peace operation, such as when a mandate is to be changed, when there are serious developments in the peace operation, and when it is determined to terminate a mission.[53]

If a Member State agrees to contribute troops to the operation, it is sent Guidelines for Troop Contributing Countries Deploying Military Units. These Guidelines typically cover such matters as general background information concerning the host country, the mandate and mission objectives, the Concept of Operations, the organisational structure, administrative and logistical matters, training requirements, and requirements concerning the conduct of personnel on the operation including issues relating to the prohibition of sexual exploitation and sexual abuse, and the Soldier's Pocket Card. Other documents that are developed include the Concepts of Operations, and directives to key appointments responsible for the management and conduct of the operation in the field.[54]

The Concepts of Operations are developed for military peacekeepers and provide details on how the mandate will be implemented, command and control, administrative and logistical matters. The mission specific Concept of Operations is one of the core documents for the peace operation together with Guidelines for Troop Contributing Countries, Rules of Engagement (ROE), operations plans, information operations plans, contingency and risk management plans, and extraction plans for the safety of those serving on the operation. The ROE are directives which are based on the mandate of the operation and issued to military peacekeepers concerning the use of force. The ROE are often reduced to more simple rules for soldiers to use in situations where a soldier is likely to use lethal or non-lethal force. In a UN peace operation, these are referred to as 'Rules of Engagement—Soldiers Pocket Card'.[55] The use of force rules and guidelines for civilian police deployed in peace operations are referred to as Directives on the Use of Force (DUF).[56]

UN-Authorised Peace Operations

Where the Security Council authorises a peace operation (by for example, authorising a multinational force under a unified command structure to conduct the operation) the UN has little involvement in the day-to-day management and control of the operation. The Secretary-General's role in such operations will usually be to act as the conduit by which the multinational force or the lead country for that force reports to the Security Council. Examples of such operations include the US-led Unified Task Force (UNITAF) in Somalia authorised in 1992, the French-led Operation Turquoise in Rwanda authorised in 1994, the NATO-led International Force (IFOR) and Stabilisation Force (SFOR) in Bosnia and Herzegovina authorised in 1995 and 1996 respectively, the NATO-led Kosovo Force (KFOR) in Kosovo authorised in 1999, the Australian-led International Force in East Timor (INTERFET) authorised in 1999, the African Union Mission in Somalia (AMISOM) in 2007, the French Forces supporting the United Nations Operations in Cote d'Ivoire authorised in 2010, and the European Union Force in the Central African Republic (EUFOR RCA) authorised in 2014.

Non-UN Peace Operations

In some circumstances, such as when the Security Council is unable to act, for example, because of the threat or use of the veto power by one of the permanent five members on the Security Council, States, regional arrangements, or agencies create peace operations. Such non-UN peace

---

53 UN Principles and Guidelines (n 3), 52.

54 It is the usual practice of the UN to restrict the access of these operational documents and, consequently, many are not available to the public. Generally, such documents are not binding on peacekeepers unless the MOU or individual undertakings create obligations to comply with the documents.

55 See ch 33 below.

56 See UN Principles and Guidelines (n 3), 14.

operations are usually established at the request of the host country and pursuant to a regional agreement or an ad hoc multilateral agreement. Often the Security Council acknowledges or endorses, either by way of a resolution or by way of a Security Council President's statement, that a peace operation has been established. Such endorsement is considered important because it reinforces the legitimacy of the operation in the context of the UN collective security system. It is therefore expected that even non-UN operations are established, managed, and conducted in accordance with the purposes and principles of the Charter. An example of such a multilateral peace operation that was endorsed by the Security Council is RAMSI. There are also circumstances where a peace operation that has been established does not get Security Council endorsement such as the MFO. There is no direct UN involvement in the management and conduct of non-UN peace operations.

3. Principles of UN Peace Operations

Regardless of the tasks carried out by peacekeepers, UN peace operations have traditionally applied three basic principles to the establishment, management, and conduct of peace operations. These principles were first articulated by Secretary-General Dag Hammarskjold in his report to the UN concerning the lessons learned from establishing and operating the first armed UN peace operation, UNEF I, in 1956.[57] The principles are:

- consent of the parties;
- impartiality; and
- the non-use of force except in self-defence and defence of the mandate.

Consent of the Parties

The term 'consent of the parties' refers to the requirement that one of the preconditions for deploying a peace operation is that it must be with the consent of the relevant parties in the host country. This in turn 'requires a commitment by the parties to a political process and their acceptance of a peacekeeping operation mandated to support that process'.[58] The High Panel explained that:

> Clearly the consent of the Government is fundamental for the deployment of a mission, and that should be reinforced. Obtaining and maintaining the consent of the other parties remains an important objective of any mission and should be pursued to the extent possible. That strengthens the view of the Panel that any peacekeeping operation must be a part of a robust political process in which the United Nations is deeply involved, and must continuously seek to build consent to the United Nations role and presence through an impartial posture.[59]

Impartiality

The term 'impartiality' refers to the requirement that peacekeepers 'implement their mandate without favour or prejudice to any party'.[60] Impartiality, in this context therefore refers to peacekeepers being 'impartial in their dealings with the parties to the conflict, but not neutral in the execution of their mandate'.[61] The High Panel was of the view that:

---

57 See 'Report of the Secretary-General: United Nations Emergency Force: Summary Study of the Experience derived from the Establishment and Operation of the Force', UN Doc A/3943, 9 October 1958. The UN considers that the 'principles are inter-related and mutually reinforcing ... [and] [t]aken together, they provide a navigation aid, or compass, for practitioners both in the field and at United Nations Headquarters'. See UN Principles and Guidelines (n 3), 31. The importance of the three 'core principles of peacekeeping to guide successful United Nations peacekeeping operations in ceasefires and implementing peace agreements' was also reaffirmed in the High Panel Report (n 2), [124].

58 UN Principles and Guidelines (n 3), 31.

59 High Panel Report (n 2), [127].

60 UN Principles and Guidelines (n 3), 33.

61 Ibid.

> 'impartiality' is not the same as neutrality or equal treatment of all parties in all cases for all time, when in some cases local parties consist not of moral equals but of obvious aggressors and victims. Impartiality must mean adherence to the principles of the Charter and to the objectives of a mission mandate that is rooted in Charter principles. On the ground, the impartiality of United Nations missions should be judged by its determination to respond even-handedly to the actions of different parties based not on who has acted but by the nature of their actions. Missions should protect civilians irrespective of the origin of the threat. They should promote respect by all actors for the human rights of the local population and the combatants regardless of affiliation. They should seek political solutions respectful of the legitimate interests and grievances of all parties and society at large.[62]

Self-defence

Self-defence in the context of peace operations has evolved to have a very broad meaning. Not only does the term refer to self-defence in the sense that peacekeepers may use force to protect themselves and others whom they have been authorised to protect, it also extends to using force in defence of the mandate or mission.[63]

The right to self-defence has been explained by the OLA as:

> not limited to States and applies as an inherent right also to the United Nations. United Nations forces have, accordingly, always been regarded as entitled to the right of self-defence and, expressly for this purpose, have been provided with light infantry weapons. This right has been consistently provided for in the rules of engagement established for each peacekeeping operation since its inception ... the use of force in self-defence is an inherent right of United Nations forces exercised to preserve a collective and individual defence.[64]

The UN has also pointed out that the Security Council's willingness to give peacekeepers the authority to proactively use force in self-defence through '"robust" mandates authorising them to "use all necessary means" to ... protect civilians ...'[65] has permitted peacekeepers to improve the security situation and contribute to peacebuilding.

The High Panel considered that the 'concept of "defence of the mandate" requires clarity as to which tasks within the mandate may require the use of force'.[66] The Panel went on to state that defence of the mandate should

> always include the responsibility to protect civilians and missions should be proactive in doing so. Different threats must be met with the appropriate use of military force, ranging from containment via deterrence and coercion to direct confrontation, particularly when civilians or peacekeepers are at risk. The actual use of force may not be necessary if the potential attackers perceive and know United Nations troops have the determination and capabilities to respond forcefully in case of attack.[67]

The use of force in individual self-defence and defence of the mandate is likely to be dealt with in the ROE for armed military personnel and DUF issued to formed police units (FPU) and UN civilian police.[68] Regardless of whether force is used in self-defence or more broadly, it is accepted that such force must 'always be calibrated in a precise, proportional, and appropriate manner, within the principle of the minimum force necessary to achieve the desired effect, while

---

62 High Panel Report (n 2), [126].

63 UN Principles and Guidelines (n 3), 34. See also, 'Report of the High-Panel on Threats, Challenges and Change, *A more secure world: our shared responsibility*' in the Note by Secretary-General to the General Assembly, UN Doc A/59/565, 2 December 2004, [213].

64 UN Juridical Yearbook 1993, 371–2 on 'The Right of Self-defence of United Nations Peacekeeping Forces and the Exercise of this Right – Article 51 of the Charter of the United Nations (19 July 1993)'.

65 UN Principles and Guidelines (n 3), 34.

66 High Panel Report (n 2), [128].

67 Ibid.

68 See ch 33 below.

sustaining consent for the mission and its mandate'.[69] Furthermore, even where self-defence is addressed in the ROE or in other UN policy, its actual relevance to individual military peacekeepers is founded in the domestic criminal law of the State contributing the peacekeeper. As such it arises as a defence to a criminal law charge such as assault or murder. As a doctrine, the use of force in self-defence, could also operate as a circumstance precluding wrongfulness in respect of a claim of international responsibility.[70]

Other Key Principles of UN Peacekeeping: Protection of Civilians and Rule of Law

In addition to the above-mentioned three fundamental principles the UN Security Council, General Assembly, and the Secretary-General have referred to two other principles: the protection of civilians (POC) and the rule of law. The UN's first practice in relation to protecting civilians can be traced to the ONUC in 1961 where peacekeepers provided protection and asylum to civilians.[71] Since then the UN has developed policies which require peacekeepers to take measures for the protection of civilians within the UN's area of operation, and to mitigate risks to civilians before, during, and after any military operation.[72] The majority of contemporary UN peace operations are mandated to protect civilians against physical violence irrespective of the source of the violence. Peacekeepers 'have the authority and responsibility to ... [protect] civilians within their capabilities and areas of deployment where the government is unable or unwilling to protect'.[73]

In relation to the rule of law, the Security Council has, since at least 1999, explicitly mandated peacekeepers to work with host countries to strengthen the rule of law.[74] The Security Council has emphasised, such as in resolution 2151 of 28 April 2014, that the rule of law is 'one of the key elements of conflict prevention, peacekeeping, conflict resolution and peacebuilding'.[75]

The Secretary-General has stated:

> [t]he 'rule of law' is a concept at the very heart of the Organization's mission. It refers to a principle of governance in which all persons, institutions and entities, public and private, including the State itself, are accountable to laws that are publicly promulgated, equally enforced and independently adjudicated, and which are consistent with international human rights norms and standards. It requires, as well, measures to ensure adherence to the principles of supremacy of law, equality before the law, accountability to the law, fairness in the application of the law, separation of powers, participation in decision-making, legal certainty, avoidance of arbitrariness and procedural and legal transparency.[76]

The rule of law architecture relevant to peace operations includes international and hybrid criminal courts, UN and regional commission of inquiries, an Office of Rule of Law and Security Institutions (OROLSI),[77] and peacekeepers mandated with functions and tasks such as undertaking law enforcement (including arresting those accused of serious international law crimes such as genocide) functions and tasks, protecting civilians and their property, and supporting

69 UN Principles and Guidelines (n 3), 35.

70 See International Law Commission, Responsibility of International Organizations: Comments and Observations received from International Organisations, A/CN4/737/Add1, 17 February 2011, 25.

71 Report on Protected Areas by the Special Representative of the Secretary-General, UN Doc S/4757, 2 March 1961, [1].

72 See ch 19 below. See also the Kigali Principles on the Protection of Civilians <http://www.globalr2p.org/media/files/kp-principles-17-november-2016.pdf> accessed 1 November 2017; and UN Department of Peacekeeping Operations/Department of Field Support; 'Use of Force by Military Components in United Nations Peacekeeping Operations', effective date 1 February 2017.

73 Protection of Civilians Mandate https://peacekeeping.un.org/en/protection-of-civilians-mandate accessed 1 November 2017. See also ch 19 below.

74 For more detail concerning UN peace operations and the rule of law, see <https://www.un.org/ruleoflaw/un-and-the-rule-of-law/> accessed 8 April 2019; and for key documents, see <https://www.un.org/ruleoflaw/key-documents/> accessed 1 November 2017.

75 SC Res 2151 (2014) of 28 February 2014, Preamble.

76 'Report of the Secretary-General: The Rule of Law and Transitional Justice in Conflict and Post-Conflict Societies', UN Doc S/2004/616, 23 August 2004, [6].

77 For more details about the Office, see <https://www.un.org/ruleoflaw/un-and-the-rule-of-law/> accessed 8 April 2019.

reform for national law enforcement institutions. The application of the rule of law to peacekeepers is also evidenced by the regimes of accountability they are subjected to.[78]

When providing rule of law assistance, the Secretary-General has issued a policy concerning the guiding principles and a framework for strengthening the rule of law that should govern the UN's approach.[79] The 2008 policy emphasises principles such as the need to advance human rights and gender justice, and to ensure national ownership. The framework concerns, among other things, developing a legal framework which is consistent with international norms and standards.

In addition to the principles described above there are other factors that also need to be considered when undertaking peace operations. These are the requirements for international legitimacy,[80] the credibility of the operation in the sense of maintaining its effectiveness,[81] and promotion of national and local ownership for the operation and any relevant peace process.[82]

4. Sources of Law Applicable to UN Peace Operations

Three legal regimes govern, to varying degrees, the activities undertaken during peace operations:

- international law;
- the law of the host country; and
- the law of the contributing State.

Each of these regimes contains legal norms relevant to establishing, managing, and conducting peace operations, and requires separate and careful examination. In considering the application of the relevant regime, the entity of the peace operation must be identified. In this context, there are three classes of entities: the peace operation, the contributing States, and the individual peacekeepers. Each of these entities will have a different relationship with the legal regime under examination. For example, while a peace operation may be subject to international legal obligations, its members are usually not bound to the laws of the host country but are expected to respect all local laws and regulations.[83] Contributing States will be bound by their international legal obligations but may not be bound by the host country's legal regime. Individual peacekeepers will be bound by the laws of the host country to the extent that they are not inconsistent with the peace operation's mandate and the provision of the applicable SOFA. They will also be bound by their own contributing State's relevant laws and any relevant undertakings pursuant to their service with the UN. Members of a peacekeeping operation are covered by the privileges and immunities as set forth in the SOFA as agreed between the UN and the host country. Such privileges and immunities apply in the interests of the United Nations and are not for the personal benefit of the individuals themselves. While members of the military component are immune from the criminal laws of the host country, their contributing States undertake to exercise jurisdiction in respect of any criminal offences which may be committed by them in the host country.[84]

International Legal Regime

The international legal sources relevant to peace operations are wide ranging. They include international treaties, agreements, binding resolutions of the Security Council and General Assembly,

78 See chs 21–33 below.
79 Guidance Note of the Secretary-General, 'UN Approach to Rule of Law Assistance', April 2008.
80 Ibid, 36.
81 Ibid, 37.
82 Ibid, 38.
83 See ch 2 below.
84 See ch 2 below.

international customary law and *jus cogens* norms, judicial decisions, and binding directives from the UN Secretary-General.

Significant Treaties

The significant treaties included in this book are 'international agreement[s] concluded between States in written form and governed by international law. These may be embodied in a single instrument, in two or more related instruments or in a range of particular designations.'[85] They are a product of negotiation and are binding on those States that are party to them. The treaties fall into a variety of categories including those that are general in nature, such as the Charter, those that concern special legal regimes such as international humanitarian law, and those that deal with specific situations relevant to peace operations, such as the Convention on the Safety of United Nations and Associated Personnel.[86]

Agreements

The agreements that are dealt with in this book are instruments that are not considered treaties. In some instances, agreements are binding. Examples of binding agreements include a SOFA or MOU. In many cases however, agreements do not, by themselves, create legal obligations. Non-binding agreements do nonetheless promulgate norms and standards. They may also serve several purposes including establishing best practice, assisting in the interpretation of the law, and developing a better understanding of various legal regimes. Such agreements are given a variety of names including Guidelines, Principles, Declarations, and Codes of Practice. In this book, examples of such agreements include the Basic Principles on the Use of Force and Firearms by Law Enforcement Officials, and the Code of Conduct for Law Enforcement Officials.[87]

Resolutions of the Security Council and General Assembly

Security Council resolutions may be an important source of law when examining matters relating to peace operations. There are two types of Security Council resolutions that are relevant. The first relates specifically to the establishment, management, and conduct of peace operations. These include resolutions that establish or authorise peace operations, and those that are concerned with the ongoing management and conduct of such operations. The second type of Security Council resolutions are those that deal with themes that are relevant to peace operations. These resolutions include, for example, those dealing with the protection of civilians.

General Assembly resolutions are also highly relevant. There are two types of General Assembly resolutions applicable. The first type concerns agreements such as the Universal Declaration of Human Rights. The second relates to resolutions which are specifically directed to peace operations such as the General Assembly resolution 52/247 on Third-party liability: temporal and financial limitations,[88] and resolutions concerning the administrative and budgetary aspects of peacekeeping.[89]

Administrative Issuances from the Secretariat

There are two types of UN administrative issuances: Secretary-General's bulletins and administrative instructions. The authority to issue these documents derives from the Secretary-General's appointment as the chief administrative officer of the UN. The general rules regarding their preparation, content, and effect can be found in the Secretary-General's Bulletin entitled 'Procedures for the Promulgation of Administrative Issuances'.[90] These issuances establish rules, policies, or procedures of the UN and are binding on peace operations and relevant staff members serving

---

85 Vienna Convention on the Law of Treaties (opened for signature 23 May 1969, entered into force 27 January 1980) 1155 UNTS 331, Article 2(1)(a) (hereafter Vienna Convention).

86 See ch 14 below.

87 See ch 13 below.

88 GA Res 52/247 of 26 June 1998.

89 See for example, 'Report of the Fifth Committee: Administrative and Budgetary Aspects of the Financing of the United Nations Peacekeeping Operations', UN Doc A/71/708/Add1, 29 June 2017.

90 UN Doc ST/SGB/1991/1, 28 May 1997, entered into force 1 June 1997.

on those operations. Examples of bulletins relevant to peace operations include the Bulletin on the application of international humanitarian law to peace operations[91] and the Bulletin on the prohibition of sexual exploitation and sexual abuse.[92]

Administrative instructions concern procedures for the implementation of UN financial regulations and rules and UN staff regulations and rules. Examples of such instructions in relation to UN peace operations include the Administration of the Staff Regulations and Rules.[93] If administrative issuances create obligations for Member States or peacekeepers then they will be binding on those to whom they are directed.

International Customary Law and Jus Cogens *Norms*

Other sources of law relevant to peace operations are customary international law and *jus cogens* norms. Customary international law has two essential elements: State practice and *opinio juris*. Together these elements indicate 'a clear and continuous habit of doing certain actions which has grown up under the aegis of the conviction that these actions are, according to international law, obligatory or right'.[94]

As stated by Sir Michael Wood in his capacity as Special Rapporteur for the ILC study on the identification of customary international law: '[r]esolutions adopted by international organisations at international conferences may, in some circumstances, be evidence of customary international law or contribute to its development; they cannot in and of themselves, constitute it'.[95] Perhaps one example of the evidence of customary international law in the context of UN peacekeeping operations is the requirement in all Security Council resolutions establishing UN peace operations that where a SOFA has not been signed for a specific operation the model SOFA shall apply.[96]

A *jus cogens* norm is a peremptory norm of general international law that is 'accepted and recognised by the international community of States as a whole as a norm from which no derogation is permitted and which can be modified only by a subsequent norm of general international law having the same character'.[97] *Jus cogens* norms are said to include:

> (a) the prohibition of aggressive use of force; (b) the right of a State to self-defence; (c) the prohibition of genocide; (d) the prohibition of torture; (e) crimes against humanity; (f) the prohibition of slavery and slave trade; (g) the prohibition of piracy; (h) the prohibition of racial discrimination and apartheid, and (i) the prohibition of hostilities directed at the civilian population ('basic rules of international humanitarian law').[98]

Judicial Decisions

The decisions of the ICJ are another important source of law for peace operations. The Court's opinions in relation to the establishment, management, and conduct of peace operations and the application of privileges and immunities of experts on mission are examples of how the ICJ

---

91 UN Doc ST/SGB/1999/13, 6 August 1999, entered into force 12 August 1999. See ch 15 below.

92 UN Doc ST/SGB/2003/13, 9 October 2003, entered into force 15 October 2003. See ch 30 below.

93 Secretariat, Administrative Instruction: Administration of the Staff Regulations and Staff Rules, ST/AI/234/Rev1/Amend2, 4 September 2014.

94 Robert Jennings and Arthur Watts (eds), *Oppenheim's International Law* (9th edn, Oxford University Press 2008) vol 1, 27. See also International Law Commission, 'Identification of Customary International Law: Text of the Draft Conclusions provisionally adopted by the Drafting Committee', UN Doc A/CN4/L872, 30 May 2016. For a more detailed discussion of customary international law, see the memorandum by the International Law Commission Secretariat, 'Formation and Evidence of Customary International Law: Elements in the Previous Work of the International Law Commission that could be particularly relevant to the topic', UN Doc A/CN4/659, 14 March 2013; and the memorandum by the International Law Commission Secretariat, 'Identification of Customary International Law: The Role of Decisions of National Courts in the Case Law of International Courts and Tribunals of a Universal Character for the Purpose of the Determination of Customary International Law', UN Doc A/CN4/691, 9 February 2016.

95 International Law Commission, 'Third Report on Identification of Customary International Law', UN Doc A/CN4/682, 27 March 2015, Draft Conclusion 13.

96 See ch 2 below.

97 Vienna Convention (n 85), Article 53. See also International Law Commission, 'First report on *jus cogens*', UN Doc A/CN4/693, 8 March 2016, Draft Conclusion 3. That report also has a detailed discussion of both the historical evolution of the concept of *jus cogens* and its legal nature.

98 'Report of the Study Group of the International Law Commission: Fragmentation of International Law: Difficulties Arising from the Diversification and Expansion of International Law', UN Doc A/CN.4/L.628, 13 April 2006, [374].

has developed a body of jurisprudence which guides peace operations. The Court also clarifies a range of issues such as those concerning the legal basis for the General Assembly or the Security Council establishing peace operations.[99]

The judgements of other courts or tribunals will also influence peace operations, particularly in relation to the application of the legal obligations of States and individuals under relevant international or domestic law.[100] Similarly, jurisprudence arising from international criminal prosecutions has an impact upon peace operations.[101]

General Principles of Law

These are legal principles that are found in most national systems of law and which are, therefore, generally accepted rules that are applicable to international organisations. In relation to peace operations, two such general principles are the requirement to act in good faith and the requirement to honour obligations legally incurred.[102] These general principles would apply in relation to the SOFAs and MOUs entered between the UN, host country, and contributing States. It is also arguable that the right of peacekeepers to use force to defend themselves is a general principle of law.

Law of the Host Country

The law of the host country impacts upon peace operations in two ways. First, it impacts on peace operations to the extent that the peace operation and peacekeepers must comply with the laws of the host country. That is to say, that a determination must be made as to the extent to which both the peace operation and peacekeepers are subject to the jurisdiction of host country laws when fulfilling their mandates. Generally, the impact of the host country's law in peace operations is subject to the application of the SOFA, including with respect to the application of privileges and immunities.

The second way in which the law of the host country impacts on peace operations relates to the influence that the law has on the interaction between peacekeepers and the local population. For example, host country laws will influence the way certain functions are undertaken by peacekeepers, particularly where those functions involve working closely with local law and order institutions. In situations where peacekeepers are engaged in law and order functions, such as investigating crimes against humanity,[103] it may be the case that the evidence gathered will be used to prosecute alleged offenders in the host country using the host country's national court system. Consequently, peacekeepers will need to ensure that they adhere to national criminal law and procedural requirements. In these types of situations, the conduct of peace operations can be dependent upon the laws of the host country for practical reasons.

Law of the Contributing State

The law of the contributing State will have considerable impact on peacekeepers where such laws apply extraterritorially and the extent to which the contributing State directs peacekeepers to comply with their State's international legal obligations. Military peacekeepers, for example, will need to comply with both the domestic military and criminal law of their State where those laws have extraterritorial application. The directions or orders given by a State to its peacekeepers will determine whether there are other legal obligations with which peacekeepers will need to comply. MOUs with troop contributing countries oblige troop contributing countries to investigate and prosecute any crimes committed by their personnel in the host country.[104]

---

99 See chs 33–35 below.

100 See for example, Decision as to the Admissibility: *Behrami and Behrami v France*, App no 71466/01, 2 May 2007; *Saramati v France, Germany and Norway*, App no 78166/01, 2 May 2007 [147]; and *The State of Netherlands v Hasan Nuhanovic*, Supreme Court of the Netherlands, 12/03324, 6 September 2013.

101 *Prosecutor v Issa Hassan Sesay, Morris Kallon, and Augustine Gbao* (Appeal Judgment) [2009] SCSL-04-15-A, [233]; *Prosecutor v Bahar Idriss Abu Garda* (Public Redacted Version, Decision on the Confirmation of Charges) [2010] ICC-02/05-02/09.

102 See UN Juridical Yearbook 2001, 381–385 on 'Payment of Settlement Claims—Liabilities of a Private Law Nature—Procedures for settlement—Budget considerations'.

103 See, for example, SC Res 2295 (2016), of 29 June 2016, Operative Part [19(f)(i)].

104 See ch 3 below.

5. Application of Law

In applying law to peace operations, it is not enough to identify the sources of law. It is also necessary to identify whether a source of law will apply to the peace operation, contributing States, or individual peacekeepers.

Application of Law to Peace Operations

Peace operations that are established by the Security Council are subsidiary organs of the Security Council. As subsidiary organs, they have the international legal personality of the UN and are subject to internal and external laws relevant to a peace operation.[105] For example, a Security Council established peace operation will be governed by internal laws which include those derived from the Charter and Security Council resolutions. External laws include those derived from treaties, such as the Convention on the Privileges and Immunities of the United Nations,[106] agreements such as SOFAs, customary international law, *jus cogens* norms, and general principles of law.

The most important legal instruments applicable to peace operations established by the Security Council are the Charter, Security Council resolutions that mandate the operation with powers and functions, the SOFA which establishes the relationship between the operation and the host country, the individual MOUs which establish the relationship between the operation and each contributing State, and where relevant individual agreements exist such as those entered between the UN and civilian police.

The Charter sets out several key provisions relevant to peace operations including the purposes and principles of the UN, the powers and functions of the Security Council, the General Assembly, and the Secretariat, as well as the privileges and immunities of the UN and the obligations of Member States in relation to the decisions of the Security Council.

The Security Council resolution establishing the mandate for the operation or governing the ongoing powers and functions of the operation will state principles and rules with which the operation will be required to comply. For example, it is the practice of the Security Council in resolutions relevant to specific peace operations to reaffirm its commitment to respect the sovereignty, territorial integrity, and political independence of the host country.

The SOFA and MOU are binding documents that establish the relationship, in the case of the SOFA, between the UN and the host country, and, in the case of the MOU, between the UN and the contributing State. The SOFA deals with matters such as the laws applicable to the peace operation, the privileges and immunities of the peace operation and peacekeepers serving on that operation, and the settlement of disputes arising from the operation. The MOU deals with matters such as discipline, investigations, and UN standards of conduct for personnel provided by national governments contributing personnel to the peace operation. MOUs also deal with administrative, financial, and logistics terms and conditions that govern the contribution of personnel, equipment, and services provided by contributing States to specific peace operations.

There are several treaties which are relevant to peace operations. Their relevance depends on whether they are binding on peace operations such as the Convention on the Privileges and Immunities of the United Nations,[107] or whether they serve the purpose of assisting the UN and contributing States to interpret legal commitments and to develop a better understanding of the legal principles, rules, and standards that may be applied, such as the International Covenant on Civil and Political Rights (ICCPR).[108]

Identifying customary international law is sometimes challenging because of the dual requirements of evidence of State practice and *opinio juris* before a legal norm can be recognised as

---

105 See Philippe Sands and Pierre Klein, *Bowett's Law of International Institutions* (5th edn, Sweet & Maxwell 2001) ch 14.

106 See ch 21 below.

107 See ch 21 below.

108 See ch 6 below.

customary international law. In relation to peace operations established by the Security Council the UN has not stated which customary international law norms are applicable to its peace operations. It may be possible, however, to argue that by analogy, where a customary norm is accepted as applying to States it should, *ipso facto*, apply to international organisations, such as the UN.

While the UN has not stated that the list of *jus cogens* norms mentioned above apply to peace operations, it is generally accepted that because these norms are superior to both treaties and customary international law, they should be binding in peace operations. Similarly, while there is no explicit statement by the UN as to the applicability of general principles of law to peace operations, it is logical that the UN would apply a general principle of law, such as the obligation to act in good faith, to the management and conduct of peace operations.

The attribution of the responsibility to the UN for its acts and omissions in peace operations has been determined by practice. Based on that practice the UN has accepted that its international responsibility for its actions stems from the fact that 'forces placed at the disposal of the United Nations are "transformed" into a United Nations subsidiary organ and, as such, entail the responsibility of the Organization'.[109] Insofar as the States contributing personnel retain some control (i.e. residual control) over their personnel concerning matters such as pay and discipline, the UN still maintains exclusive command and control as long as the residual control of the State 'does not interfere with the United Nations operational control'.[110] One would now also assume that the attribution of responsibility would be greatly influenced by the Articles on the Responsibility for International Organizations (ARIO).[111]

Application of Law to States

States engaged in peace operations, whether they are the host country or contributing States, will be bound by their treaty obligations, customary international law, *jus cogens* norms, and general principles. The key treaty obligation for States, in relation to peace operations established by the Security Council, is to comply with the Charter. Consequently, pursuant to Article 103 of the Charter, in the event of a conflict between the obligations of Member States under the Charter and the obligations of a State under any other international agreement, their obligations under the Charter will prevail.[112]

For those operations that are established by the Security Council, the host country is expected to comply with the relevant provisions of the Security Council resolution that create legal obligations for it. Furthermore, the host country will also need to comply with any legal obligations created from agreements with the UN or with other States or entities in relation to an operation. Such obligations might include those arising from the SOFA entered between the UN and the host country.

Contributing States also have similar obligations at different levels in relation to peace operations. At one level, they have obligations to comply with those parts of the Security Council resolution that create obligations for them. At another level, they have obligations pursuant to the MOU that they enter with the UN concerning the contribution of personnel and equipment.

Application of Law to Peacekeeping Personnel

The application of law to individual peacekeepers will vary depending on several factors, such as the obligation of peacekeepers to comply with the law of their own State, their obligations in relation to complying with UN regulations and directives, and the extent to which they are immune from the jurisdiction of the laws of the host country.

---

109 International Law Commission, 'Responsibility of International Organizations: Comments and Observations received from International Organizations', UN Doc A/CN4/637/Add1 of 17 February 2011, 13.

110 Ibid, 14.

111 See ch 24 below.

112 See *Questions of Interpretation and Application of the 1971 Montreal Convention arising from the Aerial Incident at Lockerbie* (*Libyan Arab Jamahiriya v United Kingdom*) (Order of 14 April 1992) [39]–[41].

Peacekeepers will be bound by the application of their State's extraterritorial laws such as military discipline law. Where the international obligations of the contributing State are not reflected in the extraterritorial application of that State's domestic law, obligations may still be created for peacekeepers by the contributing State issuing regulations and directives to their peacekeepers. Such regulations and directives might relate to the use of force by peacekeepers and, consequently, might include aspects of the State's obligations in relation to IHL or IHRL.

In situations where the UN has established a peace operation it will issue regulations and directives. All UN peacekeepers are expected to comply with the UN standards of conduct and mission-specific rules and regulations that are relevant to the operation. National authorities that contribute peacekeepers are obliged to ensure that the UN standards of conduct, and mission-specific rules and regulations can be enforced. In the context of peace operations that are established by the UN, the applicable standards of conduct are set out in 'We Are United Nations Peacekeeping Personnel',[113] and the regulations would include the Secretary-General's Bulletin on 'Observance by United Nations forces of international humanitarian law'[114] and the Secretary General's Bulletin on 'Special Measures for Protection from Sexual Exploitation and Sexual Abuse'.[115]

The accountability regime for activities in the field from a UN Secretariat perspective rests on the Secretary-General delegating operational authority over the operation to the Special Representative of the Secretary General (SRSG), also sometimes known as the Head of Mission (HOM), who then becomes the senior UN representative in the State where the peace operation is deployed. The SRSG has operational authority and therefore control over all activities of the UN in the State concerned. The SRSG delegates operational control of the peace operation to the Force Commander (FC) for the military, and the Police Commissioner (PC) for the police. In some peace operations the FC might be appointed the senior most UN representative of the UN.[116] The next level of control is at the tactical level and is the responsibility of area military and police commanders and their subordinate commanders who report to the FC or PC as appropriate. A Deputy Special Representative of the Secretary-General/Resident Coordinator/ Humanitarian Coordinator (DSRSG/RC/HC) and a Deputy Special Representative of the Secretary-General are usually appointed to assist the SRSG with the coordination of humanitarian activities and liaison.[117] The application of law to the above mentioned appointments is determined by the SOFA.

Military and civilian police peacekeepers required for the operation are recruited either through contributions from Member States of the UN or individual recruitments. Armed military peacekeepers that are contributed by their States are deployed as a contingent and commanded by a contingent commander usually from their State. Consequently, military members serving as a part of national contingents are under operational control of the FC, but remain part of their respective national armed forces and under national command. Thus, there is no direct contractual relationship between contingent members and the UN. The national governments undertake to ensure that national contingent commanders have the necessary authority over their command to maintain discipline. The requirement concerning the maintenance

113 'Report of the Special Committee on Peacekeeping Operations and its Working Group: 2007 Resumed Session (New York, 11 June 2007)', UN Doc A/61/19 (Part III), 12 June 2007, 7. Now published in the 2008 Contingent-Owned Equipment Manual, UN Doc A/ C5/63/18, 9 June 2008, Chapter 9, Annex H. See ch 27 below.

114 UN Doc ST/SGB/1999/13, 6 August 1999, entered into force 12 August 1999. See ch 15 below.

115 UN Doc ST/SGB/2003/13, 9 October 2003, entered into force 15 October 2003. See ch 30 below.

116 See, for example, Agreement between the United Nations and the Government of Sudan concerning the Status of the United Nations Interim Security Force for Abyei, signed 1 October 2012, reproduced in UN Juridical Yearbook 2012, 63–78.

117 See Note from the Secretary-General, 'Guidance on Integrated Missions: Clarifying the Role, Responsibility and Authority of the Special Representative of the Secretary-General and the Deputy Special Representative of the Secretary-General/Resident Coordinator/Humanitarian Coordinator', 17 January 2006.

of discipline is articulated in the MOU between the UN and contributing States. The UN Secretariat policy concerning conduct and discipline reinforces that:

> Member States agree that, while their military personnel remain subject to the exclusive jurisdiction of respective Troop Contributing Countries, they will comply with United Nations standards of conduct and such other documents adopted by the United Nations that regulate the conduct of this category of personnel, including the exemplification provided in Annex H of this MOU.[118]

Military personnel who are not a part of a military contingent, such as military observers, are recruited from Member States by the Secretary-General. They are seconded by their national governments to serve on the peace operation and are granted the status of experts on mission by the relevant SOFA entered between the UN and the host country. They are expected to serve as independent and impartial international officials responsible to the UN. Their service in the peace operation is established pursuant to signing an undertaking, which requires them to comply with all relevant UN rules, regulations, and directives.

Similarly, civilian police are seconded to serve on the UN peace operation, and are granted the status of experts on mission by the relevant SOFA between the UN and the host country. They are under the operational control of the PC. However, it is usual for police personnel to also report back to their national governments. Civilian police are employed to serve on UN peace operations based on individual undertakings. Consequently, they are required to comply with all relevant UN rules, regulations, and directives. National governments may also require their police personnel to comply with national laws, regulations, and directives.

Where civilian police are deployed as FPUs, they are subject to individual undertakings and an MOU may also be entered between the UN and the contributing State. The effect for FPUs being subject to an MOU is that national contingent commanders of those units must have necessary authority over their command to maintain discipline. The requirement concerning the maintenance of discipline is articulated in the MOU between the UN and contributing States which requires contributing States to ensure that members of its FPUs comply with rules and regulations.

The UN's accountability policy summarises the UN's application of standards of conduct on military observers, UN civilian police and FPUs as:

> [i]ndividual military and police personnel and members of FPUs ... are deployed with the legal status of experts on mission. They individually sign an undertaking upon commencement of service with the United Nations, through which they agree to be bound by the provisions contained in this undertaking, including the Regulations governing the Status, Basic Rights and Duties of Officials other than Secretariat Officials, and Experts on Mission (ST/SGB/2002/9), and such other documents adopted by the United Nations that regulate the conduct of this category of personnel.[119]

As civilian peacekeepers are employed on an individual basis they do not serve on peace operations pursuant to agreements with contributing States. Civilian personnel who are considered UN staff are governed by relevant UN rules, regulations, and directives. UN volunteers (UNVs) who serve on UN peace operations are bound by their conditions of service. UNVs are not UN staff members but nonetheless are under the authority of the UN and responsible to the Secretary-General for the exercise of their functions, and have the status of 'UN officials' for the purposes of the application of privileges and immunities in accordance with the SOFA.[120] Other civilian personnel are subject to the obligations arising from their individual contracts.

---

118 United Nations Policy on Accountability for Conduct and Discipline in Field Missions, UN Doc 2015.10, approved by USG/DPA, USG/DPKO, and USG/DFS, effective 1 August 2015, review date 31 July 2017, [11.6]. See chs 21–33 below.

119 Ibid, [11.5].

120 For the rules that govern UN volunteers visit their website at <http://www.unv.org/> accessed 1 November 2017. See also UN Juridical Yearbook 1991, 305–7 on 'Status of Members of the United Nations Volunteers—Question whether they are considered as "officials" or "experts on mission" for the Purposes of the Privileges and Immunities of the United Nations'. See also ch 31 below.

Local staff are also a component of UN operations and their relationship with the UN is determined by the contract that they sign with the UN. Their privileges and immunities are dealt with in the SOFA applicable to the peace operation in which they are serving.

Corporate contractors are not considered UN personnel. Their relationship to the UN is determined by the contracts that they enter with the UN. The General Conditions of Contract that frames the employment of corporate contractors states:

> [t]he Contractor shall be responsible for the professional and technical competence of the personnel it assigns to perform work under the Contract and will select reliable and competent individuals who will be able to effectively perform the obligations under the Contract and who, while doing so, will respect the local laws and customs and conform to a high standard of moral and ethical conduct.[121]

Individual contractors and consultants enter agreements between themselves and the United Nations, which contain provisions on the obligation to respect the United Nations standards of conduct.[122] If they have the status of experts on mission they are accorded the relevant privileges under the SOFA. Such privileges are for the benefit of the UN rather than for the contractor or the consultant.

Irrespective of the levels of authority or control that the UN has over peacekeepers, individuals serving on peace operations may be subject to their own domestic laws. These laws can incorporate their State's international legal obligations (for example, obligations arising from the State's ratification of the Rome Statute of the International Criminal Court), or the extra-territorial application of domestic laws. It is in this way that certain obligations found in areas of IHRL, IHL, and international criminal law (ICL) are highly relevant to the legal regime applicable to peace operations. As a minimum, all personnel serving in a UN peace operation are required to comply with UN standards of conduct.

6. Principles of Selection of Documents

Documents Included

The documents included in this book are those that are in the public domain and are most relevant to the establishment, management, and conduct of peace operations. This book has only reproduced the most relevant extracts of the key documents relating to the UN, contributing States, and peacekeepers. The documents range from those that are binding as a matter of law, to those that, while not binding, nonetheless deal with issues of normative importance. Thus, there are four categories of documents included in this book.

The first category is treaties, such as the Charter,[123] the ICCPR,[124] and the Geneva Conventions of 1949.[125] While they do not focus on peace operations, they are nonetheless relevant to how such operations are established, managed, and conducted.

The second category of documents is general international instruments. While not having treaty status, they are nonetheless relevant to peace operations either because such documents deal with matters of general relevance to such operations or because they deal specifically with peace operations. Documents that fall into the general relevance category include those such as the Basic Principles on the Use of Force and Firearms by Law Enforcement Officials.[126] The documents that fall into the category of dealing specifically with peace operations include the

---

121 United Nations Policy on Accountability for Conduct and Discipline in Field Missions, UN Doc 2015.10, approved by USG/DPA, USG/DPKO and USG/DFS, effective 1 August 2015, review date 31 July 2017, [11.8]. See also ch 31 below.

122 Ibid, [11.7]. See also ch 2 below.

123 See ch 1 below.

124 See ch 6 below.

125 See ch 16 below.

126 See ch 13 below.

General Assembly resolution on Third-party liability: temporal and financial limitations[127] and the UN model SOFA.

The third category of documents are internal UN documents which are issued by UN entities such as the Secretary-General, the DPKO, and the Department of Political Affairs. Some of these documents, such as the Secretary-General's Bulletin on UN forces observing international humanitarian law[128] focus on UN peace operations and others, such as the Status, Basic Rights and Duties of United Nations Staff Members[129] have a broader reach.

The fourth category of documents are ICJ cases, which deal either generally with matters relevant to peace operations or deal specifically with matters that have arisen in the context of peace operations. Examples of the former cases include the ICJ Advisory Opinion concerning the *Difference Relating to Immunity from Legal Process of a Special Rapporteur of the Commission of Human Rights*. Cases that fall into the latter category of dealing specifically with matters that have arisen in the context of peace operations include the Advisory Opinion concerning *Certain Expenses of the United Nations (Article 17, Paragraph 2, of the Charter)*.[130]

Documents Excluded

Documents which have not been included in this book are those relating to regional or multinational peace operations. These documents have been excluded to ensure that this book does not become too unwieldy, and to allow a focus to be placed upon those operations established by the UN. However, where appropriate the prefatory note to a document refers to any relevant regional organisation documents that deal with the same subject matter.

Other documents excluded from this collection are those developed by the UN for peace operations which are not in the public domain. Such documents include rules of engagement, directives concerning the use of force, and other material considered by the UN or peace operations as restricted or classified.

This volume does not include the actual Security Council resolutions establishing peace operations. These are too numerous to be included in a book of this nature and are found on the UN website or, in the case of more recent operations, on the website for that operation. This book has also omitted documents and material developed by contributing States for application by their peacekeepers. Thus, military doctrine, State-specific rules of engagement, use of force directives, and other such documents have been omitted.

7. Arrangement, Title, and Texts of Documents

This book is arranged in four parts. Part One is concerned with the establishment and management of peace operations. It includes treaties, agreements, and documents that are relevant to the institutional framework for establishing peace operations and the agreements relevant to States contributing personnel to such operations. Part Two relates to the conduct of peace operations and contains documents relevant to the key legal regimes applicable to peace operations. These regimes are IHRL, IHL, the protection of United Nations and associated personnel, and landmark Security Council resolutions. Part Three, while also relevant to the management and conduct of peace operations, is concerned with treaties and documents that relate to responsibility and accountability in peace operations. Part Four focuses on ICJ cases, such as the *Certain Expenses* case, which are relevant to the establishment, management, and conduct of peace operations.

127 GA Res 52/247 of 26 June 1998. See ch 22 below.
128 See ch 15 below.
129 See ch 25 below.
130 See chs 34–36 below.

8. Prefatory Notes to Documents

Before each document, a prefatory note has been included. The note outlines the historical development of the document as well as its relevance to peace operations. These notes provide the reader with a better understanding of the evolution of the document, and the key principles, rules, and standards contained in the excerpts that are relevant to UN peace operations. Where relevant the note also makes brief reference to how regional organisations, such as the AU, have reacted to the document. There are several instances where the prefatory notes quote or refer to an advice from the OLA. It should be noted that such advice reflects the OLA's view of the legal position and may not amount to establishing a principle or rule of law for the UN as an organisation.

The prefatory notes are not intended to be a full historical, political, or legal commentary on the document. Nor do they aim to provide a full explanation of the various controversial elements that might arise in interpreting or applying the document to a situation.

After each document, a few details relating to the document are provided. In the case of treaties, there is information concerning the location of the document on the Internet, the date the treaty was opened for signature and when it entered into force, the number of signatories and parties, and the depository and source. Where a document is not a treaty, there is a reference to the location of the document on the Internet, the institution or author responsible for the creation of the document, the date of the document, and its reference number.

9. Bibliography

The book provides a select bibliography for those who want additional sources of information and reading on establishing, managing, and conducting UN peace operations and related topics.

PART ONE

Establishment and Management of Peace Operations

I

Charter of the United Nations

Prefatory Note

1. Background

All UN peace operations are founded on the Charter of the United Nations (Charter).[1] The Charter is the multilateral treaty that created the UN. The treaty sets out the purposes, principles, and powers of the UN, and stipulates the rights and obligations of the States that have signed it.[2] The UN is an institution with four major purposes: the maintenance of international peace and security; the development of friendly relations between States; the achievement of international cooperation; and the harmonising of State actions.[3]

As well as the four purposes expressed in the Charter, the UN as an institution is also based on several principles. These principles include: the sovereign equality of States; the settlement of disputes by peaceful means; the requirement to refrain from the threat or use of force; and the prohibition of intervening in matters within the domestic jurisdiction of States.[4] The UN can engage with the preservation of international peace and security either through collective methods[5] or via peaceful resolution of disputes.[6] Within this context, it should be noted that Member States may maintain international peace and security pursuant to Article 51 of the Charter which provides for the right of individual or collective self-defence, or through regional arrangements pursuant to Chapter VIII of the Charter.

After World War II, the predecessor to the UN, the League of Nations, was deemed unsuccessful in its aim of achieving international peace and security. Consequently, it was decided that a new institution was required to reflect the political landscape and the pressing issues of the time. Determined to avoid the perceived failures of the League of Nations, the Charter is clear in establishing a Member State's supreme obligation to the UN, with Article 103 requiring decisions made by the Security Council under Article 25 of the Charter to prevail over any other international agreements.

The Security Council is the organ with primary responsibility for the maintenance of international peace and security, and can make decisions which all Member States of the UN are required to accept and implement pursuant to Article 25 of the Charter. This obligation was confirmed by the International Court of Justice (ICJ) in *Legal Consequences for States of the Continued Presence of South Africa in Namibia (South West Africa) notwithstanding Security Council Resolution 276* (Advisory Opinion) (*Namibia Case*):[7]

> when the Security Council adopts a decision under Article 25 in accordance with the Charter, it is for member States to comply with that decision, including those members of the Security Council which voted against it and those Members of the United Nations who are not members of the Council. To hold otherwise would be to deprive this principal organ of its essential functions and powers under the Charter.[8]

---

1 Charter of the United Nations (opened for signature 26 June 1945, entered into force 24 October 1945) 1 UNTS XVI (hereafter Charter).

2 *Certain Expenses of the United Nations (Article 17, Paragraph 2, of the Charter)* (Advisory Opinion) [1962] ICJ Rep 151, 157 (hereafter *Certain Expenses Case*) where the Court 'recognised that the Charter is a multilateral treaty, albeit a treaty having certain special characteristics'. See ch 35 below.

3 Charter (n 1), Article 1.

4 Ibid, Article 2.

5 Ibid, Chapter VII, Articles 41 and 42.

6 Ibid, Chapter VI.

7 *Legal Consequences for States of the Continued Presence of South Africa in Namibia (South West Africa) notwithstanding Security Council Resolution 276* (Advisory Opinion) [1971] ICJ Rep 16 (hereafter *Namibia Case*).

8 Ibid, 54.

It is important to note that this obligation is limited to 'decisions' of the Security Council and does not apply to broad pronouncements made by the organ. It has been determined that words used in Security Council resolutions such as 'urges' and 'invites' are non-binding, whereas the use of the term 'decides' is binding. Terms such as 'calls upon' and 'endorses' are less clear in relation to their binding nature. In situations of peace operations not requiring the consent of the parties involved, such as those created under Chapter VII of the Charter, a careful review of the exact wording of the UN resolution is required to ascertain whether the stated obligations are intended to be binding upon Member States.[9] This was confirmed by the ICJ in the *Namibia Case* where the Court stated that the language of a Security Council resolution needs to be carefully analysed before its binding effect can be determined. In carrying out this analysis the following may be considered:

> the terms of the resolution to be interpreted, the discussions leading to it, the Charter provisions invoked and, in general, all circumstances that might assist in determining the legal consequences of the resolution of the Security Council.[10]

Security Council resolutions are generally addressed to Member States but such resolutions are nevertheless also applicable by implication to the UN.[11]

2. Pacific Settlement of Disputes

Chapter VI of the Charter provides for the pacific settlement of disputes. The essence of the system is found in Article 33 of the Charter. This Article states that parties to any dispute that threatens the maintenance of international peace and security shall seek solutions to that dispute using peaceful means of their own choice such as negotiation, enquiry, mediation, judicial settlement, or resort to regional agencies or arrangements. Where disputes concern legal matters, as opposed to purely political matters, it is expected that the parties to the dispute will refer the matter to the ICJ.

Within this system of the peaceful settlement of disputes, the Security Council may investigate any dispute to determine whether the dispute is likely to endanger international peace and security, and may make recommendations to the disputing parties as to methods they may use to resolve their disagreements. The Security Council cannot, however, pursuant to Chapter VI, impose obligations on the parties. It may only make recommendations to the disputing parties. Disputing parties may also bring the dispute to the attention of the General Assembly. The powers and functions of the General Assembly in this context are limited by the requirements imposed by Articles 11 and 12 of the Charter. For example, Article 11 restricts the powers of the General Assembly to questions relating to international peace and security. Article 12 stipulates that the General Assembly shall not make any 'recommendations with respect to a dispute or situation while the Security Council is exercising its functions with respect to that dispute or situation, absent a Council request to the Assembly that it do so'.[12] The General Assembly has interpreted the words 'is exercising' narrowly as meaning 'is exercising at this moment' to avoid two organs of the UN dealing with the same matter simultaneously.[13]

---

9 See UN Juridical Yearbook 1994, 502–3 on 'Resolutions under Chapter VII adopted by the Security Council—Practice of the Council'. See also Security Council Report, 'Security Council Action under Chapter VII: Myths and Realities', Special Research Report No 1, 23 June 2008, <http://www.securitycouncilreport.org/> accessed 1 November 2017.

10 *Namibia Case* (n 7), 53.

11 See UN Juridical Yearbook 2006, 472, 'Note to the Under-Secretary-General for Peacekeeping Operations relating to the Applicability of Security Council Decisions to the United Nations Organizations operating in Afghanistan', 24 March 2006.

12 Memorandum to the Secretary of the Fourth Committee, 'Restriction imposed on the General Assembly by Article 12, paragraph 1, of the Charter of the United Nations whereby "While the Security Council is exercising in respect of any dispute or situation the functions assigned to it in the present Charter, the General Assembly shall not make any recommendation with regard to that dispute or situation unless the Security Council so requests"—interpretation of that restriction in the practice of the General Assembly, 8 October 1991' (hereafter Memorandum).

13 Ibid.

3. Enforcement Measures

The enforcement measures that may be taken by the UN and Member States to maintain international peace and security are found in Chapter VII of the Charter. The UN organ central to the system of maintaining international peace and security is the Security Council. The Security Council has the power to determine whether a situation is a threat to international peace and security. Once it makes such a determination it can, pursuant to its Article 39 powers, make recommendations, or decide what measures shall be taken to maintain or restore international peace and security. The measures that may be taken are escalatory in nature and are found in Articles 41 and 42 of the Charter. Article 41 envisages the use of non-military measures such as the interruption of economic and diplomatic relations, whilst Article 42 extends to the use of military measures including blockades. Since the 1990s, most UN peace operations have been established pursuant to the Security Council's Chapter VII powers.

4. Right of Self-Defence of States

The UN system of maintaining international peace and security does not limit the inherent right of individual or collective self-defence. However, the right of self-defence, as expressed by Article 51 of the Charter, is limited in two ways. First, Member States exercising the right of self-defence must report the exercise of the right immediately to the Security Council. Secondly, the exercise of the right is limited to the extent that once the Security Council has taken measures necessary to maintain international peace and security, the right of Member States is then limited to the actions that the Security Council believes necessary to maintain or restore international peace and security.

5. The Security Council

The Security Council consists of 15 Member States of the UN. There are five permanent members of the Council: China, France, Russia, the United Kingdom, and the United States of America. Each of these States has a veto power. The remaining ten members are elected by the General Assembly. In *Certain Expenses of the United Nations (Article 17, Paragraph 2, of the Charter)* (Advisory Opinion) (*Certain Expenses Case*),[14] the ICJ addressed the various functions of the UN's organs and determined that whilst the Security Council has primary responsibility for the maintenance of international peace and security, it does not have exclusive responsibility.

Key provisions governing the Security Council's role in this area are Articles 24 and 25 of the Charter. Article 24 stipulates that the Security Council has 'primary responsibility for the maintenance of international peace and security' and, that in carrying out its duties in relation to the maintenance of international peace and security, the Security Council 'shall act in accordance with the Purposes and Principles of the United Nations'. Article 25 establishes the principle that Members of the UN 'agree to accept and carry out the decisions of the Security Council'. Article 25 further develops the principle expressed in Article 2(5) of the Charter which requires Member States of the UN to render all possible assistance to the UN in the performance of its functions. The functions and powers of the Security Council in the context of peace operations are relevant to the Security Council acting to deal with 'Pacific Settlement of Disputes',[15] 'Action with Respect to Threats to the Peace, Breaches of the Peace, and Acts of Aggression',[16] or 'Regional Arrangements'.[17]

The clear majority of UN peace operations have been created pursuant to the powers of the Security Council. This is highlighted by the fact that the authorisation of UN peace operations has been the exclusive domain of the Security Council since the United Nations Security Force in West New Guinea (UNSF) in 1962. The Security Council is the only UN organ that may establish a peace operation if the mission requires a binding decision or the use of force is contemplated.

---

14 *Certain Expenses Case* (n 2).
15 Charter (n 1), Chapter VI.
16 Ibid, Chapter VII.
17 Ibid, Chapter VIII.

6. The General Assembly

The General Assembly consists of all the Member States of the UN and is therefore the most representative organ of the UN. The key powers and functions of the General Assembly that are relevant to UN peace operations are found in Articles 10 to 15 and Article 17. The ICJ in the *Certain Expenses Case* affirmed that the General Assembly is also concerned with international peace and security and can recommend 'measures' pursuant to Article 14 of the Charter. Pursuant to Article 11 the General Assembly may also bring to the attention of the Security Council any matter that is likely to endanger international peace and security. However, the powers of the General Assembly are restricted pursuant to Article 12(1) of the Charter which states that:

> While the Security Council is exercising in respect of any dispute or situation the functions assigned to it in the present Charter, the General Assembly shall not make any recommendation with regard to that dispute or situation unless the Security Council so requests.[18]

The General Assembly may debate, discuss, or make recommendations on 'matters that the [Security Council] is exercising its functions on'.[19]

An example of such a situation occurred during the early days of the Cold War when the Security Council was effectively stopped from exercising its primary responsibility owing to disagreements between its five permanent members and the use of the veto power to stop Security Council resolutions. This led to the General Assembly passing resolution 377 A (V), also known as the 'Uniting for Peace' resolution, which states that

> if the Security Council, because of lack of unanimity of the permanent members, fails to exercise its primary responsibility for the maintenance of international peace and security in any case where there appears to be a threat to the peace, breach of the peace, or act of aggression, the General Assembly shall consider the matter immediately with a view to making appropriate recommendations to Members for collective measures, including in the case of a breach of the peace or act of aggression, the use of armed force when necessary, to maintain or restore international peace and security.[20]

The resolution created the mechanism of the 'emergency special session' (ESS), ten of which have been convened.[21] It was under this procedure that the first armed UN peace operation, the First United Nations Emergency Force in the Middle East (UNEF I), was established during the Suez crisis in 1956. This is the only instance of the establishment of such a peace operation pursuant to the 'Uniting for Peace' resolution.

The 'Uniting for Peace' resolution was used in operations in the United Nations Observation Group in Lebanon (UNOGIL) in 1958 and the United Nations Operation in the Congo (ONUC) in 1960. Its use in these cases merely altered the tasks of peace operations which had already been established by the Security Council. The only other peace operation established by the General Assembly was UNSF in 1962. UNSF was created by General Assembly resolution 1752 (XVII)[22] as part of the peace agreement between Indonesia and the Netherlands regarding West New Guinea (West Irian). UNSF effectively provided the security for the United Nations Temporary Executive Authority (UNTEA), the first operation where the UN conducted a transitional administration. All other peace operations have been created by the Security Council.

Peace operations are funded as certain expenses of the UN under Article 17 of the Charter. This is confirmed in the annual reports of the General Assembly's Special Committee on Peacekeeping Operations (C34) which continually reaffirm

> the obligation of Member States under Article 17 of the Charter to bear the expenses of the Organization as apportioned by the General Assembly, bearing in mind the special responsibilities of the permanent members of the Security Council for the maintenance of peace and security as indicated in General Assembly resolution 1874 (S-IV) of 27 June 1963.[23]

---

18 Ibid, Article 12(1).

19 Memorandum (n 12).

20 GA Res 377 A (V) of 3 November 1950, Operative Part [1].

21 See <https://library.un.org/index-proceedings/general-assembly-emergency-special-sessions> accessed 1 November 2017. The Rules of Procedure of the General Assembly, in particular Rules 8(b), 9(b), and 10, regulate the manner of calling an emergency special session <https://www.un.org/en/ga/about/ropga/sessions.shtml> accessed 8 April 2019.

22 GA Res 1752 (XVII) of 21 September 1962.

23 See, for example, 'Report of the Special Committee on Peacekeeping Operations and its Working Group, 2009 Substantive Session (23 February–20 March 2009)', UN Doc A/63/19, 24 March 2009, [174].

7. The Secretariat

Pursuant to Article 99 of the Charter, the Secretary-General may 'bring to the attention of the Security Council any matter which in his opinion may threaten the maintenance of international peace and security'.

Regarding UN peace operations, and in accordance with the appointment of the Secretary-General as the chief administrative officer of the UN,[24] '[t]he Secretary-General is responsible to the Security Council for the organisation, conduct and direction of the [peace operation] ... and keeps the Council fully informed of developments relating to the functioning of the [peace operation]'.[25]

In exercising these delegated powers, the Secretary-General must act in the best interests of the UN itself and independently of any Member State.[26] Whilst the Secretary-General has this discretionary power delegated to him and his interpretation of it can only be challenged in the Security Council, making it binding on Member States, it is not without its limitations. For instance, the Secretary-General does not have the power to unilaterally terminate a peace operation or change its mandate. This is because the legal basis for a peace operation is a Security Council, or possibly a General Assembly, resolution and only the principal organ which passed the resolution can terminate or alter the mandate of the peace operation.

8. The International Court of Justice

The ICJ is, pursuant to Article 92 of the Charter, the principal judicial organ of the UN. The Court's jurisdiction includes 'all cases which the parties refer to it and all matters specially provided for in the Charter ... or in treaties and conventions in force'.[27] The Court may also give advisory opinions concerning legal questions referred to it by the General Assembly, Security Council, other organs of the UN, and specialised agencies, authorised by the General Assembly.[28]

It plays an integral part in how the UN achieves its primary purpose of maintaining international peace and security by resolving legal disputes between States that threaten the peace or where a breach of the peace has already occurred. This is explicitly spelt out in Article 36 of the Charter:

> In making recommendations under this Article the Security Council should also take into consideration that legal disputes should as a general rule be referred by the parties to the International Court of Justice in accordance with the provisions of the Statute of the Court.[29]

The Court's main role in relation to peace operations has been in providing advisory opinions on matters relating to peacekeeping, an example being the advisory opinion the Court delivered in the *Certain Expenses Case*. The Court also has a role to play in resolving differences in the interpretation or application of the Convention on the Privileges and Immunities of the United Nations under Section 30 of the Convention, as can be seen in the advisory opinion of the ICJ in *Difference Relating to Immunity from Legal Process of a Special Rapporteur of the Commission of Human Rights* (Advisory Opinion) (*Cumaraswamy Case*).[30]

Finally, the Court, in the form of the President, is mentioned in Section VII of the model Status-of-Forces Agreement[31] (model SOFA) which concerns the settlement of disputes. The President of the Court is to appoint the chairman of the standing claims commission or arbitration tribunal

---

24 Charter (n 1), Article 97.

25 UN Juridical Yearbook 1990, 269–70, 269 on the 'Award of the 1988 Nobel Peace Prize to the United Nations Peacekeeping Forces—Practical and Legal Obstacles to the Exercise by the United Nations Peacekeeping Forces of the Right to Nominate Candidates provided for by the Special Regulations governing the Award of the Prize'.

26 Charter (n 1), Article 100.

27 Statute of the International Court of Justice (adopted 18 April 1946), Article 36.

28 Charter (n 1), Article 96.

29 Ibid, Article 36.

30 *Difference Relating to Immunity from Legal Process of a Special Rapporteur of the Commission of Human Rights* (Advisory Opinion) [1999] ICJ Rep 62 (hereafter *Cumaraswamy Case*). See ch 36 below.

31 See ch 2 below.

where no agreement on the chairman can be reached between the Secretary-General and the government of the host country. Notwithstanding that a claims commission has never been established, the provision does demonstrate the role that the Court has in resolving disputes involving the UN.

9. Regional Arrangements

Article 52 of the Charter allows for regional arrangements or agencies to deal with matters relating to the maintenance of international peace and security if their activities are consistent with the purposes and principles of the UN. Such activities may include the peaceful settlement of disputes, such as conflict prevention, or may include enforcement action. Other than the limitation that peace operations pursuant to regional arrangements or by regional agencies must comply with the principles and purposes of the Charter there are two other caveats imposed by Chapter VIII. First, Article 53 stipulates that no enforcement action may be undertaken under regional arrangements or by regional agencies without the authorisation of the Security Council. Further, Article 54 requires the Security Council to be fully informed of activities undertaken or contemplated under regional arrangements or by regional agencies. Both Articles 53 and 54 reinforce that the primary responsibility for the maintenance of international peace and security rests with the Security Council. The relationship between the Security Council and regional arrangements and agencies is that of cooperation to improve collective security.

While the Charter does not define the terms 'regional arrangements or agencies' it is accepted that the following organisations meet the Chapter VII requirements to engage in the maintenance of international peace and security:

> African Union [AU], the European Union [EU], the Economic Community of Central African States (ECCAS), and the Economic Community of West African States (ECOWAS), the Southern African Development Community (SADC) and the Eastern African Community (EAC), the Organization of American States (OAS), the Union of South American Nations (UNASUR), the Community of Latin America and Caribbean States (CELAC), the Caribbean Community and Common Market (CARICOM), the Collective Security Treaty Organization (CSTO), the League of Arab States (LAS), the Association of Southeast Asian Nations (ASEAN) and the Arab Maghreb Union (UMA).[32]

The role of organisations such as the abovementioned is also viewed by the Security Council as a means 'to enable timely responses to disputes and emerging crises and to strengthen the role of the UN in the prevention of conflict'.[33] Furthermore, there is a broad recognition that in some circumstances regional organisations are better suited to dealing with threats to international peace and security in their region due to their better understanding of the dynamics giving rise to those threats.[34]

10. Other Relevant Provisions in the Charter

There are three other relevant provisions in the Charter concerning UN peace operations. The first is Article 103, which provides that '[i]n the event of a conflict between the obligations of the Members of the United Nations under the ... Charter and their obligations under any other international agreement, their obligations under the ... Charter shall prevail'. The importance of this provision is highlighted by, for example, the view of the European Court of Human Rights (ECtHR) in the case of *Behrami and Behrami v France and Saramati v France, Germany and Norway*. In that case, the ECtHR stated that Article 103 establishes the primacy of the UN legal order[35] on the basis that the ICJ had concluded that 'the Charter obligations of UN member states prevail over

---

32 SC Res 2167 (2014) of 28 July 2014, Preamble.

33 SC Res 2320 (2016) of 18 November 2016, Preamble.

34 SC Res 2167 (2014) of 28 July 2014, Preamble.

35 Decision as to the Admissibility: *Behrami and Behrami v France*, App no 71466/01, 2 May 2007; *Saramati v France, Germany and Norway*, App no 78166/01, 2 May 2007 [147].

conflicting obligations from another international treaty'.[36] Another way of looking at Article 103 is that it 'is a treaty rule specifying priority, and not per se a norm of *jus cogens*'.[37]

Another important provision of the Charter is Article 105, which provides for the privileges and immunities of the UN as an organisation and its staff. These privileges and immunities provide for the independent exercise of the functions of the UN. The Article 105 provisions have been consolidated in more detail in the Convention on Privileges and Immunities of the United Nations[38] and the model SOFA.

Finally, Article 101, which states the importance of the UN securing staff with the 'highest standards of efficiency, competence, and integrity', is important to UN peace operations and especially to personnel classified as experts on mission. This requirement is reflected in the Regulations Governing the Status, Basic Rights, and Duties of Officials other than Secretariat Officials, and Experts on Mission,[39] which states that '[o]fficials and experts on mission shall uphold the highest standards of efficiency, competence and integrity'.[40] This wording is also reflected in the individual undertaking signed by civilian police when joining the police component of a UN peace operation.

11. UN Peace Operations

Whilst the Charter contains no express provisions relating to peace operations, the power to establish such operations is implied in the functions and powers of the Security Council, and, to a more limited extent, the General Assembly. Peace operations are subsidiary organs of the UN as confirmed by the model SOFA.[41] Even if a peace operation, such as a regional peace operation, is established outside of the institutional framework of the Security Council, it is expected that the operation will comply with the purposes and principles enshrined in the Charter.

When the Charter was being developed, it was intended that the use of armed force under the Charter was going to be based on 'special agreement or agreements' between the Security Council and Member States of the UN under Article 43. No such agreements have even been concluded. In the *Certain Expenses Case* the ICJ considered Article 43 and found that its implementation was not a prerequisite for the establishment of UN peace operations. The UN Office of Legal Affairs (OLA) stated in a 1982 legal opinion that

> The Court thus excluded the peace-keeping operations of the United Nations from the applicability of Article 43. It further confirmed that the United Nations is not precluded from the use of military forces through procedures other than those envisaged in Article 43 of the Charter for purposes other than enforcement action.[42]

As a matter of practice, UN peace operations are established by the Security Council pursuant to a Security Council resolution. Where an operation is established by the Security Council it is a subsidiary organ of the Council and is expected to adhere to the purposes and principles found in Articles 1 and 2 of the Charter. This expectation has resulted in the development of three principles fundamental to any UN mission.[43] These principals are consent, impartiality, and the use of force only in self-defence. The importance of these principles to UN peace operations was first identified by Secretary-General Dag Hammarskjöld in his report to the UN concerning the experiences derived from the establishment and operation of the UNEF I.[44] These elements are considered 'inter-related and mutually reinforcing … [and] [t]aken together, they provide a navigation aid, or compass,

---

36 Ibid, [27].

37 International Law Commission, 'First Report on Jus Cogens by Dire Tladi, Special Rapporteur', UN Doc A/CN.4/693, 8 March 2016, [28].

38 See ch 21 below.

39 UN Doc ST/SGB/2002/9, 18 June 2002, entered into force 1 July 2002. See ch 26 below.

40 Ibid, 4, Regulation 2, Conduct (a).

41 UN Doc A/45/594, 9 October 1990, [15]. See ch 2 below.

42 UN Juridical Yearbook 1982, 183–5, 184, 'Implementation of Article 43 of the Charter of the United Nations regarding the Provision of Armed Forces, Assistance and Facilities to the Security Council for the Maintenance of International Peace and Security'.

43 See the Introduction chapter to this book, above, for a more detailed discussion concerning the three principles.

44 'Report of the Secretary-General: United Nations Emergency Force: Summary Study of the Experience derived from the Establishment and Operation of the Force', UN Doc A/3943, 9 October 1958.

for practitioners both in the field and at United Nations Headquarters'.[45] The importance of the three 'core principles of peacekeeping to guide successful United Nations peacekeeping operations in ceasefires and implementing peace agreements' was emphasised by the 2015 Report of the High-level Independent Panel on Peace Operations on Uniting Our Strengths for Peace: Politics, Partnership, and People (High Panel Report).[46]

The principle of consent refers to the 'consent of the parties' and means that UN peacekeepers are deployed with the 'consent of the main parties to the conflict'.[47] The term 'impartiality' refers to the requirement that UN peacekeepers 'implement their mandate without favour or prejudice to any party'.[48] Self-defence in the context of UN peace operations includes resistance to attempts by forceful means to prevent the mission from discharging its duties under the mandate of the Security Council (so-called 'defence of the mandate').[49] It is also arguable that there are now two further principles that form the core of UN peace operations: the protection of civilians and the application of the rule of law.[50]

The violation by an operation of these elements can cast strong questions of legitimacy over the peace operation. Respect for these elements is a crucial part in distinguishing between the use of force for acts of aggression and that which is used for peace operations. The application of the principles of consent and impartiality in UN peace operations is consistent with some key principles articulated in Article 2 of the Charter, such as the principle of the equality of States[51] and the principle of non-intervention in matters essentially within the domestic jurisdiction of any State.[52]

12. Regional Peace Operations

As stated above, the UN has recognised the value of regional organisations engaging with matters relating to the maintenance of international peace and security.[53] The Security Council reinforced in 2016 the importance of regional and sub-regional organisations in conducting peace operations and its readiness to consider proposals for such operations.[54] The Security Council has also reaffirmed that such operations must be conducted in accordance with international law:

> Reaffirming its commitment to uphold the purposes and principles of the Charter of the United Nations, including its commitment and respect to the principles of political independence, sovereign equality and territorial integrity of all States in conducting all peacekeeping activities and the need for States to comply with their obligations under international law.[55]

More specifically the Security Council has encouraged the AU

> to finalize its human rights and Conduct and Discipline Compliance frameworks for AU peace support operations, to achieve greater accountability, transparency, and compliance with international human rights law and international humanitarian law, as applicable, and with UN conduct and discipline standards, and underscores the importance of these commitments as well as the requirement for oversight by the Security Council for operations authorized by the Security Council and under the Security Council's authority consistent with Chapter VIII of the Charter.[56]

The Security Council has also emphasised that it be kept fully informed of activities undertaken by regional or sub-regional organisations in efforts to maintain international peace and security.[57]

---

45 United Nations, 'United Nations Peacekeeping Operations: Principles and Guidelines', 2008, Annex 2 (hereafter UN Principles and Guidelines, but also known as the 'Capstone Doctrine').

46 'Report of the High-level Independent Panel on Peace Operations on Uniting our Strengths for Peace: Politics, Partnership and People' attached to the Identical letters dated 17 June 2015 from the Secretary-General addressed to the President of the General Assembly and the President of the Security Council, UN Doc A/70/95-S/2015/466, 17 June 2015, [124]. See the Introduction to this book, above, for a more detailed discussion concerning these three principles.

47 UN Principles and Guidelines (n 45), 31.

48 Ibid, 33.

49 Ibid, 34.

50 See the Introduction to this book, above, for a more detailed discussion.

51 Charter (n 1), Article 2(1).

52 Ibid, Article 2(7).

53 See, for example, SC Res 2033 (2012) of 12 January 2012; SC Res 2167 (2014) of 28 July 2014; and SC Res 2320 (2016) of 18 November 2016.

54 SC Res 2320 (2016) of 18 November 2016.

55 Ibid, Preamble.

56 Ibid, [6].

57 SC Res 2167 (2014) of 28 July 2014, Operative Part [1].

Reference

Title	Charter of the United Nations
Opened for Signature	26 June 1945
Entered into Force	24 October 1945 (in accordance with Article 110)
Signatories	51 (50 of the original 51 Members signed the Charter on 26 June 1945. Poland, which signed the Charter on 15 October 1945 (being a date subsequent to the date on which the Charter of the United Nations Act 1945 received the Royal Assent), is also an original Member. 49 remain Members with two, Czechoslovakia and the former Yugoslavia, having been dissolved).[58]
Parties	193 Member States[59]
Depository	United States of America (Article 111 of the Charter)
Source	59 Stat. 1031; T.S. No. 993; 3 Bevans 1153
Full Text	<http://www.un.org/en/charter-united-nations/>[60]

Charter of the United Nations[61]

(Extracts)

PREAMBLE

WE THE PEOPLES OF THE UNITED NATIONS DETERMINED

to save succeeding generations from the scourge of war, which twice in our lifetime has brought untold sorrow to mankind, and

to reaffirm faith in fundamental human rights, in the dignity and worth of the human person, in the equal rights of men and women and of nations large and small, and

to establish conditions under which justice and respect for the obligations arising from treaties and other sources of international law can be maintained, and

to promote social progress and better standards of life in larger freedom,

AND FOR THESE ENDS

to practice tolerance and live together in peace with one another as good neighbours, and

to unite our *strength* to maintain international peace and security, and

to ensure, by the *acceptance* of principles and the institution of methods, that armed force shall not be used, save in the common interest, and

to employ international machinery for the promotion of the economic and social advancement of all peoples,

HAVE RESOLVED TO COMBINE OUR EFFORTS TO ACCOMPLISH THESE AIMS.

Accordingly, our *respective* Governments, through representatives assembled in the city of San Francisco, who have exhibited their full powers found to be in good and due form, have agreed

---

58 For a history showing the growth of UN membership, see <http://www.un.org/en/sections/member-states/growth-united-nations-membership-1945-present/index.html> accessed 16 August 2018.

59 Montenegro was accepted as the 192nd Member State of the UN by GA Res 60/264 of 28 June 2006.

60 Accessed 18 August 2018.

61 From Charter of the United Nations, © 1945 United Nations. Reprinted with the permission of the United Nations.

to the present Charter of the United Nations and do hereby establish an international organization to be known as the United Nations.

CHAPTER I – Purposes and Principles

Article 1 – The Purposes of the United Nations are:

1. To maintain international peace and security, and to that end: to take effective collective measures for the prevention and removal of threats to the peace, and for the suppression of acts of aggression or other breaches of the peace, and to bring about by peaceful means, and in conformity with the principles of justice and international law, adjustment or settlement of international disputes or situations which might lead to a breach of the peace;
2. To develop friendly relations among nations based on respect for the principle of equal rights and self-determination of peoples, and to take other appropriate measures to strengthen universal peace;
3. To achieve international co-operation in solving international problems of an economic, social, cultural, or humanitarian character, and in promoting and encouraging respect for human rights and for fundamental freedoms for all without distinction as to race, sex, language, or religion; and
4. To be a centre for harmonizing the actions of nations in the attainment of these common ends.

Article 2

The Organization and its Members, in pursuit of the Purposes stated in Article 1, shall act in accordance with the following Principles:

1. The Organization is based on the principle of the sovereign equality of all its Members.
2. All Members, in order to ensure to all of them the rights and benefits resulting from membership, shall fulfill in good faith the obligations assumed by them in accordance with the present Charter.
3. All Members shall settle their international disputes by peaceful means in such a manner that international peace and security, and justice, are not endangered.
4. All Members shall refrain in their international relations from the threat or use of force against the territorial integrity or political independence of any state, or in any other manner inconsistent with the Purposes of the United Nations.
5. All Members shall give the United Nations every assistance in any action it takes in accordance with the present Charter, and shall refrain from giving assistance to any state against which the United Nations is taking preventive or enforcement action.
6. The Organization shall ensure that states which are not Members of the United Nations act in accordance with these Principles so far as may be necessary for the maintenance of international peace and security.
7. Nothing contained in the present Charter shall authorize the United Nations to intervene in matters which are essentially within the domestic jurisdiction of any state or shall require the Members to submit such matters to settlement under the present Charter; but this principle shall not prejudice the application of enforcement measures under Chapter VII.

CHAPTER II – Membership

...

Article 4

1. Membership in the United Nations is open to all other peace-loving states which accept the obligations contained in the present Charter and, in the judgment of the Organization, are able and willing to carry out these obligations.
2. The admission of any such state to membership in the United Nations will be effected by a decision of the General Assembly upon the recommendation of the Security Council.

...

CHAPTER III – Organs

Article 7

1. There are established as the principal organs of the United Nations: a General Assembly, a Security Council, an Economic and Social Council, a Trusteeship Council, an International Court of Justice, and a Secretariat.
2. Such subsidiary organs as may be found necessary may be established in accordance with the present Charter.

...

CHAPTER IV – The General Assembly

Composition

...

Functions and Powers

Article 10

The General Assembly may discuss any questions or any matters within the scope of the present Charter or relating to the powers and functions of any organs provided for in the present Charter, and, except as provided in Article 12, may make recommendations to the Members of the United Nations or to the Security Council or to both on any such questions or matters.

Article 11

1. The General Assembly may consider the general principles of co-operation in the maintenance of international peace and security, including the principles governing disarmament and the regulation of armaments, and may make recommendations with regard to such principles to the Members or to the Security Council or to both.
2. The General Assembly may discuss any questions relating to the maintenance of international peace and security brought before it by any Member of the United Nations, or by the Security Council, or by a state which is not a Member of the United Nations in accordance with Article 35, paragraph 2, and, except as provided in Article 12, may make recommendations with regard to any such questions to the state or states concerned or to the Security Council or to both. Any such question on which action is necessary shall be referred to the Security Council by the General Assembly either before or after discussion.
3. The General Assembly may call the attention of the Security Council to situations which are likely to endanger international peace and security.
4. The powers of the General Assembly set forth in this Article shall not limit the general scope of Article 10.

Article 12

1. While the Security Council is exercising in respect of any dispute or situation the functions assigned to it in the present Charter, the General Assembly shall not make any recommendation with regard to that dispute or situation unless the Security Council so requests.
2. The Secretary-General, with the consent of the Security Council, shall notify the General Assembly at each session of any matters relative to the maintenance of international peace and security which are being dealt with by the Security Council and shall similarly notify the General Assembly, or the Members of the United Nations if the General Assembly is not in session, immediately the Security Council ceases to deal with such matters.

Article 13

1. The General Assembly shall initiate studies and make recommendations for the purpose of:
   (a) promoting international co-operation in the political field and encouraging the progressive development of international law and its codification;
   (b) promoting international co-operation in the economic, social, cultural, educational, and health fields, and assisting in the realization of human rights and fundamental freedoms for all without distinction as to race, sex, language, or religion.
2. The further responsibilities, functions and powers of the General Assembly with respect to matters mentioned in paragraph 1 (b) above are set forth in Chapters IX and X.

Article 14

Subject to the provisions of Article 12, the General Assembly may recommend measures for the peaceful adjustment of any situation, regardless of origin, which it deems likely to impair the general welfare or friendly relations among nations, including situations resulting from a violation of the provisions of the present Charter setting forth the Purposes and Principles of the United Nations.

. . .

Article 17

1. The General Assembly shall consider and approve the budget of the Organization.
2. The expenses of the Organization shall be borne by the Members as apportioned by the General Assembly.
3. The General Assembly shall consider and approve any financial and budgetary arrangements with specialized agencies referred to in Article 57 and shall examine the administrative budgets of such specialized agencies with a view to making recommendations to the agencies concerned.

. . .

Voting

. . .

Procedure

. . .

Article 22

The General Assembly may establish such subsidiary organs as it deems necessary for the performance of its functions.

Chapter V – *The Security Council*

Composition
Article 23

1. The Security Council shall consist of fifteen Members of the United Nations. The Republic of China, France, the Union of Soviet Socialist Republics, the United Kingdom of Great Britain and Northern Ireland, and the United States of America shall be permanent members of the Security Council. The General Assembly shall elect ten other Members of the United Nations to be non-permanent members of the Security Council, due regard being specially paid, in the first instance to the contribution of Members of the United Nations to the maintenance of international peace and security and to the other purposes of the Organization, and also to equitable geographical distribution.
2. The non-permanent members of the Security Council shall be elected for a term of two years. In the first election of the non-permanent members after the increase of the membership of the Security Council from eleven to fifteen, two of the four additional members shall be chosen for a term of one year. A retiring member shall not be eligible for immediate re-election.
3. Each member of the Security Council shall have one representative.

Functions and Powers
Article 24

1. In order to ensure prompt and effective action by the United Nations, its Members confer on the Security Council primary responsibility for the maintenance of international peace and security, and agree that in carrying out its duties under this responsibility the Security Council acts on their behalf.
2. In discharging these duties the Security Council shall act in accordance with the Purposes and Principles of the United Nations. The specific powers granted to the Security Council for the discharge of these duties are laid down in Chapters VI, VII, VIII, and XII.
3. The Security Council shall submit annual and, when necessary, special reports to the General Assembly for its consideration.

Article 25
The Members of the United Nations agree to accept and carry out the decisions of the Security Council in accordance with the present Charter.

Article 26
In order to promote the establishment and maintenance of international peace and security with the least diversion for armaments of the world's human and economic resources, the Security Council shall be responsible for formulating, with the assistance of the Military Staff Committee referred to in Article 47, plans to be submitted to the Members of the United Nations for the establishment of a system for the regulation of armaments.

Voting
...

Procedure
...

Article 29
The Security Council may establish such subsidiary organs as it deems necessary for the performance of its functions.

...

Article 32

Any Member of the United Nations which is not a member of the Security Council or any state which is not a Member of the United Nations, if it is a party to a dispute under consideration by the Security Council, shall be invited to participate, without vote, in the discussion relating to the dispute. The Security Council shall lay down such conditions as it deems just for the participation of a state which is not a Member of the United Nations.

CHAPTER VI – Pacific Settlement of Disputes

Article 33

1. The parties to any dispute, the continuance of which is likely to endanger the maintenance of international peace and security, shall, first of all, seek a solution by negotiation, enquiry, mediation, conciliation, arbitration, judicial settlement, resort to regional agencies or arrangements, or other peaceful means of their own choice.
2. The Security Council shall, when it deems necessary, call upon the parties to settle their dispute by such means.

Article 34

The Security Council may investigate any dispute, or any situation which might lead to international friction or give rise to a dispute, in order to determine whether the continuance of the dispute or situation is likely to endanger the maintenance of international peace and security.

Article 35

1. Any Member of the United Nations may bring any dispute, or any situation of the nature referred to in Article 34, to the attention of the Security Council or of the General Assembly.
2. A state which is not a Member of the United Nations may bring to the attention of the Security Council or of the General Assembly any dispute to which it is a party if it accepts in advance, for the purposes of the dispute, the obligations of pacific settlement provided in the present Charter.
3. The proceedings of the General Assembly in respect of matters brought to its attention under this Article will be subject to the provisions of Articles 11 and 12.

Article 36

1. The Security Council may, at any stage of a dispute of the nature referred to in Article 33 or of a situation of like nature, recommend appropriate procedures or methods of adjustment.
2. The Security Council should take into consideration any procedures for the settlement of the dispute which have already been adopted by the parties.
3. In making recommendations under this Article the Security Council should also take into consideration that legal disputes should as a general rule be referred by the parties to the International Court of Justice in accordance with the provisions of the Statute of the Court.

Article 37

1. Should the parties to a dispute of the nature referred to in Article 33 fail to settle it by the means indicated in that Article, they shall refer it to the Security Council.

2. If the Security Council deems that the continuance of the dispute is in fact likely to endanger the maintenance of international peace and security, it shall decide whether to take action under Article 36 or to recommend such terms of settlement as it may consider appropriate.

Article 38

Without prejudice to the provisions of Articles 33 to 37, the Security Council may, if all the parties to any dispute so request, make recommendations to the parties with a view to a pacific settlement of the dispute.

Chapter VII – Action with Respect to Threats to the Peace, Breaches of the Peace, and Acts of Aggression

Article 39

The Security Council shall determine the existence of any threat to the peace, breach of the peace, or act of aggression and shall make recommendations, or decide what measures shall be taken in accordance with Articles 41 and 42, to maintain or restore international peace and security.

Article 40

In order to prevent an aggravation of the situation, the Security Council may, before making the recommendations or deciding upon the measures provided for in Article 39, call upon the parties concerned to comply with such provisional measures as it deems necessary or desirable. Such provisional measures shall be without prejudice to the rights, claims, or position of the parties concerned. The Security Council shall duly take account of failure to comply with such provisional measures.

Article 41

The Security Council may decide what measures not involving the use of armed force are to be employed to give effect to its decisions, and it may call upon the Members of the United Nations to apply such measures. These may include complete or partial interruption of economic relations and of rail, sea, air, postal, telegraphic, radio, and other means of communication, and the severance of diplomatic relations.

Article 42

Should the Security Council consider that measures provided for in Article 41 would be inadequate or have proved to be inadequate, it may take such action by air, sea, or land forces as may be necessary to maintain or restore international peace and security. Such action may include demonstrations, blockade, and other operations by air, sea, or land forces of Members of the United Nations.

Article 43

1. All Members of the United Nations, in order to contribute to the maintenance of international peace and security, undertake to make available to the Security Council, on its call and in accordance with a special agreement or agreements, armed forces, assistance, and facilities, including rights of passage, necessary for the purpose of maintaining international peace and security.
2. Such agreement or agreements shall govern the numbers and types of forces, their degree of readiness and general location, and the nature of the facilities and assistance to be provided.
3. The agreement or agreements shall be negotiated as soon as possible on the initiative of the Security Council. They shall be concluded between the Security Council and

Members or between the Security Council and groups of Members and shall be subject to ratification by the signatory states in accordance with their respective constitutional processes.

Article 44

When the Security Council has decided to use force it shall, before calling upon a Member not represented on it to provide armed forces in fulfillment of the obligations assumed under Article 43, invite that Member, if the Member so desires, to participate in the decisions of the Security Council concerning the employment of contingents of that Member's armed forces.

...

Article 48

1. The action required to carry out the decisions of the Security Council for the maintenance of international peace and security shall be taken by all the Members of the United Nations or by some of them, as the Security Council may determine.
2. Such decisions shall be carried out by the Members of the United Nations directly and through their action in the appropriate international agencies of which they are members.

Article 49

The Members of the United Nations shall join in affording mutual assistance in carrying out the measures decided upon by the Security Council.

Article 50

If preventive or enforcement measures against any state are taken by the Security Council, any other state, whether a Member of the United Nations or not, which finds itself confronted with special economic problems arising from the carrying out of those measures shall have the right to consult the Security Council with regard to a solution of those problems.

Article 51

Nothing in the present Charter shall impair the inherent right of individual or collective self-defence if an armed attack occurs against a Member of the United Nations, until the Security Council has taken measures necessary to maintain international peace and security. Measures taken by Members in the exercise of this right of self-defence shall be immediately reported to the Security Council and shall not in any way affect the authority and responsibility of the Security Council under the present Charter to take at any time such action as it deems necessary in order to maintain or restore international peace and security.

Chapter VIII – Regional Arrangements

Article 52

1. Nothing in the present Charter precludes the existence of regional arrangements or agencies for dealing with such matters relating to the maintenance of international peace and security as are appropriate for regional action provided that such arrangements or agencies and their activities are consistent with the Purposes and Principles of the United Nations.
2. The Members of the United Nations entering into such arrangements or constituting such agencies shall make every effort to achieve pacific settlement of local disputes through such regional arrangements or by such regional agencies before referring them to the Security Council.

3. The Security Council shall encourage the development of pacific settlement of local disputes through such regional arrangements or by such regional agencies either on the initiative of the states concerned or by reference from the Security Council.
4. This Article in no way impairs the application of Articles 34 and 35.

Article 53

1. The Security Council shall, where appropriate, utilize such regional arrangements or agencies for enforcement action under its authority. But no enforcement action shall be taken under regional arrangements or by regional agencies without the authorization of the Security Council, with the exception of measures against any enemy state, as defined in paragraph 2 of this Article, provided for pursuant to Article 107 or in regional arrangements directed against renewal of aggressive policy on the part of any such state, until such time as the Organization may, on request of the Governments concerned, be charged with the responsibility for preventing further aggression by such a state.
2. The term enemy state as used in paragraph 1 of this Article applies to any state which during the Second World War has been an enemy of any signatory of the present Charter.

Article 54

The Security Council shall at all times be kept fully informed of activities undertaken or in contemplation under regional arrangements or by regional agencies for the maintenance of international peace and security.

...

CHAPTER XIV – The International Court of Justice

Article 92

The International Court of Justice shall be the principal judicial organ of the United Nations. It shall function in accordance with the annexed Statute, which is based upon the Statute of the Permanent Court of International Justice and forms an integral part of the present Charter.

Article 93

1. All Members of the United Nations are ipso facto parties to the Statute of the International Court of Justice.
2. A state which is not a Member of the United Nations may become a party to the Statute of the International Court of Justice on conditions to be determined in each case by the General Assembly upon the recommendation of the Security Council.

Article 94

1. Each Member of the United Nations undertakes to comply with the decision of the International Court of Justice in any case to which it is a party.
2. If any party to a case fails to perform the obligations incumbent upon it under a judgment rendered by the Court, the other party may have recourse to the Security Council, which may, if it deems necessary, make recommendations or decide upon measures to be taken to give effect to the judgment.

Article 95

Nothing in the present Charter shall prevent Members of the United Nations from entrusting the solution of their differences to other tribunals by virtue of agreements already in existence or which may be concluded in the future.

Article 96

(a) The General Assembly or the Security Council may request the International Court of Justice to give an advisory opinion on any legal question.

(b) Other organs of the United Nations and specialized agencies, which may at any time be so authorized by the General Assembly, may also request advisory opinions of the Court on legal questions arising within the scope of their activities.

CHAPTER XV – The Secretariat

Article 97

The Secretariat shall comprise a Secretary-General and such staff as the Organization may require. The Secretary-General shall be appointed by the General Assembly upon the recommendation of the Security Council. He shall be the chief administrative officer of the Organization.

Article 98

The Secretary-General shall act in that capacity in all meetings of the General Assembly, of the Security Council, of the Economic and Social Council, and of the Trusteeship Council, and shall perform such other functions as are entrusted to him by these organs. The Secretary-General shall make an annual report to the General Assembly on the work of the Organization.

Article 99

The Secretary-General may bring to the attention of the Security Council any matter which in his opinion may threaten the maintenance of international peace and security.

Article 100

1. In the performance of their duties the Secretary-General and the staff shall not seek or receive instructions from any government or from any other authority external to the Organization. They shall refrain from any action which might reflect on their position as international officials responsible only to the Organization.
2. Each Member of the United Nations undertakes to respect the exclusively international character of the responsibilities of the Secretary-General and the staff and not to seek to influence them in the discharge of their responsibilities.

Article 101

1. The staff shall be appointed by the Secretary-General under regulations established by the General Assembly.
2. Appropriate staffs shall be permanently assigned to the Economic and Social Council, the Trusteeship Council, and, as required, to other organs of the United Nations. These staffs shall form a part of the Secretariat.
3. The paramount consideration in the employment of the staff and in the determination of the conditions of service shall be the necessity of securing the highest standards of efficiency, competence, and integrity. Due regard shall be paid to the importance of recruiting the staff on as wide a geographical basis as possible.

CHAPTER XVI – Miscellaneous Provisions

. . .

Article 103

In the event of a conflict between the obligations of the Members of the United Nations under the present Charter and their obligations under any other international agreement, their obligations under the present Charter shall prevail.

Article 104

The Organization shall enjoy in the territory of each of its Members such legal capacity as may be necessary for the exercise of its functions and the fulfillment of its purposes.

Article 105

1. The Organization shall enjoy in the territory of each of its Members such privileges and immunities as are necessary for the fulfillment of its purposes.
2. Representatives of the Members of the United Nations and officials of the Organization shall similarly enjoy such privileges and immunities as are necessary for the independent exercise of their functions in connexion with the Organization.
3. The General Assembly may make recommendations with a view to determining the details of the application of paragraphs 1 and 2 of this Article or may propose conventions to the Members of the United Nations for this purpose.

...

2

Status-of-Forces Agreement between the United Nations and Host Countries

Prefatory Note

On 8 December 1989, in resolution 44/49, the General Assembly requested the Secretary-General to prepare a model Status-of-Forces Agreement (model SOFA) between the UN and host States and to make it available to Member States. The model SOFA is included in the annex to the 'Report of the Secretary-General on the Model Status-of-Forces Agreement for Peace-keeping Operations'[1] of 9 October 1990. It pertains exclusively to UN peace operations.

In some UN peace operations Status-of-Mission Agreements (SOMAs) are also entered between the UN and the host country. Such agreements are generally signed where the focus of the UN's contribution is political or civilian police rather than a military force. They are written in similar terms to SOFAs.[2]

SOFAs are one of the key documents that govern a UN peace operation. Other significant documents include the Security Council resolution establishing the peace operation's mandate and the Memorandum of Understanding (MOU)[3] concluded between the UN and each contributing State. SOFAs are negotiated formal agreements between the UN and the host country that define the legal status of both the peace operation and the individuals serving on that operation. Consequently, SOFAs are the crucial documents that grant the use of facilities, including the privileges and immunities, required by peacekeepers to enable them to fulfil the peace operation's mandate. Based on the language used in SOFAs, such as the term 'shall', the provisions relating to the entry into force, and the settlement of disputes provisions, it is clear that they are legally binding documents.

The model SOFA is intended to serve as a basis for the drafting of individual agreements to be concluded between the UN and host countries and is subject to modifications agreed to between the parties in each individual case. The 1990 model SOFA remains applicable as the starting point when negotiating a specific SOFA between the UN and a host country. Recent Security Council resolutions have provided that the model SOFA applies until a specific SOFA is signed between the parties. The General Assembly, in resolution 52/12B,[4] endorsed a recommendation to the Security Council that, pending the conclusion of a specific SOFA between the UN and the host country, the model SOFA should apply provisionally. The Security Council accepted this recommendation and has started including a paragraph to this effect in resolutions establishing UN peace operations.[5] For example, the Security Council, in resolution 2100, establishing the UN Multidimensional Integrated Stabilization Mission in the Central African Republic (MINUSCA), requested

> the Secretary-General and the transitional authorities of Mali to conclude, within 30 days of the adoption of this resolution, a status-of-forces agreement with regards to MINUSCA, taking into consideration General Assembly resolution 58/82 on the scope of legal protection under the Convention on the Safety of United Nations and Associated Personnel and ***decides*** that pending the conclusion of such

---

1 'Report of the Secretary-General on the Model Status-of-Forces Agreement for Peace-keeping Operations', UN Doc A/45/594, 9 October 1990, Annex (hereafter model SOFA).

2 See, for example, the United Nations Integrated Office in Sierra Leone SOMA 2005, and the United Nations Office in Timor-Leste SOMA 2006. Generally, SOMAs are similar in nature to SOFAs and consequently, this chapter does not address SOMAs.

3 See ch 3 below.

4 GA Res 52/12B of 19 December 1997, Operative Part [7].

5 SC Res 1159 (1998) of 27 March 1998, establishing the United Nations Mission in the Central African Republic (MINURCA), was the first Security Council resolution to provide for the model SOFA to apply provisionally until a specific SOFA was agreed with the host country.

an agreement, the model status-of-forces agreement dated 9 October 1990 (A/45/594), shall apply provisionally.[6]

If the model SOFA does not apply and no operation-specific SOFA has been concluded between the UN and the host country, then the status of the operation and most of the members of that operation, except for the military contingent and locally recruited personnel, will be governed by the Convention on the Privileges and Immunities of the United Nations (Convention).[7] This was confirmed in a legal opinion by the UN Office of Legal Affairs (OLA) in 2004.[8]

The model SOFA develops the principles of law articulated in Articles 104 and 105 of the Charter.[9] These Articles provide that the UN shall enjoy legal capacity, and such privileges and immunities in the territory of each of its Member States, as are necessary for the fulfilment of its purposes. The model SOFA also builds on the privileges and immunities as provided for in the Convention as well as providing a whole set of facilities to the peace operation. In light of the Charter and the Convention, the privileges and immunities granted to the peace operation and its members are for the purpose of carrying out the functions authorised by the mandate for the particular operation. Thus, privileges and immunities are granted in the interests of the UN and the peace operation, and not in the interests of the individual member serving on the operation.

The model SOFA deals with matters such as the status of the peace operation, the status of the members of that operation, responsibility for criminal and civil jurisdiction over the members of the operation, and the settlement of disputes or claims. It outlines the privileges and immunities that apply to both the UN peace operation itself as well as to the differing types of personnel involved in the operation. Recent SOFAs, whilst using the model SOFA as a basis, include a few important amendments and additions which are highlighted as footnotes to the text of the model SOFA included at the end of this chapter. It is therefore important when reviewing the model SOFA reprinted below to take note of the changes reflected in the footnotes to get a clearer understanding of the provisions that are reflected in contemporary SOFAs.

In relation to the privileges and immunities of the peace operation, Paragraph 15 of the model SOFA confirms that a UN peace operation is a subsidiary organ of the UN and enjoys the status, privileges, and immunities of the UN as provided for in the SOFA (where the host country is not a party to the Convention) or in accordance with the Convention (where the host country is a party to the Convention). Pursuant to Article II of the Convention, the UN, its property, and assets are immune from every form of legal process except where the UN has expressly waived its immunity. This is understood as organisational immunity as compared to individual immunities for differing categories of peacekeepers.

In relation to the privileges and immunities of peacekeepers, there are five specific categories of UN personnel in the model SOFA, each of whom is granted a different legal status in regard to privileges and immunities:

1) The Special Representative of the Secretary-General (SRSG), the Commander of the military component, and the head of the UN civilian police component are accorded diplomatic immunity as specified in Section 19 and Section 27 of the Convention;
2) UN civilian staff are granted 'officials' of the UN status and are entitled to the privileges and immunities of 'officials' under Articles V and VII of the Convention. Recent SOFAs specifically state that UN volunteers are also to be regarded as 'officials' in regard to privileges and immunities;
3) Military observers and UN civilian police, including members of formed police units, are accorded the privileges and immunities of 'experts on mission' under Article VI of the Convention;
4) Military personnel of national contingents only have those privileges and immunities specifically provided for in the SOFA; and

6 SC Res 2100 (2013) of 25 April 2013, Operative Part [33]. See also, for example, SC Res 1778 (2007) of 25 September 2007 establishing the United Nations Mission in the Central African Republic and Chad (MINURCAT), Operative Part [4]. See, for example, SC Res 1991 (2011) of 28 June 2011 establishing the United Nations Mission in South Sudan (UNMISS) where the Security Council in Operative Paragraph 26 decided 'that pending the conclusion of such an agreement [SOFA with the Republic of South Sudan], the model status-of-forces agreement dated 9 October 1990 (A/45/594), shall apply provisionally'.

7 See ch 21 below.

8 See UN Juridical Yearbook 2004, 323–5 in the 'Letter to the Acting Chair of the Special Committee on Peacekeeping Operations, United Nations, regarding immunities of civilian police and military personnel'.

9 See ch 1 above.

5) Locally recruited staff enjoy the immunities specified in Sections 18(a), (b), and (c) of the Convention unless otherwise specified in the SOFA.

Paragraph 46 of the model SOFA specifies that '[a]ll members of the United Nations peace-keeping operation, including locally recruited personnel, shall be immune from legal process in respect of words spoken or written and all acts performed by them in their official capacity'. This reflects the immunity granted to officials in Section 18(a) and experts on mission in Section 22(b) of the Convention. Pursuant to the model SOFA and UN practice, the SRSG determines whether the acts of the member of the peace operation are related to 'official duties'. If the SRSG so determines, the Secretary-General can still waive immunity regarding that act.

This determination by the SRSG is important because the UN has made it clear that it does not accept responsibility for the 'off-duty' acts of members of UN peacekeeping forces, that is, for acts carried out in an 'unofficial capacity'. It only accepts responsibility for 'official acts' carried out during the mission. In the determination of 'off-duty' versus 'on-duty' status, the OLA has stated:

> We consider the primary factor in determining an 'off-duty' situation to be whether the member of the peacekeeping mission was acting in a non-official/non-operational capacity when the incident occurred and not whether he/she was in military or civilian attire at the time of the incident or whether the incident occurred inside or outside the area of operations.[10]

The principle was reflected in a domestic Israeli case in 1979 where the court held that a Senegalese member of the United Nations Interim Force in Lebanon (UNIFIL) accused of smuggling explosives into Israeli territory could not claim immunity because 'the defendant was not in the framework of his job during the time he allegedly perpetrated the transfer of explosives for the PLO'.[11]

In terms of criminal offences, the model SOFA provides that if local authorities wish to bring criminal charges against a member of the peace operation who is a civilian, such as UN officials and experts on mission, they need the permission of the SRSG. In such cases the SRSG must carry out his or her own enquiry and then agree with the government of the host country on whether criminal proceedings should be instituted.[12] If agreement cannot be reached, the dispute resolution mechanism contained in the SOFA will be activated.[13]

Whilst the general position is that civilian members are subject to the jurisdiction of the host country in respect of any criminal offences that may be committed by them in the host country, the SRSG may not give permission for criminal proceedings to be commenced if there are concerns with the human rights standards of the local justice system or if the host country does not have a well-functioning court system. In this case, there may be a lacuna in terms of who is responsible for criminally prosecuting civilian members, since the UN can only take administrative disciplinary measures such as redeployment and the removal of benefits, or instigate an administrative sanction such as repatriation of the member to his or her own country. Currently, there is no requirement in international law for the contributing State to criminally prosecute the repatriated civilian member for offences committed on a peace operation. This gap in the law was identified in a March 2005 report entitled 'A Comprehensive Strategy to Eliminate Future Sexual Exploitation and Abuse in United Nations Peacekeeping Operations', commonly known as the 'Zeid Report'.[14] In response to the Zeid Report, the General Assembly appointed a group of legal experts to discuss how best to resolve this problem. One of the recommendations of the group of legal experts was the adoption of a Draft Convention on the criminal accountability of United Nations officials and experts on mission.[15] In the meantime, the General Assembly, in resolution 62/63,[16] strongly urged Member States

---

10 UN Juridical Yearbook 1986, 300–1, 300 on the 'Liability of the United Nations for Claims involving Off-duty Acts of Members of Peace-keeping Forces—Determination of "off-duty" versus "on-duty" status'.

11 UN Juridical Yearbook 1979, 205–10, 207 in the case of 'The Government of Israel against Papa Coli Ben Dista Saar, District Court of Haifa, Judgment of 10 May 1979'.

12 Model SOFA (n 1), [47(a)].

13 Ibid, [53].

14 UN Doc A/59/710, 24 March 2005.

15 'Report of the Group of Legal Experts: Ensuring the Accountability of United Nations Staff and Experts on Mission with Respect to Criminal Acts Committed in Peacekeeping Operations', UN Doc A/60/980, 16 August 2006. Annex III of the report contains a draft convention on the criminal accountability of United Nations officials and experts on mission. Report noted by the General Assembly in resolution 61/29 of 4 December 2006 in which they decided to establish an Ad Hoc Committee to consider it. In its resolutions 62/63 of 6 December 2007 and 63/119 of 11 December 2008, the General Assembly decided that consideration of the report of the group of legal experts, in particular its legal aspects, taking into account the views of Member States, should be continued.

16 GA Res 62/63 of 6 December 2007.

to take appropriate measures to ensure that crimes committed by officials and experts on mission do not go unpunished.[17]

The model SOFA provides that military members of the military component of the peace operation are subject to the exclusive criminal jurisdiction of their contributing State in respect of any criminal offences which may be committed by them in the host country.[18] However, as an administrative measure, the Secretary-General may order the repatriation of any military member of a contingent who has been found culpable of serious misconduct. The recent revisions to the model MOU now include explicit assurances by the contributing State that they will exercise the required criminal and disciplinary jurisdiction over their military personnel. The basis for granting absolute immunity to military personnel of military components from the host country's criminal process is that military personnel are subject to their own military judicial systems for acts committed while serving on peace operations.

In terms of civil offences instituted against a member of the peace operation, it is up to the SRSG to certify whether the alleged offences relate to an official activity of the member. If the SRSG certifies that a civil claim is unrelated to official duties then the proceeding in the local courts may continue.[19] If the SRSG certifies that a civil claim is related to official duties, the proceeding must be discontinued, and the UN and the host country shall settle the dispute by a standing claims commission established for that purpose.[20] In practice, such standing claims commissions have never been set up and claims are settled through internal claims review boards established by the UN.[21] It is important to note that the procedure in relation to civil matters applies to officials, experts on mission, military personnel of national contingents, and locally recruited staff.

Due to the rising number and complexity of third-party claims, the time being taken to process such claims, and the increasing financial burden placed on the UN as a result, the Secretary-General put forward proposals and recommendations regarding ways of limiting the liability of the UN in a 1996 report.[22] The report noted that exemption from liability for third-party claims due to 'operational necessity' was applied in practice by claims review boards. The term 'operational necessity' applies to situations 'where damage results from necessary actions taken by a peacekeeping force in the course of carrying out its operations in pursuance of its mandates'.[23] The report recommended that the principle of 'operational necessity' should be formally incorporated into Paragraph 51 of the model SOFA. Recent SOFAs have included such a reference to 'operational necessity'.

The report also recommended that the General Assembly consider looking at applying temporal and financial limitations to third-party claims. In response, the General Assembly requested the Secretary-General to develop specific guidelines on the principles and scope of application for proposed temporal and financial limitations, and how these could be established in a legally binding way. In a subsequent 1997 report,[24] the Secretary-General concluded that three things were required to establish the proposed temporal and financial limitations in a legally binding way: (i) a General Assembly resolution; (ii) a new liability clause in the SOFA; and (iii) similar provisions in the terms of reference of the claims review board for each mission.

General Assembly resolution 52/247 entitled 'Third-Party Liability: Temporal and Financial Limitations'[25] approved the temporal and financial limitations that would apply to third-party claims against the UN for personal injury, illness, or death. It also approved limitations for property loss or damage resulting from the acts of peacekeepers in the performance of their official duties on UN peace operations. The resolution also endorsed the exemption from liability due to

---

17 The General Assembly repeated this call in GA Res 63/119 of 11 December 2008 and again in GA Res 68/105 of 13 December 2013.

18 Model SOFA (n 1), [47(b)].

19 Ibid, [49(b)].

20 Ibid, [51].

21 For more information on standing claims commissions and claims review boards, see 'Reports of the Secretary-General: Administrative and Budgetary Aspects of the Financing of the United Nations Peacekeeping Operations: Financing of the United Nations Peacekeeping Operations', UN Doc A51/389, 20 September 1996 and UN Doc 51/903, 21 May 1997.

22 See 'Report of the Secretary-General: Administrative and Budgetary Aspects of the Financing of the United Nations Peacekeeping Operations: Financing of United Nations Peacekeeping Operations', UN Doc A/51/389, 20 September 1996.

23 Ibid, [13].

24 See 'Report of the Secretary-General: Administrative and Budgetary Aspects of the Financing of the United Nations Peacekeeping Operations: Financing of United Nations Peacekeeping Operations', UN Doc A/51/903, 21 May 1997.

25 See ch 22 below.

'operational necessity'. Recent SOFAs have included a liability clause applying the temporal and financial limitations approved in resolution 52/247.

Claims under the SOFA are limited to 'disputes of a private law character [which] have been understood to be disputes of the type that arise between two private parties ... [such] as claims arising from vehicle accidents'.[26] Such claims are to be distinguished from those 'based on political or policy-related grievances, such as those "related to actions taken by the Security Council or General Assembly" [which] are excluded from the scope of any obligation to provide an appropriate mode of settlement'.[27]

In the section covering the status of a UN peace operation, the model SOFA requires the UN peace operation and its members to refrain from any action incompatible with the impartial and international nature of their duties and to respect all local laws and regulations of the host country.[28] The requirement to respect local laws and regulations is also reinforced in UN documents such as the 'Secretary-General's Bulletin: Status, Basic Rights and Duties of United Nations Staff Members',[29] and the 'Secretary-General's Bulletin: Regulations Governing the Status Basic Rights and Duties of Officials other than Secretariat Officials, and Experts on Mission'.[30] Both Bulletins emphasise complying with local laws and honouring private legal obligations including orders of competent courts.[31] In return, the government of the host country agrees to respect the exclusively international nature of the UN peace operation.[32]

The model SOFA makes no reference to international humanitarian law (IHL) due to the historical position of the UN not recognising international treaties as being binding upon the institution. This changed in 1993 with the Agreement on the Status of the United Nations Assistance Mission for Rwanda (UNAMIR),[33] which was the first SOFA to include a requirement that the UN peacekeeping forces should conduct their operations in host countries with 'full respect for the principles and spirit of the general conventions applicable to the conduct of military personnel'.[34] However, this 'principles and spirit' clause soon proved inadequate and too imprecise to be of practical use. It was against this background that the Secretary-General promulgated his Bulletin entitled 'Observance by United Nations Forces of International Humanitarian Law'.[35] Section 3 of the Bulletin refers to SOFAs and uses the stronger term 'principles and rules' instead of 'principles and spirit'. The term 'principles and rules' is replicated in recent SOFAs where the UN now undertakes to ensure its peace operations are conducted 'with full respect for the principles and rules of the international conventions applicable to the conduct of military personnel'.[36]

A new section concerned with the safety and security of the peace operation and peacekeepers has been added to recent SOFAs. In this section, the government of the host country agrees to ensure that the provisions of the Convention on the Safety of United Nations and Associated Personnel are applied, and to take all appropriate measures to ensure the safety and security of all peacekeepers.[37] Where the Security Council believes that the government of the host country is not meeting its obligations to protect peacekeepers, the Council has stated, for example: 'the continued obstruction of UNMISS [United Nations Mission in the Republic of South Sudan] by the TGNU [Transitional Government of National Unity], including severe restrictions on freedom of

---

26 Letter from the Assistant Secretary-General, Senior Coordinator for Cholera Response to Ms Farha, Mr Gallon, Mr Puras, and Ms de Albuquerque, 25 November 2014, [87] (hereafter the Letter) <https://spdb.ohchr.org/hrdb/28th/Haiti_ASG_25.11.14_(3.2014).pdf> accessed 9 August 2018 . The Letter concerned the responsibility of the United Nations Stabilization Mission in Haiti (MINUSTAH) for the cholera epidemic that broke out in Haiti in October 2010 which led to the death of 9,145 persons and the infection of 780,000. For further details see: Note by the Secretary General, 'Report of the Special Rapporteur on Extreme Poverty and Human Rights', UN Doc A/71/40823, 26 August 2016 (advanced unedited version), Summary.

27 The Letter (n 26), [89].

28 Model SOFA (n 1), [6].

29 See ch 25 below.

30 See ch 26 below.

31 'Secretary-General's Bulletin: the Status, Basic Rights and Duties of United Nations Staff Members', UN Doc ST/SGB/2002/13, 1 November 2002, Rule 1.2(b); and 'Secretary-General's Bulletin: Regulations Governing Status, Basic Rights, and Duties of Officials other than Secretariat Officials, and Experts on Mission', UN Doc ST/SGB/2002/9, 18 June 2002, Regulation 2(j).

32 Model SOFA (n 1), [7].

33 See Agreement on the Status of the United Nations Assistance Mission for Rwanda (signed 5 November 1993) 1748 UNTS 257.

34 Ibid, [7](a).

35 UN Doc ST/SGB/1999/13, 6 August 1999, entered into force 12 August 1999. See ch 15 below.

36 The exact wording of this phrase may differ slightly between different SOFAs.

37 See ch 14 below.

movement and constraints on mission operations ... may be in violation of its obligations under the Status of Forces Agreement (SOFA).'[38]

Two other major changes in recent SOFAs are the right given to a UN peace operation to establish and operate its own radio station, and the inclusion of certain rights and facilities for contractors. Regarding contractors, it must be stressed that their inclusion in recent SOFAs does not grant them any special privileges or immunities. They are still subject to the civil and criminal jurisdiction of the host country.

There are several other paragraphs which set out the rights and duties that apply to the peace operation and its members. These include the rights of members of the peace operation to enter into, reside in, and depart from the host country;[39] the issuing of numbered identification cards to each member of the peace operation as well as locally recruited personnel, showing full name, date of birth, title or rank, and a photograph;[40] and the wearing of uniforms and carrying of arms by military members and UN civilian police.[41] The model SOFA also gives the SRSG the right to take charge of and dispose of the body of a deceased member of the peace operation.[42]

A further addition to recent SOFAs is a reference to the International Covenant on Civil and Political Rights (ICCPR)[43] in the equivalent of Paragraph 47(a) of the model SOFA concerning the criminal prosecution of members of the civilian component or civilian members of the military component of the UN peace operation.[44] The reference to the ICCPR is to the fair trial provisions in Articles 14 and 15, and the equality before the law provision in Article 26.

As provided for in Paragraph 16 of the model SOFA, UN premises, such as camps, are inviolable. One effect of that inviolability is that 'no local officer or official may enter these premises without the consent of, and under the conditions agreed to, by the United Nations'.[45] However, the UN has recognised that there is no right to claim inviolability of its premises where such premises are used 'as a place of refuge for persons evading justice or of diplomatic asylum. There is no legal basis for the United Nations to assert such a right ... law and practice points to a contrary conclusion'.[46] The United Nations Interim Security Force for Abyei (UNISFA) SOFA reinforces that approach:

> Without prejudice to the mandate of UNISFA, the Force Commander shall not permit the premises to become a refuge for persons seeking to avoid arrest under the law of Sudan for crimes that they are alleged to have committed and evidence of which has been provided to the Force Commander by the relevant national authorities.[47]

The UN may also sign a SOFA with another international organisation and host State, for example, the Agreement between the United Nations and the African Union and the Government of South Sudan concerning the status of the African Union/United Nations Hybrid Operation in Darfur.[48] That SOFA has a similar structure to that of the model SOFA.

Reference

Title	Draft Model Status-of-Forces Agreement between the United Nations and Host Countries
Author	General Assembly
Date	9 October 1990
Source	UN Doc A/45/594, Annex
Full Text	<http://www.un.org/Docs/journal/asp/ws.asp?m=A/45/594>[49]

---

38 SC Res 2327 (2016) of 16 December 2016, Preamble and [19]. See also SC Res 2301 of 20 July 2016, [51], regarding the United Nations Multidimensional Integrated Stabilization Mission in the Central African Republic (MINUSCA) SOFA.

39 Model SOFA (n 1), [32].

40 Ibid, [35].

41 Ibid, [37].

42 Ibid, [50].

43 See ch 6.

44 See, for example, 'Agreement between the Government of Sudan and the United Nations concerning the Status of the United Nations Mission in Sudan (UNMIS)' (signed 28 December 2005).

45 See Note to the Assistant Secretary-General for Political Affairs, concerning the legal status of the United Nations premises and the handing over of political leaders to the competent authorities of a Member State, signed 11 September 1998, [4].

46 Ibid, [5].

47 Agreement between the United Nations and the Government of South Sudan concerning the Status of the United Nations Interim Security Force for Abyei (UNISFA SOFA) (signed 1 October 2012) [16].

48 Agreement between the United Nations and the African Union and the Government of South Sudan concerning the status of the African Union/United Nations Hybrid Operation in Darfur (UNAMID SOFA), signed on 9 February 2008 (copy on file with the author).

49 Accessed 1 November 2017.

Draft Model Status-of-Forces Agreement between the United Nations and Host Countries[50]

I. Definitions

1. For the purpose of the present Agreement the following definitions shall apply:[51]

II. Application of the Present Agreement

2. Unless specifically provided otherwise, the provisions of the present Agreement and any obligation undertaken by [Government][52] or any privilege, immunity, facility or concession granted to the United Nations peace-keeping operation or any member thereof apply in [the area of operations/territory] only.[53]

---

50 From Draft Model Status-of-Forces Agreement between the United Nations and Host Countries, by General Assembly, © 1990 United Nations. Reprinted with the permission of the United Nations.
The footnotes have been added here to explain how SOFAs have developed since the model SOFA was first promulgated. To do this the model SOFA has been compared with the following five more recent SOFAs and the major changes highlighted (minor textual changes are ignored):

a. Agreement between the United Nations and the Government of Haiti concerning the Status of the United Nations Operation in Haiti (MINUSTAH SOFA), signed on 9 July 2004 (reproduced in the UN Juridical Yearbook 2004, 28–40);
b. Agreement between the Government of Sudan and the United Nations concerning the Status of the United Nations Mission in Sudan (UNMIS SOFA), signed on 28 December 2005 (reproduced in the UN Juridical Yearbook 2005, 44–60);
c. Agreement between the United Nations and the African Union and the Government of Sudan concerning the Status of the African Union/United Nations Hybrid Operation in Sudan (UNAMID SOFA), signed on 9 February 2008 (copy on file with authors);
d. The Status of Forces Agreement between the United Nations and the Government of the Republic of South Sudan concerning the United Nations Mission in South Sudan, signed on 8 August 2011 (UNMISS SOFA) (reproduced in the UN Juridical Yearbook 2011, 50–65); and
e. The Agreement between the United Nations and the Government of South Sudan concerning the status of the United Nations Interim Security Force for Abyei (UNIFSA SOFA) signed on 1 October 2012 (reproduced in UN Juridical Yearbook 2012, 63–78).

51 The model SOFA leaves the definitions section blank but includes a footnote stating:

'This section will contain definitions of the main terms used in the agreement such as:

'Participating State' means a State contributing personnel to the military and/or civilian components of the United Nations peace keeping operation.

'Convention' means the Convention on the Privileges and Immunities of the United Nations adopted by the General Assembly of the United Nations on 13 February 1946.'

Recent SOFAs include a definition of the peace operation itself and what it consists of: Special Representative, civilian component and military component, as well as definitions for a 'member of the [Peace Operation]', 'the Government', 'the territory', a 'participating State' and 'the Convention'. There are additional definitions for 'contractors', 'vehicles', 'vessels' and 'aircraft'. The term 'contractors' has been defined in the UNMIS SOFA as follows:

'contractors' means persons, other than members of UNMIS, engaged by the United Nations, including juridical as well as natural persons and their employees and sub-contractors, to perform services for UNMIS and/or to supply equipment, provisions, supplies, materials and other goods, including spare parts and means of transport, in support of UNMIS activities. Such contractors shall not be considered third party beneficiaries to this Agreement.

52 The model SOFA includes the footnote:

'The term Government as used in the present Agreement will be defined to mean the Government of the host country or Administration having de facto authority over the territory and/or area of operations in question.'

The UNMIS SOFA defines 'Government' to mean 'the Government of Sudan, the Government of National Unity of Sudan and any successor Government of Sudan', whilst in the UNAMID SOFA, it is now defined as 'the Government of the Republic of Sudan'. The MINUSTAH SOFA simply defines 'Government' to mean the Government of Haiti.

53 Recent SOFAs add contractors in here so the phrase becomes 'granted to [Peace Operation] or any member thereof or to contractors shall apply in [the area of operations/territory] only'.

III. Application of the Convention

3. The Convention on the Privileges and Immunities of the United Nations of 13 February 1946 shall apply to the United Nations peace-keeping operation subject to the provisions specified in the present Agreement.[54]

   or

4. The United Nations peace-keeping operation, its property, funds and assets, and its members, including the Special Representative/Commander, shall enjoy the privileges and immunities specified in the present Agreement as well as those provided for in the Convention, to which [host country] is a Party.[55]
5. Article II of the Convention, which applies to the United Nations peace-keeping operation, shall also apply to the property, funds and assets of participating States used in connection with the United Nations peace-keeping operation.

IV. Status of the Peace-Keeping Operation[56]

6. The United Nations peace-keeping operation and its members shall refrain from any action or activity incompatible with the impartial and international nature of their duties or inconsistent with the spirit of the present arrangements. The United Nations peace-keeping operation and its members shall respect all local laws and regulations.[57] The Special Representative/ Commander shall take all appropriate measures to ensure the observance of those obligations.
7. The Government undertakes to respect the exclusively international nature of the United Nations peace-keeping operation.

United Nations Flag and Vehicle Markings

8. The Government recognizes the right of the United Nations peace-keeping operation to display within [host country/territory] the United Nations flag on its headquarters, camps or other premises, vehicles, vessels and otherwise as decided by the Special Representative/ Commander. Other flags or pennants may be displayed only in exceptional cases. In these cases, the United Nations peace-keeping operation shall give sympathetic consideration to observations or requests of the Government of [host country].

---

54 The model SOFA includes the footnote:

> As a general rule, the basic privileges and immunities of a United Nations peace-keeping operation consist of provisions that flow from the Convention on the Privileges and Immunities of the United Nations adopted by the General Assembly on 13 February 1946. However, while the Convention is in force with respect to 124 Member States, there are a number of States that are not a party to it and there may also be United Nations operations involving relations with entities other than States. Thus, in such cases, the Status Agreement itself must provide specifically for the application of the Convention.

55 The model SOFA includes the footnote: 'Provision to be used where the host country is a party to the said Convention.' In the MINUSTAH, UNMIS, and UNAMID SOFAs, and all UN SOFAs looked at by the authors, it is the second option in Paragraph 4 of the model SOFA that is used. The only difference is that the phrase 'to which [host country] is a Party' is no longer included here but is added to the definition of 'Convention' in the definitions section.

56 Recent SOFAs include an important new Paragraph in this section between Paragraphs 6 and 7 of the model SOFA concerning the application of international humanitarian law. For example, the UNMIS SOFA states:

> 6. Without prejudice to the mandate of UNMIS and its international status:
>
> (a) The United Nations shall ensure that UNMIS shall conduct its operation in Sudan with full respect for the principles and rules of the international conventions applicable to the conduct of military personnel. These international conventions include the four Geneva Conventions of 12 August 1949 and their Additional Protocols of 8 June 1977 and the UNESCO Convention of 14 May 1954 for the Protection of Cultural Property in the Event of Armed Conflict;
>
> (b) The Government undertakes to treat at all times the military personnel of UNMIS with full respect for the principles and rules of the international conventions applicable to the treatment of military personnel. These international conventions include the four Geneva Conventions of 12 August 1949 and their Additional Protocols of 8 June 1977.
>
> UNMIS and the Government shall ensure accordingly that members of their respective military personnel are fully acquainted with the principles and rules of the above-mentioned international instruments.

57 The UNAMID SOFA states 'shall respect relevant rules and principles of international law as well as all local laws and regulations'. MINUSTAH and UNMIS SOFAs use the same wording as the model SOFA, 'shall respect all local laws and regulations'.

9. Vehicles, vessels and aircraft of the United Nations peace-keeping operation shall carry a distinctive United Nations identification, which shall be notified to the Government.

Communications

10. The United Nations peace-keeping operation shall enjoy the facilities in respect to communications provided in article III of the Convention and shall, in co-ordination with the Government, use such facilities as may be required for the performance of its task. Issues with respect to communications which may arise and which are not specifically provided for in the present Agreement shall be dealt with pursuant to the relevant provisions of the Convention.

11. Subject to the provisions of paragraph 10:[58]

(a) The United Nations peace-keeping operation shall have authority to install and operate radio sending and receiving stations as well as satellite systems to connect appropriate points within the territory of [host country/territory] with each other and with United Nations offices in other countries, and to exchange traffic with the United Nations global telecommunications network. The telecommunications services shall be operated in accordance with the International Telecommunication Convention and Regulations and the frequencies on which any such station may be operated shall be decided upon in co-operation with the Government and shall be communicated by the United Nations to the International Frequency Registration Board.

(b) The United Nations peace-keeping operation shall enjoy, within the territory of [host country/territory], the right to unrestricted communication by radio (including satellite, mobile and hand-held radio), telephone, telegraph, facsimile or any other means,[59] and of establishing the necessary facilities for maintaining such communications within and between premises of the United Nations peace-keeping operation, including the laying of cables and land lines and the establishment of fixed and mobile radio sending, receiving and repeater stations. The frequencies on which the radio will operate shall be decided upon in co-operation with the Government. It is understood that connections with the local system of telegraphs, telex and telephones may be made only after consultation and in accordance with arrangements with the Government, it being further understood that the use of the local system of telegraphs, telex and telephones will be charged at the most favourable rate.

(c) The United Nations peace-keeping operation may make arrangements through its own facilities for the processing and transport of private mail addressed to or emanating from members of the United Nations peace-keeping operation. The Government shall be informed of the nature of such arrangements and shall not interfere with or apply

---

58 Paragraph 11 of the model SOFA has been added to in recent SOFAs to include the right of the UN to establish its own radio stations for disseminating information related to its mandate. For example, the MINUSTAH SOFA states:

> MINUSTAH shall have the right to install and operate United Nations radio stations to disseminate information relating to its mandate.

The UNMIS and UNAMID SOFAs significantly expand upon this. For example, the UNMIS SOFA states:

> UNMIS shall have the right to establish, install and operate United Nations radio stations under its exclusive control to disseminate to the public in Sudan information relating to its mandate. Programmes broadcast on such stations shall be under the exclusive editorial control of UNMIS and shall not be subject to any form of censorship ...

The UNMIS and UNAMID SOFAs also include the 'right to disseminate to the public in Sudan information relating to its mandate through official printed materials and publications, which UNMIS [or UNAMID] may produce itself or through private publishing companies in Sudan'.

The UNISFA SOFA states that 'UNISFA shall have the right to disseminate information in the Mission Area through official materials and publications relating to its mandated activities in support of the implementation of the 20 June and 30 July 2011 Agreements'.

59 Due to the explosion of the Internet and new technology, electronic mail is now one of the communication methods specified in recent SOFAs along with radio communication, telephone, and fax from the model SOFA. Telegraph is another method of communication specified in the model SOFA that is outdated and no longer referred to in recent SOFAs.

censorship to the mail of the United Nations peace-keeping operation or its members. In the event that postal arrangements applying to private mail of members of the United Nations peace-keeping operation are extended to transfer of currency or the transport of packages and parcels, the conditions under which such operations are conducted shall be agreed with the Government.

Travel and Transport[60]

12. The United Nations peace-keeping operation and its members shall enjoy, together with its vehicles, vessels, aircraft and equipment, freedom of movement throughout the [host country/territory]. That freedom shall, with respect to large movements of personnel, stores or vehicles through airports or on railways or roads used for general traffic within the [host country/territory], be co-ordinated with the Government. The Government undertakes to supply the United Nations peace-keeping operation, where necessary, with maps and other information, including locations of mine fields and other dangers and impediments, which may be useful in facilitating its movements.
13. Vehicles, including all military vehicles, vessels and aircraft of the United Nations peace-keeping operation shall not be subject to registration or licensing by the Government provided that all such vehicles shall carry the third party insurance required by relevant legislation.
14. The United Nations peace-keeping operation may use roads, bridges, canals and other waters, port facilities and airfields without the payment of dues, tolls or charges, including wharfage charges. However, the United Nations peace-keeping operation will not claim exemption from charges which are in fact charges for services rendered.

Privileges and Immunities of the United Nations Peace-Keeping Operation

15. The United Nations peace-keeping operation, as a subsidiary organ of the United Nations, enjoys the status, privileges and immunities of the United Nations [as provided for in the present agreement][61] [in accordance with the Convention].[62] The provision of article II of the Convention which applies to the United Nations peace-keeping operation shall also apply to the property, funds and assets of participating States used in [host country/territory] in connection with the national contingents serving in the United Nations peace-keeping operation, as provided for in paragraph 5 of the present Agreement. The Government recognizes the right of the United Nations peace-keeping operation in particular:[63]
    (a) To import, free of duty or other restrictions, equipment, provisions, supplies and other goods which are for the exclusive and official use of the United Nations peace-keeping operation and for resale in the commissaries provided hereinafter;
    (b) To establish, maintain and operate commissaries at its headquarters, camps and posts for the benefit of the members of the United Nations peace-keeping operation, but not of locally recruited personnel. Such commissaries may provide goods

---

60 This section is substantially the same in recent SOFAs except contractors now also enjoy freedom of movement throughout the host country. For example, the UNMIS SOFA states:

> UNMIS, its members and contractors, together with their property, equipment, provisions, supplies, materials and other goods, including spare parts, as well as vehicles, vessels and aircraft of contractors used exclusively in the performance of their services for UNMIS, shall enjoy full and unrestricted freedom of movement without delay throughout Sudan by the most direct route possible . . .

61 The model SOFA includes the footnote: 'In case the other party is not party to the Convention.'

62 The model SOFA includes the footnote: 'In case the other party is a party to the Convention.' (Recent SOFAs use the phrase 'in accordance with the Convention'.)

63 The rights granted to the UN Peace Operation in (a) to import free of duty, in (c) to clear ex customs and excise warehouse free of duty, and in (d) to re-export or dispose of such equipment are also now accorded to contractors. This is a very recent addition found in the 2005 UNMIS, 2008 UNAMID, and 2011 UNMISS SOFAs, but not in the 2004 MINUSTAH SOFA.

of a consumable nature and other articles to be specified in advance. The Special Representative/Commander shall take all necessary measures to prevent abuse of such commissaries and the sale or resale of such goods to persons other than members of the United Nations peace-keeping operation, and he shall give sympathetic consideration to observation or requests of the Government concerning the operation of the commissaries;

(c) To clear ex customs and excise warehouse, free of duty or other restrictions, equipment, provisions, supplies and other goods which are for the exclusive and official use of the United Nations peace-keeping operation or for resale in the commissaries provided for above;

(d) To re-export or otherwise dispose of such equipment, as far as it is still usable, all unconsumed provisions, supplies and other goods so imported or cleared ex customs and excise warehouse which are not transferred, or otherwise disposed of, on terms and conditions to be agreed upon, to the competent local authorities of the [host country/territory] or to an entity nominated by them.

To the end that such importation, clearances, transfer or exportation may be effected with the least possible delay, a mutually satisfactory procedure, including documentation, shall be agreed between the United Nations peace-keeping operation and the Government at the earliest possible date.

V. Facilities for the United Nations Peace-Keeping Operation[64]

Premises Required for Conducting the Operational and Administrative Activities of the United Nations Peace-Keeping Operation and for Accommodating Members of the Peace-Keeping Operation

16. The Government of [host country] shall provide without cost to the United Nations peace-keeping operation and in agreement with the Special Representative/Commander such areas for headquarters, camps or other premises as may be necessary for the conduct of the operational and administrative activities of the United Nations peace-keeping operation and for the accommodation of the members of the United Nations peace-keeping operation. Without prejudice to the fact that all such premises remain [host country] territory, they shall be inviolable and subject to the exclusive control and authority of the United Nations. Where United Nations troops are co-located with military personnel of the host country, a permanent, direct and immediate access by the United Nations peace-keeping operation to those premises shall be guaranteed.[65]

17. The Government undertakes to assist the United Nations peace-keeping operation as far as possible in obtaining and making available, where applicable, water, electricity and other facilities free of charge, or, where this is not possible, at the most favourable rate and in the case of interruption or threatened interruption of service, to give as far as is within its powers the same priority to the needs of the United Nations peace-keeping operation as to essential government services. Where such utilities or facilities are not provided free of charge, payment shall be made by the United Nations peace-keeping operation on terms to be agreed with the competent authority. The United Nations

64 Recent SOFAs append 'and its Contractors'.

65 The UNISFA SOFA has an extra sentence which provides:

> Without prejudice to the mandate of UNISFA, the Force Commander shall not permit the premises to become a refuge for persons seeking to avoid arrest under the law of Sudan for crimes that they are alleged to have committed and evidence of which has been provided to the Force Commander by the relevant national authorities.

peace-keeping operation shall be responsible for the maintenance and upkeep of facilities so provided.[66]

18. The United Nations peace-keeping operation shall have the right, where necessary, to generate, within its premises, electricity for its use and to transmit and distribute such electricity.

19. The United Nations alone may consent to the entry of any government officials or of any other person not member of the United Nations peace-keeping operation to such premises.

Provisions, Supplies and Services, and Sanitary Arrangements[67]

20. The Government undertakes to assist the United Nations peace-keeping operation as far as possible in obtaining equipment, provisions, supplies and other goods and services from local sources required for its subsistence and operations. In making the purchases on the local market, the United Nations peace-keeping operation shall, on the basis of observations made and information provided by the Government in that respect, avoid any adverse effect on the local economy. The Government shall exempt the United Nations peace-keeping operation from general sales taxes in respect of all official local purchases.[68]

21. The United Nations peace-keeping operation and the Government shall co-operate with respect to sanitary services and shall extend to each other the fullest co-operation in matters concerning health, particularly with respect to the control of communicable diseases, in accordance with international conventions.

Recruitment of Local Personnel

22. The United Nations peace-keeping operation may recruit locally such personnel as it requires. Upon the request of the Special Representative/Commander, the Government undertakes to facilitate the recruitment of qualified local staff by the United Nations peace-keeping operation and to accelerate the process of such recruitment.[69]

---

66 The UNMISS SOFA goes on to state: 'In the event of interruption or threatened interruption of service, the Government undertakes to give as far as is within its powers the same priority to the needs of UNMISS as to essential government services.'

67 In recent SOFAs, there are two additional paragraphs in this section, one coming before Paragraph 20 and one between Paragraphs 20 and 21 of the model SOFA. The Paragraph inserted before Paragraph 20 of the model SOFA concerns the Government providing all the necessary authorisations, permits, and licences required for the import of equipment, provisions, supplies, and other equipment for both the Peace Operation and contractors. The paragraph inserted between Paragraphs 20 and 21 of the model SOFA concerns contractors exclusively and includes, *inter alia*, agreement by the Government that they will provide facilities for the repatriation of contractors in times of crisis.

For example, the UNMIS and UNMISS SOFAs state:

> For the proper performance of the services provided by contractors, other than Sudan nationals resident in Sudan, in support of UNMIS, the Government agrees to provide contractors with facilities for their entry into and departure from Sudan, without delay or hindrance, and for their residence in Sudan, as well as for their repatriation in time of crisis. For this purpose, the Government shall promptly issue to contractors, free of charge and without any restrictions and within forty-eight (48) hours of application, all necessary visas, licenses, permits and registrations. Contractors, other than Sudan nationals resident in Sudan, shall be accorded exemption from taxes and monetary contributions in Sudan on services, equipment, provisions, supplies, fuel, materials and other goods, including spare parts and means of transport, provided to UNMIS, including corporate, income, social security and other similar taxes arising directly from or related directly to the provision of such services or goods.

68 The UNMISS SOFA has a more detailed paragraph:

> The Government undertakes to assist UNMISS as far as possible in obtaining equipment, provisions, supplies, fuel, materials and other goods and services from local sources required for its subsistence and operations. In respect of equipment, provisions, supplies, fuel, materials and other goods and services purchased locally by UNMISS or by contractors for the official and exclusive use of UNMISS, the Government shall make appropriate administrative arrangements for the remission or return of any excise, tax or monetary contribution payable as part of the price. The Government shall exempt UNMISS and contractors from general sales taxes in respect of all local purchases for official use. In making purchases on the local market, UNMISS shall, on the basis of observations made and information provided by the Government in that respect, avoid any adverse effect on the local economy.

69 The UNISFA SOFA adds an extra sentence:

> Without prejudice to UNISFA's right to recruit such local personnel as it requires in accordance with the United Nations Staff Regulations and Rules as well as relevant United Nations policies and procedures, in the event the alleged activities of such personnel pose serious concerns for the Governments of Sudan and South Sudan, UNISFA and the two Governments as far as the implementation of the 20 June Agreement is concerned, and UNISFA and the Government of Sudan, as far as the implementation of the 30 July agreement is concerned, shall cooperate in a spirit of good faith and partnership to address such concerns when they are supported by evidence.

Currency

23. The Government undertakes to make available to the United Nations peace-keeping operation, against reimbursement in mutually acceptable currency, [local] currency required for the use of the United Nations peace-keeping operation, including the pay of its members, at the rate of exchange most favourable to the United Nations peace-keeping operation.

VI. Status of the Members of the United Nations Peace-Keeping Operation[70]

Privileges and Immunities

24. The Special Representative, the Commander of the military component of the United Nations peace-keeping operation, the head of the United Nations civilian police, and such high-ranking members of the Special Representative/Commander's staff as may be agreed upon with the Government shall have the status specified in sections 19 and 27 of the Convention, provided that the privileges and immunities therein referred to shall be those accorded to diplomatic envoys by [national or international] law.
25. Members of the United Nations Secretariat assigned to the civilian component to serve with the United Nations peace-keeping operation remain officials of the United Nations entitled to the privileges and immunities of articles V and VII of the Convention.[71]
26. Military observers, United Nations civilian police and civilian personnel other than United Nations officials whose names are for the purpose notified to the Government by the Special Representative/Commander shall be considered as experts on mission within the meaning of article VI of the Convention.[72]
27. Military personnel of national contingents assigned to the military component of the United Nations peace-keeping operation shall have the privileges and immunities specifically provided for in the present Agreement.
28. Unless otherwise specified in the present Agreement, locally recruited members of the United Nations peace-keeping operation shall enjoy the immunities concerning official acts and exemptions from taxation and national service obligations provided for in sections 18 (a), (b) and (c) of the Convention.[73]
29. Members of the United Nations peace-keeping operation shall be exempt from taxation on the pay and emoluments received from the United Nations or from a participating State and any income received from outside [host country/territory]. They shall also be exempt from all other direct taxes, except municipal rates for services enjoyed, and from all registration fees and charges.
30. Members of the United Nations peace-keeping operation shall have the right to import free of duty their personal effects in connection with their arrival in [host country/territory]. They shall be subject to the laws and regulations of [host country/territory] governing customs and foreign exchange with respect to personal property not required by them by reason of their presence in [host country/territory] with the United Nations peace-keeping

---

70 The status of members of a Peace Operation remains almost identical in recent SOFAs. One reason for this is because the status of officials and experts on mission is defined in the Convention on the Privileges and Immunities of the United Nations.

71 UN Volunteers are now included in this Paragraph, giving them the status of 'officials' with regard to their privileges and immunity. For example, the UNMIS SOFA states:

> Officials of the United Nations assigned to the civilian component to serve with UNMIS, as well as United Nations Volunteers, who shall be assimilated thereto, remain officials of the United Nations entitled to the privileges and immunities of Articles V and VII of the Convention.

72 Other categories of UN personnel who have been accorded expert on mission status may be inserted in here. For example, the UNMISS and UNISFA SOFAs include the additional category of 'military liaison officers'.

73 The UNISFA SOFA adds: 'UNISFA agrees to coordinate with the Government with a view to the deferral of any national service obligations of locally recruited personnel of UNISFA during the period of their employment. UNISFA shall accordingly notify the Government when such employment begins and ends.'

operation. Special facilities will be granted by the Government for the speedy processing of entry and exit formalities for all members of the United Nations peace-keeping operation, including the military component, upon prior written notification. On departure from [host country/territory], members of the United Nations peace-keeping operation may, notwithstanding the above-mentioned exchange regulations, take with them such funds as the Special Representative/Commander certifies were received in pay and emoluments from the United Nations or from a participating State and are a reasonable residue thereof. Special arrangements shall be made for the implementation of the present provisions in the interests of the Government and the members of the United Nations peace-keeping operation.

31. The Special Representative/Commander shall co-operate with the Government and shall render all assistance within his power in ensuring the observation of the customs and fiscal laws and regulations of [host country/territory] by the members of the United Nations peace-keeping operation, in accordance with the present Agreement.

Entry, Residence and Departure

32. The Special Representative/Commander and members of the United Nations peace-keeping operation shall, whenever so required by the Special Representative/Commander, have the right to enter into, reside in and depart from [host country/territory].

33. The Government of [host country/territory] undertakes to facilitate the entry into and departure from [host country/territory] of the Special Representative/Commander and members of the United Nations peace-keeping operation and shall be kept informed of such movement. For that purpose, the Special Representative/Commander and members of the United Nations peace-keeping operation shall be exempt from passport and visa regulations and immigration inspection and restrictions on entering into or departing from [host country/territory]. They shall also be exempt from any regulations governing the residence of aliens in [host country/territory], including registration, but shall not be considered as acquiring any right to permanent residence or domicile in [host country/territory].

34. For the purpose of such entry or departure, members of the United Nations peace-keeping operation shall only be required to have: (a) an individual or collective movement order issued by or under the authority of the Special Representative/Commander or any appropriate authority of a participating State; and (b) a personal identity card issued in accordance with paragraph 35 of the present Agreement, except in the case of first entry, when the personal identity card issued by the appropriate authorities of a participating State shall be accepted in lieu of the said identity card.

Identification

35. The Special Representative/Commander shall issue to each member of the United Nations peace-keeping operation before or as soon as possible after such member's first entry into [host country/territory], as well as to all locally recruited personnel, a numbered identity card, which shall show full name, date of birth, title or rank, service (if appropriate) and photograph. Except as provided for in paragraph 34 of the present Agreement, such identity card shall be the only document required of a member of the United Nations peace-keeping operation.[74]

36. Members of the United Nations peace-keeping operation as well as locally recruited personnel shall be required to present, but not to surrender, their [United Nations peace-keeping operation] identity cards upon demand of an appropriate official of the Government.

---

74 In recent SOFAs, the Special Representative issues a numbered identity card to contractors as well as each member of the Peace Operation and locally recruited personnel.

Uniform and Arms

37. Military members and the United Nations civilian police of the United Nations peace-keeping operation shall wear, while informing official duties, the national military or police uniform of their respective States with standard United Nations accoutrements.[75] United Nations Security Officers and Field Service Officers may wear the United Nations uniform. The wearing of civilian dress by the above-mentioned members of the United Nations peace-keeping operation may be authorized by the Special Representative/Commander at other times. Military members and civilian police of the United Nations peace-keeping operation and United Nations Security Officers designated by the Special Representative/Commander may possess and carry arms while on duty in accordance with their orders.[76]

Permits and Licences

38. The Government agrees to accept as valid, without tax or fee, a permit or licence issued by the Special Representative/Commander for the operation by any member of the United Nations peace-keeping operation, including locally recruited personnel, of any [United Nations peace-keeping operation] transport or communication equipment and for the practice of any profession or occupation in connection with the functioning of the United Nations peace-keeping operation, provided that no licence to drive a vehicle or pilot an aircraft shall be issued to any person who is not already in possession of an appropriate and valid licence.[77]

39. Without prejudice to the provisions of paragraph 37, the Government further agrees to accept as valid, without tax or fee, a permit or licence issued by the Special Representative/Commander to a member of the United Nations peace-keeping operation for the carrying or use of firearms or ammunition in connection with the functioning of the United Nations peace-keeping operation.

Military Police, Arrest and Transfer of Custody, and Mutual Assistance

40. The Special Representative shall take all appropriate measures to ensure the maintenance of discipline and good order among members of the United Nations peace-keeping operation, as well as locally recruited personnel. To this end personnel designated by the Special Representative/Commander shall police the premises of the United Nations peace-keeping operation and such areas where its members are deployed. Elsewhere such personnel shall be employed only subject to arrangements with the Government and in liaison with it in so far as such employment is necessary to maintain discipline and order among members of the United Nations peace-keeping operation.

41. The military police of the United Nations peace-keeping operation shall have the power of arrest over the military members of the United Nations peace-keeping operation. Military personnel placed under arrest outside their own contingent areas shall be transferred to their contingent Commander for appropriate disciplinary action. The personnel mentioned in paragraph 40 above may take into custody any other person on the premises of the United Nations peace-keeping operation. Such other person shall be delivered immediately to the nearest appropriate official of the Government for the purpose of dealing with any offence or disturbance on such premises.

---

75 Recent SOFAs include extra categories of personnel in United Nations military observers and United Nations military liaison officers.

76 Recent SOFAs expand upon the text in regard to the carrying of arms. For example, the UNMIS SOFA states:

> Military members, military observers, and civilian police of UNMIS, United Nations Security Officers and United Nations close protection officers designated by the Special Representative may possess and carry arms, ammunition and other items of military equipment, including global positioning devices, while on official duty in accordance with their orders. Those carrying weapons while on official duty other than those undertaking close protection duties must be in uniform at that time.

77 The privilege in this Paragraph now extends to contractors.

42. Subject to the provisions of paragraphs 24 and 26, officials of the Government may take into custody any member of the United Nations peace-keeping operation:
    (a) When so requested by the Special Representative/Commander; or
    (b) When such a member of the United Nations peace-keeping operation is apprehended in the commission or attempted commission of a criminal offence. Such person shall be delivered immediately, together with any weapons or other item seized, to the nearest appropriate representative of the United Nations peace-keeping operation, whereafter the provisions of paragraph 47 shall apply *mutatis mutandis.*

43. When a person is taken into custody under paragraph 41 or paragraph 42 (b), the United Nations peace-keeping operation or the Government, as the case may be, may make a preliminary interrogation but may not delay the transfer of custody. Following such transfer, the person concerned shall be made available upon request to the arresting authority for further interrogation.

44. The United Nations peace-keeping operation and the Government shall assist each other in carrying out all necessary investigations into offences in respect of which either or both have an interest, in the production of witnesses and in the collection and production of evidence, including the seizure of and, if appropriate, the handing over of items connected with an offence. The handing over of any such items may be made subject to their return within the terms specified by the authority delivering them. Each shall notify the other of the disposition of any case in the outcome of which the other may have an interest or in which there has been a transfer of custody under the provisions of paragraphs 41–43.

45. The Government shall ensure the prosecution of persons subject to its criminal jurisdiction who are accused of acts in relation to the United Nations peace-keeping operation or its members which, if committed in relation to the forces of the Government, would have rendered such acts liable to prosecution.[78]

---

78 This paragraph is not included in this section in recent SOFAs because it is now included in a new section on 'Safety and Security' which brings the provisions of the Convention on the Safety of United Nations and Associated Personnel into recent SOFAs. For example, the UNMIS SOFA states:

> 48. The Government shall ensure that the provisions of the Convention on the Safety of United Nations and Associate Personnel are applied to and in respect of UNMIS, its members and associated personnel and their equipment and premises. In particular:
> (i) the Government shall take all appropriate measures within its capabilities to ensure the safety, security and freedom of movement of UNMIS, its members and associated personnel and their property and assets. It shall take all appropriate steps within its capabilities, to protect members of UNMIS and its associated personnel and their equipment and premises from attack or any action that prevents them from discharging their mandate. This is without prejudice to the fact that all premises of UNMIS are inviolable and subject to the exclusive control and authority of the United Nations;
> (ii) if members of UNMIS or its associated personnel are captured, detained or taken hostage in the course of the performance of their duties and their identification has been established, they shall not be subjected to interrogation and they shall be promptly released and returned to United Nations or other appropriate authorities. Pending their release such personnel shall be treated in accordance with universally recognized standards of human rights and the principles and spirit of the Geneva Conventions of 1949;
> (iii) the Government shall ensure that the following acts are established as crimes under its national law and make them punishable by appropriate penalties, taking into account their grave nature:
> a) a murder, kidnapping or other attack upon the person or liberty of any member of UNMIS or its associated personnel;
> b) a violent attack upon the official premises, the private accommodation or the means of transportation of any member of UNMIS or its associated personnel likely to endanger his or her person or liberty;
> c) a threat to commit any such attack with the objective of compelling a physical or juridical person to do or to refrain from doing any act;
> d) an attempt to commit any such attack; and
> e) an act constituting participation as an accomplice in any such attack, or in an attempt to commit such attack, or in organizing or ordering others to commit such attack;
> (iv) the Government shall establish its jurisdiction over the crimes set out in paragraph 48 (iii) above: (a) when the crime was committed on the territory of Sudan; (b) when the alleged offender is a national of Sudan; (c) when the alleged offender, other than a member of UNMIS, is present in the territory of Sudan, unless it has extradited such a person to the State on whose territory the crime was committed, or to the State of his or her nationality, or to the State of his or her habitual residence if he or she is a stateless person, or to the State of the nationality of the victim;
> (v) the Government shall ensure the prosecution, without exception and without delay, of persons accused of acts described in paragraph 48 (iii) above who are present in the territory of Sudan (if the Government does not extradite

Jurisdiction

46. All members of the United Nations peace-keeping operation including locally recruited personnel shall be immune from legal process in respect of words spoken or written and all acts performed by them in their official capacity. Such immunity shall continue even after they cease to be members of or employed by the United Nations peace-keeping operation and after the expiration of the other provisions of the present Agreement.[79]

47. Should the Government consider that any member of the United Nations peace-keeping operation has committed a criminal offence, it shall promptly inform the Special Representative/Commander and present to him any evidence available to it. Subject to the provisions of paragraph 24:
    (a) If the accused person is a member of the civilian component or a civilian member of the military component, the Special Representative/Commander shall conduct any necessary supplementary inquiry and then agree with the Government whether or not criminal proceedings should be instituted. Failing such agreement, the question shall be resolved as provided in paragraph 53 of the present Agreement.[80]
    (b) Military members of the military component of the United Nations peace-keeping operation shall be subject to the exclusive jurisdiction of their respective participating States in respect of any criminal offences which may be committed by them in [host country/territory].

48. The Secretary-General of the United Nations will obtain assurances from Governments of participating States that they will be prepared to exercise jurisdiction with respect to crimes or offences which may be committed by members of their national contingents serving with the peace-keeping operation.[81]

49. If any civil proceeding is instituted against a member of the United Nations peace-keeping operation before any court of [host country/territory], the Special Representative/Commander shall be notified immediately, and he shall certify to the court whether or not the proceeding is related to the official duties of such member:
    (a) If the Special Representative/Commander certifies that the proceeding is related to official duties, such proceeding shall be discontinued and the provisions of paragraph 51 of the present Agreement shall apply.

---

them), as well as those persons that are subject to its criminal jurisdiction who are accused of other acts in relation to UNMIS or its members or associated personnel which, if committed in relation to the forces of the Government or against the local civilian population, would have rendered such acts liable to prosecution.

49. Upon the request of the Special Representative, the Government shall provide such security as necessary to protect UNMIS, its members and associated personnel and their equipment during the exercise of their functions.

SOFAs prior to the UNMIS SOFA did not include the term 'captured, detained or taken hostage' in Paragraph 48(ii) but instead simply used 'captured or detained' as copied directly from Article 8 of the Convention on the Safety of United Nations and Associated Personnel. The addition of 'taken hostage' is in response to the number of peacekeepers taken hostage in recent operations and the need to explicitly provide for this in the SOFA.

79 This important section providing the main 'functional immunity' for members of a peace operation remains the same in recent SOFAs.

80 The UNMIS and UNAMID SOFAs refer to the International Covenant on Civil and Political Rights. For example, the UNMIS SOFA states:

> In the event that criminal proceedings are instituted in accordance with the present Agreement, the courts and authorities of Sudan shall ensure that the member of UNMIS concerned is brought to trial and tried in accordance with international standards of justice, fairness and due process of law, as set out in the International Covenant on Civil and Political Rights, to which Sudan is a Party.

81 The model SOFA included the following footnote:

> This provision has been inserted in the model agreement in order that all issues pertaining to this section be covered. Upon conclusion of a specific agreement, the provision in question could instead be inserted in a memorandum of understanding where further clarifications on the terms of an agreement are usually provided.

This paragraph is not included in recent SOFAs but the revised 2008 model memorandum of understanding does now includes the required assurances.

(b) If the Special Representative certifies that the proceeding is not related to official duties, the proceeding may continue.[82] If the Special Representative/Commander certifies that a member of the United Nations peace-keeping operation is unable because of official duties or authorized absence to protect his interests in the proceeding, the court shall at the defendant's request suspend the proceeding until the elimination of the disability, but for not more than ninety days. Property of a member of the United Nations peace-keeping operation that is certified by the Special Representative/Commander to be needed by the defendant for the fulfilment of his official duties shall be free from seizure for the satisfaction of a judgment, decision or order. The personal liberty of a member of the United Nations peace-keeping operation shall not be restricted in a civil proceeding, whether to enforce a judgment, decision or order, to compel an oath or for any other reason.

Deceased Members

50. The Special Representative/Commander shall have the right to take charge of and dispose of the body of a member of the United Nations peace-keeping operation who dies in [host country/territory], as well as that member's personal property located within [host country/territory], in accordance with United Nations procedures.

VII. Settlement of Disputes[83]

51. Except as provided in paragraph 53, any dispute or claim of a private law character[84] to which the United Nations peace-keeping operation or any member thereof is a party and over which the courts of [host country/territory] do not have jurisdiction because of any provision of the present Agreement, shall be settled by a standing claims commission to be established for that purpose. One member of the commission shall be appointed by the Secretary-General of the United Nations, one member by the Government and a chairman jointly by the Secretary-General and the Government. If no agreement as to the chairman is reached within thirty days of the appointment of the first member of the commission, the President of the International Court of Justice may, at the request of either the Secretary-General of the United Nations or the Government, appoint the chairman. Any vacancy on the commission shall be filled by the same method prescribed for the original appointment, provided that the thirty-day period there prescribed shall start as soon as there is a vacancy in the chairmanship. The commission shall determine its own procedures, provided that any two members shall constitute a quorum for all purposes (except for a period of thirty days after the creation of a vacancy) and all decisions shall require the approval of any two members. The awards of the commission shall be final and binding, unless the Secretary-General

---

82 Extra text is added in the UNMIS and UNAMID SOFAs. For example, the UNMIS SOFA states: 'In that event, the court and authorities of Sudan shall grant the member of UNMIS concerned sufficient opportunity to safeguard his or her rights in accordance with due process of law.'

83 In recent SOFAs, Section VII 'Settlement of Disputes' has been renumbered as Section VIII because a new Section VII 'Limitation of Liability of the United Nations' has been included in response to General Assembly resolution 52/247 of 26 June 1998 on 'Third-party liability: temporal and financial limitations'. For example, the UNMIS SOFA states in Section VII 'Limitation of Liability of the United Nations':

> Third party claims for property loss or damage and for personal injury, illness or death arising from or directly attributed to UNMIS, except for those arising from operational necessity, and which cannot be settled through the internal procedures of the United Nations, shall be settled by the United Nations in the manner provided for in paragraph 55 of the present Agreement, provided that the claim is submitted within six (6) months following the occurrence of the loss, damage or injury or, if the claimant did not know or could not reasonably have know of such loss or injury, within six (6) months from the time he or she had discovered the loss or injury, but in any event not later than one year after the termination of the mandate of the operation. Upon determination of liability as provided in this Agreement, the United Nations shall pay compensation within such financial limitations as have been approved by the General Assembly in its resolution 52/247 of 26 June 1998.

84 Recent SOFAs include at this point the phrase 'not resulting from the operational necessity of [Peace Operation]'.

of the United Nations and the Government permit an appeal to a tribunal established in accordance with paragraph 53.[85] The awards of the commission shall be notified to the parties and, if against a member of the United Nations peace-keeping operation, the Special Representative/Commander or the Secretary-General of the United Nations shall use his best endeavours to ensure compliance.

52. Disputes concerning the terms of employment and conditions of service locally recruited personnel shall be settled by the administrative procedures to be established by the Special Representative/Commander.

53. Any other dispute between the United Nations peace-keeping operation and the Government,[86] and any appeal that both of them agree to allow from the award of the claims commission established pursuant to paragraph 51[87] shall, unless otherwise agreed by the parties, be submitted to a tribunal of three arbitrators. The provisions relating to the establishment and procedures of the claims commission shall apply, *mutatis mutandis*, to the establishment and procedures of the tribunal. The decisions of the tribunal shall be final and binding on both parties.

54. All differences between the United Nations and the Government of [host country/territory] arising out of the interpretation or application of the present arrangements which involve a question of principle concerning the Convention shall be dealt with in accordance with the procedure of section 30 of the Convention.[88]

VIII. Supplemental Arrangements

55. The Special Representative/Commander and the Government may conclude supplemental arrangements to the present Agreement.

IX. Liaison

56. The Special Representative/Commander and the Government shall take appropriate measures to ensure close and reciprocal liaison at every appropriate level.

X. Miscellaneous Provisions

57. Wherever the present Agreement refers to the privileges, immunities and rights of the United Nations peace-keeping operation and to the facilities the [host country/territory] undertakes to provide to the United Nations peace-keeping operation, the Government shall have the ultimate responsibility for the implementation and fulfilment of such privileges, immunities, rights and facilities by the appropriate local [host country/territory] authorities.

58. The present Agreement is concluded for the sole purpose of assisting in the implementation of Security Council/General Assembly resolution [number and date of resolution] and has no bearing upon the respective positions of the parties concerning the status of [territory].[89]

---

85 This possibility of an appeal is removed from recent SOFAs where the corresponding text simply states '[t]he awards of the commission shall be final'.

86 Recent SOFAs include the extra text 'concerning the interpretation and application of the present Agreement'. The wording in the model SOFA suggested that this paragraph concerned any dispute between the Government and the Peace Operation, not only those specifically related to the terms of the SOFA. The addition of the extra text clarifies that this is not the case.

87 Since recent SOFAs do not allow an appeal this part of the text of Paragraph 53 is no longer included.

88 The model SOFA includes the footnote: 'In case the other party to the present Agreement is a party to the Convention.' The recent SOFAs looked at all include this clause as the majority of States are now parties to the Convention.

89 The model SOFA includes the footnote: 'The insertion of this provision in an agreement is subject to its relevancy.' Recent SOFAs do not include it.

59. The present Agreement shall enter into force on ...

60. The present Agreement shall remain in force until the departure of the final element of the United Nations peace-keeping operation from [host country/territory] except that:
  (a) The provisions of paragraphs 46 and 53 [and 54][90] shall remain in force.
  (b) The provisions of paragraph 51 shall remain in force until all claims have been settled that arose prior to the termination of the present Agreement and were submitted prior to or within three months of such termination.

90 The model SOFA includes the footnote: 'see footnote i' (which in this document refers to the footnote to Paragraph 54 of the model SOFA).

3

Agreements between the United Nations and Contributing States

Prefatory Note

A model agreement between the UN and Member States contributing personnel and equipment to UN peace operations was created in 1991.[1] This agreement was subsequently rewritten in 1996[2] and renamed the model Memorandum of Understanding (model MOU) in 1997.[3] The 1997 version was amended in 2007,[4] with the General Assembly endorsing these amendments in resolution 61/267B.[5] The extant version of the model MOU can be found in Chapter 9 of the most recent edition of the Contingent-Owned Equipment (COE) Manual.[6] The model MOU that is included here is taken from the 2011 COE Manual.[7]

The MOU is a crucial document which forms the basis for agreements between the UN and States contributing resources to UN peace operations. It establishes several regulations designed to enhance the legitimacy of peace operations. It is one of the three key documents that govern UN peace operations. The other two documents are the Security Council resolution establishing the peace operation's mandate and the Status-of-Forces Agreement (SOFA) between the UN and the host country.[8]

The MOU is a formal agreement between the UN and the contributing State entailing legally binding rights and obligations. It has two key purposes. The first purpose is to establish the administrative, logistics, and financial terms and conditions to govern the contribution of personnel, equipment, and services provided by Member States in support of UN peace operations. The second is to specify UN standards of conduct for personnel provided by those Member States. The provisions compelling all peacekeepers to abide by the strengthened UN standards of conduct, especially in regard to sexual exploitation and abuse, coupled with the new accountability measures and requirements for contributing States to exercise their jurisdiction in criminal and disciplinary matters, makes the MOU an important document for contemporary peace operations. The MOU only applies to military contingents. Consequently, it does not apply to military observers, civilian police, or Formed Police Units (FPUs). Those categories of personnel are considered experts on mission and their obligations are found in the personal undertaking signed by them, and other documents such as the Regulations Governing the Status, Basic Rights and Duties of Officials other than Secretariat Officials and Experts on Mission.[9]

In relation to the historical development of the model MOU, the 1991 model agreement focused on a broad range of issues including applicable law, command and control, and accountability, but problems quickly began to emerge. After a 1994 report by the Secretary-General on the problems related to the planning, budgeting, and administration of peace operations,[10] the General Assembly authorised the Secretary-General to proceed with a reform of the methodology and procedures used for determining reimbursements to Member States for COE provided to peace

---

1 UN Doc A/46/185, 23 May 1991.
2 UN Doc A/50/995, 9 July 1996.
3 UN Doc A/51/967, 27 August 1997.
4 UN Doc A/61/19 (Part III), 12 June 2007.
5 GA Res 61/267B of 24 July 2007, Operative Part [2].
6 Letter dated 25 February 2011 from the Chair of the 2011 Working Group on Contingent-Owned Equipment to the Chair of the Fifth Committee, UN Doc A/C.5/66/8, 27 October 2011 (hereafter model COE Manual).
7 Ibid, ch 9.
8 See ch 2 above.
9 See ch 26 below.
10 UN Doc A/48/945, 25 May 1994.

operations.[11] This reform led the General Assembly to authorise the implementation of new procedures for determining reimbursement to contributing States for COE.[12] The new procedures formed the basis for the current COE system.[13] The first document produced was the 'Contribution Agreement between the United Nations and [participating State] Contributing Resources to [the United Nations Peace-Keeping Operation]'.[14] However, due to concerns by Member States about the term 'Contribution Agreement', its name was changed in 1997 to 'Model Memorandum of Understanding'.[15] The 1997 model MOU was amended in 2007[16] in response to growing concerns about sexual exploitation and abuse by peacekeepers and the damaging effect this has on the legitimacy and reputation of UN peace operations.[17]

The 2011 version of the model MOU:

> eliminates the need for detailed surveys of equipment, spare parts and consumables, and places the responsibility for asset management on the troop/police contributor. The United Nations responsibility is to ensure that the peacekeeping mission has the personnel and equipment required to fulfil its mandate, that the troop/police contributors provide personnel, equipment and services as detailed in the specific MOU, and that the contingents perform according to the established standards. The revised model MOU, including all Working Group recommendations approved by the General Assembly, is at chapter 9 of the present document.[18]

The main body of the model MOU deals with issues such as the contributions of governments to a peace operation, the basis on which the UN will reimburse governments for their contributions, the standards of conduct the UN expects of national contingents, the responsibilities of governments to maintain discipline over their national contingents, and the command and control mechanisms relating to the discipline of national contingents.

The model MOU relies heavily on annexes. Annexes A to E deal with administrative, logistical, and financial terms and conditions that govern the contributions of personnel, equipment, and services provided by the government in support of the peace operation. Annex F provides the definitions used in the MOU, and Annex G includes mission-specific Guidelines. Annex H contains the UN standards of conduct as provided for in the 'We are United Nations Peacekeeping Personnel' document. The definitions for acts such as sexual abuse, sexual exploitation, and serious misconduct in Annex F, and the new Annex H, were updated in the 2007 amendments and are reprinted below. Together these amendments effectively incorporate the Secretary-General's Bulletin on 'Special Measures for Protection from Sexual Exploitation and Sexual Abuse'[19] into the model MOU.

The 2007 amendments to the model MOU also introduced several additional Articles between Articles 7 and 8 of the 1997 version. These additional Articles include provisions on discipline, investigations, accountability, and the exercise of jurisdiction by contributing States. Several of these Articles need to be read in the light of the model SOFA,[20] the Directives for Disciplinary Matters Involving Military Members of National Contingents,[21] the 'Secretary-General's Bulletin: Special Measures for Protection from Sexual Exploitation and Sexual Abuse',[22] and the policy concerning Accountability for Conduct and Discipline in Field Missions.[23]

In relation to the conduct of investigations, the UN has confirmed that the State contributing the contingent has the responsibility to undertake the investigation. For example, the UN Office of Legal Affairs (OLA) has stated that, pursuant to the MOU, 'the responsibility to investigate the

---

11 GA Res 49/233 A of 23 December 1994.

12 GA Res 50/222 of 11 April 1996 stated that the reformed procedures would be effective from 1 July 1996.

13 For more information on the UN COE system visit its website <http://www.un.org/ar/peacekeeping/sites/coe/> accessed 1 November 2017.

14 UN Doc A/50/995, 9 July 1996.

15 UN Doc A/51/967, 27 August 1997.

16 UN Doc A/61/19 (Part III), 12 June 2007.

17 See 'Report of the Secretary-General: A Comprehensive Strategy to Eliminate Future Sexual Exploitation and Abuse in United Nations Peacekeeping Operations', UN Doc A/59/710, 24 March 2005 (commonly known as the 'Zeid Report').

18 Letter dated 25 February 2011 from the Chair of the 2011 Working Group on Contingent-Owned Equipment to the Chair of the Fifth Committee, UN Doc A/C.5/66/8, 27 October 2011, [12].

19 UN Doc ST/SGB/2003/13, 9 October 2003, entered into force 15 October 2003. See ch 30 below.

20 UN Doc A/45/594, 9 October 1990. See ch 2 below.

21 See ch 28 below.

22 See ch 30 below.

23 See ch 31 below.

theft allegedly committed by a member of the [Troop Contributing Country (TCC)] contingent of [United Nations Mission]—whether viewed from a disciplinary or a criminal law perspective—lies with the Government of [TCC]'.[24] Investigations are to be completed promptly and professionally by the TCC, and, where the investigation concerns sexual exploitation and abuse, the investigation must be completed within six months.

The model MOU provision concerning investigations by the UN where there has been an allegation of misconduct by a member of a UN military contingent has been interpreted to also apply outside the mission area. In an inter-office memorandum to the Director of the Investigation Division, Office of Internal Oversight Services (OIOS), it was concluded that:

> Article 7.12 of the MOU does not draw a distinction as to whether the alleged misconduct was committed in the mission area, or in another country. Thus, as a legal matter, article 7.12 of the MOU would apply in respect of any misconduct committed by a member of the contingent, irrespective of where it may have been committed. In this regard, we would also note that in articles 7.22 and 7.23 of the MOU the Government provides assurances to the United Nations that it will exercise jurisdiction in respect of crimes, offences or other acts of misconduct committed by the members of the military contingent while they are assigned to the military component of [United Nations Mission]. Again, articles 7.22 and 7.23 of the MOU do not draw a distinction as to the location of the crime, offence or other misconduct. Rather, the determining criterion here is that the crime, offence or other misconduct must have been committed by the member of the contingent whilst on assignment with [United Nations Mission]. In this regard, we would note that, even if the members of the contingent concerned were on vacation in [State], as stated in your memorandum, we do not think that this fact would negate their status as being on assignment with [United Nations Mission].[25]

Article 9 of the model MOU, which deals with claims by third-parties, makes it clear that the UN is responsible for dealing with any third-party claims but only where the loss or damage was caused 'in the performance of services or any other activity or operation under this MOU'. At present, third-party claims that the UN is responsible for have the temporal and financial limitations outlined in General Assembly resolution 52/247,[26] which is not referred to explicitly in the model MOU though it is in recent SOFAs.

Resolution 52/247 also endorsed the view of the Secretary-General that no financial limits will apply to claims involving gross negligence or wilful misconduct.[27] In these cases, the UN will assume liability to compensate the injured parties but retains the right to seek recovery of these monies from the individual or contributing State concerned. In relation to the term 'gross negligence', the OLA has advised that:

(a) 'Gross negligence' is negligence of a very high degree involving willfulness, recklessness or drunkenness and, in consequence, manifest disregard for the safety of life and property.
(b) It is necessary that all the facts of a case, including all mitigating circumstances, be considered.
(c) 'Necessity' may excuse conduct that might otherwise be regarded as 'gross negligence'.
(d) Gross negligence should not be inferred *solely* from:
    (i) a failure to take a precautionary measures [sic]; or
    (ii) a violation of a rule of the road or traffic regulation or other directive although either of the above should be taken into account in reaching a determination.[28]

The COE Manual states that the above approach to defining elements of gross negligence is to be given consideration, as appropriate, when applying the term 'gross negligence'.[29]

---

24 Note concerning an allegation of attempted theft against a member of a military contingent, signed 6 February 2012, reproduced in the UN Juridical Yearbook 2012, 480, [5].

25 Inter-office memorandum to the Director of the Investigation Division, Office of Internal Oversight Services (OIOS) concerning a report of possible misconduct involving members of a military contingent, signed 25 May 2012, reproduced in the UN Juridical Yearbook 2012, 482, [4].

26 GA Res 52/247 of 26 June 1998. See ch 22 below and ch 2 above.

27 'Report of the Secretary-General: Administrative and Budgetary Aspects of the Financing of United Nations Peacekeeping Operations: Financing of the United Nations Peacekeeping Operations', UN Doc A/51/903, 21 May 1997, [14].

28 UN Juridical Yearbook 1981, 165–6 on '"Gross Negligence" on the part of a staff member, resulting in damage to United Nations property—Criteria to be applied in determining whether gross negligence is involved'.

29 2011 COE Manual, ch 6, 132, [16].

The dispute settlement mechanism as provided for in the model MOU is founded on the principle that the UN and the Member State in dispute will 'discuss and resolve, amicably by negotiation in a spirit of cooperation, differences arising from the application of this MOU'.[30]

When settling disputes there are essentially two levels: the first is in the mission; and the second is in New York Headquarters.[31] Should the dispute not be resolved at the second level, the Member State and the UN may settle on a mutually agreed conciliator or mediator, and, failing that, by arbitration.[32]

The MOU that follows may be amended by agreement between the TCC and the UN. Such amendments might be referred to as 'terms of assistance' and annexed to the MOU for that peace operation.

Reference

Title	Manual on Policies and Procedures Concerning the Reimbursement and Control of Contingent-Owned Equipment of Troop/Police Contributors Participating in Peacekeeping Missions (COE Manual); Chapter 9, Memorandum of understanding between the United Nations and [participating State] contributing resources to [the United Nations Peacekeeping Operation]
Author	2011 Working Group on Contingent-Owned Equipment
Date	27 October 2011
Source	UN Doc A/C.5/66/8, Chapter 9
Full Text	<https://digitallibrary.un.org/record/722524/files/A_C-5_66_8-EN.pdf>[33]

Memorandum of Understanding between the United Nations and [participating State] contributing resources to [the United Nations Peacekeeping Operation][34]

(Extracts)

Whereas, [the United Nations peacekeeping operation] was established pursuant to the United Nations Security Council resolution ________.

Whereas, at the request of the United Nations, the Government of ______ (hereinafter referred to as the Government) has agreed to contribute personnel, equipment, and services for a [type of contingent/unit] to assist [United Nations peacekeeping mission] to carry out its mandate,

Whereas, the United Nations and the Government wish to establish the terms and conditions of the contribution.

Now therefore, the United Nations and the Government (hereinafter collectively referred to as the Parties) agree as follows:

---

30 Model MOU (n 6), [13.1].

31 Ibid, [13.1(a)], [13.1(b)].

32 Ibid, [13.2].

33 Accessed 8 April 2019.

34 From Manual on Policies and Procedures Concerning the Reimbursement and Control of Contingent-Owned Equipment of Troop/Police Contributors Participating in Peacekeeping Missions (COE Manual), by 2011 Working Group on Contingent-Owned Equipment, © 2011 United Nations. Reprinted with the permission of the United Nations.

Article 1

Definitions

1. For the purpose of this Memorandum of Understanding, the definitions listed in annex F shall apply.

Article 2

Documents constituting the memorandum of understanding

2.1 This document, including all of its annexes, constitutes the entire memorandum of understanding (hereinafter referred to as the MOU) between the Parties for the provision of personnel, equipment and services in support of [United Nations peacekeeping mission].

2.2 Annexes:

A. Personnel
   1. Requirements
   2. Reimbursement
   3. General conditions for personnel

   Appendix. Soldier's kit—mission-specific recommended requirement

B. Major equipment
   1. Requirements
   2. General conditions for major equipment
   3. Verification and control procedures
   4. Transportation
   5. Mission usage factors
   6. Loss and damage
   7. Loss and damage in transit
   8. Special case equipment
   9. Liability for damage to major equipment owned by one troop/police contributor and used by another troop/police contributor

C. Self-sustainment
   1. Requirements
   2. General conditions for self-sustainment
   3. Verification and control procedures
   4. Transportation
   5. Mission-related usage factors
   6. Loss and damage

D. Principles of verification and performance standards for major equipment provided under the wet/dry lease arrangements

E. Principles of verification and performance standards for minor equipment and consumables provided under self-sustainment

F. Definitions

G. Guidelines (aide-mémoire) to Troop-Contributing Countries[35]

H. We are United Nations Peacekeeping Personnel

---

35 Annex G is mission specific and is not included in the present document. It is distributed separately in advance of the deployment. [Note: this footnote appears in the original document as footnote '1'].

Article 3

Purpose

3. The purpose of the present memorandum of understanding is to establish the administrative, logistics and financial terms and conditions to govern the contribution of personnel, equipment, and services provided by the Government in support of [United Nations peacekeeping mission] and to specify United Nations standards of conduct for personnel provided by the Government.

Article 4

Application

4. The present MOU shall be applied in conjunction with the Guidelines to Troop-Contributing Countries.

Article 5

Contribution of the Government

5.1 The Government shall contribute to [United Nations peacekeeping mission] the personnel listed at annex A. Any personnel above the level indicated in this MOU shall be a national responsibility and thus not subject to reimbursement or other kind of support by the United Nations.

5.2 The Government shall contribute to [United Nations peacekeeping mission] the major equipment listed in annex B. The Government shall ensure that the major equipment and related minor equipment meet the performance standards set out in annex D for the duration of the deployment of such equipment to [United Nations peacekeeping mission]. Any equipment above the level indicated in this MOU shall be a national responsibility and thus not subject to reimbursement or other kind of support by the United Nations.

5.3 The Government shall contribute to [United Nations peacekeeping mission] the minor equipment and consumables related to self-sustainment as listed in annex C. The Government shall ensure that the minor equipment and consumables meet the performance standards set out in annex E for the duration of the deployment of such equipment to [United Nations peacekeeping mission]. Any equipment above the level indicated in this MOU shall be a national responsibility and thus not subject to reimbursement or other kind of support by the United Nations.

Article 6

Reimbursement and support from the United Nations

6.1 The United Nations shall reimburse the Government in respect of the personnel provided under this MOU at the rates stated in article 2 of annex A.

6.2 The United Nations shall reimburse the Government for the major equipment provided as listed in annex B. The reimbursement for the major equipment shall be reduced in the event that such equipment does not meet the required performance standards set out in annex D or in the event that the equipment listing is reduced.

6.3 The United Nations shall reimburse the Government for the provision of self-sustainment goods and services at the rates and levels stated in annex C. The reimbursement for self-sustainment shall be reduced in the event that the contingent does not meet the required performance standards set out in annex E, or in the event that the level of self-sustainment is reduced.

6.4 Reimbursement for troop/police costs will continue at full rates until departure of the personnel.

6.5 Reimbursement for major equipment will be in effect at full rates until the date of cessation of operations by a troop/police contributor or termination of the mission and thereafter be calculated at 50 per cent of the rates agreed in this MOU until the equipment departure date.

6.6 Reimbursement for self-sustainment will be in effect at full rates until the date of cessation of operations by a troop/police contributor or termination of the mission and thereafter be reduced to 50 per cent of the rates agreed in this MOU calculated upon the remaining actual deployed troop/police strengths until all troop/police personnel have departed the mission area.

6.7 When the United Nations negotiates a contract for the repatriation of equipment and the carrier exceeds a 14-day grace period after the expected arrival date, the troop/police contributor will be reimbursed by the United Nations at the dry-lease rate from the expected arrival date until the actual arrival date.

Article 7

General conditions

7.1 The parties agree that the contribution of the Government as well as the support from the United Nations shall be governed by the general conditions set out in the relevant annexes.

Article 7 bis

United Nations standards of conduct

7.2 The Government shall ensure that all members of the Government's national contingent are required to comply with the United Nations standards of conduct set out in annex H to the present memorandum of understanding.

7.3 The Government shall ensure that all members of its national contingent are made familiar with and fully understand the United Nations standards of conduct. To this end, the Government shall, inter alia, ensure that all members of its national contingent receive adequate and effective pre-deployment training in those standards.

7.4 The United Nations shall continue to provide to national contingents mission-specific training material on United Nations standards of conduct, mission-specific rules and regulations, and relevant local laws and regulations. Further, the United Nations shall conduct adequate and effective induction training and training during mission assignment to complement predeployment training.

Article 7 ter

Discipline

7.5 The Government acknowledges that the Commander of its national contingent is responsible for the discipline and good order of all members of the contingent while assigned to [United Nations Peacekeeping Mission]. The Government accordingly undertakes to ensure that the Commander of its national contingent is vested with the necessary authority and takes all reasonable measures to maintain discipline and good order among all members of the national contingent to ensure compliance with the United Nations standards of conduct, mission-specific rules and regulations and the obligations towards national and local laws and regulations in accordance with the status-of-forces agreement.

7.6 The Government undertakes to ensure, subject to any applicable national laws, that the Commander of its national contingent regularly informs the Force Commander of any serious matters involving the discipline and good order of members of its national contingent, including any disciplinary action taken for violations of the United Nations standards of conduct or mission-specific rules and regulations or for failure to respect the local laws and regulations.

7.7 The Government shall ensure that the Commander of its national contingent receives adequate and effective predeployment training in the proper discharge of his or her responsibility for maintaining discipline and good order among all members of the contingent.

7.8 The United Nations shall assist the Government in fulfilling its requirements under paragraph 7.3 above by organizing training sessions for commanders upon their arrival in the mission on the United Nations standards of conduct, mission-specific rules and regulations and the local laws and regulations.

7.9 The Government shall use its welfare payments to provide adequate welfare and recreation facilities to its contingent members in the mission.

Article 7 quater
Investigations

7.10 It is understood that the Government has the primary responsibility for investigating any acts of misconduct or serious misconduct committed by a member of its national contingent.

7.11 In the event that the Government has prima facie grounds indicating that any member of its national contingent has committed an act of serious misconduct, it shall without delay inform the United Nations and forward the case to its appropriate national authorities for the purposes of investigation.

7.12 In the event that the United Nations has prima facie grounds indicating that any member of the Government's national contingent has committed an act of misconduct or serious misconduct, the United Nations shall without delay inform the Government. If necessary to preserve evidence and where the Government does not conduct fact-finding proceedings, the United Nations may, in cases of serious misconduct, as appropriate, where the United Nations has informed the Government of the allegation, initiate a preliminary fact-finding inquiry of the matter, until the Government starts its own investigation. It is understood in this connection that any such preliminary fact-finding inquiry will be conducted by the appropriate United Nations investigative office, including the Office of Internal Oversight Services, in accordance with the rules of the Organization. Any such preliminary fact-finding inquiry shall include as part of the investigation team a representative of the Government. The United Nations shall provide a complete report of its preliminary fact-finding inquiry to the Government at its request without delay.

7.13 In the event that the Government does not notify the United Nations as soon as possible, but no later than 10 working days from the time of notification by the United Nations, that it will start its own investigation of the alleged serious misconduct, the Government is considered to be unwilling or unable to conduct such an investigation and the United Nations may, as appropriate, initiate an administrative investigation of alleged serious misconduct without delay. The administrative investigation conducted by the United Nations in regard to any member of the national contingent shall respect those legal rights of due process that are provided to him or her by national and international law. Any such administrative investigation includes as part of the investigation team a representative of the Government if the Government provides one. In case the Government nevertheless decides to start its own investigation, the United Nations provides all available materials of the case to the Government without delay. In cases where a United Nations administrative investigation is completed, the United Nations shall provide the Government with the findings of the investigation, and the evidence gathered in the course of said investigation.

7.14 In the case of a United Nations administrative investigation into possible serious misconduct by any member of the national contingent, the Government agrees to instruct the Commander of its national contingent to cooperate and to share documentation and information, subject to applicable national laws, including military laws. The Government also undertakes, through the Commander of its national contingent, to instruct the members of its national contingent to cooperate with such United Nations investigation, subject to applicable national laws, including military laws.

7.15 When the Government decides to start its own investigation and to identify or send one or more officials to investigate the matter, it shall immediately inform the United Nations of that decision, including the identities of the official or officials concerned (hereafter "National Investigations Officers").

7.16 The United Nations agrees to cooperate fully and to share documentation and information with appropriate authorities of the Government, including any National Investigations Officers, who are investigating possible misconduct or serious misconduct by any member of the national contingent of the Government.

7.17 Upon the request of the Government, the United Nations shall cooperate with the competent authorities of the Government, including any National Investigations Officers, that are investigating possible misconduct or serious misconduct by any members of its national contingent, by liaising with other Governments that are contributing personnel in support of [a United Nations peacekeeping mission], as well as with the competent authorities in the mission area, with a view to facilitating the conduct of those investigations. To this end, the United Nations shall take all possible measures to obtain consent from the host authorities. The competent authorities of the Government shall ensure that prior authorization for access to any victim or witness who is not a member of the national contingent, as well as for the collection or securing of evidence not under the ownership and control of the national contingent, is obtained from the host nation competent authorities.

7.18 In cases where National Investigations Officers are dispatched to the mission areas, they lead the investigations. The role of the United Nations investigators in such cases will be to assist the National Investigations Officers, if necessary, in the conduct of their investigations in terms of identification and interviewing of witnesses, recording witness statements, collection of documentary and forensic evidence and provision of administrative as well as logistical assistance.

7.19 Subject to its national laws and regulations, the Government shall provide the United Nations with the findings of investigations conducted by its competent authorities, including any National Investigations Officers, into possible misconduct or serious misconduct by any member of its national contingent.

7.20 When National Investigations Officers are deployed in the mission area, they will enjoy the same legal status as if they were members of their respective contingent while they are in the mission area, or host country.

7.21 Upon the request of the Government, the United Nations shall provide administrative and logistics support to the National Investigations Officers while they are in the mission area or host country. The Secretary-General will provide, in accordance with his authority, financial support as appropriate for the deployment of National Investigations Officers in situations where their presence is requested by the United Nations, normally the Department of Peacekeeping Operations, and where financial support is requested by the Government. The United Nations will request the Government to deploy National Investigations Officers in high-risk, complex matters and in cases of serious misconduct. This paragraph is without prejudice to the sovereign right of the Government to investigate any misconduct of its contingent members.

Article 7 quinquiens

Exercise of jurisdiction by the Government

7.22 Military members and any civilian members subject to national military law of the national contingent provided by the Government are subject to the Government's exclusive jurisdiction in respect of any crimes or offences that might be committed by them while they are assigned to the military component of [United Nations peacekeeping mission]. The Government assures the United Nations that it shall exercise such jurisdiction with respect to such crimes or offences.

7.23 The Government further assures the United Nations that it shall exercise such disciplinary jurisdiction as might be necessary with respect to all other acts of misconduct committed by any members of the Government's national contingent while they are assigned to the military component of [United Nations peacekeeping mission] that do not amount to crimes or offences.

Article 7 sexiens

Accountability

7.24 If either a United Nations investigation or an investigation conducted by the competent authorities of the Government concludes that suspicions of misconduct by any member of the Government's national contingent are well founded, the Government shall ensure that the case is forwarded to its appropriate authorities for due action. The Government agrees that those authorities shall take their decision in the same manner as they would in respect of any other offence or disciplinary infraction of a similar nature under its laws or relevant disciplinary code. The Government agrees to notify the Secretary-General of progress on a regular basis, including the outcome of the case.

7.25 If a United Nations investigation, in accordance with appropriate procedures, or the Government's investigation concludes that suspicions of failure by the contingent Commander to:

(a) Cooperate with a United Nations investigation in accordance with article 7 quater, paragraph 7.14, it being understood that the Commander will not have failed to cooperate merely by complying with his or her national laws and regulations, or the Government's investigation; or

(b) Exercise effective command and control; or

(c) Immediately report to appropriate authorities or take action in respect of allegations of misconduct that are reported to him are well founded;

The Government shall ensure that the case is forwarded to its appropriate authorities for due action. The fulfilment of these aspects shall be evaluated in the contingent Commander's performance appraisal.

7.26 The Government understands the importance of settling matters relating to paternity claims involving a member of its contingent. The Government will, to the extent of its national laws, seek to facilitate such claims provided to it by the United Nations to be forwarded to the appropriate national authorities. In the case that the Government's national law does not recognize the legal capacity of the United Nations to provide such claims, these shall be provided to the Government by the appropriate authorities of the host country, in accordance with applicable procedures. The United Nations must ensure that such claims are accompanied by the necessary conclusive evidence, such as a DNA sample of the child when prescribed by the Government's national law.

7.27 Bearing in mind the contingent Commander's obligation to maintain the discipline and good order of the contingent, the United Nations, through the Force Commander, shall ensure that the contingent is deployed in the mission in accordance with the agreement between the United Nations and the Government. Any redeployment outside the agreement will be made with the consent of the Government or contingent Commander, in accordance with applicable national procedures.

Article 8

Specific conditions

8.1 Environmental condition factor: _____

8.2 Intensity of operations factor: ______

8.3 Hostile action/forced abandonment factor: _________

8.4 Incremental transportation factor: The distance between the port of embarkation in the home country and the port of entry in the mission area is estimated at ________ miles (____ kilometers). The factor is set at ____ per cent of the reimbursement rates.

8.5 The following locations are the agreed originating locations and ports of entry and exit for the purpose of transportation arrangements for the movement of troops/police and equipment:

Troops/Police:
Airport/port of entry/exit: ______________________
(in the troop/police-contributing country)
Airport/port of entry/exit: ______________________________
(in the area of operations)

Note: The troops/police may be returned to another location nominated by the troop/police contributor, however, the maximum cost to the United Nations will be the cost to the agreed originating location. Where a rotation uplifts troops/police from a different port of exit this port shall become the agreed port of entry for these troops/police.

Equipment:
Originating location: _____________________________
Port of embarkation/disembarkation: _____________________
(in the contributing country)

or

Border crossing at embarkation/disembarkation:____________
(in the contributing country when landlocked or moving by road/rail)
Port of embarkation/disembarkation: _____________________
(in the mission area)

Article 9

Claims by third parties

9. The United Nations will be responsible for dealing with any claims by third parties where the loss of or damage to their property, or death or personal injury, was caused by the personnel or equipment provided by the Government in the performance of services or any other activity or operation under this MOU. However, if the loss, damage, death or injury arose from gross negligence or wilful misconduct of the personnel provided by the Government, the Government will be liable for such claims.

Article 10

Recovery

10. The Government will reimburse the United Nations for loss of or damage to United Nations-owned equipment and property caused by the personnel or equipment provided by the Government if such loss or damage (a) occurred outside the performance of services or

any other activity or operation under this MOU, or (b) arose or resulted from gross negligence or wilful misconduct of the personnel provided by the Government.

Article 11

Supplementary arrangements

11. The parties may conclude written supplementary arrangements to the present MOU.

Article 12

Amendments

12. Either of the Parties may initiate a review of the level of contribution subject to reimbursement by the United Nations or to the level of national support to ensure compatibility with the operational requirements of the mission and of the Government. The present MOU may only be amended by written agreement of the Government and the United Nations.

Article 13

Settlement of disputes

13.1 The [United Nations peacekeeping operation] shall establish a mechanism within the mission to discuss and resolve, amicably by negotiation in a spirit of cooperation, differences arising from the application of this MOU. This mechanism shall be comprised of two levels of dispute resolution:

(a) First level. The Director/Chief, Mission Support, in consultation with the Force Commander/Police Commissioner and the Contingent Commander will attempt to reach a negotiated settlement of the dispute;

(b) Second level. Should negotiations at the first level not resolve the dispute, a representative of the Permanent Mission of the Member State and the Under-Secretary-General, Department of Field Support, or his or her representative shall, at the request of either Party, attempt to reach a negotiated settlement of the dispute.

13.2 Disputes that have not been resolved as provided in paragraph 13.1 above may be submitted to a mutually agreed conciliator or mediator appointed by the President of the International Court of Justice, failing which the dispute may be submitted to arbitration at the request of either Party. Each Party shall appoint one arbitrator, and the two arbitrators so appointed shall appoint a third, who shall be the Chairman. If within thirty days of the request for arbitration either Party has not appointed an arbitrator or if within thirty days of the appointment of two arbitrators the third arbitrator has not been appointed, either Party may request the President of the International Court of Justice to appoint an arbitrator. The procedures for the arbitration shall be fixed by the arbitrators, and each Party shall bear its own expenses. The arbitral award shall contain a statement of reasons on which it is based and shall be accepted by the Parties as the final adjudication of the dispute. The arbitrators shall have no authority to award interest or punitive damages.

Article 14

Entry into force

14. The present MOU shall become effective on [date]. The financial obligations of the United Nations with respect to reimbursement of personnel, major equipment and self-sustainment rates start from the date of arrival of personnel or equipment in the mission area, and will remain in effect until the date personnel, and serviceable equipment depart the mission area as per the agreed withdrawal plan or the date of effective departure where the delay is attributable to the United Nations.

Article 15
Termination

15. The modalities for termination shall be as agreed to by the Parties following consultations between the Parties.
IN WITNESS WHEREOF, the United Nations and the Government of ______________ have signed this memorandum of understanding.
Signed in New York, on ____________________, in two originals in the English language.
For the United Nations For the Government of [troop/police contributor]

______________________________	______________________________
Under-Secretary-General	Permanent Representative
Department of Field Support	Permanent Mission of [troop/police contributor]

...

Annex F

Definitions

1. **Accepted United Nations readiness standards** means that every unit/formation, ship, weapon system or equipment must be capable of performing the missions or functions for which it is organized or designed to enable the mission's mandate to be achieved.
2. **Consumables** means supplies of a general nature, consumed on a routine basis. Consumables include combat supplies, general and technical stores, defence stores, ammunition/explosives and other basic commodities in support of major equipment as well as in support of minor equipment and personnel.
3. **Contingent** means all formed units, personnel and equipment of the troop/police contributor deployed to the mission area under this memorandum.
4. **Contingent-owned equipment** means major equipment, and minor equipment and consumables, deployed and operated by the troop/police contributor's contingent in the performance of peacekeeping operations.
5. **Environmental conditions factor** means a factor applicable to the reimbursement rates for major equipment and for self-sustainment to take into account the increased costs borne by the troop/police contributor for extreme mountainous, climatic and terrain conditions. This factor is only applicable under conditions of significant anticipated additional costs to the troop/police contributor. The factor is determined at the outset of the mission by the technical survey team, and is applied universally within the mission. The factor is not to exceed 5 per cent of the rates.
6. **Explosive ordnance disposal** (EOD) means, in the context of force EOD, the detection, identification, onsite evaluation, rendering safe, recovery and final disposal of unexploded ammunition. It is conducted on behalf of the mission by a specialist unit as a force asset. Force EOD operations may conduct activities in all or part of the mission area. It may also include ammunition that has become hazardous by damage or deterioration.
7. **Explosive ordnance disposal** (EOD) means, in the context of self-sustainment, EOD conducted by a unit within its accommodation/camp area.

8. **Force Commander** means the officer, appointed under the authority of the Secretary-General, responsible for all military operations within the mission.
9. **Forced abandonment** means actions resulting from a decision approved by the Force Commander/Police Commissioner or his authorized representative or a provision in the rules of engagement which results in the loss of custody and control of equipment and supplies.
10. **Force majeure** means acts of God, war, insurrection or other acts of a similar nature or force.
11. **Generic fair market value (GFMV)** means equipment valuations for reimbursement purposes. It is computed as the average initial purchase price plus any major capital improvements, adjusted for inflation and discounted for any prior usage, or the replacement value, whichever is less. The generic fair market value includes all issue items associated with the equipment in the performance of its operational role.
12. **Government** means the Government of the participating State.
13. **Head of Mission** means the Special Representative/Commander appointed by the Secretary-General with the consent of the Security Council responsible for all United Nations activities within the mission.
14. **Hostile action** means an incident from the action(s) of one or more belligerents, which has a direct and significant negative impact on the personnel and/or equipment of a troop/police contributor. Different activities may be characterized as a single hostile action when these activities can be related to each other on common ground.
15. **Hostile action/forced abandonment factor** means a factor applied to each category of self-sustainment rates and to the spares element (or half of the estimated maintenance rate) of the wet lease rate to compensate the troop/police contributor for loss and damage. The factor is determined at the outset of the mission by the technical survey team, and is applied universally within the mission. The factor is not to exceed 5 per cent of the rates.
16. **Incremental transportation factor** means a factor to cover the incremental costs of transportation of spare parts and consumables under the wet lease system or lease for maintenance in increments of 0.25 per cent of the leasing rate for each complete 800 kilometres (500 miles) distance, beyond the first 800 kilometres (500 miles), along a consignment route between the port of embarkation in the home country and the port of entry in the mission area. For landlocked countries or countries where equipment is moved by road or rail to and from the mission area, the port of entry in the mission area will be an agreed border crossing point.
17. **Initial provisioning** means a logistics support arrangement in a peacekeeping mission whereby the contributing State provides rations, water and petrol, oil and lubricants to the contingent/unit on a reimbursable basis. Reimbursement will be made to troop/police contributors upon submission of invoices. Normally, initial provisioning for contingents/units is required only upon the initial deployment of the contingent/unit, and for a limited period (30–60 days), until the United Nations is able to provide these consumables. The requirement for initial provision of water, rations and fuel will be specified in troop/police contributors Guidelines.
18. **Intensified operational condition factor** means a factor applicable to the reimbursement rates for major equipment and for self-sustainment rates to compensate the troop/police contributor for increased costs resulting from the scope of the task assigned, the length of logistics chains, non-availability of commercial repair and support facilities, and other operational hazards and conditions. The factor is determined at the outset of the mission by the technical survey team, and is applied universally within the mission. The factor is not to exceed 5 per cent of the rates.
19. **Lease of major equipment**
    (a) **Dry lease** means a contingent-owned equipment reimbursement system where the troop/police contributor provides equipment to the mission and the United Nations assumes responsibility for maintaining the equipment. The troop/police contributor is

reimbursed for the non-availability of its military resources for its national interest of deployed major and associated minor equipment.

(b) **Wet lease** means a contingent-owned reimbursement system where the troop/police contributor provides and assumes responsibility for maintaining and supporting deployed major items of equipment, together with the associated minor equipment. The troop/police contributor is entitled to reimbursement for providing this support.

20. **Loss or damage** means a total or partial elimination of equipment and/or supplies resulting from:
   (a) A no-fault incident;
   (b) The actions of one or more belligerents;
   (c) A decision approved by the Force Commander/Police Commissioner.
21. **Maintenance rate** means the reimbursement rate to compensate the Government for maintenance costs comprising spare parts, contracted repair, and third and fourth line maintenance that is required to keep major equipment items operational to the specified standards, and return the item to operational condition upon return from the mission area. The costs of personnel involved in first and second line maintenance is excluded from the rate, as they are reimbursed separately. The rate includes an incremental transportation rate to cover general transportation costs of spare parts. This rate forms part of the "wet lease" rate.
22. **Major equipment** means major items directly related to the unit mission as mutually determined by the United Nations and the troop/police contributor. Major equipment is accounted for either by category or individually. Separate reimbursement rates apply for each category of items of major equipment. These rates include reimbursement for minor equipment and consumables in support of the item of major equipment.
23. **Minor equipment** means equipment in support of contingents, such as catering, accommodation, non-specialist communication and engineering and other mission-related activities. Specific accounting of minor equipment is not required. Minor equipment is divided into two categories: items designed to support major equipment; and items that directly or indirectly support personnel. For personnel-related minor equipment, rates of reimbursement for self-sustainment apply.
24. **Misconduct** means any act or omission that is a violation of United Nations standards of conduct, mission-specific rules and regulations or the obligations towards national and local laws and regulations in accordance with the status-of-forces agreement where the impact is outside the national contingent.
25. **Mission-specific rules and regulations** means, mindful of national caveats, standard operating procedures, directives and other regulations, orders and instructions issued by the Head of Mission, Force Commander or Director/Chief of Mission Support of the United Nations peacekeeping mission in accordance with the United Nations standards of conduct; they shall contain information on applicable national and local laws and regulations.
26. **No-fault incident** means an incident resulting from an accidental occurrence or negligent conduct, but not including acts attributable to wilful misconduct or gross negligence, on the part of an operator/custodian of equipment.
27. **Operational ammunition** means ammunition (including aircraft self-defence systems such as chaff or infrared flares) that the United Nations and troop/police contributors agree to deploy to the mission area so that it is readily available for use in the event of need. Ammunition expended for operational training/exercise beyond accepted United Nations readiness standards on the authority of and at the specific direction of the Force Commander, in anticipation of an operational requirement, will be considered operational ammunition.

28. **Police Commissioner** means the officer, appointed under the authority of the Secretary-General, responsible for all police operations within the mission.
29. **Predeployment visits** are visits by the Department of Peacekeeping Operations/Department of Field Support/field mission teams, comprising representatives from appropriate functional areas (Force Generation Service, Field Budget and Finance Division, Logistics Support Division etc.), to Member States' countries. They are undertaken to assist Member States to prepare their contingents for deployment and to ensure that Member State contributions meet the operational requirements of the mission and deployment timings.
30. **Preliminary fact-finding inquiry** means the preservation of evidence necessary to ensure that a national or United Nations investigation can be successfully carried out at a later stage. While this inquiry may involve the collection of written statements, it will not normally include the interviewing of witnesses or other involved persons.
31. **Self-sustainment** means a logistics support concept for troop contingent/police unit in a peacekeeping mission whereby the contributing State provides some specific or all logistics support to the contingent on a reimbursable basis.
32. **Serious misconduct** is misconduct, including criminal acts, that results in, or is likely to result in, serious loss, damage or injury to an individual or to a mission. Sexual exploitation and abuse constitute serious misconduct.
33. **Sexual abuse** means the actual or threatened physical intrusion of a sexual nature, whether by force or under unequal or coercive conditions.
34. **Sexual exploitation** means any actual or attempted abuse of a position of vulnerability, differential power or trust for sexual purposes, including, but not limited to, profiting monetarily, socially or politically from the sexual exploitation of another.
35. **Unique equipment** means any special minor equipment or consumables not covered in the above self-sustainment rates and will be handled as unique equipment. These items will be handled on a bilateral special case arrangement between the troop contributor and the United Nations.

Annex G

Guidelines (aide-mémoire) to troop-contributing countries

Annex G is mission-specific and is not included in the present document. It is distributed in advance of deployment.

Annex H[36]

We are United Nations peacekeeping personnel

The United Nations Organization embodies the aspirations of all the people of the world for peace.

In this context, the Charter of the United Nations requires that all personnel must maintain the highest standards of integrity and conduct.

We will comply with the Guidelines on International Humanitarian Law for Forces Undertaking United Nations Peacekeeping Operations and the applicable portions of the Universal Declaration of Human Rights as the fundamental basis of our standards.

36 See also ch 27 below.

We, as peacekeeping personnel, represent the United Nations and are present in the country to help it recover from the trauma of a conflict. As a result, we must consciously be prepared to accept special constraints in our public and private lives in order to do the work and to pursue the ideals of the United Nations Organization.

We will be accorded certain privileges and immunities arranged through agreements negotiated between the United Nations and the host country solely for the purpose of discharging our peacekeeping duties. Expectations of the international community and the local population will be high, and our actions, behaviour and speech will be closely monitored.

We will always:

- Conduct ourselves in a professional and disciplined manner, at all times;
- Dedicate ourselves to achieving the goals of the United Nations;
- Understand the mandate and mission and comply with their provisions;
- Respect the environment of the host country;
- Respect local laws, customs and practices and be aware of and respect culture, religion, traditions and gender issues;
- Treat the inhabitants of the host country with respect, courtesy and consideration;
- Act with impartiality, integrity and tact;
- Support and aid the infirm, sick and weak;
- Obey our United Nations superiors/supervisors and respect the chain of command;
- Respect all other peacekeeping members of the mission regardless of status, rank, ethnic or national origin, race, gender, or creed;
- Support and encourage proper conduct among our fellow peacekeeping personnel;
- Report all acts involving sexual exploitation and abuse;
- Maintain proper dress and personal deportment at all times;
- Properly account for all money and property assigned to us as members of the mission; and
- Care for all United Nations equipment placed in our charge.

We will never:

- Bring discredit upon the United Nations or our nations through improper personal conduct, failure to perform our duties or abuse of our positions as peacekeeping personnel;
- Take any action that might jeopardize the mission;
- Abuse alcohol, use or traffic in drugs;
- Make unauthorized communications to external agencies, including unauthorized press statements;
- Improperly disclose or use information gained through our employment;
- Use unnecessary violence or threaten anyone in custody;
- Commit any act that could result in physical, sexual or psychological harm or suffering to members of the local population, especially women and children;
- Commit any act involving sexual exploitation and abuse, sexual activity with children under 18, or exchange of money, employment, goods or services for sex;
- Become involved in sexual liaisons which could affect our impartiality, or the well-being of others;
- Be abusive or uncivil to any member of the public;
- Wilfully damage or misuse any United Nations property or equipment;
- Use a vehicle improperly or without authorization;
- Collect unauthorized souvenirs;

- Participate in any illegal activities, corrupt or improper practices; or
- Attempt to use our positions for personal advantage, to make false claims or accept benefits to which we are not entitled.

We realize that the consequences of failure to act within these guidelines may:

- Erode confidence and trust in the United Nations;
- Jeopardize the achievement of the mission;
- Jeopardize our status and security as peacekeeping personnel; and
- Result in administrative, disciplinary or criminal action.

PART TWO

Conduct of Peace Operations

A. General Human Rights Instruments

Introduction

In terms of legal frameworks, international human rights law (IHRL) is an integral component of UN peace operations. Peacekeepers are expected to comply with their State's and the UN's human rights principles, rules, and standards. They are also expected to protect human rights by, for example, reporting violations. The UN continues to emphasise the importance of human rights to peace operations.

This introduction provides an understanding of the range of issues involved in the application of IHRL to UN peace operations. It allows those engaged at all levels of peacekeeping operations to better comprehend the relevance of human rights documents included in Part Two of this book. It does not provide a comprehensive analysis of IHRL.

The Office of the United Nations High Commissioner for Human Rights (OHCHR), the principal UN office mandated to protect human rights,[1] defines human rights as:

> rights inherent to all human beings, whatever our nationality, place of residence, sex, national or ethnic origin, colour, religion, language, or any other status. We are all equally entitled to our human rights without discrimination. These rights are all interrelated, interdependent and indivisible.[2]

The Preamble to the Charter of the United Nations (Charter)[3] expresses the determination of the drafters 'to reaffirm faith in fundamental human rights, in the dignity and worth of the human person, in the equal rights of men and women and of nations large and small'. The Charter states in Article 1(3) that one of the key purposes of the UN is:

> To achieve international co-operation in solving international problems of an economic, social, cultural, or humanitarian character, and in promoting and encouraging respect for human rights and for fundamental freedoms for all without distinction as to race, sex, language, or religion.[4]

These themes are reflected in Article 55(c) of the Charter which states that the UN shall promote 'universal respect for, and observance of, human rights and fundamental freedoms for all without distinction as to race, sex, language, or religion', and in Article 56, which requires Member States to 'take joint and separate action in co-operation with the Organization for the achievement of the purposes set forth in Article 55'. Articles 1(3), 55(c), and 56 of the Charter, therefore, bind all Member States of the UN to promote and encourage respect for, and observance of, human rights and fundamental freedoms for all, without distinction as to race, sex, language, or religion.

All the human rights treaties and standards are based on the Universal Declaration of Human Rights (UDHR).[5] The UDHR signalled rights that each State should strive to promote and protect for its own people and the peoples of territories under its jurisdiction. The UDHR affirmed the inherent dignity and worth of every person without distinction. The UDHR is now considered the foundational

---

1 For more details of the OHCHR, see <http://www.ohchr.org/EN/AboutUs/Pages/WhoWeAre.aspx> accessed 1 November 2017.

2 See <http://www.ohchr.org/EN/Issues/Pages/WhatareHumanRights.aspx> accessed 1 November 2017. Human rights have also been described as:

> rights held simply by virtue of being a human person. They are part and parcel of the integrity and dignity of the human being. They are thus rights that cannot be given or withdrawn at will by any domestic legal system. And, although they may most effectively be implemented by the domestic legal system, that system is not the source of the right. International human rights law is the source of the obligation, albeit that obligation is reflected in the content of domestic law: Rosalyn Higgins, *Problems and Processes: International Law and How We Use It* (Oxford University Press 1994) 96.

3 See ch 1 above.

4 Ibid, Article 1(3).

5 For detailed discussion of each recital in the Preamble and each individual article including its definition, concept, and drafting history, as well as a history of the complete UDHR, see <http://www.columbia.edu/ccnmtl/projects/mmt/udhr/index.html> accessed 1 November 2017. See also Bruce Oswald, Helen Durham, and Adrian Bates, *Documents on the Law of UN Peace Operations* (Oxford University Press 2010) ch 4.

document of IHRL and has led directly to the adoption of numerous other human rights treaties and instruments.

IHRL continues to develop at the universal, regional, and State levels. There are treaties such as the International Covenant on Civil and Political Rights (ICCPR)[6] and the Convention on the Rights of the Child (CRC)[7] that deal generally with human rights; and treaties such as the Convention against Torture and Other Cruel, Inhuman or Degrading Treatment or Punishment (CAT)[8] which deal with specific areas of human rights. There are also universal legal instruments that do not have the status of treaties but, nonetheless, provide useful guidance as to human rights standards that States should aspire to uphold. Such instruments include the Body of Principles for the Protection of All Persons under Any Form of Detention or Imprisonment,[9] the Code of Conduct for Law Enforcement Officials,[10] and the Basic Principles on the Use of Force and Firearms by Law Enforcement Officials.[11]

The International Court of Justice (ICJ) reaffirmed the extraterritorial application of human rights treaties in its judgment of 19 December 2005 in the *Case concerning Armed Activities on the Territory of the Congo (Democratic Republic of Congo v Uganda)* (Judgment) ('*Congo Case*')[12] when it held, citing its findings from the *Legal Consequences of the Construction of a Wall in the Occupied Palestinian Territory* (Advisory Opinion) (hereafter '*Israeli Wall Case*'),[13] 'that international human rights instruments are applicable "in respect of acts done by a State in the exercise of its jurisdiction outside its own territory", particularly in occupied territories'.[14]

In both the *Congo Case* and the *Israeli Wall Case* the ICJ stated that in situations of armed conflict, including occupation, the

> protections afforded by human rights conventions does not cease ... save through the effect of provisions for derogation of the kind to be found in Article 4 of the International Covenant on Civil and Political Rights. As regards the relationship between international humanitarian law and human rights law, there are thus three possible situations: some rights may be exclusively matters of international humanitarian law; other may be exclusively matters of human rights law; and yet others may be matters of both these branches of international law.[15]

IHRL has also been developed through regional arrangements in Africa, the Americas, and Europe.[16] In Africa, the African Charter on Human and Peoples' Rights (also known as the Banjul Charter)[17] is the central African human rights document along with a Protocol to the Charter establishing the African Court on Human and Peoples' Rights.[18] The African human rights framework is supported by other instruments such as the African Charter on the Rights and Welfare of the Child;[19] the Protocol to the African Charter on Human and Peoples' Rights on the Rights of Women in Africa;[20] and the Principles and Guidelines on the Right to a Fair Trial and Legal Assistance in Africa.[21]

---

6 See ch 6 below.

7 See ch 9 below.

8 See ch 8 below.

9 See ch 12 below.

10 See ch 13 below.

11 See ch 13 below.

12 *Case concerning Armed Activities on the Territory of the Congo (Democratic Republic of Congo v Uganda)* (Judgment) [2005] ICJ Rep 116 (hereafter *Congo Case*).

13 Legal Consequences of the Construction of a Wall in the Occupied Palestinian Territory (Advisory Opinion) [2004] ICJ Rep 136 (hereafter *Israeli Wall Case*).

14 *Congo Case* (n 12), 243.

15 *Israeli Wall Case* (n 12), [106]; *Congo Case* (n 13), [216].

16 Relevant human rights instruments may be accessed from the University of Minnesota's Human Rights Library at <http://www1.umn.edu/humanrts/instree/auoz.htm> accessed 1 November 2017.

17 African Charter on Human and Peoples' Rights (opened for signature 27 June 1981, entered into force 21 October 1996) 21 ILM 58.

18 Protocol to the African Charter on Human and Peoples' Rights on the Establishment of an African Court on Human and Peoples' Rights (9 June 1998) OAU Doc OAU/LEG/EXP/AFCHPR/PROT (III). For more information about the Court, see <http://en.african-court.org/> accessed 1 November 2017.

19 African Charter on the Rights and Welfare of the Child (opened for signature 11 July 1990, entered into force 29 November 1999) OAU Doc CAB/LEG/24.9/49 (1990).

20 Protocol to the African Charter on Human and Peoples' Rights on the Rights of Women in Africa (adopted 13 September 2000, entered into force 25 November 2005) OAU Doc CAB/LEG/66.6 (13 September 2000), reprinted in 1 African Human Rights Law Journal 40.

21 Principles and Guidelines on the Right to a Fair Trial and Legal Assistance in Africa, DOC/OS(XXX) 247, *reprinted in* 12 International Human Rights Reports 1180.

The Americas also have several instruments concerning IHRL: the American Declaration on the Rights and Duties of Man;[22] the American Convention on Human Rights;[23] the Inter-American Convention on Forced Disappearance of Persons;[24] the Inter-American Convention to Prevent and Punish Torture;[25] and the Inter-American Convention on the Prevention, Punishment, and Eradication of Violence Against Women[26] are some of the key documents which support the IHRL framework in the Americas.

The European IHRL framework is founded on the European Convention for the Protection of Human Rights and Fundamental Freedoms, as amended by Protocols Nos. 11 and 14 (ECHR).[27] Other documents relevant to the application of the ECHR include Protocol No 6 to the Convention for the Protection of Human Rights and Fundamental Freedoms concerning the Abolition of the Death Penalty,[28] and the European Convention for the Prevention of Torture and Inhuman or Degrading Treatment or Punishment.[29]

Notwithstanding the fact that this book does not contain regional human rights instruments, it might be that in certain peace operations reference will need to be made to regional human rights instruments. For instance, this will be the case where a State participating in a peacekeeping operation is a member of a regional organisation that has adopted its own human rights instruments which are viewed as binding peacekeepers of that State. For example, the European Court of Human Rights (ECtHR) has stated that where a military force has total and exclusive legal and factual control over an area such as a detention facility,[30] or where it has authority and control over an individual,[31] the rights and obligations of States under the ECHR will apply extraterritorially to those forces. The ECtHR has also stated, in relation to UN peace operations, that where the UN has command and control over the military forces of a State Party to the ECHR, the ECHR could not be interpreted in a manner which would subject that State's acts to the scrutiny of the ECtHR.[32]

In addition to universal and regional human rights instruments, States are increasingly developing and applying domestic human rights legislation. While such legislation is not included in this book, it may nonetheless be relevant to peacekeepers from those States. For example, the Canadian Charter of Rights and Freedoms 1982[33] and the United Kingdom's Human Rights Act 1998[34] may, in certain circumstances, be applied to peacekeepers from those States.

The matter of the extraterritorial application of human rights instruments has also arisen in domestic courts. The Supreme Court of the Netherlands, in its judgment about a case concerning the Dutch Battalion's involvement in the massacre of Srebrenica inhabitants by Bosnian Serbs in July 1995, determined that in some exceptional circumstances the ECHR might have extraterritorial jurisdiction.[35] The Supreme Court concluded:

---

22 American Declaration of the Rights and Duties of Man (adopted 2 May 1948) OAS Res XXX, *reprinted in* Basic Documents Pertaining to Human Rights in the Inter-American System, OEA/Ser.L.V/II.82 doc6 rev1, 17 (1992).

23 American Convention on Human Rights (opened for signature 22 November 1969, entered into force 18 July 1978) 1144 UNTS 123, *reprinted in* Basic Documents Pertaining to Human Rights in the Inter-American System, OEA/Ser.L.V/II.82 doc6 rev1, 25 (1992).

24 Inter-American Convention on Forced Disappearance of Persons (opened for signature 9 June 1994, entered into force 28 March 1996) 33 ILM 1429.

25 Inter-American Convention to Prevent and Punish Torture (opened for signature 9 December 1985, entered into force 28 February 1987) 25 ILM 519, *reprinted in* Basic Documents Pertaining to Human Rights in the Inter-American System, OEA/Ser.L.V/II.82 doc6 rev1, 83 (1992).

26 Inter-American Convention on the Prevention, Punishment and Eradication of Violence Against Women (opened for signature 9 June 1994, entered into force 5 March 1995) 33 ILM 1534.

27 European Convention for the Protection of Human Rights and Fundamental Freedoms, as amended by Protocols Nos. 11 and 14 (opened for signature 4 November 1950, entered into force 3 September 1953) ETS 5.

28 Protocol No 6 to the Convention for the Protection of Human Rights and Fundamental Freedoms concerning the Abolition of the Death Penalty (opened for signature 18 April 1983, entered into force 1 March 1985) ETS 114.

29 European Convention for the Prevention of Torture and Inhuman or Degrading Treatment or Punishment (opened for signature 26 November 1987, entered into force 1 February 1989) ETS 126.

30 *Al-Saadoon and Mufdhi v United Kingdom* (Admissibility), App No 61498/08, 30 June 2009, [88]; *Al-Saadoon and Mufdhi v United Kingdom* (Judgement), App No 61498/08, 2 March 2010; *Al-Jedda v United Kingdom*, App No 27021/08, 7 July 2011, [149] (hereafter *Al-Jedda v United Kingdom*).

31 *Al-Jedda v United Kingdom* (n 30), [149].

32 Decision as to Admissibility: *Behrami and Behrami v France,* App no 71466/01, 2 May 2007; *Saramati v France, Germany and Norway*, App no 78166/01, 2 May 2007, [144]–[152].

33 Canadian Charter of Rights and Freedoms <http://laws-lois.justice.gc.ca/eng/Const/page-15.html> accessed 1 November 2017.

34 Human Rights Act 1998 <http://www.opsi.gov.uk/acts/acts1998/ukpga_19980042_en_1> accessed 1 November 2017.

35 *State of Netherlands v Mastafić-Mujić, Mustafić, Mustafić*, Case no 12/03329, 6 September 2013. See also *State of the Netherlands v Nuhanović*, 12/03324, 6 September 2013.

In this case Dutchbat's presence in Srebrenica and in the compound in Potocari resulted from the participation of the Netherlands in UNPROFOR [United Nations Protection Force], and UNPROFOR derived its right to take action in Srebrenica from the Agreement on the status of the United Nations Protection Force in Bosnia and Herzegovina concluded between the United Nations and Bosnia and Herzegovina (see finding of law 2.6 of the interim judgment). This means that the State was competent, through Dutchbat, to exercise jurisdiction within the meaning of article 1 ECHR in the compound.

Nor can it be said that, after the fall of the enclave on 11 July 1995 and, in particular, at the moment of Dutchbat's disputed conduct, it was de facto impossible for the State to exercise jurisdiction as referred to above in the compound. According to the facts on which it has based its judgment, the Court of Appeal has assumed that the Bosnian Serb army respected Dutchbat's authority over the compound to which it had withdrawn until the departure of Dutchbat on 21 July 1995. These facts provide a sufficient basis for the view that the State, through Dutchbat, was actually able to ensure compliance with the human rights enshrined in articles 2 [protecting the right to life] and 3 [prohibiting torture, and inhuman or degrading treatment or punishment] ECHR and articles 6 [protecting the right to fair trial] and 7 [prohibiting punishment not recognised by law] in relation to Muhamed and Ibro Nukhanovic.[36]

The reach of IHRL includes protecting the fundamental rights and freedoms of individuals and extends to the right to self-determination, the right to enjoy the highest attainable standard of physical and mental health, the prohibition against the arbitrary deprivation of life, the prohibition against slavery, the right to liberty and security of the person, the prohibition against torture, the right for women to be equal with men before the law, and the interests of the child being a primary consideration in all actions concerning children. IHRL is also relevant to a range of activities such as policing, the use of force, detention operations, Disarmament, Demobilization and Reintegration (DDR), and post-conflict peacebuilding.

The increasing role of IHRL at the universal, regional, and State levels has led to a greater emphasis on the application of IHRL in UN peace operations. In the broadest sense, it may be argued that because of the provisions of the Charter and the view of the ICJ in relation to the application of IHRL instruments such as the UDHR and the ICCPR, any mandate authorising a UN peace operation should be seen as promoting and encouraging respect for human rights and fundamental freedoms within the human rights framework, even if the protection of human rights and fundamental freedoms is not explicitly mentioned. This point is reinforced by Annex H of the revised model Memorandum of Understanding (MOU)[37] and the aide-memoire (blue card) 'We are United Nations Peacekeepers', which both requires UN peacekeepers to:

> comply with the Guidelines on International Humanitarian Law for Forces Undertaking United Nations Peacekeeping Operations and the applicable portions of the Universal Declaration of Human Rights as the fundamental basis of our standards.[38]

Furthermore, Rule 5 of the Code of Conduct for Blue Helmets requires UN peacekeepers to '[r]espect and regard the human rights of all. Support and aid the infirm, sick and weak. Do not act in revenge or with malice, in particular when dealing with prisoners, detainees or people in your custody'.[39]

At an operational level, it is important to understand that human rights is one of the three pillars of the UN's work—the other two pillars being peace and security, and development.[40] Human rights is also an essential pillar of the UN's protection framework. As stated by the High-Level Independent Panel on Peace Operations:

> Over the past two decades, concerted efforts have been made to strengthen international protection frameworks. Those include the increasing prominence of human rights and protection-related mandates for United Nations peace operations, the responsibility to protect, as set out in General Assembly resolution 60/1 on the 2005 World Summit Outcome, and most recently the Human Rights Up Front initiative of

---

36 *State of the Netherlands v Nuhanović*, 12/03324, 6 September 2013, [3.17.3].

37 See ch 3 above.

38 Ad Hoc Working Group of Experts of the Special Committee on Peacekeeping Operations, 'We are United Nations Peacekeeping Personnel', UN Doc A/61/19 (Part III) 12 June 2007, 7. Now published in the 2008 Contingent-Owned Equipment Manual, UN Doc A/C.5/63/18, 9 June 2008, Chapter 9, Annex H. See ch 27 below.

39 See UN Standards of Conduct, 'Ten Rules: Code of Personal Conduct for Blue Helmets', Rule 5 <https://conduct.unmissions.org/documents-standards> accessed 1 November 2017. See ch 27 below.

40 See <http://www.un.org/un70/en/content/videos/three-pillars> accessed 1 November 2017.

the Secretary-General. In addition to the mandate of the United Nations High Commissioner for Human Rights, mechanisms of the Human Rights Council and the human rights treaty bodies, the Office of the Special Adviser on the Prevention of Genocide and the Office of the Special Adviser on the Responsibility to Protect, mandatory monitoring and reporting arrangements have been set out in General Assembly and Security Council resolutions on children in armed conflict and sexual violence in conflict. Policies, guidance and training have been developed on ways to implement human rights and protection-related mandates. Many United Nations peace operations now include protection of civilians advisers, child protection officers and women's protection advisers working alongside the mission's human rights component. But that growth in concepts, standards, advocacy and specialized personnel has yet to transform reality on the ground, where it matters.[41]

This emphasis is manifested in Security Council resolutions and in the conduct of specific operations. It is now the practice of the Security Council to include specific reference to UN peace operations promoting and encouraging respect for human rights and fundamental freedoms in resolutions establishing such operations. For example, Security Council resolution 2155 relating to the establishment of the United Nations Mission in South Sudan (UNMISS), included as one of UNMISS's tasks:

(i) To monitor, investigate, verify, and report publicly and regularly on abuses and violations of human rights and violations of international humanitarian law, including those that may amount to war crimes or crimes against humanity;

(ii) To monitor, investigate, verify and report specifically and publicly on violations and abuses committed against children and women, including all forms of sexual and gender-based violence in armed conflict by accelerating the implementation of monitoring, analysis and reporting arrangements on conflict-related sexual violence and by strengthening the monitoring and reporting mechanism for grave violations against children;

(iii) To coordinate with, and offer technical support to, where appropriate, the African Union's Commission of Inquiry for South Sudan.[42]

Similarly, the mandate of the United Nations Mission in Sudan (UNMIS) includes a contribution 'towards international efforts to protect and promote human rights in Sudan'.[43]

In resolution 2211 concerning the United Nations Organization Stabilization Mission in the Democratic Republic of the Congo (MONUSCO) the Security Council stressed the need for host nation military forces supported by UN peacekeepers to 'carry out operations in accordance with international law, including international humanitarian law and international human rights law, as applicable'.[44]

The Security Council has also emphasised the importance of IHRL in the context of thematic resolutions such as those dealing with women, peace and security,[45] and children and armed conflict.[46] For example, Security Council resolution 1674 on the protection of civilians in armed conflict states that the Security Council:

Reaffirms also its condemnation in the strongest terms of all acts of violence or abuses committed against civilians in situations of armed conflict in violation of applicable international obligations with respect in particular to (i) torture and other prohibited treatment, (ii) gender-based and sexual violence, (iii) violence against children, (iv) the recruitment and use of child soldiers, (v) trafficking in humans, (vi) forced displacement, and (vii) the intentional denial of humanitarian assistance, and ***demands*** [emphasis in original] that all parties put an end to such practices.[47]

When interpreting Security Council resolutions there is a presumption that the Security Council does not intend to impose obligations on States to breach fundamental provisions of human rights. As explained by the ECtHR in *Al-Jedda*:

the Court must have regard to the purposes for which the United Nations was created. As well as the purpose of maintaining international peace and security, set out in the first sub-paragraph of Article 1 of the Charter of the United Nations, the third sub-paragraph provides that the United Nations was

41 United Nations, 'Identical Letters dated 17 June 2015 from the Secretary-General addressed to the President of the General Assembly and the President of the Security Council', UN Doc A/70/95–S/2015/446 of 17 June 2015, [84].

42 SC Res 2155 (2014) of 27 May 2014, Operative Part [4](b).

43 SC Res 1590 (2005) of 24 March 2005, Operative Part [4](d).

44 SC Res 2211 (2015) of 26 March 2015, Operative Part [24].

45 See ch 17 below.

46 See ch 18 below.

47 SC Res 1674 (2006) of 28 April 2006, Operative Part [5].

> established to 'achieve international cooperation in ... promoting and encouraging respect for human rights and for fundamental freedoms'. Article 24 § 2 of the Charter requires the Security Council, in discharging its duties with respect to its primary responsibility for the maintenance of international peace and security, to 'act in accordance with the Purposes and Principles of the United Nations'. Against this background, the Court considers that, in interpreting its resolutions, there must be a presumption that the Security Council does not intend to impose any obligation on member States to breach fundamental principles of human rights. In the event of any ambiguity in the terms of a United Nations Security Council resolution, the Court must therefore choose the interpretation which is most in harmony with the requirements of the Convention and which avoids any conflict of obligations. In the light of the United Nations' important role in promoting and encouraging respect for human rights, it is to be expected that clear and explicit language would be used were the Security Council to intend States to take particular measures which would conflict with their obligations under international human rights law.[48]

The General Assembly's Special Committee on Peacekeeping Operations (C34) has also emphasised the importance of IHRL to peace operations. For example, the C34 has stated:

> Particularly with regard to the conduct of military, civilian police and civilian personnel in United Nations peacekeeping missions managed by the Department of Peacekeeping Operations, the Special Committee reiterates its insistence on the need for compliance with obligations under international human rights law and international humanitarian law, and underlines again that all acts of exploitation, including sexual exploitation, and all forms of abuse by military, civilian police and civilian personnel in United Nations peacekeeping missions managed by the Department are intolerable.[49]

The 2008 UN Principles and Guidelines confirm that:

> International human rights law is an integral part of the normative framework for United Nations peacekeeping operations. The Universal Declaration of Human Rights, which sets the cornerstone of international human rights standards, emphasizes that human rights and fundamental freedoms are universal and guaranteed to everybody. United Nations peacekeeping operations should be conducted in full respect of human rights and should seek to advance human rights through the implementation of their mandates ... United Nations peacekeeping personnel—whether military, police or civilian—should act in accordance with international human rights law and understand how the implementation of their tasks intersects with human rights.[50]

A further and more recent affirmation of the importance of human rights in UN peace operations is the Human Rights Due Diligence Policy on United Nations Support to Non-United Nations Security Forces[51] which concerns the human rights and international humanitarian law[52] obligations of the UN and its peacekeepers when supporting, for example, regional or host nation military forces to conduct operations.[53]

At another level, the importance and relevance of IHRL to peace operations is evidenced by a MOU between the OHCHR and the Department of Peacekeeping Operations (DPKO).[54] This MOU aims to increase the effectiveness of UN peace operations when carrying out their human rights mandates through increased cooperation between OHCHR and DPKO. Paragraph 5 of the Annex to the MOU states that:

> The activities of human rights components of peace-keeping operations shall be based on international human rights standards, as defined in the relevant international treaties, declarations, guidelines and other instruments. In the implementation of their activities ... and within the framework of their mandate, human rights components of peace-keeping operations will seek to promote an integrated approach to human rights promotion and monitoring, paying due attention to civil, cultural, economic,

---

48 *Al-Jedda v United Kingdom* (n 30), [102].

49 Special Committee on Peacekeeping Operations, 'Report of the Special Committee on Peacekeeping Operations and its Working Group at the 2005 substantive session', UN Doc A/59/19, 1 March 2005, [52].

50 United Nations, 'United Nations Peacekeeping Operations: Principles and Guidelines', 2008, 14–15 (hereafter referred to as UN Principles and Guidelines, but also known as the 'Capstone Doctrine') <https://www.un.org/ruleoflaw/blog/document/united-nations-peacekeeping-operations-principles-and-guidelines-the-capstone-doctrine/> accessed 8 April 2019.

51 See ch 32 below.

52 See ch 16 below.

53 The UN has also developed a policy entitled 'Human Rights in UN Peace Operations and Political Missions dated 31 August 2011'. Unfortunately, that policy is not in the public domain and can only be accessed through the UN intranet system.

54 Memorandum of Understanding between the Office of the High Commissioner for Human Rights and the Department of Peacekeeping Operations of 5 November 1999.

political and social rights, including the right to development, and to the special needs of women, children, minorities, internally displaced persons, and other groups requiring special protection.[55]

To reinforce the importance of human rights at an institutional level, the former UN Secretary-General Ban Ki-Moon developed the Human Rights up Front (HRuP) initiative to ensure that the UN prioritises human rights in its work on peace and security, and development.[56] The initiative brings together:

- Cultural change: (i) All staff and UN entities to conduct their work with an awareness of their wider responsibility to support the UN Charter and overall UN mandates; (ii) Staff to take principled positions and act with moral courage; (iii) UNHQ to back staff who uphold overall UN responsibilities; (iv) greater accountability for UN action.
- Operational change: (i) Bring the UN's three pillars together; (ii) Joint analysis and strategy by the UN system, in the field and UNHQ; (iii) Better early warning and response.
- Change to UN engagement with Member States: (i) Proactive engagement with national authorities about concerns identified in analysis; (ii) early and full engagement with Member States to prevent large-scale human rights violations.[57]

Specific peace operations may also develop an IHRL framework to apply to the conduct of their operations. For example, the transitional administrations in Kosovo and East Timor emphasised the application of several human rights instruments to the conduct of their administrations. The United Nations Interim Administration Mission in Kosovo (UNMIK) was given a broad mandate to provide Kosovo with a 'transitional administration while establishing and overseeing the development of provisional democratic self-governing institutions to ensure conditions for a peaceful and normal life for all inhabitants in Kosovo'.[58] Within this broad mandate one of UNMIK's main responsibilities included 'protecting and promoting human rights'.[59] This is reflected in UNMIK regulation 1999/24 on the law applicable in Kosovo, which states in section 1.3 that:

> In exercising their functions, all persons undertaking public duties or holding public office in Kosovo shall observe internationally recognized human rights standards, as reflected in particular in:
>
> (a) The Universal Declaration on Human Rights of 10 December 1948;
>
> (b) The European Convention for the Protection of Human Rights and Fundamental Freedoms of 4 November 1950 and the Protocols thereto;
>
> (c) The International Covenant on Civil and Political Rights of 16 December 1966 and the Protocols thereto;
>
> (d) The International Covenant on Economic, Social and Cultural Rights of 16 December 1966;
>
> (e) The Convention on the Elimination of All Forms of Racial Discrimination of 21 December 1965;
>
> (f) The Convention on Elimination of All Forms of Discrimination Against Women of 17 December 1979;
>
> (g) The Convention Against Torture and Other Cruel, Inhumane or Degrading Treatment or Punishment of 17 December 1984; and
>
> (h) The International Convention on the Rights of the Child of 20 December 1989.[60]

It is appropriate that peacekeepers address how they might best ensure that their conduct does not breach the rights of the population in their area of operations, particularly in light of the UN's emphasis on protecting and promoting fundamental human rights and freedoms. In this context IHRL is relevant in at least four ways.

First, IHRL is a very useful body of law for peacekeepers when they are undertaking capacity building and mentoring national police in the host State. In such situations, peacekeepers can use international human rights instruments to develop a State's capacity to adhere to fundamental

---

55 Ibid, Annex [5].

56 General Assembly, 'Letter dated 24 December 2015 from the Secretary-General addressed to the President of the General Assembly', UN Doc A/70/656 of 6 January 2016.

57 'Human Rights up Front: A Summary for Staff', see <http://www.un.org/News/dh/pdf/english/2016/Human-Rights-up-Front.pdf> accessed 1 November 2017.

58 SC Res 1244 (1999) of 10 June 1999, Operative Part [5].

59 Ibid, Operative Part [11](j).

60 United Nations Interim Administration Mission in Kosovo (UNMIK), Reg 1999/24 of 12 December 1999 on the law applicable in Kosovo, Section 1.3 <http://www.unmikonline.org/regulations/unmikgazette/02english/E1999regs/RE1999_24.htm> accessed 1 November 2017.

principles of human rights such as the prohibitions against discrimination and torture, as well as to develop best practices in relation to matters such as the treatment of refugees, internally displaced persons, persons in custody, and other vulnerable individuals.

Second, when dealing with the local population the legal norms found in IHRL instruments will be highly relevant for peacekeepers. For example, in situations where peacekeepers take and handle detainees they will need to apply relevant norms found in documents such as the ICCPR, CAT, and the Body of Principles for the Protection of All Persons Under Any Form of Detention or Imprisonment, to ensure that they do not breach the legal obligations of their States, the fundamental rights of detainees, and that their dealings with detainees meet best practice standards.

Third, when UN peacekeepers are working with non-UN forces, such as regional or host State security forces, they cannot support those forces 'where there are substantial grounds for believing there is a real risk of the receiving entities committing grave violations of international humanitarian law, human rights or refugee law and where the relevant authorities fail to take the necessary corrective or mitigating measures'.[61]

Fourth, IHRL is also relevant in relation to the accountability of peacekeepers. For example, in situations where the UN adversely interferes with the human rights of individuals in the host country the only formal mechanism for financial compensation is via the UN's third-party liability framework, which is an internal process.[62]

61 United Nations, 'Human Rights Due Diligence Policy on United Nations Support to Non-Judicial Nations Security Forces of 5 March 2013', UN Doc A/67/775–S/2013/110, Annex [1]. See ch 32 below.

62 See Introduction to Part Three and chs 22–24 below.

4

Convention on the Prevention and Punishment of the Crime of Genocide

Prefatory Note

Peacekeeping missions are sometimes established to deal with situations of genocide or the effects of genocide. The Convention on the Prevention and Punishment of the Crime of Genocide (Genocide Convention)[1] concerns one of the most serious crimes in international law. The prohibition of genocide is recognised as a *jus cogens* norm of international law.[2] The crime of genocide is also recognised as an international crime in the Rome Statute of the International Criminal Court (Rome Statute).[3] As stipulated in the Genocide Convention and in the Rome Statute, the crime is committed when a person acts with:

> intent to destroy, in whole or in part, a national, ethical, racial or religious group . . . [by]:
>
> a. Killing members of the group;
>
> b. Causing serious bodily or mental harm to members of the group;
>
> c. Deliberately inflicting on the group conditions of life calculated to bring about its physical destruction in whole or in part;
>
> d. Imposing measures intended to prevent births within the group;
>
> e. Forcibly transferring children of the group to another group.[4]

The difference between the crimes of genocide and ethnic cleansing was addressed by the International Court of Justice (ICJ) in *Application of the Convention on the Prevention and Punishment of the Crime of Genocide (Bosnia and Herzegovina v Serbia and Montenegro)* (Judgment) (*Genocide Case*):

> Neither the intent, as a matter of policy, to render an area 'ethnically homogeneous', nor the operations that may be carried out to implement such policy, can as such be designated as genocide . . . As the ICTY has observed, while 'there are obvious similarities between a genocidal policy and the policy commonly known as "ethnic cleansing" ' (*Krstić*, IT-98-33-T, Trial Chamber Judgment, 2 August 2001, para. 562), yet '[a] clear distinction must be drawn between physical destruction and mere dissolution of a group. The expulsion of a group or part of a group does not in itself suffice for genocide.' (*Stakić*, IT-97-24-T, Trial Chamber Judgment, 31 July 2003, para. 519.) In other words, whether a particular operation described as 'ethnic cleansing' amounts to genocide depends on the presence or absence of acts listed in Article II of the Genocide Convention, and of the intent to destroy the group as such. In fact, in the context of the Convention, the term 'ethnic cleansing' has no legal significance of its own.[5]

Article I of the Genocide Convention confirms that genocide is a crime under international law in both war and peacetime which State Parties pledge to prevent and punish. Article VII obliges States in cases of genocide to 'grant extradition in accordance with their laws and treaties in force'.[6]

---

1 Convention on the Prevention and Punishment of the Crime of Genocide (opened for signature 9 December 1948, entered into force 12 January 1951) 78 UNTS 277 (hereafter Genocide Convention).

2 *Application of the Convention on the Prevention and Punishment of the Crime of Genocide (Bosnia and Herzegovina v Serbia and Montenegro)* (Judgment) [2007] ICJ Rep 1, 161 (hereafter *Genocide Case*); *Case concerning the Armed Activities on the Territory of the Congo (Democratic Republic of the Congo v Rwanda)* (Judgment) [2006] ICJ Rep [64].

3 Rome Statute of the International Criminal Court (opened for signature 17 July 1998, entered into force 1 July 2002) 2187 UNTS 3, Articles 5 and 6 (hereafter Rome Statute).

4 Genocide Convention (n 1), Article II.

5 *Genocide Case* (n 2), 190. In relation to ethnic cleansing, see also UN Security Council, 'Interim Report of the Commission of Experts Established Pursuant to Security Council Resolution 780 (1992)', UN Doc S/25274 (26 January 1993); and 'Final Report of the Commission of Experts Established Pursuant to United Nations Security Council Resolution 780 (1992)', UN Doc S/1994/674 (27 May 1994), Annex.

6 Genocide Convention (n 1), Article VII.

Although not explicit, Article VII, when read together with Articles V and VI, has been taken to impose an 'extradite or prosecute' (*aut dedere aut judicare*) obligation on State Parties.[7] If the arresting State is not the territory where the alleged act was committed, the State must extradite the person to the State where the act occurred for prosecution or to the appropriate international criminal tribunal if it has jurisdiction.

The ICJ in the *Genocide Case* found that Article I of the Genocide Convention places a direct obligation on a State Party to prevent genocide.[8]

The ICJ also found that the obligation of a State to prevent and punish the crime of genocide under Article I is not territorially limited by the Genocide Convention.[9] The Court stated:

> The substantive obligations arising from Articles I and III are not on their face limited by territory. They apply to a State wherever it may be acting or may be able to act in ways appropriate to meeting the obligations in question.[10]

Later in its judgment the Court discussed the obligation to prevent genocide under Article I not as a requirement to succeed in preventing genocide, but rather to 'employ all means reasonably available to them, to prevent genocide so far as possible'.[11] Responsibility is not incurred simply because the attempt to prevent genocide failed. Rather, responsibility is incurred 'if the State manifestly failed to take all measures to prevent genocide which were within its power, and which might have contributed to preventing the genocide'.[12]

Peace operations have been deployed in situations where genocide has occurred or allegations of the crime of genocide have arisen. For example, the United Nations Mission for Rwanda II (UNAMIR II),[13] and United Nations Organization Stabilization Mission in the Democratic Republic of the Congo (MONUSCO)[14] were created in large part to deal with the genocide that occurred in Rwanda in 1994. More recently, the UN's Special Adviser on the Prevention of Genocide has monitored the risk of genocide in South Sudan and has recommended that the Security Council consider specifically requesting the United Nations Mission in South Sudan (UNMISS):

> monitor, investigate and report on all incidents of hate speech and incitement to violence, and be provided full access by the Government of South Sudan to do so ... [and] [a]ll support should be given to UNMISS to carry out all the Mission's mandated tasks, in particularly tasks that relate to the protection of civilians and human rights monitoring, which could contribute to preventing future violence. The Government should be pressed to ensure that freedom of movement is granted to all United Nations personnel, both civilians and military, to conduct patrols, investigate and report on incidents, and conduct community based conflict prevention and resolution initiatives.[15]

The Security Council has also reaffirmed that the crime of genocide as 'recognized [in the Genocide Convention] is an odious scourge ... and that further international cooperation is required to facilitate the timely prevention and punishment of the crime of genocide'.[16]

In peace operations, the Genocide Convention is relevant in at least three ways. First, the Convention is relevant in the use of armed force by peacekeepers to prevent any act of genocide. Such actions would at the very least be consistent with the general mandate of protecting civilians. Second, the broad obligation to prevent genocide means that peacekeepers must report and, where appropriate, investigate allegations concerning genocide. For example, as mentioned above, the Secretary-General's Special Adviser on the Prevention of Genocide has encouraged the Security Council to 'specifically request that UNMISS [United Nations Mission in South Sudan] monitor, investigate and report on all incidents of hate speech and incitement to violence, and be

---

7 See Final Report of the International Law Commission, 'The Obligation to Extradite or Prosecute (*aut dedere aut judicare*)', 2014.

8 *Genocide Case* (n 2), 165.

9 Ibid, 153–4.

10 Ibid, 183.

11 Ibid, 430.

12 Ibid.

13 For more detail about UNAMIR II, see <https://peacekeeping.un.org/en> accessed 1 November 2017.

14 See <https://monusco.unmissions.org/en> accessed 1 November 2017.

15 Statement to the Security Council by Adama Dieng, United Nations Special Adviser on the Prevention of Genocide, on his visit to South Sudan, 17 November 2016, Press Release (hereafter Special Adviser on the Prevention of Genocide Press Release). For more detail about the role of the Special Adviser on the Prevention of Genocide, see <https://www.un.org/en/genocideprevention/> accessed 8 April 2019.

16 SC Res 2150 (2014) of 16 April 2014, Preamble.

provided full access by the Government of South Sudan to do so'.[17] Third, the obligation to prevent and punish those who commit the act of genocide might give rise to peacekeepers detaining any person accused of genocide until such time that the person can be handed to the appropriate national or international organisations. For example, Security Council resolution 2211 concerning MONUSCO, authorised peacekeepers to:

> Support and work with the authorities of the DRC to arrest and bring to justice those allegedly responsible for genocide, war crimes and crimes against humanity and violations of international humanitarian law and violations or abuses of human rights in the country, including leaders of armed groups, including through cooperation with States of the region and the ICC.[18]

Reference

Title	Convention on the Prevention and Punishment of the Crime of Genocide
Date of Adoption	9 December 1948
Opened for Signature	9 December 1948
Entered into Force	12 January 1951 in accordance with article XIII
Signatories	41
Parties	149
Depository	United Nations
Treaty Series	78 UNTS 277
Full Text	<https://www.ohchr.org/en/professionalinterest/pages/crimeofgenocide.aspx>[19]

Convention on the Prevention and Punishment of the Crime of Genocide[20]

(Extracts)

The Contracting Parties,

Having considered the declaration made by the General Assembly of the United Nations in its resolution 96 (I) dated 11 December 1946 that genocide is a crime under international law, contrary to the spirit and aims of the United Nations and condemned by the civilized world,

Recognizing that at all periods of history genocide has inflicted great losses on humanity, and

Being convinced that, in order to liberate mankind from such an odious scourge, international co-operation is required,

Hereby agree as hereinafter provided:

Article I

The Contracting Parties confirm that genocide, whether committed in time of peace or in time of war, is a crime under international law which they undertake to prevent and to punish.

17 Special Adviser on the Prevention of Genocide Press Release (n 15).

18 See also SC Res 2211 (2015) of 26 March 2016, Operative Part [9](d). In relation to the United Nations Multidimensional Integrated Stabilization Mission in the Central African Republic (MINUSCA), where the mandate to assist the authorities of the Central African Republic might be implied to extend to bringing those accused of genocide to justice, see SC Res 2301 (2016) of 26 July 2016, Operative Part [35](a).

19 Accessed 1 November 2017.

20 From Convention on the Prevention and Punishment of the Crime of Genocide, © 1948 United Nations. Reprinted with the permission of the United Nations.

Article II

In the present Convention, genocide means any of the following acts committed with intent to destroy, in whole or in part, a national, ethnical, racial or religious group, as such:

(a) Killing members of the group;
(b) Causing serious bodily or mental harm to members of the group;
(c) Deliberately inflicting on the group conditions of life calculated to bring about its physical destruction in whole or in part;
(d) Imposing measures intended to prevent births within the group;
(e) Forcibly transferring children of the group to another group.

Article III

The following acts shall be punishable:

(a) Genocide;
(b) Conspiracy to commit genocide;
(c) Direct and public incitement to commit genocide;
(d) Attempt to commit genocide;
(e) Complicity in genocide.

Article IV

Persons committing genocide or any of the other acts enumerated in article III shall be punished, whether they are constitutionally responsible rulers, public officials or private individuals.

Article V

The Contracting Parties undertake to enact, in accordance with their respective Constitutions, the necessary legislation to give effect to the provisions of the present Convention, and, in particular, to provide effective penalties for persons guilty of genocide or any of the other acts enumerated in article III.

Article VI

Persons charged with genocide or any of the other acts enumerated in article III shall be tried by a competent tribunal of the State in the territory of which the act was committed, or by such international penal tribunal as may have jurisdiction with respect to those Contracting Parties which shall have accepted its jurisdiction.

Article VII

Genocide and the other acts enumerated in article III shall not be considered as political crimes for the purpose of extradition.

The Contracting Parties pledge themselves in such cases to grant extradition in accordance with their laws and treaties in force.

Article VIII

Any Contracting Party may call upon the competent organs of the United Nations to take such action under the Charter of the United Nations as they consider appropriate for the prevention and suppression of acts of genocide or any of the other acts enumerated in article III.

Article IX

Disputes between the Contracting Parties relating to the interpretation, application or fulfilment of the present Convention, including those relating to the responsibility of a State for genocide or for any of the other acts enumerated in article III, shall be submitted to the International Court of Justice at the request of any of the parties to the dispute.

. . .

Article XII

Any Contracting Party may at any time, by notification addressed to the Secretary-General of the United Nations, extend the application of the present Convention to all or any of the territories for the conduct of whose foreign relations that Contracting Party is responsible.

5

Refugees and Internally Displaced Persons

Prefatory Note

Peacekeepers are often mandated with functions and tasks requiring them to protect or assist refugees and internally displaced persons (IDPs). Such mandates arise because one of the many adverse consequences of conflict and natural disasters is the displacement of people either across State borders or within States. In order to address such displacements two instruments exist. The first is the Convention relating to the Status of Refugees (Refugee Convention)[1] and the Protocol relating to the Status of Refugees (Refugee Protocol).[2] The second is entitled Guiding Principles on Internal Displacement (Guiding Principles).[3] Extracts of the Refugee Convention, the Refugee Protocol, and the Guiding Principles are reprinted below.

1. The Refugee Convention

The Refugee Convention defines the term 'refugee' to be any person who:

> As a result of events occurring before 1 January 1951 and owing to well-founded fear of being persecuted for reasons of race, religion, nationality, membership of a particular social group or political opinion, is outside the country of his nationality and is unable or, owing to such fear, is unwilling to avail himself of the protection of that country; or who, not having a nationality and being outside the country of his former habitual residence as a result of such events, is unable or, owing to such fear, is unwilling to return to it.[4]

One of the most important phrases in this definition is 'outside the country of his nationality'. This means that to trigger refugee status a person must have crossed an international border and be outside their country of origin. Thus, the rights contained in the Refugee Convention do not apply to IDPs, who are people who have had to flee their homes due to reasons such as internal conflict or human rights abuses, but who have not crossed an international border. Whilst the needs of IDPs and refugees can be similar, the provisions of the Refugee Convention do not extend to IDPs.

The Refugee Convention identifies those categories of people who cannot claim refugee status, including those who are suspected of committing 'a crime against peace, a war crime, or a crime against humanity'.[5] It provides that '[e]very refugee has duties to the country in which he finds himself, which require in particular that he conform to its laws and regulations as well as to measures taken for the maintenance of public order'.[6] It also puts an obligation on State Parties to apply the Refugee Convention without discrimination as to race, religion, or country of origin.[7] The Refugee Convention outlines the rights that State Parties should accord to refugees present in their country including freedom of religion,[8] freedom of association,[9] and the right to work,[10] housing,[11] and education.[12]

---

1 Convention relating to the Status of Refugees (opened for signature 28 July 1951, entered into force 22 April 1954) 189 UNTS 137 (hereafter Refugee Convention).

2 Protocol relating to the Status of Refugees (opened for signature 31 January 1967, entered into force 4 October 1967) 606 UNTS 267 (hereafter Refugee Protocol).

3 United Nations Office for the Coordination of Humanitarian Affairs, 'Guiding Principles on Internal Displacement', <https://www.brookings.edu/wp-content/uploads/2016/07/GPEnglish.pdf> accessed 1 November 2017. Copies of the Guiding Principles in all the available languages can be downloaded from the Brookings-Bern Project on Internal Displacement at <https://www.brookings.edu/project/brookings-lse-project-on-internal-displacement/> accessed 1 November 2017.

4 Refugee Convention (n 1), Article 1A(2).

5 Ibid, Article 1F(a).

6 Ibid, Article 2.

7 Ibid, Article 3.

8 Ibid, Article 4.

9 Ibid, Article 15.

10 Ibid, Article 17.

11 Ibid, Article 21.

12 Ibid, Article 22.

A significant section of the Refugee Convention is Chapter V on Administrative Measures. This covers such matters as identity papers,[13] access to travel documents,[14] and freedom of movement.[15] This Chapter also includes the fundamental principle of non-refoulement, that is, that no State Party shall expel or return ('refouler') a refugee against his or her will, in any manner whatsoever, to a territory 'where his life or freedom would be threatened on account of his race, religion, nationality, membership of a particular social group or political opinion'.[16] That right is however subject to the State's assessment that the person claiming refugee status is not a threat to the security of the State or a danger to the community in which they are seeking asylum.[17]

Whilst the definition of 'refugee' in Article 1 of the Refugee Convention was couched in general terms, a fundamental problem is that it only applies to people who became refugees '[a]s a result of events occurring before 1 January 1951'.[18] This temporal limitation means that the Refugee Convention does not apply to people becoming refugees after 1951. A further problem in the Refugee Convention is that it allows State Parties to make a declaration as to whether the words 'events occurring before 1 January 1951' mean 'events occurring in Europe before 1 January 1951' or 'events occurring in Europe or elsewhere before 1 January 1951'.[19] At the time this allowed States to limit their obligations under the Refugee Convention to those who became refugees due to events in Europe. These temporal and geographical limitations made little sense as time passed and new refugees emerged. Furthermore, the mandate of the Office of the United Nations High Commissioner for Refugees (UNHCR) was universal and had no similar limitations. To deal with these temporal and geographical limitations the Refugee Protocol[20] was developed. Article 1(2) of the Protocol removes the temporal limitation:

> For the purpose of the present Protocol, the term 'refugee' shall, except as regards the application of paragraph 3 of this article, mean any person within the definition of article I of the Convention as if the words 'As a result of events occurring before 1 January 1951 and ...' and the words '... as a result of such events', in article 1 A (2) were omitted.[21]

Article 1(3) provides that '[t]he present Protocol shall be applied by the States Parties hereto without any geographic limitation'. Article 1(1) provides that State Parties to the Protocol 'undertake to apply Articles 2 to 34 inclusive of the Convention to refugees as hereinafter defined' in Article 1(2) of the Protocol. These are substantive provisions from the Refugee Convention. The result of the Protocol is to turn the Refugee Convention into a universal instrument for the protection of refugees anywhere in the world.

The UNHCR was established in 1950 by the United Nations General Assembly 'to lead and co-ordinate international action to protect refugees and resolve refugee problems worldwide'.[22] In the UN system, it therefore has the lead in all matters concerning refugees. A useful web-based resource is the UNHCR Protection Manual which provides guidance on a range of issues including refugee protection for those fleeing armed conflict and other situations of violence.[23]

A further overlay of legal protection to refugees is provided by regional instruments such as the Convention Governing the Specific Aspects of Refugee Problems in Africa,[24] the San José Declaration on Refugees and Displaced Persons,[25] and the European Union Directive on standards for the qualification of third-country nationals or stateless persons as beneficiaries of international

---

13 Ibid, Article 27.

14 Ibid, Article 28.

15 Ibid, Article 26.

16 Ibid, Article 33(1).

17 Ibid, Article 33(2). See also UNHCR Protection Manual <http://www.unhcr.org/en-au/protection-manual.html> available at 1 November 2017 (hereafter UNHCR Protection Manual).

18 Refugee Convention (n 1), Article 1A(2).

19 Ibid, Article 1B.

20 See <http://www.unhcr.org/en-au/protection/basic/3b66c2aa10/convention-protocol-relating-status-refugees.html> accessed 1 November 2017.

21 Refugee Protocol (n 2), Article 1(2).

22 See Statute of the Office of the United Nations High Commissioner for Refugees, GA Res 428(V) of 14 December 1950 <http://www.unhcr.org/en-au/protection/basic/3b66c39e1/statute-office-united-nations-high-commissioner-refugees.html> accessed 1 November 2017. See also <http://www.unhcr.org/pages/49c3646c2.html> for further information about the Office and its work.

23 UNHCR Protection Manual (n 17).

24 Organization of African Unity (OAU), Convention Governing the Specific Aspects of Refugee Problems in Africa, 10 September 1969, entered into force 20 June 1974, 1001 UNTS 45.

25 San Jose Declaration on Refugees and Displaced Persons, 7 December 1994.

protection, for a uniform status for refugees or for persons eligible for subsidiary protection, and for the content of the protection granted.[26]

2. Internally Displaced Persons

The Guiding Principles were completed in 1998. They are annexed to the 1998 Report of the Representative of the Secretary-General on Internally Displaced Persons (Representative), Mr Francis Deng, which was submitted pursuant to the Commission on Human Rights (Commission) resolution 1997/39.[27] The Guiding Principles are published by the UN and fall within the purview of the Office for the Coordination of Humanitarian Affairs (OCHA).[28] The Guiding Principles define IDPs as:

> persons or groups of persons who have been forced or obliged to flee or to leave their homes or places of habitual residence, in particular as a result of or in order to avoid the effects of armed conflict, situations of generalized violence, violations of human rights or natural or human-made disasters, and who have not crossed an internationally recognized state border.[29]

Whilst IDPs and refugees have both been forced to flee their homes, IDPs remain within their country of origin whereas refugees cross an international boundary into another country.

In 1996, the Representative prepared, in collaboration with a team of international legal experts, a 'Compilation and Analysis of Legal Norms' (Compilation) relevant to IDPs.[30] The Compilation examined international human rights law (IHRL), international humanitarian law (IHL), and refugee law by analogy, and considered the extent to which existing law covers the needs and rights of IDPs through the imposition of corresponding obligations on States to provide for their protection and assistance. The analysis showed that the existing legal framework left many gaps in regard to the protection and assistance of IDPs and that it is difficult to identify which laws applied and when. To remedy these gaps, the Representative and the legal experts developed the Guiding Principles. The General Assembly, in resolution 54/167, welcomed 'the publication and the wide dissemination of the compilation and analysis of legal norms prepared by the representative of the Secretary-General, in particular the Guiding Principles on Internal Displacement'.[31] Resolution 54/167 emphasised that whilst national authorities have the primary responsibility to provide protection and assistance to IDPs, responsibility also belongs to the international community because of the human rights and humanitarian issues involved.

Since resolution 54/167, there have been later General Assembly resolutions concerning protection and assistance for displaced persons. For example, resolution 58/177 notes that the Rome Statute of the International Criminal Court 'defines the deportation or forcible transfer of population as a crime against humanity and the unlawful deportation or transfer of the civilian population, as well as ordering the displacement of the civilian population, as war crimes'.[32] Resolution 58/177 also expresses particular concern at the issues surrounding IDPs who are women and children, and makes reference to Security Council resolution 1325 on women, peace, and security.[33]

The Guiding Principles, while not legally binding on States, address the specific needs of IDPs worldwide by identifying rights and guarantees relevant to their protection.[34] The Guiding

---

26 Directive 2011/95/EU of the European Parliament and of the Council of 13 December 2011 on Standards for the Qualification of Third-Country Nationals or Stateless Persons as Beneficiaries of International Protection, for a Uniform Status for Refugees or for Persons Eligible for Subsidiary Protection, and for the Content of the Protection Granted (recast) [2011] OJ L 337/9-337/26 <https://www.ecre.org/wp-content/uploads/2016/07/ECRE-Information-Note-on-the-Qualification-Directive-recast_October-2013.pdf> accessed 1 November 2017.

27 Report of the Representative of the Secretary-General, Mr Francis M Deng, submitted pursuant to Commission resolution 1997/39, 'Further Promotion and Encouragement of Human Rights and Fundamental Freedoms, including the Question of the Programme and Methods of Work of the Commission: Human Rights, Mass Exodus and Displaced Persons', UN Doc E/CN4/1998/53/Add.2, 11 February 1998, Addendum: Guiding Principles on Internal Displacement (hereafter Guiding Principles).

28 See <http://ochaonline.un.org/> accessed 1 November 2017.

29 Guiding Principles (n 27), Introduction: Scope and Purpose [2].

30 Report of the Representative of the Secretary-General, Mr Francis M Deng, 'Further Promotion and Encouragement of Human Rights and Fundamental Freedoms, including the Question of the Programme and Methods of Work of the Commission: Human Rights, Mass Exodus and Displaced Persons', UN Doc E/CN4/1996/52/Add2, 5 December 1995.

31 GA Res 54/167 of 17 December 1999, Preamble [8].

32 GA Res 58/177 of 22 December 2003, Preamble [9].

33 SC Res 1325 (2000) of 31 October 2000. See ch 17 below.

34 Guiding Principles (n 27), Introduction: Scope, and Purpose [1].

Principles emphasise the vulnerability of IDPs, and serve to reaffirm principles, rules, and standards that should be applied to the treatment of IDPs. They reflect principles of protection found in IHRL and IHL,[35] and are consistent with refugee law.

A key component of the Guiding Principles is their emphasis on 'national authorities hav[ing] the primary duty and responsibility to provide protection and humanitarian assistance to ... [IDPs] within their jurisdiction'.[36] The Guiding Principles also address protection during displacement, humanitarian assistance, and return, resettlement, and reintegration.

The General Assembly, in resolution 62/153, recognises:

> the Guiding Principles on Internal Displacement as an important international framework for the protection of internally displaced persons, welcomes the fact that an increasing number of States, United Nations agencies and regional and non-governmental organizations are applying them as a standard, and encourages all relevant actors to make use of the Guiding Principles when dealing with situations of internal displacement.[37]

Principle 1 provides that IDPs 'shall enjoy, in full equality, the same rights and freedoms under international and domestic law as do other persons in their country'. Principle 5 requires authorities and international actors to 'respect and ensure respect for their obligations under international law, including human rights and humanitarian law, in all circumstances, so as to prevent and avoid conditions that might lead to displacement of persons'.

Principle 27 is relevant to peace operations as it provides that:

> International humanitarian organizations and other appropriate actors when providing assistance should give due regard to the protection needs and human rights of internally displaced persons and take appropriate measures in this regard. In so doing, these organizations and actors should respect relevant international standards and codes of conduct.[38]

Principle 28 is also relevant to peacekeepers as it deals with the return of IDPs to areas under their effective control. It states that:

> Competent authorities have the primary duty and responsibility to establish conditions, as well as provide the means, which allow internally displaced persons to return voluntarily, in safety and with dignity, to their homes or places of habitual residence, or to resettle voluntarily in another part of the country. Such authorities shall endeavour to facilitate the reintegration of returned or resettled internally displaced persons.[39]

The Guiding Principles are supported by a variety of documents which provide guidance as to how to deal with IDPs and the situations in which they find themselves. For example, the Handbook for the Protection of Internally Displaced Persons,[40] which was promulgated in 2010, operationalises the Guiding Principles in the context of peace operations by emphasising how peacekeepers can protect and assist IDPs. It describes the role of peacekeepers in the protection of IDPs by providing security, having a presence to deter attacks, sharing information concerning humanitarian matters such as the level and type of assistance required, and assisting with contingency planning and early warning analysis.[41] Also of use to peacekeepers are the Protection Checklist[42] and the Camp Closure Guidelines.[43]

In the UN system, there is no single office responsible for the protection of IDPs. The OCHA is mandated to provide the Emergency Relief Coordinator with support in coordinating protection and assistance to IDPs. In the field, OCHA supports the Resident Coordinator/Humanitarian

---

35 Ibid, [3].

36 Ibid, Principle 3(1).

37 See GA Res 62/153 of 18 December 2007, Operative Part [10]. See also GA Res 70/165 of 22 February 2016.

38 Guiding Principles (n 27), Principle 27.

39 Ibid, Principle 28.

40 Handbook for the Protection of Internally Displaced Persons <http://www.unhcr.org/4c2355229.html> accessed 1 November 2017; see also UNHCR Protection Manual (n 17).

41 See Handbook for the Protection of Internally Displaced Persons, 55–7 <https://docs.unocha.org/sites/dms/Documents/IDP%20Handbook_FINAL%20All%20document_NEW.pdf> accessed 1 November 2017.

42 Organization for Security and Co-operation in Europe Secretariat and the Office of the High Commissioner for Refugees, 'Protection Checklist: Addressing Displacement and Protection of Displaced Populations and Affected Communities along the Conflict Cycle: A Collaborative Approach' (2012) <http://www.osce.org/cpc/111464?download=true> accessed 1 November 2017.

43 Global CCCM Cluster, 'Camp Closure Guidelines 2014', see <http://www.globalcccmcluster.org/tools-and-guidance/publications/camp-closure-guidelines> accessed 1 November 2017.

Coordinator to protect the interest of IDPs through advocacy, technical guidance, and interagency coordination.[44] More importantly, from a peacekeeping perspective, the OCHA 'also takes the lead in addressing challenges in accessing IDPs, including negotiating with relevant parties in order to secure humanitarian access ... [and] supports monitoring and reporting on IDP issues'.[45]

A further overlay of legal protections for IDPs is provided for by regional agreements such as the African Union Convention for the Protection and Assistance of Internally Displaced Persons in Africa.[46]

Peacekeepers can be mandated with a variety of functions and tasks that require engagement with refugees and IDPs. They might be mandated to support the host State's efforts to assist or resettle refugees and IDPs. For example, in 2015, peacekeepers serving with the United Nations Organization Stabilization Mission in the Democratic Republic of the Congo (MONUSCO) were tasked with:

> Support[ing] the Government's efforts, along with international partners and neighbouring countries, to create an environment conducive to the voluntary, safe and dignified return of internally displaced persons and refugees, or voluntary local integration or resettlement.[47]

Peacekeepers might be required to prevent violations of international law in refugee and IDP camps as shown by the terms of Security Council resolution 1834 concerning the United Nations Mission in the Central African Republic and Chad (MINURCAT). That resolution emphasised:

> the need to respect international refugee law, preserve the civilian and humanitarian nature of the refugee camps and internally displaced persons sites and prevent any recruitment of individuals, including children, which might be carried out in or around the camps by armed groups.[48]

In other situations, the role of peacekeepers might be to protect refugees and IDPs and their camps. For example, one of the tasks given to peacekeepers serving with the United Nations Mission in South Sudan (UNMISS) is to:

> deter violence against civilians ... especially through proactive deployment, active patrolling with particular attention to IDPs, including, but not limited to, those in protection sites and refugee camps ... [and] foster a secure environment for the eventual safe and voluntary return of IDPs and refugees including through monitoring of, ensuring respect for human rights ...[49]

The UNHCR will be operating in peace operation areas as part of their role as the UN agency tasked with the protection of refugees. Peacekeepers should do all they can to cooperate with UNHCR staff. This requirement can be made explicit in the mandate of a peace operation. For example, the Security Council, in resolution 1778, gave MINURCAT the mandate to:

> liaise with the Chadian Government and the Office of the United Nations High Commissioner for Refugees (UNHCR) in support of their efforts to relocate refugee camps which are in close proximity to the border, and to provide to UNHCR, on availability and [a] cost-reimbursable basis, logistical assistance for that purpose.[50]

The Refugee Convention and Refugee Protocol are also relevant to peace operations because Security Council resolutions on women, peace, and security,[51] children and armed conflict,[52] and the protection of civilians in armed conflict,[53] deal with the specific rights of refugees including safety in refugee camps, provisions for the safe return of refugees, and respect for international refugee

---

44 See OCHA, 'OCHA on Message: Internal Displacement' <https://docs.unocha.org/sites/dms/Documents/OOM_InternalDisplacement_English.pdf> accessed 1 November 2017.

45 Ibid.

46 African Union Convention for the Protection and Assistance of Internally Displaced Persons in Africa (opened for signature 22 October 2009, entered into force 6 December 2012) (hereafter Kampala Convention) <http://www.unhcr.org/en-au/about-us/background/4ae9bede9/african-union-convention-protection-assistance-internally-displaced-persons.html> accessed 1 November 2017. See also International Conference on the Great Lakes Region, Regional Treaties, Agreements, Declarations and Related, Protocol on the Protection and Assistance to Internally Displaced Persons (adopted 30 November 2006) <http://www.refworld.org/docid/52384fe44.html> accessed 1 November 2017.

47 SC Res 1925 (2010) of 28 May 2010, Operative Part [12](g).

48 SC Res 1834 (2008) of 24 September 2008, Preamble [12].

49 SC Res 2327 (2016) of 16 December 2016, Operative Part [7](a)(ii).

50 SC Res 1778 (2007) of 25 September 2007, Operative Part [2](c).

51 See, for example, SC Res 1325 (2000) of 31 October 2000; and SC Res 1820 (2008) of 19 June 2008. See ch 17 below.

52 See, for example, SC Res 1612 (2005) of 26 July 2005; and SC Res 1882 (2009) of 4 August 2009. See ch 18 below.

53 See, for example, SC Res 1674 (2006) of 28 April 2006; and SC Res 1894 (2009) of 11 November 2009. See ch 19 below.

law. For example, the Security Council, in resolution 1325 on women, peace, and security, called upon all parties to

> respect fully international law applicable to the rights and protection of women and girls, especially as civilians, in particular the obligations applicable to them under … the Refugee Convention of 1951 and the Protocol thereto of 1967 …[54]

Resolution 1325 also called upon all parties to armed conflict to 'respect the civilian and humanitarian character of refugee camps and settlements'.[55] The Security Council, in resolution 1674 on the protection of civilians in armed conflict, reaffirmed:

> the need to maintain the security and civilian character of refugee and internally displaced person camps, ***stresses*** the primary responsibility of States in this regard, and ***encourages*** the Secretary-General where necessary and in the context of existing peacekeeping operations and their respective mandates, to take all feasible measures to ensure security in and around such camps and of their inhabitants.[56]

The Security Council, in resolution 1674, also reaffirmed its practice of:

> ensuring that the mandates of United Nations peacekeeping, political and peacebuilding missions include, where appropriate and on a case-by-case basis, provisions regarding … (iii) the creation of conditions conducive to the voluntary, safe, dignified and sustainable return of refugees and internally displaced persons, and ***expresses its intention*** of ensuring that (i) such mandates include clear guidelines as to what missions can and should do to achieve those goals …[57]

The Security Council has requested the Secretary-General to ensure peacekeepers have appropriate training in refugee law, which will include the Refugee Convention and Protocol. For example, in resolution 1265, on the protection of civilians in armed conflict, the Security Council requested the Secretary-General:

> to ensure that United Nations personnel involved in peacemaking, peacekeeping and peace-building activities have appropriate training in international humanitarian, human rights and refugee law …[58]

When considering mandates for peace operations the Security Council has stated that it would:

> ***Help*** to establish the necessary security conditions to ***facilitate*** delivery of humanitarian assistance, taking into account the special needs of refugees, IDPs, women, children, elderly and disabled people, and to create conditions necessary for voluntary, safe, dignified and sustainable return of refugees and IDPs.[59]

References

Title	Convention relating to the Status of Refugees
Date of Adoption	28 July 1951
Entered into Force	22 April 1954 in accordance with Article 43
Signatories	19
Parties	145
Depository	United Nations
Treaty Series	189 UNTS 137
Full Text	<https://www.ohchr.org/en/professionalinterest/pages/statusofrefugees.aspx>[60]

Title	Protocol relating to the Status of Refugees
Date of Adoption	31 January 1967, authentic text signed by the President of the General Assembly and Secretary-General in New York and transmitted to Governments
Entered into Force	4 October 1967 in accordance with Article VIII
Parties	146
Depository	United Nations
Treaty Series	606 UNTS 267
Full Text	<https://www.ohchr.org/EN/ProfessionalInterest/Pages/ProtocolStatusOfRefugees.aspx>[61]

54 SC Res 1325 (2000) of 31 October 2000, Operative Part [9].
55 Ibid, Operative Part [12].
56 SC Res 1674 (2006) of 28 April 2006, Operative Part [14].
57 Ibid, Operative Part [16].
58 SC Res 1265 (1999) of 17 September 1999, Operative Part [14].
59 SC Res 2086 (2013) of 21 January 2013, Operative Part [8] (f).
60 Accessed 9 August 2018.
61 Accessed 1 November 2017.

Title	Guiding Principles on Internal Displacement
Author	Representative of the Secretary-General on Internally Displaced Persons
Adopted by	UN Commission on Human Rights
Date of Adoption	11 February 1998
Meeting	Fifty-fourth session, Commission on Human Rights
Source	UN Doc E/CN.4/1998/53/Add.2, Annex
Full Text	<https://www.brookings.edu/wp-content/uploads/2016/07/GPEnglish.pdf> (versions in over 35 languages)[62]

Convention relating to the Status of Refugees[63]

(Extracts)

Preamble

The High Contracting Parties,

Considering that the Charter of the United Nations and the Universal Declaration of Human Rights approved on 10 December 1948 by the General Assembly have affirmed the principle that human beings shall enjoy fundamental rights and freedoms without discrimination,

Considering that the United Nations has, on various occasions, manifested its profound concern for refugees and endeavoured to assure refugees the widest possible exercise of these fundamental rights and freedoms,

Considering that it is desirable to revise and consolidate previous international agreements relating to the status of refugees and to extend the scope of and the protection accorded by such instruments by means of a new agreement,

Considering that the grant of asylum may place unduly heavy burdens on certain countries, and that a satisfactory solution of a problem of which the United Nations has recognized the international scope and nature cannot therefore be achieved without international co-operation,

Expressing the wish that all States, recognizing the social and humanitarian nature of the problem of refugees, will do everything within their power to prevent this problem from becoming a cause of tension between States,

Noting that the United Nations High Commissioner for Refugees is charged with the task of supervising international conventions providing for the protection of refugees, and recognizing that the effective co-ordination of measures taken to deal with this problem will depend upon the co-operation of States with the High Commissioner,

Have agreed as follows:

62 Accessed 1 November 2017.

63 From Convention relating to the Status of Refugees © 1951 United Nations. Reprinted with the permission of the United Nations.

Chapter I – General Provisions

Article 1 – Definition of the term 'refugee'

A. For the purposes of the present Convention, the term 'refugee' shall apply to any person who:

(1) Has been considered a refugee under the Arrangements of 12 May 1926 and 30 June 1928 or under the Conventions of 28 October 1933 and 10 February 1938, the Protocol of 14 September 1939 or the Constitution of the International Refugee Organization;

Decisions of non-eligibility taken by the International Refugee Organization during the period of its activities shall not prevent the status of refugee being accorded to persons who fulfil the conditions of paragraph 2 of this section;

(2) As a result of events occurring before 1 January 1951 and owing to well-founded fear of being persecuted for reasons of race, religion, nationality, membership of a particular social group or political opinion, is outside the country of his nationality and is unable, or owing to such fear, is unwilling to avail himself of the protection of that country; or who, not having a nationality and being outside the country of his former habitual residence, is unable or, owing to such fear, is unwilling to return to it.

In the case of a person who has more than one nationality, the term 'the country of his nationality' shall mean each of the countries of which he is a national, and a person shall not be deemed to be lacking the protection of the country of his nationality if, without any valid reason based on well-founded fear, he has not availed himself of the protection of one of the countries of which he is a national.

B. (1) For the purposes of this Convention, the words 'events occurring before 1 January 1951' in article 1, section A, shall be understood to mean either:

(a) 'events occurring in Europe before 1 January 1951'; or

(b) 'events occurring in Europe or elsewhere before 1 January 1951'; and each Contracting State shall make a declaration at the time of signature, ratification or accession, specifying which of these meanings it applies for the purpose of its obligations under this Convention.

(2) Any Contracting State which has adopted alternative (a) may at any time extend its obligations by adopting alternative (b) by means of a notification addressed to the Secretary-General of the United Nations.

C. This Convention shall cease to apply to any person falling under the terms of section A if:

(1) He has voluntarily re-availed himself of the protection of the country of his nationality; or

(2) Having lost his nationality, he has voluntarily reacquired it; or

(3) He has acquired a new nationality, and enjoys the protection of the country of his new nationality; or

(4) He has voluntarily re-established himself in the country which he left or outside which he remained owing to fear of persecution; or

(5) He can no longer, because the circumstances in connection with which he has been recognized as a refugee have ceased to exist, continue to refuse to avail himself of the protection of the country of his nationality.

Provided that this paragraph shall not apply to a refugee falling under section A (1) of this article who is able to invoke compelling reasons arising out of previous persecution for refusing to avail himself of the protection of the country of nationality;

(6) Being a person who has no nationality he is, because the circumstances in connection with which he has been recognized as a refugee have ceased to exist, able to return to the country of his former habitual residence;

Provided that this paragraph shall not apply to a refugee falling under section A (1) of this article who is able to invoke compelling reasons arising out of previous persecution for refusing to return to the country of his former habitual residence.

D. This Convention shall not apply to persons who are at present receiving from organs or agencies of the United Nations other than the United Nations High Commissioner for Refugees protection or assistance.

When such protection or assistance has ceased for any reason, without the position of such persons being definitively settled in accordance with the relevant resolutions adopted by the General Assembly of the United Nations, these persons shall ipso facto be entitled to the benefits of this Convention.

E. This Convention shall not apply to a person who is recognized by the competent authorities of the country in which he has taken residence as having the rights and obligations which are attached to the possession of the nationality of that country.

F. The provisions of this Convention shall not apply to any person with respect to whom there are serious reasons for considering that:

(a) He has committed a crime against peace, a war crime, or a crime against humanity, as defined in the international instruments drawn up to make provision in respect of such crimes;

(b) He has committed a serious non-political crime outside the country of refuge prior to his admission to that country as a refugee;

(c) He has been guilty of acts contrary to the purposes and principles of the United Nations.

...

Article 3 – Non-discrimination

The Contracting States shall apply the provisions of this Convention to refugees without discrimination as to race, religion or country of origin.

...

Chapter II – Juridical Status

Article 12 – Personal Status

1. The personal status of a refugee shall be governed by the law of the country of his domicile or, if he has no domicile, by the law of the country of his residence.
2. Rights previously acquired by a refugee and dependent on personal status, more particularly rights attaching to marriage, shall be respected by a Contracting State, subject to compliance, if this be necessary, with the formalities required by the law of that State, provided that the right in question is one which would have been recognized by the law of that State had he not become a refugee.

...

Chapter V – *Administrative Measures*

...

Article 31 – Refugees unlawfully in the country of refuge

1. The Contracting States shall not impose penalties, on account of their illegal entry or presence, on refugees who, coming directly from a territory where their life or freedom was threatened in the sense of article 1, enter or are present in their territory without authorization, provided they present themselves without delay to the authorities and show good cause for their illegal entry or presence.

2. The Contracting States shall not apply to the movements of such refugees restrictions other than those which are necessary and such restrictions shall only be applied until their status in the country is regularized or they obtain admission into another country. The Contracting States shall allow such refugees a reasonable period and all the necessary facilities to obtain admission into another country.

Article 32 – Expulsion

1. The Contracting States shall not expel a refugee lawfully in their territory save on grounds of national security or public order.
2. The expulsion of such a refugee shall be only in pursuance of a decision reached in accordance with due process of law. Except where compelling reasons of national security otherwise require, the refugee shall be allowed to submit evidence to clear himself, and to appeal to and be represented for the purpose before competent authority or a person or persons specially designated by the competent authority.
3. The Contracting States shall allow such a refugee a reasonable period within which to seek legal admission into another country. The Contracting States reserve the right to apply during that period such internal measures as they may deem necessary.

Article 33 – Prohibition of expulsion or return ('refoulement')

1. No Contracting State shall expel or return ('refouler') a refugee in any manner whatsoever to the frontiers of territories where his life or freedom would be threatened on account of his race, religion, nationality, membership of a particular social group or political opinion.
2. The benefit of the present provision may not, however, be claimed by a refugee whom there are reasonable grounds for regarding as a danger to the security of the country in which he is, or who, having been convicted by a final judgement of a particularly serious crime, constitutes a danger to the community of that country.

...

Protocol relating to the Status of Refugees[64]

(Extracts)

Preamble

The States Parties to the present Protocol,

Considering that the Convention relating to the Status of Refugees done at Geneva on 28 July 1951 (hereinafter referred to as the Convention) covers only those persons who have become refugees as a result of events occurring before 1 January 1951,

Considering that new refugee situations have arisen since the Convention was adopted and that the refugees concerned may therefore not fall within the scope of the Convention,

64 From Protocol relating to the Status of Refugees © 1967 United Nations. Reprinted with the permission of the United Nations.

Considering that it is desirable that equal status should be enjoyed by all refugees covered by the definition in the Convention irrespective of the dateline 1 January 1951,

Have agreed as follows:

Article 1 – General Provision

1. The States Parties to the present Protocol undertake to apply articles 2 to 34 inclusive of the Convention to refugees as hereinafter defined.
2. For the purpose of the present Protocol, the term "refugee" shall, except as regards the application of paragraph 3 of this article, mean any person within the definition of article I of the Convention as if the words "As a result of events occurring before 1 January 1951 and . . ." and the words ". . . as a result of such events", in article 1 A (2) were omitted.
3. The present Protocol shall be applied by the States Parties hereto without any geographic limitation, save that existing declarations made by States already Parties to the Convention in accordance with article I B (I) (a) of the Convention, shall, unless extended under article I B (2) thereof, apply also under the present Protocol.

. . .

Guiding Principles on Internal Displacement[65]

. . .

Introduction: Scope and Purpose

1. These Guiding Principles address the specific needs of internally displaced persons worldwide. They identify rights and guarantees relevant to the protection of persons from forced displacement and to their protection and assistance during displacement as well as during return or resettlement and reintegration.
2. For the purposes of these Principles, internally displaced persons are persons or groups of persons who have been forced or obliged to flee or to leave their homes or places of habitual residence, in particular as a result of or in order to avoid the effects of armed conflict, situations of generalized violence, violations of human rights or natural or human-made disasters, and who have not crossed an internationally recognized state border.
3. These Principles reflect and are consistent with international human rights law and international humanitarian law. They provide guidance to:
   (a) The Representative of the Secretary-General on internally displaced persons in carrying out his mandate;
   (b) States when faced with the phenomenon of internal displacement;
   (c) All other authorities, groups and persons in their relations with internally displaced persons; and
   (d) Intergovernmental and non-governmental organizations when addressing internal displacement.
4. These Guiding Principles should be disseminated and applied as widely as possible.

65 From Guiding Principles on Internal Displacement, Francis Deng, the Representative of the Secretary-General on Internally Displaced Persons, © 1998 United Nations. Reprinted with the permission of the United Nations.

SECTION I – General Principles

Principle 1

1. Internally displaced persons shall enjoy, in full equality, the same rights and freedoms under international and domestic law as do other persons in their country. They shall not be discriminated against in the enjoyment of any rights and freedoms on the ground that they are internally displaced.
2. These Principles are without prejudice to individual criminal responsibility under international law, in particular relating to genocide, crimes against humanity and war crimes.

Principle 2

1. These Principles shall be observed by all authorities, groups and persons irrespective of their legal status and applied without any adverse distinction. The observance of these Principles shall not affect the legal status of any authorities, groups or persons involved.
2. These Principles shall not be interpreted as restricting, modifying or impairing the provisions of any international human rights or international humanitarian law instrument or rights granted to persons under domestic law. In particular, these Principles are without prejudice to the right to seek and enjoy asylum in other countries.

Principle 3

1. National authorities have the primary duty and responsibility to provide protection and humanitarian assistance to internally displaced persons within their jurisdiction.
2. Internally displaced persons have the right to request and to receive protection and humanitarian assistance from these authorities. They shall not be persecuted or punished for making such a request.

Principle 4

1. These Principles shall be applied without discrimination of any kind, such as race, colour, sex, language, religion or belief, political or other opinion, national, ethnic or social origin, legal or social status, age, disability, property, birth, or on any other similar criteria.
2. Certain internally displaced persons, such as children, especially unaccompanied minors, expectant mothers, mothers with young children, female heads of household, persons with disabilities and elderly persons, shall be entitled to protection and assistance required by their condition and to treatment which takes into account their special needs.

SECTION II – Principles Relating to Protection from Displacement

Principle 5

All authorities and international actors shall respect and ensure respect for their obligations under international law, including human rights and humanitarian law, in all circumstances, so as to prevent and avoid conditions that might lead to displacement of persons.

Principle 6

1. Every human being shall have the right to be protected against being arbitrarily displaced from his or her home or place of habitual residence.
2. The prohibition of arbitrary displacement includes displacement:
   - (a) When it is based on policies of apartheid, "ethnic cleansing" or similar practices aimed at/or resulting in altering the ethnic, religious or racial composition of the affected population;
   - (b) In situations of armed conflict, unless the security of the civilians involved or imperative military reasons so demand;

(c) In cases of large-scale development projects, which are not justified by compelling and overriding public interests;

(d) In cases of disasters, unless the safety and health of those affected requires their evacuation; and

(e) When it is used as a collective punishment.

3. Displacement shall last no longer than required by the circumstances.

Principle 7

1. Prior to any decision requiring the displacement of persons, the authorities concerned shall ensure that all feasible alternatives are explored in order to avoid displacement altogether. Where no alternatives exist, all measures shall be taken to minimize displacement and its adverse effects.
2. The authorities undertaking such displacement shall ensure, to the greatest practicable extent, that proper accommodation is provided to the displaced persons, that such displacements are effected in satisfactory conditions of safety, nutrition, health and hygiene, and that members of the same family are not separated.
3. If displacement occurs in situations other than during the emergency stages of armed conflicts and disasters, the following guarantees shall be complied with:

(a) A specific decision shall be taken by a State authority empowered by law to order such measures;

(b) Adequate measures shall be taken to guarantee to those to be displaced full information on the reasons and procedures for their displacement and, where applicable, on compensation and relocation;

(c) The free and informed consent of those to be displaced shall be sought;

(d) The authorities concerned shall endeavour to involve those affected, particularly women, in the planning and management of their relocation;

(e) Law enforcement measures, where required, shall be carried out by competent legal authorities; and

(f) The right to an effective remedy, including the review of such decisions by appropriate judicial authorities, shall be respected.

Principle 8

Displacement shall not be carried out in a manner that violates the rights to life, dignity, liberty and security of those affected.

Principle 9

States are under a particular obligation to protect against the displacement of indigenous peoples, minorities, peasants, pastoralists and other groups with a special dependency on and attachment to their lands.

SECTION III – Principles Relating to Protection During Displacement

Principle 10

1. Every human being has the inherent right to life which shall be protected by law. No one shall be arbitrarily deprived of his or her life. Internally displaced persons shall be protected in particular against:

(a) Genocide;

(b) Murder;

(c) Summary or arbitrary executions; and
(d) Enforced disappearances, including abduction or unacknowledged detention, threatening or resulting in death.

Threats and incitement to commit any of the foregoing acts shall be prohibited.

2. Attacks or other acts of violence against internally displaced persons who do not or no longer participate in hostilities are prohibited in all circumstances. Internally displaced persons shall be protected, in particular, against:
   (a) Direct or indiscriminate attacks or other acts of violence, including the creation of areas wherein attacks on civilians are permitted;
   (b) Starvation as a method of combat;
   (c) Their use to shield military objectives from attack or to shield, favour or impede military operations;
   (d) Attacks against their camps or settlements; and
   (e) The use of anti-personnel landmines.

Principle 11

1. Every human being has the right to dignity and physical, mental and moral integrity.
2. Internally displaced persons, whether or not their liberty has been restricted, shall be protected in particular against:
   (a) Rape, mutilation, torture, cruel, inhuman or degrading treatment or punishment, and other outrages upon personal dignity, such as acts of gender-specific violence, forced prostitution and any form of indecent assault;
   (b) Slavery or any contemporary form of slavery, such as sale into marriage, sexual exploitation, or forced labour of children; and
   (c) Acts of violence intended to spread terror among internally displaced persons.

   Threats and incitement to commit any of the foregoing acts shall be prohibited.

Principle 12

1. Every human being has the right to liberty and security of person. No one shall be subjected to arbitrary arrest or detention.
2. To give effect to this right for internally displaced persons, they shall not be interned in or confined to a camp. If in exceptional circumstances such internment or confinement is absolutely necessary, it shall not last longer than required by the circumstances.
3. Internally displaced persons shall be protected from discriminatory arrest and detention as a result of their displacement.
4. In no case shall internally displaced persons be taken hostage.

Principle 13

1. In no circumstances shall displaced children be recruited nor be required or permitted to take part in hostilities.
2. Internally displaced persons shall be protected against discriminatory practices of recruitment into any armed forces or groups as a result of their displacement. In particular any cruel, inhuman or degrading practices that compel compliance or punish non-compliance with recruitment are prohibited in all circumstances.

Principle 14

1. Every internally displaced person has the right to liberty of movement and freedom to choose his or her residence.

2. In particular, internally displaced persons have the right to move freely in and out of camps or other settlements.

Principle 15

Internally displaced persons have:

(a) The right to seek safety in another part of the country;
(b) The right to leave their country;
(c) The right to seek asylum in another country; and
(d) The right to be protected against forcible return to or resettlement in any place where their life, safety, liberty and/or health would be at risk.

Principle 16

1. All internally displaced persons have the right to know the fate and whereabouts of missing relatives.
2. The authorities concerned shall endeavour to establish the fate and whereabouts of internally displaced persons reported missing, and cooperate with relevant international organizations engaged in this task. They shall inform the next of kin on the progress of the investigation and notify them of any result.
3. The authorities concerned shall endeavour to collect and identify the mortal remains of those deceased, prevent their despoliation or mutilation, and facilitate the return of those remains to the next of kin or dispose of them respectfully.
4. Grave sites of internally displaced persons should be protected and respected in all circumstances. Internally displaced persons should have the right of access to the grave sites of their deceased relatives.

Principle 17

1. Every human being has the right to respect of his or her family life.
2. To give effect to this right for internally displaced persons, family members who wish to remain together shall be allowed to do so.
3. Families which are separated by displacement should be reunited as quickly as possible. All appropriate steps shall be taken to expedite the reunion of such families, particularly when children are involved. The responsible authorities shall facilitate inquiries made by family members and encourage and cooperate with the work of humanitarian organizations engaged in the task of family reunification.
4. Members of internally displaced families whose personal liberty has been restricted by internment or confinement in camps shall have the right to remain together.

Principle 18

1. All internally displaced persons have the right to an adequate standard of living.
2. At the minimum, regardless of the circumstances, and without discrimination, competent authorities shall provide internally displaced persons with and ensure safe access to:

   (a) Essential food and potable water;
   (b) Basic shelter and housing;
   (c) Appropriate clothing; and
   (d) Essential medical services and sanitation.

3. Special efforts should be made to ensure the full participation of women in the planning and distribution of these basic supplies.

Principle 19

1. All wounded and sick internally displaced persons as well as those with disabilities shall receive to the fullest extent practicable and with the least possible delay, the medical care and attention they require, without distinction on any grounds other than medical ones. When necessary, internally displaced persons shall have access to psychological and social services.
2. Special attention should be paid to the health needs of women, including access to female health care providers and services, such as reproductive health care, as well as appropriate counselling for victims of sexual and other abuses.
3. Special attention should also be given to the prevention of contagious and infectious diseases, including AIDS, among internally displaced persons.

Principle 20

1. Every human being has the right to recognition everywhere as a person before the law.
2. To give effect to this right for internally displaced persons, the authorities concerned shall issue to them all documents necessary for the enjoyment and exercise of their legal rights, such as passports, personal identification documents, birth certificates and marriage certificates. In particular, the authorities shall facilitate the issuance of new documents or the replacement of documents lost in the course of displacement, without imposing unreasonable conditions, such as requiring the return to one's area of habitual residence in order to obtain these or other required documents.
3. Women and men shall have equal rights to obtain such necessary documents and shall have the right to have such documentation issued in their own names.

Principle 21

1. No one shall be arbitrarily deprived of property and possessions.
2. The property and possessions of internally displaced persons shall in all circumstances be protected, in particular, against the following acts:
   (a) Pillage;
   (b) Direct or indiscriminate attacks or other acts of violence;
   (c) Being used to shield military operations or objectives;
   (d) Being made the object of reprisal; and
   (e) Being destroyed or appropriated as a form of collective punishment.
3. Property and possessions left behind by internally displaced persons should be protected against destruction and arbitrary and illegal appropriation, occupation or use.

Principle 22

1. Internally displaced persons, whether or not they are living in camps, shall not be discriminated against as a result of their displacement in the enjoyment of the following rights:
   (a) The rights to freedom of thought, conscience, religion or belief, opinion and expression;
   (b) The right to seek freely opportunities for employment and to participate in economic activities;
   (c) The right to associate freely and participate equally in community affairs;
   (d) The right to vote and to participate in governmental and public affairs, including the right to have access to the means necessary to exercise this right; and
   (e) The right to communicate in a language they understand.

Principle 23

1. Every human being has the right to education.
2. To give effect to this right for internally displaced persons, the authorities concerned shall ensure that such persons, in particular displaced children, receive education which shall be free and compulsory at the primary level. Education should respect their cultural identity, language and religion.
3. Special efforts should be made to ensure the full and equal participation of women and girls in educational programmes.
4. Education and training facilities shall be made available to internally displaced persons, in particular adolescents and women, whether or not living in camps, as soon as conditions permit.

SECTION IV – Principles Relating to Humanitarian Assistance

Principle 24

1. All humanitarian assistance shall be carried out in accordance with the principles of humanity and impartiality and without discrimination.
2. Humanitarian assistance to internally displaced persons shall not be diverted, in particular for political or military reasons.

Principle 25

1. The primary duty and responsibility for providing humanitarian assistance to internally displaced persons lies with national authorities.
2. International humanitarian organizations and other appropriate actors have the right to offer their services in support of the internally displaced. Such an offer shall not be regarded as an unfriendly act or an interference in a State's internal affairs and shall be considered in good faith. Consent thereto shall not be arbitrarily withheld, particularly when authorities concerned are unable or unwilling to provide the required humanitarian assistance.
3. All authorities concerned shall grant and facilitate the free passage of humanitarian assistance and grant persons engaged in the provision of such assistance rapid and unimpeded access to the internally displaced.

Principle 26

Persons engaged in humanitarian assistance, their transport and supplies shall be respected and protected. They shall not be the object of attack or other acts of violence.

Principle 27

1. International humanitarian organizations and other appropriate actors when providing assistance should give due regard to the protection needs and human rights of internally displaced persons and take appropriate measures in this regard. In so doing, these organizations and actors should respect relevant international standards and codes of conduct.
2. The preceding paragraph is without prejudice to the protection responsibilities of international organizations mandated for this purpose, whose services may be offered or requested by States.

SECTION V – Principles Relating to Return, Resettlement and Reintegration

Principle 28

1. Competent authorities have the primary duty and responsibility to establish conditions, as well as provide the means, which allow internally displaced persons to return voluntarily, in

safety and with dignity, to their homes or places of habitual residence, or to resettle voluntarily in another part of the country. Such authorities shall endeavour to facilitate the reintegration of returned or resettled internally displaced persons.

2. Special efforts should be made to ensure the full participation of internally displaced persons in the planning and management of their return or resettlement and reintegration.

Principle 29

1. Internally displaced persons who have returned to their homes or places of habitual residence or who have resettled in another part of the country shall not be discriminated against as a result of their having been displaced. They shall have the right to participate fully and equally in public affairs at all levels and have equal access to public services.
2. Competent authorities have the duty and responsibility to assist returned and/or resettled internally displaced persons to recover, to the extent possible, their property and possessions which they left behind or were dispossessed of upon their displacement. When recovery of such property and possessions is not possible, competent authorities shall provide or assist these persons in obtaining appropriate compensation or another form of just reparation.

Principle 30

All authorities concerned shall grant and facilitate for international humanitarian organizations and other appropriate actors, in the exercise of their respective mandates, rapid and unimpeded access to internally displaced persons to assist in their return or resettlement and reintegration.

6

The International Covenants on Human Rights

Prefatory Note

The International Covenant on Economic, Social and Cultural Rights (ICESCR),[1] and the International Covenant on Civil and Political Rights (ICCPR)[2] form what is sometimes known as the International Bill of Human Rights. Both documents are relevant to the planning and conduct of peace operations in a variety of situations including where peacekeepers are engaged in State building, supporting local authorities to maintain law and order, or considering how to engage with other non-UN military forces.

The ICESCR and the ICCPR are founded on the Charter of the United Nations (Charter) which states in Article 1(3) that one of the purposes of the UN is to promote and encourage 'respect for human rights and for fundamental freedoms for all'.[3] The ICESCR and ICCPR translate the principles of the Universal Declaration of Human Rights (UDHR)[4] into legally binding form. Both the ICESCR and the ICCPR reinforce the broad human rights aim that 'freedom from fear and want can only be achieved if conditions are created whereby everyone may enjoy his economic, social and cultural rights as well as his civil and political rights'.[5] Extracts from the ICESCR and the ICCPR are reprinted below.

The International Court of Justice (ICJ) reaffirmed the extraterritorial application of human rights treaties in its judgment of 19 December 2005 in the *Case concerning Armed Activities on the Territory of the Congo (Democratic Republic of the Congo v Uganda)* (Judgment) (*Congo Case*),[6] when the court held 'that international human rights instruments are applicable "in respect of acts done by a State in the exercise of its jurisdiction outside its own territory", particularly in occupied territories'.[7]

1. The ICESCR

The ICESCR further develops those principles in the UDHR concerning economic, social, and cultural rights. These rights are regarded as relative or positive rights and obligations that must be progressively achieved, as opposed to the civil and political rights in the ICCPR that need to be protected immediately.

An Optional Protocol to the ICESCR was adopted by the General Assembly on 10 December 2008 in resolution 63/117.[8] The Optional Protocol expands the ICESCR's role in human rights protection

---

1 International Covenant on Economic, Social and Cultural Rights (opened for signature 16 December 1966, entered into force 3 January 1976) 993 UNTS 3 (hereafter ICESCR).

2 International Covenant on Civil and Political Rights (opened for signature 16 December 1966, entered into force 23 March 1976) 999 UNTS 171 (hereafter ICCPR).

3 Charter of the United Nations (opened for signature 26 June 1945, entered into force 24 October 1945) 1 UNTS XVI, Article 1(3) (hereafter Charter). See ch 1 above.

4 Universal Declaration of Human Rights, adopted by GA Res 217A (III) of 10 December 1948. See <http://www.un.org/en/universal-declaration-human-rights/index.html> accessed 1 November 2017. See also Bruce Oswald, Helen Durham, and Adrian Bates, *Documents on the Law of UN Peace Operations* (Oxford University Press 2010) ch 4.

5 Preamble common to both the ICESCR and ICCPR.

6 *Case concerning Armed Activities on the Territory of the Congo (Democratic Republic of the Congo v Uganda)* (Judgment) [2005] ICJ Rep 116 (hereafter *Congo Case*).

7 Ibid, 243.

8 GA Res 63/117 of 10 December 2008. The text of the Optional Protocol is annexed to the resolution. It entered into force on 5 May 2013.

by allowing the Human Rights Council to receive complaints about violations of the rights protected by the ICESCR from individuals of State Parties to the Optional Protocol.

Contributing States that are party to the ICESCR are to act in conformity with the UN Charter.[9] The ICESCR obliges State Parties to:

> take steps, individually and through international assistance and co-operation, especially economic and technical, to the maximum of its available resources, with a view to achieving progressively the full realization of the rights recognized in the present Covenant by all appropriate means, including particularly the adoption of legislative measures.[10]

The ICJ discussed the scope of application of the ICESCR in its Advisory Opinion of 9 July 2004 on the *Legal Consequences of the Construction of a Wall in the Occupied Palestinian Territory* (Advisory Opinion) (*Israeli Wall Case*).[11] The Court stated that:

> The International Covenant on Economic, Social and Cultural Rights contains no provision on its scope of application. This may be explicable by the fact that this Covenant guarantees rights which are essentially territorial. However, it is not to be excluded that it applies both to territories over which a State party has sovereignty and to those over which that State exercises territorial jurisdiction.[12]

The ICESCR assigns monitoring functions to the United Nations Economic and Social Council (ECOSOC),[13] which, in turn, established the Committee on Economic, Social and Cultural Rights (CESCR) to carry out this role.[14] The CESCR issues General Comments to assist in interpreting various provisions of the ICESCR.[15]

2. The ICCPR

The ICCPR is concerned with fulfilling the 'ideal of free human beings enjoying civil and political freedom'.[16] It has two Optional Protocols. The First Optional Protocol establishes the individual complaints mechanism for the ICCPR.[17] The Second Optional Protocol concerns the abolition of the death penalty.[18]

In terms of the scope of application of the ICCPR, Article 2(1) states:

> Each State Party to the present Covenant undertakes to respect and to ensure to all individuals within its territory and subject to its jurisdiction the rights recognized in the present Covenant, without distinction of any kind, such as race, colour, sex, language, religion, political or other opinion, national or social origin, property, birth or other status.[19]

There has been much argument about the interpretation of the phrase 'within its territory and subject to its jurisdiction'. One interpretation takes both territory and jurisdiction together and limits the reach of the ICCPR to those areas that are both part of the territory of the State Party as well as those areas under its effective control. Another splits the phrase into two, so that State Parties have to ensure the rights in the ICCPR apply to both individuals within its territory, and individuals subject to its jurisdiction regardless of whether they are in its territory or not. The UN Human Rights Committee (HRC) in its 2004 General Comment[20] on the general legal obligations on State Parties to the ICCPR specifically addressed this issue:

---

9 ICESCR (n 1), Article 1(3). For UN Charter see ch 1 above.

10 Ibid, Article 2(1).

11 *Legal Consequences of the Construction of a Wall in the Occupied Palestinian Territory* (Advisory Opinion) [2004] ICJ Rep 136 (hereafter *Israeli Wall Case*).

12 Ibid, 180.

13 See ICESCR (n 1), Articles 16–22.

14 Ibid.

15 For more detail concerning General Comments by the Committee on Economic, Social and Cultural Rights, see <http://tbinternet.ohchr.org/_layouts/treatybodyexternal/TBSearch.aspx?Lang=en&TreatyID=9&DocTypeID=11> accessed 1 November 2017.

16 ICCPR (n 2), Preamble.

17 First Optional Protocol to the International Covenant on Civil and Political Rights (opened for signature 16 December 1966, 23 March 1976) 999 UNTS 171 (hereafter First Optional Protocol).

18 Second Optional Protocol to the International Covenant on Civil and Political Rights, Aiming at the Abolition of the Death Penalty (opened for signature 15 December 1989, entered into force 11 July 1991) A/RES/44/128 (hereafter Second Optional Protocol)

19 ICCPR (n 2), Article 2(1).

20 The Human Rights Committee (hereafter HRC) has issued a number of General Comments. Such Comments include: General Comment 35—Article 9 (Liberty and Security of Person); General Comment 31—Article 29 (States of Emergency): and General Comment 20—Article 7 (Prohibition of torture, or other cruel, inhuman or degrading treatment or punishment). For more detail

> States Parties are required by article 2, paragraph 1, to respect and to ensure the Covenant rights to all persons who may be within their territory and to all persons subject to their jurisdiction. This means that a State party must respect and ensure the rights laid down in the Covenant to anyone within the power or effective control of that State Party, even if not situated within the territory of the State Party ... This principle also applies to those within the power or effective control of the forces of a State Party acting outside its territory, regardless of the circumstances in which such power or effective control was obtained, such as forces constituting a national contingent of a State Party assigned to an international peace-keeping or peace-enforcement operation.[21]

The ICJ also discussed this issue in the *Israeli Wall Case* and accepted the broad interpretation of Article 2. The ICJ stated:

> The Court would observe that, while the jurisdiction of States is primarily territorial, it may sometimes be exercised outside the national territory. Considering the object and purpose of the International Covenant on Civil and Political Rights, it would seem natural that, even when such is the case, States parties to the Covenant should be bound to comply with its provisions ... [22]

The ICJ went on to state:

> In conclusion, the Court considers that the International Covenant on Civil and Political Rights is applicable in respect of acts done by a State in the exercise of its jurisdiction outside its own territory.[23]

The ICJ reaffirmed this principle in the *Congo Case*[24] when it held, citing its findings from the *Israeli Wall Case*, 'that international human rights instruments are applicable "in respect of acts done by a State in the exercise of its jurisdiction outside its own territory", particularly in occupied territories'.[25] The ICJ held that the ICCPR was therefore applicable to the actions of Uganda in the territory of the Democratic Republic of the Congo, as was the Convention on the Rights of the Child and the relevant Geneva Conventions.[26]

Article 4 of the ICCPR, which allows State Parties to derogate from some of their obligations under the ICCPR in certain circumstances, states:

> 1. In time of public emergency which threatens the life of the nation and the existence of which is officially proclaimed, the States Parties to the present Covenant may take measures derogating from their obligations under the present Covenant to the extent strictly required by the exigencies of the situation, provided that such measures are not inconsistent with their other obligations under international law and do not involve discrimination solely on the ground of race, colour, sex, language, religion or social origin.
> 2. No derogation from articles 6, 7, 8 (paragraphs I and 2), 11, 15, 16 and 18 may be made under this provision.[27]

The ICJ discussed the issue of whether the ICCPR continued to apply during an armed conflict in its Advisory Opinion of 8 July 1996 on the *Legality of the Threat or Use of Nuclear Weapons* (Advisory Opinion) (*Nuclear Weapons Case*).[28] The ICJ's conclusion, which was reaffirmed in the *Israeli Wall Case* and the *Congo Case*, was that:

> the protection of the International Covenant of Civil and Political Rights does not cease in times of war, except by operation of Article 4 of the Covenant whereby certain provisions may be derogated from in a time of national emergency.[29]

To ensure the proper implementation of the ICCPR, the instrument sets up a framework which is monitored by the HRC and the Office of the United Nations High Commissioner for Human Rights (OHCHR). The HRC, which is made up of independent experts, undertakes a range of roles and

---

concerning the HRC General Comments, see <http://tbinternet.ohchr.org/_layouts/treatybodyexternal/TBSearch.aspx?Lang=en&TreatyID=8&DocTypeID=11> accessed 1 November 2017.

21 UN Human Rights Committee, 'General Comment 31' in 'Nature of the General Legal Obligation on States Parties to the Covenant' (2004), UN Doc CCPR/C/21/Rev.1/Add.13, [10].

22 *Israeli Wall Case* (n 11), 179.

23 Ibid, 180.

24 *Congo Case* (n 6).

25 Ibid, 243.

26 Ibid.

27 ICCPR (n 2), Article 4.

28 *Legality of the Threat or Use of Nuclear Weapons* (Advisory Opinion) [1996] ICJ Rep 226.

29 Ibid, 240.

functions, which includes assessing the adherence of State Parties in relation to their implementation of rights under the ICCPR, considering interstate complaints,[30] dealing with individual complaints in accordance with the First Optional Protocol, and non-compliance by State Parties bound by the Second Optional Protocol.

The First Optional Protocol expands the HRC's role in human rights protection by allowing it to receive complaints about violations of the rights protected by the ICCPR from individuals of State Parties to the First Optional Protocol. The HRC, and other human rights treaty monitoring bodies such as the Committee for the Elimination of Discrimination Against Women, form part of the overall UN framework for the protection of human rights along with the High Commissioner for Human Rights, who heads the OHCHR[31] and the Human Rights Council.[32]

The Second Optional Protocol is specifically aimed at the abolition of the death penalty. The death penalty is viewed in contradistinction to Article 3 of the UDHR (all human beings have the right to life) and Article 6 of the ICCPR (all human beings have the inherent right to life). However, pursuant to Article 2(1) of the Second Optional Protocol, State Parties are permitted to make a reservation allowing for use of the death penalty 'in time of war pursuant to a conviction for a most serious crime of a military nature committed during wartime'.

The rights which the ICESCR and ICCPR seek to protect are reinforced by regional human rights agreements. These include the African Charter on Human and Peoples' Rights,[33] the American Convention on Human Rights,[34] with the Additional Protocol to the American Convention on Human Rights in the Area of Economic, Social and Cultural Rights (Protocol of San Salvador),[35] the Arab Charter on Human Rights,[36] the European Convention for the Protection of Human Rights and Fundamental Freedoms,[37] and the European Social Charter.[38]

There are several provisions in the ICESCR that are relevant to peace operations, particularly in situations where peacekeepers are responsible for the well-being of the national population. For example, provisions relating to employment,[39] and the right to enjoy the highest attainable standard of physical and mental health,[40] provide peacekeepers with a benchmark as to the minimum standards that they need to apply when employing local staff. The right to enjoy the highest attainable standard of physical and mental health[41] is also relevant to situations where peacekeepers are responsible for persons in detention. The abovementioned rights are also relevant to peace operations where the operation is mandated to undertake post-conflict State building (for example, in the Democratic Republic of the Congo and Timor-Leste),[42] or to govern a territory (for example, Timor-Leste).[43]

The ICCPR is very relevant to the planning, managing, and conducting of peace operations. For example, in the context of the use of force and law enforcement, the ICCPR sets standards concerning the right to life,[44] the right to liberty and security of the person,[45] the prohibition from torture or cruel, inhuman, or degrading treatment or punishment,[46] and respect for the inherent dignity of any person deprived of their liberty.[47] The ICCPR is also useful for advocating minimum

---

30 For further details, see <http://www.ohchr.org/EN/HRBodies/CCPR/Pages/CCPRIndex.aspx> accessed 1 November 2017.

31 See <http://www.ohchr.org> accessed 1 November 2017.

32 See <http://www.ohchr.org/en/hrbodies/hrc/pages/hrcindex.aspx> accessed 1 November 2017.

33 African Charter on Human and Peoples' Rights (opened for signature 27 June 1981, entered into force 21 October 1996) 21 ILM 58.

34 American Convention on Human Rights (opened for signature 22 November 1969, entered into force 18 July 1978) 1144 UNTS 123, reprinted in Basic Documents Pertaining to Human Rights in the Inter-American System, OEA/Ser.L.V/II.82 doc.6 rev.1, 25 (1992).

35 Additional Protocol to the American Convention on Human Rights in the Area of Economic, Social and Cultural Rights (opened for signature 16 November 1999) A-52.

36 Arab Charter on Human Rights (adopted 15 September 2004), reprinted in 12 International Human Rights Report 893 (2005).

37 European Convention for the Protection of Human Rights and Fundamental Freedoms, as amended by Protocols Nos 11 and 14 (opened for signature 4 November 1950, entered into force 3 September 1953) ETS 5.

38 European Social Charter (revised 3 May 1996) ETS 163.

39 ICESCR (n 1), Article 7.

40 Ibid, Article 12.

41 Ibid.

42 See SC Res 2277 (2016) of 30 March 2016; and SC Res 1969 (2011) of 24 February 2011.

43 See, for example, SC Res 1272 of 22 October 1999.

44 ICCPR (n 2), Article 6.

45 Ibid, Article 9.

46 Ibid, Article 7.

47 Ibid, Article 10.

standards when peacekeepers are involved in capacity building. For example, the provisions relating to the prohibition from arbitrary or unlawful interference with a person's privacy,[48] the prohibition against inciting national, racial, or religious hatred,[49] and the right to peaceful assembly[50] are relevant to ensuring that acts of national authorities do not breach fundamental human rights standards.

Many peacekeeping operations have specifically mandated peacekeepers to support host State authorities to protect and monitor human rights. For example, the United Nations Mission in Liberia (UNMIL) mandated peacekeepers:

> To support the Government of Liberia in carrying out promotion, protection and monitoring activities of human rights in Liberia, with special attention to violations and abuses committed against children and women.[51]

In some cases, the mandate given to peacekeepers might extend to assisting authorities to deal with human rights violations by bringing those accused of such crimes to justice. For example, peacekeepers serving in the Central African Republic (CAR) are to:

> Support the restoration and maintenance of public safety and the rule of law, including through apprehending and handing over to the CAR authorities ... those in the country responsible for crimes involving serious human rights violations ... so that they can be brought to justice.[52]

Another level of relevance stems from situations where peacekeepers commit human rights violations, such as when they commit sexual exploitation and abuse.[53] The UN has also, through its Human Rights Due Diligence Policy,[54] sought to ensure that peacekeepers have a framework to engage with supporting non-UN forces (such as the forces of the host State authorities) to ensure that the UN does not assist those forces to commit grave human rights violations many of which are prohibited by the ICCPR, such as unlawful detention or torture.

A number of peace operations have a Human Rights Component.[55] This Component carries out a variety of tasks including monitoring, investigating, and reporting on the human rights situation, assisting a host State to prevent human rights violations, building human rights capabilities in the host State, and ensuring that peace processes promote justice and equity.[56] In much of the Component's work, such as reporting on arbitrary detention, or the arbitrary deprivation of life, the ICCPR will be the foundation. The OHCHR has a policy on the integration of human rights in UN peace operations which it developed with the UN Secretariat's Department of Peacekeeping Operations (DPKO), the Department of Political Affairs (DPA), and Department of Field Support (DFS).[57]

References

Title	International Covenant on Economic, Social and Cultural Rights
Date of Adoption	16 December 1966 in General Assembly Resolution 2200A (XXI)
Opened for Signature	19 December 1966
Entered into Force	3 January 1976 in accordance with Article 27
Signatories	71
Parties	166
Depository	United Nations
Treaty Series	993 UNTS 3
Full Text	<https://www.ohchr.org/en/professionalinterest/pages/cescr.aspx>[58]

48 Ibid, Article 17.

49 Ibid, Article 20.

50 Ibid, Article 21.

51 SC Res 2333 (2016) of 23 December 2016, Operative Part [11](c)(i).

52 SC Res 2301 (2016) of 29 July 2016, Operative Part [35](a)(iii).

53 See, for example, SC Res 2272 (2016) of 11 March 2016. See ch 20 below. See also SC Res 2242 (2015) of 13 October 2015.

54 Identical letters dated 25 February 2013 from the Secretary-General addressed to the President of the General Assembly and the President of the Security Council, UN Doc A/67/775-S/2013/110, 5 March 2013. See ch 32 below.

55 In 2016, there were 17 UN peace missions that had a Human Rights Component. See <http://www.ohchr.org/EN/newyork/Stories/Pages/Strengtheninghumanrightsinpeaceoperations.aspx> accessed 1 November 2017.

56 For more details about the HRC work, see <http://www.ohchr.org/EN/Countries/Pages/PeaceMissionsIndex.aspx> accessed 1 November 2017 and <http://www2.ohchr.org/english/ohchrreport2014_2017/omp_web_version/index.html#/downloads> accessed 1 November 2017.

57 The policy is not in the public domain.

58 Accessed 9 August 2018.

Title	International Covenant on Civil and Political Rights
Date of Adoption	16 December 1966 in General Assembly Resolution 2200A (XXI)
Opened for Signature	19 December 1966
Entered into Force	23 March 1976 in accordance with Article 49, except for Article 41 (Human Rights Committee) which came into force on 28 March 1979 in accordance with paragraph 2 of Article 41
Signatories	74
Parties	169
Depository	United Nations
Treaty Series	999 UNTS 171
Full Text	<https://www.ohchr.org/en/professionalinterest/pages/ccpr.aspx>[59]

International Covenant on Economic, Social, and Cultural Rights[60]

(Extracts)

Preamble

The States Parties to the present Covenant,

Considering that, in accordance with the principles proclaimed in the Charter of the United Nations, recognition of the inherent dignity and of the equal and inalienable rights of all members of the human family is the foundation of freedom, justice and peace in the world,

Recognizing that these rights derive from the inherent dignity of the human person,

Recognizing that, in accordance with the Universal Declaration of Human Rights, the ideal of free human beings enjoying freedom from fear and want can only be achieved if conditions are created whereby everyone may enjoy his economic, social and cultural rights, as well as his civil and political rights,

Considering the obligation of States under the Charter of the United Nations to promote universal respect for, and observance of, human rights and freedoms,

Realizing that the individual, having duties to other individuals and to the community to which he belongs, is under a responsibility to strive for the promotion and observance of the rights recognized in the present Covenant,

Agree upon the following articles:

...

Part II

Article 2

1. Each State Party to the present Covenant undertakes to take steps, individually and through international assistance and co-operation, especially economic and technical, to the maximum

59 Accessed 9 August 2018.

60 From International Covenant on Civil and Political Rights, © 1966 United Nations. Reprinted with the permission of the United Nations.

of its available resources, with a view to achieving progressively the full realization of the rights recognized in the present Covenant by all appropriate means, including particularly the adoption of legislative measures.

2. The States Parties to the present Covenant undertake to guarantee that the rights enunciated in the present Covenant will be exercised without discrimination of any kind as to race, colour, sex, language, religion, political or other opinion, national or social origin, property, birth or other status.
3. Developing countries, with due regard to human rights and their national economy, may determine to what extent they would guarantee the economic rights recognized in the present Covenant to non-nationals.

...

Article 4

The States Parties to the present Covenant recognize that, in the enjoyment of those rights provided by the State in conformity with the present Covenant, the State may subject such rights only to such limitations as are determined by law only in so far as this may be compatible with the nature of these rights and solely for the purpose of promoting the general welfare in a democratic society.

Article 5

1. Nothing in the present Covenant may be interpreted as implying for any State, group or person any right to engage in any activity or to perform any act aimed at the destruction of any of the rights or freedoms recognized herein, or at their limitation to a greater extent than is provided for in the present Covenant.
2. No restriction upon or derogation from any of the fundamental human rights recognized or existing in any country in virtue of law, conventions, regulations or custom shall be admitted on the pretext that the present Covenant does not recognize such rights or that it recognizes them to a lesser extent.

Part III

Article 6

1. The States Parties to the present Covenant recognize the right to work, which includes the right of everyone to the opportunity to gain his living by work which he freely chooses or accepts, and will take appropriate steps to safeguard this right.
2. The steps to be taken by a State Party to the present Covenant to achieve the full realization of this right shall include technical and vocational guidance and training programmes, policies and techniques to achieve steady economic, social and cultural development and full and productive employment under conditions safeguarding fundamental political and economic freedoms to the individual.

Article 7

The States Parties to the present Covenant recognize the right of everyone to the enjoyment of just and favourable conditions of work which ensure, in particular:

(a) Remuneration which provides all workers, as a minimum, with:
   (i) Fair wages and equal remuneration for work of equal value without distinction of any kind, in particular women being guaranteed conditions of work not inferior to those enjoyed by men, with equal pay for equal work;
   (ii) A decent living for themselves and their families in accordance with the provisions of the present Covenant;

(b) Safe and healthy working conditions;
(c) Equal opportunity for everyone to be promoted in his employment to an appropriate higher level, subject to no considerations other than those of seniority and competence;
(d) Rest, leisure and reasonable limitation of working hours and periodic holidays with pay, as well as remuneration for public holidays

Article 8

1. The States Parties to the present Covenant undertake to ensure:
   (a) The right of everyone to form trade unions and join the trade union of his choice, subject only to the rules of the organization concerned, for the promotion and protection of his economic and social interests. No restrictions may be placed on the exercise of this right other than those prescribed by law and which are necessary in a democratic society in the interests of national security or public order or for the protection of the rights and freedoms of others;
   (b) The right of trade unions to establish national federations or confederations and the right of the latter to form or join international trade-union organizations;
   (c) The right of trade unions to function freely subject to no limitations other than those prescribed by law and which are necessary in a democratic society in the interests of national security or public order or for the protection of the rights and freedoms of others;
   (d) The right to strike, provided that it is exercised in conformity with the laws of the particular country.
2. This article shall not prevent the imposition of lawful restrictions on the exercise of these rights by members of the armed forces or of the police or of the administration of the State.
3. Nothing in this article shall authorize States Parties to the International Labour Organisation Convention of 1948 concerning Freedom of Association and Protection of the Right to Organize to take legislative measures which would prejudice, or apply the law in such a manner as would prejudice, the guarantees provided for in that Convention.

Article 9

The States Parties to the present Covenant recognize the right of everyone to social security, including social insurance.

Article 10

The States Parties to the present Covenant recognize that:

1. The widest possible protection and assistance should be accorded to the family, which is the natural and fundamental group unit of society, particularly for its establishment and while it is responsible for the care and education of dependent children. Marriage must be entered into with the free consent of the intending spouses.
2. Special protection should be accorded to mothers during a reasonable period before and after childbirth. During such period working mothers should be accorded paid leave or leave with adequate social security benefits.
3. Special measures of protection and assistance should be taken on behalf of all children and young persons without any discrimination for reasons of parentage or other conditions. Children and young persons should be protected from economic and social exploitation. Their employment in work harmful to their morals or health or dangerous to life or likely to hamper their normal development should be punishable by law. States should also set age limits below which the paid employment of child labour should be prohibited and punishable by law.

Article 11

1. The States Parties to the present Covenant recognize the right of everyone to an adequate standard of living for himself and his family, including adequate food, clothing and housing, and to the continuous improvement of living conditions. The States Parties will take appropriate steps to ensure the realization of this right, recognizing to this effect the essential importance of international co-operation based on free consent.
2. The States Parties to the present Covenant, recognizing the fundamental right of everyone to be free from hunger, shall take, individually and through international co-operation, the measures, including specific programmes, which are needed:
   (a) To improve methods of production, conservation and distribution of food by making full use of technical and scientific knowledge, by disseminating knowledge of the principles of nutrition and by developing or reforming agrarian systems in such a way as to achieve the most efficient development and utilization of natural resources;
   (b) Taking into account the problems of both food-importing and food-exporting countries, to ensure an equitable distribution of world food supplies in relation to need.

Article 12

1. The States Parties to the present Covenant recognize the right of everyone to the enjoyment of the highest attainable standard of physical and mental health.
2. The steps to be taken by the States Parties to the present Covenant to achieve the full realization of this right shall include those necessary for:
   (a) The provision for the reduction of the stillbirth-rate and of infant mortality and for the healthy development of the child;
   (b) The improvement of all aspects of environmental and industrial hygiene;
   (c) The prevention, treatment and control of epidemic, endemic, occupational and other diseases;
   (d) The creation of conditions which would assure to all medical service and medical attention in the event of sickness.

Article 13

1. The States Parties to the present Covenant recognize the right of everyone to education. They agree that education shall be directed to the full development of the human personality and the sense of its dignity, and shall strengthen the respect for human rights and fundamental freedoms. They further agree that education shall enable all persons to participate effectively in a free society, promote understanding, tolerance and friendship among all nations and all racial, ethnic or religious groups, and further the activities of the United Nations for the maintenance of peace.
2. The States Parties to the present Covenant recognize that, with a view to achieving the full realization of this right:
   (a) Primary education shall be compulsory and available free to all;
   (b) Secondary education in its different forms, including technical and vocational secondary education, shall be made generally available and accessible to all by every appropriate means, and in particular by the progressive introduction of free education;
   (c) Higher education shall be made equally accessible to all, on the basis of capacity, by every appropriate means, and in particular by the progressive introduction of free education;

(d) Fundamental education shall be encouraged or intensified as far as possible for those persons who have not received or completed the whole period of their primary education;

(e) The development of a system of schools at all levels shall be actively pursued, an adequate fellowship system shall be established, and the material conditions of teaching staff shall be continuously improved.

3. The States Parties to the present Covenant undertake to have respect for the liberty of parents and, when applicable, legal guardians to choose for their children schools, other than those established by the public authorities, which conform to such minimum educational standards as may be laid down or approved by the State and to ensure the religious and moral education of their children in conformity with their own convictions.

4. No part of this article shall be construed so as to interfere with the liberty of individuals and bodies to establish and direct educational institutions, subject always to the observance of the principles set forth in paragraph I of this article and to the requirement that the education given in such institutions shall conform to such minimum standards as may be laid down by the State.

Article 14

Each State Party to the present Covenant which, at the time of becoming a Party, has not been able to secure in its metropolitan territory or other territories under its jurisdiction compulsory primary education, free of charge, undertakes, within two years, to work out and adopt a detailed plan of action for the progressive implementation, within a reasonable number of years, to be fixed in the plan, of the principle of compulsory education free of charge for all.

Article 15

1. The States Parties to the present Covenant recognize the right of everyone:

(a) To take part in cultural life;

(b) To enjoy the benefits of scientific progress and its applications;

(c) To benefit from the protection of the moral and material interests resulting from any scientific, literary or artistic production of which he is the author.

2. The steps to be taken by the States Parties to the present Covenant to achieve the full realization of this right shall include those necessary for the conservation, the development and the diffusion of science and culture.

3. The States Parties to the present Covenant undertake to respect the freedom indispensable for scientific research and creative activity.

4. The States Parties to the present Covenant recognize the benefits to be derived from the encouragement and development of international contacts and co-operation in the scientific and cultural fields.

International Covenant on Civil and Political Rights[61]

(Extracts)

Preamble

The States Parties to the present Covenant,

Considering that, in accordance with the principles proclaimed in the Charter of the United Nations, recognition of the inherent dignity and of the equal and inalienable rights of all members of the human family is the foundation of freedom, justice and peace in the world,

Recognizing that these rights derive from the inherent dignity of the human person,

Recognizing that, in accordance with the Universal Declaration of Human Rights, the ideal of free human beings enjoying civil and political freedom and freedom from fear and want can only be achieved if conditions are created whereby everyone may enjoy his civil and political rights, as well as his economic, social and cultural rights,

Considering the obligation of States under the Charter of the United Nations to promote universal respect for, and observance of, human rights and freedoms,

Realizing that the individual, having duties to other individuals and to the community to which he belongs, is under a responsibility to strive for the promotion and observance of the rights recognized in the present Covenant,

Agree upon the following articles:

Part I

Article 1

1. All peoples have the right of self-determination. By virtue of that right they freely determine their political status and freely pursue their economic, social and cultural development.
2. All peoples may, for their own ends, freely dispose of their natural wealth and resources without prejudice to any obligations arising out of international economic co-operation, based upon the principle of mutual benefit, and international law. In no case may a people be deprived of its own means of subsistence.
3. The States Parties to the present Covenant, including those having responsibility for the administration of Non-Self-Governing and Trust Territories, shall promote the realization of the right of self-determination, and shall respect that right, in conformity with the provisions of the Charter of the United Nations.

Part II

Article 2

1. Each State Party to the present Covenant undertakes to respect and to ensure to all individuals within its territory and subject to its jurisdiction the rights recognized in the present Covenant, without distinction of any kind, such as race, colour, sex, language, religion, political or other opinion, national or social origin, property, birth or other status.

2. Where not already provided for by existing legislative or other measures, each State Party to the present Covenant undertakes to take the necessary steps, in accordance with its constitutional processes and with the provisions of the present Covenant, to adopt such laws or other measures as may be necessary to give effect to the rights recognized in the present Covenant.
3. Each State Party to the present Covenant undertakes:
   (a) To ensure that any person whose rights or freedoms as herein recognized are violated shall have an effective remedy, notwithstanding that the violation has been committed by persons acting in an official capacity;
   (b) To ensure that any person claiming such a remedy shall have his right thereto determined by competent judicial, administrative or legislative authorities, or by any other competent authority provided for by the legal system of the State, and to develop the possibilities of judicial remedy;
   (c) To ensure that the competent authorities shall enforce such remedies when granted.

Article 3

The States Parties to the present Covenant undertake to ensure the equal right of men and women to the enjoyment of all civil and political rights set forth in the present Covenant.

Article 4

1. In time of public emergency which threatens the life of the nation and the existence of which is officially proclaimed, the States Parties to the present Covenant may take measures derogating from their obligations under the present Covenant to the extent strictly required by the exigencies of the situation, provided that such measures are not inconsistent with their other obligations under international law and do not involve discrimination solely on the ground of race, colour, sex, language, religion or social origin.
2. No derogation from articles 6, 7, 8 (paragraphs 1 and 2), 11, 15, 16 and 18 may be made under this provision.
3. Any State Party to the present Covenant availing itself of the right of derogation shall immediately inform the other States Parties to the present Covenant, through the intermediary of the Secretary-General of the United Nations, of the provisions from which it has derogated and of the reasons by which it was actuated. A further communication shall be made, through the same intermediary, on the date on which it terminates such derogation.

Article 5

1. Nothing in the present Covenant may be interpreted as implying for any State, group or person any right to engage in any activity or perform any act aimed at the destruction of any of the rights and freedoms recognized herein or at their limitation to a greater extent than is provided for in the present Covenant.
2. There shall be no restriction upon or derogation from any of the fundamental human rights recognized or existing in any State Party to the present Covenant pursuant to law, conventions, regulations or custom on the pretext that the present Covenant does not recognize such rights or that it recognizes them to a lesser extent.

Part III

Article 6

1. Every human being has the inherent right to life. This right shall be protected by law. No one shall be arbitrarily deprived of his life.

2. In countries which have not abolished the death penalty, sentence of death may be imposed only for the most serious crimes in accordance with the law in force at the time of the commission of the crime and not contrary to the provisions of the present Covenant and to the Convention on the Prevention and Punishment of the Crime of Genocide. This penalty can only be carried out pursuant to a final judgement rendered by a competent court.
3. When deprivation of life constitutes the crime of genocide, it is understood that nothing in this article shall authorize any State Party to the present Covenant to derogate in any way from any obligation assumed under the provisions of the Convention on the Prevention and Punishment of the Crime of Genocide.
4. Anyone sentenced to death shall have the right to seek pardon or commutation of the sentence. Amnesty, pardon or commutation of the sentence of death may be granted in all cases.
5. Sentence of death shall not be imposed for crimes committed by persons below eighteen years of age and shall not be carried out on pregnant women.
6. Nothing in this article shall be invoked to delay or to prevent the abolition of capital punishment by any State Party to the present Covenant.

Article 7

No one shall be subjected to torture or to cruel, inhuman or degrading treatment or punishment. In particular, no one shall be subjected without his free consent to medical or scientific experimentation.

Article 8

1. No one shall be held in slavery; slavery and the slave-trade in all their forms shall be prohibited.
2. No one shall be held in servitude.
3. (a) No one shall be required to perform forced or compulsory labour;
   (b) Paragraph 3 (a) shall not be held to preclude, in countries where imprisonment with hard labour may be imposed as a punishment for a crime, the performance of hard labour in pursuance of a sentence to such punishment by a competent court;
   (c) For the purpose of this paragraph the term "forced or compulsory labour" shall not include:
      (i) Any work or service, not referred to in subparagraph (b), normally required of a person who is under detention in consequence of a lawful order of a court, or of a person during conditional release from such detention;
      (ii) Any service of a military character and, in countries where conscientious objection is recognized, any national service required by law of conscientious objectors;
      (iii) Any service exacted in cases of emergency or calamity threatening the life or well-being of the community;
      (iv) Any work or service which forms part of normal civil obligations.

Article 9

1. Everyone has the right to liberty and security of person. No one shall be subjected to arbitrary arrest or detention. No one shall be deprived of his liberty except on such grounds and in accordance with such procedure as are established by law.
2. Anyone who is arrested shall be informed, at the time of arrest, of the reasons for his arrest and shall be promptly informed of any charges against him.
3. Anyone arrested or detained on a criminal charge shall be brought promptly before a judge or other officer authorized by law to exercise judicial power and shall be entitled to trial within a reasonable time or to release. It shall not be the general rule that persons awaiting

trial shall be detained in custody, but release may be subject to guarantees to appear for trial, at any other stage of the judicial proceedings, and, should occasion arise, for execution of the judgement.

4. Anyone who is deprived of his liberty by arrest or detention shall be entitled to take proceedings before a court, in order that that court may decide without delay on the lawfulness of his detention and order his release if the detention is not lawful.
5. Anyone who has been the victim of unlawful arrest or detention shall have an enforceable right to compensation.

Article 10

1. All persons deprived of their liberty shall be treated with humanity and with respect for the inherent dignity of the human person.
2. (a) Accused persons shall, save in exceptional circumstances, be segregated from convicted persons and shall be subject to separate treatment appropriate to their status as unconvicted persons;

   (b) Accused juvenile persons shall be separated from adults and brought as speedily as possible for adjudication.
3. The penitentiary system shall comprise treatment of prisoners the essential aim of which shall be their reformation and social rehabilitation. Juvenile offenders shall be segregated from adults and be accorded treatment appropriate to their age and legal status.

Article 11

No one shall be imprisoned merely on the ground of inability to fulfil a contractual obligation.

Article 12

1. Everyone lawfully within the territory of a State shall, within that territory, have the right to liberty of movement and freedom to choose his residence.
2. Everyone shall be free to leave any country, including his own.
3. The above-mentioned rights shall not be subject to any restrictions except those which are provided by law, are necessary to protect national security, public order (ordre public), public health or morals or the rights and freedoms of others, and are consistent with the other rights recognized in the present Covenant.
4. No one shall be arbitrarily deprived of the right to enter his own country.

Article 13

An alien lawfully in the territory of a State Party to the present Covenant may be expelled therefrom only in pursuance of a decision reached in accordance with law and shall, except where compelling reasons of national security otherwise require, be allowed to submit the reasons against his expulsion and to have his case reviewed by, and be represented for the purpose before, the competent authority or a person or persons especially designated by the competent authority.

Article 14

1. All persons shall be equal before the courts and tribunals. In the determination of any criminal charge against him, or of his rights and obligations in a suit at law, everyone shall be entitled to a fair and public hearing by a competent, independent and impartial tribunal established by law. The press and the public may be excluded from all or part of a trial for reasons of morals, public order (ordre public) or national security in a democratic society, or when the interest of the private lives of the parties so requires, or to the extent strictly necessary in the opinion of the court in special circumstances where publicity would prejudice the interests of justice; but any judgement rendered in a criminal case or in a suit at law shall be

made public except where the interest of juvenile persons otherwise requires or the proceedings concern matrimonial disputes or the guardianship of children.

2. Everyone charged with a criminal offence shall have the right to be presumed innocent until proved guilty according to law.
3. In the determination of any criminal charge against him, everyone shall be entitled to the following minimum guarantees, in full equality:
   (a) To be informed promptly and in detail in a language which he understands of the nature and cause of the charge against him;
   (b) To have adequate time and facilities for the preparation of his defence and to communicate with counsel of his own choosing;
   (c) To be tried without undue delay;
   (d) To be tried in his presence, and to defend himself in person or through legal assistance of his own choosing; to be informed, if he does not have legal assistance, of this right; and to have legal assistance assigned to him, in any case where the interests of justice so require, and without payment by him in any such case if he does not have sufficient means to pay for it;
   (e) To examine, or have examined, the witnesses against him and to obtain the attendance and examination of witnesses on his behalf under the same conditions as witnesses against him;
   (f) To have the free assistance of an interpreter if he cannot understand or speak the language used in court;
   (g) Not to be compelled to testify against himself or to confess guilt.
4. In the case of juvenile persons, the procedure shall be such as will take account of their age and the desirability of promoting their rehabilitation.
5. Everyone convicted of a crime shall have the right to his conviction and sentence being reviewed by a higher tribunal according to law.
6. When a person has by a final decision been convicted of a criminal offence and when subsequently his conviction has been reversed or he has been pardoned on the ground that a new or newly discovered fact shows conclusively that there has been a miscarriage of justice, the person who has suffered punishment as a result of such conviction shall be compensated according to law, unless it is proved that the non-disclosure of the unknown fact in time is wholly or partly attributable to him.
7. No one shall be liable to be tried or punished again for an offence for which he has already been finally convicted or acquitted in accordance with the law and penal procedure of each country.

Article 15

1. No one shall be held guilty of any criminal offence on account of any act or omission which did not constitute a criminal offence, under national or international law, at the time when it was committed. Nor shall a heavier penalty be imposed than the one that was applicable at the time when the criminal offence was committed. If, subsequent to the commission of the offence, provision is made by law for the imposition of the lighter penalty, the offender shall benefit thereby.
2. Nothing in this article shall prejudice the trial and punishment of any person for any act or omission which, at the time when it was committed, was criminal according to the general principles of law recognized by the community of nations.

Article 16

Everyone shall have the right to recognition everywhere as a person before the law.

Article 17

1. No one shall be subjected to arbitrary or unlawful interference with his privacy, family, home or correspondence, nor to unlawful attacks on his honour and reputation.
2. Everyone has the right to the protection of the law against such interference or attacks.

Article 18

1. Everyone shall have the right to freedom of thought, conscience and religion. This right shall include freedom to have or to adopt a religion or belief of his choice, and freedom, either individually or in community with others and in public or private, to manifest his religion or belief in worship, observance, practice and teaching.
2. No one shall be subject to coercion which would impair his freedom to have or to adopt a religion or belief of his choice.
3. Freedom to manifest one's religion or beliefs may be subject only to such limitations as are prescribed by law and are necessary to protect public safety, order, health, or morals or the fundamental rights and freedoms of others.
4. The States Parties to the present Covenant undertake to have respect for the liberty of parents and, when applicable, legal guardians to ensure the religious and moral education of their children in conformity with their own convictions.

...

Article 19

1. Everyone shall have the right to hold opinions without interference.
2. Everyone shall have the right to freedom of expression; this right shall include freedom to seek, receive and impart information and ideas of all kinds, regardless of frontiers, either orally, in writing or in print, in the form of art, or through any other media of his choice.
3. The exercise of the rights provided for in paragraph 2 of this article carries with it special duties and responsibilities. It may therefore be subject to certain restrictions, but these shall only be such as are provided by law and are necessary:
   (a) For respect of the rights or reputations of others;
   (b) For the protection of national security or of public order (ordre public), or of public health or morals.

Article 20

1. Any propaganda for war shall be prohibited by law.
2. Any advocacy of national, racial or religious hatred that constitutes incitement to discrimination, hostility or violence shall be prohibited by law.

Article 21

The right of peaceful assembly shall be recognized. No restrictions may be placed on the exercise of this right other than those imposed in conformity with the law and which are necessary in a democratic society in the interests of national security or public safety, public order (ordre public), the protection of public health or morals or the protection of the rights and freedoms of others.

...

Article 26

All persons are equal before the law and are entitled without any discrimination to the equal protection of the law. In this respect, the law shall prohibit any discrimination and guarantee to all persons equal and effective protection against discrimination on any ground such as race, colour, sex, language, religion, political or other opinion, national or social origin, property, birth or other status.

...

7

Convention on the Elimination of All Forms of Discrimination against Women

Prefatory Note

The Convention on the Elimination of All Forms of Discrimination against Women (CEDAW)[1] continues to be a foundation for the UN's approach to dealing with gender issues—particularly women, peace, and security—on peace operations.

The genesis of CEDAW can be found in the Charter of the United Nations (Charter).[2] The Preamble to the Charter states that the peoples of the United Nations were determined to 'reaffirm faith … in the equal rights of men and women'.[3] The Charter further states in Article 1(3) that one of the purposes of the UN is to promote and encourage 'respect for human rights and for fundamental freedoms for all without distinction as to … sex'. The principle of non-discrimination, including on the basis of sex, is included in the Universal Declaration of Human Rights (UDHR),[4] the International Covenant on Civil and Political Rights (ICCPR),[5] and the International Covenant on Economic, Social and Cultural Rights (ICESCR).[6]

In resolution 31/136,[7] the General Assembly approved the Programme for the UN Decade for Women. One of the aims of the programme was the adoption of a Convention on the Elimination of Discrimination against Women during the first half of the 1970s. The final text of CEDAW was adopted by the General Assembly in resolution 34/180.[8] The adoption of CEDAW was the culmination of over thirty years of work by the Commission on the Status of Women (CSW). CEDAW entered into force on 3 September 1981 during the UN's Decade for Women.

Article 1 of CEDAW defines discrimination against women as:

> any distinction, exclusion or restriction made on the basis of sex which has the effect or purpose of impairing or nullifying the recognition, enjoyment or exercise by women, irrespective of their marital status, on a basis of equality of men and women, of human rights and fundamental freedoms in the political, economic, social, cultural, civil or any other field.[9]

Article 2 outlines what State Parties are required to do to eliminate discrimination. This includes embodying 'the principle of the equality of men and women in their national constitutions',[10] and adopting 'appropriate legislative and other measures, including sanctions where appropriate, prohibiting all discrimination against women'.[11] Requirements also include establishing 'legal protection of the rights of women on an equal basis with men';[12] taking 'all appropriate measures, including legislation, to modify or abolish existing laws, regulations, customs, and practices which constitute discrimination against women';[13]

---

1 Convention on the Elimination of All Forms of Discrimination against Women (opened for signature 18 December 1979, entered into force 3 September 1981) 1249 UNTS 13 (hereafter CEDAW).

2 Charter of the United Nations (opened for signature 26 June 1945, entered into force 24 October 1945) 1 UNTS XVI (hereafter Charter). See ch 1 above.

3 Charter (n 2), Preamble [2].

4 Universal Declaration of Human Rights, adopted by GA Res 217(III) of 10 December 1948. See also Bruce Oswald, Helen Durham and Adrian Bates, *Documents on the Law of UN Peace Operations* (Oxford University Press 2010) ch 4.

5 See ch 6 above.

6 See ch 6 above.

7 GA Res 31/136 of 16 December 1976, Operative Part [1].

8 GA Res 34/180 of 18 December 1979.

9 CEDAW (n 1), Article 1.

10 Ibid, Article 2(a).

11 Ibid, Article 2(b).

12 Ibid, Article 2(c).

13 Ibid, Article 2(f).

and repealing 'all national penal provisions which constitute discrimination against women'.[14]

In General Recommendation 30 on women in conflict prevention, conflict, and post-conflict situations, the Committee on the Elimination of Discrimination against Women[15] stated:

> In conflict and post-conflict situations, States parties are bound to apply the Convention and other international human rights and humanitarian law when they exercise territorial or extraterritorial jurisdiction, whether individually, for example, in unilateral military action, or as members of international or intergovernmental organizations or coalitions, for example, as part of an international peacekeeping force. The Convention applies to a wide range of situations, including wherever a State exercises jurisdiction, such as occupation and other forms of administration of foreign territory, for example, United Nations administration of territory; to national contingents that form part of an international peacekeeping or peace-enforcement operation; to persons detained by agents of a State, such as the military or mercenaries, outside its territory; to lawful or unlawful military actions in another State; to bilateral or multilateral donor assistance for conflict prevention and humanitarian aid, mitigation or post-conflict reconstruction; in involvement as third parties in peace or negotiation processes; and in the formation of trade agreements with conflict-affected countries.[16]

In Article 3, CEDAW gives positive affirmation to the principle of equality by requiring State Parties to take 'all appropriate measures, including legislation, to ensure the full development and advancement of women, for the purpose of guaranteeing them the exercise and enjoyment of human rights and fundamental freedoms on a basis of equality with men'.

The Optional Protocol to the Convention on the Elimination of All Forms of Discrimination against Women (Optional Protocol)[17] creates two new procedures to enhance compliance with CEDAW. Most significant is the communications procedure in Article 2 of the Optional Protocol which permits complaints from those 'claiming to be victims of a violation of any of the rights set out in ... [CEDAW]'.[18]

As well as CEDAW, there are a number of other important international human rights instruments dealing with the rights of women including the Declaration on the Protection of Women and Children in Emergency and Armed Conflict proclaimed by General Assembly resolution 3318 (XXIX),[19] and the Declaration on the Elimination of Violence against Women proclaimed by General Assembly resolution 48/104.[20]

The Committee on the Elimination of Discrimination against Women has issued a number of general recommendations other than General Recommendation 30, such as General Recommendation 28 on the core obligations of States parties under Article 2 of the CEDAW.[21]

The rights of women are also dealt with by a number of regional instruments such as the Inter-American Convention on the Prevention, Punishment and Eradication of Violence Against Women,[22] the Protocol to the African Charter on Human and Peoples' Rights on the Rights of Women in Africa,[23] and the Kampala Declaration on Sexual and Gender-Based Violence.[24] The

---

14 Ibid, Article 2(g).

15 The Committee on the Elimination of Discrimination against Women (hereafter Committee) is a body of independent experts who are mandated to: (1) receive communications from individuals or groups of individuals submitting claims of violations of rights protected under the CEDAW to the Committee; and (2) initiate inquiries into situations of grave or systematic violations of women's rights. These procedures are optional and are only available where the State concerned has accepted them. The Committee also formulates general recommendations and suggestions. General recommendations are directed to States and concern articles or themes in the CEDAW. For more information about the Committee, see <http://www.ohchr.org/EN/HRBodies/CEDAW/Pages/Introduction.aspx> accessed 1 November 2017.

16 Committee on the Elimination of Discrimination against Women, 'General Recommendation No 30 on Women in Conflict Prevention, Conflict and Post-Conflict Situations', UN Doc CEDAW/C/GC/30, 1 November 2013 [9].

17 Optional Protocol to the Convention on the Elimination of All Forms of Discrimination against Women (opened for signature 6 October 1999, entered into force 22 December 2000) 2131 UNTS 83 (hereafter Optional Protocol).

18 Ibid, Article 2.

19 GA Res 3318 (XXIX) of 14 December 1974 <http://www.un.org/documents/ga/res/29/ares29.htm> accessed 1 November 2017.

20 GA Res 48/104 of 20 December 1993 <http://www.un.org/documents/ga/res/48/a48r104.htm> accessed 1 November 2017.

21 For other General Recommendations from the Committee, see <http://tbinternet.ohchr.org/_layouts/treatybodyexternal/TBSearch.aspx?Lang=en&TreatyID=3&DocTypeID=11> accessed 1 November 2017.

22 Inter-American Convention on the Prevention, Punishment and Eradication of Violence Against Women (opened for signature 9 June 1994, entered into force 5 March 1995) 33 ILM 1534.

23 Protocol to the African Charter on Human and Peoples' Rights on the Rights of Women in Africa (adopted 13 September 2000, entered into force 25 November 2005) OAU Doc CAB/LEG/66.6 (13 September 2000).

24 Declaration of the Heads of State and Government of the Member States of the International Conference on the Great Lakes Region (Kampala, 15 December 2011) <http://www.acordinternational.org/silo/files/declaration-by-heads-of-state-from-icglr.pdf> accessed 1 November 2017.

African Union (AU) has reinforced the rights of women in peace and security through policies such as the AU Gender Policy of 2009,[25] the AU policy on Women and Disarmament, Demobilisation, and Reintegration,[26] and the AU-UN Framework Agreement,[27] and the AU Five-Year Gender Peace and Security Programme.[28] The European Union (EU) has also developed policies to mainstream gender in its security and defence policy.[29]

CEDAW is relevant to UN peace operations for a variety of reasons. For example, the protection and respect for the human rights of women are increasingly referred to in Security Council resolutions concerning peace operations. In resolution 2252, the Security Council gave the United Nations Mission in South Sudan (UNMISS) the mandate to:

> [P]rotect civilians under threat of physical violence, irrespective of the source of such violence, within its capacity and areas of deployment, with specific protection for women and children, including through the continued use of the Mission's Child Protection and Women Protection Advisers.[30]

Other tasks with which peacekeepers might be mandated include supporting the host State to 'combat sexual and gender-based violence, including ... to combat impunity for perpetrators of such crimes'.[31]

There are several thematic Security Council resolutions on women, peace, and security that deal with the specific rights of women.[32] For example, the Security Council, in resolution 1325, called upon all parties to armed conflict to:

> [R]espect fully international law applicable to the rights and protection of women and girls, especially as civilians, in particular the obligations applicable to them under ... the Convention on the Elimination of All Forms of Discrimination against Women of 1979 and the Optional Protocol thereto of 1999 ...[33]

Resolution 1325 led to a greater focus on the role of women in peace operations. In particular, the Security Council has expressed its willingness to incorporate a gender perspective into peace operations, and has urged the Secretary-General to ensure that field operations include a gender component with trained staff and appropriate funding.[34] The General Assembly has also recognised the importance of the role of women and has expressed concerns about the number of women serving in peace operations.[35] This emphasis on including a gender perspective in peace operations is reflected in the mandates for a number of UN peace operations. For example, in resolution 1704, the Security Council gave the United Nations Integrated Mission in Timor-Leste (UNMIT) the mandate to:

> [M]ainstream gender perspectives and those of children and youth throughout the Mission's policies, programmes and activities, and, working together with United Nations agencies, funds and programmes, support the development of a national strategy to promote gender equality and empowerment of women.[36]

In resolution 2242, on women, peace, and security, the Security Council urged:

> DPKO [Department of Peacekeeping Operations] and DPA [Department of Political Affairs] to ensure the necessary gender analysis and technical gender expertise is included throughout all stages of mission

---

25 African Union Gender Policy (2009) <http://www.un.org/en/africa/osaa/pdf/au/gender_policy_2009.pdf> accessed 1 November 2017.

26 African Union Disarmament, Demobilisation, and Reintegration Capacity Program, Operational Guidelines on DDR for Women (2014) <http://www.peaceau.org/uploads/au-operational-guideline-on-ddr-for-women.pdf> accessed 1 November 2017.

27 See <http://www.peaceau.org/en/article/african-union-launches-five-year-gender-peace-and-security-programme-2015-2020> accessed 1 November 2017.

28 African Union Five-Year Gender Peace and Security Programme 2015–2020 <http://www.peaceau.org/en/article/african-union-launches-five-year-gender-peace-and-security-programme-2015-2020> accessed 1 November 2017.

29 See, for example, 'Checklist to Ensure Gender Mainstreaming and Implementation of UNSCR 1325 in the Planning and Conduct of ESDP Operations', Doc 12068/06, 2008, reprinted in General Secretariat of the Council, 'Mainstreaming Human Rights and Gender into European Security and Defence Policy: Compilation of Relevant Documents'.

30 SC Res 2252 (2015) of 15 December 2015, Operative Part [8](a)(i).

31 See, for example, SC Res 2333 (2016) of 23 December 2016, Operative Part [11](c)(ii).

32 See, for example, SC Res 1325 (2000) of 31 October 2000; SC Res 1820 (2008) of 19 June 2008. See ch 17 below.

33 SC Res 1325 (2000) of 31 October 2000, Operative Part [9].

34 For more information on the gender component of UN peace operations, see <https://peacekeeping.un.org/en/promoting-women-peace-and-security> accessed 8 April 2019.

35 GA Res 70/286 (2016) of 8 July 2016, Operative Part [25].

36 SC Res 1704 (2006) of 25 August 2006, Operative Part [4](k).

> planning, mandate development, implementation, review and mission drawdown, ensuring the needs and participation of women are integrated in all sequenced stages of mission mandates.[37]

Other thematic Security Council resolutions, such as those on children and armed conflict,[38] the protection of civilians in armed conflict,[39] and sexual exploitation and abuse,[40] also refer to the protection of women. For example, the Security Council, in resolution 1674 on the protection of civilians in armed conflict, reaffirmed its condemnation:

> of all acts of violence or abuses committed against civilians in situations of armed conflict in violation of applicable international obligations with respect in particular to ... (ii) gender-based and sexual violence ... (v) trafficking in humans ... and ***demands*** [emphasis in original] that all parties put an end to such practices.[41]

The UN has also expressed concern over the continuing and serious allegations of sexual exploitation and abuse by UN peacekeepers. In resolution 2272 the Security Council urged 'all troop-contributing countries to take the steps necessary to conduct investigations of allegations of sexual exploitation and abuse by their personnel'.[42]

Also relevant to the framework on the protection of women are documents such as the Secretary-General's Bulletin on 'Special measures for protection from sexual exploitation and sexual abuse',[43] the Protocol to Prevent, Suppress and Punish Trafficking in Persons, Especially Women and Children,[44] the Recommended Principles and Guidelines on Human Rights and Human Trafficking,[45] the UN's Department of Peacekeeping Operations and Department of Field Support Policy on Gender Equality in UN Peacekeeping Operations,[46] and the Framework of Cooperation between the United Nations Office of the Special Representative of the Secretary-General on Sexual Violence in Conflict and the African Union Commission Concerning the Prevention and Response to Conflict-related Sexual Violence in Africa.[47]

Reference

Title	Convention on the Elimination of All Forms of Discrimination against Women (CEDAW)
Date of Adoption	18 December 1979
Opened for Signature	1 March 1980
Entered into Force	3 September 1981 in accordance with Article 27(1)
Signatories	99
Parties	189
Depository	United Nations
Treaty Series	1249 UNTS 13
Full Text	<https://www.ohchr.org/en/professionalinterest/pages/cedaw.aspx>[48]

37 SC Res 2242 (2015) of 13 October 2015, Operative Part [7]. See ch 17 below.
38 See ch 18 below.
39 See ch 19 below.
40 See ch 20 below.
41 SC Res 1674 (2006) of 28 April 2006, Operative Part [5].
42 SC Res 2272 (2016) of 11 Mar 2016, Operative Part [11].
43 Secretary-General's Bulletin, 'Special Measures for Protection from Sexual Exploitation and Sexual Abuse', UN Doc ST/SGB/2003/13, 9 October 2003, entered into force 15 October 2003. See ch 30 below.
44 Protocol to Prevent, Suppress and Punish Trafficking in Persons, Especially Women and Children, supplementing the United Nations Convention against Transnational Organized Crime (adopted 15 November 2000) 2225 UNTS 209.
45 Addendum to the Report of the United Nations Office of the High Commissioner for Human Rights to the Economic and Social Council, 'Recommended Principles and Guidelines on Human Rights and Human Trafficking', UN Doc E/2002/68/Add.1, 20 May 2002.
46 Department of Peacekeeping Operations and Department of Field Support, 'Gender Equality in UN Peacekeeping Operations', 26 July 2010.
47 Adopted on 31 January 2014.
48 Accessed 9 August 2018.

Convention on the Elimination of All Forms of Discrimination against Women[49]

(Extracts)

PREAMBLE

The States Parties to the present Convention,

Noting that the Charter of the United Nations reaffirms faith in fundamental human rights, in the dignity and worth of the human person and in the equal rights of men and women,

Noting that the Universal Declaration of Human Rights affirms the principle of the inadmissibility of discrimination and proclaims that all human beings are born free and equal in dignity and rights and that everyone is entitled to all the rights and freedoms set forth therein, without distinction of any kind, including distinction based on sex,

Noting that the States Parties to the International Covenants on Human Rights have the obligation to ensure the equal rights of men and women to enjoy all economic, social, cultural, civil and political rights,

Considering the international conventions concluded under the auspices of the United Nations and the specialized agencies promoting equality of rights of men and women,

Noting also the resolutions, declarations and recommendations adopted by the United Nations and the specialized agencies promoting equality of rights of men and women,

Concerned, however, that despite these various instruments extensive discrimination against women continues to exist,

Recalling that discrimination against women violates the principles of equality of rights and respect for human dignity, is an obstacle to the participation of women, on equal terms with men, in the political, social, economic and cultural life of their countries, hampers the growth of the prosperity of society and the family and makes more difficult the full development of the potentialities of women in the service of their countries and of humanity,

Concerned that in situations of poverty women have the least access to food, health, education, training and opportunities for employment and other needs,

Convinced that the establishment of the new international economic order based on equity and justice will contribute significantly towards the promotion of equality between men and women,

Emphasizing that the eradication of apartheid, all forms of racism, racial discrimination, colonialism, neo-colonialism, aggression, foreign occupation and domination and interference in the internal affairs of States is essential to the full enjoyment of the rights of men and women,

Affirming that the strengthening of international peace and security, the relaxation of international tension, mutual co-operation among all States irrespective of their social and economic systems, general and complete disarmament, in particular nuclear disarmament under

49 From Convention on the Elimination of All Forms of Discrimination against Women © 1979 United Nations. Reprinted with the permission of the United Nations.

strict and effective international control, the affirmation of the principles of justice, equality and mutual benefit in relations among countries and the realization of the right of peoples under alien and colonial domination and foreign occupation to self-determination and independence, as well as respect for national sovereignty and territorial integrity, will promote social progress and development and as a consequence will contribute to the attainment of full equality between men and women,

Convinced that the full and complete development of a country, the welfare of the world and the cause of peace require the maximum participation of women on equal terms with men in all fields,

Bearing in mind the great contribution of women to the welfare of the family and to the development of society, so far not fully recognized, the social significance of maternity and the role of both parents in the family and in the upbringing of children, and aware that the role of women in procreation should not be a basis for discrimination but that the upbringing of children requires a sharing of responsibility between men and women and society as a whole,

Aware that a change in the traditional role of men as well as the role of women in society and in the family is needed to achieve full equality between men and women,

Determined to implement the principles set forth in the Declaration on the Elimination of Discrimination against Women and, for that purpose, to adopt the measures required for the elimination of such discrimination in all its forms and manifestations,

Have agreed on the following:

PART I

Article 1

For the purposes of the present Convention, the term "discrimination against women" shall mean any distinction, exclusion or restriction made on the basis of sex which has the effect or purpose of impairing or nullifying the recognition, enjoyment or exercise by women, irrespective of their marital status, on a basis of equality of men and women, of human rights and fundamental freedoms in the political, economic, social, cultural, civil or any other field.

Article 2

States Parties condemn discrimination against women in all its forms, agree to pursue by all appropriate means and without delay a policy of eliminating discrimination against women and, to this end, undertake:

(a) To embody the principle of the equality of men and women in their national constitutions or other appropriate legislation if not yet incorporated therein and to ensure, through law and other appropriate means, the practical realization of this principle;

(b) To adopt appropriate legislative and other measures, including sanctions where appropriate, prohibiting all discrimination against women;

(c) To establish legal protection of the rights of women on an equal basis with men and to ensure through competent national tribunals and other public institutions the effective protection of women against any act of discrimination;

(d) To refrain from engaging in any act or practice of discrimination against women and to ensure that public authorities and institutions shall act in conformity with this obligation;

(e) To take all appropriate measures to eliminate discrimination against women by any person, organization or enterprise;

(f) To take all appropriate measures, including legislation, to modify or abolish existing laws, regulations, customs and practices which constitute discrimination against women;

(g) To repeal all national penal provisions which constitute discrimination against women.

Article 3

States Parties shall take in all fields, in particular in the political, social, economic and cultural fields, all appropriate measures, including legislation, to ensure the full development and advancement of women, for the purpose of guaranteeing them the exercise and enjoyment of human rights and fundamental freedoms on a basis of equality with men.

. . .

Article 5

States Parties shall take all appropriate measures:

(a) To modify the social and cultural patterns of conduct of men and women, with a view to achieving the elimination of prejudices and customary and all other practices which are based on the idea of the inferiority or the superiority of either of the sexes or on stereotyped roles for men and women;

(b) To ensure that family education includes a proper understanding of maternity as a social function and the recognition of the common responsibility of men and women in the upbringing and development of their children, it being understood that the interest of the children is the primordial consideration in all cases.

Article 6

States Parties shall take all appropriate measures, including legislation, to suppress all forms of traffic in women and exploitation of prostitution of women.

PART II

Article 7

States Parties shall take all appropriate measures to eliminate discrimination against women in the political and public life of the country and, in particular, shall ensure to women, on equal terms with men, the right:

(a) To vote in all elections and public referenda and to be eligible for election to all publicly elected bodies;

(b) To participate in the formulation of government policy and the implementation thereof and to hold public office and perform all public functions at all levels of government;

(c) To participate in non-governmental organizations and associations concerned with the public and political life of the country.

. . .

PART III

. . .

Article 11

1. States Parties shall take all appropriate measures to eliminate discrimination against women in the field of employment in order to ensure, on a basis of equality of men and women, the same rights, in particular:

   (a) The right to work as an inalienable right of all human beings;

   (b) The right to the same employment opportunities, including the application of the same criteria for selection in matters of employment;

(c) The right to free choice of profession and employment, the right to promotion, job security and all benefits and conditions of service and the right to receive vocational training and retraining, including apprenticeships, advanced vocational training and recurrent training;

(d) The right to equal remuneration, including benefits, and to equal treatment in respect of work of equal value, as well as equality of treatment in the evaluation of the quality of work;

(e) The right to social security, particularly in cases of retirement, unemployment, sickness, invalidity and old age and other incapacity to work, as well as the right to paid leave;

(f) The right to protection of health and to safety in working conditions, including the safeguarding of the function of reproduction.

...

Part IV

Article 15

1. States Parties shall accord to women equality with men before the law.
2. States Parties shall accord to women, in civil matters, a legal capacity identical to that of men and the same opportunities to exercise that capacity. In particular, they shall give women equal rights to conclude contracts and to administer property and shall treat them equally in all stages of procedure in courts and tribunals.
3. States Parties agree that all contracts and all other private instruments of any kind with a legal effect which is directed at restricting the legal capacity of women shall be deemed null and void.
4. States Parties shall accord to men and women the same rights with regard to the law relating to the movement of persons and the freedom to choose their residence and domicile.

...

Part VI

Article 23

Nothing in the present Convention shall affect any provisions that are more conducive to the achievement of equality between men and women which may be contained:

(a) In the legislation of a State Party; or

(b) In any other international convention, treaty or agreement in force for that State.

Article 24

States Parties undertake to adopt all necessary measures at the national level aimed at achieving the full realization of the rights recognized in the present Convention.

...

8

Convention against Torture and Other Cruel, Inhuman, or Degrading Treatment or Punishment

Prefatory Note

The Convention against Torture and Other Cruel, Inhuman or Degrading Treatment or Punishment (CAT)[1] is particularly relevant to peace operations where peacekeepers are engaged in assisting host State law authorities to maintain law and order, or when peacekeepers are undertaking State building. In situations where peacekeepers take detainees they must ensure that they do not breach the provisions of the CAT.

The CAT is directed at making more 'effective the struggle against torture and other cruel, inhuman or degrading treatment or punishment throughout the world'.[2]

The prohibition of torture is found in numerous treaties and international instruments: Article 2 of the CAT, Article 5 of the Universal Declaration of Human Rights (UDHR),[3] Article 7 of the International Covenant on Civil and Political Rights (ICCPR),[4] Principles 6 and 33 of the Body of Principles for the Protection of All Persons under Any Form of Detention or Imprisonment (Body of Principles),[5] and Articles 2 and 5 of the Code of Conduct for Law Enforcement Officials (Code of Conduct).[6] Torture is also prohibited in international and non-international armed conflicts through the grave breach provisions in Geneva Conventions I–IV,[7] Common Article 3 to Geneva Conventions I–IV, Article 75 of Additional Protocol I,[8] and Article 4 of Additional Protocol II.[9] Under the Rome Statute of the International Criminal Court (Rome Statute), torture is a war crime in both international and non-international armed conflicts,[10] and a crime against humanity.[11] The prohibition against torture is also a peremptory norm of general international law.[12]

---

1 Convention against Torture and Other Cruel, Inhuman or Degrading Treatment or Punishment (opened for signature 10 December 1984, entered into force 26 June 1987) 1465 UNTS 85 (hereafter CAT).

2 Ibid, Preamble.

3 Universal Declaration of Human Rights, adopted by GA Res 217A (III) of 10 December 1948. See <http://www.un.org/en/universal-declaration-human-rights/index.html> accessed 1 November 2017.

4 See ch 6 above.

5 See ch 12 below.

6 See ch 13 below.

7 Geneva Conventions I–IV are: Geneva Convention for the Amelioration of the Condition of the Wounded and Sick in Armed Forces in the Field (opened for signature 12 August 1949, entered into force 21 October 1950) 75 UNTS 31, Article 50 (Geneva Convention I); Geneva Convention for the Amelioration of the Condition of Wounded, Sick and Shipwrecked Members of Armed Forces at Sea (opened for signature 12 August 1949, entered into force 21 October 1950) 75 UNTS 85, Article 51 (Geneva Convention II); Geneva Convention Relative to the Treatment of Prisoners of War (opened for signature 12 August 1949, entered into force 21 October 1950) 75 UNTS 135, Article 130 (Geneva Convention III); and Geneva Convention Relative to the Protection of Civilian Persons in Time of War (opened for signature 12 August 1949, entered into force 21 October 1950) 75 UNTS 287, Article 147 (Geneva Convention IV). See ch 16 below.

8 Protocol Additional to the Geneva Conventions of 12 August 1949, and relating to the Protection of Victims of International Armed Conflicts (Protocol I) (opened for signature 8 June 1977, entered into force 7 December 1978) 1125 UNTS 3, Article 75(2)(a)(ii).

9 Protocol Additional to the Geneva Conventions of 12 August 1949, and relating to the Protection of Victims of Non-International Armed Conflicts (Protocol II) (opened for signature 8 June 1977, entered into force 7 December 1978) 1125 UNTS 609, Article 4(2)(a).

10 Rome Statute of the International Criminal Court (opened for signature 17 July 1998, entered into force 1 July 2002), 2187 UNTS 3, Article 8 (hereafter Rome Statute). See ch 23 below.

11 Ibid, Article 7.

12 The International Tribunal for the Former Yugoslavia (ICTY) in *Prosecutor v Furundzija* (Judgment) (Trial Chamber) Case No ICTY-95-17/1-T (10 December 1988) 154 confirmed the *jus cogens* character of the norm by stating: '[c]learly, the *jus cogens* nature of the prohibition against torture articulates the notion that the prohibition has now become one of the most fundamental standards of the international community'. See also International Law Commission, 'First Report on *jus cogens*', UN Doc A/CN4/693, 8 March 2016 [48].

The foundations of the CAT are Article 5 of the UDHR and Article 7 of the ICCPR, both of which state that '[n]o one shall be subjected to torture or to cruel, inhuman or degrading treatment or punishment'. More specifically, the CAT had its genesis in General Assembly resolution 3059 (XXVII)[13] in which the General Assembly, gravely concerned that torture was still practised in various parts of the world, rejected any form of torture or other cruel, inhuman, or degrading treatment or punishment.

In 2002, the General Assembly adopted the Optional Protocol to the Convention against Torture and Other Cruel, Inhuman or Degrading Treatment or Punishment (Optional Protocol) in resolution 57/199,[14] which came into force on 22 June 2006. The Optional Protocol's objective is to establish 'a system of regular visits undertaken by independent international and national bodies to places where people are deprived of their liberty, to prevent torture and other cruel, inhuman or degrading treatment or punishment'.[15] To that end, the Optional Protocol obliges State Parties to establish independent National Preventive Mechanisms with the power to monitor all places of deprivation of liberty under their jurisdiction. It also provides for the establishment of a Subcommittee on Prevention of Torture and Other Cruel, Inhuman or Degrading Treatment or Punishment to carry out international monitoring functions outlined in the Optional Protocol.

Article 1 of the CAT defines torture to mean:

> any act by which severe pain or suffering, whether physical or mental, is intentionally inflicted on a person for such purposes as obtaining from him or a third person information or a confession, punishing him for an act he or a third person has committed or is suspected of having committed, or intimidating or coercing him or a third person, or for any reason based on discrimination of any kind, when such pain or suffering is inflicted by or at the instigation of or with the consent or acquiescence of a public official or other person acting in an official capacity. It does not include pain or suffering arising only from, inherent in or incidental to lawful sanctions.[16]

Article 2 commits State Parties to taking 'effective legislative, administrative, judicial or other measures to prevent acts of torture in any territory under its jurisdiction'. The scope of application for the CAT is therefore any territory under each State Party's jurisdiction.

The Committee Against Torture[17] has interpreted the phrase 'any territory under its jurisdiction' to not only include the State's sovereign territory, but also:

> all areas where the State party exercises, directly or indirectly, in whole or in part, de jure or de facto effective control, in accordance with international law. The reference to 'any territory' in article 2, like that in articles 5, 11, 12, 13 and 16, refers to prohibited acts committed not only on board a ship or aircraft registered by a State party, but also during military occupation or peacekeeping operations and in such places as embassies, military bases, detention facilities, or other areas over which a State exercises factual or effective control.[18]

Article 2(2) of the CAT provides that there is no derogation, including in times of war, from the prohibition against torture:

> No exceptional circumstances whatsoever, whether a state of war or a threat of war, internal political instability or any other public emergency, may be invoked as a justification of torture.[19]

Pursuant to the CAT, State Parties cannot 'expel, return ("refouler") or extradite a person to another State where there are substantial grounds for believing that he would be in danger of being subjected to torture'.[20] State Parties must also 'ensure that all acts of torture are offences under its

---

13 GA Res 3059 (XXVIII) of 2 November 1973.

14 GA Res 57/199 of 18 December 2002 (Optional Protocol) .

15 Ibid, Article 1.

16 CAT (n 1), Article 1.

17 The Committee Against Torture (Committee) is an independent body of experts. For more details concerning the Committee, see <http://www.ohchr.org/EN/HRBodies/CAT/Pages/CATIntro.aspx> accessed 1 November 2017. The Committee has issued General Comments concerning the implementation of Article 3 of the CAT in the context of Article 2 (General Comment No 1), and the implementation of Article 14(b) (General Comment No 3).

18 Committee Against Torture, General Comment No 2, Implementation of Article 2 by States Parties, UN Doc CAT/C/GC/2, 24 January 2008, [16].

19 CAT (n 1) , Article 2(2).

20 Ibid, Article 3(1).

criminal law',[21] establish jurisdiction over acts of torture committed by or against a party's citizens or on territory under its jurisdiction, as well as universal jurisdiction over alleged torturers arrested in territory under its jurisdiction when they cannot be extradited,[22] and ensure that torture is an extraditable offence.[23]

In terms of acts not amounting to torture but being other cruel, inhuman or degrading treatment or punishment, Article 16 obliges States to

> undertake to prevent in any territory under its jurisdiction other acts of cruel, inhuman or degrading treatment or punishment which do not amount to torture as defined in article I, when such acts are committed by or at the instigation of or with the consent or acquiescence of a public official or other person acting in an official capacity. In particular, the obligations contained in articles 10, 11, 12 and 13 shall apply with the substitution for references to torture of references to other forms of cruel, inhuman or degrading treatment or punishment.[24]

The General Assembly has also drawn the attention of governments to the Principles on the Effective Investigation and Documentation of Torture and Other Cruel, Inhuman or Degrading Treatment or Punishment (Principles), and has strongly encouraged them to 'reflect upon the Principles as a useful tool in efforts to combat torture'.[25] The Principles are intended to provide substance and tools for States in interpreting their obligations under Articles 12 and 13 of the CAT in regard to investigating and documenting allegations of torture. For example, Principle 2 states that:

> States shall ensure that complaints and reports of torture or ill-treatment are promptly and effectively investigated. Even in the absence of an express complaint, an investigation shall be undertaken if there are other indications that torture or ill-treatment might have occurred.[26]

The Principles further provide specific guidelines on how States should investigate allegations of torture in such a way as to ensure the impartiality and the safety of the victim and witnesses.

There are several regional treaties and standards which reinforce the principles and rules found in the CAT. In Africa, the Robben Island Guidelines provide guidance to African States as to how to prevent torture and provide avenues of redress for victims,[27] as do the African Commission on Human and Peoples' Rights Guidelines on the Conditions of Arrest, Police Custody, and Pre-Trial Detention in Africa.[28] In the Americas, there is the Inter-American Convention to Prevent and Punish Torture,[29] and the guidelines developed by the Inter-American Commission on Human Rights concerning principles on the rights of persons deprived of liberty.[30] In Europe, Article 3 of the European Convention for the Protection of Human Rights and Fundamental Freedoms, (ECHR), prohibits torture.[31] Article 13 of the Arab Charter on Human Rights addresses the prohibition and prevention of torture.[32]

---

21 Ibid, Article 4(1).

22 Ibid, Article 5.

23 Ibid, Article 8.

24 Ibid, Article 16(1).

25 See GA Res 55/89 of 4 December 2000, Operative Part [3]. The Principles are annexed to the resolution. The Principles reinforce the Manual on the Effective Investigation and Documentation of Torture and Other Cruel, Inhuman or Degrading Treatment or Punishment (Istanbul Protocol) which was submitted to the United Nations High Commissioner for Human Rights, 9 August 1999 <http://www.ohchr.org/Documents/Publications/training8Rev1en.pdf> accessed 1 November 2017.

26 Principles (n 25), Principle 2.

27 Resolution on Guidelines and Measures for the Prohibition and Prevention of Torture, Cruel, Inhuman or Degrading Treatment or Punishment in Africa (The Robben Island Guidelines) of May 2003, and the 2nd edition of 2008 <http://www.apt.ch/en/resources/the-robben-island-guidelines-2003-2008/> accessed 1 November 2017.

28 African Commission on Human and Peoples' Rights, Guidelines on the Conditions of Arrest, Police Custody and Pre-Trial Detention in Africa of 2014 <http://www.achpr.org/instruments/guidelines_arrest_detention/> accessed 3 September 2018.

29 Inter-American Convention to Prevent and Punish Torture (opened for signature 9 December 1985, entered into force 28 February 1987) OAS Treaty Series 67.

30 Principles and Best Practices on the Protection of Persons Deprived of Liberty in the Americas (approved by the Inter-American Commission on Human Rights during its 131st regular period of sessions, 3–14 March 2008).

31 European Convention on Human Rights, as amended by Protocols Nos. 11 and 14 (opened for signature 4 November 1950, entered into force 3 September 1953) ETS 5, Article 3. See also Council of Europe European Prison Rules, June 2006 <https://rm.coe.int/16806f3d4f> accessed 1 March 2017.

32 Arab Charter on Human Rights (May 22, 2004, reprinted in 12 International Human Rights Report 893 (2005), entered into force 15 March 2008) <http://www.humanrights.se/wp-content/uploads/2012/01/Arab-Charter-on-Human-Rights.pdf> accessed 14 March 2017.

As a matter of international criminal law, the Rome Statute has broadened the definition of torture by defining it as 'the intentional infliction of severe pain or suffering, whether physical or mental, upon a person in the custody or under the control of the accused; except that torture shall not include pain or suffering arising only from, inherent in or incidental to, lawful sanctions'.[33] Thus, the Rome Statute definition in relation to crimes against humanity does not require the severe pain or suffering to be inflicted by a public official or other person acting in an official capacity.

In UN peace operations, peacekeepers may face situations where individuals in the area of operations may be subjected to torture, cruel, inhuman or degrading treatment or punishment either by a State or by a non-State armed group. Peacekeepers in such situations may be required to prevent such crimes or to investigate and to bring to justice any individual accused of such ill-treatment. This will be the case where, for example, peacekeepers are authorised to monitor human rights violations and abuses which, by implication, would require them to monitor, report, and where appropriate investigate acts of torture committed by local authorities.[34] UN peace operations should also ensure that the treatment of any individual held in detention by peacekeepers does not breach the provisions of the CAT. For example, peacekeepers should know what is likely to amount to torture, cruel, inhuman or degrading treatment or punishment. In this context, Article 10 of the CAT requires State Parties to educate and inform members of their police and military forces, medical personnel, public officials, and others involved in the custody, interrogation, or treatment of individuals subjected to arrest, detention, or imprisonment regarding the prohibition against torture.

In situations where peacekeepers are involved in dealing with detainees, matters such as the continual systematic review of standard operating procedures for the treatment of detainees so as to prevent torture,[35] and undertaking investigations where there are reasonable grounds to believe that an act of torture has been committed,[36] are required. The prohibition against expelling, returning, or extraditing a detainee to another State where there are substantial grounds for believing that the detainee would be subjected to torture[37] will be relevant to ensure that peacekeepers do not abuse the rights of detainees.

Reference

Title	Convention against Torture and Other Cruel, Inhuman or Degrading Treatment or Punishment
Date of Adoption	10 December 1984
Opened for Signature	10 December 1984
Entered into Force	26 June 1987 in accordance with Article 27(1)
Signatories	83
Parties	162
Depository	United Nations
Treaty Series	1465 UNTS 85
Full Text	<https://www.ohchr.org/EN/ProfessionalInterest/Pages/CAT.aspx>[38]

33 Rome Statute (n 10), Article 7(2)(e).
34 See, for example, SC Res 2303 (2016) of 29 July 2016; SC Res 2211 (2015) of 26 March 2015.
35 CAT (n 1), Article 11.
36 Ibid, Article 12.
37 Ibid, Article 3.
38 Accessed 3 September 2018.

Convention against Torture and Other Cruel, Inhuman or Degrading Treatment or Punishment[39]

(Extracts)

Preamble

The States Parties to this Convention,

Considering that, in accordance with the principles proclaimed in the Charter of the United Nations, recognition of the equal and inalienable rights of all members of the human family is the foundation of freedom, justice and peace in the world,

Recognizing that those rights derive from the inherent dignity of the human person,

Considering the obligation of States under the Charter, in particular Article 55, to promote universal respect for, and observance of, human rights and fundamental freedoms,

Having regard to article 5 of the Universal Declaration of Human Rights and article 7 of the International Covenant on Civil and Political Rights, both of which provide that no one shall be subjected to torture or to cruel, inhuman or degrading treatment or punishment,

Having regard also to the Declaration on the Protection of All Persons from Being Subjected to Torture and Other Cruel, Inhuman or Degrading Treatment or Punishment, adopted by the General Assembly on 9 December 1975,

Desiring to make more effective the struggle against torture and other cruel, inhuman or degrading treatment or punishment throughout the world,

Have agreed as follows:

Part I

Article I

1. For the purposes of this Convention, the term "torture" means any act by which severe pain or suffering, whether physical or mental, is intentionally inflicted on a person for such purposes as obtaining from him or a third person information or a confession, punishing him for an act he or a third person has committed or is suspected of having committed, or intimidating or coercing him or a third person, or for any reason based on discrimination of any kind, when such pain or suffering is inflicted by or at the instigation of or with the consent or acquiescence of a public official or other person acting in an official capacity. It does not include pain or suffering arising only from, inherent in or incidental to lawful sanctions.
2. This article is without prejudice to any international instrument or national legislation which does or may contain provisions of wider application.

39 From Convention against Torture and Other Cruel, Inhuman or Degrading Treatment or Punishment © 1984 United Nations. Reprinted with the permission of the United Nations.

Article 2

1. Each State Party shall take effective legislative, administrative, judicial or other measures to prevent acts of torture in any territory under its jurisdiction.
2. No exceptional circumstances whatsoever, whether a state of war or a threat of war, internal political instability or any other public emergency, may be invoked as a justification of torture.
3. An order from a superior officer or a public authority may not be invoked as a justification of torture.

Article 3

1. No State Party shall expel, return ("refouler") or extradite a person to another State where there are substantial grounds for believing that he would be in danger of being subjected to torture.
2. For the purpose of determining whether there are such grounds, the competent authorities shall take into account all relevant considerations including, where applicable, the existence in the State concerned of a consistent pattern of gross, flagrant or mass violations of human rights.

Article 4

1. Each State Party shall ensure that all acts of torture are offences under its criminal law. The same shall apply to an attempt to commit torture and to an act by any person which constitutes complicity or participation in torture.
2. Each State Party shall make these offences punishable by appropriate penalties which take into account their grave nature.

Article 5

1. Each State Party shall take such measures as may be necessary to establish its jurisdiction over the offences referred to in article 4 in the following cases:
    (a) When the offences are committed in any territory under its jurisdiction or on board a ship or aircraft registered in that State;
    (b) When the alleged offender is a national of that State;
    (c) When the victim is a national of that State if that State considers it appropriate.
2. Each State Party shall likewise take such measures as may be necessary to establish its jurisdiction over such offences in cases where the alleged offender is present in any territory under its jurisdiction and it does not extradite him pursuant to article 8 to any of the States mentioned in paragraph 1 of this article.
3. This Convention does not exclude any criminal jurisdiction exercised in accordance with internal law.

Article 6

1. Upon being satisfied, after an examination of information available to it, that the circumstances so warrant, any State Party in whose territory a person alleged to have committed any offence referred to in article 4 is present shall take him into custody or take other legal measures to ensure his presence. The custody and other legal measures shall be as provided in the law of that State but may be continued only for such time as is necessary to enable any criminal or extradition proceedings to be instituted.
2. Such State shall immediately make a preliminary inquiry into the facts.
3. Any person in custody pursuant to paragraph 1 of this article shall be assisted in communicating immediately with the nearest appropriate representative of the State of which he is a

national, or, if he is a stateless person, with the representative of the State where he usually resides.

4. When a State, pursuant to this article, has taken a person into custody, it shall immediately notify the States referred to in article 5, paragraph 1, of the fact that such person is in custody and of the circumstances which warrant his detention. The State which makes the preliminary inquiry contemplated in paragraph 2 of this article shall promptly report its findings to the said States and shall indicate whether it intends to exercise jurisdiction.

Article 7

1. The State Party in the territory under whose jurisdiction a person alleged to have committed any offence referred to in article 4 is found shall in the cases contemplated in article 5, if it does not extradite him, submit the case to its competent authorities for the purpose of prosecution.
2. These authorities shall take their decision in the same manner as in the case of any ordinary offence of a serious nature under the law of that State. In the cases referred to in article 5, paragraph 2, the standards of evidence required for prosecution and conviction shall in no way be less stringent than those which apply in the cases referred to in article 5, paragraph 1.
3. Any person regarding whom proceedings are brought in connection with any of the offences referred to in article 4 shall be guaranteed fair treatment at all stages of the proceedings.

Article 8

1. The offences referred to in article 4 shall be deemed to be included as extraditable offences in any extradition treaty existing between States Parties. States Parties undertake to include such offences as extraditable offences in every extradition treaty to be concluded between them.
2. If a State Party which makes extradition conditional on the existence of a treaty receives a request for extradition from another State Party with which it has no extradition treaty, it may consider this Convention as the legal basis for extradition in respect of such offences. Extradition shall be subject to the other conditions provided by the law of the requested State.
3. States Parties which do not make extradition conditional on the existence of a treaty shall recognize such offences as extraditable offences between themselves subject to the conditions provided by the law of the requested State.
4. Such offences shall be treated, for the purpose of extradition between States Parties, as if they had been committed not only in the place in which they occurred but also in the territories of the States required to establish their jurisdiction in accordance with article 5, paragraph 1.

Article 9

1. States Parties shall afford one another the greatest measure of assistance in connection with criminal proceedings brought in respect of any of the offences referred to in article 4, including the supply of all evidence at their disposal necessary for the proceedings.
2. States Parties shall carry out their obligations under paragraph I of this article in conformity with any treaties on mutual judicial assistance that may exist between them.

Article 10

1. Each State Party shall ensure that education and information regarding the prohibition against torture are fully included in the training of law enforcement personnel, civil or military, medical personnel, public officials and other persons who may be involved in the custody,

interrogation or treatment of any individual subjected to any form of arrest, detention or imprisonment.

2. Each State Party shall include this prohibition in the rules or instructions issued in regard to the duties and functions of any such person.

Article 11

Each State Party shall keep under systematic review interrogation rules, instructions, methods and practices as well as arrangements for the custody and treatment of persons subjected to any form of arrest, detention or imprisonment in any territory under its jurisdiction, with a view to preventing any cases of torture.

Article 12

Each State Party shall ensure that its competent authorities proceed to a prompt and impartial investigation, wherever there is reasonable ground to believe that an act of torture has been committed in any territory under its jurisdiction.

Article 13

Each State Party shall ensure that any individual who alleges he has been subjected to torture in any territory under its jurisdiction has the right to complain to, and to have his case promptly and impartially examined by, its competent authorities. Steps shall be taken to ensure that the complainant and witnesses are protected against all ill-treatment or intimidation as a consequence of his complaint or any evidence given.

. . .

Article 15

Each State Party shall ensure that any statement which is established to have been made as a result of torture shall not be invoked as evidence in any proceedings, except against a person accused of torture as evidence that the statement was made.

Article 16

1. Each State Party shall undertake to prevent in any territory under its jurisdiction other acts of cruel, inhuman or degrading treatment or punishment which do not amount to torture as defined in article 1, when such acts are committed by or at the instigation of or with the consent or acquiescence of a public official or other person acting in an official capacity. In particular, the obligations contained in articles 10, 11, 12 and 13 shall apply with the substitution for references to torture of references to other forms of cruel, inhuman or degrading treatment or punishment.
2. The provisions of this Convention are without prejudice to the provisions of any other international instrument or national law which prohibits cruel, inhuman or degrading treatment or punishment or which relates to extradition or expulsion.

. . .

9

Rights of the Child

Prefatory Note

The relevance of the Convention on the Rights of the Child (CRC)[1] arises in UN peace operations at many levels. For example, peacekeepers responsible for planning peace operations will need to consider how to best deal with child soldiers. Peacekeepers will also need to consider the rights of children when assisting local authorities in State building. The Security Council continues to emphasise the importance of protecting children in the mandates issued to peacekeepers.

The CRC rests on the premise that children are particularly vulnerable and therefore require special protection. A child, as defined in the CRC, is a person below the age of eighteen years unless the law applicable to that person sets the age of attaining majority earlier.[2] The CRC applies to all children within the jurisdiction of State Parties to the CRC.

The four foundational principles of the CRC are non-discrimination,[3] that the primary consideration in all actions concerning children is the best interests of the child,[4] the obligation on a State to ensure to the maximum extent possible the survival and development of the child as well as recognising the child's inherent right to life,[5] and the child's right to express his or her opinion and to have that opinion considered in matters concerning the child.[6]

In 2000, the General Assembly adopted the Optional Protocol to the Convention on the Rights of the Child on the Involvement of Children in Armed Conflict (Optional Protocol) in resolution 54/263.[7] That resolution also annexed a second optional protocol entitled 'Optional Protocol to the Convention on the Rights of the Child on the Sale of Children, Child Prostitution and Child Pornography, as well as the Basic Measures Needed for their Prevention and Eradication' (Second Optional Protocol).[8] Article 2(1) of the CRC states that 'States Parties shall respect and ensure the rights set forth in the present Convention to each child within their jurisdiction'. Article 6(1) of the Optional Protocol states that '[e]ach State Party shall take all necessary legal, administrative and other measures to ensure the effective implementation and enforcement of the provisions of the present Protocol within its jurisdiction'. The use of the phrases 'within their jurisdiction' and 'within its jurisdiction' suggests that the CRC and the Optional Protocol have extraterritorial application, and would therefore apply in peace operations in those areas of the host country that are within the effective control of a military contingent of a contributing State that is also a State Party to the CRC and the Optional Protocol. There are no phrases in the Second Optional Protocol which suggest that it has extraterritorial application for State Parties. Extracts from both the CRC and the Optional Protocol are reprinted below.

The International Court of Justice (ICJ) discussed the extraterritorial application of the CRC, along with the International Covenant on Civil and Political Rights (ICCPR)[9] and the International Covenant on Economic, Social and Cultural Rights (ICESCR),[10] in *Legal Consequences of the Construction of a*

---

1 Convention on the Rights of the Child (opened for signature 20 November 1989, entered into force 2 September 1990) 1577 UNTS 3 (hereafter CRC). The CRC was adopted by the UN General Assembly in resolution 44/25 of 20 November 1989 and entered into force on 2 September 1990. The CRC was annexed to that resolution.

2 Ibid, Article 1.

3 Ibid, Article 2.

4 Ibid, Article 3.

5 Ibid, Article 6.

6 Ibid, Article 12.

7 Optional Protocol to the Convention on the Rights of the Child on the Involvement of Children in Armed Conflict (opened for signature 25 May 2000, entered into force 12 February 2002) UN Doc A/RES/54/263 (hereafter Optional Protocol). The Optional Protocol was annexed to the resolution and entered into force on 12 February 2002.

8 Optional Protocol to the Convention on the Rights of the Child on the Sale of Children, Child Prostitution, and Child Pornography (opened for signature 8 March 1995, entered into force 18 January 2002) UN Doc UN Doc A/RES/54/263.

9 See ch 6 above.

10 See ch 6 above.

Wall in the Occupied Palestinian Territory (Advisory Opinion) (*Israeli Wall Case*).[11] After finding that the ICCPR and ICESCR applied extraterritorially, the ICJ stated:

> As regards the Convention on the Rights of the Child of 20 November 1989, that instrument contains an Article 2 according to which 'States Parties shall respect and ensure the rights set forth in the . . . Convention to each child within their jurisdiction . . .' That Convention is therefore applicable within the Occupied Palestinian Territory.[12]

The ICJ reaffirmed this principle in its judgment in the *Case concerning Armed Activities on the Territory of the Congo (Democratic Republic of the Congo v Uganda)* (Judgment) (*Congo Case*)[13] when the court held, citing its findings from the *Israeli Wall Case*, 'that international human rights instruments are applicable "in respect of acts done by a State in the exercise of its jurisdiction outside its own territory", particularly in occupied territories'.[14] The court then went on to hold that a number of international human rights instruments, including the CRC and its Optional Protocol, were therefore applicable to the actions of Uganda in the territory of the Democratic Republic of the Congo.[15]

The CRC and the Optional Protocol focus on the rights of the child in situations of armed conflict by limiting the age at which a child can take part directly in hostilities, or be recruited to serve in an armed force or with an armed group. Article 38(2) of the CRC requires State Parties to 'take all feasible measures to ensure that persons who have not attained the age of fifteen years do not take a direct part in hostilities'. Article 38(3) requires State Parties to 'refrain from recruiting any person who has not attained the age of fifteen years into their armed forces'.

This requirement in Article 38(3)—to refrain from the recruitment of children under the age of fifteen—is in tension with the CRC's definition of a 'child' in Article 1 as anyone under the age of eighteen. However, by setting the minimum age as fifteen years for the recruitment of children and their participation in hostilities, Article 38 is consistent with international humanitarian law (IHL).[16] The Rome Statute[17] includes as a war crime the conscription or enlistment of children under the age of fifteen years into armed forces, or using them to actively participate in hostilities.[18]

The Optional Protocol to the CRC is a direct response to concerns raised about the inconsistent use of the definition of child in the CRC discussed above. Under the Optional Protocol, State Parties agree to 'take all feasible measures to ensure that members of their armed forces who have not attained the age of 18 years do not take a direct part in hostilities',[19] and to ensure 'that persons who have not attained the age of 18 years are not compulsorily recruited into their armed forces'.[20]

The Optional Protocol does not put a positive obligation on State Parties not to recruit children of less than eighteen years into their armed forces, but rather requires that any such recruitment should be voluntary and that any member of their armed forces under eighteen years should not take part directly in hostilities. In regard to armed groups that are distinct from the armed forces of a State,[21] the language of the Optional Protocol is even stronger by stating that such armed groups 'should not, under any circumstances, recruit or use in hostilities persons under the age of 18 years'.[22] There is also an obligation on State Parties to 'take all feasible measures to prevent such

---

11 *Legal Consequences of the Construction of a Wall in the Occupied Palestinian Territory* (Advisory Opinion) [2004] ICJ Rep 136 (hereafter *Israeli Wall Case*).

12 Ibid, 181.

13 *Case concerning Armed Activities on the Territory of the Congo (Democratic Republic of the Congo v Uganda)* (Judgment) [2005] ICJ Rep 116 (hereafter *Congo Case*).

14 Ibid, 243.

15 Ibid.

16 The age of fifteen is consistent with international humanitarian law. See Protocol Additional to the Geneva Conventions of 12 August 1949, and relating to the Protection of Victims of International Armed Conflicts (Protocol I) (opened for signature 8 June 1977, entered into force 7 December 1978) 1125 UNTS 3, Article 77(2) (hereafter Additional Protocol I); Protocol Additional to the Geneva Conventions of 12 August 1949, and relating to the Protection of Victims of Non-International Armed Conflicts (Protocol II) (opened for signature 8 June 1977, entered into force 7 December 1978) 1125 UNTS 609, Article 4(3)(c) (hereafter Additional Protocol II). See ch 16 below.

17 See Rome Statute of the International Criminal Court (opened for signature 17 July 1998, entered into force 1 July 2002) 2187 UNTS (hereafter Rome Statute). See ch 23 below.

18 Ibid, Article 8(2)(b)(xxvi) in regard to international armed conflicts; and Article 8(2)(e)(vii) in regard to non-international armed conflicts.

19 Optional Protocol (n 7), Article 1.

20 Ibid, Article 2.

21 For information on non-State armed groups, as distinct from the armed forces of a State, visit the Rule of Law in Armed Conflicts Project <http://www.rulac.org/> accessed 1 November 2017.

22 Optional Protocol (n 7), Article 4(1).

recruitment and use, including the adoption of legal measures necessary to prohibit and criminalize such practices'.[23]

International criminal law (ICL) prohibits conscripting or enlisting children under the age of fifteen years into the armed forces or groups or using them to participate actively in hostilities.[24] That prohibition was addressed in the case of the *Situation in the Democratic Republic of the Congo, in the Case of the Prosecutor v Thomas Lubanga Dyilo*.[25] The International Criminal Court (ICC) Trial Chamber noted that the principal objective of the provisions is to protect:

> children under the age of 15 from the risks that are associated with armed conflict, and first and foremost they are directed at securing their physical and psychological well-being. This includes not only protection from violence and fatal or non-fatal injuries during fighting, but also the potentially serious trauma that can accompany recruitment (including separating children from their families, interrupting or disrupting their schooling and exposing them to an environment of violence and fear) ... [such trauma including exposure to] rape, sexual enslavement and other forms of sexual violence, cruel and inhumane treatment, as well as further kinds of hardship that are incompatible with their fundamental rights.[26]

In relation to children associated with armed forces and armed groups, the Paris Commitments and the Paris Principles add a layer of non-binding protections to situations where children are undergoing disarmament, demobilisation, and reintegration.[27]

Regional and subregional organisations have also devoted their attention to the protection of children during peace operations. For example, the Office of the Special Representative of the Secretary-General for Children and Armed Conflict has signed a declaration with the African Union (AU) Commission which outlines its areas of collaboration with the AU Department of Peace and Security, with the support of the United Nations Children's Fund (UNICEF) in areas such as the 'development of improved and harmonized training programs on child protection for troop contributing countries to African Union Peace Missions'.[28] The AU also has a set of guidelines for the disarming, demobilisation, and reintegration of children.[29] More specifically, the African Union Mission in Somalia (AMISOM) has developed standard operating procedures 'for caring for and arranging handover of defecting and captured children'[30] detained by AMISOM.

The European Union (EU) has also developed guidelines on children affected by armed conflict and has developed a Checklist for the Integration of the Protection of Children affected by Armed Conflict (Checklist).[31] The Checklist is intended to ensure that the rights of children and their protection are addressed during the planning for a mission and during the implementation phase of the mission.

The UN and the North Atlantic Treaty Organization (NATO) have developed a training course to 'ensure that NATO troops are better prepared to prevent violations and to assist in reducing the effects of armed conflicts on children'.[32]

---

23 Ibid, Article 4(2).

24 See Rome Statute (n 17), Article 8(2)(b)(xxvi) concerning international armed conflicts; and Article 8(2)(e)(vii) with regard to non-international armed conflicts.

25 *Situation in the Democratic Republic of the Congo, in the case of the Prosecutor v Thomas Lubanga Dyilo* (Judgment) (Trial Chamber I) ICC-01/04-01/06, 14 March 2012.

26 Ibid, [605]–[606].

27 For more information on children associated with armed forces or armed groups see UNICEF, 'Paris Principles: Principles and Guidelines on Children Associated with Armed Forces or Armed Groups', February 2007 <https:// https://www.unicef.org/emerg/files/ParisPrinciples310107English.pdf > accessed 20 Septemeber 2018.

28 Joint Press Statement by the African Union and the Special Representative of the Secretary-General for Children and Armed Conflict and United Nations Children's Fund (UNICEF), 'The United Nations Working Together with the African Union to Protect Children in Armed Conflict', 19 September 2014 <https://childrenandarmedconflict.un.org/press-release/the-un-working-together-with-au/> accessed 1 November 2017.

29 African Union Disarmament, Demobilisation and Reintegration Capacity Program, 'DDR and Children Operational Guideline' (2014) <http://www.peaceau.org/en/article/african-union-operational-guideline-on-ddr-and-children> accessed 1 November 2017.

30 Working Group on Children and Armed Conflict, 'Conclusions on Children and Armed Conflict in Somalia', S/AC.51.2011/2, 1 March 2011 [6]. See also UN Doc A/69/926–UN Doc S/2015/409 of 5 June 2015 [156].

31 See Council of European Union, 'General Review of the Implementation of the Checklist for the Integration of the Protection of Children affected by Armed Conflict into ESDP Operations', Doc no 9638/08, 21 May 2008, Annex I.

32 See Office of the Special Representative of the Secretary-General for Children and Armed Conflict, 'NATO and the United Nations launch a training module on Children and Armed Conflict', 10 June 2013 <https://childrenandarmedconflict.un.org/nato-and-the-united-nations-launch-a-training-module-on-children-and-armed-conflict/> accessed 1 November 2017.

The CRC's relevance in peace operations stems primarily from the recognition that children are amongst the most vulnerable individuals during times of conflict and therefore require protection. The matters dealt with in Articles 33 to 41 of the CRC are particularly relevant because they establish fundamental norms concerning the protection of children. Such norms include the protection of children from all forms of sexual exploitation and sexual abuse.[33] This would include protection from the acts of peacekeepers, a respect for the rules of IHL applicable to children in armed conflict,[34] and the protection and care for children affected by armed conflict.[35] Such norms also include ensuring that no child is subject to torture or other cruel, inhuman, or degrading treatment or punishment, including a prohibition on the use of capital punishment,[36] ensuring that no child is arbitrarily deprived of his or her liberty,[37] and that children who are arrested are treated with humanity and measures are taken as to ensure the safety of children, such as keeping detained children away from detained adults.[38]

Article 6(3) of the Optional Protocol is also relevant to UN peace operations as it requires peacekeepers to take all feasible measures to provide children associated with armed forces or armed groups, who are found or captured within the jurisdiction of peacekeepers, with appropriate assistance for their demobilisation and social reintegration.[39] Furthermore, peacekeepers should assist children to reintegrate into their communities, including reuniting them with their families, in areas under their effective control.

At the institutional level, the UN Secretary-General, the Security Council Working Group on Children and Armed Conflict, and the Office of the Special Representative for Children and Armed Conflict are also important in ensuring that peacekeepers are aware of, and better prepared to deal with, child protection issues. For example, the Secretary-General's annual reports on children and armed conflict highlight key matters arising from peace operations relevant to the protection of children.[40] The Working Group on Children and Armed Conflict reports to the Security Council on a variety of issues including how best to manage the protection of children in areas where UN peacekeepers are serving.[41] The Special Representative for Children and Armed Conflict plays an important role in monitoring and reporting on the six grave violations against children during armed conflict: killing and maiming children; recruitment or use of children as soldiers; sexual violence against children; attacks against schools or hospitals; denial of humanitarian access for children; and abduction of children.[42] UNICEF has also been instrumental in developing UN and regional mechanisms to protect children.[43] The Department of Peacekeeping Operations (DPKO) has a policy entitled 'Mainstreaming the Protection, Rights and Well-being of Children affected by Armed Conflict within UN Peacekeeping Operations'.[44]

The relevance of the CRC to UN peace operations also arises due to thematic Security Council resolutions which also concern children's rights. The Security Council, in resolution 2225 on children and armed conflict, covered the particular rights of children in armed conflict. In relation to UN peace operations, the Security Council recognised:

---

33 CRC (n 1), Article 34.

34 Ibid, Article 38(1).

35 Ibid, Article 38(4).

36 Ibid, Article 37(a).

37 Ibid, Article 37(b).

38 Ibid, Article 37(c).

39 Optional Protocol (n 7), Article 6(3).

40 See, for example, UN Doc A/69/926–S/2015/409 of 5 June 2015. Such reports are made by the Secretary-General pursuant to SC Res 2068 (2012) of 19 September 2012.

41 See, for example Security Council Working Group on Children and Armed Conflict, 'Letter dated 8 September 2006 from the Permanent Representative of France to the United Nations addressed to the President of the Security Council', UN Doc S/2006/724, 11 September 2006; Working Group on Children and Armed Conflict, 'Conclusions on Children and Armed Conflict in Somalia', UN Doc S/AC.51.2011/2, 1 March 2011 [6].

42 See Office of the Special Representative of the Secretary-General for Children and Armed Conflict, Working Paper No 1, 'The Six Grave Violations Against Children During Armed Conflict: The Legal Foundation', October 2009 (updated November 2013) <https://childrenandarmedconflict.un.org/publications/WorkingPaper-1_SixGraveViolationsLegalFoundation.pdf> accessed 1 November 2017.

43 See, for example, SC Res 2143 (2014) of 7 March 2014, Preamble.

44 Department of Peacekeeping Operations and Department of Field Support, 'Policy on Mainstreaming the Protection, Rights, and Well-being of Children affected by Armed Conflict within UN Peacekeeping Operations', 1 June 2009, reviewed 1 June 2011 <https://peacekeeping.un.org/sites/default/files/peacekeeping/en/dpkodfs_child_protection_policy.pdf> accessed 8 April 2019.

> the role of United Nations peacekeeping operations ... in the protection of children, particularly the crucial role of child protection advisers in mainstreaming child protection and leading monitoring, prevention and reporting efforts in missions, and in this regard reiterates its decision to continue the inclusion of specific provisions for the protection of children in the mandates of all relevant United Nations peacekeeping operations and political missions, encourages deployment of child protection advisers to such missions, and calls upon the Secretary-General to ensure that the need for and the number and roles of such advisers are systematically assessed during the preparation and renewal of each United Nations peacekeeping operation and political mission.[45]

The Security Council, in resolution 1820 on women, peace and security, encouraged:

> troop and police contributing countries, in consultation with the Secretary-General, to consider steps they could take to heighten awareness and the responsiveness of their personnel participating in UN peacekeeping operations to protect civilians, including women and children, and prevent sexual violence against women and girls in conflict and post-conflict situations, including wherever possible the deployment of a higher percentage of women peacekeepers or police.[46]

The Security Council has, on a number of occasions, reaffirmed its commitment to include 'specific provisions for the protection of children in the mandates of all relevant United Nations peacekeeping operations'.[47] In 2014, for example, it mandated the United Nations Multidimensional Integrated Stabilization Mission in the Central African Republic (MINUSCA) '[t]o provide specific protection for women and children affected by armed conflict[48] ... [and] [t]o monitor, help investigate and report specifically on violations and abuses committed against children ... and to contribute to efforts to identify and prosecute perpetrators, and to prevent such violations and abuses'.[49] Furthermore, MINUSCA was also mandated to support the Central African Republic authorities to arrest and bring to justice those responsible for war crimes and crimes against humanity.[50] It was pursuant to those mandates that the UN Secretary-General reported to the Security Council that MINUSCA police had arrested two members of a non-State armed group for allegedly raping a fourteen-year-old girl.[51] Finally, in relation to the MINUSCA mandate, the Security Council also requested the force:

> [T]o take fully into account child protection as a cross-cutting issue throughout its mandate and to assist the Transitional Authorities in ensuring that the protection of children's rights is taken into account, inter alia, in DDR [disarmament, demobilization and reintegration] and DDRR [disarmament, demobilization, reintegration and repatriation] processes and in security sector reform in order to end and prevent violations and abuses against children.[52]

In relation to the United Nations Organization Stabilization Mission in the Democratic Republic of the Congo (MONUSCO), the Council called upon

> the Government of the DRC to pursue the full implementation, with the support of MONUSCO as appropriate, of the action plan to prevent and end the recruitment and use of children and sexual violence by the FARDC [Congolese Armed Forces], and to strengthen its efforts to combat impunity for conflict-related sexual violence, including sexual violence committed by the FARDC.[53]

The Security Council may mandate peacekeepers to engage in a range of tasks specifically directed towards children. MONUSCO was requested to protect children to assist local authorities to separate children from non-State armed actors.[54]

---

45 SC Res 2225 (2015) of 18 June 2015, Operative Part [15]. See also SC Res 2427 (2018) of 9 July 2018, Operative Part [33]. See also SC Res 1612 (2005) of 26 July 2005, Operative Part [12] and [15]; SC Res 1674 (2006) of 28 April 2006, Operative Part [19]. See ch 18 below.

46 SC Res 1820 (2008) of 19 June 2008, Operative Part [8]. See ch 17 below.

47 SC Res 2143 (2014) of 7 March 2014, Operative Part [24].

48 SC Res 2149 (2014) of 10 April 2014, Operative Part [30](a)(ii). See, for example, in relation to the United Nations Transitional Administration in East Timor (UNTAET): SC Res 1272 (1999) of 25 October 1999, Operative Part [10]; in relation to the United Nations Mission in Liberia (UNMIL): SC Res 1509 (2003) of 19 September 2003, Operative Part [3](l); and in relation to the United Nations Organization Mission in the Democratic Republic of the Congo (MONUC) SC Res 1756 (2007) of 15 May 2007, Operative Part [3](c).

49 SC Res 2149 (2014), Operative Part [30](e)(ii).

50 Ibid, Operative Part [30](f)(i).

51 UN Doc A/69/926–S/2015/409, 5 June 2015, [51].

52 SC Res 2149 (2014) of 10 April 2014, Operative Part [34].

53 SC Res 2211 (2015) of 26 March 2015, Operative Part [32].

54 SC Res 2277 (2016) of 30 March 2016, Operative Part [37].

The Security Council has reiterated the importance of mainstreaming child protection, the crucial role of child protection advisers, the training of peacekeepers in relation to child protection,[55] and giving 'full attention to violations against children in the application of the Human Rights Due Diligence Policy on United Nations Support to non-United Nations Security Forces'.[56] The President of the Council has also stated that:

> The Security Council recognizes the valuable contribution pertinent regional and subregional organizations and arrangements make for the protection of children affected by armed conflict. In this regard, the Security Council encourages the continued mainstreaming of child protection into the advocacy, policies, programmes and mission planning of these organizations and arrangements as well as training of personnel and inclusion of child protection staff in their peacekeeping and field operations and establishment, within their secretariats, of child protection mechanisms, including through the appointment of child protection focal points.[57]

In light of the allegations of sexual exploitation and abuse against peacekeepers, the Security Council has also called for:

> continued implementation by United Nations peacekeeping operations of the Secretary-General's zero-tolerance policy on sexual exploitation and abuse and to ensure full compliance of their personnel with the United Nations code of conduct, reiterates its request to the Secretary-General to continue to take all necessary action in this regard and to keep the Security Council informed, and urges troop-contributing countries to continue taking appropriate preventive action, such as mandatory pre-deployment child protection training including on sexual exploitation and abuse, and to ensure full accountability in cases of such conduct involving their personnel.[58]

References

Title	Convention on the Rights of the Child
Date of Adoption	20 November 1989
Opened for Signature	20 November 1989
Entered into Force	2 September 1990 in accordance with Article 49(1)
Signatories	140
Parties	196
Depository	United Nations
Treaty Series	1577 UNTS 3
Full Text	<https://www.ohchr.org/en/professionalinterest/pages/crc.aspx>[59]

Title	Optional Protocol to the Convention on the Rights of the Child on the Involvement of Children in Armed Conflict
Date of Adoption	25 May 2000
Opened for Signature	25 May 2000
Entered into Force	12 February 2002 in accordance with Article 10(1)
Signatories	130
Parties	167
Depository	United Nations
Source	UN Doc A/RES/54/263, Annex
Full Text	<https://www.ohchr.org/en/professionalinterest/pages/opaccrc.aspx>[60]

55 SC Res 2225 (2015) of 18 June 2015, Operative Part [15]–[16].
56 Ibid, Operative Part [17].
57 Statement by the President of the Security Council, UN Doc S/PRST/2013/12, 6 August 2013, 3.
58 SC Res 2225 (2015) of 18 June 2015, Operative Part [16].
59 Accessed 9 August 2018.
60 Accessed 9 August 2018.

Convention on the Rights of the Child[61]

(Extracts)

PREAMBLE

The States Parties to the present Convention,

Considering that, in accordance with the principles proclaimed in the Charter of the United Nations, recognition of the inherent dignity and of the equal and inalienable rights of all members of the human family is the foundation of freedom, justice and peace in the world,

Bearing in mind that the peoples of the United Nations have, in the Charter, reaffirmed their faith in fundamental human rights and in the dignity and worth of the human person, and have determined to promote social progress and better standards of life in larger freedom,

Recognizing that the United Nations has, in the Universal Declaration of Human Rights and in the International Covenants on Human Rights, proclaimed and agreed that everyone is entitled to all the rights and freedoms set forth therein, without distinction of any kind, such as race, colour, sex, language, religion, political or other opinion, national or social origin, property, birth or other status,

Recalling that, in the Universal Declaration of Human Rights, the United Nations has proclaimed that childhood is entitled to special care and assistance,

Convinced that the family, as the fundamental group of society and the natural environment for the growth and well-being of all its members and particularly children, should be afforded the necessary protection and assistance so that it can fully assume its responsibilities within the community,

Recognizing that the child, for the full and harmonious development of his or her personality, should grow up in a family environment, in an atmosphere of happiness, love and understanding,

Considering that the child should be fully prepared to live an individual life in society, and brought up in the spirit of the ideals proclaimed in the Charter of the United Nations, and in particular in the spirit of peace, dignity, tolerance, freedom, equality and solidarity,

Bearing in mind that the need to extend particular care to the child has been stated in the Geneva Declaration of the Rights of the Child of 1924 and in the Declaration of the Rights of the Child adopted by the General Assembly on 20 November 1959 and recognized in the Universal Declaration of Human Rights, in the International Covenant on Civil and Political Rights (in particular in articles 23 and 24), in the International Covenant on Economic, Social and Cultural Rights (in particular in article 10) and in the statutes and relevant instruments of specialized agencies and international organizations concerned with the welfare of children,

Bearing in mind that, as indicated in the Declaration of the Rights of the Child, "the child, by reason of his physical and mental immaturity, needs special safeguards and care, including appropriate legal protection, before as well as after birth",

Recalling the provisions of the Declaration on Social and Legal Principles relating to the Protection and Welfare of Children, with Special Reference to Foster Placement and Adoption Nationally and Internationally; the United Nations Standard Minimum Rules for the Administration of Juvenile Justice (The Beijing Rules); and the Declaration on the Protection of Women and Children in Emergency and Armed Conflict,

Recognizing that, in all countries in the world, there are children living in exceptionally difficult conditions, and that such children need special consideration,

Taking due account of the importance of the traditions and cultural values of each people for the protection and harmonious development of the child,

Recognizing the importance of international co-operation for improving the living conditions of children in every country, in particular in the developing countries,

Have agreed as follows:

Part I

Article 1

For the purposes of the present Convention, a child means every human being below the age of eighteen years unless under the law applicable to the child, majority is attained earlier.

Article 2

1. States Parties shall respect and ensure the rights set forth in the present Convention to each child within their jurisdiction without discrimination of any kind, irrespective of the child's or his or her parent's or legal guardian's race, colour, sex, language, religion, political or other opinion, national, ethnic or social origin, property, disability, birth or other status.
2. States Parties shall take all appropriate measures to ensure that the child is protected against all forms of discrimination or punishment on the basis of the status, activities, expressed opinions, or beliefs of the child's parents, legal guardians, or family members.

Article 3

1. In all actions concerning children, whether undertaken by public or private social welfare institutions, courts of law, administrative authorities or legislative bodies, the best interests of the child shall be a primary consideration.
2. States Parties undertake to ensure the child such protection and care as is necessary for his or her well-being, taking into account the rights and duties of his or her parents, legal guardians, or other individuals legally responsible for him or her, and, to this end, shall take all appropriate legislative and administrative measures.
3. States Parties shall ensure that the institutions, services and facilities responsible for the care or protection of children shall conform with the standards established by competent authorities, particularly in the areas of safety, health, in the number and suitability of their staff, as well as competent supervision.

...

Article 6

1. States Parties recognize that every child has the inherent right to life.
2. States Parties shall ensure to the maximum extent possible the survival and development of the child.

...

Article 9

1. States Parties shall ensure that a child shall not be separated from his or her parents against their will, except when competent authorities subject to judicial review determine, in accordance with applicable law and procedures, that such separation is necessary for the best interests of the child. Such determination may be necessary in a particular case such as one involving abuse or neglect of the child by the parents, or one where the parents are living separately and a decision must be made as to the child's place of residence.
2. In any proceedings pursuant to paragraph 1 of the present article, all interested parties shall be given an opportunity to participate in the proceedings and make their views known.
3. States Parties shall respect the right of the child who is separated from one or both parents to maintain personal relations and direct contact with both parents on a regular basis, except if it is contrary to the child's best interests.
4. Where such separation results from any action initiated by a State Party, such as the detention, imprisonment, exile, deportation or death (including death arising from any cause while the person is in the custody of the State) of one or both parents or of the child, that State Party shall, upon request, provide the parents, the child or, if appropriate, another member of the family with the essential information concerning the whereabouts of the absent member(s) of the family unless the provision of the information would be detrimental to the well-being of the child. States Parties shall further ensure that the submission of such a request shall of itself entail no adverse consequences for the person(s) concerned.

. . .

Article 11

1. States Parties shall take measures to combat the illicit transfer and non-return of children abroad.
2. To this end, States Parties shall promote the conclusion of bilateral or multilateral agreements or accession to existing agreements.

Article 12

1. States Parties shall assure to the child who is capable of forming his or her own views the right to express those views freely in all matters affecting the child, the views of the child being given due weight in accordance with the age and maturity of the child.
2. For this purpose, the child shall in particular be provided the opportunity to be heard in any judicial and administrative proceedings affecting the child, either directly, or through a representative or an appropriate body, in a manner consistent with the procedural rules of national law.

. . .

Article 16

1. No child shall be subjected to arbitrary or unlawful interference with his or her privacy, family, home or correspondence, nor to unlawful attacks on his or her honour and reputation.
2. The child has the right to the protection of the law against such interference or attacks.

. . .

Article 19

1. States Parties shall take all appropriate legislative, administrative, social and educational measures to protect the child from all forms of physical or mental violence, injury or abuse, neglect or negligent treatment, maltreatment or exploitation, including sexual abuse, while in the care of parent(s), legal guardian(s) or any other person who has the care of the child.

2. Such protective measures should, as appropriate, include effective procedures for the establishment of social programmes to provide necessary support for the child and for those who have the care of the child, as well as for other forms of prevention and for identification, reporting, referral, investigation, treatment and follow-up of instances of child maltreatment described heretofore, and, as appropriate, for judicial involvement.

Article 20

1. A child temporarily or permanently deprived of his or her family environment, or in whose own best interests cannot be allowed to remain in that environment, shall be entitled to special protection and assistance provided by the State.
2. States Parties shall in accordance with their national laws ensure alternative care for such a child.
3. Such care could include, inter alia, foster placement, kafalah of Islamic law, adoption or if necessary placement in suitable institutions for the care of children. When considering solutions, due regard shall be paid to the desirability of continuity in a child's upbringing and to the child's ethnic, religious, cultural and linguistic background.

...

Article 22

1. States Parties shall take appropriate measures to ensure that a child who is seeking refugee status or who is considered a refugee in accordance with applicable international or domestic law and procedures shall, whether unaccompanied or accompanied by his or her parents or by any other person, receive appropriate protection and humanitarian assistance in the enjoyment of applicable rights set forth in the present Convention and in other international human rights or humanitarian instruments to which the said States are Parties.
2. For this purpose, States Parties shall provide, as they consider appropriate, co-operation in any efforts by the United Nations and other competent intergovernmental organizations or non-governmental organizations co-operating with the United Nations to protect and assist such a child and to trace the parents or other members of the family of any refugee child in order to obtain information necessary for reunification with his or her family. In cases where no parents or other members of the family can be found, the child shall be accorded the same protection as any other child permanently or temporarily deprived of his or her family environment for any reason, as set forth in the present Convention.

...

Article 32

1. States Parties recognize the right of the child to be protected from economic exploitation and from performing any work that is likely to be hazardous or to interfere with the child's education, or to be harmful to the child's health or physical, mental, spiritual, moral or social development.
2. States Parties shall take legislative, administrative, social and educational measures to ensure the implementation of the present article. To this end, and having regard to the relevant provisions of other international instruments, States Parties shall in particular:
   (a) Provide for a minimum age or minimum ages for admission to employment;
   (b) Provide for appropriate regulation of the hours and conditions of employment;
   (c) Provide for appropriate penalties or other sanctions to ensure the effective enforcement of the present article.

Article 33

States Parties shall take all appropriate measures, including legislative, administrative, social and educational measures, to protect children from the illicit use of narcotic drugs and psychotropic substances as defined in the relevant international treaties, and to prevent the use of children in the illicit production and trafficking of such substances.

Article 34

States Parties undertake to protect the child from all forms of sexual exploitation and sexual abuse. For these purposes, States Parties shall in particular take all appropriate national, bilateral and multilateral measures to prevent:

(a) The inducement or coercion of a child to engage in any unlawful sexual activity;

(b) The exploitative use of children in prostitution or other unlawful sexual practices;

(c) The exploitative use of children in pornographic performances and materials.

Article 35

States Parties shall take all appropriate national, bilateral and multilateral measures to prevent the abduction of, the sale of or traffic in children for any purpose or in any form.

Article 36

States Parties shall protect the child against all other forms of exploitation prejudicial to any aspects of the child's welfare.

Article 37

States Parties shall ensure that:

(a) No child shall be subjected to torture or other cruel, inhuman or degrading treatment or punishment. Neither capital punishment nor life imprisonment without possibility of release shall be imposed for offences committed by persons below eighteen years of age;

(b) No child shall be deprived of his or her liberty unlawfully or arbitrarily. The arrest, detention or imprisonment of a child shall be in conformity with the law and shall be used only as a measure of last resort and for the shortest appropriate period of time;

(c) Every child deprived of liberty shall be treated with humanity and respect for the inherent dignity of the human person, and in a manner which takes into account the needs of persons of his or her age. In particular, every child deprived of liberty shall be separated from adults unless it is considered in the child's best interest not to do so and shall have the right to maintain contact with his or her family through correspondence and visits, save in exceptional circumstances;

(d) Every child deprived of his or her liberty shall have the right to prompt access to legal and other appropriate assistance, as well as the right to challenge the legality of the deprivation of his or her liberty before a court or other competent, independent and impartial authority, and to a prompt decision on any such action.

Article 38

1. States Parties undertake to respect and to ensure respect for rules of international humanitarian law applicable to them in armed conflicts which are relevant to the child.
2. States Parties shall take all feasible measures to ensure that persons who have not attained the age of fifteen years do not take a direct part in hostilities.
3. States Parties shall refrain from recruiting any person who has not attained the age of fifteen years into their armed forces. In recruiting among those persons who have attained the age of fifteen years but who have not attained the age of eighteen years, States Parties shall endeavour to give priority to those who are oldest.

4. In accordance with their obligations under international humanitarian law to protect the civilian population in armed conflicts, States Parties shall take all feasible measures to ensure protection and care of children who are affected by an armed conflict.

Article 39

States Parties shall take all appropriate measures to promote physical and psychological recovery and social reintegration of a child victim of: any form of neglect, exploitation, or abuse; torture or any other form of cruel, inhuman or degrading treatment or punishment; or armed conflicts. Such recovery and reintegration shall take place in an environment which fosters the health, self-respect and dignity of the child.

Article 40

1. States Parties recognize the right of every child alleged as, accused of, or recognized as having infringed the penal law to be treated in a manner consistent with the promotion of the child's sense of dignity and worth, which reinforces the child's respect for the human rights and fundamental freedoms of others and which takes into account the child's age and the desirability of promoting the child's reintegration and the child's assuming a constructive role in society.
2. To this end, and having regard to the relevant provisions of international instruments, States Parties shall, in particular, ensure that:
   (a) No child shall be alleged as, be accused of, or recognized as having infringed the penal law by reason of acts or omissions that were not prohibited by national or international law at the time they were committed;
   (b) Every child alleged as or accused of having infringed the penal law has at least the following guarantees:
      (i) To be presumed innocent until proven guilty according to law;
      (ii) To be informed promptly and directly of the charges against him or her, and, if appropriate, through his or her parents or legal guardians, and to have legal or other appropriate assistance in the preparation and presentation of his or her defence;
      (iii) To have the matter determined without delay by a competent, independent and impartial authority or judicial body in a fair hearing according to law, in the presence of legal or other appropriate assistance and, unless it is considered not to be in the best interest of the child, in particular, taking into account his or her age or situation, his or her parents or legal guardians;
      (iv) Not to be compelled to give testimony or to confess guilt; to examine or have examined adverse witnesses and to obtain the participation and examination of witnesses on his or her behalf under conditions of equality;
      (v) If considered to have infringed the penal law, to have this decision and any measures imposed in consequence thereof reviewed by a higher competent, independent and impartial authority or judicial body according to law;
      (vi) To have the free assistance of an interpreter if the child cannot understand or speak the language used;
      (vii) To have his or her privacy fully respected at all stages of the proceedings.
3. States Parties shall seek to promote the establishment of laws, procedures, authorities and institutions specifically applicable to children alleged as, accused of, or recognized as having infringed the penal law, and, in particular:
   (a) The establishment of a minimum age below which children shall be presumed not to have the capacity to infringe the penal law;

(b) Whenever appropriate and desirable, measures for dealing with such children without resorting to judicial proceedings, providing that human rights and legal safeguards are fully respected.

4. A variety of dispositions, such as care, guidance and supervision orders; counselling; probation; foster care; education and vocational training programmes and other alternatives to institutional care shall be available to ensure that children are dealt with in a manner appropriate to their well-being and proportionate both to their circumstances and the offence.

Article 41

Nothing in the present Convention shall affect any provisions which are more conducive to the realization of the rights of the child and which may be contained in:

(a) The law of a State party; or

(b) International law in force for that State.

...

Optional Protocol to the Convention on the Rights of the Child on the Involvement of Children in Armed Conflict[62]

(Extracts)

PREAMBLE

The States Parties to the present Protocol,

Encouraged by the overwhelming support for the Convention on the Rights of the Child, demonstrating the widespread commitment that exists to strive for the promotion and protection of the rights of the child,

Reaffirming that the rights of children require special protection, and calling for continuous improvement of the situation of children without distinction, as well as for their development and education in conditions of peace and security,

Disturbed by the harmful and widespread impact of armed conflict on children and the long-term consequences it has for durable peace, security and development,

Condemning the targeting of children in situations of armed conflict and direct attacks on objects protected under international law, including places that generally have a significant presence of children, such as schools and hospitals,

Noting the adoption of the Rome Statute of the International Criminal Court, in particular, the inclusion therein as a war crime, of conscripting or enlisting children under the age of 15 years

62 From Optional Protocol to the Convention on the Rights of the Child on the Involvement of Children in Armed Conflict © 2000 United Nations. Reprinted with the permission of the United Nations.

or using them to participate actively in hostilities in both international and non-international armed conflicts,

Considering therefore that to strengthen further the implementation of rights recognized in the Convention on the Rights of the Child there is a need to increase the protection of children from involvement in armed conflict,

Noting that article 1 of the Convention on the Rights of the Child specifies that, for the purposes of that Convention, a child means every human being below the age of 18 years unless, under the law applicable to the child, majority is attained earlier,

Convinced that an optional protocol to the Convention that raises the age of possible recruitment of persons into armed forces and their participation in hostilities will contribute effectively to the implementation of the principle that the best interests of the child are to be a primary consideration in all actions concerning children,

Noting that the twenty-sixth International Conference of the Red Cross and Red Crescent in December 1995 recommended, inter alia, that parties to conflict take every feasible step to ensure that children below the age of 18 years do not take part in hostilities,

Welcoming the unanimous adoption, in June 1999, of International Labour Organization Convention No. 182 on the Prohibition and Immediate Action for the Elimination of the Worst Forms of Child Labour, which prohibits, inter alia, forced or compulsory recruitment of children for use in armed conflict,

Condemning with the gravest concern the recruitment, training and use within and across national borders of children in hostilities by armed groups distinct from the armed forces of a State, and recognizing the responsibility of those who recruit, train and use children in this regard,

Recalling the obligation of each party to an armed conflict to abide by the provisions of international humanitarian law,

Stressing that the present Protocol is without prejudice to the purposes and principles contained in the Charter of the United Nations, including Article 51, and relevant norms of humanitarian law,

Bearing in mind that conditions of peace and security based on full respect of the purposes and principles contained in the Charter and observance of applicable human rights instruments are indispensable for the full protection of children, in particular during armed conflicts and foreign occupation,

Recognizing the special needs of those children who are particularly vulnerable to recruitment or use in hostilities contrary to the present Protocol owing to their economic or social status or gender,

Mindful of the necessity of taking into consideration the economic, social and political root causes of the involvement of children in armed conflicts,

Convinced of the need to strengthen international cooperation in the implementation of the present Protocol, as well as the physical and psychosocial rehabilitation and social reintegration of children who are victims of armed conflict,

Encouraging the participation of the community and, in particular, children and child victims in the dissemination of informational and educational programmes concerning the implementation of the Protocol,

Have agreed as follows:

Article 1

States Parties shall take all feasible measures to ensure that members of their armed forces who have not attained the age of 18 years do not take a direct part in hostilities.

Article 2

States Parties shall ensure that persons who have not attained the age of 18 years are not compulsorily recruited into their armed forces.

Article 3

1. States Parties shall raise the minimum age for the voluntary recruitment of persons into their national armed forces from that set out in article 38, paragraph 3, of the Convention on the Rights of the Child, taking account of the principles contained in that article and recognizing that under the Convention persons under the age of 18 years are entitled to special protection.
2. Each State Party shall deposit a binding declaration upon ratification of or accession to the present Protocol that sets forth the minimum age at which it will permit voluntary recruitment into its national armed forces and a description of the safeguards it has adopted to ensure that such recruitment is not forced or coerced.
3. States Parties that permit voluntary recruitment into their national armed forces under the age of 18 years shall maintain safeguards to ensure, as a minimum, that:
   (a) Such recruitment is genuinely voluntary;
   (b) Such recruitment is carried out with the informed consent of the person's parents or legal guardians;
   (c) Such persons are fully informed of the duties involved in such military service;
   (d) Such persons provide reliable proof of age prior to acceptance into national military service.
4. Each State Party may strengthen its declaration at any time by notification to that effect addressed to the Secretary-General of the United Nations, who shall inform all States Parties. Such notification shall take effect on the date on which it is received by the Secretary-General.
5. The requirement to raise the age in paragraph 1 of the present article does not apply to schools operated by or under the control of the armed forces of the States Parties, in keeping with articles 28 and 29 of the Convention on the Rights of the Child.

Article 4

1. Armed groups that are distinct from the armed forces of a State should not, under any circumstances, recruit or use in hostilities persons under the age of 18 years.
2. States Parties shall take all feasible measures to prevent such recruitment and use, including the adoption of legal measures necessary to prohibit and criminalize such practices.
3. The application of the present article shall not affect the legal status of any party to an armed conflict.

Article 5

Nothing in the present Protocol shall be construed as precluding provisions in the law of a State Party or in international instruments and international humanitarian law that are more conducive to the realization of the rights of the child.

Article 6

1. Each State Party shall take all necessary legal, administrative and other measures to ensure the effective implementation and enforcement of the provisions of the present Protocol within its jurisdiction.
2. States Parties undertake to make the principles and provisions of the present Protocol widely known and promoted by appropriate means, to adults and children alike.
3. States Parties shall take all feasible measures to ensure that persons within their jurisdiction recruited or used in hostilities contrary to the present Protocol are demobilized or otherwise

released from service. States Parties shall, when necessary, accord to such persons all appropriate assistance for their physical and psychological recovery and their social reintegration.

...

Article 8

1. Each State Party shall, within two years following the entry into force of the present Protocol for that State Party, submit a report to the Committee on the Rights of the Child providing comprehensive information on the measures it has taken to implement the provisions of the Protocol, including the measures taken to implement the provisions on participation and recruitment.
2. Following the submission of the comprehensive report, each State Party shall include in the reports it submits to the Committee on the Rights of the Child, in accordance with article 44 of the Convention, any further information with respect to the implementation of the Protocol. Other States Parties to the Protocol shall submit a report every five years.
3. The Committee on the Rights of the Child may request from States Parties further information relevant to the implementation of the present Protocol.

...

10

International Convention for the Protection of All Persons from Enforced Disappearance

Prefatory Note

In UN peace operations, peacekeepers may face situations where individuals may be subjected to enforced disappearances either by a State or a non-State armed group. In such cases, the International Convention for the Protection of All Persons from Enforced Disappearance (Convention)[1] is, at the very least, a useful benchmark to ensure that the State or armed group does not breach the fundamental protections articulated in the Convention. In situations where peacekeepers might be responsible for taking or handling detainees the Convention also provides useful principles, rules, and standards to ensure that detainees are appropriately accounted for.

The Convention seeks to prevent enforced disappearances, combat impunity for the crime of enforced disappearance, and provide remedies for victims of enforced disappearances.[2] It reinforces the principle that the enforced disappearance of any person is a human rights violation. The Convention was adopted by the General Assembly in resolution 61/177 of 20 December 2006. The text of the Convention is annexed to the resolution.

The Convention is based on General Assembly resolution 47/133[3] and the Charter of the United Nations (Charter),[4] and recalls a long list of international instruments that are relevant to enforced disappearances including the Convention against Torture and Other Cruel, Inhuman or Degrading Treatment or Punishment,[5] the Declaration of Basic Principles of Justice for Victims of Crime and Abuse of Power,[6] the United Nations Standard Minimum Rules for the Treatment of Prisoners,[7] the Body of Principles for the Protection of All Persons under Any Form of Detention or Imprisonment,[8] and the Code of Conduct for Law Enforcement Officials.[9] The resolution states that whilst acts of enforced disappearance constitute violations of the prohibitions in the above human rights instruments, it is still necessary to develop a specific instrument on enforced disappearances—the Convention—as a body of principles for all States.

Article 1 of the Convention states that '[n]o one shall be subjected to enforced disappearance'. This is a principle from which no derogation is permissible, even in times of war. Article 2 defines 'enforced disappearance' to mean:

> the arrest, detention, abduction or any other form of deprivation of liberty by agents of the State or by persons or groups of persons acting with the authorization, support or acquiescence of the State, followed by a refusal to acknowledge the deprivation of liberty or by concealment of the fate or whereabouts of the disappeared person, which place such a person outside the protection of the law.[10]

The Convention implicitly refers to the Rome Statute of the International Criminal Court (Rome Statute)[11] when it states in Article 5 that '[t]he widespread or systematic practice of enforced disappearance constitutes a crime against humanity as defined in applicable international law and shall attract the consequences provided for under such applicable international law'. The applicable

---

1 International Convention for the Protection of All Persons from Enforced Disappearance (opened for signature 20 December 2006, entered into force 23 December 2010) (Convention).

2 GA Res 61/177 of 12 January 2007, Preamble.

3 GA Res 47/133 of 18 December 1992.

4 See ch 1 above.

5 See ch 8 above.

6 See ch 11 below.

7 See ch 12 below.

8 See ch 12 below.

9 See ch 13 below.

10 Convention (n 1), Article 2.

11 See ch 23 below.

international law will include the Rome Statute, which contains, in Article 7(1)(i), enforced disappearance as a crime against humanity.

Each State Party should take appropriate measures 'to ensure that enforced disappearance constitutes an offence under its criminal law',[12] and make the offence of enforced disappearance 'punishable by appropriate penalties which take into account its extreme seriousness'.[13] In terms of the enforced disappearance of persons by non-State actors, Article 3 obliges State Parties to 'take appropriate measures to investigate acts defined in article 2 committed by persons or groups of persons acting without the authorization, support or acquiescence of the State and to bring those responsible to justice'. The Convention provides that the offence of enforced disappearance is one of universal jurisdiction and that State Parties who arrest an offender in their territory have to either prosecute or extradite the offender to another State or international criminal tribunal.[14] Article 16 provides that '[n]o State Party shall expel, return ("refouler"), surrender or extradite a person to another State where there are substantial grounds for believing that he or she would be in danger of being subjected to enforced disappearance'.

Article 17 provides that '[n]o one shall be held in secret detention' and State Parties are obliged to pass legislation that provides for a number of specified conditions for people deprived of their liberty. This includes keeping certain information on the deprivation of liberty of a person and providing it, when requested, to relatives of the person deprived of liberty, their representatives, or their counsel.[15]

Article 23 provides for the training of law enforcement personnel, both civilian and military, medical personnel, public officials, and other persons who may be involved in the custody or treatment of any person deprived of liberty so that they do not participate in an enforced disappearance. Article 24 defines 'victim' to mean 'the disappeared person and any individual who has suffered harm as the direct result of an enforced disappearance' and affirms the right of any victim to know the truth about the circumstances of an enforced disappearance and the fate of the disappeared person. Article 25 covers the special circumstances surrounding children and enforced disappearances.

In line with the other core human rights treaties, Article 26 provides that a Committee on Enforced Disappearances shall be established to carry out the functions provided for under the Convention. This includes receiving communications from or on behalf of individuals claiming to be victims if the State Party makes a declaration that it recognises the competence of the Committee to receive and consider complaints from individuals subject to its jurisdiction.[16] The Working Group on Enforced or Involuntary Disappearances[17] also deals with the subject of enforced disappearances.

In UN peace operations, peacekeepers may face situations where individuals are subjected to enforced disappearances either by a State or a non-State armed group.[18] Peacekeepers in such situations may be required to prevent any further enforced disappearances and to investigate and resolve existing cases of enforced disappearance.

UN peace operations should also ensure that the detention of any individual by peacekeepers is consistent with the provisions of the Convention. For example, peacekeepers should follow the accountability mechanisms laid down in Article 17 of the Convention, such as the compilation and maintenance of one or more up-to-date official registers and/or records of persons deprived of liberty. Ensuring that appropriate steps are taken to account for individuals held in custody by peacekeepers will assist in avoiding concerns such as those expressed by the Office of the UN High Commissioner for Human Rights 'involving the enforced disappearance 15 months ago of at least 11 people, including five women and one child, by troops from the Republic of Congo that were

12 Convention (n 1), Article 4.

13 Ibid, Article 7(1).

14 Ibid, Articles 9, 10, and 11.

15 Ibid, Article 18.

16 Ibid, Article 31. For further detail concerning the Committee see <http://www.ohchr.org/EN/HRBodies/CED/Pages/CEDIntro.aspx> accessed 1 November 2017. At the time of writing the Committee has not issued any General Comments.

17 Established pursuant to the Commission on Human Rights resolution 20 (XXXVI) of 29 January 1980. For further detail of the Working Group see <http://www.ohchr.org/EN/Issues/Disappearances/Pages/DisappearancesIndex.aspx> accessed 1 November 2017.

18 In relation to the Democratic Republic of the Congo (where United Nations Organization Stabilization Mission in the Democratic Republic of the Congo (MONUSCO) is currently carrying out its mission) the Working Group on Enforced or Involuntary Disappearances noted 47 outstanding cases of enforced disappearances between 16 May 2015 and 18 May 2016: see Report of the Working Group on Enforced or Involuntary Disappearances, UN Doc A/HRC/33/51, 28 July 2016, p 14.

part of MISCA [Mission internationale de soutien à la Centrafrique sous conduite africaine, also sometimes referred to as the African-led International Support Mission in the CAR], the AU-led peacekeeping force at the time'.[19]

One area of law and practice that will be relevant to UN peacekeepers who handle detainees is whether the records they keep of detainees can be released. The UN Office of Legal Affairs (OLA) dealt with this matter in an inter-office memorandum in relation to a 'request for information regarding the ... [UN's] involvement in an exchange of detainees'.[20] OLA stated:

> We note that the information and documentation requested is internal and confidential and relates to official United Nations work, and moreover that the documentation contains politically sensitive information concerning the exchange of detainees (including) [Name 3] between [Member State B] and [Member State A], and the procedure of such exchange. The documentation is United Nations property and forms part of the United Nations archives, and inviolable in terms of sections 3 and 4 of the Convention on the Privileges and Immunities of the United Nations. In this case we see no reason for departing from our normal policy and practice of declining to provide internal and confidential information relating to official matters to private persons.[21]

Reference

Title	International Convention for the Protection of All Persons from Enforced Disappearance
Date of Adoption	20 December 2006 in General Assembly Resolution 61/177
Opened for Signature	6 February 2007
Entered into Force	23 December 2010
Signatories	97
Parties	58
Depository	United Nations
Source	2716 UNTS 3
Full Text	<https://www.ohchr.org/en/hrbodies/ced/pages/conventionced.aspx>[22]

International Convention for the Protection of All Persons from Enforced Disappearance[23]

(Extracts)

PREAMBLE

The States Parties to this Convention,

Considering the obligation of States under the Charter of the United Nations to promote universal respect for, and observance of, human rights and fundamental freedoms,

Having regard to the Universal Declaration of Human Rights,

---

19 Security Council Report, 'August 2015 Monthly Forecast: Central African Republic', 31 July 2015 <http://www.securitycouncilreport.org/monthly-forecast/2015-08/central_african_republic_13.php> accessed 1 November 2017.

20 Inter-office memorandum to the Director of the Executive Office of the Secretary-General, concerning a request for information regarding the Organization's involvement in an exchange of detainees, signed 11 January 1995, reprinted in the UN Juridical Yearbook: Special Edition, 1.

21 Ibid.

22 Accessed 9 August 2018.

23 From International Convention for the Protection of All Persons from Enforced Disappearance © 2006 United Nations. Reprinted with the permission of the United Nations.

Recalling the International Covenant on Economic, Social and Cultural Rights, the International Covenant on Civil and Political Rights and the other relevant international instruments in the fields of human rights, humanitarian law and international criminal law,

Also recalling the Declaration on the Protection of All Persons from Enforced Disappearance adopted by the General Assembly of the United Nations in its resolution 47/133 of 18 December 1992,

Aware of the extreme seriousness of enforced disappearance, which constitutes a crime and, in certain circumstances defined in international law, a crime against humanity,

Determined to prevent enforced disappearances and to combat impunity for the crime of enforced disappearance,

Considering the right of any person not to be subjected to enforced disappearance, the right of victims to justice and to reparation,

Affirming the right of any victim to know the truth about the circumstances of an enforced disappearance and the fate of the disappeared person, and the right to freedom to seek, receive and impart information to this end,

Have agreed on the following articles:

PART I

Article 1

1. No one shall be subjected to enforced disappearance.
2. No exceptional circumstances whatsoever, whether a state of war or a threat of war, internal political instability or any other public emergency, may be invoked as a justification for enforced disappearance.

Article 2

For the purposes of this Convention, "enforced disappearance" is considered to be the arrest, detention, abduction or any other form of deprivation of liberty by agents of the State or by persons or groups of persons acting with the authorization, support or acquiescence of the State, followed by a refusal to acknowledge the deprivation of liberty or by concealment of the fate or whereabouts of the disappeared person, which place such a person outside the protection of the law.

Article 3

Each State Party shall take appropriate measures to investigate acts defined in article 2 committed by persons or groups of persons acting without the authorization, support or acquiescence of the State and to bring those responsible to justice.

Article 4

Each State Party shall take the necessary measures to ensure that enforced disappearance constitutes an offence under its criminal law.

Article 5

The widespread or systematic practice of enforced disappearance constitutes a crime against humanity as defined in applicable international law and shall attract the consequences provided for under such applicable international law.

Article 6

1. Each State Party shall take the necessary measures to hold criminally responsible at least:
   (a) Any person who commits, orders, solicits or induces the commission of, attempts to commit, is an accomplice to or participates in an enforced disappearance;

(b) A superior who:

(i) Knew, or consciously disregarded information which clearly indicated, that subordinates under his or her effective authority and control were committing or about to commit a crime of enforced disappearance;

(ii) Exercised effective responsibility for and control over activities which were concerned with the crime of enforced disappearance; and

(iii) Failed to take all necessary and reasonable measures within his or her power to prevent or repress the commission of an enforced disappearance or to submit the matter to the competent authorities for investigation and prosecution;

(c) Subparagraph (b) above is without prejudice to the higher standards of responsibility applicable under relevant international law to a military commander or to a person effectively acting as a military commander.

2. No order or instruction from any public authority, civilian, military or other, may be invoked to justify an offence of enforced disappearance.

Article 7

1. Each State Party shall make the offence of enforced disappearance punishable by appropriate penalties which take into account its extreme seriousness.

2. Each State Party may establish:

(a) Mitigating circumstances, in particular for persons who, having been implicated in the commission of an enforced disappearance, effectively contribute to bringing the disappeared person forward alive or make it possible to clarify cases of enforced disappearance or to identify the perpetrators of an enforced disappearance;

(b) Without prejudice to other criminal procedures, aggravating circumstances, in particular in the event of the death of the disappeared person or the commission of an enforced disappearance in respect of pregnant women, minors, persons with disabilities or other particularly vulnerable persons.

...

Article 9

1. Each State Party shall take the necessary measures to establish its competence to exercise jurisdiction over the offence of enforced disappearance:

(a) When the offence is committed in any territory under its jurisdiction or on board a ship or aircraft registered in that State;

(b) When the alleged offender is one of its nationals;

(c) When the disappeared person is one of its nationals and the State Party considers it appropriate.

2. Each State Party shall likewise take such measures as may be necessary to establish its competence to exercise jurisdiction over the offence of enforced disappearance when the alleged offender is present in any territory under its jurisdiction, unless it extradites or surrenders him or her to another State in accordance with its international obligations or surrenders him or her to an international criminal tribunal whose jurisdiction it has recognized.

3. This Convention does not exclude any additional criminal jurisdiction exercised in accordance with national law.

Article 10

1. Upon being satisfied, after an examination of the information available to it, that the circumstances so warrant, any State Party in whose territory a person suspected of having committed an offence of enforced disappearance is present shall take him or her into custody or take such

other legal measures as are necessary to ensure his or her presence. The custody and other legal measures shall be as provided for in the law of that State Party but may be maintained only for such time as is necessary to ensure the person's presence at criminal, surrender or extradition proceedings.

2. A State Party which has taken the measures referred to in paragraph 1 of this article shall immediately carry out a preliminary inquiry or investigations to establish the facts. It shall notify the States Parties referred to in article 9, paragraph 1, of the measures it has taken in pursuance of paragraph 1 of this article, including detention and the circumstances warranting detention, and of the findings of its preliminary inquiry or its investigations, indicating whether it intends to exercise its jurisdiction.
3. Any person in custody pursuant to paragraph 1 of this article may communicate immediately with the nearest appropriate representative of the State of which he or she is a national, or, if he or she is a stateless person, with the representative of the State where he or she usually resides.

Article 11

1. The State Party in the territory under whose jurisdiction a person alleged to have committed an offence of enforced disappearance is found shall, if it does not extradite that person or surrender him or her to another State in accordance with its international obligations or surrender him or her to an international criminal tribunal whose jurisdiction it has recognized, submit the case to its competent authorities for the purpose of prosecution.
2. These authorities shall take their decision in the same manner as in the case of any ordinary offence of a serious nature under the law of that State Party. In the cases referred to in article 9, paragraph 2, the standards of evidence required for prosecution and conviction shall in no way be less stringent than those which apply in the cases referred to in article 9, paragraph 1.
3. Any person against whom proceedings are brought in connection with an offence of enforced disappearance shall be guaranteed fair treatment at all stages of the proceedings. Any person tried for an offence of enforced disappearance shall benefit from a fair trial before a competent, independent and impartial court or tribunal established by law.

Article 12

1. Each State Party shall ensure that any individual who alleges that a person has been subjected to enforced disappearance has the right to report the facts to the competent authorities, which shall examine the allegation promptly and impartially and, where necessary, undertake without delay a thorough and impartial investigation. Appropriate steps shall be taken, where necessary, to ensure that the complainant, witnesses, relatives of the disappeared person and their defence counsel, as well as persons participating in the investigation, are protected against all ill-treatment or intimidation as a consequence of the complaint or any evidence given.
2. Where there are reasonable grounds for believing that a person has been subjected to enforced disappearance, the authorities referred to in paragraph 1 of this article shall undertake an investigation, even if there has been no formal complaint.
3. Each State Party shall ensure that the authorities referred to in paragraph 1 of this article:
   (a) Have the necessary powers and resources to conduct the investigation effectively, including access to the documentation and other information relevant to their investigation;
   (b) Have access, if necessary with the prior authorization of a judicial authority, which shall rule promptly on the matter, to any place of detention or any other place where there are reasonable grounds to believe that the disappeared person may be present.

4. Each State Party shall take the necessary measures to prevent and sanction acts that hinder the conduct of an investigation. It shall ensure in particular that persons suspected of having committed an offence of enforced disappearance are not in a position to influence the progress of an investigation by means of pressure or acts of intimidation or reprisal aimed at the complainant, witnesses, relatives of the disappeared person or their defence counsel, or at persons participating in the investigation.

Article 13

1. For the purposes of extradition between States Parties, the offence of enforced disappearance shall not be regarded as a political offence or as an offence connected with a political offence or as an offence inspired by political motives. Accordingly, a request for extradition based on such an offence may not be refused on these grounds alone.
2. The offence of enforced disappearance shall be deemed to be included as an extraditable offence in any extradition treaty existing between States Parties before the entry into force of this Convention.
3. States Parties undertake to include the offence of enforced disappearance as an extraditable offence in any extradition treaty subsequently to be concluded between them.
4. If a State Party which makes extradition conditional on the existence of a treaty receives a request for extradition from another State Party with which it has no extradition treaty, it may consider this Convention as the necessary legal basis for extradition in respect of the offence of enforced disappearance.
5. States Parties which do not make extradition conditional on the existence of a treaty shall recognize the offence of enforced disappearance as an extraditable offence between themselves.
6. Extradition shall, in all cases, be subject to the conditions provided for by the law of the requested State Party or by applicable extradition treaties, including, in particular, conditions relating to the minimum penalty requirement for extradition and the grounds upon which the requested State Party may refuse extradition or make it subject to certain conditions.
7. Nothing in this Convention shall be interpreted as imposing an obligation to extradite if the requested State Party has substantial grounds for believing that the request has been made for the purpose of prosecuting or punishing a person on account of that person's sex, race, religion, nationality, ethnic origin, political opinions or membership of a particular social group, or that compliance with the request would cause harm to that person for any one of these reasons.

...

Article 15

States Parties shall cooperate with each other and shall afford one another the greatest measure of mutual assistance with a view to assisting victims of enforced disappearance, and in searching for, locating and releasing disappeared persons and, in the event of death, in exhuming and identifying them and returning their remains.

Article 16

1. No State Party shall expel, return ("refouler"), surrender or extradite a person to another State where there are substantial grounds for believing that he or she would be in danger of being subjected to enforced disappearance.
2. For the purpose of determining whether there are such grounds, the competent authorities shall take into account all relevant considerations, including, where applicable, the existence in the State concerned of a consistent pattern of gross, flagrant or mass violations of human rights or of serious violations of international humanitarian law.

Article 17

1. No one shall be held in secret detention.
2. Without prejudice to other international obligations of the State Party with regard to the deprivation of liberty, each State Party shall, in its legislation:
   (a) Establish the conditions under which orders of deprivation of liberty may be given;
   (b) Indicate those authorities authorized to order the deprivation of liberty;
   (c) Guarantee that any person deprived of liberty shall be held solely in officially recognized and supervised places of deprivation of liberty;
   (d) Guarantee that any person deprived of liberty shall be authorized to communicate with and be visited by his or her family, counsel or any other person of his or her choice, subject only to the conditions established by law, or, if he or she is a foreigner, to communicate with his or her consular authorities, in accordance with applicable international law;
   (e) Guarantee access by the competent and legally authorized authorities and institutions to the places where persons are deprived of liberty, if necessary with prior authorization from a judicial authority;
   (f) Guarantee that any person deprived of liberty or, in the case of a suspected enforced disappearance, since the person deprived of liberty is not able to exercise this right, any persons with a legitimate interest, such as relatives of the person deprived of liberty, their representatives or their counsel, shall, in all circumstances, be entitled to take proceedings before a court, in order that the court may decide without delay on the lawfulness of the deprivation of liberty and order the person's release if such deprivation of liberty is not lawful.
3. Each State Party shall assure the compilation and maintenance of one or more up-to-date official registers and/or records of persons deprived of liberty, which shall be made promptly available, upon request, to any judicial or other competent authority or institution authorized for that purpose by the law of the State Party concerned or any relevant international legal instrument to which the State concerned is a party. The information contained therein shall include, as a minimum:
   (a) The identity of the person deprived of liberty;
   (b) The date, time and place where the person was deprived of liberty and the identity of the authority that deprived the person of liberty;
   (c) The authority that ordered the deprivation of liberty and the grounds for the deprivation of liberty;
   (d) The authority responsible for supervising the deprivation of liberty;
   (e) The place of deprivation of liberty, the date and time of admission to the place of deprivation of liberty and the authority responsible for the place of deprivation of liberty;
   (f) Elements relating to the state of health of the person deprived of liberty;
   (g) In the event of death during the deprivation of liberty, the circumstances and cause of death and the destination of the remains;
   (h) The date and time of release or transfer to another place of detention, the destination and the authority responsible for the transfer.

Article 18

1. Subject to articles 19 and 20, each State Party shall guarantee to any person with a legitimate interest in this information, such as relatives of the person deprived of liberty, their representatives or their counsel, access to at least the following information:
   (a) The authority that ordered the deprivation of liberty;
   (b) The date, time and place where the person was deprived of liberty and admitted to the place of deprivation of liberty;

(c) The authority responsible for supervising the deprivation of liberty;
(d) The whereabouts of the person deprived of liberty, including, in the event of a transfer to another place of deprivation of liberty, the destination and the authority responsible for the transfer;
(e) The date, time and place of release;
(f) Elements relating to the state of health of the person deprived of liberty;
(g) In the event of death during the deprivation of liberty, the circumstances and cause of death and the destination of the remains.

2. Appropriate measures shall be taken, where necessary, to protect the persons referred to in paragraph 1 of this article, as well as persons participating in the investigation, from any ill-treatment, intimidation or sanction as a result of the search for information concerning a person deprived of liberty.

Article 19

1. Personal information, including medical and genetic data, which is collected and/or transmitted within the framework of the search for a disappeared person shall not be used or made available for purposes other than the search for the disappeared person. This is without prejudice to the use of such information in criminal proceedings relating to an offence of enforced disappearance or the exercise of the right to obtain reparation.
2. The collection, processing, use and storage of personal information, including medical and genetic data, shall not infringe or have the effect of infringing the human rights, fundamental freedoms or human dignity of an individual.

Article 20

1. Only where a person is under the protection of the law and the deprivation of liberty is subject to judicial control may the right to information referred to in article 18 be restricted, on an exceptional basis, where strictly necessary and where provided for by law, and if the transmission of the information would adversely affect the privacy or safety of the person, hinder a criminal investigation, or for other equivalent reasons in accordance with the law, and in conformity with applicable international law and with the objectives of this Convention. In no case shall there be restrictions on the right to information referred to in article 18 that could constitute conduct defined in article 2 or be in violation of article 17, paragraph 1.
2. Without prejudice to consideration of the lawfulness of the deprivation of a person's liberty, States Parties shall guarantee to the persons referred to in article 18, paragraph 1, the right to a prompt and effective judicial remedy as a means of obtaining without delay the information referred to in article 18, paragraph 1. This right to a remedy may not be suspended or restricted in any circumstances.

Article 21

Each State Party shall take the necessary measures to ensure that persons deprived of liberty are released in a manner permitting reliable verification that they have actually been released. Each State Party shall also take the necessary measures to assure the physical integrity of such persons and their ability to exercise fully their rights at the time of release, without prejudice to any obligations to which such persons may be subject under national law.

. . .

Article 23

1. Each State Party shall ensure that the training of law enforcement personnel, civil or military, medical personnel, public officials and other persons who may be involved in the custody or treatment of any person deprived of liberty includes the necessary education and information regarding the relevant provisions of this Convention, in order to:

   (a) Prevent the involvement of such officials in enforced disappearances;

(b) Emphasize the importance of prevention and investigations in relation to enforced disappearances;

(c) Ensure that the urgent need to resolve cases of enforced disappearance is recognized.

2. Each State Party shall ensure that orders or instructions prescribing, authorizing or encouraging enforced disappearance are prohibited. Each State Party shall guarantee that a person who refuses to obey such an order will not be punished.

3. Each State Party shall take the necessary measures to ensure that the persons referred to in paragraph 1 of this article who have reason to believe that an enforced disappearance has occurred or is planned report the matter to their superiors and, where necessary, to the appropriate authorities or bodies vested with powers of review or remedy.

Article 24

1. For the purposes of this Convention, "victim" means the disappeared person and any individual who has suffered harm as the direct result of an enforced disappearance.

2. Each victim has the right to know the truth regarding the circumstances of the enforced disappearance, the progress and results of the investigation and the fate of the disappeared person. Each State Party shall take appropriate measures in this regard.

3. Each State Party shall take all appropriate measures to search for, locate and release disappeared persons and, in the event of death, to locate, respect and return their remains.

4. Each State Party shall ensure in its legal system that the victims of enforced disappearance have the right to obtain reparation and prompt, fair and adequate compensation.

5. The right to obtain reparation referred to in paragraph 4 of this article covers material and moral damages and, where appropriate, other forms of reparation such as:

   (a) Restitution;

   (b) Rehabilitation;

   (c) Satisfaction, including restoration of dignity and reputation;

   (d) Guarantees of non-repetition.

6. Without prejudice to the obligation to continue the investigation until the fate of the disappeared person has been clarified, each State Party shall take the appropriate steps with regard to the legal situation of disappeared persons whose fate has not been clarified and that of their relatives, in fields such as social welfare, financial matters, family law and property rights.

7. Each State Party shall guarantee the right to form and participate freely in organizations and associations concerned with attempting to establish the circumstances of enforced disappearances and the fate of disappeared persons, and to assist victims of enforced disappearance.

Article 25

1. Each State Party shall take the necessary measures to prevent and punish under its criminal law:

   (a) The wrongful removal of children who are subjected to enforced disappearance, children whose father, mother or legal guardian is subjected to enforced disappearance or children born during the captivity of a mother subjected to enforced disappearance;

   (b) The falsification, concealment or destruction of documents attesting to the true identity of the children referred to in subparagraph (a) above.

2. Each State Party shall take the necessary measures to search for and identify the children referred to in paragraph 1 (a) of this article and to return them to their families of origin, in accordance with legal procedures and applicable international agreements.

3. States Parties shall assist one another in searching for, identifying and locating the children referred to in paragraph 1 (a) of this article.

4. Given the need to protect the best interests of the children referred to in paragraph 1 (a) of this article and their right to preserve, or to have re-established, their identity, including their nationality, name and family relations as recognized by law, States Parties which recognize a system of adoption or other form of placement of children shall have legal procedures in place to review the adoption or placement procedure, and, where appropriate, to annul any adoption or placement of children that originated in an enforced disappearance.
5. In all cases, and in particular in all matters relating to this article, the best interests of the child shall be a primary consideration, and a child who is capable of forming his or her own views shall have the right to express those views freely, the views of the child being given due weight in accordance with the age and maturity of the child.

Part II

Article 26

1. A Committee on Enforced Disappearances (hereinafter referred to as "the Committee") shall be established to carry out the functions provided for under this Convention. The Committee shall consist of ten experts of high moral character and recognized competence in the field of human rights, who shall serve in their personal capacity and be independent and impartial. The members of the Committee shall be elected by the States Parties according to equitable geographical distribution. Due account shall be taken of the usefulness of the participation in the work of the Committee of persons having relevant legal experience and of balanced gender representation.

...

Part III

Article 37

Nothing in this Convention shall affect any provisions which are more conducive to the protection of all persons from enforced disappearance and which may be contained in:

(a) The law of a State Party;

(b) International law in force for that State.

...

Article 43

This Convention is without prejudice to the provisions of international humanitarian law, including the obligations of the High Contracting Parties to the four Geneva Conventions of 12 August 1949 and the two Additional Protocols thereto of 8 June 1977, or to the opportunity available to any State Party to authorize the International Committee of the Red Cross to visit places of detention in situations not covered by international humanitarian law.

...

II

Justice and Remedies

Prefatory Note

UN peacekeepers will often be involved in issues relating to justice and providing remedies to victims. For example, in some peace operations, peacekeepers are mandated to assist the host State to bring individuals accused of gross violations of human rights or grave breaches of international humanitarian law (IHL) to justice. The matter of the UN providing remedies to victims who have been adversely affected by the conduct of its peacekeepers has also arisen.

International human rights law (IHRL),[1] IHL,[2] and international criminal law (ICL)[3] provide for a right to justice and remedies for victims of crime, abuses of power, and gross violations of IHRL and serious violations of IHL. To give effect to a right to justice and remedies, the UN General Assembly has adopted a Declaration of Basic Principles of Justice for Victims of Crime and Abuse of Power (Declaration),[4] and the Basic Principles and Guidelines on the Right to a Remedy and Reparation for Victims of Gross Violations of International Human Rights Law and Serious Violations of International Humanitarian Law (Basic Principles).[5] Extracts from the Declaration and the Basic Principles are reprinted below.

1. Declaration of Basic Principles of Justice for Victims of Crime and Abuse of Power

On 29 November 1985, the General Assembly adopted the Declaration in resolution 40/34.[6] This document had been approved several months earlier by the Seventh United Nations Congress on the Prevention of Crime and the Treatment of Offenders. According to resolution 40/34, the Declaration was 'designed to assist Governments and the international community in their efforts to secure justice and assistance for victims of crime and victims of abuse of power'.[7]

In adopting the Declaration, the General Assembly called upon Member States to take the necessary steps to give effect to its provisions and recommended at the international and regional levels that all appropriate measures be taken to 'promote training activities designed to foster adherence to United Nations standards and norms and to curtail possible abuses',[8] and to 'develop ways and means of providing recourse for victims where national channels may be insufficient'.[9] The General Assembly urged specialised agencies, other entities and bodies of the UN system, other relevant inter-governmental and non-government organisations, and the public to cooperate in the implementation of the provisions of the Declaration.

A victim of crime is defined in Section A, Article 1 of the Declaration as:

> persons who, individually or collectively, have suffered harm, including physical or mental injury, emotional suffering, economic loss or substantial impairment of their fundamental rights, through acts or

---

1 See, for example, chs 6, 8, and 10 above.

2 See, for example, ch 16 below.

3 See, for example, ch 23 below.

4 Declaration of Basic Principles of Justice for Victims of Crime and Abuse of Power, adopted by the General Assembly in GA Res 40/34 of 29 November 1985. The text of the Declaration is annexed to the resolution (hereafter Declaration).

5 Basic Principles and Guidelines on the Right to a Remedy and Reparation for Victims of Gross Violations of International Human Rights Law and Serious Violations of International Humanitarian Law, adopted by the General Assembly in GA Res 60/147 of 16 December 2005 (hereafter Basic Principles). The text of the Basic Principles is annexed to the Resolution.

6 GA Res 40/34 of 29 November 1985.

7 Ibid, Operative Part [3].

8 Ibid, Operative Part [5](a).

9 Ibid, [5](d).

> omissions that are in violation of criminal laws operative within Member States, including those laws proscribing criminal abuse of power.[10]

This definition can also include, where appropriate, the immediate family or dependants of the victim.[11] To qualify as a victim there is no requirement that the perpetrator be identified or prosecuted.[12] Article 4 of the Declaration also makes clear that all victims, rather than just those impacted by a UN peacekeeping mission, should be treated with compassion and respect for their dignity.

After defining a victim, Section A deals with access to justice and fair treatment, restitution, compensation, and assistance. Article 4 requires victims to be granted access to mechanisms of justice and prompt redress as provided for by national legislation. Article 5 encourages States to inform victims of their rights in seeking redress through judicial and administrative mechanisms. Article 8 deals with restitution and proposes that, where appropriate, fair restitution should be made available to victims, their families, or dependents. Compensation is raised in Articles 12 and 13 and requires States to endeavour to provide such compensation if other sources of funding are not available.

A victim of an abuse of power is defined in Section B, Article 18 as:

> persons who, individually or collectively, have suffered harm, including physical or mental injury, emotional suffering, economic loss or substantial impairment of their fundamental rights, through acts or omissions that do not yet constitute violations of national criminal laws but of internationally recognized norms relating to human rights.[13]

2. Basic Principles and Guidelines on the Right to a Remedy and Reparation for Victims of Gross Violations of International Human Rights Law and Serious Violations of International Humanitarian Law

When adopting the Basic Principles, the General Assembly affirmed a victim-oriented perspective and 'its human solidarity with victims of violations of international law, including violations of international human rights law and international humanitarian law'.[14] Furthermore, the General Assembly emphasised that the Basic Principles do not constitute new international or domestic legal obligations, but should be viewed as being complimentary to existing IHRL and IHL.[15]

The scope of the obligations found in the Basic Principles include investigating violations, taking action against those allegedly responsible for violations in accordance with domestic and international law, providing access to justice for victims, and providing effective remedies to victims.[16] The right to effective remedies includes: '(a) Equal and effective access to justice; (b) Adequate, effective and prompt reparation for harm suffered; [and] (c) Access to relevant information concerning violations and reparation mechanisms'.[17] Reparation for harm suffered includes restitution,[18] compensation,[19] rehabilitation,[20] satisfaction,[21] and guarantees of non-repetition.[22]

The Declaration and the Basic Principles are not binding on UN peace operations and were not developed to specifically address issues relating to peacekeepers. However, they set appropriate standards of behaviour that are relevant to all peace operations and therefore require consideration by those engaged in implementing UN mandates.

---

10 Declaration (n 4), Article 1.
11 Ibid, Article 2.
12 Ibid.
13 Ibid, Article 18.
14 GA Res 60/147 of 21 March 2006, Preamble.
15 Ibid.
16 Basic Principles (n 5), Article 3.
17 Ibid, Article 11.
18 Ibid, Article 19.
19 Ibid, Article 20.
20 Ibid, Article 21.
21 Ibid, Article 22.
22 Ibid, Article 23.

The Declaration is of relevance to those engaged in UN peace operations in two distinct ways. The first relates to instances when peacekeepers are dealing with victims of crime or abuse of power. In such a situation, the Declaration provides information in relation to the legal rights and obligations of victims and the redress procedure they should receive. The second concerns guidelines on the obligations relating to any victims who are created by peacekeepers during the implementation of the mandate, whether this is due to actions or abuses of power.

In relation to both the Declaration and the Basic Principles, the provisions dealing with access to justice and fair treatment, restitution, and compensation are of relevance to peacekeepers. That relevance is reinforced by the United Nations Secretary-General's Guidance Note on Reparations for Conflict-Related Sexual Violence.[23] That note offers operational guidance on the consideration of different forms of reparations[24] and extrapolates eight principles to guide UN engagement in reparations for victims of conflict-related sexual violence:

1. Adequate reparation for victims of conflict-related sexual violence entails a combination of different forms of reparations
2. Judicial and/or administrative reparations should be available to victims of conflict-related sexual violence as part of their right to obtain prompt, adequate and effective remedies
3. Individual and collective reparations should complement and reinforce each other
4. Reparations should strive to be transformative, including in design, implementation and impact
5. Development cooperation should support States' obligation to ensure access to reparations
6. Meaningful participation and consultation of victims in the mapping, design, implementation, monitoring and evaluation of reparations should be ensured
7. Urgent interim reparations to address immediate needs and avoid irreparable harm should be made available
8. Adequate procedural rules for proceedings involving sexual violence and reparations should be in place[25]

Part Three of the International Law Commission (ILC) Articles on the Responsibility of International Organizations[26] deals with the legal consequences of the wrongful acts of international organisations, including the UN. In relation to reparations, the ILC notes in its commentary the difficulties facing international organisations in making reparations because of the 'inadequacy of the financial resources that are generally available ... for meeting this type of expense'.[27]

The UN has argued that the 'obligation to make reparation, as well as the scope of such reparation, must be subject, in the case of the United Nations, to such rules of the organization, and more particularly to the *lex specialis* rule'.[28] In relation to third-party claims against the UN, General Assembly resolution 52/247 sets the following framework for compensation: claims arising from personal injury; illness or death; property loss or damage; and non-consensual use of privately owned property.[29] Claims arising because of 'operational necessity' (i.e. claims for property loss or damage caused in the ordinary course of the peace operation and in the pursuit of the mandate) are precluded from being compensated for under that resolution. The following limitations apply to the payment of compensation in respect of third-party claims for personal injury, illness or death resulting from UN peace operations:

(a) Compensable types of injury or loss are limited to economic loss, such as medical and rehabilitation expenses, loss of earnings, loss of financial support, transportation expenses associated with the injury, illness or medical care, as well as legal and burial expenses;

23 'Guidance Note of the Secretary-General: Reparations for Conflict-Related Sexual Violence', June 2014 <http://www.ohchr.org/Documents/Press/GuidanceNoteReparationsJune-2014.pdf> accessed 1 November 2017.

24 Ibid, 15–20.

25 Ibid, 1.

26 See ch 24 below.

27 Articles on the Responsibility of International Organizations with Commentaries, 2011 Article 31, Commentary [4], http://legal.un.org/ilc/texts/instruments/english/commentaries/9_11_2011.pdf> accessed 9 August 2018.

28 International Law Commission, 'Responsibility of International Organizations: Comments and Observations Received from International Organizations', UN Doc A/CN4/637/Add1, 17 February 2011, 30 [8].

29 See ch 22 below.

(b) No compensation is payable by the United Nations for non-economic loss, such as pain and suffering or moral anguish, as well as punitive or moral damages;

(c) Except in exceptional circumstances, and subject to requisite approval (including approval by the General Assembly), the amount of compensation payable for injury, illness or death must not exceed a maximum of US$ 50,000, provided, however, that within such limitation, the actual amount is to be determined by reference to local compensation standards;

(d) Compensation for loss or damage to personal property shall cover the reasonable costs of repair or replacement;

(e) The payment of compensation is excluded in the event of operational necessity.[30]

The UN noted in its submission to the ILC that 'in the practice of the Organization [i.e. UN] to date, compensation would appear to be the only form of reparation, although restitution and satisfaction remain possible forms of reparation'.[31] The Secretariat also pointed out that the financial limitations stipulated in resolution 52/247 'do not apply to claims of gross negligence or wilful misconduct, or in particular areas, such as vehicle accidents and aircraft accidents, where the ... [UN] has made arrangements for commercial insurance to cover third-party claims for personal injury or death'.[32] Limitations on liability are also placed in the UN Status-of-Forces Agreements (SOFAs).[33]

The UN has also noted that its obligation to settle claims in UN peace operations is based on section 29(a) of the Convention on the Privileges and Immunities of the United Nations,[34] and the model SOFA,[35] and that those provisions are restricted to the payment of private claims.[36] The UN also holds the view that claims which are political in nature or are related to decisions or actions of the Security Council are 'excluded from the scope of any obligation to provide an appropriate mode of settlement'.[37]

References

Title	Declaration of Basic Principles of Justice for Victims of Crime and Abuse of Power
Author	Text approved by consensus at the Seventh United Nations Congress on the Prevention of Crime and Treatment of Offenders, Milan, Italy, 26 August to 6 September 1985
Adopted by	General Assembly (without a vote)
Date of Adoption	29 November 1985
Source	UN Doc A/RES/40/34, Annex
Full Text	<http://www.un.org/documents/ga/res/40/a40r034.htm>[38]

Title	Basic Principles and Guidelines on the Right to a Remedy and Reparation for Victims of Gross Violations of International Human Rights Law and Serious Violations of International Humanitarian Law
Depository	United Nations
Adopted by	General Assembly (without a vote)
Date of Adoption	16 December 2005
Source	UN Doc A/RES/60/147
Full Text	<http://www.ohchr.org/EN/ProfessionalInterest/Pages/RemedyAndReparation.aspx>[39]

30 International Law Commission, 'Responsibility of International Organizations: Comments and Observations Received from International Organizations', UN Doc A/CN4/637/Add1, 17 February 2011, 29–30.

31 Ibid, 29 [16.2].

32 Ibid, 30 [16.5].

33 Ibid, 30 [16.6]. See also ch 2 above.

34 See ch 21 below.

35 See ch 2 above.

36 Letter from Pedro Medrano, Assistant Secretary-General, to Ms Farha, Mr Gallón, Mr Pūras, and Ms de Albuquerque dated 25 November 2014 concerning the cholera outbreak in Haiti, [87] <https://spdb.ohchr.org/hrdb/28th/Haiti_ASG_25.11.14_(3.2014).pdf> accessed 1 November 2017.

37 Ibid, [89].

38 Accessed 1 November 2017.

39 Accessed 1 November 2017.

Declaration of Basic Principles of Justice for Victims of Crime and Abuse of Power[40]

A. VICTIMS OF CRIME

1. "Victims" means persons who, individually or collectively, have suffered harm, including physical or mental injury, emotional suffering, economic loss or substantial impairment of their fundamental rights, through acts or omissions that are in violation of criminal laws operative within Member States, including those laws proscribing criminal abuse of power.
2. A person may be considered a victim, under this Declaration, regardless of whether the perpetrator is identified, apprehended, prosecuted or convicted and regardless of the familial relationship between the perpetrator and the victim. The term "victim" also includes, where appropriate, the immediate family or dependants of the direct victim and persons who have suffered harm in intervening to assist victims in distress or to prevent victimization.
3. The provisions contained herein shall be applicable to all, without distinction of any kind, such as race, colour, sex, age, language, religion, nationality, political or other opinion, cultural beliefs or practices, property, birth or family status, ethnic or social origin, and disability.

Access to Justice and Fair Treatment

4. Victims should be treated with compassion and respect for their dignity. They are entitled to access to the mechanisms of justice and to prompt redress, as provided for by national legislation, for the harm that they have suffered.
5. Judicial and administrative mechanisms should be established and strengthened where necessary to enable victims to obtain redress through formal or informal procedures that are expeditious, fair, inexpensive and accessible. Victims should be informed of their rights in seeking redress through such mechanisms.
6. The responsiveness of judicial and administrative processes to the needs of victims should be facilitated by:
   (a) Informing victims of their role and the scope, timing and progress of the proceedings and of the disposition of their cases, especially where serious crimes are involved and where they have requested such information;
   (b) Allowing the views and concerns of victims to be presented and considered at appropriate stages of the proceedings where their personal interests are affected, without prejudice to the accused and consistent with the relevant national criminal justice system;
   (c) Providing proper assistance to victims throughout the legal process;
   (d) Taking measures to minimize inconvenience to victims, protect their privacy, when necessary, and ensure their safety, as well as that of their families and witnesses on their behalf, from intimidation and retaliation;

(e) Avoiding unnecessary delay in the disposition of cases and the execution of orders or decrees granting awards to victims.

7. Informal mechanisms for the resolution of disputes, including mediation, arbitration and customary justice or indigenous practices, should be utilized where appropriate to facilitate conciliation and redress for victims.

Restitution

8. Offenders or third parties responsible for their behaviour should, where appropriate, make fair restitution to victims, their families or dependants. Such restitution should include the return of property or payment for the harm or loss suffered, reimbursement of expenses incurred as a result of the victimization, the provision of services and the restoration of rights.

9. Governments should review their practices, regulations and laws to consider restitution as an available sentencing option in criminal cases, in addition to other criminal sanctions.

10. In cases of substantial harm to the environment, restitution, if ordered, should include, as far as possible, restoration of the environment, reconstruction of the infrastructure, replacement of community facilities and reimbursement of the expenses of relocation, whenever such harm results in the dislocation of a community.

11. Where public officials or other agents acting in an official or quasi-official capacity have violated national criminal laws, the victims should receive restitution from the State whose officials or agents were responsible for the harm inflicted. In cases where the Government under whose authority the victimizing act or omission occurred is no longer in existence, the State or Government successor in title should provide restitution to the victims.

Compensation

12. When compensation is not fully available from the offender or other sources, States should endeavour to provide financial compensation to:

(a) Victims who have sustained significant bodily injury or impairment of physical or mental health as a result of serious crimes;

(b) The family, in particular dependants of persons who have died or become physically or mentally incapacitated as a result of such victimization.

13. The establishment, strengthening and expansion of national funds for compensation to victims should be encouraged. Where appropriate, other funds may also be established for this purpose, including in those cases where the State of which the victim is a national is not in a position to compensate the victim for the harm.

Assistance

14. Victims should receive the necessary material, medical, psychological and social assistance through governmental, voluntary, community-based and indigenous means.

15. Victims should be informed of the availability of health and social services and other relevant assistance and be readily afforded access to them.

16. Police, justice, health, social service and other personnel concerned should receive training to sensitize them to the needs of victims, and guidelines to ensure proper and prompt aid.

17. In providing services and assistance to victims, attention should be given to those who have special needs because of the nature of the harm inflicted or because of factors such as those mentioned in paragraph 3 above.

B. VICTIMS OF ABUSE OF POWER

18. "Victims" means persons who, individually or collectively, have suffered harm, including physical or mental injury, emotional suffering, economic loss or substantial impairment of their fundamental rights, through acts or omissions that do not yet constitute violations of national criminal laws but of internationally recognized norms relating to human rights.
19. States should consider incorporating into the national law norms proscribing abuses of power and providing remedies to victims of such abuses. In particular, such remedies should include restitution and/or compensation, and necessary material, medical, psychological and social assistance and support.
20. States should consider negotiating multilateral international treaties relating to victims, as defined in paragraph 18.
21. States should periodically review existing legislation and practices to ensure their responsiveness to changing circumstances, should enact and enforce, if necessary, legislation proscribing acts that constitute serious abuses of political or economic power, as well as promoting policies and mechanisms for the prevention of such acts, and should develop and make readily available appropriate rights and remedies for victims of such acts.

Basic Principles and Guidelines on the Right to a Remedy and Reparation for Victims of Gross Violations of International Human Rights Law and Serious Violations of International Humanitarian Law[41]

(Extracts)

...

Recalling the Declaration of Basic Principles of Justice for Victims of Crime and Abuse of Power emanating from the deliberations of the Seventh United Nations Congress on the Prevention of Crime and the Treatment of Offenders and General Assembly resolution 40/34 of 29 November 1985 by which the Assembly adopted the text recommended by the Congress,

---

41 From Basic Principles and Guidelines on the Right to a Remedy and Reparation for Victims of Gross Violations of International Human Rights Law and Serious Violations of International Humanitarian Law, General Assembly © 2005 United Nations. Reprinted with the permission of the United Nations.

Reaffirming the principles enunciated in the Declaration of Basic Principles of Justice for Victims of Crime and Abuse of Power, including that victims should be treated with compassion and respect for their dignity, have their right to access to justice and redress mechanisms fully respected, and that the establishment, strengthening and expansion of national funds for compensation to victims should be encouraged, together with the expeditious development of appropriate rights and remedies for victims,

Noting that the Rome Statute of the International Criminal Court requires the establishment of "principles relating to reparations to, or in respect of, victims, including restitution, compensation and rehabilitation", requires the Assembly of States Parties to establish a trust fund for the benefit of victims of crimes within the jurisdiction of the Court, and of the families of such victims, and mandates the Court "to protect the safety, physical and psychological well-being, dignity and privacy of victims" and to permit the participation of victims at all "stages of the proceedings determined to be appropriate by the Court",

Affirming that the Basic Principles and Guidelines contained herein are directed at gross violations of international human rights law and serious violations of international humanitarian law which, by their very grave nature, constitute an affront to human dignity,

Emphasizing that the Basic Principles and Guidelines contained herein do not entail new international or domestic legal obligations but identify mechanisms, modalities, procedures and methods for the implementation of existing legal obligations under international human rights law and international humanitarian law which are complementary though different as to their norms,

Recalling that international law contains the obligation to prosecute perpetrators of certain international crimes in accordance with international obligations of States and the requirements of national law or as provided for in the applicable statutes of international judicial organs, and that the duty to prosecute reinforces the international legal obligations to be carried out in accordance with national legal requirements and procedures and supports the concept of complementarity,

Noting that contemporary forms of victimization, while essentially directed against persons, may nevertheless also be directed against groups of persons who are targeted collectively,

Recognizing that, in honouring the victims' right to benefit from remedies and reparation, the international community keeps faith with the plight of victims, survivors and future human generations and reaffirms the international legal principles of accountability, justice and the rule of law,

Convinced that, in adopting a victim-oriented perspective, the international community affirms its human solidarity with victims of violations of international law, including violations of international human rights law and international humanitarian law, as well as with humanity at large, in accordance with the following Basic Principles and Guidelines,

Adopts the following Basic Principles and Guidelines:

I. Obligation to respect, ensure respect for and implement international human rights law and international humanitarian law

1. The obligation to respect, ensure respect for and implement international human rights law and international humanitarian law as provided for under the respective bodies of law eqqmanates from:

(*a*) Treaties to which a State is a party;

(*b*) Customary international law;

(*c*) The domestic law of each State.

2. If they have not already done so, States shall, as required under international law, ensure that their domestic law is consistent with their international legal obligations by:

(a) Incorporating norms of international human rights law and international humanitarian law into their domestic law, or otherwise implementing them in their domestic legal system;
(b) Adopting appropriate and effective legislative and administrative procedures and other appropriate measures that provide fair, effective and prompt access to justice;
(c) Making available adequate, effective, prompt and appropriate remedies, including reparation, as defined below;
(d) Ensuring that their domestic law provides at least the same level of protection for victims as that required by their international obligations.

II. Scope of the obligation

3. The obligation to respect, ensure respect for and implement international human rights law and international humanitarian law as provided for under the respective bodies of law, includes, inter alia, the duty to:
(a) Take appropriate legislative and administrative and other appropriate measures to prevent violations;
(b) Investigate violations effectively, promptly, thoroughly and impartially and, where appropriate, take action against those allegedly responsible in accordance with domestic and international law;
(c) Provide those who claim to be victims of a human rights or humanitarian law violation with equal and effective access to justice, as described below, irrespective of who may ultimately be the bearer of responsibility for the violation;

and

(d) Provide effective remedies to victims, including reparation, as described below.

III. Gross violations of international human rights law and serious violations of international humanitarian law that constitute crimes under international law

4. In cases of gross violations of international human rights law and serious violations of international humanitarian law constituting crimes under international law, States have the duty to investigate and, if there is sufficient evidence, the duty to submit to prosecution the person allegedly responsible for the violations and, if found guilty, the duty to punish her or him. Moreover, in these cases, States should, in accordance with international law, cooperate with one another and assist international judicial organs competent in the investigation and prosecution of these violations.

5. To that end, where so provided in an applicable treaty or under other international law obligations, States shall incorporate or otherwise implement within their domestic law appropriate provisions for universal jurisdiction. Moreover, where it is so provided for in an applicable treaty or other international legal obligations, States should facilitate extradition or surrender offenders to other States and to appropriate international judicial bodies and provide judicial assistance and other forms of cooperation in the pursuit of international justice, including assistance to, and protection of, victims and witnesses, consistent with international human rights legal standards and subject to international legal requirements such as those relating to the prohibition of torture and other forms of cruel, inhuman or degrading treatment or punishment.

IV. Statutes of limitations

6. Where so provided for in an applicable treaty or contained in other international legal obligations, statutes of limitations shall not apply to gross violations of international human rights law and serious violations of international humanitarian law which constitute crimes under international law.

7. Domestic statutes of limitations for other types of violations that do not constitute crimes under international law, including those time limitations applicable to civil claims and other procedures, should not be unduly restrictive.

V. Victims of gross violations of international human rights law and serious violations of international humanitarian law

8. For purposes of the present document, victims are persons who individually or collectively suffered harm, including physical or mental injury, emotional suffering, economic loss or substantial impairment of their fundamental rights, through acts or omissions that constitute gross violations of international human rights law, or serious violations of international humanitarian law. Where appropriate, and in accordance with domestic law, the term "victim" also includes the immediate family or dependants of the direct victim and persons who have suffered harm in intervening to assist victims in distress or to prevent victimization.

9. A person shall be considered a victim regardless of whether the perpetrator of the violation is identified, apprehended, prosecuted, or convicted and regardless of the familial relationship between the perpetrator and the victim.

VI. Treatment of victims

10. Victims should be treated with humanity and respect for their dignity and human rights, and appropriate measures should be taken to ensure their safety, physical and psychological well-being and privacy, as well as those of their families. The State should ensure that its domestic laws, to the extent possible, provide that a victim who has suffered violence or trauma should benefit from special consideration and care to avoid his or her re-traumatization in the course of legal and administrative procedures designed to provide justice and reparation.

VII. Victims' right to remedies

11. Remedies for gross violations of international human rights law and serious violations of international humanitarian law include the victim's right to the following as provided for under international law:

(a) Equal and effective access to justice;

(b) Adequate, effective and prompt reparation for harm suffered;

(c) Access to relevant information concerning violations and reparation mechanisms.

VIII. Access to justice

12. A victim of a gross violation of international human rights law or of a serious violation of international humanitarian law shall have equal access to an effective judicial remedy as provided for under international law. Other remedies available to the victim include access to administrative and other bodies, as well as mechanisms, modalities and proceedings conducted in accordance with domestic law. Obligations arising under international law to secure the right to access justice and fair and impartial proceedings shall be reflected in domestic laws. To that end, States should:

(a) Disseminate, through public and private mechanisms, information about all available remedies for gross violations of international human rights law and serious violations of international humanitarian law;

(b) Take measures to minimize the inconvenience to victims and their representatives, protect against unlawful interference with their privacy as appropriate and ensure their safety from intimidation and retaliation, as well as that of their families and witnesses, before, during and after judicial, administrative, or other proceedings that affect the interests of victims;

(c) Provide proper assistance to victims seeking access to justice;

(d) Make available all appropriate legal, diplomatic and consular means to ensure that victims can exercise their rights to remedy for gross violations of international human rights law or serious violations of international humanitarian law.

13. In addition to individual access to justice, States should endeavour to develop procedures to allow groups of victims to present claims for reparation and to receive reparation, as appropriate.

14. An adequate, effective and prompt remedy for gross violations of international human rights law or serious violations of international humanitarian law should include all available and appropriate international processes in which a person may have legal standing and should be without prejudice to any other domestic remedies.

IX. Reparation for harm suffered

15. Adequate, effective and prompt reparation is intended to promote justice by redressing gross violations of international human rights law or serious violations of international humanitarian law. Reparation should be proportional to the gravity of the violations and the harm suffered. In accordance with its domestic laws and international legal obligations, a State shall provide reparation to victims for acts or omissions which can be attributed to the State and constitute gross violations of international human rights law or serious violations of international humanitarian law. In cases where a person, a legal person, or other entity is found liable for reparation to a victim, such party should provide reparation to the victim or compensate the State if the State has already provided reparation to the victim.

16. States should endeavour to establish national programmes for reparation and other assistance to victims in the event that the parties liable for the harm suffered are unable or unwilling to meet their obligations.

17. States shall, with respect to claims by victims, enforce domestic judgements for reparation against individuals or entities liable for the harm suffered and endeavour to enforce valid foreign legal judgements for reparation in accordance with domestic law and international legal obligations. To that end, States should provide under their domestic laws effective mechanisms for the enforcement of reparation judgements.

18. In accordance with domestic law and international law, and taking account of individual circumstances, victims of gross violations of international human rights law and serious violations of international humanitarian law should, as appropriate and proportional to the gravity of the violation and the circumstances of each case, be provided with full and effective reparation, as laid out in principles 19 to 23, which include the following forms: restitution, compensation, rehabilitation, satisfaction and guarantees of non-repetition.

19. *Restitution* should, whenever possible, restore the victim to the original situation before the gross violations of international human rights law or serious violations of international humanitarian law occurred. Restitution includes, as appropriate: restoration of liberty, enjoyment of human rights, identity, family life and citizenship, return to one's place of residence, restoration of employment and return of property.

20. *Compensation* should be provided for any economically assessable damage, as appropriate and proportional to the gravity of the violation and the circumstances of each case, resulting from gross violations of international human rights law and serious violations of international humanitarian law, such as:

(a) Physical or mental harm;

(b) Lost opportunities, including employment, education and social benefits;
(c) Material damages and loss of earnings, including loss of earning potential;
(d) Moral damage;
(e) Costs required for legal or expert assistance, medicine and medical services, and psychological and social services.

21. *Rehabilitation* should include medical and psychological care as well as legal and social services.

22. *Satisfaction* should include, where applicable, any or all of the following:
(a) Effective measures aimed at the cessation of continuing violations;
(b) Verification of the facts and full and public disclosure of the truth to the extent that such disclosure does not cause further harm or threaten the safety and interests of the victim, the victim's relatives, witnesses, or persons who have intervened to assist the victim or prevent the occurrence of further violations;
(c) The search for the whereabouts of the disappeared, for the identities of the children abducted, and for the bodies of those killed, and assistance in the recovery, identification and reburial of the bodies in accordance with the expressed or presumed wish of the victims, or the cultural practices of the families and communities;
(d) An official declaration or a judicial decision restoring the dignity, the reputation and the rights of the victim and of persons closely connected with the victim;
(e) Public apology, including acknowledgement of the facts and acceptance of responsibility;
(f) Judicial and administrative sanctions against persons liable for the violations;
(g) Commemorations and tributes to the victims;
(h) Inclusion of an accurate account of the violations that occurred in international human rights law and international humanitarian law training and in educational material at all levels.

23. *Guarantees of non-repetition* should include, where applicable, any or all of the following measures, which will also contribute to prevention:
(a) Ensuring effective civilian control of military and security forces;
(b) Ensuring that all civilian and military proceedings abide by international standards of due process, fairness and impartiality;
(c) Strengthening the independence of the judiciary;
(d) Protecting persons in the legal, medical and health-care professions, the media and other related professions, and human rights defenders;
(e) Providing, on a priority and continued basis, human rights and international humanitarian law education to all sectors of society and training for law enforcement officials as well as military and security forces;
(f) Promoting the observance of codes of conduct and ethical norms, in particular international standards, by public servants, including law enforcement, correctional, media, medical, psychological, social service and military personnel, as well as by economic enterprises;
(g) Promoting mechanisms for preventing and monitoring social conflicts and their resolution;
(h) Reviewing and reforming laws contributing to or allowing gross violations of international human rights law and serious violations of international humanitarian law.

X. Access to relevant information concerning violations and reparation mechanisms

24. States should develop means of informing the general public and, in particular, victims of gross violations of international human rights law and serious violations of international humanitarian law of the rights and remedies addressed by these Basic Principles and Guidelines and of all available legal, medical, psychological, social, administrative and all other services to which victims may have a right of access. Moreover, victims and their representatives should be entitled to seek and obtain information on the causes leading to their victimization and on the causes and conditions pertaining to the gross violations of international human rights law and serious violations of international humanitarian law and to learn the truth in regard to these violations.

XI. Non-discrimination

25. The application and interpretation of these Basic Principles and Guidelines must be consistent with international human rights law and international humanitarian law and be without any discrimination of any kind or on any ground, without exception.

XII. Non-derogation

26. Nothing in these Basic Principles and Guidelines shall be construed as restricting or derogating from any rights or obligations arising under domestic and international law. In particular, it is understood that the present Basic Principles and Guidelines are without prejudice to the right to a remedy and reparation for victims of all violations of international human rights law and international humanitarian law. It is further understood that these Basic Principles and Guidelines are without prejudice to special rules of international law.

XIII. Rights of others

27. Nothing in this document is to be construed as derogating from internationally or nationally protected rights of others, in particular the right of an accused person to benefit from applicable standards of due process.

12

The Protection of Persons under Detention or Imprisonment

Prefatory Note

UN peacekeepers have detained individuals since the first UN armed operation—the United Nations Emergency Force (UNEF I)—in 1956. Since that operation, the UN has had to consider its obligations in relation to the treatment of detainees in many peace operations.

Both international human rights law (IHRL)[1] and international humanitarian law (IHL)[2] provide protection for persons detained or imprisoned. In IHRL, Article 9 of the International Covenant on Civil and Political Rights (ICCPR), for example, prohibits arbitrary arrest or detention.[3] In situations of international armed conflict, Article 42 of Geneva Convention IV limits the internment of protected persons to cases where 'the security of the Detaining Power makes it absolutely necessary'.[4] Both bodies of law also create obligations to treat those detained humanely.[5]

In the *Case concerning United States Diplomatic and Consular Staff in Tehran (USA v Iran)* (Judgment) (*Hostages Case*),[6] the International Court of Justice (ICJ) referred to the 'fundamental principles enunciated in the Universal Declaration of Human Rights'[7] in respect of the arbitrary deprivation of a person's freedom, prohibited under Article 9 of the Universal Declaration of Human Rights (UDHR) which states that '[n]o one shall be subjected to arbitrary arrest, detention, or exile'.[8] The Court stated:

> Wrongfully to deprive human beings of their freedom and to subject them to physical constraint in conditions of hardship is in itself manifestly incompatible with the principles of the Charter of the United Nations, as well as with the fundamental principles enunciated in the Universal Declaration of Human Rights.[9]

The broad prohibition of arbitrary arrest or detention, and the obligation to treat those arrested or detained humanely, have been further developed by a range of international instruments such as United Nations Standard Minimum Rules for the Treatment of Prisoners (the Nelson Mandela Rules),[10] the Body of Principles for the Protection of All Persons under Any Form of Detention or Imprisonment (Body of Principles),[11] the Basic Principles for the Treatment of Prisoners (Basic

---

1 See, for example, chs 6, 8, and 10 above.

2 See chs 15 and 16 below.

3 International Covenant on Civil and Political Rights (opened for signature 16 December 1966, entered into force 23 March 1976) 999 UNTS 171 (hereafter ICCPR). See ch 6 above. See also regional human rights instruments such as the European Convention for the Protection of Human Rights and Fundamental Freedoms, as amended by Protocols Nos 11 and 14 (opened for signature 4 November 1950, entered into force 3 September 1953) ETS 5, Article 5; African Charter on Human and Peoples' Rights (opened for signature 27 June 1981, entered into force 21 October 1996) 21 ILM 58, Article 6; American Convention on Human Rights (opened for signature 22 November 1969, entered into force 18 July 1978) 1144 UNTS 123, Article 7; and Arab Charter on Human Rights (adopted 15 September 2004), reprinted in 12 International Human Rights Report 893 (2005), Article 14.

4 See also Geneva Convention Relative to the Protection of Civilian Persons in Times of War (opened for signature 12 August 1949, entered into force 21 October 1950) 75 UNTS 287, Article 78, which applies during occupation. See ch 16 below.

5 See, for example, ICCPR (n 3), Article 10; and Protocol Additional to the Geneva Conventions of 1949, and relating to the Protection of Victims in Non-International Armed Conflicts (Protocol II) (opened for signature 8 June 1977, entered into force 7 December 1978) 1125 UNTS 609, Article 5(3). See ch 16 below.

6 *Case concerning United States Diplomatic and Consular Staff in Tehran (USA v Iran)* (Judgment) [1980] ICJ Rep 3 (hereafter *Hostages Case*).

7 Ibid, 91.

8 GA Res 217 A (III) (1948) of 10 December 1948. See also Bruce Oswald, Helen Durham, and Adrian Bates, *Documents on the Law of UN Peace Operations* (Oxford University Press 2010) ch 4.

9 *Hostages Case* (n 6), 91.

10 GA Res 70/175 of 8 January 2016, Annex, 'United Nations Standard Minimum Rules for the Treatment of Prisoners' (hereafter Nelson Mandela Rules).

11 GA Res 43/173 of 9 December 1988, Annex, 'Body of Principles for the Protection of All Persons under Any Form of Detention or Imprisonment' (hereafter Body of Principles).

Principles),[12] the United Nations Rules for the Protection of Juveniles Deprived of their Liberty, [13] the United Nations Standard Minimum Rules for Non-custodial Measures (the Tokyo Rules),[14] the United Nations Standard Minimum Rules for the Administration of Juvenile Justice (the Beijing Rules),[15] the United Nations Basic Principles and Guidelines on Remedies and Procedures on the Right of Anyone Deprived of His or Her Liberty by Arrest or Detention to Bring Proceedings before Court (Basic Principles and Guidelines),[16] and the United Nations Rules for the Treatment of Women Prisoners and Non-Custodial Measures for Women Offenders (the Bangkok Rules).[17] The Working Group on Arbitrary Detention has submitted to the General Assembly its Basic Principles and Guidelines, which deal with situations where a person has been deprived of their liberty.[18] The Copenhagen Process Principles and Guidelines on the Handling of Detainees in International Military Operations (Copenhagen Principles)[19] is another recent addition to the above documents. The Human Rights Committee in General Comment 35 also addressed the matter of the deprivation of liberty in the context of interpreting Article 9 of the ICCPR.[20]

There are several regional instruments that deal with the treatment of prisoners such as the Principles and Best Practices on the Protection of Persons deprived of Liberty in the Americas,[21] the revised European Prison Rules,[22] the Kampala Declaration on Prison Conditions in Africa,[23] the Arusha Declaration on Good Prison Practice,[24] the Principles and Guidelines on the Right to a Fair Trial and Legal Assistance in Africa,[25] and the African Commission Guidelines on the Conditions of Arrest, Police Custody, and Pre-Trial Detention in Africa.[26]

The treatment of those who are detained or imprisoned raises significant issues and this is reflected in the wide range of documents dealing with the subject matter. For the purposes of this book, two key instruments have been included: the Nelson Mandela Rules and the Body of Principles.

1. The Nelson Mandela Rules

The UN's desire to develop standards to protect the interests of all persons held in detention or imprisonment may be traced to the First United Nations Congress on the Prevention of Crime and the Treatment of Offenders in 1955.[27] The Standard Minimum Rules for the Treatment of Prisoners were subsequently approved by the Economic and Social Council by resolution 663 C (XXIV), and resolution 2076 (LXII).[28]

12 UN Doc A/RES/45/111, 14 December 1990.

13 Adopted by GA Res 45/113 of 14 December 1990, see <http://www.un.org/documents/ga/res/45/a45r113.htm> accessed 1 November 2017.

14 Adopted by GA Res 45/110 of 14 December 1990, see <http://www.ohchr.org/Documents/ProfessionalInterest/tokyorules.pdf> accessed 1 November 2017.

15 Adopted by GA Res 40/33 of 29 November 1985, see <http://www.ohchr.org/Documents/ProfessionalInterest/beijingrules.pdf> accessed 1 November 2017.

16 'Report of the Working Group on Arbitrary Detention: United Nations Basic Principles and Guidelines on the Right of Anyone Deprived of Their Liberty to Bring Proceedings before a Court', UN Doc WGAD/CRP.1/2015, 4 May 2015 (hereafter Basic Principles and Guidelines) <http://www.ohchr.org/EN/Issues/Detention/Pages/DraftBasicPrinciples.aspx> accessed 1 November 2017.

17 United Nations Rules for the Treatment of Women Prisoners and Non-Custodial Measures for Women Offenders, adopted by GA Res 65/229 of 21 December 2010 <https://www.unodc.org/documents/justice-and-prison-reform/Bangkok_Rules_ENG_22032015.pdf>.

18 Basic Principles and Guidelines (n 16).

19 Copenhagen Process on the Handling of Detainees in International Military Operations, 'Copenhagen Process Principles and Guidelines', concluded in Copenhagen on 19 October 2012 (Copenhagen Principles).

20 Human Rights Committee, General Comment No. 35, 'Article 9 (Liberty and security of person)', UN Doc CCPR/C/GC/35 of 16 December 2014.

21 Inter-American Commission on Human Rights, 'Principles and Best Practices on the Protection of Persons deprived of Liberty in the Americas', approved by the Commission during its 131st regular period of sessions held from 3 March to 14 March 2008.

22 Council of Europe, European Prison Rules, June 2006.

23 ECOSOC Res 1997/36 (1997) of 21 July 1997, Annex.

24 Arusha Decalaration on Good Prison Practice (27 February 1999, Arusha Tanzania).

25 Principles and Guidelines on the Right to a Fair Trial and Legal Assistance in Africa, DOC/OS(XXX) 247, reprinted in 12 International Human Rights Reports 1180.

26 African Commission on Human and Peoples' Rights, Guidelines on the Conditions of Arrest, Police Custody, and Pre-Trial Detention in Africa <http://www.achpr.org/instruments/guidelines_arrest_detention/> accessed 1 November 2017.

27 United Nations Office of Drugs and Crime, First United Nations Congress on the Prevention of Crime and the Treatment of Offenders in 1955 (Geneva, 22 August–3 September 1955).

28 ECOSOC Res 663 C (XXIV) of 31 July 1957; and ECOSOC Res 2076 (LXII) of 13 May 1977.

On 17 December 2015, a revised version of the Rules was adopted by the General Assembly, and the Rules are now known as the Nelson Mandela Rules to honour the legacy of Nelson Mandela.[29] The revised version of the Rules was developed by the Expert Group on the Standard Minimum Rules for the Treatment of Prisoners pursuant to a number of General Assembly resolutions.[30]

The Nelson Mandela Rules have no binding authority on States or the UN, but nonetheless have normative value because they have been adopted by the General Assembly. Furthermore, they are important because they '[t]hey set out what is generally accepted as being good principle and practice in the treatment of prisoners and prison management'.[31]

The Rules have two parts. Part I concerns the treatment of those held in prisons and includes matters such as the obligation to treat prisoners humanely,[32] accommodation for prisoners,[33] health care services for prisoners and sanctions,[34] and the use of restraints that may be applied against prisoners.[35] Part II concerns the rules applicable to special categories of prisoners such as 'prisoners under sentence',[36] 'prisoners with mental disabilities and/or health conditions',[37] and 'persons arrested or detained without charge'.[38]

2. Body of Principles

In 1979, the Sub-Commission on Prevention of Discrimination and Protection of Minorities,[39] a subsidiary body of the UN Commission on Human Rights, adopted the Declaration on the Protection of All Persons under Any Form of Detention or Imprisonment annexed to General Assembly resolution 3453 (XXX).[40] In 1980, the General Assembly established an open-ended working group with the task of finalising the draft Body of Principles.[41]

The Working Group on the Draft Body of Principles for the Protection of All Persons under Any Form of Detention or Imprisonment met between 1981 and 1988 before finally submitting the text of the draft Body of Principles to the Sixth Committee of the General Assembly where final drafting took place. Final drafting involved not only Member States but also non-governmental organisations (NGOs) such as Amnesty International.

In 1988, the General Assembly approved the Body of Principles in resolution 43/173.[42] The Body of Principles is annexed to resolution 43/173[43] and has no binding force on States or the UN. The Working Group on Arbitrary Detention, established by the Commission on Human Rights and entrusted with the investigation of instances of alleged arbitrary detention, has stated that the Body of Principles 'is an instrument declaratory of pre-existing rights, in as much as the main purpose of many of its provisions is to set forth, and sometimes develop, principles already recognized under customary law'.[44]

The Body of Principles is comprised of a section specifying the scope of its principles, which 'apply for the protection of all persons under any form of detention or imprisonment',[45] a section

---

29 Nelson Mandela Rules (n 10), Operative Part [6].

30 See, for example, GA Res 68/188 of 20 December 2012; GA Res 68/190 of 18 December 2013; and GA Res 69/192 of 26 January 2015. For an analysis of how the Nelson Mandela rules differ from the 1957 version of the Standard Minimum Rules for the Treatment of Prisoners, see <https://www.penalreform.org/priorities/prison-conditions/standard-minimum%20rules/> accessed 1 November 2017.

31 Nelson Mandela Rules (n 10), Preliminary Observation 1.

32 Ibid, Rule 1.

33 Ibid, Rules 12–17.

34 Ibid, Rules 24–35.

35 Ibid. Rules 36–49.

36 Ibid, Part II, Section A.

37 Ibid, Part II, Section B.

38 Ibid, Part II, Section E.

39 This commission was renamed the Sub-Commission on the Promotion and Protection of Human Rights in 1999.

40 GA Res 3453 (XXX) of 9 December 1975.

41 GA Res 35/177 of 15 December 1980 [3].

42 GA Res 43/173 of 9 December 1988.

43 Ibid.

44 Report of the Working Group on Arbitrary Detention, 'Question of the Human Rights of All Persons Subjected to Any Form of Detention or Imprisonment', UN Doc E/CN.4/1993/24, 12 January 1993, 12, [20].

45 GA Res 43/173 of 9 December 1988, Annex. See <http://www.un.org/documents/ga/res/43/a43r173.htm> accessed 1 November 2017.

defining the meaning of several terms used, and a section containing the 39 principles. The Body of Principles ends with a General Clause stating that '[n]othing in this Body of Principles shall be construed as restricting or derogating from any right defined in the International Covenant on Civil and Political Rights'.[46]

Key provisions of the Body of Principles include those concerning the treatment of detained persons, procedural safeguards concerning persons arrested or detained, and accountability mechanisms. They reinforce areas of human rights law such as the requirement to treat any person arrested, detained, or imprisoned 'in a humane manner and with respect for the inherent dignity of the human person'.[47] The principle of humane treatment is further supported by Principle 6 which prohibits 'torture or ... cruel, inhuman or degrading treatment or punishment'. The term 'cruel, inhuman or degrading treatment or punishment' is interpreted in a footnote to the Body of Principles which states that:

> The term 'cruel, inhuman or degrading treatment or punishment' should be interpreted so as to extend the widest possible protection against abuses, whether physical or mental, including the holding of a detained or imprisoned person in conditions which deprive him, temporarily or permanently, of the use of any of his natural senses, such as sight or hearing, or of his awareness of place and the passing of time.[48]

Thus, if Principle 6 were to be relied upon, the hooding and blindfolding of detainees would be prohibited because such acts deprive the detainee of sight. Other key provisions relating to treatment of detainees outline the right of detainees to be provided with 'information on and an explanation of [their] rights and how to avail [themselves] of such rights' by the authority responsible for the detention,[49] the entitlement to legal counsel,[50] the opportunity to receive a 'proper medical examination ... after [their] admission to the place of detention or imprisonment',[51] and 'a right to make a request or complaint regarding [their] treatment'.[52]

Principle 2 of the Body of Principles requires that any form of detention must only be carried out in accordance with the provisions of the law and by competent officials authorised by law. This principle therefore prohibits arbitrary detention. Principle 4 requires that any detention or imprisonment and measures affecting the human rights of a person detained or imprisoned 'shall be ordered by, or be subject to the effective control of, a judicial or other authority'. In the context of UN peace operations these two principles prohibit peacekeepers from arbitrarily arresting, detaining, or imprisoning a person; and require appropriate command and control mechanisms to be put in place. Accountability through mechanisms such as directives dealing with the taking and handling of detainees and rules of engagement are therefore essential to compliance with Principles 2 and 4.

In addition to the accountability requirements provided for by Principles 2 and 4, the right of *habeas corpus* enshrined in Principle 11 provides that a person detained must be given an effective opportunity to be heard by a judicial or other authority. This reinforces Principles 2 and 4, and the requirement that the continuance of a person's detention is reviewed. Principle 11 must be read in conjunction with Principle 32 which permits a detained person or their counsel to instigate proceedings to challenge the lawfulness of detention and to secure the release of the detainee if detention is found to be unlawful. This right of *habeas corpus* is fundamental to all national and international legal systems and no justification can be used to abrogate the right.

The Body of Principles also provides for places of detention to be 'visited regularly by qualified and experienced persons appointed by, and responsible to, a competent authority distinct from the authority directly in charge of the administration of the place of detention or imprisonment'.[53] Such visits are essential to ensure that places of detention comply with relevant laws and regulations.

---

46 Ibid, Annex, General Clause.
47 Body of Principles (n 11), Principle 1.
48 Ibid, Annex, footnote 1.
49 Ibid, Principle 13.
50 Ibid, Principles 17 and 18.
51 Ibid, Principle 24.
52 Ibid, Principle 33.
53 Ibid, Principle 29.

In terms of the abovementioned instruments dealing with the treatment of persons detained or imprisoned, it is also important to recognise that, pursuant to Article 10 of the Convention against Torture and Other Cruel, Inhuman or Degrading Treatment or Punishment (CAT),[54] State Parties must ensure all persons who may be involved in the custody, interrogation, or treatment of any individual are fully trained and provided with information regarding the prohibition against torture. States must also 'keep under systematic review interrogation rules, instructions, methods and practices as well as arrangements for the custody and treatment of persons subjected to any form of arrest, detention or imprisonment in any territory under its jurisdiction, with a view to preventing any cases of torture'.[55]

The Nelson Mandela Rules and Body of Principles are relevant to UN peace operations because, in combination with international human rights instruments such as the ICCPR and the CAT, they establish a framework for ensuring that persons deprived of their liberty have their fundamental human rights protected. The framework is particularly relevant where peacekeepers have detained civilians or where peacekeepers are responsible for law and order functions, including mentoring local law and order officials.

Peacekeepers have taken detainees in a variety of operations. The UN has, for example, taken detainees during the first UN armed operation—UNEF I.[56] UN forces have also detained persons when undertaking joint operations. In Somalia, UN peacekeepers, along with US military personnel, detained a 'total of 740 Somalis' during operations conducted by the Second United Nations Operation in Somalia (UNOSOM II).[57] The United Nations Organization Stabilization Mission in the Democratic Republic of the Congo (MONUSCO) registered over 45 arrests of individuals in Goma, Kinshasa, Lubumbashi, and Uvira in relation to protests.[58] On other operations, such as the United Nations Multidimensional Integrated Stabilization Mission in the Central African Republic (MINUSCA), the Security Council has mandated the force to 'support the restoration and maintenance of public safety and the rule of law, including through apprehending and handing over to the CAR [Central African Republic] authorities'.[59]

UN peacekeepers may also detain persons who are undergoing Disarmament, Demobilization and Reintegration (DDR) programs. For example, peacekeepers may detain a former non-State armed actor because they have been accused of committing gross human rights violations. To deal with such situations, the African Union (AU) has developed guidelines[60] to assist its peacekeepers to devise mission or operation specific detention orders. The guidelines recognise that the very act of disarming surrendering fighters will often lead to detention. The guidelines also extend to situations where AU peacekeepers are mandated to arrest or capture individuals, or transfer detainees to another detaining authority. The guidelines provide a useful framework for undertaking detention operations by UN peacekeepers.

The Nelson Mandela Rules and the Body of Principles provide peacekeepers with guidance on matters such as registering detainees,[61] allocating accommodation to detainees,[62] the inspection of detention facilities,[63] the investigation of complaints by detainees,[64] advising detainees with information on and explanation of their rights,[65] and the right to be visited by members of the detainee's family.[66] It is also expected that the Nelson Mandela Rules and Body of Principles are

---

54 See ch 8 above.

55 Convention against Torture and Other Cruel, Inhuman or Degrading Treatment or Punishment (opened for signature 10 December 1984, entered into force 26 June 1987) 1465 UNTS 85, Article 11.

56 Secretary-General, 'United Nations Emergency Force: Summary of Study of the Experience Derived from the Establishment and Operations of the Force', UN Doc A/3943 (1958) [54].

57 Further Report of the Secretary-General Submitted in Pursuance of paragraph 19 of resolution 814 (1993) and paragraph 5 of resolution 865 (1993) on the Situation in Somalia, including the 3 October 1993 Incident in Mogadishu, and Presenting Three Options for the Continuation of UNOMSOM II, UN Doc S/26738, 12 November 1993, [74].

58 Report of the Secretary-General on the United Nations Organization Stabilization Mission in the Democratic Republic of the Congo, UN Doc S/2016/233, 9 March 2016, [10].

59 SC Res 2301 (2016) of 26 July 2016, Operative Part [35](a)(iii). See also Operative Part [34](d)(i).

60 African Union Commission, African Union Disarmament, Demobilization and Reintegration Capacity Program, AU Guidelines on Detention and DDR (2014).

61 Nelson Mandela Rules (n 10), Rule 7.

62 Ibid, Rules 12–17.

63 Ibid, Rule 83.

64 Body of Principles (n 11), Principle 7.

65 Ibid, Principle 13.

66 Ibid, Principle 19.

reinforced by internal UN documents relevant to specific peace operations. For example, to ensure that those detained by UN peacekeepers are treated humanely and consistently with international human rights obligations the Department of Peacekeeping Operations (DPKO) has issued an Interim Standard Operating Procedure: Detention in United Nations Peace Operations.[67]

The Nelson Mandela Rules and Body of Principles are also useful to peacekeepers when they are mandated to undertake rule of law tasks such as assisting or supporting local authorities undertaking law reform. For example, Security Council resolution 1702 decided that, consistent with its mandate, the United Nations Stabilization Mission in Haiti (MINUSTAH):

> will provide assistance and advice to the Haitian authorities, in consultation with relevant actors, in monitoring, restructuring, reforming and strengthening of the justice sector, including through ... the rapid identification and implementation of mechanisms to address prison overcrowding and prolonged pre-trial detention and the coordination and planning of these activities ...[68]

The Nelson Mandela Rules and Body of Principles are also relevant in situations where UN peacekeepers are managing 'holding facilities' where local persons are held in detention.[69]

As such, both documents provide a realistic foundation for mentoring local authorities in further developing the capacity of national penal institutions.

In some situations, the UN has entered agreements with the host State concerning the handover of detainees by peacekeepers to the law enforcement authorities of that country. Such agreements are based on the Status of Forces Agreement (SOFA) which requires the UN to hand over detainees taken by peacekeepers.[70] The agreements might also require assurances from the host state as to how they will deal with those detainees handed to them by the UN. For example, in relation to United Nations Organization Mission in the Democratic Republic of the Congo (MONUC), the UN entered discussions with the government of the Democratic Republic of the Congo that they would not apply the death penalty to rebels that had been detained by the UN and handed over to the government. On other peace operations, such as MINUSCA, the obligation to hand over detainees to local authorities was mandated by the Security Council[71] and followed up with a detailed supplemental agreement concerning how detainees are to be handled by both the UN and by the Government of Mali.[72]

On the matter of providing documents about detainees to third-parties, the UN has stated that such 'documentation is United Nations property and forms part of the United Nations archives, and inviolable in terms of sections 3 and 4 of the Convention on the Privileges and Immunities of the United Nations',[73] and has declined to release the information to private persons.

References

Title	United Nations Standard Minimum Rules for the Treatment of Prisoners (the Nelson Mandela Rules)
Author	General Assembly
Adopted by	General Assembly
Source	GA Res 70/175 of 8 January 2016
Full Text	<http://www.un.org/en/ga/search/view_doc.asp?symbol=A/RES/70/175>[74]
Title	Body of Principles for the Protection of All Persons under Any Form of Detention or Imprisonment
Author	Working Group on the Draft Body of Principles for the Protection of All Persons under Any Form of Detention or Imprisonment

67 The Interim Standard Operating Procedures are not in the public domain. For the link to the full document, see <http://dag.un.org/handle/11176/89521?show=full> accessed 1 November 2017.

68 SC Res 1702 (2006) of 15 August 2006, Operative Part [14].

69 Report of the Secretary-General on South Sudan, S/2016/341, 13 April 2016 [41].

70 See ch 2 above.

71 See, for example, SC Res 2217 (2015), of 28 April 2015, Operative Part [33(a)(iii)].

72 Supplementary Arrangement to the Status of Forces Agreement between the United Nations and the Government of the Republic of Mali Concerning the Treatment of Individuals Detained and Handed over to the Government of Mali by the United Nations Multidimensional Integrated Stabilization Mission in Mali (MINUSA) of 1 July 2013 UNTS A-51015.

73 Inter-office memorandum to the Director of the Executive Office of the Secretary-General, concerning a request for information regarding the Organization's involvement in an exchange for detainees signed 11 January 1995, reproduced in the UN Juridical Yearbook 2015, 1.

74 Accessed 15 September 2018.

Adopted by General Assembly (without a vote)
Date of Adoption 9 December 1988
Source GA Res 43/173 of 9 December 1988, Annex
Full Text <https://www.ohchr.org/Documents/ProfessionalInterest/bodyprinciples.pdf>[75]

United Nations Standard Minimum Rules for the Treatment of Prisoners (the Nelson Mandela Rules)[76]

(Extracts)

Preliminary observation 1

The following rules are not intended to describe in detail a model system of penal institutions. They seek only, on the basis of the general consensus of contemporary thought and the essential elements of the most adequate systems of today, to set out what is generally accepted as being good principles and practice in the treatment of prisoners and prison management.

Preliminary observation 2

1. In view of the great variety of legal, social, economic and geographical conditions in the world, it is evident that not all of the rules are capable of application in all places and at all times. They should, however, serve to stimulate a constant endeavour to overcome practical difficulties in the way of their application, in the knowledge that they represent, as a whole, the minimum conditions which are accepted as suitable by the United Nations.
2. On the other hand, the rules cover a field in which thought is constantly developing. They are not intended to preclude experiment and practices, provided these are in harmony with the principles and seek to further the purposes which derive from the text of the rules as a whole. It will always be justifiable for the central prison administration to authorize departures from the rules in this spirit.

Preliminary observation 3

1. Part I of the rules covers the general management of prisons, and is applicable to all categories of prisoners, criminal or civil, untried or convicted, including prisoners subject to "security measures" or corrective measures ordered by the judge.
2. Part II contains rules applicable only to the special categories dealt with in each section. Nevertheless, the rules under section A, applicable to prisoners under sentence, shall be equally applicable to categories of prisoners dealt with in sections B, C and D, provided they do not conflict with the rules governing those categories and are for their benefit.

75 Accessed 15 September 2018.
76 United Nations Standard Minimum Rules for the Treatment of Prisoners, by General Assembly © 2016 United Nations. Reprinted with the permission of the United Nations.

Preliminary observation 4

1. The rules do not seek to regulate the management of institutions set aside for young persons such as juvenile detention facilities or correctional schools, but in general part I would be equally applicable in such institutions.
2. The category of young prisoners should include at least all young persons who come within the jurisdiction of juvenile courts. As a rule, such young persons should not be sentenced to imprisonment.

I. Rules of general application

Basic principles

Rule 1

All prisoners shall be treated with the respect due to their inherent dignity and value as human beings. No prisoner shall be subjected to, and all prisoners shall be protected from, torture and other cruel, inhuman or degrading treatment or punishment, for which no circumstances whatsoever may be invoked as a justification. The safety and security of prisoners, staff, service providers and visitors shall be ensured at all times.

Rule 2

1. The present rules shall be applied impartially. There shall be no discrimination on the grounds of race, colour, sex, language, religion, political or other opinion, national or social origin, property, birth or any other status. The religious beliefs and moral precepts of prisoners shall be respected.
2. In order for the principle of non-discrimination to be put into practice, prison administrations shall take account of the individual needs of prisoners, in particular the most vulnerable categories in prison settings. Measures to protect and promote the rights of prisoners with special needs are required and shall not be regarded as discriminatory.

Rule 3

Imprisonment and other measures that result in cutting off persons from the outside world are afflictive by the very fact of taking from these persons the right of self-determination by depriving them of their liberty. Therefore the prison system shall not, except as incidental to justifiable separation or the maintenance of discipline, aggravate the suffering inherent in such a situation.

Rule 4

1. The purposes of a sentence of imprisonment or similar measures deprivative of a person's liberty are primarily to protect society against crime and to reduce recidivism. Those purposes can be achieved only if the period of imprisonment is used to ensure, so far as possible, the reintegration of such persons into society upon release so that they can lead a law-abiding and self-supporting life.
2. To this end, prison administrations and other competent authorities should offer education, vocational training and work, as well as other forms of assistance that are appropriate and available, including those of a remedial, moral, spiritual, social and health- and sports-based nature. All such programmes, activities and services should be delivered in line with the individual treatment needs of prisoners.

Rule 5

1. The prison regime should seek to minimize any differences between prison life and life at liberty that tend to lessen the responsibility of the prisoners or the respect due to their dignity as human beings.

2. Prison administrations shall make all reasonable accommodation and adjustments to ensure that prisoners with physical, mental or other disabilities have full and effective access to prison life on an equitable basis.

Prisoner file management

Rule 6

There shall be a standardized prisoner file management system in every place where persons are imprisoned. Such a system may be an electronic database of records or a registration book with numbered and signed pages. Procedures shall be in place to ensure a secure audit trail and to prevent unauthorized access to or modification of any information contained in the system.

Rule 7

No person shall be received in a prison without a valid commitment order. The following information shall be entered in the prisoner file management system upon admission of every prisoner:

(a) Precise information enabling determination of his or her unique identity, respecting his or her self-perceived gender;
(b) The reasons for his or her commitment and the responsible authority, in addition to the date, time and place of arrest;
(c) The day and hour of his or her admission and release as well as of any transfer;
(d) Any visible injuries and complaints about prior ill-treatment;
(e) An inventory of his or her personal property;
(f) The names of his or her family members, including, where applicable, his or her children, the children's ages, location and custody or guardianship status;
(g) Emergency contact details and information on the prisoner's next of kin.

Rule 8

The following information shall be entered in the prisoner file management system in the course of imprisonment, where applicable:

(a) Information related to the judicial process, including dates of court hearings and legal representation;
(b) Initial assessment and classification reports;
(c) Information related to behaviour and discipline;
(d) Requests and complaints, including allegations of torture or other cruel, inhuman or degrading treatment or punishment, unless they are of a confidential nature;
(e) Information on the imposition of disciplinary sanctions;
(f) Information on the circumstances and causes of any injuries or death and, in the case of the latter, the destination of the remains.

Rule 9

All records referred to in rules 7 and 8 shall be kept confidential and made available only to those whose professional responsibilities require access to such records. Every prisoner shall be granted access to the records pertaining to him or her, subject to redactions authorized under domestic legislation, and shall be entitled to receive an official copy of such records upon his or her release.

Rule 10

Prisoner file management systems shall also be used to generate reliable data about trends relating to and characteristics of the prison population, including occupancy rates, in order to create a basis for evidence-based decision-making.

Separation of categories

Rule 11

The different categories of prisoners shall be kept in separate institutions or parts of institutions, taking account of their sex, age, criminal record, the legal reason for their detention and the necessities of their treatment; thus:

(a) Men and women shall so far as possible be detained in separate institutions; in an institution which receives both men and women, the whole of the premises allocated to women shall be entirely separate;

(b) Untried prisoners shall be kept separate from convicted prisoners;

(c) Persons imprisoned for debt and other civil prisoners shall be kept separate from persons imprisoned by reason of a criminal offence;

(d) Young prisoners shall be kept separate from adults.

Accommodation

Rule 12

1. Where sleeping accommodation is in individual cells or rooms, each prisoner shall occupy by night a cell or room by himself or herself. If for special reasons, such as temporary overcrowding, it becomes necessary for the central prison administration to make an exception to this rule, it is not desirable to have two prisoners in a cell or room.
2. Where dormitories are used, they shall be occupied by prisoners carefully selected as being suitable to associate with one another in those conditions. There shall be regular supervision by night, in keeping with the nature of the prison.

Rule 13

All accommodation provided for the use of prisoners and in particular all sleeping accommodation shall meet all requirements of health, due regard being paid to climatic conditions and particularly to cubic content of air, minimum floor space, lighting, heating and ventilation.

Rule 14

In all places where prisoners are required to live or work:

(a) The windows shall be large enough to enable the prisoners to read or work by natural light and shall be so constructed that they can allow the entrance of fresh air whether or not there is artificial ventilation;

(b) Artificial light shall be provided sufficient for the prisoners to read or work without injury to eyesight.

Rule 15

The sanitary installations shall be adequate to enable every prisoner to comply with the needs of nature when necessary and in a clean and decent manner.

Rule 16

Adequate bathing and shower installations shall be provided so that every prisoner can, and may be required to, have a bath or shower, at a temperature suitable to the climate, as frequently as necessary for general hygiene according to season and geographical region, but at least once a week in a temperate climate.

Rule 17

All parts of a prison regularly used by prisoners shall be properly maintained and kept scrupulously clean at all times.

Personal hygiene

Rule 18

1. Prisoners shall be required to keep their persons clean, and to this end they shall be provided with water and with such toilet articles as are necessary for health and cleanliness.

2. In order that prisoners may maintain a good appearance compatible with their self-respect, facilities shall be provided for the proper care of the hair and beard, and men shall be able to shave regularly.

Clothing and bedding

Rule 19

1. Every prisoner who is not allowed to wear his or her own clothing shall be provided with an outfit of clothing suitable for the climate and adequate to keep him or her in good health. Such clothing shall in no manner be degrading or humiliating.
2. All clothing shall be clean and kept in proper condition. Underclothing shall be changed and washed as often as necessary for the maintenance of hygiene.
3. In exceptional circumstances, whenever a prisoner is removed outside the prison for an authorized purpose, he or she shall be allowed to wear his or her own clothing or other inconspicuous clothing.

Rule 20

If prisoners are allowed to wear their own clothing, arrangements shall be made on their admission to the prison to ensure that it shall be clean and fit for use.

Rule 21

Every prisoner shall, in accordance with local or national standards, be provided with a separate bed and with separate and sufficient bedding which shall be clean when issued, kept in good order and changed often enough to ensure its cleanliness.

Food

Rule 22

1. Every prisoner shall be provided by the prison administration at the usual hours with food of nutritional value adequate for health and strength, of wholesome quality and well prepared and served.
2. Drinking water shall be available to every prisoner whenever he or she needs it.

Exercise and sport

Rule 23

1. Every prisoner who is not employed in outdoor work shall have at least one hour of suitable exercise in the open air daily if the weather permits.
2. Young prisoners, and others of suitable age and physique, shall receive physical and recreational training during the period of exercise. To this end, space, installations and equipment should be provided.

Health-care services

Rule 24

1. The provision of health care for prisoners is a State responsibility. Prisoners should enjoy the same standards of health care that are available in the community, and should have access to necessary health-care services free of charge without discrimination on the grounds of their legal status.
2. Health-care services should be organized in close relationship to the general public health administration and in a way that ensures continuity of treatment and care, including for HIV, tuberculosis and other infectious diseases, as well as for drug dependence.

Rule 25

1. Every prison shall have in place a health-care service tasked with evaluating, promoting, protecting and improving the physical and mental health of prisoners, paying particular

attention to prisoners with special health-care needs or with health issues that hamper their rehabilitation.

2. The health-care service shall consist of an interdisciplinary team with sufficient qualified personnel acting in full clinical independence and shall encompass sufficient expertise in psychology and psychiatry. The services of a qualified dentist shall be available to every prisoner.

Rule 26

1. The health-care service shall prepare and maintain accurate, up-to-date and confidential individual medical files on all prisoners, and all prisoners should be granted access to their files upon request. A prisoner may appoint a third party to access his or her medical file.
2. Medical files shall be transferred to the health-care service of the receiving institution upon transfer of a prisoner and shall be subject to medical confidentiality.

Rule 27

1. All prisons shall ensure prompt access to medical attention in urgent cases. Prisoners who require specialized treatment or surgery shall be transferred to specialized institutions or to civil hospitals. Where a prison service has its own hospital facilities, they shall be adequately staffed and equipped to provide prisoners referred to them with appropriate treatment and care.
2. Clinical decisions may only be taken by the responsible health-care professionals and may not be overruled or ignored by non-medical prison staff.

Rule 28

In women's prisons, there shall be special accommodation for all necessary prenatal and postnatal care and treatment. Arrangements shall be made wherever practicable for children to be born in a hospital outside the prison. If a child is born in prison, this fact shall not be mentioned in the birth certificate.

Rule 29

1. A decision to allow a child to stay with his or her parent in prison shall be based on the best interests of the child concerned. Where children are allowed to remain in prison with a parent, provision shall be made for:
   (a) Internal or external childcare facilities staffed by qualified persons, where the children shall be placed when they are not in the care of their parent;
   (b) Child-specific health-care services, including health screenings upon admission and ongoing monitoring of their development by specialists.
2. Children in prison with a parent shall never be treated as prisoners.

Rule 30

A physician or other qualified health-care professionals, whether or not they are required to report to the physician, shall see, talk with and examine every prisoner as soon as possible following his or her admission and thereafter as necessary. Particular attention shall be paid to:

(a) Identifying health-care needs and taking all necessary measures for treatment;

(b) Identifying any ill-treatment that arriving prisoners may have been subjected to prior to admission;

(c) Identifying any signs of psychological or other stress brought on by the fact of imprisonment, including, but not limited to, the risk of suicide or self-harm and withdrawal symptoms resulting from the use of drugs, medication or alcohol; and undertaking all appropriate individualized measures or treatment;

(d) In cases where prisoners are suspected of having contagious diseases, providing for the clinical isolation and adequate treatment of those prisoners during the infectious period;

(e) Determining the fitness of prisoners to work, to exercise and to participate in other activities, as appropriate.

Rule 31

The physician or, where applicable, other qualified health-care professionals shall have daily access to all sick prisoners, all prisoners who complain of physical or mental health issues or injury and any prisoner to whom their attention is specially directed. All medical examinations shall be undertaken in full confidentiality.

Rule 32

1. The relationship between the physician or other health-care professionals and the prisoners shall be governed by the same ethical and professional standards as those applicable to patients in the community, in particular:
   (a) The duty of protecting prisoners' physical and mental health and the prevention and treatment of disease on the basis of clinical grounds only;
   (b) Adherence to prisoners' autonomy with regard to their own health and informed consent in the doctor-patient relationship;
   (c) The confidentiality of medical information, unless maintaining such confidentiality would result in a real and imminent threat to the patient or to others;
   (d) An absolute prohibition on engaging, actively or passively, in acts that may constitute torture or other cruel, inhuman or degrading treatment or punishment, including medical or scientific experimentation that may be detrimental to a prisoner's health, such as the removal of a prisoner's cells, body tissues or organs.
2. Without prejudice to paragraph 1 (d) of this rule, prisoners may be allowed, upon their free and informed consent and in accordance with applicable law, to participate in clinical trials and other health research accessible in the community if these are expected to produce a direct and significant benefit to their health, and to donate cells, body tissues or organs to a relative.

Rule 33

The physician shall report to the prison director whenever he or she considers that a prisoner's physical or mental health has been or will be injuriously affected by continued imprisonment or by any condition of imprisonment.

Rule 34

If, in the course of examining a prisoner upon admission or providing medical care to the prisoner thereafter, health-care professionals become aware of any signs of torture or other cruel, inhuman or degrading treatment or punishment, they shall document and report such cases to the competent medical, administrative or judicial authority. Proper procedural safeguards shall be followed in order not to expose the prisoner or associated persons to foreseeable risk of harm.

Rule 35

1. The physician or competent public health body shall regularly inspect and advise the prison director on:
   (a) The quantity, quality, preparation and service of food;
   (b) The hygiene and cleanliness of the institution and the prisoners;
   (c) The sanitation, temperature, lighting and ventilation of the prison;
   (d) The suitability and cleanliness of the prisoners' clothing and bedding;
   (e) The observance of the rules concerning physical education and sports, in cases where there is no technical personnel in charge of these activities.
2. The prison director shall take into consideration the advice and reports provided in accordance with paragraph 1 of this rule and rule 33 and shall take immediate steps to give effect to the advice and the recommendations in the reports. If the advice or recommendations do not fall within the prison director's competence or if he or she does not concur with them, the director shall immediately submit to a higher authority his or her own report and the advice or recommendations of the physician or competent public health body.

Restrictions, discipline and sanctions

Rule 36

Discipline and order shall be maintained with no more restriction than is necessary to ensure safe custody, the secure operation of the prison and a well ordered community life.

Rule 37

The following shall always be subject to authorization by law or by the regulation of the competent administrative authority:

(a) Conduct constituting a disciplinary offence;

(b) The types and duration of sanctions that may be imposed;

(c) The authority competent to impose such sanctions;

(d) Any form of involuntary separation from the general prison population, such as solitary confinement, isolation, segregation, special care units or restricted housing, whether as a disciplinary sanction or for the maintenance of order and security, including promulgating policies and procedures governing the use and review of, admission to and release from any form of involuntary separation.

Rule 38

1. Prison administrations are encouraged to use, to the extent possible, conflict prevention, mediation or any other alternative dispute resolution mechanism to prevent disciplinary offences or to resolve conflicts.
2. For prisoners who are, or have been, separated, the prison administration shall take the necessary measures to alleviate the potential detrimental effects of their confinement on them and on their community following their release from prison.

Rule 39

1. No prisoner shall be sanctioned except in accordance with the terms of the law or regulation referred to in rule 37 and the principles of fairness and due process. A prisoner shall never be sanctioned twice for the same act or offence.
2. Prison administrations shall ensure proportionality between a disciplinary sanction and the offence for which it is established, and shall keep a proper record of all disciplinary sanctions imposed.
3. Before imposing disciplinary sanctions, prison administrations shall consider whether and how a prisoner's mental illness or developmental disability may have contributed to his or her conduct and the commission of the offence or act underlying the disciplinary charge. Prison administrations shall not sanction any conduct of a prisoner that is considered to be the direct result of his or her mental illness or intellectual disability.

Rule 40

1. No prisoner shall be employed, in the service of the prison, in any disciplinary capacity.
2. This rule shall not, however, impede the proper functioning of systems based on self-government, under which specified social, educational or sports activities or responsibilities are entrusted, under supervision, to prisoners who are formed into groups for the purposes of treatment.

Rule 41

1. Any allegation of a disciplinary offence by a prisoner shall be reported promptly to the competent authority, which shall investigate it without undue delay.
2. Prisoners shall be informed, without delay and in a language that they understand, of the nature of the accusations against them and shall be given adequate time and facilities for the preparation of their defence.
3. Prisoners shall be allowed to defend themselves in person, or through legal assistance when the interests of justice so require, particularly in cases involving serious disciplinary charges.

If the prisoners do not understand or speak the language used at a disciplinary hearing, they shall be assisted by a competent interpreter free of charge.

4. Prisoners shall have an opportunity to seek judicial review of disciplinary sanctions imposed against them.
5. In the event that a breach of discipline is prosecuted as a crime, prisoners shall be entitled to all due process guarantees applicable to criminal proceedings, including unimpeded access to a legal adviser.

Rule 42

General living conditions addressed in these rules, including those related to light, ventilation, temperature, sanitation, nutrition, drinking water, access to open air and physical exercise, personal hygiene, health care and adequate personal space, shall apply to all prisoners without exception.

Rule 43

1. In no circumstances may restrictions or disciplinary sanctions amount to torture or other cruel, inhuman or degrading treatment or punishment. The following practices, in particular, shall be prohibited:
   (a) Indefinite solitary confinement;
   (b) Prolonged solitary confinement;
   (c) Placement of a prisoner in a dark or constantly lit cell;
   (d) Corporal punishment or the reduction of a prisoner's diet or drinking water;
   (e) Collective punishment.
2. Instruments of restraint shall never be applied as a sanction for disciplinary offences.
3. Disciplinary sanctions or restrictive measures shall not include the prohibition of family contact. The means of family contact may only be restricted for a limited time period and as strictly required for the maintenance of security and order.

Rule 44

For the purpose of these rules, solitary confinement shall refer to the confinement of prisoners for 22 hours or more a day without meaningful human contact. Prolonged solitary confinement shall refer to solitary confinement for a time period in excess of 15 consecutive days.

Rule 45

1. Solitary confinement shall be used only in exceptional cases as a last resort, for as short a time as possible and subject to independent review, and only pursuant to the authorization by a competent authority. It shall not be imposed by virtue of a prisoner's sentence.
2. The imposition of solitary confinement should be prohibited in the case of prisoners with mental or physical disabilities when their conditions would be exacerbated by such measures. The prohibition of the use of solitary confinement and similar measures in cases involving women and children, as referred to in other United Nations standards and norms in crime prevention and criminal justice,[77] continues to apply.

Rule 46

1. Health-care personnel shall not have any role in the imposition of disciplinary sanctions or other restrictive measures. They shall, however, pay particular attention to the health of prisoners held under any form of involuntary separation, including by visiting such prisoners on

---

77 The Rules include the footnote: 'See rule 67 of the United Nations Rules for the Protection of Juveniles Deprived of their Liberty (resolution 45/113, annex); and rule 22 of the United Nations Rules for the Treatment of Women Prisoners and Non-custodial Measures for Women Offenders (the Bangkok Rules) (resolution 65/229, annex).

a daily basis and providing prompt medical assistance and treatment at the request of such prisoners or prison staff.

2. Health-care personnel shall report to the prison director, without delay, any adverse effect of disciplinary sanctions or other restrictive measures on the physical or mental health of a prisoner subjected to such sanctions or measures and shall advise the director if they consider it necessary to terminate or alter them for physical or mental health reasons.
3. Health-care personnel shall have the authority to review and recommend changes to the involuntary separation of a prisoner in order to ensure that such separation does not exacerbate the medical condition or mental or physical disability of the prisoner.

Instruments of restraint

Rule 47

1. The use of chains, irons or other instruments of restraint which are inherently degrading or painful shall be prohibited.
2. Other instruments of restraint shall only be used when authorized by law and in the following circumstances:
   (a) As a precaution against escape during a transfer, provided that they are removed when the prisoner appears before a judicial or administrative authority;
   (b) By order of the prison director, if other methods of control fail, in order to prevent a prisoner from injuring himself or herself or others or from damaging property; in such instances, the director shall immediately alert the physician or other qualified health-care professionals and report to the higher administrative authority.

Rule 48

1. When the imposition of instruments of restraint is authorized in accordance with paragraph 2 of rule 47, the following principles shall apply:
   (a) Instruments of restraint are to be imposed only when no lesser form of control would be effective to address the risks posed by unrestricted movement;
   (b) The method of restraint shall be the least intrusive method that is necessary and reasonably available to control the prisoner's movement, based on the level and nature of the risks posed;
   (c) Instruments of restraint shall be imposed only for the time period required, and they are to be removed as soon as possible after the risks posed by unrestricted movement are no longer present.
2. Instruments of restraint shall never be used on women during labour, during childbirth and immediately after childbirth.

Rule 49

The prison administration should seek access to, and provide training in the use of, control techniques that would obviate the need for the imposition of instruments of restraint or reduce their intrusiveness.

Searches of prisoners and cells

Rule 50

The laws and regulations governing searches of prisoners and cells shall be in accordance with obligations under international law and shall take into account international standards and norms, keeping in mind the need to ensure security in the prison. Searches shall be conducted in a manner that is respectful of the inherent human dignity and privacy of the individual being searched, as well as the principles of proportionality, legality and necessity.

Rule 51

Searches shall not be used to harass, intimidate or unnecessarily intrude upon a prisoner's privacy. For the purpose of accountability, the prison administration shall keep appropriate records of searches, in particular strip and body cavity searches and searches of cells, as well as the reasons for the searches, the identities of those who conducted them and any results of the searches.

Rule 52

1. Intrusive searches, including strip and body cavity searches, should be undertaken only if absolutely necessary. Prison administrations shall be encouraged to develop and use appropriate alternatives to intrusive searches. Intrusive searches shall be conducted in private and by trained staff of the same sex as the prisoner.
2. Body cavity searches shall be conducted only by qualified health-care professionals other than those primarily responsible for the care of the prisoner or, at a minimum, by staff appropriately trained by a medical professional in standards of hygiene, health and safety.

Rule 53

Prisoners shall have access to, or be allowed to keep in their possession without access by the prison administration, documents relating to their legal proceedings.

Information to and complaints by prisoners

Rule 54

Upon admission, every prisoner shall be promptly provided with written information about:

(a) The prison law and applicable prison regulations;
(b) His or her rights, including authorized methods of seeking information, access to legal advice, including through legal aid schemes, and procedures for making requests or complaints;
(c) His or her obligations, including applicable disciplinary sanctions; and
(d) All other matters necessary to enable the prisoner to adapt himself or herself to the life of the prison.

Rule 55

1. The information referred to in rule 54 shall be available in the most commonly used languages in accordance with the needs of the prison population. If a prisoner does not understand any of those languages, interpretation assistance should be provided.
2. If a prisoner is illiterate, the information shall be conveyed to him or her orally. Prisoners with sensory disabilities should be provided with information in a manner appropriate to their needs.
3. The prison administration shall prominently display summaries of the information in common areas of the prison.

Rule 56

1. Every prisoner shall have the opportunity each day to make requests or complaints to the prison director or the prison staff member authorized to represent him or her.
2. It shall be possible to make requests or complaints to the inspector of prisons during his or her inspections. The prisoner shall have the opportunity to talk to the inspector or any other inspecting officer freely and in full confidentiality, without the director or other members of the staff being present.
3. Every prisoner shall be allowed to make a request or complaint regarding his or her treatment, without censorship as to substance, to the central prison administration and to the judicial or other competent authorities, including those vested with reviewing or remedial power.
4. The rights under paragraphs 1 to 3 of this rule shall extend to the legal adviser of the prisoner. In those cases where neither the prisoner nor his or her legal adviser has the possibility of

exercising such rights, a member of the prisoner's family or any other person who has knowledge of the case may do so.

Rule 57

1. Every request or complaint shall be promptly dealt with and replied to without delay. If the request or complaint is rejected, or in the event of undue delay, the complainant shall be entitled to bring it before a judicial or other authority.
2. Safeguards shall be in place to ensure that prisoners can make requests or complaints safely and, if so requested by the complainant, in a confidential manner. A prisoner or other person mentioned in paragraph 4 of rule 56 must not be exposed to any risk of retaliation, intimidation or other negative consequences as a result of having submitted a request or complaint.
3. Allegations of torture or other cruel, inhuman or degrading treatment or punishment of prisoners shall be dealt with immediately and shall result in a prompt and impartial investigation conducted by an independent national authority in accordance with paragraphs 1 and 2 of rule 71.

Contact with the outside world

Rule 58

1. Prisoners shall be allowed, under necessary supervision, to communicate with their family and friends at regular intervals:
   (a) By corresponding in writing and using, where available, telecommunication, electronic, digital and other means; and
   (b) By receiving visits.
2. Where conjugal visits are allowed, this right shall be applied without discrimination, and women prisoners shall be able to exercise this right on an equal basis with men. Procedures shall be in place and premises shall be made available to ensure fair and equal access with due regard to safety and dignity.

Rule 59

Prisoners shall be allocated, to the extent possible, to prisons close to their homes or their places of social rehabilitation.

Rule 60

1. Admission of visitors to the prison facility is contingent upon the visitor's consent to being searched. The visitor may withdraw his or her consent at any time, in which case the prison administration may refuse access.
2. Search and entry procedures for visitors shall not be degrading and shall be governed by principles at least as protective as those outlined in rules 50 to 52. Body cavity searches should be avoided and should not be applied to children.

Rule 61

1. Prisoners shall be provided with adequate opportunity, time and facilities to be visited by and to communicate and consult with a legal adviser of their own choice or a legal aid provider, without delay, interception or censorship and in full confidentiality, on any legal matter, in conformity with applicable domestic law. Consultations may be within sight, but not within hearing, of prison staff.
2. In cases in which prisoners do not speak the local language, the prison administration shall facilitate access to the services of an independent competent interpreter.
3. Prisoners should have access to effective legal aid.

Rule 62

1. Prisoners who are foreign nationals shall be allowed reasonable facilities to communicate with the diplomatic and consular representatives of the State to which they belong.

2. Prisoners who are nationals of States without diplomatic or consular representation in the country and refugees or stateless persons shall be allowed similar facilities to communicate with the diplomatic representative of the State which takes charge of their interests or any national or international authority whose task it is to protect such persons.

Rule 63

Prisoners shall be kept informed regularly of the more important items of news by the reading of newspapers, periodicals or special institutional publications, by hearing wireless transmissions, by lectures or by any similar means as authorized or controlled by the prison administration.

Books

Rule 64

Every prison shall have a library for the use of all categories of prisoners, adequately stocked with both recreational and instructional books, and prisoners shall be encouraged to make full use of it.

Religion

Rule 65

1. If the prison contains a sufficient number of prisoners of the same religion, a qualified representative of that religion shall be appointed or approved. If the number of prisoners justifies it and conditions permit, the arrangement should be on a full-time basis.
2. A qualified representative appointed or approved under paragraph 1 of this rule shall be allowed to hold regular services and to pay pastoral visits in private to prisoners of his or her religion at proper times.
3. Access to a qualified representative of any religion shall not be refused to any prisoner. On the other hand, if any prisoner should object to a visit of any religious representative, his or her attitude shall be fully respected.

Rule 66

So far as practicable, every prisoner shall be allowed to satisfy the needs of his or her religious life by attending the services provided in the prison and having in his or her possession the books of religious observance and instruction of his or her denomination.

Retention of prisoners' property

Rule 67

1. All money, valuables, clothing and other effects belonging to a prisoner which he or she is not allowed to retain under the prison regulations shall on his or her admission to the prison be placed in safe custody. An inventory thereof shall be signed by the prisoner. Steps shall be taken to keep them in good condition.
2. On the release of the prisoner, all such articles and money shall be returned to him or her except in so far as he or she has been authorized to spend money or send any such property out of the prison, or it has been found necessary on hygienic grounds to destroy any article of clothing. The prisoner shall sign a receipt for the articles and money returned to him or her.
3. Any money or effects received for a prisoner from outside shall be treated in the same way.
4. If a prisoner brings in any drugs or medicine, the physician or other qualified health-care professionals shall decide what use shall be made of them.

Notifications

Rule 68

Every prisoner shall have the right, and shall be given the ability and means, to inform immediately his or her family, or any other person designated as a contact person, about his or her imprisonment, about his or her transfer to another institution and about any serious illness or injury. The sharing of prisoners' personal information shall be subject to domestic legislation.

Rule 69

In the event of a prisoner's death, the prison director shall at once inform the prisoner's next of kin or emergency contact. Individuals designated by a prisoner to receive his or her health information shall be notified by the director of the prisoner's serious illness, injury or transfer to a health institution. The explicit request of a prisoner not to have his or her spouse or nearest relative notified in the event of illness or injury shall be respected.

Rule 70

The prison administration shall inform a prisoner at once of the serious illness or death of a near relative or any significant other. Whenever circumstances allow, the prisoner should be authorized to go, either under escort or alone, to the bedside of a near relative or significant other who is critically ill, or to attend the funeral of a near relative or significant other.

Investigations

Rule 71

1. Notwithstanding the initiation of an internal investigation, the prison director shall report, without delay, any custodial death, disappearance or serious injury to a judicial or other competent authority that is independent of the prison administration and mandated to conduct prompt, impartial and effective investigations into the circumstances and causes of such cases. The prison administration shall fully cooperate with that authority and ensure that all evidence is preserved.
2. The obligation in paragraph 1 of this rule shall equally apply whenever there are reasonable grounds to believe that an act of torture or other cruel, inhuman or degrading treatment or punishment has been committed in prison, irrespective of whether a formal complaint has been received.
3. Whenever there are reasonable grounds to believe that an act referred to in paragraph 2 of this rule has been committed, steps shall be taken immediately to ensure that all potentially implicated persons have no involvement in the investigation and no contact with the witnesses, the victim or the victim's family.

Rule 72

The prison administration shall treat the body of a deceased prisoner with respect and dignity. The body of a deceased prisoner should be returned to his or her next of kin as soon as reasonably possible, at the latest upon completion of the investigation. The prison administration shall facilitate a culturally appropriate funeral if there is no other responsible party willing or able to do so and shall keep a full record of the matter.

Removal of prisoners

Rule 73

1. When prisoners are being removed to or from an institution, they shall be exposed to public view as little as possible, and proper safeguards shall be adopted to protect them from insult, curiosity and publicity in any form.
2. The transport of prisoners in conveyances with inadequate ventilation or light, or in any way which would subject them to unnecessary physical hardship, shall be prohibited.
3. The transport of prisoners shall be carried out at the expense of the prison administration and equal conditions shall apply to all of them.

Institutional personnel

Rule 74

1. The prison administration shall provide for the careful selection of every grade of the personnel, since it is on their integrity, humanity, professional capacity and personal suitability for the work that the proper administration of prisons depends.

2. The prison administration shall constantly seek to awaken and maintain in the minds both of the personnel and of the public the conviction that this work is a social service of great importance, and to this end all appropriate means of informing the public should be used.
3. To secure the foregoing ends, personnel shall be appointed on a full-time basis as professional prison staff and have civil service status with security of tenure subject only to good conduct, efficiency and physical fitness. Salaries shall be adequate to attract and retain suitable men and women; employment benefits and conditions of service shall be favourable in view of the exacting nature of the work.

Rule 75

1. All prison staff shall possess an adequate standard of education and shall be given the ability and means to carry out their duties in a professional manner.
2. Before entering on duty, all prison staff shall be provided with training tailored to their general and specific duties, which shall be reflective of contemporary evidence-based best practice in penal sciences. Only those candidates who successfully pass the theoretical and practical tests at the end of such training shall be allowed to enter the prison service.
3. The prison administration shall ensure the continuous provision of in service training courses with a view to maintaining and improving the knowledge and professional capacity of its personnel, after entering on duty and during their career.

Rule 76

1. Training referred to in paragraph 2 of rule 75 shall include, at a minimum, training on:
   (a) Relevant national legislation, regulations and policies, as well as applicable international and regional instruments, the provisions of which must guide the work and interactions of prison staff with inmates;
   (b) Rights and duties of prison staff in the exercise of their functions, including respecting the human dignity of all prisoners and the prohibition of certain conduct, in particular torture and other cruel, inhuman or degrading treatment or punishment;
   (c) Security and safety, including the concept of dynamic security, the use of force and instruments of restraint, and the management of violent offenders, with due consideration of preventive and defusing techniques, such as negotiation and mediation;
   (d) First aid, the psychosocial needs of prisoners and the corresponding dynamics in prison settings, as well as social care and assistance, including early detection of mental health issues.
2. Prison staff who are in charge of working with certain categories of prisoners, or who are assigned other specialized functions, shall receive training that has a corresponding focus.

Rule 77

All prison staff shall at all times so conduct themselves and perform their duties as to influence the prisoners for good by their example and to command their respect.

Rule 78

1. So far as possible, prison staff shall include a sufficient number of specialists such as psychiatrists, psychologists, social workers, teachers and trade instructors.
2. The services of social workers, teachers and trade instructors shall be secured on a permanent basis, without thereby excluding part-time or voluntary workers.

Rule 79

1. The prison director should be adequately qualified for his or her task by character, administrative ability, suitable training and experience.
2. The prison director shall devote his or her entire working time to official duties and shall not be appointed on a part-time basis. He or she shall reside on the premises of the prison or in its immediate vicinity.

3. When two or more prisons are under the authority of one director, he or she shall visit each of them at frequent intervals. A responsible resident official shall be in charge of each of these prisons.

Rule 80

1. The prison director, his or her deputy, and the majority of other prison staff shall be able to speak the language of the greatest number of prisoners, or a language understood by the greatest number of them.
2. Whenever necessary, the services of a competent interpreter shall be used.

Rule 81

1. In a prison for both men and women, the part of the prison set aside for women shall be under the authority of a responsible woman staff member who shall have the custody of the keys of all that part of the prison.
2. No male staff member shall enter the part of the prison set aside for women unless accompanied by a woman staff member.
3. Women prisoners shall be attended and supervised only by women staff members. This does not, however, preclude male staff members, particularly doctors and teachers, from carrying out their professional duties in prisons or parts of prisons set aside for women.

Rule 82

1. Prison staff shall not, in their relations with the prisoners, use force except in self-defence or in cases of attempted escape, or active or passive physical resistance to an order based on law or regulations. Prison staff who have recourse to force must use no more than is strictly necessary and must report the incident immediately to the prison director.
2. Prison staff shall be given special physical training to enable them to restrain aggressive prisoners.
3. Except in special circumstances, prison staff performing duties which bring them into direct contact with prisoners should not be armed. Furthermore, prison staff should in no circumstances be provided with arms unless they have been trained in their use.

Internal and external inspections

Rule 83

1. There shall be a twofold system for regular inspections of prisons and penal services:
   (a) Internal or administrative inspections conducted by the central prison administration;
   (b) External inspections conducted by a body independent of the prison administration, which may include competent international or regional bodies.
2. In both cases, the objective of the inspections shall be to ensure that prisons are managed in accordance with existing laws, regulations, policies and procedures, with a view to bringing about the objectives of penal and corrections services, and that the rights of prisoners are protected.

Rule 84

1. Inspectors shall have the authority:
   (a) To access all information on the numbers of prisoners and places and locations of detention, as well as all information relevant to the treatment of prisoners, including their records and conditions of detention;
   (b) To freely choose which prisons to visit, including by making unannounced visits at their own initiative, and which prisoners to interview;
   (c) To conduct private and fully confidential interviews with prisoners and prison staff in the course of their visits;

(d) To make recommendations to the prison administration and other competent authorities.

2. External inspection teams shall be composed of qualified and experienced inspectors appointed by a competent authority and shall encompass health-care professionals. Due regard shall be given to balanced gender representation.

Rule 85

1. Every inspection shall be followed by a written report to be submitted to the competent authority. Due consideration shall be given to making the reports of external inspections publicly available, excluding any personal data on prisoners unless they have given their explicit consent.
2. The prison administration or other competent authorities, as appropriate, shall indicate, within a reasonable time, whether they will implement the recommendations resulting from the external inspection.

II. Rules applicable to special categories

A. Prisoners under sentence

Guiding principles

Rule 86

The guiding principles hereafter are intended to show the spirit in which penal institutions should be administered and the purposes at which they should aim, in accordance with the declaration made under preliminary observation 1 of these rules.

Rule 87

Before the completion of the sentence, it is desirable that the necessary steps be taken to ensure for the prisoner a gradual return to life in society. This aim may be achieved, depending on the case, by a pre-release regime organized in the same prison or in another appropriate institution, or by release on trial under some kind of supervision which must not be entrusted to the police but should be combined with effective social aid.

Rule 88

1. The treatment of prisoners should emphasize not their exclusion from the community but their continuing part in it. Community agencies should therefore be enlisted wherever possible to assist the prison staff in the task of social rehabilitation of the prisoners.
2. There should be in connection with every prison social workers charged with the duty of maintaining and improving all desirable relations of a prisoner with his or her family and with valuable social agencies. Steps should be taken to safeguard, to the maximum extent compatible with the law and the sentence, the rights relating to civil interests, social security rights and other social benefits of prisoners.

Rule 89

1. The fulfilment of these principles requires individualization of treatment and for this purpose a flexible system of classifying prisoners in groups. It is therefore desirable that such groups should be distributed in separate prisons suitable for the treatment of each group.
2. These prisons do not need to provide the same degree of security for every group. It is desirable to provide varying degrees of security according to the needs of different groups. Open prisons, by the very fact that they provide no physical security against escape but rely on the self-discipline of the inmates, provide the conditions most favourable to the rehabilitation of carefully selected prisoners.
3. It is desirable that the number of prisoners in closed prisons should not be so large that the individualization of treatment is hindered. In some countries it is considered that the

population of such prisons should not exceed 500. In open prisons the population should be as small as possible.

4. On the other hand, it is undesirable to maintain prisons which are so small that proper facilities cannot be provided.

Rule 90

The duty of society does not end with a prisoner's release. There should, therefore, be governmental or private agencies capable of lending the released prisoner efficient aftercare directed towards the lessening of prejudice against him or her and towards his or her social rehabilitation.

Treatment

Rule 91

The treatment of persons sentenced to imprisonment or a similar measure shall have as its purpose, so far as the length of the sentence permits, to establish in them the will to lead law-abiding and self-supporting lives after their release and to fit them to do so. The treatment shall be such as will encourage their self-respect and develop their sense of responsibility.

Rule 92

1. To these ends, all appropriate means shall be used, including religious care in the countries where this is possible, education, vocational guidance and training, social casework, employment counselling, physical development and strengthening of moral character, in accordance with the individual needs of each prisoner, taking account of his or her social and criminal history, physical and mental capacities and aptitudes, personal temperament, the length of his or her sentence and prospects after release.
2. For every prisoner with a sentence of suitable length, the prison director shall receive, as soon as possible after his or her admission, full reports on all the matters referred to in paragraph 1 of this rule. Such reports shall always include a report by the physician or other qualified health-care professionals on the physical and mental condition of the prisoner.
3. The reports and other relevant documents shall be placed in an individual file. This file shall be kept up to date and classified in such a way that it can be consulted by the responsible personnel whenever the need arises.

Classification and individualization

Rule 93

1. The purposes of classification shall be:
   (a) To separate from others those prisoners who, by reason of their criminal records or characters, are likely to exercise a bad influence;
   (b) To divide the prisoners into classes in order to facilitate their treatment with a view to their social rehabilitation.
2. So far as possible, separate prisons or separate sections of a prison shall be used for the treatment of different classes of prisoners.

Rule 94

As soon as possible after admission and after a study of the personality of each prisoner with a sentence of suitable length, a programme of treatment shall be prepared for him or her in the light of the knowledge obtained about his or her individual needs, capacities and dispositions.

Privileges

Rule 95

Systems of privileges appropriate for the different classes of prisoners and the different methods of treatment shall be established at every prison, in order to encourage good conduct, develop a sense of responsibility and secure the interest and cooperation of prisoners in their treatment.

Work

Rule 96

1. Sentenced prisoners shall have the opportunity to work and/or to actively participate in their rehabilitation, subject to a determination of physical and mental fitness by a physician or other qualified health-care professionals.
2. Sufficient work of a useful nature shall be provided to keep prisoners actively employed for a normal working day.

Rule 97

1. Prison labour must not be of an afflictive nature.
2. Prisoners shall not be held in slavery or servitude.
3. No prisoner shall be required to work for the personal or private benefit of any prison staff.

Rule 98

1. So far as possible the work provided shall be such as will maintain or increase the prisoners' ability to earn an honest living after release.
2. Vocational training in useful trades shall be provided for prisoners able to profit thereby and especially for young prisoners.
3. Within the limits compatible with proper vocational selection and with the requirements of institutional administration and discipline, prisoners shall be able to choose the type of work they wish to perform.

Rule 99

1. The organization and methods of work in prisons shall resemble as closely as possible those of similar work outside of prisons, so as to prepare prisoners for the conditions of normal occupational life.
2. The interests of the prisoners and of their vocational training, however, must not be subordinated to the purpose of making a financial profit from an industry in the prison.

Rule 100

1. Preferably, institutional industries and farms should be operated directly by the prison administration and not by private contractors.
2. Where prisoners are employed in work not controlled by the prison administration, they shall always be under the supervision of prison staff. Unless the work is for other departments of the government, the full normal wages for such work shall be paid to the prison administration by the persons to whom the labour is supplied, account being taken of the output of the prisoners.

Rule 101

1. The precautions laid down to protect the safety and health of free workers shall be equally observed in prisons.
2. Provision shall be made to indemnify prisoners against industrial injury, including occupational disease, on terms not less favourable than those extended by law to free workers.

Rule 102

1. The maximum daily and weekly working hours of the prisoners shall be fixed by law or by administrative regulation, taking into account local rules or custom in regard to the employment of free workers.
2. The hours so fixed shall leave one rest day a week and sufficient time for education and other activities required as part of the treatment and rehabilitation of prisoners.

Rule 103

1. There shall be a system of equitable remuneration of the work of prisoners.

2. Under the system, prisoners shall be allowed to spend at least a part of their earnings on approved articles for their own use and to send a part of their earnings to their family.
3. The system should also provide that a part of the earnings should be set aside by the prison administration so as to constitute a savings fund to be handed over to the prisoner on his or her release.

Education and recreation

Rule 104

1. Provision shall be made for the further education of all prisoners capable of profiting thereby, including religious instruction in the countries where this is possible. The education of illiterate prisoners and of young prisoners shall be compulsory and special attention shall be paid to it by the prison administration.
2. So far as practicable, the education of prisoners shall be integrated with the educational system of the country so that after their release they may continue their education without difficulty.

Rule 105

Recreational and cultural activities shall be provided in all prisons for the benefit of the mental and physical health of prisoners.

Social relations and aftercare

Rule 106

Special attention shall be paid to the maintenance and improvement of such relations between a prisoner and his or her family as are desirable in the best interests of both.

Rule 107

From the beginning of a prisoner's sentence, consideration shall be given to his or her future after release and he or she shall be encouraged and provided assistance to maintain or establish such relations with persons or agencies outside the prison as may promote the prisoner's rehabilitation and the best interests of his or her family.

Rule 108

1. Services and agencies, governmental or otherwise, which assist released prisoners in re-establishing themselves in society shall ensure, so far as is possible and necessary, that released prisoners are provided with appropriate documents and identification papers, have suitable homes and work to go to, are suitably and adequately clothed having regard to the climate and season and have sufficient means to reach their destination and maintain themselves in the period immediately following their release.
2. The approved representatives of such agencies shall have all necessary access to the prison and to prisoners and shall be taken into consultation as to the future of a prisoner from the beginning of his or her sentence.
3. It is desirable that the activities of such agencies shall be centralized or coordinated as far as possible in order to secure the best use of their efforts.

B. Prisoners with mental disabilities and/or health conditions

Rule 109

1. Persons who are found to be not criminally responsible, or who are later diagnosed with severe mental disabilities and/or health conditions, for whom staying in prison would mean an exacerbation of their condition, shall not be detained in prisons, and arrangements shall be made to transfer them to mental health facilities as soon as possible.
2. If necessary, other prisoners with mental disabilities and/or health conditions can be observed and treated in specialized facilities under the supervision of qualified health-care professionals.

3. The health-care service shall provide for the psychiatric treatment of all other prisoners who are in need of such treatment.

Rule 110

It is desirable that steps should be taken, by arrangement with the appropriate agencies, to ensure if necessary the continuation of psychiatric treatment after release and the provision of social-psychiatric aftercare.

C. Prisoners under arrest or awaiting trial

Rule 111

1. Persons arrested or imprisoned by reason of a criminal charge against them, who are detained either in police custody or in prison custody (jail) but have not yet been tried and sentenced, will be referred to as "untried prisoners" hereinafter in these rules.
2. Unconvicted prisoners are presumed to be innocent and shall be treated as such.
3. Without prejudice to legal rules for the protection of individual liberty or prescribing the procedure to be observed in respect of untried prisoners, these prisoners shall benefit from a special regime which is described in the following rules in its essential requirements only.

Rule 112

1. Untried prisoners shall be kept separate from convicted prisoners.
2. Young untried prisoners shall be kept separate from adults and shall in principle be detained in separate institutions.

Rule 113

Untried prisoners shall sleep singly in separate rooms, with the reservation of different local custom in respect of the climate.

Rule 114

Within the limits compatible with the good order of the institution, untried prisoners may, if they so desire, have their food procured at their own expense from the outside, either through the administration or through their family or friends. Otherwise, the administration shall provide their food.

Rule 115

An untried prisoner shall be allowed to wear his or her own clothing if it is clean and suitable. If he or she wears prison dress, it shall be different from that supplied to convicted prisoners.

Rule 116

An untried prisoner shall always be offered the opportunity to work, but shall not be required to work. If he or she chooses to work, he or she shall be paid for it.

Rule 117

An untried prisoner shall be allowed to procure at his or her own expense or at the expense of a third party such books, newspapers, writing material and other means of occupation as are compatible with the interests of the administration of justice and the security and good order of the institution.

Rule 118

An untried prisoner shall be allowed to be visited and treated by his or her own doctor or dentist if there are reasonable grounds for the application and he or she is able to pay any expenses incurred.

Rule 119

1. Every untried prisoner has the right to be promptly informed about the reasons for his or her detention and about any charges against him or her.
2. If an untried prisoner does not have a legal adviser of his or her own choice, he or she shall be entitled to have a legal adviser assigned to him or her by a judicial or other authority in all

cases where the interests of justice so require and without payment by the untried prisoner if he or she does not have sufficient means to pay. Denial of access to a legal adviser shall be subject to independent review without delay.

Rule 120

1. The entitlements and modalities governing the access of an untried prisoner to his or her legal adviser or legal aid provider for the purpose of his or her defence shall be governed by the same principles as outlined in rule 61.
2. An untried prisoner shall, upon request, be provided with writing material for the preparation of documents related to his or her defence, including confidential instructions for his or her legal adviser or legal aid provider.

D. Civil prisoners

Rule 121

In countries where the law permits imprisonment for debt, or by order of a court under any other non-criminal process, persons so imprisoned shall not be subjected to any greater restriction or severity than is necessary to ensure safe custody and good order. Their treatment shall be not less favourable than that of untried prisoners, with the reservation, however, that they may possibly be required to work.

E. Persons arrested or detained without charge

Rule 122

Without prejudice to the provisions of article 9 of the International Covenant on Civil and Political Rights,[78] persons arrested or imprisoned without charge shall be accorded the same protection as that accorded under part I and part II, section C, of these rules. Relevant provisions of part II, section A, of these rules shall likewise be applicable where their application may be conducive to the benefit of this special group of persons in custody, provided that no measures shall be taken implying that re-education or rehabilitation is in any way appropriate to persons not convicted of any criminal offence.

Body of Principles for the Protection of All Persons under Any Form of Detention or Imprisonment[79]

Scope of the Body of Principles

These principles apply for the protection of all persons under any form of detention or imprisonment.

78 The Rules include the footnote: See resolution 2200 A (XXI), annex.

79 From Body of Principles for the Protection of All Persons Under Any Form of Denteion or Imprisonment © 1988 United Nations. Reprinted with the permission of the United Nations.

Use of Terms

For the purposes of the Body of Principles:

(a) "Arrest" means the act of apprehending a person for the alleged commission of an offence or by the action of an authority;
(b) "Detained person" means any person deprived of personal liberty except as a result of conviction for an offence;
(c) "Imprisoned person" means any person deprived of personal liberty as a result of conviction for an offence;
(d) "Detention" means the condition of detained persons as defined above;
(e) "Imprisonment" means the condition of imprisoned persons as defined above;
(f) The words "a judicial or other authority" means a judicial or other authority under the law whose status and tenure should afford the strongest possible guarantees of competence, impartiality and independence.

Principle 1

All persons under any form of detention or imprisonment shall be treated in a humane manner and with respect for the inherent dignity of the human person.

Principle 2

Arrest, detention or imprisonment shall only be carried out strictly in accordance with the provisions of the law and by competent officials or persons authorized for that purpose.

Principle 3

There shall be no restriction upon or derogation from any of the human rights of persons under any form of detention or imprisonment recognized or existing in any State pursuant to law, conventions, regulations or custom on the pretext that this Body of Principles does not recognize such rights or that it recognizes them to a lesser extent.

Principle 4

Any form of detention or imprisonment and all measures affecting the human rights of a person under any form of detention or imprisonment shall be ordered by, or be subject to the effective control of, a judicial or other authority.

Principle 5

1. These principles shall be applied to all persons within the territory of any given State, without distinction of any kind, such as race, colour, sex, language, religion or religious belief, political or other opinion, national, ethnic or social origin, property, birth or other status.
2. Measures applied under the law and designed solely to protect the rights and special status of women, especially pregnant women and nursing mothers, children and juveniles, aged, sick or handicapped persons shall not be deemed to be discriminatory. The need for, and the application of, such measures shall always be subject to review by a judicial or other authority.

Principle 6

No person under any form of detention or imprisonment shall be subjected to torture or to cruel, inhuman or degrading treatment or punishment.[80] No circumstance whatever may be invoked as a justification for torture or other cruel, inhuman or degrading treatment or punishment.

80 The term 'cruel, inhuman or degrading treatment or punishment' should be interpreted so as to extend the widest possible protection against abuses, whether physical or mental, including the holding of a detained or imprisoned person in conditions which deprive him, temporarily or permanently, of the use of any of his natural senses, such as sight or hearing, or of his awareness of place and the passing of time. [Note: this footnote appears in the original document as footnote '1'].

Principle 7

1. States should prohibit by law any act contrary to the rights and duties contained in these principles, make any such act subject to appropriate sanctions and conduct impartial investigations upon complaints.
2. Officials who have reason to believe that a violation of this Body of Principles has occurred or is about to occur shall report the matter to their superior authorities and, where necessary, to other appropriate authorities or organs vested with reviewing or remedial powers.
3. Any other person who has ground to believe that a violation of this Body of Principles has occurred or is about to occur shall have the right to report the matter to the superiors of the officials involved as well as to other appropriate authorities or organs vested with reviewing or remedial powers.

Principle 8

Persons in detention shall be subject to treatment appropriate to their unconvicted status. Accordingly, they shall, whenever possible, be kept separate from imprisoned persons.

Principle 9

The authorities which arrest a person, keep him under detention or investigate the case shall exercise only the powers granted to them under the law and the exercise of these powers shall be subject to recourse to a judicial or other authority.

Principle 10

Anyone who is arrested shall be informed at the time of his arrest of the reason for his arrest and shall be promptly informed of any charges against him.

Principle 11

1. A person shall not be kept in detention without being given an effective opportunity to be heard promptly by a judicial or other authority. A detained person shall have the right to defend himself or to be assisted by counsel as prescribed by law.
2. A detained person and his counsel, if any, shall receive prompt and full communication of any order of detention, together with the reasons therefor.
3. A judicial or other authority shall be empowered to review as appropriate the continuance of detention.

Principle 12

1. There shall be duly recorded:
    (a) The reasons for the arrest;
    (b) The time of the arrest and the taking of the arrested person to a place of custody as well as that of his first appearance before a judicial or other authority;
    (c) The identity of the law enforcement officials concerned;
    (d) Precise information concerning the place of custody.
2. Such records shall be communicated to the detained person, or his counsel, if any, in the form prescribed by law.

Principle 13

Any person shall, at the moment of arrest and at the commencement of detention or imprisonment, or promptly thereafter, be provided by the authority responsible for his arrest, detention or imprisonment, respectively with information on and an explanation of his rights and how to avail himself of such rights.

Principle 14

A person who does not adequately understand or speak the language used by the authorities responsible for his arrest, detention or imprisonment is entitled to receive promptly in a language which he understands the information referred to in principle 10, principle 11, paragraph 2, principle 12, paragraph 1, and principle 13 and to have the assistance, free of charge, if necessary, of an interpreter in connection with legal proceedings subsequent to his arrest.

Principle 15

Notwithstanding the exceptions contained in principle 16, paragraph 4, and principle 18, paragraph 3, communication of the detained or imprisoned person with the outside world, and in particular his family or counsel, shall not be denied for more than a matter of days.

Principle 16

1. Promptly after arrest and after each transfer from one place of detention or imprisonment to another, a detained or imprisoned person shall be entitled to notify or to require the competent authority to notify members of his family or other appropriate persons of his choice of his arrest, detention or imprisonment or of the transfer and of the place where he is kept in custody.
2. If a detained or imprisoned person is a foreigner, he shall also be promptly informed of his right to communicate by appropriate means with a consular post or the diplomatic mission of the State of which he is a national or which is otherwise entitled to receive such communication in accordance with international law or with the representative of the competent international organization, if he is a refugee or is otherwise under the protection of an intergovernmental organization.
3. If a detained or imprisoned person is a juvenile or is incapable of understanding his entitlement, the competent authority shall on its own initiative undertake the notification referred to in the present principle. Special attention shall be given to notifying parents or guardians.
4. Any notification referred to in the present principle shall be made or permitted to be made without delay. The competent authority may however delay a notification for a reasonable period where exceptional needs of the investigation so require.

Principle 17

1. A detained person shall be entitled to have the assistance of a legal counsel. He shall be informed of his right by the competent authority promptly after arrest and shall be provided with reasonable facilities for exercising it.
2. If a detained person does not have a legal counsel of his own choice, he shall be entitled to have a legal counsel assigned to him by a judicial or other authority in all cases where the interests of justice so require and without payment by him if he does not have sufficient means to pay.

Principle 18

1. A detained or imprisoned person shall be entitled to communicate and consult with his legal counsel.
2. A detained or imprisoned person shall be allowed adequate time and facilities for consultation with his legal counsel.
3. The right of a detained or imprisoned person to be visited by and to consult and communicate, without delay or censorship and in full confidentiality, with his legal counsel may not be suspended or restricted save in exceptional circumstances, to be specified by law or lawful regulations, when it is considered indispensable by a judicial or other authority in order to maintain security and good order.

4. Interviews between a detained or imprisoned person and his legal counsel may be within sight, but not within the hearing, of a law enforcement official.
5. Communications between a detained or imprisoned person and his legal counsel mentioned in the present principle shall be inadmissible as evidence against the detained or imprisoned person unless they are connected with a continuing or contemplated crime.

Principle 19

A detained or imprisoned person shall have the right to be visited by and to correspond with, in particular, members of his family and shall be given adequate opportunity to communicate with the outside world, subject to reasonable conditions and restrictions as specified by law or lawful regulations.

Principle 20

If a detained or imprisoned person so requests, he shall if possible be kept in a place of detention or imprisonment reasonably near his usual place of residence.

Principle 21

1. It shall be prohibited to take undue advantage of the situation of a detained or imprisoned person for the purpose of compelling him to confess, to incriminate himself otherwise or to testify against any other person.
2. No detained person while being interrogated shall be subject to violence, threats or methods of interrogation which impair his capacity of decision or his judgement.

Principle 22

No detained or imprisoned person shall, even with his consent, be subjected to any medical or scientific experimentation which may be detrimental to his health.

Principle 23

1. The duration of any interrogation of a detained or imprisoned person and of the intervals between interrogations as well as the identity of the officials who conducted the interrogations and other persons present shall be recorded and certified in such form as may be prescribed by law.
2. A detained or imprisoned person, or his counsel when provided by law, shall have access to the information described in paragraph 1 of the present principle.

Principle 24

A proper medical examination shall be offered to a detained or imprisoned person as promptly as possible after his admission to the place of detention or imprisonment, and thereafter medical care and treatment shall be provided whenever necessary. This care and treatment shall be provided free of charge.

Principle 25

A detained or imprisoned person or his counsel shall, subject only to reasonable conditions to ensure security and good order in the place of detention or imprisonment, have the right to request or petition a judicial or other authority for a second medical examination or opinion.

Principle 26

The fact that a detained or imprisoned person underwent a medical examination, the name of the physician and the results of such an examination shall be duly recorded. Access to such records shall be ensured. Modalities therefore shall be in accordance with relevant rules of domestic law.

Principle 27

Non-compliance with these principles in obtaining evidence shall be taken into account in determining the admissibility of such evidence against a detained or imprisoned person.

Principle 28

A detained or imprisoned person shall have the right to obtain within the limits of available resources, if from public sources, reasonable quantities of educational, cultural and informational material, subject to reasonable conditions to ensure security and good order in the place of detention or imprisonment.

Principle 29

1. In order to supervise the strict observance of relevant laws and regulations, places of detention shall be visited regularly by qualified and experienced persons appointed by, and responsible to, a competent authority distinct from the authority directly in charge of the administration of the place of detention or imprisonment.
2. A detained or imprisoned person shall have the right to communicate freely and in full confidentiality with the persons who visit the places of detention or imprisonment in accordance with paragraph 1 of the present principle, subject to reasonable conditions to ensure security and good order in such places.

Principle 30

1. The types of conduct of the detained or imprisoned person that constitute disciplinary offences during detention or imprisonment, the description and duration of disciplinary punishment that may be inflicted and the authorities competent to impose such punishment shall be specified by law or lawful regulations and duly published.
2. A detained or imprisoned person shall have the right to be heard before disciplinary action is taken. He shall have the right to bring such action to higher authorities for review.

Principle 31

The appropriate authorities shall endeavour to ensure, according to domestic law, assistance when needed to dependent and, in particular, minor members of the families of detained or imprisoned persons and shall devote a particular measure of care to the appropriate custody of children left with out supervision.

Principle 32

1. A detained person or his counsel shall be entitled at any time to take proceedings according to domestic law before a judicial or other authority to challenge the lawfulness of his detention in order to obtain his release without delay, if it is unlawful.
2. The proceedings referred to in paragraph 1 of the present principle shall be simple and expeditious and at no cost for detained persons without adequate means. The detaining authority shall produce without unreasonable delay the detained person before the reviewing authority.

Principle 33

1. A detained or imprisoned person or his counsel shall have the right to make a request or complaint regarding his treatment, in particular in case of torture or other cruel, inhuman or degrading treatment, to the authorities responsible for the administration of the place of detention and to higher authorities and, when necessary, to appropriate authorities vested with reviewing or remedial powers.
2. In those cases where neither the detained or imprisoned person nor his counsel has the possibility to exercise his rights under paragraph 1 of the present principle, a member of the family of the detained or imprisoned person or any other person who has knowledge of the case may exercise such rights.
3. Confidentiality concerning the request or complaint shall be maintained if so requested by the complainant.
4. Every request or complaint shall be promptly dealt with and replied to without undue delay. If the request or complaint is rejected or, in case of inordinate delay, the complainant shall be

entitled to bring it before a judicial or other authority. Neither the detained or imprisoned person nor any complainant under paragraph 1 of the present principle shall suffer prejudice for making a request or complaint.

Principle 34

Whenever the death or disappearance of a detained or imprisoned person occurs during his detention or imprisonment, an inquiry into the cause of death or disappearance shall be held by a judicial or other authority, either on its own motion or at the instance of a member of the family of such a person or any person who has knowledge of the case. When circumstances so warrant, such an inquiry shall be held on the same procedural basis whenever the death or disappearance occurs shortly after the termination of the detention or imprisonment. The findings of such inquiry or a report thereon shall be made available upon request, unless doing so would jeopardize an ongoing criminal investigation.

Principle 35

1. Damage incurred because of acts or omissions by a public official contrary to the rights contained in these principles shall be compensated according to the applicable rules or liability provided by domestic law.
2. Information required to be recorded under these principles shall be available in accordance with procedures provided by domestic law for use in claiming compensation under the present principle.

Principle 36

1. A detained person suspected of or charged with a criminal offence shall be presumed innocent and shall be treated as such until proved guilty according to law in a public trial at which he has had all the guarantees necessary for his defence.
2. The arrest or detention of such a person pending investigation and trial shall be carried out only for the purposes of the administration of justice on grounds and under conditions and procedures specified by law. The imposition of restrictions upon such a person which are not strictly required for the purpose of the detention or to prevent hindrance to the process of investigation or the administration of justice, or for the maintenance of security and good order in the place of detention shall be forbidden.

Principle 37

A person detained on a criminal charge shall be brought before a judicial or other authority provided by law promptly after his arrest. Such authority shall decide without delay upon the lawfulness and necessity of detention. No person may be kept under detention pending investigation or trial except upon the written order of such an authority. A detained person shall, when brought before such an authority, have the right to make a statement on the treatment received by him while in custody.

Principle 38

A person detained on a criminal charge shall be entitled to trial within a reasonable time or to release pending trial.

Principle 39

Except in special cases provided for by law, a person detained on a criminal charge shall be entitled, unless a judicial or other authority decides otherwise in the interest of the administration of justice, to release pending trial subject to the conditions that may be imposed in accordance with the law. Such authority shall keep the necessity of detention under review.

General clause

Nothing in this Body of Principles shall be construed as restricting or derogating from any right defined in the International Covenant on Civil and Political Rights.

13

Public Safety and the Use of Force

Prefatory Note

In contemporary UN peace operations UN civilian police officers and formed police units (FPUs) are often mandated to assist local authorities to maintain public safety and the rule of law. It is only by exception, such as during the United Nations Transitional Administration in East Timor (UNTAET),[1] that UN civilian police and FPUs have been mandated with executive law enforcement functions and tasks. Unless UN police and FPUs have been mandated with executive powers they do not have the authority to exercise powers such as arrest or to enforce local laws. Those authorities remain with the host State law enforcement authorities.

Human rights instruments, such as the International Covenant on Civil and Political Rights (ICCPR),[2] the Convention against Torture and Other Cruel, Inhuman or Degrading Treatment or Punishment (CAT),[3] and the International Convention for the Protection of All Persons from Enforced Disappearance,[4] affect the powers, duties, and obligations of those involved in law enforcement during peace operations. They do so by stipulating principles, rules, and standards concerning arbitrary detention, treatment of persons in custody, and record keeping to ensure accountability and transparency. There are also two key non-binding instruments that are directed to law enforcement officials which reaffirm fundamental principles, rules, and standards that officials should abide by. Those instruments are the Code of Conduct for Law Enforcement Officials (Code of Conduct)[5] and Basic Principles on the Use of Force and Firearms by Law Enforcement Officials (Basic Principles),[6] and are founded on key human rights instruments such as the ICCPR. The UN also has several policy documents that are relevant to law enforcement in peace operations, such as United Nations Police in Peacekeeping Operations and Special Political Missions (Policing Policy),[7] the Formed Police Units in United Nations Peacekeeping Operations (FPU Policy),[8] and the Directive on the Use of Force (DUF),[9] that apply to its police peacekeepers. Both the Policing Policy and the FPU Policy reinforce that the Code of Conduct and the Basic Principles are foundation documents in relation to UN police or FPUs using force or firearms.[10]

In relation to UN military peacekeepers, their obligations and rights when undertaking security and public order tasks such as detention are stipulated in rules of engagement (ROE), the Soldiers Pocket Card or standard operating procedures.[11]

This chapter reprints extracts from two documents which are directly relevant to UN police of FPUs assisting local authorities to maintain public safety and the rule of law, undertaking law enforcement tasks, or where the use of force by military forces is contemplated to maintain security and public order. Those documents are the Code of Conduct and the Basic Principles.

---

1 See SC Res 1272 (1999) of 25 October 1999.

2 See ch 6 above.

3 See ch 8 above.

4 See ch 10 above.

5 Code of Conduct for Law Enforcement Officials, GA Res 34/169 of 17 December 1979, Annex (hereafter Code of Conduct).

6 Basic Principles on the Use of Force and Firearms by Law Enforcement Officials (adopted by the Eighth United Nations Congress on the Prevention of Crime and the Treatment of Offenders 27 August–7 September 1990, welcomed by GA Res 45/121 of 18 December 1990) (hereafter Basic Principles).

7 Department of Peacekeeping Operations and Department of Field Support, 'Policy: United Nations Police in Peacekeeping Operations and Special Political Missions', 1 February 2014 <https://police.un.org/sites/default/files/sgf-policy-police-2014.pdf> accessed 26 March 2019 (hereafter Policing Policy).

8 Department of Peacekeeping Operations and Department of Field Support, 'Policy (revised): Formed Police Units in United Nations Peacekeeping Operations', 1 January 2017 <https://police.un.org/sites/default/files/fpu_policy_2016.pdf> accessed 26 March 2019 (hereafter FPU Policy).

9 The Directive on the Use of Force is not available in the public domain.

10 Policing Policy (n 7), [106]; FPU Policy (n 8), [67].

11 See ch 33 below.

1. Code of Conduct for Law Enforcement Officials

On 17 December 1979, the General Assembly adopted the Code of Conduct in resolution 34/169. The Code was disseminated to governments with the recommendation that 'favourable consideration should be given to its use within the framework of national legislation or practice as a body of principles for observance by law enforcement officials'.[12] Containing eight articles, with commentary relating to its application, the Code of Conduct aims to create and reinforce the obligations of law enforcement officials to respect and protect human dignity, and provides mechanisms for accountability.

The Code of Conduct is focused on law enforcement officials working within the jurisdiction of their own State. The term 'law enforcement officials' is widely defined in Article 1 and includes all officers of the law, military authorities and State security forces exercising police powers, especially the powers of arrest or detention.

Article 3 of the Code of Conduct limits the use of force by law enforcement officials to when it is 'strictly necessary and to the extent required for the performance of their duty'. This concept of 'necessary force' is clarified in the commentaries as 'exceptional',[13] and to be understood in accordance with 'national principles of proportionality'.[14] The Code of Conduct is specific in relation to weapons and states that the 'use of firearms is considered an extreme measure'.[15]

Article 4 deals with issues of confidentiality and should be understood in the context of the fundamental rights of those detained during peace operations, particularly in relation to information obtained from those in custody. Article 7 provides useful guidance to peacekeepers who are responsible for mentoring national law and order personnel. Article 8 is a useful benchmark as it emphasises the need for law enforcement officials to respect the Code of Conduct and to prevent or oppose violations of it. This article also deals with the creation of review procedures and requires law enforcement officials who believe violations of the Code have occurred or may occur to report such matters to superior authorities or organs vested with reviewing and remedial powers. As the commentary states:

> The article seeks to preserve the balance between the need for internal discipline of the agency on which public safety is largely dependent, on the one hand, and the need for dealing with violations of basic human rights, on the other.[16]

2. Basic Principles on the Use of Force and Firearms by Law Enforcement Officials

On 18 December 1990, the General Assembly welcomed the Basic Principles in resolution 45/166.[17] The Basic Principles were originally developed by an Interregional Preparatory Meeting for the Eighth United Nations Congress on the Prevention of Crime and the Treatment of Offenders (Eighth Congress), the Committee on Crime Prevention and Control, and the International Expert Meeting on United Nations and Law Enforcement. The Basic Principles were later adopted by the Eighth Congress in 1990.[18]

The Basic Principles build upon Article 3 of the Code of Conduct, and provide further detail on the use of force and firearms by law enforcement officials. The Basic Principles, like the Code of Conduct, are an integral part of the overall framework guiding personnel engaged in UN peace operations.[19] They were formulated to assist Member States to ensure and promote the duties imposed on law enforcement officials.

---

12 GA Res 34/169 of 17 December 1979, Preamble [9].

13 Code of Conduct (n 5), Article 3(a).

14 Ibid, Article 3(b).

15 Ibid, Article 3(c).

16 Ibid, Article 8(b).

17 GA Res 45/166 of 18 December 1990, Operative Part [4].

18 See Report prepared by the Secretariat on the Eighth United Nations Congress on the Prevention of Crime and Treatment of Offenders, UN Doc A/CONF.144/28/Rev.1, 27 August–7 September 1990, 110.

19 See, for example, United Nations Department of Peacekeeping Operations, Department of Field Support, Guidelines: Police Operations in United Nations Peacekeeping Operations and Special Political Missions, 1 January 2016 [87].

Encouraging Member States to bring the Basic Principles to the attention of law enforcement officials, the judiciary, government, and the public at large, the Eighth Congress recommended the Basic Principles 'for national, regional and interregional action and implementation, taking into account the political, economic, social and cultural circumstances and traditions of each country'.[20]

As noted in the preamble, the Basic Principles expand and develop existing best practice and express standards.[21] The scope of application of these Basic Principles is the same as the Code of Conduct, with the terms applying to all officers of the law, as well as members of the military and State security forces who exercise police powers, in particular, the powers of arrest or detention.

Principle 1 urges government and law enforcement agencies to use force and firearms in accordance with the law, and to continue to review the use of force and firearms. Principles 2 to 5 concern proportionality and the escalation of the use of force. Principle 5, for example, notes that if the use of force and firearms is unavoidable, issues of proportionality, minimal damage/injury, and the provision of medical assistance apply. In relation to the provision of this assistance, Principle 5(d) notes that relatives or friends of the affected person are to be notified 'at the earliest possible moment', which could be interpreted to mean as soon as reasonably practicable.

In the event of injury or death caused by force or firearms, a report and investigation is required under Principle 6 and Principle 22. A state of emergency or other 'exceptional circumstances' cannot be invoked to justify breaches of the Basic Principles pursuant to Principle 8.

Principle 9 deals with issues relating to self-defence. The Basic Principles apply only to law enforcement officials and the concept of self-defence is more limited than the definition which applies to personnel engaged in UN peace operations. For such personnel, the definition of self-defence is often articulated in broader terms as it encompasses defence of the mission or the mandate as well as personal safety.[22]

The guidelines for the development of rules and regulations on the use of firearms found in Principle 11 are very useful for the creation of ROE and DUF. These guidelines include the circumstances, accountability, warnings, and reporting systems to be considered in the event that permission is given to carry and use firearms.

Other features of the Basic Principles which have high relevance to UN peace operations include Principle 14 on the dispersal of riots. A number of principles specifically regulate the treatment of persons in custody or detention, with Principle 15 requiring law enforcement officials not to use force against those in custody or detention 'except when strictly necessary' for security or personal safety. Principle 16 echoes these requirements in relation to the use of firearms.

There are also a range of principles which deal with the obligations to establish reporting and review procedures,[23] and to allow persons affected by use of force or firearms access to an independent review process.[24] Superior officers can be held responsible for abuses,[25] and the defence of superior orders is not applicable to cases involving the use of force or firearms against the Basic Principles.[26]

The Security Council has recognised the importance of UN policing in 'peacekeeping, post-conflict peacebuilding, security, the rule of law, and the creation of [stability as] a basis for development'.[27] The Security Council has also noted that the UN Police Component can support host States by undertaking security sector reform such as 'restructuring and rebuilding of such institutions including through technical assistance, co-location, training and mentoring programs, in the context of broader efforts to strengthen the rule of law and reform the security sector, where mandated'.[28]

Some of the specific mandates given to UN police and FPUs include supporting and restoring 'public safety and the rule of law'[29] and reforming host State law and order authorities.[30] Some

---

20 Ibid.
21 Ibid, 112.
22 See ch 33 below.
23 Basic Principles (n 6), Principle 22.
24 Ibid, Principle 23.
25 Ibid, Principle 24.
26 Ibid, Principle 26.
27 SC Res 2185 (2014) of 20 November 2014, Preamble.
28 Ibid, Operative Part [8].
29 SC Res 2217 (2015) of 28 April 2015, Operative Part [33(a)(iii)].
30 See, for example, SC Res 2348 (2017) of 31 March 2017, Operative Part [35(ii)(a)].

of the functions and tasks carried out by UN police and FPUs include assisting local authorities to counter transnational organised crime and terrorism,[31] monitoring situations where law and order has broken down,[32] and protecting UN facilities from criminal threats.[33] FPUs have also undertaken riot control, protection of civilians and property, and have detained individuals accused of serious crimes.

In light of those mandates and tasks it is now generally accepted that in UN peace operations the Code of Conduct and the Basic Principles are foundational documents in setting out the minimum standards for law enforcement.[34] Both the Policing Policy and the FPU Policy require, consistent with Principle 1 of the Basic Principles, that mission-specific guidance is issued to clarify the use of force and firearms and other police equipment.[35] Both the Policing Policy and FPU Policy also state that the use of force by UN police and FPUs is to be consistent with the Code of Conduct and the Basic Principles.[36] The FPU Policy makes it clear that 'exceptional circumstances' do not warrant deviation from the Code of Conduct and the Basic Principles.[37]

Due to the Code of Conduct's broad definition of 'law enforcement officials' it is reasonable to conclude that its provisions should also apply as a benchmark of minimum standards to military peacekeepers undertaking law and order functions and tasks. For example, where military peacekeepers are required to assist a host State to bring individuals accused of grave breaches of international humanitarian law (IHL) or gross violations of international human rights law (IHRL) to justice, the Code of Conduct provides useful guidance on the professional standard required in treating those detained as well as the use of force in carrying out an arrest or detention. Similarly, when military peacekeepers are mentoring or working with local law and order officials, the Code of Conduct and the Basic Principles provide a very useful benchmark.

References

Title	Code of Conduct for Law Enforcement Officials
Adopted by	General Assembly (without a vote)
Date of Adoption	17 December 1979
Source	GA Res 34/169, Annex
Full Text	<http://www.ohchr.org/EN/ProfessionalInterest/Pages/LawEnforcementOfficials.aspx>[38]

Title	Basic Principles on the Use of Force and Firearms by Law Enforcement Officials
Author	Originally developed by an Interregional Preparatory Meeting for the Eighth United Nations Congress on the Prevention of Crime and the Treatment of Offenders
Adopted by	Eighth United Nations Congress on the Prevention of Crime and the Treatment of Offenders, Havana, Cuba
Date of Adoption	27 August to 7 September 1990
Source	UN Doc A/CONF144/28/Rev1, 110 (Annex, 112)
Full Text	<http://www.ohchr.org/EN/ProfessionalInterest/Pages/UseOfForceAndFirearms.aspx>[39]

31 Report of the Secretary-General on the Situation in Mali, S/2015/1030 of 24 December 2014, [50].
32 Twenty-ninth progress report of the Secretary-General on the United Nations Mission in Liberia, S/2015/275, 23 April 2015 [22].
33 Report of the Secretary-General on South Sudan, S/2016/341, 13 April 2016 [26].
34 Policing Policy (n 7), [106]; FPU Policy (n 8), [67].
35 Policing Policy (n 7), [107]; FPU Policy (n 8), [67].
36 Policing Policy (n 7), [108]; FPU Policy (n 8), [68].
37 FPU Policy (n 8), [68].
38 Accessed 16 September 2018.
39 Accessed 16 September 2018.

Code of Conduct for Law Enforcement Officials[40]

Article 1

Law enforcement officials shall at all times fulfil the duty imposed upon them by law, by serving the community and by protecting all persons against illegal acts, consistent with the high degree of responsibility required by their profession.

Commentary:

(a) The term "law enforcement officials", includes all officers of the law, whether appointed or elected, who exercise police powers, especially the powers of arrest or detention.

(b) In countries where police powers are exercised by military authorities, whether uniformed or not, or by State security forces, the definition of law enforcement officials shall be regarded as including officers of such services.

(c) Service to the community is intended to include particularly the rendition of services of assistance to those members of the community who by reason of personal, economic, social or other emergencies are in need of immediate aid.

(d) This provision is intended to cover not only all violent, predatory and harmful acts, but extends to the full range of prohibitions under penal statutes. It extends to conduct by persons not capable of incurring criminal liability.

Article 2

In the performance of their duty, law enforcement officials shall respect and protect human dignity and maintain and uphold the human rights of all persons.

Commentary:

(a) The human rights in question are identified and protected by national and international law. Among the relevant international instruments are the Universal Declaration of Human Rights, the International Covenant on Civil and Political Rights, the Declaration on the Protection of All Persons from Being Subjected to Torture and Other Cruel, Inhuman or Degrading Treatment or Punishment, the United Nations Declaration on the Elimination of All Forms of Racial Discrimination, the International Convention on the Elimination of All Forms of Racial Discrimination, the International Convention on the Suppression and Punishment of the Crime of Apartheid, the Convention on the Prevention and Punishment of the Crime of Genocide, the Standard Minimum Rules for the Treatment of Prisoners and the Vienna Convention on Consular Relations.

(b) National commentaries to this provision should indicate regional or national provisions identifying and protecting these rights.

Article 3

Law enforcement officials may use force only when strictly necessary and to the extent required for the performance of their duty.

40 From Code of Conduct for Law Enforcement Officials, by General Assembly © 1979 United Nations. Reprinted with the permission of the United Nations.

Commentary:

(a) This provision emphasizes that the use of force by law enforcement officials should be exceptional; while it implies that law enforcement officials may be authorized to use force as is reasonably necessary under the circumstances for the prevention of crime or in effecting or assisting in the lawful arrest of offenders or suspected offenders, no force going beyond that may be used.

(b) National law ordinarily restricts the use of force by law enforcement officials in accordance with a principle of proportionality. It is to be understood that such national principles of proportionality are to be respected in the interpretation of this provision. In no case should this provision be interpreted to authorize the use of force which is disproportionate to the legitimate objective to be achieved.

(c) The use of firearms is considered an extreme measure. Every effort should be made to exclude the use of firearms, especially against children. In general, firearms should not be used except when a suspected offender offers armed resistance or otherwise jeopardizes the lives of others and less extreme measures are not sufficient to restrain or apprehend the suspected offender. In every instance in which a firearm is discharged, a report should be made promptly to the competent authorities.

Article 4

Matters of a confidential nature in the possession of law enforcement officials shall be kept confidential, unless the performance of duty or the needs of justice strictly require otherwise.

Commentary:

By the nature of their duties, law enforcement officials obtain information which may relate to private lives or be potentially harmful to the interests, and especially the reputation, of others. Great care should be exercised in safeguarding and using such information, which should be disclosed only in the performance of duty or to serve the needs of justice. Any disclosure of such information for other purposes is wholly improper.

Article 5

No law enforcement official may inflict, instigate or tolerate any act of torture or other cruel, inhuman or degrading treatment or punishment, nor may any law enforcement official invoke superior orders or exceptional circumstances such as a state of war or a threat of war, a threat to national security, internal political instability or any other public emergency as a justification of torture or other cruel, inhuman or degrading treatment or punishment.

Commentary:

(a) This prohibition derives from the Declaration on the Protection of All Persons from Being Subjected to Torture and Other Cruel, Inhuman or Degrading Treatment or Punishment, adopted by the General Assembly, according to which:

> "[Such an act is] an offence to human dignity and shall be condemned as a denial of the purposes of the Charter of the United Nations and as a violation of the human rights and fundamental freedoms proclaimed in the Universal Declaration of Human Rights [and other international human rights instruments]."

(b) The Declaration defines torture as follows:

> "... torture means any act by which severe pain or suffering, whether physical or mental, is intentionally inflicted by or at the instigation of a public official on a person for such purposes as obtaining from him or a third person information or confession, punishing him for an act he has committed or is suspected of having committed, or intimidating him or other persons. It does not include pain or suffering arising only from, inherent in or

incidental to, lawful sanctions to the extent consistent with the Standard Minimum Rules for the Treatment of Prisoners."

(c) The term "cruel, inhuman or degrading treatment or punishment" has not been defined by the General Assembly but should be interpreted so as to extend the widest possible protection against abuses, whether physical or mental.

Article 6
Law enforcement officials shall ensure the full protection of the health of persons in their custody and, in particular, shall take immediate action to secure medical attention whenever required.

Commentary:

(a) "Medical attention", which refers to services rendered by any medical personnel, including certified medical practitioners and paramedics, shall be secured when needed or requested.
(b) While the medical personnel are likely to be attached to the law enforcement operation, law enforcement officials must take into account the judgement of such personnel when they recommend providing the person in custody with appropriate treatment through, or in consultation with, medical personnel from outside the law enforcement operation.
(c) It is understood that law enforcement officials shall also secure medical attention for victims of violations of law or of accidents occurring in the course of violations of law.

Article 7
Law enforcement officials shall not commit any act of corruption. They shall also rigorously oppose and combat all such acts.

Commentary:

(a) Any act of corruption, in the same way as any other abuse of authority, is incompatible with the profession of law enforcement officials. The law must be enforced fully with respect to any law enforcement official who commits an act of corruption, as Governments cannot expect to enforce the law among their citizens if they cannot, or will not, enforce the law against their own agents and within their agencies.
(b) While the definition of corruption must be subject to national law, it should be understood to encompass the commission or omission of an act in the performance of or in connection with one's duties, in response to gifts, promises or incentives demanded or accepted, or the wrongful receipt of these once the act has been committed or omitted.
(c) The expression "act of corruption" referred to above should be understood to encompass attempted corruption.

Article 8
Law enforcement officials shall respect the law and the present Code. They shall also, to the best of their capability, prevent and rigorously oppose any violations of them.

Law enforcement officials who have reason to believe that a violation of the present Code has occurred or is about to occur shall report the matter to their superior authorities and, where necessary, to other appropriate authorities or organs vested with reviewing or remedial power.

Commentary:

(a) This Code shall be observed whenever it has been incorporated into national legislation or practice. If legislation or practice contains stricter provisions than those of the present Code, those stricter provisions shall be observed.
(b) The article seeks to preserve the balance between the need for internal discipline of the agency on which public safety is largely dependent, on the one hand, and the need for dealing with violations of basic human rights, on the other. Law enforcement officials shall

report violations within the chain of command and take other lawful action outside the chain of command only when no other remedies are available or effective. It is understood that law enforcement officials shall not suffer administrative or other penalties because they have reported that a violation of this Code has occurred or is about to occur.

(c) The term "appropriate authorities or organs vested with reviewing or remedial power" refers to any authority or organ existing under national law, whether internal to the law enforcement agency or independent thereof, with statutory, customary or other power to review grievances and complaints arising out of violations within the purview of this Code.

(d) In some countries, the mass media may be regarded as performing complaint review functions similar to those described in subparagraph (c) above. Law enforcement officials may, therefore, be justified if, as a last resort and in accordance with the laws and customs of their own countries and with the provisions of article 4 of the present Code, they bring violations to the attention of public opinion through the mass media.

(e) Law enforcement officials who comply with the provisions of this Code deserve the respect, the full support and the co-operation of the community and of the law enforcement agency in which they serve, as well as the law enforcement profession.

Basic Principles on the Use of Force and Firearms by Law Enforcement Officials[41]

Whereas the work of law enforcement officials is a social service of great importance and there is, therefore, a need to maintain and, whenever necessary, to improve the working conditions and status of these officials,

Whereas a threat to the life and safety of law enforcement officials must be seen as a threat to the stability of society as a whole,

Whereas law enforcement officials have a vital role in the protection of the right to life, liberty and security of the person, as guaranteed in the Universal Declaration of Human Rights and reaffirmed in the International Covenant on Civil and Political Rights,

Whereas the Standard Minimum Rules for the Treatment of Prisoners provide for the circumstances in which prison officials may use force in the course of their duties,

Whereas article 3 of the Code of Conduct for Law Enforcement Officials provides that law enforcement officials may use force only when strictly necessary and to the extent required for the performance of their duty,

Whereas the preparatory meeting for the Seventh United Nations Congress on the Prevention of Crime and the Treatment of Offenders, held at Varenna, Italy, agreed on elements to be considered in the course of further work on restraints on the use of force and firearms by law enforcement officials,

41 From Basic Principles on the Use of Force and Firearms by Law Enforcement Officials © 1990 United Nations. Reprinted with the permission of the United Nations.

Whereas the Seventh Congress, in its resolution 14, inter alia, emphasizes that the use of force and firearms by law enforcement officials should be commensurate with due respect for human rights,

Whereas the Economic and Social Council, in its resolution 1986/10, section IX, of 21 May 1986, invited Member States to pay particular attention in the implementation of the Code to the use of force and firearms by law enforcement officials, and the General Assembly, in its resolution 41/149 of 4 December 1986, inter alia, welcomed this recommendation made by the Council,

Whereas it is appropriate that, with due regard to their personal safety, consideration be given to the role of law enforcement officials in relation to the administration of justice, to the protection of the right to life, liberty and security of the person, to their responsibility to maintain public safety and social peace and to the importance of their qualifications, training and conduct,

The basic principles set forth below, which have been formulated to assist Member States in their task of ensuring and promoting the proper role of law enforcement officials, should be taken into account and respected by Governments within the framework of their national legislation and practice, and be brought to the attention of law enforcement officials as well as other persons, such as judges, prosecutors, lawyers, members of the executive branch and the legislature, and the public.

General provisions

1. Governments and law enforcement agencies shall adopt and implement rules and regulations on the use of force and firearms against persons by law enforcement officials. In developing such rules and regulations, Governments and law enforcement agencies shall keep the ethical issues associated with the use of force and firearms constantly under review.
2. Governments and law enforcement agencies should develop a range of means as broad as possible and equip law enforcement officials with various types of weapons and ammunition that would allow for a differentiated use of force and firearms. These should include the development of non-lethal incapacitating weapons for use in appropriate situations, with a view to increasingly restraining the application of means capable of causing death or injury to persons. For the same purpose, it should also be possible for law enforcement officials to be equipped with self-defensive equipment such as shields, helmets, bullet-proof vests and bullet-proof means of transportation, in order to decrease the need to use weapons of any kind.
3. The development and deployment of non-lethal incapacitating weapons should be carefully evaluated in order to minimize the risk of endangering uninvolved persons, and the use of such weapons should be carefully controlled.
4. Law enforcement officials, in carrying out their duty, shall, as far as possible, apply non-violent means before resorting to the use of force and firearms. They may use force and firearms only if other means remain ineffective or without any promise of achieving the intended result.
5. Whenever the lawful use of force and firearms is unavoidable, law enforcement officials shall:
   (a) Exercise restraint in such use and act in proportion to the seriousness of the offence and the legitimate objective to be achieved;
   (b) Minimize damage and injury, and respect and preserve human life;
   (c) Ensure that assistance and medical aid are rendered to any injured or affected persons at the earliest possible moment;
   (d) Ensure that relatives or close friends of the injured or affected person are notified at the earliest possible moment.

6. Where injury or death is caused by the use of force and firearms by law enforcement officials, they shall report the incident promptly to their superiors, in accordance with principle 22.
7. Governments shall ensure that arbitrary or abusive use of force and firearms by law enforcement officials is punished as a criminal offence under their law.
8. Exceptional circumstances such as internal political instability or any other public emergency may not be invoked to justify any departure from these basic principles.

Special provisions

9. Law enforcement officials shall not use firearms against persons except in self-defence or defence of others against the imminent threat of death or serious injury, to prevent the perpetration of a particularly serious crime involving grave threat to life, to arrest a person presenting such a danger and resisting their authority, or to prevent his or her escape, and only when less extreme means are insufficient to achieve these objectives. In any event, intentional lethal use of firearms may only be made when strictly unavoidable in order to protect life.
10. In the circumstances provided for under principle 9, law enforcement officials shall identify themselves as such and give a clear warning of their intent to use firearms, with sufficient time for the warning to be observed, unless to do so would unduly place the law enforcement officials at risk or would create a risk of death or serious harm to other persons, or would be clearly inappropriate or pointless in the circumstances of the incident.
11. Rules and regulations on the use of firearms by law enforcement officials should include guidelines that:
    (a) Specify the circumstances under which law enforcement officials are authorized to carry firearms and prescribe the types of firearms and ammunition permitted;
    (b) Ensure that firearms are used only in appropriate circumstances and in a manner likely to decrease the risk of unnecessary harm;
    (c) Prohibit the use of those firearms and ammunition that cause unwarranted injury or present an unwarranted risk;
    (d) Regulate the control, storage and issuing of firearms, including procedures for ensuring that law enforcement officials are accountable for the firearms and ammunition issued to them;
    (e) Provide for warnings to be given, if appropriate, when firearms are to be discharged;
    (f) Provide for a system of reporting whenever law enforcement officials use firearms in the performance of their duty.

Policing unlawful assemblies

12. As everyone is allowed to participate in lawful and peaceful assemblies, in accordance with the principles embodied in the Universal Declaration of Human Rights and the International Covenant on Civil and Political Rights, Governments and law enforcement agencies and officials shall recognize that force and firearms may be used only in accordance with principles 13 and 14.
13. In the dispersal of assemblies that are unlawful but non-violent, law enforcement officials shall avoid the use of force or, where that is not practicable, shall restrict such force to the minimum extent necessary.
14. In the dispersal of violent assemblies, law enforcement officials may use firearms only when less dangerous means are not practicable and only to the minimum extent necessary. Law enforcement officials shall not use firearms in such cases, except under the conditions stipulated in principle 9.

Policing persons in custody or detention

15. Law enforcement officials, in their relations with persons in custody or detention, shall not use force, except when strictly necessary for the maintenance of security and order within the institution, or when personal safety is threatened.
16. Law enforcement officials, in their relations with persons in custody or detention, shall not use firearms, except in self-defence or in the defence of others against the immediate threat of death or serious injury, or when strictly necessary to prevent the escape of a person in custody or detention presenting the danger referred to in principle 9.
17. The preceding principles are without prejudice to the rights, duties and responsibilities of prison officials, as set out in the Standard Minimum Rules for the Treatment of Prisoners, particularly rules 33, 34 and 54.

Qualifications, training and counselling

18. Governments and law enforcement agencies shall ensure that all law enforcement officials are selected by proper screening procedures, have appropriate moral, psychological and physical qualities for the effective exercise of their functions and receive continuous and thorough professional training. Their continued fitness to perform these functions should be subject to periodic review.
19. Governments and law enforcement agencies shall ensure that all law enforcement officials are provided with training and are tested in accordance with appropriate proficiency standards in the use of force. Those law enforcement officials who are required to carry firearms should be authorized to do so only upon completion of special training in their use.
20. In the training of law enforcement officials, Governments and law enforcement agencies shall give special attention to issues of police ethics and human rights, especially in the investigative process, to alternatives to the use of force and firearms, including the peaceful settlement of conflicts, the understanding of crowd behaviour, and the methods of persuasion, negotiation and mediation, as well as to technical means, with a view to limiting the use of force and firearms. Law enforcement agencies should review their training programmes and operational procedures in the light of particular incidents.
21. Governments and law enforcement agencies shall make stress counselling available to law enforcement officials who are involved in situations where force and firearms are used.

Reporting and review procedures

22. Governments and law enforcement agencies shall establish effective reporting and review procedures for all incidents referred to in principles 6 and 11 (f). For incidents reported pursuant to these principles, Governments and law enforcement agencies shall ensure that an effective review process is available and that independent administrative or prosecutorial authorities are in a position to exercise jurisdiction in appropriate circumstances. In cases of death and serious injury or other grave consequences, a detailed report shall be sent promptly to the competent authorities responsible for administrative review and judicial control.
23. Persons affected by the use of force and firearms or their legal representatives shall have access to an independent process, including a judicial process. In the event of the death of such persons, this provision shall apply to their dependants accordingly.
24. Governments and law enforcement agencies shall ensure that superior officers are held responsible if they know, or should have known, that law enforcement officials under their command are resorting, or have resorted, to the unlawful use of force and firearms, and they did not take all measures in their power to prevent, suppress or report such use.
25. Governments and law enforcement agencies shall ensure that no criminal or disciplinary sanction is imposed on law enforcement officials who, in compliance with the Code of

Conduct for Law Enforcement Officials and these basic principles, refuse to carry out an order to use force and firearms, or who report such use by other officials.

26. Obedience to superior orders shall be no defence if law enforcement officials knew that an order to use force and firearms resulting in the death or serious injury of a person was manifestly unlawful and had a reasonable opportunity to refuse to follow it. In any case, responsibility also rests on the superiors who gave the unlawful orders.

B. Protection of United Nations and Associated Personnel

14

Safety of United Nations and Associated Personnel

Prefatory Note

There have been more than 3700 peacekeepers killed on UN peace operations between 1948 and September 2018.[1] Of them, 1002 peacekeepers were killed maliciously.[2] The three missions that gave rise to the highest number of peacekeepers killed by malicious acts are: the United Nations Operations in the Congo (ONUC) during which 104 peacekeepers were killed in 1961; the Second United Nations Operation in Somalia (UNOSOM II) during which 112 were killed between 1992 and 1994; and the United Nations Protection Force in Croatia and Bosnia Herzegovina (UNPROFOR) during which 74 were killed between 1992 and 1995.[3] To address the attacks on peacekeepers, particularly those like the attacks against UNOSOM II and UNPROFOR, the UN developed the Convention on the Safety of United Nations and Associated Personnel (Safety Convention).[4]

The Safety Convention and the Optional Protocol to the Convention on the Safety of United Nations and Associated Personnel (Optional Protocol)[5] are concerned with the protection and safety of UN and associated personnel in certain peace operations. The framework of protection is reinforced in UN Status-of-Forces Agreements (SOFAs)[6] and, since 2003, by Security Council resolutions concerning the establishment of peacekeeping operations.[7] The focus on protecting UN and associated personnel is a part of the broader issue of protecting civilians in UN peace operations.

In 1993, the Security Council requested the Secretary-General to prepare a report on the security of UN peace operations.[8] One recommendation from the report was the development of a convention relating to the safety and security of UN forces and personnel. The Security Council, in resolution 868, welcomed the Secretary-General's report and the initiatives of the General Assembly to 'consider the elaboration of new instruments relating to the security and safety of United Nations forces and personnel'.[9]

In 2000, the Secretary-General, prompted by both the Security Council and the General Assembly, submitted a report which dealt specifically with the scope of legal protection afforded to

1 See <https://peacekeeping.un.org/sites/default/files/statsbyyear_1_15.pdf> accessed 6 October 2018. These fatalities include both Department of Peacekeepig Operations and non-Department of Peackeeping Operations peacekeepers.

2 Between 1948 and 30 November 2016, the UN recorded a total of 922 fatalities by malicious acts. For further details, see <https://peacekeeping.un.org/sites/default/files/statsbymissionincidenttype_4_17.pdf > accessed 6 October 2018.

3 See <https://peacekeeping.un.org/sites/default/files/statsbyyearmissionincidenttype_5a_14.pdf> accessed 6 October 2018.

4 Convention on the Safety of United Nations and Associated Personnel (opened for signature 9 December 1994, entered into force 15 January 1999) 2051 UNTS 363 (hereafter Safety Convention).

5 Optional Protocol to the Convention on the Safety of United Nations and Associated Personnel (adopted by the General Assembly in GA Res 60/42 of 8 December 2005, entered into force on 19 August 2010) (hereafter Optional Protocol).

6 See ch 2 above. See also, for example, SC Res 2327 (2016) of 16 December 2016, Preamble and [19]; and SC Res 2301 (2016) of 20 July 2016, [51].

7 See, for example, SC Res 1778 (2007) of 25 September 2007.

8 Report of the Secretary-General, 'Security of United Nations Operations', UN Doc S/26358, 27 August 1993.

9 SC Res 868 (1993) of 29 September 1993, Preamble [5].

UN peacekeepers and associated personnel under the Safety Convention.[10] The Secretary-General identified the inadequacies of the Safety Convention and proposed a protocol to extend its legal protection to all UN and associated personnel who were not covered by the Safety Convention.

In 2001, the General Assembly, in resolution 56/89,[11] recommended the inclusion of key provisions of the Safety Convention in SOFAs. Resolution 56/89 also established an Ad Hoc Committee on the Scope of Legal Protection under the Convention on the Safety of United Nations and Associated Personnel (Ad Hoc Committee) to 'consider the recommendations made by the Secretary-General in his Report on measures to strengthen and enhance the protective legal regime for United Nations and associated personnel'.[12]

The Security Council, in resolution 1502, adopted the recommendation of the General Assembly when it requested:

> the Secretary-General to seek the inclusion of, and that host countries include, key provisions of the Convention on the Safety of United Nations and Associated Personnel, among others, those regarding the prevention of attacks against members of United Nations operations, the establishment of such attacks as crimes punishable by law and the prosecution or extradition of offenders, in future as well as, if necessary, in existing status-of-forces, status-of-missions and host country agreements negotiated between the United Nations and those countries, mindful of the importance of the timely conclusion of such agreements.[13]

The Rome Statute of the International Criminal Court (Rome Statute) provides, as does the Statute of the Special Court for Sierra Leone (SCSL), that it is a war crime in both international and non-international armed conflicts to intentionally direct attacks against:

> personnel, installations, material, units or vehicles involved in a humanitarian assistance or peace-keeping mission in accordance with the Charter of the United Nations, as long as they are entitled to the protection given to civilians or civilian objects under the international law of armed conflict.[14]

The prohibition against attacking peacekeepers is reflected in the jurisprudence of both the SCSL and the International Criminal Court (ICC). The SCSL, in *Prosecutor v Sesay, Kallon and Gbao* ('*RUF Case*'), concluded that peacekeepers become combatants when they take a direct part in the hostilities.[15] The ICC, in the pre-trial hearings of cases against Nourain and Jamus,[16] and Garda,[17] reached similar conclusions in relation to attacks on African peacekeepers.

Since 2003, the Security Council has, as a matter of practice, reaffirmed the applicability of resolution 1502 when establishing peace operations. For example, Security Council resolution 1778 relating to the United Nations Mission in the Central African Republic and Chad (MINURCAT) reaffirms 'resolutions ... 1502 (2003) on the protection of humanitarian and United Nations personnel'.[18]

SOFAs concluded after resolution 1502 have included the key provisions of the Safety Convention through the insertion of an additional paragraph where the government of the host State undertakes to ensure that the provisions of the Safety Convention are applied to the UN peace operation, its members, and associated personnel and their equipment and premises.

Whilst it is generally accepted that the nature of working on peace operations involves inherent dangers, the Safety Convention seeks to stop 'sanctioned attacks' where a community or State specifically targets such personnel to achieve particular aims. The Safety Convention also guides participants on UN peace operations as to some of their rights and obligations. The Safety Convention extends the law concerning the protection of certain categories of persons found in several international conventions. Some of these conventions include the Convention on the

---

10 Report of the Secretary-General, 'Scope of Legal Protection under the Convention on the Safety of United Nations and Associated Personnel', UN Doc A/55/637, 21 November 2000.

11 GA Res 56/89 of 12 December 2001.

12 Ibid, Operative Part [7].

13 SC Res 1502 (2003) of 26 August 2003, Operative Part [5](a).

14 Rome Statute of the International Criminal Court (opened for signature 17 July 1998, entered into force 1 July 2002) 2187 UNTS 3, Articles 8(2)(b)(iii) and (e)(iii) (hereafter Rome Statute) see ch 23 below. See also Statute of the Special Court for Sierra Leone (adopted 16 January 2002 pursuant to SC Res 1315 (2000) of 14 August 2000) Article 4(b).

15 *Prosecutor v Sesay, Kallon and Gbao* (Judgment) [2009] Special Court for Sierra Leone, Trial Chamber I, Case No SCSL-04-15 [233] (hereafter *RUF Case*).

16 *Prosecutor v Abdallah Banda Abakaer Nourain and Saleh Mohammed Jerbo Jamus*, Second Decision on the Proscutor's Application under Article 58, [27 August 2009] ICC-02/05-03/09, [18]–[22].

17 *Prosecutor v Bahar Idriss Abu Garda*, Decision on the Confirmation of the Charges [8 February 2010] ICC-02/05-02/09, [83]–[84].

18 SC Res 1778 (2007) of 25 September 2007, Preamble [9].

Privileges and Immunities of the United Nations,[19] the Convention on the Privileges and Immunities of the Specialized Agencies,[20] and the Vienna Convention on Diplomatic Relations.[21] These treaties recognise that certain categories of persons, due to the nature of their work, require international protection. Other international treaties such as the Geneva Conventions of 1949 and their 1977 Additional Protocols[22] are also relevant in circumstances involving armed conflict, as they protect peacekeepers when the UN is not a party to the conflict, or its peacekeepers are not active participants in hostilities.

The Safety Convention applies in respect of UN and associated personnel and UN operations.[23] The terms 'United Nations personnel', 'officials and experts on mission', 'associated personnel', and 'United Nations operation' are defined in Article 1 of the Safety Convention.

It should be noted that the Safety Convention does not apply to UN-authorised peace operations that are not conducted under the authority and control of the UN. Nor does the Safety Convention apply to enforcement action under Chapter VII of the Charter of the United Nations.[24]

Article 9 of the Safety Convention provides a list of intentional acts committed against UN or associated personnel which require domestic implementation and prosecution. These acts include those of a violent physical nature (murder, kidnapping, or other attacks upon the person or liberty of any UN or associated personnel), as well as violent attacks upon official premises, private accommodation, and transportation. This article also deals with the threat and attempt to commit such attacks as well as acts of participation as an accomplice.

As well as providing protection, the Safety Convention imposes obligations on the part of UN and associated personnel. Military and police components of a UN peace operation and their transportation are required to have distinct identification,[25] and UN and associated personnel are obliged to respect the laws and regulations of the host State and transit States, as well as refrain from actions incompatible with the nature of their duties.[26] In relation to States, the Safety Convention obliges State Parties to enforce provisions as well as to take 'all appropriate measures to ensure the safety and security of United Nations and associated personnel'.[27]

The savings clause states that nothing in the Safety Convention shall affect:

> The applicability of international humanitarian law and universally recognized standards of human rights as contained in international instruments in relation to the protection of United Nations operations and United Nations and associated personnel or the responsibility of such personnel to respect such law and standards.[28]

The Optional Protocol is significant as it supplements and expands the scope of the Safety Convention and provides legal protection for UN and associated personnel in peacebuilding missions going beyond peace operations. The Optional Protocol protects personnel delivering humanitarian, political, or development assistance in peacebuilding, or delivering emergency humanitarian assistance.[29] A competent organ[30] of the UN is required to establish these activities, which must then be conducted under the authority and control of the UN.[31] The Optional Protocol also permits the host State to make an 'opt-out' declaration to the Secretary-General that it will not apply the Optional Protocol in relation to the delivery of emergency humanitarian assistance for natural disasters.[32]

---

19 See ch 21 below.

20 Convention on the Privileges and Immunities of the Specialized Agencies (opened for signature 21 November 1947, entered into force 2 December 1948) 33 UNTS 261.

21 Vienna Convention on Diplomatic Relations (opened for signature 18 April 1961, entered into force 24 April 1964) 500 UNTS 95.

22 See ch 16 below.

23 Safety Convention (n 4), Article 2(1).

24 Ibid, Article 2(2).

25 Ibid, Article 3.

26 Ibid, Article 6.

27 Ibid, Article 7.

28 Ibid, Article 20(a).

29 Optional Protocol (n 5), Article II(1).

30 Charter of the United Nations (opened for signature 26 June 1945, entered into force 24 October 1945) 1 UNTS XVI, Article 7 (hereafter Charter).

31 Optional Protocol (n 5), Article II(1).

32 Ibid, Article II(3).

However, it has been argued that the 'opt-out' provision 'requires an opt-out declaration for every time that such an operation is planned to take place in a host country'.[33]

The Safety Convention and the reference to it in SOFAs are relevant to UN peace operations due to the subject matter that they cover, and the numerous referrals made to them by the Security Council in resolutions concerning peace operations. For example, Security Council resolution 2149 relating to the United Nations Multidimensional Integrated Stabilization Mission in the Central African Republic (MINUSCA) requests:

> the Secretary-General and the Transitional Authorities of the Central African Republic to conclude, within 30 days of the adoption of this resolution, a status-of-forces agreement with regard to MINUSCA, taking into consideration General Assembly resolution 58/82 on the scope of legal protection under the Convention on the Safety of United Nations and Associated Personnel ...[34]

The Safety Convention and Optional Protocol are also relevant to UN peace operations when the Security Council has made the protection of peacekeepers and humanitarian personnel a specific component of an operation's mandate. An example is resolution 1828 where the Security Council decided to extend the mandate of the African Union/United Nations Hybrid Operation in Darfur (UNAMID), and demanded:

> an end to violence by all sides, to attacks on civilians, peacekeepers and humanitarian personnel, and to other violations of human rights and international humanitarian law in Darfur ...[35]

The UN has also argued that, in situations where UN peacekeepers are taking no direct or active part in hostilities, or are not engaged as combatants in an armed conflict, peacekeepers do not have:

> the status of a 'protected group' (similar to the one enjoyed by medical personnel and units), [however,] the cumulative effect of the 'protective clauses' in a series of legal instruments—namely, the protected and protective status of the United Nations emblem,[36] the obligation to protect peacekeeping missions from the effects of mines,[37] the duty to ensure their safety and security[38] and the criminalization and internationalization of attacks against peacekeepers[39] when in an armed conflict ... [UN peacekeepers] are entitled to protection given to civilians ... [this] is an indication that a customary international humanitarian law principle has emerged, whereby peacekeeping personnel performing functions under the United Nations Charter in an area and situation of armed conflict and taking no part in the hostilities, are entitled the status of a 'protected group'; with the correlative obligation on the Parties to the conflict to take precautionary measures to respect their protected status.[40]

Crucially, however, the Safety Convention is now relevant in all UN peace operations because of its inclusion in the SOFAs concluded between the UN and States.[41]

References

Title	Convention on the Safety of United Nations and Associated Personnel
Date of Adoption	9 December 1994
Open for Signature	15 December 1994 to 31 December 1995
Entered into Force	15 January 1999 in accordance with article 27
Signatories	43
Parties	94
Depository	United Nations
Treaty Series	2051 UNTS 363

33 Mahnoush H Arsanjani, 'Introductory Note: Convention on the Safety of United Nations and Associated Personnel' and 'Introductory Note: Optional Protocol to the Convention on the Safety of United Nations and Associated Personnel' <http://legal.un.org/avl/ha/csunap/csunap.html> accessed 1 November 2017.

34 SC Res 2149 (2014) of 10 April 2014, Operative Part [41].

35 SC Res 1828 (2008) of 31 July 2008, Operative Part [11].

36 See Protocol Additional to the Geneva Conventions of 12 August 1949, and relating to the Protection of Victims of International Armed Conflict (Protocol I) (opened for signature 8 June 1977, entered into force 7 December 1978) 1125 UNTS 3, Articles 37(1)(d) and 38(2).

37 See Convention on Prohibitions or Restrictions on the Use of Certain Conventional Weapons which may be deemed to be Excessively Injurious or to have Indiscriminate Effects (and Protocols I, II and III) (as amended on 21 December 2001) (opened for signature 10 October 1980, entered into force 2 December 1983) 1342 UNTS 137, Additional Protocol II, Article 8.

38 See Safety Convention (n 4), Articles 7 and 9.

39 See Rome Statute (n 14), Article 8(2)(b)(iii).

40 United Nations Juridical Yearbook (2006), 521, Note on the Protection of Peacekeeping Personnel under International Humanitarian Law, 9 August 2006.

41 For an overview of SOFAs, see ch 2 above.

Full Text	<http://www.un.org/law/cod/safety.htm>[42]
Title	Optional Protocol to the Convention on the Safety of United Nations and Associated Personnel
Date of Adoption	8 December 2005
Open for Signature	16 January 2006 to 16 January 2007
Entered into Force	19 August 2010
Signatories	34
Parties	32
Depository	United Nations
Source	UN Doc A/RES/60/42, Annex (adopted with a vote)
Full Text	<lang= https://treaties.un.org/Pages/ViewDetails.aspx?src=IND&mtdsg_no=XVIII-8-a&chapter=18&en>[43]

Convention on the Safety of United Nations and Associated Personnel[44]

(Extracts)

The States Parties to this Convention,

Deeply concerned over the growing number of deaths and injuries resulting from deliberate attacks against United Nations and associated personnel,

Bearing in mind that attacks against, or other mistreatment of, personnel who act on behalf of the United Nations are unjustifiable and unacceptable, by whomsoever committed,

Recognizing that United Nations operations are conducted in the common interest of the international community and in accordance with the principles and purposes of the Charter of the United Nations,

Acknowledging the important contribution that United Nations and associated personnel make in respect of United Nations efforts in the fields of preventive diplomacy, peacemaking, peace-keeping, peace-building and humanitarian and other operations,

Conscious of the existing arrangements for ensuring the safety of United Nations and associated personnel, including the steps taken by the principal organs of the United Nations, in this regard,

Recognizing none the less that existing measures of protection for United Nations and associated personnel are inadequate,

Acknowledging that the effectiveness and safety of United Nations operations are enhanced where such operations are conducted with the consent and cooperation of the host State,

Appealing to all States in which United Nations and associated personnel are deployed and to all others on whom such personnel may rely, to provide comprehensive support aimed at facilitating the conduct and fulfilling the mandate of United Nations operations,

Convinced that there is an urgent need to adopt appropriate and effective measures for the prevention of attacks committed against United Nations and associated personnel and for the punishment of those who have committed such attacks,

---

42 Accessed 17 September 2018.

43 Accessed 1 November 2017.

44 From Convention on the Safety of United Nations and Associated Personnel © 1994 United Nations. Reprinted with the permission of the United Nations.

Have agreed as follows:

Article 1 – Definitions

For the purposes of this Convention:

(a) "United Nations personnel" means:
   (i) Persons engaged or deployed by the Secretary-General of the United Nations as members of the military, police or civilian components of a United Nations operation;
   (ii) Other officials and experts on mission of the United Nations or its specialized agencies or the International Atomic Energy Agency who are present in an official capacity in the area where a United Nations operation is being conducted;

(b) "Associated personnel" means:
   (i) Persons assigned by a Government or an intergovernmental organization with the agreement of the competent organ of the United Nations;
   (ii) Persons engaged by the Secretary-General of the United Nations or by a specialized agency or by the International Atomic Energy Agency;
   (iii) Persons deployed by a humanitarian non-governmental organization or agency under an agreement with the Secretary-General of the United Nations or with a specialized agency or with the International Atomic Energy Agency, to carry out activities in support of the fulfilment of the mandate of a United Nations operation;

(c) "United Nations operation" means an operation established by the competent organ of the United Nations in accordance with the Charter of the United Nations and conducted under United Nations authority and control:
   (i) Where the operation is for the purpose of maintaining or restoring international peace and security; or
   (ii) Where the Security Council or the General Assembly has declared, for the purposes of this Convention, that there exists an exceptional risk to the safety of the personnel participating in the operation;

(d) "Host State" means a State in whose territory a United Nations operation is conducted;

(e) "Transit State" means a State, other than the host State, in whose territory United Nations and associated personnel or their equipment are in transit or temporarily present in connection with a United Nations operation.

Article 2 – Scope of application

1. This Convention applies in respect of United Nations and associated personnel and United Nations operations, as defined in article 1.
2. This Convention shall not apply to a United Nations operation authorized by the Security Council as an enforcement action under Chapter VII of the Charter of the United Nations in which any of the personnel are engaged as combatants against organized armed forces and to which the law of international armed conflict applies.

Article 3 – Identification

1. The military and police components of a United Nations operation and their vehicles, vessels and aircraft shall bear distinctive identification. Other personnel, vehicles, vessels and aircraft involved in the United Nations operation shall be appropriately identified unless otherwise decided by the Secretary-General of the United Nations.
2. All United Nations and associated personnel shall carry appropriate identification documents.

Article 4 – Agreements on the status of the operation

The host State and the United Nations shall conclude as soon as possible an agreement on the status of the United Nations operation and all personnel engaged in the operation including, inter alia, provisions on privileges and immunities for military and police components of the operation.

Article 5 – Transit

A transit State shall facilitate the unimpeded transit of United Nations and associated personnel and their equipment to and from the host State.

Article 6 – Respect for laws and regulations

1. Without prejudice to such privileges and immunities as they may enjoy or to the requirements of their duties, United Nations and associated personnel shall:
   (a) Respect the laws and regulations of the host State and the transit State; and
   (b) Refrain from any action or activity incompatible with the impartial and international nature of their duties.
2. The Secretary-General of the United Nations shall take all appropriate measures to ensure the observance of these obligations.

Article 7 – Duty to ensure the safety and security of United Nations and associated personnel

1. United Nations and associated personnel, their equipment and premises shall not be made the object of attack or of any action that prevents them from discharging their mandate.
2. States Parties shall take all appropriate measures to ensure the safety and security of United Nations and associated personnel. In particular, States Parties shall take all appropriate steps to protect United Nations and associated personnel who are deployed in their territory from the crimes set out in article 9.
3. States Parties shall cooperate with the United Nations and other States Parties, as appropriate, in the implementation of this Convention, particularly in any case where the host State is unable itself to take the required measures.

Article 8 – Duty to release or return United Nations and associated personnel captured or detained

Except as otherwise provided in an applicable status-of-forces agreement, if United Nations or associated personnel are captured or detained in the course of the performance of their duties and their identification has been established, they shall not be subjected to interrogation and they shall be promptly released and returned to United Nations or other appropriate authorities. Pending their release such personnel shall be treated in accordance with universally recognized standards of human rights and the principles and spirit of the Geneva Conventions of 1949.

Article 9 – Crimes against United Nations and associated personnel

1. The intentional commission of:
   (a) A murder, kidnapping or other attack upon the person or liberty of any United Nations or associated personnel;
   (b) A violent attack upon the official premises, the private accommodation or the means of transportation of any United Nations or associated personnel likely to endanger his or her person or liberty;
   (c) A threat to commit any such attack with the objective of compelling a physical or juridical person to do or to refrain from doing any act;
   (d) An attempt to commit any such attack; and
   (e) An act constituting participation as an accomplice in any such attack, or in an attempt to commit such attack, or in organizing or ordering others to commit such attack, shall be made by each State Party a crime under its national law.
2. Each State Party shall make the crimes set out in paragraph 1 punishable by appropriate penalties which shall take into account their grave nature.

Article 10 – Establishment of jurisdiction

1. Each State Party shall take such measures as may be necessary to establish its jurisdiction over the crimes set out in article 9 in the following cases:
   (a) When the crime is committed in the territory of that State or on board a ship or aircraft registered in that State;
   (b) When the alleged offender is a national of that State.
2. A State Party may also establish its jurisdiction over any such crime when it is committed:
   (a) By a stateless person whose habitual residence is in that State; or
   (b) With respect to a national of that State; or
   (c) In an attempt to compel that State to do or to abstain from doing any act.
3. Any State Party which has established jurisdiction as mentioned in paragraph 2 shall notify the Secretary-General of the United Nations. If such State Party subsequently rescinds that jurisdiction, it shall notify the Secretary-General of the United Nations.
4. Each State Party shall take such measures as may be necessary to establish its jurisdiction over the crimes set out in article 9 in cases where the alleged offender is present in its territory and it does not extradite such person pursuant to article 15 to any of the States Parties which have established their jurisdiction in accordance with paragraph 1 or 2.
5. This Convention does not exclude any criminal jurisdiction exercised in accordance with national law.

Article 11 – Prevention of crimes against United Nations and associated personnel

States Parties shall cooperate in the prevention of the crimes set out in article 9, particularly by:

(a) Taking all practicable measures to prevent preparations in their respective territories for the commission of those crimes within or outside their territories; and

(b) Exchanging information in accordance with their national law and coordinating the taking of administrative and other measures as appropriate to prevent the commission of those crimes.

Article 12 – Communication of information

1. Under the conditions provided for in its national law, the State Party in whose territory a crime set out in article 9 has been committed shall, if it has reason to believe that an alleged offender has fled from its territory, communicate to the Secretary-General of the United Nations and, directly or through the Secretary-General, to the State or States concerned all the pertinent facts regarding the crime committed and all available information regarding the identity of the alleged offender.
2. Whenever a crime set out in article 9 has been committed, any State Party which has information concerning the victim and circumstances of the crime shall endeavour to transmit such information, under the conditions provided for in its national law, fully and promptly to the Secretary-General of the United Nations and the State or States concerned.

Article 13 – Measures to ensure prosecution or extradition

1. Where the circumstances so warrant, the State Party in whose territory the alleged offender is present shall take the appropriate measures under its national law to ensure that person's presence for the purpose of prosecution or extradition.
2. Measures taken in accordance with paragraph 1 shall be notified, in conformity with national law and without delay, to the Secretary-General of the United Nations and, either directly or through the Secretary-General, to:

(a) The State where the crime was committed;
(b) The State or States of which the alleged offender is a national or, if such person is a stateless person, in whose territory that person has his or her habitual residence;
(c) The State or States of which the victim is a national; and
(d) Other interested States.

Article 14 – Prosecution of alleged offenders

The State Party in whose territory the alleged offender is present shall, if it does not extradite that person, submit, without exception whatsoever and without undue delay, the case to its competent authorities for the purpose of prosecution, through proceedings in accordance with the law of that State. Those authorities shall take their decision in the same manner as in the case of an ordinary offence of a grave nature under the law of that State.

Article 15 – Extradition of alleged offenders

1. To the extent that the crimes set out in article 9 are not extraditable offences in any extradition treaty existing between States Parties, they shall be deemed to be included as such therein. States Parties undertake to include those crimes as extraditable offences in every extradition treaty to be concluded between them.
2. If a State Party which makes extradition conditional on the existence of a treaty receives a request for extradition from another State Party with which it has no extradition treaty, it may at its option consider this Convention as the legal basis for extradition in respect of those crimes. Extradition shall be subject to the conditions provided in the law of the requested State.
3. States Parties which do not make extradition conditional on the existence of a treaty shall recognize those crimes as extraditable offences between themselves subject to the conditions provided in the law of the requested State.
4. Each of those crimes shall be treated, for the purposes of extradition between States Parties, as if it had been committed not only in the place in which it occurred but also in the territories of the States Parties which have established their jurisdiction in accordance with paragraph 1 or 2 of article 10.

Article 16 – Mutual assistance in criminal matters

1. States Parties shall afford one another the greatest measure of assistance in connection with criminal proceedings brought in respect of the crimes set out in article 9, including assistance in obtaining evidence at their disposal necessary for the proceedings. The law of the requested State shall apply in all cases.
2. The provisions of paragraph 1 shall not affect obligations concerning mutual assistance embodied in any other treaty.

Article 17 – Fair treatment

1. Any person regarding whom investigations or proceedings are being carried out in connection with any of the crimes set out in article 9 shall be guaranteed fair treatment, a fair trial and full protection of his or her rights at all stages of the investigations or proceedings.
2. Any alleged offender shall be entitled:
   (a) To communicate without delay with the nearest appropriate representative of the State or States of which such person is a national or which is otherwise entitled to protect that person's rights or, if such person is a stateless person, of the State which, at that person's request, is willing to protect that person's rights; and
   (b) To be visited by a representative of that State or those States.

Article 18 – Notification of outcome of proceedings

The State Party where an alleged offender is prosecuted shall communicate the final outcome of the proceedings to the Secretary-General of the United Nations, who shall transmit the information to other States Parties.

Article 19 – Dissemination

The States Parties undertake to disseminate this Convention as widely as possible and, in particular, to include the study thereof, as well as relevant provisions of international humanitarian law, in their programmes of military instruction.

Article 20 – Savings clauses

Nothing in this Convention shall affect:

(a) The applicability of international humanitarian law and universally recognized standards of human rights as contained in international instruments in relation to the protection of United Nations operations and United Nations and associated personnel or the responsibility of such personnel to respect such law and standards;

(b) The rights and obligations of States, consistent with the Charter of the United Nations, regarding the consent to entry of persons into their territories;

(c) The obligation of United Nations and associated personnel to act in accordance with the terms of the mandate of a United Nations operation;

(d) The right of States which voluntarily contribute personnel to a United Nations operation to withdraw their personnel from participation in such operation; or

(e) The entitlement to appropriate compensation payable in the event of death, disability, injury or illness attributable to peace-keeping service by persons voluntarily contributed by States to United Nations operations.

Article 21 – Right of self-defence

Nothing in this Convention shall be construed so as to derogate from the right to act in self-defence.

Article 22 – Dispute settlement

1. Any dispute between two or more States Parties concerning the interpretation or application of this Convention which is not settled by negotiation shall, at the request of one of them, be submitted to arbitration. If within six months from the date of the request for arbitration the parties are unable to agree on the organization of the arbitration, any one of those parties may refer the dispute to the International Court of Justice by application in conformity with the Statute of the Court.
2. Each State Party may at the time of signature, ratification, acceptance or approval of this Convention or accession thereto declare that it does not consider itself bound by all or part of paragraph 1. The other States Parties shall not be bound by paragraph 1 or the relevant part thereof with respect to any State Party which has made such a reservation.
3. Any State Party which has made a reservation in accordance with paragraph 2 may at any time withdraw that reservation by notification to the Secretary-General of the United Nations.

...

Optional Protocol to the Convention on the Safety of United Nations and Associated Personnel[45]

(Extracts)

The States Parties to this Protocol,

Recalling the terms of the Convention on the Safety of United Nations and Associated Personnel, done at New York on 9 December 1994,

Deeply concerned over the continuing pattern of attacks against United Nations and associated personnel,

Recognizing that United Nations operations conducted for the purposes of delivering humanitarian, political or development assistance in peacebuilding and of delivering emergency humanitarian assistance which entail particular risks for United Nations and associated personnel require the extension of the scope of legal protection under the Convention to such personnel,

Convinced of the need to have in place an effective regime to ensure that the perpetrators of attacks against United Nations and associated personnel engaged in United Nations operations are brought to justice,

Have agreed as follows:

Article I – Relationship

This Protocol supplements the Convention on the Safety of United Nations and Associated Personnel, done at New York on 9 December 1994 (hereinafter referred to as 'the Convention'), and as between the Parties to this Protocol, the Convention and the Protocol shall be read and interpreted together as a single instrument.

Article II – Application of the Convention to United Nations Operations

1. The Parties to this Protocol shall, in addition to those operations as defined in article 1 (c) of the Convention, apply the Convention in respect of all other United Nations operations established by a competent organ of the United Nations in accordance with the Charter of the United Nations and conducted under United Nations authority and control for the purposes of:

   (a) Delivering humanitarian, political or development assistance in peacebuilding, or

   (b) Delivering emergency humanitarian assistance.

2. Paragraph 1 does not apply to any permanent United Nations office, such as headquarters of the Organization or its specialized agencies established under an agreement with the United Nations.

3. A host State may make a declaration to the Secretary-General of the United Nations that it shall not apply the provisions of this Protocol with respect to an operation under article II

45 From Optional Protocol to the Convention on the Safety of United Nations and Associated Personnel © 2005 United Nations. Reprinted with the permission of the United Nations.

(1) (b) which is conducted for the sole purpose of responding to a natural disaster. Such a declaration shall be made prior to the deployment of the operation.

Article III – Duty of a State Party with respect to Article 8 of the Convention

The duty of a State Party to this Protocol with respect to the application of article 8 of the Convention to United Nations operations defined in article II of this Protocol shall be without prejudice to its right to take action in the exercise of its national jurisdiction over any United Nations or associated personnel who violates the laws and regulations of that State, provided that such action is not in violation of any other international law obligation of the State Party.

. . .

C. International Humanitarian Law

Introduction

International humanitarian law (IHL) is integral to planning and conducting UN peace operations, particularly as mandates become more robust and as UN peacekeepers may become engaged in the conduct of hostilities of such a nature in which IHL would apply.

This introduction provides an overall understanding of the importance of the IHL documents included in this section. It is not intended to provide comprehensive coverage of the multitude of issues relating to IHL, nor examine in detail the debates on the application of certain legal norms to elements of UN peace operations.

IHL is the area of international law which regulates conduct during times of armed conflict and during military occupation. As a body of law, it applies to all belligerent parties engaged in the conflict. The foundational documents for this body of law are the four Geneva Conventions of 12 August 1949 which are collectively referred to as the 'Geneva Conventions'.[1] There are also three Additional Protocols[2] to those Conventions. The four Geneva Conventions apply to international armed conflicts, as does Additional Protocol I. Common Article 3 to the four Geneva Conventions and Additional Protocol II apply to non-international armed conflicts. Additional Protocol III applies to both international and non-international armed conflicts.

IHL is also sometimes referred to as *jus in bello*, the laws of armed conflict, or the laws of war. It operates when a specific threshold of armed conflict occurs either between States, or in certain circumstances, within States. At a broad level, IHL aims to strike a balance between permitting military forces to undertake legitimate operations whilst ensuring the protection of the victims of armed conflict. IHL reinforces the general principle that 'the right of the Parties to the conflict to choose methods or means of warfare is not unlimited'.[3] Stemming from that principle there are four other principles of IHL: military necessity, humanity, distinction, and proportionality. The principle of military necessity is said to contain the following elements:

a. the force used can be and is being controlled;

b. since military necessity permits the use of force only if it is 'not otherwise prohibited by the law of armed conflict', necessity cannot excuse a departure from the law;[4]

c. the use of force in ways that are not otherwise prohibited is legitimate if it is necessary to achieve, as quickly as possible, the complete or partial submission of the enemy;

---

1 Geneva Convention for the Amelioration of the Condition of the Wounded and Sick in Armed Forces in the Field (opened for signature 12 August 1949, entered into force 21 October 1950) 75 UNTS 31 (hereafter Geneva Convention I); Geneva Convention for the Amelioration of the Condition of Wounded, Sick and Shipwrecked Members of Armed Forces at Sea (opened for signature 12 August 1949, entered into force 21 October 1950) 75 UNTS 85 (hereafter Geneva Convention II); Geneva Convention Relative to the Treatment of Prisoners of War (opened for signature 12 August 1949, entered into force 21 October 1950) 75 UNTS 135 (hereafter Geneva Convention III); Geneva Convention Relative to the Protection of Civilian Persons in Time of War (opened for signature 12 August 1949, entered into force 21 October 1950) 75 UNTS 287 (hereafter Geneva Convention IV). See ch 16 below.

2 Protocol Additional to the Geneva Conventions of 12 August 1949, and relating to the Protection of Victims of International Armed Conflicts (Protocol I) (opened for signature 8 June 1977, entered into force 7 December 1978) 1125 UNTS 3 (hereafter Additional Protocol I); Protocol Additional to the Geneva Conventions of 12 August 1949, and relating to the Protection of Victims of Non-International Armed Conflicts (Protocol II) (opened for signature 8 June 1977, entered into force 7 December 1978) 1125 UNTS 609 (hereafter Additional Protocol II); Protocol Additional to the Geneva Conventions of 12 August 1949, and relating to the Adoption of an Additional Distinctive Emblem (Additional Protocol III) (opened for signature 8 December 2005, entered into force 14 January 2007) 2404 UNTS 261 (hereafter Additional Protocol III). See ch 16 below.

3 Additional Protocol I (n 2), Article 35(1).

4 Note that the UN uses the term 'operational necessity' about third-party claims and this term should not be confused with the meaning of 'necessity' under IHL.

d. conversely, the use of force which is not necessary is unlawful, since it involves wanton killing or destruction.[5]

The principle of humanity 'forbids the infliction of suffering, injury or destruction not actually necessary for the accomplishment of legitimate military purposes'.[6] The principle of distinction requires military forces when using force to distinguish between combatants and non-combatants and legitimate military targets from civilian objects.[7] The principle of proportionality 'requires that the losses resulting from a military action should not be excessive in relation to the expected military advantage'.[8]

The legal framework concerning the use of armed force, sometimes referred to as *jus ad bellum*, pursuant to, for example, the UN Charter,[9] must be distinguished from *jus in bello* or IHL.

The first detailed IHL treaty was the 1907 Hague Regulations,[10] which concerned the law of land warfare. That treaty was subsequently built upon by the four Geneva Conventions and their Additional Protocols. In addition to the Geneva Conventions and their Additional Protocols, there are several other treaties and instruments that deal specifically with protecting the victims of armed conflict, methods and means of warfare, naval and air warfare, and cultural property.[11]

The four Geneva Conventions, along with their Additional Protocols, are pivotal to IHL. The Geneva Conventions are universally ratified and it is widely agreed that many elements of these treaties and their Additional Protocols have crystallised into customary international law.[12]

In some cases, the interpretation and application of those treaties have been influenced by developments in international human rights law (IHRL) and international criminal law (ICL). For example, Common Article 3 to the four Geneva Conventions prohibits 'torture' but does not define what constitutes 'torture'. The Convention against Torture and Other Cruel, Inhuman or Degrading Treatment or Punishment (CAT)[13] and the Rome Statute of the International Criminal Court (Rome Statute)[14] provide a definition of torture to give effect to the prohibition against torture in the context of war crimes. The Optional Protocol to the Convention on the Rights of the Child on the Involvement of Children in Armed Conflict,[15] and the Basic Principles and Guidelines on the Right to a Remedy and Reparation for Victims of Gross Violations of International Human Rights Law and Serious Violations of International Humanitarian Law,[16] are other examples of the interplay between human rights instruments and IHL.

The interplay between IHL and IHRL has been addressed by the International Court of Justice (ICJ) in both *Legal Consequences of the Construction of a Wall in the Occupied Palestinian Territory* (Advisory Opinion) (*Israeli Wall Case*)[17] and the *Case concerning Armed Activities on the Territory of the Congo (Democratic Republic of the Congo v Uganda)* (Judgment) (*Congo Case*).[18] The ICJ has stated that in situations of armed conflict, including occupation, the:

> protection offered by human rights conventions does not cease … save through the effect of provisions for derogation of the kind to be found in Article 4 of the International Covenant on Civil and Political Rights. As regards the relationship between international humanitarian law and human rights

---

5 United Kingdom Ministry of Defence, 'The Manual of the Law of Armed Conflict' (2005) [2.2.1].

6 Ibid, [2.4].

7 Ibid, [2.5]–[2.5.3].

8 Ibid, [2.6].

9 See ch 1 above.

10 Hague Convention (IV) respecting the Laws and Customs of War on Land and Its Annex: Regulations concerning the Laws and Customs of War on Land (opened for signature 18 October 1907, entered into force 26 January 1910) (hereafter 1907 Hague Regulations).

11 For a list of those treaties, see <https://www.icrc.org/en/icrc-databases-international-humanitarian-law> and <https://www.icrc.org/en/document/what-treaties-make-ihl-what-customary-ihl> accessed 2 October 2018.

12 For an analysis of the customary international law status of the Geneva Conventions and their Additional Protocols, see the International Committee of the Red Cross, 'Study on Customary International Humanitarian Law', ICRC Doc 30IC/07/8.3, October 2007 <https://www.icrc.org/eng/assets/files/other/30ic_8-3_customaryihl_report_final_eng.pdf > accessed 6 October 2018.

13 See ch 8 above.

14 See ch 23 below.

15 See ch 9 above.

16 See ch 11 above.

17 *Legal Consequences of the Construction of a Wall in the Occupied Palestinian Territory* (Advisory Opinion) [2004] ICJ Rep 136 (hereafter *Israeli Wall Case*).

18 *Case concerning Armed Activities on the Territory of the Congo (Democratic Republic of Congo v Uganda)* (Judgment) [2005] ICJ Rep 168 (hereafter *Congo Case*).

> law, there are thus three possible situations: some rights may be exclusively matters of international humanitarian law; other may be exclusively matters of human rights law; yet others may be matters of both these branches of international law.[19]

The application of IHL treaties to the UN as an organisation has been controversial. One of the key reasons for this controversy is the question of the accession of the UN to the four Geneva Conventions and Additional Protocols. On this matter, the UN Office of Legal Affairs (OLA) has traditionally:

> maintained ... that the United Nations is not substantively in a position to become a party to the 1949 Conventions ... [because] the United Nations is unable to fulfill obligations which for the execution require the exercise of powers not granted to the [UN] ... [20]

Notwithstanding the legal concerns regarding accession to the Geneva Conventions and their Additional Protocols expressed by OLA, in 1978 the UN exchanged letters with the International Committee of the Red Cross (ICRC) acknowledging the UN's duty to comply with the 'principles and spirit' of IHL. A circular letter to this effect was sent to all Force Commanders (FCs) on 24 May 1978 and has not been withdrawn. In a further letter to the President of the ICRC in 1992, the UN explained that the Secretariat was working on a formula regarding respect for IHL to insert into Status-of-Forces Agreements (SOFAs).[21] The letter outlined the problem of describing IHL to be observed by the UN and suggested that 'the description must not be too narrow but for practical purposes it must also not be too broad'.[22] In 1993, with the Agreement on the Status of the United Nations Assistance Mission for Rwanda (UNAMIR), a specific provision was finally included in a SOFA which required UN peace operations to conduct their operations in host countries with 'full respect for the principles and spirit of general conventions applicable to the conduct of military personnel',[23] which, by implication, would include IHL.

However, the reference to respecting the principles and spirit of the international conventions applicable to the conduct of military personnel was considered insufficient, especially after international outrage at the actions of some peacekeepers in the early 1990s, when accusations surfaced of military members of national contingents engaging in killings, sexual violence, and torture. It was against this background that the 1995 report of the General Assembly's Special Committee on Peacekeeping Operations (C34) called on the Secretary-General to 'complete the elaboration of a code of conduct for United Nations peace-keeping personnel consistent with applicable international humanitarian law, so as to ensure the highest standards of performance and conduct'.[24]

The ICRC took the initiative in this and organised two meetings of experts in 1995 to discuss the issue of the applicability of IHL to UN peace operations and the elaboration of a suitable code of conduct for UN peacekeepers. After discussions between the ICRC and the UN Secretariat, draft Guidelines for UN Forces Regarding Respect for International Humanitarian Law (Guidelines) were drawn up and given to the Secretary-General by the ICRC President.[25]

At the same time as the Guidelines were being drafted, the UN released 'We are United Nations Peacekeepers'.[26] The 'We are United Nations Peacekeepers' card states that peacekeepers 'will comply with the Guidelines on International Humanitarian Law for Forces Undertaking United Nations Peacekeeping Operations ... as the fundamental basis of our standards'.[27] It is logical that the Guidelines referred to in the 'We are United Nations Peacekeepers' card are the same Guidelines as those drawn up by the ICRC and UN Secretariat in May 1996.

---

19 *Israeli Wall Case* (n 17), [106].

20 UN Juridical Yearbook 1972, 153–4, 'Question of the possible accession of intergovernmental organizations to the Geneva Conventions for the protection of war victims'.

21 UN Juridical Yearbook 1992, 430–1, 'Question of the application of the 1949 Geneva Conventions for the protection of war victims and their 1977 Additional Protocols in peacekeeping operations of the United Nations'.

22 Ibid, 431.

23 See Agreement on the Status of the United Nations Assistance Mission for Rwanda (5 November 1993, 1748 UNTS 17) [7](a). <https://treaties.un.org/doc/Publication/UNTS/Volume%201748/volume-1748-I-30482-English.pdf> accessed 2 October 2018.

24 Report of the Special Committee on Peace-keeping Operations, 'Comprehensive Review of the Whole Question of Peace-keeping Operations in All their Aspects', UN Doc A/50/230, 22 June 1995, [73].

25 Yves Sandoz, The International Committee of the Red Cross as guardian of international humanitarian law, 13 December 1998 <https://www.icrc.org/eng/resources/documents/misc/about-the-icrc-311298.htm> accessed 2 October 2018.

26 'We are United Nations Peacekeepers.' Available at <http://dag.un.org/handle/11176/89516?show=full> accessed 2 October 2018.

27 Ibid. See ch 27 below.

The work of the ICRC and the UN Secretariat, specifically the OLA, led to the Secretary-General promulgating an administrative bulletin (Bulletin) relating to the application of IHL to UN peace operations entitled 'Secretary-General's Bulletin: Observance by United Nations Forces of International Humanitarian Law'.[28] That Bulletin is founded on the principles and rules stated in the four Geneva Conventions and Additional Protocols I and II.[29]

Regardless of the UN's position concerning the application of IHL to its peace operations, contributing States are bound by their national and international obligations concerning the application of IHL obligations in peace operations. Thus, contributing States must ensure that members of their armed forces adhere to the provisions found in this international legal regime.

The Security Council has condemned all violations of IHL and has emphasised the:

> obligations of all States to ensure respect for international humanitarian law ... and ... the responsibility of States to comply with their obligations to end impunity and to prosecute those responsible for war crimes, genocide, crimes against humanity or other serious violations of international humanitarian law.[30]

IHL is integral to the planning and conduct of UN peace operations at several levels. First, in situations where peacekeepers are engaged in armed conflict, both the UN and its peacekeepers are bound by IHL. Even when not in an armed conflict the UN has, in recent SOFAs, stated that it shall conduct its operations with 'full respect for the principles and rules ... [of] the four Geneva Conventions ... and their Additional Protocols'[31]—a point also emphasised in the Bulletin.[32] Furthermore, as noted above, peacekeepers are also bound by their State's obligations under IHL. Where peacekeepers meet the threshold for the application of IHL set out in the Bulletin, they will also need to apply the provisions of the Bulletin.

The relevance of IHL to UN peace operations also extends to situations where the Security Council has made specific pronouncements of the applicability of this law to the operation's mandate. For example, Security Council resolution 1778 relating to the United Nations Mission in the Central African Republic and Chad (MINURCAT) reaffirmed the:

> obligation of all parties to implement fully the rules and principles of international humanitarian law, particularly those regarding the protection of humanitarian personnel ...[33]

More specifically, the Security Council has stressed the need for UN peacekeepers conducting joint operations with the armed forces of the Democratic Republic of the Congo to carry out their 'operations in accordance with international law, including [IHL] and [IHRL], as applicable'.[34]

The Security Council has also stated that, where appropriate, it will consider requesting

> regular reporting by United Nations peacekeeping and other relevant missions authorized by the Security Council on concrete steps taken to ensure the protection of the civilian population in the conduct of hostilities and on measures to ensure accountability for violations of applicable international humanitarian law.[35]

In this context, IHL is relevant to peace operations where peacekeepers are mandated to 'co-operate in national and international efforts to bring to justice perpetrators of grave violations of ... international humanitarian law'.[36] This mandate is consistent with the Security Council's aim

---

28 United Nations Secretariat, 'Secretary-General's Bulletin: Observance by United Nations Forces of International Humanitarian Law', UN Doc ST/SGB/1999/13, 6 August 1999, entered into force 12 August 1999 (hereafter Bulletin). See ch 15 below.

29 The updated 'We are United Nations Peacekeeping Personnel' document that now forms the UN standards of conduct in Annex H to the revised model Memorandum of Understanding (see ch 3 above) still has peacekeepers undertaking to comply with the Guidelines on International Humanitarian Law for Forces Undertaking United Nations Peacekeeping Operations rather than undertaking to comply with the Bulletin. See <https://conduct.unmissions.org/> accessed 1 November 2017. It is unclear why the updated 'We are United Nations Peacekeeping Personnel' does not refer to the Bulletin, as it is the more recent standard setting document for compliance with IHL by peacekeepers.

30 Statement of the President of the Security Council, UN Doc S/PRST/2009/1, 14 January 2009, 1 [3].

31 See, for example, Agreement between the United Nations and the Government of Sudan concerning the Status of the United Nations Mission in Sudan (UNMIS SOFA), signed on 28 December 2005 (reproduced in the UN Juridical Yearbook 2005, 44–60), [6(a)]. See ch 2 above.

32 Bulletin (n 28), Section 3.

33 SC Res 1778 (2007) of 25 September 2007, Operative Part [17].

34 SC Res 2277 (2016) of 30 March 2016, Operative Part [18].

35 Statement by the President of the Security Council, UN Doc S/PRST/2009/1, 14 January 2009, Annex, [D].

36 SC Res 1794 (2007) of 21 December 2007, Operative Part [16]. See also SC Res 2211 (2015) of 26 March 2015, Operative Part [24].

'to promote ... the establishment of effective arrangements for investigating and prosecuting violations' of IHL.[37]

The Human Rights Due Diligence Policy on United Nations Support to Non-United Nations Security Forces (Policy) also reinforces that the UN cannot provide support to local or regional forces where 'there are substantial grounds for believing there is a real risk of the receiving entities committing [among other things] grave violations of international humanitarian ... law'.[38] This Policy could be read as reinforcing the principle in Common Article 1 to the four Geneva Conventions to 'respect and ensure respect' for those Conventions.

Even if the Geneva Conventions are not applicable as a matter of law to an operation, many provisions contained therein are useful in establishing best practice standards when dealing with the civilian population of the host country. For example, the provisions in Geneva Conventions I and IV concerning the establishment of protected areas, such as neutral hospital zones, may be useful for peacekeepers where they have been mandated to protect the local population. Furthermore, in relation to peacekeeping practice of taking and handling detainees, Geneva Conventions III and IV provide several provisions that may be useful. The provisions relating to the humane treatment of prisoners of war in Geneva Convention III and internees in Geneva Convention IV may be used by analogy in peace operations. The provisions found in Common Article 3 concerning minimum treatment guarantees must, at the very least, be adhered to if peacekeepers are engaged in armed hostilities.

The UN Rules of Engagement (ROE), a primary document developed by the Department of Peacekeeping Operations (DPKO) governing the use of force by peacekeepers,[39] also incorporates IHL principles, rules, and standards. For example, in relation to the UN Organization Stabilization Mission in the Democratic Republic of the Congo (MONUSCO) the UN has stated that 'the rules of engagement ... have ... been adapted to the new mandate of MONUSCO, and [the Office of Legal Affairs] has ensured that they are in full compliance with the IHL rules relating to the conduct of hostilities'.[40]

The question of whether it is lawful for a belligerent to target peacekeepers as combatants when the peacekeepers are engaged in hostilities where IHL applies has arisen under ICL. In the case of *Prosecutor v Sesay, Kallon and Gbao*, the Special Court for Sierra Leone (SCSL) concluded that peacekeepers are only considered combatants when they take a direct part in the hostilities.[41] The International Criminal Court (ICC), in the pre-trial hearings of cases against Nourain and Jamus,[42] and Garda,[43] reached similar conclusions concerning the combatant status of African Union (AU) peacekeepers. Considering the Secretary-General's Bulletin, the Rome Statute, and the jurisprudence from the tribunals, it is arguable that UN peacekeepers may be a civilian one moment and a combatant another. The practical effect of such a conclusion is that peacekeepers may only be targeted when they are taking a direct or active part in hostilities.[44]

In situations where UN peacekeepers are taking no direct or active part in hostilities, or are not engaged as combatants in an armed conflict, the UN has argued that there is no international instrument that:

> explicitly grant[s] peacekeeping operations the status of a "protected group" (similar to the one enjoyed by medical personnel and units), [however,] the cumulative effect of the "protective clauses" in a series of legal instruments—namely, the protected and protective status of the United Nations emblem, the obligation to protect peacekeeping missions from the effects of mines, the duty to ensure their safety and security and the criminalization and internationalization of attacks against peacekeepers when in an armed conflict [UN peacekeepers] are entitled to protection given to civilians ... [This] is

---

37 Statement of the President of the Security Council, UN Doc S/PRST/2009/1, 14 January 2009, Annex, [F].

38 Human Rights Due Diligence Policy on United Nations Support to Non-United Nations Security Forces, UN Doc A/67/775–S/2013/110, 5 March 2013, Annex [1]. See ch 32 below.

39 See ch 33 below.

40 Patricia O'Brien, 'Respecting IHL: Challenges and Responses', 36th Round-table on Current Issues of International Law, 5 September 2013, <http://legal.un.org/ola/media/info_from_lc/POB-San-Remo-36th-Roundtable-5-September-2013.pdf> accessed 2 October 2018.

41 *Prosecutor v Sesay, Kallon and Gbao* (Judgment) [2009] Special Court for Sierra Leone, Trial Chamber I, Case No SCSL-04-15, [233].

42 *Prosecutor v Abdallah Banda Abakaer Nourain and Saleh Mohammed Jerbo Jamus*, Second Decision on the Proscutor's Application under Article 58, [27 August 2009] ICC-02/05-03/09, [19].

43 *Prosecutor v Bahar Idriss Abu Garda*, Decision on the Confirmation of the Charges [8 February 2010] ICC-02/05-02/09, [83]–[84].

44 For a more detailed discussion on this matter see ch 16 below.

> an indication that a customary international humanitarian law principle has emerged, whereby peacekeeping personnel performing functions under the United Nations Charter in an area and situation of armed conflict and taking no part in the hostilities, are entitled the status of a "protected group"; with the correlative obligation on the Parties to the conflict to take precautionary measures to respect their protected status.[45]

The Security Council, when referring to the safety of UN and associated personnel[46] in its resolutions concerning peace operations, often emphasises the fact that peacekeepers are not combatants. In the resolutions concerning the UN Organization Stabilization Mission in the Democratic Republic of Congo (MONUSCO), for example, the Security Council demands that 'all relevant parties cooperate fully in the deployment ... by guaranteeing the safety, security ... of United Nations and associated personnel'.[47] That 'demand' implies that peacekeepers are not to be targeted.

Regional organisations have also considered the application of IHL to peace operations. The Protocol relating to the Establishment of the Peace and Security Council of the AU[48] emphasises the importance of international law, including IHL, in maintaining peace and security. More specifically, Article 13(13) provides for the African Standby Force to have training on IHL and IHRL, with emphasis in that training on the protection of women and children. The Solemn Declaration on a Common African Defence and Security Policy also emphasises the importance of providing a 'framework for humanitarian action to ensure that international humanitarian law is applied during conflicts between and among African states'.[49] The AU Operational Guidelines, such as those dealing with children and DDR,[50] and detention and DDR,[51] also refer to the application of IHL in AU operations. For example, the AU has stated that the AU Mission in Somalia (AMISOM), 'cognisant of its obligations under international humanitarian law (IHL) ... has continued to make considerable efforts to ensure that its operations are conducted in compliance with applicable IHL'.[52] The UN has also underlined the importance of AMISOM 'abiding by all requirements applicable to it under ... [IHL, particularly] the need for AMISOM to ensure that any detainees in their custody, including disengaged combatants, are treated in strict compliance with applicable obligations under international humanitarian law and human rights law'.[53] In relation to specific violations of IHL, for example in Somalia, the AU has condemned 'all acts of violence perpetrated against humanitarian workers, as well as attacks against civilians, in violation of international humanitarian law'.[54]

The European Union (EU) and its Member States have accepted that IHL applies in situations where 'EU-led forces become engaged in an armed conflict'.[55] Furthermore, in 2009 the EU issued its Updated European Union Guidelines on Promoting Compliance with International Humanitarian Law which aims to 'address compliance with IHL by third States, and, as appropriate, non-State actors operating in third States'.[56] The EU, in at least one of its peace operations, has emphasised the importance of 'training on International Humanitarian Law, protection of civilians and human rights'.[57]

---

45 Note on the Protection of Peacekeeping Personnel under International Humanitarian Law, 9 August 2006, United Nations Juridical Yearbook (2006), 521 [11]. See ch 14 above for details concerning the references in this quote.

46 See ch 14 above.

47 SC Res 2211 (2015) of 26 March 2015, Operative Part [37]. See also SC Res 1925 (2010) of 28 May 2010, Operative Part [21]; and SC Res 2277 (2016) of 30 March 2016, Operative Part [35](iv).

48 Protocol relating to the Establishment of the Peace and Security Council of the African Union (adopted 9 July 2002, entered into force 26 December 2003).

49 Solemn Declaration on a Common African Defence and Security Policy (adopted 28 February 2004) Article 13(v).

50 See, for example, African Union Disarmament, Demobilisation and Reintegration Capacity Program, 'DDR and Children: Operational Guideline', 2014, 9.

51 See, for example, African Union Disarmament, Demobilisation and Reintegration Capacity Program, 'AU Guidelines on Detention and DDR', 2014, 10.

52 African Union Peace and Security Council, 'Report of the Chairperson of the Commission on the Situation in Somalia', PSC/PR/2.(CDLXII), 16 October 2014, [34].

53 SC Res 2124 (2013) of 12 November 2013, [12].

54 African Union Peace and Security Council, Communique, 18 January 2008, PSC/PR/Comm(CV), [8].

55 See Frederik Naert, 'Observance of International Humanitarian Law by Forces under the Command of the European Union' (2013) 95 (891/892) IRRC 639.

56 Updated European Union Guidelines on Promoting Compliance with International Humanitarian Law [2009] *Official Journal of the European Union* C 303/06 15.12.2009, [2].

57 EU Council Decision 2013/34/CFSP of 17 January 2013 on a European Union Military Mission to Contribute to the Training of the Malian Armed Forces (EUTM Mali) [2013] OJ L 14/19, Article 1(2)(b).

The ICRC's most recent view concerning the application of the four Geneva Conventions to UN peace operations is that:

> a case-by-case approach is required in order to determine which entity has effective or overall control over the military operations, and therefore who should be considered a party to the international armed conflict. In some cases, both the international organization and some or all of the States contributing troops to the operation may be Parties to the armed conflict.[58]

58 International Committee of the Red Cross, *Commentary on the First Geneva Convention: Convention (I) for the Amelioration of the Condition of the Wounded and Sick in Armed Forces in the Field* (Cambridge University Press 2016), Commentary to Common Article 2, [252].

15

Secretary-General's Bulletin: Observance by United Nations Forces of International Humanitarian Law

Prefatory Note

The Secretary-General's Bulletin entitled 'Observance by United Nations Forces of International Humanitarian Law' (Bulletin)[1] was entered into force on 12 August 1999. The Bulletin is a set of fundamental principles and rules of international humanitarian law (IHL) applicable to 'United Nations forces when in situations of armed conflict they are actively engaged therein as combatants, to the extent and for the duration of their engagement'.[2] The rules of IHL included in the Bulletin are sourced from the four Geneva Conventions of 1949 and their Additional Protocols of 1977,[3] as well as the 1954 Hague Convention for the Protection of Cultural Property in the Event of Armed Conflict (1954 Hague Convention).[4]

As the Chief Administrative Officer of the UN, under Article 97 of the UN Charter,[5] the Secretary-General has the power to promulgate administrative issuances in the form of bulletins or administrative instructions.[6] Secretary-General's bulletins therefore have authority within the UN as part of its internal regulations. This includes within peace operations as subsidiary organs of the UN. In terms of peacekeepers, the Bulletin binds UN staff directly since all staff are governed by relevant UN rules, regulations, and administrative issuances under the Staff Regulations and Rules.[7] This includes the Force Commander (FC) who remains a UN staff member and, consequently, is bound to consider his or her obligations under the Bulletin when issuing operational orders during a peace operation. The Bulletin binds military observers through the individual undertakings they sign in which they agree to comply with all mission directives and other administrative issuances.

Military members of national contingents have no individual contractual link with the UN and remain administratively attached to their respective national militaries. The obligations of military personnel in a UN peace operation are provided for in the Memorandum of Understanding (MOU) agreed to between the UN and the contributing State.[8] Prior to the revised model MOU of 2007 (Revised Model MOU),[9] military personnel of national contingents were only bound by the

---

1 'Secretary-General's Bulletin: Observance by United Nations Forces of International Humanitarian Law', UN Doc ST/SGB/1999/13, 6 August 1999, entered into force 12 August 1999 (hereafter Bulletin).

2 Ibid, Section 1.1.

3 Geneva Convention for the Amelioration of the Condition of the Wounded and Sick in Armed Forces in the Field (opened for signature 12 August 1949, entered into force 21 October 1950) 75 UNTS 31 (hereafter Geneva Convention I); Geneva Convention for the Amelioration of the Condition of Wounded, Sick and Shipwrecked Members of Armed Forces at Sea (opened for signature 12 August 1949, entered into force 21 October 1950) 75 UNTS 85 (hereafter Geneva Convention II); Geneva Convention Relative to the Treatment of Prisoners of War (opened for signature 12 August 1949, entered into force 21 October 1950) 75 UNTS 135 (hereafter Geneva Convention III); Geneva Convention Relative to the Protection of Civilian Persons in Time of War (opened for signature 12 August 1949, entered into force 21 October 1950) 75 UNTS 287 (hereafter Geneva Convention IV); Protocol Additional to the Geneva Conventions of 12 August 1949, and relating to the Protection of Victims of International Armed Conflicts (Protocol I) (opened for signature 8 June 1977, entered into force 7 December 1978) 1125 UNTS 3; and Protocol Additional to the Geneva Conventions of 12 August 1949, and relating to the Protection of Victims of Non-International Armed Conflicts (Protocol II) (opened for signature 8 June 1977, entered into force 7 December 1978) 1125 UNTS 609. See ch 16 below.

4 Convention for the Protection of Cultural Property in the Event of Armed Conflict (opened for signature 14 May 1954, entered into force 7 August 1956) 249 UNTS 215.

5 See ch 1 above.

6 See 'Secretary-General's Bulletin: Procedures for the Promulgation of Administrative Issuances', UN Doc ST/SGB/1997/1, 28 May 1997, entered into force 1 June 1997.

7 See ch 25 below.

8 See ch 3 above.

9 UN Doc A/61/19 (Part III), 12 June 2007. See ch 3 above.

IHL provisions incorporated into their national laws and not by any obligations in the Bulletin. This has changed with the Revised Model MOU, if it is accepted that the requirement to comply with the 'Guidelines on International Humanitarian Law for Forces Undertaking United Nations Peacekeeping Operations' in Annex H of the Revised Model MOU actually refers to the Bulletin.

One of the results of the promulgation of this Bulletin is the clarification of the application of IHL to UN peacekeepers engaged in specific activities during peace operations. Prior to 1999, UN Status-of-Forces Agreements (SOFAs) which were negotiated between a host State and the UN used the term 'full respect for the principles and spirit' of IHL. After the Secretary-General's Bulletin, the stronger and more definitive term 'full respect for the principle and rules' of IHL was adopted.

The preamble of the Bulletin specifies that it is only 'applicable to United Nations forces conducting operations under United Nations command and control'.[10] This means the Bulletin only applies to UN peace operations. The phrase 'command and control' is not strictly correct as contributing States usually place their national contingents under the UN's operational authority and control whilst retaining national command for such matters as discipline and administration over their military personnel, and thus they are not fully under the command and control of the UN.[11] The Bulletin is also not applicable in UN-authorised peace operations under the command and control of another entity such as a State, regional arrangement, or agency. The Bulletin makes this clear in its preamble. UN-authorised peace operations, unlike UN peace operations, are not subsidiary organs of the UN and do not fall under the operational authority and control of the UN even though they do remain under the ultimate authority and control of the Security Council. As a result, UN-authorised peace operations are not bound by administrative issuances of the Secretary-General such as the Bulletin.

The applicability of IHL to UN forces is outlined in Section 1.1:

> The fundamental principles and rules of international humanitarian law set out in the present bulletin are applicable to United Nations forces when in situations of armed conflict they are actively engaged therein as combatants, to the extent and for the duration of their engagement. They are accordingly applicable in enforcement actions, or in peacekeeping operations when the use of force is permitted in self-defence.[12]

The Bulletin does not provide a definition of the term 'armed conflict'. However, the 'threshold' for applicability under Section 1.1 is higher than that found in the 1949 Geneva Conventions and the 1977 Additional Protocols. The Geneva Conventions and Additional Protocols are more broadly applied during an armed conflict and protection obligations are not premised upon a combatant being 'actively engaged'.

Section 1.1 also articulates a so-called 'dual-key' test for the application of the Bulletin: first, there must be an armed conflict in the area in which peacekeepers are deployed. Second, the Bulletin will only apply for the time and to the extent that peacekeepers are engaged in the conflict. That interpretation of the Bulletin is consistent with the approach taken by the Rome Statute of the International Criminal Court (Rome Statute)[13] and international criminal tribunals.[14] The International Criminal Court (ICC) in the pre-trial hearings of cases against Nourain and Jamus,[15] and Garda,[16] concluded that African Union peacekeepers were only combatants when taking a

---

10 Bulletin (n 1), Preamble.

11 The UN, in relation to UN peace operations, distinguishes between three levels of command. These levels are: (1) overall political direction, the purview of the Security Council; (2) executive direction and control, provided by the Secretary-General; and (3) command in the field, residing in the chief of the mission. See 'Report of the Secretary-General: Command and Control of United Nations Peace-keeping Operations', UN Doc A/49/681, 21 November 1994, [4]. More recently the UN Secretariat has argued that the UN 'maintains, in principle, exclusive "operational command and control" and the lending State such other residual control': International Law Commission, 'Responsibility of International Organizations: Comments and Observations received from International Organizations', 17 February 2011, UN Doc A/CN4/637/Add1, 14 [4].

12 Bulletin (n 1), Section 1.1.

13 See ch 23 below.

14 For the jurisprudence of the Special Court for Sierra Leone on this point, see *Prosecutor v Sesay, Kallon and Gbao* (Judgment) [2009] Special Court for Sierra Leone, Trial Chamber I, Case No SCSL-04-15, (hereafter *RUF Case*). For the jurisprudence of the International Criminal Court, see *Prosecutor v Abdallah Banda Abakaer Nourain and Saleh Mohammed Jerbo Jamus*, Second Decision on the Proscutor's Application under Article 58, [27 August 2009] ICC-02/05-03/09 (hereafter *Nourain and Jamus*); and *Prosecutor v Bahar Idriss Abu Garda*, Decision on the Confirmation of the Charges [8 February 2010] ICC-02/05-02/09 (hereafter *Garda*).

15 *Nourain and Jamus* (n 14), [18]–[21].

16 *Garda* (n 14), [83]–[84].

direct part in hostilities. It should be noted that in *Prosecutor v Sesay, Kallon and Gbao* (*RUF Case*), before the Special Court for Sierra Leone (SCSL), the court also concluded that peacekeepers only become combatants when they take a direct part in the hostilities.[17] The conclusion that is drawn from the Bulletin, the Rome Statute, and the tribunals is that peacekeepers may be a civilian one moment and a combatant another.

The concept of 'self-defence' within the Bulletin is applicable to the defence of the UN mission and its mandate as well as the personal safety of those under the operational command and control of the UN.[18]

Section 2 confirms that the Bulletin does not replace obligations imposed by State ratification of IHL treaties, and thus UN personnel will be bound by their own national laws relating to the laws of war. Section 3 of the Bulletin notes that SOFAs are now required to include the obligation of UN forces to provide 'full respect for the principles and rules' of general international humanitarian law applicable to military operations. In considering applicability, the obligation for the UN to adhere to principles of customary international law is a further consideration in determining the relevance of IHL to UN peace operations.

Whilst some of the sections in the Bulletin mirror obligations found in treaty and customary law, in several instances the Bulletin must be seen as a 'best practice' doctrine where the obligation is beyond that found in IHL. For example, in Section 6.2 a larger range of weapons are prohibited from being used than are permitted under treaty or customary law. In dealing with cultural property, Section 6.6 requires a higher obligation of protection and prohibition when compared with the 1954 Hague Convention as issues such as military necessity are not included in the Bulletin. In a similar manner, Section 6.7, which deals with the destruction of objects indispensable to the survival of the civilian population, is not fettered by the principle of military necessity or proportionately and is thus a blanket prohibition.

In relation to the treatment of detainees, Section 8 of the Bulletin accords protections and privileges found in Geneva Convention III (such as visits by the International Committee of the Red Cross) upon all individuals detained irrespective of the type of armed conflict or the classification of the detainee.

The Bulletin, in conjunction with IHL treaties and principles of customary international law, provides a foundation for the rules of engagement drafted by the UN for each peace operation.

In the case of breaches of the Bulletin by military members of national contingents, the UN can only take administrative action such as repatriation under the Directives for Disciplinary Matters Involving Military Members of National Contingents.[19] Any necessary disciplinary or criminal action against military members of their national contingent must be undertaken by the contributing State pursuant to the assurances given to the UN under the Revised Model MOU. Thus, Section 4 of the Bulletin provides that '[i]n case of violations of international humanitarian law, members of the military personnel of a United Nations force are subject to prosecution in their national courts'.

There is also the possibility of prosecuting peacekeepers before the ICC if their crimes fall within the jurisdiction of the court, and the contributing State shows itself unwilling or unable to prosecute.

Reference

Title	Secretary-General's Bulletin: Observance by United Nations Forces of International Humanitarian Law
Author	Secretary-General of the United Nations
Date of Bulletin	6 August 1999
Entered force	12 August 1999 (in accordance with Section 10)
Source	UN Doc ST/SGB/1999/13
Full Text	<https://conduct.unmissions.org/secretary-general%E2%80%99s-bulletin-observance-united-nations-forces-international-humanitarian-law>[20]

17 *RUF Case* (n 14), [233]. See ch 16 below for a more detailed discussion.

18 See United Nations, 'United Nations Peacekeeping Operations: Principles and Guidelines', 2008, 34–5.

19 The limited jurisdiction of the UN to deal with military personnel is also reinforced by the model SOFA, which provides that military members of the military component of the peace operation are subject to the exclusive criminal jurisdiction of their contributing State. See ch 28 below.

20 Accessed 19 September 2018.

Secretary-General's Bulletin: Observance by United Nations Forces of International Humanitarian Law[21]

(Extracts)

The Secretary-General, for the purpose of setting out fundamental principles and rules of international humanitarian law applicable to United Nations forces conducting operations under United Nations command and control, promulgates the following:

Section 1

Field of application

1.1 The fundamental principles and rules of international humanitarian law set out in the present bulletin are applicable to United Nations forces when in situations of armed conflict they are actively engaged therein as combatants, to the extent and for the duration of their engagement. They are accordingly applicable in enforcement actions, or in peacekeeping operations when the use of force is permitted in self-defence.

1.2 The promulgation of this bulletin does not affect the protected status of members of peacekeeping operations under the 1994 Convention on the Safety of United Nations and Associated Personnel or their status as non-combatants, as long as they are entitled to the protection given to civilians under the international law of armed conflict.

Section 2

Application of national law

The present provisions do not constitute an exhaustive list of principles and rules of international humanitarian law binding upon military personnel, and do not prejudice the application thereof, nor do they replace the national laws by which military personnel remain bound throughout the operation.

Section 3

Status-of-forces agreement

In the status-of-forces agreement concluded between the United Nations and a State in whose territory a United Nations force is deployed, the United Nations undertakes to ensure that the force shall conduct its operations with full respect for the principles and rules of the general conventions applicable to the conduct of military personnel. The United Nations also undertakes to ensure that members of the military personnel of the force are fully acquainted with the principles and rules of those international instruments. The obligation to respect the said principles and rules is applicable to United Nations forces even in the absence of a status-of-forces agreement.

---

21 From Secretary-General's Bulletin: Observance by United Nations Forces of International Humanitarian Law © 1999 United Nations. Reprinted with the permission of the United Nations.

Section 4
Violations of international humanitarian law

In case of violations of international humanitarian law, members of the military personnel of a United Nations force are subject to prosecution in their national courts.

Section 5
Protection of the civilian population

5.1 The United Nations force shall make a clear distinction at all times between civilians and combatants and between civilian objects and military objectives. Military operations shall be directed only against combatants and military objectives. Attacks on civilians or civilian objects are prohibited.

5.2 Civilians shall enjoy the protection afforded by this section, unless and for such time as they take a direct part in hostilities.

5.3 The United Nations force shall take all feasible precautions to avoid, and in any event to minimize, incidental loss of civilian life, injury to civilians or damage to civilian property.

5.4 In its area of operation, the United Nations force shall avoid, to the extent feasible, locating military objectives within or near densely populated areas, and take all necessary precautions to protect the civilian population, individual civilians and civilian objects against the dangers resulting from military operations. Military installations and equipment of peacekeeping operations, as such, shall not be considered military objectives.

5.5 The United Nations force is prohibited from launching operations of a nature likely to strike military objectives and civilians in an indiscriminate manner, as well as operations that may be expected to cause incidental loss of life among the civilian population or damage to civilian objects that would be excessive in relation to the concrete and direct military advantage anticipated.

5.6 The United Nations force shall not engage in reprisals against civilians or civilian objects.

Section 6
Means and methods of combat

6.1 The right of the United Nations force to choose methods and means of combat is not unlimited.

6.2 The United Nations force shall respect the rules prohibiting or restricting the use of certain weapons and methods of combat under the relevant instruments of international humanitarian law. These include, in particular, the prohibition on the use of asphyxiating, poisonous or other gases and biological methods of warfare; bullets which explode, expand or flatten easily in the human body; and certain explosive projectiles. The use of certain conventional weapons, such as non-detectable fragments, anti-personnel mines, booby traps and incendiary weapons, is prohibited.

6.3 The United Nations force is prohibited from employing methods of warfare which may cause superfluous injury or unnecessary suffering, or which are intended, or may be expected to cause, widespread, long-term and severe damage to the natural environment.

6.4 The United Nations force is prohibited from using weapons or methods of combat of a nature to cause unnecessary suffering.

6.5 It is forbidden to order that there shall be no survivors.

6.6 The United Nations force is prohibited from attacking monuments of art, architecture or history, archaeological sites, works of art, places of worship and museums and libraries which constitute the cultural or spiritual heritage of peoples. In its area of operation, the United Nations force shall not use such cultural property or their immediate surroundings for purposes which might expose them to destruction or damage. Theft, pillage, misappropriation and any act of vandalism directed against cultural property is strictly prohibited.

6.7 The United Nations force is prohibited from attacking, destroying, removing or rendering useless objects indispensable to the survival of the civilian population, such as foodstuff, crops, livestock and drinking-water installations and supplies.

6.8 The United Nations force shall not make installations containing dangerous forces, namely dams, dikes and nuclear electrical generating stations, the object of military operations if such operations may cause the release of dangerous forces and consequent severe losses among the civilian population.

6.9 The United Nations forces shall not engage in reprisals against objects and installations protected under this section.

Section 7
Treatment of civilians and persons *hors de combat*

7.1 Persons not, and no longer, taking part in military operations, including civilians, members of armed forces who have laid down their weapons and persons placed *hors de combat* by reason of sickness, wounds or detention, shall, in all circumstances, be treated humanely and without any adverse distinction based on race, sex, religious convictions or any other ground. They shall be accorded full respect for their person, honour and religious and other convictions.

7.2 The following acts against any of the persons mentioned in section 7.1 are prohibited at any time and in any place: violence to life or physical integrity; murder as well as cruel treatment such as torture, mutilation or any form of corporal punishment; collective punishment; reprisals; the taking of hostages; rape; enforced prostitution; any form of sexual assault and humiliation and degrading treatment; enslavement; and pillage.

7.3 Women shall be especially protected against any attack, in particular against rape, enforced prostitution or any other form of indecent assault.

7.4 Children shall be the object of special respect and shall be protected against any form of indecent assault.

Section 8
Treatment of detained persons

The United Nations force shall treat with humanity and respect for their dignity detained members of the armed forces and other persons who no longer take part in military operations by reason of detention. Without prejudice to their legal status, they shall be treated in accordance with the relevant provisions of the Third Geneva Convention of 1949, as may be applicable to them *mutatis mutandis*. In particular:

(a) Their capture and detention shall be notified without delay to the party on which they depend and to the Central Tracing Agency of the International Committee of the Red Cross (ICRC), in particular in order to inform their families;

(b) They shall be held in secure and safe premises which provide all possible safeguards of hygiene and health, and shall not be detained in areas exposed to the dangers of the combat zone;

(c) They shall be entitled to receive food and clothing, hygiene and medical attention;

(d) They shall under no circumstances be subjected to any form of torture or ill-treatment;

(e) Women whose liberty has been restricted shall be held in quarters separated from men's quarters, and shall be under the immediate supervision of women;

(f) In cases where children who have not attained the age of sixteen years take a direct part in hostilities and are arrested, detained or interned by the United Nations force, they shall continue to benefit from special protection. In particular, they shall be held in quarters separate from the quarters of adults, except when accommodated with their families;

(g) ICRC's right to visit prisoners and detained persons shall be respected and guaranteed.

Section 9

Protection of the wounded, the sick, and medical and relief personnel

9.1 Members of the armed forces and other persons in the power of the United Nations force who are wounded or sick shall be respected and protected in all circumstances. They shall be treated humanely and receive the medical care and attention required by their condition, without adverse distinction. Only urgent medical reasons will authorize priority in the order of treatment to be administered.

9.2 Whenever circumstances permit, a suspension of fire shall be arranged, or other local arrangements made, to permit the search for and identification of the wounded, the sick and the dead left on the battlefield and allow for their collection, removal, exchange and transport.

9.3 The United Nations force shall not attack medical establishments or mobile medical units. These shall at all times be respected and protected, unless they are used, outside their humanitarian functions, to attack or otherwise commit harmful acts against the United Nations force.

9.4 The United Nations force shall in all circumstances respect and protect medical personnel exclusively engaged in the search for, transport or treatment of the wounded or sick, as well as religious personnel.

9.5 The United Nations force shall respect and protect transports of wounded and sick or medical equipment in the same way as mobile medical units.

9.6 The United Nations force shall not engage in reprisals against the wounded, the sick or the personnel, establishments and equipment protected under this section.

9.7 The United Nations force shall in all circumstances respect the Red Cross and Red Crescent emblems. These emblems may not be employed except to indicate or to protect medical units and medical establishments, personnel and material. Any misuse of the Red Cross or Red Crescent emblems is prohibited.

9.8 The United Nations force shall respect the right of the families to know about the fate of their sick, wounded and deceased relatives. To this end, the force shall facilitate the work of the ICRC Central Tracing Agency.

9.9 The United Nations force shall facilitate the work of relief operations which are humanitarian and impartial in character and conducted without any adverse distinction, and shall respect personnel, vehicles and premises involved in such operations.

...

16

The Four Geneva Conventions of 1949 and their Additional Protocols

Prefatory Note

The four Geneva Conventions of 12 August 1949 are collectively termed the 'Geneva Conventions'.[1] There are also three Additional Protocols[2] to those Conventions. The four Geneva Conventions apply to international armed conflicts, as does Additional Protocol I. Common Article 3 to the four Conventions and Additional Protocol II apply to non-international armed conflicts. Additional Protocol III applies to both international and non-international armed conflicts. Extracts from the Conventions and their Additional Protocols are reprinted below.

The Geneva Conventions and their Additional Protocols are relevant to UN peace operations in several ways. For example, peacekeepers are expected to comply with the principles and rules stated in the Conventions and Additional Protocols. Peacekeepers are also expected to monitor and sometimes bring to justice those accused of committing serious breaches of the Conventions and Additional Protocols. Additionally, the provisions in the Conventions and the Additional Protocols determine when peacekeepers might be lawfully targeted. Furthermore, knowing when to use, and how to protect, the emblems dealt with in the Geneva Conventions and Additional Protocols is essential to better protecting the victims of armed conflict.

1. The Four Geneva Conventions

Each of the four Geneva Conventions deals with specific subject matter reflected in the titles of the treaties. Geneva Convention I covers armed forces in the field, Geneva Convention II deals with shipwrecked members of armed forces at sea, Geneva Convention III focuses on prisoners of war, and Geneva Convention IV pertains to civilian persons. Whilst each of the Conventions deals with different categories of individuals, the four Geneva Conventions are thematically united by the aim of protecting victims during times of armed conflict. The four Geneva Conventions also contain several Common Articles which are replicated in each Convention.

Common Articles of the Four Geneva Conventions

Common Article 1 requires State Parties to respect, and ensure respect, for the Geneva Conventions in all circumstances. Common Article 2 limits the application of the circumstances in which the Geneva Conventions apply to those situations of armed conflict which may arise between two or more States. In situations of armed conflict not of an international character (i.e. between a State and one or more non-State armed groups or between non-State armed groups) Common Article 3 is particularly important as it is the only Article in the Geneva Conventions dealing with armed

---

1 Geneva Convention for the Amelioration of the Condition of the Wounded and Sick in Armed Forces in the Field (opened for signature 12 August 1949, entered into force 21 October 1950) 75 UNTS 31 (hereafter Geneva Convention I); Geneva Convention for the Amelioration of the Condition of Wounded, Sick and Shipwrecked Members of Armed Forces at Sea (opened for signature 12 August 1949, entered into force 21 October 1950) 75 UNTS 85 (hereafter Geneva Convention II); Geneva Convention Relative to the Treatment of Prisoners of War (opened for signature 12 August 1949, entered into force 21 October 1950) 75 UNTS 135 (hereafter Geneva Convention III); Geneva Convention Relative to the Protection of Civilian Persons in Time of War (opened for signature 12 August 1949, entered into force 21 October 1950) 75 UNTS 287 (hereafter Geneva Convention IV).

2 Protocol Additional to the Geneva Conventions of 12 August 1949, and relating to the Protection of Victims of International Armed Conflicts (Protocol I) (opened for signature 8 June 1977, entered into force 7 December 1978) 1125 UNTS 3 (hereafter Additional Protocol I); Protocol Additional to the Geneva Conventions of 12 August 1949, and relating to the Protection of Victims of Non-International Armed Conflicts (Protocol II) (opened for signature 8 June 1977, entered into force 7 December 1978) 1125 UNTS 609 (hereafter Additional Protocol II); Protocol Additional to the Geneva Conventions of 12 August 1949, and relating to the Adoption of an Additional Distinctive Emblem (Protocol III) (opened for signature 8 December 2005, entered into force 14 January 2007) 2404 UNTS 261 (hereafter Additional Protocol III).

conflict of a 'non-international' nature. Common Article 3 provides some minimum obligations concerning the humane treatment of persons taking no active part in hostilities. The standards of humane treatment required include prohibitions on cruel treatment and torture, the taking of hostages, and outrages on personal dignity.

Articles Dealing with the ICRC and the Requirement for Enforcement

The four Geneva Conventions contain specific provisions relating to the special position of the International Committee of the Red Cross (ICRC). Common Article 3(2) permits the ICRC to offer its services to the parties of the conflict. Article 9 in Geneva Conventions I, II, and III, and Article 10 in Geneva Convention IV also permit the ICRC to carry out humanitarian activities for the benefit of the victims of armed conflict.

There are also provisions that are consistent throughout the Geneva Conventions relating to the obligation of States to enact legislation permitting the prosecution of persons committing, or ordering to be committed, grave breaches of the Geneva Conventions. In each of the Geneva Conventions, States 'shall be under the obligation to search for persons alleged to have committed, or to have ordered to be committed, such grave breaches, and shall bring such persons, regardless of their nationality, before its own courts'.[3]

The three Common Articles to the four Geneva Conventions, as well as the similar Articles dealing with the position of the ICRC and the obligation to prosecute those accused of committing grave breaches, are extracted below in a separate section for ease of reference. The extracts of the four Geneva Conventions follow with a short summary of each Convention. Due to the large number of relevant articles within each of the Geneva Conventions, if a theme or principle is replicated within the treaties it is only included once in the extracts below.

Geneva Convention I for the Amelioration of the Condition of the Wounded and Sick in Armed Forces in the Field

As well as the focus upon the wounded and sick on the battlefield, defined as 'protected persons', Geneva Convention I requires State Parties to protect medical units and establishments, and their personnel. It also contains specific obligations relating to the use of the red cross and red crescent emblems (distinctive emblems which, with Additional Protocol III, will now include the red crystal) including the creation of legislation to prevent the abuse of these emblems. An Annex deals with hospital zones and localities.

Geneva Convention II for the Amelioration of the Condition of Wounded, Sick and Shipwrecked Members of Armed Forces at Sea

In addition to the Common Articles found in all four treaties, Geneva Convention II provides a definition of 'protected persons' to include those wounded, sick and shipwrecked. It also requires States to respect and protect military hospital ships and associated personnel.

Geneva Convention III Relative to the Treatment of Prisoners of War

Ensuring the humane treatment of prisoners of war is an important part of international humanitarian law (IHL) and the original international laws relating to this area can be found in the specific regulations annexed to the 1899 Hague Convention II and the 1907 Hague Convention IV.

Geneva Convention III provides a definition for those to be accorded prisoners of war (PW) status and significant details on the humane treatment of prisoners including matters such as questioning, discipline measures, conditions of internment, and release and repatriation at the close of hostilities. This Convention also deals with matters of correspondence and contains a provision on the rights of the ICRC to visit places of internment.

Geneva Convention IV Relative to the Protection of Civilian Persons in Time of War

Geneva Convention IV deals with the treatment of civilians in the hands of an adversary whether in an occupied territory or in internment, and aims to protect civilians during times of armed conflict.

3 See Geneva Convention I (n 1), Article 49; Geneva Convention II (n 1), Article 50; Geneva Convention III (n 1), Article 129; Geneva Convention IV (n 1), Article 146.

The Convention also provides some regulations relating to the conduct of hostilities; however, these obligations can be found more fully developed in Additional Protocol I.

Geneva Convention IV contains references to the protections accorded to particular categories of civilians (such as women and children), prohibits deportations, deals with ensuring food and medical supplies to the population, and regulates the treatment of internees. Geneva Convention IV also grants rights to the ICRC to visit places of internment. The annexes concern hospital and safety zones, collective relief, and model internment cards, letters, and correspondence cards.

2. Additional Protocols

Protocol I Additional to the Geneva Conventions of 1949

Additional Protocol I develops and extends the four Geneva Conventions. In particular, it supplements Geneva Convention III by its elaboration of who is entitled to the status of combatant and PW, and the treatment of persons during armed conflict. Additional Protocol I also supplements Geneva Convention IV by dealing more directly and extensively with the protection of civilians from the effects of hostilities and by providing regulation on the conduct of military attacks. The Additional Protocol also deals with 'armed conflicts in which peoples are fighting against colonial domination and alien occupation and against racist régimes in the exercise of their right of self-determination'.[4]

Many of the provisions in this Protocol can be found in earlier IHL treaties including the 1907 Hague Convention and its Regulations.[5] The adoption of Additional Protocol I was seen to incorporate rules relating to the conduct of hostilities, which were previously part of the Hague Regulations, into the Geneva Conventions.

A key provision in Additional Protocol I requires parties to the conflict at all times to direct their operations only against military objectives at all times and in doing so 'distinguish between the civilian population and combatants and between civilian objects and military objectives'.[6] Another key provision is the principle that the means and methods used by any party to an armed conflict are not unlimited. Consequently, pursuant to Article 35, the use of means and methods of warfare which cause superfluous injury and unnecessary suffering are prohibited. Article 75 in Additional Protocol I also develops a range of fundamental guarantees to be applied to persons who are in the power of a party to a conflict. Such guarantees include requirements to treat protected persons humanely in all circumstances.

Additional Protocol I also provides greater clarity concerning the treatment of particular categories of civilians. For example, it is more detailed in the measures concerning the protection of women in situations such as arrest or detention when women are pregnant or have dependent infants.[7] Similarly, the regime dealing with the protection of children found in Article 77 of this Additional Protocol provides that children 'shall be the object of special respect and shall be protected against any form of indecent assault'.

Protocol II Additional to the Geneva Conventions of 1949

Additional Protocol II develops Common Article 3 to the four Geneva Conventions, which relates to armed conflict of a non-international nature such as 'internal' or civil wars. The scope of this Additional Protocol is limited. It is not applicable in 'situations of internal disturbances and tensions, such as riots, isolated and sporadic acts of violence'.[8] There is also a requirement for the conflict to be fought between armed forces and 'other armed groups' under responsible command, exercising control of territory, and implementing Additional Protocol II. Additional Protocol II expands several of the protections found in Common Article 3, including the fundamental guarantees of detained individuals and the protection of the civilian population.

---

4 Additional Protocol I (n 2), Article 1(4).

5 Hague Convention (IV) respecting the Laws and Customs of War on Land and Its Annex: Regulations concerning the Laws and Customs of War on Land (opened for signature 18 October 1907, entered into force 26 January 1910).

6 Additional Protocol I (n 2), Article 48.

7 Ibid, Article 76.

8 Additional Protocol II (n 2), Article 1(2).

Protocol III Additional to the Geneva Conventions of 12 August 1949

Protocol III deals exclusively with the creation of an additional distinctive emblem of protection—a red crystal—which is additional to the red cross, the red crescent, and the red lion and sun emblems.

There are a range of reasons why these instruments are highly relevant to peace operations. In particular, many of the obligations found in the Secretary-General's Bulletin entitled 'Observance by United Nations Forces of International Humanitarian Law'[9] are drawn directly from the four Geneva Conventions and the Additional Protocols I and II.

The ICRC's most recent view concerning the application of the four Geneva Conventions to UN peace operations is that:

> a case-by-case approach is required in order to determine which entity has effective or overall control over the military operations and therefore who should be considered a Party to the international armed conflict. In some cases, both the international organization and some or all of the States contributing troops to the operation may be Parties to the armed conflict.[10]

There are situations where the Security Council has stressed the importance of peacekeepers adhering to IHL in the conduct of their operations. In resolution 2277, for example, the Security Council emphasised that the United Nations Organization Stabilization Mission in the Democratic Republic of the Congo (MONUSCO) forces undertaking operations with the armed forces of the Democratic Republic of the Congo are 'to carry out operations in accordance with international law, including international humanitarian law and international human rights law, as applicable'.[11]

In specific instances the Security Council makes pronouncements of the applicability of IHL, including elements of the Geneva Conventions, into peace operation mandates. The General Assembly and the Security Council have also acknowledged the possibility of using the International Fact-Finding Commission pursuant to Article 90 of Additional Protocol I to gather information on alleged violations of IHL.[12]

The issue of whether it is lawful to attack peacekeepers has arisen in the jurisprudence of several tribunals. The Special Court for Sierra Leone (SCSL) has stated that:

> common sense dictates that peacekeepers are considered to be civilians only insofar as they fall within the definition of civilians laid down for non-combatants in customary international law and under Additional Protocol II . . . namely, that they do not take a direct part in hostilities. It is also the Chamber's view that by force of logic, personnel of peacekeeping missions are entitled to protection as long as they are not taking a direct part in the hostilities—and thus have become combatants—at the time of the alleged offence. Where peacekeepers become combatants, they can be legitimate targets for the extent of their participation in accordance with international humanitarian law. As with all civilians, their protection would not cease if the personnel use armed force only in exercising their right to individual self-defence. Likewise, the Chambers opines that the use of force by peacekeepers in self-defence in the discharge of their mandate, provided that it is limited to such use, would not alter or diminish the protection afforded to peacekeepers.[13]

Thus, UN peacekeepers who take a direct part in hostilities lose the protection afforded to civilians pursuant to Article 50 in Additional Protocol I, and Article 13 of Additional Protocol II.

However, to conclude that peacekeepers are in fact taking a direct part in hostilities the SCSL opined that it is necessary to:

> consider the totality of the circumstances existing at the time of the alleged offence, including, *inter alia*, the relevant Security Council resolutions for the operation, the specific operational mandates, the role and practices actually adopted by the peacekeeping mission during the particular conflict, their rules of engagement and operational orders, the nature of the arms and equipment used by the peacekeeping force, the interaction between the peacekeeping force and the parties involved in the conflict,

---

9 See ch 15 above.

10 International Committee of the Red Cross, *Commentary on the First Geneva Convention: Convention (I) for the Amelioration of the Condition of the Wounded and Sick in Armed Forces in the Field* (Cambridge University Press 2016), Commentary to Common Article 2, [252].

11 SC Res 2277 (2016) of 30 March 2016, Operative Part [18].

12 See, for example, General Assembly, 'Status of the Protocols Additional to the Geneva Conventions of 1949 and relating to the Protection of Victims of Armed Conflicts', UN Doc A/C.6/69/L.12, 10 November 2014, Preamble. For the Security Council, see SC Res 1894 (2009) of 11 November 2009, Operative Part [9].

13 *Prosecutor v Issa Hassan Sesay, Morris Kallon and Augustine Gbao* (Trial Judgment) [2009] SCSL-04-15-A, [233].

> any use of force between the peacekeeping force and the parties in the conflict, the nature and frequency of such force and the conduct of the alleged victim(s) and their fellow personnel.[14]

The above non-exhaustive list of indicia as to when a peacekeeper might be taking a direct part in hostilities should be compared with the test suggested by the ICRC. The ICRC has argued that a civilian must meet the following cumulative criteria to be considered as 'taking a direct or active part in hostilities':

1. The act must be likely to adversely affect the military operations or military capacity of a party to an armed conflict or, alternatively, to inflict death, injury, or destruction on persons or objects protected against direct attack (threshold of harm); and
2. there must be a direct causal link between the act and the harm likely to result either from that act, or from a coordinated military operation of which that act constitutes an integral part (direct causation); and
3. the act must be specifically designed to directly cause the required threshold of harm in support of a party to the conflict and to the detriment of another (belligerent nexus).[15]

In *Prosecutor v Bahar Idriss Abu Garda*, the International Criminal Court (ICC) reinforced the views of the SCSL in relation to attacks on African Union peacekeepers.[16] The ICC also stated that in situations where attacks are carried out in a non-international armed conflict against objects such as UN peacekeeping installations, materials, units, or vehicles, those objects:

> shall be entitled to the protection given to civilian objects, unless and for such time as their nature, location, purpose or use make an effective contribution to the military action of a party to the conflict and insofar as their total or partial destruction, capture or neutralization, in the circumstances ruling at the time, offers a definite military advantage.[17]

The ICC reached that conclusion on the basis that even though Additional Protocol I has no prohibition against attacking civilian objects, such attacks are prohibited as a matter of customary international law.[18]

The approaches taken by both the SCSL and the ICC in relation to attacks on peacekeepers is consistent with the offence of war crimes against peacekeepers found in Article 8(2)(e)(iii) of the Rome Statute of the International Criminal Court (Rome Statute).[19]

The SCSL has also discussed the law concerning the issue of when holding peacekeepers hostage might be considered a breach of Common Article 3 and of Additional Protocol II.[20] A further offence, explicitly dealt with by Additional Protocol I, Article 37 is the act of 'feigning ... protected status by the use of signs, emblems or uniforms of the United Nations'.

The UN has also argued that there is no international instrument that:

> explicitly grant[s] peacekeeping operations the status of a 'protected group' (similar to the one enjoyed by medical personnel and units), [however] the cumulative effect of the 'protective clauses' in a series of legal instruments—namely, the protected and protective status of the United Nations emblem, the obligation to protect peacekeeping missions from the effects of mines, the duty to ensure their safety and security and the criminalization and internationalization of attacks against peacekeepers when in an armed conflict ... [UN peacekeepers] are entitled to protection given to civilians ... [This] is an indication that a customary international humanitarian law principle has emerged, whereby peacekeeping personnel performing functions under the United Nations Charter in an area and situation of armed conflict and taking no part in the hostilities, are entitled the status of a 'protected group': with the correlative obligation on the Parties to the conflict to take precautionary measures to respect their protected status.[21]

---

14 Ibid, [234].

15 'Interpretive Guidance on the Notion of Direct Participation in Hostilities under International Humanitarian Law, Adopted by the Assembly of the International Committee of the Red Cross on 26 February 2009' (2008) 90 *IRRC* 995–6.

16 Situation in Darfur, Sudan, in the case of the *Prosecutor v Bahar Idriss Abu Garda* (Public Redacted Version, Decision on the Confirmation of Charges) [2010] ICC-02/05-02/09, [83].

17 Ibid, [89].

18 Ibid, [88].

19 Rome Statute of the International Criminal Court (opened for signature 17 July 1998, entered into force 1 July 2002) 2187 UNTS 3.

20 See the discussion in *Prosecutor v Issa Hassan Sesay, Morris Kallon and Augustine Gbao* (Appeal judgment) [2009] Case No SCSL-04-15-A [550]–[609] concerning the elements concerning the prohibition against taking of hostages as a war crime.

21 'Note on the Protection of Peacekeeping Personnel under International Humanitarian Law', 9 August 2006, United Nations Juridical Yearbook (2006), 521 [11]. See ch 14 above for more detail concerning the references in this quote.

The Additional Protocols are relevant in situations where the Security Council has included in the mission's mandate specific obligations relating to IHL. For example, in Security Council resolution 1794 concerning the mandate for the United Nations Organization Mission in the Democratic Republic of the Congo (MONUC), peacekeepers were requested by the Security Council 'to strengthen prevention, protection, and response to sexual violence'.[22] Both Additional Protocols I and II provide a more detailed articulation of what is meant by the term 'sexual violence'. In particular, sexual violence would include, pursuant to Additional Protocol II, Article 4(2)(e), 'outrages upon personal dignity, in particular, humiliating and degrading treatment, rape, enforced prostitution and any form of indecent assault'.

Many of the provisions of the Geneva Conventions and their Additional Protocols are useful in establishing appropriate standards for peacekeepers when they are dealing with the civilian population of the host State. For example, the provisions in Geneva Conventions I and IV concerning the establishment of protected areas such as neutral hospital zones may be useful for peacekeepers in circumstances where they have been mandated to protect the local population. Furthermore, where peacekeepers take and handle detainees, Geneva Conventions III and IV provide several provisions that may be useful. The provisions relating to the humane treatment of prisoners of war in Geneva Convention III and internees in Geneva Convention IV may be used by analogy in peace operations. Furthermore, even in situations where a peace operation is not deployed during an armed conflict but is undertaking an 'administration of territory mandate' such as in Kosovo or Timor-Leste, peacekeepers might draw inspiration from provisions concerning the law of occupation in Geneva Convention IV to deal with such matters as changing the penal law of the territory appropriate provisions.[23] Article 35 in Geneva Convention IV is also important to reinforce the principle that civilians should be permitted to leave a territory before or during armed conflict.

If the Additional Protocols do not apply to peace operations as a matter of law, they nonetheless are useful in establishing appropriate standards for peacekeepers in their dealings with the national population of the host State. For example, the provisions relating to fundamental guarantees found in Additional Protocol I, Article 75, provide minimum standards concerning treatment that peacekeepers should comply with. Similarly, the provisions in both Article 75 in Additional Protocol I and Article 5 in Additional Protocol II provide fundamental standards that should be applied by peacekeepers when they are required to deal with persons who have been detained.

It is important for peacekeepers to know and respect the emblems dealt with in Additional Protocol III which are legally utilised by military, medical, and religious personnel, as well humanitarian workers with the International Red Cross/Crescent Movement. Misuse of these emblems to gain a military advantage is the war crime of perfidy. Article 5 of this Additional Protocol is concerned with missions under UN auspices and provides that medical and religious personnel in UN operations may use the red cross, the red crescent, red lion and sun, or the red crystal.

More broadly, the Security Council has also stated that, where appropriate, it will consider requesting:

> regular reporting by United Nations peacekeeping and other relevant missions authorized by the Security Council on concrete steps taken to ensure the protection of the civilian population in the conduct of hostilities and on measures to ensure accountability for violations of applicable international humanitarian law.[24]

References[25]

Title	Geneva Convention for the Amelioration of the Condition of the Wounded and Sick in Armed Forces in the Field of August 12, 1949 (Geneva Convention I)
Date of Adoption	12 August 1949
Period for Signature	12 August 1949 to 12 February 1950 (see Article 56)
Entered into Force	21 October 1950 in accordance with Article 58
Parties	196

22 SC Res 1794 (2007) of 21 December 2007, Operative Part [18].

23 See Geneva Convention IV (n 1), Article 64.

24 Statement by the President of the Security Council, UN Doc S/PRST/2009/1, 14 January 2009, Annex, [D].

25 The International Committee of the Red Cross (ICRC) maintains an IHL database which contains the full text, commentaries and up to date status on the four Geneva Conventions of 1949 <http://www.icrc.org/ihl.nsf> accessed 18 November 2018.

Depository Switzerland
Treaty Series 75 UNTS 31
Full Text <http://www.icrc.org/ihl.nsf/FULL/365?OpenDocument>[26]

Title Geneva Convention for the Amelioration of the Condition of Wounded, Sick and Shipwrecked Members of Armed Forces at Sea of August 12, 1949 (Geneva Convention II)
Date of Adoption 12 August 1949
Period for Signature 12 August 1949 to 12 February 1950 (see Article 55)
Entered into Force 21 October 1950 in accordance with Article 57
Parties 196
Depository Switzerland
Treaty Series 75 UNTS 85
Full Text <http://www.icrc.org/ihl.nsf/FULL/370?OpenDocument>[27]

Title Geneva Convention Relative to the Treatment of Prisoners of War of August 12, 1949 (Geneva Convention III)
Date of Adoption 12 August 1949
Period for Signature 12 August 1949 to 12 February 1950 (see Article 136)
Entered into Force 21 October 1950 in accordance with Article 138
Parties 196
Depository Switzerland
Treaty Series 75 UNTS 135
Full Text <http://www.icrc.org/ihl.nsf/FULL/375?OpenDocument>[28]

Title Geneva Convention Relative to the Protection of Civilian Persons in Time of War of August 12, 1949 (Geneva Convention IV)
Date of Adoption 12 August 1949
Period for Signature 12 August 1949 to 12 February 1950 (see Article 151)
Entered into Force 21 October 1950 in accordance with Article 153
Parties 196
Depository Switzerland
Treaty Series 75 UNTS 287
Full Text <http://www.icrc.org/ihl.nsf/FULL/380?OpenDocument>[29]

Title Protocol Additional to the Geneva Conventions of 12 August 1949, and relating to the Protection of Victims of International Armed Conflicts (Protocol I)
Date of Adoption 8 June 1977
Period for Signature 12 months from 12 December 1977 (Article 92)
Entered into Force 7 December 1978 in accordance with Article 95(1)
Parties 174
Depository Switzerland
Treaty Series 1125 UNTS 3
Full Text <http://www.icrc.org/ihl.nsf/FULL/470?OpenDocument>[30]

Title Protocol Additional to the Geneva Conventions of 12 August 1949, and relating to the Protection of Victims of Non-International Armed Conflicts (Protocol II)
Date of Adoption 8 June 1977
Period for Signature 12 months from 12 December 1977 (Article 20)
Entered into Force 7 December 1978 in accordance with Article 23(1)
Parties 168
Depository Switzerland
Treaty Series 1125 UNTS 609
Full Text <http://www.icrc.org/ihl.nsf/FULL/475?OpenDocument>[31]

Title Protocol Additional to the Geneva Conventions of 12 August 1949, and relating to the Adoption of an Additional Distinctive Emblem (Protocol III)

---

26 Accessed 18 November 2018.
27 Accessed 18 November 2018.
28 Accessed 18 November 2018.
29 Accessed 18 November 2018.
30 Accessed 18 November 2018.
31 Accessed 18 November 2018.

Open for Signature 8 December 2005
Entered into Force 14 January 2007 in accordance with Article 11
Parties 73
Depository Switzerland
Treaty Series 2404 UNTS 261
Full Text <http://www.icrc.org/ihl.nsf/FULL/615?OpenDocument>[32]

Common Articles to the Four Geneva Conventions

(Extracts)

Article 1

The High Contracting Parties undertake to respect and to ensure respect for the present Convention in all circumstances.

Article 2

In addition to the provisions which shall be implemented in peacetime, the present Convention shall apply to all cases of declared war or of any other armed conflict which may arise between two or more of the High Contracting Parties, even if the state of war is not recognized by one of them.

The Convention shall also apply to all cases of partial or total occupation of the territory of a High Contracting Party, even if the said occupation meets with no armed resistance.

Although one of the Powers in conflict may not be a party to the present Convention, the Powers who are parties thereto shall remain bound by it in their mutual relations. They shall furthermore be bound by the Convention in relation to the said Power, if the latter accepts and applies the provisions thereof.

Article 3

In the case of armed conflict not of an international character occurring in the territory of one of the High Contracting Parties, each Party to the conflict shall be bound to apply, as a minimum, the following provisions:

1. Persons taking no active part in the hostilities, including members of armed forces who have laid down their arms and those placed *hors de combat* by sickness, wounds, detention, or any other cause, shall in all circumstances be treated humanely, without any adverse distinction founded on race, colour, religion or faith, sex, birth or wealth, or any other similar criteria.

To this end, the following acts are and shall remain prohibited at any time and in any place whatsoever with respect to the above-mentioned persons:

(a) violence to life and person, in particular murder of all kinds, mutilation, cruel treatment and torture;

(b) taking of hostages;

(c) outrages upon personal dignity, in particular, humiliating and degrading treatment;

32 Accessed 18 November 2018.

(d) the passing of sentences and the carrying out of executions without previous judgment pronounced by a regularly constituted court, affording all the judicial guarantees which are recognized as indispensable by civilized peoples.

2. The wounded and sick shall be collected and cared for.[33]

An impartial humanitarian body, such as the International Committee of the Red Cross, may offer its services to the Parties to the conflict.

The Parties to the conflict should further endeavour to bring into force, by means of special agreements, all or part of the other provisions of the present Convention.

The application of the preceding provisions shall not affect the legal status of the Parties to the conflict.

. . .

Articles dealing with the ICRC and the requirements of enforcing IHL

(Extracts)

Article 9(GC1)[34]

The provisions of the present Convention constitute no obstacle to the humanitarian activities which the International Committee of the Red Cross or any other impartial humanitarian organization may, subject to the consent of the Parties to the conflict concerned, undertake for the protection of wounded and sick, medical personnel and chaplains, and for their relief.

. . .

Chapter IX – Repression of Abuses and Infractions

Article 49(GCI)[35]

The High Contracting Parties undertake to enact any legislation necessary to provide effective penal sanctions for persons committing, or ordering to be committed, any of the grave breaches of the present Convention defined in the following Article.

Each High Contracting Party shall be under the obligation to search for persons alleged to have committed, or to have ordered to be committed, such grave breaches, and shall bring such persons, regardless of their nationality, before its own courts. It may also, if it prefers, and in accordance with the provisions of its own legislation, hand such persons over for trial to another High Contracting Party concerned, provided such High Contracting Party has made out a *prima facie* case.

Each High Contracting Party shall take measures necessary for the suppression of all acts contrary to the provisions of the present Convention other than the grave breaches defined in the following Article.

33 In Geneva Convention II, Common Article 3(2) also mentions the 'shipwrecked'.

34 See also Geneva Convention II and III, Article 9; Geneva Convention IV, Article 10.

35 See also Geneva Convention II, Article 50; Geneva Convention III, Article 129; Geneva Convention IV, Article 146.

In all circumstances, the accused persons shall benefit by safeguards of proper trial and defence, which shall not be less favourable than those provided by Article 105 and those following of the Geneva Convention relative to the Treatment of Prisoners of War of August 12, 1949.

Article 50 (GCI)[36]

Grave breaches to which the preceding Article relates shall be those involving any of the following acts, if committed against persons or property protected by the Convention: wilful killing, torture or inhuman treatment, including biological experiments, wilfully causing great suffering or serious injury to body or health, and extensive destruction and appropriation of property, not justified by military necessity and carried out unlawfully and wantonly.

Article 51 (GCI)[37]

No High Contracting Party shall be allowed to absolve itself or any other High Contracting Party of any liability incurred by itself or by another High Contracting Party in respect of breaches referred to in the preceding Article.

Article 52 (GCI)[38]

At the request of a Party to the conflict, an enquiry shall be instituted, in a manner to be decided between the interested Parties, concerning any alleged violation of the Convention.

If agreement has not been reached concerning the procedure for the enquiry, the Parties should agree on the choice of an umpire who will decide upon the procedure to be followed.

Once the violation has been established, the Parties to the conflict shall put an end to it and shall repress it with the least possible delay.

. . .

Geneva Convention for the Amelioration of the Condition of the Wounded and Sick in Armed Forces in the Field of August 12, 1949 (Geneva Convention I)

(Extracts)

. . .

Article 12

Members of the armed forces and other persons mentioned in the following Article, who are wounded or sick, shall be respected and protected in all circumstances.

They shall be treated humanely and cared for by the Party to the conflict in whose power they may be, without any adverse distinction founded on sex, race, nationality, religion, political opinions, or any other similar criteria. Any attempts upon their lives, or violence to their persons, shall be strictly prohibited; in particular, they shall not be murdered or exterminated,

36 See also Geneva Convention II, Article 51; Geneva Convention III, Article 130; Geneva Convention IV, Article 147.

37 See also Geneva Convention II, Article 52; Geneva Convention III, Article 131; Geneva Convention IV, Article 148.

38 See also Geneva Convention II, Article 53; Geneva Convention III, Article 132; Geneva Convention IV, Article 149.

subjected to torture or to biological experiments; they shall not wilfully be left without medical assistance and care, nor shall conditions exposing them to contagion or infection be created.

Only urgent medical reasons will authorize priority in the order of treatment to be administered.

Women shall be treated with all consideration due to their sex.

The Party to the conflict which is compelled to abandon wounded or sick to the enemy shall, as far as military considerations permit, leave with them a part of its medical personnel and material to assist in their care.

...

Article 14

Subject to the provisions of Article 12, the wounded and sick of a belligerent who fall into enemy hands shall be prisoners of war, and the provisions of international law concerning prisoners of war shall apply to them.

...

Article 19

Fixed establishments and mobile medical units of the Medical Service may in no circumstances be attacked, but shall at all times be respected and protected by the Parties to the conflict. Should they fall into the hands of the adverse Party, their personnel shall be free to pursue their duties, as long as the capturing Power has not itself ensured the necessary care of the wounded and sick found in such establishments and units.

The responsible authorities shall ensure that the said medical establishments and units are, as far as possible, situated in such a manner that attacks against military objectives cannot imperil their safety.

...

Article 23

In time of peace, the High Contracting Parties and, after the outbreak of hostilities, the Parties to the conflict, may establish in their own territory and, if the need arises, in occupied areas, hospital zones and localities so organized as to protect the wounded and sick from the effects of war, as well as the personnel entrusted with the organization and administration of these zones and localities and with the care of the persons therein assembled.

Upon the outbreak and during the course of hostilities, the Parties concerned may conclude agreements on mutual recognition of the hospital zones and localities they have created. They may for this purpose implement the provisions of the Draft Agreement annexed to the present Convention, with such amendments as they may consider necessary.

The Protecting Powers and the International Committee of the Red Cross are invited to lend their good offices in order to facilitate the institution and recognition of these hospital zones and localities.

Article 24

Medical personnel exclusively engaged in the search for, or the collection, transport or treatment of the wounded or sick, or in the prevention of disease, staff exclusively engaged in the administration of medical units and establishments, as well as chaplains attached to the armed forces, shall be respected and protected in all circumstances.

...

Article 26

The staff of National Red Cross Societies and that of other Voluntary Aid Societies, duly recognized and authorized by their Governments, who may be employed on the same duties as the personnel named in Article 24, are placed on the same footing as the personnel named in the said Article, provided that the staff of such societies are subject to military laws and regulations.

Each High Contracting Party shall notify to the other, either in time of peace or at the commencement of or during hostilities, but in any case before actually employing them, the names of the societies which it has authorized, under its responsibility, to render assistance to the regular medical service of its armed forces.

...

Article 38

As a compliment to Switzerland, the heraldic emblem of the red cross on a white ground, formed by reversing the Federal colours, is retained as the emblem and distinctive sign of the Medical Service of armed forces.

Nevertheless, in the case of countries which already use as emblem, in place of the red cross, the red crescent or the red lion and sun on a white ground, those emblems are also recognized by the terms of the present Convention.

...

Geneva Convention for the Amelioration of the Condition of Wounded, Sick and Shipwrecked Members of Armed Forces at Sea of August 12, 1949 (Geneva Convention II)

(Extracts)

...

Article 12

Members of the armed forces and other persons mentioned in the following Article, who are at sea and who are wounded, sick or shipwrecked, shall be respected and protected in all circumstances, it being understood that the term "shipwreck" means shipwreck from any cause and includes forced landings at sea by or from aircraft.

Such persons shall be treated humanely and cared for by the Parties to the conflict in whose power they may be, without any adverse distinction founded on sex, race, nationality, religion, political opinions, or any other similar criteria. Any attempts upon their lives, or violence to their persons, shall be strictly prohibited; in particular, they shall not be murdered or exterminated, subjected to torture or to biological experiments; they shall not wilfully be left without medical assistance and care, nor shall conditions exposing them to contagion or infection be created.

Only urgent medical reasons will authorize priority in the order of treatment to be administered. Women shall be treated with all consideration due to their sex.

...

Geneva Convention Relative to the Treatment of Prisoners of War of August 12, 1949 (Geneva Convention III)

(Extracts)

...

Article 4

A. Prisoners of war, in the sense of the present Convention, are persons belonging to one of the following categories, who have fallen into the power of the enemy:

1. Members of the armed forces of a Party to the conflict as well as members of militias or volunteer corps forming part of such armed forces.
2. Members of other militias and members of other volunteer corps, including those of organized resistance movements, belonging to a Party to the conflict and operating in or outside their own territory, even if this territory is occupied, provided that such militias or volunteer corps, including such organized resistance movements, fulfil the following conditions:
   (a) that of being commanded by a person responsible for his subordinates;
   (b) that of having a fixed distinctive sign recognizable at a distance;
   (c) that of carrying arms openly;
   (d) that of conducting their operations in accordance with the laws and customs of war.
3. Members of regular armed forces who profess allegiance to a government or an authority not recognized by the Detaining Power.
4. Persons who accompany the armed forces without actually being members thereof, such as civilian members of military aircraft crews, war correspondents, supply contractors, members of labour units or of services responsible for the welfare of the armed forces, provided that they have received authorization from the armed forces which they accompany, who shall provide them for that purpose with an identity card similar to the annexed model.
5. Members of crews, including masters, pilots and apprentices, of the merchant marine and the crews of civil aircraft of the Parties to the conflict, who do not benefit by more favourable treatment under any other provisions of international law.
6. Inhabitants of a non-occupied territory, who on the approach of the enemy spontaneously take up arms to resist the invading forces, without having had time to form themselves into regular armed units, provided they carry arms openly and respect the laws and customs of war.

B. The following shall likewise be treated as prisoners of war under the present Convention:

1. Persons belonging, or having belonged, to the armed forces of the occupied country, if the occupying Power considers it necessary by reason of such allegiance to intern them, even though it has originally liberated them while hostilities were going on outside the territory it occupies, in particular where such persons have made an unsuccessful attempt to rejoin the armed forces to which they belong and which are engaged in combat, or where they fail to comply with a summons made to them with a view to internment.

2. The persons belonging to one of the categories enumerated in the present Article, who have been received by neutral or non-belligerent Powers on their territory and whom these Powers are required to intern under international law, without prejudice to any more favourable treatment which these Powers may choose to give and with the exception of Articles 8, 10, 15, 30, fifth paragraph, 58–67, 92, 126 and, where diplomatic relations exist between the Parties to the conflict and the neutral or non-belligerent Power concerned, those Articles concerning the Protecting Power. Where such diplomatic relations exist, the Parties to a conflict on whom these persons depend shall be allowed to perform towards them the functions of a Protecting Power as provided in the present Convention, without prejudice to the functions which these Parties normally exercise in conformity with diplomatic and consular usage and treaties.

C. This Article shall in no way affect the status of medical personnel and chaplains as provided for in Article 33 of the present Convention.

Article 5

The present Convention shall apply to the persons referred to in Article 4 from the time they fall into the power of the enemy and until their final release and repatriation.

Should any doubt arise as to whether persons, having committed a belligerent act and having fallen into the hands of the enemy, belong to any of the categories enumerated in Article 4, such persons shall enjoy the protection of the present Convention until such time as their status has been determined by a competent tribunal.

...

Article 12

Prisoners of war are in the hands of the enemy Power, but not of the individuals or military units who have captured them. Irrespective of the individual responsibilities that may exist, the Detaining Power is responsible for the treatment given them.

Prisoners of war may only be transferred by the Detaining Power to a Power which is a party to the Convention and after the Detaining Power has satisfied itself of the willingness and ability of such transferee Power to apply the Convention. When prisoners of war are transferred under such circumstances, responsibility for the application of the Convention rests on the Power accepting them while they are in its custody.

Nevertheless if that Power fails to carry out the provisions of the Convention in any important respect, the Power by whom the prisoners of war were transferred shall, upon being notified by the Protecting Power, take effective measures to correct the situation or shall request the return of the prisoners of war. Such requests must be complied with.

Article 13

Prisoners of war must at all times be humanely treated. Any unlawful act or omission by the Detaining Power causing death or seriously endangering the health of a prisoner of war in its custody is prohibited, and will be regarded as a serious breach of the present Convention. In particular, no prisoner of war may be subjected to physical mutilation or to medical or scientific experiments of any kind which are not justified by the medical, dental or hospital treatment of the prisoner concerned and carried out in his interest.

Likewise, prisoners of war must at all times be protected, particularly against acts of violence or intimidation and against insults and public curiosity.

Measures of reprisal against prisoners of war are prohibited.

Article 14

Prisoners of war are entitled in all circumstances to respect for their persons and their honour.

Women shall be treated with all the regard due to their sex and shall in all cases benefit by treatment as favourable as that granted to men.

Prisoners of war shall retain the full civil capacity which they enjoyed at the time of their capture. The Detaining Power may not restrict the exercise, either within or without its own territory, of the rights such capacity confers except in so far as the captivity requires.

. . .

Article 17

Every prisoner of war, when questioned on the subject, is bound to give only his surname, first names and rank, date of birth, and army, regimental, personal or serial number, or failing this, equivalent information.

If he wilfully infringes this rule, he may render himself liable to a restriction of the privileges accorded to his rank or status.

Each Party to a conflict is required to furnish the persons under its jurisdiction who are liable to become prisoners of war, with an identity card showing the owner's surname, first names, rank, army, regimental, personal or serial number or equivalent information, and date of birth. The identity card may, furthermore, bear the signature or the fingerprints, or both, of the owner, and may bear, as well, any other information the Party to the conflict may wish to add concerning persons belonging to its armed forces. As far as possible the card shall measure 6.5 x 10 cm. and shall be issued in duplicate. The identity card shall be shown by the prisoner of war upon demand, but may in no case be taken away from him.

No physical or mental torture, nor any other form of coercion, may be inflicted on prisoners of war to secure from them information of any kind whatever. Prisoners of war who refuse to answer may not be threatened, insulted, or exposed to any unpleasant or disadvantageous treatment of any kind.

Prisoners of war who, owing to their physical or mental condition, are unable to state their identity, shall be handed over to the medical service. The identity of such prisoners shall be established by all possible means, subject to the provisions of the preceding paragraph.

The questioning of prisoners of war shall be carried out in a language which they understand.

Article 18

All effects and articles of personal use, except arms, horses, military equipment and military documents, shall remain in the possession of prisoners of war, likewise their metal helmets and gas masks and like articles issued for personal protection. Effects and articles used for their clothing or feeding shall likewise remain in their possession, even if such effects and articles belong to their regulation military equipment.

At no time should prisoners of war be without identity documents. The Detaining Power shall supply such documents to prisoners of war who possess none.

. . .

The Detaining Power may withdraw articles of value from prisoners of war only for reasons of security; when such articles are withdrawn, the procedure laid down for sums of money impounded shall apply.

Such objects, likewise the sums taken away in any currency other than that of the Detaining Power and the conversion of which has not been asked for by the owners, shall be kept in the custody of the Detaining Power and shall be returned in their initial shape to prisoners of war at the end of their captivity.

. . .

Article 23

No prisoner of war may at any time be sent to, or detained in areas where he may be exposed to the fire of the combat zone, nor may his presence be used to render certain points or areas immune from military operations.

Prisoners of war shall have shelters against air bombardment and other hazards of war, to the same extent as the local civilian population. With the exception of those engaged in the protection of their quarters against the aforesaid hazards, they may enter such shelters as soon as possible after the giving of the alarm. Any other protective measure taken in favour of the population shall also apply to them.

Detaining Powers shall give the Powers concerned, through the intermediary of the Protecting Powers, all useful information regarding the geographical location of prisoner of war camps.

Whenever military considerations permit, prisoner of war camps shall be indicated in the day-time by the letters PW or PG, placed so as to be clearly visible from the air. The Powers concerned may, however, agree upon any other system of marking. Only prisoner of war camps shall be marked as such.

...

Article 25

Prisoners of war shall be quartered under conditions as favourable as those for the forces of the Detaining Power who are billeted in the same area. The said conditions shall make allowance for the habits and customs of the prisoners and shall in no case be prejudicial to their health.

The foregoing provisions shall apply in particular to the dormitories of prisoners of war as regards both total surface and minimum cubic space, and the general installations, bedding and blankets.

The premises provided for the use of prisoners of war individually or collectively, shall be entirely protected from dampness and adequately heated and lighted, in particular between dusk and lights out. All precautions must be taken against the danger of fire.

In any camps in which women prisoners of war, as well as men, are accommodated, separate dormitories shall be provided for them.

Article 26

The basic daily food rations shall be sufficient in quantity, quality and variety to keep prisoners of war in good health and to prevent loss of weight or the development of nutritional deficiencies. Account shall also be taken of the habitual diet of the prisoners.

The Detaining Power shall supply prisoners of war who work with such additional rations as are necessary for the labour on which they are employed.

Sufficient drinking water shall be supplied to prisoners of war. The use of tobacco shall be permitted.

Prisoners of war shall, as far as possible, be associated with the preparation of their meals; they may be employed for that purpose in the kitchens. Furthermore, they shall be given the means of preparing, themselves, the additional food in their possession.

Adequate premises shall be provided for messing.

Collective disciplinary measures affecting food are prohibited.

...

Article 29

The Detaining Power shall be bound to take all sanitary measures necessary to ensure the cleanliness and healthfulness of camps and to prevent epidemics.

Prisoners of war shall have for their use, day and night, conveniences which conform to the rules of hygiene and are maintained in a constant state of cleanliness. In any camps in which women prisoners of war are accommodated, separate conveniences shall be provided for them.

Also, apart from the baths and showers with which the camps shall be furnished, prisoners of war shall be provided with sufficient water and soap for their personal toilet and for washing their personal laundry; the necessary installations, facilities and time shall be granted them for that purpose.

...

Article 31

Medical inspections of prisoners of war shall be held at least once a month. They shall include the checking and the recording of the weight of each prisoner of war. Their purpose shall be, in particular, to supervise the general state of health, nutrition and cleanliness of prisoners and to detect contagious diseases, especially tuberculosis, malaria and venereal disease. For this purpose the most efficient methods available shall be employed, e.g. periodic mass miniature radiography for the early detection of tuberculosis.

...

Article 34

Prisoners of war shall enjoy complete latitude in the exercise of their religious duties, including attendance at the service of their faith, on condition that they comply with the disciplinary routine prescribed by the military authorities.

Adequate premises shall be provided where religious services may be held.

...

Article 38

While respecting the individual preferences of every prisoner, the Detaining Power shall encourage the practice of intellectual, educational, and recreational pursuits, sports and games amongst prisoners, and shall take the measures necessary to ensure the exercise thereof by providing them with adequate premises and necessary equipment.

Prisoners shall have opportunities for taking physical exercise, including sports and games, and for being out of doors. Sufficient open spaces shall be provided for this purpose in all camps.

...

Article 46

The Detaining Power, when deciding upon the transfer of prisoners of war, shall take into account the interests of the prisoners themselves, more especially so as not to increase the difficulty of their repatriation.

The transfer of prisoners of war shall always be effected humanely and in conditions not less favourable than those under which the forces of the Detaining Power are transferred. Account shall always be taken of the climatic conditions to which the prisoners of war are accustomed and the conditions of transfer shall in no case be prejudicial to their health.

The Detaining Power shall supply prisoners of war during transfer with sufficient food and drinking water to keep them in good health, likewise with the necessary clothing, shelter and medical attention. The Detaining Power shall take adequate precautions especially in case of transport by sea or by air, to ensure their safety during transfer, and shall draw up a complete list of all transferred prisoners before their departure.

Article 47

Sick or wounded prisoners of war shall not be transferred as long as their recovery may be endangered by the journey, unless their safety imperatively demands it.

If the combat zone draws closer to a camp, the prisoners of war in the said camp shall not be transferred unless their transfer can be carried out in adequate conditions of safety, or if they are exposed to greater risks by remaining on the spot than by being transferred.

...

Article 69

Immediately upon prisoners of war falling into its power, the Detaining Power shall inform them and the Powers on which they depend, through the Protecting Power, of the measures taken to carry out the provisions of the present Section. They shall likewise inform the parties concerned of any subsequent modifications of such measures.

...

Article 71

Prisoners of war shall be allowed to send and receive letters and cards. If the Detaining Power deems it necessary to limit the number of letters and cards sent by each prisoner of war, the said number shall not be less than two letters and four cards monthly, exclusive of the capture cards provided for in Article 70, and conforming as closely as possible to the models annexed to the present Convention. Further limitations may be imposed only if the Protecting Power is satisfied that it would be in the interests of the prisoners of war concerned to do so owing to difficulties of translation caused by the Detaining Power's inability to find sufficient qualified linguists to carry out the necessary censorship. If limitations must be placed on the correspondence addressed to prisoners of war, they may be ordered only by the Power on which the prisoners depend, possibly at the request of the Detaining Power. Such letters and cards must be conveyed by the most rapid method at the disposal of the Detaining Power; they may not be delayed or retained for disciplinary reasons.

Prisoners of war who have been without news for a long period, or who are unable to receive news from their next of kin or to give them news by the ordinary postal route, as well as those who are at a great distance from their homes, shall be permitted to send telegrams, the fees being charged against the prisoners of war's accounts with the Detaining Power or paid in the currency at their disposal. They shall likewise benefit by this measure in cases of urgency.

As a general rule, the correspondence of prisoners of war shall be written in their native language. The Parties to the conflict may allow correspondence in other languages.

Sacks containing prisoner of war mail must be securely sealed and labelled so as clearly to indicate their contents, and must be addressed to offices of destination.

...

Article 78

Prisoners of war shall have the right to make known to the military authorities in whose power they are, their requests regarding the conditions of captivity to which they are subjected.

They shall also have the unrestricted right to apply to the representatives of the Protecting Powers either through their prisoners' representative or, if they consider it necessary, direct, in order to draw their attention to any points on which they may have complaints to make regarding their conditions of captivity.

These requests and complaints shall not be limited nor considered to be a part of the correspondence quota referred to in Article 71. They must be transmitted immediately. Even if they are recognized to be unfounded, they may not give rise to any punishment.

Prisoners' representatives may send periodic reports on the situation in the camps and the needs of the prisoners of war to the representatives of the Protecting Powers.

...

Article 82

A prisoner of war shall be subject to the laws, regulations and orders in force in the armed forces of the Detaining Power; the Detaining Power shall be justified in taking judicial or disciplinary measures in respect of any offence committed by a prisoner of war against such laws, regulations or orders. However, no proceedings or punishments contrary to the provisions of this Chapter shall be allowed.

If any law, regulation or order of the Detaining Power shall declare acts committed by a prisoner of war to be punishable, whereas the same acts would not be punishable if committed by a member of the forces of the Detaining Power, such acts shall entail disciplinary punishments only.

...

Article 99

No prisoner of war may be tried or sentenced for an act which is not forbidden by the law of the Detaining Power or by international law, in force at the time the said act was committed.

No moral or physical coercion may be exerted on a prisoner of war in order to induce him to admit himself guilty of the act of which he is accused.

No prisoner of war may be convicted without having had an opportunity to present his defence and the assistance of a qualified advocate or counsel.

...

Article 121

Every death or serious injury of a prisoner of war caused or suspected to have been caused by a sentry, another prisoner of war, or any other person, as well as any death the cause of which is unknown, shall be immediately followed by an official enquiry by the Detaining Power.

A communication on this subject shall be sent immediately to the Protecting Power. Statements shall be taken from witnesses, especially from those who are prisoners of war, and a report including such statements shall be forwarded to the Protecting Power.

If the enquiry indicates the guilt of one or more persons, the Detaining Power shall take all measures for the prosecution of the person or persons responsible.

Geneva Convention Relative to the Protection of Civilian Persons in Time of War of August 12, 1949 (Geneva Convention IV)

(Extracts)

...

Article 4

Persons protected by the Convention are those who, at a given moment and in any manner whatsoever, find themselves, in case of a conflict or occupation, in the hands of a Party to the conflict or Occupying Power of which they are not nationals.

Nationals of a State which is not bound by the Convention are not protected by it. Nationals of a neutral State who find themselves in the territory of a belligerent State, and nationals of a co-belligerent State, shall not be regarded as protected persons while the State of which they are nationals has normal diplomatic representation in the State in whose hands they are.

The provisions of Part II are, however, wider in application, as defined in Article 13.

Persons protected by the Geneva Convention for the Amelioration of the Condition of the Wounded and Sick in Armed Forces in the Field of August 12, 1949, or by the Geneva Convention for the Amelioration of the Condition of Wounded, Sick and Shipwrecked Members of Armed Forces at Sea of August 12, 1949, or by the Geneva Convention relative to the Treatment of Prisoners of War of August 12, 1949, shall not be considered as protected persons within the meaning of the present Convention.

Article 5

Where, in the territory of a Party to the conflict, the latter is satisfied that an individual protected person is definitely suspected of or engaged in activities hostile to the security of the State, such individual person shall not be entitled to claim such rights and privileges under the present Convention as would, if exercised in the favour of such individual person, be prejudicial to the security of such State.

Where in occupied territory an individual protected person is detained as a spy or saboteur, or as a person under definite suspicion of activity hostile to the security of the Occupying Power, such person shall, in those cases where absolute military security so requires, be regarded as having forfeited rights of communication under the present Convention.

In each case, such persons shall nevertheless be treated with humanity, and in case of trial, shall not be deprived of the rights of fair and regular trial prescribed by the present Convention. They shall also be granted the full rights and privileges of a protected person under the present Convention at the earliest date consistent with the security of the State or Occupying Power, as the case may be.

...

Article 14

In time of peace, the High Contracting Parties and, after the outbreak of hostilities, the Parties thereto, may establish in their own territory and, if the need arises, in occupied areas, hospital and safety zones and localities so organized as to protect from the effects of war, wounded, sick and aged persons, children under fifteen, expectant mothers and mothers of children under seven.

Upon the outbreak and during the course of hostilities, the Parties concerned may conclude agreements on mutual recognition of the zones and localities they have created. They may for this purpose implement the provisions of the Draft Agreement annexed to the present Convention, with such amendments as they may consider necessary.

The Protecting Powers and the International Committee of the Red Cross are invited to lend their good offices in order to facilitate the institution and recognition of these hospital and safety zones and localities.

Article 15

Any Party to the conflict may, either directly or through a neutral State or some humanitarian organization, propose to the adverse Party to establish, in the regions where fighting is taking place, neutralized zones intended to shelter from the effects of war the following persons, without distinction:

(a) wounded and sick combatants or non-combatants;

(b) civilian persons who take no part in hostilities, and who, while they reside in the zones, perform no work of a military character.

When the Parties concerned have agreed upon the geographical position, administration, food supply and supervision of the proposed neutralized zone, a written agreement shall be concluded and signed by the representatives of the Parties to the conflict. The agreement shall fix the beginning and the duration of the neutralization of the zone.

Article 16

The wounded and sick, as well as the infirm, and expectant mothers, shall be the object of particular protection and respect.

As far as military considerations allow, each Party to the conflict shall facilitate the steps taken to search for the killed and wounded, to assist the shipwrecked and other persons exposed to grave danger, and to protect them against pillage and ill-treatment.

Article 17

The Parties to the conflict shall endeavour to conclude local agreements for the removal from besieged or encircled areas, of wounded, sick, infirm, and aged persons, children and maternity cases, and for the passage of ministers of all religions, medical personnel and medical equipment on their way to such areas.

...

Article 24

The Parties to the conflict shall take the necessary measures to ensure that children under fifteen, who are orphaned or are separated from their families as a result of the war, are not left to their own resources, and that their maintenance, the exercise of their religion and their education are facilitated in all circumstances. Their education shall, as far as possible, be entrusted to persons of a similar cultural tradition.

The Parties to the conflict shall facilitate the reception of such children in a neutral country for the duration of the conflict with the consent of the Protecting Power, if any, and under due safeguards for the observance of the principles stated in the first paragraph.

They shall, furthermore, endeavour to arrange for all children under twelve to be identified by the wearing of identity discs, or by some other means.

...

Article 26

Each Party to the conflict shall facilitate enquiries made by members of families dispersed owing to the war, with the object of renewing contact with one another and of meeting, if possible. It shall encourage, in particular, the work of organizations engaged on this task provided they are acceptable to it and conform to its security regulations.

Article 27

Protected persons are entitled, in all circumstances, to respect for their persons, their honour, their family rights, their religious convictions and practices, and their manners and customs. They shall at all times be humanely treated, and shall be protected especially against all acts of violence or threats thereof and against insults and public curiosity.

Women shall be especially protected against any attack on their honour, in particular against rape, enforced prostitution, or any form of indecent assault.

Without prejudice to the provisions relating to their state of health, age and sex, all protected persons shall be treated with the same consideration by the Party to the conflict in whose power they are, without any adverse distinction based, in particular, on race, religion or political opinion.

However, the Parties to the conflict may take such measures of control and security in regard to protected persons as may be necessary as a result of the war.

...

Article 30

Protected persons shall have every facility for making application to the Protecting Powers, the International Committee of the Red Cross, the National Red Cross (Red Crescent, Red Lion and Sun) Society of the country where they may be, as well as to any organization that might assist them.

These several organizations shall be granted all facilities for that purpose by the authorities, within the bounds set by military or security considerations.

Apart from the visits of the delegates of the Protecting Powers and of the International Committee of the Red Cross, provided for by Article 143, the Detaining or Occupying Powers shall facilitate as much as possible visits to protected persons by the representatives of other organizations whose object is to give spiritual aid or material relief to such persons.

Article 31

No physical or moral coercion shall be exercised against protected persons, in particular to obtain information from them or from third parties.

Article 32

The High Contracting Parties specifically agree that each of them is prohibited from taking any measure of such a character as to cause the physical suffering or extermination of protected persons in their hands. This prohibition applies not only to murder, torture, corporal punishment, mutilation and medical or scientific experiments not necessitated by the medical treatment of a protected person, but also to any other measures of brutality whether applied by civilian or military agents.

Article 33

No protected person may be punished for an offence he or she has not personally committed. Collective penalties and likewise all measures of intimidation or of terrorism are prohibited.

Pillage is prohibited.

Reprisals against protected persons and their property are prohibited.

Article 34

The taking of hostages is prohibited.

Article 35

All protected persons who may desire to leave the territory at the outset of, or during a conflict, shall be entitled to do so, unless their departure is contrary to the national interests of the State. The applications of such persons to leave shall be decided in accordance with regularly established procedures and the decision shall be taken as rapidly as possible. Those persons permitted to leave may provide themselves with the necessary funds for their journey and take with them a reasonable amount of their effects and articles of personal use.

If any such person is refused permission to leave the territory, he shall be entitled to have such refusal reconsidered as soon as possible by an appropriate court or administrative board designated by the Detaining Power for that purpose.

Upon request, representatives of the Protecting Power shall, unless reasons of security prevent it, or the persons concerned object, be furnished with the reasons for refusal of any request for permission to leave the territory and be given, as expeditiously as possible, the names of all persons who have been denied permission to leave.

...

Article 37

Protected persons who are confined pending proceedings or serving a sentence involving loss of liberty, shall during their confinement be humanely treated.

As soon as they are released, they may ask to leave the territory in conformity with the foregoing Articles.

...

Article 39

Protected persons who, as a result of the war, have lost their gainful employment, shall be granted the opportunity to find paid employment. That opportunity shall, subject to security considerations and to the provisions of Article 40, be equal to that enjoyed by the nationals of the Power in whose territory they are. Where a Party to the conflict applies to a protected person methods of control which result in his being unable to support himself, and especially if such a person is prevented for reasons of security from finding paid employment on reasonable conditions, the said Party shall ensure his support and that of his dependents. Protected persons may in any case receive allowances from their home country, the Protecting Power, or the relief societies referred to in Article 30.

...

Article 42

The internment or placing in assigned residence of protected persons may be ordered only if the security of the Detaining Power makes it absolutely necessary.

If any person, acting through the representatives of the Protecting Power, voluntarily demands internment, and if his situation renders this step necessary, he shall be interned by the Power in whose hands he may be.

Article 43

Any protected person who has been interned or placed in assigned residence shall be entitled to have such action reconsidered as soon as possible by an appropriate court or administrative board designated by the Detaining Power for that purpose. If the internment or placing in assigned residence is maintained, the court or administrative board shall periodically, and at least twice yearly, give consideration to his or her case, with a view to the favourable amendment of the initial decision, if circumstances permit.

Unless the protected persons concerned object, the Detaining Power shall, as rapidly as possible, give the Protecting Power the names of any protected persons who have been interned or subjected to assigned residence, or who have been released from internment or assigned residence. The decisions of the courts or boards mentioned in the first paragraph of the present Article shall also, subject to the same conditions, be notified as rapidly as possible to the Protecting Power.

. . .

Article 47

Protected persons who are in occupied territory shall not be deprived, in any case or in any manner whatsoever, of the benefits of the present Convention by any change introduced, as the result of the occupation of a territory, into the institutions or government of the said territory, nor by any agreement concluded between the authorities of the occupied territories and the Occupying Power, nor by any annexation by the latter of the whole or part of the occupied territory.

Article 48

Protected persons who are not nationals of the Power whose territory is occupied, may avail themselves of the right to leave the territory subject to the provisions of Article 35, and decisions thereon shall be taken according to the procedure which the Occupying Power shall establish in accordance with the said Article.

Article 49

Individual or mass forcible transfers, as well as deportations of protected persons from occupied territory to the territory of the Occupying Power or to that of any other country, occupied or not, are prohibited, regardless of their motive.

Nevertheless, the Occupying Power may undertake total or partial evacuation of a given area if the security of the population or imperative military reasons do demand. Such evacuations may not involve the displacement of protected persons outside the bounds of the occupied territory except when for material reasons it is impossible to avoid such displacement. Persons thus evacuated shall be transferred back to their homes as soon as hostilities in the area in question have ceased.

The Occupying Power undertaking such transfers or evacuations shall ensure, to the greatest practicable extent, that proper accommodation is provided to receive the protected persons, that the removals are effected in satisfactory conditions of hygiene, health, safety and nutrition, and that members of the same family are not separated.

The Protecting Power shall be informed of any transfers and evacuations as soon as they have taken place.

The Occupying Power shall not detain protected persons in an area particularly exposed to the dangers of war unless the security of the population or imperative military reasons so demand.

The Occupying Power shall not deport or transfer parts of its own civilian population into the territory it occupies.

Article 50

The Occupying Power shall, with the cooperation of the national and local authorities, facilitate the proper working of all institutions devoted to the care and education of children.

The Occupying Power shall take all necessary steps to facilitate the identification of children and the registration of their parentage. It may not, in any case, change their personal status, nor enlist them in formations or organizations subordinate to it.

Should the local institutions be inadequate for the purpose, the Occupying Power shall make arrangements for the maintenance and education, if possible by persons of their own nationality, language and religion, of children who are orphaned or separated from their parents as a result of the war and who cannot be adequately cared for by a near relative or friend.

A special section of the Bureau set up in accordance with Article 136 shall be responsible for taking all necessary steps to identify children whose identity is in doubt. Particulars of their parents or other near relatives should always be recorded if available.

The Occupying Power shall not hinder the application of any preferential measures in regard to food, medical care and protection against the effects of war, which may have been adopted prior to the occupation in favour of children under fifteen years, expectant mothers, and mothers of children under seven years.

...

Article 53

Any destruction by the Occupying Power of real or personal property belonging individually or collectively to private persons, or to the State, or to other public authorities, or to social or cooperative organizations, is prohibited, except where such destruction is rendered absolutely necessary by military operations.

...

Article 55

To the fullest extent of the means available to it the Occupying Power has the duty of ensuring the food and medical supplies of the population; it should, in particular, bring in the necessary foodstuffs, medical stores and other articles if the resources of the occupied territory are inadequate.

The Occupying Power may not requisition foodstuffs, articles or medical supplies available in the occupied territory, except for use by the occupation forces and administration personnel, and then only if the requirements of the civilian population have been taken into account. Subject to the provisions of other international Conventions, the Occupying Power shall make arrangements to ensure that fair value is paid for any requisitioned goods.

The Protecting Power shall, at any time, be at liberty to verify the state of the food and medical supplies in occupied territories, except where temporary restrictions are made necessary by imperative military requirements.

...

Article 59

If the whole or part of the population of an occupied territory is inadequately supplied, the Occupying Power shall agree to relief schemes on behalf of the said population, and shall facilitate them by all the means at its disposal.

Such schemes, which may be undertaken either by States or by impartial humanitarian organizations such as the International Committee of the Red Cross, shall consist, in particular, of the provision of consignments of foodstuffs, medical supplies and clothing.

All Contracting Parties shall permit the free passage of these consignments and shall guarantee their protection.

A Power granting free passage to consignments on their way to territory occupied by an adverse Party to the conflict shall, however, have the right to search the consignments, to regulate their passage according to prescribed times and routes, and to be reasonably satisfied through the Protecting Power that these consignments are to be used for the relief of the needy population and are not to be used for the benefit of the Occupying Power.

...

Article 63

Subject to temporary and exceptional measures imposed for urgent reasons of security by the Occupying Power:

(a) recognized National Red Cross (Red Crescent, Red Lion and Sun) Societies shall be able to pursue their activities in accordance with Red Cross principles, as defined by the International Red Cross Conferences. Other relief societies shall be permitted to continue their humanitarian activities under similar conditions;

(b) the Occupying Power may not require any changes in the personnel or structure of these societies, which would prejudice the aforesaid activities.

The same principles shall apply to the activities and personnel of special organizations of a non-military character, which already exist or which may be established, for the purpose of ensuring the living conditions of the civilian population by the maintenance of the essential public utility services, by the distribution of relief and by the organization of rescues.

Article 64

The penal laws of the occupied territory shall remain in force, with the exception that they may be repealed or suspended by the Occupying Power in cases where they constitute a threat to its security or an obstacle to the application of the present Convention. Subject to the latter consideration and to the necessity for ensuring the effective administration of justice, the tribunals of the occupied territory shall continue to function in respect of all offences covered by the said laws.

The Occupying Power may, however, subject the population of the occupied territory to provisions which are essential to enable the Occupying Power to fulfil its obligations under the present Convention, to maintain the orderly government of the territory, and to ensure the security of the Occupying Power, of the members and property of the occupying forces or administration, and likewise of the establishments and lines of communication used by them.

...

Article 68

Protected persons who commit an offence which is solely intended to harm the Occupying Power, but which does not constitute an attempt on the life or limb of members of the occupying forces or administration, nor a grave collective danger, nor seriously damage the property of the occupying forces or administration or the installations used by them, shall be liable to internment or simple imprisonment, provided the duration of such internment or imprisonment is proportionate to the offence committed. Furthermore, internment or imprisonment shall, for such offences, be the only measure adopted for depriving protected persons of liberty. The courts provided for under Article 66 of the present Convention may at their discretion convert a sentence of imprisonment to one of internment for the same period.

The penal provisions promulgated by the Occupying Power in accordance with Articles 64 and 65 may impose the death penalty on a protected person only in cases where the person is guilty of espionage, of serious acts of sabotage against the military installations of the Occupying Power or of intentional offences which have caused the death of one or more persons, provided that such offences were punishable by death under the law of the occupied territory in force before the occupation began.

The death penalty may not be pronounced against a protected person unless the attention of the court has been particularly called to the fact that since the accused is not a national of the Occupying Power, he is not bound to it by any duty of allegiance.

In any case, the death penalty may not be pronounced against a protected person who was under eighteen years of age at the time of the offence.

...

Article 70

Protected persons shall not be arrested, prosecuted or convicted by the Occupying Power for acts committed or for opinions expressed before the occupation, or during a temporary interruption thereof, with the exception of breaches of the laws and customs of war.

Nationals of the Occupying Power who, before the outbreak of hostilities, have sought refuge in the territory of the occupied State, shall not be arrested, prosecuted, convicted or deported from the occupied territory, except for offences committed after the outbreak of hostilities, or for offences under common law committed before the outbreak of hostilities which, according to the law of the occupied State, would have justified extradition in time of peace.

...

Article 76

Protected persons accused of offences shall be detained in the occupied country, and if convicted they shall serve their sentences therein. They shall, if possible, be separated from other detainees and shall enjoy conditions of food and hygiene which will be sufficient to keep them in good health, and which will be at least equal to those obtaining in prisons in the occupied country.

They shall receive the medical attention required by their state of health.

They shall also have the right to receive any spiritual assistance which they may require.

Women shall be confined in separate quarters and shall be under the direct supervision of women.

Proper regard shall be paid to the special treatment due to minors.

Protected persons who are detained shall have the right to be visited by delegates of the Protecting Power and of the International Committee of the Red Cross, in accordance with the provisions of Article 143.

Such persons shall have the right to receive at least one relief parcel monthly.

Article 77

Protected persons who have been accused of offences or convicted by the courts in occupied territory shall be handed over at the close of occupation, with the relevant records, to the authorities of the liberated territory.

Article 78

If the Occupying Power considers it necessary, for imperative reasons of security, to take safety measures concerning protected persons, it may, at the most, subject them to assigned residence or to internment.

Decisions regarding such assigned residence or internment shall be made according to a regular procedure to be prescribed by the Occupying Power in accordance with the provisions of the present Convention. This procedure shall include the right of appeal for the parties concerned. Appeals shall be decided with the least possible delay. In the event of the decision being upheld, it shall be subject to periodical review, if possible every six months, by a competent body set up by the said Power.

Protected persons made subject to assigned residence and thus required to leave their homes shall enjoy the full benefit of Article 39 of the present Convention.

...

Article 80

Internees shall retain their full civil capacity and shall exercise such attendant rights as may be compatible with their status.

...

Article 82

The Detaining Power shall, as far as possible, accommodate the internees according to their nationality, language and customs. Internees who are nationals of the same country shall not be separated merely because they have different languages.

Throughout the duration of their internment, members of the same family, and in particular parents and children, shall be lodged together in the same place of internment, except when separation of a temporary nature is necessitated for reasons of employment or health or for the purposes of enforcement of the provisions of Chapter IX of the present Section. Internees may request that their children who are left at liberty without parental care shall be interned with them.

Wherever possible, interned members of the same family shall be housed in the same premises and given separate accommodation from other internees, together with facilities for leading a proper family life.

...

Article 84

Internees shall be accommodated and administered separately from prisoners of war and from persons deprived of liberty for any other reason.

Article 85

The Detaining Power is bound to take all necessary and possible measures to ensure that protected persons shall, from the outset of their internment, be accommodated in buildings or quarters which afford every possible safeguard as regards hygiene and health, and provide efficient protection against the rigours of the climate and the effects of the war. In no case shall permanent places of internment be situated in unhealthy areas or in districts the climate of which is injurious to the internees. In all cases where the district, in which a protected person is temporarily interned, is in an unhealthy area or has a climate which is harmful to his health, he shall be removed to a more suitable place of internment as rapidly as circumstances permit.

The premises shall be fully protected from dampness, adequately heated and lighted, in particular between dusk and lights out. The sleeping quarters shall be sufficiently spacious and well ventilated, and the internees shall have suitable bedding and sufficient blankets, account being taken of the climate, and the age, sex, and state of health of the internees.

Internees shall have for their use, day and night, sanitary conveniences which conform to the rules of hygiene and are constantly maintained in a state of cleanliness. They shall be provided with sufficient water and soap for their daily personal toilet and for washing their personal laundry; installations and facilities necessary for this purpose shall be granted to them. Showers or baths shall also be available. The necessary time shall be set aside for washing and for cleaning.

Whenever it is necessary, as an exceptional and temporary measure, to accommodate women internees who are not members of a family unit in the same place of internment as men, the provision of separate sleeping quarters and sanitary conveniences for the use of such women internees shall be obligatory.

...

Article 89

Daily food rations for internees shall be sufficient in quantity, quality and variety to keep internees in a good state of health and prevent the development of nutritional deficiencies. Account shall also be taken of the customary diet of the internees.

Internees shall also be given the means by which they can prepare for themselves any additional food in their possession.

Sufficient drinking water shall be supplied to internees. The use of tobacco shall be permitted.

Internees who work shall receive additional rations in proportion to the kind of labour which they perform.

Expectant and nursing mothers and children under fifteen years of age, shall be given additional food, in proportion to their physiological needs.

Article 90

When taken into custody, internees shall be given all facilities to provide themselves with the necessary clothing, footwear and change of underwear, and later on, to procure further supplies if required. Should any internees not have sufficient clothing, account being taken of the climate, and be unable to procure any, it shall be provided free of charge to them by the Detaining Power.

The clothing supplied by the Detaining Power to internees and the outward markings placed on their own clothes shall not be ignominious nor expose them to ridicule.

Workers shall receive suitable working outfits, including protective clothing, whenever the nature of their work so requires.

Article 91

Every place of internment shall have an adequate infirmary, under the direction of a qualified doctor, where internees may have the attention they require, as well as an appropriate diet. Isolation wards shall be set aside for cases of contagious or mental diseases.

Maternity cases and internees suffering from serious diseases, or whose condition requires special treatment, a surgical operation or hospital care, must be admitted to any institution where adequate treatment can be given and shall receive care not inferior to that provided for the general population.

Internees shall, for preference, have the attention of medical personnel of their own nationality.

Internees may not be prevented from presenting themselves to the medical authorities for examination. The medical authorities of the Detaining Power shall, upon request, issue to every internee who has undergone treatment an official certificate showing the nature of his illness or injury, and the duration and nature of the treatment given. A duplicate of this certificate shall be forwarded to the Central Agency provided for in Article 140.

Treatment, including the provision of any apparatus necessary for the maintenance of internees in good health, particularly dentures and other artificial appliances and spectacles, shall be free of charge to the internee.

...

Article 97

Internees shall be permitted to retain articles of personal use. Monies, cheques, bonds, etc., and valuables in their possession may not be taken from them except in accordance with established procedure. Detailed receipts shall be given therefor.

...

A woman internee shall not be searched except by a woman.

On release or repatriation, internees shall be given all articles, monies or other valuables taken from them during internment and shall receive in currency the balance of any credit to their accounts kept in accordance with Article 98, with the exception of any articles or amounts withheld by the Detaining Power by virtue of its legislation in force. If the property of an internee is so withheld, the owner shall receive a detailed receipt.

Family or identity documents in the possession of internees may not be taken away without a receipt being given. At no time shall internees be left without identity documents. If they have none, they shall be issued with special documents drawn up by the detaining authorities, which will serve as their identity papers until the end of their internment.

Internees may keep on their persons a certain amount of money, in cash or in the shape of purchase coupons, to enable them to make purchases.

...

Article 99

Every place of internment shall be put under the authority of a responsible officer, chosen from the regular military forces or the regular civil administration of the Detaining Power. The officer in charge of the place of internment must have in his possession a copy of the present Convention in the official language, or one of the official languages, of his country and shall be responsible for its application. The staff in control of internees shall be instructed in the provisions of the present Convention and of the administrative measures adopted to ensure its application.

The text of the present Convention and the texts of special agreements concluded under the said Convention shall be posted inside the place of internment, in a language which the internees understand, or shall be in the possession of the Internee Committee.

Regulations, orders, notices and publications of every kind shall be communicated to the internees and posted inside the places of internment, in a language which they understand.

Every order and command addressed to internees individually must likewise be given in a language which they understand.

Article 100

The disciplinary regime in places of internment shall be consistent with humanitarian principles, and shall in no circumstances include regulations imposing on internees any physical exertion dangerous to their health or involving physical or moral victimization. Identification by tattooing or imprinting signs or markings on the body, is prohibited.

In particular, prolonged standing and roll-calls, punishment drill, military drill and manoeuvres, or the reduction of food rations, are prohibited.

Article 101

Internees shall have the right to present to the authorities in whose power they are, any petition with regard to the conditions of internment to which they are subjected.

They shall also have the right to apply without restriction through the Internee Committee or, if they consider it necessary, direct to the representatives of the Protecting Power, in order to indicate to them any points on which they may have complaints to make with regard to the conditions of internment.

Such petitions and complaints shall be transmitted forthwith and without alteration, and even if the latter are recognized to be unfounded, they may not occasion any punishment.

Periodic reports on the situation in places of internment and as to the needs of the internees may be sent by the Internee Committees to the representatives of the Protecting Powers.

...

Article 107

Internees shall be allowed to send and receive letters and cards. If the Detaining Power deems it necessary to limit the number of letters and cards sent by each internee, the said number shall not be less than two letters and four cards monthly; these shall be drawn up so as to conform as closely as possible to the models annexed to the present Convention. If limitations must be placed on the correspondence addressed to internees, they may be ordered only by the Power to which such internees owe allegiance, possibly at the request of the Detaining Power. Such letters and cards must be conveyed with reasonable despatch; they may not be delayed or retained for disciplinary reasons.

Internees who have been a long time without news, or who find it impossible to receive news from their relatives, or to give them news by the ordinary postal route, as well as those who are at a considerable distance from their homes, shall be allowed to send telegrams, the charges being paid by them in the currency at their disposal. They shall likewise benefit by this provision in cases which are recognized to be urgent.

As a rule, internees' mail shall be written in their own language. The Parties to the conflict may authorize correspondence in other languages.

. . .

Article 116

Every internee shall be allowed to receive visitors, especially near relatives, at regular intervals and as frequently as possible.

As far as is possible, internees shall be permitted to visit their homes in urgent cases, particularly in cases of death or serious illness of relatives.

Article 117

Subject to the provisions of the present Chapter, the laws in force in the territory in which they are detained will continue to apply to internees who commit offences during internment.

If general laws, regulations or orders declare acts committed by internees to be punishable, whereas the same acts are not punishable when committed by persons who are not internees, such acts shall entail disciplinary punishments only.

No internee may be punished more than once for the same act, or on the same count.

. . .

Article 127

The transfer of internees shall always be effected humanely. As a general rule, it shall be carried out by rail or other means of transport, and under conditions at least equal to those obtaining for the forces of the Detaining Power in their changes of station. If, as an exceptional measure, such removals have to be effected on foot, they may not take place unless the internees are in a fit state of health, and may not in any case expose them to excessive fatigue.

The Detaining Power shall supply internees during transfer with drinking water and food sufficient in quantity, quality and variety to maintain them in good health, and also with the necessary clothing, adequate shelter and the necessary medical attention. The Detaining Power shall take all suitable precautions to ensure their safety during transfer, and shall establish before their departure a complete list of all internees transferred.

Sick, wounded or infirm internees and maternity cases shall not be transferred if the journey would be seriously detrimental to them, unless their safety imperatively so demands.

If the combat zone draws close to a place of internment, the internees in the said place shall not be transferred unless their removal can be carried out in adequate conditions of safety, or unless they are exposed to greater risks by remaining on the spot than by being transferred.

When making decisions regarding the transfer of internees, the Detaining Power shall take their interests into account and, in particular, shall not do anything to increase the difficulties of repatriating them or returning them to their own homes.

. . .

Article 131

Every death or serious injury of an internee, caused or suspected to have been caused by a sentry, another internee or any other person, as well as any death the cause of which is unknown, shall be immediately followed by an official enquiry by the Detaining Power.

A communication on this subject shall be sent immediately to the Protecting Power. The evidence of any witnesses shall be taken, and a report including such evidence shall be prepared and forwarded to the said Protecting Power.

If the enquiry indicates the guilt of one or more persons, the Detaining Power shall take all necessary steps to ensure the prosecution of the person or persons responsible.

Article 132

Each interned person shall be released by the Detaining Power as soon as the reasons which necessitated his internment no longer exist.

The Parties to the conflict shall, moreover, endeavour during the course of hostilities, to conclude agreements for the release, the repatriation, the return to places of residence or the accommodation in a neutral country of certain classes of internees, in particular children, pregnant women and mothers with infants and young children, wounded and sick, and internees who have been detained for a long time.

Article 133

Internment shall cease as soon as possible after the close of hostilities.

Internees, in the territory of a Party to the conflict, against whom penal proceedings are pending for offences not exclusively subject to disciplinary penalties, may be detained until the close of such proceedings and, if circumstances require, until the completion of the penalty. The same shall apply to internees who have been previously sentenced to a punishment depriving them of liberty.

By agreement between the Detaining Power and the Powers concerned, committees may be set up after the close of hostilities, or of the occupation of territories, to search for dispersed internees.

Article 134

The High Contracting Parties shall endeavour, upon the close of hostilities or occupation, to ensure the return of all internees to their last place of residence, or to facilitate their repatriation.

...

Article 136

Upon the outbreak of a conflict and in all cases of occupation, each of the Parties to the conflict shall establish an official Information Bureau responsible for receiving and transmitting information in respect of the protected persons who are in its power. Each of the Parties to the conflict shall, within the shortest possible period, give its Bureau information of any measure taken by it concerning any protected persons who are kept in custody for more than two weeks, who are subjected to assigned residence or who are interned. It shall, furthermore, require its various departments concerned with such matters to provide the aforesaid Bureau promptly with information concerning all changes pertaining to these protected persons, as, for example, transfers, releases, repatriations, escapes, admittances to hospitals, births and deaths.

Annex I – Draft Agreement relating to Hospital and Safety Zones and Localities

Article 1

Hospital and safety zones shall be strictly reserved for the persons mentioned in Article 23 of the Geneva Convention for the Amelioration of the Condition of the Wounded and Sick in Armed Forces in the Field of 12 August, 1949, and in Article 14 of the Geneva Convention relative to the Protection of Civilian Persons in Time of War of 12 August, 1949, and for the personnel entrusted with the organization and administration of these zones and localities and with the care of the persons therein assembled.

Nevertheless, persons whose permanent residence is within such zones shall have the right to stay there.

Article 2
No persons residing, in whatever capacity, in a hospital and safety zone shall perform any work, either within or without the zone, directly connected with military operations or the production of war material.

Article 3
The Power establishing a hospital and safety zone shall take all necessary measures to prohibit access to all persons who have no right of residence or entry therein.

Article 4
Hospital and safety zones shall fulfil the following conditions:

(a) They shall comprise only a small part of the territory governed by the Power which has established them.
(b) They shall be thinly populated in relation to the possibilities of accommodation.
(c) They shall be far removed and free from all military objectives, or large industrial or administrative establishments.
(d) They shall not be situated in areas which, according to every probability, may become important for the conduct of the war.

Article 5
Hospital and safety zones shall be subject to the following obligations:

(a) The lines of communication and means of transport which they possess shall not be used for the transport of military personnel or material, even in transit.
(b) They shall in no case be defended by military means.

Article 6
Hospital and safety zones shall be marked by means of oblique red bands on a white ground, placed on the buildings and outer precincts.

Zones reserved exclusively for the wounded and sick may be marked by means of the Red Cross (Red Crescent, Red Lion and Sun) emblem on a white ground.

They may be similarly marked at night by means of appropriate illumination.

Article 7
The Powers shall communicate to all the High Contracting Parties in peacetime or on the outbreak of hostilities, a list of the hospital and safety zones in the territories governed by them. They shall also give notice of any new zones set up during hostilities.

As soon as the adverse Party has received the above-mentioned notification, the zone shall be regularly established.

If, however, the adverse Party considers that the conditions of the present agreement have not been fulfilled, it may refuse to recognize the zone by giving immediate notice thereof to the Party responsible for the said zone, or may make its recognition of such zone dependent upon the institution of the control provided for in Article 8.

Article 8
Any Power having recognized one or several hospital and safety zones instituted by the adverse Party shall be entitled to demand control by one or more Special Commissions, for the purpose of ascertaining if the zones fulfil the conditions and obligations stipulated in the present agreement.

For this purpose, members of the Special Commissions shall at all times have free access to the various zones and may even reside there permanently. They shall be given all facilities for their duties of inspection.

Article 9

Should the Special Commissions note any facts which they consider contrary to the stipulations of the present agreement, they shall at once draw the attention of the Power governing the said zone to these facts, and shall fix a time limit of five days within which the matter should be rectified. They shall duly notify the Power who has recognized the zone.

If, when the time limit has expired, the Power governing the zone has not complied with the warning, the adverse Party may declare that it is no longer bound by the present agreement in respect of the said zone.

Article 10

Any Power setting up one or more hospital and safety zones, and the adverse Parties to whom their existence has been notified, shall nominate or have nominated by the Protecting Powers or by other neutral Powers, persons eligible to be members of the Special Commissions mentioned in Articles 8 and 9.

Article 11

In no circumstances may hospital and safety zones be the object of attack. They shall be protected and respected at all times by the Parties to the conflict.

Article 12

In the case of occupation of a territory, the hospital and safety zones therein shall continue to be respected and utilized as such.

Their purpose may, however, be modified by the Occupying Power, on condition that all measures are taken to ensure the safety of the persons accommodated.

Article 13

The present agreement shall also apply to localities which the Powers may utilize for the same purposes as hospital and safety zones.

...

Protocol Additional to the Geneva Conventions of 12 August 1949, and relating to the Protection of Victims of International Armed Conflicts (Protocol I)

(Extracts)

PREAMBLE

The High Contracting Parties,

Proclaiming their earnest wish to see peace prevail among peoples,

Recalling that every State has the duty, in conformity with the Charter of the United Nations, to refrain in its international relations from the threat or use of force against the sovereignty, territorial integrity or political independence of any State, or in any other manner inconsistent with the purposes of the United Nations.

Believing it necessary nevertheless to reaffirm and develop the provisions protecting the victims of armed conflicts and to supplement measures intended to reinforce their application,

Expressing their conviction that nothing in this Protocol or in the Geneva Conventions of 12 August 1949 can be construed as legitimizing or authorizing any act of aggression or any other use of force inconsistent with the Charter of the United Nations,

Reaffirming further that the provisions of the Geneva Conventions of 12 August 1949 and of this Protocol must be fully applied in all circumstances to all persons who are protected by those instruments, without any adverse distinction based on the nature or origin of the armed conflict or on the causes espoused by or attributed to the Parties to the conflicts,

Have agreed on the following:

Part I. General Provisions

Article 1 – General principles and scope of application

1. The High Contracting Parties undertake to respect and to ensure respect for this Protocol in all circumstances.
2. In cases not covered by this Protocol or by other international agreements, civilians and combatants remain under the protection and authority of the principles of international law derived from established custom, from the principles of humanity and from the dictates of public conscience.
3. This Protocol, which supplements the Geneva Conventions of 12 August 1949 for the protection of war victims, shall apply in the situations referred to in Article 2 common to those Conventions.
4. The situations referred to in the preceding paragraph include armed conflicts in which peoples are fighting against colonial domination and alien occupation and against racist regimes in the exercise of their right of self-determination, as enshrined in the Charter of the United Nations and the Declaration on Principles of International Law concerning Friendly Relations and Co-operation among States in accordance with the Charter of the United Nations.

...

Part II. Wounded, Sick and Shipwrecked

Section I. General Protection

...

Article 11 – Protection of persons

1. The physical or mental health and integrity of persons who are in the power of the adverse Party or who are interned, detained or otherwise deprived of liberty as a result of a situation referred to in Article I shall not be endangered by any unjustified act or omission. Accordingly, it is prohibited to subject the persons described in this Article to any medical procedure which is not indicated by the state of health of the person concerned and which is not consistent with generally accepted medical standards which would be applied under similar medical circumstances to persons who are nationals of the Party conducting the procedure and who are in no way deprived of liberty.

2. It is, in particular, prohibited to carry out on such persons, even with their consent:
   (a) Physical mutilations;
   (b) Medical or scientific experiments;
   (c) Removal of tissue or organs for transplantation, except where these acts are justified in conformity with the conditions provided for in paragraph 1.
3. Exceptions to the prohibition in paragraph 2 (c) may be made only in the case of donations of blood for transfusion or of skin for grafting, provided that they are given voluntarily and without any coercion or inducement, and then only for therapeutic purposes, under conditions consistent with generally accepted medical standards and controls designed for the benefit of both the donor and the recipient.
4. Any wilful act or omission which seriously endangers the physical or mental health or integrity of any person who is in the power of a Party other than the one on which he depends and which either violates any of the prohibitions in paragraphs 1 and 2 or fails to comply with the requirements of paragraph 3 shall be a grave breach of this Protocol.
5. The persons described in paragraph I have the right to refuse any surgical operation. In case of refusal, medical personnel shall endeavour to obtain a written statement to that effect, signed or acknowledged by the patient.
6. Each Party to the conflict shall keep a medical record for every donation of blood for transfusion or skin for grafting by persons referred to in paragraph 1, if that donation is made under the responsibility of that Party. In addition, each Party to the conflict shall endeavour to keep a record of all medical procedures undertaken with respect to any person who is interned, detained or otherwise deprived of liberty as a result of a situation referred to in Article 1. These records shall be available at all times for inspection by the Protecting Power.

...

Section III. Missing and Dead Persons

Article 32 – General Principle

In the implementation of this Section, the activities of the High Contracting Parties, of the Parties to the conflict and of the international humanitarian organizations mentioned in the Conventions and in this Protocol shall be prompted mainly by the right of families to know the fate of their relatives.

...

Part III. Methods and Means of Warfare Combatant and Prisoner-Of-War Status

Section I. Methods and Means of Warfare

Article 35 – Basic rules

1. In any armed conflict, the right of the Parties to the conflict to choose methods or means of warfare is not unlimited.
2. It is prohibited to employ weapons, projectiles and material and methods of warfare of a nature to cause superfluous injury or unnecessary suffering.
3. It is prohibited to employ methods or means of warfare which are intended, or may be expected, to cause widespread, long-term and severe damage to the natural environment.

...

Article 37 – Prohibition of perfidy

1. It is prohibited to kill, injure or capture an adversary by resort to perfidy. Acts inviting the confidence of an adversary to lead him to believe that he is entitled to, or is obliged to accord, protection under the rules of international law applicable in armed conflict, with intent to betray that confidence, shall constitute perfidy. The following acts are examples of perfidy:
   (a) The feigning of an intent to negotiate under a flag of truce or of a surrender;
   (b) The feigning of an incapacitation by wounds or sickness;
   (c) The feigning of civilian, non-combatant status; and
   (d) The feigning of protected status by the use of signs, emblems or uniforms of the United Nations or of neutral or other States not Parties to the conflict.
2. Ruses of war are not prohibited. Such ruses are acts which are intended to mislead an adversary or to induce him to act recklessly but which infringe no rule of international law applicable in armed conflict and which are not perfidious because they do not invite the confidence of an adversary with respect to protection under that law. The following are examples of such ruses: the use of camouflage, decoys, mock operations and misinformation.

...

Section II. Combatants and Prisoner-of-War Status

Article 43 – Armed forces

1. The armed forces of a Party to a conflict consist of all organized armed forces, groups and units which are under a command responsible to that Party for the conduct of its subordinates, even if that Party is represented by a government or an authority not recognized by an adverse Party. Such armed forces shall be subject to an internal disciplinary system which, *inter alia*, shall enforce compliance with the rules of international law applicable in armed conflict.
2. Members of the armed forces of a Party to a conflict (other than medical personnel and chaplains covered by Article 33 of the Third Convention) are combatants, that is to say, they have the right to participate directly in hostilities.
3. Whenever a Party to a conflict incorporates a paramilitary or armed law enforcement agency into its armed forces it shall so notify the other Parties to the conflict.

Article 44 – Combatants and prisoners of war

1. Any combatant, as defined in Article 43, who falls into the power of an adverse Party shall be a prisoner of war.
2. While all combatants are obliged to comply with the rules of international law applicable in armed conflict, violations of these rules shall not deprive a combatant of his right to be a combatant or, if he falls into the power of an adverse Party, of his right to be a prisoner of war, except as provided in paragraphs 3 and 4.
3. In order to promote the protection of the civilian population from the effects of hostilities, combatants are obliged to distinguish themselves from the civilian population while they are engaged in an attack or in a military operation preparatory to an attack. Recognizing, however, that there are situations in armed conflicts where, owing to the nature of the hostilities an armed combatant cannot so distinguish himself, he shall retain his status as a combatant, provided that, in such situations, he carries his arms openly:
   (a) During each military engagement, and
   (b) During such time as he is visible to the adversary while he is engaged in a military deployment preceding the launching of an attack in which he is to participate.

Acts which comply with the requirements of this paragraph shall not be considered as perfidious within the meaning of Article 37, paragraph 1 (c).

4. A combatant who falls into the power of an adverse Party while failing to meet the requirements set forth in the second sentence of paragraph 3 shall forfeit his right to be a prisoner of war, but he shall, nevertheless, be given protections equivalent in all respects to those accorded to prisoners of war by the Third Convention and by this Protocol. This protection includes protections equivalent to those accorded to prisoners of war by the Third Convention in the case where such a person is tried and punished for any offences he has committed.
5. Any combatant who falls into the power of an adverse Party while not engaged in an attack or in a military operation preparatory to an attack shall not forfeit his rights to be a combatant and a prisoner of war by virtue of his prior activities.
6. This Article is without prejudice to the right of any person to be a prisoner of war pursuant to Article 4 of the Third Convention.
7. This Article is not intended to change the generally accepted practice of States with respect to the wearing of the uniform by combatants assigned to the regular, uniformed armed units of a Party to the conflict.
8. In addition to the categories of persons mentioned in Article 13 of the First and Second Conventions, all members of the armed forces of a Party to the conflict, as defined in Article 43 of this Protocol, shall be entitled to protection under those Conventions if they are wounded or sick or, in the case of the Second Convention, shipwrecked at sea or in other waters.

Article 45 – Protection of persons who have taken part in hostilities

1. A person who takes part in hostilities and falls into the power of an adverse Party shall be presumed to be a prisoner of war, and therefore shall be protected by the Third Convention, if he claims the status of prisoner of war, or if he appears to be entitled to such status, or if the Party on which he depends claims such status on his behalf by notification to the detaining Power or to the Protecting Power. Should any doubt arise as to whether any such person is entitled to the status of prisoner of war, he shall continue to have such status and, therefore, to be protected by the Third Convention and this Protocol until such time as his status has been determined by a competent tribunal.
2. If a person who has fallen into the power of an adverse Party is not held as a prisoner of war and is to be tried by that Party for an offence arising out of the hostilities, he shall have the right to assert his entitlement to prisoner-of-war status before a judicial tribunal and to have that question adjudicated. Whenever possible under the applicable procedure, this adjudication shall occur before the trial for the offence. The representatives of the Protecting Power shall be entitled to attend the proceedings in which that question is adjudicated, unless, exceptionally, the proceedings are held in camera in the interest of State security. In such a case the detaining Power shall advise the Protecting Power accordingly.
3. Any person who has taken part in hostilities, who is not entitled to prisoner-of-war status and who does not benefit from more favourable treatment in accordance with the Fourth Convention shall have the right at all times to the protection of Article 75 of this Protocol. In occupied territory, any such person, unless he is held as a spy, shall also be entitled, notwithstanding Article 5 of the Fourth Convention, to his rights of communication under that Convention.

...

Article 47 – Mercenaries

1. A mercenary shall not have the right to be a combatant or a prisoner of war.
2. A mercenary is any person who:

(a) Is specially recruited locally or abroad in order to fight in an armed conflict;
(b) Does, in fact, take a direct part in the hostilities;
(c) Is motivated to take part in the hostilities essentially by the desire for private gain and, in fact, is promised, by or on behalf of a Party to the conflict, material compensation substantially in excess of that promised or paid to combatants of similar ranks and functions in the armed forces of that Party;
(d) Is neither a national of a Party to the conflict nor a resident of territory controlled by a Party to the conflict;
(e) Is not a member of the armed forces of a Party to the conflict; and
(f) Has not been sent by a State which is not a Party to the conflict on official duty as a member of its armed forces.

Part IV. Civilian Population

Section I. General Protection Against Effects of Hostilities

Chapter I. Basic rule and field of application

Article 48 – Basic rule

In order to ensure respect for and protection of the civilian population and civilian objects, the Parties to the conflict shall at all times distinguish between the civilian population and combatants and between civilian objects and military objectives and accordingly shall direct their operations only against military objectives.

Article 49 – Definition of attacks and scope of application

1. "Attacks" means acts of violence against the adversary, whether in offence or in defence.
2. The provisions of this Protocol with respect to attacks apply to all attacks in whatever territory conducted, including the national territory belonging to a Party to the conflict but under the control of an adverse Party.
3. The provisions of this Section apply to any land, air or sea warfare which may affect the civilian population, individual civilians or civilian objects on land. They further apply to all attacks from the sea or from the air against objectives on land but do not otherwise affect the rules of international law applicable in armed conflict at sea or in the air.
4. The provisions of this Section are additional to the rules concerning humanitarian protection contained in the Fourth Convention, particularly in Part II thereof, and in other international agreements binding upon the High Contracting Parties, as well as to other rules of international law relating to the protection of civilians and civilian objects on land, at sea or in the air against the effects of hostilities.

Chapter II. Civilians and Civilian Population

Article 50 – Definition of civilians and civilian population

1. A civilian is any person who does not belong to one of the categories of persons referred to in Article 4 A (1), (2), (3) and (6) of the Third Convention and in Article 43 of this Protocol. In case of doubt whether a person is a civilian, that person shall be considered to be a civilian.
2. The civilian population comprises all persons who are civilians.
3. The presence within the civilian population of individuals who do not come within the definition of civilians does not deprive the population of its civilian character.

Article 51 – Protection of the civilian population

1. The civilian population and individual civilians shall enjoy general protection against dangers arising from military operations. To give effect to this protection, the following rules, which are additional to other applicable rules of international law, shall be observed in all circumstances.
2. The civilian population as such, as well as individual civilians, shall not be the object of attack. Acts or threats of violence the primary purpose of which is to spread terror among the civilian population are prohibited.
3. Civilians shall enjoy the protection afforded by this Section, unless and for such time as they take a direct part in hostilities.
4. Indiscriminate attacks are prohibited. Indiscriminate attacks are:
   (a) Those which are not directed at a specific military objective;
   (b) Those which employ a method or means of combat which cannot be directed at a specific military objective; or
   (c) Those which employ a method or means of combat the effects of which cannot be limited as required by this Protocol; and consequently, in each such case, are of a nature to strike military objectives and civilians or civilian objects without distinction.
5. Among others, the following types of attacks are to be considered as indiscriminate:
   (a) An attack by bombardment by any methods or means which treats as a single military objective a number of clearly separated and distinct military objectives located in a city, town, village or other area containing a similar concentration of civilians or civilian objects; and
   (b) An attack which may be expected to cause incidental loss of civilian life, injury to civilians, damage to civilian objects, or a combination thereof, which would be excessive in relation to the concrete and direct military advantage anticipated.
6. Attacks against the civilian population or civilians by way of reprisals are prohibited.
7. The presence or movements of the civilian population or individual civilians shall not be used to render certain points or areas immune from military operations, in particular in attempts to shield military objectives from attacks or to shield, favour or impede military operations. The Parties to the conflict shall not direct the movement of the civilian population or individual civilians in order to attempt to shield military objectives from attacks or to shield military operations.
8. Any violation of these prohibitions shall not release the Parties to the conflict from their legal obligations with respect to the civilian population and civilians, including the obligation to take the precautionary measures provided for in Article 57.

Chapter III. Civilian Objects

Article 52 – General protection of civilian objects

1. Civilian objects shall not be the object of attack or of reprisals. Civilian objects are all objects which are not military objectives as defined in paragraph 2.
2. Attacks shall be limited strictly to military objectives. In so far as objects are concerned, military objectives are limited to those objects which by their nature, location, purpose or use make an effective contribution to military action and whose total or partial destruction, capture or neutralization, in the circumstances ruling at the time, offers a definite military advantage.

3. In case of doubt whether an object which is normally dedicated to civilian purposes, such as a place of worship, a house or other dwelling or a school, is being used to make an effective contribution to military action, it shall be presumed not to be so used.

...

Article 54 – Protection of objects indispensable to the survival of the civilian population

1. Starvation of civilians as a method of warfare is prohibited.
2. It is prohibited to attack, destroy, remove or render useless objects indispensable to the survival of the civilian population, such as foodstuffs, agricultural areas for the production of foodstuffs, crops, livestock, drinking water installations and supplies and irrigation works, for the specific purpose of denying them for their sustenance value to the civilian population or to the adverse Party, whatever the motive, whether in order to starve out civilians, to cause them to move away, or for any other motive.
3. The prohibitions in paragraph 2 shall not apply to such of the objects covered by it as are used by an adverse Party:
   (a) As sustenance solely for the members of its armed forces; or
   (b) If not as sustenance, then in direct support of military action, provided, however, that in no event shall actions against these objects be taken which may be expected to leave the civilian population with such inadequate food or water as to cause its starvation or force its movement.
4. These objects shall not be made the object of reprisals.
5. In recognition of the vital requirements of any Party to the conflict in the defence of its national territory against invasion, derogation from the prohibitions contained in paragraph 2 may be made by a Party to the conflict within such territory under its own control where required by imperative military necessity.

Article 55 – Protection of the natural environment

1. Care shall be taken in warfare to protect the natural environment against widespread, long-term and severe damage. This protection includes a prohibition of the use of methods or means of warfare which are intended or may be expected to cause such damage to the natural environment and thereby to prejudice the health or survival of the population.
2. Attacks against the natural environment by way of reprisals are prohibited.

...

Chapter IV. Precautionary Principles

Article 57 – Precautions in attack

1. In the conduct of military operations, constant care shall be taken to spare the civilian population, civilians and civilian objects.
2. With respect to attacks, the following precautions shall be taken:
   (a) Those who plan or decide upon an attack shall:
      (i) Do everything feasible to verify that the objectives to be attacked are neither civilians nor civilian objects and are not subject to special protection but are military objectives within the meaning of paragraph 2 of Article 52 and that it is not prohibited by the provisions of this Protocol to attack them;
      (ii) Take all feasible precautions in the choice of means and methods of attack with a view to avoiding, and in any event to minimizing, incidental loss of civilian life, injury to civilians and damage to civilian objects;

(iii) Refrain from deciding to launch any attack which may be expected to cause incidental loss of civilian life, injury to civilians, damage to civilian objects, or a combination thereof, which would be excessive in relation to the concrete and direct military advantage anticipated;

(b) An attack shall be cancelled or suspended if it becomes apparent that the objective is not a military one or is subject to special protection or that the attack may be expected to cause incidental loss of civilian life, injury to civilians, damage to civilian objects, or a combination thereof, which would be excessive in relation to the concrete and direct military advantage anticipated;

(c) Effective advance warning shall be given of attacks which may affect the civilian population, unless circumstances do not permit.

3. When a choice is possible between several military objectives for obtaining a similar military advantage, the objective to be selected shall be that the attack on which may be expected to cause the least danger to civilian lives and to civilian objects.

4. In the conduct of military operations at sea or in the air, each Party to the conflict shall, in conformity with its rights and duties under the rules of international law applicable in armed conflict, take all reasonable precautions to avoid losses of civilian lives and damage to civilian objects.

5. No provision of this Article may be construed as authorizing any attacks against the civilian population, civilians or civilian objects.

Article 58 – Precautions against the effects of attacks

The Parties to the conflict shall, to the maximum extent feasible:

(a) Without prejudice to Article 49 of the Fourth Convention, endeavour to remove the civilian population, individual civilians and civilian objects under their control from the vicinity of military objectives;

(b) Avoid locating military objectives within or near densely populated areas;

(c) Take the other necessary precautions to protect the civilian population, individual civilians and civilian objects under their control against the dangers resulting from military operations.

Chapter V. Localities and zones under special protection

Article 59 – Non-defended localities

1. It is prohibited for the Parties to the conflict to attack, by any means whatsoever, non-defended localities.

2. The appropriate authorities of a Party to the conflict may declare as a non-defended locality any inhabited place near or in a zone where armed forces are in contact which is open for occupation by an adverse Party. Such a locality shall fulfil the following conditions:

   (a) All combatants, as well as mobile weapons and mobile military equipment must have been evacuated;

   (b) No hostile use shall be made of fixed military installations or establishments;

   (c) No acts of hostility shall be committed by the authorities or by the population; and

   (d) No activities in support of military operations shall be undertaken.

3. The presence, in this locality, of persons specially protected under the Conventions and this Protocol, and of police forces retained for the sole purpose of maintaining law and order, is not contrary to the conditions laid down in paragraph 2.

4. The declaration made under paragraph 2 shall be addressed to the adverse Party and shall define and describe, as precisely as possible, the limits of the non-defended locality. The Party

to the conflict to which the declaration is addressed shall acknowledge its receipt and shall treat the locality as a non-defended locality unless the conditions laid down in paragraph 2 are not in fact fulfilled, in which event it shall immediately so inform the Party making the declaration. Even if the conditions laid down in paragraph 2 are not fulfilled, the locality shall continue to enjoy the protection provided by the other provisions of this Protocol and the other rules of international law applicable in armed conflict.

5. The Parties to the conflict may agree on the establishment of non- defended localities even if such localities do not fulfil the conditions laid down in paragraph 2. The agreement should define and describe, as precisely as possible, the limits of the non-defended locality; if necessary, it may lay down the methods of supervision.
6. The Party which is in control of a locality governed by such an agreement shall mark it, so far as possible, by such signs as may be agreed upon with the other Party, which shall be displayed where they are clearly visible, especially on its perimeter and limits and on highways.
7. A locality loses its status as a non-defended locality when it ceases to fulfil the conditions laid down in paragraph 2 or in the agreement referred to in paragraph 5. In such an eventuality, the locality shall continue to enjoy the protection provided by the other provisions of this Protocol and the other rules of international law applicable in armed conflict.

Article 60 – Demilitarized zones

1. It is prohibited for the Parties to the conflict to extend their military operations to zones on which they have conferred by agreement the status of demilitarized zone, if such extension is contrary to the terms of this agreement.
2. The agreement shall be an express agreement, may be concluded verbally or in writing, either directly or through a Protecting Power or any impartial humanitarian organization, and may consist of reciprocal and concordant declarations. The agreement may be concluded in peacetime, as well as after the outbreak of hostilities, and should define and describe, as precisely as possible, the limits of the demilitarized zone and, if necessary, lay down the methods of supervision.
3. The subject of such an agreement shall normally be any zone which fulfils the following conditions:
   (a) All combatants, as well as mobile weapons and mobile military equipment, must have been evacuated;
   (b) No hostile use shall be made of fixed military installations or establishments;
   (c) No acts of hostility shall be committed by the authorities or by the population; and
   (d) Any activity linked to the military effort must have ceased.

The Parties to the conflict shall agree upon the interpretation to be given to the condition laid down in sub-paragraph (d) and upon persons to be admitted to the demilitarized zone other than those mentioned in paragraph 4.

4. The presence, in this zone, of persons specially protected under the Conventions and this Protocol, and of police forces retained for the sole purpose of maintaining law and order, is not contrary to the conditions laid down in paragraph 3.
5. The Party which is in control of such a zone shall mark it, so far as possible, by such signs as may be agreed upon with the other Party, which shall be displayed where they are clearly visible, especially on its perimeter and limits and on highways.
6. If the fighting draws near to a demilitarized zone, and if the Parties to the conflict have so agreed, none of them may use the zone for purposes related to the conduct of military operations or unilaterally revoke its status.
7. If one of the Parties to the conflict commits a material breach of the provisions of paragraphs 3 or 6, the other Party shall be released from its obligations under the agreement conferring

upon the zone the status of demilitarized zone. In such an eventuality, the zone loses its status but shall continue to enjoy the protection provided by the other provisions of this Protocol and the other rules of international law applicable in armed conflict.

...

Section III. Treatment of Persons in the Power of a Party to the Conflict

Chapter I. Field of application and protection of persons and objects

...

Article 74 – Reunion of dispersed families

The High Contracting Parties and the Parties to the conflict shall facilitate in every possible way the reunion of families dispersed as a result of armed conflicts and shall encourage in particular the work of the humanitarian organizations engaged in this task in accordance with the provisions of the Conventions and of this Protocol and in conformity with their respective security regulations.

Article 75 – Fundamental guarantees

1. In so far as they are affected by a situation referred to in Article 1 of this Protocol, persons who are in the power of a Party to the conflict and who do not benefit from more favourable treatment under the Conventions or under this Protocol shall be treated humanely in all circumstances and shall enjoy, as a minimum, the protection provided by this Article without any adverse distinction based upon race, colour, sex, language, religion or belief, political or other opinion, national or social origin, wealth, birth or other status, or on any other similar criteria. Each Party shall respect the person, honour, convictions and religious practices of all such persons.
2. The following acts are and shall remain prohibited at any time and in any place whatsoever, whether committed by civilian or by military agents:
   (a) Violence to the life, health, or physical or mental well-being of persons, in particular:
      (i) Murder;
      (ii) Torture of all kinds, whether physical or mental;
      (iii) Corporal punishment; and
      (iv) Mutilation;
   (b) Outrages upon personal dignity, in particular humiliating and degrading treatment, enforced prostitution and any form of indecent assault;
   (c) The taking of hostages;
   (d) Collective punishments; and
   (e) Threats to commit any of the foregoing acts.
3. Any person arrested, detained or interned for actions related to the armed conflict shall be informed promptly, in a language he understands, of the reasons why these measures have been taken. Except in cases of arrest or detention for penal offences, such persons shall be released with the minimum delay possible and in any event as soon as the circumstances justifying the arrest, detention or internment have ceased to exist.
4. No sentence may be passed and no penalty may be executed on a person found guilty of a penal offence related to the armed conflict except pursuant to a conviction pronounced by an impartial and regularly constituted court respecting the generally recognized principles of regular judicial procedure, which include the following:

(a) The procedure shall provide for an accused to be informed without delay of the particulars of the offence alleged against him and shall afford the accused before and during his trial all necessary rights and means of defence;
(b) No one shall be convicted of an offence except on the basis of individual penal responsibility;
(c) No one shall be accused or convicted of a criminal offence on account of any act or omission which did not constitute a criminal offence under the national or international law to which he was subject at the time when it was committed; nor shall a heavier penalty be imposed than that which was applicable at the time when the criminal offence was committed; if, after the commission of the offence, provision is made by law for the imposition of a lighter penalty, the offender shall benefit thereby;
(d) Anyone charged with an offence is presumed innocent until proved guilty according to law;
(e) Anyone charged with an offence shall have the right to be tried in his presence;
(f) No one shall be compelled to testify against himself or to confess guilt;
(g) Anyone charged with an offence shall have the right to examine, or have examined, the witnesses against him and to obtain the attendance and examination of witnesses on his behalf under the same conditions as witnesses against him;
(h) No one shall be prosecuted or punished by the same Party for an offence in respect of which a final judgement acquitting or convicting that person has been previously pronounced under the same law and judicial procedure;
(i) Anyone prosecuted for an offence shall have the right to have the judgement pronounced publicly; and
(j) A convicted person shall be advised on conviction of his judicial and other remedies and of the time-limits within which they may be exercised.

5. Women whose liberty has been restricted for reasons related to the armed conflict shall be held in quarters separated from men's quarters. They shall be under the immediate supervision of women. Nevertheless, in cases where families are detained or interned, they shall, whenever possible, be held in the same place and accommodated as family units.
6. Persons who are arrested, detained or interned for reasons related to the armed conflict shall enjoy the protection provided by this Article until their final release, repatriation or re-establishment, even after the end of the armed conflict.
7. In order to avoid any doubt concerning the prosecution and trial of persons accused of war crimes or crimes against humanity, the following principles shall apply:
(a) Persons who are accused of such crimes should be submitted for the purpose of prosecution and trial in accordance with the applicable rules of international law; and
(b) Any such persons who do not benefit from more favourable treatment under the Conventions or this Protocol shall be accorded the treatment provided by this Article, whether or not the crimes of which they are accused constitute grave breaches of the Conventions or of this Protocol.
8. No provision of this Article may be construed as limiting or infringing any other more favourable provision granting greater protection, under any applicable rules of international law, to persons covered by paragraph 1.

Chapter II. Measures in favour of women and children

Article 76 – Protection of women

1. Women shall be the object of special respect and shall be protected in particular against rape, forced prostitution and any other form of indecent assault.

2. Pregnant women and mothers having dependent infants who are arrested, detained or interned for reasons related to the armed conflict, shall have their cases considered with the utmost priority.
3. To the maximum extent feasible, the Parties to the conflict shall endeavour to avoid the pronouncement of the death penalty on pregnant women or mothers having dependent infants, for an offence related to the armed conflict. The death penalty for such offences shall not be executed on such women.

Article 77 – Protection of children

1. Children shall be the object of special respect and shall be protected against any form of indecent assault. The Parties to the conflict shall provide them with the care and aid they require, whether because of their age or for any other reason.
2. The Parties to the conflict shall take all feasible measures in order that children who have not attained the age of fifteen years do not take a direct part in hostilities and, in particular, they shall refrain from recruiting them into their armed forces. In recruiting among those persons who have attained the age of fifteen years but who have not attained the age of eighteen years, the Parties to the conflict shall endeavour to give priority to those who are oldest.
3. If, in exceptional cases, despite the provisions of paragraph 2, children who have not attained the age of fifteen years take a direct part in hostilities and fall into the power of an adverse Party, they shall continue to benefit from the special protection accorded by this Article, whether or not they are prisoners of war.
4. If arrested, detained or interned for reasons related to the armed conflict, children shall be held in quarters separate from the quarters of adults, except where families are accommodated as family units as provided in Article 75, paragraph 5.
5. The death penalty for an offence related to armed conflict shall not be executed on persons who had not attained the age of eighteen years at the time the offence was committed.

Article 78 – Evacuation of children

1. No Party to the conflict shall arrange for the evacuation of children, other than its own nationals, to a foreign country except for a temporary evacuation where compelling reasons of the health or medical treatment of the children or, except in occupied territory, their safety, so require. Where the parents or legal guardians can be found, their written consent to such evacuation is required. If these persons cannot be found, the written consent to such evacuation of the persons who by law or custom are primarily responsible for the care of the children is required. Any such evacuation shall be supervised by the Protecting Power in agreement with the Parties concerned, namely, the Party arranging for the evacuation, the Party receiving the children and any Parties whose nationals are being evacuated. In each case, all Parties to the conflict shall take all feasible precautions to avoid endangering the evacuation.
2. Whenever an evacuation occurs pursuant to paragraph 1, each child's education, including his religious and moral education as his parents desire, shall be provided while he is away with the greatest possible continuity.
3. With a view to facilitating the return to their families and country of children evacuated pursuant to this Article, the authorities of the Party arranging for the evacuation and, as appropriate, the authorities of the receiving country shall establish for each child a card with photographs, which they shall send to the Central Tracing Agency of the International Committee of the Red Cross. Each card shall bear, whenever possible, and whenever it involves no risk of harm to the child, the following information:

   (a) Surname(s) of the child;
   (b) The child's first name(s);
   (c) The child's sex;

(d) The place and date of birth (or, if that date is not known, the approximate age);
(e) The father's full name;
(f) The mother's full name and her maiden name;
(g) The child's next-of-kin;
(h) The child's nationality;
(i) The child's native language, and any other languages he speaks;
(j) The address of the child's family;
(k) Any identification number for the child;
(l) The child's state of health;
(m) The child's blood group;
(n) Any distinguishing features;
(o) The date on which and the place where the child was found;
(p) The date on which and the place from which the child left the country;
(q) The child's religion, if any;
(r) The child's present address in the receiving country;
(s) Should the child die before his return, the date, place and circumstances of death and place of interment.

...

Part V. Execution of the Conventions and of this Protocol

Section I. General Provisions

...

Article 81 – Activities of the Red Cross and other humanitarian organizations

1. The Parties to the conflict shall grant to the International Committee of the Red Cross all facilities within their power so as to enable it to carry out the humanitarian functions assigned to it by the Conventions and this Protocol in order to ensure protection and assistance to the victims of conflicts; the International Committee of the Red Cross may also carry out any other humanitarian activities in favour of these victims, subject to the consent of the Parties to the conflict concerned.
2. The Parties to the conflict shall grant to their respective Red Cross (Red Crescent, Red Lion and Sun) organizations the facilities necessary for carrying out their humanitarian activities in favour of the victims of the conflict, in accordance with the provisions of the Conventions and this Protocol and the fundamental principles of the Red Cross as formulated by the International Conferences of the Red Cross.
3. The High Contracting Parties and the Parties to the conflict shall facilitate in every possible way the assistance which Red Cross (Red Crescent, Red Lion and Sun) organizations and the League of Red Cross Societies extend to the victims of conflicts in accordance with the provisions of the Conventions and this Protocol and with the fundamental principles of the Red Cross as formulated by the International Conferences of the Red Cross.
4. The High Contracting Parties and the Parties to the conflict shall, as far as possible, make facilities similar to those mentioned in paragraphs 2 and 3 available to the other humanitarian organizations referred to in the Conventions and this Protocol which are duly authorized by the respective Parties to the conflict and which perform their humanitarian activities in accordance with the provisions of the Conventions and this Protocol.

...

SECTION II. REPRESSION OF BREACHES OF THE CONVENTIONS AND OF THIS PROTOCOL

Article 85 – Repression of breaches of this Protocol

1. The provisions of the Conventions relating to the repression of breaches and grave breaches, supplemented by this Section, shall apply to the repression of breaches and grave breaches of this Protocol.
2. Acts described as grave breaches in the Conventions are grave breaches of this Protocol if committed against persons in the power of an adverse Party protected by Articles 44, 45 and 73 of this Protocol, or against the wounded, sick and shipwrecked of the adverse Party who are protected by this Protocol, or against those medical or religious personnel, medical units or medical transports which are under the control of the adverse Party and are protected by this Protocol.
3. In addition to the grave breaches defined in Article 11, the following acts shall be regarded as grave breaches of this Protocol, when committed wilfully, in violation of the relevant provisions of this Protocol, and causing death or serious injury to body or health:
   (a) Making the civilian population or individual civilians the object of attack;
   (b) Launching an indiscriminate attack affecting the civilian population or civilian objects in the knowledge that such attack will cause excessive loss of life, injury to civilians or damage to civilian objects, as defined in Article 57, paragraph 2 (a) (iii);
   (c) Launching an attack against works or installations containing dangerous forces in the knowledge that such attack will cause excessive loss of life, injury to civilians or damage to civilian objects, as defined in Article 57, paragraph 2 (a) (iii);
   (d) Making non-defended localities and demilitarized zones the object of attack;
   (e) Making a person the object of attack in the knowledge that he is *hors de combat*;
   (f) The perfidious use, in violation of Article 37, of the distinctive emblem of the red cross, red crescent or red lion and sun or of other protective signs recognized by the Conventions or this Protocol.
4. In addition to the grave breaches defined in the preceding paragraphs and in the Conventions, the following shall be regarded as grave breaches of this Protocol, when committed wilfully and in violation of the Conventions or the Protocol:
   (a) The transfer by the Occupying Power of parts of its own civilian population into the territory it occupies, or the deportation or transfer of all or parts of the population of the occupied territory within or outside this territory, in violation of Article 49 of the Fourth Convention;
   (b) Unjustifiable delay in the repatriation of prisoners of war or civilians;
   (c) Practices of *apartheid* and other inhuman and degrading practices involving outrages upon personal dignity, based on racial discrimination;
   (d) Making the clearly-recognized historic monuments, works of art or places of worship which constitute the cultural or spiritual heritage of peoples and to which special protection has been given by special arrangement, for example, within the framework of a competent international organization, the object of attack, causing as a result extensive destruction thereof, where there is no evidence of the violation by the adverse Party of Article 53, sub-paragraph (b), and when such historic monuments, works of art and places of worship are not located in the immediate proximity of military objectives:
   (e) Depriving a person protected by the Conventions or referred to in paragraph 2 of this Article of the rights of fair and regular trial.
5. Without prejudice to the application of the Conventions and of this Protocol, grave breaches of these instruments shall be regarded as war crimes.

. . .

Article 87 – Duty of commanders

1. The High Contracting Parties and the Parties to the conflict shall require military commanders, with respect to members of the armed forces under their command and other persons under their control, to prevent and, where necessary, to suppress and to report to competent authorities breaches of the Conventions and of this Protocol.
2. In order to prevent and suppress breaches, High Contracting Parties and Parties to the conflict shall require that, commensurate with their level of responsibility, commanders ensure that members of the armed forces under their command are aware of their obligations under the Conventions and this Protocol.
3. The High Contracting Parties and Parties to the conflict shall require any commander who is aware that subordinates or other persons under his control are going to commit or have committed a breach of the Conventions or of this Protocol, to initiate such steps as are necessary to prevent such violations of the Conventions or this Protocol, and, where appropriate, to initiate disciplinary or penal action against violators thereof.

...

Article 89 – Co-operation

In situations of serious violations of the Conventions or of this Protocol, the High Contracting Parties undertake to act, jointly or individually, in co-operation with the United Nations and in conformity with the United Nations Charter.

...

Article 91 – Responsibility

A Party to the conflict which violates the provisions of the Conventions or of this Protocol shall, if the case demands, be liable to pay compensation. It shall be responsible for all acts committed by persons forming part of its armed forces.

...

Protocol Additional to the Geneva Conventions of 12 August 1949, and relating to the Protection of Victims of Non-International Armed Conflicts (Protocol II)

(Extracts)

PREAMBLE

The High Contracting Parties,

Recalling that the humanitarian principles enshrined in Article 3 common to the Geneva Conventions of 12 August 1949, constitute the foundation of respect for the human person in cases of armed conflict not of an international character,

Recalling furthermore that international instruments relating to human rights offer a basic protection to the human person,

Emphasizing the need to ensure a better protection for the victims of those armed conflicts,

Recalling that, in cases not covered by the law in force, the human person remains under the protection of the principles of humanity and the dictates of the public conscience,

Have agreed on the following:

Part I. Scope of the Protocol

Article 1 – Material field of application

1. This Protocol, which develops and supplements Article 3 common to the Geneva Conventions of 12 August 1949 without modifying its existing conditions of application, shall apply to all armed conflicts which are not covered by Article 1 of the Protocol Additional to the Geneva Conventions of 12 August 1949, and relating to the Protection of Victims of International Armed Conflicts (Protocol I) and which take place in the territory of a High Contracting Party between its armed forces and dissident armed forces or other organized armed groups which, under responsible command, exercise such control over a part of its territory as to enable them to carry out sustained and concerted military operations and to implement this Protocol.
2. This Protocol shall not apply to situations of internal disturbances and tensions, such as riots, isolated and sporadic acts of violence and other acts of a similar nature, as not being armed conflicts.

Article 2 – Personal field of application

1. This Protocol shall be applied without any adverse distinction founded on race, colour, sex, language, religion or belief, political or other opinion, national or social origin, wealth, birth or other status, or on any other similar criteria (hereinafter referred to as "adverse distinction") to all persons affected by an armed conflict as defined in Article 1.
2. At the end of the armed conflict, all the persons who have been deprived of their liberty or whose liberty has been restricted for reasons related to such conflict, as well as those deprived of their liberty or whose liberty is restricted after the conflict for the same reasons, shall enjoy the protection of Articles 5 and 6 until the end of such deprivation or restriction of liberty.

. . .

Part II. Humane Treatment

Article 4 – Fundamental guarantees

1. All persons who do not take a direct part or who have ceased to take part in hostilities, whether or not their liberty has been restricted, are entitled to respect for their person, honour and convictions and religious practices. They shall in all circumstances be treated humanely, without any adverse distinction. It is prohibited to order that there shall be no survivors.
2. Without prejudice to the generality of the foregoing, the following acts against the persons referred to in paragraph I are and shall remain prohibited at any time and in any place whatsoever:
   (a) Violence to the life, health and physical or mental well-being of persons, in particular murder as well as cruel treatment such as torture, mutilation or any form of corporal punishment;
   (b) Collective punishments;
   (c) Taking of hostages;
   (d) Acts of terrorism;

(e) Outrages upon personal dignity, in particular humiliating and degrading treatment, rape, enforced prostitution and any form of indecent assault;
(f) Slavery and the slave trade in all their forms;
(g) Pillage;
(h) Threats to commit any of the foregoing acts.

3. Children shall be provided with the care and aid they require, and in particular:
(a) They shall receive an education, including religious and moral education, in keeping with the wishes of their parents, or in the absence of parents, of those responsible for their care;
(b) All appropriate steps shall be taken to facilitate the reunion of families temporarily separated;
(c) Children who have not attained the age of fifteen years shall neither be recruited in the armed forces or groups nor allowed to take part in hostilities;
(d) The special protection provided by this Article to children who have not attained the age of fifteen years shall remain applicable to them if they take a direct part in hostilities despite the provisions of sub-paragraph (c) and are captured;
(e) Measures shall be taken, if necessary, and whenever possible with the consent of their parents or persons who by law or custom are primarily responsible for their care, to remove children temporarily from the area in which hostilities are taking place to a safer area within the country and ensure that they are accompanied by persons responsible for their safety and well-being.

Article 5 – Persons whose liberty has been restricted

1. In addition to the provisions of Article 4, the following provisions shall be respected as a minimum with regard to persons deprived of their liberty for reasons related to the armed conflict, whether they are interned or detained:
(a) The wounded and the sick shall be treated in accordance with Article 7;
(b) The persons referred to in this paragraph shall, to the same extent as the local civilian population, be provided with food and drinking water and be afforded safeguards as regards health and hygiene and protection against the rigours of the climate and the dangers of the armed conflict;
(c) They shall be allowed to receive individual or collective relief;
(d) They shall be allowed to practise their religion and, if requested and appropriate, to receive spiritual assistance from persons, such as chaplains, performing religious functions;
(e) They shall, if made to work, have the benefit of working conditions and safeguards similar to those enjoyed by the local civilian population.

2. Those who are responsible for the internment or detention of the persons referred to in paragraph I shall also, within the limits of their capabilities, respect the following provisions relating to such persons:
(a) Except when men and women of a family are accommodated together, women shall be held in quarters separated from those of men and shall be under the immediate supervision of women;
(b) They shall be allowed to send and receive letters and cards, the number of which may be limited by the competent authority if it deems necessary;
(c) Places of internment and detention shall not be located close to the combat zone. The persons referred to in paragraph 1 shall be evacuated when the places where they are interned or detained become particularly exposed to danger arising out of the armed conflict, if their evacuation can be carried out under adequate conditions of safety;
(d) They shall have the benefit of medical examinations;

(e) Their physical or mental health and integrity shall not be endangered by an unjustified act or omission. Accordingly, it is prohibited to subject the persons described in this Article to any medical procedure which is not indicated by the state of health of the person concerned, and which is not consistent with the generally accepted medical standards applied to free persons under similar medical circumstances.

3. Persons who are not covered by paragraph I but whose liberty has been restricted in any way whatsoever for reasons related to the armed conflict shall be treated humanely in accordance with Article 4 and with paragraphs 1 (a), (c) and (d), and 2 (b) of this Article.

4. If it is decided to release persons deprived of their liberty, necessary measures to ensure their safety shall be taken by those so deciding.

Article 6 – Penal prosecutions

1. This Article applies to the prosecution and punishment of criminal offences related to the armed conflict.

2. No sentence shall be passed and no penalty shall be executed on a person found guilty of an offence except pursuant to a conviction pronounced by a court offering the essential guarantees of independence and impartiality. In particular:

   (a) The procedure shall provide for an accused to be informed without delay of the particulars of the offence alleged against him and shall afford the accused before and during his trial all necessary rights and means of defence;

   (b) No one shall be convicted of an offence except on the basis of individual penal responsibility;

   (c) No one shall be held guilty of any criminal offence on account of any act or omission which did not constitute a criminal offence, under the law, at the time when it was committed; nor shall a heavier penalty be imposed than that which was applicable at the time when the criminal offence was committed; if, after the commission of the offence, provision is made by law for the imposition of a lighter penalty, the offender shall benefit thereby;

   (d) Anyone charged with an offence is presumed innocent until proved guilty according to law;

   (e) Anyone charged with an offence shall have the right to be tried in his presence;

   (f) No one shall be compelled to testify against himself or to confess guilt.

3. A convicted person shall be advised on conviction of his judicial and other remedies and of the time-limits within which they may be exercised.

4. The death penalty shall not be pronounced on persons who were under the age of eighteen years at the time of the offence and shall not be carried out on pregnant women or mothers of young children.

5. At the end of hostilities, the authorities in power shall endeavour to grant the broadest possible amnesty to persons who have participated in the armed conflict, or those deprived of their liberty for reasons related to the armed conflict, whether they are interned or detained.

...

Part III. Wounded, Sick and Shipwrecked

Article 9 – Protection of medical and religious personnel

1. Medical and religious personnel shall be respected and protected and shall be granted all available help for the performance of their duties. They shall not be compelled to carry out tasks which are not compatible with their humanitarian mission.

2. In the performance of their duties medical personnel may not be required to give priority to any person except on medical grounds.

Article 10 – General protection of medical duties

1. Under no circumstances shall any person be punished for having carried out medical activities compatible with medical ethics, regardless of the person benefiting therefrom.
2. Persons engaged in medical activities shall neither be compelled to perform acts or to carry out work contrary to, nor be compelled to refrain from acts required by, the rules of medical ethics or other rules designed for the benefit of the wounded and sick, or this Protocol.
3. The professional obligations of persons engaged in medical activities regarding information which they may acquire concerning the wounded and sick under their care shall, subject to national law, be respected.
4. Subject to national law, no person engaged in medical activities may be penalized in any way for refusing or failing to give information concerning the wounded and sick who are, or who have been, under his care.

Article 11 – Protection of medical units and transports

1. Medical units and transports shall be respected and protected at all times and shall not be the object of attack.
2. The protection to which medical units and transports are entitled shall not cease unless they are used to commit hostile acts, outside their humanitarian function. Protection may, however, cease only after a warning has been given setting, whenever appropriate, a reasonable time-limit, and after such warning has remained unheeded.

Article 12 – The distinctive emblem

Under the direction of the competent authority concerned, the distinctive emblem of the red cross, red crescent or red lion and sun on a white ground shall be displayed by medical and religious personnel and medical units, and on medical transports. It shall be respected in all circumstances. It shall not be used improperly.

Part IV. Civilian Population

Article 13 – Protection of the civilian population

1. The civilian population and individual civilians shall enjoy general protection against the dangers arising from military operations. To give effect to this protection, the following rules shall be observed in all circumstances.
2. The civilian population as such, as well as individual civilians, shall not be the object of attack. Acts or threats of violence the primary purpose of which is to spread terror among the civilian population are prohibited.
3. Civilians shall enjoy the protection afforded by this Part, unless and for such time as they take a direct part in hostilities.

Article 14 – Protection of objects indispensable to the survival of the civilian population

Starvation of civilians as a method of combat is prohibited. It is therefore prohibited to attack, destroy, remove or render useless, for that purpose, objects indispensable to the survival of the civilian population, such as foodstuffs, agricultural areas for the production of foodstuffs, crops, livestock, drinking water installations and supplies and irrigation works.

Article 15 – Protection of works and installations containing dangerous forces

Works or installations containing dangerous forces, namely dams, dykes and nuclear electrical generating stations, shall not be made the object of attack, even where these objects are military objectives, if such attack may cause the release of dangerous forces and consequent severe losses among the civilian population.

Article 16 – Protection of cultural objects and of places of worship

Without prejudice to the provisions of The Hague Convention for the Protection of Cultural Property in the Event of Armed Conflict of 14 May 1954, it is prohibited to commit any acts of hostility directed against historic monuments, works of art or places of worship which constitute the cultural or spiritual heritage of peoples, and to use them in support of the military effort.

Article 17 – Prohibition of forced movement of civilians

1. The displacement of the civilian population shall not be ordered for reasons related to the conflict unless the security of the civilians involved or imperative military reasons so demand. Should such displacements have to be carried out, all possible measures shall be taken in order that the civilian population may be received under satisfactory conditions of shelter, hygiene, health, safety and nutrition.
2. Civilians shall not be compelled to leave their own territory for reasons connected with the conflict.

Article 18 – Relief societies and relief actions

1. Relief societies located in the territory of the High Contracting Party, such as Red Cross (Red Crescent, Red Lion and Sun) organizations, may offer their services for the performance of their traditional functions in relation to the victims of the armed conflict. The civilian population may, even on its own initiative, offer to collect and care for the wounded, sick and shipwrecked.
2. If the civilian population is suffering undue hardship owing to a lack of the supplies essential for its survival, such as foodstuffs and medical supplies, relief actions for the civilian population which are of an exclusively humanitarian and impartial nature and which are conducted without any adverse distinction shall be undertaken subject to the consent of the High Contracting Party concerned.

...

Protocol Additional to the Geneva Conventions of 12 August 1949, and relating to the Adoption of an Additional Distinctive Emblem (Protocol III)

(Extracts)

Preamble

The High Contracting Parties,

Reaffirming the provisions of the Geneva Conventions of 12 August 1949 (in particular Articles 26, 38, 42 and 44 of the First Geneva Convention) and, where applicable, their Additional Protocols of 8 June 1977 (in particular Articles 18 and 38 of Additional Protocol I and Article 12 of Additional Protocol II), concerning the use of distinctive emblems,

Desiring to supplement the aforementioned provisions so as to enhance their protective value and universal character,

Noting that this Protocol is without prejudice to the recognized right of High Contracting Parties to continue to use the emblems they are using in conformity with their obligations under the Geneva Conventions and, where applicable, the Protocols additional thereto,

Recalling that the obligation to respect persons and objects protected by the Geneva Conventions and the Protocols additional thereto derives from their protected status under international law and is not dependent on use of the distinctive emblems, signs or signals,

Stressing that the distinctive emblems are not intended to have any religious, ethnic, racial, regional or political significance,

Emphasizing the importance of ensuring full respect for the obligations relating to the distinctive emblems recognized in the Geneva Conventions, and, where applicable, the Protocols additional thereto,

Recalling that Article 44 of the First Geneva Convention makes the distinction between the protective use and the indicative use of the distinctive emblems,

Recalling further that National Societies undertaking activities on the territory of another State must ensure that the emblems they intend to use within the framework of such activities may be used in the country where the activity takes place and in the country or countries of transit,

Recognizing the difficulties that certain States and National Societies may have with the use of the existing distinctive emblems,

Noting the determination of the International Committee of the Red Cross, the International Federation of Red Cross and Red Crescent Societies and the International Red Cross and Red Crescent Movement to retain their current names and emblems,

Have agreed on the following:

Article 1 – Respect for and scope of application of this Protocol

1. The High Contracting Parties undertake to respect and to ensure respect for this Protocol in all circumstances.
2. This Protocol reaffirms and supplements the provisions of the four Geneva Conventions of 12 August 1949 ("the Geneva Conventions") and, where applicable, of their two Additional Protocols of 8 June 1977 ("the 1977 Additional Protocols") relating to the distinctive emblems, namely the red cross, the red crescent and the red lion and sun, and shall apply in the same situations as those referred to in these provisions.

Article 2 – Distinctive emblems

1. This Protocol recognizes an additional distinctive emblem in addition to, and for the same purposes as, the distinctive emblems of the Geneva Conventions. The distinctive emblems shall enjoy equal status.
2. This additional distinctive emblem, composed of a red frame in the shape of a square on edge on a white ground, shall conform to the illustration in the Annex to this Protocol. This distinctive emblem is referred to in this Protocol as the "third Protocol emblem".
3. The conditions for use of and respect for the third Protocol emblem are identical to those for the distinctive emblems established by the Geneva Conventions and, where applicable, the 1977 Additional Protocols.
4. The medical services and religious personnel of armed forces of High Contracting Parties may, without prejudice to their current emblems, make temporary use of any distinctive emblem referred to in paragraph 1 of this Article where this may enhance protection.

Article 3 – Indicative use of the third Protocol emblem

1. National Societies of those High Contracting Parties which decide to use the third Protocol emblem may, in using the emblem in conformity with relevant national legislation, choose to incorporate within it, for indicative purposes:
   (a) a distinctive emblem recognized by the Geneva Conventions or a combination of these emblems; or
   (b) another emblem which has been in effective use by a High Contracting Party and was the subject of a communication to the other High Contracting Parties and the International Committee of the Red Cross through the depositary prior to the adoption of this Protocol.

   Incorporation shall conform to the illustration in the Annex to this Protocol.
2. A National Society which chooses to incorporate within the third Protocol emblem another emblem in accordance with paragraph 1 above, may, in conformity with national legislation, use the designation of that emblem and display it within its national territory.
3. National Societies may, in accordance with national legislation and in exceptional circumstances and to facilitate their work, make temporary use of the distinctive emblem referred to in Article 2 of this Protocol.
4. This Article does not affect the legal status of the distinctive emblems recognized in the Geneva Conventions and in this Protocol, nor does it affect the legal status of any particular emblem when incorporated for indicative purposes in accordance with paragraph 1 of this Article.

Article 4 – International Committee of the Red Cross and International Federation of Red Cross and Red Crescent Societies

The International Committee of the Red Cross and the International Federation of Red Cross and Red Crescent Societies, and their duly authorized personnel, may use, in exceptional circumstances and to facilitate their work, the distinctive emblem referred to in Article 2 of this Protocol.

Article 5 – Missions under United Nations auspices

The medical services and religious personnel participating in operations under the auspices of the United Nations may, with the agreement of participating States, use one of the distinctive emblems mentioned in Articles 1 and 2.

Article 6 – Prevention and repression of misuse

1. The provisions of the Geneva Conventions and, where applicable, the 1977 Additional Protocols, governing prevention and repression of misuse of the distinctive emblems shall apply equally to the third Protocol emblem. In particular, the High Contracting Parties shall take measures necessary for the prevention and repression, at all times, of any misuse of the distinctive emblems mentioned in Articles 1 and 2 and their designations, including the perfidious use and the use of any sign or designation constituting an imitation thereof.
2. Notwithstanding paragraph 1 above, High Contracting Parties may permit prior users of the third Protocol emblem, or of any sign constituting an imitation thereof, to continue such use, provided that the said use shall not be such as would appear, in time of armed conflict, to confer the protection of the Geneva Conventions and, where applicable, the 1977 Additional Protocols, and provided that the rights to such use were acquired before the adoption of this Protocol.

...

Annex – Third Protocol Emblem

(Article 2(2) and Article 3(1) of the Protocol)

Article 1 – Distinctive emblem

Article 2 – Indicative use of the third Protocol emblem

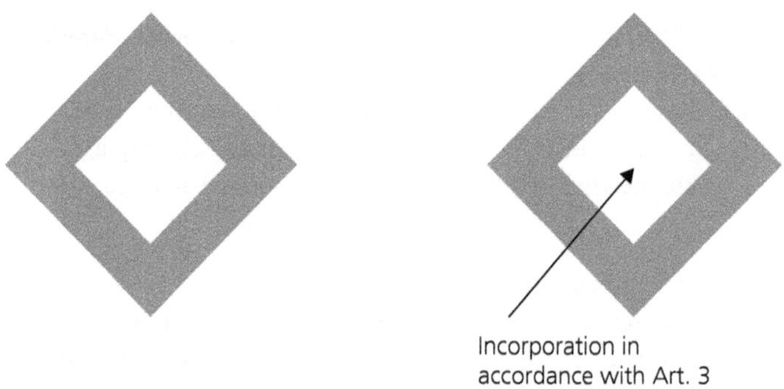

D. Thematic Security Council Resolutions

Introduction

The Security Council, through what are often referred to as thematic (sometimes referred to as 'cross-cutting') resolutions, has raised how UN peace operations and UN peacekeepers might do more to protect civilians. These resolutions differ from the more specific country related resolutions, such as those establishing peace operations, by addressing general issues or themes which relate to the maintenance of international peace and security.

The list of themes dealt with by the Security Council in thematic resolutions is quite extensive. They range from very broad topics, such as the maintenance of international peace and security, climate change, peacebuilding, and the pacific settlements of disputes, to more narrow topics such as HIV/AIDS.[1] Each of the issues is dealt with by a 'landmark resolution'.[2]

The thematic resolutions covered in this part of the book concern four issues: (1) women, peace, and security; (2) children in armed conflict; (3) protection of civilians in armed conflict; and (4) sexual exploitation and abuse. The landmark Security Council resolutions for each of these four themes are: resolution 1325 of 31 October 2000 for women, peace, and security; resolution 1612 of 26 July 2005 for children in armed conflict; resolution 1674 of 28 April 2006 for the protection of civilians in armed conflict; and resolution of 2272 of 11 March 2016 on sexual exploitation and abuse by UN peacekeepers.

These resolutions are mutually reinforcing under the overarching theme of the protection of civilians by UN peacekeepers. Broadly speaking, they address (1) reinforcing international legal norms concerning principles and rules such as the prohibitions against targeting civilians, and violence against women and children; (2) condemning those who breach fundamental legal norms protecting civilians; (3) obligations, roles, and functions that peacekeepers have or should have to protect civilians; and (4) the primary obligation of Member States to hold those who attack or threaten to attack civilians accountable for those attacks or threats.

Landmark resolutions and subsequent thematic resolutions are binding if they are phrased as decisions of the Security Council.[3] Even if they are not binding such resolutions carry some normative strength because they are issued by the Security Council—the peak international body that deals with threats to international peace and security. They also have normative value because they reaffirm or reinforce fundamental legal principles such as the prohibitions against targeting civilians, gender and sexual violence, and sexual exploitation and abuse. Furthermore, the resolutions, such as resolution 1325 and resolution 1612, have influenced the peacekeeping policies of regional organisations such as the African Union (AU) and the European Union (EU). As such, the thematic resolutions discussed in this Part should be viewed as contributing to the planning for, and conduct of, peace operations by providing peacekeepers with guidelines and standards to apply when protecting civilians.

The importance of the thematic resolutions is also reinforced by the fact that it is now common practice that every year the General Assembly's Special Committee on Peacekeeping Operations (C34) devotes sections of its report to the General Assembly to addressing 'gender and peacekeeping', 'children and peacekeeping', 'protection of civilians', and 'conduct and discipline'.

The four themes dealt with in this Part are continually evolving as the Security Council seeks to better understand and engage with how peacekeepers might better protect civilians.

---

1 For a complete list of themes, see Repertoire of the Practice of the Security Council <http://www.un.org/en/sc/repertoire/studies/general_studies.shtml> accessed 3 October 2018.

2 The phrase 'landmark resolution' refers to the first resolution of the Council to deal with a thematic issue.

3 See Introduction to this book for a discussion concerning binding Security Council resolutions.

17

Women, Peace, and Security

Prefatory Note

The Security Council has focused on women, peace, and security in the context of peace operations from several perspectives including the role of women in peacebuilding, the protection of women from violence, and undertaking gender analysis when planning and conducting UN peace operations. As part of that work, the Security Council adopted several resolutions concerning 'women, peace, and security'. These resolutions, along with the resolutions concerning children and armed conflict,[1] civilians in armed conflict,[2] and sexual exploitation and sexual abuse,[3] are thematic resolutions and mutually reinforce each other.

The first resolution dealing with women, peace, and security—the landmark resolution 1325—was adopted in 2000. The following resolutions on women, peace and security have since been adopted: 1820, 1888, 1889, 1960, 2106, 2122, and 2242. Each is concerned with enhancing the protection of women in armed conflict and their role in the maintenance of international peace and security. These resolutions should also be viewed as a part of the framework that reinforces the principles and rules found in the Convention on the Elimination of All Forms of Discrimination against Women (CEDAW).[4]

The four Security Council resolutions reproduced in this chapter are resolution 1325 adopted on 31 October 2000, resolution 1820 adopted on 19 June 2008, resolution 1888 adopted on 30 September 2009, and resolution 2242 adopted on 13 October 2015. Resolutions 1889, 1960, 2106, and 2122 have not been included because they do not focus on peace operations.

All the resolutions on women, peace, and security reinforce the Security Council's resolve to deal with gender-based issues in the context of armed conflict and international peace and security. Gender equality has been an issue on the agenda of the UN since its inception in 1945. In the Preamble to the Charter of the United Nations (Charter), the peoples of the United Nations were determined to 'reaffirm faith ... in the equal rights of men and women',[5] and Article 2 of the Universal Declaration of Human Rights states that 'everyone is entitled to the rights and freedoms set forth in this Declaration, without distinction of any kind, such as ... sex'. These rights were given legally binding force in the CEDAW.

In the 1990s, awareness developed of the importance of considering women's rights in matters of international law and policy. Documents such as the Beijing Declaration and Platform for Action adopted by the Fourth World Conference on Women in 1995[6] contributed to debates on these matters.[7] Concurrently, developments in international criminal prosecutions, in particular the inclusion of gender-based crimes in subject matter jurisdiction, added weight to the recognition of the impact of political tensions and armed conflict upon women.

It was within this context that in 1999 the Secretary-General issued the Bulletin entitled 'Observance by United Nations Forces of International Humanitarian Law'[8] which included specific reference to women. In 2000, the Windhoek Declaration and the Namibia Plan of Action on Mainstreaming a Gender Perspective in Multidimensional Peace Support Operations (Namibia Plan)

---

1 See ch 18 below.
2 See ch 19 below.
3 See ch 20 below.
4 See ch 7 above.
5 Charter of the United Nations (opened for signature 26 June 1945, entered into force 24 October 1945) 1 UNTS XVI, Preamble. See ch 1 above.
6 Fourth World Conference on Women, Beijing Declaration and Platform for Action (Beijing, 15 September 1995) <http://www.un.org/womenwatch/daw/beijing/beijingdeclaration.html> accessed 26 December 2018.
7 See 'Report of the Fourth World Conference on Women', UN Doc A/CONF177/20, 17 October 1995.
8 'Secretary-General's Bulletin: Observance by United Nations Forces of International Humanitarian Law', UN Doc ST/SGB/1999/13, 6 August 1999, entered into force 12 August 1999. See ch 15 above.

also emphasised the role of gender in peace operations.[9] The Windhoek Declaration and Namibia Plan were adopted at a seminar organised by the Lessons Learned Unit[10] of the Department of Peacekeeping Operations (DPKO) and the Office of the Special Adviser on Gender Issues and Advancement of Women. The Windhoek Declaration stresses that, in order to ensure the effectiveness of peace operations, the principle of gender equality must become part of the operation at all levels so that women can fully participate, equally with men, in all aspects of the peace process from peacekeeping to peacebuilding, and in the future political life of the country.

The increased focus on gender issues in peace operations led to the adoption of resolution 1325. The Security Council had previously indicated concern about the issue of women and girls in situations of armed conflict in a number of earlier resolutions.[11] In the late 1990s, for example, the Security Council adopted a series of thematic resolutions covering the area of human security starting with resolution 1261 on children and armed conflict. In resolution 1261, the Security Council urged 'all parties to armed conflicts to take special measures to protect children, in particular girls, from rape and other forms of sexual abuse and gender-based violence in situations of armed conflict'.[12]

This was followed by Security Council resolution 1265 on the protection of civilians in armed conflict which noted 'the importance of including in the mandates of peacemaking, peacekeeping and peace-building operations special protection and assistance provisions for groups requiring particular attention, including women and children'.[13] A range of other resolutions dealing with issues surrounding the protection of women, children and other vulnerable groups were adopted in 2000[14] including resolution 1308 on HIV/AIDS and international peacekeeping operations.[15]

In resolution 1325, the Security Council expressed 'concern that civilians, particularly women and children, account for the vast majority of those adversely affected by armed conflict, including as refugees and internally displaced persons'.[16] This concern led the Security Council to reaffirm the need for States to fully implement international humanitarian law[17] and international human rights law[18] relating to the protection of women and girls during and after armed conflicts. The Security Council also reaffirmed 'the important role of women in the prevention and resolution of conflicts and in peace-building', and stressed 'the importance of their equal participation and full involvement in all efforts for the maintenance and promotion of peace and security, and the need to increase their role in decision-making with regard to conflict prevention and resolution'.[19] The requirement of recognising women's agency as well as their vulnerabilities resulted in the Security Council identifying the urgent need to 'mainstream a gender perspective into peacekeeping operations'.[20]

A significant element of resolution 1325 is the Security Council's articulation of its willingness to incorporate a gender perspective into peacekeeping operations. This involves ensuring that field operations include a gender component as well as addressing the particular vulnerabilities of women in armed conflict.[21] The resolution, in its Operative Part, also urges that a range of measures be taken by all relevant actors, such as Member States and the UN, to increase the participation of women in decision-making roles in peace processes, as well as within UN field-based peace operations. These measures include: increasing the representation of women at all decision-making

9 'Letter dated 12 July 2000 from the Permanent Representative of Namibia to the United Nations addressed to the Secretary-General', UN Doc A/55/138–S/2000/693, 14 July 2000, Annexes I and II.

10 Now known as the Peacekeeping Best Practices Section (PBPS). The PBPS maintain the Peacekeeping Resource Hub <http://research.un.org/en/peacekeeping-community> accessed 26 December 2018.

11 See, for example, SC Res 1208 (1998) of 19 November 1998 on the situation in African refugee camps.

12 SC Res 1261 (1999) of 25 August 1999, Operative Part [10]. See ch 18 below.

13 SC Res 1265 (1999) of 17 September 1999, Operative Part [13]. See ch 19 below.

14 See SC Res 1296 (2000) of 19 April 2000; SC Res 1314 (2000) of 11 August 2000.

15 SC Res 1308 (2000) of 17 July 2000. See Bruce Oswald, Helen Durham, and Adrian Bates, *Documents on the Law of UN Peace Operations* (Oxford University Press 2010) ch 4.

16 SC Res 1325 (2000) of 31 October 2000, Preamble [4].

17 See chs 15–16 above.

18 See chs 4–13 above.

19 SC Res 1325 (2000) of 31 October 2000, Preamble [5].

20 Ibid, Preamble [8].

21 For further information on Gender and UN Peacekeeping, visit <https://peacekeeping.un.org/en/promoting-women-peace-and-security> accessed 31 December 2018, which includes fact sheets on women, peace, and security, gender mainstreaming, and gender advisers in peace operations.

levels; the Secretary-General appointing an increased number of women as special representatives; expanding the role of women in UN field operations; adopting a gender perspective when negotiating peace agreements; and supporting local initiatives of women involved in the peace process.

In terms of international law, resolution 1325 called upon all parties to an armed conflict to:

> respect fully international law applicable to the rights and protection of women and girls, especially as civilians, in particular the obligations applicable to them under the Geneva Conventions of 1949 and the Additional Protocols thereto of 1977, the Refugee Convention of 1951 and the Protocol thereto of 1967, the Convention on the Elimination of All Forms of Discrimination against Women of 1979 and the Optional Protocol thereto of 1999 and the United Nations Convention on the Rights of the Child of 1989 and the two Optional Protocols thereto of 25 May 2000, and to bear in mind the relevant provisions of the Rome Statute of the International Criminal Court.[22]

Resolution 1325 also called on all parties to an armed conflict to protect women and children from gender-based violence, in particular rape and other forms of sexual abuse, emphasising the responsibility of States to end impunity for, and to prosecute, acts of genocide, crimes against humanity, and war crimes including those relating to sexual violence against women and children. Finally, it requested the 'Secretary-General, where appropriate, to include in his reporting to the Security Council progress on gender mainstreaming throughout peacekeeping missions and all other aspects relating to women and girls'.[23]

In 2001, the Security Council adopted resolution 1366 which reiterated 'its recognition of the role of women in conflict prevention and *requests* the Secretary-General to give greater attention to gender perspectives in the implementation of peacekeeping and peace-building mandates as well as in conflict prevention efforts'.[24]

Since resolution 1325, the General Assembly's Special Committee on Peacekeeping Operations (C34) has included a section on gender and peacekeeping in its annual reports starting with the 2001 report.[25] In its 2014 report, the C34 requested the DPKO:

> to continue working in a cooperative and coordinated manner with UN-Women and all other relevant United Nations actors in order to ensure the full implementation of its mandate relating to the promotion of gender perspectives in peacekeeping operations, as well as Security Council resolution 1325 (2000) and all subsequent resolutions relating to women, peace and security, so as to optimize the effectiveness and impact of United Nations work in the area of women and peace and security.[26]

The next resolution on the theme of women, peace, and security was resolution 1820 in 2008.[27] That resolution concerned sexual violence against women and children during armed conflict and how this could be prevented. The Security Council reaffirmed its commitment to its earlier resolutions dealing with women, peace, and security and recalled that the Rome Statute of the International Criminal Court[28] included a range of sexual violence offences, noting that 'rape and other forms of sexual violence can constitute a war crime, a crime against humanity, or a constitutive act with respect to genocide'.[29] Resolution 1820 called upon all Member States to:

> comply with their obligations for prosecuting persons responsible for such acts, to ensure that all victims of sexual violence, particularly women and girls, have equal protection under the law and equal access to justice . . .[30]

With respect to peace operations, resolution 1820 requested the Secretary-General, working with the C34, to develop training programmes for peacekeepers to enable them to recognise, respond

---

22 SC Res 1325 (2000) of 31 October 2000, Operative Part [9].

23 Ibid, Operative Part [17].

24 SC Res 1366 (2001) of 30 August 2001, Operative Part [17].

25 'Report of the Special Committee on Peacekeeping Operations: Comprehensive Review of the Whole Question of Peacekeeping Operations in all their Aspects', UN Doc A/55/1024, 31 July 2001.

26 'Report of the Special Committee on Peacekeeping Operations, 2015 Substantive Session (17 February–13 March 2015)', UN Doc A/69/19, 17 March 2015, [191].

27 SC Res 1820 (2008) of 19 June 2008.

28 See ch 23 below.

29 SC Res 1820 (2008) of 19 June 2008, Operative Part [4].

30 Ibid.

to and prevent sexual violence in mission areas, to continue to work on strengthening the policy of zero tolerance of sexual exploitation in UN peace operations, and to develop guidelines to

> enhance the ability of relevant UN peacekeeping operations, consistent with their mandates, to protect civilians, including women and girls, from all forms of sexual violence and to systematically include in his written reports to the Council on conflict situations his observations concerning the protection of women and girls and recommendations in this regard.[31]

Resolution 1820 urged contributing States to consider steps they could take to raise awareness of the issue of sexual violence amongst their personnel on UN peace operations to better protect women and children in conflict and post-conflict situations. It also urged contributing States to ensure full accountability in respect of any of their own personnel suspected of involvement in acts of sexual exploitation and abuse.

The Security Council's concerns that 'violence against women and children including all forms of sexual violence in situations of armed conflict ... continue to occur, and in some situations have become systematic or widespread'[32] led the Security Council to issue resolution 1888 on 30 September 2009. A key component of that resolution is the Security Council's demand that:

> all parties to armed conflict immediately take appropriate measures to protect civilians, including women and children, from all forms of sexual violence, including measures such as, inter alia, enforcing appropriate military disciplinary measures and upholding the principle of command responsibility, training troops on the categorical prohibition of all forms of sexual violence against civilians, debunking myths that fuel sexual violence and vetting candidates for national armies and security forces to ensure the exclusion of those associated with serious violations of international humanitarian and human rights law, including sexual violence.[33]

The Security Council's focus on taking appropriate measures to stop sexual violence is further demonstrated by the Security Council urging all parties to a conflict:

> to ensure that all reports of sexual violence committed by civilians or by military personnel are thoroughly investigated and the alleged perpetrators brought to justice, and that civilian superiors and military commanders, in accordance with international humanitarian law, use their authority and powers to prevent sexual violence, including by combating impunity.[34]

In resolution 1888 the Security Council reinforced its intention to ensure that when establishing or renewing mandates for peace operations, those mandates should include, where appropriate, provisions 'on the prevention of, and response to, sexual violence, with corresponding reporting requirements to the Council'.[35] One reporting requirement highlighted in resolution 1888 relates to the Secretary-General in his regular reports on individual peace operations to include, where appropriate, 'information on steps taken to implement measures to protect civilians, particularly women and children, against sexual violence'.[36] Resolution 1888 also articulates the Security Council's decision to 'include specific provisions, as appropriate, for the protection of women and children from rape and other sexual violence in the mandates'[37] of UN peace operations.

Security Council resolution 2242 emphasises the importance of the DPKO taking the necessary steps to ensure that gender analysis is undertaken in all its peace operations.[38] The Security Council also expresses its concern over

> continuing allegations of sexual exploitation and abuse by United Nations peacekeepers and non-United Nations forces, including military, civilian and police personnel, urges police- and troop-contributing countries to provide robust pre-deployment training on sexual exploitation and abuse and vetting of their peacekeeping personnel, to conduct swift and thorough investigations of their uniformed personnel and, if appropriate, to prosecute, and to inform the United Nations in a timely manner of the status and outcome of investigations, ***calls upon*** the United Nations to cooperate as appropriate and

---

31 Ibid, Operative Part [9].
32 SC Res 1888 (2009) of 30 September 2009, Preamble [3].
33 Ibid, Operative Part [3].
34 Ibid, Operative Part [7].
35 Ibid, Operative Part [11].
36 Ibid, Operative Part [25].
37 Ibid, Operative Part [12].
38 SC Res 2242 (2015) of 13 October 2015, Operative Part [7].

> in a timely manner with national authorities, including courts responsible for investigating such allegations, when requested for that purpose ...[39]

The General Assembly has added its focus to the matter of women, peace, and security in several resolutions[40] which focus on the intensification of efforts to eliminate all forms of violence against women in all their manifestations including in conflict and conflict-related situations.

The C34 started considering gender issues in peace operations in its 1998 report which stated that:

> The Special Committee, noting the increasingly close and direct contact between United Nations peacekeeping personnel and local populations during peacekeeping operations, stresses the importance of participants in peacekeeping operations being given specific training, including gender-sensitive training, in managing those contacts.[41]

In their 1999 report, delegates to the C34 expressed concern that 'the growing contact of peacekeepers with the civilian population, including women and children creates a need for personnel that are more gender sensitive', stressing the need for integrating a gender perspective into peacekeeping operations.[42] The report stated that one of the DPKO's four long-term priorities was to 'promote gender balance at Headquarters and in the field'.[43]

The women, peace, and security resolutions are fundamental resolutions which must be considered in all aspects of the establishment, management, and conduct of such operations. Specific reference to these resolutions can be found in cases such as resolution 2333 concerning the United Nations Mission in Liberia (UNMIL), where the Security Council emphasised: 'the important role of women in the prevention and resolution of conflicts and in peacebuilding, as recognized in resolution 1325 (2000), *underlines* that a gender perspective should be taken into account in implementing all aspects of the mandate of UNMIL ...'[44]

The women, peace, and security resolutions are also relevant to UN peace operations because it is now the practice of the Security Council to give UN peace operations a specific mandate to promote and protect the human rights of women. For example, in resolution 2327 the Security Council mandated the United Nations Mission in South Sudan:

> To protect civilians under threat of physical violence, irrespective of the source of such violence, within its capacity and areas of deployment, with specific protection for women and children, including through the continued use of the Mission's Child Protection and Women Protection Advisers[45] ... [and] [t]o monitor, investigate, verify and report specifically and publicly on violations and abuses committed against children and women, including those involving all forms of sexual and gender-based violence in armed conflict by accelerating the implementation of monitoring, analysis and reporting arrangements on conflict-related sexual violence and by strengthening the monitoring and reporting mechanism for violations and abuses against children.[46]

Furthermore, the women, peace, and security resolutions are also important because they require peace operations to mainstream gender issues into their operational activities both by ensuring the protection of women and children's rights, as well as ensuring arrangements are made whereby they can participate fully in the peace process at all levels. This includes in decision-making roles within the management structure of a peace operation. The objectives of a peace operation are more likely to be achieved if everyone involved in the peace operation including civilian and military peacekeepers observes a gender perspective. Resolution 1820 is also crucial in stressing that sexual violence as a tactic of war can significantly exacerbate situations of armed conflict, demanding that all parties to an armed conflict immediately protect civilians from all forms of sexual violence, and affirming the Security Council's intention to consider targeted sanctions against perpetrators.

39 Ibid, Operative Part [9]. See also SC Res 2272 (2016) of 11 March 2016, which reinforces those concerns of the Security Council.

40 See, for example, GA Res 61/143 of 19 December 2006; GA Res 62/133 of 18 December 2007; GA Res 63/155 of 18 December 2008.

41 'Report of the Special Committee on Peacekeeping Operations: Comprehensive Review of the Whole Question of Peacekeeping Operations in all their Aspects', UN Doc A/53/127, 21 May 1998, [92].

42 'Report of the Special Committee on Peacekeeping Operations: Comprehensive Review of the Whole Question of Peacekeeping Operations in all their Aspects', UN Doc A/54/87, 23 June 1999, [15].

43 Ibid, [9].

44 SC Res 2333 (2016) of 23 December 2016, Operative Part [8]. See also SC Res 1769 (2007) of 31 July 2007, Preamble [4]; SC Res 1828 (2008) of 31 July 2008, Operative Part [15]; and SC Res 2301 of 26 July 2016, Preamble.

45 SC Res 2327 (2016) of 16 December 2016, Operative Part [7](a)(i).

46 Ibid, Operative Part [7](b)(ii). See also SC Res 1509 (2003) of 19 September 2003, Operative Part [3](l), relating to the United Nations Mission in Liberia (UNMIL); and SC Res 1756 (2007) of 15 May 2007, Operative Part [3](c), relating to the United Nations Organization Mission in the Democratic Republic of the Congo.

The emphasis on peacekeepers protecting women from all forms of sexual violence requires that peacekeepers receive appropriate training on what behaviour is considered sexual exploitation and abuse. Resolution 1888 adds to the mechanisms for protecting women by requiring, where appropriate, the 'identification of women's protection advisers (WPAs) among gender advisers and human rights protection units'.[47]

One of the outcomes of resolution 1325 is the Gender Resource Package for Peacekeeping Operations produced in 2004.[48] It is

> designed to explain the concept of 'gender mainstreaming' to peacekeeping personnel at Headquarters and in missions. It is a reference guide that includes background information and highlights key gender issues in each functional area of peacekeeping operations.[49]

It is intended to be used by all peacekeepers, including civilian staff, police, and military members of national contingents.

A 2006 report of the Secretary-General stated that '[a] policy directive on gender equality in peacekeeping was adopted on 3 November 2006 and transmitted to missions and Member States'.[50] The DPKO Policy Directive on Gender Equality in UN Peacekeeping Operations (Directive)[51] is targeted to all categories of peacekeepers with implementation to be tailored to the specific mandate of each peace operation. The Directive obliges all uniformed and civilian staff to ensure equal participation of women, men, girls, and boys in all peacekeeping activities. The Directive includes the following definition of gender mainstreaming:

> Mainstreaming a gender perspective is the process of assessing the implications for women and men of any planned action, including legislation, policies or programmes, in all areas and at all levels. It is a strategy for making women's as well as men's concerns and experiences an integral dimension of the design, implementation, monitoring and evaluation of policies and programmes in all political, economic and societal spheres so that women and men benefit equally and inequality is not perpetuated. The ultimate goal is to achieve gender equality.[52]

In 2010, the effort to mainstream and integrate gender perspectives into peace operations was bolstered by the DPKO and Department of Field Support issuing guidelines to be applied by military peacekeepers.[53] Those guidelines are intended to assist peacekeepers to enhance the role played by women in peace operations, and to develop a greater awareness of gender at the strategic, operational, and tactical levels of peace operations.

Using the Security Council women, peace, and security resolutions as inspiration, some regional organisations have developed policies concerning the protection of women in armed conflict and post-conflict situations. For example, the African Union (AU) Gender Policy reinforces its commitment to 'promoting effective participation of women in peacekeeping and security including efforts aimed at reconciliation in post conflict reconstruction and development'.[54] The AU's operational guidelines on Disarmament, Demobilization and Reintegration (DDR) for women is also a useful resource tool when planning for, and conducting, DDR for women and girls in Africa because it deals with matters such as gender equality and women's full participation in DDR and respect for women's rights.

---

47 SC Res 1888 (2009) of 30 September 2009, Operative Part [12].

48 See Peacekeeping Best Practices Unit, Department of Peacekeeping Operations, 'Gender Resource Package for Peacekeeping Operations' (2004) (Gender Resources Package) at <https://www.un.org/ruleoflaw/blog/document/gender-resource-package-for-peacekeeping-operations/> accessed 31 December 2018. The Gender Advisory Area at <https://peacekeeping.un.org/en/promoting-women-peace-and-security> accessed 31 December 2018, also contains many documents of relevance to gender and peacekeeping.

49 Gender Resource Package for Peacekeeping Operations, Introduction, xi.

50 See 'Report of the Secretary-General: Implementation of the Recommendations of the Special Committee on Peacekeeping Operations', UN Doc A/61/668/Add1, 22 December 2006, [40].

51 Department of Peacekeeping Operations, 'DPKO Policy Directive on Gender Equality in UN Peacekeeping Operations', 3 November 2006. The policy directive is available at <http://www.un.org/womenwatch/feature/wps/Policy%20directive%20gender%20equality%20FINAL%202006.pdf> accessed 26 December 2018.

52 Ibid, Terms and Definitions, 8. The definition is taken from the Economic and Social Council (ECOSOC), 'Report of the Economic and Social Council for 1997', UN Doc A/52/3, 18 September 1997, 28. See also the discussion on gender mainstreaming on the UN's Women Watch website concerning the implementation of SC Res 1325 (2000) <http://www.un.org/womenwatch/feature/wps/index.html> accessed 26 December 2018.

53 Department of Peacekeeping/Department of Field Support, 'Integrating a Gender Perspective into the Work of the United Nations Military in Peacekeeping Operations', March 2010 <https://peacekeeping.un.org/sites/default/files/dpko_dfs_gender_military_perspective.pdf > accessed 28 November 2018.

54 African Union Gender Policy (2009) Commitment 8, 19–21 <http://www.un.org/en/africa/osaa/pdf/au/gender_policy_2009.pdf> accessed 26 December 2018.

In 2012, the Security Council stressed the 'need for the United Nations and the African Union to work to ensure that women and gender perspectives are fully integrated into all peace and security efforts undertaken by the two organizations, including by building the necessary capacity'.[55]

The European Union (EU) has also taken measures to implement resolution 1325 through its decision to promote gender equality and gender mainstream in crisis management.[56] The EU policy reinforces standards such as the requirement to train its peacekeepers on matters concerning gender equality, and the need to undertake operational planning where specific guidance on gender issues is provided for tasks identified in operational documents.

The North Atlantic Treaty Organization (NATO) has also incorporated the Security Council's women, peace and security resolutions by agreeing that:

> NATO and its partners aim to ensure that a gender perspective is mainstreamed into policies, activities and efforts to prevent and resolve conflicts. Due regard will be given to the social roles of both men and women and how these may lead to different risks and security needs. Attention will also be paid to how these roles may translate into different contributions to conflict prevention and resolution.[57]

The women, peace, and security resolutions are closely linked to the resolutions concerning children and armed conflict, the protection of civilians in armed conflict, and sexual exploitation and sexual abuse. All four thematic topics provide a framework for the protection of civilians, particularly women and children. Consequently, all UN peacekeepers should be aware of these resolutions and the requirements they place on peacekeepers in regard to the protection of women and children.

References

Title	Security Council Resolution 1325 (2000) on Women, Peace and Security
Author	Security Council
Meeting	4213th Meeting
Date	31 October 2000
Source	UN Doc S/RES/1325 (2000)
Full Text	<https://undocs.org/S/RES/1325(2000)>[58]

Title	Security Council Resolution 1820 (2008) on Women, Peace and Security
Author	Security Council
Meeting	5916th Meeting
Date	19 June 2008
Source	UN Doc S/RES/1820 (2008)
Full Text	<https://undocs.org/S/RES/1820(2008)>[59]

Title	Security Council Resolution 1888 (2009) on Women, Peace and Security
Author	Security Council
Meeting	6195th Meeting
Date	30 September 2009
Source	UN Doc S/RES/1888 (2009)
Full Text	<https://undocs.org/S/RES/1888(2009)>[60]

Title	Security Council Resolution 2242 (2015) on Women, Peace and Security
Author	Security Council
Meeting	7533th Meeting
Date	13 October 2015
Source	UN Doc S/RES/2242 (2015)
Full Text	<http://undocs.org/S/RES/2242(2015)>[61]

---

55 SC Res 2033 (2012) of 12 January 2012, Operative Part [12].

56 European Council, 'Council Conclusions on Promoting Gender Equality and Gender Mainstreaming in Crisis Management', Doc 14884/1/06, 11 November 2006.

57 North Atlantic Treaty Organization/Euro-Atlantic Partnership Council Policy for the Implementation of UNSCR 1325 on Women, Peace and Security and Related Resolutions, 1 April 2014, [8] <http://www.nato.int/cps/en/natohq/official_texts_109830.htm?selectedLocale=en> accessed 26 December 2018.

58 Accessed 26 December 2018.

59 Accessed 26 December 2018.

60 Accessed 26 December 2018.

61 Accessed 26 December 2018.

Security Council Resolution 1325 (2000)[62]

The Security Council,

Recalling its resolutions 1261 (1999) of 25 August 1999, 1265 (1999) of 17 September 1999, 1296 (2000) of 19 April 2000 and 1314 (2000) of 11 August 2000, as well as relevant statements of its President, and *recalling also* the statement of its President to the press on the occasion of the United Nations Day for Women's Rights and International Peace (International Women's Day) of 8 March 2000 (SC/6816),

Recalling also the commitments of the Beijing Declaration and Platform for Action (A/52/231) as well as those contained in the outcome document of the twenty-third Special Session of the United Nations General Assembly entitled "Women 2000: Gender Equality, Development and Peace for the Twenty-First Century" (A/S-23/10/Rev1), in particular those concerning women and armed conflict,

Bearing in mind the purposes and principles of the Charter of the United Nations and the primary responsibility of the Security Council under the Charter for the maintenance of international peace and security,

Expressing concern that civilians, particularly women and children, account for the vast majority of those adversely affected by armed conflict, including as refugees and internally displaced persons, and increasingly are targeted by combatants and armed elements, and *recognizing* the consequent impact this has on durable peace and reconciliation,

Reaffirming the important role of women in the prevention and resolution of conflicts and in peace-building, and *stressing* the importance of their equal participation and full involvement in all efforts for the maintenance and promotion of peace and security, and the need to increase their role in decision-making with regard to conflict prevention and resolution,

Reaffirming also the need to implement fully international humanitarian and human rights law that protects the rights of women and girls during and after conflicts,

Emphasizing the need for all parties to ensure that mine clearance and mine awareness programmes take into account the special needs of women and girls,

Recognizing the urgent need to mainstream a gender perspective into peacekeeping operations, and in this regard *noting* the Windhoek Declaration and the Namibia Plan of Action on Mainstreaming a Gender Perspective in Multidimensional Peace Support Operations (S/2000/693),

Recognizing also the importance of the recommendation contained in the statement of its President to the press of 8 March 2000 for specialized training for all peacekeeping personnel on the protection, special needs and human rights of women and children in conflict situations,

Recognizing that an understanding of the impact of armed conflict on women and girls, effective institutional arrangements to guarantee their protection and full participation in the peace process can significantly contribute to the maintenance and promotion of international peace and security,

Noting the need to consolidate data on the impact of armed conflict on women and girls,

62 From Security Council Resolution 1325 (2000) on Women, Peace and Security, by Security Council © 2000 United Nations. Reprinted with the permission of the United Nations.

1. *Urges* Member States to ensure increased representation of women at all decision-making levels in national, regional and international institutions and mechanisms for the prevention, management, and resolution of conflict;
2. *Encourages* the Secretary-General to implement his strategic plan of action (A/49/587) calling for an increase in the participation of women at decision-making levels in conflict resolution and peace processes;
3. *Urges* the Secretary-General to appoint more women as special representatives and envoys to pursue good offices on his behalf, and in this regard *calls on* Member States to provide candidates to the Secretary-General, for inclusion in a regularly updated centralized roster;
4. *Further urges* the Secretary-General to seek to expand the role and contribution of women in United Nations field-based operations, and especially among military observers, civilian police, human rights and humanitarian personnel;
5. *Expresses* its willingness to incorporate a gender perspective into peacekeeping operations, and *urges* the Secretary-General to ensure that, where appropriate, field operations include a gender component;
6. *Requests* the Secretary-General to provide to Member States training guidelines and materials on the protection, rights and the particular needs of women, as well as on the importance of involving women in all peacekeeping and peace-building measures, *invites* Member States to incorporate these elements as well as HIV/AIDS awareness training into their national training programmes for military and civilian police personnel in preparation for deployment, and *further requests* the Secretary-General to ensure that civilian personnel of peacekeeping operations receive similar training;
7. *Urges* Member States to increase their voluntary financial, technical and logistical support for gender-sensitive training efforts, including those undertaken by relevant funds and programmes, inter alia, the United Nations Fund for Women and United Nations Children's Fund, and by the Office of the United Nations High Commissioner for Refugees and other relevant bodies;
8. *Calls on* all actors involved, when negotiating and implementing peace agreements, to adopt a gender perspective, including, inter alia:
   (a) The special needs of women and girls during repatriation and resettlement and for rehabilitation, reintegration and post-conflict reconstruction;
   (b) Measures that support local women's peace initiatives and indigenous processes for conflict resolution, and that involve women in all of the implementation mechanisms of the peace agreements;
   (c) Measures that ensure the protection of and respect for human rights of women and girls, particularly as they relate to the constitution, the electoral system, the police and the judiciary;
9. *Calls upon* all parties to armed conflict to respect fully international law applicable to the rights and protection of women and girls, especially as civilians, in particular the obligations applicable to them under the Geneva Conventions of 1949 and the Additional Protocols thereto of 1977, the Refugee Convention of 1951 and the Protocol thereto of 1967, the Convention on the Elimination of All Forms of Discrimination against Women of 1979 and the Optional Protocol thereto of 1999 and the United Nations Convention on the Rights of the Child of 1989 and the two Optional Protocols thereto of 25 May 2000, and to bear in mind the relevant provisions of the Rome Statute of the International Criminal Court;
10. *Calls on* all parties to armed conflict to take special measures to protect women and girls from gender-based violence, particularly rape and other forms of sexual abuse, and all other forms of violence in situations of armed conflict;

11. *Emphasizes* the responsibility of all States to put an end to impunity and to prosecute those responsible for genocide, crimes against humanity, and war crimes including those relating to sexual and other violence against women and girls, and in this regard *stresses* the need to exclude these crimes, where feasible from amnesty provisions;
12. *Calls upon* all parties to armed conflict to respect the civilian and humanitarian character of refugee camps and settlements, and to take into account the particular needs of women and girls, including in their design, and recalls its resolutions 1208 (1998) of 19 November 1998 and 1296 (2000) of 19 April 2000;
13. *Encourages* all those involved in the planning for disarmament, demobilization and reintegration to consider the different needs of female and male ex-combatants and to take into account the needs of their dependants;
14. *Reaffirms* its readiness, whenever measures are adopted under Article 41 of the Charter of the United Nations, to give consideration to their potential impact on the civilian population, bearing in mind the special needs of women and girls, in order to consider appropriate humanitarian exemptions;
15. *Expresses* its willingness to ensure that Security Council missions take into account gender considerations and the rights of women, including through consultation with local and international women's groups;
16. *Invites* the Secretary-General to carry out a study on the impact of armed conflict on women and girls, the role of women in peace-building and the gender dimensions of peace processes and conflict resolution, and *further invites* him to submit a report to the Security Council on the results of this study and to make this available to all Member States of the United Nations;
17. *Requests* the Secretary-General, where appropriate, to include in his reporting to the Security Council progress on gender mainstreaming throughout peacekeeping missions and all other aspects relating to women and girls;
18. *Decides* to remain actively seized of the matter.

Security Council Resolution 1820 (2008)[63]

(Extracts)

The Security Council,

Reaffirming its commitment to the continuing and full implementation of resolution 1325 (2000), 1612 (2005) and 1674 (2006) and recalling the Statements of its president of 31 October 2001 (Security Council/PRST/2001/31), 31 October 2002 (Security Council/PRST/2002/32), 28 October 2004 (Security Council/PRST/2004/40), 27 October 2005 (Security Council/PRST/2005/52), 8 November 2006 (Security Council/PRST/2006/42), 7 March 2007 (Security Council/PRST/2007/5), and 24 October 2007 (Security Council/PRST/2007/40);

63 From Security Council Resolution 1820 (2008) on Women, Peace and Security, by Security Council © 2008 United Nations. Reprinted with the permission of the United Nations.

...

Noting that civilians account for the vast majority of those adversely affected by armed conflict; that women and girls are particularly targeted by the use of sexual violence, including as a tactic of war to humiliate, dominate, instil fear in, disperse and/or forcibly relocate civilian members of a community or ethnic group; and that sexual violence perpetrated in this manner may in some instances persist after the cessation of hostilities;

Recalling its condemnation in the strongest terms of all sexual and other forms of violence committed against civilians in armed conflict, in particular women and children;

Reiterating deep concern that, despite its repeated condemnation of violence against women and children in situations of armed conflict, including sexual violence in situations of armed conflict, and despite its calls addressed to all parties to armed conflict for the cessation of such acts with immediate effect, such acts continue to occur, and in some situations have become systematic and widespread, reaching appalling levels of brutality,

Recalling the inclusion of a range of sexual violence offences in the Rome Statute of the International Criminal Court and the statutes of the ad hoc international criminal tribunals,

Reaffirming the important role of women in the prevention and resolution of conflicts and in peacebuilding, and *stressing* the importance of their equal participation and full involvement in all efforts for the maintenance and promotion of peace and security, and the need to increase their role in decision-making with regard to conflict prevention and resolution,

Deeply concerned also about the persistent obstacles and challenges to women's participation and full involvement in the prevention and resolution of conflicts as a result of violence, intimidation and discrimination, which erode women's capacity and legitimacy to participate in post-conflict public life, and acknowledging the negative impact this has on durable peace, security and reconciliation, including post-conflict peacebuilding,

Recognizing that States bear primary responsibility to respect and ensure the human rights of their citizens, as well as all individuals within their territory as provided for by relevant international law,

Reaffirming that parties to armed conflict bear the primary responsibility to take all feasible steps to ensure the protection of affected civilians,

Welcoming the ongoing coordination of efforts within the United Nations system, marked by the inter-agency initiative "United Nations Action against Sexual Violence in Conflict," to create awareness about sexual violence in armed conflicts and post-conflict situations and, ultimately, to put an end to it,

1. *Stresses* that sexual violence, when used or commissioned as a tactic of war in order to deliberately target civilians or as a part of a widespread or systematic attack against civilian populations, can significantly exacerbate situations of armed conflict and may impede the restoration of international peace and security, *affirms* in this regard that effective steps to prevent and respond to such acts of sexual violence can significantly contribute to the maintenance of international peace and security, and *expresses its readiness*, when considering situations on the agenda of the Council, to, where necessary, adopt appropriate steps to address widespread or systematic sexual violence;
2. *Demands* the immediate and complete cessation by all parties to armed conflict of all acts of sexual violence against civilians with immediate effect;
3. *Demands* that all parties to armed conflict immediately take appropriate measures to protect civilians, including women and girls, from all forms of sexual violence, which could include, inter alia, enforcing appropriate military disciplinary measures and upholding the principle of command responsibility, training troops on the categorical prohibition of all forms of sexual violence against civilians, debunking myths that fuel sexual violence, vetting armed and security forces to take into account past actions of rape and other forms of sexual violence, and evacuation of women and children under imminent threat of sexual violence to safety; and

requests the Secretary-General, where appropriate, to encourage dialogue to address this issue in the context of broader discussions of conflict resolution between appropriate UN officials and the parties to the conflict, taking into account, inter alia, the views expressed by women of affected local communities;

4. *Notes* that rape and other forms of sexual violence can constitute a war crime, a crime against humanity, or a constitutive act with respect to genocide, *stresses the need for* the exclusion of sexual violence crimes from amnesty provisions in the context of conflict resolution processes, and *calls upon* Member States to comply with their obligations for prosecuting persons responsible for such acts, to ensure that all victims of sexual violence, particularly women and girls, have equal protection under the law and equal access to justice, and *stresses* the importance of ending impunity for such acts as part of a comprehensive approach to seeking sustainable peace, justice, truth, and national reconciliation;
5. *Affirms its intention*, when establishing and renewing state-specific sanctions regimes, to take into consideration the appropriateness of targeted and graduated measures against parties to situations of armed conflict who commit rape and other forms of sexual violence against women and girls in situations of armed conflict;
6. *Requests* the Secretary-General, in consultation with the Security Council, the Special Committee on Peacekeeping Operations and its Working Group and relevant States, as appropriate, to develop and implement appropriate training programs for all peacekeeping and humanitarian personnel deployed by the United Nations in the context of missions as mandated by the Council to help them better prevent, recognize and respond to sexual violence and other forms of violence against civilians;
7. *Requests* the Secretary-General to continue and strengthen efforts to implement the policy of zero tolerance of sexual exploitation and abuse in United Nations peacekeeping operations; and *urges* troop and police contributing countries to take appropriate preventative action, including pre-deployment and in-theater awareness training, and other action to ensure full accountability in cases of such conduct involving their personnel;
8. *Encourages* troop and police contributing countries, in consultation with the Secretary-General, to consider steps they could take to heighten awareness and the responsiveness of their personnel participating in UN peacekeeping operations to protect civilians, including women and children, and prevent sexual violence against women and girls in conflict and post-conflict situations, including wherever possible the deployment of a higher percentage of women peacekeepers or police;
9. *Requests* the Secretary-General to develop effective guidelines and strategies to enhance the ability of relevant UN peacekeeping operations, consistent with their mandates, to protect civilians, including women and girls, from all forms of sexual violence and to systematically include in his written reports to the Council on conflict situations his observations concerning the protection of women and girls and recommendations in this regard;
10. *Requests* the Secretary-General and relevant United Nations agencies, inter alia, through consultation with women and women-led organizations as appropriate, to develop effective mechanisms for providing protection from violence, including in particular sexual violence, to women and girls in and around UN managed refugee and internally displaced persons camps, as well as in all disarmament, demobilization, and reintegration processes, and in justice and security sector reform efforts assisted by the United Nations;
11. *Stresses* the important role the Peacebuilding Commission can play by including in its advice and recommendations for post-conflict peacebuilding strategies, where appropriate, ways to address sexual violence committed during and in the aftermath of armed conflict, and in ensuring consultation and effective representation of women's civil society in its country-specific configurations, as part of its wider approach to gender issues;

12. *Urges* the Secretary-General and his Special Envoys to invite women to participate in discussions pertinent to the prevention and resolution of conflict, the maintenance of peace and security, and post-conflict peacebuilding, and encourages all parties to such talks to facilitate the equal and full participation of women at decision-making levels;

...

14. *Urges* appropriate regional and sub-regional bodies in particular to consider developing and implementing policies, activities, and advocacy for the benefit of women and girls affected by sexual violence in armed conflict;

...

Security Council Resolution 1888 (2009)[64]

(Extracts)

The Security Council,

Reaffirming its commitment to the continuing and full implementation of resolutions 1325 (2000), 1612 (2005), 1674 (2006), 1820 (2008) and 1882 (2009) and all relevant statements of its President,

Welcoming the report of the Secretary-General of 16 July 2009 (S/2009/362), but remaining deeply concerned over the lack of progress on the issue of sexual violence in situations of armed conflict in particular against women and children, notably against girls, and noting as documented in the Secretary-General's report that sexual violence occurs in armed conflicts throughout the world,

Reiterating deep concern that, despite its repeated condemnation of violence against women and children including all forms of sexual violence in situations of armed conflict, and despite its calls addressed to all parties to armed conflict for the cessation of such acts with immediate effect, such acts continue to occur, and in some situations have become systematic or widespread,

...

Recalling that international humanitarian law affords general protection to women and children as part of the civilian population during armed conflicts and special protection due to the fact that they can be placed particularly at risk,

Recalling the responsibilities of States to end impunity and to prosecute those responsible for genocide, crimes against humanity, war crimes and other egregious crimes perpetrated against civilians, and in this regard, noting with concern that only limited numbers of perpetrators of sexual violence have been brought to justice, while recognizing that in conflict and in post conflict situations national justice systems may be significantly weakened,

Reaffirming that ending impunity is essential if a society in conflict or recovering from conflict is to come to terms with past abuses committed against civilians affected by armed conflict and to prevent future such abuses, *drawing attention* to the full range of justice and reconciliation mechanisms to be considered, including national, international and "mixed" criminal courts and

64 From Security Council Resolution 1888 (2009) on Women, Peace and Security, by Security Council © 2009 United Nations. Reprinted with the permission of the United Nations.

tribunals and truth and reconciliation commissions, and *noting* that such mechanisms can promote not only individual responsibility for serious crimes, but also peace, truth, reconciliation and the rights of the victims,

Recalling the inclusion of a range of sexual violence offences in the Rome Statute of the International Criminal Court and the statutes of the ad hoc international criminal tribunals,

Stressing the necessity for all States and non-State parties to conflicts to comply fully with their obligations under applicable international law, including the prohibition on all forms of sexual violence,

Recognizing the need for civilian and military leaders, consistent with the principle of command responsibility, to demonstrate commitment and political will to prevent sexual violence and to combat impunity and enforce accountability, and that inaction can send a message that the incidence of sexual violence in conflicts is tolerated,

Emphasizing the importance of addressing sexual violence issues from the outset of peace processes and mediation efforts, in order to protect populations at risk and promote full stability, in particular in the areas of pre-ceasefire humanitarian access and human rights agreements, ceasefires and ceasefire monitoring, Disarmament, Demobilization and Reintegration (DDR), Security Sector Reform (SSR) arrangements, justice and reparations, post-conflict recovery and development,

...

Welcoming the inclusion of women in peacekeeping missions in civil, military and police functions, and *recognizing* that women and children affected by armed conflict may feel more secure working with and reporting abuse to women in peacekeeping missions, and that the presence of women peacekeepers may encourage local women to participate in the national armed and security forces, thereby helping to build a security sector that is accessible and responsive to all, especially women,

Welcoming the efforts of the Department of Peacekeeping Operations to develop gender guidelines for military personnel in peacekeeping operations to facilitate the implementation of resolutions 1325 (2000) and 1820 (2008), and operational guidance to assist civilian, military and police components of peacekeeping missions to effectively implement resolution 1820 (2008),

Having considered the report of the Secretary-General of 16 July 2009 (S/2009/362) and *stressing* that the present resolution does not seek to make any legal determination as to whether situations that are referred to in the Secretary-General's report are or are not armed conflicts within the context of the Geneva Conventions and the Additional Protocols thereto, nor does it prejudge the legal status of the non-State parties involved in these situations,

...

Noting the role currently assigned to the Office of the Special Adviser on Gender Issues to monitor implementation of resolution 1325 and to promote gender mainstreaming within the United Nations system, women's empowerment and gender equality, and *expressing* the importance of effective coordination within the United Nations system in these areas,

Recognizing that States bear the primary responsibility to respect and ensure the human rights of their citizens, as well as all individuals within their territory as provided for by relevant international law,

Reaffirming that parties to armed conflict bear the primary responsibility to take all feasible steps to ensure the protection of affected civilians,

...

1. *Reaffirms* that sexual violence, when used or commissioned as a tactic of war in order to deliberately target civilians or as a part of a widespread or systematic attack against civilian populations, can significantly exacerbate situations of armed conflict and may impede the restoration of international peace and security; *affirms* in this regard that effective steps to prevent and

respond to such acts of sexual violence can significantly contribute to the maintenance of international peace and security; and *expresses its readiness*, when considering situations on the agenda of the Council, to take, where necessary, appropriate steps to address widespread or systematic sexual violence in situations of armed conflict;

2. *Reiterates* its demand for the complete cessation by all parties to armed conflict of all acts of sexual violence with immediate effect;
3. *Demands* that all parties to armed conflict immediately take appropriate measures to protect civilians, including women and children, from all forms of sexual violence, including measures such as, inter alia, enforcing appropriate military disciplinary measures and upholding the principle of command responsibility, training troops on the categorical prohibition of all forms of sexual violence against civilians, debunking myths that fuel sexual violence and vetting candidates for national armies and security forces to ensure the exclusion of those associated with serious violations of international humanitarian and human rights law, including sexual violence;
4. *Requests* that the United Nations Secretary-General appoint a Special Representative to provide coherent and strategic leadership, to work effectively to strengthen existing United Nations coordination mechanisms, and to engage in advocacy efforts, inter alia with governments, including military and judicial representatives, as well as with all parties to armed conflict and civil society, in order to address, at both headquarters and country level, sexual violence in armed conflict, while promoting cooperation and coordination of efforts among all relevant stakeholders, primarily through the inter-agency initiative "United Nations Action Against Sexual Violence in Conflict";
5. *Encourages* the entities comprising UN Action Against Sexual Violence in Conflict, as well as other relevant parts of the United Nations system, to support the work of the aforementioned Special Representative of the Secretary-General and to continue and enhance cooperation and information sharing among all relevant stakeholders in order to reinforce coordination and avoid overlap at the headquarters and country levels and improve system-wide response;
6. *Urges* States to undertake comprehensive legal and judicial reforms, as appropriate, in conformity with international law, without delay and with a view to bringing perpetrators of sexual violence in conflicts to justice and to ensuring that survivors have access to justice, are treated with dignity throughout the justice process and are protected and receive redress for their suffering;
7. *Urges* all parties to a conflict to ensure that all reports of sexual violence committed by civilians or by military personnel are thoroughly investigated and the alleged perpetrators brought to justice, and that civilian superiors and military commanders, in accordance with international humanitarian law, use their authority and powers to prevent sexual violence, including by combating impunity;
8. *Calls upon* the Secretary-General to identify and take the appropriate measures to deploy rapidly a team of experts to situations of particular concern with respect to sexual violence in armed conflict, working through the United Nations presence on the ground and with the consent of the host government, to assist national authorities to strengthen the rule of law, and *recommends* making use of existing human resources within the United Nations system and voluntary contributions, drawing upon requisite expertise, as appropriate, in the rule of law, civilian and military judicial systems, mediation, criminal investigation, security sector reform, witness protection, fair trial standards, and public outreach; to, inter alia:

   (a) Work closely with national legal and judicial officials and other personnel in the relevant governments' civilian and military justice systems to address impunity, including by the strengthening of national capacity, and drawing attention to the full range of justice mechanisms to be considered;

(b) Identify gaps in national response and encourage a holistic national approach to address sexual violence in armed conflict, including by enhancing criminal accountability, responsiveness to victims, and judicial capacity;

(c) Make recommendations to coordinate domestic and international efforts and resources to reinforce the government's ability to address sexual violence in armed conflict;

(d) Work with the United Nations Mission, Country Team, and the aforementioned Special Representative of the Secretary-General as appropriate towards the full implementation of the measures called for by resolution 1820 (2008);

...

11. *Expresses its intention* to ensure that resolutions to establish or renew peacekeeping mandates contain provisions, as appropriate, on the prevention of, and response to, sexual violence, with corresponding reporting requirements to the Council;

12. *Decides* to include specific provisions, as appropriate, for the protection of women and children from rape and other sexual violence in the mandates of United Nations peacekeeping operations, including, on a case-by-case basis, the identification of women's protection advisers (WPAs) among gender advisers and human rights protection units, and requests the Secretary-General to ensure that the need for, and the number and roles of WPAs are systematically assessed during the preparation of each United Nations peacekeeping operation;

...

17. *Urges* that issues of sexual violence be included in all United Nations-sponsored peace negotiation agendas, and *also urges* inclusion of sexual violence issues from the outset of peace processes in such situations, in particular in the areas of pre-ceasefires, humanitarian access and human rights agreements, ceasefires and ceasefire monitoring, DDR and SSR arrangements, vetting of armed and security forces, justice, reparations, and recovery/development;

...

19. *Encourages* Member States to deploy greater numbers of female military and police personnel to United Nations peacekeeping operations, and to provide all military and police personnel with adequate training to carry out their responsibilities;

20. *Requests* the Secretary-General to ensure that technical support is provided to troop and police contributing countries, in order to include guidance for military and police personnel on addressing sexual violence in predeployment and induction training;

21. *Requests* the Secretary-General to continue and strengthen efforts to implement the policy of zero tolerance of sexual exploitation and abuse in United Nations peacekeeping operations; and *urges* troop and police contributing countries to take appropriate preventative action, including predeployment and in-theater awareness training, and other action to ensure full accountability in cases of such conduct involving their personnel;

22. *Requests* that the Secretary-General continue to direct all relevant United Nations entities to take specific measures to ensure systematic mainstreaming of gender issues within their respective institutions, including by ensuring allocation of adequate financial and human resources within all relevant offices and departments and on the ground, as well as to strengthen, within their respective mandates, their cooperation and coordination when addressing the issue of sexual violence in armed conflict;

...

24. *Requests* that the Secretary-General ensure more systematic reporting on incidents of trends, emerging patterns of attack, and early warning indicators of the use of sexual violence in armed conflict in all relevant reports to the Council, and *encourages* the Special Representatives of the Secretary-General, the Emergency Relief Coordinator, the High Commissioner for Human Rights, the Special Rapporteur on Violence against Women, and the Chairperson(s) of UN Action to provide, in coordination with the aforementioned

Special Representative, additional briefings and documentation on sexual violence in armed conflict to the Council;

25. *Requests* the Secretary-General to include, where appropriate, in his regular reports on individual peacekeeping operations, information on steps taken to implement measures to protect civilians, particularly women and children, against sexual violence;

26. *Requests* the Secretary-General, taking into account the proposals contained in his report as well as any other relevant elements, to devise urgently and preferably within three months, specific proposals on ways to ensure monitoring and reporting in a more effective and efficient way within the existing United Nations system on the protection of women and children from rape and other sexual violence in armed conflict and post-conflict situations, utilizing expertise from the United Nations system and the contributions of national Governments, regional organizations, non-governmental organizations in their advisory capacity and various civil society actors, in order to provide timely, objective, accurate and reliable information on gaps in United Nations entities response, for consideration in taking appropriate action;

...

29. *Decides* to remain actively seized of the matter.

Security Council Resolution 2242 (2015)[65]

(Extracts)

The Security Council,

Reaffirming its commitment to the continuing and full implementation, in a mutually reinforcing manner, of resolutions 1325 (2000), 1820 (2008), 1888 (2009), 1889 (2009), 1960 (2010), 2106 (2013), and 2122 (2013) and all relevant statements of its President,

...

Reaffirming the obligations of States Parties to the Convention on the Elimination of All Forms of Discrimination against Women and the Optional Protocol thereto and *urging* States that have not yet done so to consider ratifying or acceding to it, *further noting* General Recommendation 30 of the Committee for the Elimination of All Forms of Discrimination against Women on Women and Conflict Prevention and Post-Conflict Situations,

Welcoming the report of the Secretary-General of 17 September 2015 (S/2015/716) submitting the results of the Global Study on the implementation of resolution 1325, *recognizing* with appreciation all the work undertaken for the Global Study and *encouraging* close examination of its recommendations,

...

Taking note of the Report of the Secretary-General on the Future of United Nations peace operations: implementation of the recommendations of the High-level Independent Panel on Peace Operations (S/2015/682), and the Report of the Advisory Group of Experts for the

65 From Security Council Resolution 2242 (2015) on Women, Peace and Security, by Security Council © 2015 United Nations. Reprinted with the permission of the United Nations.

Review of the United Nations Peacebuilding Architecture (S/2015/490), and *welcoming* the recommendations contained therein relating to Women, Peace and Security, and *further urging* all actors to consider their implementation,

Reaffirming the obligations of States and all parties to armed conflict to comply with international humanitarian law and international human rights law, as applicable, and the need to end all violations of international humanitarian law and all violations and abuses of human rights,

Reaffirming that sexual violence, when used or commissioned as a method or tactic of war or as a part of a widespread or systematic attack against civilian populations, can significantly exacerbate and prolong situations of armed conflict and may impede the restoration of international peace and security,

...

3. *Encourages* Member States to increase their funding on women, peace and security including through more aid in conflict and post-conflict situations for programmes that further gender equality and women's empowerment, as well as through support to civil society, and to support countries in armed conflict and post-conflict situations, including through capacity-building, in their implementation of women, peace and security resolutions, *calls for* increased international development cooperation related to women's empowerment and gender equality and *invites* aid providers to track the gender focus of aid contributions;
4. *Urges* the Secretary-General and relevant United Nations entities, including but not limited to the Department for Peacekeeping Operations (DPKO), the Department for Political Affairs (DPA), and the Peacebuilding Support Office (PBSO) to redouble their efforts to integrate women's needs and gender perspectives into their work, including in all policy and planning processes and assessment missions, and in relation to requests made in resolution 2122 (2013), and to address deficits in accountability including through the addition by the Secretary-General of gender targets as an indicator of individual performance in all compacts with senior managers at United Nations Headquarters and in the field, including Special Envoys, Special Representatives of the Secretary-General, Resident and Humanitarian Coordinators, to be used for monitoring and to inform decision-making by the Secretary-General, including for recruiting for future posts, and *further encourages* closer working relationships within the United Nations among all those responsible for implementing the women, peace and security agenda, including UN-Women, taking into account their role on women, peace and security coordination and accountability, and the Secretary-General's Special Representative on Sexual Violence in Conflict;
5. *Recognizes* the ongoing need for greater integration of resolution 1325 (2000) in its own work in alignment with resolution 2122 (2013), including the need to address challenges linked to the provision of specific information and recommendations on the gender dimensions of situations on the Council's agenda, to inform and help strengthen the Council's decisions, and therefore in addition to elements set out in resolution 2122 (2013), and in accordance with established practice and procedure:
   (a) *Expresses its intention* to convene meetings of relevant Security Council experts as part of an Informal Experts Group on Women, Peace and Security to facilitate a more systematic approach to Women, Peace and Security within its own work and enable greater oversight and coordination of implementation efforts;
   (b) *Decides* to integrate women, peace and security concerns across all country-specific situations on the Security Council's agenda, taking into account the specific context of each country, *expresses its intention* to dedicate periodic Security Council consultations on country situations, as necessary, to the topic of Women, Peace and Security implementation, progress and challenges, and *reiterates its intention* to ensure Security Council

missions take into account gender considerations and the rights of women, including through consultation with local and international women's groups;

(c) *Expresses its intention* to invite civil society, including women's organizations, to brief the Council in country-specific considerations and relevant thematic areas, as well as the Under-Secretary-General/Executive Director of UN-Women and the Under-Secretary-General/Special Representative of the Secretary-General on Sexual Violence in Conflict to brief more regularly on country situations and relevant thematic areas of work on its agenda including on matters of urgency for women and girls in conflict and crisis;

...

7. *Urges* DPKO and DPA to ensure the necessary gender analysis and technical gender expertise is included throughout all stages of mission planning, mandate development, implementation, review and mission drawdown, ensuring the needs and participation of women are integrated in all sequenced stages of mission mandates, *welcomes* the commitment of the Secretary-General that Senior Gender Advisors will be located in the offices of his Special Representatives, *calls for* senior gender advisors and other gender officer posts to be budgeted for and speedily recruited where appointed in special political missions and multidimensional peacekeeping operations, and *encourages* greater cooperation between DPKO, DPA and UN-Women to enable more gender responsive United Nations peacekeeping operations and special political missions, including through providing field-based gender advisors and other missions' sectors with full access to the policy, substantive and technical support of these entities on the implementation of resolution 1325 (2000) and successive resolutions, making full use of respective comparative advantages;
8. *Welcomes* the Secretary-General's commitment to prioritize the appointment of more women in senior United Nations leadership positions, bearing in mind a cross-geographical representation and in accordance with existing relevant rules and regulations governing administrative and budgetary issues, and *encourages* him to review the obstacles preventing women's recruitment and professional advancement, *further welcomes* efforts to incentivize greater numbers of women in militaries and police deployed to United Nations peacekeeping operations, and *calls upon* the Secretary-General to initiate, in collaboration with Member States, a revised strategy, within existing resources, to double the numbers of women in military and police contingents of UN peacekeeping operations over the next five years;
9. *Expresses* deep concern over continuing allegations of sexual exploitation and abuse by United Nations peacekeepers and non-United Nations forces, including military, civilian and police personnel, urges police- and troop-contributing countries to provide robust pre-deployment training on sexual exploitation and abuse and vetting of their peacekeeping personnel, to conduct swift and thorough investigations of their uniformed personnel and, if appropriate, to prosecute, and to inform the United Nations in a timely manner of the status and outcome of investigations, *calls upon* the United Nations to cooperate as appropriate and in a timely manner with national authorities, including courts responsible for investigating such allegations, when requested for that purpose, and *requests* United Nations troop- and police-contributing country meetings to address sexual exploitation and abuse whenever relevant and the United Nations Military Staff Committee to discuss these issues as part of its regular programme;
10. *Welcomes* the Secretary-General's continued efforts at implementing his policy of zero tolerance of misconduct, in particular the wide-ranging proposals on prevention, enforcement and remedial action which promote greater accountability, including his commitment to bring to public light misconduct by United Nations personnel, as well as his proposal to keep the Security Council informed of developments regarding implementation of his zero tolerance policy on sexual exploitation and abuse, and his decision that all countries repeatedly listed in the annexes of his reports on Children and Armed Conflict and Sexual

Violence in Conflict are prohibited from participating in United Nations peacekeeping operations, and *urges* those troop- and police-contributing countries that are currently listed to cease such violations and implement actions plans expeditiously, thereby avoiding suspension from peace operations, *further requests* the Secretary-General to include a section on conduct and discipline including, whenever relevant, adherence to his zero tolerance policy on sexual exploitation and abuse, in all his reports on country-specific situations to the Security Council;

...

18

Children and Armed Conflict

Prefatory Note

The UN has emphasised the importance of peacekeepers protecting children during peace operations since the late 1990s. For example, UN peacekeepers have been encouraged to work with local authorities to tackle the trafficking of children. More fundamentally, it is now accepted that all UN peace operations must mainstream the protection of children.

The Security Council has adopted several resolutions concerning the protection of children affected by armed conflict. These resolutions, combined with Security Council resolutions concerning women, peace, and security,[1] the protection of civilians in armed conflict,[2] and sexual exploitation and sexual abuse,[3] are thematic resolutions which are mutually reinforcing.

Between 1999 and 2005 the Security Council passed five resolutions on the theme of children and armed conflict[4] before adopting the landmark resolution 1612.[5] The Security Council stated that these resolutions contributed 'to a comprehensive framework for addressing the protection of children affected by armed conflict'.[6] Since resolution 1612, the Security Council has passed a number of other resolutions dealing with children: resolution 1882 adopted on 4 August 2009; resolution 1998 adopted on 12 July 2011; resolution 2068 adopted on 19 September 2012; and resolution 2143 adopted on 7 March 2014. These resolutions should be viewed as a part of the framework that reinforces the principles and rules found in the Convention on the Rights of the Child,[7] the Optional Protocol to the Convention on the Rights of the Child on the Involvement of Children in Armed Conflict,[8] and the Geneva Conventions[9] and their Additional Protocols.[10]

The three Security Council resolutions reproduced in this chapter are resolution 1612 of 26 July 2005, resolution 1882 adopted on 4 August 2009, and resolution 2143 adopted on 7 March 2014. The other resolutions have not been reproduced because they do not focus on peace operations.

Resolution 1612 requested the Secretary-General to implement a monitoring and reporting mechanism on violations of children's rights in armed conflict. It further stressed that it is the responsibility of UN peacekeeping missions and UN country teams, consistent with their mandates, 'to ensure effective follow-up to Security Council resolutions ... and to monitor and report to the Secretary-General'.[11] The importance of establishing child protection was also dealt with in resolution 1882 where the Security Council requested, among other things, UN peacekeeping operations in close cooperation with the

> governments of the concerned countries, to establish appropriate strategies and coordination mechanisms for information exchange and cooperation on child protection concerns, in particular cross-border issues, bearing in mind relevant conclusions by the Security Council Working Group on Children and Armed Conflict and paragraph 2 (d) of its resolution 1612 (2005).[12]

In 2014, in resolution 2143, the Security Council recommended that peacekeepers be trained in matters relating to the protection of children so as to make peacekeepers more effective in

---

1 See ch 17 above.
2 See ch 19 below.
3 See ch 20 below.
4 See SC Res 1261 (1999) of 25 August 1999; SC Res 1314 (2000) of 11 August 2000; SC Res 1379 (2001) of 20 November 2001; SC Res 1460 (2003) of 30 January 2003; and SC Res 1539 (2004) of 22 April 2004.
5 SC Res 1612 (2005) of 26 July 2005, Preamble [1].
6 Ibid.
7 See ch 9 above.
8 See ch 9 above.
9 See ch 16 above.
10 See ch 16 above.
11 SC Res 1612 (2000) of 26 July 2005, Operative Part [10].
12 SC Res 1882 (2009) of 4 August 2009, Operative Part [12].

recognising, reporting and responding to violations and abuses committed against children.[13] That resolution reinforced the Security Council's decision in resolutions 1612 and 1882 to 'continue the inclusion of specific provisions for the protection of children in the mandates of all relevant United Nations peacekeeping operations ... [and] encourages deployment of child protection advisers to such missions'.[14] That resolution also dealt with the 'use of schools in contravention of applicable international law'.[15]

The General Assembly's Special Committee on Peacekeeping Operations (C34) has also considered the issue of children in the context of peace operations. In its 2003 report, the C34 included a specific section entitled 'Children and Peacekeeping' which welcomed resolution 1460 and the appointment of child protection advisors in the UN Mission in the Democratic Republic of the Congo and the UN Mission in Sierra Leone.[16]

The Working Group on Children and Armed Conflict (Working Group) was established pursuant to Security Council resolution 1612 to '[m]ake recommendations to the Council on possible measures to promote the protection of children affected by armed conflict, including through recommendations on appropriate mandates for peacekeeping missions and recommendations with respect to the parties to the conflict'.[17] The work of that Working Group is important in highlighting matters such as how peacekeepers treat children,[18] and the requirement for peacekeepers to 'comply with applicable international law and to respect the civilian character of schools and hospitals, including their personnel'.[19]

The Security Council has, since 1999, given the UN, including peacekeepers, a specific mandate to protect children. For example, in resolution 1272 establishing the UN Transitional Administration in East Timor, the Security Council called upon all parties:

> to cooperate with humanitarian and human rights organizations so as to ensure their safety, the protection of civilians, in particular children ... [20]

In resolution 1769 which established the African Union/United Nations Mission in Darfur, the Security Council called:

> on all concerned parties to ensure that the protection of children is addressed in the implementation of the Darfur Peace Agreement, and ***requests*** the Secretary-General to ensure continued monitoring and reporting of the situation of children and continued dialogue with parties to the conflict towards the preparations of time-bound action plans to end recruitment and use of child soldiers and other violations against children.[21]

The UN Stabilization Mission in Haiti was encouraged to work with appropriate international actors and the government of Haiti to effectively tackle the 'trafficking of persons especially children',[22] and to protect vulnerable groups including children through 'joint community policing in the camps'.[23]

Resolution 1612 has an important impact on the mandates of UN missions, by placing upon them a requirement to mainstream the protection of children into their operations, and to ensure there is an adequate monitoring and reporting mechanism in place on the situation of children, especially in regard to ending the recruitment and use of children associated with armed forces or armed groups,[24] and other grave violations of children's rights. Resolution 1882 now requires

---

13 SC Res 2143 (2014) of 7 March 2014, Operative Part [20].

14 Ibid, Operative Part [24].

15 Ibid, Operative Part [18].

16 'Report of the Special Committee on Peacekeeping Operations: Comprehensive Review of the Whole Question of Peacekeeping Operations in all their Aspects', UN Doc A/57/767, 28 March 2003, [121]–[122].

17 SC Res 1612 (2000) of 26 July 2005, Operative Part [8](a).

18 Working Group on Children and Armed Conflict, 'Conclusions on Children and Armed Conflict in the Central African Republic', UN Doc S/AC51/2016/3, 19 December 2016, [4].

19 Ibid, [8](w).

20 SC Res 1272 (1999) of 25 October 1999, Operative Part [10].

21 SC Res 1769 (2007) of 31 July 2007, Operative Part [17].

22 SC Res 2313 (2016) of 13 October 2016, Operative Part [21].

23 Ibid, Operative Part [30].

24 For more information on children associated with armed forces or armed groups see UNICEF, 'The Paris Principles: Principles and Guidelines on Children Associated with Armed Forces or Armed Groups', February 2007 <https://www.unicef.org/emerg/files/ParisPrinciples310107English.pdf> accessed 1 April 2019.

monitoring and reporting of parties to an armed conflict that engage in 'killing and maiming of children and/or rape and other sexual violence against children'.[25]

Resolution 1612 has been a foundation for some regional organisations to develop policies for the protection of children in armed conflict and post-conflict situations. The African Union (AU) signed a declaration in 2013 on protecting children in all AU activities,[26] and has developed guidelines for dealing with children who are going through the Disarmament, Demobilization and Reintegration (DDR) process.[27] Those guidelines seek to operationalise the planning for, and conduct of, DDR for children which occur within the framework of the four principles: (1) the best interest of the child; (2) voluntary participation and informed consent; (3) confidentiality and transparency; and (4) national ownership. Further evidence of the engagement of UN and regional peacekeeping forces in protecting children is the government of Somalia's Action Plan with the UN and the AU Mission in Somalia to take all necessary measures to protect children.[28] That plan concerns training Somalian security forces on child protection, and releasing children from the ranks of the Somali National Army.

The European Union (EU) also has a policy on children in armed conflict which deals with the legal and policy framework,[29] and a checklist for the integration of the protection of children affected by armed conflict into European Security and Defence Policy (ESDP) operations.[30] That checklist covers matters such as the inclusion of child protection in mission planning, and operational aspects of protecting children in ESDP operations. In March 2015, the North Atlantic Treaty Organization (NATO) issued its policy on the protection of civilians. That policy concerns how child protection practices are to be adopted in NATO-led operations and missions.[31]

References

Title	Security Council Resolution 1612 (2005) on Children and Armed Conflict
Author	Security Council
Meeting	5235th Meeting
Date	26 July 2005
Source	UN Doc S/RES/1612 (2005)
Full Text	<http://unscr.com/en/resolutions/doc/1612>[32]

Title	Security Council Resolution 1882 (2009) on Children and Armed Conflict
Author	Security Council
Meeting	6176th Meeting
Date	4 August 2009
Source	UN Doc. S/RES/1882 (2009)
Full Text	<http://unscr.com/en/resolutions/doc/1882>[33]

Title	Security Council Resolution 2143 (2014) on Children and Armed Conflict
Author	Security Council
Meeting	7129th Meeting
Date	7 March 2014
Source	UN Doc. S/RES/2143 (2014)
Full Text	<http://unscr.com/en/resolutions/doc/2143>[34]

---

25 SC Res 1882 (2009) of 4 August 2009, Operative Part [3].

26 African Union Press Release of 19 September 2013 <http://www.peaceau.org/uploads/the-un-working-together-with-the-au-to-protect-children-in-armed-conflict.pdf> accessed 27 December 2018.

27 African Union Disarmament, Demobilisation and Reintegration Capacity Program, 'DDR and Children Operational Guideline' (2014) <http://www.peaceau.org/en/article/african-union-operational-guideline-on-ddr-and-children > accessed 27 December 2018.

28 See 'We are Children not Soldiers', Fact Sheet, May 2016 <https://childrenandarmedconflict.un.org/wp-content/uploads/2016/04/Somalia-Fact-Sheet-May-2016.pdf> accessed 1 November 2017.

29 European Council, 'Update of the EU Guidelines on Children and Armed Conflict', Doc 10019/08, 5 June 2008. See also 'Revised Implementation Strategy of the EU Guidelines on Children in Armed Conflict', Doc 17488/10, 6 December 2010.

30 European Council, 'General Review of the Implementation of the Checklist for the Integration of the Protection of Children affected by Armed Conflict into ESDP Operations', Doc 9693/08, 21 May 2008.

31 North Atlantic Treaty Organization, 'NATO Policy for the Protection of Civilians', endorsed by the Heads of State and Government participating in the meeting of the North Atlantic Council in Warsaw 8–9 July 2016 <https://www.nato.int/cps/en/natohq/official_texts_133945.htm?selectedLocale=en> accessed 27 December 2018.

32 Accessed 27 December 2018.

33 Accessed 27 December 2018.

34 Accessed 27 December 2018.

Security Council Resolution 1612 (2005)[35]

(Extracts)

The Security Council,

Reaffirming its resolutions 1261 (1999) of 25 August 1999, 1314 (2000) of 11 August 2000, 1379 (2001) of 20 November 2001, 1460 (2003) of 30 January 2003, and 1539 (2004) of 22 April 2004, which contribute to a comprehensive framework for addressing the protection of children affected by armed conflict,

...

Convinced that the protection of children in armed conflict should be regarded as an important aspect of any comprehensive strategy to resolve conflict,

...

Having considered the report of the Secretary-General of 9 February 2005 (S/2005/72) and stressing that the present resolution does not seek to make any legal determination as to whether situations which are referred to in the Secretary-General's report are or are not armed conflicts within the context of the Geneva Conventions and the Additional Protocols thereto, nor does it prejudge the legal status of the non-State parties involved in these situations,

Gravely concerned by the documented links between the use of child soldiers in violation of applicable international law and the illicit trafficking of small arms and light weapons and stressing the need for all States to take measures to prevent and to put an end to such trafficking,

1. *Strongly condemns* the recruitment and use of child soldiers by parties to armed conflict in violation of international obligations applicable to them and all other violations and abuses committed against children in situations of armed conflict;
2. *Takes note* of the action plan presented by the Secretary-General relating to the establishment of a monitoring and reporting mechanism on children and armed conflict as called for in paragraph 2 of its resolution 1539 (2004) and, in this regard:
   - (a) Underlines that the mechanism is to collect and provide timely, objective, accurate and reliable information on the recruitment and use of child soldiers in violation of applicable international law and on other violations and abuses committed against children affected by armed conflict, and the mechanism will report to the working group to be created in accordance with paragraph 8 of this resolution;
   - (b) Underlines further that this mechanism must operate with the participation of and in cooperation with national Governments and relevant United Nations and civil society actors, including at the country level;
   - (c) Stresses that all actions undertaken by United Nations entities within the framework of the monitoring and reporting mechanism must be designed to support and supplement, as appropriate, the protection and rehabilitation roles of national Governments;
   - (d) Also stresses that any dialogue established under the framework of the monitoring and reporting mechanism by United Nations entities with non-State armed groups in order to ensure protection for and access to children must be conducted in the context of peace

35 From Security Council Resolution 1612 (2005) on Children and Armed Conflict, by Security Council, © 2005 United Nations. Reprinted with the permission of the United Nations.

processes where they exist and the cooperation framework between the United Nations and the concerned Government;

3. *Requests* the Secretary-General to implement without delay, the abovementioned monitoring and reporting mechanism, beginning with its application, within existing resources, in close consultation with countries concerned, to parties in situations of armed conflict listed in the annexes to the Secretary-General's report (S/2005/72) that are on the agenda of the Security Council, and then, in close consultation with countries concerned, to apply it to parties in other situations of armed conflict listed in the annexes to the Secretary-General's report (S/2005/72), bearing in mind the discussion of the Security Council and the views expressed by Member States, in particular during the annual debate on Children and Armed Conflict, and also taking into account the findings and recommendations of an independent review on the implementation of the mechanism to be reported to the Security Council by 31 July 2006. The independent review will include:
   (a) An assessment of the overall effectiveness of the mechanism, as well as the timeliness, accuracy, objectivity and reliability of the information compiled through the mechanism;
   (b) Information on how effectively the mechanism is linked to the work of the Security Council and other organs of the United Nations;
   (c) Information on the relevance and clarity of the division of responsibilities;
   (d) Information on the budgetary and other resource implications for United Nations actors and voluntary funded organizations contributing to the mechanism;
   (e) Recommendations for the full implementation of the mechanism;
4. *Stresses* that the implementation of the monitoring and reporting mechanism by the Secretary-General will be undertaken only in the context of and for the specific purpose of ensuring the protection of children affected by armed conflict and shall not thereby prejudge or imply a decision by the Security Council as to whether or not to include a situation on its agenda;
5. *Welcomes* the initiatives taken by UNICEF and other United Nations entities to gather information on the recruitment and use of child soldiers in violation of applicable international law and on other violations and abuses committed against children in situations of armed conflict and invites the Secretary-General to take due account of these initiatives during the initial phase of implementation of the mechanism referred to in paragraph 3;

...

8. *Decides* to establish a working group of the Security Council consisting of all members of the Council to review the reports of the mechanism referred to in paragraph 3 of this resolution, to review progress in the development and implementation of the action plans mentioned in paragraph 7 of this resolution and to consider other relevant information presented to it; *decides further* that the working group shall:
   (a) Make recommendations to the Council on possible measures to promote the protection of children affected by armed conflict, including through recommendations on appropriate mandates for peacekeeping missions and recommendations with respect to the parties to the conflict;
   (b) Address requests, as appropriate, to other bodies within the United Nations system for action to support implementation of this resolution in accordance with their respective mandates;
9. *Recalls* paragraph 5 (c) of its resolution 1539 (2004), and reaffirms its intention to consider imposing, through country-specific resolutions, targeted and graduated measures, such as, inter alia, a ban on the export and supply of small arms and light weapons and of other military equipment and on military assistance, against parties to situations of armed conflict which are on the Security Council's agenda and are in violation of applicable international law relating to the rights and protection of children in armed conflict;

10. *Stresses* the responsibility of United Nations peacekeeping missions and United Nations country teams, consistent with their respective mandates, to ensure effective follow-up to Security Council resolutions, ensure a coordinated response to CAAC concerns and to monitor and report to the Secretary-General;
11. *Welcomes* the efforts undertaken by United Nations peacekeeping operations to implement the Secretary-General's zero-tolerance policy on sexual exploitation and abuse and to ensure full compliance of their personnel with the United Nations code of conduct, requests the Secretary-General to continue to take all necessary action in this regard and to keep the Security Council informed, and urges troop-contributing countries to take appropriate preventive action including predeployment awareness training, and to take disciplinary action and other action to ensure full accountability in cases of misconduct involving their personnel;
12. *Decides* to continue the inclusion of specific provisions for the protection of children in the mandates of United Nations peacekeeping operations, including the deployment, on a case-by-case basis, of child-protection advisers (CPAs), and requests the Secretary-General to ensure that the need for and the number and roles of CPAs are systematically assessed during the preparation of each United Nations peacekeeping operation; welcomes the comprehensive assessment undertaken on the role and activities of CPAs with a view to drawing lessons learned and best practices;
13. *Welcomes* recent initiatives by regional and subregional organizations and arrangements for the protection of children affected by armed conflict, and encourages continued mainstreaming of child protection into their advocacy, policies and programmes; development of peer review and monitoring and reporting mechanisms; establishment, within their secretariats, of child-protection mechanisms; inclusion of child-protection staff and training in their peace and field operations; sub- and interregional initiatives to end activities harmful to children in times of conflict, in particular cross-border recruitment and abduction of children, illicit movement of small arms, and illicit trade in natural resources through the development and implementation of guidelines on children and armed conflict;
14. *Calls upon* all parties concerned to ensure that the protection, rights and well-being of children affected by armed conflict are specifically integrated into all peace processes, peace agreements and post-conflict recovery and reconstruction planning and programmes;
15. *Calls upon* all parties concerned to abide by the international obligations applicable to them relating to the protection of children affected by armed conflict as well as the concrete commitments they have made to the Special Representative of the Secretary-General for Children and Armed Conflict, to UNICEF and other United Nations agencies and to cooperate fully with the United Nations peacekeeping missions and United Nations country teams, where appropriate, in the context of the cooperation framework between the United Nations and the concerned Government, in the follow-up and implementation of these commitments;
16. *Urges* Member States, United Nations entities, regional and subregional organizations and other parties concerned, to take appropriate measures to control illicit subregional and cross-border activities harmful to children, including illicit exploitation of natural resources, illicit trade in small arms, abduction of children and their use and recruitment as soldiers as well as other violations and abuses committed against children in situations of armed conflict in violation of applicable international law;

. . .

21. *Decides* to remain actively seized of this matter.

Security Council Resolution 1882 (2009)[36]

(Extracts)

The Security Council,

Reaffirming its resolutions 1261 (1999) of 25 August 1999, 1314 (2000) of 11 August 2000, 1379 (2001) of 20 November 2001, 1460 (2003) of 30 January 2003, 1539 (2004) of 22 April 2004, and 1612 (2005) of 26 July 2005, and the Statements of its President on 24 July 2006 (S/PRST/2006/33), 28 November 2006 (S/PRST/2006/48), 12 February 2008 (S/PRST/2008/6), 17 July 2008 (S/PRST/2008/28) and 29 April 2009 (S/PRST/2009/9), which contribute to a comprehensive framework for addressing the protection of children affected by armed conflict,

Acknowledging that the implementation of its resolution 1612 (2005) has generated progress, resulting in the release and reintegration of children into their families and communities and in a more systematic dialogue between the United Nations country-level task forces and parties to the armed conflict on the implementation of time-bound action plans, *while remaining deeply concerned* over the lack of progress on the ground in some situations of concern, where parties to conflict continue to violate with impunity the relevant provisions of applicable international law relating to the rights and protection of children in armed conflict,

...

Calling on all parties to armed conflicts to comply strictly with the obligations applicable to them under international law for the protection of children in armed conflict, including those contained in the Convention on the Rights of the Child and its Optional Protocol on the involvement of Children in Armed Conflict, as well as the Geneva Conventions of 12th August 1949 and their Additional Protocols of 1977,

...

Having considered the report of the Secretary-General of 26 March 2009 (S/2009/158) and *stressing* that the present resolution does not seek to make any legal determination as to whether situations which are referred to in the Secretary-General's report are or are not armed conflicts within the context of the Geneva Conventions and the Additional Protocols thereto, nor does it prejudge the legal status of the non-State parties involved in these situations,

Deeply concerned that children continue to account for a considerable number of casualties resulting from killing and maiming in armed conflicts including as a result of deliberate targeting, indiscriminate and excessive use of force, indiscriminate use of landmines, cluster munitions and other weapons and use of children as human shields and *equally deeply concerned* about the high incidence and appalling levels of brutality of rape and other forms of sexual violence committed against children, in the context of and associated with armed conflict including the use or commissioning of rape and other forms of sexual violence in some situations as a tactic of war,

1. *Strongly condemns* all violations of applicable international law involving the recruitment and use of children by parties to armed conflict as well as their re-recruitment, killing and maiming, rape and other sexual violence, abductions, attacks against schools or hospitals and denial of humanitarian access by parties to armed conflict and all other violations of international law committed against children in situations of armed conflict;

---

36 From Security Council Resolution 1882 (2009) on Children and Armed Conflict, by Security Council, © 2009 United Nations. Reprinted with the permission of the United Nations.

2. *Reaffirms* that the monitoring and reporting mechanism will continue to be implemented in situations listed in the annexes to the reports of the Secretary-General on children and armed conflict in line with the principles set out in paragraph 2 of its resolution 1612 (2005) and that its establishment and implementation shall not prejudge or imply a decision by the Security Council as to whether or not to include a situation on its agenda;
3. *Recalls* paragraph 16 of its resolution 1379 (2001) and *requests* the Secretary-General also to include in the annexes to his reports on children and armed conflict those parties to armed conflict that engage, in contravention of applicable international law, in patterns of killing and maiming of children and/or rape and other sexual violence against children, in situations of armed conflict, bearing in mind all other violations and abuses against children, and notes that the present paragraph will apply to situations in accordance with the conditions set out in paragraph 16 of its resolution 1379 (2001);
4. *Invites* the Secretary-General through his Special Representative for Children and Armed Conflict to exchange appropriate information and maintain interaction from the earliest opportunity with the governments concerned regarding violations and abuses committed against children by parties which may be included in the annexes to his periodic report;
5. *While noting* that some parties to armed conflict have responded to its call upon them to prepare and implement concrete time-bound action plans to halt recruitment and use of children in violation of applicable international law;

   (a) *Reiterates* its call on parties to armed conflict listed in the annexes of the Secretary-General's report on children and armed conflict that have not already done so to prepare and implement, without further delay, action plans to halt recruitment and use of children in violation of applicable international law;

   (b) *Calls upon* those parties listed in the annexes of the Secretary-General's report on children and armed conflict that commit, in contravention of applicable international law, killing and maiming of children and/or rape and other sexual violence against children, in situations of armed conflict, to prepare concrete time-bound action plans to halt those violations and abuses;

   (c) *Further calls* upon all parties listed in the annexes to the Secretary-General's report on children and armed conflict to address all other violations and abuses committed against children and undertake specific commitments and measures in this regard;

   (d) *Urges* those parties listed in the annexes of the Secretary-General's report on children and armed conflict to implement the provisions contained in this paragraph in close cooperation with the Special Representative of the Secretary-General for Children and Armed Conflict and the United Nations country-level task forces on monitoring and reporting;

...

7. *Reiterates* its determination to ensure respect for its resolutions on children and armed conflict, and in this regard:

   (a) *Welcomes* the sustained activity and recommendations of its Working Group on Children and Armed Conflict as called for in paragraph 8 of its resolution 1612 (2005), and invites it to continue reporting regularly to the Security Council;

   (b) *Requests* enhanced communication between the Working Group and relevant Security Council Sanctions Committees, including through the exchange of pertinent information on violations and abuses committed against children in armed conflict;

   (c) *Reaffirms* its intention to take action against persistent perpetrators in line with paragraph 9 of its resolution 1612 (2005);

...

11. *Welcomes* the efforts of the Department of Peacekeeping Operations in mainstreaming child protection into peacekeeping missions, in line with that Department's recently adopted Child Protection Policy directive, and encourages the deployment of Child Protection Advisers to peacekeeping operations, as well as into relevant peacebuilding and political missions, and decides to continue the inclusion of specific provisions for the protection of children in such mandates;
12. *Requests* Member States, United Nations peacekeeping, peacebuilding and political missions and United Nations country teams, within their respective mandates and in close cooperation with governments of the concerned countries, to establish appropriate strategies and coordination mechanisms for information exchange and cooperation on child protection concerns, in particular cross-border issues, bearing in mind relevant conclusions by the Security Council Working Group on Children and Armed Conflict and paragraph 2 (d) of its resolution 1612 (2005);
13. *Stresses* that effective disarmament, demobilization and reintegration programmes for children, building on best practices identified by UNICEF and other relevant child protection actors, are crucial for the well-being of all children who, in contravention of applicable international law, have been recruited or used by armed forces and groups, and are a critical factor for durable peace and security, and urges national Governments and donors to ensure that these community-based programmes receive timely, sustained and adequate resources and funding;

...

Security Council Resolution 2143 (2014)[37]

(Extracts)

The Security Council,

Reaffirming its resolutions 1261 (1999) of 25 August 1999, 1314 (2000) of 11 August 2000, 1379 (2001) of 20 November 2001, 1460 (2003) of 30 January 2003, 1539 (2004) of 22 April 2004, 1612 (2005) of 26 July 2005, 1882 (2009) of 4 August 2009, 1998 (2011) of 12 July 2011 and 2068 (2012) of 19 September 2012, and the Statements of its President on 24 July 2006 (S/PRST/2006/33), 28 November 2006 (S/PRST/2006/48), 12 February 2008 (S/PRST/2008/6), 17 July 2008 (S/PRST/2008/28), 29 April 2009 (S/PRST/2009/9), 16 June 2010 (S/PRST/2010/10) and 17 June 2013 (S/PRST/2013/8), which contribute to a comprehensive framework for addressing the protection of children affected by armed conflict,

Acknowledging that its resolutions 1612 (2005), 1882 (2009), 1998 (2011) and 2068 (2012) and the Statements of its President on children and armed conflict have generated progress in preventing and responding to violations and abuses committed against children, in particular in the demobilization, rehabilitation and reintegration of thousands of children, the signing of

37 From Security Council Resolution 2143 (2014) on Children and Armed Conflict, by Security Council, by Security Council, © 2014 United Nations. Reprinted with the permission of the United Nations.

action plans between parties to armed conflict and the United Nations and the delisting of parties to conflict from the Annexes to the Secretary-General's annual report,

...

Recalling that all parties to armed conflict must comply strictly with the obligations applicable to them under international law for the protection of children in armed conflict, including those contained in the Convention on the Rights of the Child and its Optional Protocol on the involvement of Children in armed conflict, as well as the Geneva Conventions of 12 August 1949 and their Additional Protocols of 1977,

...

Expressing deep concern about the military use of schools by armed forces and non-State armed groups in contravention of applicable international law, including those involving their use as military barracks, weapons storage facilities, command centres, detention and interrogation sites and firing and observation positions,

Expressing further concern regarding the high number of children that are being killed and maimed in conflict and post-conflict situations by landmines, explosive remnants of war, improvised explosive devices and other unexploded ordnance,

Convinced that the protection of children in armed conflict should be an important aspect of any comprehensive strategy to resolve conflict and build peace,

...

Recognizing the crucial role of child protection advisers in mainstreaming child protection and leading monitoring, prevention and reporting efforts in relevant United Nations peacekeeping missions, political missions and peacebuilding offices in accordance with their mandate, including advice for and close cooperation and coordination between the missions, UNICEF and specialized NGOs for child demobilization and integration and prevention of recruitment,

Underlining the importance of providing military, police and civilian peacekeepers with adequate predeployment and in-mission training on mission-specific child protection issues and on appropriate comprehensive prevention and protection responses,

Recognizing the valuable contribution of relevant regional and subregional organizations and arrangements for the protection of children affected by armed conflict and commending in this regard the declaration signed on 17 September 2013 between the Office of the Special Representative of the Secretary-General for Children and Armed Conflict and the Peace and Security Department of the African Union Commission, in order to mainstream protection mechanisms in all peace and security activities of the African Union, in close partnership with UNICEF, as well as the EU Guidelines on Children and Armed Conflict, including its Checklist for the integration of the protection of children affected by armed conflict into EU Common Security and Defense Policy operations and the development by NATO, in close collaboration with the DPKO and the Office of the Special Representative of the Secretary-General, of training courses and military guidelines on Children and Armed Conflict,

1. *Strongly condemns* all violations of applicable international law involving the recruitment and use of children by parties to armed conflict, as well as their re-recruitment, killing and maiming, rape and other sexual violence, abductions, attacks against schools or hospitals and denial of humanitarian access by parties to armed conflict and all other violations of international law, including international humanitarian law, human rights law and refugee law, committed against children in situations of armed conflict and *demands* that all relevant parties immediately put an end to such practices and take special measures to protect children;
2. *Calls on* Member States to devise ways, in close consultations with the United Nations country-level task force on monitoring and reporting and United Nations country teams, to facilitate the development and implementation of time-bound action plans, and the review and monitoring by the United Nations country-level task force of obligations and commitments relating to the protection of children affected by armed conflict;

...

4. *Stresses* the importance of regular and timely consideration of violations and abuses committed against children in armed conflict, including through incorporating, where appropriate, a children and armed conflict dimension in the terms of reference of Security Council field visits, and *invites* its Working Group on Children and Armed Conflict to make full use of its toolkit (S/2006/724) in light of ongoing discussions on enhancing compliance, and in this regard to continue considering the issue of persistent perpetrators and action plan implementation;
5. *Recalls* the fact that the conscription or enlistment of children under the age of 15 or using them to participate actively in hostilities in both international and non-international armed conflict constitutes a war crime under the Rome Statute of the International Criminal Court, and *notes* that the Optional Protocol to the Convention on the Rights of the Child on the involvement of children in armed conflict requires State parties to set a minimum age of 18 for compulsory recruitment and participation in hostilities and to raise the minimum age for voluntary recruitment from that set out in article 38, paragraph 3, of the Convention on the Rights of the Child and to take all feasible measures to ensure that members of their armed forces who have not attained the age of 18 years do not take a direct part in hostilities;

...

9. Further urges Member States, United Nations entities and other parties concerned to ensure that child protection provisions, including those relating to the release and reintegration of children formerly associated with armed forces or armed groups, are integrated into all peace negotiations and peace agreements;

...

13. *Urges* concerned Member States, when undertaking security sector reforms, to mainstream child protection, such as the establishment of child protection units in national security forces and of effective age assessment mechanisms to prevent underage recruitment *while stressing* in this regard the importance of ensuring universal birth registration, including late birth registration;

...

18. *Expresses deep concern* at the military use of schools in contravention of applicable international law, recognizing that such use may render schools legitimate targets of attack, thus endangering children's and teachers' safety as well as children's education and in this regard:
    (a) *Urges* all parties to armed conflict to respect the civilian character of schools in accordance with international humanitarian law;
    (b) *Encourages* Member States to consider concrete measures to deter the use of schools by armed forces and armed non-State groups in contravention of applicable international law;
    (c) *Urges* Member States to ensure that attacks on schools in contravention of international humanitarian law are investigated and those responsible duly prosecuted;
    (d) *Calls upon* United Nations country-level task forces to enhance the monitoring and reporting on the military use of schools;
19. *Recalls* the obligations of all parties to an armed conflict, in accordance with international humanitarian law, to ensure that the wounded and sick, including children, receive, to the fullest extent practicable and with the least possible delay, the medical care and attention required by their condition, and to respect and protect medical and health personnel, facilities, transports and activities in accordance with international humanitarian law;
20. *Recommends* that Member States include child protection in military training and standard operating procedures, as well as in military guidance as appropriate; *recommends further* that

United Nations entities and United Nations peacekeeping troop and police-contributing countries undertake targeted and operational trainings for the preparation of United Nations mission personnel including troop and police contingents on their contribution in preventing violations against children so as to give all mission personnel the ability to effectively recognize, report and respond to violations and abuses committed against children and to successfully support child protection activities for better implementation of their respective mandates;

21. *Urges* all United Nations entities, including peacekeeping missions, political missions, peacebuilding offices, United Nations offices, agencies, funds and programmes to give full attention to violations against children in the application of the human rights due diligence policy on United Nations support to non-United Nations security forces;

. . .

23. *Urges* relevant United Nations entities to continue to take concrete steps to reduce the impact of mines, unexploded ordnance and cluster munition and explosive remnants of war on children by prioritizing mine clearance, risk education and risk reduction activities;

24. *Decides* to continue the inclusion of specific provisions for the protection of children in the mandates of all relevant United Nations peacekeeping operations and political missions, encourages deployment of child protection advisers to such missions, and calls upon the Secretary-General to ensure that the need for and the number and roles of such advisers are systematically assessed during the preparation and renewal of each United Nations peacekeeping operation and political mission and *encourages* DPKO and DPA to take into account child protection when briefing the Council on country-specific situations;

25. *Encourages* pertinent regional and subregional organizations and arrangements to help address the widespread impact of armed conflict on children, *invites* them to continue the mainstreaming of child protection into their advocacy, policies, programmes and mission planning, the development and expansion of guidelines to protect children affected by armed conflict as well as the training of personnel and the inclusion of child protection staff in their peacekeeping and field operations, and *reiterates* its call for the establishment of child protection mechanisms within their secretariats, including through the appointment of child protection focal points;

. . .

19

Protection of Civilians in Armed Conflict

Prefatory Note

Since the United Nations Mission in Sierra Leone (UNAMSIL) in 1999, UN peacekeepers have been mandated to protect civilians. In contemporary peace operations, the meaning of the term 'protection of civilians' goes beyond the use of force. The term now includes all the adherence to, and promotion of, international humanitarian law (IHL)[1] and international human rights law (IHRL),[2] the enforcement of international criminal law,[3] as well as the provision of humanitarian assistance. The matter of peacekeepers protecting civilians may be viewed as one of the fundamental principles underlying UN peace operations.

To reinforce the protection of civilians the Security Council has issued several resolutions. Some of those resolutions focus on broad issues such as the responsibility to protect,[4] while others focus more narrowly on the role that peacekeepers have in protecting civilians. All these resolutions, together with the resolutions concerning women, peace, and security,[5] children and armed conflict,[6] and sexual exploitation and sexual abuse,[7] should be considered as mutually reinforcing.

The UN's first practice of protecting civilians may be traced to the operations conducted by the United Nations Operation in the Congo (ONUC) in the early 1960s. In 1961, for example, a Special Representative of the Secretary-General (SRSG) reported on the 'efforts made by ONUC to protect individuals from arbitrary arrest and violation of fundamental human rights'.[8] He specifically mentioned how ONUC set up protected areas in provinces such as the Oriental province and Equator,[9] and how on occasions ONUC provided protection and asylum.[10]

The SRSG also explained the principles that were observed by ONUC in giving protection or asylum:

(a) Asylum is granted only to persons who can show that they are in real danger of assassination, arbitrary arrest, ill-treatment or other persecution on account of their race, tribal origin, nationality, religion, political convictions or associations.

(b) UN protection is not granted to avoid lawful prosecution on charges of common law crimes, but the benefit of the doubt is given to applicants for asylum where the charges appear to be politically motivated, or where there appears to be jeopardy to life.

(c) Once granted UN asylum, the protected persons are prohibited from conducting any outside political activities, or from sending out communications other than of a strictly humanitarian nature, e.g. information to close relatives as to their personal safety.

(d) Protected persons are free to leave UN asylum at any time at their own discretion, but once they leave the protected area, UN cannot assume any further responsibility for their safety.[11]

---

1 See chs 15–16 above.
2 See chs 4–13 above.
3 See ch 23 below.
4 See, for example, SC Res 1674 (2006) of 28 April 2006.
5 See ch 17 above.
6 See ch 18 above.
7 See ch 20 below.
8 'Report dated 2 March 1961 to the Secretary-General from his Special Representative in the Congo on United Nations Protected Areas', UN Doc S/4757, 2 March 1961, [1].
9 Ibid, [1]–[5].
10 Ibid, [7]–[8].
11 Ibid, [8].

In 1998, the UN Office of Legal Affairs added to the above principles when it stated that the UN may assist an individual in imminent danger by offering the individual temporary refuge.[12] The right to 'temporary refuge' is limited to situations protecting a person 'in acute danger of being killed or wounded until the danger has passed. A threat of arrest by the constitutional authorities of the territorial State of persons accused or sentenced for common criminal offences, however, can never constitute such a threat'.[13]

Notwithstanding that early start, the protection of civilians only became a theme on the agenda of the Security Council in 1999 when it adopted resolution 1261 on children and armed conflict,[14] which became the precursor to each of the three landmark resolutions on civilians, women, and children. The Security Council considered the issue of the protection of civilians in armed conflict in 1999 when it requested the Secretary-General to submit a report on ways in which the Security Council 'could improve the physical and legal protection of civilians in situations of armed conflict'.[15] The ensuing report of the Secretary-General[16] led the Security Council to adopt resolution 1265[17] on the protection of civilians in armed conflict, in which the Security Council:

> 4. Urges all parties concerned to comply strictly with their obligations under international humanitarian, human rights and refugee law, in particular those contained in the Hague Conventions of 1899 and 1907 and in the Geneva Conventions of 1949 and their Additional Protocols of 1977, as well as with the decisions of the Security Council;
>
> ...
>
> 6. Emphasizes the responsibility of States to end impunity and to prosecute those responsible for genocide, crimes against humanity and serious violations of international humanitarian law.
> 11. Expresses its willingness to consider how peacekeeping mandates might better address the negative impact of armed conflict on civilians
>
> ...
>
> 13. Notes the importance of including in the mandates of peacemaking, peacekeeping and peace-building operations special protection and assistance provisions for groups requiring particular attention, including women and children.[18]

Following resolution 1265, Security Council resolution 1296 continued the thematic focus on the protection of civilians in armed conflict. Resolution 1296 affirmed the Security Council's intention:

> to ensure, where appropriate and feasible, that peacekeeping missions are given suitable mandates and adequate resources to protect civilians under imminent threat of physical danger, including by strengthening the ability of the United Nations to plan and rapidly deploy peacekeeping personnel, civilian police, civil administrators, and humanitarian personnel, utilizing the stand-by arrangements as appropriate.[19]

Resolution 1296 also reiterates the importance of peacekeepers having the appropriate training in IHL,[20] IHRL,[21] and international refugee law.[22] In addition, resolution 1296 states that peacekeepers should also be trained in 'coordination and sensitivity in the prevention of HIV/AIDS and other communicable diseases'[23] and in doing so ties in with Security Council resolution 1308 on HIV/AIDS.[24]

In resolution 1674,[25] the Security Council formally adopted the 'responsibility to protect doctrine' by reaffirming 'the provisions of paragraphs 138 and 139 of the 2005 World Summit Outcome Document regarding the responsibility to protect populations from genocide, war crimes, ethnic

---

12 UN Juridical Yearbook 1998: Special Edition, 2, 'Note to the Assistant Secretary-General for Political Affairs, concerning the legal status of the United Nations premises and the handing-over of political leaders to the competent authorities of a Member State', 11 September 1998.
13 Ibid.
14 SC Res 1261 (1999) of 25 August 1999. See ch 18 above.
15 Statement by the President of the Security Council, UN Doc S/PRST/1999/6, 12 February 1999, 3.
16 'Report of the Secretary-General to the Security Council on the Protection of Civilians in Armed Conflict', UN Doc S/1999/957, 8 September 1999.
17 SC Res 1265 (1999) of 17 September 1999.
18 Ibid, Operative Parts [4], [6], [11], [13].
19 SC Res 1296 (2000) of 19 April 2000, Operative Part [13].
20 See chs 15–16 above.
21 See chs 3–14 above.
22 See ch 5 above.
23 SC Res 1296 (2000) of 19 April 2000, Operative Part [19].
24 SC Res 1308 (2000) of 17 July 2000.
25 SC Res 1674 (2006) of 28 April 2006.

cleansing and crimes against humanity'.[26] Paragraph 139 of the World Summit Outcome Document states, in part, that:

> we are prepared to take collective action, in a timely and decisive manner, through the Security Council, in accordance with the Charter, including Chapter VII, on a case-by-case basis and in cooperation with relevant regional organizations as appropriate, should peaceful means be inadequate and national authorities are manifestly failing to protect their populations from genocide, war crimes, ethnic cleansing and crimes against humanity.[27]

Resolution 1674 reaffirms the requirement for all parties involved in an armed conflict to comply with their obligations under IHL and the responsibility of all States to prosecute those responsible for war crimes, crimes against humanity, and genocide.

Since adopting resolution 1674 in 2006 the Security Council has issued a number of other resolutions that address the protection of other vulnerable groups such as journalists, media professionals and associated personnel,[28] and humanitarian personnel.[29] In 2009 the Security Council again adopted a broad resolution concerning the protection of civilians: resolution 1894.[30] The resolutions adopted since resolution 1674, with the resolutions concerning the protection of UN and associated personnel, protection of women, and children, reinforce the framework of protection afforded by the Geneva Conventions and their Additional Protocols.[31]

Resolution 1894 addressed a number of matters relating to peacekeepers undertaking protection mandates, including: 'that mandated protection activities must be given priority in decisions about the use of available capacity and resources';[32] 'the importance of entrusting peacekeeping ... missions that are tasked with the protection of civilians with clear, credible and achievable mandates';[33] and requesting the 'Secretary-General to ensure that all relevant peacekeeping missions with protection mandates incorporate comprehensive protection strategies into the overall mission implementation plans and contingency plans'.[34] This chapter reproduces resolutions 1674 and 1894 because of their focus on peace operations.

Unlike the areas of gender and children, the General Assembly's Special Committee on Peacekeeping Operations (C34) had not included a separate section on the protection of civilians in its annual reports until the 2009 report, which included a section entitled 'Other mandated tasks, including the protection of civilians'.[35] Since 2009, the C34 has continued to acknowledge that:

> the protection of civilians is currently mandated in a number of United Nations peacekeeping missions. The Special Committee recognizes that protection of civilians is the primary responsibility of the host country and accordingly emphasizes that relevant peacekeeping missions with this mandate should conduct their tasks without prejudice to the primary responsibility of the host Government to protect civilians.[36]

That acknowledgement is reinforced in Security Council resolutions, such as resolution 2301 concerning the Central African Republic (CAR), which recalls that the 'CAR authorities have the primary responsibility to protect all populations in the CAR'.[37]

The Security Council has also issued statements containing an aide-memoire to guide its decisions concerning the protection of civilians. The 2015 aide-memoire raised several matters concerning the protection of civilians, including: general protection concerns; the protection of refugees and displaced persons; specific protections of children and women; and rule of law and

---

26 Ibid, Operative Part [4].

27 See GA Res 60/1 of 16 September 2005, Operative Part [139]. All the 2005 World Summit Documents can be found online <http://www.un.org/en/events/pastevents/worldsummit_2005.shtml> accessed 28 December 2018.

28 SC Res 1738 (2006) of 23 December 2006; SC Res 2175 (2014) of 29 August 2014; and SC Res 2286 (2016) of 3 May 2016.

29 SC Res 1502 (2003) of 26 August 2003; and SC Res 2175 (2014) of 29 August 2014.

30 SC Res 1894 (2009) of 11 November 2009.

31 See ch 16 above.

32 SC Res 1894 (2009) of 11 November 2009, Operative Part [19].

33 Ibid, Operative Part [20].

34 Ibid, Operative Part [24].

35 'Report of the Special Committee on Peacekeeping Operations and its Working Group, 2009 Substantive Session (23 February–20 March 2009)', UN Doc A/63/19, 24 March 2009, [125]–[128].

36 Ibid, [127]. See also 'Report of the Special Committee on Peacekeeping Operations, 2015 Substantive Session (17 February–13 March 2015)', UN Doc A/69/19, 17 March 2015, [218].

37 SC Res 2301 (2016) of 26 July 2016, Preamble [4].

accountability measures.[38] The aide-memoire also has a very useful addendum of the language used by the Security Council in its resolutions concerning various aspects of protecting civilians.

In 2015, the Department of Peacekeeping Operations (DPKO) and the Department of Field Support (DFS) issued a policy concerning the protection of civilians in UN peacekeeping.[39] That policy defines the protection of civilians mandate as: 'all necessary means, up to and including the use of deadly force, aimed at preventing or responding to threats of physical violence against civilians, within capabilities and areas of operations, and without prejudice to the responsibility of the host government'.[40] The policy also states that a number of principles apply to protection of civilian mandates, including: grounded in international law; a priority mandate; the primary responsibility of governments; a responsibility for peacekeepers; an active duty to protect; under effective command and control; the continuing applicability of the principles of peacekeeping; a whole-of-mission activity; a comprehensive approach; cooperation with humanitarian actors and respect for humanitarian principles; a community-based approach; a gender perspective; and, mainstreaming of child protection concerns.[41]

The resolutions concerning the protection of civilians, in conjunction with other more specific resolutions protecting vulnerable groups, such as women and children, are relevant for UN peace operations due to the subject matter they cover, and the fact that they are reaffirmed in Security Council resolutions establishing peace operations. For example, in resolution 2301 concerning the United Nations Multidimensional Integrated Stabilization Mission in the Central African Republic, the Security Council recalled:

> its resolutions on the protection of civilians in armed conflict, including 2286 (2016) and 1894 (2009); its resolutions on Children and Armed Conflict including 2225 (2015) and its resolutions on Women, Peace and Security including 2106 (2013) and 2242 (2015).[42]

Since UNAMSIL, and reinforced by resolution 1894, it is now the practice of the Security Council to give UN peace operations a specific mandate to protect civilians. For example, in resolution 2313, concerning the United Nations Stabilization Mission in Haiti (MINUSTAH), the Security Council encouraged MINUSTAH to:

> continue assisting the Government of Haiti in providing adequate protection to the civilian population, with particular attention to the needs of internally displaced persons and other vulnerable groups, especially women and children, including through joint community policing in the camps, in line with Security Council resolution 1894 (2009).[43]

In some cases, the Security Council has mandated peacekeepers more explicitly to use armed force to protect civilians. For example, Security Council resolution 2211 concerning the United Nations Organization Stabilization Mission in the Democratic Republic of the Congo, mandates peacekeepers to 'take all necessary measures'[44] to:

> Ensure, within its area of operations, effective protection of civilians under threat of physical violence, including by deterring, preventing and stopping armed groups from inflicting violence on the populations, paying particular attention to civilians gathered in displaced and refugee camps, humanitarian personnel and human rights defenders, in the context of violence emerging from any of the parties engaged in the conflict, and mitigating the risk to civilians before, during and after any military operation.[45]

---

38 'Statement by the President of the Security Council', UN Doc S/PRST/2015/23, 25 November 2015.

39 Department of Peacekeeping Operations/Department of Field Support, 'DPKO/DFS Policy: The Protection of Civilians in United Nations Peacekeeping', 1 April 2015 <http://providingforpeacekeeping.org/wp-content/uploads/2017/08/2015-07-Policy-on-PoC-in-Peacekeeping-Operations.pdf> accessed 28 December 2018. This policy is to be read in conjunction with other UN guidelines, such as the DPKO/DFS 'Implementing Guidelines for Military Components of United Nations Peacekeeping Operations', and the DPKO/DFS 'Guidelines: Use of Military Force by Military Components in United Nations Peacekeeping Operations', [7].

40 Department of Peacekeeping Operations/Department of Field Support, 'DPKO/DFS Policy: The Protection of Civilians in United Nations Peacekeeping', 1 April 2015, [13] <http://providingforpeacekeeping.org/wp-content/uploads/2017/08/2015-07-Policy-on-PoC-in-Peacekeeping-Operations.pdf> accessed 28 December 2018'.

41 Ibid, [16]–[29].

42 SC Res 2301 (2016) of 26 July 2016, Preamble [29].

43 SC Res 2313 (2016) of 13 October 2016, Operative Part [30].

44 SC Res 2211 (2015) of 26 March 2015, Operative Part [9].

45 Ibid, Operative Part [9](a).

Another development in the framework for the protection of civilians is the endorsement by several States of the Kigali Principles on the Protection of Civilians.[46] Those Principles, developed in 2015, reinforce the need:

> 3. To be prepared to use force to protect civilians, as necessary and consistent with the mandate. Such action encompasses making a show of force as a deterrent; interpositioning our forces between armed actors and civilians; and taking direct military action against armed actors with clear hostile intent to harm civilians.
> 4. Not to stipulate caveats or other restrictions that prevent us from fulfilling our responsibility to protect civilians in accordance with the mandate.[47]

Blending the protection of civilian resolutions with authorities to use force to protect civilians has resulted in the DPKO and DFS issuing guidelines entitled 'Use of Force by Military Components in United Nations Peacekeeping Operations'[48] which reinforced the principle that '[p]eacekeepers should not wait for hostile elements to attack civilians'.[49]

In contemporary UN peace operations, the protection of civilians mandate is guided by the following principles:

- Protecting civilians is the primary responsibility of governments;
- Peacekeepers with a mandate to protect civilians have the authority and responsibility to provide protection within their capabilities and areas of deployment where the government is unable or unwilling to protect;
- The protection of civilians mandate is a whole-of-mission activity, not only a military task, which embodies an active duty to protect;
- Protecting civilians is done in cooperation with humanitarian actors and with respect for humanitarian principles;
- The protection of civilians mandate is consonant with the principles of peacekeeping, including the consent of the host state, impartial mandate implementation, and the use of force only in self-defence or as authorized by the Security Council;
- The protection of civilians mandate is a priority mandate, pursuant to Security Council resolutions.[50]

The African Union (AU), European Union (EU) and the North Atlantic Treaty Organization (NATO) have also adopted policies concerning the protection of civilians. In March 2012 the AU issued its policy entitled 'Draft Guidelines for the Protection of Civilians in African Union Peace Support Operations'.[51] An important dimension of the AU's approach to dealing with the protection of civilians is its Civilian Casualty Tracking, Analysis, and Response Cell (CCTARC) which 'captures and record [sic] reported events and incidents of civilian casualties within [African Union Mission in Somalia] area of operation'.[52] The CCTARC is referred to Security Council resolution 2124, which stressed the need for the African Union Mission in Somalia to 'develop further an effective approach to the protection of civilians . . .'.[53]

The EU issued its policy on the protection of civilians in peacekeeping operations in 2008.[54] More recently, in 2016, the Head of the Delegation of the EU to the UN stated that '[p]eacekeepers must protect civilians under threat of physical violence, in a manner consistent with the requirements

46 The Kigali Principles on the Protection of Civilians (hereafter Kigali Principles) (June 2015) <http://www.globalr2p.org/media/files/kp-principles-17-november-2016.pdf> accessed 28 December 2018.

47 Ibid, [3]–[4].

48 Department of Peacekeeping Operations/ Department of Field Support, 'Guidelines: Use of Force by Military Components in United Nations Peacekeeping Operations', January 2017 <https://publicintelligence.net/un-peacekeeping-forces-guidelines/> accessed 31 December 2018.

49 Ibid, [31]; see also [35](b). See ch 33 below.

50 United Nations Peacekeeping, 'Protection of Civilians Mandate' <https://peacekeeping.un.org/en/protection-of-civilians-mandate> accessed 28 December 2018.

51 African Union, 'Draft Guidelines for the Protection of Civilians in African Union Peace Support Operations' (2012) <http://www.peaceau.org/uploads/draft-au-poc-guidelines-english.pdf> accessed 28 December 2018. See also the African Union Convention for the Protection and Assistance of Internally Displaced Persons in Africa (opened for signature 22 October 2009, entered into force 6 December 2012) <http://www.unhcr.org/en-au/about-us/background/4ae9bede9/african-union-convention-protection-assistance-internally-displaced-persons.html> accessed 1 November 2017.

52 See African Union Mission in Somalia (AMISOM), Civilian Casualty Tracking, Analysis, and Response Cell (CCTARC) <http://amisom-au.org/cctarc/> accessed 28 December 2018.

53 SC Res 2124 (2013) of 12 November 2013, Operative Part [11].

54 European Parliament Policy Department, External Policies, 'The Protection of Civilians during Peacekeeping Operations', June 2008.

of their mandates. Different levels of threat must be met with the appropriate and commensurate use of force, as necessary. In many ways, training is the cornerstone of improving the protection of civilians by missions.'[55] NATO issued its policy on the protection of civilians in July 2016.[56]

Resolution 1674 is reprinted and 1894 is extracted below.

References

Title	Security Council Resolution 1674 (2006) on Protection of Civilians in Armed Conflict
Author	Security Council
Meeting	5430th Meeting
Date	28 April 2006
Source	UN Doc S/RES/1674 (2006)
Full Text	<http://unscr.com/en/resolutions/doc/1674>[57]

Title	Security Council Resolution 1894 (2009) on Protection of Civilians in Armed Conflict
Author	Security Council
Meeting	6216th Meeting
Date	11 November 2009
Source	UN Doc S/RES/1894 (2009)
Full Text	<http://unscr.com/en/resolutions/doc/1894>[58]

Security Council Resolution 1674 (2006)[59]

The Security Council,

Reaffirming its resolutions 1265 (1999) and 1296 (2000) on the protection of civilians in armed conflict, its various resolutions on children and armed conflict and on women, peace and security, as well as its resolution 1631 (2005) on cooperation between the United Nations and regional organizations in maintaining international peace and security, and further reaffirming its determination to ensure respect for, and follow-up to, these resolutions,

Reaffirming its commitment to the Purposes of the Charter of the United Nations as set out in Article 1 (1–4) of the Charter, and to the Principles of the Charter as set out in Article 2 (1–7) of the Charter, including its commitment to the principles of the political independence, sovereign equality and territorial integrity of all States, and respect for the sovereignty of all States,

Acknowledging that peace and security, development and human rights are the pillars of the United Nations system and the foundations for collective security and well-being, and *recognizing* in this regard that development, peace and security and human rights are interlinked and mutually reinforcing,

Expressing its deep regret that civilians account for the vast majority of casualties in situations of armed conflict,

55 EU Statement to the Security Council, UN Doc S/PV/7606, 19 January 2016, 57.

56 North Atlantic Treaty Organization, 'NATO Policy for the Protection of Civilians', endorsed by the Heads of State and Government participating in the meeting of the North Atlantic Council in Warsaw 8–9 July 2016 <https://www.nato.int/cps/en/natohq/official_texts_133945.htm?selectedLocale=en> accessed 28 December 2018.

57 Accessed 28 December 2018.

58 Accessed 28 December 2018.

59 From Security Council Resolution 1674 (2006) on Protection of Civilians in Armed Conflict, by Security Council © 2006 United Nations. Reprinted with the permission of the United Nations.

Gravely concerned with the effects of the illicit exploitation and trafficking of natural resources, as well as the illicit trafficking of small arms and light weapons, and the use of such weapons on civilians affected by armed conflict,

Recognizing the important contribution to the protection of civilians in armed conflict by regional organizations, and *acknowledging in this regard*, the steps taken by the African Union,

Recognizing the important role that education can play in supporting efforts to halt and prevent abuses committed against civilians affected by armed conflict, in particular efforts to prevent sexual exploitation, trafficking in humans, and violations of applicable international law regarding the recruitment and re-recruitment of child soldiers,

Recalling the particular impact which armed conflict has on women and children, including as refugees and internally displaced persons, as well as on other civilians who may have specific vulnerabilities, and stressing the protection and assistance needs of all affected civilian populations,

Reaffirming that parties to armed conflict bear the primary responsibility to take all feasible steps to ensure the protection of affected civilians,

Bearing in mind its primary responsibility under the Charter of the United Nations for the maintenance of international peace and security, and *underlining* the importance of taking measures aimed at conflict prevention and resolution,

1. *Notes with appreciation* the contribution of the Report of the Secretary-General of 28 November 2005 to its understanding of the issues surrounding the protection of civilians in armed conflict, and *takes note of* its conclusions;
2. *Emphasizes* the importance of preventing armed conflict and its recurrence, and *stresses in this context* the need for a comprehensive approach through promoting economic growth, poverty eradication, sustainable development, national reconciliation, good governance, democracy, the rule of law, and respect for, and protection of, human rights, and in this regard, *urges* the cooperation of Member States and *underlines* the importance of a coherent, comprehensive and coordinated approach by the principal organs of the United Nations, cooperating with one another and within their respective mandates;
3. *Recalls* that deliberately targeting civilians and other protected persons as such in situations of armed conflict is a flagrant violation of international humanitarian law, *reiterates* its condemnation in the strongest terms of such practices, and *demands* that all parties immediately put an end to such practices;
4. *Reaffirms* the provisions of paragraphs 138 and 139 of the 2005 World Summit Outcome Document regarding the responsibility to protect populations from genocide, war crimes, ethnic cleansing and crimes against humanity;
5. *Reaffirms also* its condemnation in the strongest terms of all acts of violence or abuses committed against civilians in situations of armed conflict in violation of applicable international obligations with respect in particular to (i) torture and other prohibited treatment, (ii) gender-based and sexual violence, (iii) violence against children, (iv) the recruitment and use of child soldiers, (v) trafficking in humans, (vi) forced displacement, and (vii) the intentional denial of humanitarian assistance, and *demands* that all parties put an end to such practices;
6. *Demands* that all parties concerned comply strictly with the obligations applicable to them under international law, in particular those contained in the Hague Conventions of 1899 and 1907 and in the Geneva Conventions of 1949 and their Additional Protocols of 1977, as well as with the decisions of the Security Council;
7. *Reaffirms* that ending impunity is essential if a society in conflict or recovering from conflict is to come to terms with past abuses committed against civilians affected by armed conflict and to prevent future such abuses, *draws attention* to the full range of justice and reconciliation mechanisms to be considered, including national, international and "mixed" criminal courts and tribunals and truth and reconciliation commissions, and *notes* that such mechanisms can

promote not only individual responsibility for serious crimes, but also peace, truth, reconciliation and the rights of the victims;

8. *Emphasizes* in this context the responsibility of States to comply with their relevant obligations to end impunity and to prosecute those responsible for war crimes, genocide, crimes against humanity and serious violations of international humanitarian law, while recognizing, for States in or recovering from armed conflict, the need to restore or build independent national judicial systems and institutions;
9. *Calls on* States that have not already done so to consider ratifying the instruments of international humanitarian, human rights and refugee law, and to take appropriate legislative, judicial and administrative measures to implement their obligations under these instruments;
10. *Demands* that all States fully implement all relevant decisions of the Security Council, and in this regard cooperate fully with United Nations peacekeeping missions and country teams in the follow-up and implementation of these resolutions;
11. *Calls upon* all parties concerned to ensure that all peace processes, peace agreements and post-conflict recovery and reconstruction planning have regard for the special needs of women and children and include specific measures for the protection of civilians including (i) the cessation of attacks on civilians, (ii) the facilitation of the provision of humanitarian assistance, (iii) the creation of conditions conducive to the voluntary, safe, dignified and sustainable return of refugees and internally displaced persons, (iv) the facilitation of early access to education and training, (v) the re-establishment of the rule of law, and (vi) the ending of impunity;
12. *Recalls* the prohibition of the forcible displacement of civilians in situations of armed conflict under circumstances that are in violation of parties' obligations under international humanitarian law;
13. *Urges* the international community to provide support and assistance to enable States to fulfil their responsibilities regarding the protection of refugees and other persons protected under international humanitarian law;
14. *Reaffirms* the need to maintain the security and civilian character of refugee and internally displaced person camps, *stresses* the primary responsibility of States in this regard, and *encourages* the Secretary-General where necessary and in the context of existing peacekeeping operations and their respective mandates, to take all feasible measures to ensure security in and around such camps and of their inhabitants;
15. *Expresses its intention* of continuing its collaboration with the United Nations Emergency Relief Coordinator, and *invites* the Secretary-General to fully associate him from the earliest stages of the planning of United Nations peacekeeping and other relevant missions;
16. *Reaffirms* its practice of ensuring that the mandates of United Nations peacekeeping, political and peacebuilding missions include, where appropriate and on a case-by-case basis, provisions regarding (i) the protection of civilians, particularly those under imminent threat of physical danger within their zones of operation, (ii) the facilitation of the provision of humanitarian assistance, and (iii) the creation of conditions conducive to the voluntary, safe, dignified and sustainable return of refugees and internally displaced persons, and *expresses its intention* of ensuring that (i) such mandates include clear guidelines as to what missions can and should do to achieve those goals, (ii) the protection of civilians is given priority in decisions about the use of available capacity and resources, including information and intelligence resources, in the implementation of the mandates, and (iii) that protection mandates are implemented;
17. *Reaffirms* that, where appropriate, United Nations peacekeeping and other relevant missions should provide for the dissemination of information about international humanitarian, human rights and refugee law and the application of relevant Security Council resolutions;

18. *Underscores* the importance of disarmament, demobilization and reintegration of ex-combatants (DDR) in the protection of civilians affected by armed conflict, and, in this regard, *emphasizes* (i) its support for the inclusion in mandates of United Nations peacekeeping and other relevant missions, where appropriate and on a case-by-case basis, of specific and effective measures for DDR, (ii) the importance of incorporating such activities into specific peace agreements, where appropriate and in consultation with the parties, and (iii) the importance of adequate resources being made available for the full completion of DDR programmes and activities;
19. *Condemns in the strongest terms* all sexual and other forms of violence committed against civilians in armed conflict, in particular women and children, and *undertakes* to ensure that all peace support operations employ all feasible measures to prevent such violence and to address its impact where it takes place;
20. *Condemns in equally strong terms* all acts of sexual exploitation, abuse and trafficking of women and children by military, police and civilian personnel involved in United Nations operations, *welcomes* the efforts undertaken by United Nations agencies and peacekeeping operations to implement a zero-tolerance policy in this regard, and *requests* the Secretary-General and personnel-contributing countries to continue to take all appropriate action necessary to combat these abuses by such personnel, including through the full implementation without delay of those measures adopted in the relevant General Assembly resolutions based upon the recommendations of the report of the Special Committee on Peacekeeping, A/59/19/Rev.1;
21. *Stresses* the importance for all, within the framework of humanitarian assistance, of upholding and respecting the humanitarian principles of humanity, neutrality, impartiality and independence;
22. *Urges* all those concerned as set forth in international humanitarian law, including the Geneva Conventions and the Hague Regulations, to allow full unimpeded access by humanitarian personnel to civilians in need of assistance in situations of armed conflict, and to make available, as far as possible, all necessary facilities for their operations, and to promote the safety, security and freedom of movement of humanitarian personnel and United Nations and its associated personnel and their assets;
23. *Condemns* all attacks deliberately targeting United Nations and associated personnel involved in humanitarian missions, as well as other humanitarian personnel, *urges* States on whose territory such attacks occur to prosecute or extradite those responsible, and *welcomes* in this regard the adoption on 8 December 2005 by the General Assembly of the Optional Protocol to the Convention on the Safety of United Nations and Associated Personnel;
24. *Recognizes* the increasingly valuable role that regional organizations and other intergovernmental institutions play in the protection of civilians, and *encourages* the Secretary-General and the heads of regional and other intergovernmental organizations to continue their efforts to strengthen their partnership in this regard;
25. *Reiterates* its invitation to the Secretary-General to continue to refer to the Council relevant information and analysis regarding the protection of civilians where he believes that such information or analysis could contribute to the resolution of issues before it, requests him to continue to include in his written reports to the Council on matters of which it is seized, as appropriate, observations relating to the protection of civilians in armed conflict, and encourages him to continue consultations and take concrete steps to enhance the capacity of the United Nations in this regard;
26. *Notes* that the deliberate targeting of civilians and other protected persons, and the commission of systematic, flagrant and widespread violations of international humanitarian and human rights law in situations of armed conflict, may constitute a threat to international

peace and security, and, *reaffirms in this regard* its readiness to consider such situations and, where necessary, to adopt appropriate steps;

27. *Requests* the Secretary-General to submit his next report on the protection of civilians in armed conflict within 18 months of the date of this resolution;

28. *Decides* to remain seized of the matter.

Security Council Resolution 1894 (2009)[60]

(Extracts)

The Security Council,

Reaffirming its commitment to the continuing and full implementation, in a mutually-reinforcing manner, of resolutions 1265 (1999), 1296 (2000), 1325 (2000), 1612 (2005), 1674 (2006), 1738 (2006), 1820 (2008), 1882 (2009), 1888 (2009) and 1889 (2009), and all relevant statements of its President,

...

Noting that this year marks the tenth anniversary of the progressive consideration by the Security Council of the protection of civilians in armed conflict as a thematic issue; and *acknowledging* the enduring need for the Security Council and Member States to strengthen further the protection of civilians in armed conflict,

Noting further that this year also marks the 60th anniversary of the Geneva Conventions of 1949, which together with their Additional Protocols constitute the basis for the legal framework for the protection of civilians in armed conflict,

Recognizing that States bear the primary responsibility to respect and ensure the human rights of their citizens, as well as all individuals within their territory as provided for by relevant international law,

Reaffirming that parties to armed conflict bear the primary responsibility to take all feasible steps to ensure the protection of civilians,

...

Stressing the particular impact that armed conflict has on women and children, including as refugees and internally displaced persons, as well as on other civilians who may have specific vulnerabilities including persons with disabilities and older persons, and *stressing* the protection and assistance needs of all affected civilian populations,

Noting the adoption of the African Union Convention for the Protection and Assistance of Internally Displaced Persons in Africa (2009),

Noting with grave concern the severity and prevalence of constraints on humanitarian access, as well as the frequency and gravity of attacks against humanitarian personnel and objects and the significant implications of such attacks for humanitarian operations,

...

60 From Security Council Resolution 1894 (2009) on Protection of Civilians in Armed Conflict, by Security Council © 2009 United Nations. Reprinted with the permission of the United Nations.

Taking note of the report of the Secretary-General on the protection of civilians of 29 May 2009 (S/2009/277) and its annex on constraints on humanitarian access, which identify the core challenges to the effective protection of civilians, namely enhancing compliance with international law; enhancing compliance by non-State armed groups with their obligations under international law; enhancing protection through more effective and better resourced United Nations peacekeeping and other relevant missions; enhancing humanitarian access; and enhancing accountability for violations,

Welcoming the proposals, conclusions and recommendations on the protection of civilians included in the report of the Special Committee on Peacekeeping Operations and its Working Group (A/63/19) and the important work conducted by the Security Council Working Group on Peacekeeping Operations, including its efforts aimed at enhancing the implementation of protection mandates,

Recalling the statement of its President of 5 August 2009 (S/PRST/2009/24) and *welcoming* ongoing efforts to strengthen UN peacekeeping,

Noting that United Nations peacekeeping missions constitute one of several means at the United Nations' disposal to protect civilians in situations of armed conflict,

1. *Demands* that parties to armed conflict comply strictly with the obligations applicable to them under international humanitarian, human rights and refugee law, as well as to implement all relevant decisions of the Security Council and in this regard, *urges* them to take all required measures to respect and protect the civilian population and meet its basic needs;
2. *Reiterates* its condemnation in the strongest terms of attacks in situations of armed conflict directed against civilians as such and other protected persons or objects as well as indiscriminate or disproportionate attacks and the utilisation of the presence of civilians to render certain points, areas or military forces immune from military operations, as flagrant violations of international humanitarian law and demands that all parties immediately put an end to such practices;
3. *Notes* that the deliberate targeting of civilians as such and other protected persons, and the commission of systematic, flagrant and widespread violations of applicable international humanitarian and human rights law in situations of armed conflict may constitute a threat to international peace and security, and *reaffirms in this regard* its readiness to consider such situations and, where necessary, to adopt appropriate steps;
4. *Reiterates* its willingness to respond to situations of armed conflict where civilians are being targeted or humanitarian assistance to civilians is being deliberately obstructed, including through the consideration of appropriate measures at the Security Council's disposal in accordance with the Charter of the United Nations;

...

7. *Calls upon* all parties concerned,
   (a) to ensure the widest possible dissemination of information about international humanitarian, human rights and refugee law;
   (b) to provide training for public officials, members of armed forces and armed groups, personnel associated to armed forces, civilian police and law enforcement personnel, and members of the judicial and legal professions; and to raise awareness among civil society and the civilian population on relevant international humanitarian, human rights and refugee law, as well as on the protection, special needs and human rights of women and children in conflict situations, to achieve full and effective compliance;
   (c) to ensure that orders and instructions issued to armed forces and other relevant actors are in compliance with applicable international law, and that they are observed, inter alia, by establishing effective disciplinary procedures, central to which must be the strict

adherence to the principle of command responsibility to support compliance with international humanitarian law;

(d) to seek, where appropriate, support from United Nations peacekeeping and other relevant missions, as well as United Nations Country Teams and the International Committee of the Red Cross and, where appropriate, other members of the International Red Cross and Red Crescent Movement, on training and awareness raising on international humanitarian, human rights and refugee law;

8. *Emphasizes* the importance of addressing in its country specific deliberations the compliance of parties to armed conflict with international humanitarian, human rights and refugee law; *notes* the range of existing methods used, on a case by case basis, for gathering information on alleged violations of applicable international law relating to the protection of civilians and *underlines* the importance in this regard of receiving information that is timely, objective, accurate and reliable;

9. *Considers* the possibility, to this end, of using the International Fact-Finding Commission established by Article 90 of the First Additional Protocol to the Geneva Conventions;

10. *Affirms* its strong opposition to impunity for serious violations of international humanitarian law and human rights law and *emphasizes* in this context the responsibility of States to comply with their relevant obligations to end impunity and to thoroughly investigate and prosecute persons responsible for war crimes, genocide, crimes against humanity or other serious violations of international humanitarian law in order to prevent violations, avoid their recurrence and seek sustainable peace, justice, truth and reconciliation;

...

14. *Stresses* the importance for all parties to armed conflict to cooperate with humanitarian personnel in order to allow and facilitate access to civilian populations affected by armed conflict;

15. *Expresses* its intention to:

    (a) Call on parties to armed conflict to comply with the obligations applicable to them under international humanitarian law to take all required steps to protect civilians and to facilitate the rapid and unimpeded passage of relief consignments, equipment and personnel,

    (b) Mandate UN peacekeeping and other relevant missions, where appropriate, to assist in creating conditions conducive to safe, timely and unimpeded humanitarian assistance,

16. *Further expresses* its intention to:

    (a) Consistently condemn and call for the immediate cessation of all acts of violence and other forms of intimidation deliberately directed against humanitarian personnel,

    (b) Call on parties to armed conflict to comply with the obligations applicable to them under international humanitarian law to respect and protect humanitarian personnel and consignments used for humanitarian relief operations,

    (c) Take appropriate steps in response to deliberate attacks against humanitarian personnel;

17. *Invites* the Secretary-General to continue the systematic monitoring and analysis of constraints on humanitarian access, to include as appropriate observations and recommendations in his briefings and country-specific reports to the Council;

18. *Recalls* its determination to upgrade the strategic oversight of peacekeeping operations mindful of the important role peacekeeping operations play for the protection of civilians and *reaffirms* its support to the efforts made by the Secretary-General to review peacekeeping operations and to provide enhanced planning and support and *renews* its encouragement to deepen these efforts, in partnership with troop and police contributing countries and other relevant stakeholders;

19. *Reaffirms* its practice of ensuring that mandates of UN peacekeeping and other relevant missions include, where appropriate and on a case-by-case basis, provisions regarding the protection of civilians, *stresses* that mandated protection activities must be given priority in decisions about the use of available capacity and resources, including information and intelligence resources, in the implementation of mandates; and *recognizes*, that the protection of civilians when and as mandated requires a coordinated response from all relevant mission components;

20. *Reaffirms also* the importance of entrusting peacekeeping and other relevant missions that are tasked with the protection of civilians with clear, credible and achievable mandates, based on accurate and reliable information on the situation on the ground, and a realistic assessment of threats against civilians and missions, made in consultation with all relevant stakeholders, and *further reaffirms* the importance of a greater awareness in the Security Council of the resource and field support implications of its decisions and *stresses* the necessity to ensure the execution of the afore-mentioned mandates to protect civilians in the field;

21. *Recognizes* the necessity to take into account the protection needs of civilians in situations of armed conflict, in particular women and children, in the early phase of mandate drafting and throughout the lifecycle of United Nations peacekeeping and other relevant missions and in this regard *underlines* the importance of engagement with the countries concerned and of close consultation with the Secretariat, troop and police contributing countries, and other relevant actors;

22. *Recognizes also* the need for comprehensive operational guidance on peacekeeping missions' tasks and responsibilities in the implementation of protection of civilians mandates and *requests* the Secretary-General to develop in close consultation with Member States including troop and police contributing countries and other relevant actors, an operational concept for the protection of civilians, and to report back on progress made;

23. *Requests* the Secretary-General, in consultation with relevant actors, to ensure that peacekeeping missions with protection of civilians' mandates, in keeping with the strategic plans that guide their deployment, conduct mission-wide planning, pre-deployment training, and senior leadership training on the protection of civilians and requests troop and police contributing countries to ensure the provision of appropriate training of their personnel participating in UN peacekeeping and other relevant missions to heighten the awareness and responsiveness to protection concerns, including training on HIV/AIDS and zero tolerance of sexual exploitation and abuse in UN peacekeeping missions;

24. *Requests* the Secretary-General to ensure that all relevant peacekeeping missions with protection mandates incorporate comprehensive protection strategies into the overall mission implementation plans and contingency plans which include assessments of potential threats and options for crisis response and risk mitigation and establish priorities, actions and clear roles and responsibilities under the leadership and coordination of the SRSG, with the full involvement of all relevant actors and in consultation with United Nations Country teams;

25. *Requests* the Secretary-General to ensure that United Nations missions provide local communities with adequate information with regard to the role of the mission and in this regard ensure coordination between a United Nations mission and relevant humanitarian agencies;

26. *Takes note* of practical measures taken by ongoing peacekeeping missions and United Nations Country Teams to enhance the protection of civilians in the field, and *requests* the Secretary-General to include best practice in his next report on protection of civilians to the Council;

27. *Reaffirms* its practice of requiring benchmarks, as and where appropriate, to measure and review progress made in the implementation of peacekeeping mandates and *stresses* the

importance of including indicators of progress regarding the protection of civilians in such benchmarks for relevant missions;

. . .

30. *Reiterates* the importance of the Aide Memoire on the protection of civilians (S/PRST/2009/1) as a practical tool that provides a basis for improved analysis and diagnosis of key protection issues, particularly during deliberations on peacekeeping mandates and *stresses* the need to implement the approaches set out therein on a more regular and consistent basis, taking into account the particular circumstances of each conflict situation;
31. *Recognizes* the important role of the Secretary-General in providing timely information to the Security Council on protection of civilians in armed conflict in particular through thematic and country specific reports and through briefings;

. . .

33. *Requests* the Secretary-General to develop guidance for UN peacekeeping and other relevant missions on the reporting on the protection of civilians in armed conflict with a view to streamlining reporting and enhancing the Council's monitoring and oversight of the implementation of protection mandates of UN peacekeeping and other missions;
34. *Stresses* the importance of consultation and cooperation between the United Nations, the International Committee of the Red Cross and other relevant organisations including regional organisations to improve the protection of civilians in armed conflict;

. . .

36. Decides *to remain seized of the matter.*

20

Sexual Exploitation and Abuse

Prefatory Note

Resolution 2272 concerning sexual exploitation and abuse was adopted by the Security Council on 11 March 2016. It is the first resolution from the Security Council which focuses on sexual exploitation and abuse by peacekeepers. As such, it may be viewed as a landmark resolution. Resolution 2272, along with the resolutions concerning women, peace, and security,[1] children and armed conflict,[2] and the protection of civilians in armed conflict,[3] should be viewed as mutually reinforcing each other in the UN's endeavour to protect civilians in peace operations.

The primary purposes of resolution 2272 are to reinforce that 'sexual exploitation and abuse by United Nations peacekeepers undermines the implementation of peacekeeping mandates, as well as the credibility of United Nations peacekeeping',[4] and to reaffirm the Security Council's 'support for the United Nations zero tolerance policy on all forms of sexual exploitation and abuse'.[5] The resolution also welcomed the UN's 'prevention, reporting, enforcement and remedial action in order to promote greater accountability'.[6] The Security Council reinforced that it remains the primary responsibility of troop-contributing States to investigate allegations of sexual exploitation and abuse, and to hold their personnel accountable where appropriate for such exploitation and abuse.[7]

The resolution is innovative in the sense that it elevates sanctions for sexual exploitation and abuse from the individual level to military or formed police units. It deals with four broad themes: (1) the repatriation of a military or formed police unit 'when there is credible evidence of widespread or systematic sexual exploitation and abuse by that unit';[8] (2) the need for non-UN forces authorised pursuant to Security Council mandates to 'take adequate measures to prevent and combat impunity for sexual exploitation and abuse by their personnel';[9] (3) the requirement for Member States to certify that pre-deployment training on the prohibition of sexual exploitation and abuse has been provided to their troops and police;[10] and (4) that appropriate UN 'mechanisms, including those related to Children and Armed Conflict, Women Peace and Security and the Office of the High Commissioner for Human Rights, to continue to include allegations of sexual exploitation and abuse in their regular reporting to the Secretary-General'.[11] The resolution reinforces the requirement for troop and police-contributing nations to 'deliver robust sexual exploitation and abuse pre-deployment training in accordance with the terms of their memoranda of understanding and other agreements with the United Nations'.[12] The Security Council also welcomed the Secretary-General's appointment of a Special Coordinator on Improving the United Nations Response to Sexual Exploitation and Abuse.[13]

Where sexual exploitation and abuse is viewed as conflict-related violence, international criminal law (ICL), particularly the Rome Statute of the International Criminal Court (Rome Statute), Article 7(g)[14] will be relevant. Similarly, the Guidance Note of the Secretary-General may also be

---

1 See ch 17 above.
2 See ch 18 above.
3 See ch 19 above.
4 SC Res 2272 (2016) of 11 March 2016, Preamble.
5 Ibid.
6 Ibid.
7 Ibid.
8 Ibid, [1].
9 Ibid, [7].
10 Ibid, [10].
11 Ibid, [13].
12 Ibid, [10].
13 Ibid, Preamble.
14 Rome Statute of the International Criminal Court (opened for signature 17 July 1998, entered into force 1 July 2002) 2187 UNTS 3. See ch 23 below.

relevant to guide reparations to victims.[15] That Note provides 'policy and operational guidance for United Nations engagement in the area of reparations for victims of conflict-related sexual violence'.[16]

Sexual exploitation and abuse by peacekeepers first entered the UN's collective consciousness during the early 1990s[17] when allegations of sexual exploitation and abuse were made against peacekeepers serving with the UN Transitional Administration for Cambodia (UNTAC).[18] It was not until 2003 however that the impetus for developing formal policies to combat sexual exploitation and abuse came about.[19] The two UN policies that were promulgated in 2003 were the Directives for Disciplinary Matters Involving Military Members of National Contingents[20] and the Secretary-General's Bulletin on Special Measures for the Protection from Sexual Exploitation and Sexual Abuse[21] (the Bulletin).

To understand the term 'sexual exploitation and abuse', as used in resolution 2272, it is necessary to refer to the Bulletin. The term 'sexual exploitation' is defined in the Bulletin as 'any actual or attempted abuse of a position of vulnerability, differential power, or trust, for sexual purposes, including, but not limited to, profiting monetarily, socially or politically from the sexual exploitation of another'.[22] The Bulletin also makes clear that the:

> Exchange of money, employment, goods or services for sex, including sexual favours or other forms of humiliating, degrading or exploitative behaviour, is prohibited. This includes any exchange of assistance that is due to beneficiaries of assistance.[23]

The term 'sexual abuse' is defined to mean 'the actual or threatened physical intrusion of a sexual nature, whether by force or under unequal or coercive conditions'.[24] The Bulletin also recognises that '[s]exual activity with children (persons under the age of 18) is prohibited regardless of the age of majority or age of consent locally. Mistaken belief in the age of a child is not a defence.'[25] The Bulletin makes clear that both sexual exploitation and sexual abuse are acts of serious misconduct and therefore grounds for disciplinary measures.[26]

The General Assembly,[27] the Security Council,[28] and the Secretariat[29] have addressed aspects of how to deal with sexual exploitation and abuse by peacekeepers. In 2005, for example, the

15 Guidance Note of the Secretary-General, 'Reparations for Conflict-Related Sexual Violence', June 2014 <http://www.ohchr.org/Documents/Press/GuidanceNoteReparationsJune-2014.pdf> accessed 21 November 2018.

16 Ibid, Summary.

17 For a timeline of the UN's initiatives to address sexual exploitation and abuse, see <https://cdu.unlb.org/Policy/EvolutionofInitiativestoAddressSexualExploitationandAbuse.a> accessed 21 November 2018. For a comprehensive list of documents issued by the UN on its efforts to address sexual exploitation and abuse by peacekeepers, see <http://www.codebluecampaign.com/un-docs/> accessed 21 November 2018.

18 For an overview of the 20 years of the UN's attempts to deal with sexual exploitation and abuse by UN peacekeepers, see Elsa Buchanan, 'UN Peacekeeping: Allegations of Sexual Exploitation and Abuse – A 20 year History of Shame', 7 March 2016, *International Business Times*, <http://www.ibtimes.co.uk/un-peacekeeping-allegations-sexual-exploitation-abuse-20-year-history-shame-1547581> accessed 21 November 2018.

19 A key factor driving that impetus was not the allegations of sexual exploitation by UN peacekeepers, but substantiated evidence of widespread sexual exploitation of refugee children in West Africa by aid workers. See Note by the Secretary-General, 'Investigation into Sexual Exploitation of Refugees by Aid Workers in West Africa', UN Doc A/57/465, 11 October 2002. That investigation was undertaken by the Inter-Agency Standing Committee Task Force on Protection from Sexual Exploitation and Abuse in Humanitarian Crisis which was established in March 2002.

20 Department of Peacekeeping Operations, Directives for Disciplinary Matters Involving Military Members of National Contingents, UN Doc DPKO/MD/03/00993, July 2003. See ch 28 below. A similar Directive was issued in relation to Police Officers and Military Observers: UN Doc DPKO/MD/03/00994. See ch 29 below.

21 'Secretary General's Bulletin: Special Measures for Protection from Sexual Exploitation and Sexual Abuse', UN Doc ST/SGB/2003/13, 9 October 2003 <https://oios.un.org/resources/2015/01/ST-SGB-2003-13.pdf> accessed 21 November 2018 (hereafter the Bulletin). See ch 30 below.

22 Ibid, Section 1.

23 Ibid, Section 3.2(c).

24 Ibid, Section 1.

25 Ibid, Section 3.2(b).

26 Ibid, Section 3.2(a).

27 See, for example, 'Comprehensive Review of a Strategy to Eliminate Future Sexual Exploitation and Abuse in United Nations Peacekeeping Operations', UN Doc A/RES/59/300, 30 June 2005; and 'United Nations Comprehensive Strategy on Assistance and Support to Victims of Sexual Exploitation and Abuse by United Nations Staff and Related Personnel', UN Doc A/Res/62/214, 7 March 2008. See also the Reports of the Special Committee on Peacekeeping Operations such as UN Doc A/69/19, 17 February–13 March 2015, [58]–[71];'Special Measures for Protection from Sexual Exploitation and Sexual Abuse', UN Doc A/71/708/Add1, 29 June 2017, Draft resolution V.

28 See, for example, Security Council Presidential Statements of 31 May 2005, UN Doc S/PRST/2005/21; 25 November 2015, UN Doc S/PRST/2015/22; and SC Res 2242 (2015) of 13 October 2015.

29 For a list of all Secretary-General Reports concerning Special Measures for Protection from Sexual Exploitation and Abuse between 2004 and 2018, see <http://www.codebluecampaign.com/un-docs> accessed 21 November 2018.

Secretary-General wrote to the General Assembly about allegations of sexual exploitation and abuse by peacekeepers and how the 'exemplary record [of peacekeepers] has been clouded by the unconscionable conduct of a few individuals'.[30] In that letter to the General Assembly, the Secretary-General provided a Comprehensive Strategy to Eliminate Future Sexual Exploitation and Abuse in United Nations Peacekeeping Operations.[31] Based on that Strategy, the United Nations, in 2007, revised its model Memorandum of Understanding[32] between troop contributing countries and the UN to include specific provisions concerning sexual exploitation and abuse. Rule 1.2(e) of the UN Staff Rules also reinforces that sexual exploitation and abuse is prohibited.[33]

In June 2015, the Secretary-General appointed an independent panel to review sexual exploitation and abuse allegations made against peacekeeping forces serving in the Central African Republic (CAR).[34] The Panel's comprehensive report identified that notwithstanding all the UN's advocacy and policy efforts since 2003, little had been achieved:

> Yet the very same problems identified by the previous reports remain unaddressed and unabated: a culture of impunity in which some leaders turn a blind-eye to sexual crimes by troops; a bureaucratic culture in which many are not willing to take responsibility for addressing the violations or to show leadership in investigating and prosecuting the criminal conduct; a disproportionate concern with protecting the image of the UN and its agencies rather than helping the victims; and routine and systematic delay at every stage of decision-making, even as the failure to act means that crimes may be reoccurring and that the chances of bringing the perpetrators to justice decrease day by day. The end result is inaction, which only feeds the perception that there is little risk or consequence for those who choose to exploit the most vulnerable members of society.[35]

In June 2016, the Secretary-General issued another report in which he detailed a six-component strategy to combat sexual exploitation and abuse. The six components are:

> (a) Member State engagement and emerging best practices in United Nations troop and police deployments; (b) enhanced unified system-wide approach; (c) strengthened prevention, including increased awareness-raising, outreach to host communities, community-based reporting mechanisms and augmented training to United Nations personnel; (d) enhanced victim-centred response, encompassing victim services and protection; (e) robust enforcement through strengthened reporting, thorough and coordinated investigation and transparent judicial and public accountability; and (f) greater focus on monitoring and reporting on sexual exploitation and abuse by non-United Nations forces.[36]

After the Secretary-General's June 2016 report, the General Assembly in its deliberations concerning 'cross-cutting' issues that affect peace operations expressed its support for the full implementation of the UN's zero tolerance policy,[37] and highlighted the importance of 'providing expeditious support to victims . . . [and] for victims to receive immediate basic assistance and support in accordance with their individual needs'.[38]

The Secretary-General, in February 2017, issued a new strategy to improve UN action on sexual exploitation and abuse. The strategy focuses on four main areas of action to deal with preventing and responding to sexual exploitation and abuse by UN personnel, including peacekeepers, and forces acting under UN mandates.[39] The areas of action are: (1) putting victims first; (2) ending impunity; (3) engaging civil society and external partners; and (4) improving strategic communications for education and transparency. The UN Secretariat has also developed a system-wide matrix which

30 Secretary-General, Letter dated 24 March 2005 from the Secretary-General to the President of the General Assembly, UN Doc A/59/710, 24 March 2005, 1.

31 Ibid, 4–41.

32 See ch 3 above.

33 Staff Regulations and Rules of the United Nations, UN Doc ST/SGB/2017/1, 30 December 2016. See ch 25 below.

34 In 2014 allegations of sexual abuse by peacekeepers serving in the CAR were raised by a Human Rights Officer deployed with the UN peacekeeping mission. Little was done about those allegations until May 2015 when the international media started to report the incidents of abuse. See Report of an Independent Review on Sexual Exploitation and Abuse by International Peacekeeping Forces in the Central African Republic, 'Taking Action on Sexual Exploitation and Abuse by Peacekeepers' (17 December 2015) (hereafter CAR Report). See also the Final Report of the Expert Mission to Evaluate Risks to SEA (Sexual Exploitation and Abuse) Prevention Efforts in MINUSTAH, UNMIL, MONUSCO, and UNMISS of 3 November 2013.

35 CAR Report (n 34), 4–5.

36 UN Doc A/71/97, 23 June 2016, [6].

37 UN Doc A/RES/70/286, 8 July 2016, [71].

38 Ibid, [75]–[76].

39 Report of the Secretary-General, 'Special Measures for Protection from Exploitation and Abuse: A New Approach', UN Doc A/71/818, 28 February 2017.

outlines the responsibilities of UN entities to respond to sexual exploitation and abuse, as well as responsibility and accountability measures to prevent sexual exploitation and abuse.[40]

The Secretary-General also developed a 'Voluntary Compact on Elimination of Sexual Exploitation and Abuse between the Secretary-General of the United Nations and Member States' (the Compact), which is 'intended to send a signal to the world of joint commitment and mutual accountability on the part of the United Nations and Member States on preventing and addressing sexual exploitation and abuse'.[41] The Compact applies to all peace operations 'whether ... in the peacekeeping, humanitarian or development context or otherwise, and whether it consists of uniformed or civilian personnel or those working directly within the United Nations system'.[42]

As a part of his initiative to put victims first the Secretary-General appointed a 'Victims' Rights Advocate' to

> support an integrated, strategic response to victim assistance in coordination with United Nations system actors with responsibility for assisting victims. She will work with government institutions, civil society, and national and legal and human rights organizations to build networks of support and to help ensure that the full effect of local laws, including remedies for victims, are brought to bear.[43]

It is now common practice for the Security Council to reinforce the UN's zero-tolerance policy concerning sexual exploitation and abuse. For example, resolution 2313 concerning the UN Stabilization Mission in Haiti (MINUSTAH), recalling resolution 2272, requested the Secretary-General to:

> continue to take the necessary measures to ensure full compliance of all MINUSTAH personnel with the United Nations zero-tolerance policy on sexual exploitation and abuse, and to continue to keep the Council informed, and urges troop- and police-contributing countries to redouble efforts in preventing cases of misconduct and to ensure that acts involving their personnel are properly investigated and punished.[44]

Added to the abovementioned 2017 initiatives by the Secretary-General is the development of the sexual exploitation and abuse 'No Excuse' pocket card. That card, developed by the Office of the Secretary-General includes 'a concise and portable statement of the UN rules and prohibitions related to sexual exploitation and abuse and provide contact details for reporting allegations. These [cards] are to be distributed to all deployed UN personnel, affiliated staff, implementing partners and contractors'.[45]

Security Council resolution 2272 is reprinted below.

Reference

Title	Security Council Resolution 2272 (2016) on Sexual Exploitation and Abuse
Author	Security Council
Meeting	7643rd Meeting
Date	11 March 2016
Source	UN Doc S/RES/2272 (2016)
Full Text	<https://undocs.org/S/RES/2272(2016)> accessed 9 April 2019[46]

40 Ibid, Summary.

41 See 'Voluntary Compact' <https://www.un.org/preventing-sexual-exploitation-and-abuse/content/voluntary-compact> accessed 21 November 2018. At the time of writing the Voluntary Compact was not available to the public.

42 Ibid.

43 See <https://www.un.org/preventing-sexual-exploitation-and-abuse/content/victims-rights-advocate> accessed 01 April 2019.

44 SC Res 2313 of 13 October 2016, Operative Part [31].

45 See <http://repository.un.org/handle/11176/400598>.

46 Accessed 1 April 2019.

Security Council Resolution 2272 (2016)[47]

The Security Council,

Recalling the purposes and principles of the Charter of the United Nations and *bearing in mind* its primary responsibility under the Charter for the maintenance of international peace and security,

Recalling the Statements by its President of 31 May 2005 (S/PRST/2005/21), 25 November 2015 (S/PRST/2015/22) and 31 December 2015 (S/PRST/2015/26), as well as its resolution 2242 (2015) and press statement of 18 August 2015,

Reaffirming that proper conduct by, and discipline over, all personnel deployed in United Nations peace operations are crucial to their effectiveness,

Stressing that sexual exploitation and abuse by United Nations peacekeepers undermines the implementation of peacekeeping mandates, as well as the credibility of United Nations peacekeeping, and *reaffirming* its support for the United Nations zero tolerance policy on all forms of sexual exploitation and abuse,

Expressing deep concern about the serious and continuous allegations and under-reporting of sexual exploitation and abuse by United Nations peacekeepers and non-United Nations forces, including military, civilian and police personnel, and *underscoring* that sexual exploitation and abuse, among other crimes and forms of serious misconduct, by any such personnel is unacceptable,

Recalling the primary responsibility of troop-contributing countries to investigate allegations of sexual exploitation and abuse by their personnel and of troop-and police-contributing countries to hold accountable, including through prosecution, where appropriate, their personnel for acts of sexual exploitation and abuse, taking into account due process,

Honouring the heroic work of tens of thousands of United Nations peacekeepers, *underscoring* that the United Nations should not let the actions of a few tarnish the achievements of the whole and *commending* the troop- and police-contributing countries that have taken steps to prevent, investigate and hold accountable their personnel for acts of sexual exploitation and abuse,

Welcoming the Secretary-General's continued efforts to implement and reinforce the United Nations zero tolerance policy on sexual exploitation and abuse, in particular to strengthen the Organisation's prevention, reporting, enforcement and remedial action in order to promote greater accountability,

Welcoming the appointment by the Secretary-General of Jane Holl Lute as his Special Coordinator on Improving the United Nations Response to Sexual Exploitation and Abuse,

Taking note of the report of the High-level Independent Panel on Peace Operations (S/2015/446), the report of the Secretary-General entitled 'The Future of United Nations Peace Operations: Implementation of the Recommendations of the High-Level Independent Panel on Peace Operations' (A/70/357-S/2015/682), the report of the External Independent Review of the United Nations Response to Allegations of Sexual Exploitation and Abuse in the Central African Republic submitted on 17 December 2015 to the Secretary-General, the report of the Secretary-General of 17 September 2015 submitting the results of the Global Study on the implementation of resolution 1325 (S/2015/716), as well as the report of 4 March 2016 of the

47 From Security Council Resolution 2272 (2016) on Sexual Exploitation and Abuse, by Security Council © 2016 United Nations. Reprinted with the permission of the United Nations.

Secretary-General on Special measures for protection and prevention of sexual exploitation and abuse (A/70/729), and *taking note* of the recommendations contained therein related to the prevention and combating of sexual exploitation and abuse,

1. *Endorses* the decision of the Secretary-General to repatriate a particular military unit or formed police unit of a contingent when there is credible evidence of widespread or systemic sexual exploitation and abuse by that unit and *requests* the Secretary-General to give immediate and ongoing effect to this decision, including by urgently finalising his guidance to United Nations peacekeeping operations to implement this decision;
2. *Requests* the Secretary-General, when a particular troop-contributing country whose personnel are the subject of an allegation or allegations of sexual exploitation and abuse has not taken appropriate steps to investigate the allegation and/or when the particular troop- or police-contributing country has not held the perpetrators accountable or informed the Secretary-General of the progress of its investigations and/or actions taken, to replace all military units and/or formed police units of the troop- or police-contributing country in the United Nations peacekeeping operation where the allegation or allegations arose with uniformed personnel from a different troop- or police-contributing country, as applicable and further *requests* the Secretary-General to ensure that the replacement troop- or police-contributing country has upheld standards of conduct and discipline and appropriately addressed allegations against or confirmed acts, if any, of sexual exploitation and abuse by its personnel;
3. Consistent with paragraph 2 above regarding repatriation, *requests* the Secretary-General to assess whether a Member State has taken the appropriate steps to investigate, hold accountable and inform him of the progress of its investigations when determining whether that Member State should participate in other current or future United Nations peacekeeping operations;
4. Requests the Secretary-General to gather and preserve evidence ahead of investigations of sexual exploitation and abuse in United Nations peace operations with due consideration for the safety, security and confidentiality of victims, to ensure that the concerned United Nations peace operation takes immediate steps to prevent, including through risk assessments, future incidents of sexual exploitation and abuse, to strengthen the accessibility, coordination and independence of processes for complaint receipt and management and to assist victims, including by maintaining confidentiality, helping to minimize trauma and facilitating access, as appropriate, to immediate care, medical and psychological support;
5. *Welcomes* the efforts of the Secretary-General to expand vetting of all United Nations peacekeeping personnel to ensure that they do not have a history of sexual misconduct in service with the United Nations and *reiterates* its support for the United Nations Human Rights Screening Policy;
6. *Expresses deep concern* over the continuing and serious allegations of sexual exploitation and abuse by United Nations peacekeepers in the United Nations Multidimensional Integrated Stabilisation Mission in the Central African Republic (MINUSCA), as well as in other United Nations peacekeeping operations and by non-United Nations forces;
7. *Urges* all non-United Nations forces authorised under a Security Council mandate to take adequate measures to prevent and combat impunity for sexual exploitation and abuse by their personnel;
8. *Calls upon* Member States deploying non-United Nations forces authorized under a Security Council mandate to take appropriate steps to investigate allegations of sexual exploitation and abuse, hold perpetrators accountable and repatriate units when there is credible evidence of widespread or systemic sexual exploitation or abuse by those units;

9. *Urges* all Member States to take concrete steps aimed at preventing and combating impunity for sexual exploitation and abuse by members of United Nations peace operations;

10. *Welcomes* the ongoing efforts by Member States to strengthen sexual exploitation and abuse pre-deployment training of troop and police contributors to United Nations peace operations, *urges* further efforts by all troop and police-contributing countries to deliver robust sexual exploitation and abuse pre-deployment training in accordance with the terms of their memoranda of understanding and other agreements with the United Nations, *encourages* further assistance by Member States and multilateral partners to troop- and police-contributing countries in this regard and *welcomes* the decision of the Secretary-General to require certificates of compliance by troop-and police-contributors to this effect;

11. *Urges* all troop-contributing countries to take the steps necessary to conduct investigations of allegations of sexual exploitation and abuse by their personnel and to conclude such investigations as expeditiously as possible, in line with the Secretary-General's request, further *urges* all troop- and police-contributing countries to take appropriate steps to hold accountable those personnel responsible for sexual exploitation and abuse and to report to the United Nations fully and promptly on actions undertaken and *welcomes* the request by the Secretary-General for troop- and police-contributing countries to deploy national investigation officers in their contingents to support these efforts;

12. *Underscores* the critical importance that civilians, in particular women and children, in internally-displaced persons and refugee sites are protected from any form of abuse or exploitation, *requests* the Secretary-General, where applicable to continue to take steps to enhance measures in United Nations peace operations against all forms of abuse and exploitation of civilians by any member of the United Nations peace operation and *encourages* the Secretary-General to ensure that United Nations peace operations, as applicable, facilitate the identification of possible abuses and mitigate against the stigmatization of victims;

13. *Encourages* the appropriate United Nations mechanisms, including those related to Children and Armed Conflict, Women, Peace and Security and the Office of the High Commissioner for Human Rights, to continue to include allegations of sexual exploitation and abuse in their regular reporting to the Secretary-General and *calls upon* the Secretary-General to immediately inform the concerned Member State about any such allegations and to take steps to improve internal information-sharing within the United Nations regarding allegations of sexual exploitation and abuse.

PART THREE

Responsibility and Accountability in Peace Operations

Introduction

The responsibility and accountability of the UN and those who serve on peace operations is of fundamental importance for the efficiency, effectiveness, and the reputations of those operations. Allegations of the UN being responsible for the cholera outbreak in Haiti, cases of sexual exploitation and abuse by peacekeepers, and the failure of UN peacekeepers to protect civilians have led to calls for the UN to be more accountable for its actions and omissions.

The purpose of this introduction is to provide a better understanding of the role that the documents included in this Part play in holding UN peace operations, and those that serve on them, responsible and accountable for their acts or omissions. This introduction therefore briefly addresses the responsibility and accountability of the UN as an organisation, of peace operations as subsidiary organs of the UN, as well as of individuals who serve on peace operations.

From the UN's perspective, the legal framework for determining the responsibility of a UN peace operation may be summarised as follows:

> The question of attribution of the conduct of a peacekeeping force to the United Nations or to contributing States is determined by the legal status of the force, the agreements between the United Nations and contributing States and their opposability to third States ... [Where] a United Nations peacekeeping force established by the Security Council or the General Assembly is a subsidiary organ of the United Nations. Members of the military personnel placed by Member States under United Nations Command, although remaining in their national service, are, for the duration of their assignment to the force considered international personnel under the authority of the United Nations and subject to the instruction of the Force Commander. The functions of the force are exclusively international and members of the force are bound to discharge their functions with the sole interest of the United Nations in view. The peacekeeping operation as a whole is subject to the executive direction and control of the Secretary-General, under the overall direction of the Council or the Assembly, as the case may be.[1]

In situations where the UN or another international organisation or entity is conducting a peace operation, responsibility is most likely to be determined by who has effective command and control over the operation.[2]

Before referring to the documents in this part it is necessary to outline some of the levels of responsibility and accountability that exist on UN peace operations. At the highest or strategic level the responsibilities of the UN as an international organisation rest on the UN Charter.[3] The UN and the peace operations it establishes are therefore subject to internal and external laws relevant to a peace operation.

To fulfil the obligations arising from the Charter, such as to ensure that the Secretary-General or the Secretariat do not act beyond their powers, a multitude of processes exist at the strategic level (i.e. the UN headquarters level), the operational level (i.e. at the mission headquarters and in the field), and the tactical level (i.e. units and individual peacekeepers). Some of the processes at the strategic level include the General Assembly overseeing peace operations through the Administrative and Budgetary Committee (Fifth Committee)[4] and the Special Committee on Peacekeeping Operations (C34), which exists within the Fourth Committee.[5] The accountability of the Secretary-General to ensure the efficient and effective exercise of the powers delegated to the Secretariat to manage peace operations is undertaken primarily through the reports that the Secretary-General makes to the Security Council and sometimes to the General Assembly.

At both the strategic and operational levels another form of responsibility and accountability is undertaken by entering into the Status-of-Forces Agreement (SOFA) between the UN and the host

---

1 International Law Commission, 'Responsibility of International Organizations: Comments and Observations received from International Organizations', UN Doc A/CN4/637 Add1, 14 February 2011, 10. See ch 24 below.

2 See ch 24 below.

3 Charter of the United Nations. See ch 1 above.

4 See <http://www.un.org/en/ga/fifth/pkofinancing.shtml> accessed 1 November 2017.

5 See <https://peacekeeping.un.org/sites/default/files/sites/ctte/CTTEE.htm> accessed 1 April 2019.

State,[6] and the Memorandum of Understanding (MOU) between the UN and the State contributing its forces to the peace operation.[7]

At another operational level, accountability of the peace operation may also be ensured through the conducting of reports, investigations, and inquiries such as those undertaken in relation to sexual exploitation and abuse by peacekeepers.[8]

At the operational and tactical levels accountability of UN peacekeepers is ensured through a variety of directives and instructions which are issued either by the UN or the State that is responsible for the peacekeepers. Where an MOU does not apply, individual peacekeepers are bound by their contractual obligations to the UN. The UN's efforts to maintain appropriate levels of behaviour by its peacekeepers is reinforced through conduct and discipline units. Those units support the Troop Contributing Countries' efforts to ensure that peacekeepers do not breach orders and become undisciplined. In relation to serious criminal offences such as crimes against humanity or war crimes the Rome Statute of the International Criminal Court (Rome Statute)[9] may also be applicable if the troop contributing countries is unwilling or unable to exercise jurisdiction.[10]

Turning now to the documents in this part. The principles and rules relevant to the responsibility and accountability of the UN and its staff in UN peace operations are founded on the Charter, the Convention on the Privileges and Immunities of the United Nations (General Convention),[11] and the jurisprudence of the International Court of Justice (ICJ).[12] The General Assembly's resolution on third-party liability[13] and the Articles on the Responsibility of International Organizations (ARIO) focus on the responsibility of the UN as an organisation.[14] The Rome Statute[15] and the Codes of Conduct, Directives, and Guidelines[16] address the accountability of individual peacekeepers.

All UN accountability documents are founded on the Charter. Articles 100, 101, 104, and 105 of the Charter provide a framework concerning the employment, responsibilities, and duties of UN staff and the UN as an organisation. Article 100(1) provides that the Secretary-General and staff of the UN Secretariat 'shall not seek or receive instructions from any government or from any other authority external to the [UN] Organization'. That Article also stipulates that both the Secretary-General and the Secretariat staff 'shall refrain from any action which might reflect on their position as international officials responsible only to the Organisation'. Pursuant to Article 101(3) of the Charter, UN staff members are to have the 'highest standards of efficiency, competence and integrity'. The privileges and immunities of the UN as an organisation are dealt with by Articles 104 and 105 of the Charter. The principle of accountability that underlies the legal capacity of the UN is that of functional immunity. In other words, the UN shall, pursuant to Article 105, 'enjoy in the territory of its Members such privileges and immunities as are necessary for the fulfilment of its purposes'.

The General Convention builds on the Charter by according particular status, immunities, and privileges to the UN, its representatives, and officials. The recognition of the UN's juridical personality and the immunity of the UN's property and assets from legal process are addressed by the General Convention. As subsidiary organs of the UN, peace operations also enjoy the status, privileges, and immunities of the UN as provided for by the General Convention. Paragraph 15 of the model SOFA confirms that position of UN peace operations.[17] The UN Office of Legal Affairs (OLA) has stated that:

> As a subsidiary organ of the United Nations, an act of a peacekeeping force is, in principle, imputable to the Organization, and if committed in violation of an international obligation entails the international responsibility of the Organization and its liability in compensation.[18]

---

6 See ch 2 above.

7 See ch 3 above.

8 See ch 20 above.

9 See ch 23 below.

10 See ch 3 above in relation the state of nationality having criminal jurisdiction over its peacekeepers.

11 See ch 21 below.

12 See chs 34–36 below.

13 See ch 22 below.

14 See ch 24 below.

15 See ch 23 below.

16 See chs 25–33 below.

17 'Report of the Secretary-General on the Model Status-of-Forces Agreement for Peace-keeping Operations', UN Doc A/45/594, 9 October 1990, Annex, Paragraph 15.

18 UN Juridical Yearbook 2004, 352–6, 354 'Interoffice memorandum to the Director of Codification Division, Office of Legal Affairs and Secretary of the International Law Commission regarding the topic Responsibility of International Organizations', 3 February 2004.

The accountability of the UN as an organisation, particularly in the context of peace operations, has been addressed by the ICJ in two cases: *Reparation for Injuries Suffered in the Service of the United Nations* (*Reparations Case*),[19] and *Certain Expenses of the United Nations (Article 17, Paragraph 2, of the Charter)* (*Certain Expenses Case*).[20] In the *Reparations Case*, the ICJ concluded that the UN is an organisation with international legal personality and opined that the UN has powers 'by necessary implication as being essential to the performance of its duties'.[21] Some of those powers include the power to bring claims against one of its Member States and to conclude agreements such as a SOFA or MOU. The *Certain Expenses Case* confirmed that while the powers of the UN are wide, they are not unlimited. The Court stated that 'when the Organization takes action which warrants the assertion that it was appropriate for the fulfilment of one of the stated purposes of the United Nations; the presumption is that such action is not ultra vires the Organization'.[22]

More recently, the International Law Commission (ILC) has in the ARIO reinforced that the UN may be held accountable for breaches of its obligations under international law, and may therefore be liable to make reparations for the injury caused by its internationally wrongful act. The UN's approach to reparations for its wrongful acts in peace operations is dealt with by the General Assembly resolution entitled 'Third-Party Liability: Temporal and Financial Limitations', which provides temporal and financial limitations that would apply to third-party claims against the UN for 'personal injury, illness or death, and for property loss or damage ... resulting from or attributable to the activities of members of the peacekeeping operations in the performance of their official duties'.[23] Furthermore, the resolution makes clear that 'liability is not engaged in relation to third-party claims resulting from or attributable to the activities of members of peacekeeping operations arising from "operational necessity"'.[24]

As stated above, the General Convention also provides certain categories of UN personnel with privileges and immunities. The extent of those privileges and immunities in relation to experts on mission, which would in the context of peace operations include military observers and UN civilian police, was dealt with by the ICJ in *Difference Relating to Immunity from Legal Process of a Special Rapporteur of the Commission of Human Rights*.[25] This case reinforced the rule, stated in Article VI, Section 23, of the General Convention, that privileges and immunities are granted to the experts in the interest of the UN and not for the personal benefit of the individual.[26] The case also stands for the rule that the 'Secretary-General has the primary responsibility and authority to protect the interests of the Organization and its agents'[27] and therefore it is for the Secretary-General to assert the individual's immunity.[28]

Individual peacekeepers might, depending on the obligations of the State they belong to, be subject to the accountability regime created by the Rome Statute. The International Criminal Court (ICC) has the capacity to try individuals for crimes such as war crimes and crimes against humanity. The UN has negotiated an agreement with the ICC to provide the framework for cooperation between the two organisations.[29]

At another level the accountability of UN personnel depends in large part on their employment category in the UN and on peace operations. They are five general employment categories: (1) UN staff members both national and international (also referred to as UN officials) and United Nations Volunteers (UNV) who are assimilated to UN officials; (2) individual military and police members and members of Formed Police Units (provided with expert on mission status); (3) other

---

19 *Reparations for Injuries Suffered in the Service of the United Nations* (Advisory Opinion) [1949] ICJ Rep 174 (hereafter *Reparations Case*). See ch 34 below.

20 *Certain Expenses of the United Nations (Article 17, Paragraph 2, of the Charter)* (Advisory Opinion) [1962] ICJ Rep 151 (hereafter *Certain Expenses Case*). See ch 35 below.

21 *Reparations Case* (n 19), 182.

22 *Certain Expenses Case* (n 20), 168.

23 See GA Res 52/247 of 17 July 1988, Operative Part [5]. See ch 22 below.

24 Ibid, Operative Part [6].

25 *Difference Relating to Immunity from Legal Process of a Special Rapporteur of the Commission on Human Rights, International Court* (Advisory Opinion) [1999] ICJ Rep 62 (hereafter *Cumaraswamy Case*). See ch 36 below.

26 *Cumaraswamy Case* (n 25), [51].

27 Ibid.

28 Ibid, [56].

29 Negotiated Relationship Agreement between the International Criminal Court and the United Nations, UN Doc A/58/874, 10 April 2004, entered into force 22 July 2004.

government provided personnel with the status of experts on mission; (4) members of military contingents; and (5) consultants or individual contractors of the UN.[30] Within these categories the accountability of UN personnel is dependent on whether there is a contractual link between the UN and the individual through a written undertaking, or the MOU between the UN and the country contributing troops. The relationship that UN officials and experts on mission (such as military observers and UN civilian police) have with the UN is founded on an individual written undertaking, whereas the UN's relationship with members of military units is through an MOU.

Once a person is designated as either a UN official or an expert on mission the General Convention sets the parameters for their accountability. Articles V and VII of the General Convention deal with UN officials and Article VI concerns experts on mission. In peace operations, the application of the General Convention is reinforced in Part IV of the model SOFA and in the Staff Regulations and Rules of the United Nations (Staff Regulations).[31]

The Staff Regulations are founded on the Charter which states that 'staff shall be appointed by the Secretary-General under regulations established by the General Assembly'.[32] After a number of provisional Staff Regulations, the General Assembly established the first permanent Staff Regulations in resolution 590 (VI).[33] The Staff Regulations have been amended and added to many times over the years through further General Assembly resolutions.[34] Once adopted by the General Assembly, the Secretary-General issues the Regulations by way of a Bulletin. The most recent Staff Regulation was issued in 2017.[35] The Staff Regulations include matters such as classification of posts and staff, salaries and related allowances, disciplinary measures, and appeals.

The Secretary-General's Bulletin entitled 'Status, Basic Rights and Duties of United Nations Staff Members' (Status of Staff Members)[36] applies to all members of the UN Secretariat including those members who are working for the principal and subsidiary organs of the UN.[37] That document therefore applies to UN staff serving in appointments such as the Special Representative of the Secretary-General (SRSG), the FC, and the Commander of the Civilian Police. The Bulletin entitled 'Status, Basic Rights and Duties of Officials other than Secretariat Officials and Experts on Mission' (Status of Experts on Mission)[38] applies to UN officials who are performing full time services for the UN but who are not staff such as UN experts on mission, military observers, or UN civilian police. Both documents were developed under the overarching structure of the Staff Regulations.

A further level of accountability which arises from the application of the model MOU is the UN Code of Conduct entitled 'We are United Nations Peacekeeping Personnel'. That document, which is given to all peacekeepers, is incorporated as Annex H of the 2011 revised model MOU and reinforces Article 103 of the UN Charter that all UN personnel must maintain the highest standards of integrity and conduct. Reinforcing the 'We are United Nations Peacekeeping Personnel' standards are the 'Ten Rules: Code of Personal Conduct for Blue Helmets'.[39]

The Directives for Disciplinary Matters Involving Military Members of National Contingents,[40] and the Directives for Disciplinary Matters Involving Civilian Police Officers and Military Observers,[41] are issued by the Secretary-General. The purpose of both Directives is to establish UN procedures to be followed when there are allegations of serious misconduct and misconduct against military members, civilian police officers and military observers deployed on UN peace operations.

A more specific form of accountability of UN peacekeepers is the Secretary-General's Bulletin on 'Special Measures for Protection from Sexual Exploitation and Sexual Abuse'.[42] The Bulletin's primary

30 See UN Policy, Accountability for Conduct and Discipline in Field Missions, 1 August 2015, [11.1].
31 See ch 25 below.
32 Charter, Article 101(1).
33 GA Res 590 (VI) of 2 February 1952.
34 See 'Secretary-General's Bulletin: Staff Regulation and Rules of the United Nations', UN Doc ST/SGB/2017/1 (amended text to include ST/SGB/2017/Corr1 issued on 18 January 2017 and effective from 1 January 2017), [3].
35 Ibid.
36 'Secretary-General's Bulletin: Status, Basic Rights and Duties of United Nations Staff Members', UN Doc ST/SGB/2016/9, 21 July 2016.
37 Ibid, Sections 2–9.
38 See ch 26 below.
39 See ch 27 below.
40 See ch 28 below.
41 See ch 29 below.
42 See ch 30 below.

focus is to prevent and address cases of sexual exploitation and sexual abuse.[43] The Bulletin should be read with Secretary-General's Bulletin on the 'Prohibition of Discrimination, Harassment, including Sexual Harassment, and Abuse of Authority' (Harassment Bulletin).[44] The Harassment Bulletin defines the terms 'discrimination', 'harassment', 'sexual harassment', and 'abuse of authority'.[45] It reinforces Article 101(3) of the Charter and the provisions in the Staff Regulations and Staff Rules concerning dignity and respect in the work place.[46] The Bulletin also specifies the duties of managers and supervisors,[47] preventative measures,[48] corrective measures,[49] and monitoring[50] in dealing with discrimination, harassment, sexual harassment, and abuse of authority.

To consolidate the accountability principles, rules, and standards directed at individuals serving on UN peace operations the Departments of Political Affairs (DPA), the Department of Peacekeeping Operations (DPKO), and the Department of Field Support (DFS) in the UN Secretariat have issued a policy entitled 'Accountability for Conduct and Discipline in Field Missions'.[51] That Policy 'sets out the framework in place to ensure accountability for the conduct and discipline of all persons serving in peacekeeping and special political missions'.[52] Compliance with the Policy is compulsory.[53] The Policy is based on the fundamental principle articulated in Staff Regulation that the Secretary-General may 'impose disciplinary measures on staff members who engage in misconduct'.[54] The disciplinary and criminal accountability measures found in the Policy compliment those found in the Staff Regulations and the model MOU. Importantly, the Policy explains the three-pronged strategy of the Secretariat in addressing misconduct: prevention, enforcement, and remedial action.[55]

This part of the book also reprints the Human Rights Due Diligence Policy on United Nations Support to Non-United Nations Security Forces (HRDDP).[56] The HRDDP was developed by the UN Secretary-General to deal with UN peacekeepers providing support to non-UN forces, such as the forces of the host state and peacekeeping forces of regional organisations.[57] The Policy articulates a responsibility and accountability mechanism which requires peacekeepers to: (1) assess the risks involved in providing or not providing the support; (2) be transparent with the receiving entity about the UN's obligations; and (3) have an effective implementation framework for ensuring that the support provided meets the UN's obligations. The effective implementation framework includes procedures to monitor the entity's compliance with international humanitarian law (IHL),[58] international human rights law (IHRL),[59] and refugee law,[60] procedures to intercede should there be grave violations of the law, and general guidelines to ensure that the policy can be implemented in the context in which it is to be applied.[61]

The final documents in Part Three are 'Use of Force by Military Components in United Nations Peacekeeping Operations' (Use of Force Guidelines) issued by DPKO and DFS, and the ROE Soldier's Pocket Card. Both documents concern the use of armed force by military peacekeepers.[62] The Use

---

43 UN Doc ST/SGB/2003/13, 9 October 2003, entered into force 15 October 2003, Preamble.

44 UN Doc ST/SGB/2008/5, 11 February 2008, entered into force 1 March 2008, Preamble.

45 Ibid, Section 1.

46 Ibid, Section 2.

47 Ibid, Section 3.

48 Ibid, Section 4.

49 Ibid, Section 5.

50 Ibid, Section 6.

51 See ch 31 below.

52 UN Policy, Accountability for Conduct and Discipline in Field Mission, 1 August 2015, [1].

53 Ibid, [4].

54 'Secretary-General's Bulletin: Staff Regulations', UN Doc ST/SGB/2016/5, 1 July 2016, [10.1].

55 UN Policy, Accountability for Conduct and Discipline in Field Mission, 1 August 2015, [10.4].

56 General Assembly and Security Council, 'Identical letters dated 25 February 2013 from the Secretary-General addresses to the President of the General Assembly and to the President of the Security Council', UN Doc A/67/775-S/2013/11, 5 March 2013 <http://www.ohchr.org/Documents/HRBodies/SP/AMeetings/20thsession/IdenticalLetterSG25Feb2013_en.pdf> accessed 1 November 2017 (hereafter HRDDP). The HRDDP is annexed to the letter. See also ch 32 below.

57 For a more detailed definition of 'non-United Nations security forces', see HRDDP (n 56), [7]. The UN has also published a Guidance Note concerning the application of the HRDDP: <http://dag.un.org/handle/11176/387415> accessed 1 November 2017.

58 See chs 15–16 above.

59 See chs 4–13 above.

60 See ch 5 above.

61 HRDDP (n 56), 2.

62 See ch 33 below.

of Force Guidelines establish an accountability framework for every instance where force is used by peacekeepers. The ROE Soldiers Pocket Card deals with key aspects concerning the individual use of force by military peacekeepers.

In its 2009 report, the C34 reaffirmed:

> that all peacekeeping personnel must be informed of and adhere to all applicable rules, regulations, provisions and guidelines provided by the United Nations for peacekeepers, as well as to national laws and regulations.[63]

There are other UN internal documents such as Staff Regulations,[64] Guidelines,[65] Administrative Instructions,[66] and Information Circulars[67] that are relevant to varying degrees to peace operations but are not included in this part.

---

63 'Report of the Special Committee on Peacekeeping Operations: 2009 Substantive Session', UN Doc A/63/19, 23 February–20 March 2009, [49].

64 'Secretary-General's Bulletin: Staff Regulations', UN Doc ST/SGB/2016/5, 1 July 2016.

65 Guidelines on Cooperation with the Business Sector, issued November 2009. See <http://www.un.org/en/ethics/relevantdocs.shtml> accessed 1 November 2017.

66 Access to these documents is limited to United Nations Staff Members.

67 Access to these documents is limited to United Nations Staff Members.

A. Privileges and Immunities of the United Nations and its Agencies

21

Convention on the Privileges and Immunities of the United Nations

Prefatory Note

Legal immunities are of significant relevance to all areas of UN peace operations. Such immunities arise from three main sources: international law, Status-of-Forces Agreements (SOFAs),[1] and domestic law. The Convention on the Privileges and Immunities of the United Nations (General Convention)[2] should be understood in the context of other treaties such as the Charter, the Vienna Convention on Diplomatic Relations,[3] and the Convention on the Privileges and Immunities of the Specialized Agencies (Specialized Agencies Convention).[4] This chapter focuses on the General Convention and its application to peace operations.

The General Convention was adopted by the General Assembly on 13 February 1946 during its first session in resolution 22 (I) A. There were no signatories to the General Convention; however, upon adoption, it was submitted to every Member State of the UN for accession.[5] The General Convention is founded on Articles 104 and 105 of the UN Charter[6] which accord a particular status, immunities, and privileges to the UN, its representatives, and officials. The UN Office of Legal Affairs (OLA) has stated that the provisions of the General Convention have now become a 'part of the general international law governing the relations of States and the United Nations'.[7]

Article I, Section 1 of the General Convention recognises that the UN shall possess juridical personality. This means that each signatory State recognises that the UN, as an international organisation, shall have the legal capacity to contract, acquire, and dispose of immovable and movable property and to institute legal proceedings in that State. The International Court of Justice (ICJ), in its Advisory Opinion on *Reparation for Injuries Suffered in the Service of the United Nations*,[8] found that the General Convention could only operate 'upon the international plane and as between parties possessing international personality'.[9] This makes it clear that the UN has international legal personality. UN peace operations have the international legal personality of the UN because they are subsidiary organs of the UN. The General Convention therefore applies to UN peace operations

---

1 See ch 2 above.

2 Convention on the Privileges and Immunities of the United Nations (opened for signature 13 February 1946, entered into force 17 September 1946) 1 UNTS 15 (hereafter General Convention). The General Convention was adopted by the General Assembly in GA Res 22 (I) A (1946) of 13 February 1946.

3 Vienna Convention on Diplomatic Relations (opened for signature 18 April 1961, entered into force 24 June 1964) 500 UNTS 95.

4 Convention on the Privileges and Immunities of the Specialized Agencies (opened for signature 21 November 1947, entered into force 2 December 1948) 33 UNTS 261 (hereafter Specialized Agencies Convention).

5 General Convention (n 2), Section 31.

6 See ch 1 above.

7 UN Juridical Yearbook 1967, 311–14, 314 on the 'Question of privileges and immunities of the United Nations, of representatives of Member States and of Officials of the Organization', 6 December 1967.

8 *Reparation for Injuries Suffered in the Service of the United Nations* (Advisory Opinion) [1949] ICJ Rep 174, (hereafter *Reparations Case*). See ch 34 below.

9 Ibid, 179.

but does not apply to operations authorised by the Security Council which are conducted under the control of States or regional organisations.

Articles II and III of the General Convention provide the privileges and immunities of the UN itself. Article II, Section 2, provides that the UN and its property and assets shall enjoy immunity from every form of legal process. This gives the UN absolute immunity from legal process unless it expressly waives its immunity.[10] Section 3 provides for the inviolability of UN premises and Section 4 for the inviolability of all UN archives and documents. Paragraph 15 of the model SOFA confirms that UN peace operations, as subsidiary organs of the UN, also enjoy the status, privileges, and immunities of the UN as provided for in the General Convention. As such, a UN peace operation, and its property and assets, enjoy immunity from every form of legal process. This must be understood as organisational immunity, in contrast to individual immunities for differing categories of personnel, such as officials and experts on mission under the General Convention, and differing categories of peacekeepers in the model SOFA. The organisational immunity is 'not ... from legal liability but only exemption from local jurisdiction'.[11] In cases where the issue of the Organisation's immunity arises it is assumed that the Secretary-General has the authority to waive the Organisation's immunity.[12]

Individual privileges and immunities under the General Convention are granted to representatives of Member States, officials, and experts on mission. The term 'representatives' includes 'delegates, deputy delegates, advisers, technical experts and secretaries of delegations'.[13] In relation to personnel covered by the General Convention, an 'official' is a person who the Secretary-General designates as such.[14] This includes 'all members of the staff of the United Nations, with the exception of those who are recruited locally and are assigned to hourly rates'.[15] Whilst the text of Article VI, Section 22, does not specifically define an 'expert', it is a term which is broad enough to include consultants,[16] military observers, and civilian police personnel. The practice of the UN has been to classify any person who is entrusted to perform a specific and important task for the UN as an 'expert on mission' if they are neither a staff member (i.e. an official) nor a representative of a Member State.[17]

Individual privileges and immunities under the General Convention are granted in the interests of the UN and not for personal benefit. In other words, the privileges and immunities are granted to ensure that officials and experts can exercise their functions to the extent necessary to fulfil the purposes of the UN. The Secretary-General's Bulletin on the Status, Basic Rights and Duties of United Nations Staff Members reinforces the principle that the privileges and immunities granted to UN staff are not an excuse for them to fail to observe the laws of the host state, and they do not 'furnish an excuse for non-performance of their private obligations'.[18]

The Secretary-General has the right and the duty to waive the immunity of any official or expert 'where, in his opinion, the immunity would impede the course of justice and can be waived without prejudice to the interests of the United Nations'.[19] The right and duty to waive immunity, and authority to do so, is 'vested exclusively (except for his own privileges and immunities, which

---

10 See UN Juridical Yearbook 1984, 188–9 on the 'Immunity of UNRWA [United Nations Relief and Works Agency for Palestine Refugees in the Near East] from every form of legal process under the Convention on the Privileges and Immunities of the United Nations—System of law by which the question of UNRWA's immunity from jurisdiction is to be judged—Nature of the immunity under that system of law', 28 February 1984.

11 'Inter-office memorandum to the Acting Director of the Legal Department, concerning the waiver of immunity—actual and implied', reprinted in U N Juridical Yearbook 1948: Special Edition, 1–7, 1, 20 December 1948.

12 Ibid, 3.

13 General Convention (n 2), Section 16.

14 Ibid, Section 17.

15 GA Res 76 (I) of 7 December 1946, Operative Part [2].

16 UN Juridical Yearbook 1996, 440–1, 441 on 'Obligations of the United Nations with respect to income tax levied by a Member State—Article II, Section 2, and Article V, Section 18, of the Convention on the Privileges and Immunities of the United Nations—Status of consultants', 8 August 1996.

17 See UN Juridical Yearbook 1998, 481–2 on the 'Question of whether contractors' personnel could be considered as "experts on mission"—Article VI, Section 22, of the 1946 Convention on the Privileges and Immunities of the United Nations', 23 March 1998.

18 'Secretary-General's Bulletin: Status, Basic Rights and Duties of United Nations Staff Members', UN Doc ST/SGB/2016/9, 21 July 2016, Regulation 1.1(f). See ch 25 below.

19 General Convention (n 2), Section 20 and see also Section 23.

the Security Council may waive) in the Secretary-General'.[20] Consequently, officials and experts on mission cannot waive their own immunities.

Military members of a UN peace operation, who, at the same time, are members of national contingents, are accorded functional immunity from jurisdiction, but this is not based on the General Convention. Rather, such immunity is based on the SOFA between the UN and the host country. SOFAs incorporate many of the elements of the General Convention and are applicable to a broader array of UN personnel. They are binding between the host country and the UN irrespective of whether the host country is a party to the General Convention.

A range of privileges are provided for officials and experts on mission under the General Convention including those relating to personal and property protection.[21]

Officials of the UN are entitled to the privileges and immunities found in Articles V and VII of the General Convention. Key aspects of the privileges and immunities granted to officials in the context of UN peace operations include immunity from legal process in respect of words spoken or written and all acts performed by them in their official capacity, and the entitlement to import items free of duty. Officials may also be issued a UN *laissez-passer* as a valid travel document.[22]

Experts on mission for the UN are entitled to the privileges and immunities found in Article VI of the General Convention. The key aspects of the privileges and immunities granted to experts include immunity from personal arrest or detention and seizure of personal baggage, immunity from legal process of every kind in respect of words spoken or written and acts done by them during the performance of their mission, and the inviolability of all papers and documents.

Section 19 provides that '[i]n addition to the immunities and privileges specified in Section 18, the Secretary-General and all Assistant Secretaries-General shall be accorded in respect of themselves, their spouses and minor children, the privileges and immunities, exemptions and facilities accorded to diplomatic envoys, in accordance with international law'.

The model SOFA incorporates these protections for some categories of peacekeepers. Paragraph 24 of the model SOFA provides that the Special Representative of the Secretary-General (SRSG), the Commander of the military component, and the head of the UN civilian police component are accorded diplomatic immunity as specified in Section 19 of the Convention. Paragraph 25 of the model SOFA provides that UN civilian staff remain 'officials' of the UN entitled to the privileges and immunities of officials under Articles V and VII of the General Convention, and in Paragraph 26 it provides that military observers and UN civilian police are 'experts on mission' for the UN entitled to the privileges and immunities of experts on mission under Article VI of the General Convention.

The authority of the UN to resolve third party claims is reflected in Article VIII, Section 29, of the General Convention where the UN undertakes to make provisions for appropriate modes of settlement of both claims against the UN itself and claims against officials when immunity has not been waived by the Secretary-General.[23] The appropriate mode of settlement for claims arising in a peace operation is provided through the dispute settlement procedure in Paragraph 51 of the model SOFA. Regarding third-party liability, the General Assembly, in Resolution 52/247,[24] adopted temporal and financial limitations on the UN outlining what kinds of injury are compensable, the maximum amount that may be paid, and the time limit within which claims can be brought. These limits are now explicitly included in current SOFAs.

In relation to Section 29 of the General Convention, the UN has stated that claims pursuant to that Section are limited to disputes that arise between two private parties—such as those arising from vehicle accidents.[25] The Section cannot be relied upon to make claims concerning political

20 UN Juridical Yearbook 1969, 224–5, 225 on the 'Exclusive authority of the Secretary-General as regards permission to execute the waivers of privileges and immunities required by a Member State from staff members maintaining or seeking permanent resident status in that State—Policy of the United Nations in that respect', 11 July 1969.

21 General Convention (n 2), Sections 18 and 22.

22 A UN *laissez-passer* (from the French 'let pass') is a valid travel document issued to UN officials to facilitate their movement across international borders when on official UN business.

23 See UN Juridical Yearbook 2001, 381–5 on 'Payment of settlement claims—Liabilities of private law nature—Procedures for settlement—Budget considerations', 23 February 2001.

24 GA Res 52/247 of 26 June 1998. See ch 22 below.

25 Letter from the Assistant Secretary-General, Senior Coordinator for Cholera Response to Ms Farha, Mr Gallon, Mr Puras, and Ms de Albuqerque, 25 November 2014, [87] <https://spdb.ohchr.org/hrdb/28th/Haiti_ASG_25.11.14_(3.2014).pdf> accessed 9 August 2018.

or policy related complaints 'such as those "related to actions or decisions taken by the Security Council or the General Assembly" '.[26]

In situations where the UN or another international organisation or entity is conducting a peace operation, third-party claims are settled according to who has effective command and control over the operation.[27] The basis for the settlement of such claims are agreements signed between the UN and the entity which contain:

> provisions to the effect that each participant will be solely responsible for handling third-party claims in respect of death, personal injury or illness caused by its personnel or agents, or for loss or damage to third-party property to the extent that such claims arise from or in connection with, acts or omissions of that party or of its personnel or agents.[28]

The issue of acts performed during an expert's functions formed the basis of the Advisory Opinion of the ICJ on the *Differences Relating to Immunity from Process of a Special Rapporteur of the Commission of Human Rights* (*Cumaraswamy Case*).[29] The issue was whether allegedly defamatory statements made by the Special Rapporteur were spoken in the course of his mission and therefore fell within the claimed immunity from legal process as 'official' acts under the General Convention. The Court identified the Secretary-General as having primacy in the process of determining whether a particular expert on mission is entitled to the immunity provided for in Section 22(b).[30] Based on Sections 20 and 23 of the General Convention, the OLA has determined that only the Secretary-General has the competence to determine what constitutes an 'official' or 'unofficial' act and not 'courts of law or any other national authorities of Member States'.[31] The ICJ, however, stated that any such finding by the Secretary-General is only 'to be given the greatest weight by national courts'.[32] In UN peace operations, the Secretary-General delegates the competence to make this determination regarding acts of peacekeepers to the SRSG. This is reflected in Paragraphs 47(a) and 49 of the model SOFA. If the SRSG does determine an act to be related to 'official duties' then only the Secretary-General can waive immunity concerning that act.

The issue of waiver of immunity has also arisen in relation to UN staff giving evidence. The OLA has stated that:

> In considering whether a request for a waiver should be granted, and if so, whether any conditions should be applied to the waiver, the Secretary-General considers whether the evidence or testimony to be provided by the witness would prejudice the interests of the United Nations; specifically whether such evidence or testimony would: (i) endanger the safety or security of current or former personnel of the United Nations or otherwise prejudice the security or proper conduct of any operation or activity of the United Nations; (ii) violate a duty of confidentiality which the United Nations owes to a third party; or (iii) compromise the confidentiality which is necessary for the effective operation of the internal decision-making processes of the United Nations, or of future United Nations peacekeeping operations.[33]

Article VIII, Section 30, of the General Convention provides that all differences arising out of the interpretation or application of the General Convention shall be referred to the ICJ. This process was followed in the ICJ Advisory Opinion in the *Cumaraswamy Case*.

There is also the Specialized Agencies Convention. Whilst UN peace operations are subsidiary organs of the UN and fall under the General Convention, specialised agencies are autonomous organisations, and therefore require a separate Convention to provide them with the necessary privileges

26 Ibid, [89].

27 International Law Commission, 'Responsibility of International Organizations: Comments and Observations received from International Organizations', 17 February 2011, UN Doc A/CN4/637/Add1, 11. See ch 24 below.

28 Ibid, 11–12.

29 *Difference Relating to Immunity from Legal Process of a Special Rapporteur of the Commission of Human Rights* (Advisory Opinion) [1999] ICJ Rep 62 (hereafter *Cumaraswamy Case*). See ch 36 below.

30 Ibid, 87.

31 UN Juridical Yearbook 1995, 403–4, 404 on the 'Question of who can determine whether the acts of United Nations officials are performed in their official capacity—Section 20 of the Convention on the Privileges and Immunities of the United Nations', 24 January 1995.

32 *Cumaraswamy Case* (n 29), 87 [61].

33 'Note to the Department of Peacekeeping Operations regarding criminal proceedings in relation to violent protest by former individual contractors of a United Nations Mission', reprinted in U N Juridical Yearbook 2008, 404–6, 405, 12 May 2008. In some cases a specific agreement may be established concerning UN personnel giving evidence—see, for example, 'Memorandum of Understanding between the United Nations and the International Criminal Court concerning cooperation between the United

and immunities. The Specialized Agencies Convention was adopted by the General Assembly in resolution 179 (II),[34] and provides similar privileges and immunities to the specialised agencies and their officials as are provided to the UN and UN officials under the General Convention. For example, the Specialized Agencies Convention provides that officials of the specialised agencies shall '[b]e immune from legal process in respect of words spoken or written and all acts performed by them in their official capacity'.[35] This mirrors the immunities provided to officials of the UN in Section 18 of the General Convention. Similar provisions can be found in respect of waiving immunity, settlement of disputes, and settling differences arising out of the interpretation or application of the Specialized Agencies Convention.

The Specialized Agencies Convention defines the words 'specialized agencies' to mean the following agencies: the International Labour Organization (ILO), the Food and Agriculture Organization of the United Nations (FAO), the United Nations Educational, Scientific and Cultural Organization (UNESCO), the International Civil Aviation Organization (ICAO), the International Monetary Fund (IMF), the International Bank for Reconstruction and Development (IBRD), the World Health Organization (WHO), the Universal Postal Union (UPU), the International Telecommunication Union (ITU), and any other agency in relationship with the UN in accordance with Articles 57 and 63 of the Charter.[36]

The Specialized Agencies Convention assumes importance in UN peace operations when a specialised agency and its officials are operating in the same territory as a peace operation. Officials of specialised agencies are not covered by the SOFA between the UN and host country which only refers to officials of the UN and the privileges and immunities they are entitled to under Articles V and VII of the General Convention. Consequently, the only privileges that apply to officials of specialised agencies are those outlined in the Specialized Agencies Convention if the host country is a signatory.

Since the International Law Commission (ILC) adopted its Articles on the Responsibility of International Organizations,[37] several principles arising from the Specialized Agencies Convention have been reinforced. For example, Article 6 (conduct of organs or agents of an international organ), Article 7 (conduct of organs of a State or organs or agents of an international organisation placed at the disposal of another international organ), and Article 36 (compensation) reinforce general principles arising from the Convention concerning the conduct of United Nations officials,[38] the criteria for attribution between the acts of States contributing troops and the United Nations,[39] and compensation for breaches of obligations under international law.[40]

In the context of UN peace operations, the General Convention also applies to matters such as access to UN compounds. The OLA has stated that, pursuant to Section 3 of the General Convention, the 'United Nations alone is competent to exercise control over its premises and the activities conducted therein. It follows, therefore, that no local officer or official may enter these premises without the consent of, and under the conditions agreed to, by the United Nations.'[41]

The reach of the General Convention also extends to cases brought against the UN before international tribunals and domestic courts. For example, in *Behrami and Behrami v France and Saramati v France, Germany and Norway*,[42] the European Court of Human Rights (ECtHR) concluded that because the UN Interim Administration Mission in Kosovo (UNMIK) 'was a subsidiary organ of the UN created under Chapter VII and KFOR [International Security Force in Kosovo] was exercising

---

Nations Operation in Côte d'Ivoire (UNOCI) and the Prosecutor of the International Criminal Court, New York, 20 and 23 January 2012', Article 11, reprinted in the U N Juridical Yearbook 2012, 78–96, 89.

34 GA Res 179 (II) of 21 November 1947.

35 Specialized Agencies Convention (n 4), Section 19(a).

36 Ibid, Section 1(ii). There are now several other specialised agencies in relationship with the UN in accordance with Articles 57 and 63 of the Charter, such as the United Nations Industrial Development Organization (UNIDO).

37 International Law Commission, 'Draft Articles on the Responsibility of International Organizations, and Commentaries' submitted to the General Assembly as part of the work of UN Doc A/66/10, 3 October 2011.

38 Ibid, Commentary to Article 6.

39 Ibid, Commentary to Article 7.

40 Ibid, Commentary to Articles 7 and 36.

41 U N Juridical Yearbook 1998: Special Edition, 1–2, [3], 'Note to the Assistant Secretary-General for Political Affairs, concerning the legal status of the United Nations premises and the handing-over of political leaders to the competent authority of a Member State', 11 September 1998.

42 Decision as to the Admissibility: *Behrami and Behrami v France*, App no 71412/01, 2 May 2007; *Saramati v France, Germany and Norway*, App no 78166/01, 2 May 2007.

powers lawfully delegated under Chapter VII of the Charter ... the applicants'[43] complaints must be declared incompatible *ratione personae* with the provisions of the [European] Convention [for the Protection of Human Rights and Fundamental Freedoms].'[44]

In relation to cases involving United Nations peace operations brought before national courts the immunity of the UN and its staff has been absolute. For example, in *Georges v United Nations*, which arose from the cholera outbreak caused by peacekeepers serving with the UN Stabilization Mission in Haiti (MINUSTAH), the United States Federal Court concluded that MINUSTAH enjoyed absolute immunity under the General Convention from any action alleging that United Nations personnel were responsible for the cholera epidemic in Haiti.[45] The Federal Court also concluded in that case that the UN immunity is not dependent on the UN establishing settlement of disputes mechanisms pursuant to Section 29 of the General Convention.[46] The only exception from that absolute immunity is if the UN expressly waives its immunity.[47] The Federal Court also dismissed any suit against the UN Secretary-General and his Special Representative in Haiti on the basis that Article 105 of the Charter and Article 19 of the General Convention provided them with immunity from civil and administrative jurisdiction.[48]

Reference

Title	Convention on the Privileges and Immunities of the United Nations
Date of Adoption	13 February 1946
Entered into Force	17 September 1946 (in accordance with Section 32, the Convention entered into force upon deposit of the first instrument of accession by the UK)
Signatories	None (in accordance with Section 31, the Convention was submitted to every Member of the UN for accession)
Parties	162
Depository	United Nations
Treaty Series	1 UNTS 15
Full Text	<http://www.un.org/en/ethics/pdf/convention.pdf>[49]

Convention on the Privileges and Immunities of the United Nations[50]

(Extracts)

Whereas Article 104 of the Charter of the United Nations provides that the Organization shall enjoy in the territory of each of its Members such legal capacity as may be necessary for the exercise of its functions and the fulfilment of its purposes and

Whereas Article 105 of the Charter of the United Nations provides that the Organization shall enjoy in the territory of each of its Members such privileges and immunities as are necessary for the fulfilment of its purposes and that representatives of the Members of the United Nations and officials of the Organization shall similarly enjoy such privileges and immunities as are necessary for the independent exercise of their functions in connection with the Organization.

43 Ibid, [151] and [152].

44 European Convention for the Protection of Human Rights and Fundamental Freedoms, as amended by Protocols Nos 11 and 14 (opened for signature 4 November 1950, entered into force 3 September 1953) ETS 5.

45 *Georges v United Nations* 84 FSupp 3d 246, 248–9 (SD NY, 2015).

46 Ibid, 249.

47 Ibid.

48 Ibid, 250.

49 Accessed 1 November 2017.

50 From Convention on the Privileges and Immunities of the United Nations © 1946 United Nations. Reprinted with the permission of the United Nations.

Consequently the General Assembly by a Resolution adopted on the 13 February 1946, approved the following Convention and proposed it for accession by each Member of the United Nations.

ARTICLE I – Juridical Personality

Section 1

The United Nations shall possess juridical personality. It shall have the capacity:

(a) To contract;

(b) To acquire and dispose of immovable and movable property;

(c) To institute legal proceedings.

ARTICLE II – Property, Funds and Assets

Section 2

The United Nations, its property and assets wherever located and by whomsoever held, shall enjoy immunity from every form of legal process except insofar as in any particular case it has expressly waived its immunity shall extend to any particular case it has expressly waived its immunity. It is, however, understood that no waiver of immunity shall extend to any measure of execution.

Section 3

The premises of the United Nations shall be inviolable. The property and assets of the United Nations, wherever located and by whomsoever held, shall be immune from search, requisition, confiscation, expropriation and any other form of interference, whether by executive, administrative, judicial or legislative action.

Section 4

The archives of the United Nations, and in general all documents belonging to it or held by it, shall be inviolable wherever located.

...

Section 7

The United Nations, its assets, income and other property shall be:

(a) Exempt from all direct taxes; it is understood, however, that the United Nations will not claim exemption from taxes which are, in fact, no more than charges for public utility services;

(b) Exempt from customs duties and prohibitions and restrictions on imports and exports in respect of articles imported or exported by the United Nations for its official use. It is understood, however, that articles imported under such exemption will not be sold in the country into which they were imported except under conditions agreed with the Government of that country;

(c) Exempt from customs duties and prohibitions and restrictions on imports and exports in respect of its publications.

...

ARTICLE III – Facilities in Respect of Communications

Section 9

The United Nations shall enjoy in the territory of each Member for its official communications treatment not less favourable than that accorded by the Government of that Member to any other Government including its diplomatic mission in the matter of priorities, rates and taxes on mails, cables, telegrams, radiograms, telephotos, telephone and other communications; and press rates for information to the press and radio. No censorship shall be applied to the official correspondence and other official communications of the United Nations.

Section 10

The United Nations shall have the right to use codes and to despatch and receive its correspondence by courier or in bags, which shall have the same immunities and privileges as diplomatic couriers and bags.

ARTICLE IV – The Representatives of Members

Section 11

Representatives of Members to the principal and subsidiary organs of the United Nations and to conferences convened by the United Nations, shall, while exercising their functions and during the journey to and from the place of meeting, enjoy the following privileges and immunities:

(a) Immunity from personal arrest or detention and from seizure of their personal baggage, and, in respect of words spoken or written and all acts done by them in their capacity as representatives, immunity from legal process of every kind;

(a) [sic] Inviolability for all papers and documents;

(c) The right to use codes and to receive papers or correspondence by courier or in sealed bags;

(d) Exemption in respect of themselves and their spouses from immigration restrictions, aliens registration or national service obligations in the state they are visiting or through which they are passing in the exercise of their functions;

(e) The same facilities in respect of currency or exchange restrictions as are accorded to representatives of foreign governments on temporary official missions;

(f) The same immunities and facilities in respect of their personal baggage as are accorded to diplomatic envoys, and also;

(g) Such other privileges, immunities and facilities not inconsistent with the foregoing as diplomatic envoys enjoy, except that they shall have no right to claim exemption from customs duties on goods imported (otherwise than as part of their personal baggage) or from excise duties or sales taxes.

Section 12

In order to secure, for the representatives of Members to the principal and subsidiary organs of the United Nations and to conferences convened by the United Nations, complete freedom of speech and independance [sic] in the discharge of their duties, the immunity from legal process in respect of words spoken or written and all acts done by them in discharging their duties shall continue to be accorded, notwithstanding that the persons concerned are no longer the representatives of Members.

Section 13

Where the incidence of any form of taxation depends upon residence, periods during which the representatives of Members to the principal and subsidiary organs of the United Nations and to conferences convened by the United Nations are present in a state for the discharge of their duties shall not be considered as periods of residence.

Section 14

Privileges and immunities are accorded to the representatives of Members not for the personal benefit of the individuals themselves, but in order to safeguard the independent exercise of their functions in connection with the United Nations. Consequently a Member not only has the right but is under a duty to waive the immunity of its representative in any case where in the opinion of the Member the immunity would impede the course of justice, and it can be waived without prejudice to the purpose for which the immunity is accorded.

Section 15

The provisions of Sections 11, 12 and 13 are not applicable as between a representative and the authorities of the state of which he is a national or of which he is or has been the representative.

Section 16

In this article the expression "representatives" shall be deemed to include all delegates, deputy delegates, advisers, technical experts and secretaries of delegations.

Article V – *Officials*

Section 17

The Secretary-General will specify the categories of officials to which the provisions of this Article and Article VII shall apply. He shall submit these categories to the General Assembly. Thereafter these categories shall be communicated to the Governments of all Members. The names of the officials included in these categories shall from time to time be made known to the Governments of Members.

Section 18

Officials of the United Nations shall:

(a) Be immune from legal process in respect of words spoken or written and all acts performed by them in their official capacity;
(b) Be exempt from taxation on the salaries and emoluments paid to them by the United Nations;
(c) Be immune from national service obligations;
(d) Be immune, together with their spouses and relatives dependent on them, from immigration restrictions and alien registration;
(e) Be accorded the same privileges in respect of exchange facilities as are accorded to the officials of comparable ranks forming part of diplomatic missions to the Government concerned;
(f) Be given, together with their spouses and relatives dependent on them, the same repatriation facilities in time of international crisis as diplomatic envoys;
(g) Have the right to import free of duty their furniture and effects at the time of first taking up their post in the country in question.

Section 19

In addition to the immunities and privileges specified in Section 18, the Secretary-General and all Assistant Secretaries-General shall be accorded in respect of themselves, their spouses and minor children, the privileges and immunities, exemptions and facilities accorded to diplomatic envoys, in accordance with international law.

Section 20

Privileges and immunities are granted to officials in the interests of the United Nations and not for the personal benefit of the individuals themselves. The Secretary-General shall have the right and the duty to waive the immunity of any official in any case where, in his opinion, the immunity would impede the course of justice and can be waived without prejudice to the interests of the United Nations. In the case of the Secretary-General, the Security Counsil [sic] shall have the right to waive immunity.

Section 21

The United Nations shall co-operate at all times with the appropriate authorities of Members to facilitate the proper administration of justice, secure the observance of police regulations and prevent the occurrence of any abuse in connection with the privileges, immunities and facilities mentioned in this Article.

Article VI – Experts on Missions for the United Nations

Section 22

Experts (other than officials coming within the scope of Article V) performing missions for the United Nations shall be accorded such privileges and immunities as are necessary for the independent exercise of their functions during the period of their missions, including the time spent on journeys in connection with their missions. In particular they shall be accorded:

(a) Immunity from personal arrest or detention and from seizure of their personal baggage;

(b) In respect of words spoken or written and acts done by them in the course of the performance of their mission, immunity from legal process of every kind. This immunity from legal process shall continue to be accorded notwithstanding that the persons concerned are no longer employed on missions for the United Nations;

(c) Inviolability for all papers and documents;

(d) For the purpose of their communications with the United Nations, the right to use codes and to receive papers or correspondence by courier or in sealed bags;

(e) The Same [sic] facilities in respect of currency or exchange restrictions as are accorded to representatives of foreign governments on temporary official missions;

(f) The same immunities and facilities in respect of their personal baggage as are accorded to diplomatic envoys.

Section 23

Privileges and immunities are granted to experts in the interests of the United Nations and not for the personal benefit of the individuals themselves. The Secretary-General shall have the right and the duty to waive the immunity of any expert in any case where, in his opinion, the immunity would impede the course of justice and it can be waived without prejudice to the interests of the United Nations.

Article VII – United Nations Laissez-Passer

Section 24

The United Nations may issue United Nations laissez-passer to its officials. These laissez-passer shall be recognized and accepted as valid travel documents by the authorities of Members, taking into account the provisions of Section 25.

Section 25

Applications for visas (where required) from the holders of United Nations laissez-passer, when accompanied by a certificate that they are travelling on the business of the United Nations, shall be dealt with as speedily as possible. In addition, such persons shall be granted facilities for speedy travel.

Section 26

Similar facilities to those specified in Section 25 shall be accorded to experts and other persons who, though not the holders of United Nations laissez-passer, have a certificate that they are travelling on the business of the United Nations.

...

Article VIII – Settlement of Disputes

Section 29

The United Nations shall make provisions for appropriate modes of settlement of:

(a) Disputes arising out of contracts or other disputes of a private law character to which the United Nations is a party;

(b) Disputes involving any official of the United Nations who by reason of his official position enjoys immunity, if immunity has not been waived by the Secretary-General.

Section 30

All differences arising out of the interpretation or application of the present convention shall be referred to the International Court of Justice, unless in any case it is agreed by the parties to have recourse to another mode of settlement. If a difference arises between the United Nations on the one hand and a Member on the other hand, a request shall be made for an advisory opinion on any legal question involved in accordance with Article 96 of the Charter and Article 65 of the Statute of the Court. The opinion given by the Court shall be accepted as decisive by the parties.

Final Article

...

Section 36

The Secretary-General may conclude with any Member or Members supplementary agreements adjusting the provisions of this convention so far as that Member or those Members are concerned. These supplementary agreements shall in each case be subject to the approval of the General Assembly.

B. Third-Party Liability

22

Third-Party Liability: Temporal and Financial Limitations

Prefatory Note

The General Assembly adopted resolution 52/247 on 'Third-party liability: temporal and financial limitations' on 26 June 1998.[1] The resolution sets temporal and financial limitations on the liability of the UN to third parties resulting or arising from incidents that occur during UN peace operations. Specifically, the resolution sets out a regime for dealing with third-party claims against the UN for 'personal injury, illness or death, and for property loss or damage ... resulting from or attributable to the activities of members of peacekeeping operations in the performance of their official duties'.[2] Liability, however, will not arise in situations where a third-party claim results from, or is, attributable to acts of peacekeepers arising from 'operational necessity'.[3]

The UN can incur liabilities in relation to third parties as it has an international legal personality. The UN Office of Legal Affairs (OLA) stated in 2001 that:

> as an attribute of the international legal and juridical personality of the United Nations, it is established that the Organization is capable of incurring obligations and liabilities of a private law nature.[4]

The UN has immunity from all legal process under Article II, Section 2 of the Convention on Privileges and Immunities of the United Nations (General Convention)[5] unless it expressly waives such immunity. However, pursuant to Section 29 of the General Convention, the UN should make provisions for the settlement of '[d]isputes arising out of contracts or other disputes of a private law character to which the United Nations is a party'. The UN has interpreted Section 29 to mean that such claims are limited to 'disputes of the type that arise between two *private* parties'.[6] The Secretary-General has argued that 'claims "based on political or policy-related grievances," such as those "related to actions or decisions taken by the Security Council or the General Assembly", are excluded from the scope of any obligation to provide an appropriate mode of settlement'.[7]

The UN has accepted its responsibility to pay compensation to third parties in UN peace operations since the First United Nations Emergency Force in the Middle East (UNEF I) in 1956,[8] and the United Nations Operation in the Congo (ONUC) in 1960. The UN settled several claims by Belgian nationals arising from the operations of ONUC.[9] A letter from the Acting Permanent Representative

1 GA Res 52/247 of 26 June 1998.

2 Ibid, Operative Part [5].

3 Ibid, Operative Part [6].

4 UN Juridical Yearbook 2001, 381–5, 381, 'Payment of settlement claims—Liabilities of private law nature—Procedures for settlement—Budget considerations', 23 February 2001.

5 See ch 21 above.

6 Letter from Assistant Secretary-General, Senior Coordinator for Cholera Response to Ms Farha, Mr Gallon, Mr Puras, and Ms de Albuquerque, 25 November 2014, [87] <https://spdb.ohchr.org/hrdb/28th/Haiti_ASG_25.11.14_(3.2014).pdf> accessed 9 August 2018 (emphasis added).

7 Ibid, [89].

8 See 'Report of the Secretary-General: United Nations Emergency Force: Summary Study of the Experience derived from the Establishment and Operation of the Force', UN Doc A/3943, 9 October 1958, [141]–[143].

9 See UN Juridical Yearbook 1965, 39–42 reproducing the 'Exchange of letters constituting an Agreement between the United Nations and Belgium relating to the settlement of claims filed against the United Nations in the Congo by Belgian nationals, New York, 20 February 1965'.

of the Union of Soviet Socialist Republics addressed to the Secretary-General indicated that the UN should not pay these claims and that the Secretary-General did not have the authority in any case to make these payments without authorisation from the Security Council.[10] In response to this letter, the Secretary-General replied:

> It has always been the policy of the United Nations, acting through the Secretary-General, to compensate individuals who have suffered damages for which the Organization was legally liable. This policy is in keeping with generally recognized legal principles and with the Convention on Privileges and Immunities of the United Nations. In addition ... it is reinforced ... by considerations of equity and humanity which the United Nations cannot ignore.[11]

The OLA has also stated that:

> As a subsidiary organ of the United Nations, an act of a peacekeeping force is, in principle, imputable to the Organization, and if committed in violation of an international obligation entails the international responsibility of the Organization and its liability in compensation.[12]

Therefore, although the General Assembly has the authority under Article 17 of the UN Charter,[13] 'it has no alternative but to honour obligations incurred by the Organization'.[14]

The 1990 model Status-of-Forces Agreement (model SOFA)[15] between the UN and host countries includes a standard clause outlining the appropriate mode of settlement for claims arising in a UN peace operation.[16] The standard clause provides that the UN and the host country shall settle disputes by means of a standing claims commission established for that purpose.[17] In practice, the commissions have never been set up and such claims are settled through internal claims review boards established by the UN.

In 1996, the General Assembly's Advisory Committee on Administrative and Budgetary Questions (ACABQ), concerned that third-party claims against the UN were estimated at $15.5 million[18] asked the Secretary-General to

> develop and propose ... appropriate measures and procedures that would provide for a simple, efficient and prompt settlement of third-party claims, secure United Nations interests, limit its liabilities and allow for a coordinated approach to the issue on the part of the United Nations organizations, agencies and programmes.[19]

The General Assembly endorsed that request in resolution 50/235 and instructed the Secretary-General to 'develop revised cost estimates for third-party claims and adjustments, following completion of the thorough study to be completed by the Legal Counsel'.[20] The Secretary-General's 1996 report, submitted pursuant to resolution 50/235, distinguished between

> the tortious liability of the Organization for damage in the ordinary operation of the force regardless of the type of operation and its liability for combat-related damage whether in the course of a Chapter VII operation or in a peacekeeping operation where force has been used in self-defence.[21]

In that report, the Secretary-General also identified that the UN's most commonly incurred liability was for activities relating to 'non-consensual use and occupancy of premises, personal injury and

---

10 Ibid, 40, footnote 26, reproducing the 'Letter dated 2 August 1965 from the Acting Permanent Representative of the Union of Soviet Socialist Republics addressed to the Secretary-General', UN Doc S/6589, 2 August 1965.

11 Ibid.

12 UN Juridical Yearbook 2004, 352–6, 354, 'Interoffice memorandum to the Director of Codification Division, Office of Legal Affairs and Secretary of the International Law Commitssion regarding the topic Responsibility of International Organizations', 3 February 2004.

13 See ch 1.

14 UN Juridical Yearbook 2001, 381–5, 383, 'Payment of settlement claims—Liabilities of private law nature—Procedures for settlement—Budget considerations', 23 February 2001.

15 See ch 2 above.

16 'Report of the Secretary-General on the Model Status-of-Forces Agreement for Peace-keeping Operations', UN Doc A/45/594, 9 October 1990, [51].

17 Ibid.

18 'Report of the Secretary-General: Financing of the United Nations Protection Force, the United Nations Confidence Restoration Operation in Croatia, the United Nations Preventive Deployment Force and the United Nations Peace Forces Headquarters; Administrative and Budgetary Aspects of the Financing of the United Nations Peacekeeping Operations: Financing of the United Nations Peacekeeping Operations', UN Doc A/51/389, 20 September 1996, Summary (hereafter Secretary-General's Report: Financing the United Nations Peacekeeping Operations).

19 Ibid, [1].

20 GA Res 50/235 of 7 June 1996, Operative Part [16].

21 Secretary-General's Report: Financing the United Nations Peacekeeping Operations (n 18), [4].

property loss or damage arising from the ordinary operation of the force, and such injury and damage as result from combat operations'.[22]

In relation to damage resulting from non-consensual use and occupancy of privately owned property the Secretary-General stated that the organisation was not exempted from paying adequate compensation.[23] However, in relation to State-owned property, pursuant to Paragraph 16 of the model SOFA, the State need not be compensated if the property is used temporarily.[24]

On the topic of property loss and damage caused by UN forces during ordinary operations, the Secretary-General concluded that the liability of the UN is subject to the exception of 'operational necessity', that is, where damage results from necessary actions taken by a peacekeeping force in carrying out its operations in pursuance of its mandates.[25]

The report also outlines what must be considered in deciding whether 'operational necessity' applies. The Secretary-General, noting that what constitutes 'operational necessity' must be considered on a case by case basis, also added that the commander 'must attempt to strike a balance between the operational necessity of the force and the respect for private property'.[26] Some of the specific factors identified by the Secretary-General as relevant to deciding whether an act would be justified as 'operational necessity' included:

(a) There must be a good-faith conviction on the part of the force commander that an "operational necessity" exists;
(b) The operational need that prompted the action must be strictly necessary and not a matter of mere convenience or expediency. It must also leave little or no time for the commander to pursue another, less destructive option;
(c) The act must be executed in pursuance of an operational plan and not the result of a rash individual action;
(d) The damage caused should be proportional to what is strictly necessary in order to achieve the operational goal.[27]

The report further noted that exemption from liability for third-party claims due to 'operational necessity' is already applied in practice by claims review boards, but recommended that this should be formally incorporated into Paragraph 51 of the model SOFA.[28] Recent SOFAs have included a reference to 'operational necessity' in their equivalent to Paragraph 51. The doctrine of operational necessity as described above is now considered by the UN Secretariat as an example of *lex specialis* in the practice of the UN.[29] The report also recommended that the General Assembly consider applying temporal and financial limitations to third-party claims.

Having considered the Secretary-General's report, the General Assembly, in resolution 51/13, requested 'the Secretary-General to develop specific measures, including criteria and guidelines for implementing the principles outlined in his report'.[30] In the 1997 report submitted pursuant to resolution 51/13, the Secretary-General looked at the principle and scope of application of temporal and financial limitations and how these could be established in a legally binding manner.[31] The Secretary-General concluded that three things were necessary and sufficient to do this: a General Assembly resolution; a new liability clause in the model SOFA; and similar provisions in the terms of reference of the claims review board for each mission.[32]

---

22 Ibid, [3].
23 Ibid, [12].
24 Ibid.
25 Ibid, [13].
26 Ibid, [14].
27 Ibid.
28 Ibid, [15].
29 International Law Commission, 'Responsibility of International Organizations: Comments and Observations received from International Organizations', UN Doc A/CN4/637/Add1, 17 February 2011, 35.
30 GA Res 51/13 of 4 November 1996, Operative Part [2].
31 'Report of the Secretary-General: Administrative and Budgetary Aspects of the Financing of the United Nations Peacekeeping Operations: Financing of United Nations Peacekeeping Operations', UN Doc A/51/903, 21 May 1997 (hereafter Secretary-General's Report: Administrative and Budgetary Aspects).
32 Ibid, [38].

A General Assembly resolution is necessary to give the UN 'the legislative authority for limiting its liability vis-à-vis Member States'.[33] The power of the General Assembly to do this comes from its exclusive authority over the budget of the UN under Article 17 of the Charter. The International Court of Justice (ICJ) in *Certain Expenses of the United Nations (Article 17, Paragraph 2, of the Charter)* (Advisory Opinion) (*Certain Expenses Case*)[34] confirmed the exclusive power of the General Assembly over the budget of the UN. Article 17 is the only Article in the Charter which refers to budgetary authority and in Paragraph 1, it is the General Assembly which is given the power to consider and approve the budget of the organisation. However, a General Assembly resolution is only binding within the UN itself and a new clause in the SOFA between the UN and host country is required to bind the host country, by its express consent, to the financial and temporal limitations.[35] Recent SOFAs have included a new section titled 'Limitation of Liability of the United Nations', which incorporates the financial and temporal limitations and makes specific reference to General Assembly resolution 52/247. The temporal and financial limitations should also be 'included in the terms of reference of the local claims review boards as a basis for their jurisdiction'.[36] This ensures that the temporal and financial limits are binding between the UN and third-party claimants who 'institute proceedings before such boards'.[37]

Resolution 52/247, which was adopted on the advice of the Secretary-General,[38] approved the temporal and financial limitations that would apply to third-party claims against the UN for 'personal injury, illness or death, and for property loss or damage (including non-consensual use of premises) resulting from or attributable to the activities of members of peacekeeping operations in the performance of their official duties'.[39] This makes it clear that the UN only accepts liability for acts of peacekeepers 'in the performance of their official duties'.[40]

The matter of peacekeepers committing crimes while 'off-duty' has arisen several times. In such cases the UN Secretariat has, in a submission to the International Law Commission, advised that the UN might accept responsibility for such actions. The test proposed by the Secretariat focuses on the functions undertaken by the UN peacekeeper rather than their on/off-duty status.[41]

The General Assembly, in resolution 52/247, also endorsed:

> the views of the Secretary-General, reflected in paragraph 14 of his [1997] report, with regard to third-party claims resulting from gross negligence or wilful misconduct of the personnel provided by troop-contributing States for peacekeeping operations . . .[42]

Paragraph 14 of the Secretary-General's 1997 report states that:

> On the other hand, no financial limitations are proposed with regard to claims arising as a result of gross negligence or wilful misconduct. If such claims are established, the Organization would assume liability to compensate a third party, retaining the right to seek recovery from the individual or the troop-contributing State concerned. In the view of the Secretary-General, the Organization cannot limit its responsibility when a member of a peacekeeping operation, while performing his duties, has committed a wrongful act wilfully or with a criminal intent or because of gross negligence. But it is precisely because of that element of gross fault or wilful or criminal intent that the Organization is justified in seeking recovery from the individual or the troop-contributing State concerned. This approach is consistent with the prevailing practice in other fields of international law where limited liability is recognized for negligence, but is not applicable in cases of gross negligence.[43]

In these cases, the UN will assume liability to compensate the injured parties but retain the right to seek recovery of these monies from the individual or contributing State concerned. This is reflected

---

33 Ibid, [39].

34 See ch 35 below.

35 Secretary-General's Report: Administrative and Budgetary Aspects (n 31), [40].

36 Ibid, [41].

37 Ibid.

38 Ibid, [47].

39 GA Res 52/247 of 26 June 1998, Operative Part [5].

40 Ibid.

41 International Law Commission, 'Responsibility of International Organizations: Comments and Observations received from International Organizations', UN Doc A/CN4/637 Add1, 17 February 2011, 16. See also ch 24 below. For an older opinion on this matter see UN Juridical Yearbook 1986, 300–1, 300, on 'Liability of the United Nations for claims involving off-duty acts of members of peace-keeping forces—Determination of "off-duty" versus "on-duty" status', 23 July 1986.

42 GA Res 52/247 of 26 June 1998, Operative Part [7].

43 Secretary-General's Report: Administrative and Budgetary Aspects (n 31), [14].

in Article 9 of the model Memorandum of Understanding (model MOU) between the UN and contributing States.[44]

In relation to the term 'gross negligence' the OLA has advised that:

(a) "Gross negligence" is negligence of a very high degree involving wilfulness, recklessness or drunkenness and, in consequence, manifest disregard for the safety of life and property.

(b) It is necessary that all the facts of a case, including all mitigating circumstances, be considered.

(c) "Necessity" may excuse conduct that might otherwise be regarded as "gross negligence".

(d) Gross negligence should not be inferred *solely* from:

   (i) a failure to take a [sic] precautionary measures; or

   (ii) a violation of a rule of the road or traffic regulation or other directive although either of the above should be taken into account in reaching a determination.[45]

Some general examples of grossly negligent conduct are then given and include: racing of vehicles; using a vehicle to frighten someone; drink driving; as well as some real life examples from UN peace operations of gross negligence and negligence cases.[46] The matter of whether conduct amounts to gross negligence must therefore be assessed on a case-by-case basis.

No compensation is payable for third-party claims arising out of actions that are attributable to 'operational necessity'. In resolution 52/247, the General Assembly endorsed the exemption from liability due to 'operational necessity'.[47]

It also establishes a temporal limit as to when the UN will pay compensation.[48] In exceptional circumstances, the Secretary-General can accept claims falling outside this temporal limit.[49]

Resolution 52/247 also provides that in respect of third-party claims for personal injury, illness, or death, compensation is only payable for economic loss such as medical expenses, loss of earnings, and loss of financial support. Compensation is not payable for non-economic loss 'such as pain and suffering or moral anguish'.[50] The amount of compensation payable for these claims shall not exceed US$50,000.00 determined 'by reference to local compensation standards'.[51] In exceptional circumstances the Secretary-General can recommend to the General Assembly, for approval, a payout of more than US$50,000.00.[52]

In respect of third-party claims against the UN for property loss or damage, resolution 52/247 includes non-consensual use of premises, stating that compensation shall be based on criteria such as the fair rental value and the cost of repair.[53] In addition, in respect of third-party claims against the UN for loss or damage to personal property, compensation 'shall cover the reasonable costs of repair or replacement'.[54]

Finally, the General Assembly, in resolution 52/247, requested the Secretary-General to 'implement the present resolution in respect of the status-of-forces agreements'[55] and to 'ensure that the terms of reference of the local review boards include the temporal and financial limitations'.[56]

It should be noted that the UN is only liable to third parties for claims resulting or arising from UN peace operations where the conduct of the peacekeeping force is attributable to the UN. In UN-authorised peace operations, where the conduct is imputable to the State or States concerned, it is the responsibility of these States to settle any third-party claims. The OLA has explained that:

> The principle of attribution of the conduct of a peacekeeping force to the United Nations is premised on the assumption that the operation in question is conducted under United Nations command and

44 See ch 3 above.
45 UN Juridical Yearbook 1981, 165–6, 166 on '"Gross negligence" on the part of a staff member, resulting in damage to United Nations property – Criteria to be applied in determining whether gross negligence is involved', 30 June 1981.
46 Ibid.
47 GA Res 52/247 of 26 June 1998, Operative Part [6].
48 Ibid, Operative Part [8].
49 Ibid.
50 Ibid, Operative Part [9](b).
51 Ibid, Operative Part [9](d).
52 Ibid, Operative Part [9](e).
53 Ibid, Operative Part [10].
54 Ibid, Operative Part [11](a).
55 Ibid, Operative Part [12].
56 Ibid, Operative Part [13].

control, and thus having the legal status of a United Nations subsidiary organ. In authorized chapter VII operations conducted under national command and control, the conduct of the operation is imputable to the State or States conducting the operation. In joint operations, namely, those conducted by a United Nations peacekeeping operation and an operation conducted under national or regional command and control, international responsibility lies where effective command and control is vested and practically exercised.[57]

The resolution on third-party liability is considered by the UN Secretariat an example of *lex specialis*, and therefore is seen as prevailing 'over the duty to provide full reparation',[58] as provided for in the Articles on the Responsibility of International Organizations.[59]

Reference

Title	Third-party liability: temporal and financial limitations
Author	General Assembly
Adopted by	General Assembly (without a vote)
Date of Adoption	26 June 1998
Meeting	88th plenary meeting
Source	UN Doc A/RES/52/247
Full Text	<http://www.un.org/Docs/journal/asp/ws.asp?m=A/RES/52/247>[60]

General Assembly Resolution 52/247[61] Third-party liability: temporal and financial limitations

The General Assembly,

Recalling its resolution 51/13 of 4 November 1996 on third-party liability against the United Nations resulting or arising from peacekeeping operations conducted by the Organization, in which the Assembly requested the Secretary-General to develop specific measures, including criteria and guidelines for implementing the principles of temporal and financial limitations on the liability of the United Nations,

Having considered the report of the Secretary-General on third-party liability and the related report of the Advisory Committee on Administrative and Budgetary Questions,

1. *Takes note* of the report of the Secretary-General on third-party liability;
2. *Also takes note* of the observations contained in the report of the Advisory Committee on Administrative and Budgetary Questions;
3. *Endorses* the proposals of the Secretary-General for implementing the principles of temporal and financial limitations on the liability of the Organization;
4. *Also endorses* the recommendations of the Advisory Committee on Administrative and Budgetary Questions;

57 UN Juridical Yearbook 2004, 352–6, 355 on the 'Responsibility of International Organizations', 3 February 2004.

58 International Law Commission, 'Responsibility of International Organizations: Comments and Observations received from International Organizations', UN Doc A/CN4/637/Add1, 17 February 2011, [25](2).

59 International Law Commission, 'Draft Articles on the Responsibility of International Organizations, and Commentaries', submitted to the General Assembly as part of the work of UN Doc A/66/10, 3 October 2011.

60 Accessed 1 November 2017.

61 From Third-party liability: temporal and financial limitations, by General Assembly © 1998 United Nations. Reprinted with the permission of the United Nations.

5. *Decides* that the temporal and financial limitations set out in paragraphs 8 to 11 below shall apply to third-party claims against the Organization for personal injury, illness or death, and for property loss or damage (including non-consensual use of premises) resulting from or attributable to the activities of members of peacekeeping operations in the performance of their official duties, as described in paragraph 13 of the report of the Secretary-General;
6. *Endorses* the view of the Secretary-General that liability is not engaged in relation to third-party claims resulting from or attributable to the activities of members of peacekeeping operations arising from "operational necessity", as described in paragraph 14 of the first report of the Secretary-General on third-party liability;
7. *Also endorses* the views of the Secretary-General, reflected in paragraph 14 of his report, with regard to third-party claims resulting from gross negligence or wilful misconduct of the personnel provided by troop-contributing States for peacekeeping operations, and requests him to report on their implementation in the relevant performance reports;
8. *Decides* that, where the liability of the Organization is engaged in relation to third-party claims against the Organization resulting from peacekeeping operations, the Organization will not pay compensation in regard to such claims submitted after six months from the time the damage, injury or loss was sustained, or from the time it was discovered by the claimant, and in any event after one year from the termination of the mandate of the peacekeeping operation, provided that in exceptional circumstances, such as described in paragraph 20 of the report of the Secretary-General, the Secretary-General may accept for consideration a claim made at a later date;
9. *Decides also*, in respect of third-party claims against the Organization for personal injury, illness or death resulting from peacekeeping operations, that:
   (a) Compensable types of injury or loss shall be limited to economic loss, such as medical and rehabilitation expenses, loss of earnings, loss of financial support, transportation expenses associated with the injury, illness or medical care, legal and burial expenses;
   (b) No compensation shall be payable by the United Nations for non-economic loss, such as pain and suffering or moral anguish, as well as punitive or moral damages;
   (c) No compensation shall be payable by the United Nations for homemaker services and other such damages that, in the sole opinion of the Secretary-General, are impossible to verify or are not directly related to the injury or loss itself;
   (d) The amount of compensation payable for injury, illness or death of any individual, including for the types of loss and expenses described in subparagraph (*a*) above, shall not exceed a maximum of 50,000 United States dollars, provided, however, that within such limitation the actual amount is to be determined by reference to local compensation standards;
   (e) In exceptional circumstances, the Secretary-General may recommend to the General Assembly, for its approval, that the limitation of 50,000 dollars provided for in subparagraph (*d*) above be exceeded in a particular case if the Secretary-General, after carrying out the required investigation, finds that there are compelling reasons for exceeding the limitation;
10. *Decides further* in respect of third-party claims against the Organization for property loss or damage resulting from peacekeeping operations that:
   (*a*) Compensation for non-consensual use of premises shall either: (i) be calculated on the basis of the fair rental value, determined on the basis of the local rental market prices that prevailed prior to the deployment of the peacekeeping operation as established by the United Nations pre-mission technical survey team; or (ii) not exceed a maximum ceiling

amount payable per square metre or per hectare as established by the United Nations pre-mission technical survey team on the basis of available relevant information; the Secretary-General will decide on the appropriate method for calculating compensation payable for non-consensual use of premises at the conclusion of the pre-mission technical survey;

(*b*) Compensation for loss or damage to premises shall either: (i) be calculated on the basis of the equivalent of a number of months of the rental value, or a fixed percentage of the rental amount payable for the period of United Nations occupancy; or (ii) be set at a fixed percentage of the cost of repair; the Secretary-General will decide on the appropriate method for calculating compensation payable for loss or damage to premises at the conclusion of the pre-mission technical survey;

(*c*) No compensation shall be payable by the United Nations for loss or damages that, in the sole opinion of the Secretary-General, are impossible to verify or are not directly related to the loss of or damage to the premises;

11. *Decides* that:

(*a*) Compensation for loss or damage to personal property of third parties arising from the activities of the operation or in connection with the performance of official duties by its members shall cover the reasonable costs of repair or replacement;

(*b*) No compensation shall be payable by the United Nations for loss or damages that, in the sole opinion of the Secretary-General, are impossible to verify or are not directly related to the loss of or damage to the personal property;

12. *Requests* the Secretary-General to take the necessary measures to implement the present resolution in respect of the status-of-forces agreements in accordance with paragraph 40 of his report;

13. *Also requests* the Secretary-General to ensure that the terms of reference of the local review boards include the temporal and financial limitations on the liability of the Organization, as set out in paragraphs 8 to 11 above, and that those boards rely on those temporal and financial limitations as a basis for their jurisdiction and recommendations for compensation for third-party claims against the Organization resulting from its peacekeeping operations.

C. International Criminal Law

23

Rome Statute of the International Criminal Court

Prefatory Note

The Rome Statute of the International Criminal Court (Rome Statute)[1] seeks to ensure that the most serious crimes of concern to the international community as a whole do not go unpunished. Such crimes include genocide and war crimes such as attacks on peacekeepers. Article 1 of the Statute establishes the International Criminal Court (ICC).[2] The ICC is a permanent court with the capacity to try individuals for the crimes of aggression, crimes of genocide, crimes against humanity, and war crimes. It is a court of last resort and will not act if relevant cases are being genuinely investigated or prosecuted by a State with jurisdiction.

The creation of the ICC was influenced by the International Military Tribunals established post-WWII (termed the Nuremberg[3] and Tokyo[4] Tribunals). Other key influences were the ad hoc international criminal tribunals for the Former Yugoslavia[5] and Rwanda,[6] established by the Security Council in 1993 and 1994 respectively. The Rome Statute is based on the Draft Statute for an International Criminal Court, adopted by the International Law Commission (ILC) in 1994. Following the ILC's adoption of the Draft Statute, the General Assembly established a Preparatory Committee on the Establishment of an International Criminal Court, which, in turn, led to the Rome Conference at which the Rome Statute was adopted in 2002.[7]

The ICC has jurisdiction to try individuals for the most serious international crimes of concern to the international community committed after the Rome Statute's entry into force. The subject matter of these crimes is found in Part II of the Rome Statute, which defines genocide,[8] crimes against humanity,[9] war crimes,[10] and the crime of aggression.[11]

---

1 Rome Statute of the International Criminal Court (opened for signature 17 July 1998, entered into force 1 July 2002) 2187 UNTS 3 (hereafter Rome Statute).

2 Ibid, Article 1.

3 Agreement for the Prosecution and Punishment of the Major War Criminals of the European Axis Powers (signed and entered into force 8 August 1945) 82 UNTS 279.

4 Charter of the International Military Tribunal for the Far East (signed and entered into force 19 January 1946, amended 26 April 1948) 4 Bevans 20.

5 International Criminal Tribunal for the former Yugoslavia (ICTY), established by SC Res 827 (1993) of 25 May 1993. For more information, visit <http://www.icty.org/> accessed 1 November 2017.

6 International Criminal Tribunal for Rwanda (ICTR), established by SC Res 955 (1994) of 8 November 1994. For more information, visit <http://unictr.irmct.org/ /> accessed 1 November 2017.

7 Since the establishment of the ICC, several international and mixed criminal tribunals have been established. See, for example, the Extraordinary Chambers in the Courts of Cambodia (ECCC) which were set up by the government of Cambodia and the UN to try serious crimes committed during the rule of the Khmer Rouge from 1975 to 1979. For more information, visit <http://www.eccc.gov.kh/> accessed 1 November 2017. See also the Special Tribunal for Lebanon, which was set up to prosecute those persons responsible for the attack of 14 February 2005 that killed the former Lebanese Prime Minister Rafiq Hariri and related terrorism attacks. For more information, visit <http://www.stl-tsl.org/> accessed 1 November 2017. In 2016, the Security Council encouraged the Central African Republic authorities to operationalise the Special Criminal Court which the Republic had agreed to establish to deal with international crimes perpetrated in the Republic: see SC Res 2301 (2016) of 26 July 2016, Operative Part [10].

8 Rome Statute (n 1), Article 6.

9 Ibid, Article 7.

10 Ibid, Article 8.

11 See 'Draft resolution proposed by the Vice-Presidents of the Assembly Activation of the jurisdiction of the Court over the crime of aggression', ICC-ASP/16/L10, 14 December 2017 which was passed at the sixteenth session of the Assembly of State Parties meeting in New York. The ICC's jurisdiction of this crime will be activated as of 17 July 2018.

For the Court to exercise jurisdiction, Article 13 requires either a referral from a State Party, a referral from the Security Council, or the Prosecutor to initiate an investigation *proprio motu*.[12] Article 12 deals with the preconditions to the exercise of jurisdiction and requires either the acceptance of the ICC's jurisdiction by the State on whose territory the crime in question occurred, or by the State of the nationality of the accused.[13] If the case has been referred to the Court by the Security Council pursuant to Chapter VII, no State consent is required.[14] In addition, Article 12 allows non-State Parties to make a declaration to accept the jurisdiction of the Court, and States Parties to accept the jurisdiction of the Court over acts committed after entry into force of the Rome Statute generally, but before entry into force of the Rome Statute for the State concerned.

For those involved in peace operations these developments are important to understand both in relation to the mandate of specific missions and in relation to issues arising from immunity and privileges. The Negotiated Relationship Agreement between the International Criminal Court and the United Nations (Relationship Agreement)[15] includes a range of provisions in which the UN 'undertakes to cooperate with the Court'.[16] These include the provision of information and documentation, and the UN's principles concerning the release of documents which have been provided to the UN under an expectation of confidentiality.[17] The Relationship Agreement also deals with situations when the ICC seeks to exercise jurisdiction over individuals with immunity and privileges granted by the UN and notes that the UN undertakes '[t]o cooperate fully with the Court ... in particular by waiving any such privileges and immunities in accordance with the Convention on the Privileges and Immunities of the United Nations and the relevant rules of international law'.[18]

A Memorandum of Understanding between the UN and the ICC (ICC MOU) concerning cooperation between the UN Mission in the Democratic Republic of Congo (MONUC) and the ICC was signed in 2005,[19] and deals with issues such as cooperation and legal assistance, services, facilities, and support as well as security arrangements. A similar MOU was signed between the UN and the ICC concerning cooperation between the UN Operation in Côte d'Ivoire (UNOCI) and the Prosecutor of the ICC (UNOCI MOU).[20] In broad terms, the UNOCI MOU modalities for cooperation and assistance are founded on UNOCI's mandate 'to support national and international efforts to bring to justice perpetrators of grave violations of human rights and international humanitarian law in Côte d'Ivoire'.[21] Chapter III of that MOU addresses matters concerning cooperation and legal assistance to the Prosecutor and provides details concerning the following matters: the Prosecutor interviewing members of UNOCI;[22] testimony by members of UNOCI;[23] UNOCI assistance to trace witnesses;[24] preserved physical evidence;[25] and carrying out arrests, searches and seizures, and securing of crime scenes.[26]

The issue of the prosecution of peacekeepers, especially those from non-State Parties of the Rome Statute, was the subject of two Security Council resolutions. Resolution 1422 requested that:

> the ICC, if a case arises involving current or former officials or personnel from a contributing State not a Party to the Rome Statute over acts or omissions relating to a United Nations established or authorized operation, shall for a twelve-month period ... not commence or proceed with investigation or prosecution of any such case ...[27]

---

12 Under his or her own initiative.

13 The jurisdiction provisions relating to the crime of aggression are set out in the Rome Statute (n 1), Articles 15 *bis* and 15 *ter*.

14 In 2011, for example, the Security Council referred the situation in the Libyan Arab Jamahiriya to the Prosecutor of the ICC: see SC Res 1970 (2011) of 26 February 2011, Operative Part [4].

15 Negotiated Relationship Agreement between the International Criminal Court and the United Nations, UN Doc A/58/874, 10 April 2004, entered into force 22 July 2004.

16 Ibid, Article 15(1).

17 Ibid, Article 20.

18 Ibid, Article 19.

19 Reproduced in UN Juridical Yearbook 2005, 71–90, 'Memorandum of Understanding between the United Nations and International Criminal Court concerning cooperation between the United Nations Organization Mission in the Democratic Republic of the Congo (MONUC) and the International Criminal Court', 8 November 2005.

20 Reproduced in the UN Juridical Yearbook 2012, 78–96, 'Memorandum of Understanding between the United Nations and the International Criminal Court concerning cooperation between the United Nations Operation in Côte d'Ivoire (UNOCI) and the Prosecutor of the International Criminal Court', 23 January 2012.

21 Ibid, Preamble [5].

22 Ibid, Article 10.

23 Ibid, Article 11.

24 Ibid, Article 12.

25 Ibid, Article 14.

26 Ibid, Article 15.

27 SC Res 1422 (2002) of 12 July 2002, Operative Part [1].

Resolution 1487[28] renewed this request to the ICC for another 12 months starting 1 July 2003. There have been no further Security Council resolutions renewing this request, which lapsed in 2004.

In resolution 1593,[29] the Security Council referred the situation of Darfur to the ICC and made specific mention of the importance of cooperation by all States and regional and international organisations with the Court.[30] The Security Council also decided that personnel on UN-established or UN-authorised peace operations from contributing States not a party to the Rome Statute 'shall be subject to the exclusive jurisdiction of that contributing State'.[31]

Article 98 of the Rome Statute deals with the Court not proceeding with a request for the surrender of an individual into its jurisdiction if the surrender would require the requested State to 'act inconsistently with its obligations under international agreements'.[32] Such international agreements can include Status-of-Forces Agreements (SOFAs),[33] which often involve host countries granting immunity to UN personnel engaged in actions relevant to the mandate of specific missions. However, a Troop Contributing Country (TCC) that is a State Party to the Rome Statute would not be able to circumvent its obligations under the Rome Statute by claiming such immunities for its peacekeepers.

Peacekeepers have been mandated on occasion to assist the ICC in bringing individuals accused of war crimes and crimes against humanity to justice. The UN Organization Stabilization Mission in the Democratic Republic of the Congo (MONUSCO) was authorised to '[s]upport and work with the Government of the DRC to arrest and bring to justice those responsible for war crimes and crimes against humanity in the country, including through cooperation with States of the region and the ICC'.[34] A similar mandate was given to peacekeepers serving with the UN Multidimensional Integrated Stabilization Mission in the Central African Republic (MINUSCA).[35] Pursuant to that mandate MINUSCA supported and cooperated with the ICC in transferring Dominic Ongwen, an alleged commander in the Lord's Resistance Army, to the ICC.[36]

The UN had adopted a policy prohibiting non-essential contact with persons subject to an ICC warrant of arrest. Where peacekeepers must interact with persons who have been indicted by the ICC (in practice, those who have an ongoing role in the government of a host State), the OLA has emphasised that such interaction must be 'limited to what is strictly required for carrying out'[37] the peace operation's mandate. Such a restriction or limitation is important to avoid any allegation or perception of undermining the role of the ICC.

The Rome Statute is also relevant to peace operations in that the ICC has jurisdiction over the war crime of intentionally directing an attack 'against personnel, installations, material, units or vehicles involved in a humanitarian assistance or peacekeeping mission in accordance with the Charter of the United Nations, as long as they are entitled to the protection given to civilians or civilian objects under the international law of armed conflict'.[38] Such attacks are unlawful in both international and non-international armed conflicts. The ICC in the pre-trial hearings of cases against Nourain and Jamus,[39] and Garda,[40] concerning the combatant status of African Union peacekeepers, reinforced the conclusion of the Special Court for Sierra Leone (SCSL) that peacekeepers are civilians unless they are taking a direct part in hostilities.[41] The ICC also stated that in a non-international armed conflict, under customary international law, objects such as UN peacekeeping installations, materials, units, or vehicles:

---

28 SC Res 1487 (2003) of 12 June 2003.

29 SC Res 1593 (2005) of 31 March 2005.

30 Ibid, Operative Part [2].

31 Ibid, Operative Part [6].

32 Rome Statute (n 1), Article 98(2).

33 See ch 2 above.

34 SC Res 2147 (2014) of 28 March 2014, Operative Part [4](d).

35 SC Res 2301 (2016) of 26 July 2016, Operative Part [35](a)(iii); see also Operative Part [33](b)(i).

36 See International Criminal Court Press Release, 'Dominic Ongwen transferred to the Hague' 20 January 2015 <https://www.icc-cpi.int/pages/item.aspx?name=pr1084> accessed 31 December 2018.

37 Reproduced in the UN Juridical Yearbook 2006, 493–7, 494, 'Note to the Under-Secretary General for Political Affairs regarding activities of the Special Envoy in [Rebel Group]-affected areas', 31 August 2006.

38 Rome Statute (n 1), Articles 8(b)(iii) and 8(e)(iii).

39 *Prosecutor v Abdallah Banda Abakaer Nourain and Saleh Mohammed Jerbo Jamus* [2009] ICC-02/05-03/09.

40 *Prosecutor v Bahar Idriss Abu Garda* [2010] ICC-02/05-02/09 (hereafter *Garda*).

41 Ibid, [83]. For a more detailed discussion of the status of peacekeepers in armed conflict see chs 15–16 above.

shall be entitled to the protection given to civilian objects, unless and for such time as their nature, location, purpose or use make an effective contribution to the military action of a party to the conflict and insofar as their total or partial destruction, capture or neutralization, in the circumstances ruling at the time, offers a definite military advantage.[42]

The ICC Office of the Prosecutor has also sought to investigate attacks against non-UN peacekeepers. In 2015, the Office of the Prosecutor, pursuant to Article 15 of the Statute, sought authorisation to investigate attacks by South Ossetia forces and Georgian armed forces in August 2008.[43] Pursuant to that request the ICC, on 27 January 2016, authorised the Prosecutor to proceed with an investigation for the crimes within the ICC jurisdiction.[44]

Reference

Title	Rome Statute of the International Criminal Court
Date of Adoption	17 July 1998
Period for Signature	17 July 1998 to 31 December 2000
Entered into Force	1 July 2002 (in accordance with Article 126)
Signatories	138
Parties	123
Depository	United Nations
Treaty Series	2187 UNTS 3
Full Text	<https://www.icc-cpi.int/nr/rdonlyres/add16852-aee9-4757-abe7-9cdc7cf02886/283503/romestatuteng1.pdf >[45]

Rome Statute of the International Criminal Court[46]

(Extracts)

...

Part II – Jurisdiction, Admissibility and Applicable Law

Article 5 – Crimes within the jurisdiction of the Court

1. The jurisdiction of the Court shall be limited to the most serious crimes of concern to the international community as a whole. The Court has jurisdiction in accordance with this Statute with respect to the following crimes:
   (a) The crime of genocide;
   (b) Crimes against humanity;
   (c) War crimes;
   (d) The crime of aggression.

42 Ibid, [89].

43 Office of the Prosecutor, 'Situation in Georgia: Summary of Prosecution's Request for Authorisation of an Investigation Pursuant to Article 15', 13 October 2015 <https://www.icc-cpi.int/iccdocs/otp/Art_15_Application_Summary-ENG.pdf> accessed 1 November 2017.

44 International Criminal Court, 'ICC Pre-Trial Chamber I authorises the Prosecutor to open an investigation into the situation in Georgia, 27 January 2016 <https://www.icc-cpi.int/Pages/item.aspx?name=pr1183> accessed 1 November 2017.

45 Last visited 31 December 2018.

46 From Rome Statute of the International Criminal Court © 1998 United Nations. Reprinted with the permission of the United Nations.

2. The Court shall exercise jurisdiction over the crime of aggression once a provision is adopted in accordance with articles 121 and 123 defining the crime and setting out the conditions under which the Court shall exercise jurisdiction with respect to this crime. Such a provision shall be consistent with the relevant provisions of the Charter of the United Nations.

Article 6 – Genocide

For the purpose of this Statute, "genocide" means any of the following acts committed with intent to destroy, in whole or in part, a national, ethnical, racial or religious group, as such:

(a) Killing members of the group;
(b) Causing serious bodily or mental harm to members of the group;
(c) Deliberately inflicting on the group conditions of life calculated to bring about its physical destruction in whole or in part;
(d) Imposing measures intended to prevent births within the group;
(e) Forcibly transferring children of the group to another group.

Article 7 – Crimes against humanity

1. For the purpose of this Statute, "crime against humanity" means any of the following acts when committed as part of a widespread or systematic attack directed against any civilian population, with knowledge of the attack:
   (a) Murder;
   (b) Extermination;
   (c) Enslavement;
   (d) Deportation or forcible transfer of population;
   (e) Imprisonment or other severe deprivation of physical liberty in violation of fundamental rules of international law;
   (f) Torture;
   (g) Rape, sexual slavery, enforced prostitution, forced pregnancy, enforced sterilization, or any other form of sexual violence of comparable gravity;
   (h) Persecution against any identifiable group or collectivity on political, racial, national, ethnic, cultural, religious, gender as defined in paragraph 3, or other grounds that are universally recognized as impermissible under international law, in connection with any act referred to in this paragraph or any crime within the jurisdiction of the Court;
   (i) Enforced disappearance of persons;
   (j) The crime of apartheid;
   (k) Other inhumane acts of a similar character intentionally causing great suffering, or serious injury to body or to mental or physical health.
2. For the purpose of paragraph 1:
   (a) "Attack directed against any civilian population" means a course of conduct involving the multiple commission of acts referred to in paragraph 1 against any civilian population, pursuant to or in furtherance of a State or organizational policy to commit such attack;
   (b) "Extermination" includes the intentional infliction of conditions of life, inter alia the deprivation of access to food and medicine, calculated to bring about the destruction of part of a population;
   (c) "Enslavement" means the exercise of any or all of the powers attaching to the right of ownership over a person and includes the exercise of such power in the course of trafficking in persons, in particular women and children;

(d) "Deportation or forcible transfer of population" means forced displacement of the persons concerned by expulsion or other coercive acts from the area in which they are lawfully present, without grounds permitted under international law;

(e) "Torture" means the intentional infliction of severe pain or suffering, whether physical or mental, upon a person in the custody or under the control of the accused; except that torture shall not include pain or suffering arising only from, inherent in or incidental to, lawful sanctions;

(f) "Forced pregnancy" means the unlawful confinement of a woman forcibly made pregnant, with the intent of affecting the ethnic composition of any population or carrying out other grave violations of international law. This definition shall not in any way be interpreted as affecting national laws relating to pregnancy;

(g) "Persecution" means the intentional and severe deprivation of fundamental rights contrary to international law by reason of the identity of the group or collectivity;

(h) "The crime of apartheid" means inhumane acts of a character similar to those referred to in paragraph 1, committed in the context of an institutionalized regime of systematic oppression and domination by one racial group over any other racial group or groups and committed with the intention of maintaining that regime;

(i) "Enforced disappearance of persons" means the arrest, detention or abduction of persons by, or with the authorization, support or acquiescence of, a State or a political organization, followed by a refusal to acknowledge that deprivation of freedom or to give information on the fate or whereabouts of those persons, with the intention of removing them from the protection of the law for a prolonged period of time.

3. For the purpose of this Statute, it is understood that the term "gender" refers to the two sexes, male and female, within the context of society. The term "gender" does not indicate any meaning different from the above.

Article 8 – War crimes

1. The Court shall have jurisdiction in respect of war crimes in particular when committed as part of a plan or policy or as part of a large-scale commission of such crimes.

2. For the purpose of this Statute, "war crimes" means:

(a) Grave breaches of the Geneva Conventions of 12 August 1949, namely, any of the following acts against persons or property protected under the provisions of the relevant Geneva Convention:

(i) Wilful killing;

(ii) Torture or inhuman treatment, including biological experiments;

(iii) Wilfully causing great suffering, or serious injury to body or health;

(iv) Extensive destruction and appropriation of property, not justified by military necessity and carried out unlawfully and wantonly;

(v) Compelling a prisoner of war or other protected person to serve in the forces of a hostile Power;

(vi) Wilfully depriving a prisoner of war or other protected person of the rights of fair and regular trial;

(vii) Unlawful deportation or transfer or unlawful confinement;

(viii) Taking of hostages.

(b) Other serious violations of the laws and customs applicable in international armed conflict, within the established framework of international law, namely, any of the following acts:

(i) Intentionally directing attacks against the civilian population as such or against individual civilians not taking direct part in hostilities;

(ii) Intentionally directing attacks against civilian objects, that is, objects which are not military objectives;

(iii) Intentionally directing attacks against personnel, installations, material, units or vehicles involved in a humanitarian assistance or peacekeeping mission in accordance with the Charter of the United Nations, as long as they are entitled to the protection given to civilians or civilian objects under the international law of armed conflict;

(iv) Intentionally launching an attack in the knowledge that such attack will cause incidental loss of life or injury to civilians or damage to civilian objects or widespread, long-term and severe damage to the natural environment which would be clearly excessive in relation to the concrete and direct overall military advantage anticipated;

(v) Attacking or bombarding, by whatever means, towns, villages, dwellings or buildings which are undefended and which are not military objectives;

(vi) Killing or wounding a combatant who, having laid down his arms or having no longer means of defence, has surrendered at discretion;

(vii) Making improper use of a flag of truce, of the flag or of the military insignia and uniform of the enemy or of the United Nations, as well as of the distinctive emblems of the Geneva Conventions, resulting in death or serious personal injury;

(viii) The transfer, directly or indirectly, by the Occupying Power of parts of its own civilian population into the territory it occupies, or the deportation or transfer of all or parts of the population of the occupied territory within or outside this territory;

(ix) Intentionally directing attacks against buildings dedicated to religion, education, art, science or charitable purposes, historic monuments, hospitals and places where the sick and wounded are collected, provided they are not military objectives;

(x) Subjecting persons who are in the power of an adverse party to physical mutilation or to medical or scientific experiments of any kind which are neither justified by the medical, dental or hospital treatment of the person concerned nor carried out in his or her interest, and which cause death to or seriously endanger the health of such person or persons;

(xi) Killing or wounding treacherously individuals belonging to the hostile nation or army;

(xii) Declaring that no quarter will be given;

(xiii) Destroying or seizing the enemy's property unless such destruction or seizure be imperatively demanded by the necessities of war;

(xiv) Declaring abolished, suspended or inadmissible in a court of law the rights and actions of the nationals of the hostile party;

(xv) Compelling the nationals of the hostile party to take part in the operations of war directed against their own country, even if they were in the belligerent's service before the commencement of the war;

(xvi) Pillaging a town or place, even when taken by assault;

(xvii) Employing poison or poisoned weapons;

(xviii) Employing asphyxiating, poisonous or other gases, and all analogous liquids, materials or devices;

(xix) Employing bullets which expand or flatten easily in the human body, such as bullets with a hard envelope which does not entirely cover the core or is pierced with incisions;

(xx) Employing weapons, projectiles and material and methods of warfare which are of a nature to cause superfluous injury or unnecessary suffering or which are inherently indiscriminate in violation of the international law of armed conflict, provided that such weapons, projectiles and material and methods of warfare are the subject of a comprehensive prohibition and are included in an annex to this Statute, by an amendment in accordance with the relevant provisions set forth in articles 121 and 123;

(xxi) Committing outrages upon personal dignity, in particular humiliating and degrading treatment;

(xxii) Committing rape, sexual slavery, enforced prostitution, forced pregnancy, as defined in article 7, paragraph 2 (f), enforced sterilization, or any other form of sexual violence also constituting a grave breach of the Geneva Conventions;

(xxiii) Utilizing the presence of a civilian or other protected person to render certain points, areas or military forces immune from military operations;

(xxiv) Intentionally directing attacks against buildings, material, medical units and transport, and personnel using the distinctive emblems of the Geneva Conventions in conformity with international law;

(xxv) Intentionally using starvation of civilians as a method of warfare by depriving them of objects indispensable to their survival, including wilfully impeding relief supplies as provided for under the Geneva Conventions;

(xxvi) Conscripting or enlisting children under the age of fifteen years into the national armed forces or using them to participate actively in hostilities.

(c) In the case of an armed conflict not of an international character, serious violations of article 3 common to the four Geneva Conventions of 12 August 1949, namely, any of the following acts committed against persons taking no active part in the hostilities, including members of armed forces who have laid down their arms and those placed hors de combat by sickness, wounds, detention or any other cause:

(i) Violence to life and person, in particular murder of all kinds, mutilation, cruel treatment and torture;

(ii) Committing outrages upon personal dignity, in particular humiliating and degrading treatment;

(iii) Taking of hostages;

(iv) The passing of sentences and the carrying out of executions without previous judgement pronounced by a regularly constituted court, affording all judicial guarantees which are generally recognized as indispensable.

(d) Paragraph 2 (c) applies to armed conflicts not of an international character and thus does not apply to situations of internal disturbances and tensions, such as riots, isolated and sporadic acts of violence or other acts of a similar nature.

(e) Other serious violations of the laws and customs applicable in armed conflicts not of an international character, within the established framework of international law, namely, any of the following acts:

(i) Intentionally directing attacks against the civilian population as such or against individual civilians not taking direct part in hostilities;

(ii) Intentionally directing attacks against buildings, material, medical units and transport, and personnel using the distinctive emblems of the Geneva Conventions in conformity with international law;

(iii) Intentionally directing attacks against personnel, installations, material, units or vehicles involved in a humanitarian assistance or peacekeeping mission in accordance with the Charter of the United Nations, as long as they are entitled to the protection given to civilians or civilian objects under the international law of armed conflict;

(iv) Intentionally directing attacks against buildings dedicated to religion, education, art, science or charitable purposes, historic monuments, hospitals and places where the sick and wounded are collected, provided they are not military objectives;

(v) Pillaging a town or place, even when taken by assault;

(vi) Committing rape, sexual slavery, enforced prostitution, forced pregnancy, as defined in article 7, paragraph 2 (f), enforced sterilization, and any other form of sexual violence also constituting a serious violation of article 3 common to the four Geneva Conventions;

(vii) Conscripting or enlisting children under the age of fifteen years into armed forces or groups or using them to participate actively in hostilities;

(viii) Ordering the displacement of the civilian population for reasons related to the conflict, unless the security of the civilians involved or imperative military reasons so demand;

(ix) Killing or wounding treacherously a combatant adversary;

(x) Declaring that no quarter will be given;

(xi) Subjecting persons who are in the power of another party to the conflict to physical mutilation or to medical or scientific experiments of any kind which are neither justified by the medical, dental or hospital treatment of the person concerned nor carried out in his or her interest, and which cause death to or seriously endanger the health of such person or persons;

(xii) Destroying or seizing the property of an adversary unless such destruction or seizure be imperatively demanded by the necessities of the conflict;

(f) Paragraph 2 (e) applies to armed conflicts not of an international character and thus does not apply to situations of internal disturbances and tensions, such as riots, isolated and sporadic acts of violence or other acts of a similar nature. It applies to armed conflicts that take place in the territory of a State when there is protracted armed conflict between governmental authorities and organized armed groups or between such groups.

3. Nothing in paragraph 2 (c) and (e) shall affect the responsibility of a Government to maintain or re-establish law and order in the State or to defend the unity and territorial integrity of the State, by all legitimate means.

Article 9 – Elements of Crimes

1. Elements of Crimes shall assist the Court in the interpretation and application of articles 6, 7 and 8. They shall be adopted by a two-thirds majority of the members of the Assembly of States Parties.

2. Amendments to the Elements of Crimes may be proposed by:

   (a) Any State Party;

   (b) The judges acting by an absolute majority;

   (c) The Prosecutor.

Such amendments shall be adopted by a two-thirds majority of the members of the Assembly of States Parties.

3. The Elements of Crimes and amendments thereto shall be consistent with this Statute.

Article 10

Nothing in this Part shall be interpreted as limiting or prejudicing in any way existing or developing rules of international law for purposes other than this Statute.

Article 11 – Jurisdiction ratione temporis

1. The Court has jurisdiction only with respect to crimes committed after the entry into force of this Statute.
2. If a State becomes a Party to this Statute after its entry into force, the Court may exercise its jurisdiction only with respect to crimes committed after the entry into force of this Statute for that State, unless that State has made a declaration under article 12, paragraph 3.

Article 12 – Preconditions to the exercise of jurisdiction

1. A State which becomes a Party to this Statute thereby accepts the jurisdiction of the Court with respect to the crimes referred to in article 5.
2. In the case of article 13, paragraph (a) or (c), the Court may exercise its jurisdiction if one or more of the following States are Parties to this Statute or have accepted the jurisdiction of the Court in accordance with paragraph 3:
   (a) The State on the territory of which the conduct in question occurred or, if the crime was committed on board a vessel or aircraft, the State of registration of that vessel or aircraft;
   (b) The State of which the person accused of the crime is a national.
3. If the acceptance of a State which is not a Party to this Statute is required under paragraph 2, that State may, by declaration lodged with the Registrar, accept the exercise of jurisdiction by the Court with respect to the crime in question. The accepting State shall cooperate with the Court without any delay or exception in accordance with Part 9.

Article 13 – Exercise of jurisdiction

The Court may exercise its jurisdiction with respect to a crime referred to in article 5 in accordance with the provisions of this Statute if:

(a) A situation in which one or more of such crimes appears to have been committed is referred to the Prosecutor by a State Party in accordance with article 14;
(b) A situation in which one or more of such crimes appears to have been committed is referred to the Prosecutor by the Security Council acting under Chapter VII of the Charter of the United Nations; or
(c) The Prosecutor has initiated an investigation in respect of such a crime in accordance with article 15.

Article 14 – Referral of a situation by a State Party

1. A State Party may refer to the Prosecutor a situation in which one or more crimes within the jurisdiction of the Court appear to have been committed requesting the Prosecutor to investigate the situation for the purpose of determining whether one or more specific persons should be charged with the commission of such crimes.
2. As far as possible, a referral shall specify the relevant circumstances and be accompanied by such supporting documentation as is available to the State referring the situation.

Article 15 – Prosecutor

1. The Prosecutor may initiate investigations proprio motu on the basis of information on crimes within the jurisdiction of the Court.
2. The Prosecutor shall analyse the seriousness of the information received. For this purpose, he or she may seek additional information from States, organs of the United Nations, intergovernmental or non-governmental organizations, or other reliable sources that he or she deems appropriate, and may receive written or oral testimony at the seat of the Court.
3. If the Prosecutor concludes that there is a reasonable basis to proceed with an investigation, he or she shall submit to the Pre-Trial Chamber a request for authorization of an investigation,

together with any supporting material collected. Victims may make representations to the Pre-Trial Chamber, in accordance with the Rules of Procedure and Evidence.

4. If the Pre-Trial Chamber, upon examination of the request and the supporting material, considers that there is a reasonable basis to proceed with an investigation, and that the case appears to fall within the jurisdiction of the Court, it shall authorize the commencement of the investigation, without prejudice to subsequent determinations by the Court with regard to the jurisdiction and admissibility of a case.
5. The refusal of the Pre-Trial Chamber to authorize the investigation shall not preclude the presentation of a subsequent request by the Prosecutor based on new facts or evidence regarding the same situation.
6. If, after the preliminary examination referred to in paragraphs 1 and 2, the Prosecutor concludes that the information provided does not constitute a reasonable basis for an investigation, he or she shall inform those who provided the information. This shall not preclude the Prosecutor from considering further information submitted to him or her regarding the same situation in the light of new facts or evidence.

Article 16 – Deferral of investigation or prosecution

No investigation or prosecution may be commenced or proceeded with under this Statute for a period of 12 months after the Security Council, in a resolution adopted under Chapter VII of the Charter of the United Nations, has requested the Court to that effect; that request may be renewed by the Council under the same conditions.

...

Article 20 – Ne bis in idem

1. Except as provided in this Statute, no person shall be tried before the Court with respect to conduct which formed the basis of crimes for which the person has been convicted or acquitted by the Court.
2. No person shall be tried by another court for a crime referred to in article 5 for which that person has already been convicted or acquitted by the Court.
3. No person who has been tried by another court for conduct also proscribed under article 6, 7 or 8 shall be tried by the Court with respect to the same conduct unless the proceedings in the other court:
   (a) Were for the purpose of shielding the person concerned from criminal responsibility for crimes within the jurisdiction of the Court; or
   (b) Otherwise were not conducted independently or impartially in accordance with the norms of due process recognized by international law and were conducted in a manner which, in the circumstances, was inconsistent with an intent to bring the person concerned to justice.

Article 21 – Applicable law

1. The Court shall apply:
   (a) In the first place, this Statute, Elements of Crimes and its Rules of Procedure and Evidence;
   (b) In the second place, where appropriate, applicable treaties and the principles and rules of international law, including the established principles of the international law of armed conflict;
   (c) Failing that, general principles of law derived by the Court from national laws of legal systems of the world including, as appropriate, the national laws of States that would normally exercise jurisdiction over the crime, provided that those principles are not

inconsistent with this Statute and with international law and internationally recognized norms and standards.

2. The Court may apply principles and rules of law as interpreted in its previous decisions.
3. The application and interpretation of law pursuant to this article must be consistent with internationally recognized human rights, and be without any adverse distinction founded on grounds such as gender as defined in article 7, paragraph 3, age, race, colour, language, religion or belief, political or other opinion, national, ethnic or social origin, wealth, birth or other status.

...

Part IX – International cooperation and judicial assistance

...

Article 98 – Cooperation with respect to waiver of immunity and consent to surrender

1. The Court may not proceed with a request for surrender or assistance which would require the requested State to act inconsistently with its obligations under international law with respect to the State or diplomatic immunity of a person or property of a third State, unless the Court can first obtain the cooperation of that third State for the waiver of the immunity.
2. The Court may not proceed with a request for surrender which would require the requested State to act inconsistently with its obligations under international agreements pursuant to which the consent of a sending State is required to surrender a person of that State to the Court, unless the Court can first obtain the cooperation of the sending State for the giving of consent for the surrender.

...

D. Articles on the Responsibility of International Organizations

24

Articles on the Responsibility of International Organizations

Prefatory Note

The Articles on the Responsibility of International Organizations (ARIO)[1] address wrongful acts of an international organisation and the consequences of those acts or omissions in international law. They are therefore relevant to organisations such as the UN and to its subsidiary organs including UN peace operations (i.e. those that are commanded and controlled by the UN). In relation to UN peace operations, there are several pertinent issues addressed by the ARIO and their accompanying commentaries. These issues include the circumstances in which the conduct of the peace operation or a peacekeeper will be attributable to the UN, the legal responsibility of the UN in connection with an act of another State or international organisation, and the application of the principles of reparation for injury.

The International Law Commission (ILC) was established in 1947 by the General Assembly[2] to promote the 'progressive development of international law and its codification'.[3] In 2000, the ILC proposed to include the topic 'responsibility of international organisations' in its programme of long-term works and, in resolution 56/82 of 12 December 2001, the General Assembly requested the ILC to begin its work on this topic.[4] The ILC commenced its work in 2003, and concluded in 2011 when it adopted the Draft Articles.[5] The Draft Articles and commentaries were submitted to the General Assembly and, in resolution 66/100, the Assembly took note of the ARIO 'with a view to examining, inter alia, the question of the form that might be given to the articles'.[6] The final version of the ARIO with their commentaries are annexed to resolution 66/100. At the time of writing this edition, the ARIO have not been adopted by States nor have they been the subject of intergovernmental negotiations, but are nonetheless considered persuasive on the responsibility of international organisations.[7]

When the ILC was developing the Draft Articles, the UN Secretariat made submissions in relation to its practice and understanding of the law applicable to the attribution of conduct to the UN. The submissions included matters such as attribution to the UN for the conduct of peacekeepers; the conduct of organs or agents working in conjunction with the UN; the distinction between 'binding' and 'authorising' resolutions of the UN;[8] self-defence; necessity; reparations; and *lex specialis*. What

1 GA Res 66/100 of 9 December 2011, (hereafter ARIO).

2 For more details about the ILC, see <http://legal.un.org/ilc/> accessed 1 November 2017.

3 Statute of the International Law Commission 1947 as adopted by the General Assembly in resolution 174 (II) of 21 November 1947 Article 1(1), as amended by resolutions 485 (V) of 12 December 1950, 984 (X) of 3 December 1955, 985 (X) of 3 December 1955 and 36/39 of 18 November 1981.

4 GA Res 56/82 of 18 January 2002, Operative Part [8].

5 For more details concerning the development of the ILC's work on the topic of responsibility of international organisations see <http://legal.un.org/ilc/summaries/9_11.shtml> accessed 1 November 2017.

6 ARIO (n 1), Operative Part [4].

7 For the views of several states and international organisations concerning the persuasiveness of the Draft Articles see 'Report of the Secretary-General: Responsibility of International Organisations: Comments and Information received from Governments and International Organizations', UN Doc A/72/80, 26 April 2017.

8 See the Introduction to this book and ch 1 above for further discussion concerning 'binding' and 'authorising' resolutions.

follows here are excerpts from the submissions made by the UN on the attribution of responsibility, *ultra vires* conduct, and *lex specialis*. The focus on the UN's submissions is necessary to better understand how the UN might view the application of the ARIO to UN peacekeeping operations.

Article 7 concerns the conduct of the organs of a State, or organs or agents of an international organisation placed at the disposal of another international organisation, and reaffirms that, in such cases, the acts of the organs or agents are considered the acts of the latter organisation, if that organisation exercises 'effective control'. The commentary accompanying this Article makes it quite clear that the doctrine of effective control is particularly important in applying principles of attribution in situations where military contingents are placed at the disposal of the UN or where the UN undertakes operations with another international organisation. Based on the submissions made by the UN Secretariat it is clear that the doctrine of effective control is controversial.

In relation to the attribution of acts of UN operations to the UN, the UN Secretariat made a detailed submission in 2004 and a further submission in 2011. Both submissions argued for a test of 'effective command and control' for the attribution of conduct to the UN, rather than the test that was settled upon by the ILC, namely that of 'effective control'.

The 2004 submission reinforces that UN peace operations are subsidiary organs of the UN, and that the attribution of the conduct of a peacekeeping force to the UN or to a contributing State is determined by the legal status of the force. The full submission follows:

1. The question of attribution of the conduct of a peacekeeping force to the United Nations or to contributing States is determined by the legal status of the force, the agreements between the United Nations and contributing States and their opposability to third States.
2. A United Nations peacekeeping force established by the Security Council or the General Assembly is a subsidiary organ of the United Nations. Members of the military personnel placed by Member States under United Nations command, although remaining in their national service, are, for the duration of their assignment to the force, considered international personnel under the authority of the United Nations and subject to the instructions of the force commander. The functions of the force are exclusively international and members of the force are bound to discharge their functions with the sole interest of the United Nations in view. The peacekeeping operation as a whole is subject to the executive direction and control of the Secretary-General, under the overall direction of the Council or the Assembly, as the case may be.
3. As a subsidiary organ of the United Nations, an act of a peacekeeping force is, in principle, imputable to the Organization, and, if committed in violation of an international obligation, entails the international responsibility of the Organization and its liability in compensation. The fact that any such act may have been performed by members of a national military contingent forming part of the peacekeeping operation does not affect the international responsibility of the United Nations *vis-à-vis* third States or individuals.
4. Agreements concluded between the United Nations and States contributing troops to the Organization contain a standard clause on third-party liability delineating the respective responsibilities of the Organization and contributing States for loss, damage, injury or death caused by the personnel or equipment of the contributing State. Article 9 of the Model Memorandum of Understanding between the United Nations and [participating State] contributing resources to [the United Nations Peacekeeping Operation] provides in this regard:

   The United Nations will be responsible for dealing with any claims by third parties where the loss of or damage to their property, or death or personal injury, was caused by the personnel or equipment provided by the Government in the performance of services or any other activity or operation under this Memorandum. However, if the loss, damage, death or injury arose from gross negligence or wilful misconduct of the personnel provided by the Government, the Government will be liable for such claims.[9]

5. While the agreements between the United Nations and contributing States divide the responsibility in the relationship between them, they are not opposable to third States. *Vis-à-vis* third States and

9 The footnote accompanying this quote states:

A similar provision is contained in article 6 of the Memorandum of agreement used by the Organization to obtain gratis personnel (ST/AI/1999/6), annex. It reads:

"The United Nations shall be responsible for dealing with claims by third parties where the loss of or damage to their property, or death or personal injury, was caused by the actions or omissions of the ... personnel in the performance of services to the United Nations under the agreement with the Government. However, if the loss, damage, death or injury arose from gross negligence or wilful misconduct of the ... personnel provided by the donor, the Government shall be liable to the United Nations for all amounts paid by the United Nations to the claimants and all costs incurred by the United Nations in settling such claims." [Note: this footnote appears in the original as footnote '10'].

individuals, therefore, where the international responsibility of the Organization is engaged, liability in compensation is, in the first place, entailed for the United Nations, which may then revert to the contributing State concerned and seek recovery on the basis of the agreement between them.

6. The principle of attribution of the conduct of a peacekeeping force to the United Nations is premised on the assumption that the operation in question is conducted under United Nations command and control, and thus has the legal status of a United Nations subsidiary organ. In Chapter VII-authorized operations conducted under national command and control, the conduct of the operation is imputable to the State or States conducting the operation. In joint operations, namely, those conducted by a United Nations peacekeeping operation and an operation conducted under national or regional command and control, international responsibility lies where *effective* command and control is vested and practically exercised.[10]

The 2011 submission from the Secretariat on the matter of attribution reinforces the 'effective command and control test' and explains the UN's views concerning attribution when the UN authorises another international organisation or State to undertake peace operations. The submission explains:

> 2. In the practice of the United Nations a clear distinction is made between two kinds of military operations: (a) United Nations operations conducted under United Nations command and control, and (b) United Nations-authorized operations conducted under national or regional command and control. *United Nations operations* conducted under United Nations command and control are subsidiary organs of the United Nations. They are accountable to the Secretary-General under the political direction of the Security Council. *United Nations-authorized operations* are conducted under national or regional command and control, and while authorized by the Security Council they are independent of the United Nations or the Security Council in the conduct and funding of the operation. Having *authorized* the operation, the Security Council does not ***control*** any aspect of the operation, nor does it monitor it for its duration. Its role following the authorization of the operation is limited to receiving periodic reports through the lead nation or organization conducting the operation.
>
> 3. In determining the attributability of an act or an omission of members of a military operation to the United Nations, the Organization has been guided by the principle of "command and control" over the operation or the action in question. Its position on the scope of its responsibility for the operational activities of military operations, including for combat-related activities, was set out in the report of the Secretary-General on the financing of the United Nations Protection Force and other peacekeeping operations, according to which:[11]
>
> "17. The international responsibility of the United Nations for combat-related activities of United Nations forces is premised on the assumption that the operation in question is under the exclusive command and control of the United Nations. Where a Chapter VII-authorized operation is conducted under national command and control, international responsibility for the activities of the force is vested in the State or States conducting the operation. [. . .]
>
> 18. In joint operations, international responsibility for the conduct of the troops lies where operational command and control is vested according to the arrangements establishing the modalities of cooperation between the State or States providing the troops and the United Nations. In the absence of formal arrangements between the United Nations and the State or States providing troops, responsibility would be determined in each and every case according to the degree of effective control exercised by either party in the conduct of the operation."
>
> 4. Questions about attribution of responsibility to a United Nations or a United Nations-authorized operation have arisen in the practice of the United Nations in only two cases: the operation in the Republic of Korea, and the Somalia operation. But while the operation in the Republic of Korea was conducted under national command and control, in the case of Somalia, the simultaneous or consecutive deployment of two operations—a United Nations and a United Nations-authorized operation—and the proximity in time and place between the two have given rise to questions about attribution of responsibility for damage or injury caused in the course of either operation.
>
> . . .
>
> 7. The practical arrangements put in place for settling third-party claims in Somalia, where multiple operations were conducted sequentially or simultaneously, reflects the principle that each State or

10 The referenced footnote states: 'See the report of the Secretary-General on financing United Nations peacekeeping operations (A/51/389), paras. 17–18. See also the annex to the present report, attachment No. 80.' See International Law Commission, 'Responsibility of International Organisations: Comments and Observations received from International Organizations', UN Doc A/CN4/545, 25 June 2004, 28.

11 A/51/389. [Note: this footnote appears in the original as footnote '7'].

organization is responsible for damage caused by forces under its command and control, regardless of the fact that in both cases the Security Council, as the "source of authority" ', had either mandated or authorized the operation. In settling a large number of third-party claims for damage caused by forces under its command and control, the United States as well as other States contributing troops have accepted responsibility and liability in compensation. In the case of Somalia, as in that of the Republic of Korea, while the United Nations cannot attest to the settlement of all such claims by the United States, it can confirm that no such claims were attributed to the United Nations, or otherwise compensated by the Organization.

8. The principle that responsibility is entailed where command and control is vested is now reflected in a host of recently concluded bilateral agreements and arrangements between the United Nations and Member States cooperating with United Nations operations under separate command and control structure. Such agreements contain provisions to the effect that each participant will be solely responsible for handling third-party claims in respect of death, personal injury or illness caused by its personnel or agents, or for loss or damage to third-party property to the extent that such claims arise from or in connection with, acts or omissions of that party or of its personnel or agents.[12]

9. The recent jurisprudence of the European Court of Human Rights, beginning with the ***Behrami and Saramati***[13] case disregarded this fundamental distinction between the two kinds of operation for purposes of attribution. In attributing to the United Nations acts of a United Nations-authorized operation International Security Force in Kosovo (KFOR) conducted under ***regional command and control***, solely on the grounds that the Security Council had "delegated" its powers to the said operation and had "ultimate authority and control" over it, the Court disregarded the test of "effective command and control" which for over six decades has guided the United Nations and Member States in matters of attribution.

10. Consistent with the long-standing principle that responsibility lies where command and control is vested, the responsibility of the United Nations cannot be entailed by acts or omissions of those not subject to its command and control. Since the early days of peacekeeping operations the United Nations has recognized its responsibility and liability in compensation for acts or omissions of members of its peacekeeping operations, and by the same token, it has refused to entertain claims against other military operations—notwithstanding the fact that they were authorized by the Security Council. This practice has been uniform, consistent and without exception.[14]

In relation to the conduct of organs or agents placed at the disposal of the UN by a State or another international organisation, the UN Secretariat went on to emphasise why the 'effective command and control test' is a more appropriate test for the UN:

1. The test of "effective control" proposed by the International Law Commission is a factual test of actual control over the conduct in question, and is to be applied in the relationship between the organization and the lending State, or in the case of United Nations operations, between the United Nations and troop-contributing States. In the latter case, conditioning the attribution of an act of a national contingent to the United Nations on the degree of the "effective control" over the act or conduct in question implies, in fact, that, where the lending State continues to exercise operational control over the imputed act, responsibility should be attributed to the lending State and not to the receiving organization.

---

12 These include the Agreement between the United Nations Organization and the Government of the United States of America Concerning the Establishment of Security for the United Nations Assistance Mission for Iraq, 2005; the arrangement between the United Nations and the European Union concluded further to the Arrangement on the European Union Force in the Democratic Republic of the Congo (EUFOR RD Congo) support to the United Nations Organization Mission in the Democratic Republic of the Congo (MONUC), 2006; the Technical Arrangement between the United Nations and the Government of Australia Concerning Cooperation with and Assistance to the United Nations Integrated Mission in Timor-Leste (UNMIT), 2007; and the Arrangements between the United Nations and the European Union Governing the Cooperation between the United Nations Mission in the Central African Republic and Chad (MINURCAT) and the European Union Force EUFOR Tchad/RCA, 2008. The case of the African Union/United Nations Hybrid Operation in Darfur (UNAMID) is the exception. Established by Security Council resolution 1769 (2007) as a joint operation, UNAMID is a joint subsidiary organ of both the United Nations and the African Union. Responsibility for third-party claims for personal injury, death and property damage attributable to UNAMID is "settled by the United Nations" only (para. 54 of the Agreement between the United Nations and the African Union and the Government of the Sudan Concerning the Status of the African Union/United Nations Hybrid Operation in Darfur, 2008). [Note: this footnote appears in the original as footnote '10].

13 *Behrami and Saramati*, Application No. 71412/01, European Court of Human Rights, 2 May 2007. The *Behrami and Saramati* case was followed by a string of cases in which the question of attribution was similarly decided by the European Court. *Kasumaj v. Greece*, Application No. 6974/05, European Court of Human Rights, 5 July 2007; *Gajic v. Germany*, Application No. 31446/02, European Court of Human Rights, 28 August 2008; *Beric v. Bosnia and Herzegovina*, Application No. 36357/04, European Court of Human Rights, 16 October 2007. [Note: this footnote appears in the original as footnote '11'].

14 International Law Commission, 'Responsibility of International Organizations: Comments and Observations received from International Organizations', UN Doc A/CN4/637/Add1, 17 February 2011, 10–12 (hereafter 2011 Submission).

2. In the practice of the United Nations the test of "effective command and control" applies "horizontally" to distinguish between a United Nations operation conducted under United Nations command and control and a United Nations authorized operation conducted under national or regional command and control. In contrast, the test of "effective control" proposed by the Commission would apply "vertically" in the relations between the United Nations and its troop-contributing States to condition the responsibility of the Organization on the extent of its effective control over the conduct of the troops in question.
3. It has been the long-established position of the United Nations, however, that forces placed at the disposal of the United Nations are "transformed" into a United Nations subsidiary organ[15] and, as such, entail the responsibility of the Organization, just like any other subsidiary organ, regardless of whether the control exercised over all aspects of the operation was, in fact, "effective". In the practice of the United Nations, therefore, the test of "effective control" within the meaning of that, draft article 6 has never been used to determine the division of responsibilities for damage caused in the course of any given operation between the United Nations and any of its troop-contributing States. This position continued to obtain even in cases — such as UNOSOM II in Somalia — where the United Nations command and control structure had broken down.
4. In this connection, the Secretariat notes that the residual control exercised by the lending State in matters of disciplinary and criminal prosecution, salaries and promotion for the duration of the operation, is inherent in the institution of United Nations peacekeeping, where the United Nations maintains, in principle, exclusive "operational command and control" and the lending State such other residual control. However, as long as such residual control does not interfere with the United Nations operational control, it is of no relevance for the purpose of attribution.
5. Mindful of the realities of peacekeeping operations but keen to maintain the integrity of the United Nations operation vis-à-vis third parties, the United Nations has struck a balance, whereby it remains responsible vis-à-vis third parties, but reserves the right in cases of gross negligence or wilful misconduct to revert to the lending State. Under article 9 of the memorandum of understanding between the United Nations and the [participating State] contributing resources to [the United Nations peacekeeping operation],

   "[t]he United Nations will be responsible for dealing with any claims by third parties where the loss of or damage to their property, or death or personal injury, was caused by the personnel or equipment provided by the Government in the performance of services or any other activity or operation under this MOU. However, if the loss, damage, death or injury arose from gross negligence or wilful misconduct of the personnel provided by the Government, the Government will be liable for such claims".[16]
6. For a number of reasons, notably political, the United Nations practice of maintaining the principle of United Nations responsibility vis-à-vis third parties in connection with peacekeeping operations and reverting as appropriate to the lending State is likely to continue. The Secretariat nevertheless supports the inclusion of draft article 6 as a general guiding principle in the determination of responsibilities between the United Nations and its Member States with respect to organs or agents placed at the disposal of the Organization, including possibly in connection with activities of the Organization in other contexts.[17]

The ILC did not accept the UN's more nuanced approach concerning the relationship between 'command and control' and 'effective control' on UN peace operations. As demonstrated by Article 8 the ILC settled on the broader 'effective control test'. Nor did the ILC take account of the principle of 'residual control', where the sending State exercises criminal and administrative jurisdiction over its members.

---

15 Paragraph 15 of the 1990 model status-of-forces agreement for peacekeeping operations provides that, "[t]he United Nations peacekeeping operation, as a subsidiary organ of the United Nations, enjoys the status, privileges and immunities of the United Nations ..." (A/45/594, annex). [Note: this footnote appears in the original as footnote '15'].

16 A/C.5/60/26, chap. 9, art. 9. In another context, administrative instruction ST/AI/1999/6 on gratis personnel provides in section 13, on third-party claims, as follows: "The United Nations shall be responsible for dealing with claims by third parties where the loss of or damage to their property, or death or personnel injury was caused by the actions or omissions of the gratis personnel in the performance of services to the United Nations under the agreement with the donor. However, if the loss, damage, death or injury arose from gross negligence or wilful misconduct of the gratis personnel provided by the donor, the donor shall be liable to the United Nations for all amounts paid by the United Nations to the claimants and all costs incurred by the United Nations in settling such claims".' [Note: this footnote appears in the original as footnote '16'].

17 2011 submission (n 16), 13–14.

The UN Secretariat also made submissions concerning the application of the consequences to an international organisation if the conduct of an organ or agent exceeds the authority of that organ or agent (i.e. acting *ultra vires*).

2. There appears to be scant practice concerning actual claims against the Organization in respect of alleged *ultra vires* acts by its organs or agents. The practice we have identified requires a strong link between the impugned act or omission and the official functions of the organ or agent ... There is practice to suggest that when an organ or an agent identified as such by the Organization acts in its official capacity and within the overall functions of the Organization, but outside the scope of its authorization, such act may nevertheless be considered an act of the Organization ...
4. In this connection, the Secretariat notes that the 1986 opinion quoted by the Commission[18] does not reflect the consistent practice of the Organization. In 1974, the Office of Legal Affairs advised the Field Operations Service as to whether the United Nations Emergency Force (UNEF) Claims Review Board was authorized to handle and settle claims in respect of tortious acts committed during the Force members' off-duty periods. It advised that "there may well be situations involving actions by Force members off duty which the United Nations could appropriately recognize as engaging its responsibility", and made a distinction between off-duty acts of Force members in circumstances closely related to the functions of the Force member (i.e., the use of a Government-issued weapon), and actions entirely unrelated to the Force member's status as such. Accordingly, the test for the attribution of the act was whether it related to the functions of the Organization, irrespective of whether the Force member was on or off duty at the time.
5. The limited practice of the United Nations in the context of responsibility for *ultra vires* acts suggests that, at a minimum, the text of draft article 7 [in the final Draft Articles this is Draft Article 8] should be modified so as to provide that attribution in any such case could exist only where an organ or agent "acts in an official capacity and within the overall functions of the organization". In addition, the United Nations recommends that the International Law Commission give additional consideration to the question of whether the standard for attribution in respect of such acts should be the same for agents as for organs of the organization, in the light of the fact that an agent may have a more remote institutional link to the organization than an organ.
6. In the interest of clarity, the United Nations also recommends that the Commission not include in the commentary the excerpt of the legal opinion from the 1986 *United Nations Juridical Yearbook* concerning on-duty and off-duty acts in peacekeeping operations.[19]

Article 8 demonstrates that both the ILC and the UN Secretariat agree that the 'functionality' test is the most appropriate for deciding whether conduct of an official is *ultra vires*. The Secretariat went on to recommend that the ILC develop a separate standard of attribution for agents because agents have a more remote link to the organisation. The ILC does not appear to have accepted that suggestion in its commentary.

When responding to the suggestion that the Draft Articles should include a provision concerning *lex specialis* the UN stated:

The most notable examples of ***lex specialis*** in the practice of the United Nations include the principle of "operational necessity", which precludes responsibility for property loss or damage caused in the course of United Nations peacekeeping operations under the conditions set out by the Secretary-General and endorsed by the General Assembly[20] (see the comments on draft article 24), and the temporal and financial limitations adopted in the same resolution for injury or damage caused in the course of the same operations. Resolution 52/247 on third-party liability: temporal and financial limitations, adopted on 26 June 1998, sets temporal and financial limitations on the liability of the United Nations in respect of third-party claims arising out of United Nations peacekeeping operations, and as such prevails over the duty to provide full reparation under draft article 33. The resolution specifies, inter alia, that "no compensation shall be payable by the United Nations for non-economic loss", and that the amount of compensation payable for injury, illness or death of any individual, including for medical and rehabilitation expenses, loss of earnings, loss of financial support etc., "shall not exceed a maximum of 50,000 United States dollars". Pursuant to paragraph 12 of General Assembly resolution 52/247,

---

18 In para. (9) of the commentary. [Note: this footnote appears in the original as footnote '17'].

19 2011 submission (n 16), 15–16.

20 In paragraph 6 of resolution 52/247 the General Assembly endorsed "the view of the Secretary-General that liability is not engaged in relation to third-party claims resulting from or attributable to the activities of members of peacekeeping operations arising from 'operational necessity', as described in paragraph 14 of the first report of the Secretary-General on third-party liability [(A/51/389)]". [Note: this footnote appears in the original as footnote '48'].

> the Secretary-General consistently includes the limitations on liability in the status-of-force agreements concluded between the United Nations and the States where peacekeeping operations are deployed.[21]

During the drafting phase of the Draft Articles, two States expressed their views concerning the responsibility of international organisations in the context of UN peace operations. Mexico argued that:

> attribution of conduct to the United Nations would be the general rule when ... the forces involved are under United Nations control ... the actions and omissions were committed within the framework of a United Nations mandate, including ultra vires and ... the conduct derived from a status-of-forces or status-of-mission agreement.[22]

The emphasis on responsibility being regulated by agreements entered between host States and the UN was also made by the Democratic Republic of the Congo in its submissions to the ILC.[23]

The Articles have been reprinted below. The commentary to each article has been reprinted to the extent that the commentary is relevant to peace operations. The document extracted below is still titled Draft Articles, and refers to itself in the text and commentary as the 'draft articles'.

Reference[24]

Title	Draft articles on the responsibility of international organizations, with commentaries
Author	International Law Commission
Adopted by	International Law Commission
Date of Adoption	2011
Meeting	Sixty-third session
Source	Yearbook of the International Law Commission 2011, vol. II, Part Two
Full Text	<http://legal.un.org/ilc/texts/instruments/english/commentaries/9_11_2011.pdf>[25]

Draft Articles on the Responsibility of International Organizations, with Commentaries[26]

(Extracts)

Responsibility of international organizations

General commentary

(1) In 2001 the International Law Commission adopted a set of articles on the responsibility of States for internationally wrongful acts. As stated in those articles, they "are without prejudice to any question of the responsibility under international law of an international

21 2011 submission (n 16), 35.

22 International Law Commission, 'Responsibility of International Organizations: Comments and Observations received from Governments', UN Doc A/CN4/547, 6 August 2004, 9.

23 International Law Commission, 'Responsibility of International Organizations: Comments and Observations received from Governments', UN Doc A/CN4/556, 12 May 2005, 43.

24 The Draft Articles on the responsibility of international organisations were adopted by the ILC at its sixty-third session, in 2011, and submitted to the General Assembly as a part of the ILC's report covering the work of that session (UN Doc A/66/10). The report, which also contains commentaries to the Draft Articles, appears in Yearbook of the International Law Commission 2011, Volume II, Part Two.

25 Accessed 1 November 2017.

26 From Draft Articles on the Responsibility of International Organizations, with Commentaries, by International Law Commission © 2011 United Nations. Reprinted with the permission of the United Nations.

organization, or of any State for the conduct of an international organization" (art. 57). Given the number of existing international organizations and their ever increasing functions, these issues appeared to be of particular importance. Thus the Commission decided in 2002 to pursue its work for the codification and the progressive development of the law of international responsibility by taking up the two questions that had been left without prejudice in article 57 on State responsibility. The present draft articles represent the result of this further study. In conducting the study, the Commission was assisted by the comments and suggestions received from States and international organizations.

(2) The scope of application of the present draft articles reflects what was left open in article 57 of the draft articles on State responsibility. Most of the present draft articles consider the first issue that was mentioned in that provision: the responsibility of an international organization for an act which is internationally wrongful. Only a few draft articles, mainly those contained in Part Five, consider the second issue: the responsibility of a State for the conduct of an international organization. The second issue is closely connected with the first one because the conduct in question of an international organization will generally be internationally wrongful and entail the international responsibility of the international organization concerned. However, under certain circumstances which are considered in articles 60 and 61 and the related commentaries, the conduct of an international organization may not be wrongful and no international responsibility would arise for that organization.

...

(4) While the present draft articles are in many respects similar to the articles on State responsibility, they represent an autonomous text. Each issue has been considered from the specific perspective of the responsibility of international organizations. Some provisions address questions that are peculiar to international organizations. When, in the study of the responsibility of international organizations, the conclusion is reached that an identical or similar solution to the one expressed in the articles on State responsibility should apply with respect to international organizations, this is based on appropriate reasons and not on a general presumption that the same principles apply.

...

(7) International organizations are quite different from States, and in addition present great diversity among themselves. In contrast with States, they do not possess a general competence and have been established in order to exercise specific functions ("principle of speciality"). There are very significant differences among international organizations with regard to their powers and functions, size of membership, relations between the organization and its members, procedures for deliberation, structure and facilities, as well as the primary rules including treaty obligations by which they are bound. Because of this diversity and its implications, the draft articles where appropriate give weight to the specific character of the organization, especially to its functions, as for instance article 8 on excess of authority or contravention of instructions. The provision on *lex specialis* (art. 64) has particular importance in this context. Moreover, the diversity of international organizations may affect the application of certain articles, some of which may not apply to certain international organizations in the light of their powers and functions.

...

(9) The present draft articles are divided into Six Parts. Part One defines the scope of the articles and gives the definition of certain terms. Parts Two to Four (arts. 3 to 57) follow the general layout of the articles on State responsibility. Part Two sets forth the preconditions for the international responsibility of an international organization to arise. Part Three addresses the legal consequences flowing for the responsible organization, in particular the obligation to make reparation. Part Four concerns the implementation of

responsibility of an international organization, especially the question of which States or international organizations are entitled to invoke that responsibility. Part Five addresses the responsibility of States in connection with the conduct of an international organization. Finally, Part Six contains certain general provisions applicable to the whole set of draft articles.

Part One

Introduction

Article 1

Scope of the present draft articles

1. The present draft articles apply to the international responsibility of an international organization for an internationally wrongful act.
2. The present draft articles also apply to the international responsibility of a State for an internationally wrongful act in connection with the conduct of an international organization.

Commentary

(1) The definition of the scope of the draft articles in article 1 is intended to be as comprehensive and accurate as possible. While article 1 covers all the issues that are to be addressed in the following articles, this is without prejudice to any solution that will be given to those issues. Thus, for instance, the reference in paragraph 2 to the international responsibility of a State in connection with the conduct of an international organization does not imply that such a responsibility will be held to exist.

...

Article 2

Use of terms

For the purposes of the present draft articles:

(a) "international organization" means an organization established by a treaty or other instrument governed by international law and possessing its own international legal personality. International organizations may include as members, in addition to States, other entities;

(b) "rules of the organization" means, in particular, the constituent instruments, decisions, resolutions and other acts of the international organization adopted in accordance with those instruments, and established practice of the organization;

(c) "organ of an international organization" means any person or entity which has that status in accordance with the rules of the organization;

(d) "agent of an international organization" means an official or other person or entity, other than an organ, who is charged by the organization with carrying out, or helping to carry out, one of its functions, and thus through whom the organization acts.

Commentary

(1) The definition of "international organization" given in article 2, subparagraph (*a*), is considered as appropriate for the purposes of the present draft articles and is not intended as a definition for all purposes. It outlines certain common characteristics of the international organizations to which the following articles apply. The same characteristics may be relevant for purposes other than the international responsibility of international organizations.

(2) The fact that an international organization does not possess one or more of the characteristics set forth in article 2, subparagraph (*a*), and thus is not within the definition for the purposes of the present articles, does not imply that certain principles and rules stated in the following articles do not apply also to that organization.

(3) Starting with the 1969 Vienna Convention,[27] several codification conventions have succinctly defined the term "international organization" as "intergovernmental organization".[28] In each case, the definition was given only for the purposes of the relevant convention and not for all purposes. The text of some of these codification conventions added some further elements to the definition: for instance, the 1986 Vienna Conventiononly applies to those intergovernmental organizations which have the capacity to conclude treaties.[29] No additional element would be required in the case of international responsibility apart from possessing an obligation under international law. However, the adoption of a different definition is preferable for several reasons. First, it is questionable whether by defining an international organization as an intergovernmental organization one provides much information: it is not even clear whether the term "intergovernmental organization" refers to the constituent instrument or to actual membership. Second, the term "intergovernmental" is in any case inappropriate to a certain extent, because several important international organizations have been established with the participation also of State organs other than Governments. Third, an increasing number of international organizations include among their members entities other than States as well as States; the term "intergovernmental organization" might be thought to exclude these organizations, although with regard to international responsibility it is difficult to see why one should reach solutions that differ from those applying to organizations of which only States are members.

...

(7) Article 2 also requires the international organization to possess "international legal personality". The acquisition of legal personality under international law does not depend on the inclusion in the constituent instrument of a provision such as Article 104 of the Charter of the United Nations, which reads as follows:

> "The Organization shall enjoy in the territory of each of its Members such legal capacity as may be necessary for the exercise of its functions and the fulfilment of its purposes."

The purpose of this type of provision in the constituent instrument is to impose on the member States an obligation to recognize the organization's legal personality under their internal laws. A similar obligation is imposed on the host State when a similar text is included in the headquarters agreement.[30]

...

27 The relevant provision is article 2, paragraph (1) (*i*). [Note: this footnote appears in the original document as footnote '57'].

28 See article 1, paragraph 1 (1), of the Vienna Convention on the Representation of States in their Relations with International Organizations of a Universal Character; article 2, paragraph 1 (*n*), of the 1978 Vienna Convention; and article 2, paragraph 1 (*i*), of the 1986 Vienna Convention. [Note: this footnote appears in the original document as footnote '58'].

29 See article 6 of the Convention. As the Commission noted with regard to the draft articles on treaties concluded between States and international organizations or between two or more international organizations (paragraph (22) of the commentary to article 2),

> "Either an international organization has the capacity to conclude *at least* one treaty, in which case the rules in the draft articles will be applicable to it, or, despite its title, it does not have that capacity, in which case it is pointless to state explicitly that the draft article do not apply to it."

(*Yearbook ... 1981*, vol. II (Part Two), p. 124).

[Note: this footnote appears in the original document as footnote '59'].

30 Thus, in its judgment No. 149 of 18 March 1999 in *Istituto Universitario Europeo* v. *Piette*, the Italian Court of Cassation found that "[t]he provision in an international agreement of the obligation to recognize legal personality to an organization and the implementation by law of that provision only mean that the organization acquires legal personality under the municipal law of the contracting States" (*Giustizia civile*, vol. 49 (1999), p. 1313). [Note: this footnote appears in the original document as footnote '66'].

(9) In the passages quoted in the previous paragraph, and more explicitly in its advisory opinion on *Reparation for Injuries*,[31] the Court appeared to favour the view that when legal personality of an organization exists, it is an "objective" personality. Thus, it would not be necessary to enquire whether the legal personality of an organization has been recognized by an injured State before considering whether the organization may be held internationally responsible according to the present articles.

(10) The legal personality of an organization, which is a precondition of the international responsibility of that organization, needs to be "distinct from that of its member States".[32] This element is reflected in the requirement in article 2, subparagraph (*a*), that the international legal personality should be the organization's "own", a term that the Commission considers as synonymous with the phrase "distinct from that of its member States". The existence for the organization of a distinct legal personality does not exclude the possibility of a certain conduct being attributed both to the organization and to one or more of its members or to all its members.

(11) The second sentence of article 2, subparagraph (*a*), seeks first of all to emphasize the role that States play in practice with regard to all the international organizations which are covered by the present articles. This key role was expressed by the International Court of Justice, albeit incidentally, in its advisory opinion on the *Legality of the Use by a State of Nuclear Weapons in Armed Conflict*, in the following sentence:

> International organizations are governed by the "principle of speciality", that is to say, they are invested by the States which create them with powers, the limits of which are a function of the common interests whose promotion those States entrust to them.[33]

Many international organizations have only States as members. In other organizations, which have a different membership, the presence of States among the members is essential for the organization to be considered in the present articles.[34] This requirement is intended to be conveyed by the words "in addition to States".

...

(16) The definition of "rules of the organization" in subparagraph (*b*) is to a large extent based on the definition of the same term that is included in the 1986 Vienna Convention.[35] Apart from a few minor stylistic changes, the definition in subparagraph (*b*) differs from the one contained in that codification convention only because it refers, together with "decisions" and "resolutions", to "other acts of the organization". This addition is intended to cover more comprehensively the great variety of acts that international organizations adopt. The words "in particular" have nevertheless been retained, since the rules of the organization may also include such instruments as agreements concluded by the organization with third parties and judicial or arbitral decisions binding the organization. For the purpose of attribution of conduct, decisions, resolutions and other acts of the organization are relevant, whether they are regarded as binding or not, insofar as they give functions to organs or

31 *Reparation for injuries suffered in the service of the United Nations, Advisory Opinion: I.C.J. Reports 1949*, p. 174, at p. 185. [Note: this footnote appears in the original document as footnote '69'].

32 This wording was used by G. G. Fitzmaurice in the definition of the term "international organization" that he proposed in his first report on the law of treaties (*Yearbook ... 1956*, vol. II, document A/CN.4/101, p. 108) and by the Institute of International Law in its 1995 Lisbon resolution on "The legal consequences for member states of the non-fulfilment by international organizations of their obligations toward third parties" (Institute of International Law, *Yearbook*, vol. 66, Part II, Session of Lisbon (1995), p. 445; available from www.idi-iil.org, "Resolutions"). [Note: this footnote appears in the original document as footnote '70'].

33 See footnote 68 above. [Note: this footnote appears in the original document as footnote '71'].

34 Thus, the definition in article 2 does not cover international organizations whose membership only comprises international organizations. An example of this type of organization is the Joint Vienna Institute, which was established on the basis of an agreement between five international organizations. See www.jvi.org. [Note: this footnote appears in the original document as footnote '72'].

35 Article 2, paragraph 1 (*j*) states that " 'rules of the organization' means, in particular, the constituent instruments, decisions and resolutions adopted in accordance with them, and established practice of the organization". [Note: this footnote appears in the original document as footnote '79'].

agents in accordance with the constituent instruments of the organization. The latter instruments are referred to in the plural, following the wording of the Vienna Convention, although a given organization may well possess a single constituent instrument.

(17) One important feature of the definition of "rules of the organization" in subparagraph (*b*) is that it gives considerable weight to practice. The influence that practice may have in shaping the rules of the organization was described in a comment by the North Atlantic Treaty Organization (NATO), which noted that NATO was an organization where "the fundamental internal rule governing the functioning of the organization—that of consensus decision-making—is to be found neither in the treaties establishing NATO nor in any formal rules and is, rather, the result of the practice of the organization".[36]

(18) The definition seeks to strike a balance between the rules enshrined in the constituent instruments and formally accepted by the members of the organization, on the one hand, and the need for the organization to develop as an institution, on the other hand. As the International Court of Justice said in its advisory opinion on *Reparation for Injuries*:

> Whereas a State possesses the totality of international rights and duties recognized by international law, the rights and duties of an entity such as the Organization must depend upon its purposes and functions as specified or implied in its constituent documents and developed in practice.[37]

(19) The definition of "rules of the organization" is not intended to imply that all the rules pertaining to a given international organization are placed at the same level. The rules of the organization concerned will provide, expressly or implicitly, for a hierarchy among the different kinds of rules. For instance, the acts adopted by an international organization will generally not be able to derogate from its constituent instruments.

(20) A definition of the term "organ [of the organization]" is given in subparagraph (*c*). International organizations show a variety of approaches with regard to the use of this term. Some constituent instruments contain a list of organs, which may be more or less broad,[38] while in the rules of certain other organizations the term "organ" is not used.

(21) Notwithstanding this variety of approaches, it is preferable not to adopt a uniform definition which would be at odds with the rules of various organizations. The different scope that the term "organ" may have according to the rules of the organization concerned does not affect attribution of conduct to the organization, given the fact that also the conduct of agents is attributed to the organization according to article 6. Thus, subparagraph (*c*) refers to the rules of the organization and considers that an organ is "any person or entity which has that status according to the rules of the organization".

(22) The definition in subparagraph (*c*) is similar to the one of organ of State, which is given in article 4, paragraph 2, of the articles on responsibility of States for internationally wrongful acts. According to this text, "[a]n organ includes any person or entity which has that status in accordance with the internal law of the State".[39] Subparagraph (*c*) leaves it to the international organization concerned to define its own organs.

---

36 A/CN.4/637 and Add.1 (under the section entitled "Draft article 63 … North Atlantic Treaty Organization". [Note: this footnote appears in the original document as footnote '80'].

37 *Reparation for injuries suffered in the service of the United Nations* (see footnote 69 above), p. 180). [Note: this footnote appears in the original document as footnote '81'].

38 Examples of broader lists are provided by the constituent instruments of the Organization of American States (OAS) and the International Criminal Police Organization (INTERPOL). Article 53 of the Charter of the Organization of American States lists as organs the General Assembly, the Meeting of Consultation of Ministers of Foreign Affairs, the Councils, the IAJC, the Inter-American Commission on Human Rights, the General Secretariat, the Specialized Conferences and the Specialized Organizations. According to article 5 of the ICPO-INTERPOL Constitution and General Regulations, the organization comprises the General Assembly, the Executive Committee, the General Secretariat, the National Central Bureaus, the Advisers and the Commission for the Control of Files. An example of a very economical list is provided by NATO. Article 9 of the North Atlantic Treaty establishes a single organ, the Council, which is given the competence to create "such subsidiary bodies as may be necessary". [Note: this footnote appears in the original document as footnote '82'].

39 *Yearbook … 2001*, vol. II (Part Two) and corrigendum, p. 40. [Note: this footnote appears in the original as footnote '83'].

(23) Subparagraph (*d*) provides a definition of the term "agent" which is based on a passage in the advisory opinion of the International Court of Justice on *Reparation for Injuries*. When considering the capacity of the United Nations to bring a claim in case of an injury, the Court said that it

> understands the word "agent" in the most liberal sense, that is to say, any person who, whether a paid official or not, and whether permanently employed or not, has been charged by an organ of the organization with carrying out, or helping to carry out, one of its functions—in short, any person through whom it acts.[40]

(24) When the Court referred to one of the functions of the organization, it did not exclude that the agent be charged with carrying out, or helping to carry out, more than one function. The reference to "one of its functions" in subparagraph (*d*) should be understood in the same way.

(25) International organizations do not act only through natural persons, whether officials or not. Thus, the definition of "agent" also covers all the entities through whom the organization acts.

(26) The definition of "agent" is of particular relevance to the question of attribution of conduct to an international organization. It is therefore preferable to develop the analysis of various aspects of this definition in the context of attribution, especially in article 6 and the related commentary.

(27) In order to avoid a possible overlap between the definition of "organ of an international organization" and that of "agent of an international organization", the latter phrase only covers persons or entities that do not come within the definition under subparagraph (*c*).

...

Chapter I

General Principles

Article 3

Responsibility of an international organization for its internationally wrongful acts

Every internationally wrongful act of an international organization entails the international responsibility of that organization.

Commentary

(1) The general principle, as stated in article 3, applies to whichever entity commits an internationally wrongful act. The same may be said of the principle stated in article 4.[41] The formulation of article 3 is modelled on that applicable to States according to the articles on responsibility of States for internationally wrongful acts. There seems to be little reason for formulating these principles in another manner. It is noteworthy that in a report on peacekeeping operations the Secretary-General of the United Nations referred to

> the principle of State responsibility—widely accepted to be applicable to international organizations—that damage caused in breach of an international obligation and which is attributable to the State (or to the Organization) entails the international responsibility of the State (or of the Organization).[42]

---

40 *Reparation for injuries suffered in the service of the United Nations* (see footnote 69 above), p. 177. [Note: this footnote appears in the original document as footnote '84'].

41 *Yearbook ... 2001*, vol. II (Part Two) and corrigendum, pp. 26 and 32–34. The classical analysis that led the Commission to adopt articles 1 and 2 on the responsibility of States for internationally wrongful acts is contained in Roberto Ago's third report on State responsibility, *Yearbook ... 1971*, vol. II (Part One), document A/CN.4/246 and Add. 1–3, pp. 214–223, paras. 49–75. [Note: this footnote appears in the original document as footnote '85'].

42 A/51/389, p. 4, para 6. [Note: this footnote appears in the original document as footnote '86'].

...

(3) When an international organization commits a wrongful act, its responsibility is entailed. One may find a statement of this principle in the advisory opinion of the International Court of Justice on *Difference Relating to Immunity from Legal Process of a Special Rapporteur of the Commission on Human Rights*, in which the Court said that it

> wishes to point out that the question of immunity from legal process is distinct from the issue of compensation for any damages incurred as a result of acts performed by the United Nations or by its agents acting in their official capacity.
>
> The United Nations may be required to bear responsibility for the damage arising from such acts.[43]

(4) The meaning of international responsibility is not defined in article 3, nor is it in the corresponding provisions of the draft articles on responsibility of States for internationally wrongful acts. There the consequences of an internationally wrongful act are dealt with in Part Two of the text, which concerns the "content of the international responsibility of a State".[44]

...

(6) The fact that an international organization is responsible for an internationally wrongful act does not exclude the existence of parallel responsibility of other subjects of international law in the same set of circumstances. For instance, an international organization may have co-operated with a State in the breach of an obligation imposed on both. Another example may be that of conduct which is simultaneously attributed to an international organization and a State and which entails the international responsibility of both the organization and the State.

Article 4
Elements of an internationally wrongful act of an international organization

There is an internationally wrongful act of an international organization when conduct consisting of an action or omission:

(a) is attributable to that organization under international law; and
(b) constitutes a breach of an international obligation of that organization.

Commentary

(1) Article 4 expresses with regard to international organizations a general principle that applies to every internationally wrongful act, whoever its author. As in the case of States, the attribution of conduct to an international organization is one of the two essential elements for an internationally wrongful act to occur. The term "conduct" is intended to cover both acts and omissions on the part of the international organization. The rules pertaining to attribution of conduct to an international organization are set forth in chapter II.

(2) A second essential element, to be examined in chapter III, is that conduct constitutes the breach of an obligation under international law. The obligation may result either from a treaty binding the international organization or from any other source of international law applicable to the organization. As the International Court of Justice noted in its advisory opinion on the *Interpretation of the Agreement of 25 March 1951 between the WHO and Egypt*, international organizations are

---

43 *Difference Relating to Immunity from Legal Process of a Special Rapporteur of the Commission on Human Rights, Advisory Opinion, I.C.J. Reports 1999*, p. 62, at pp. 88–89, para. 66. [Note: this footnote appears in the original document as footnote '87'].

44 *Yearbook ... 2001*, vol. II (Part Two) and corrigendum, pp. 86–116. [Note: this footnote appears in the original document as footnote '88'].

bound by any obligations incumbent upon them under general rules of international law, under their constitutions or under international agreements to which they are parties.[45] A breach is thus possible with regard to any of these international obligations.

(3) Again as in the case of States, damage does not appear to be an element necessary for international responsibility of an international organization to arise. In most cases, an internationally wrongful act will entail material damage. However, it is conceivable that the breach of an international obligation occurs in the absence of any material damage. Whether the damage will be required or not depends on the content of the primary obligation.

Article 5

Characterization of an act of an international organization as internationally wrongful

The characterization of an act of an international organization as internationally wrongful is governed by international law.

Commentary

(1) By setting forth that the characterization of an act of an international organization as internationally wrongful depends on international law, article 5 adapts to international organizations a statement made for States in the first sentence of article 3 on the responsibility of States for internationally wrongful acts. This statement may appear obvious and already be implied in article 4 of the present draft articles, which refers to international law for determining both whether an action or omission is attributable to an international organization and whether it constitutes a breach of an international obligation. However, the need to refer to international law in order to characterize an act as internationally wrongful is an important point which warrants a specific statement.

...

(4) The question of the legal nature and possible effects of the rules of the organization is examined in greater detail to the commentary to article 10, concerning the existence of a breach of an international obligation.

Chapter II

Attribution of conduct to an international organization

Commentary

(1) According to article 4 of the present articles, attribution of conduct under international law to an international organization is one condition for an international wrongful act of that international organization to arise, the other condition being that the same conduct constitutes a breach of an obligation that exists under international law for the international organization. Articles 6 to 9 below address the question of attribution of conduct to an international organization. As stated in article 4, conduct is intended to include actions and omissions.

(2) The responsibility of an international organization may in certain cases arise also when conduct is not attributable to that international organization.[46] In these cases, conduct would be attributed to a State or to another international organization. In the latter case, rules on attribution of conduct to an international organization are also relevant.

...

45 See footnote 67 above. [Note: this footnote appears in the original document as footnote '89'].

46 Some examples are given in Chapter IV. [Note: this footnote appears in the original document as footnote '92'].

(4) Although it may not frequently occur in practice, dual or even multiple attribution of conduct cannot be excluded. Thus, attribution of a certain conduct to an international organization does not imply that the same conduct cannot be attributed to a State, nor does attribution of conduct to a State rule out attribution of the same conduct to an international organization. One could also envisage conduct being simultaneously attributed to two or more international organizations, for instance when they establish a joint organ and act through that organ.

...

Article 6

Conduct of organs or agents of an international organization

1. The conduct of an organ or agent of an international organization in the performance of functions of that organ or agent shall be considered an act of that organization under international law, whatever position the organ or agent holds in respect of the organization.
2. The rules of the organization shall apply in the determination of the functions of its organs and agents.

Commentary

...

(2) It is noteworthy that, while some provisions of the Charter of the United Nations use the term "organs",[47] the International Court of Justice, when dealing with the status of persons acting for the United Nations, considered relevant only the fact that a person had been conferred functions by an organ of the United Nations. The Court used the term "agent" and did not consider relevant the fact that the person in question had or did not have an official status. In its advisory opinion on *Reparation for Injuries*, the Court noted that the question addressed by the General Assembly concerned the capacity of the United Nations to bring a claim in case of injury caused to one of its agents and said that it

> understands the word "agent" in the most liberal sense, that is to say, any person who, whether a paid official or not, and whether permanently employed or not, has been charged by an organ of the organization with carrying out, or helping to carry out, one of its functions—in short, any person through whom it acts.[48]

In the later advisory opinion on the *Applicability of Article VI, section 22, of the Convention on the Privileges and Immunities of the United Nations*, the Court noted that

> [i]n practice, according to the information supplied by the Secretary-General, the United Nations has had occasion to entrust missions—increasingly varied in nature—to persons not having the status of United Nations officials.[49]

With regard to privileges and immunities, the Court also said in the same opinion that

> [t]he essence of the matter lies not in their administrative position but in the nature of their mission.[50]

(3) More recently, in its advisory opinion on *Difference Relating to Immunity from Legal Process of a Special Rapporteur of the Commission on Human Rights*, the Court noted that in case of

---

47 Article 7 of the Charter of the United Nations refers to "principal organs" and to "subsidiary organs". This latter term appears also in Articles 22 and 29 of the Charter of the United Nations. [Note: this footnote appears in the original document as footnote '98'].

48 *Reparation for injuries suffered in the service of the United Nations* (see footnote 69 above), p. 177. This passage was already quoted in the text corresponding to footnote 84 above. [Note: this footnote appears in the original document as footnote '99'].

49 *Applicability of Article VI, Section 22, of the Convention on the Privileges and Immunities of the United Nations, Advisory Opinion, I.C.J. Reports 1989*, p. 177, at p. 194, para. 48. [Note: this footnote appears in the original document as footnote '100'].

50 *Ibid.*, para. 47. [Note: this footnote appears in the original document as footnote '101'].

> damages incurred as a result of acts performed by the United Nations or by its agents acting in their official capacity ... [t]he United Nations may be required to bear responsibility for the damage arising from such acts.[51]

(4) What was said by the International Court of Justice with regard to the United Nations applies more generally to international organizations, most of which act through their organs (whether so defined or not) and a variety of agents to which the carrying out of the organization's functions is entrusted. As was stated in a decision of the Swiss Federal Council of 30 October 1996,

> [a]s a rule, one attributes to an international organization acts and omissions of its organs of all rank and nature and of its agents in the exercise of their competences.[52]

(5) The distinction between organs and agents does not appear to be relevant for the purpose of attribution of conduct to an international organization. The conduct of both organs and agents is attributable to the organization.

(6) An organ or agent of an international organization may be an organ or agent who has been seconded by a State or another international organization. The extent to which the conduct of the seconded organ or agent has to be attributed to the receiving organization is discussed in the commentary to article 7.

(7) The requirement in paragraph 1 that the organ or agent acts "in the performance of functions of that organ or agent" is intended to make it clear that conduct is attributable to the international organization when the organ or agent exercises functions that have been given to that organ or agent, and at any event is not attributable when the organ or agent acts in a private capacity. The question of attribution of *ultra vires* conduct is addressed in article 8.

(8) According to draft article 4, paragraph 1, of the articles on responsibility of States for internationally wrongful acts, attribution to a State of conduct of an organ takes place "whether the organ exercises legislative, executive, judicial or any other functions, whatever position it holds in the organization of the State, and whatever its character as an organ of the central Government or of a territorial unit of the State".[53] The latter specification could hardly apply to an international organization. The other elements could be retained, but it is preferable to use simpler wording, also in view of the fact that, while all States may be held to exercise all the above-mentioned functions, organizations vary significantly from one another also in this regard. Thus paragraph 1 simply states "whatever position the organ or agent holds in respect of the organization".

(9) The international organization concerned establishes which functions are entrusted to each organ or agent. This is generally done, as indicated in paragraph 2, by the "rules of the organization". By not making the rules of the organization the only criterion, the wording of paragraph 2 is intended to leave the possibility open that, in exceptional circumstances, functions may be considered as given to an organ or agent even if this could not be said to be based on the rules of the organization.

(10) Article 5 of the articles on responsibility of States for internationally wrongful acts concerns "[c]onduct of persons or entities exercising elements of governmental authority".[54]

---

51 *Difference Relating to Immunity from Legal Process of a Special Rapporteur of the Commission on Human Rights* (see footnote 87 above), pp. 88–89, para. 66. [Note: this footnote appears in the original document as footnote '102'].

52 This is a translation from the original French, which reads as follows: *En règle générale, sont imputables à une organisation internationale les actes et omissions de ses organes de tout rang et de toute nature et de ses agents dans l'exercice de leurs compétences* (document VPB 61.75, published on the Swiss Federal Council's website: www.vpb.admin.ch). [Note: this footnote appears in the original document as footnote '103'].

53 *Yearbook ... 2001*, vol. II (Part Two) and corrigendum, pp. 40–42; see also paragraphs. (6)–(7) of the related commentary, pp. 40–41. [Note: this footnote appears in the original document as footnote '104'].

54 *Ibid.*, pp. 42–43. [Note: this footnote appears in the original document as footnote '105'].

This terminology is generally not appropriate for international organizations. One would have to express in a different way the link that an entity may have with an international organization. It is, however, superfluous to put in the present draft articles an additional provision in order to include persons or entities in a situation corresponding to the one envisaged in article 5 of the articles on responsibility of States for internationally wrongful acts. The term "agent" is given in subparagraph (*d*) of article 2 a wide meaning that adequately covers these persons or entities.

(11) A similar conclusion may be reached with regard to the persons or groups of persons referred to in article 8 of the articles on responsibility of States for internationally wrongful acts.[55] This provision concerns persons or groups of persons acting in fact on the instructions, or under the direction or control, of a State. Should persons or groups of persons act under the instructions, or the direction or control, of an international organization, they would have to be regarded as agents according to the definition given in subparagraph (*d*) of article 2. As was noted above in paragraph (9) of the present commentary, in exceptional cases, a person or entity would be considered, for the purpose of attribution of conduct, as entrusted with functions of the organization, even if this was not pursuant to the rules of the organization.

Article 7

Conduct of organs of a State or organs or agents of an international organization placed at the disposal of another international organization

The conduct of an organ of a State or an organ or agent of an international organization that is placed at the disposal of another international organization shall be considered under international law an act of the latter organization if the organization exercises effective control over that conduct.

Commentary

(1) When an organ of a State is placed at the disposal of an international organization, the organ may be fully seconded to that organization. In this case, the organ's conduct would clearly be attributable only to the receiving organization. The same consequence would apply when an organ or agent of one international organization is fully seconded to another organization. In these cases, the general rule set out in article 6 would apply. Article 7 deals with the different situation in which the seconded organ or agent still acts to a certain extent as organ of the seconding State or as organ or agent of the seconding organization. This occurs for instance in the case of military contingents that a State places at the disposal of the United Nations for a peacekeeping operation, since the State retains disciplinary powers and criminal jurisdiction over the members of the national contingent.[56] There, the problem arises whether a specific conduct of the seconded organ or agent is to be attributed to the receiving organization or to the seconding State or organization.

(2) Since the articles on responsibility of States for internationally wrongful acts do not use the term "agent" within this context, article 7 only considers the case of an organ of a State being placed at the disposal of the organization. However, the term "organ", with reference to a State, has to be understood in a wide sense, as comprising those entities and persons whose conduct is attributable to a State according to articles 5 and 8 of the articles on responsibility of States for internationally wrongful acts.

55 *Ibid.*, pp. 47–49. [Note: this footnote appears in the original document as footnote '106'].

56 This is generally specified in the agreement that the United Nations concludes with the contributing State. See the Secretary-General's report on Command and control of United Nations peace-keeping operations (A/49/681), para. 6. [Note: this footnote appears in the original document as footnote '107'].

(3) The seconding State or organization may conclude an agreement with the receiving organization over placing an organ or agent at the latter organization's disposal. The agreement may state which State or organization would be responsible for conduct of that organ or agent. For example, according to the model contribution agreement relating to military contingents placed at the disposal of the United Nations by one of its Member States, the United Nations is regarded as liable towards third parties, but has a right of recovery from the contributing State under circumstances such as "loss, damage, death or injury [arising] from gross negligence or wilful misconduct of the personnel provided by the Government".[57] The agreement appears to deal only with distribution of responsibility and not with attribution of conduct. At any event, this type of agreement is not conclusive because it governs only the relations between the contributing State or organization and the receiving organization and could thus not have the effect of depriving a third party of any right that this party may have towards the State or organization that is responsible under the general rules.

(4) The criterion for attribution of conduct either to the contributing State or organization or to the receiving organization is based, according to article 7, on the factual control that is exercised over the specific conduct taken by the organ or agent placed at the receiving organization's disposal. As was noted in the comment by one State, account needs to be taken of the "full factual circumstances and particular context".[58] Article 6 of the articles on responsibility of States for internationally wrongful acts[59] takes a similar approach, although it is differently worded. According to the latter article, what is relevant is that "the organ is acting in the exercise of elements of the governmental authority of the State at whose disposal it is placed". However, the commentary on article 6 on the responsibility of States for internationally wrongful acts explains that, for conduct to be attributed to the receiving State, it must be "under its exclusive direction and control, rather than on instructions from the sending State".[60] In any event, the wording of article 6 cannot be replicated here, because the reference to "the exercise of elements of governmental authority" is unsuitable to international organizations.

(5) With regard to States, the existence of control has been mainly discussed in relation to the question whether conduct of persons or of groups of persons, especially irregular armed forces, is attributable to a State.[61] In the context of the placing of an organ or agent at the disposal of an international organization, control plays a different role. It does not concern the issue whether a certain conduct is attributable at all to a State or an international organization, but rather to which entity—the contributing State or organization or the receiving organization—conduct has to be attributed.

(6) The United Nations assumes that in principle it has exclusive control of the deployment of national contingents in a peacekeeping force. This premise led the United Nations Legal Counsel to state that

> [a]s a subsidiary organ of the United Nations, an act of a peacekeeping force is, in principle, imputable to the Organization, and if committed in violation of an international obligation entails the international responsibility of the Organization and its liability in compensation.[62]

---

57 Article 9 of the model contribution agreement (A/50/995, annex; A/51/967, annex; A/51/967, annex). [Note: this footnote appears in the original document as footnote '109'].

58 United Kingdom (*Official Records of the General Assembly, Sixty-fourth Session, Sixth Committee*, 16th meeting (A/C.6/64/SR.16), para. 23). [Note: this footnote appears in the original document as footnote '110'].

59 *Yearbook . . . 2001*, vol. II (Part Two) and corrigendum, pp. 43–45 [Note: this footnote appears in the original document as footnote '111'].

60 *Ibid.*, p. 44, paragraph (2) of the commentary to article 6. [Note: this footnote appears in the original document as footnote '112'].

61 See article 8 of the draft articles on responsibility of States for internationally wrongful acts and commentary thereto (*ibid.*, pp. 47–49). [Note: this footnote appears in the original document as footnote '113'].

62 Memorandum of 3 February 2004 by the United Nations Legal Counsel to the Director of the Codification Division, *Yearbook . . . 2004*, vol. II (Part One), document A/CN.4/545, p. 28. [Note: this footnote appears in the original document as footnote '114'].

This statement sums up United Nations practice relating to the United Nations Operation in the Congo,[63] the United Nations Peacekeeping Force in Cyprus[64] and later peacekeeping forces.[65] In a recent comment, the United Nations Secretariat observed that "[f]or a number of reasons, notably political", the practice of the United Nations had been that of "maintaining the principle of United Nations responsibility *vis-à-vis* third parties" in connection with peacekeeping operations.[66]

(7) Practice relating to peacekeeping forces is particularly significant in the present context because of the control that the contributing State retains over disciplinary and criminal matters.[67] This may have consequences with regard to attribution of conduct. For instance, the United Nations Office of Legal Affairs took the following line with regard to compliance with obligations under the 1973 Convention on international trade in endangered species of wild fauna and flora:

> Since the Convention places the responsibility for enforcing its provisions on the States parties and since the troop-contributing States retain jurisdiction over the criminal acts of their military personnel, the responsibility for enforcing the provisions of the Convention rests with those troop-contributing States which are parties to the Convention.[68]

Attribution of conduct to the contributing State is clearly linked with the retention of some powers by that State over its national contingent and thus on the control that the State possesses in the relevant respect.

(8) As has been held by several scholars,[69] when an organ or agent is placed at the disposal of an international organization, the decisive question in relation to attribution of a particular conduct appears to be who has effective control over the conduct in question. For instance, it would be difficult to attribute to the United Nations conduct of forces in circumstances such as those described in the report of the Commission of Inquiry which was established in order to investigate armed attacks on the United Nations Operation in Somalia II (UNOSOM II):

> The Force Commander of UNOSOM II was not in effective control of several national contingents which, in varying degrees, persisted in seeking orders from their home authorities before executing orders of the Forces Command.

63 See the agreements providing for compensation that were concluded by the United Nations with Belgium (United Nations, *Treaty Series*, vol. 535, No. 7779, p. 191), Greece (*ibid.*, vol. 565, No. 8230, p. 3), Italy (*ibid.*, vol. 588, No. 8525, p. 197), Luxembourg (*ibid.*, vol. 585, No. 8487, p. 147) and Switzerland (*ibid.*, vol. 564, No. 621, p. 193). [Note: this footnote appears in the original document as footnote '115'].

64 United Nations, *Juridical Yearbook 1980* (Sales No. E.83.V.1), pp. 184–185. [Note: this footnote appears in the original document as footnote '116'].

65 See Report of the Secretary-General on financing of United Nations peacekeeping operations (A/51/389), paras. 7–8. [Note: this footnote appears in the original document as footnote '117'].

66 A/CN.4/637 and Add. 1 (under the section entitled "Draft article 6 . . . United Nations"), para. 6. [Note: this footnote appears in the original document as footnote '118'].

67 See above, paragraph (1) of the commentary to the present draft article and footnote 107. [Note: this footnote appears in the original document as footnote '119'].

68 United Nations, *Juridical Yearbook 1994* (Sales No. E.00.V.8), p. 450. [Note: this footnote appears in the original document as footnote '120'].

69 See J.-P. Ritter, "La protection diplomatique à l'égard d'une organisation internationale", AFDI, vol. 8 (1962), pp. 427 *et seq.*, at p. 442; R. Simmonds, *Legal Problems Arising from the United Nations Military Operations in the Congo* ,The Hague, Martinus Nijhoff, 1968, p. 229; B. Amrallah, "The international responsibility of the United Nations for activities carried out by U.N. peace-keeping forces", *Revue égyptienne de droit international*, vol. 32 (1976), pp. 57 *et seq.*, at pp. 62–63 and 73–79; E. Butkiewicz, "The premises of international responsibility of inter-governmental organizations", *Polish Yearbook of International Law*, vol. 11 (1981–1982), pp. 117 *et seq.*, at pp. 123–125 and 134–135; M. Pérez González, "Les organisations internationales et le droit de la responsabilité", RGDIP, vol. 92 (1988), pp. 63 *et seq.*, at p. 83; M. Hirsch, *The Responsibility of International Organizations toward Third Parties,* Dordrecht, Martinus Nijhoff, 1995, pp. 64–67; C. F. Amerasinghe, *Principles of the Institutional Law of International Organizations*, Cambridge University Press, 1996, pp. 241–243; P. Klein, *La responsabilité des organisations internationales dans les ordres juridiques internes et en droit des gens,* Brussels, Bruylant/Editions de l'Université de Bruxelles, 1998, pp. 379–380; I. Scobbie, "International organizations and international relations", in R.-J. Dupuy (ed.), *A Handbook of International Organizations*, 2nd ed., Dordrecht, Martinus Nijhoff, 1998, p. 891; C. Pitschas, *Die völkerrechtliche Verantwortlichkeit der Europäischen Gemeinschaft und ihrer Mitgliedstaaten,* Berlin, Duncker and Humblot, 2001, p. 51; and J.-M. Sorel, "La responsabilité des Nations Unies dans les opérations de maintien de la paix", *International Law Forum*, vol. 3, No. 2 (2001), pp. 127 *et seq.*, at p. 129. Some authors refer to "effective control", some others to "operational control". The latter concept

Many major operations undertaken under the United Nations flag and in the context of UNOSOM's mandate were totally outside the command and control of the United Nations, even though the repercussions impacted crucially on the mission of UNOSOM and the safety of its personnel."[70]

Taking the same approach, the Court of First Instance of Brussels found that the decision by the commander of the Belgian contingent of the United Nations Assistance Mission for Rwanda (UNAMIR) to abandon a *de facto* refugee camp at Kigali in April 1994 was "taken under the aegis of Belgium and not of UNAMIR".[71]

(9) The Secretary-General of the United Nations held that the criterion of the "degree of effective control" was decisive with regard to joint operations:

> The international responsibility of the United Nations for combat-related activities of United Nations forces is premised on the assumption that the operation in question is under the exclusive command and control of the United Nations ... In joint operations, international responsibility for the conduct of the troops lies where operational command and control is vested according to the arrangements establishing the modalities of co-operation between the State or States providing the troops and the United Nations. In the absence of formal arrangements between the United Nations and the State or States providing troops, responsibility would be determined in each and every case according to the degree of effective control exercised by either party in the conduct of the operation.[72]

What has been held with regard to joint operations, such as those involving UNOSOM II and the Quick Reaction Force in Somalia, should also apply to peacekeeping operations, insofar as it is possible to distinguish in their regard areas of effective control respectively pertaining to the United Nations and the contributing State. While it is understandable that, for the sake of efficiency of military operations, the United Nations insists on claiming exclusive command and control over peacekeeping forces, attribution of conduct should also in this regard be based on a factual criterion.

(10) The European Court of Human Rights considered, first in *Behrami and Behrami* v. *France* and *Saramati* v. *France, Germany and Norway*,[73] its jurisdiction *ratione personae* in relation to the conduct of forces placed in Kosovo at the disposal of the United Nations (United Nations Interim Administration Mission in Kosovo (UNMIK)) or authorized by the United Nations (Kosovo Force (KFOR)). The Court referred to the present work of the International Law Commission and in particular to the criterion of "effective control" that had been provisionally adopted by the Commission. While not formulating any criticism to this criterion, the Court considered that the decisive factor was whether the United Nations Security Council "retained ultimate authority and control so that operational command only was delegated".[74] While acknowledging "the effectiveness or unity of [the]

was used also by Bothe (see M. Bothe, *Streitkräfte internationaler Organisationen,* Cologne/Berlin, Heymanns Verlag, 1968, p. 87). Difficulties in drawing a line between operational and organizational control were underlined by Condorelli (L. Condorelli, "Le statut des forces de l'ONU et le droit international humanitaire", *Rivista di Diritto Internazionale*, vol. 78 (1995), pp. 881 *et seq.,* at pp. 887–888). The draft suggested by the Committee on Accountability of International Organisations of the International Law Association referred to a criterion of "effective control (operational command and control)" (International Law Association, *Report of the Seventy-first Conference Held in Berlin, 16–21 August 2004*, London, 2004, p. 200). [Note: this footnote appears in the original document as footnote '121'].

70 S/1994/653, paras. 243–244. [Note: this footnote appears in the original document as footnote '122'].

71 *Mukeshimana-Ngulinzira and Others v. Belgium and Others*, RG Nos. 04/4807/A and 07/15547/A, Judgment of 8 December 2010, Court of First Instance of Brussels, *Oxford Reports on International Law in Domestic Courts,* vol. 1604 (BE 2010), para. 38; available from www.oxfordlawreports.com. In the original French the quoted passage reads as follows: *une décision prise sous l'égide de la Belgique et non de la MINUAR*. [Note: this footnote appears in the original document as footnote '123'].

72 A/51/389, paras. 17–18. [Note: this footnote appears in the original document as footnote '124'].

73 Grand Chamber decision of 2 May 2007 (Admissibility), Application nos. 71412/01 and 78166/01, European Court of Human Rights (available from the Court's HUDOC database: http://hudoc.echr.coe.int). [Note: this footnote appears in the original document as footnote '125'].

74 *Ibid.*, para. 133. [Note: this footnote appears in the original document as footnote '126'].

operational command [of NATO]" concerning KFOR,[75] the Court noted that the presence of KFOR in Kosovo was based on a resolution adopted by the Security Council and concluded that "KFOR was exercising lawfully delegated Chapter VII [of the Charter of the United Nations] powers of the [United Nations Security Council] so that the impugned action was, in principle, 'attributable' to the [United Nations] within the meaning of the word outlined [in article 4 of the present articles]".[76] One may note that, when applying the criterion of effective control, "operational" control would seem more significant than "ultimate" control, since the latter hardly implies a role in the act in question.[77] It is therefore not surprising that in his report of June 2008 on the UNMIK, the Secretary-General of the United Nations distanced himself from the latter criterion and stated, "It is understood that the international responsibility of the United Nations will be limited in the extent of its effective operational control."[78]

(11) In *Kasumaj* v. *Greece*[79] and *Gajić* v. *Germany*[80] the European Court of Human Rights reiterated its view concerning the attribution to the United Nations of conduct taken by national contingents allocated to KFOR. Likewise in *Berić and others* v. *Bosnia and Herzegovina*[81] the same Court quoted verbatim and at length its previous decision in *Behrami* and *Saramati* when reaching the conclusion that the conduct of the High Representative in Bosnia and Herzegovina had to be attributed to the United Nations.

(12) Also the decision of the House of Lords in the *Al-Jedda* case[82] contained ample references to the present work of the Commission. One of the majority opinions stated that "[i]t was common ground between the parties that the governing principle [was] that expressed by the International Law Commission in article [7] of its draft articles on Responsibility of International Organizations".[83] The House of Lords was confronted with a claim arising from the detention of a person by British troops in Iraq. In its resolution 1546 (2004) of 8

75 *Ibid.*, para. 139. [Note: this footnote appears in the original document as footnote '127'].

76 *Ibid.*, para. 141 [Note: this footnote appears in the original document as footnote '128'].

77 Various authors pointed out that the European Court did not apply the criterion of effective control in the way that had been envisaged by the Commission. See C. A. Bell, "Reassessing multiple attribution: the International Law Commission and the *Behrami* and *Saramati* decision", *New York University Journal of International Law and Politics*, vol. 42, No. 2 (2010), p. 501; P. Bodeau-Livinec, G. P. Buzzini and S. Villalpando, Note, AJIL, vol. 102, No. 2 (2008), pp. 323 *et seq.*, at pp. 328–329; P. Klein, "Responsabilité pour les faits commis dans le cadre d'opérations de paix et étendue du pouvoir de contrôle de la Cour européenne des droits de l'homme: quelques considérations critiques sur l'arrêt *Behrami* et *Saramati*", AFDI, vol. 53 (2007), pp. 43 *et seq.*, at p. 55; P. Lagrange, "Responsabilité des Etats pour actes accomplis en application du chapitre VII de la Charte des Nations Unies", RGDIP, vol. 112 (2008), pp. 85 *et* seq., at pp. 94–95; C. Laly-Chevalier, "Les opérations militaires et civiles des Nations Unies et la Convention européenne des droits de l'homme", *Revue belge de droit international*, vol. 40 (2007), pp. 627 *et seq.*, at pp. 642–644; K. M. Larsen, "Attribution of conduct in peace operations: The 'ultimate authority and control' test", *European Journal of International Law*, vol. 19, No. 3 (2008), pp. 509 *et seq.*, at pp. 521–522; F. Messineo, "The House of Lords in *Al-Jedda* and public international law: attribution of conduct to UN-authorized forces and the power of the Security Council to displace human rights", *Netherlands International Law Review*, vol. 56, No. 1 (2009), pp. 35 *et seq.*, at pp. 39–43; M. Milanović and T. Papić, "As bad as it gets: The European Court of Human Rights's *Behrami* and *Saramati* decision and general international law", *International and Comparative Law Quarterly*, vol. 58 (2009), pp. 267 *et seq.*, at pp. 283–286; A. Orakhelashvili, Note, AJIL, vol. 102 (2008), pp. 337 *et seq.*, at p. 341; P. Palchetti, "Azioni di forze istituite o autorizzate dalle Nazioni Unite davanti alla Corte europea dei diritti dell'uomo: i casi *Behrami* e *Saramati*", *Rivista di diritto internazionale*, vol. 90 (2007), pp. 681 *et seq.*, at pp. 689–690; A. Sari, "Jurisdiction and international responsibility in peace support operations: the *Behrami* and *Saramati* cases", *Human Rights Law Review*, vol. 8, No. 1 (2008), pp. 151 *et seq.*, at p. 164; L.-A. Sicilianos, "L'(ir)responsabilité des forces multilatérales?", in L. Boisson de Chazournes and M. Kohen (eds.), *International Law and the Quest for its Implementation*; Liber Amicorum *Vera Gowlland-Debbas*, Leiden, Brill, 2010, pp. 95 *et seq.*, at pp. 98–106; and H. Strydom, "The responsibility of international organisations for conduct arising out of armed conflict situations", *South African Yearbook of International Law*, vol. 34 (2009), pp. 101 *et seq.*, at pp. 116–120. [Note: this footnote appears in the original document as footnote '129'].

78 S/2008/354, para. 16. [Note: this footnote appears in the original document as footnote '130'].

79 Decision of 5 July 2007 on the admissibility of Application no. 6974/05. [Note: this footnote appears in the original document as footnote '131'].

80 Decision of 28 August 2007 on the admissibility of Application no. 31446/02. [Note: this footnote appears in the original document as footnote '132'].

81 Decision of 16 October 2007 on the admissibility of Application nos. 36357/04, 36360/04, 38346/04, 41705/04, 45190/04, 45578/04, 45579/04, 45580/04, 91/05, 97/05, 100/05, 1121/05, 1123/05, 1125/05, 1129/05, 1132/05, 1133/05, 1169/05, 1172/05, 1175/05, 1177/05, 1180/05, 1185/05, 20793/05 and 25496/05. [Note: this footnote appears in the original document as footnote '133'].

82 *R. (on the application of Al-Jedda)* v. *Secretary of State for Defence*, Judgment of 12 December 2007, House of Lords [2007] UKHL 58. [Note: this footnote appears in the original document as footnote '134'].

83 *Ibid.*, paragraph 5 of the opinion of Lord Bingham of Cornhill. [Note: this footnote appears in the original document as footnote '135'].

June 2004, the Security Council had previously authorized the presence of the multinational force in that country. The majority opinions appeared to endorse the views expressed by the European Court of Human Rights in *Behrami* and *Saramati*, but distinguished the facts of the case and concluded that it could not "realistically be said that US and UK forces were under the effective command and control of the [United Nations], or that UK forces were under such command and control when they detained the appellant".[84] This conclusion appears to be in line with the way in which the criterion of effective control was intended.

(13) After the judgment of the House of Lords, an application was made by Mr. Al-Jedda to the European Court of Human Rights. In *Al-Jedda* v. *the United Kingdom,* this Court quoted several texts concerning attribution, including the article (identical to the present article) which had been adopted by the Commission on first reading and some paragraphs of the commentary.[85] The Court considered that "the United Nations Security Council had neither effective control nor ultimate authority and control over the acts and omissions of foreign troops within the Multinational Force and that the applicant's detention was not, therefore, attributable to the United Nations".[86] The Court unanimously concluded that the applicant's detention had to be attributed to the respondent State.[87]

(14) (14) The question of attribution was also considered in a judgment of the District Court of The Hague concerning the attribution of the conduct of the Dutch contingent in the United Nations Protection Force (UNPROFOR) in relation to the massacre in Srebrenica. This judgment contained only a general reference to the Commission's articles.[88] The Court found that "the reprehended acts of Dutchbat should be assessed as those of an UNPROFOR contingent" and that "these acts and omissions should be attributed strictly, as a matter of principle, to the United Nations".[89] The Court then considered that if "Dutchbat was instructed by the Dutch authorities to ignore [United Nations] orders or to go against them, and Dutchbat behaved in accordance with this instruction from the Netherlands, this constitutes a violation of the factual basis on which the attribution to the [United Nations] rests."[90] The Court did not find that there was sufficient evidence for reaching such a conclusion. On appeal from the judgment of the District Court, the Hague Court of Appeal referred to the draft article (identical to the present article) which had been adopted by the Commission on first reading. The Court applied the criterion of "effective control" to the circumstances of the case and reached the conclusion that the respondent State was responsible for its involvement in the events at Srebrenica which had led to the killing of three Bosnian Muslim men after they had been evicted from the compound of Dutchbat.[91]

---

84 See the opinion of Lord Bingham of Cornhill, *ibid.*, paras. 22–24 (the quotation is taken from paragraph 23). Baroness Hale of Richmond (para. 124), Lord Carswell (para. 131) and Lord Brown of Eaton-under-Heywood (paras. 141–149, with his own reasons) concurred on this conclusion, while Lord Rodger of Earlsferry dissented. [Note: this footnote appears in the original document as footnote '136'].

85 Application no. 2702/08, Judgment of 7 July 2011, Grand Chamber, European Court of Human Rights, *Reports of Judgments and Decisions* 2011, para. 56 (available from the Court's HUDOC database: http://hudoc.echr.coe.int). [Note: this footnote appears in the original document as footnote '137'].

86 *Ibid.*, para. 84. The Court found that Al-Jedda's "internment took place within a detention facility in Basrah City, controlled exclusively by British forces, and [that] the applicant was therefore within the authority and control of the United Kingdom throughout" (para. 85). [Note: this footnote appears in the original document as footnote '139'].

87 *Ibid.*, paragraph 3 of the operative part. [Note: this footnote appears in the original document as footnote '139'].

88 *H. N.* v. *the Netherlands*, Case No. 265615/HA ZA 06-1671, Judgment of 10 September 2008, District Court of The Hague, para. 4.8. English translation available from http://deeplink.rechtspraak.nl/uitspr aak?id=ECLI:NL:RBSGR:2008:BF0181. [Note: this footnote appears in the original document as footnote '140].

89 *Ibid.*, para. 4.11. [Note: this footnote appears in the original document as footnote '141'].

90 *Ibid.*, para. 4.14.1. [Note: this footnote appears in the original document as footnote '142'].

91 *Nuhanović* v. *Netherlands*, Case No. LJN:BR5388, Judgment of 5 July 2011, The Hague Court of Appeal (Civil Law Section), especially paragraphs 5.8–5.9. English translation available from http://zoeken.rechtspraak.nl; also available from www.oxfordlawreports.com (International Law in Domestic Courts (ILDC) 1742 (NL 2011)). The Court argued that the Netherlands had been able to prevent the removal of the victims. When giving a wide meaning to the concept of "effective control" so as to include also the ability to prevent, the Court followed the approach taken by T. Dannenbaum, "Translating the standard of effective control into a system of effective accountability: how liability should be apportioned for violations of human rights by Member State troop contingents serving as United Nations peacekeepers", *Harvard International Law Journal*, vol. 51, No. 1 (2010), pp. 113 *et seq.*,

(15) The principles applicable to peacekeeping forces may be extended to other State organs placed at the disposal of the United Nations, such as disaster relief units, about which the United Nations Secretary-General wrote that

> [i]f the disaster relief unit is itself established by the United Nations, the unit would be a subsidiary organ of the United Nations. A disaster relief unit of this kind would be similar in legal status to, for example, the United Nations [Peacekeeping] Force in Cyprus (UNFICYP).[92]

(16) Similar conclusions would have to be reached in the rarer case that an international organization places one of its organs at the disposal of another international organization. An example is provided by the Pan American Sanitary Conference, which, as a result of an agreement between WHO and the Pan American Health Organization, serves "respectively as the Regional Committee and the Regional Office of the World Health Organization for the Western Hemisphere, within the provisions of the Constitution of the World Health Organization".[93] The Legal Counsel of WHO noted that

> [o]n the basis of that arrangement, acts of [the Pan American Health Organization] and of its staff could engage the responsibility of WHO.[94]

Article 8

Excess of authority or contravention of instructions

The conduct of an organ or agent of an international organization shall be considered an act of that organization under international law if the organ or agent acts in an official capacity and within the overall functions of that organization, even if the conduct exceeds the authority of that organ or agent or contravenes instructions.

Commentary

(1) Article 8 deals with *ultra vires* conduct of organs or agents of an international organization. *Ultra vires* conduct may be within the competence of the organization, but exceed the authority of the acting organ or agent. It also may exceed the competence of the organization,[95] in which case it will also exceed the authority of the organ or of the agent who performed it.

(2) Article 8 has to be read in the context of the other provisions relating to attribution, especially article 6. It is to be understood that, in accordance with article 6, organs and agents are persons and entities exercising functions of the organization. Apart from exceptional cases (paragraph (11) of the commentary to article 6), the rules of the organization, as defined in article 2, subparagraph (*b*), will govern the issue whether an organ or agent has authority to undertake a certain conduct. It is implied that instructions are relevant to the purpose of attribution of conduct only if they are binding the organ or agent. Also in this regard the rules of the organization will generally be decisive.

---

at p. 157. The Court considered the possibility of a dual attribution of conduct to the State of origin and the United Nations. This solution had been advocated by C. Leck, "International responsibility in United Nations peacekeeping operations: command and control arrangements and the attribution of conduct", *Melbourne Journal of International Law*, vol. 10 (2009), pp. 346 *et seq.*, at pp. 362–364. [Note: this footnote appears in the original document as footnote '143'].

92 United Nations, *Juridical Yearbook 1971* (Sales No. E.73.V.1), p. 187. [Note: this footnote appears in the original document as footnote '144'].

93 Article 2 of the Agreement concerning the integration of the Pan American Sanitary Organization with the World Health Organization, signed at Washington, D.C. on 24 May 1949 (United Nations, *Treaty Series*, vol. 32, No. 178, p. 387, at p. 388). [Note: this footnote appears in the original document as footnote '145'].

94 Letter of 19 December 2003 from the Legal Counsel of WHO to the United Nations Legal Counsel, *Yearbook . . . 2004*, vol. II (Part One), document A/CN.4/545, p. 34. [Note: this footnote appears in the original document as footnote '146'].

95 As the International Court of Justice said in its advisory opinion on *Legality of the Use by a State of Nuclear Weapons in Armed Conflict*

(3) The wording of article 8 closely follows that of draft article 7 on the responsibility of States for internationally wrongful acts.[96] One textual difference is due to the fact that the latter article takes the wording of draft articles 4 and 5 on State responsibility into account and thus considers the *ultra vires* conduct of "an organ of a State or a person or entity empowered to exercise elements of governmental authority", while the present article only needs to be aligned with article 6 and thus more simply refers to "an organ or an agent of an international organization".

(4) The key element for attribution in draft article 7 on the responsibility of States for internationally wrongful acts is the requirement that the organ or agent acts "in that capacity". This wording is intended to convey the need for a close link between the *ultra vires* conduct and the organ's or agent's functions. As was said in the commentary to draft article 7 on State responsibility, the text "indicates that the conduct referred to comprises only the actions and omissions of organs purportedly or apparently carrying out their official functions, and not the private actions or omissions of individuals who happen to be organs or agents of the State".[97] In order to make this point clearer, the present article expressly specifies the requirement that the organ or agent of an international organization "acts in an official capacity and within the overall functions of that organization".[98]

(5) Article 8 only concerns attribution of conduct and does not prejudice the question whether an *ultra vires* act is valid or not under the rules of the organization. Even if the act was considered to be invalid, it may entail the responsibility of the organization. The need to protect third parties requires attribution not to be limited to acts that are regarded as valid.

(6) The possibility of attributing to an international organization acts that an organ takes *ultra vires* has been admitted by the International Court of Justice in its advisory opinion on *Certain expenses of the United Nations*, in which the Court stated as follows:

> If it is agreed that the action in question is within the scope of the functions of the Organization but it is alleged that it has been initiated or carried out in a manner not in conformity with the division of functions among the several organs which the Charter [of the United Nations] prescribes, one moves to the internal plane, to the internal structure of the Organization. If the action was taken by the wrong organ, it was irregular as a matter of that internal structure, but this would not necessarily mean that the expense incurred was not an expense of the Organization. Both national or international law contemplate cases in which the body corporate or politic may be bound, as to third parties, by an *ultra vires* act of an agent.[99]

The fact that the Court considered that the United Nations would have to bear expenses deriving from *ultra vires* acts of an organ reflects policy considerations that appear even stronger in relation to wrongful conduct. Denying attribution of conduct may deprive third parties of all redress, unless conduct could be attributed to a State or to another organization.

(7) A distinction between the conduct of organs and officials and that of other agents would find little justification in view of the limited significance that the distinction carries in the

---

> international organizations ... do not, unlike States, possess a general competence. International organizations are governed by the 'principle of speciality', that is to say, they are invested by the States which create them with powers, the limits of which are a function of the common interests whose promotion those States entrust to them.

(*Legality of the Use by a State of Nuclear Weapons in Armed Conflict* (see footnote 68 above), p. 78, para. 25). [Note: this footnote appears in the original document as footnote '147'].

96 *Yearbook ... 2001*, vol. II (Part Two) and corrigendum, pp. 45–47. [Note: this footnote appears in the original document as footnote '148'].

97 *Ibid.*, p. 46, paragraph (8) of the commentary to article 7. [Note: this footnote appears in the original document as footnote '149'].

98 The inclusion of a reference to the functions of the organization was advocated by J. M. Cortés Martín, *Las Organizaciones Internacionales: Codificación y Desarrollo Progresivo de su Responsabilidad Internacional*, Seville, Instituto Andaluz de Administración Pública, 2008), pp. 211–223. [Note: this footnote appears in the original document as footnote '150'].

99 *Certain expenses of the United Nations (Article 17, paragraph 2, of the Charter), Advisory Opinion of 20 July 1962: I.C.J. Reports 1962*, p. 151, at p. 168. [Note: this footnote appears in the original document as footnote '151'].

practice of international organizations.[100] The International Court of Justice appears to have asserted the organization's responsibility for *ultra vires* acts also of persons other than officials. In its advisory opinion on *Difference Relating to Immunity from Legal Process of a Special Rapporteur of the Commission on Human Rights*, the Court stated that

> it need hardly be said that all agents of the United Nations, in whatever official capacity they act, must take care not to exceed the scope of their functions, and should so comport themselves as to avoid claims against the United Nations.[101]

One obvious reason why an agent—in this case an expert on mission—should take care not to exceed the scope of his or her functions in order to avoid that claims be preferred against the organization is that the organization could well be held responsible for the agent's conduct.

(8) The rule stated in article 8 also finds support in the following statement of the General Counsel of the International Monetary Fund (IMF):

> Attribution may apply even though the official exceeds the authority given to him, he failed to follow rules or he was negligent. However, acts of an official that were not performed in his official capacity would not be attributable to the organization.[102]

(9) Practice of international organizations confirms that *ultra vires* conduct of an organ or agent is attributable to the organization when that conduct is linked with the organ's or agent's official functions. This appears to underlie the position taken by the Office of Legal Affairs of the United Nations in a memorandum concerning claims involving off-duty acts of members of peacekeeping forces:

> United Nations policy in regard to off-duty acts of the members of peace-keeping forces is that the Organization has no legal or financial liability for death, injury or damage resulting from such acts ... We consider the primary factor in determining an "off-duty" situation to be whether the member of a peace-keeping mission was acting in a non-official/non-operational capacity when the incident occurred and not whether he/she was in military or civilian attire at the time of the incident or whether the incident occurred inside or outside the area of operation ... [W]ith regard to United Nations legal and financial liability a member of the Force on a state of alert may nonetheless assume an off-duty status if he/she independently acts in an individual capacity, not attributable to the performance of official duties, during that designated "state-of-alert" period... [W]e wish to note that the factual circumstances of each case vary and, hence, a determination of whether the status of a member of a peace-keeping mission is on duty or off duty may depend in part on the particular factors of the case, taking into consideration the opinion of the Force Commander or Chief of Staff.[103]

While the "off-duty" conduct of a member of a national contingent would not be attributed to the organization,[104] the "on-duty" conduct may be so attributed. One would then have to

---

100 The Committee on Accountability of International Organizations of the International Law Association suggested the following rule:

> "The conduct of organs, officials, or agents of an [international organization] shall be considered an act of that [international organization] under international law if the organ, official, or agent was acting in its official capacity, even if that conduct exceeds the authority granted or contravenes instructions given (*ultra vires*)."

(International Law Association, *Report of the Seventy-first Conference* ... (see footnote 121 above), p. 200. [Note: this footnote appears in the original document as footnote '152'].

101 *Difference Relating to Immunity from Legal Process of a Special Rapporteur of the Commission on Human Rights* (see footnote 87 above), p. 89, para. 66. [Note: this footnote appears in the original document as footnote '153'].

102 *Yearbook ... 2004*, vol. II (Part One), document A/CN.4/545, p. 33. [Note: this footnote appears in the original document as footnote '154'].

103 United Nations, *Juridical Yearbook 1986* (Sales No. E.94.V.2), p. 300. [Note: this footnote appears in the original document as footnote '155'].

104 A clear case of an "off-duty" act of a member of the United Nations Interim Force in Lebanon, who had engaged in moving explosives to the territory of Israel, was considered by the District Court of Haifa in a judgment of 10 May 1979 (see United

examine whether the *ultra vires* conduct in question is related to the functions entrusted to the person concerned.

(10) The fact that conduct is taken by an organ or agent off duty does not necessarily exclude the responsibility of the international organization if the latter breached an obligation of prevention that may exist under international law. This is likely to be the situation to which the Office of Legal Affairs of the United Nations referred in 1974 when it considered, with reference to off-duty conduct of members of the United Nations Emergency Force, that "there may well be situations involving actions by Force members off duty which the United Nations could appropriately recognise as engaging its responsibility".[105]

Article 9

Conduct acknowledged and adopted by an international organization as its own

Conduct which is not attributable to an international organization under articles 6 to 8 shall nevertheless be considered an act of that organization under international law if and to the extent that the organization acknowledges and adopts the conduct in question as its own.

Commentary

(1) Article 9 concerns the case in which an international organization "acknowledges and adopts" as its own certain conduct which would not be attributable to that organization under the preceding articles. Attribution is then based on the attitude taken by the organization with regard to a certain conduct. The reference to the "extent" reflects the possibility that acknowledgement and adoption relate only to part of the conduct in question.

(2) Article 9 mirrors the content of article 11 on the responsibility of States for internationally wrongful acts,[106] which is identically worded but for the reference to a State instead of an international organization. As the commentary on article 11 explains, attribution can be based on acknowledgement and adoption of conduct also when that conduct "may not have been attributable".[107] In other words, the criterion of attribution now under consideration may be applied even when it has not been established whether attribution may be effected on the basis of other criteria.

(3) In certain instances of practice, relating both to States and to international organizations, it may not be clear whether what is involved by the acknowledgement is attribution of conduct or responsibility. This is not altogether certain, for instance, with regard to the following statement made on behalf of the European Community in the oral pleading before a World Trade Organization (WTO) panel in the case *European Communities—Customs Classification of Certain Computer Equipment*. The European Community declared that it was

> ready to assume the entire international responsibility for all measures in the area of tariff concessions, whether the measure complained about has been taken at the [European Community] level or at the level of Member States.[108]

(4) The question of attribution was clearly addressed by a decision of Trial Chamber II of the International Criminal Tribunal for the former Yugoslavia in *Prosecutor* v. *Dragan Nikolić*.

Nations, *Juridical Yearbook 1979* (Sales No. E.82.V.1), p. 205). [Note: this footnote appears in the original document as footnote '156'].

105 This passage of an unpublished opinion was quoted in the comment of the Secretariat of the United Nations, A/CN.4/637 and Add.1 (in the section "Draft article 7 ... United Nations", para. 4). [Note: this footnote appears in the original document as footnote '157'].

106 *Yearbook ... 2001*, vol. II (Part Two) and corrigendum, p. 52. [Note: this footnote appears in the original document as footnote '158'].

107 *Ibid.*, paragraph (1) of the commentary to article 11. [Note: this footnote appears in the original document as footnote '159'].

108 Unpublished document. [Note: this footnote appears in the original document as footnote '160'].

The question was raised whether the arrest of the accused was attributable to the Stabilization Force (SFOR). The Chamber first noted that the Commission's articles on responsibility of States for internationally wrongful acts were "not binding on States". It then referred to article 57 and observed that the articles were "primarily directed at the responsibility of States and not at those of international organizations or entities".[109] However, the Chamber found that, "[p]urely as *general* legal guidance", it would "use the principles laid down in the draft articles insofar as they may be helpful for determining the issue at hand".[110] This led the Chamber to quote extensively article 11 and the related commentary.[111] The Chamber then added:

> The Trial Chamber observes that both Parties use the same and similar criteria of "acknowledgement", "adoption", "recognition", "approval" and "ratification", as used by the [International Law Commission]. The question is therefore whether on the basis of the assumed facts SFOR can be considered to have "acknowledged and adopted" the conduct undertaken by the individuals "as its own".[112]

The Chamber concluded that the conduct of SFOR did not "amount to an 'adoption' or 'acknowledgement' of the illegal conduct 'as their own' ".[113]

(5) No policy reasons appear to militate against applying to international organizations the criterion for attribution based on acknowledgement and adoption. The question may arise regarding the competence of the international organization in making that acknowledgement and adoption, and concerning which organ or agent would be competent to do so. Although the existence of a specific rule is highly unlikely, the rules of the organization govern also this issue.

Chapter III

Breach of an international obligation

Commentary

(1) Articles 6 to 9 of the present draft articles address the question of attribution of conduct to an international organization. According to article 4, attribution of conduct is one of the two conditions for an internationally wrongful act of an international organization to arise. The other condition is that the same conduct "constitutes a breach of an international obligation of that organization". This condition is examined in the present Chapter.

(2) As specified in article 4, conduct of an international organization may consist of "an action or omission". An omission constitutes a breach when the international organization is under an international obligation to take some positive action and fails to do so. A breach may also consist in an action that is inconsistent with what the international organization is required to do, or not to do, under international law.

(3) To a large extent, the four articles included in the present chapter correspond, in their substance and wording, to articles 12 to 15 on the responsibility of States for internationally

---

109 *Prosecutor v. Dragan Nikolić*, Case No. IT-94-2-PT, *Decision on defence motion challenging the exercise of jurisdiction by the Tribunal*, 9 October 2002, International Tribunal for the Former Yugoslavia, *Judicial Supplement*, No. 37, para. 60. [Note: this footnote appears in the original document as footnote '161'].

110 *Ibid.*, para. 61. [Note: this footnote appears in the original document as footnote '162'].

111 *Ibid.*, paras. 62–63. [Note: this footnote appears in the original document as footnote '163'].

112 *Ibid.*, para. 64. [Note: this footnote appears in the original document as footnote '164'].

113 *Ibid.*, para. 66. The appeal was rejected on a different basis. On the point here at issue, the Appeals Chamber only noted that "the exercise of jurisdiction should not be declined in case of abductions carried out by private individuals whose actions, unless instigated, acknowledged or condoned by a State or an international organization, or other entity, do not necessarily in themselves violate State sovereignty" (*Prosecutor v. Dragan Nikolić*, Case No. IT-94-2-AR73, *Decision on interlocutory appeal concerning legality*

wrongful acts.[114] Those articles express principles of a general nature that appear to be applicable to the breach of an international obligation on the part of any subject of international law. There would thus be little reason to take a different approach in the present articles, although available practice relating to international organizations is limited with regard to the various issues addressed in the present chapter.

Article 10

Existence of a breach of an international obligation

1. There is a breach of an international obligation by an international organization when an act of that international organization is not in conformity with what is required of it by that obligation, regardless of the origin or character of the obligation concerned.
2. Paragraph 1 includes the breach of an international obligation that may arise for an international organization towards its members under the rules of the organization.

Commentary

...

(2) As in the case of State responsibility, the term "international obligation" means an obligation under international law "regardless of the origin" of the obligation concerned. As mentioned in the commentary on article 12 on the responsibility of States for internationally wrongful acts, this is intended to convey that the international obligation "may be established by a customary rule of international law, by a treaty or by a general principle applicable within the international legal order".[115]

(3) An international obligation may be owed by an international organization to the international community as a whole, one or several States, whether members or non-members, another international organization or other international organizations and any other subject of international law.

...

(7) Although the question of the legal nature of the rules of the organization is far from theoretical for the purposes of the present draft articles, since it affects the applicability of the principles of international law with regard to responsibility for breaches of certain obligations arising from the rules of the organization, paragraph 2 does not attempt to express a clear-cut view on the issue. It simply intends to say that, to the extent that an obligation arising from the rules of the organization has to be regarded as an obligation under international law, the principles expressed in the present article apply. Breaches of obligations under the rules of the organization are not always breaches of obligations under international law.

...

Article 11

International obligation in force for an international organization

An act of an international organization does not constitute a breach of an international obligation unless the organization is bound by the obligation in question at the time the act occurs.

...

of arrest, 5 June 2003, International Tribunal for the Former Yugoslavia, *Judicial Supplement*, No. 42, para. 26). [Note: this footnote appears in the original document as footnote '165'].

114 *Yearbook ... 2001*, vol. II (Part Two) and corrigendum, pp. 54–64. [Note: this footnote appears in the original document as footnote '166'].

115 *Ibid.*, p. 55, paragraph (3) of the commentary to article 12. [Note: this footnote appears in the original document as footnote '168'].

Article 12
Extension in time of the breach of an international obligation

1. The breach of an international obligation by an act of an international organization not having a continuing character occurs at the moment when the act is performed, even if its effects continue.
2. The breach of an international obligation by an act of an international organization having a continuing character extends over the entire period during which the act continues and remains not in conformity with that obligation.
3. The breach of an international obligation requiring an international organization to prevent a given event occurs when the event occurs and extends over the entire period during which the event continues and remains not in conformity with that obligation.

...

Article 13
Breach consisting of a composite act

1. The breach of an international obligation by an international organization through a series of actions and omissions defined in aggregate as wrongful occurs when the action or omission occurs which, taken with the other actions or omissions, is sufficient to constitute the wrongful act.
2. In such a case, the breach extends over the entire period starting with the first of the actions or omissions of the series and lasts for as long as these actions or omissions are repeated and remain not in conformity with the international obligation.

...

Chapter IV

Responsibility of an international organization in connection with the act of a State or another international organization

Commentary

(1) Articles 16 to 18 on the responsibility of States for internationally wrongful acts[116] cover the cases in which a State aids or assists, directs and controls, or coerces another State in the commission of an internationally wrongful act. Article 16 was described as "reflecting a customary rule" by the International Court of Justice in its judgment on the merits in *Application of the Convention on the Prevention and Punishment of the Crime of Genocide.*[117] Parallel situations could be envisaged with regard to international organizations. For instance, an international organization may aid or assist a State or another international organization in the commission of an internationally wrongful act. For the purposes of international responsibility, there would be no reason for distinguishing the case of an international organization aiding or assisting a State or another international organization from that of a State aiding or assisting another State. Thus, even if available practice with regard to international organizations is limited, there is some justification for including in the present articles provisions that are parallel to articles 16 to 18 on the responsibility of States for internationally wrongful acts.

(2) The pertinent provisions of the draft articles on responsibility of States for internationally wrongful acts are based on the premise that aid or assistance, direction and control, and coercion do not affect attribution of conduct to the State which is aided or assisted, under the

---

116 *Ibid.*, pp. 65–69. [Note: this footnote appears in the original document as footnote '178'].

117 *Application of the Convention on the Prevention and Punishment of the Crime of Genocide (Bosnia and Herzegovina* v. *Serbia and Montenegro), Judgment, I.C.J. Reports 2007*, p. 43, at p. 150, para. 420. [Note: this footnote appears in the original document as footnote '179'].

direction or control, or under coercion. It is that State which commits an internationally wrongful act, although in the case of coercion wrongfulness could be excluded, while the other State is held responsible not for having actually committed the wrongful act but for its causal contribution to the commission of the act.

(3) The relations between an international organization and its member States or international organizations may allow the former organization to influence the conduct of members also in cases that are not envisaged in articles 16 to 18 on the responsibility of States for internationally wrongful acts. Some international organizations have the power to take decisions binding their members, while most organizations may only influence their members' conduct through non-binding acts. The consequences that this type of relation, which does not have a parallel in the relations between States, may entail with regard to an international organization's responsibility is also examined in the present Chapter.

...

Article 14

Aid or assistance in the commission of an internationally wrongful act

An international organization which aids or assists a State or another international organization in the commission of an internationally wrongful act by the State or the latter organization is internationally responsible for doing so if:

(*a*) the former organization does so with knowledge of the circumstances of the internationally wrongful act; and

(*b*) the act would be internationally wrongful if committed by that organization.

Commentary

(1) The international responsibility that an entity may incur under international law for aiding or assisting another entity in the commission of an internationally wrongful act does not appear to depend on the nature and character of the entities concerned.[118] Thus, notwithstanding the limited practice specifically relating to international organizations, the rules applicable to the relations between States should also apply when an international organization aids and assists a State or another international organization in the commission of an internationally wrongful act.

...

(6) An example of practice of aid or assistance concerning an international organization is provided by an internal document issued on 12 October 2009 by the United Nations Legal Counsel. This concerned the support given by the United Nations Organization Mission in the Democratic Republic of the Congo (MONUC) to the Armed Forces of the Democratic Republic of the Congo (FARDC), and the risk, to which an internal memorandum had referred, of violations by the latter forces of international humanitarian law, human rights law and refugee law. The Legal Counsel wrote:

> If MONUC has reason to believe that FARDC units involved in an operation are violating one or the other of those bodies of law and if, despite MONUC's intercession with the FARDC and with the Government of the [Democratic Republic of the Congo], MONUC has reason to believe that such violations are still being committed, then MONUC may not lawfully continue to support that operation, but must cease its participation in it

---

118 The Committee on Accountability of International Organizations of the International Law Association stated that "[t]here is also an internationally wrongful act of an [international organization] when it aids or assists a State or another [international organization] in the commission of an internationally wrongful act by that State or other [international organization]" (International Law Association, *Report of the Seventy-first Conference* ... (see footnote 121 above), pp. 200–201). This text does not refer to the conditions listed in article 14 under subparagraphs (*a*) and (*b*) of the present articles. [Note: this footnote appears in the original document as footnote '187'].

completely... MONUC may not lawfully provide logistic or "service" support to any FARDC operation if it has reason to believe that the FARDC units involved are violating any of those bodies of law... This follows directly from the Organization's obligations under customary international law and from the Charter to uphold, promote and encourage respect for human rights, international humanitarian law and refugee law.[119]

Article 15

Direction and control exercised over the commission of an internationally wrongful act

An international organization which directs and controls a State or another international organization in the commission of an internationally wrongful act by the State or the latter organization is internationally responsible for that act if:

(*a*) the former organization does so with knowledge of the circumstances of the internationally wrongful act; and

(*b*) the act would be internationally wrongful if committed by that organization.

Commentary

(1) The text of article 15 corresponds to article 17 on the responsibility of States for internationally wrongful acts,[120] for reasons similar to those explained in the commentary to article 14 of the present draft articles. The appropriate modifications to the text have been introduced. Thus, the reference to the directing and controlling State has been replaced by that to an international organization which directs and controls; moreover, the term "State" has been replaced with "State or another international organization" in the reference to the entity which is directed and controlled.

(2) Article 15 provides that international responsibility will arise when an international organization "directs and controls a State or another international organization in the commission of an internationally wrongful act".

(3) If one assumes that KFOR is an international organization, an example of two international organizations allegedly exercising direction and control in the commission of a wrongful act may be taken from the preliminary objections by the Government of France in *Legality of Use of Force (Yugoslavia* v. *France)* before the International Court of Justice, when the Government argued that

"NATO is responsible for the 'direction' of KFOR and the United Nations for 'control' of it."[121]

A joint exercise of direction and control was probably envisaged.

(4) In the relations between an international organization and its member States and international organizations the concept of "direction and control" could conceivably be extended so as to encompass cases in which an international organization takes a decision binding its members. The commentary on article 17 on the responsibility of States for internationally wrongful acts explains that "[a]rticle 17 is limited to cases where a dominant State actually directs and controls conduct which is a breach of an international obligation of the

119 The documents were published in *The New York Times*, 9 December 2009, www.nytimes.com. [Note: this footnote appears in the original document as footnote '192'].

120 *Yearbook ... 2001*, vol. II (Part Two) and corrigendum, pp. 67–68. [Note: this footnote appears in the original document as footnote '193'].

121 *Legality of Use of Force (Yugoslavia* v. *France), Preliminary objections of the French Republic (5 July 2000), I.C.J. Reports 2001*, p. 13, at p. 33, para. 46. The argument was made for the purpose of attributing the allegedly wrongful conduct to the international organizations concerned. A similar view with regard to NATO and KFOR was held by Alain Pellet in his article "L'imputabilité d'éventuels actes illicites: responsabilité de l'OTAN ou des États membres", in C. Tomuschat (ed.), *Kosovo and the International Community: a Legal Assessment*, The Hague, Kluwer Law International, 2002, pp. 193 *et seq.*, at p. 199. [Note: this footnote appears in the original document as footnote '194'].

dependent State",[122] that "the term 'controls' refers to cases of domination over the commission of wrongful conduct and not simply the exercise of oversight, still less mere influence or concern",[123] and that "the word 'directs' does not encompass mere incitement or suggestion but rather connotes actual direction of an operative kind".[124] If one interprets the provision in the light of the passages quoted above, the adoption of a binding decision on the part of an international organization could constitute, under certain circumstances, a form of direction or control in the commission of an internationally wrongful act. The assumption is that the State or international organization which is the addressee of the decision is not given discretion to carry out conduct that, while complying with the decision, would not constitute an internationally wrongful act.

(5) If the adoption of a binding decision were to be regarded as a form of direction and control within the purview of the present article, this provision would overlap with article 17 of the present draft articles. The overlap would only be partial: it is sufficient to point out that article 17 also covers the case where a binding decision requires a member State or international organization to commit an act which is not unlawful for that State or international organization. In any case, the possible overlap between articles 15 and 17 would not create any inconsistency, since both provisions assert, albeit under different conditions, the international responsibility of the international organization which has taken a decision binding its member States or international organizations.

(6) The requirements set forth under subparagraphs (*a*) and (*b*) respectively refer to "knowledge of the circumstances of the internationally wrongful act" and to the fact that "the act would be internationally wrongful if committed by that organization". These requirements are identical to those listed in article 14 concerning aid or assistance in the commission of an internationally wrongful act. The same commentary applies.

Article 16

Coercion of a State or another international organization

An international organization which coerces a State or another international organization to commit an act is internationally responsible for that act if:

(*a*) the act would, but for the coercion, be an internationally wrongful act of the coerced State or international organization; and

(*b*) the coercing international organization does so with knowledge of the circumstances of the act.

Commentary

(1) Article 16 envisages coercion on the part of the international organization in the commission of an internationally wrongful act. The nature and character of the coercing or of the coerced entities do not significantly alter the situation. Thus, one may apply also to international organizations a rule similar to article 18 on the responsibility of States for internationally wrongful acts.

...

122 *Yearbook ... 2001*, vol. II (Part Two) and corrigendum, p. 68, paragraph (6) of the commentary to article 17. [Note: this footnote appears in the original document as footnote '195'].

123 *Ibid.*, p. 69, paragraph (7) of the commentary to article 17. [Note: this footnote appears in the original document as footnote '196'].

124 *Ibid.* [Note: this footnote appears in the original document as footnote '197'].

Article 17

Circumvention of international obligations through decisions and authorizations addressed to members

1. An international organization incurs international responsibility if it circumvents one of its international obligations by adopting a decision binding member States or international organizations to commit an act that would be internationally wrongful if committed by the former organization.
2. An international organization incurs international responsibility if it circumvents one of its international obligations by authorizing member States or international organizations to commit an act that would be internationally wrongful if committed by the former organization and the act in question is committed because of that authorization.
3. Paragraphs 1 and 2 apply whether or not the act in question is internationally wrongful for the member States or international organizations to which the decision or authorization is addressed.

Commentary

(1) The fact that an international organization is a subject of international law distinct from its members opens up the possibility for the organization to try to influence its members in order to achieve through them a result that the organization could not lawfully achieve directly, and thus circumvent one of its international obligations. As was noted by the delegation of Austria during the debate in the Sixth Committee,

> "an international organization should not be allowed to escape responsibility by 'outsourcing' its actors."[125]

(2) The Legal Counsel of the World Intellectual Property Organization (WIPO) considered the case of an international organization requiring a member State to commit an internationally unlawful act, and wrote that

> "in the event a certain conduct, which a member State takes in compliance with a request on the part of an international organization, appears to be in breach of an international obligation both of that State and of that organization, then the organization should also be regarded as responsible under international law."[126]

(3) The opportunity for circumvention is likely to be higher when the conduct of the member State or international organization would not be in breach of an international obligation, for instance because the circumventing international organization is bound by a treaty with a non-member State and the same treaty does not produce effects for the organization's members.

(4) The term "circumvention" implies an intention on the part of the international organization to take advantage of the separate legal personality of its members in order to avoid compliance with an international obligation. The evidence of such an intention will depend on the circumstances.

(5) In the case of a binding decision, paragraph 1 does not stipulate as a precondition, for the international responsibility of an international organization to arise, that the required act be committed by member States or international organizations. Since compliance by members with a binding decision is to be expected, the likelihood of a third party being injured would

---

125 *Official Records of the General Assembly, Fifty-ninth Session, Sixth Committee*, 22nd meeting (A/C.6/59/SR.22), para. 24. [Note: this footnote appears in the original document as footnote '200'].

126 *Yearbook ... 2005*, vol. II (Part One), document A/CN.4/556, p. 52. [Note: this footnote appears in the original document as footnote '201'].

then be high. It appears therefore preferable to hold the organization already responsible and thus allow the third party that would be injured to seek a remedy even before the act is committed. Moreover, if international responsibility arises at the time the decision is taken, the international organization would have to refrain from placing its members in the uncomfortable position of either infringing their obligations under the decision or causing the international responsibility of the international organization, as well as possibly incurring their own responsibility.

(6) A member State or international organization may be given discretion with regard to implementation of a binding decision adopted by an international organization. In its judgment on the merits in *Bosphorus Hava Yollari Turizm ve Ticaret Şirketi* v. *Ireland*, the European Court of Human Rights considered conduct that member States of the European Community take when implementing binding acts of the European Community and observed that

> a State would be fully responsible under the Convention for all acts falling outside its strict international legal obligations ... [N]umerous Convention cases ... confirm this. Each case (in particular, *Cantoni*, at para. 26) concerned a review by this Court of the exercise of State discretion for which Community law provided.[127]

(7) Paragraph 1 assumes that compliance with the binding decision of the international organization necessarily entails circumvention of one of its international obligations. As was noted in a statement in the Sixth Committee by the delegation of Denmark on behalf of the five Nordic countries,

> it appeared essential to find the point where the member State could be said to have so little "room for manoeuvre" that it would seem unreasonable to make it solely responsible for certain conduct.[128]

Should, on the contrary, the decision allow the member State or international organization some discretion to take an alternative course which does not imply circumvention, responsibility could arise for the international organization that has taken the decision only if circumvention actually occurs, as stated in paragraph 2.

(8) Paragraph 2 covers the case in which an international organization circumvents one of its international obligations by authorizing a member State or international organization to commit a certain act. When a member State or organization is authorized to commit an act, it is apparently free not to avail itself of the authorization received. However, this may be only in theory, because an authorization often implies the conferral by an organization of certain functions to the member or members concerned so that they would exercise these functions instead of the organization. Moreover, by authorizing an act, the organization generally expects the authorization to be acted upon.

(9) While paragraph 2 uses the term "authorization", it does not require an act of an international organization to be so defined under the rules of the organization concerned. The principle expressed in paragraph 2 also applies to acts of an international organization which may be defined by different terms but present a similar character to an authorization as described above.

(10) For international responsibility to arise, the first condition in paragraph 2 is that the international organization authorizes an act that would be wrongful for that organization and moreover would allow it to circumvent one of its international obligations. Since the

---

127 *Bosphorus Hava Yollari Turizm ve Ticaret Anonim Şirketi* v. *Ireland*, Judgment of 30 June 2005 (see footnote 184 above), para. 157. [Note: this footnote appears in the original document as footnote '202'].

128 *Offical Records of the General Assembly, Fifty-ninth Session, Sixth Committee*, 22nd meeting (A/C.6/59/SR.22), para. 66. [Note: this footnote appears in the original document as footnote '203'].

authorization may not prompt any conduct which conforms to it, a further condition laid out in paragraph 2 is that the act which is authorized is actually committed.

(11) Moreover, it is specified that the act in question be committed "because of that authorization". This condition requires a contextual analysis of the role that the authorization actually plays in determining the conduct of the member State or international organization.

(12) For the purposes of establishing responsibility, reliance on the authorization should not be unreasonable. The responsibility of the authorizing international organization cannot arise if, for instance, the authorization is outdated and not intended to apply to the current circumstances, because of substantial changes that have intervened since the adoption.

(13) While the authorizing international organization would be responsible if it requested, albeit implicitly, the commission of an act that would represent a circumvention of one of its obligations, that organization would clearly not be responsible for any other breach that the member State or international organization to which the authorization is addressed might commit. To that extent, the following statement contained in a letter addressed on 11 November 1996 by the United Nations Secretary-General to the Prime Minister of Rwanda appears accurate:

> [I]nsofar as "Opération Turquoise" is concerned, although that operation was "authorized" by the Security Council, the operation itself was under national command and control and was not a United Nations operation. The United Nations is, therefore, not internationally responsible for acts and omissions that might be attributable to "Opération Turquoise".[129]

(14) Paragraph 3 makes it clear that, unlike articles 14 to 16, the present article does not make the international responsibility of the international organization dependent on the unlawfulness of the conduct of the member State or international organization to which the decision or authorization is addressed.

(15) As was noted in the commentaries on articles 15 and 16, when the conduct is unlawful and other conditions are fulfilled, there is the possibility of an overlap between the cases covered in those provisions and those to which article 17 applies. However, the consequence would only be the existence of alternative bases for holding an international organization responsible.

Article 18

Responsibility of an international organization member of another international organization

Without prejudice to articles 14 to 17, the international responsibility of an international organization that is a member of another international organization also arises in relation to an act of the latter under the conditions set out in articles 61 and 62 for States that are members of an international organization.

...

Article 19

Effect of this chapter

This chapter is without prejudice to the international responsibility of the State or international organization which commits the act in question, or of any other State or international organization.

---

129 Unpublished letter. "Opération Turquoise" was established by Security Council resolution 929 (1994) of 22 June 1994. [Note: this footnote appears in the original document as footnote '204'].

Commentary

The present article is a "without prejudice" clause relating to the whole chapter. It corresponds in part to article 19 on the responsibility of States for internationally wrongful acts. The latter provision intends to leave unprejudiced "the international responsibility, under other provisions of these articles, of the State which commits the act in question, or of any other State".[130] References to international organizations have been added in the present article. Moreover, since the international responsibility of States committing a wrongful act is covered by the articles on the responsibility of States for internationally wrongful acts and not by the present articles, the wording of the clause has been made more general.

Chapter V

Circumstances precluding wrongfulness

...

Article 20

Consent

Valid consent by a State or an international organization to the commission of a given act by another international organization precludes the wrongfulness of that act in relation to that State or the former organization to the extent that the act remains within the limits of that consent.

Commentary

...

(3) As an example of consent that renders a specific conduct on the part of an international organization lawful, one could give that of a State allowing an investigation to be carried out on its territory by a commission of inquiry set up by the United Nations Security Council.[131] Another example is consent by a State to the verification of the electoral process by an international organization.[132] A further, and specific, example is consent to the deployment of the European Union Aceh Monitoring Mission in Indonesia, following an invitation addressed in July 2005 by the Government of Indonesia to the European Union and seven contributing States.[133]

(4) Consent given by an international organization concerns compliance with an international obligation that exists towards that organization. It does not affect international obligations to the extent that they may also exist towards the members of the consenting organization, unless that organization has been empowered to express consent also on behalf of the members.

(5) Consent dispensing an international organization with the performance of an obligation in a particular case must be "valid". This term refers to matters "addressed by international law rules outside the framework of State responsibility"[134] or of the responsibility of an international organization, such as whether the organ or agent who gave the consent was authorized to do so on behalf of the relevant State or international organization, or whether

---

130 *Yearbook ... 2001*, vol. II (Part Two) and corrigendum, p. 70. [Note: this footnote appears in the original document as footnote '205'].

131 For the requirement of consent, see paragraph 6 of the Declaration on Fact-fnding by the United Nations in the Field of the Maintenance of International Peace and Security annexed to General Assembly resolution 46/59 of 9 December 1991. [Note: this footnote appears in the original document as footnote '211'].

132 With regard to the role of consent in relation to the function of verifying an electoral process, see the report of the Secretary-General on enhancing the effectiveness of the principle of periodic and genuine elections (A/49/675), para. 16. [Note: this footnote appears in the original document as footnote '212'].

133 A reference to the invitation by the Government of Indonesia may be found in the preambular paragraph of the European Union Council Joint Action 2005/643/CFSP of 9 September 2005, *Official Journal of the European Union*, No. L 234, 10 September 2005, p. 13. [Note: this footnote appears in the original document as footnote '213'].

134 *Yearbook ... 2001*, vol. II (Part Two) and corrigendum, p. 73, paragraph (4) of the commentary to article 20 of the draft articles on responsibility of States for internationally wrongful acts. [Note: this footnote appears in the original document as footnote '214'].

the consent was vitiated by coercion or some other factor. The competence of the consenting organ or agent will generally depend on the internal law of the State concerned or, as the case may be, on the rules of organization concerned. The requirement that consent does not affect compliance with peremptory norms is stated in article 26. This is a general provision covering all the circumstances precluding wrongfulness.

...

Article 21

Self-defence

The wrongfulness of an act of an international organization is precluded if and to the extent that the act constitutes a lawful measure of self-defence under international law.

Commentary

(1) According to the commentary on the corresponding article (art. 21) on the responsibility of States for internationally wrongful acts, that article concerns "self-defence as an exception to the prohibition against the use of force".[135] The reference in that article to the "lawful" character of the measure of self-defence is explained as follows:

> [T]he term "lawful" implies that the action taken respects those obligations of total restraint applicable in international armed conflict, as well as compliance with the requirements of proportionality and of necessity inherent in the notion of self-defence. Article 21 simply reflects the basic principle for the purposes of chapter V, leaving questions of the extent and application of self-defence to the applicable primary rules referred to in the Charter [of the United Nations]."[136]

...

(3) In the practice relating to United Nations forces, the term "self-defence" has often been used in a different sense, with regard to situations other than those contemplated in Article 51 of the Charter of the United Nations. References to "self-defence" have been made also in relation to the "defence of the mission".[137] For instance, in relation to UNPROFOR, a memorandum of the Legal Bureau of the Canadian Department of Foreign Affairs and International Trade held that

> "self-defence could well include the defence of the safe areas and the civilian population in those areas.[138]

While these references to "self-defence" confirm that self-defence represents a circumstance precluding wrongfulness of conduct by an international organization, the term is given a meaning that encompasses cases other than those in which a State or an international organization responds to an armed attack by a State. At any event, the question of the extent to which United Nations forces are entitled to resort to force depends on the primary rules concerning the scope of the mission and need not be discussed here.

(4) Also, the conditions under which an international organization may resort to self-defence pertain to the primary rules and need not be examined in the present context.

---

135 *Ibid.*, p. 74, paragraph (1) of the commentary to article 21. [Note: this footnote appears in the original document as footnote '215'].

136 *Ibid.*, p. 75, paragraph (6) of the commentary to article 21. [Note: this footnote appears in the original document as footnote '216'].

137 As was noted by the High-level Panel on Threats, Challenges and Change, "the right to use force in self-defence ... is widely understood to extend to the 'defence of the mission' " (report of the High-level Panel on Threats, Challenges and Change, "A more secure world: our shared responsibility", document A/59/565 and Corr.1, para. 213). [Note: this footnote appears in the original document as footnote '217'].

138 *The Canadian Yearbook of International Law*, vol. 34 (1996), p. 389. [Note: this footnote appears in the original document as footnote '218'].

Those rules will set forth to what extent an international organization may invoke self-defence. One of the issues relates to the "invocability" of collective self-defence on the part of an international organization when one of its member States is the object of an armed attack and the international organization has the power to act in collective self-defence.[139]

...

Article 22

Countermeasures

1. Subject to paragraphs 2 and 3, the wrongfulness of an act of an international organization not in conformity with an international obligation towards a State or another international organization is precluded if and to the extent that the act constitutes a countermeasure taken in accordance with the substantive and procedural conditions required by international law, including those set forth in chapter II of Part Four for countermeasures taken against another international organization.
2. Subject to paragraph 3, an international organization may not take countermeasures against a responsible member State or international organization unless:
   (a) the conditions referred to in paragraph 1 are met;
   (b) the countermeasures are not inconsistent with the rules of the organization; and
   (c) no appropriate means are available for otherwise inducing compliance with the obligations of the responsible State or international organization concerning cessation of the breach and reparation.
3. Countermeasures may not be taken by an international organization against a member State or international organization in response to a breach of an international obligation under the rules of the organization unless such countermeasures are provided for by those rules.

...

Article 23

Force majeure

1. The wrongfulness of an act of an international organization not in conformity with an international obligation of that organization is precluded if the act is due to *force majeure*, that is, the occurrence of an irresistible force or of an unforeseen event, beyond the control of the organization, making it materially impossible in the circumstances to perform the obligation.
2. Paragraph 1 does not apply if:
   (*a*) the situation of *force majeure* is due, either alone or in combination with other factors, to the conduct of the organization invoking it; or
   (*b*) the organization has assumed the risk of that situation occurring.

...

Article 24

Distress

1. The wrongfulness of an act of an international organization not in conformity with an international obligation of that organization is precluded if the author of the act in question has no other reasonable way, in a situation of distress, of saving the author's life or the lives of other persons entrusted to the author's care.

139 A positive answer is implied in article 25 (a) of the Protocol Relating to the Mechanism for Conflict Prevention, Management, Resolution, Peacekeeping and Security, adopted on 10 December 1999 by the members of the Economic Community of West

2. Paragraph 1 does not apply if:

   (a) the situation of distress is due, either alone or in combination with other factors, to the conduct of the organization invoking it; or

   (b) the act in question is likely to create a comparable or greater peril.

   ...

Article 25
Necessity

1. Necessity may not be invoked by an international organization as a ground for precluding the wrongfulness of an act not in conformity with an international obligation of that organization unless the act:

   (*a*) is the only means for the organization to safeguard against a grave and imminent peril an essential interest of its member States or of the international community as a whole, when the organization has, in accordance with international law, the function to protect that interest; and

   (*b*) does not seriously impair an essential interest of the State or States towards which the international obligation exists, or of the international community as a whole.

2. In any case, necessity may not be invoked by an international organization as a ground for precluding wrongfulness if:

   (*a*) the international obligation in question excludes the possibility of invoking necessity; or

   (*b*) the organization has contributed to the situation of necessity.

Commentary

...

(4) While the conditions set by article 25 on the responsibility of States for internationally wrongful acts would be applicable also with regard to international organizations, the scarcity of practice and the considerable risk that invocability of necessity entails for compliance with international obligations suggest that, as a matter of policy, necessity should not be invocable by international organizations as widely as by States. This may be achieved by limiting the essential interests which may be protected by the invocation of necessity to those of the member States and of the international community as a whole, to the extent that the organization has, in accordance with international law, the function to protect them. Thus, when an international organization has been given powers over certain matters, it may, in the use of these powers, invoke the need to safeguard an essential interest of the international community or of its member States, provided that this is consistent with the principle of speciality. On the other hand, an international organization may invoke one of its own essential interests only if it coincides with an essential interest of the international community or of its member States. This solution may be regarded as an attempt to reach a compromise between two opposite positions with regard to necessity: the view of those who favour placing international organizations on the same level as States and the opinion of those who would totally rule out the invocability of necessity by international organizations.

...

African States (ECOWAS), which provides for the application of the "Mechanism" "in cases of aggression or conflict in any Member State or threat thereof". The text of this provision is reproduced by A. Ayissi (ed.), *Cooperating for Peace in West Africa: an Agenda for the 21st Century*, Geneva, UNIDIR, 2001 (UNIDIR/2001/9, United Nations publication, Sales No. GV.E/F.01.0.19), p. 127. [Note: this footnote appears in the original document as footnote '219'].

Article 26

Compliance with peremptory norms

Nothing in this Chapter precludes the wrongfulness of any act of an international organization which is not in conformity with an obligation arising under a peremptory norm of general international law.

Commentary

(1) Chapter V of Part One of the draft articles on responsibility of States for internationally wrongful acts contains a "without prejudice" provision which applies to all the circumstances precluding wrongfulness considered in that chapter. The purpose of this provision—article 26—is to "make it clear that the circumstances precluding wrongfulness in chapter V of Part One do not authorize or excuse any derogation from a peremptory norm of general international law".[140]

(2) The commentary on article 26 on the responsibility of States for internationally wrongful acts states that "peremptory norms that are clearly accepted and recognized include the prohibitions of aggression, genocide, slavery, racial discrimination, crimes against humanity and torture, and the right to self-determination".[141] In its judgment in the *Armed Activities on the Territory of the Congo* case, the International Court of Justice found that the prohibition of genocide "assuredly" was a peremptory norm.[142]

(3) It is clear that, like States, international organizations could not invoke a circumstance precluding wrongfulness in the case of non-compliance with an obligation arising under a peremptory norm. Thus, there is the need for a "without prejudice" provision matching the one applicable to States.

(4) The present article reproduces the text of article 26 on the responsibility of States for internationally wrongful acts with the replacement of the term "State" by "international organization".

Article 27

Consequences of invoking a circumstance precluding wrongfulness

The invocation of a circumstance precluding wrongfulness in accordance with this Chapter is without prejudice to:

(*a*) compliance with the obligation in question, if and to the extent that the circumstance precluding wrongfulness no longer exists;

(*b*) the question of compensation for any material loss caused by the act in question.

...

Part Three

Content of the international responsibility of an international organization

Commentary

(1) Part Three of the present draft articles defines the legal consequences of internationally wrongful acts of international organizations. This Part is organized in three chapters, which follow the general pattern of the articles on responsibility of States for internationally wrongful acts.[143]

---

140 *Yearbook ... 2001*, vol. II (Part Two) and corrigendum, p. 85, paragraph (4) of the commentary to article 26. [Note: this footnote appears in the original document as footnote '239'].

141 *Ibid.*, p. 85, paragraph (5) of the commentary to article 26. [Note: this footnote appears in the original document as footnote '240'].

142 *Armed Activities on the Territory of the Congo (New Application: 2002) (Democratic Republic of the Congo* v. *Rwanda), Jurisdiction and Admissibility, Judgment, I.C.J. Reports 2006*, p. 6, at p. 32, para. 64. The text of the judgment is also available from www.icj-cij.org. [Note: this footnote appears in the original document as footnote '241'].

143 *Yearbook ... 2001*, vol. II (Part Two) and corrigendum, pp. 86–116. [Note: this footnote appears in the original document as footnote '244'].

(2) Chapter I (arts. 28 to 33) lays down certain general principles and sets out the scope of Part Three. Chapter II (arts. 34 to 40) specifies the obligation of reparation in its various forms. Chapter III (arts. 41 and 42) considers the additional consequences that are attached to internationally wrongful acts consisting of serious breaches of obligations under peremptory norms of general international law.

Chapter I

General principles

Article 28

Legal consequences of an internationally wrongful act

The international responsibility of an international organization which is entailed by an internationally wrongful act in accordance with the provisions of Part Two involves legal consequences as set out in this Part.

...

Article 29

Continued duty of performance

The legal consequences of an internationally wrongful act under this Part do not affect the continued duty of the responsible international organization to perform the obligation breached.

...

Article 30

Cessation and non-repetition

The international organization responsible for the internationally wrongful act is under an obligation:

(a) to cease that act, if it is continuing;

(b) to offer appropriate assurances and guarantees of non-repetition, if circumstances so require.

... Article 31

Reparation

1. The responsible international organization is under an obligation to make full reparation for the injury caused by the internationally wrongful act.
2. Injury includes any damage, whether material or moral, caused by the internationally wrongful act of an international organization.

Commentary

(1) The present article sets out the principle that the responsible international organization is required to make full reparation for the injury caused. This principle seeks to protect the injured party from being adversely affected by the internationally wrongful act.

(2) Injury is defined as including "any damage, whether material or moral, caused by the internationally wrongful act". According to the judgment of the European Court of Justice in *Walz* v. *Clickair*, this wording, as it appears in paragraph 2 of article 31 on the responsibility of States for internationally wrongful acts,[144] expresses a concept which "is common to all

144 *Ibid.*, p. 91. [Note: this footnote appears in the original document as footnote '247'].

the international law sub-systems" and expresses "the ordinary meaning to be given to the concept of damage in international law".[145]

(3) As in the case of States, the principle of full reparation is often applied in practice in a flexible manner. The injured party may be mainly interested in the cessation of a continuing wrongful act or in the non-repetition of the wrongful act. The ensuing claim to reparation may therefore be limited. This especially occurs when the injured State or organization puts forward a claim for its own benefit and not for that of individuals or entities whom it seeks to protect. However, the restraint on the part of the injured State or organization in the exercise of its rights does not generally imply that the same party would not regard itself as entitled to full reparation. Thus the principle of full reparation is not put in question.

(4) It may be difficult for an international organization to have all the necessary means for making the required reparation. This fact is linked to the inadequacy of the financial resources that are generally available to international organizations for meeting this type of expense. However, that inadequacy cannot exempt a responsible organization from the legal consequences resulting from its responsibility under international law.

(5) The fact that international organizations sometimes grant compensation *ex gratia* is not due to abundance of resources, but rather to a reluctance, which organizations share with States, to admit their own international responsibility.

(6) When an international organization intends to undertake an activity in a country where its international responsibility may be engaged, one option for the organization is to conclude with the territorial State an agreement limiting its responsibility for wrongful acts occurring in relation to that activity. An example may be offered by the United Nations practice concerning peacekeeping operations, to the extent that the agreements with States to whose territory peacekeeping missions are deployed also cover claims arising out of international responsibility.[146]

(7) In setting out the principle of full reparation, the present article mainly refers to the more frequent case in which an international organization is solely responsible for an internationally wrongful act. The assertion of a duty of full reparation for the organization does not necessarily imply that the same principle applies when the organization is held responsible in connection with a certain act together with one or more States or one or more other organizations: for instance, when the organization aids or assists a State in the commission of the wrongful act.[147]

(8) The present article reproduces article 31 on the responsibility of States for internationally wrongful acts, with the replacement in both paragraphs of the term "State" with "international organization".

Article 32

Relevance of the rules of the organization

1. The responsible international organization may not rely on its rules as justification for failure to comply with its obligations under this Part.
2. Paragraph 1 is without prejudice to the applicability of the rules of an international organization to the relations between the organization and its member States and organizations.

145 *Axel Walz* v. *Clickair SA*, Case No. C-63/09, Judgment of 6 May 2010, Third Chamber, Court of Justice of the European Union, paras. 27–28. [Note: this footnote appears in the original document as footnote '249'].

146 The Secretariat of the United Nations referred in this context to that practice. See A/CN.4/637 and Add. 1 (under the section entitled "Draft article 30 … United Nations"), para. 6. [Note: this footnote appears in the original document as footnote '250'].

147 See article 14 of the present draft articles. [Note: this footnote appears in the original document as footnote '251'].

Commentary

(1) Paragraph 1 states the principle that an international organization cannot invoke its rules in order to justify non-compliance with its obligations under international law entailed by the commission of an internationally wrongful act. This principle finds a parallel in the principle that a State may not rely on its internal law as a justification for failure to comply with its obligations under Part Two of the articles on the responsibility of States for internationally wrongful acts. The text of paragraph 1 replicates article 32 on State responsibility,[148] with two changes: the term "international organization" replaces "State" and the reference to the rules of the organization replaces that to the internal law of the State.

(2) A similar approach was taken by article 27, paragraph 2, of the 1986 Vienna Convention, which parallels the corresponding provision of the 1969 Vienna Convention on the Law of Treaties by saying that "[a]n international organization party to a treaty may not invoke the rules of the organization as justification for its failure to perform the treaty".

...

(4) Rules of the organization may also affect the application of the principles and rules set out in Part Two in the relations between an international organization and its members, for instance in the matter of attribution. They would be regarded as special rules and need not be made the object of a special reference in that Part. On the contrary, in Part Three a "without prejudice" provision concerning the application of the rules of the organization in respect of members seems useful in view of the implications that may otherwise be inferred from the principle of irrelevance of the rules of the organization. The presence of such a "without prejudice" provision will serve as a reminder of the fact that the general statement in paragraph 1 may admit exceptions in the relations between an international organization and its member States and organizations.

(5) The provision in question, which is set out in paragraph 2, only applies insofar as the obligations in Part Three relate to the international responsibility that an international organization may have towards its member States and organizations. It cannot affect in any manner the legal consequences entailed by an internationally wrongful act towards a non-member State or organization, nor can it affect the consequences relating to breaches of obligations under peremptory norms as these breaches would affect the international community as a whole.

Article 33
Scope of international obligations set out in this Part

1. The obligations of the responsible international organization set out in this Part may be owed to one or more States, to one or more other organizations, or to the international community as a whole, depending in particular on the character and content of the international obligation and on the circumstances of the breach.
2. This Part is without prejudice to any right, arising from the international responsibility of an international organization, which may accrue directly to any person or entity other than a State or an international organization.

Commentary

(1) In the articles on responsibility of States for internationally wrongful acts, Part One concerns any breach of an obligation under international law that may be attributed to a State, irrespective of the nature of the entity or person to whom the obligation is owed. The scope

148 *Yearbook ... 2001*, vol. II (Part Two) and corrigendum, p. 94. [Note: this footnote appears in the original document as footnote '252'].

of Part Two of those articles is limited to obligations that arise for a State towards another State. This seems to be because of the difficulty of considering the consequences of an internationally wrongful act and thereafter the implementation of responsibility in respect of an injured party whose breaches of international obligations are not covered in Part One. The reference to responsibility existing towards the international community as a whole does not raise a similar problem, since it is hardly conceivable that the international community as a whole would incur international responsibility.

(2) Should one take a similar approach with regard to international organizations in the present draft articles, one would have to limit the scope of Part Three to obligations arising for international organizations towards other international organizations or towards the international community as a whole. However, it seems logical to include also obligations that organizations have towards States, given the existence of the articles on responsibility of States for internationally wrongful acts. As a result, Part Three of the present draft articles encompasses obligations that a responsible international organization may have towards one or more other organizations, one or more States, or the international community as a whole. This is meant to include the possibility that an international organization incurs international responsibility, and therefore acquires the obligations set out in Part Three, towards one State and one organization, two or more States and one organization, two or more States and two more organizations, or one State and two or more organizations.

(3) With the change in the reference to the responsible entity and with the addition explained above, paragraph 1 follows the wording of article 33, paragraph 1, on State responsibility.[149]

(4) While the scope of Part Three is limited according to the definition in paragraph 1, this does not mean that obligations entailed by an internationally wrongful act do not arise towards persons or entities other than States and international organizations. Like article 33, paragraph 2, on State responsibility, paragraph 2 provides that Part Three is without prejudice to any right that arises out of international responsibility and may accrue directly to those persons and entities.

(5) With regard to the international responsibility of international organizations, one significant area in which rights accrue to persons other than States or organizations is that of breaches by international organizations of their obligations under international law concerning employment. Another area is that of breaches committed by peacekeeping forces and affecting individuals.[150] The consequences of these breaches with regard to individuals, as stated in paragraph (1), are not covered by the present draft articles.

Chapter II

Reparation for injury

Article 34

Forms of reparation

Full reparation for the injury caused by the internationally wrongful act shall take the form of restitution, compensation and satisfaction, either singly or in combination, in accordance with the provisions of this chapter.

149 *Ibid.*, pp. 94–95. [Note: this footnote appears in the original document as footnote '253'].

150 See, for instance, General Assembly resolution 52/247 of 26 June 1998, on "Third-party liability: temporal and fnancial limitations". [Note: this footnote appears in the original document as footnote '254'].

Commentary

(1) The above provision is identical to article 34 on the responsibility of States for internationally wrongful acts.[151] This seems justified since the forms of reparation consisting of restitution, compensation and satisfaction are applied in practice to international organizations as well as to States. Certain examples relating to international organizations are given in the commentaries to the following articles, which specifically address the various forms of reparation.

(2) A note by the Director General of the International Atomic Energy Agency provides an instance in which the three forms of reparation are considered to apply to a responsible international organization. Concerning the "international responsibility of the Agency in relation to safeguards", he wrote on 24 June 1970 the following:

> Although there may be circumstances when the giving of satisfaction by the Agency may be appropriate, it is proposed to give consideration only to reparation properly so called. Generally speaking, reparation properly so called may be either restitution in kind or payment of compensation.[152]

Article 35
Restitution

An international organization responsible for an internationally wrongful act is under an obligation to make restitution, that is, to re-establish the situation which existed before the wrongful act was committed, provided and to the extent that restitution:

(*a*) is not materially impossible;

(*b*) does not involve a burden out of all proportion to the benefit deriving from restitution instead of compensation.

Commentary

(1) Restitution is a form of reparation that involves the re-establishment as far as possible of the situation which existed before the internationally wrongful act was committed by the responsible international organization.

(2) The concept and forms of restitution and the related conditions, as defined in article 35 on the responsibility of States for internationally wrongful acts,[153] appear to be applicable also to international organizations. There is no reason that would suggest a different approach with regard to the latter. The text above therefore reproduces article 35 on State responsibility, the only difference being that the term "State" is replaced by "international organization".

Article 36
Compensation

1. The international organization responsible for an internationally wrongful act is under an obligation to compensate for the damage caused thereby, insofar as such damage is not made good by restitution.

---

151 *Yearbook ... 2001*, vol. II (Part Two) and corrigendum, pp. 95–96. [Note: this footnote appears in the original document as footnote '255'].

152 GOV/COM.22/27, para. 27. See *Yearbook ... 2004*, vol. II (Part One), document A/CN.4/545, annex. The note is on file with the Codifcation Division of the Office of Legal Affairs. It has to be noted that, according to the prevailing use, which is reflected in article 34 on the responsibility of States for internationally wrongful acts and the article above, reparation is considered to include satisfaction. [Note: this footnote appears in the original document as footnote '256'].

153 *Yearbook ... 2001*, vol. II (Part Two), p. 96 [Note: this footnote appears in the original document as footnote '257'].

2. The compensation shall cover any financially assessable damage including loss of profits insofar as it is established.

Commentary

(1) Compensation is the form of reparation most frequently made by international organizations. The most well-known instance of practice concerns the settlement of claims arising from the United Nations operation in the Congo. Compensation to nationals of Belgium, Greece, Italy, Luxembourg and Switzerland was granted through exchanges of letters between the Secretary-General and the permanent missions of the respective States in keeping with the United Nations declaration contained in these letters according to which the United Nations stated as follows:

> [I]t would not evade responsibility where it was established that United Nations agents had in fact caused unjustifiable damage to innocent parties.[154]

With regard to the same operation, further settlements were made with France, the United Kingdom of Great Britain and Northern Ireland, the United States of America, and Zambia,[155] and also with the International Committee of the Red Cross.[156]

(2) The fact that such compensation was given as reparation for breaches of obligations under international law may be gathered not only from some of the claims but also from a letter, dated 6 August 1965, addressed by the Secretary-General to the Acting Permanent Representative of the Union of Soviet Socialist Republics.. In this letter, the Secretary-General said the followng:

> It has always been the policy of the United Nations, acting through the Secretary-General, to compensate individuals who have suffered damages for which the Organization was legally liable. This policy is in keeping with generally recognized legal principles and with the Convention on Privileges and Immunities of the United Nations. In addition, in regard to the United Nations activities in the Congo, it is reinforced by the principles set forth in the international conventions concerning the protection of the life and property of the civilian population during hostilities as well as by considerations of equity and humanity which the United Nations cannot ignore.[157]

(3) A reference to the obligation on the United Nations to pay compensation was also made by the International Court of Justice in its advisory opinion on *Difference Relating to Immunity from Legal Process of a Special Rapporteur of the Commission on Human Rights.*[158]

---

154 Exchange of letters constituting an agreement relating to the settlement of claims filed against the United Nations in the Congo by Belgian nationals (New York, 20 February 1965), United Nations, *Treaty Series*, vol. 535, No. 7780, p. 197; exchange of letters (with annex) constituting an agreement relating to the settlement of claims fled against the United Nations in the Congo by Swiss nationals (New York, 3 June 1966), *ibid.*, vol. 564, No. 621, p. 193; exchange of letters constituting an agreement relating to the settlement of claims filed against the United Nations in the Congo by Greek nationals (New York, 20 June 1966), *ibid.*, vol. 565, No. 8230, p. 3; exchange of letters constituting an agreement relating to the settlement of claims filed against the United Nations in the Congo by Luxembourg nationals (New York, 28 December 1966), *ibid.*, vol. 585, No. 8487, p. 147; and exchange of letters constituting an agreement relating to the settlement of claims filed against the United Nations in the Congo by Italian nationals (New York, 18 January 1967), *ibid.*, vol. 588, No. 8525, p. 197. [Note: this footnote appears in the original document as footnote '258'].

155 See K. Schmalenbach, *Die Haftung Internationaler Organisationen: im Rahmen von Militäreinsätzen und Territorialverwaltungen*, Frankfurt am Main, Peter Lang, 2004, at pp. 314–321. [Note: this footnote appears in the original document as footnote '259'].

156 The text of this agreement was reproduced by K. Ginther, *Die völkerrechtliche Verantwortlichkeit Internationaler Organisationen gegenüber Drittstaaten*, Vienna/New York, Springer, 1969, pp. 166–167. [Note: this footnote appears in the original document as footnote '260'].

157 United Nations, *Juridical Yearbook 1965* (Sales No. 67.V.3), p. 41, footnote 26 (document S/6597). The view that the United Nations placed its responsibility at the international level was maintained by J. J. A. Salmon, "Les accords Spaak–U Thant du 20 février 1965", AFDI, vol. 11 (1965), p. 468, at pp. 483 and 487. [Note: this footnote appears in the original document as footnote '261'].

158 *Difference Relating to Immunity from Legal Process of a Special Rapporteur of the Commission on Human Rights* (see footnote 87 above), pp. 88–89, para. 66. [Note: this footnote appears in the original document as footnote '262'].

(4) There is no reason to depart from the text of article 36 on the responsibility of States for internationally wrongful acts,[159] apart from replacing the term "State" by "international organization".

Article 37
Satisfaction

1. The international organization responsible for an internationally wrongful act is under an obligation to give satisfaction for the injury caused by that act insofar as it cannot be made good by restitution or compensation.
2. Satisfaction may consist in an acknowledgement of the breach, an expression of regret, a formal apology or another appropriate modality.
3. Satisfaction shall not be out of proportion to the injury and may not take a form humiliating to the responsible international organization.

Commentary

(1) Practice offers some examples of satisfaction on the part of international organizations, generally in the form of an apology or an expression of regret. Although the examples that follow do not expressly refer to the existence of a breach of an obligation under international law, they at least imply that an apology or an expression of regret by an international organization would be one of the appropriate legal consequences for such a breach.

(2) With regard to the fall of Srebrenica, the United Nations Secretary-General said:

> The United Nations experience in Bosnia was one of the most difficult and painful in our history. It is with the deepest regret and remorse that we have reviewed our own actions and decisions in the face of the assault on Srebrenica.[160]

(3) On 16 December 1999, upon receiving the report of the Independent Inquiry into the actions of the United Nations during the 1994 genocide in Rwanda, the Secretary-General stated:

> All of us must bitterly regret that we did not do more to prevent it. There was a United Nations force in the country at the time, but it was neither mandated nor equipped for the kind of forceful action which would have been needed to prevent or halt the genocide. On behalf of the United Nations, I acknowledge this failure and express my deep remorse.[161]

(4) Shortly after the NATO bombing of the Chinese embassy in Belgrade, a NATO spokesman said in a press conference:

> I think we have done what anybody would do in these circumstances, first of all we have acknowledged responsibility clearly, unambiguously, quickly; we have expressed our regrets to the Chinese authorities.[162]

A further apology was addressed on 13 May 1999 by German Chancellor Gerhard Schröder on behalf of Germany, NATO and NATO Secretary General Javier Solana to Foreign Minister Tang Jiaxuan and Premier Zhu Rongji.[163]

---

159 *Yearbook ... 2001*, vol. II (Part Two) and corrigendum, pp. 98–105. [Note: this footnote appears in the original document as footnote '263'].

160 Report of the Secretary-General pursuant to General Assembly resolution 53/35: the fall of Srebrenica (A/54/549), para. 503. [Note: this footnote appears in the original document as footnote '264'].

161 www.un.org (Press Release SG/SM/7263). See also the report of the Independent Inquiry into the actions of the United Nations during the 1994 genocide in Rwanda, S/1999/1257, Enclosure. [Note: this footnote appears in the original document as footnote '265'].

162 www.nato.int/kosovo/press/p990509b.htm. [Note: this footnote appears in the original document as footnote '266'].

163 "NATO apologises to Beijing", http://news.bbc.co.uk/2/hi/asiapacific/341533.stm. [Note: this footnote appears in the original document as footnote '267'].

(5) As with regard to other forms of reparation, the rules of the responsible international organization will determine which organ or agent is competent to give satisfaction on behalf of the organization.

(6) The modalities and conditions of satisfaction that concern States are applicable also to international organizations. A form of satisfaction intended to humiliate the responsible international organization may be unlikely, but is not unimaginable. A theoretical example would be that of the request of a formal apology in terms that would be demeaning to the organization or one of its organs. The request could also refer to the conduct taken by one or more member States or organizations within the framework of the responsible organization. Although the request for satisfaction might then specifically target one or more members, the responsible organization would be asked to give it and would necessarily be affected.

(7) Thus, the paragraphs of article 37 on the responsibility of States for internationally wrongful acts[164] may be transposed, with the replacement of the term "State" with "international organization" in paragraphs 1 and 3.

Article 38

Interest

1. Interest on any principal sum due under this chapter shall be payable when necessary in order to ensure full reparation. The interest rate and mode of calculation shall be set so as to achieve that result.
2. Interest runs from the date when the principal sum should have been paid until the date the obligation to pay is fulfilled.

Commentary

The rules contained in article 38 on the responsibility of States for internationally wrongful acts[165] with regard to interest are intended to ensure application of the principle of full reparation. Similar considerations in this regard apply to international organizations. Therefore, both paragraphs of article 38 on State responsibility are here reproduced without change.

Article 39

Contribution to the injury

In the determination of reparation, account shall be taken of the contribution to the injury by wilful or negligent action or omission of the injured State or international organization or of any person or entity in relation to whom reparation is sought.

Commentary

(1) No apparent reason would preclude extending to international organizations the provision set out in article 39 on the responsibility of States for internationally wrongful acts.[166] Such an extension is made in two directions: first, international organizations are also entitled to invoke contribution to the injury in order to diminish their responsibility; second, the entities that may have contributed to the injury include international organizations. The latter extension requires the addition of the words "or international organization" after "State" in the corresponding article on State responsibility.

(2) One instance of relevant practice in which contribution to the injury was invoked concerns the shooting of a civilian vehicle in the Congo. In this case compensation by the United Nations was reduced because of the contributory negligence by the driver of the vehicle.[167]

---

164 *Yearbook . . . 2001*, vol. II (Part Two) and corrigendum, pp. 105–107. [Note: this footnote appears in the original document as footnote '268'].

165 *Ibid.*, pp. 107–109. [Note: this footnote appears in the original document as footnote '269'].

166 *Ibid.*, pp. 109–110. [Note: this footnote appears in the original document as footnote '270'].

167 See Klein, *La responsabilité des organisations internationales dans les ordres juridiques internes et en droit des gens* (footnote 121 above), p. 606. [Note: this footnote appears in the original document as footnote '271'].

(3) This article is without prejudice to any obligation to mitigate the injury that the injured party may have under international law. The existence of such an obligation would arise under a primary rule. Thus, it does not need to be discussed here.

(4) The reference to "any person or entity in relation to whom reparation is sought" has to be read in conjunction with the definition given in article 33 of the scope of the international obligations set out in Part Three. This scope is limited to obligations arising for a responsible international organization towards States, other international organizations or the international community as a whole. The above reference seems appropriately worded in this context. The existence of rights that directly accrue to other persons or entities is thereby not prejudiced.

Article 40

Ensuring the fulfilment of the obligation to make reparation

1. The responsible international organization shall take all appropriate measures in accordance with its rules to ensure that its members provide it with the means for effectively fulfilling its obligations under this chapter.
2. The members of a responsible international organization shall take all the appropriate measures that may be required by the rules of the organization in order to enable the organization to fulfil its obligations under this chapter.

Commentary

(1) International organizations having a separate legal personality are in principle the only subjects that bear international responsibility for their international wrongful acts. When an international organization is responsible for an internationally wrongful act, States and other organizations incur responsibility because of their membership of a responsible organization only according to the conditions stated in articles 18, 61 and 62. The present article does not envisage any further instance in which States and international organizations would be held internationally responsible for the act of the organization of which they are members.

(2) Consistent with the views expressed by several States that responded to a question raised by the Commission in its 2006 report to the General Assembly,[168] no subsidiary obligation of members towards the injured party is considered to arise when the responsible organization is not in a position to make reparation.[169] The same opinion was expressed in statements by the IMF and the Organization for the Prohibition of Chemical Weapons.[170] This approach

168 *Yearbook … 2006*, vol. II (Part Two), p. 21, para. 28. [Note: this footnote appears in the original document as footnote '272'].

169 The delegation of the Netherlands noted that there would be "no basis for such an obligation" (*Offical Records of the General Assembly, Sixty-frst Session, Sixth Committee*, 14th meeting (A/C.6/61/ SR.14), para. 23). Similar views were expressed by Denmark, on behalf of the Nordic countries (Denmark, Finland, Iceland, Norway and Sweden) (*ibid.*, 13th meeting (A/C.6/61/SR.13), para. 32); Belgium (*ibid.*, 14th meeting (A/C.6/61/SR.14), paras. 41–42); Spain (*ibid.*, paras. 52–53); France (*ibid.*, para. 63); Italy (*ibid.*, para. 66); the United States (*ibid.*, para. 83); Belarus (*ibid.*, para. 100); Switzerland (*ibid.*, 15th meeting (A/C.6/61/SR.15), para. 5); Cuba (*ibid.*, 16th meeting (A/C.6/61/SR.16), para. 13); and Romania (*ibid.*, 19th meeting (A/C.6/61/SR.19), para. 60). The delegation of Belarus, however, suggested that a "scheme of subsidiary responsibility for compensation could be established as a special rule, for example in cases where the work of the organization was connected with the exploitation of dangerous resources" (*ibid.*, 14th meeting (A/C.6/61/SR.14), para. 100). Although sharing the prevailing view, the delegation of Argentina requested the Commission to "analyse whether the special characteristics and rules of each organization, as well as considerations of justice and equity, called for exceptions to the basic rule, depending on the circumstances of each case" (*ibid.*, 13th meeting (A/C.6/61/ SR.13), para. 49). More recently, see the statement by Belarus (*ibid., Sixty-fourth Session, Sixth Committee*, 15th meeting (A/C.6/64/SR.15), para. 36), Hungary (*ibid.*, 16th meeting (A/C.6/64/SR.16), para. 40), Portugal (*ibid.*, para. 46) and Greece (*ibid.*, para. 62) and the written comments by Germany (A/CN.4/636 and Add.1–2 (under the section entitled "Draft article 39 … "), para. 3) and the Republic of Korea (*ibid.*). A similar position was taken by Austria (*ibid.*, para. 4). The Islamic Republic of Iran, while sharing the same view, maintained that "the brunt of responsibility in such cases should be borne by those members which, on account of their decision-making role or overall position within the organization, had contributed to the injurious act" (*Offical Records of the General Assembly, Sixty-fourth Session, Sixth Committee*, 16th meeting (A/C.6/64/SR.16), para. 53). [Note: this footnote appears in the original document as footnote '273'].

170 *Yearbook … 2007*, vol. II (Part One), A/CN.4/582, p. 29. Several international organizations suggested that the Commission state an obligation for members as "an exercise in progressive development" (A/ CN.4/637 and Add.1 (under the section entitled "Draft article 39 … ")). [Note: this footnote appears in the original document as footnote '274'].

appears to conform to practice, which does not show any support for the existence of such an obligation under international law.

(3) Thus, the injured party would have to rely on the fulfilment by the responsible international organization of its obligations. It is clear that if no budget line is provided for the event that the organization incurs international responsibility, the effective fulfilment of the obligation to make reparation will be at risk. Thus, paragraph 1 stresses the need for an international organization to take all appropriate measures so as to be in a position of complying with its obligations should it incur responsibility. This will generally imply that the members of the organization should be requested to provide the necessary means.

(4) Paragraph 2 is essentially of an expository character. It intends to remind members of a responsible international organization that they are required to take, in accordance with the rules of the organization, all appropriate measures in order to provide the organization with the means for effectively fulfilling its obligation to make reparation.

(5) In both paragraphs, the reference to the rules of the organization is meant to define the basis of the requirements in question.[171] While the rules of the organization do not necessarily deal with the matter expressly, an obligation for members to finance the organization as part of the general duty to cooperate with the organization may be implied under the relevant rules. As was noted by Judge Sir Gerald Fitzmaurice in his separate opinion in the *Certain expenses of the United Nations* advisory opinion:

> Without finance, the Organization could not perform its duties. Therefore, even in the absence of Article 17, paragraph 2, a general obligation for Member States collectively to finance the Organization would have to be read into the Charter [of the United Nations], on the basis of the same principle as the Court applied in the [*Reparation for Injuries*] case, namely "by necessary implication as being essential to the performance of its [i.e. the Organization's] duties" (*I.C.J. Reports 1949*, at p. 182).[172]

Chapter III

Serious breaches of obligations under peremptory norms of general international law

Article 41

Application of this Chapter

1. This Chapter applies to the international responsibility which is entailed by a serious breach by an international organization of an obligation arising under a peremptory norm of general international law.
2. A breach of such an obligation is serious if it involves a gross or systematic failure by the responsible international organization to fulfil the obligation.

...

Article 42

Particular consequences of a serious breach of an obligation under this Chapter

1. States and international organizations shall cooperate to bring to an end through lawful means any serious breach within the meaning of article 41.

---

171 See the statements by the delegations of Denmark, on behalf of the Nordic countries (Denmark, Finland, Iceland, Norway and Sweden) (*Official Records of the General Assembly, Sixty-first Session, Sixth Committee*, 13th meeting (A/C.6/61/SR.13), para. 32); Belgium (*ibid.*, 14th meeting (A/C.6/61/SR.14), para. 42); Spain (*ibid.*, para. 53); France (*ibid.*, para. 63); and Switzerland (*ibid.*, 15th meeting (A/C.6/61/SR.15), para. 5). Also, the Institute of International Law held that an obligation to put a responsible organization in funds only existed "pursuant to its Rules" (Institute of International Law, *Yearbook*, vol. 66, Part II, Session of Lisbon (1995), p. 451). [Note: this footnote appears in the original document as footnote '275].

172 *Certain expenses of the United Nations* (see footnote 151 above), p. 208. [Note: this footnote appears in the original document as footnote '276'].

2. No State or international organization shall recognize as lawful a situation created by a serious breach within the meaning of article 41, nor render aid or assistance in maintaining that situation.
3. This article is without prejudice to the other consequences referred to in this Part and to such further consequences that a breach to which this chapter applies may entail under international law.

Commentary

...

(6) In this context it may be useful to recall that, in the operative part of its advisory opinion on the *Legal Consequences of the Construction of a Wall in the Occupied Palestinian Territory*, the International Court of Justice first stated the obligation incumbent upon Israel to cease forthwith the works of the construction of the wall and, "[g]iven the character and the importance of the rights and obligations involved", the obligation for all States "not to recognize the illegal situation resulting from the construction of the wall ... [and] not to render aid or assistance in maintaining the situation created by such construction".[173] The Court then added:

> The United Nations, and especially the General Assembly and the Security Council, should consider what further action is required to bring to an end the illegal situation resulting from the construction of the wall and the associated regime, taking due account of the present Advisory Opinion.[174]

...

Part Four

The implementation of the international responsibility of an international organization

Commentary

(1) Part Four of the present articles concerns the implementation of the international responsibility of international organizations. This Part is subdivided into two chapters, according to the general pattern of the articles on responsibility of States for internationally wrongful acts.[175] Chapter I deals with the invocation of international responsibility and with certain associated issues. These do not include questions relating to remedies that may be available for implementing international responsibility. Chapter II considers countermeasures taken in order to induce the responsible international organization to cease the unlawful conduct and to provide reparation.

(2) Issues relating to the implementation of international responsibility are here considered insofar as they concern the invocation of the responsibility of an international organization. Thus, while the present draft articles consider the invocation of responsibility by a State or an international organization, they do not address questions relating to the invocation of responsibility of States.[176] However, one provision (art. 48) refers to the case in which the

---

173 *Legal Consequences of the Construction of a Wall in the Occupied Palestinian Territory, Advisory Opinion, I.C.J. Reports 2004*, p. 136, at p. 200, para. 159. See also subparagraph (3) B and D of the operative paragraph, ibid., pp. 201–202, para. 163. [Note: this footnote appears in the original document as footnote '284'].

174 *Ibid.*, p. 202, para. 163, subparagraph (3) E of the operative paragraph. The same language appears in paragraph 160 of the advisory opinion, *ibid.*, p. 200. [Note: this footnote appears in the original document as footnote '285'].

175 *Yearbook ... 2001*, vol. II (Part Two) and corrigendum, pp. 116–139. [Note: this footnote appears in the original document as footnote '288'].

176 See article 1 and in particular paragraph (10) of the commentary thereto. [Note: this footnote appears in the original document as footnote '289'].

responsibility of one or more States is concurrent with that of one or more international organizations for the same wrongful act.

Chapter I

Invocation of the responsibility of an international organization

Article 43

Invocation of responsibility by an injured State or international organization

A State or an international organization is entitled as an injured State or an injured international organization to invoke the responsibility of another international organization if the obligation breached is owed to:

(*a*) that State or the former international organization individually;

(*b*) a group of States or international organizations including that State or the former international organization, or the international community as a whole, and the breach of the obligation:

(i) specially affects that State or that international organization; or

(ii) is of such a character as radically to change the position of all the other States and international organizations to which the obligation is owed with respect to the further performance of the obligation.

Commentary

...

(3) Practice concerning the entitlement of an international organization to invoke international responsibility because of the breach of an obligation owed to that organization individually mainly concerns breaches of obligations that are committed by States. Since the present draft articles do not address questions relating to the invocation of responsibility of States, this practice is here relevant only indirectly. The obligations breached to which practice refers were imposed either by a treaty or by general international law. It was in the latter context that in its advisory opinion on *Reparation for Injuries,* the International Court of Justice stated that it was "established that the Organization has capacity to bring claims on the international plane".[177] Also in the context of breaches of obligations under general international law that were committed by a State, the Governing Council of the United Nations Compensation Commission envisaged compensation "with respect to any direct loss, damage, or injury to Governments or international organizations as a result of Iraq's unlawful invasion and occupation of Kuwait".[178] On this basis, several entities that were expressly defined as international organizations were, as a result of their claims, awarded compensation by the Panel of Commissioners: the Arab Planning Institute, the Inter-Arab Investment Guarantee Corporation, the Gulf Arab States Educational Research Center, the Arab Fund for Economic and Social Development, the Joint Program Production Institution for the Arab Gulf Countries and the Arab Towns Organization.[179]

...

(5) Breaches of this type, which rarely affect States, are even less likely to be relevant for international organizations. However, one cannot rule out that an international organization

177 *Reparation for injuries suffered in the service of the United Nations* (see footnote 69 above), pp. 184–185. [Note: this footnote appears in the original document as footnote '291'].

178 S/AC.26/1991/7/Rev.1, para. 34. [Note: this footnote appears in the original document as footnote '292'].

179 Report and recommendations made by the Panel of Commissioners concerning the Sixth Instalment of "F1" Claims (S/AC.26/2002/6), paras. 213–371. [Note: this footnote appears in the original document as footnote '293'].

may commit a breach that falls into one or the other category and that a State or an international organization may then be entitled to invoke responsibility as an injured State or international organization. It is therefore preferable to include in the present article the possibility that a State or an international organization may invoke responsibility of an international organization as an injured State or international organization under similar circumstances. This is provided in subparagraph (*b*) (i) and (ii).

...

Article 44

Notice of claim by an injured State or international organization

1. An injured State or international organization which invokes the responsibility of another international organization shall give notice of its claim to that organization.
2. The injured State or international organization may specify in particular:
   (a) the conduct that the responsible international organization should take in order to cease the wrongful act, if it is continuing;
   (b) what form reparation should take in accordance with the provisions of Part Three.

Commentary

...

(2) Paragraph 1 does not specify what form the invocation of responsibility should take. The fact that, according to paragraph 2, the State or international organization invoking responsibility may specify some elements, and in particular "what form reparation should take", does not imply that the responsible international organization is bound to conform to those specifications.

...

Article 45

Admissibility of claims

1. An injured State may not invoke the responsibility of an international organization if the claim is not brought in accordance with any applicable rule relating to the nationality of claims.
2. When the rule of exhaustion of local remedies applies to a claim, an injured State or international organization may not invoke the responsibility of another international organization if any available and effective remedy has not been exhausted.

...

Article 46

Loss of the right to invoke responsibility

The responsibility of an international organization may not be invoked if:

(a) the injured State or international organization has validly waived the claim;

(b) the injured State or international organization is to be considered as having, by reason of its conduct, validly acquiesced in the lapse of the claim.

...

Article 47

Plurality of injured States or international organizations

Where several States or international organizations are injured by the same internationally wrongful act of an international organization, each injured State or international organization may separately invoke the responsibility of the international organization for the internationally wrongful act.

Commentary

...

(2) Any injured State or international organization is entitled to invoke responsibility independently from any other injured State or international organization. This does not preclude some or all of the injured entities invoking responsibility jointly, if they so wish. Coordination of claims would contribute to avoid the risk of a double recovery.

(3) An instance of claims that may be concurrently preferred by an injured State and an injured international organization was envisaged by the International Court of Justice in its advisory opinion on *Reparation for Injuries*. The Court found that both the United Nations and the national State of the victim could claim "in respect of the damage caused ... to the victim or to persons entitled through him" and noted that there was "no rule of law which assigns priority to the one or to the other, or which compels either the State or the Organization to refrain from bringing an international claim. The Court sees no reason why the parties concerned should not find solutions inspired by goodwill and common sense".[180]

(4) An injured State or international organization could undertake to refrain from invoking responsibility, leaving other injured States or international organizations to do so. If this undertaking is not only an internal matter between the injured entities, it could lead to the loss for the former State or international organization of the right to invoke responsibility according to article 46.

(5) When an international organization and one or more of its members are both injured as the result of the same wrongful act, the rules of the organization could similarly attribute to the organization or to its members the exclusive function of invoking responsibility.

Article 48

Responsibility of an international organization and one or more States or international organizations

1. Where an international organization and one or more States or other international organizations are responsible for the same internationally wrongful act, the responsibility of each State or organization may be invoked in relation to that act.
2. Subsidiary responsibility may be invoked insofar as the invocation of the primary responsibility has not led to reparation.
3. Paragraphs 1 and 2:
   (a) do not permit any injured State or international organization to recover, by way of compensation, more than the damage it has suffered;
   (b) are without prejudice to any right of recourse that the State or international organization providing reparation may have against the other responsible States or international organizations.

...

Article 49

Invocation of responsibility by a State or an international organization other than an injured State or international organization

1. A State or an international organization other than an injured State or international organization is entitled to invoke the responsibility of another international organization in accordance with paragraph 4 if the obligation breached is owed to a group of States or international

180 *Reparation for injuries suffered in the service of the United Nations* (see footnote 69 above), pp. 184–186. [Note: this footnote appears in the original document as footnote '312'].

organizations, including the State or organization that invokes responsibility, and is established for the protection of a collective interest of the group.

2. A State other than an injured State is entitled to invoke the responsibility of an international organization in accordance with paragraph 4 if the obligation breached is owed to the international community as a whole.
3. An international organization other than an injured international organization is entitled to invoke the responsibility of another international organization in accordance with paragraph 4 if the obligation breached is owed to the international community as a whole and safeguarding the interest of the international community as a whole underlying the obligation breached is within the functions of the international organization invoking responsibility.
4. A State or an international organization entitled to invoke responsibility under paragraphs 1 to 3 may claim from the responsible international organization:
   (a) cessation of the internationally wrongful act, and assurances and guarantees of non-repetition in accordance with article 30; and
   (b) performance of the obligation of reparation in accordance with Part Three, in the interest of the injured State or international organization or of the beneficiaries of the obligation breached.
5. The requirements for the invocation of responsibility by an injured State or international organization under draft articles 44, 45, paragraph 2, and 46 apply to an invocation of responsibility by a State or international organization entitled to do so under paragraphs 1 to 4.

...

Article 50
Scope of this Chapter

This Chapter is without prejudice to the entitlement that a person or entity other than a State or an international organization may have to invoke the international responsibility of an international organization.

Commentary

(1) Articles 43 to 49 above address the implementation of the responsibility of an international organization only to the extent that responsibility is invoked by a State or another international organization. This accords with article 33, which defines the scope of the international obligations set out in Part Three by stating that these only relate to the breach of an obligation under international law that an international organization owes to a State, another international organization or the international community as a whole. The same article further specifies that this is "without prejudice to any right, arising from the international responsibility of an international organization, which may accrue directly to any person or entity other than a State or an international organization". Thus, by referring only to the invocation of responsibility by a State or an international organization, the scope of the present chapter reflects that of Part Three. Invocation of responsibility is considered only insofar as it concerns the obligations set out in Part Three.

(2) While it could be taken as implied that the articles concerning invocation of responsibility are without prejudice to the entitlement that a person or entity other than a State or an international organization may have to invoke responsibility of an international organization, an express statement to this effect serves the purpose of conveying more clearly that the present chapter is not intended to exclude any such entitlement.

Chapter II

Countermeasures

Article 51

Object and limits of countermeasures

1. An injured State or an injured international organization may only take countermeasures against an international organization which is responsible for an internationally wrongful act in order to induce that organization to comply with its obligations under Part Three.
2. Countermeasures are limited to the non-performance for the time being of international obligations of the State or international organization taking the measures towards the responsible international organization.
3. Countermeasures shall, as far as possible, be taken in such a way as to permit the resumption of performance of the obligations in question.
4. Countermeasures shall, as far as possible, be taken in such a way as to limit their effects on the exercise by the responsible international organization of its functions.

...

Article 52

Conditions for taking countermeasures by members of an international organization

1. Subject to paragraph 2, an injured State or international organization which is a member of a responsible international organization may not take countermeasures against that organization unless:
   (*a*) the conditions referred to in article 51 are met;
   (*b*) the countermeasures are not inconsistent with the rules of the organization; and
   (*c*) no appropriate means are available for otherwise inducing compliance with the obligations of the responsible international organization concerning cessation of the breach and reparation.
2. Countermeasures may not be taken by an injured State or international organization which is a member of a responsible international organization against that organization in response to a breach of an international obligation under the rules of the organization unless such countermeasures are provided for by those rules.

...

Article 53

Obligations not affected by countermeasures

1. Countermeasures shall not affect:
   (*a*) the obligation to refrain from the threat or use of force as embodied in the Charter of the United Nations;
   (*b*) obligations for the protection of human rights;
   (*c*) obligations of a humanitarian character prohibiting reprisals;
   (*d*) other obligations under peremptory norms of general international law.
2. An injured State or international organization taking countermeasures is not relieved from fulfilling its obligations:
   (*a*) under any dispute settlement procedure applicable between it and the responsible international organization;
   (*b*) to respect any inviolability of organs or agents of the responsible international organization and of the premises, archives and documents of that organization.

...

Article 54

Proportionality of countermeasures

Countermeasures must be commensurate with the injury suffered, taking into account the gravity of the internationally wrongful act and the rights in question.

...

Article 55

Conditions relating to resort to countermeasures

1. Before taking countermeasures, an injured State or international organization shall:
   (*a*) call upon the responsible international organization, in accordance with draft article 44, to fulfil its obligations under Part Three;
   (*b*) notify the responsible international organization of any decision to take countermeasures and offer to negotiate with that organization.
2. Notwithstanding paragraph 1 (*b*), the injured State or international organization may take such urgent countermeasures as are necessary to preserve its rights.
3. Countermeasures may not be taken, and if already taken must be suspended without undue delay if:
   (*a*) the internationally wrongful act has ceased; and
   (*b*) the dispute is pending before a court or tribunal which has the authority to make decisions binding on the parties.
4. Paragraph 3 does not apply if the responsible international organization fails to implement the dispute settlement procedures in good faith.

...

Article 56

Termination of countermeasures

Countermeasures shall be terminated as soon as the responsible international organization has complied with its obligations under Part Three in relation to the internationally wrongful act.

...

Article 57

Measures taken by States or international organizations other than an injured State or international organization

This chapter does not prejudice the right of any State or international organization, entitled under article 49, paragraphs 1 to 3, to invoke the responsibility of another international organization, to take lawful measures against that organization to ensure cessation of the breach and reparation in the interest of the injured State or organization or of the beneficiaries of the obligation breached.

...

Part Five

Responsibility of a State in connection with the conduct of an international organization

Commentary

(1) In accordance with article 1, paragraph 2, the present draft articles are intended to fill a gap that was deliberately left in the articles on responsibility of States for internationally wrongful acts. As stated in article 57 on the responsibility of States for internationally wrongful acts,

those articles are "without prejudice to any question of the responsibility ... of any State for the conduct of an international organization".[181]

(2) Not all the questions that may affect the responsibility of a State in connection with the act of an international organization are examined in the present draft articles. For instance, questions relating to attribution of conduct to a State are covered only in the articles on responsibility of States for internationally wrongful acts. Thus, if an issue arises as to whether certain conduct is to be attributed to a State or to an international organization or to both, the present articles will provide criteria for ascertaining whether conduct is to be attributed to the international organization, while the articles on the responsibility of States for internationally wrongful acts will regulate attribution of conduct to the State.

(3) The present Part assumes that there exists conduct attributable to an international organization. In most cases, that conduct will also be internationally wrongful. However, exceptions are provided for the cases envisaged in articles 60 and 61, which deal respectively with coercion of an international organization by a State and with international responsibility in case of a member State circumventing one of its international obligations by taking advantage of the competence of an international organization.

(4) According to articles 61 and 62, the State that incurs responsibility in connection with the act of an international organization is necessarily a member of that organization. In the cases envisaged in articles 58, 59 and 60, the responsible State may or may not be a member.

(5) The present Part does not address the question of responsibility that may arise for entities other than States that are also members of an international organization. Chapter IV of Part Two of the present draft articles already considers the responsibility that an international organization may incur when it aids or assists or directs and controls in the commission of an internationally wrongful act of another international organization of which the former organization is a member. The same chapter also deals with coercion by an international organization that is a member of the coerced organization. Article 18 considers further cases of responsibility of international organizations as members of another international organization. Questions relating to the responsibility of entities, other than States or international organizations, that are also members of international organizations fall outside the scope of the present draft articles.

Article 58

Aid or assistance by a State in the commission of an internationally wrongful act by an international organization

1. A State which aids or assists an international organization in the commission of an internationally wrongful act by the latter is internationally responsible for doing so if:
   (*a*) the State does so with knowledge of the circumstances of the internationally wrongful act; and
   (*b*) the act would be internationally wrongful if committed by that State.
2. An act by a State member of an international organization done in accordance with the rules of the organization does not as such engage the international responsibility of that State under the terms of this article.

181 *Yearbook ... 2001*, vol. II (Part Two) and corrigendum, p. 141. [Note: this footnote appears in the original document as footnote '350'].

Commentary

(1) The present article addresses a situation parallel to the one covered in article 14, which concerns aid or assistance by an international organization in the commission of an internationally wrongful act by another international organization. Both articles closely follow the text of article 16 on the responsibility of States for internationally wrongful acts.[182]

(2) Aid or assistance by a State could constitute a breach of an obligation that the State has acquired under a primary norm. For example, a nuclear-weapon State Party to the Treaty on the Non-Proliferation of Nuclear Weapons would have to refrain from assisting a non-nuclear-weapon State in the acquisition of nuclear weapons, and the same would seem to apply to assistance given to an international organization of which some non-nuclear-weapon States are members.

(3) The present article uses the same wording as article 16 on the responsibility of States for internationally wrongful acts, because it would be hard to find reasons for applying a different rule when the aided or assisted entity is an international organization rather than a State. Paragraph 1 sets in subparagraphs (*a*) and (*b*) the conditions for international responsibility to arise for the aiding or assisting State. It is to be noted that no distinction is made with regard to the temporal relation between the conduct of the State and the internationally wrongful act of the international organization.

(4) A State aiding or assisting an international organization in the commission of an internationally wrongful act may or may not be a member of that organization. Should the State be a member, the possibility that aid or assistance could result from conduct taken by the State within the framework of the organization cannot be totally excluded. However, as specified in paragraph 2, an act by a member State which is done in accordance with the rules of the organization does not as such engage the international responsibility of that State for aid or assistance. These criteria could entail some difficulties in ascertaining whether aid or assistance has taken place in borderline cases. The factual context such as the size of membership and the nature of the involvement will probably be decisive.

(5) The fact that a State does not *per se* incur international responsibility for aiding or assisting an international organization of which it is a member when it acts in accordance with the rules of the organization does not imply that the State would then be free to ignore its international obligations. These obligations may well encompass the conduct of a State when it acts within an international organization. Should a breach of an international obligation be committed by a State in this capacity, the State would not incur international responsibility under the present article, but rather under the articles on the responsibility of States for internationally wrongful acts.

(6) The heading of article 16 on the responsibility of States for internationally wrongful acts has been slightly adapted, by adding "by a State" to the words "aid or assistance", in order to distinguish the heading of the present article from that of article 14 of the present draft articles.

Article 59
Direction and control exercised by a State over the commission of an internationally wrongful act by an international organization

1. A State which directs and controls an international organization in the commission of an internationally wrongful act by the latter is internationally responsible for that act if:
   (*a*) the State does so with knowledge of the circumstances of the internationally wrongful act; and

182 *Ibid.*, p. 65. [Note: this footnote appears in the original document as footnote '351'].

(*b*) the act would be internationally wrongful if committed by that State.

2. An act by a State member of an international organization done in accordance with the rules of the organization does not as such engage the international responsibility of that State under the terms of this draft article.

Commentary

(1) While article 15 relates to direction and control exercised by an international organization in the commission of an internationally wrongful act by another international organization, the present article considers the case in which direction and control are exercised by a State. Both articles closely follow the text of article 17 on the responsibility of States for internationally wrongful acts.[183]

(2) The State directing and controlling an international organization in the commission of an internationally wrongful act may or may not be a member of that organization. As in the case of aid or assistance, which is considered in article 58 and the related commentary, a distinction has to be made between participation by a member State in the decision-making process of the organization according to its pertinent rules, and direction and control which would trigger the application of the present article. Since the latter conduct could take place within the framework of the organization, in borderline cases one would face the same problems that have been referred to in the commentary on the previous article.

(3) Paragraph 1 sets in (*a*) and (*b*) the conditions for the responsibility of the State to arise with the same wording that is used in article 17 on the responsibility of States for internationally wrongful acts. There are no reasons for making a distinction between the case in which a State directs and controls another State in the commission of an internationally wrongful act and the case in which the State similarly directs and controls an international organization.

(4) As in article 58, paragraph 2 of the present draft article specifies that an act of a member State done in accordance with the rules of the organization does not as such cause the responsibility of that State for direction and control in the commission of an internationally wrongful act.

(5) The heading of the present article has been slightly adapted from article 17 on the responsibility of States for internationally wrongful acts by adding the words "by a State", in order to distinguish it from the heading of article 15 of the present articles.

Article 60

Coercion of an international organization by a State

A State which coerces an international organization to commit an act is internationally responsible for that act if:

(*a*) the act would, but for the coercion, be an internationally wrongful act of the coerced international organization; and

(*b*) the coercing State does so with knowledge of the circumstances of the act.

...

Article 61

Circumvention of international obligations of a State member of an international organization

1. A State member of an international organization incurs international responsibility if, by taking advantage of the fact that the organization has competence in relation to the subject matter of one of the State's international obligations, it circumvents that obligation by causing

183 *Ibid.*, pp. 67–69. [Note: this footnote appears in the original document as footnote '352'].

the organization to commit an act that, if committed by the State, would have constituted a breach of the obligation.

2. Paragraph 1 applies whether or not the act in question is internationally wrongful for the international organization.

Commentary

...

(3) The jurisprudence of the European Court of Human Rights provides a few examples of *dicta* affirming the possibility of States being held responsible when they fail to ensure compliance with their obligations under the European Convention on Human Rights in a field where they have attributed competence to an international organization. In *Waite and Kennedy* v. *Germany*, the Court examined the question of whether the right of access to justice had been unduly impaired by a State that granted immunity to the European Space Agency, of which it was a member, in relation to claims concerning employment. The Court said that

> where States establish international organisations in order to pursue or strengthen their cooperation in certain fields of activities, and where they attribute to these organisations certain competences and accord them immunities, there may be implications as to protection of fundamental rights. It would be incompatible with the purpose and object of the [European Convention on Human Rights], however, if the Contracting States were thereby absolved from their responsibility under the Convention in relation to the field of activity covered by such attribution.[184]

(4) In *Bosphorus Hava Yollary Turizm ve Ticaret Anonim Sirketi* v. *Ireland*, the Court took a similar approach with regard to a State measure implementing a regulation of the European Community. The Court said that a State could not free itself from its obligations under the European Convention on Human Rights by transferring functions to an international organization, because

> absolving Contracting States completely from their Convention responsibility in the areas covered by such a transfer would be incompatible with the purpose and object of the Convention; the guarantees of the Convention could be limited or excluded at will, thereby depriving it of its peremptory character and undermining the practical and effective nature of its safeguards ... The State is considered to retain Convention liability in respect of treaty commitments subsequent to the entry into force of the Convention ....[185]

(5) In a more recent case before the European Court of Human Rights, *Gasparini* v. *Italy and Belgium*, an application had been made against these two States by two employees of NATO alleging the inadequacy of the settlement procedure concerning employment disputes with

---

184 *Waite and Kennedy* v. *Germany*, Application no. 26083/94, Judgment of 18 February 1999, Grand Chamber, European Court of Human Rights, *Reports of Judgments and Decisions* 1999-I, p. 393, at p. 410, para. 67. The Court concluded that the "essence of [the applicant's] 'right to a court' " under the Convention had not been impaired (p. 412, para. 73). After examining the *dictum* in this case, Ian Brownlie noted that, "[w]hilst the context is that of human rights, the principle invoked would seem to be general in its application" (I. Brownlie, "The responsibility of States for the acts of international organizations", in M. Ragazzi (ed.), *International Responsibility Today: Essays in Memory of Oscar Schachter*, Leiden/Boston, Martinus Nijhoff, 2005, p. 355, at p. 361). Views similar to those of the European Court of Human Rights were expressed by A. Di Blase, "Sulla responsabilità internazionale per attività dell'ONU", *Rivista di Diritto Internazionale*, vol. 57 (1974), p. 250, at pp. 275–276; M. Hirsch, *The Responsibility of International Organizations toward Third Parties* (footnote 121 above), p. 179; K. Zemanek, Institute of International Law, *Yearbook*, vol. 66, Part I, Session of Lisbon (1995), p. 329; P. Sands, in P. Sands and P. Klein (eds.), *Bowett's Law of International Institutions*, London, Sweet and Maxwell, 2001, p. 524; D. Sarooshi, *International Organizations and their Exercise of Sovereign Powers*, Oxford University Press, 2005, p. 64; and O. De Schutter, "Human rights and the rise of international organisations: the logic of sliding scales in the law of international responsibility", in J. Wouters *et al.* (eds.), *Accountability for Human Rights Violations by International Organisations*, Antwerp, Intersentia, 2010, p. 51. [Note: this footnote appears in the original document as footnote '356'].

185 *Bosphorus Hava Yollari Turizm ve Ticaret Anonim Şirketi* v. *Ireland*, Application no. 45036/98, Judgment of 30 June 2005 (see footnote 184 above), para. 154. The Court found that the defendant State had not incurred responsibility because the relevant fundamental rights were protected within the European Community "in a manner which can be considered at least equivalent to that for which the Convention provides" (para. 155). [Note: this footnote appears in the original document as footnote '357'].

NATO. The Court said that States, when they transfer part of their sovereign powers to an organization of which they are members, are under an obligation to see that the rights guaranteed by the Convention receive within the organization an "equivalent protection" to that ensured by the Convention mechanism. As in the two previous decisions referred to in the preceding paragraphs, the Court found that this obligation had not been breached, in this case because the procedure within NATO was not tainted with "manifest insufficiency".[186]

(6) According to the present article, three conditions are required for international responsibility to arise for a member State circumventing one of its international obligations. The first one is that the international organization has competence in relation to the subject matter of an international obligation of a State. This could occur through the transfer of State functions to an organization of integration. However, the cases covered are not so limited. Moreover, an international organization could be established in order to exercise functions that States may not have. What is relevant for international responsibility to arise under the present article is that the international obligation covers the area in which the international organization is provided with competence. The obligation may specifically relate to that area or be more general, as in the case of obligations under treaties for the protection of human rights.

(7) A second condition for international responsibility to arise according to the present article is that there be a significant link between the conduct of the circumventing member State and that of the international organization. The act of the international organization has to be caused by the member State.

(8) The third condition for international responsibility to arise is that the international organization commits an act that, if committed by the State, would have constituted a breach of the obligation. An act that would constitute a breach of the obligation has to be committed.

(9) Paragraph 2 explains that the present article does not require the act to be internationally wrongful for the international organization concerned. Circumvention is more likely to occur when the international organization is not bound by the international obligation. However, the mere existence of an international obligation for the organization does not necessarily exempt the State from international responsibility.

(10) Should the act of the international organization be wrongful and be caused by the member State, there could be an overlap between the cases covered in article 61 and those considered in articles 58, 59 and 60. This would occur when the conditions set by one of these articles are fulfilled. However, such an overlap would not be problematic, because it would only imply the existence of a plurality of bases for holding the State responsible.

Article 62
Responsibility of a State member of an international organization for an internationally wrongful act of that organization

1. A State member of an international organization is responsible for an internationally wrongful act of that organization if:
   (*a*) it has accepted responsibility for that act towards the injured party; or
   (*b*) it has led the injured party to rely on its responsibility.
2. Any international responsibility of a State under paragraph 1 is presumed to be subsidiary.

186 *Gasparini* v. *Italy and Belgium*, Application no. 10750/03, Decision of 12 May 2009, European Court of Human Rights (issued in French). The text is available from http://hudoc.echr.coe.int/ fre?i=001-92899. [Note: this footnote appears in the original document as footnote '358'].

Commentary

(1) A State member of an international organization may be held responsible in accordance with articles 58 to 61. The present article envisages two additional cases in which member States incur responsibility. Member States may furthermore be responsible according to the articles on the responsibility of States for internationally wrongful acts,[187] but this lies beyond the scope of the present draft articles.

(2) Consistently with the approach generally taken by the present draft articles as well as by the articles on the responsibility of States for internationally wrongful acts, article 62 positively identifies those cases in which a State incurs responsibility and does not say when responsibility is not deemed to arise. While it would be thus inappropriate to include in the draft a provision stating a residual, and negative, rule for those cases in which responsibility is not considered to arise for a State in connection with the act of an international organization, such a rule is clearly implied. Therefore, membership does not as such entail for member States international responsibility when the organization commits an internationally wrongful act.

(3) The view that member States cannot generally be regarded as internationally responsible for the internationally wrongful acts of the organization has been defended by several States in contentious cases. The German Government recalled in a written comment that it had

> advocated the principle of separate responsibility before the European Commission of Human Rights (*M. & Co.*), the European Court of Human Rights (*Senator Lines*) and the [International Court of Justice] (*Legality of Use of Force*) and [had] rejected responsibility for reason of membership for measures taken by the European Community, NATO and the United Nations.[188]

...

(6) The view that member States are not in general responsible does not rule out that there are certain cases, other than those considered in the previous articles, in which a State would be responsible for the internationally wrongful act of the organization. The least controversial case is that of acceptance of international responsibility by the States concerned. This case is stated in subparagraph (*a*). No qualification is given to acceptance. This is intended to mean that acceptance may be expressly stated or implied and may occur either before or after the time when responsibility arises for the organization.

...

Article 63

Effect of this Part

This Part is without prejudice to the international responsibility of the international organization which commits the act in question, or of any State or other international organization.

...

Article 64

Lex specialis

These draft articles do not apply where and to the extent that the conditions for the existence of an internationally wrongful act or the content or implementation of the international responsibility of an international organization, or a State in connection with the conduct of an

187 This would apply to the case envisaged by the Institute of International Law in article 5 (c) (ii) of its resolution on "The legal consequences for member States of the non-fulfilment by international organizations of their obligations toward third parties" that "the international organization has acted as the agent of the State, in law or in fact" (Institute of International Law, *Yearbook*, vol. 66, Part II (see footnote 70 above), p. 449).

188 *Yearbook* ... *2005*, vol. II (Part One), document A/CN.4/556, p. 61. [Note: this footnote appears in the original document as footnote '360'].

international organization, are governed by special rules of international law. Such special rules of international law may be contained in the rules of the organization applicable to the relations between an international organization and its members.

Commentary

(1) Special rules relating to international responsibility may supplement more general rules or may replace them, in whole or in part. These special rules may concern the relations that certain categories of international organizations or one specific international organization have with some or all States or other international organizations. They may also concern matters addressed in Part Five of the present articles.

...

(8) Given the particular importance that the rules of the organization are likely to have as special rules concerning international responsibility in the relations between an international organization and its members, a specific reference to the rules of the organization has been added at the end of the present article. The rules of the organization may, expressly or implicitly, govern various aspects of the issues dealt with in Parts Two to Five. For instance, they may affect the consequences of a breach of international law that an international organization may commit when the injured party is a member State or international organization. The relevance of special rules with regard to the issue of countermeasures has been considered in articles 22 and 52 and the related commentaries.

Article 65
Questions of international responsibility not regulated by these draft articles
The applicable rules of international law continue to govern questions concerning the responsibility of an international organization or a State for an internationally wrongful act to the extent that they are not regulated by these draft articles.

...

Article 66
Individual responsibility
These draft articles are without prejudice to any question of the individual responsibility under international law of any person acting on behalf of an international organization or a State.

Commentary

...

(2) Thus, the fact that the conduct of an individual is attributed to an international organization or a State does not exempt that individual from the international criminal responsibility that he or she may incur for his or her conduct. On the other hand, when an internationally wrongful act of an international organization or a State is committed, the international responsibility of individuals that have been instrumental to the wrongful act cannot be taken as implied. However, in certain cases the international criminal responsibility of some individuals may arise, for instance when they have been instrumental to the serious breach of an obligation under a peremptory norm in the circumstances envisaged in article 41.

(3) Individual responsibility could also relate to damage caused by an act of a person acting on behalf of an international organization. For instance, when the victims of an international crime suffer damage, the responsible individual may have an obligation to make reparation.

Article 67
Charter of the United Nations
These draft articles are without prejudice to the Charter of the United Nations.

Commentary

(1) The present article reproduces article 59 on the responsibility of States for internationally wrongful acts,[189] which sets forth a "without prejudice" provision concerning the Charter of the United Nations. The reference to the Charter of the United Nations includes obligations that are directly stated therein as well as those flowing from binding decisions of the Security Council, which, according to the International Court of Justice, similarly prevail over other obligations under international law on the basis of article 103 of the Charter of the United Nations.[190] According to article 103, "[i]n the event of a conflict between the obligations of the Members of the United Nations under the present Charter and their obligations under any other international agreement, their obligations under the Charter shall prevail".

(2) Insofar as issues of State responsibility are covered in the present draft articles, there could be no reason to query the applicability of the same "without prejudice" provision as the corresponding article on the responsibility of States for internationally wrongful acts. A question may be raised with regard to the responsibility of international organizations, since they are not members of the United Nations and therefore have not formally agreed to be bound by the Charter of the United Nations. However, even if the prevailing effect of obligations under the Charter of the United Nations may have a legal basis for international organizations that differs from the legal basis applicable to States,[191] one may reach the conclusion that the Charter of the United Nations has a prevailing effect also with regard to international organizations. For instance, when establishing an arms embargo which requires all its addressees not to comply with an obligation to supply arms that they may have accepted under a treaty, the Security Council does not distinguish between States and international organizations.[192] It is at any event not necessary, for the purpose of the present draft articles, to determine the extent to which the international responsibility of an international organization is affected, directly or indirectly, by the Charter of the United Nations.

(3) The present article is not intended to exclude the applicability of the principles and rules set forth in the preceding articles to the international responsibility of the United Nations.

---

189 *Ibid.*, p. 143. [Note: this footnote appears in the original document as footnote '383'].

190 See the orders on provisional measures in the cases *Questions of Interpretation and Application of the 1971 Montreal Convention [for the suppression of unlawful acts against the safety of civil aviation] arising from the Aerial Incident at Lockerbie (Libyan Arab Jamahiriya* v. *United Kingdom; Libyan Arab Jamahiriya* v. *United States of America), Provisional Measures, Order of 14 April 1992, I.C.J. Reports 1992*, at pp. 15 and 126. [Note: this footnote appears in the original document as footnote '384'].

191 One explanation is that Article 103 of the Charter of the United Nations prevails over the constituent instruments of the international organizations. See R. H. Lauwaars, "The interrelationship between United Nations law and the law of other international organizations", *Michigan Law Review*, vol. 82 (1983–1984), p. 1604 *et seq.* [Note: this footnote appears in the original document as footnote '385'].

192 As was noted by B. Fassbender, "The United Nations Charter as constitution of the international Community", *Columbia Journal of Transnational Law*, vol. 36, No. 3 (1998), p. 529 *et seq.*, at p. 609, "intergovernmental organizations are generally required to comply with Council resolutions". [Note: this footnote appears in the original document as footnote '386'].

E. Codes of Conduct, Directives, and Guidelines

25

Secretary-General's Bulletin: Status, Basic Rights and Duties of United Nations Staff Members

Prefatory Note

The Secretary-General's Bulletin on the 'Status, Basic Rights and Duties of United Nations Staff Members' (Bulletin) was promulgated on 1 November 2002 and entered into force on 1 December 2002.[1] The Bulletin was updated most recently in 2016[2] and it applies to all UN staff members serving on UN peace operations. One of its primary purposes is to hold UN staff members accountable. It does this by setting out their status, basic rights, and duties.[3]

The Bulletin is founded on the UN Charter[4] and the Convention on the Privileges and Immunities of the United Nations.[5]

After several provisional Staff Regulations, the General Assembly established the first permanent Staff Regulations in resolution 590 (VI).[6] The Staff Regulations have been amended and added to many times over the years through further General Assembly resolutions.[7]

The Staff Regulations 'embody the fundamental conditions of service and the basic rights, duties and obligations of the United Nations Secretariat'.[8] A UN staff member is someone whose:

> employment and contractual relationship are defined by a letter of appointment subject to regulations promulgated by the General Assembly pursuant to Article 101, paragraph 1, of the Charter.[9]

The letter of appointment is pursuant to Staff Regulation 4.1. Annex II of the Staff Regulations provides that a letter of appointment shall state:

> the appointment is subject to the provisions of the Staff Regulations and of the Staff Rules . . . and to changes which may be duly made in such regulations and rules from time to time.[10]

The Secretary-General, as the chief administrative officer of the UN, issues Staff Rules that expand on the broad principles outlined in the Staff Regulations. Whilst the Staff Regulations apply to all

---

1 'Secretary-General's Bulletin: Status, Basic Rights and Duties of United Nations Staff Members', UN Doc ST/SGB/2002/13, 1 November 2002 (hereafter Bulletin).

2 'Secretary-General's Bulletin: Staff Regulations', UN Doc ST/SGB/2016/5, 1 July 2016.

3 Ibid, 6.

4 See ch 1 above.

5 See ch 21 above.

6 GA Res 590 (VI) of 2 February 1952.

7 See, for example, 'Secretary-General's Bulletin: Status, Basic Rights and Duties of United Nations Staff Members', UN Doc ST/SGB/1998/19, 10 December 1998. Promulgated in GA Res 52/252 of 8 September 1998.

8 'Secretary-General's Bulletin: Staff Regulations', UN Doc ST/SGB/2009/6, 27 May 2009, 1.

9 Ibid.

10 Ibid, Annex II(a)(i).

staff, there were three series of Staff Rules applicable to different categories of staff. These were the 100, 200, and 300 series of the Staff Rules. In 2009, the 100, 200, and 300 series were abolished in favour of a single set of Staff Rules.[11]

In August 1994, the Secretary-General announced that a UN 'Code of Conduct' for staff would be developed as part of a transparent and effective system of accountability.[12] In 1997, the Secretary-General released a report on the proposed Code of Conduct.[13] The Code was to be implemented through revisions to Article 1 of the Staff Regulations and Chapter 1 of the 100 series of the Staff Rules. Reference was also made to the 1954 report of the International Civil Service Advisory Board entitled 'Standards of Conduct in the International Civil Service' (1954 standards) as providing an illustrative guide for staff of expected standards of conduct rather than a set of rules that bind staff.[14]

The General Assembly, in resolution 52/12B on 'Renewing the United Nations: A Programme for Reform', noted that the Secretary-General had submitted a draft Code of Conduct for UN Staff to the General Assembly and agreed to expedite its consideration.[15] Following resolution 52/12B, an addendum to the Secretary-General's report on the proposed Code of Conduct was published where it was proposed to replace the term 'Code of Conduct' with the term 'Status, Basic Rights and Duties of Staff'.[16]

The General Assembly, in resolution 52/252, adopted the revised text of Article 1 of the Staff Regulations and took note of the revised text of Chapter 1 of the 100 series of the Staff Rules.[17] The resolution also outlined the provisions governing the status, basic rights, and duties of staff members.[18] The text of all of the provisions outlined in the resolution was included in the 1998 Secretary-General's Bulletin entitled 'Status, Basic Rights and Duties of United Nations Staff Members'.[19] The 1998 Bulletin was replaced by the 2002 Bulletin which, in turn, was replaced by the 2016 Bulletin. The 2016 Bulletin not only updates the 2002 Bulletin but also reflects the changes made to the 2016 Staff Regulations[20] and Staff Rules.[21]

The contents of the Bulletin reproduced in this chapter include the revised text of Article 1 of the Staff Regulations with some provisions from the Staff Rules. The regulations and rules in the Bulletin are accompanied by a commentary. It should be noted, however, that the commentary 'is not part of the Staff Regulations and Rules and so is not a legal norm, nor does it have the legal force of a rule'.[22] However, staff may 'safely rely on the commentary to guide their actions, since it provides a more detailed understanding of and guidance on the statutory provisions and of staff members' basic rights and obligations'.[23] Consequently, the Bulletin provides Staff with a guide for their actions.[24]

The Bulletin is directly relevant to UN peace operations because it requires that UN staff assigned to a peace operation to adhere to certain standards of conduct concerning the discharge of their duties and their relationships with sources external to the organisation. It also requires UN staff assigned to peace operations to 'uphold and respect the principles set out in the Charter, including faith in fundamental human rights'.[25]

---

11 See the 'Secretary-General's Bulletin: Staff Rules: Staff Regulations of the United Nations and provisional Staff Rules', UN Doc ST/SGB/2009/7, 16 June 2009.

12 'Report of the Secretary-General: Establishment of a Transparent and Effective System of Accountability and Responsibility', UN Doc A/C.5/49/1, 5 August 1994, [28]–[31].

13 'Report of the Secretary-General: Proposed United Nations Code of Conduct', UN Doc A/52/488, 17 October 1997.

14 Ibid, [4].

15 GA Res 52/12B of 19 December 1997, Operative Part [23].

16 'Report of the Secretary-General: Proposed United Nations Code of Conduct', UN Doc A/52/488/Add.1, 28 July 1998, [3].

17 GA Res 52/252 of 8 September 1998.

18 Ibid, Operative Part [8].

19 UN Doc ST/SGB/1998/19, 10 December 1998.

20 UN Doc ST/SGB/2016/5, 1 July 2016.

21 UN Doc ST/SGB/2017/1, 30 December 2016.

22 'Secretary-General's Bulletin: Status, Basic Rights and Duties of United Nations Staff Members', UN Doc ST/SGB/2016/9, 21 July 2016, Annex, Introduction, [4].

23 Ibid.

24 Ibid.

25 Bulletin (n 1), Regulation 1.2(a).

The Bulletin also states that '[s]taff members are international civil servants. Their responsibilities as staff members are not national but exclusively international'.[26] This emphasis on the international nature of their responsibilities is further reinforced by the requirement that UN staff shall not 'seek or accept instructions ... from any Government or other source external to the Organisation'.[27] Bulletin Regulation 1.3(a) deals with accountability and provides that UN staff members 'are accountable to the Secretary-General for the proper discharge of their functions'.

The standards of conduct expected of UN staff members are founded on the Charter. Pursuant to Article 101(3) of the Charter, UN staff members are to have the 'highest standards of efficiency, competence and integrity'.[28] In this context, integrity 'embraces all aspects of behaviour of an international civil servant, including such qualities as honesty, truthfulness, impartiality and incorruptibility'.[29] UN Staff are also required to be loyal to the 'aims, principles and purposes' of the UN.[30] They are prohibited from any form of sexual exploitation and abuse[31] and '[a]ny form of discrimination or harassment, including sexual or gender harassment, as well as physical or verbal abuse at the workplace or in connection with work'.[32] These prohibitions have been expanded upon in the Secretary-General's Bulletins concerning 'Special Measures for Protection from Sexual Exploitation and Sexual Abuse'[33] and the 'Prohibition of Discrimination, Harassment, including Sexual Harassment, and Abuse of Authority'[34] respectively.

The privileges and immunities of UN staff 'furnish no excuse to the staff members who are covered by them to fail to observe laws and police regulations of the State in which they are located'.[35] Furthermore, the privileges and immunities afforded to staff members do not provide an 'excuse for non-performance of their private obligations'.[36] If an issue arises which concerns the application of privileges and immunities, a staff member is obligated to report the matter to the Secretary-General and, where the privileges and immunities apply, it is for the Secretary-General to waive them.[37]

Where a staff member fails to comply with their obligations, Rule 101.2(a) provides for disciplinary proceedings being instituted:

> Disciplinary procedures set out in article X of the Staff Regulations and chapter X of the Staff Rules may be instituted against a staff member who fails to comply with his or her obligations and the standards of conduct set out in the Charter of the United Nations, the Staff Regulations and Rules, the Financial Regulations and Rules and all administrative issuances.

The right of UN staff to appeal administrative decisions is provided for in Article XI of the Staff Regulations whilst Chapter XI of the Staff Rules outlines the procedures for such appeals.

In terms of criminal offences, the general position is that UN staff members are subject to the jurisdiction of the host country, subject to the application of relevant privileges and immunities found in the Convention. On a peace operation, however, the model Status-of-Forces Agreement (model SOFA) provides that if the local authorities wish to bring criminal charges against a member of the peace operation who is a civilian, such as UN staff members (officials), then they need the permission of the Special Representative of the Secretary-General (SRSG).[38] If the SRSG decides not to give permission for criminal proceedings to be commenced in the host country there may be a lacuna in terms of who is responsible for criminally prosecuting the UN staff member since the UN can only take the disciplinary measures outlined in the Staff Regulations and Rules.

---

26 Ibid, Regulation 1.1(a).
27 Ibid, Regulation 1.1(b).
28 Ibid, Regulations 1.1(d) and 1.2(b).
29 Ibid, Regulation 1.2(b) and Commentary [2].
30 Ibid, Regulation 1.2(e).
31 Ibid, Rule 1.2(a).
32 Ibid, Rule 101.2(d).
33 See ch 30 below.
34 UN Doc ST/SGB/2008/5, 11 February 2008.
35 Bulletin (n 1), Regulation 1.1(f).
36 Ibid.
37 Ibid.
38 'Report of the Secretary-General on the Model Status-of-Forces Agreement for Peace-keeping Operations', UN Doc A/45/594, 9 October 1990, Annex, [47](a). See ch 2 above.

The Secretariat's policy concerning accountability for the conduct of UN personnel serving in field missions[39] reinforces the disciplinary and accountability processes described above.[40]

Reference[41]

Title	Secretary-General's Bulletin: Status, Basic Rights and Duties of United Nations Staff Members
Author	Secretary-General of the United Nations
Date of Bulletin	21 July 2016
Entered into force	21 July 2016
Source	UN Doc ST/SGB/2016/9
Full Text	<http://www.undp.org/content/dam/undp/library/corporate/ethics/Status,%20basic%20 rights%20and%20duties%20of%20United%20Nations%20staff%20members.pdf>[42]

Secretary-General's Bulletin: Status, Basic Rights and Duties of United Nations Staff Members[43]

(Extracts)

...

III. Scope and purpose of the Staff Regulations of the United Nations

Article I of the Staff Regulations of the United Nations and related rules from chapter I of the Staff Rules, with commentary

Staff Regulations of the United Nations

Scope and purposeThe Staff Regulations embody the fundamental conditions of service and the basic rights, duties and obligations of the United Nations Secretariat. They represent the broad principles of human resources policy for the staffing and administration of the Secretariat. For the purposes of these Regulations, the expressions "United Nations Secretariat", "staff members" or "staff" shall refer to all the staff members of the Secretariat, within the meaning of Article 97 of the Charter of the United Nations, whose employment and contractual relationship are defined by a letter of appointment subject to regulations promulgated by the General Assembly pursuant to Article 101, paragraph 1, of the Charter. The Secretary-General, as the chief administrative officer, shall provide and enforce such staff rules consistent with these principles as he or she considers necessary.

39 Department of Political Affairs, Department of Peacekeeping Operations, and Department of Field Support, 'Accountability for Conduct and Discipline in Field Missions', 1 August 2015. See ch 31 below.

40 Ibid: see, for example, [11] and [12].

41 The United Nations Human Resource Handbook contains the latest Staff Regulations, Staff Rules, Secretary-General's Bulletins and Administrative Instructions plus any amendments and updates <https://hr.un.org/handbook> accessed 2 April 2019.

42 Accessed 15 August 2018.

43 From the Secretary-General's Bulletin: Status, Basic Rights and Duties of United Nations Staff Members, by the Secretary-General,

Article I

Duties, obligations and privileges

Staff regulation 1.1

Status of staffRegulation 1.1 (a)

Staff members are international civil servants. Their responsibilities as staff members are not national but exclusively international.

Commentary

Staff regulation 1.1 (a) clarifies that the responsibilities of staff are exclusively international owing to their status as international civil servants (see paras. 3–15, 33 and 34 of the 2013 standards of conduct, reproduced in the present annex). This requisite international outlook stems from an understanding of and loyalty to the objectives and purposes of the United Nations itself. The term "international civil servants" and the inherent rights and obligations that attach to this status apply to all staff, whether locally or internationally recruited.

Regulation 1.1 (b)

Staff members shall make the following written declaration witnessed by the Secretary-General or his or her authorized representative:

"I solemnly declare and promise to exercise in all loyalty, discretion and conscience the functions entrusted to me as an international civil servant of the United Nations, to discharge these functions and regulate my conduct with the interests of the United Nations only in view, and not to seek or accept instructions in regard to the performance of my duties from any Government or other source external to the Organization.

"I also solemnly declare and promise to respect the obligations incumbent upon me as set out in the Staff Regulations and Rules."

Commentary

1. Staff regulation 1.1 (b) contains the declaration of office of staff, and its opening words incorporate the text of former staff regulation 1.9 insofar as it relates to staff members (see paras. 3–15 of the 2013 standards of conduct). It requests staff members upon entry on duty to expressly declare that they will act with the interests of the Organization only in view in the discharge of their functions.
2. The second paragraph of the declaration refers specifically to the Staff Regulations and Rules.

Regulation 1.1 (c)

The Secretary-General shall ensure that the rights and duties of staff members, as set out in the Charter and the Staff Regulations and Rules and in the relevant resolutions and decisions of the General Assembly, are respected.

Commentary

The regulation codifies a duty that falls on the Secretary-General, that is, to ensure that the rights and duties of staff members are respected.

Regulation 1.1 (d)

The Secretary-General shall seek to ensure that the paramount consideration in the determination of the conditions of service shall be the necessity of securing staff of the highest standards of efficiency, competence and integrity.

Commentary

1. Staff regulation 1.1 (d) places on the Secretary-General an affirmative duty to seek to ensure that the criteria set out in Article 101, paragraph 3, of the Charter for the determination of the

conditions of service of the staff are implemented. This provision is not intended to affect the role of legislative bodies involved in the process of establishing conditions of service. It does, however, seek to formulate the responsibility of the Secretary-General to advocate, in the appropriate forums, the adoption of what he or she considers to be the appropriate conditions of service to secure the recruitment and retention of staff possessing the highest standards of efficiency, competence and integrity.

2. The salaries of staff in the Professional and higher categories are determined by reference to the best paying national civil service under what is known as the Noblemaire principle. The salaries of staff in the General Service and related categories are established by the Secretary-General on the basis of the best prevailing conditions of employment in the locality where the United Nations office concerned is located under what is commonly referred to as the Flemming principle. The determination of the conditions of service of staff in the Field Service category follows the same pattern as the Professional category.

Regulation 1.1 (e)

The Staff Regulations apply to all staff at all levels, including staff of the separately funded organs, holding appointments under the Staff Rules.

Commentary

Regulation 1.1 (e) makes clear that the Staff Regulations apply to all staff members, irrespective of levels, including staff members of the separately funded organs within the meaning of Article 97 of the Charter whose contractual link with the Organization is through a letter of appointment issued pursuant to regulations promulgated by the General Assembly.

Regulation 1.1 (f)

The privileges and immunities enjoyed by the United Nations by virtue of Article 105 of the Charter are conferred in the interests of the Organization. These privileges and immunities furnish no excuse to the staff members who are covered by them to fail to observe laws and police regulations of the State in which they are located nor do they furnish an excuse for non-performance of their private obligations. In any case where an issue arises regarding the application of these privileges and immunities, the staff member shall immediately report the matter to the Secretary-General, who alone may decide whether such privileges and immunities exist and whether they shall be waived in accordance with the relevant instruments.

Commentary

1. Staff regulation 1.1 (f) defines the scope and extent of the privileges and immunities of the United Nations that are enjoyed by staff in the interest of the Organization (see also paras. 43 and 44 of the 2013 standards of conduct).
2. Staff rule 1.2 (b) (see below) deals with the obligation of staff to honour their private legal obligations.

Staff rule 1.1

Status of staff

Rule 1.1 (a)

The declaration made by a staff member on appointment pursuant to staff regulation 1.1 (b) shall be placed in his or her official status file. A new declaration shall be made after a break in service that exceeds three months.

Commentary

Staff rule 1.1 (a) codifies that the written declaration made on appointment is placed in the official status file. The second sentence seeks to ensure that a new declaration is made after a break in service that exceeds three months unless the staff member is reinstated and the staff member's services are considered continuous under current staff rule 4.18 (b).

Rule 1.1 (b)

The declaration administered under staff regulation 1.1 (b) shall not prevent the close collaboration of staff with a Government pursuant to an agreement between the Government and the United Nations.

Commentary

Staff rule 1.1 (b) clarifies that the written declaration does not prevent staff members from liaising and working with a Government where there has been an agreement, such as a technical cooperation agreement, between the Government and the United Nations. Staff members remain bound by their declaration towards the Organization and the principles guiding the international civil service.

Staff regulation 1.2

Basic rights and obligations of staff

Core values

Regulation 1.2 (a)

Staff members shall uphold and respect the principles set out in the Charter, including faith in fundamental human rights, in the dignity and worth of the human person and in the equal rights of men and women. Consequently, staff members shall exhibit respect for all cultures; they shall not discriminate against any individual or group of individuals or otherwise abuse the power and authority vested in them.

Commentary

This provision describes the basic values and behaviours expected of international civil servants because of their status. At the heart of those values are the principles set out in the preamble to the Charter. The first sentence is a quotation from those opening words, and the second sentence sets out the obligation of staff flowing from a commitment to those values (see also paras. 2–6, 14, 15, 21 and 22 of the 2013 standards of conduct).

Regulation 1.2 (b)

Staff members shall uphold the highest standards of efficiency, competence and integrity. The concept of integrity includes, but is not limited to, probity, impartiality, fairness, honesty and truthfulness in all matters affecting their work and status.

Commentary

1. This provision describes more basic values expected of international civil servants because of their status. It is derived from Article 101, paragraph 3, of the Charter and affirmatively places on staff the obligation to uphold the highest standards of efficiency, competence and integrity after appointment to the Secretariat.
2. At the heart of those values is integrity, allied with a dedication to the values and principles set out in the Charter. As discussed in paragraph 5 of the 2013 standards of conduct, the concept of integrity "embraces all aspects of behaviour of an international civil servant, including such qualities as honesty, truthfulness, impartiality and incorruptibility".
3. Various other provisions deal with particular manifestations of this set of basic values in different circumstances, for example, staff regulations 1.2 (d)–(i), (m) and (n).

General rights and obligations

Regulation 1.2 (c)

Staff members are subject to the authority of the Secretary-General and to assignment by him or her to any of the activities or offices of the United Nations. In exercising this authority the

Secretary-General shall seek to ensure, having regard to the circumstances, that all necessary safety and security arrangements are made for staff carrying out the responsibilities entrusted to them.

Commentary

1. The Secretary-General, as the chief administrative officer of the Organization, has an inherent responsibility to seek to ensure the safety of staff. This regulation recognizes that responsibility as a basic right of staff (see also para. 41 of the 2013 standards of conduct).
2. In exercising his or her authority to assign staff to any of the activities of the Organization, the Secretary-General shall seek to ensure that, while assigned to hardship areas, staff are afforded reasonable conditions of life and work having regard to the existing conditions.
3. Furthermore, since staff are subject to assignment, measures should be taken to ensure that staff are advised of conditions prevailing at the duty station to which they are assigned.

Regulation 1.2 (d)

In the performance of their duties staff members shall neither seek nor accept instructions from any Government or from any other source external to the Organization.

Commentary

1. Staff regulation 1.2 (d) flows from the first sentence of Article 100, paragraph 1, of the Charter (see paras. 8, 12, 33 and 34 of the 2013 standards of conduct).
2. This regulation makes clear that directions or instructions to staff come from the Secretary-General, who must fulfil only the legislative mandates of the Organization. This is true in all areas, including, for example, decisions relating to the appointment and promotion of staff, which are for the Secretary-General to make as the chief administrative officer of the Organization. In this context, it is improper for staff to request or allow a Government to intervene in a selection or appointment decision.

Regulation 1.2 (e)

By accepting appointment, staff members pledge themselves to discharge their functions and regulate their conduct with the interests of the Organization only in view. Loyalty to the aims, principles and purposes of the United Nations, as set forth in its Charter, is a fundamental obligation of all staff members by virtue of their status as international civil servants.

Commentary

1. The first sentence of staff regulation 1.2 (e) reiterates the oath or declaration of office and sets out the principle that staff must regulate their conduct with only the interests of the Organization in view (see paras. 4 and 7 of the 2013 standards of conduct). The second sentence of staff regulation 1.2 (e) focuses on the concept of loyalty to the aims, principles and purposes of the Organization as set out in the Charter (which is alluded to in the declaration contained in staff regulation 1.1 (b)) (ibid., paras. 4, 7 and 34). It highlights those obligations which arise from the very status of a staff member and which, at present, are set out only in the declaration subscribed to by staff upon their entry on duty.
2. The Secretary-General, and those to whom he or she has delegated decision-making authority, has the responsibility to make decisions as to whether the staff have complied with the provisions of the Staff Regulations and Rules. Since no set of rules, no matter how long or complex, can cover all situations, it is clear that there must be discretion in the application of the rules. This is common to all systems of administrative law. However, the discretionary authority of the Secretary-General is not unlimited, and relevant jurisprudence has consistently held that decisions cannot be tainted by prejudice, arbitrariness, improper motive or discrimination.

Regulation 1.2 (f)

While staff members' personal views and convictions, including their political and religious convictions, remain inviolable, staff members shall ensure that those views and convictions do not adversely affect their official duties or the interests of the United Nations. They shall conduct themselves at all times in a manner befitting their status as international civil servants and shall not engage in any activity that is incompatible with the proper discharge of their duties with the United Nations. They shall avoid any action and, in particular, any kind of public pronouncement that may adversely reflect on their status, or on the integrity, independence and impartiality that are required by that status.

Commentary

1. As stated in paragraph 2 of the 2013 standards of conduct:

> ".... international civil servants have a special calling: to serve the ideals of peace, respect for fundamental rights, economic and social progress, and international cooperation. It is therefore incumbent on international civil servants to adhere to the highest standards of conduct; for, ultimately, it is the international civil service that will enable the United Nations system to bring about a just and peaceful world."

(See also para. 5 on the integrity expected of international civil servants; paras. 4, 7 and 37 on loyalty; paras. 6, 9 and 14 on tolerance and understanding; paras. 9 and 10 on impartiality; paras. 11 and 12 on independence; paras. 4, 14 and 40 on international outlook; and para.15 on freedom from discrimination.)

2. The 2013 standards of conduct state, in paragraph 9:

> "Impartiality implies tolerance and restraint, particularly in dealing with political or religious convictions. While their personal views remain inviolate, international civil servants do not have the freedom of private persons to take sides or to express their convictions publicly on controversial matters, either individually or as members of a group, irrespective of the medium used. This can mean that, in certain situations, personal views should be expressed only with tact and discretion."

3. As noted in the commentary on regulation 1.2 (e), it is for the Secretary-General to decide whether a staff member has met the standards set out in this provision. While the Secretary-General has the responsibility and discretion to assess a staff member's conduct, such discretion must be exercised reasonably, without improper motives and in accordance with the requirements of due process. The United Nations Dispute and Appeals Tribunals have reiterated this principle in their jurisprudence.

Regulation 1.2 (g)

Staff members shall not use their office or knowledge gained from their official functions for private gain, financial or otherwise, or for the private gain of any third party, including family, friends and those they favour. Nor shall staff members use their office for personal reasons to prejudice the positions of those they do not favour.

Commentary

1. Staff regulation 1.2 (g) is consistent with principles set out in the 2013 standards of conduct (paras. 23–26 29, 38 and 39). The use of one's office for personal gain is unacceptable. This includes conducting business from a United Nations office or using the Organization's property, such as information technology resources. As such, it includes using the United Nations facilities for a business, using the United Nations name, logo or address for a business or approving a contract for a family business, as well as conducting business for private gain through a personal e-mail using the Organization's information technology infrastructure or equipment. It also reflects the principle that staff members shall not use

information that has not been made public for the private advantage of the staff member or any third party.

2. Staff regulation 1.2 (g), for the sake of clarity, makes specific reference to the prohibition on a staff member favouring a third party, including family or friends, from profiting from a staff member's position or the exercise of his or her functions. The terms "family" and "friends" are broad and intended to encompass not only family members and friends as normally understood, but also relationships that are not recognized by the Staff Regulations and Rules as creating a dependency.
3. The regulation also prohibits the use of office or knowledge gained from that office for personal reasons to prejudice or harm the careers of individual staff members or harm third parties.
4. This regulation also applies to and prohibits using one's office or the Organization's property or resources, including information technology, to advertise or otherwise advance private or political interests of others, including, but not limited to, private companies or political parties. This includes the use of private e-mail in the office or through the Organization's infrastructure or equipment for such purposes.

Regulation 1.2 (h)

Staff members may exercise the right to vote but shall ensure that their participation in any political activity is consistent with, and does not reflect adversely upon, the independence and impartiality required by their status as international civil servants.

Commentary

1. Staff regulation 1.2 (h) reiterates the principle addressed in the 2013 standards of conduct (paras. 9, 10, 33, 48 and 49) emphasizing the need to ensure that political activities do not have an impact on the independence and impartiality of staff. This provision clarifies that staff members may have political views in general, but need to ensure that political views and activities do not have an impact on their independence and impartiality.
2. The notion of consistency with the status of an international civil servant is to be determined by the Secretary-General in view of the necessity of staff being, and appearing to be, independent and impartial. Thus, it is clear that staff members cannot be candidates for political office. In case of doubt, inquiries could be made by staff pursuant to staff rule 1.2 (t) and relevant administrative issuances governing outside activities, as well as to the Ethics Office.
3. Staff members have the right to form staff representative bodies in accordance with staff regulations 8.1 and 8.2 in order to ensure, in the words of staff regulation 8.1, "the effective participation of staff in identifying, examining and resolving issues relating to staff welfare, including conditions of work, general conditions of life and other human resources policies".
4. Staff regulation 1.2 (h) also addresses participation in political events in public such as a political rally. While staff may have political views, their status as impartial international civil servants never ceases while in service, and expression of a particular political opinion or opinion about a particularly sensitive political matter in public may not be compatible with that status.

Regulation 1.2 (i)

Staff members shall exercise the utmost discretion with regard to all matters of official business. They shall not communicate to any Government, entity, person or any other source any information known to them by reason of their official position that they know or ought to have known has not been made public, except as appropriate in the normal course of their duties or by authorization of the Secretary-General. These obligations do not cease upon separation from service.

Commentary

1. Staff regulation 1.2 (i) reflects the fact that official information cannot be used for private purposes, except with authorization. This flows from the idea that staff members should place the interests of the Organization above their own (see para. 4 of the 2013 standards of conduct and the wording of the declaration under staff regulation 1.1) and is intended to protect sensitive and confidential information where the disclosure would have an adverse impact on the Organization's interests, operations and activities. It follows that permission must be obtained for disclosure to third parties of information that has not been made public, unless such disclosure is in the normal course of the duties of the staff member (for example, a press officer) or a staff member was specifically authorized to make such disclosure in the circumstances in question (see also staff regulation 1.2 (r) regarding the duty of staff to cooperate with United Nations investigations).
2. The last sentence of the regulation provides that the obligations set out in the provision do not cease upon separation from service. If a former staff member were to ignore the regulation, a note could be placed in his or her official status file to prevent re-employment.

Honours, gifts or remuneration

Regulation 1.2 (j)

No staff member shall accept any honour, decoration, favour, gift or remuneration from any Government.

Commentary

1. Staff regulations 1.2 (j), (k) and (l) provide the basic provisions regulating the issue of acceptance by staff members of any honour, decoration, favour, gift or remuneration from outside sources (see paras. 50 and 51 of the 2013 standards of conduct).[44] The purpose of these regulations is to ensure the independence and impartiality of staff members.
2. Staff regulation 1.2 (j) contains the basic rule that staff may not accept any honour, decoration, gift or remuneration from any Government (ibid., para. 47),[45] whereby the term "Government" is to be understood broadly, including national, state and municipal authorities and any government representative or other agent as well as intergovernmental organizations.
3. This rule applies whatever the reason for the award, even if the award is unrelated to the staff member's service with the Organization, since it is imperative that an international civil servant be perceived as independent from any national Government or other international organization. This includes governmental housing supplements or other support payments or perquisites, which in all cases can be deemed as a possible conflict of interest and infringement into the staff member's impartial status. It does not apply, however, to subsidies or perquisites offered locally to all United Nations staff members at a duty station such as state-subsidized childcare facilities or other aspects addressed in the host country agreement context such as tax or duty exemptions.
4. Staff regulation 1.2 (j) stresses the importance of the appearance of strict independence and impartiality of staff and thus reaffirms the absolute prohibition on acceptance of benefits from Governments. No exception to this prohibition beyond staff regulation 1.2 (k) (see below) is foreseen, and there is no basis for the Secretary-General to grant approval for acceptance.

---

44 Even though para. 50 envisages the possibility of authorization by the executive head of an organization of an honour, decoration, gift, favour or remuneration from a Government, this is precluded by staff regulation 1.2 (j), as explained in paras. 2 and 3 of the commentary on regulation 1.2 (j). [Note: this footnote appears in the orginal as footnote 'a'].

45 Staff regulation 3.4 (c) envisages that staff members may accept child benefits from their Governments but that, in such a case, United Nations dependency benefits will be reduced. The United Nations may also consider accepting housing provided from Governments, and when staff are assigned to such housing, rental deductions from emoluments are applicable. [Note: this footnote appears in the orginal as footnote 'b'].

5. This provision does not include receipt of remuneration in the form of salary from another international organization where staff are serving under an approved contractual modality such as secondment or loan on the basis of the Inter-Organization Agreement concerning Transfer, Secondment or Loan of Staff among the Organizations Applying the United Nations Common System of Salaries and Allowances or bilateral agreements.

Regulation 1.2 (k)

If refusal of an unanticipated honour, decoration, favour or gift from a Government would cause embarrassment to the Organization, the staff member may receive it on behalf of the Organization and then report and entrust it to the Secretary-General, who will either retain it for the Organization or arrange for its disposal for the benefit of the Organization or for a charitable purpose.[46]

Commentary

It can happen that a staff member is given an unanticipated honour, decoration, favour or gift, perhaps in public, by a minister or even a head of State. In such cases, a public refusal could cause a needlessly unpleasant incident. In such cases, regulation 1.2 (k) clarifies that the unanticipated honour, decoration, favour or gift may be received by the staff member, but only and expressly on behalf of the United Nations. The honour, decoration, favour or gift must then be given to the Secretary-General for retention or disposal by the Organization.[47] Remuneration from a Government must always be refused, and such refusal, as staff are paid by the Organization, could hardly cause embarrassment.

Regulation 1.2 (l)

No staff member shall accept any honour, decoration, favour, gift or remuneration from any non-governmental source without first obtaining the approval of the Secretary-General.

Commentary

1. Staff regulation 1.2 (l) requires that a staff member not accept any honour, decoration, favour, gift or remuneration from a non-governmental source without first obtaining the approval of the Secretary-General (see also paras. 50 and 51 of the 2013 standards of conduct).
2. A non-governmental source means any non-governmental organization or any private source. Educational institutions, even though at times publicly or government-funded, are considered to be a non-governmental source.[48]
3. Approval is not granted where the honour, decoration, favour, gift or remuneration is incompatible with the status of an international civil servant; or may be granted with conditions such as the obligation to entrust it to the Organization upon receipt, in particular when the honour, decoration, favour, gift or remuneration is related to the official function of the staff member.
4. Staff rule 1.2 (l) allows for acceptance of an unanticipated honour, decoration, favour or gift under similar circumstances of acceptance of gifts from Governments.

Conflict of interest

Regulation 1.2 (m)

A conflict of interest occurs when, by act or omission, a staff member's personal interests interfere with the performance of his or her official duties and responsibilities or with the integrity, independence and impartiality required by the staff member's status as an international civil

46 See ST/AI/2010/1 on reporting, retaining and disposing of honours, decorations, favours, gifts or remuneration from governmental and non-governmental sources. [Note: this footnote appears in the orginal as footnote 'c'].

47 Ibid. [Note: this footnote appears in the orginal as footnote 'd'].

48 Ibid. [Note: this footnote appears in the orginal as footnote 'e'].

servant. When an actual or possible conflict of interest does arise, the conflict shall be disclosed by staff members to their head of office, mitigated by the Organization and resolved in favour of the interests of the Organization.

Commentary

1. The purpose of staff regulation 1.2 (m) is to inform staff that they cannot allow personal interests to interfere with the performance of their duties or their status as international civil servants. The regulation clarifies that actual as well as potential conflicts must be avoided, disclosed and resolved. The key interest is the interest of the Organization. It will be for the Secretary-General and heads of departments to assess whether a particular act or omission raises a potential conflict of interest situation. Staff are obliged to disclose even possible conflicts and to follow instructions on how to resolve the situation, including to avoid and remove the conflict or the circumstances that make it a possible conflict. Failure by a staff member to disclose an actual or possible conflict can seriously disrupt operations of the Organization and pose detriment to the Organization's integrity and reputation as a whole, and may lead to the imposition of disciplinary measures against the staff member.
2. The definition of "conflict of interest" is complemented by the similar but more comprehensive definition set out in paragraph 23 of the 2013 standards of conduct, as follows:

   > "Conflicts of interest may occur when an international civil servant's personal interests interfere with the performance of his/her official duties or call into question the qualities of integrity, independence and impartiality required by the status of an international civil servant. Conflicts of interest include circumstances in which international civil servants, directly or indirectly, may benefit improperly, or allow a third party to benefit improperly, from their association with their organization. Conflicts of interest can arise from an international civil servant's personal or familial dealings with third parties, individuals, beneficiaries, or other institutions. If a conflict of interest or possible conflict of interest does arise, the conflict shall be disclosed, addressed and resolved in the best interest of the organization. Questions entailing a conflict of interest can be very sensitive and need to be treated with care."

3. This provision does not seek to affect the efforts of staff associations established under staff regulation 8.1 to raise funds from staff for their activities.

Regulation 1.2 (n)

All staff members at the D-1 level and above shall be required to file financial disclosure statements on appointment and at intervals therefore as prescribed by the Secretary-General, in respect of themselves, their spouses and their dependent children, and to assist the Secretary-General in verifying the accuracy of the information submitted when so requested. The financial disclosure statements shall include certification that the assets and economic activities of the staff members, their spouses and their dependent children do not pose a conflict of interest with their official duties or the interests of the United Nations. The financial disclosure statements will remain confidential and will only be used, as prescribed by the Secretary-General, in making determinations pursuant to staff regulation 1.2 (m). The Secretary-General may require other staff to file financial disclosure statements as he or she deems necessary in the interest of the Organization.

Commentary

1. Staff regulation 1.2 (n) includes all staff at the D-1 level and above in the obligation to submit financial disclosure statements on appointment and at intervals as prescribed by the Secretary-General (see also para. 24 of the 2013 standards of conduct), in respect of themselves, their spouses and dependent children. This requirement is designed to minimize the risk of officials being perceived as using their position for personal gain and to detect, manage or mitigate

reputational and conflict of interest risks to the Organization. The regulation makes it clear that these financial disclosure statements will remain confidential and will only be used by the Secretary-General in assessing whether an actual or possible conflict of interest as per staff regulation 1.2 (m) exists. Staff are in all cases obliged to also inform their head of office or department in case of any actual or possible conflict of interest under staff regulation 1.2 (m), regardless of whether or not they are required to file a financial disclosure statement.

2. Staff regulation 1.2 (n) places the burden of the initial assessment on the staff members themselves: staff members have to certify that no conflict of interest exists. Staff members must fully cooperate with the Secretary-General's efforts to verify any submitted information. Where in doubt, staff members should contact the Ethics Office to seek advice about risks for conflicts of interest and how to manage them. Where there is even a possibility of an actual or potential conflict of interest, staff are obliged to inform their head of office or department; this is independent and separate from the disclosure mechanism under staff regulation 1.2 (n).[49] Further, filing a financial disclosure statement does not substitute for the obligation to inform the head of office or department of any actual or potential conflict of interest.
3. Staff regulation 1.2 (n) also gives to the Secretary-General the authority to prescribe the form and periodic interval of such disclosure statements, to establish procedures to ensure that the statements remain confidential, and to require other staff to file financial disclosure statements.
4. The Secretariat's mechanism for financial disclosure statements under staff regulation 1.2 (n) is detailed in Secretary-General's bulletin ST/SGB/2006/6, entitled "Financial disclosure and declaration of interest statements".[50]

Outside employment and activities
Regulation 1.2 (o)

Staff members shall not engage in any outside occupation or employment, whether remunerated or not, without the approval of the Secretary-General.

Commentary

1. Staff regulation 1.2 (o) reflects the Organization's long-standing policy on outside occupation or employment, whether during or outside the work week (see also paras. 45–49 of the 2013 standards of conduct).
2. The notion of occupation includes, but is not limited to, the practice of a profession or calling (whether as an employee or on an independent contract) or any concern in the nature of trade. Employment is generally understood as a legal relationship pursuant to which one person is providing work and skill at the control and direction of another. At the same time, self-employment, ownership of an entity, undertaking management responsibilities for an entity, or serving in any management capacity, e.g., on any non-United Nations entity or freelance work are also covered by the notion of "occupation" and "employment" and require the approval of the Secretary-General. Renting out immovable or movable properties may constitute an occupation, depending on factors such as the number of properties and the income derived from such activity.
3. Being on a leave arrangement from an employer other than the United Nations is also considered "employment" or "occupation" within the meaning of this provision, even if no directions are given. Such a leave arrangement would constitute a conflict of interest and contradict

49 The Secretary-General, by his bulletin ST/SGB/2005/22, entitled "Ethics Office—establishment and terms of reference", entrusted the Ethics Office with the task of administering the financial disclosure programme. [Note: this footnote appears in the orginal as footnote 'f'].

50 Throughout the bulletin, any references to administrative issuances include any amendment or superseding issuance on the subject. [Note: this footnote appears in the orginal as footnote 'g'].

the status of international civil servants; therefore, it must be disclosed and resolved in the interest of the Organization. Leave arrangements from government service while working for the United Nations are addressed in tripartite agreements among the United Nations, the Government and the staff member. Secondment from government service is addressed in staff regulation 4.1 and annex II, paragraph (c), of the Staff Regulations, which provide for the need for supporting documentation on the terms and conditions of such secondment agreed to by the Member State and the staff member. Without such agreement, the staff member may be required to cancel the leave arrangement in the light of his or her status as an international civil servant.

4. The 2013 standards of conduct clarify that staff members on leave, with or without pay, from the United Nations should bear in mind that they remain international civil servants and remain subject to the Organization's regulations and rules. Therefore, staff may engage in an outside occupation or employment or outside activity only with express permission from the Organization, including when on leave (para. 47).
5. No approval is possible for outside occupation or employment in governmental service in a political office, in a diplomatic or other representational post or in any other function not compatible with the staff member's continued status as an international civil servant. This cannot be authorized in the context of special leave arrangements under staff rule 5.3 (b). In exceptional circumstances, however, purely technical functions could be approved at the request of a Government.

Regulation 1.2 (p)

The Secretary-General may authorize staff members to engage in an outside occupation or employment, whether remunerated or not, if:

(i) The outside occupation or employment does not conflict with the staff member's official functions or the status of an international civil servant;

(ii) The outside occupation or employment is not against the interest of the United Nations; and

(iii) The outside occupation or employment is permitted by local law at the duty station or where the occupation or employment occurs.

Commentary

1. Staff regulation 1.2 (p) sets out in specific terms the Organization's long-standing requirements that must be met before a staff member may be given permission to engage in an outside occupation or employment. The key factors in determining whether permission should be granted relate to the compatibility of that occupation or employment with the status of and the functions being discharged by the staff member and with the interests of the United Nations (see also paras. 45–49 of the 2013 standards of conduct). In addition, the occupation or employment must be permitted by local law. If the Secretary-General decides under his discretionary authority that permission for such occupation or employment should be denied, a reason will be given.
2. The first requirement is that there be no conflict with the staff member's official functions or with the staff member's status as an international civil servant. For example, it would not be appropriate for a member of the Office of Legal Affairs to be working part-time in an outside law firm. Another example would be outside employment with an organization, including a non-governmental one, that might wish to enter into contractual or other relations with the United Nations. A conflict between official functions and outside employment can also exist simply in the need for the staff member to dedicate time to the outside employment, as staff members are expected—and remunerated—to devote their entire work time to the interest and work of the United Nations and to be available when exigencies of service so require.

3. The second requirement is that such occupation or employment not be against the interest of the United Nations, primarily, that the occupation or employment does not reflect adversely upon the United Nations. For example, permission would not be granted for a staff member to work with an organization the goals of which are incompatible with those of the United Nations or to work in a capacity that could call into question the impartiality and independence of the staff member. This is often the case where staff are asked by Governments or public officials to work for them or organizations or companies related to them while remaining staff members of the United Nations. Other examples include working for entities the objectives or work methods or practices of which contradict or are not compatible with the goals, objectives or values of the Organization. In addition, non-governmental organizations often follow political interests or seek contractual links to the Organization that may have to be reviewed when assessing a request by a staff member. The key element is safeguarding the impartiality of the international civil servant (see paras. 3–14 of the 2013 standards of conduct).
4. The third requirement is that the occupation or employment be permitted under the law of the duty station concerned. For example, in the United States of America, staff holding G-4 visas are not permitted under local law to accept outside employment or to earn money from an occupation, so no permission would be granted.
5. Outside activities that relate to the United Nations are regulated through staff rule 1.2 (t). Outside non-remunerated activities that have nothing to do with a staff member's official functions would remain at the discretion of the staff member (for example, the secretary of a stamp club) and normally do not require the approval of the Secretary-General, unless they have an impact on the staff member's performance of official duties (see para. 45 of the 2013 standards of conduct).

Use of property and assets

Regulation 1.2 (q)

Staff members shall use the property and assets of the Organization only for official purposes and shall exercise reasonable care when utilizing such property and assets.

Commentary

1. Staff regulation 1.2 (q) makes explicit the duty to use reasonable care when utilizing the property and assets of the Organization; this duty is behind several provisions in the Financial Rules and the Staff Rules. It includes all property and assets, including information and communications technology (ICT) that is provided for official purposes only. As per ST/SGB/2004/15 on use of information and communication technology resources and data, this also encompasses the ICT resources and data itself.
2. Management accountability for the way in which staff resources are utilized is discussed in the commentary on staff rule 1.3 (a).

Regulation 1.2 (r)

Staff members must respond fully to requests for information from staff members and other officials of the Organization authorized to investigate the possible misuse of funds, waste or abuse.

Commentary

1. Staff regulation 1.2 (r) builds on the obligation to supply information set out in current staff rule 1.5. This provision seeks to ensure that staff members clearly understand that they must cooperate with official investigations by the Organization and must supply information on their official actions to, for example, the internal or external auditors or internal investigators or ad hoc inquiry panels. Such requests are not in the nature of criminal inquiries where an individual may refuse to answer on the basis of self-incrimination. The issue in the employment relationship between a staff member and the Organization is whether the highest

standards of competence, efficiency and integrity required of United Nations staff members have been met.

2. The Secretary-General has the authority to request staff to supply information, and the staff have a duty to do so. This is without prejudice to the rights of staff under article X of the Staff Regulations and chapter X of the Staff Rules.

Staff rule 1.2

Basic rights and obligations of staff

General

Rule 1.2 (a)

Staff members shall follow the directions and instructions properly issued by the Secretary-General and by their supervisors.

Commentary

1. Staff rule 1.2 (a) deals with the obligation of staff to follow directions properly given by supervising officials (see paras. 16–20 of the 2013 standards of conduct).
2. As per the 2013 standards of conduct, staff members must follow the instructions they receive in connection with their official functions, but also have a right to ask for written instructions if they have doubts as to the consistency of the instruction with the Charter or any other constitutional instrument, decisions of the governing bodies or administrative rules and regulations (para. 19). Although it is clear that staff must follow instructions, it should also be noted that they have a right to challenge instructions that they consider to violate their contract of employment or terms of appointment pursuant to chapter XI of the Staff Rules.
3. Staff do not have to follow instructions that are manifestly inconsistent with their official functions or threaten their safety or have nothing to do with their official activities, since such instructions are not proper. The use of the word "properly" in staff rule 1.2 (a) means that a supervisor who gives improper instructions will be held accountable. Such cases are rare and can usually be handled by seeking a review from the supervisor at the next level or by consulting the Office of Human Resources Management.

Rule 1.2 (b)

Staff members must comply with local laws and honour their private legal obligations, including, but not limited to, the obligation to honour orders of competent courts.

Commentary

1. Staff rule 1.2 (b) is an amplification of staff regulation 1.1 (f), which provides that the privileges and immunities of the Organization afford no excuse to staff for non-performance of their private obligations (see paras. 43 and 44 of the 2013 standards of conduct). The Secretary-General shall determine in any particular case whether such privileges and immunities exist and, if so, whether they shall be waived.
2. Staff rule 1.2 (b) makes clear to staff that they have an obligation to honour such private legal obligations. This provision assists the Organization effectively in ensuring that staff respect the applicable laws and court orders relating to their private obligations, including, but not limited to, obligations under civil (contract/tort, etc.), family or immigration laws. In the event that a plaintiff forwards to the Organization a court order against a staff member, the Administration will seek the views of the staff member before taking any action on the basis of that order. It is the responsibility of staff who have an order against them that they contest to avail themselves of all existing means under the applicable national law to appeal the order and/or obtain relief from the obligation to comply with the order pending its appeal.
3. Failure to honour such private obligations may be treated as a disciplinary matter under article X of the Staff Regulations and chapter X of the Staff Rules. In cases of non-compliance

with family support court orders, deductions from staff members' salaries, wages and other emoluments may be made in accordance with the procedures set out in Secretary-General's bulletin ST/SGB/1999/4. Other indebtedness to third parties may also result in deductions made from a staff member's emoluments under staff rule 3.18 (c).

4. Non-compliance with private legal obligations can also amount to a staff member bringing the Organization into disrepute, and staff must act in accordance with their status at all times.

Rule 1.2 (c)

Staff members have the duty to report any breach of the Organization's regulations and rules to the officials whose responsibility it is to take appropriate action and to cooperate with duly authorized audits and investigations. Staff members shall not be retaliated against for complying with these duties.

Commentary

Staff rule 1.2 (c) emphasizes the obligation of all staff members to report breaches of the Organization's regulations and rules through the designated reporting channels. At the same time, it manifests the principle of non-retaliation against staff for having reported breaches of rules by others. Both the duty to report and the protection from retaliation encourage efforts on the part of all to further the United Nations as an Organization driven by integrity and transparency. It ensures that breaches such as embezzlement are brought to the attention of the Organization by staff who may know about such breaches and who do not have to fear retaliation for their honesty.

Rule 1.2 (d)

Disciplinary procedures set out in article X of the Staff Regulations and chapter X of the Staff Rules may be instituted against a staff member who fails to comply with his or her obligations and the standards of conduct set out in the Charter of the United Nations, the Staff Regulations and Rules, the Financial Regulations and Rules, and administrative issuances.

Commentary

Staff rule 1.2 (d) ensures that staff are held accountable through disciplinary procedures for failure to comply with their obligations and the standards of conduct set out in the Charter of the United Nations, the Staff Regulations and Rules, the Financial Regulations and Rules and all related issuances. Administrative issuances refer to issuances promulgated by the Secretary-General, or by those who hold authority delegated by the Secretary-General, in furtherance of the Staff Regulations and Rules and the Financial Regulations and Rules (see ST/SGB/2009/4).

Specific instances of prohibited conduct

Rule 1.2 (e)

Sexual exploitation and abuse is prohibited. Sexual activity with children (persons under the age of 18) is prohibited regardless of the age of majority or the age of consent locally, except where a staff member is legally married to a person who is under the age of 18 but over the age of majority or consent in his or her country of citizenship. Mistaken belief in the age of a child is not a defence. The exchange of money, employment, goods or services for sex, including sexual favours or other forms of humiliating, degrading or exploitative behaviour, is prohibited. United Nations staff members are obliged to create and maintain an environment that prevents sexual exploitation and sexual abuse.

Commentary

Staff rules 1.2 (e)–(k) address specific instances of prohibited conduct. Staff rule 1.2 (e) was added to address the Organization's serious and growing concern over sexual exploitation and abuse. Sexual exploitation and abuse is listed as a matter of serious misconduct under staff regulation 10.1 (b). Staff rule 1.2 (e) reflects the importance that the Organization attaches to preventing and addressing cases of exploitation and abuse, in line with the Secretary-General's zero-tolerance policy.

Rule 1.2 (f)

Any form of discrimination or harassment, including sexual or gender harassment, as well as abuse in any form at the workplace or in connection with work, is prohibited.

Commentary

1. Staff rule 1.2 (f) reproduces the core of Secretary-General's bulletin ST/SGB/2008/5, which sets out United Nations policy on equal treatment of men and women in the Secretariat, and which also prohibits all forms of discrimination, harassment, including sexual harassment, and abuse of authority (see also paras. 15, 21 and 22 of the 2013 standards of conduct). The clarification "in any form" emphasizes that acts of abuse and harassment may take many forms and are not limited to physical or verbal abuse.
2. All dealings among staff members should be governed by the principles of dignity and mutual respect. Inappropriate behaviour that does not comport with these standards should be addressed by managers and supervisors, irrespective of whether the behaviour may rise to the level of abuse. This follows from their obligation in positions of leadership to ensure a harmonious workplace based on mutual respect (see paras. 16 and 21 of the 2013 standards of conduct).

Rule 1.2 (g)

Staff members shall not disrupt or otherwise interfere with any meeting or other official activity of the Organization, including activity in connection with the administration of justice system, nor shall staff members threaten, intimidate or otherwise engage in any conduct intended, directly or indirectly, to interfere with the ability of other staff members to discharge their official functions. Staff members shall not threaten, retaliate or attempt to retaliate against such individuals or against staff members exercising their rights and duties under the present Rules.

Commentary

1. Staff rule 1.2 (g) prohibits actions that threaten, intimidate or interfere with official functions and activities, as well as any act that would constitute retaliation or attempted retaliation.
2. The rule is not intended to prevent permitted activities in the exercise of rights such as the right of staff to peaceful assembly, the right of representatives of staff bodies to address the Fifth Committee or other organs that have authorized such procedures, or the right of staff to meet in authorized meeting rooms. What is prohibited are actions by staff members that prevent Member States, departments, offices, staff and other authorized persons from holding a meeting or carrying out an official activity. Ultimately, the applicability of the rule will be determined on a case-by-case basis, but the test is reasonably clear in that conduct which prevents others from performing official functions is not permitted.
3. It is noted that at times staff representatives have for certain periods suspended participation in joint bodies. Withdrawal by staff representatives from joint bodies does not constitute interference with official functions, as in such cases the Administration may proceed without the consultation normally needed pursuant to article VIII of the Staff Regulations and chapter VIII of the Staff Rules.
4. The last sentence of staff rule 1.2 (g) emphasizes the importance of the Organization's policy prohibiting acts or attempts of retaliation (see also staff rule 1.2 (c)).

Rule 1.2 (h)

Staff members shall not intentionally misrepresent their functions, official title or the nature of their duties to Member States or to any entities or persons external to the United Nations.

Commentary

1. Staff rule 1.2 (h) prohibits the intentional misrepresentation of official title or duties to outside parties, for example, by placing misleading titles on business cards, usually for private advantage. The use of the word "intentional" makes clear that this prohibition does not extend to accidental or inadvertent actions.
2. While the rule expressly prohibits misrepresentation towards third parties, such intentional misrepresentation towards other staff members is also prohibited.
3. Accordingly, staff members should use the functional or official title associated with the position they hold within the Organization, and refrain from using academic, professional or honorific titles such as prefixes or suffixes in their presentation towards others when acting on official business.

Rule 1.2 (i)

Staff members shall not intentionally alter, destroy, falsify or misplace or render useless any official document, record or file entrusted to them by virtue of their functions, which document, record or file is intended to be kept as part of the records of the Organization.

Commentary

Staff rule 1.2 (i) puts staff on notice that the intentional unauthorized destruction, alteration, falsification or misplacement or other means of rendering useless any records that were intended to form part of the official files of the Organization, or a department or office, is prohibited. This has been a problem from time to time in disciplinary cases or audits when key documents have been found to be missing from official files of the Organization. The use of the word "intentional" makes clear that this is not a careless or accidental act. The word "falsify" has been added to include cases where staff members may forge records or falsify documents, for example, to claim benefits to which they were not entitled. Such prohibited acts may also constitute fraud. Records or files include electronic records or files and e-mail or other server-based records.

Rule 1.2 (j)

Staff members shall not seek to influence Member States, principal or subsidiary organs of the United Nations or expert groups in order to obtain a change from a position or decision taken by the Secretary-General, including decisions relating to the financing of Secretariat programmes or units, or in order to secure support for improving their personal situation or the personal situation of other staff members or for blocking or reversing unfavourable decisions regarding their status or their colleagues' status.

Commentary

1. Staff rule 1.2 (j) seeks to make clear that the lobbying of Member States by individual staff members against positions taken by the Secretary-General is not permitted (see also paras. 27–29 and 31 of the 2013 standards of conduct). This includes lobbying Member States to intervene in the administration of justice on behalf of a staff member.
2. The General Assembly has recognized the importance of its informal interaction with staff representatives in human resources management issues. Such informal interactions with Member States by elected officials acting in staff representative functions are not prohibited by staff rule 1.2 (j).

Rule 1.2 (k)

Staff members shall neither offer nor promise any favour, gift, remuneration or any other personal benefit to another staff member or to any third party with a view to causing him or her to perform, fail to perform or delay the performance of any official act. Similarly, staff members shall neither seek nor accept any favour, gift, remuneration or any other personal benefit from another staff member or from any third party in exchange for performing, failing to perform or delaying the performance of any official act.

Commentary

The prohibition in staff rule 1.2 (k) applies to a staff member's relations with other staff members and with third parties. While the general proposition is that the practices described in the rule violate the highest standards of integrity required of staff members (see paras. 17, 50 and 51 of the 2013 standards of conduct), the purpose of this rule is specifically to deal with the perversion and abuse of power, influence-peddling and other improper or even corrupt practices. Offering or accepting any favour, gift, remuneration or other incentive with the intention of obtaining the performance, non-performance or delaying of official duties by the staff member may, and in most cases does, constitute bribery and/or other forms of misconduct.

Honours, gifts or remuneration

Rule 1.2 (l)

No staff member shall accept any honour, decoration, favour, gift or remuneration from any Government. However, if refusal of an unanticipated honour, decoration, favour or gift from a Government would cause embarrassment to the Organization, the staff member may receive it on behalf of the Organization provided that it is reported and entrusted to the Secretary-General through established procedures.

Commentary

Rule 1.2 (l) reiterates the prohibition on accepting any honour, decoration, favour, gift or remuneration from any Government stipulated in staff regulation 1.2 (j) and (k). The only possible exception is a situation in which a staff member is presented with an unanticipated honour, decoration, etc., by a government official and refusal to accept it would cause unnecessary embarrassment to the Organization. In such a situation, the presented gift or award, etc., may be accepted formally on behalf of the Organization, rather than on behalf of the individual staff member. Staff members must report such receipt of gifts or honours, etc., and entrust them to the Secretary-General through the established procedures.[51] See also staff regulation 1.2 (j) above and the commentary on staff rule 1.2 (m) below.

Rule 1.2 (m)

Acceptance by staff members of any honour, decoration, favour, gift or remuneration from non-governmental sources requires the prior approval of the Secretary-General. Approval shall be granted only in exceptional cases and where such acceptance is not incompatible with the interests of the Organization and with the staff member's status as an international civil servant. If circumstances do not allow for prior approval or if refusal of an unanticipated honour, decoration, favour or gift, including a minor gift of essentially nominal value, would cause embarrassment to the Organization, staff members may receive it on behalf of the Organization provided that it is reported and entrusted to the Secretary-General through established procedures. See also staff regulation 1.2 (l) and the commentary thereon.

Commentary

1. The intended purpose of the staff regulations and rules dealing with honours, decorations, favours, gifts or remuneration from governmental and non-governmental sources is to ensure the independence and impartiality of staff members. Latitude is allowed in connection with such honours, decorations, etc., from non-governmental sources only when the prior approval of the Secretary-General is obtained for accepting an honour, decoration, favour,

51 See ST/AI/2010/1 on reporting, retaining and disposing of honours, decorations, favours, gifts or remuneration from governmental and non-governmental sources. [Note: this footnote appears in the orginal as footnote 'h'].

gift or remuneration, as stipulated in staff rule 1.2 (m), which implements staff regulation 1.2 (l). Staff rule 1.2 (m) provides guidance on the conditions under which honours, decorations, favours, gifts or remuneration may be accepted from non-governmental sources (see also paras. 50 and 51 of the 2013 standards of conduct). In essence, advance approval is required and will be granted only in exceptional cases and only where acceptance would not compromise the interests of the Organization or the status of the staff member as an international civil servant. The only exceptions are situations in which obtaining prior approval is not possible, as may be the case with honours, decorations, favours, gifts or remuneration from Governments (see staff regulation 1.2 (j) and (k) above) and refusal of the unanticipated honour, etc., would cause embarrassment to the Organization. Only in such a case may the honour, etc., be accepted by the staff member, but only and expressly on behalf of the Organization. Honours, decorations, favours, gifts or remuneration must in all cases be reported to the Secretary-General and entrusted to him through the established procedures.[52]

2. Acceptance of a gift, etc., outside these parameters may result in an instruction to the staff member to return it, unless in turn this may cause embarrassment to the Organization. Staff members are, therefore, expected to consult with their administering official prior to accepting any gifts, etc., under this rule.
3. Any honour, decoration, favour, gift or remuneration relating to the performance of official functions should be directed to the Organization, not to an individual staff member, and should be so designated.

Rule 1.2 (n)

The Secretary-General may authorize staff members to accept from a non-governmental source or a university or a related institution, academic awards, distinctions and tokens of a commemorative or honorary character, such as scrolls, certificates, trophies or other items of essentially nominal monetary value.

Commentary

Staff rule 1.2 (n) provides the Secretary-General with limited authority to allow staff members to accept certain awards, distinctions and tokens from a non-governmental source or from a university. The rule provides that, for the purpose of the rule, universities or related institutions are not considered governmental sources since, in many countries, they are not so considered and it would be incongruous for a staff member to be authorized to accept an honorary degree or certification from universities in some, but not all, countries. Therefore, the Secretary-General would normally grant authorization to accept an honorary degree or certificate from any university or related institution that is recognized as an academic institution by the Secretary-General. For example, no approval would be granted for honours from so-called "diploma mills" or institutions not recognized by a competent national authority.

Rule 1.2 (o)

Staff members, as part of their official functions, will be expected from time to time to attend governmental or other functions such as meetings, conferences, meals and diplomatic receptions. Such attendance is not considered receipt of a favour, gift or remuneration within the meaning of the Staff Regulations and Rules.

Commentary

Staff rule 1.2 (o) addresses the issue of attendance at various official functions. It is clear that international officials are required from time to time to attend governmental or other luncheons, dinners and diplomatic receptions. Such attendance will not be considered by the Secretary-General

52 Ibid. [Note: this footnote appears in the orginal as footnote 'i'].

to be a favour, gift or remuneration within the meaning of staff regulation 1.2 (j)–(l). However, such attendance or receipt of hospitality favours from non-governmental sources is limited under staff rule 1.2 (p) (see below).

Rule 1.2 (p)

Staff members shall not accept any gift, remuneration or favour from any source having or seeking to have any type of contractual relationship with the Organization.

Commentary

Staff rule 1.2 (p) emphasizes the importance of staff not accepting any gift, remuneration or favour from any source (governmental or non-governmental, including universities) that has sought or seeks a contractual relationship with the Organization. This includes gifts from vendors or implementing partners, such as non-governmental organizations. The acceptance of hospitality favours from sources that have sought or seek such contractual relations is prohibited. In addition, for staff performing relevant functions that would enable them to influence such contractual relations, the acceptance of any favour, including meals or participation in a reception sponsored by a relevant party, could also be seen as creating a possible conflict of interest under staff rule 1.2 (q) and must be avoided.

Conflict of interest

Rule 1.2 (q)

A staff member whose personal interests interfere with the performance of his or her official duties and responsibilities or with the integrity, independence and impartiality required by the staff member's status as an international civil servant shall disclose any such actual or possible interest to the head of office and, except as otherwise authorized by the Secretary-General, formally excuse himself or herself from participating with regard to any involvement in that matter which might give rise to a conflict of interest situation.

Commentary

Staff rule 1.2 (q) contains a definition of "conflict of interest" that is aligned with the Staff Regulations. The objective of the provision is to compel the disclosure and disposition of any actual or possible conflict of interest in a transparent manner. Where a conflict is so identified, the staff member must comply with instructions on how to resolve the matter, as all staff have the obligation to avoid conflicts of interest. This definition is complemented by the definition set out in the 2013 standards of conduct (para. 23). See also the commentary on staff regulation 1.2 (m) above.

Rule 1.2 (r)

Pursuant to staff regulation 1.2 (n), the Secretary-General shall establish procedures for the filing and utilization of financial disclosure statements.

Commentary

On the basis of staff rule 1.2 (r), the Secretary-General has established procedures to implement the filing of financial disclosure statements with due regard to the necessary confidentiality of such forms. The programme is administered by the Ethics Office.[53] See also the commentary on staff regulation 1.2 (n) above.

Outside activities

Rule 1.2 (s)

Staff members shall not engage in any outside occupation or employment, whether remunerated or not, without the approval of the Secretary-General.

---

53 See ST/SGB/2005/22, entitled "Ethics Office—establishment and terms of reference". [Note: this footnote appears in the orginal as footnote 'j'].

Rule 1.2 (t)

Staff members shall not, except in the normal course of official duties or with the prior approval of the Secretary-General, engage in any outside activities that relate to the purpose, activities or interests of the United Nations. Outside activities include but are not limited to:

(i) Issuing statements to the press, radio or other agencies of public information;

(ii) Accepting speaking engagements;

(iii) Taking part in film, theatre, radio or television productions;

(iv) Submitting articles, books or other material for publication, or for any electronic dissemination.

Approval may be granted in accordance with staff regulation 1.2 (p).

Commentary

1. Staff rules 1.2 (s) and (t) distinguish between outside occupation or employment and outside activities that relate to the purpose, activities or interests of the United Nations. In either case, the staff member must request the approval of the Secretary-General. If a request is denied, a reason for that refusal will be given (see paras. 45–49 of the 2013 standards of conduct).
2. Staff rule 1.2 (t) includes in its scope any type of outside activity that relates to the purpose, activities or interests of the Organization, not limited to the list of examples of specific events or engagements provided in the rule. Staff rule 1.2 (t) (iv) further clarifies that the electronic dissemination of material for publication, for example, via e-mail or on public websites, also requires the approval of the Secretary-General. This includes contemporary means of dissemination of information through the Internet and social media. Where approved, public dissemination in any form must bear appropriate disclaimers, such as "The views expressed herein are those of the author(s) and do not necessarily reflect the views of the United Nations," unless the staff member has been requested, as part of the approval, not to disclose his or her affiliation with the Organization. Further, any publication in any form that can be associated with the author as a staff member of the Organization should bear an appropriate disclaimer.
3. Outside activities that are of benefit to the Organization or the achievement of its goals and contribute to the development of the professional skills of staff members are usually not only permitted, but also encouraged, for example, the approved publication of scholarly articles or participation in symposiums. Publicly available statements of United Nations officials, even in their private capacity, may have a significant impact on the image and reputation of the Organization. For publications, approval not only for the activity as such, but also for the manuscript prior to publication, is required if it relates to the purpose, activities or interests of the United Nations.
4. For approved outside activities that relate to the purpose, activities or interests of the Organization, only subsistence allowances similar to those payable by the United Nations may be accepted by the staff member. No other remuneration may be accepted. This serves to support the independence and impartiality expected of staff members when they engage in United Nations-related activities, given their status as international civil servants (see also staff rule 1.2 (w) below).
5. Staff members are reminded that outside activities shall not compromise the confidentiality of the Organization's information. They shall not communicate to any person any information known to them by reason of their official position that has not been made public, except with the permission of the Secretary-General. This obligation does not cease upon separation from the Organization. In this context, staff members may be required to sign an appropriate confidentiality statement prior to engaging in the activity or to ensure that no references to their affiliation with the Organization will be displayed in relevant public forums.
6. Approval is a discretionary decision by the Secretary-General and may take into account information and assessments by the employing office or department, the Ethics Office, the

Office of Human Resources Management and/or the Office of Legal Affairs as well as any other relevant substantive offices or departments.

Rule 1.2 (u)

Membership in a political party is permitted, provided that such membership does not entail action, or an obligation to take action, by the staff member contrary to staff regulation 1.2 (h). The payment of normal financial contributions to a political party shall not be construed as an activity inconsistent with the principles set out in staff regulation 1.2 (h).

Commentary

Staff rule 1.2 (u) clarifies the staff member's rights and obligations vis-à-vis political activities (see also paras. 48 and 49 of the 2013 standards of conduct and the commentary on staff regulation 1.2 (h) above).

Rule 1.2 (v)

The Secretary-General shall establish procedures whereby staff may seek in confidence clarification as to whether proposed outside activities would conflict with their status as international civil servants.

Commentary

Staff rule 1.2 (v) seeks to assist staff in determining whether there are conflict situations by requiring the establishment of procedures to enable the staff to seek confidential guidance on such issues (see also paras. 45 and 48 of the 2013 standards of conduct). Staff members may reach out to the Ethics Office for guidance.[54]

Travel and per diem for outside activities

Rule 1.2 (w)

Staff members who are authorized by the Secretary-General to participate in activities related to the work of the Organization which are organized by a Government, intergovernmental organization, non-governmental organization or other private source may receive from that organizing entity accommodation, travel and subsistence allowance generally in line with those payable by the United Nations. In such cases the daily subsistence allowance that may otherwise be payable by the United Nations shall be reduced as envisaged in staff rule 7.10 (a).

Commentary

Staff rule 1.2 (w) addresses invitations routinely extended by Governments, intergovernmental organizations, non-governmental institutions or other private sources to the Secretary-General and staff members to attend conferences or meetings or undertake other activities dealing with United Nations-related matters. Attendance at such events is normally authorized by the Secretary-General, and the rule reflects that current practice. It also provides an opportunity for the Organization to save on allowances that may be payable by the Organization by having the accommodation or travel and subsistence allowance provided by the Government, intergovernmental organization, non-governmental organization or private source and by reducing the travel subsistence allowance that may otherwise be payable to the staff member. The rule limits the permissible compensation that staff members may accept, when participating in United Nations-related activities, from sources other than the United Nations for travel, accommodation and subsistence to ensure the independence and impartiality expected of staff members, given their status as international civil servants. In this regard, it would be improper to accept from governmental or non-governmental sources higher levels of compensation than are allowed by the United Nations for its staff for travel on official business.

54 See ST/SGB/2005/22, entitled "Ethics Office—establishment and terms of reference". [Note: this footnote appears in the orginal as footnote 'k'].

Staff regulation 1.3
Performance of staff
Regulation 1.3 (a)

Staff members are accountable to the Secretary-General for the proper discharge of their functions. Staff members are required to uphold the highest standards of efficiency, competence and integrity in the discharge of their functions. Their performance will be appraised periodically to ensure that the required standards of performance are met.

Commentary

1. Much of staff regulation 1.3 deals with the standards of performance required of staff members and provides that they will be evaluated and held accountable for meeting the required standards established by the Charter. Since the separately administered funds and programmes have systems for assessing performance that are adapted to meet their special needs, the provisions of staff regulation 1.3 (a) must remain very general. The regulation places on managers the responsibility to make proper appraisals of performance, which reinforces the solid legislative basis for such procedures and practices.
2. Staff regulation 1.3 (a) makes it clear that staff members are required to uphold the highest standards of efficiency, competence and integrity in the discharge of their functions (see Article 101 of the Charter and paras. 3–14 and 52–54 of the 2013 standards of conduct). The regulation emphasizes the concept of accountability for performance as a fundamental condition of service. In this context, the General Assembly adopted a definition of accountability in its resolution 64/259:

   "Accountability is the obligation of the Secretariat and its staff members to be answerable for all decisions made and actions taken by them, and to be responsible for honouring their commitments, without qualification or exception.

   "Accountability includes achieving objectives and high-quality results in a timely and cost-effective manner, in fully implementing and delivering on all mandates to the Secretariat approved by the United Nations intergovernmental bodies and other subsidiary organs established by them in compliance with all resolutions, regulations, rules and ethical standards; truthful, objective, accurate and timely reporting on performance results; responsible stewardship of funds and resources; all aspects of performance, including a clearly defined system of rewards and sanctions; and with due recognition to the important role of the oversight bodies and in full compliance with accepted recommendations."
3. The relationship between integrity and performance is discussed in the commentary on staff rule 1.3 (a) below.
4. An integral part of the performance of managers is to manage properly the human, financial and other resources entrusted to them. It should be emphasized that the higher level of responsibility associated with the managerial functions of managers entails a commensurate increase in their accountability for the proper performance of all their duties in managing the human and financial resources entrusted to them.

Regulation 1.3 (b)

The whole time of staff members shall be at the disposal of the Secretary-General for the performance of official functions. The Secretary-General shall establish a normal working week and shall establish official holidays for each duty station. Exceptions may be made by the Secretary-General as the needs of the service may require, and staff members shall be required to work beyond the normal tour of duty when requested to do so.

Commentary

Staff regulation 1.3 (b) makes it clear that, although staff normally work an ordinary working week, they must work in excess of that working week when so directed. Any requests to work additional hours must be reasonable and must be related to the needs of the service.

Staff rule 1.3

Performance of staff members
Rule 1.3 (a)

Staff members shall be evaluated for their efficiency, competence and integrity through performance appraisal mechanisms that shall assess the staff member's compliance with the standards set out in the Staff Regulations and Staff Rules for purposes of accountability.

Commentary

1. Staff rule 1.3 (a) makes explicit that the efficiency, competence and integrity required of staff by the Charter and staff regulation 1.3 (a) will be evaluated and that they will be held accountable to maintain the required standards.
2. Generally speaking, an appraisal relates primarily to efficiency and competence, but integrity is part of the essential characteristic of an international civil servant and may have an impact on the performance of official duties. For example, abusive conduct by a staff member towards his or her colleagues is not excused even if the staff member is efficient. On the other hand, the staff member's personal life is generally of no concern to a supervisor unless there is an impact on the discharge of his or her functions or on his or her role as an international civil servant. As noted in the 2013 standards of conduct:

   "4. International civil servants should share the vision of their organizations. It is loyalty to this vision that ensures the integrity and international outlook of international civil servants; a shared vision guarantees that they will place the interests of their organization above their own and use its resources in a responsible manner.

   "5. The concept of integrity enshrined in the Charter of the United Nations embraces all aspects of an international civil servant's behaviour, including such qualities as honesty, truthfulness, impartiality and incorruptibility. These qualities are as basic as those of competence and efficiency, also enshrined in the Charter."

3. It is important to note that competence and efficiency of staff include not only the way in which they perform their tasks, but the way in which they interact with others. As noted in the 2013 standards of conduct, the obligations of staff towards their supervisors, and of supervisors towards their staff, are of crucial importance. Those duties and obligations bear repeating in this commentary:

   "16. Managers and supervisors are in positions of leadership and it is their responsibility to ensure a harmonious workplace based on mutual respect; they should be open to all views and opinions and make sure that the merits of staff are properly recognized. They need to provide support to them; this is particularly important when staff are subject to criticism arising from the performance of their duties. Managers are also responsible for guiding and motivating their staff and promoting their development.

   "17. Managers and supervisors serve as role models and they have therefore a special obligation to uphold the highest standards of conduct. It is quite improper for them to solicit favours, gifts or loans from their staff; they must act impartially, without favouritism and intimidation. In matters relating to the appointment or career of others, international civil servants should not try to influence colleagues for personal reasons.

   "18. Managers and supervisors should communicate effectively with their staff and share relevant information with them. International civil servants have a reciprocal responsibility to provide all pertinent facts and information to their supervisors and to abide by and defend any decisions taken, even when those do not accord with their personal views.

   "19. International civil servants must follow the instructions they receive in connection with their official functions and, if they have doubts as to whether an instruction is consistent with the Charter or any other constitutional instrument, decisions of the governing bodies or administrative rules and regulations, they should first consult their supervisors. If the international civil servant and supervisor cannot agree, the international civil servant may ask for written instructions. These may be challenged through the proper institutional mechanisms, but any challenge should not delay carrying out the instruction. International civil servants may also record their views in official files. They should not follow verbal or written instructions that are manifestly inconsistent with their official functions or that threaten their safety or that of others.

"20. International civil servants have the duty to report any breach of the organization's regulations and rules to the official or entity within their organizations whose responsibility it is to take appropriate action, and to cooperate with duly authorized audits and investigations. An international civil servant who reports such a breach in good faith or who cooperates with an audit or investigation has the right to be protected against retaliation for doing so."

4. It should be emphasized that supervisors will be assessed not only on their technical competence, but also on the way in which they utilize the staff placed under their direction.

Rule 1.3 (b)

The Secretary-General shall seek to ensure that appropriate learning and development programmes are available for the benefit of staff.

Commentary

As staff are required to uphold the highest standards of efficiency, competence and integrity, it follows that during their careers the Secretary-General must seek to ensure that staff are provided with appropriate learning and development opportunities to assist them in meeting the challenges of responding effectively to the changing mandates of the Organization.

Rule 1.3 (c)

Performance reports shall be prepared regularly for all staff members, including at the Assistant Secretary-General level and above, in accordance with procedures promulgated by the Secretary-General.

Commentary

Staff rule 1.3 (c) provides that performance appraisal will be pursuant to procedures promulgated by the Secretary-General.

IV. Standards of conduct for the international civil service, 2013

Introduction

1. The United Nations and the specialized agencies embody the highest aspirations of the peoples of the world. Their aim is to save succeeding generations from the scourge of war and to enable every man, woman and child to live in dignity and freedom.
2. The international civil service bears responsibility for translating these ideals into reality. It relies on the great traditions of public administration that have grown up in member States: competence, integrity, impartiality, independence and discretion. But over and above this, international civil servants have a special calling: to serve the ideals of peace, respect for fundamental rights, economic and social progress, and international cooperation. It is therefore incumbent on international civil servants to adhere to the highest standards of conduct; for, ultimately, it is the international civil service that will enable the United Nations system to bring about a just and peaceful world.

Guiding principles

3. The values that are enshrined in the United Nations organizations must also be those that guide international civil servants in all their actions: fundamental human rights, social justice, the dignity and worth of the human person and respect for the equal rights of men and women and of nations great and small.

4. International civil servants should share the vision of their organizations. It is loyalty to this vision that ensures the integrity and international outlook of international civil servants; a shared vision guarantees that they will place the interests of their organization above their own and use its resources in a responsible manner.
5. The concept of integrity enshrined in the Charter of the United Nations embraces all aspects of an international civil servant's behaviour, including such qualities as honesty, truthfulness, impartiality and incorruptibility. These qualities are as basic as those of competence and efficiency, also enshrined in the Charter.
6. Tolerance and understanding are basic human values. They are essential for international civil servants, who must respect all persons equally, without any distinction whatsoever. This respect fosters a climate and a working environment sensitive to the needs of all. To achieve this in a multicultural setting calls for a positive affirmation going well beyond passive acceptance.
7. International loyalty means loyalty to the whole United Nations system and not only to the organization for which one works; international civil servants have an obligation to understand and exemplify this wider loyalty. The need for a cooperative and understanding attitude towards international civil servants of other United Nations organizations is obviously most important where international civil servants of several organizations are serving in the same country or region.
8. If the impartiality of the international civil service is to be maintained, international civil servants must remain independent of any authority outside their organization; their conduct must reflect that independence. In keeping with their oath of office, they should not seek nor should they accept instructions from any Government, person or entity external to the organization. It cannot be too strongly stressed that international civil servants are not, in any sense, representatives of Governments or other entities, nor are they proponents of their policies. This applies equally to those on secondment from Governments and to those whose services have been made available from elsewhere. International civil servants should be constantly aware that through their allegiance to the Charter and the corresponding instruments of each organization, member States and their representatives are committed to respect this independent status.
9. Impartiality implies tolerance and restraint, particularly in dealing with political or religious convictions. While their personal views remain inviolate, international civil servants do not have the freedom of private persons to take sides or to express their convictions publicly on controversial matters, either individually or as members of a group, irrespective of the medium used. This can mean that, in certain situations, personal views should be expressed only with tact and discretion.
10. This does not mean that international civil servants have to give up their personal political views or national perspectives. It does mean, however, that they must at all times maintain a broad international outlook and an understanding of the international community as a whole.
11. The independence of the international civil service does not conflict with, or obscure, the fact that it is the member States that collectively make up—in some cases with other constituents—the organization. Conduct that furthers good relations with individual member States and that contributes to their trust and confidence in the organizations' secretariat strengthens the organizations and promotes their interest.
12. International civil servants who are responsible for projects in particular countries or regions may be called upon to exercise special care in maintaining their independence. At times they might receive instructions from the host country but this should not compromise their independence. If at any time they consider that such instructions threaten their independence, they must consult their supervisors.

13. International civil servants at all levels are accountable and answerable for all actions carried out, as well as decisions taken, and commitments made by them in performing their functions.
14. An international outlook stems from an understanding of and loyalty to the objectives and purposes of the organizations of the United Nations system as set forth in their legal instruments. It implies, inter alia, respect for the right of others to hold different points of view and follow different cultural practices. It requires a willingness to work without bias with persons of all nationalities, religions and cultures; it calls for constant sensitivity as to how words and actions may look to others. It requires avoidance of any expressions that could be interpreted as biased or intolerant. As working methods can be different in different cultures, international civil servants should not be wedded to the attitudes, working methods or work habits of their own country or region.
15. Freedom from discrimination is a basic human right. International civil servants are expected to respect the dignity, worth and equality of all people without any distinction whatsoever. Assumptions based on stereotypes must be assiduously avoided. One of the main tenets of the Charter is the equality of men and women, and organizations should therefore do their utmost to promote gender equality.

Working relations

16. Managers and supervisors are in positions of leadership and it is their responsibility to ensure a harmonious workplace based on mutual respect; they should be open to all views and opinions and make sure that the merits of staff are properly recognized. They need to provide support to them; this is particularly important when staff are subject to criticism arising from the performance of their duties. Managers are also responsible for guiding and motivating their staff and promoting their development.
17. Managers and supervisors serve as role models and they have therefore a special obligation to uphold the highest standards of conduct. It is quite improper for them to solicit favours, gifts or loans from their staff; they must act impartially, without favouritism and intimidation. In matters relating to the appointment or career of others, international civil servants should not try to influence colleagues for personal reasons.
18. Managers and supervisors should communicate effectively with their staff and share relevant information with them. International civil servants have a reciprocal responsibility to provide all pertinent facts and information to their supervisors and to abide by and defend any decisions taken, even when those do not accord with their personal views.
19. International civil servants must follow the instructions they receive in connection with their official functions and, if they have doubts as to whether an instruction is consistent with the Charter or any other constitutional instrument, decisions of the governing bodies or administrative rules and regulations, they should first consult their supervisors. If the international civil servant and supervisor cannot agree, the international civil servant may ask for written instructions. These may be challenged through the proper institutional mechanisms, but any challenge should not delay carrying out the instruction. International civil servants may also record their views in official files. They should not follow verbal or written instructions that are manifestly inconsistent with their official functions or that threaten their safety or that of others.
20. International civil servants have the duty to report any breach of the organization's regulations and rules to the official or entity within their organizations whose responsibility it is to take appropriate action, and to cooperate with duly authorized audits and investigations. An international civil servant who reports such a breach in good faith or who cooperates with an audit or investigation has the right to be protected against retaliation for doing so.

Harassment and abuse of authority

21. Harassment in any shape or form is an affront to human dignity and international civil servants must not engage in any form of harassment. International civil servants have the right to a workplace environment free of harassment or abuse. All organizations must prohibit any kind of harassment. Organizations have a duty to establish rules and provide guidance on what constitutes harassment and abuse of authority and how unacceptable behaviour will be addressed.
22. International civil servants must not abuse their authority or use their power or position in a manner that is offensive, humiliating, embarrassing or intimidating to another person.

Conflict of interest

23. Conflicts of interest may occur when an international civil servant's personal interests interfere with the performance of his/her official duties or call into question the qualities of integrity, independence and impartiality required by the status of an international civil servant. Conflicts of interest include circumstances in which international civil servants, directly or indirectly, may benefit improperly, or allow a third party to benefit improperly, from their association with their organization. Conflicts of interest can arise from an international civil servant's personal or familial dealings with third parties, individuals, beneficiaries, or other institutions. If a conflict of interest or possible conflict of interest does arise, the conflict shall be disclosed, addressed and resolved in the best interest of the organization. Questions entailing a conflict of interest can be very sensitive and need to be treated with care.

Disclosure of information

24. International civil servants should avoid assisting third parties in their dealings with their organization where this might lead to actual or perceived preferential treatment. This is particularly important in procurement matters or when negotiating prospective employment. At times, international civil servants may, owing to their position or functions in accordance with the organization's policies, be required to disclose certain personal assets if this is necessary to enable their organizations to make sure that there is no conflict. The organizations must ensure confidentiality of any information so disclosed, and must use it only for defined purposes or as authorized by the international civil servant concerned. International civil servants should also disclose in advance possible conflicts of interest that may arise in the course of carrying out their duties and seek advice on mitigation and remediation. They should perform their official duties and conduct their personal affairs in a manner that preserves and enhances public confidence in their own integrity and that of their organization.

Use of the resources of United Nations organizations

25. International civil servants are responsible for safeguarding the resources of United Nations organizations which are to be used for the purpose of delivering an organization's mandate and to advance the best interests of the organization. International civil servants shall use the assets, property, information and other resources of their organizations for authorized purposes only and with care. Limited personal use of the resources of an organization, such as electronic and communications resources, may be permitted by the organization in accordance with applicable policies.

Post-employment restrictions

26. After leaving service with organizations of the United Nations system, international civil servants should not take improper advantage of their former official functions and positions, including through unauthorized use or distribution of privileged or confidential information; nor should international civil servants, including those working in procurement services and as requisitioning officers, attempt to unduly influence the decisions of

the organization in the interest or at the request of third parties with a view to seeking an opportunity to be employed by such third parties.

Role of the secretariats (headquarters and field duty stations)

27. The main function of all secretariats is to assist legislative bodies in their work and to carry out their decisions. The executive heads are responsible for directing and controlling the work of the secretariats. Accordingly, when submitting proposals or advocating positions before a legislative body or committee, international civil servants are presenting the position of the executive head, not that of an individual or organizational unit.
28. In providing services to a legislative or representative body, international civil servants should serve only the interests of the organization, not that of an individual or organizational unit. It would not be appropriate for international civil servants to prepare for government or other international civil service representatives any speeches, arguments or proposals on questions under discussion without approval of the executive head. It could, however, be quite appropriate to provide factual information, technical advice or assistance with such tasks as the preparation of draft resolutions.
29. It is entirely improper for international civil servants to lobby or seek support from government representatives or members of legislative organs to obtain advancement either for themselves or for others or to block or reverse unfavourable decisions regarding their status. By adhering to the Charter and the constitutions of the organizations of the United Nations system, Governments have undertaken to safeguard the independence of the international civil service; it is therefore understood that government representatives and members of legislative bodies will neither accede to such requests nor intervene in such matters. The proper method for an international civil servant to address such matters is through administrative channels; each organization is responsible for providing these.

Staff-management relations

30. An enabling environment is essential for constructive staff-management relations and serves the interests of the organizations. Relations between management and staff should be guided by mutual respect. Elected staff representatives have a cardinal role to play in the consideration of conditions of employment and work, as well as in matters of staff welfare. Freedom of association is a fundamental human right and international civil servants have the right to form and join associations, unions or other groupings to promote and defend their interests. Continuing dialogue between staff and management is indispensable. Management should facilitate this dialogue.
31. Elected staff representatives enjoy rights that derive from their status; this may include the opportunity to address legislative organs of their organization. These rights should be exercised in a manner that is consistent with the Charter of the United Nations, the Universal Declaration of Human Rights and the international covenants on human rights, and does not undermine the independence and integrity of the international civil service. In using the broad freedom of expression they enjoy, staff representatives must exercise a sense of responsibility and avoid undue criticism of the organization.
32. Staff representatives must be protected against discriminatory or prejudicial treatment based on their status or activities as staff representatives, both during their term of office and after it has ended. Organizations should avoid unwarranted interference in the administration of their staff unions or associations.

Relations with member States and legislative bodies

33. It is the clear duty of all international civil servants to maintain the best possible relations with Governments and avoid any action that might impair this. They should not interfere in the policies or affairs of Governments. It is unacceptable for them, either individually or

collectively, to criticize or try to discredit a Government. At the same time, it is understood that international civil servants may speak freely in support of their organizations' policies. Any activity, direct or indirect, to undermine or overthrow a Government constitutes serious misconduct.

34. International civil servants are not representatives of their countries, nor do they have authority to act as liaison agents between organizations of the United Nations system and their Governments. The executive head may, however, request an international civil servant to undertake such duties, a unique role for which international loyalty and integrity are essential. For their part, neither Governments nor organizations should place international civil servants in a position where their international and national loyalties may conflict.

Relations with the public

35. For an organization of the United Nations system to function successfully, it must have the support of the public. All international civil servants therefore have a continuing responsibility to promote a better understanding of the objectives and work of their organizations. This requires them to be well informed of the achievements of their own organizations and to familiarize themselves with the work of the United Nations system as a whole.

36. There is a risk that on occasion international civil servants may be subject to criticism from outside their organizations; in keeping with their responsibility as international civil servants, they should respond with tact and restraint. It is the obligation of their organizations to defend them against criticism for actions taken in fulfilment of their duties.

37. It would not be proper for international civil servants to air personal grievances or criticize their organizations in public. International civil servants should endeavour at all times to promote a positive image of the international civil service, in conformity with their oath of loyalty.

Relations with the media

38. Openness and transparency in relations with the media are effective means of communicating the organizations' messages. The organizations should have guidelines and procedures in place for which the following principles should apply: international civil servants should regard themselves as speaking in the name of their organizations and avoid personal references and views; in no circumstances should they use the media to further their own interests, to air their own grievances, to reveal unauthorized information or to attempt to influence their organizations' policy decisions.

Use and protection of information

39. Because disclosure of confidential information may seriously jeopardize the efficiency and credibility of an organization, international civil servants are responsible for exercising discretion in all matters of official business. They must not divulge confidential information without authorization. International civil servants should not use information to personal advantage that has not been made public and is known to them by virtue of their official position. These obligations do not cease upon separation from service. Organizations must maintain guidelines for the use and protection of confidential information, and it is equally necessary for such guidelines to keep pace with developments in communications and other new technology. It is understood that these provisions do not affect established practices governing the exchange of information between the secretariats and member States, which ensure the fullest participation of member States in the life and work of the organizations.

Respect for different customs and culture

40. The world is home to a myriad of different peoples, languages, cultures, customs and traditions. A genuine respect for them all is a fundamental requirement for an international civil servant. Any behaviour that is not acceptable in a particular cultural context must

be avoided. However, if a tradition is directly contrary to any human rights instrument adopted by the United Nations system, the international civil servant must be guided by the latter. International civil servants should avoid an ostentatious lifestyle and any display of an inflated sense of personal importance.

Security and safety

41. While an executive head assigns staff in accordance with the exigencies of the service, it is the responsibility of organizations to ensure that the health, well-being, security and lives of their staff, without any discrimination whatsoever, will not be subject to undue risk. The organizations should take measures to protect the safety of their staff and that of their family members. At the same time, it is incumbent on international civil servants to comply with all instructions designed to protect their safety.

Personal conduct

42. The private life of international civil servants is their own concern and organizations should not intrude upon it. There can be situations, however, in which the behaviour of an international civil servant may reflect on the organization. International civil servants must therefore bear in mind that their conduct and activities outside the workplace, even if unrelated to official duties, can compromise the image and the interests of the organizations. This can also result from the conduct of members of international civil servants' households and it is the responsibility of international civil servants to make sure that their households are fully aware of this.
43. The privileges and immunities that international civil servants enjoy are conferred upon them solely in the interests of the organizations. They do not exempt international civil servants from observing local laws, nor do they provide an excuse for ignoring private legal or financial obligations. It should be remembered that only the executive head is competent to waive the immunity accorded to international civil servants or to determine its scope.
44. Violations of the law can range from serious criminal activities to trivial offences, and organizations may be called upon to exercise judgment depending on the nature and circumstances of individual cases. A conviction by a national court will usually, although not always, be persuasive evidence of the act for which an international civil servant was prosecuted; acts that are generally recognized as offences by national criminal laws will normally also be considered violations of the standards of conduct for the international civil service.

Outside employment and activities

45. The primary obligation of international civil servants is to devote their energies to the work of their organizations. Therefore, international civil servants should not engage, without prior authorization, in any outside activity, whether remunerated or not, that interferes with that obligation or is incompatible with their status or conflicts with the interests of the organization. Any questions about this should be referred to the executive head.
46. Subject to the above, outside activities may, of course, be beneficial both to staff members and to their organizations. Organizations should allow, encourage and facilitate the participation of international civil servants in professional activities that foster contacts with private and public bodies and thus serve to maintain and enhance their professional and technical competencies.
47. International civil servants on leave, whether with or without pay, should bear in mind that they remain international civil servants in the employ of their organization and remain subject to its rules. They may, therefore, accept employment, paid or unpaid, during their leave only with proper authorization.

48. In view of the independence and impartiality that they must maintain, international civil servants, while retaining the right to vote, should not participate in political activities, such as standing for or holding local or national political office. This does not, however, preclude participation in local community or civic activities, provided that such participation is consistent with the oath of service in the United Nations system. It is necessary for international civil servants to exercise discretion in their support for a political party or campaign, and they should not accept or solicit funds, write articles or make public speeches or statements to the press. These cases require the exercise of judgment and, in case of doubt, should be referred to the executive head.

49. The significance of membership in a political party varies from country to country and it is difficult to formulate standards that will apply in all cases. In general, international civil servants may be members of a political party, provided its prevailing views and the obligations imposed on its members are consistent with the oath of service in the United Nations system.

Gifts, honours and remuneration from outside sources

50. To protect the international civil service from any appearance of impropriety, international civil servants must not accept, without authorization from the executive head, any honour, decoration, gift, remuneration, favour or economic benefit of more than nominal value from any source external to their organizations; it is understood that this includes Governments as well as commercial firms and other entities.

51. International civil servants should not accept supplementary payments or other subsidies from a Government or any other source prior to, during or after their assignment with an organization of the United Nations system if the payment is related to that assignment. Balancing this requirement, it is understood that Governments or other entities, recognizing that they are at variance with the spirit of the Charter and the constitutions of the organizations of the United Nations system, should not make or offer such payments.

Conclusion

52. The attainment of the standards of conduct for the international civil service requires the highest commitment of all parties. International civil servants must be committed to the values, principles and standards set forth herein. They are expected to uphold them in a positive and active manner. They should feel responsible for contributing to the broad ideals to which they dedicated themselves in joining the United Nations system. Organizations have the obligation to implement these standards through their policy framework, including rules, regulations and other administrative instruments. For their part, member States are expected, through their allegiance to the Charter and other constituent instruments, to preserve the independence and impartiality of the international civil service.

53. For these standards to be effectively applied, it is essential that they be widely disseminated and that measures be taken and mechanisms put in place to ensure that their scope and importance are understood throughout the international civil service, the member States and the organizations of the United Nations system.

54. Respect for these standards assures that the international civil service will continue to be an effective instrument in fulfilling its responsibilities and in meeting the aspirations of the peoples of the world.

26

Secretary General's Bulletin: Regulations Governing the Status, Basic Rights and Duties of Officials other than Secretariat Officials, and Experts on Mission

Prefatory Note

The General Assembly, in resolution 56/280 of 27 March 2002, adopted the draft regulations governing the status, basic rights, and duties of officials other than Secretariat officials and experts on mission (officials and experts). On 18 June 2002, the Secretary-General's Bulletin entitled 'Regulations Governing the Status, Basic Rights and Duties of Officials other than Secretariat Officials, and Experts on Mission' (Regulations) was promulgated.[1] The purpose of the Regulations is to assist officials and experts in understanding their status, basic rights, and duties.

The genesis of the Regulations can be traced to the history of the Staff Regulations and Rules of the United Nations[2] and the promulgation of the Secretary-General's Bulletin on the 'Status, Basic Rights and Duties of United Nations Staff Members'.[3]

The term 'officials other than Secretariat officials' is used by the General Assembly to refer to persons performing full time services for the UN who are not staff.[4] Such persons are entitled to the privileges and immunities accorded to officials in Articles V and VII of the Convention on the Privileges and Immunities of the United Nations (General Convention)[5] and would be regarded as officials under the model Status-of-Forces Agreement (model SOFA) between the UN and host countries.[6]

The term 'experts on mission' has no precise definition. The practice of the UN has been to classify any person who is entrusted to perform a specific and important task for the UN as an 'expert on mission' as long as they are neither a staff member (i.e. an official), nor a representative of a Member State.[7] Experts on mission for the UN are entitled to the privileges and immunities found in Article VI of the General Convention. Whilst the text of Article VI, Section 22 of the General Convention does not specifically define an 'expert on mission', it is a term which in practice is considered to include military observers, civilian police, and consultants. That interpretation is reinforced by the model SOFA which provides that military observers and civilian police on UN peace operations are 'experts on mission' for the UN.[8]

The Regulations form part of the contract of employment of experts on mission and officials other than Secretariat officials.[9] The contents of the Regulations reproduced here include the

---

1 'Secretary-General's Bulletin: Regulations Governing the Status, Basic Rights and Duties of Officials other than Secretariat Officials, and Experts on Mission', UN Doc ST/SGB/2002/9, 18 June 2002 (hereafter Regulations).

2 See ch 25 above.

3 'Secretary-General's Bulletin: Status, Basic Rights and Duties of United Nations Staff Members', UN Doc ST/SGB/2002/13, 1 November 2002.

4 Regulations (n 1), Introduction, [2].

5 Convention on the Privileges and Immunities of the United Nations (opened for signature 13 February 1946, entered into force 17 September 1946) 1 UNTS 15. See ch 21 above.

6 'Report of the Secretary-General on the Model Status-of-Forces Agreement for Peace-keeping Operations', UN Doc A/45/594, 9 October 1990, [25] (hereafter model SOFA).

7 See the UN Juridical Yearbook 1998, 481–2 on the 'Question of whether contractors' personnel could be considered as "experts on mission"—Article VI, Section 22, of the 1946 Convention on the Privileges and Immunities of the United Nations', 23 March 1998.

8 Model SOFA (n 6), Annex, [26]. See ch 2 above.

9 Regulations (n 1), Introduction, [5].

commentary accompanying the Regulations. It should be noted, however, that the commentary 'is not part of the Regulations adopted by the Assembly, and so is not a legal norm; nor does it have the legal force of a rule'.[10]

In 1994, the Secretary-General announced that a UN 'Code of Conduct' for staff would be developed as part of a transparent and effective system of accountability.[11] In 1997, the Secretary-General released a report on the proposed Code of Conduct.[12] The report briefly refers to the status of officials other than Secretariat officials, experts on mission, and the Secretary-General themselves. It states that, since officials other than Secretariat officials also perform duties for the UN, the General Assembly might consider that they should be subject to a similar code of conduct. This Code could then also apply to experts on mission and the Secretary-General.[13]

In resolution 52/252, which adopted the provisions governing the status and basic rights and duties of staff members, the General Assembly also requested the Secretary-General to:

> expedite the submission to the General Assembly, by its fifty-fourth session, of appropriate regulations and rules governing the status, basic rights and duties of the Secretary-General, officials other than Secretariat officials and experts on mission.[14]

This led to two reports by the Secretary-General, one on proposed regulations governing the status, basic rights, and duties of officials other than Secretariat officials and experts on mission,[15] and another on regulations governing the status, basic rights, and duties of the Secretary-General.[16] The report concerning the Secretary-General's status, basic rights, and duties concluded that the provisions of the UN Charter[17] relating to the Secretary-General appropriately address the Secretary-General's status, basic rights, and duties, and there was no need for additional regulations and rules in this area.

The report on the proposed regulations governing the status, basic rights, and duties of officials other than Secretariat officials and experts on mission included the text of draft regulations in Annex I and the same text with an explanatory commentary in Annex II. The text of the draft regulations was modelled on the revised Article I of the Staff Regulations and the Staff Rules as promulgated in the Secretary-General's Bulletin on the 'Status, Basic Rights and Duties of United Nations Staff Members'.[18] The draft regulations were adjusted in two further reports of the Secretary-General[19] before a final version was submitted to the General Assembly. The General Assembly adopted the Regulations, with a few minor modifications, in resolution 56/280.[20]

The Regulations are directly relevant to UN peace operations in at least three ways. First, they require that officials and experts adhere to certain standards of conduct concerning the discharge of their duties and their relationships with sources external to the Organization. They also reinforce that the privileges and immunities that are afforded to officials and experts are in the interests of the UN, and establish a process for dealing with situations where such privileges and immunities might be threatened. Finally, the Regulations outline the accountability standards of officials and experts.

---

10 Ibid, Introduction, [6].

11 'Report of the Secretary-General: Establishment of a Transparent and Effective System of Accountability and Responsibility', UN Doc A/C5/49/1, 5 August 1994, [28]–[31].

12 'Report of the Secretary-General: Proposed United Nations Code of Conduct', UN Doc A/52/488, 17 October 1997.

13 Ibid, [2].

14 GA Res 52/252 of 8 September 1998, Operative Part [9].

15 'Report of the Secretary-General: Proposed Regulations Governing the Status, Basic Rights and Duties of Officials other than Secretariat Officials and Experts on Mission', UN Doc A/54/695, 29 December 1999.

16 'Report of the Secretary-General: Regulations governing the Status, Basic Rights and Duties of the Secretary-General', UN Doc A/54/710, 24 February 2000.

17 See ch 1 above.

18 'Secretary-General's Bulletin: Status, Basic Rights and Duties of United Nations Staff Members', UN Doc ST/SGB/2002/13, 1 November 2002.

19 'Report of the Secretary-General: Proposed Regulations governing the Status, Basic Rights and Duties of Officials other than Secretariat Officials and Experts on Mission and Regulations governing the Status, Basic Rights and Duties of the Secretary-General', UN Doc A/55/928, 5 May 2001; 'Report of the Secretary-General: Proposed Regulations governing the Status, Basic Rights and Duties of Officials other than Secretariat Officials and Experts on Mission and Regulations governing the Status, Basic Rights and Duties of the Secretary-General', UN Doc A/56/437, 4 October 2001.

20 GA Res 56/280 of 27 March 2002.

The standards of conduct expected of officials and experts are founded on the UN Charter. Pursuant to Article 101(3) of the Charter, officials and experts are to have the 'highest standards of efficiency, competence and integrity'.[21] In this context, integrity includes 'probity, impartiality, fairness, honesty and truthfulness in all matters affecting their work and status'.[22] Officials and experts are also required to be loyal to the 'aims, principles and purposes' of the UN,[23] which includes promoting and respecting human rights and fundamental freedoms. They are prohibited from '[a]ny form of discrimination or harassment, including sexual or gender harassment, as well as physical or verbal abuse, at the workplace or in connection with work'.[24]

The Regulations also state that the responsibilities of officials and experts are international and not national.[25] This emphasis on the international nature of their responsibilities is further reinforced by the requirement that officials and experts 'shall neither seek nor accept instructions from any Government or from any other source external to the Organization'.[26]

Both the requirement to adhere to the standards expected by the UN and the independent nature of being employed as an official or expert are reinforced by the Regulations requiring officials and experts to make a written declaration in which they promise to exercise the functions entrusted to them by the UN and to ensure that they regulate their conduct in the interests of the UN.[27]

The privileges and immunities of officials and experts are dealt with in Regulation 1(e). That Regulation reinforces the principle that the privileges and immunities conferred on officials and experts are in the interests of the Organization, as is articulated in Article 105 of the Charter and the General Convention. The Regulation also states that these 'privileges and immunities furnish no excuse to those who are covered by them to fail to observe the laws and police regulations of the State in which they are located; nor do they furnish an excuse for non-performance of their private obligations'.[28] Where the application of the privileges and immunities of officials or experts does arise the matter is to be immediately reported to the Secretary-General, 'who alone may decide whether such privileges and immunities exist and whether they shall be waived, in accordance with the relevant instruments'.[29] Officials and experts on mission must also 'comply with local laws and honour their private legal obligations'.[30]

Regulation 3 deals with accountability and provides that officials and experts 'are accountable to the United Nations for the proper discharge of their functions'. The administrative and disciplinary measures that can be taken against civilian police and military observers on UN peace operations is covered in the chapter on the Directives for Disciplinary Matters involving Civilian Police Officers and Military Observers, which are also reinforced by the policy on the accountability of UN field personnel.

In terms of criminal offences, the general position is that officials and experts are subject to the jurisdiction of the host country, subject to the application of relevant privileges and immunities found in the Convention. On a peace operation, however, the model SOFA provides that if the local authorities wish to bring criminal charges against a member of the peace operation who is a civilian, such as officials and experts, then they need the permission of the Special Representative of the Secretary-General (SRSG).[31] If the SRSG decides not to give permission for criminal proceedings to be commenced in the host country there may be a lacuna in terms of who is responsible for prosecuting officials or experts, such as civilian police and military observers, since the UN can only institute administrative or disciplinary measures such as repatriation.

In 2013, the General Assembly adopted a resolution on the criminal accountability of UN officials and experts on mission which emphasised that crimes committed by officials and experts on

21 Regulations (n 1), Regulation 2(a).
22 Ibid.
23 Ibid, Regulation 2(c).
24 Ibid, Regulation 2(k). For a more comprehensive overview, see the discussion in the Introduction to this Part.
25 Ibid, Regulation 1(a).
26 Ibid, Regulation 2(b).
27 Ibid, Regulation 1(b).
28 Ibid, Regulation 1(e).
29 Ibid.
30 Ibid, Regulation 2(j).
31 Model SOFA (n 6), [47](a).

mission are unacceptable[32] and strongly urged 'States to take all appropriate measures to ensure that … [such crimes] do not go unpunished and that the perpetrators of such crimes are brought to justice, without prejudice to the privileges and immunities of such persons …'[33]

In terms of UN peace operations, the Regulations are most relevant in regard to experts on mission since peace operations include a significant civilian police component and military observers. Civilian police and military observers are employed to serve on UN peace operations as experts on mission on the basis of individual undertakings. Consequently, they are required to comply with all applicable UN rules, regulations, directives, and other issuances. These include the Directives for Disciplinary Matters involving Civilian Police Officers and Military Observers, and the two aide-mémoires (blue cards) issued to all peacekeepers entitled 'Ten Rules: Code of Personal Conduct for Blue Helmets' and 'We are United Nations Peacekeepers'.[34]

They are also bound by the Secretary-General's Bulletin on 'Special Measures for Protection from Sexual Exploitation and Sexual Abuse'[35] due to a revision of the individual undertaking they sign. This was confirmed in the 2006 report of the Special Committee on Peacekeeping Operations (C34), where the C34 noted:

> that the undertaking for experts on mission, such as United Nations police and military observers, has also been revised to include the standards of bulletin ST/SGB/2003/13.[36]

The Secretariat's policy concerning accountability for the conduct of UN personnel serving in field missions[37] reinforces the disciplinary and accountability processes described above.

Reference[38]

Title	Secretary-General's Bulletin: Regulations Governing the Status, Basic Rights and Duties of Officials other than Secretariat Officials, and Experts on Mission
Author	Secretary-General of the United Nations
Date of Bulletin	18 June 2002
Entered into force	1 July 2002
Source	UN Doc ST/SGB/2002/9
Full Text	<https://hr.un.org/content/ regulations-governing-status-basic-rights-and-duties-officials-other-secretariat-officials>[39]

32 GA Res 68/105 of 16 December 2013, Preamble.

33 Ibid, Operative Part [2].

34 See ch 27 below.

35 See ch 30 below.

36 'Report of the Special Committee on Peacekeeping Operations and its Working Group, 2006 Substantive Session', UN Doc A/60/19, 22 March 2006, [65].

37 Department of Political Affairs, Department of Peacekeeping Operatoins, and Department of Field Support, 'Accountability for Conduct and Discipline in Field Missions', 1 August 2015. See ch 31 below.

38 The United Nations Human Resource Handbook contains Staff Regulations, Staff Rules, Secretary-General's Bulletins and Administrative Instructions plus any amendments and updates <https://hr.un.org/handbook> accessed 24 December 2018.

39 Accessed 24 December 2018.

Secretary-General's Bulletin: Regulations Governing the Status, Basic Rights and Duties of Officials other than Secretariat Officials, and Experts on Mission, with commentary[40]

(Extracts)

...

III. Regulations Governing the Status, Basic Rights and Duties of Officials other than Secretariat Officials, and Experts on Mission with Commentary

Regulation 1

Status

Regulation 1 (a)

The responsibilities of officials other than Secretariat officials (hereinafter referred to as "officials") and of experts on mission are not national but exclusively international.

Commentary

1. The United Nations has persons who perform services for it on a substantially full-time basis but who are not staff members. These persons have consistently been referred to by the General Assembly as "officials other than Secretariat officials". In addition, pursuant to article V, section 17, of the General Convention, the Secretary-General has specified and submitted to the Assembly proposals that a number of persons who occupy certain positions within the Organization be accorded the privileges and immunities under articles V and VII of the General Convention, even though they are not staff members. These persons have also been referred to as "officials other than Secretariat officials".
2. The United Nations also has experts who perform assignments for the Organization. Article VI of the General Convention provides that experts (other than officials coming within the scope of article V) shall be accorded privileges and immunities necessary to enable them to carry out their missions for the United Nations and specifies a number of those privileges and immunities. These experts have been referred to as "experts on mission".
3. The Regulations and the commentary, as applied to the Chairman and the Vice-Chairman of the International Civil Service Commission, the Inspectors of the Joint Inspection Unit and other officials and experts who perform functions in respect of the common system, in accordance with the statute of the International Civil Service Commission or that of the Joint Inspection Unit, respectively, or other mandates approved by the General Assembly or other

40 From Regulations Governing the Status, Basic Rights and Duties of Officials other than Secretariat Officials, and Experts on Mission, with commentary, by the Secretary-General © 2002 United Nations. Reproduced with the permission of the United Nations.

relevant main bodies and organs of the United Nations, should be construed in the light of those functions and mandates. References to the United Nations or the United Nations Organization in the context of these Regulations and the commentary should be applied, bearing in mind that the functions of those officials and experts are related to the common system.

4. Regulation 1 (a) is similar to the second sentence of staff regulation 1.1 (a).[41]

Regulation 1 (b)

Officials and experts on mission shall make the following written declaration witnessed by the Secretary-General or an authorized representative:

> "I solemnly declare and promise to exercise in all loyalty, discretion and conscience the functions entrusted to me by the United Nations, to discharge these functions and regulate my conduct with the interests of the United Nations only in view, and not to seek or accept instructions in regard to the performance of my duties from any Government or other source external to the Organization."

Commentary

Regulation 1 (b), which is similar to staff regulation 1.1 (b), contains the declaration of office of officials and experts on mission. In view of the system-wide functions of the International Civil Service Commission and the Joint Inspection Unit, the term "United Nations" in the written declaration will be replaced by the words "United Nations and other participating organizations", and the word "Organization" will be replaced by the word "organizations" in the case of the Chairman and Vice-Chairman of the International Civil Service Commission and the Inspectors of the Joint Inspection Unit.

Regulation 1 (c)

The Secretary-General shall seek to ensure that the rights and duties of officials and of experts on mission, as set out in the General Convention, are respected. The Secretary-General shall also seek to ensure, having regard to the circumstances, that all necessary safety and security arrangements are made for officials and experts on mission carrying out the responsibilities entrusted to them.

Commentary

1. The first sentence of regulation 1 (c), which is similar to staff regulation 1.1 (c), codifies an implicit duty that falls upon the Secretary-General, namely, to seek to ensure that the rights and duties of officials and experts on mission as set out in the General Convention are respected (as such rights are granted by Governments, the Secretary-General can only "seek to ensure" that they are respected). The protection accorded to officials and experts on mission under this provision relates to their official acts and thus does not lapse upon cessation of their service for the Organization, or, if they are part-time, on days when they are not in service.
2. The second sentence of regulation 1 (c), which reproduces the essence of the second sentence of staff regulation 1.2 (c), sets forth the responsibility of the Secretary-General to seek to ensure the safety of officials and experts on mission.

Regulation 1 (d)

Experts on mission will receive a copy of the present Regulations Governing the Status, Basic Rights and Duties of Officials other than Secretariat Officials, and Experts on Mission (hereinafter referred to as "the Regulations") when they receive documentation from the United

41 Hereinafter, references to staff regulations and rules denote the provisions contained in article I of the Staff Regulations and chapter I of the 100 series of the Staff Rules that came into effect on 1 January 1999, pursuant to General Assembly resolution 52/252. [Note: this footnote appears in the original document as footnote '2'].

Nations relating to their mission and will be required to acknowledge receipt of the Regulations. Officials will receive a copy of the Regulations at an appropriate opportunity.

Commentary

1. Experts on mission retained by the Secretariat sign a consultant contract or receive a letter or other documentation indicating the scope of their mission for the Organization. The consultant contract or other documentation will incorporate the Regulations by reference, and experts will be required to acknowledge that they will abide by the Regulations.
2. At times, legislative bodies entrust tasks to individuals to perform assignments for those bodies (for example, members and special rapporteurs of the International Law Commission and other bodies). Those individuals have the status of experts on mission. Although their appointments may have been concluded without the signature of any document of appointment, their attention will be drawn to the Regulations when they receive documentation from the Secretariat relating to their functions and/or their assignment. That documentation will include a copy of the Regulations explaining that they were adopted by the General Assembly and thus constitute part of the conditions of those individuals' assignment for the United Nations.
3. Officials will receive a copy of the Regulations at an appropriate time, such as when they make the declaration of office (see regulation 1 (b)).

Regulation 1 (e)

The privileges and immunities enjoyed by the United Nations by virtue of Article 105 of its Charter are conferred in the interests of the Organization. These privileges and immunities furnish no excuse to those who are covered by them to fail to observe the laws and police regulations of the State in which they are located; nor do they furnish an excuse for non-performance of their private obligations. In any case where an issue arises regarding the application of these privileges and immunities, an official or an expert on mission shall immediately report the matter to the Secretary-General, who alone may decide whether such privileges and immunities exist and whether they shall be waived, in accordance with the relevant instruments. The Secretary-General should inform and may take into account the views of the legislative bodies that appointed the officials or experts on mission.

Commentary

1. Regulation 1 (e), which deals with privileges and immunities, is similar to staff regulation 1.1 (f) (see paras. 32, 49, 54 and 55 of the report on standards of conduct in the international civil service 1954,[42] which was prepared by the International Civil Service Advisory Board (hereinafter referred to as "the ICSAB report")).
2. Regulation 2 (j) specifies the obligations on those who are covered by such privileges and immunities to honour their private legal obligations.
3. Pursuant to article V, section 20, and article VI, section 23, of the General Convention, it is only the Secretary-General who has the right to waive the privileges and immunities accorded to officials and experts on mission. In deciding whether such privileges and immunities exist and whether they should be waived, the Secretary-General may take into account the views of the legislative body that appointed the officials or experts on mission.

Regulation 1 (f)

These regulations are applicable to the Chairman and Vice-Chairman of the International Civil Service Commission and the Inspectors of the Joint Inspection Unit, without prejudice to and in accordance with the statutes of the International Civil Service Commission and the Joint

42 A/52/488, annex III. [Note: this footnote appears in the original document as footnote '3'].

Inspection Unit, which stipulate that these officials perform their functions in respect of the United Nations and other organizations that accept their statutes.

[There is no commentary to this provision.]

Regulation 2

Conduct

Regulation 2 (a)

Officials and experts on mission shall uphold the highest standards of efficiency, competence and integrity. The concept of integrity includes, but is not limited to, probity, impartiality, fairness, honesty and truthfulness in all matters affecting their work and status.

Commentary

1. Regulation 2 (a), which describes basic values expected of officials and experts on mission, is similar to staff regulation 1.2 (b).
2. The first sentence of regulation 2 (a) is derived from Article 101, paragraph 3, of the Charter of the United Nations by virtue of affirmatively placing upon officials and experts on mission the obligation to uphold the highest standards of efficiency, competence and integrity. As pointed out in paragraph 4 of the ICSAB report, the concept of integrity includes "honesty, truthfulness, fidelity, probity and freedom from corrupting influences".

Regulation 2 (b)

In the performance of their duties, officials and experts on mission shall neither seek nor accept instructions from any Government or from any other source external to the Organization.

Commentary

Regulation 2 (b), which is similar to staff regulation 1.2 (d), flows from the first sentence of Article 100, paragraph 1, of the Charter of the United Nations (see ICSAB report, paras. 7, 18 and 31).

Regulation 2 (c)

Officials and experts on mission shall discharge their functions and regulate their conduct with the interests of the Organization only in view. Loyalty to the aims, principles and purposes of the United Nations, as set forth in its Charter, is a fundamental obligation of all individuals covered by the present Regulations.

Commentary

1. Regulation 2 (c) in substance contains the same obligations as are contained in staff regulation 1.2 (e) applicable to staff. The first sentence of regulation 2 (c) sets forth an idea that is contained in staff regulation 1.1 (a) and in staff regulation 1.1 (b), which contains the written declaration of office, that is to say, the idea that staff must regulate their conduct with the interests of the Organization only in view (ibid., para. 4).
2. The second sentence of regulation 2 (c) focuses on the concept of loyalty to the aims, principles and purposes of the Organization as set forth in the Charter of the United Nations (which is alluded to in the declaration contained in regulation 1(b)) (ibid., paras. 5, 6 and 21).

Regulation 2 (d)

While the personal views and convictions of officials and experts on mission, including their political and religious convictions, remain inviolable, they shall ensure that those views and convictions do not adversely affect their official duties or the interests of the United Nations. Officials and experts on mission shall conduct themselves at all times in a manner befitting their status. They shall not engage in any activity that is incompatible with the proper discharge of their duties with the United Nations. They shall avoid any action and, in particular, any kind of public pronouncement that may adversely reflect on their status, or on the integrity, independence and impartiality that are required by that status.

Commentary

1. Regulation 2 (d) is similar to staff regulation 1.2 (f). The core idea of conduct befitting an international civil servant was considered by the International Civil Service Advisory Board in 1954. The Advisory Board remarked that "high standards of conduct are best attained by a universal understanding among staff members of the relation between their conduct and the success of the international organizations, and by the development of a strong tradition among men and women who are jealous of the reputation of the organizations that they serve and are anxious to safeguard it" (ICSAB report, para. 2; see also para. 4, on the integrity expected of international civil servants; paras. 5, 6 and 21, on loyalty; paras. 7 and 18, on independence; and paras. 8 and 48, on impartiality).
2. In respect of the last sentence of the regulation, it would be for the Organization to characterize an action or pronouncement as adversely reflecting on the status of an official or an expert on mission.

Regulation 2 (e)

Officials and experts on mission shall not use their office or knowledge gained from their official functions for private gain, financial or otherwise, or for the gain of any third party, including family, friends and those they favour. Nor shall they use their office for personal reasons to prejudice the positions of those they do not favour.

Commentary

1. Regulation 2 (e), which is similar to staff regulation 1.2 (g), codifies principles set out in the ICSAB report (see paras. 17, 28 and 42). The use of one's office for personal gain is clearly unacceptable. This includes not only conducting a business from a United Nations office but also such activities as using United Nations facilities for a business, using the United Nations name, logo or address for a business and approving a contract for a family business without disclosure. Regulation 2 (e) also reflects the principle set out in staff regulation 1.2 (g) that a staff member shall not use information that has not been made public for the private advantage of the staff member or of any third party.
2. The regulation, for clarity, makes specific reference to prohibiting an official or expert on mission from so favouring a third party, including family or friends, as to enable that third party to profit from the position of the official or expert on mission or from the exercise of his or her functions. The term "friends" is broad and seeks to encompass not only friends as normally understood, but also relationships that are not recognized by the United Nations as creating a dependency.
3. The regulation also prohibits the use of office or knowledge gained from that office for personal reasons to prejudice or harm third parties.

Regulation 2 (f)

Officials and experts on mission shall exercise the utmost discretion in regard to all matters of official business. Officials and experts on mission shall not communicate to any Government, entity, person or any other source any information known to them by reason of their official position that they know or ought to have known has not been made public, except as appropriate in the normal course of their duties or by authorization of the Secretary-General. If they are not appointed by the Secretary-General, such authorization shall be conferred by the body that appointed them. These obligations do not cease upon the cessation of their official functions.

Commentary

1. Regulation 2 (f), which is similar to staff regulation 1.2 (i), reflects the principle that official information may not be used for private purposes, except with authorization. This flows from

the idea that officials and experts on mission are obligated to regulate their conduct with the interests of the Organization only in view (see ICSAB report, para. 4) and also from the requirements of regulation 2 (e). It follows that permission must be obtained for disclosure to third parties of information that has not been made public, unless such disclosure is specifically authorized or is in the normal course of duties of the official or expert on mission. Authorization of the Secretary-General is not required for officials and experts on mission who have not been appointed by the Secretary-General. Those officials and experts on mission would require the authorization of the body that had appointed them if the communication of the information was not a normal part of their duties.

2. The last sentence of the regulation provides that the obligations contained in the provision do not cease upon cessation of official functions. It may be difficult to enforce such a provision, but, at the very least, if a former official or expert on mission ignored the obligations contained in this regulation, the official file of the former official or expert on mission could be noted so as to prevent his or her re-engagement.

Regulation 2 (g)

Officials and experts on mission may not accept any honour, decoration, favour, gift or remuneration from any Government or non-governmental source for activities carried out during the course of their official functions while in the service of the United Nations.

Commentary

To ensure that officials and experts are perceived as impartial, regulation 2 (g) prohibits the acceptance of any honour, decoration, favour, gift or remuneration from any Government or non-governmental source for activities carried out during the course of their official functions while in the service of the United Nations.

Regulation 2 (h)

Officials and experts on mission shall not be actively associated with the management of, or hold a financial interest in, any profit-making, business or other concern, if it were possible for them or the profit-making, business or other concern to benefit from such association or financial interest by reason of their position with the United Nations. Officials or experts on mission who are in such a situation shall either dispose of that financial interest or formally excuse themselves from participating with regard to any involvement in that matter that has given rise to the conflict-of-interest situation.

Commentary

1. The first sentence of regulation 2 (h) is similar to staff regulation 1.2 (m). The purpose of the provision is to put officials and experts on mission on notice that they cannot be actively associated with a profit-making, business or other concern, if either the concern or the official or expert on mission is to profit therefrom by reason of the association with the Organization. It will be for the Secretary-General or the appointing authority to judge whether a particular act has given rise to a conflict-of-interest situation.
2. The second sentence of regulation 2 (h) is similar to the second part of staff rule 101.2 (n), which deals with the consequences of a staff member's having a possible conflict-of-interest situation. In such cases, the official or expert on mission shall dispose of the interests or, if practicable, shall excuse himself or herself from dealing with the matter on behalf of the Organization.
3. Generally, experts on mission are appointed on a part-time basis, and it is therefore likely that they are engaged in other activities, including employment, when they are not performing services for the Organization. While there is no question that experts on mission may be so engaged, they must ensure that those activities are not incompatible with their status or functions as experts on mission.

Regulation 2 (i)

Officials and experts on mission shall file financial disclosure statements if requested to do so by the Secretary-General. The Secretary-General shall prescribe the format and information to be provided in such statements and shall establish procedures for filing them. The financial disclosure statements will remain confidential and will be used, as prescribed by the Secretary-General, only in making determinations pursuant to regulation 2 (h). It will be for the Secretary-General, in due consultation with the appointing authority in the case of officials not appointed by the Secretary-General, to judge whether a particular fact has given rise to a conflict-of-interest situation.

Commentary

Regulation 2 (i) is similar to, but more general than, staff regulation 1.2 (n), which requires all staff at the assistant secretary-general level and above to submit financial disclosure statements upon appointment and at intervals as prescribed by the Secretary-General, in respect of themselves and their dependent children, including any substantial transfers of assets and property to spouses and dependent children from the staff member or from any other source that might constitute a conflict of interest. This requirement is designed to minimize the risk of a perception of officials and experts on mission as using their position for personal gain. The regulation enables the Secretary-General to require officials and experts on mission to file financial disclosure statements, which will remain confidential and will be used only in dealing with conflict-of-interest situations (for example, in assessing whether an official was in such a situation).

Regulation 2 (j)

Officials and experts on mission must comply with local laws and honour their private legal obligations, including, but not limited to, the obligation to honour orders of competent courts.

Commentary

1. Regulation 2 (j), which is similar to staff rule 101.2 (c), is really an amplification of regulation 1 (e), which provides that the privileges and immunities of the Organization afford no excuse for non-performance of private obligations (ibid., paras. 32, 54 and 55).
2. Regulation 2 (j) makes clear that private obligations must be honoured. It is the responsibility of those subject to the present Regulations, if they have a court order against them that they contest, to avail themselves of all means existing under the applicable national law to appeal the order and/or to secure relief from the obligation to comply with the order pending its appeal.

Regulation 2 (k)

Any form of discrimination or harassment, including sexual or gender harassment, as well as physical or verbal abuse, at the workplace or in connection with work, is prohibited.

Commentary

Regulation 2 (k), which is similar to staff rule 101.2 (d), reproduces the core of Secretary-General's bulletin ST/SGB/253 of 29 October 1992, which established United Nations policy on equal treatment of men and women in the Secretariat and also prohibited all forms of discrimination or harassment.

Regulation 2 (l)

Officials and experts on mission shall not intentionally misrepresent their functions, official title or the nature of their duties to Member States or to any entities or persons external to the United Nations.

Commentary

Regulation 2 (l) is similar to staff rule 101.2 (f), which prohibits the intentional misrepresentation of an official title or duties to outside parties (for example, by placing misleading titles on business cards). The use of the word “intentional” makes clear that this does not refer to careless or accidental acts.

Regulation 2 (m)

Officials and experts on mission participating, as part of their official functions, in activities organized by a Government, intergovernmental organization, non-governmental organization or other private source may receive from the Government, intergovernmental organization, nongovernmental organization or private source accommodation and travel and subsistence allowance generally in line with those payable by the United Nations. In such cases, the travel and subsistence allowance that may otherwise be payable by the United Nations shall be reduced in the same manner as in respect of staff members of the Organization.

Commentary

1. Regulation 2 (m), which is similar to staff rule 101.2 (s), deals with the issue of participation at various official functions. Officials and experts on mission who as part of their official functions participate in activities organized by a Government, intergovernmental organization, non-governmental organization or other private source may receive from it accommodation and travel and subsistence allowance generally in line with those payable by the United Nations, and in such cases the allowances that may otherwise be payable by the United Nations shall be reduced in the same amount as in respect of staff members of the Organization. Such provisions are presently found in staff rule 107.15 (a).
2. It should be noted that accommodation and travel and subsistence allowance may be accepted only if their acceptance would be appropriate to the status of officials and experts on mission and to the integrity, independence and impartiality that are required by that status. There may therefore be situations in which it would not be appropriate to accept those allowances from a Government, intergovernmental organization, non-governmental organization or other private source.

Regulation 3

Accountability

Officials and experts on mission are accountable to the United Nations for the proper discharge of their functions.

Commentary

Regulation 3, which is similar to staff regulation 1.3 (a), makes clear that officials and experts on mission are accountable for their actions. The method of accountability may vary. For officials appointed by the General Assembly, that accountability would be a matter for the Assembly. For experts on mission, it would be the Secretary-General or the appointing authority who could terminate an assignment or otherwise admonish the expert.

27

United Nation Standards of Conduct: We are United Nations Peacekeeping Personnel

Prefatory Note

There are two UN standards of conduct that are directly relevant to UN peacekeepers undertaking their functions and tasks: 'We are United Nations Peacekeeping Personnel';[1] and 'Ten Rules: Code of Personal Conduct for Blue Helmets' (hereafter Ten Rules).[2] Both are reprinted below.

The history of the UN standards of conduct can be traced to a 1995 report of the General Assembly's Special Committee on Peacekeeping Operations (C34) in which the C34 called on the Secretary-General to 'complete the elaboration of a code of conduct for United Nations peacekeeping personnel, consistent with applicable international humanitarian law, so as to ensure the highest standards of performance and conduct'.[3] By 1997, the code of conduct for peacekeepers had been completed. In the 1997 C34 report, 'many Member States welcomed the production by the Department of Peacekeeping Operations [DPKO] of a code of conduct for peacekeepers'.[4]

In respect of the standards of conduct, the Secretary-General has stated:

> Troop-contributing countries have over the years universally accepted the general standards of conduct set out in the publications entitled 'Ten Rules: Code of Personal Conduct for Blue Helmets' and 'We Are United Nations Peacekeepers'. Practice has thus made these general standards applicable to contingent members.[5]

The standards are binding on civilian police and military observers because they serve on UN peace operations as experts on mission on the basis of individual undertakings. Consequently, they are bound by all applicable UN rules, regulations, directives, and other issuances including the Ten Rules and 'We are United Nations Peacekeepers'. On the other hand, military members of national contingents have no individual contractual link with the UN and remain administratively attached to their respective national militaries. The obligations of military personnel in a UN peace operation are provided for in the Memorandum of Understanding (MOU)[6] agreed to between the UN and contributing State.

As explained in the Report of the Secretary-General: A Comprehensive Strategy to Eliminate Future Sexual Exploitation and Abuse in United Nations Peacekeeping Operations (Zeid Report):

> The mission-specific guidelines for troop-contributing countries deploying military units, which are also made available to troop-contributing countries, are starting to include the prohibitions against sexual exploitation and abuse established in the 2003 Secretary-General's bulletin. The guidelines are annexed to the mission specific memorandum of understanding signed by the United Nations and each troop-contributing country. The provisions in a memorandum of understanding between the United Nations and the troop-contributing country are binding. The annexed troop-contributing country guidelines,

---

1 See ch 9 (entitled Memorandum of Understanding), Annex H of the most recent edition of the Contingent-Owned Equipment (COE) Manual, UN Doc A/C5/66/8, 27 October 2011 (hereafter We are United Nations Peacekeeping Personnel). <http://www.un.org/en/ga/search/view_doc.asp?symbol=A/C.5/66/8> accessed 28 November 2018.

2 United Nations Department of Peacekeeping Operations, 'Ten Rules: Code of Personal Conduct for Blue Helmets', 1997 (hereafter Ten Rules), Rule [5] <http://www.un.org/en/peacekeeping/documents/un_in.pdf > accessed 28 November 2018.

3 'Report of the Special Committee on Peace-keeping Operations: Comprehensive Review of the Whole Question of Peace-keeping Operations in all their Aspects', UN Doc A/50/230, 22 June 1995, [73].

4 'Report of the Special Committee on Peacekeeping Operations: Comprehensive Review of the Whole Question of Peacekeeping Operations in all their Aspects', UN Doc A/52/209, 28 June 1997, [26].

5 'Report of the Secretary-General: A Comprehensive Strategy to Eliminate Future Sexual Exploitation and Abuse in United Nations Peacekeeping Operations', UN Doc A/59/710, 24 March 2005, [19] (hereafter Zeid Report).

6 See ch 3 above.

however, which contain the detailed rules of the bulletin, are specifically identified as containing general administrative and financial arrangements. In legal terms, 'guidelines' can be contrasted to 'rules'. Guidelines provide a general model that may or may not be followed depending on the circumstances; rules set out norms that must be followed. But codes of conduct, in particular detailed prohibitions against sexual exploitation and abuse, must have the status of binding rules. They cannot be merely guidelines.[7]

Consequently, the first recommendation of the Zeid Report was that:

> The General Assembly should reiterate its approval of the standards set out in the 2003 bulletin and make them applicable to all categories of peacekeeping personnel, without exception ... Furthermore, the Assembly should decide that those standards and the standards contained in Ten Rules and We Are United Nations Peacekeepers be included in the model memorandums of understanding, and the troop-contributing countries should undertake to issue the standards in a form binding on their personnel.[8]

1. We are United Nations Peacekeeping Personnel

The UN standards of conduct, 'We are United Nations Peacekeeping Personnel', are set out in Annex H of the 2011 revised model Memorandum of Understanding (hereafter model MOU) between the UN and contributing States.[9]

Annex H, along with the additional definitions in Annex F for acts such as sexual abuse, sexual exploitation, and serious misconduct, seeks to incorporate the provisions of the 2003 Secretary-General's Bulletin on 'Special Measures for Protection from Sexual Exploitation and Sexual Abuse'[10] (SGB SEA) into the model MOU. This incorporation seeks to ensure that military members of national contingents are bound by the standards of conduct and prohibitions on sexual exploitation and sexual abuse as stated in the SGB SEA. UN staff members are bound by the SGB SEA directly as an administrative issuance of the Secretary-General; experts on mission are bound through changes made to the individual undertaking they sign; and military members of national contingents are now bound through the revisions to the model MOU. This is in direct response to growing concerns about sexual exploitation and abuse by peacekeepers and the consequences for the reputation of UN peace operations.[11]

Based on the recommendations in the Zeid Report, Annex H of the revised model MOU was originally going to include the Ten Rules, 'We are United Nations Peacekeepers', and 'Prohibitions on sexual exploitation and abuse'.[12] The final version of Annex H, however, is an updated version of 'We are United Nations Peacekeepers' incorporating the relevant provisions from the SGB SEA and titled 'We are United Nations Peacekeeping Personnel'.[13] Along with the additional definitions in Annex F, Annex H ensures that military members of national contingents are bound by the same standards of conduct, including the prohibitions against sexual exploitation and sexual abuse, which bind all other peacekeepers. Contributing States undertake to ensure all military members of their national contingents must comply with the UN standards of conduct in Annex H. The contents of both the Ten Rules and 'We are United Nations Peacekeeping Personnel' are issued to all peacekeepers[14] on blue cards, and are therefore often referred to as the 'Blue Cards'.

The revised model MOU states:

> The Government shall ensure that all members of the Government's national contingent are required to comply with the United Nations standards of conduct set out in annex H to the present memorandum of understanding.[15]

---

7 Zeid Report (n 5), [20].
8 Ibid, [27].
9 The extant version of the model MOU can be found in ch 9 of the most recent edition of the Contingent-Owned Equipment (COE) Manual, UN Doc A/C5/66/8, 27 October 2011 (n 1). See ch 3 above for the model MOU.
10 UN Doc ST/SGB/2003/13, 9 October 2003, entered into force 15 October 2003. See ch 30 below.
11 As highlighted in the Zeid Report (n 5).
12 'Report of the Secretary-General: Revised Draft Model Memorandum of Understanding between the United Nations and [participating State] contributing resources to [the United Nations Peacekeeping Operation]', UN Doc A/61/494, 3 October 2006, Article 2.
13 Model MOU (n 9), Annex H.
14 For the Ten Rules (n 2); and for We are United Nations Peacekeeping Personnel see (n 1).
15 Model MOU (n 9), Article 7.2.

The Preamble to 'We are United Nations Peacekeeping Personnel' requires peacekeepers to:

> comply with the Guidelines on International Humanitarian Law for Forces Undertaking United Nations Peacekeeping Operations and the applicable portions of the Universal Declaration of Human Rights as the fundamental basis of our standards.[16]

It can be assumed that the 'Guidelines on International Humanitarian Law for Forces Undertaking United Nations Peacekeeping Operations' referred to are the same as the 'Guidelines for UN Forces Regarding Respect for International Humanitarian Law' drawn up by the UN Secretariat and the International Committee of the Red Cross (ICRC) in 1996, which eventually became the 'Secretary-General's Bulletin: Observance by United Nations Forces of International Humanitarian Law'.[17]

Annex H requires peacekeepers to always '[r]espect local laws, customs and practices and be aware of and respect culture, religion, traditions and gender issues'.[18] The addition of 'respect local laws' in Annex H ensures that military members of national contingents respect local laws in the same way that other peacekeepers must. UN staff 'must comply with local laws and honour their private legal obligations' under Staff Rule 1.2(b).[19] Experts on mission 'must comply with local laws and honour their private legal obligations' under Regulation 2(j) of the 'Regulations Governing the Status, Basic Rights and Duties of Officials other than Secretariat Officials, and Experts on Mission'.[20]

It should also be noted that the model Status-of-Forces Agreement (model SOFA) provides that the 'United Nations peace-keeping operation and its members shall respect all local laws and regulations'.[21] This is reflected in the revised model MOU where the contributing State undertakes to:

> ensure that the Commander of its national contingent is vested with the necessary authority and takes all reasonable measures to maintain discipline and good order among all members of the national contingent to ensure compliance with the United Nations standards of conduct, mission-specific rules and regulations and the obligations towards national and local laws and regulations in accordance with the status-of-forces agreement.[22]

Annex H includes several additions to 'We are United Nations Peacekeepers' that incorporate the prohibitions against sexual exploitation and sexual abuse from the SGB SEA into the UN standards of conduct set out in 'We are United Nations Peacekeeping Personnel'. These include peacekeepers reporting '[a]ll acts involving sexual exploitation and abuse', and peacekeepers never committing '[a]ny act involving sexual exploitation and abuse, sexual activity with children under 18, or exchange of money, employment, goods or services for sex'.[23]

If a military member of a national contingent violates the standards of conduct in Annex H, they can face administrative, disciplinary, or criminal action.[24] Whilst administrative action in the form of repatriation can be taken by the UN, any disciplinary or criminal actions against military members of national contingents are the sole reserve of the contributing State. In the model MOU, contributing States agree to exercise their jurisdiction in criminal and disciplinary matters over military members of their national contingents.[25]

The six additional definitions in Annex F of the model MOU include definitions for sexual exploitation, sexual abuse, misconduct, and serious misconduct. The definitions of sexual exploitation and sexual abuse match those in Section 1 of the SGB SEA. Misconduct is defined in Annex F as:

> any act or omission that is a violation of United Nations standards of conduct, mission-specific rules and regulations or the obligations towards national and local laws and regulations in accordance with the status-of-forces agreement where the impact is outside the national contingent.[26]

---

16 Ibid, Annex H, Preamble.

17 See ch 15 above.

18 Model MOU (n 9), Annex H.

19 'Secretary-General's Bulletin: Status, Basic Rights and Duties of United Nations Staff Members', UN Doc ST/SGB/2016/9, 21 July 2016. See ch 25 above.

20 'Secretary-General's Bulletin: Regulations Governing the Status, Basic Rights and Duties of Officials other than Secretariat Officials, and Experts on Mission', UN Doc ST/SGB/2002/9, 18 June 2002, entered into force 1 July 2002, Annex II, [2](j). See ch 26 above.

21 Report of the Secretary-General, 'Model Status-of-Forces Agreement for Peace-keeping Operations', UN Doc A/45/594, 9 October 1990, [6]. See ch 2 above.

22 Model MOU (n 9), Article 7.5.

23 Ibid, Annex H.

24 Ibid.

25 Model MOU (n 9), Articles 7.22 and 7.23.

26 Ibid, Annex F, [24].

Serious misconduct is defined in Annex F as:

> misconduct, including criminal acts, that results in, or is likely to result in, serious loss, damage or injury to an individual or to a mission. Sexual exploitation and abuse constitute serious misconduct.[27]

These definitions of misconduct and serious misconduct apply to the acts of military members of national contingents. Based on these definitions a violation of the UN standards of conduct in Annex H by a military member of a national contingent is misconduct and could result in disciplinary action. If it involved sexual exploitation and abuse it would be serious misconduct and could result in disciplinary or criminal action. These potential consequences for a violation of the UN standards of conduct are also clearly specified in Annex H.

2. Code of Personal Conduct for Blue Helmets

The rules outlined in the Ten Rules are binding on civilian police and military observers on the basis of the individual undertakings that they sign.[28] The rules are not binding upon military members of national contingents because they do not form part of the MOU signed between the UN and the contributing State. However, the practice of contributing States over the years in accepting the rules set out in Ten Rules makes them applicable to military personnel, at least as non-binding guidelines.[29]

In any case, the rules outlined in Ten Rules are reflected in the UN standards of conduct set out in 'We are United Nations Peacekeeping Personnel'. For instance, Rule 5 states that Blue Helmets must '[r]espect and regard the human rights of all',[30] which is encompassed in the requirement of peacekeepers to comply with the applicable portions of the Universal Declaration of Human Rights (UDHR)[31] as the fundamental basis of their behaviour. Similarly, Rule 2 requires Blue Helmets to '[r]espect the law of the land of the host country, their local culture, traditions, customs and practices' whilst, pursuant to Rule 4, they must not 'indulge in immoral acts of sexual, physical or psychological abuse or exploitation of the local population or United Nations staff, especially women and children'.[32]

To ensure compliance with UN standards of conduct and discipline, UN peace operations now have dedicated Conduct and Discipline Units (CDU) which act as the principal focal points for conduct and discipline issues within the mission.[33] This includes receiving reports of misconduct by peacekeepers and referring them to the appropriate investigatory body for action.

References

Title	United Nations Standards of Conduct: We are United Nations Peacekeeping Personnel
Author	Working Group on Contingent-Owned Equipment
Date	27 October 2011
Source	UN Doc A/C5/66/8, Chapter 9, Annex H.
Full Text	< http://www.un.org/en/ga/search/view_doc.asp?symbol=A/C.5/66/8>[34]
Title	Ten Rules: Code of Personal Conduct for Blue Helmets
Author	United Nations Department of Peacekeeping Operations
Date	1997
Full Text	<https://conduct.unmissions.org/ten-rulescode-personal-conduct-blue-helmets>[35]

27 Ibid, Annex F, [32].
28 Zeid Report (n 5), [18].
29 Ibid, [19].
30 Ten Rules, (n 2) Rule [5].
31 See ch 6 above.
32 Ten Rules (n 2), Rule [2] and Rule [4].
33 See <https://conduct.unmissions.org/> accessed 28 November 2018.
34 'We are United Nations Peacekeeping Personnel' in Annex H can be compared with 'We are United Nations Peacekeepers' <http://www.un.org/Depts/dpko/dpko/Conduct/un_in.pdf> accessed 1 November 2017.
35 Accessed 28 November 2018.

We are United Nations Peacekeeping Personnel[36]

The United Nations Organization embodies the aspirations of all the people of the world for peace.

In this context the United Nations Charter requires that all personnel must maintain the highest standards of integrity and conduct.

We will comply with the Guidelines on International Humanitarian Law for Forces Undertaking United Nations Peacekeeping Operations and the applicable portions of the Universal Declaration of Human Rights as the fundamental basis of our standards.

We, as peacekeeping personnel, represent the United Nations and are present in the country to help it recover from the trauma of a conflict. As a result, we must consciously be prepared to accept special constraints in our public and private lives in order to do the work and to pursue the ideals of the United Nations Organization.

We will be accorded certain privileges and immunities arranged through agreements negotiated between the United Nations and the host country solely for the purpose of discharging our peacekeeping duties. Expectations of the international community and the local population will be high, and our actions, behaviour and speech will be closely monitored.

We will always:

- Conduct ourselves in a professional and disciplined manner, at all times
- Dedicate ourselves to achieving the goals of the United Nations
- Understand the mandate and mission and comply with their provisions
- Respect the environment of the host country
- Respect local laws, customs and practices and be aware of and respect culture, religion, traditions and gender issues
- Treat the inhabitants of the host country with respect, courtesy and consideration
- Act with impartiality, integrity and tact
- Support and aid the infirm, sick and weak
- Obey our United Nations superiors/supervisors and respect the chain of command
- Respect all other peacekeeping members of the mission regardless of status, rank, ethnic or national origin, race, gender, or creed
- Support and encourage proper conduct among our fellow peacekeeping personnel
- Report all acts involving sexual exploitation and abuse
- Maintain proper dress and personal deportment at all times
- Properly account for all money and property assigned to us as members of the mission
- Care for all United Nations equipment placed in our charge.

We will never:

- Bring discredit upon the United Nations or our nations through improper personal conduct, failure to perform our duties or abuse of our positions as peacekeeping personnel
- Take any action that might jeopardize the mission

36 From United Nations Standards of Conduct: We are United Nations Peacekeeping Personnel, by the Working Group on Contingent-Owned Equipment © 2011 United Nations. Reprinted with the permission of the United Nations.

- Abuse alcohol, use or traffic in drugs
- Make unauthorized communications to external agencies, including unauthorized press statements
- Improperly disclose or use information gained through our employment
- Use unnecessary violence or threaten anyone in custody
- Commit any act that could result in physical, sexual or psychological harm or suffering to members of the local population, especially women and children
- Commit any act involving sexual exploitation and abuse, sexual activity with children under 18, or exchange of money, employment, goods or services for sex
- Become involved in sexual liaisons which could affect our impartiality or the well-being of others
- Be abusive or uncivil to any member of the public
- Wilfully damage or misuse any United Nations property or equipment
- Use a vehicle improperly or without authorization
- Collect unauthorized souvenirs
- Participate in any illegal activities, corrupt or improper practices
- Attempt to use our positions for personal advantage, to make false claims or accept benefits to which we are not entitled.

We realize that the consequences of failure to act within these guidelines may:

- Erode confidence and trust in the United Nations
- Jeopardize the achievement of the mission
- Jeopardize our status and security as peacekeeping personnel and
- Result in administrative, disciplinary or criminal action.

Ten Rules: Code of Personal Conduct for Blue Helmets[37]

Rule 1

Dress, think, talk, act and behave in a manner befitting the dignity of a disciplined, caring, considerate, mature, respected and trusted soldier, displaying the highest integrity and impartiality. Have pride in your position as a peace-keeper and do not abuse or misuse your authority.

Rule 2

Respect the law of the land of the host country, their local culture, traditions, customs and practices.

37 From Ten Rules: Code of Personal Conduct for Blue Helmets, by United Nations Department of Peacekeeping Operations © 1997 United Nations. Reprinted with the permission of the United Nations.

Rule 3

Treat the inhabitants of the host country with respect, courtesy and consideration. You are there as a guest to help them and in so doing will be welcomed with admiration. Neither solicit or accept any material reward, honor or gift.

Rule 4

Do not indulge in immoral acts of sexual, physical or psychological abuse or exploitation of the local population or United Nations staff, especially women and children.

Rule 5

Respect and regard the human rights of all. Support and aid the infirm, sick and weak. Do not act in revenge or with malice, in particular when dealing with prisoners, detainees or people in your custody.

Rule 6

Properly care for and account for all United Nations money, vehicles, equipment and property assigned to you and do not trade or barter with them to seek personal benefits.

Rule 7

Show military courtesy and pay appropriate compliments to all members of the mission, including other United Nations contingents regardless of their creed, gender, rank or origin.

Rule 8

Show respect for and promote the environment, including the flora and fauna, of the host country.

Rule 9

Do not engage in excessive consumption of alcohol or any consumption or trafficking of drugs.

Rule 10

Exercise the utmost discretion in handling confidential information and matters of official business which can put lives into danger or soil the image of the United Nations.

28

Directives for Disciplinary Matters Involving Military Members of National Contingents

Prefatory Note

The Department of Peacekeeping Operations (DPKO) issued the Directives for Disciplinary Matters Involving Military Members of National Contingents (Directives)[1] in 2003. The Directives follow the same format, and are very similar to, the Directives for Disciplinary Matters Involving Civilian Police Officers and Military Observers. The purpose of the Directives is to:

> establish United Nations procedures to be followed for alleged breaches of conduct in the mission area by military members of national contingents assigned to United Nations peacekeeping and other field missions.[2]

The Directives are not binding on military members of national contingents. Military members of national contingents have no individual contractual link with the UN and remain administratively attached to their respective national militaries. The obligations of military personnel in a UN peace operation are provided for in the Memorandum of Understanding (MOU)[3] agreed to between the UN and contributing State.

The main purpose of the Directives is to establish UN procedures to be followed when there are allegations of misconduct and serious misconduct against military members of national contingents. The Directives do not alter the national procedures adopted by Troop Contributing Countries (TCCs). The procedures involve a preliminary investigation followed by a Board of Inquiry, with Annex A of the Directives containing the 'Procedures for Board of Inquiry for Disciplinary Cases', and Annex B containing the 'Guidelines for Preliminary Investigations'.

The definition of 'serious misconduct' in the Directives does not apply to military members of national contingents. Rather a similar but distinct definition of serious misconduct located in Annex F to the revised model MOU between the UN and contributing States applies to them. Both the definition in the Directives and Annex F, however, include sexual exploitation and abuse as serious misconduct. This should be read in conjunction with the Secretary-General's Bulletin on 'Special Measures for Protection from Sexual Exploitation and Sexual Abuse'.[4] The Directives also include 'harassment, including sexual harassment' as part of the definition of 'serious misconduct'.[5]

The summary of the legal status of military members of national contingents in the Directives is taken from the model Status-of-Forces Agreement (model SOFA).[6] The model SOFA provides that military personnel on a peace operation are subject to the exclusive criminal jurisdiction of the contributing State in respect of any criminal offences which may be committed by them in the host country, though they are subject to any civil claims unrelated to their official duties in the jurisdiction of the host country.[7]

---

1 Department of Peacekeeping Operations, 'Directives for Disciplinary Matters Involving Military Members of National Contingents', UN Doc DPKO/MD/03/00993, 1 July 2003 (hereafter Directives).

2 Ibid, [1].

3 These MOUs are based on the model MOU—see Letter dated 25 February 2011 from the Chair of the 2011 Working Group on Contingent-Owned Equipment to the Chair of the Fifth Committee, UN Doc A/C5/66/8, 27 October 2011 (hereafter model MOU). See ch 3 above.

4 See ch 30 below.

5 Directives (n 1), [4].

6 See ch 2 above.

7 See 'Report of the Secretary-General on the Model Status-of-Forces Agreement for Peace-keeping Operations', UN Doc A/45/594, 9 October 1990, Annex, [49](b) (hereafter model SOFA).

The actions that may be taken under the Directives against military members of national contingents include repatriation,[8] and while not referred to in the Directives, pursuant to practice reported by the Secretary-General, forfeiture of any payments owed to the individual where a report of sexual exploitation and abuse is substantiated.[9] Any disciplinary or criminal actions against military members of national contingents are the sole reserve of the contributing State under the model MOU. Under the model MOU, contributing States agree to exercise their jurisdiction in criminal and disciplinary matters over military members of their national contingents.[10]

The relevance of the Directives in respect of disciplinary matters involving military members of national contingents must be read in the light of General Assembly resolution 59/287[11] which gave the Office of Internal Oversight Services (OIOS)[12] the responsibility to investigate all alleged acts of sexual exploitation and abuse committed by any category of peacekeepers. As a representative of OIOS noted:

> OIOS essentially had powers to investigate possible misconduct of staff of the Organization, as well as possible misconduct by personnel of a national contingent of a troop-contributing country in cases concerning sexual exploitation and abuse.[13]

However, even these powers of the OIOS to investigate serious misconduct by military members of national contingents must be read in the light of the 2011 version of the model MOU which gave primary responsibility to investigate such acts to the contributing State.[14]

The subsidiary role of the OIOS is further reinforced by Articles 7.12 and 7.13 of the model MOU. Article 7.12 provides that any preliminary fact-finding inquiry conducted by the OIOS can only be carried out under certain circumstances, whilst Article 7.13 provides that the UN can only start an administrative investigation when the contributing State is unable or unwilling to start its own investigation. The UN investigation must stop and hand over all its evidence to the contributing State, however, if the contributing State decides to start its own investigation.

The action to be taken if either an investigation by the contributing State or a UN investigation finds that allegations of misconduct are well founded is provided for in Article 7.24 of the model MOU.

The procedures for Boards of Inquiry and preliminary investigations are contained in Annex A and Annex B of the Directives. Annex A outlines the 'Procedures for Board of Inquiry for Disciplinary Cases' whilst Annex B outlines the 'Guidelines for Preliminary Investigations'.

The procedures in the Directives for investigating acts of serious misconduct need to be read in light of General Assembly resolution 59/287,[15] which granted the OIOS the responsibility to investigate all alleged acts of sexual exploitation and abuse. The resolution re-emphasised that 'the Office of Internal Oversight Services is the internal body entrusted with investigation in the United Nations'[16] and decided that 'in cases of serious misconduct and/or criminal behaviour, investigations should be conducted by professional investigators'.[17] Boards of Inquiry, on the other hand, are 'composed of at least three impartial, senior officials appointed by the Head of Mission'.[18] General Assembly resolution 62/247 on 'Strengthening Investigations' reaffirmed that 'the Office of Internal Oversight Services is the internal body entrusted with investigation in the United Nations'.[19] Resolution 62/247 also reaffirms that:

> trained heads of offices, programme managers and boards of inquiry, as well as the Department of Safety and Security and the Ethics Office, may carry out administrative inquiries and investigations, except in cases of serious misconduct and/or criminal behaviour, in accordance with resolution 59/287.[20]

---

8 Directives (n 1), [24]. See also SC Res 2272 (2016) of 11 March 2016, Operative Part [1].

9 'Report of the Secretary-General: Combating Sexual Exploitation and Abuse', UN Doc A/71/97, 23 June 2016, [77].

10 Model MOU (n 3), Articles 7.22 and 7.23.

11 GA Res 59/287 of 13 April 2005. The Office was established pursuant to GA Res 48/218B of 29 July 1994.

12 See <https://oios.un.org/> accessed 1 November 2017. For a more detailed analysis of the role of the OIOS see the 'Report of the Office of Internal Oversight Services on strengthening the investigation functions in the United Nations', UN Doc A/58/708, 10 February 2004 (hereafter Report of OIOS).

13 'Report of the Ad Hoc Committee on criminal accountability of United Nations officials and experts on mission, Second session (7–9 and 11 April 2008)', UN Doc A/63/54, 15 April 2008, Annex I, Section B, [12].

14 Model MOU (n 3), Article 7.10.

15 GA Res 59/287 of 13 April 2005.

16 Ibid, Operative Part [3].

17 Ibid, Operative Part [9].

18 Directives (n 1), [17].

19 GA Res 62/247 of 3 April 2007, Operative Part [11].

20 Ibid, Operative Part [12].

Therefore, the Boards of Inquiry convened under the Directives cannot carry out administrative inquiries and investigations in cases of serious misconduct and/or criminal behaviour but must leave these investigations to the OIOS.[21]

The disciplinary and criminal accountability processes described above must also be read in the context of the UN Secretariat's policy concerning conduct and discipline of peacekeepers. That policy explains the role that Member States have in ensuring accountability of military members. For example, paragraph 16.2 provides that:

> Member States are responsible for informing the United Nations of instances of misconduct involving their personnel serving in United Nations field missions and ensuring that investigations conducted by them are completed promptly and professionally. In instances involving sexual exploitation and abuse, save for exceptional circumstances, investigations are expected to be completed within six months.[22]

Paragraph 18.3 also reinforces that the OIOS 'has overall responsibility for internal United Nations administrative investigations'.[23]

The Secretariat's policy concerning accountability for the conduct of UN personnel serving in field missions[24] reinforces the disciplinary and accountability framework described above.

Reference

Title	Directives for Disciplinary Matters Involving Military Members of National Contingents
Author	Department of Peacekeeping Operations
Date	1 July 2003
Source	DPKO/MD/03/00993
Full Text	<http://www.pseataskforce.org/uploads/tools/directivesfordisciplinarymattersinvolvingmilitarymembersofnationalcontingents_undpko_english.doc>[25]

Directives for Disciplinary Matters Involving Military Members of National Contingents[26]

I. Purpose

1. The purpose of the present directives is to establish United Nations procedures to be followed for alleged breaches of conduct in the mission area by military members of national contingents assigned to United Nations peacekeeping and other field missions.

II. Scope of Application

2. These directives shall apply to cases of serious misconduct as defined in section III, committed by military members of national contingents. In addition, any act of misconduct that has a detrimental effect on the image, credibility, impartiality or integrity of the United Nations,

21 Report of OIOS (n 12).

22 Department of Political Affairs, Department of Peacekeeping Operations, and Department of Field Support, 'Accountability for Conduct and Discipline in Field Missions', 1 August 2015. See ch 31 below.

23 Ibid.

24 Ibid.

25 Accessed 1 November 2017.

26 From Directives for Disciplinary Matters Involving Military Members of National Contingents, by Department of Peacekeeping Operations © 2003 United Nations. Reprinted with the permission of the United Nations.

the peacekeeping or other field operation or the national contingent concerned shall be regarded as an act of misconduct falling within the scope of these directives.

3. Cases of minor misconduct, as defined in section III, committed by military members of national contingents shall normally be dealt with by the national contingent commander, as provided for under the relevant national military laws and guidelines and in conformity with mission directives and standard operating and administrative procedures.

III. Definitions

4. For the purpose of the present directives, the following definitions shall apply:
Serious misconduct: Any act, omission or negligence, including criminal acts, that is a violation of mission standard operating procedures, directives, or any other applicable rules, regulations or administrative instructions that results in or is likely to result in serious damage or injury[27] to an individual or to the mission. Serious misconduct includes, but is not limited to:

- Sexual abuse and exploitation of any individual, particularly children;
- Harassment, including sexual harassment;[28]
- Abuse of authority;
- Breach of confidentiality;
- Abuse of United Nations privileges and immunities;
- Use, possession or distribution of illegal narcotics;
- Embezzlement or other financial malfeasance;
- Wilful disobedience of a lawful order;
- Conduct prejudicial to good order and discipline;
- Driving while intoxicated or other grossly negligent driving;
- Intoxicated while on duty or in public on repeated occasions;
- Repeatedly absent from duty without permission;
- Unlawful acts (e.g. theft, fraud, smuggling, bribery) on or off United Nations premises, with or without the involvement of United Nations vehicles, and whether or not the individual was officially on duty at the time of the offence.

Minor misconduct: Any act, omission or negligence that is a violation of mission standard operating procedures (SOPs), directives, or any other applicable rules, regulations or administrative instructions, but which does not result or is not likely to result in major damage or injury to an individual or the mission. Minor misconduct includes, but is not limited to:

- Improper uniform appearance;
- Neglect in performance of duty not amounting to a wilful or deliberate act;
- Intoxication while on duty or in public;
- Negligent driving.

---

27 The term 'injury' denotes any harm whatever illegally caused to any person, in body, mind, reputation or property. [Note: this footnote appears in the original document as footnote '1'].

28 Refer to *Directive on Sexual Harassment in United Nations Peacekeeping and Other Field Missions for Military Members of National Contingents, Military Observers and Civilian Police Officers* for a description of a formal complaint of sexual harassment. [Note: this footnote appears in the original document as footnote '2'].

IV. Standard of Conduct

5. Military members of national contingents shall refrain from any action or activity incompatible with the impartial and independent nature of their duties and inconsistent with the letter or spirit of the authorized mandate of the operation, the status of forces agreement, and other applicable legal norms and standards. Military members of national contingents shall respect all local laws and regulations.
6. Military members of national contingents are required to abide by the highest standards of integrity while in service for the United Nations. They shall refrain from any conduct that would adversely reflect on the United Nations and shall not engage in any activity that is incompatible with the aims and objectives of the United Nations. They are also required to abide by mission standard operating procedures, directives, or any other applicable rules, regulations or administrative issuances.
7. Upon deployment to the field mission, all military personnel shall receive a briefing on these directives, the types of serious misconduct prohibited and the process that will ensue should an allegation of misconduct be made. In this briefing, particular attention shall be drawn to the standard of conduct expected of members of United Nations field missions and to local laws and customs and the need to respect them.

V. Legal Status

8. Military members of national contingents assigned to the military component of a United Nations peacekeeping or other field operation shall be subject to the exclusive jurisdiction of their respective participating States in respect of any criminal offences that may be committed by them in the mission area. They shall be immune from legal process in respect of words spoken or written and all acts performed by them in their official capacity. They are, however, subject to the jurisdiction of the host country/territory in respect of any disputes/claims of a civil nature not related to the performance of their official functions.

VI. Notification

9. In cases where military members of national contingents are believed to have been involved in an act of serious misconduct or an act that has the potential to damage the image, credibility or integrity of the United Nations, the Head of Mission shall be notified immediately. Any member of the field mission who becomes aware of such acts shall report them to the Head of Mission.
10. Notification may also be made to the Personnel Conduct Officer, who shall bring it to the attention of the Head of Mission.

VII. Preliminary Investigation

11. Upon receiving a report of any serious misconduct involving a military member of a national contingent, the Head of Mission shall immediately initiate a preliminary investigation. Mission officials may be assisted in this investigation by local police or military personnel. If required, the investigation team could include a civilian member of the field mission, such as United Nations civilian police, human rights monitor, United Nations security officer, or child protection adviser, to assist in carrying out the preliminary investigation.
12. The purpose of the preliminary investigation shall be to establish the facts of the case. The investigation shall be conducted in accordance with the *Guidelines for Preliminary Investigations* contained in Annex B.

13. To the extent possible, the preliminary investigation must be completed before the individuals(s) involved and any witnesses leave the mission area due to rotation or for any other reason. No repatriation of individual(s) involved must occur before the conclusion of the preliminary investigation and a determination of the necessary administrative action to be taken. However, in normal circumstances, individuals concerned shall be allowed to depart the mission area after they have provided statements and their role in the investigation is complete.
14. The results of the preliminary investigation shall be immediately reported to the Head of Mission. The report shall contain a full account of the facts, any documentary evidence, statements made, or other relevant records. If the preliminary investigation appears to indicate that the report of serious misconduct is well-founded, the Head of Mission shall immediately report this to United Nations Headquarters in New York, who shall inform the national authorities of the country concerned through their Permanent Mission. The Head of Mission shall also convene a Board of Inquiry.

VIII. Board of Inquiry

15. Acts of serious misconduct or acts that have the potential to damage the image, credibility or integrity of the United Nations shall require the convening of a mission headquarters Board of Inquiry,[29] in accordance with the procedures set out in Annex A.
16. The purpose of the Board of Inquiry shall be to establish the facts of the case. The Board shall determine cause and responsibility in the incident under review. The Board of Inquiry may also make recommendations for appropriate administrative action, including repatriation. A Board of Inquiry shall not be a judicial body; it is a management tool to assist the Head of Mission in discharging his/her responsibilities. It may also assist the participating State concerned in its own investigation of the incident or act, for the purpose of appropriate national disciplinary proceedings. A Board of Inquiry shall not consider questions of compensation or legal liability.
17. The Board of Inquiry shall be convened within 48 to 72 hours after the findings of the preliminary investigation becoming available. The Board of Inquiry shall be convened by the Head of Mission, who shall issue its terms of reference. The Board shall be composed of at least three impartial, senior officials appointed by the Head of Mission. Due consideration shall be given to geographic and gender representation on the Board of Inquiry. All Board members shall serve in their individual capacity. In exceptional cases, the Secretary-General or the Under-Secretary-General for Peacekeeping Operations shall appoint Board members external to the mission.
18. The proceedings of the Board of Inquiry shall be conducted as speedily as possible. The members of the Board shall not proceed on other missions or on leave until the Board has completed its deliberations. (See Annex A on *Procedures for Board of Inquiry for Disciplinary Cases.*)
19. Board of Inquiry proceedings shall not preclude any interim measures that the national contingent commander may wish to take with regard to the individual(s) involved or the conduct of a national investigation, in accordance with national military rules and procedures.
20. The Head of Mission shall review the final report of the Board of Inquiry and its recommendations, if any, in consultation with the appropriate personnel (e.g. Legal Officer,

29 Other circumstances under which a mission headquarters Board of Inquiry should be instituted are described in the *Draft Field Administration Manual*. [Note: this footnote appears in the original document as footnote '3'].

Medical Adviser) before determining the action to be taken. The final report of the Board of Inquiry shall be transmitted to United Nations Headquarters in New York, along with the decision of the Head of Mission and the description of measures taken to implement that decision. Any comments that the Head of Mission may have on the recommendations of the Board or on the report in general shall also be transmitted along with the final report.

21. Any recommendations submitted by the Board of Inquiry, together with any comments thereon by the Head of Mission and his/her final decision, shall also be communicated to the commanding officer concerned.

22. The Board of Inquiry file shall be closed after the Head of Mission has approved and forwarded copies of the Board's report to United Nations Headquarters in New York. The Board of Inquiry file and all relevant documentation shall be retained in the mission archives until the closure of the mission and thereafter shall be transferred to United Nations Headquarters in New York.

23. Board of Inquiry reports shall be confidential, internal documents of the United Nations and, as a rule, shall not be made available to outside entities. The release of a Board of Inquiry report to a Government to be used for its official purposes shall be approved by United Nations Headquarters in New York.

IX. Repatriation

24. The decision to repatriate a military member of a national contingent, in all cases, shall be made by United Nations Headquarters in New York, based on the recommendation of the Head of Mission. Once decided, repatriation shall be immediate and the national authorities concerned shall be contacted at once through the Permanent Mission concerned in New York. The expenses connected with the repatriation and replacement action shall be borne by the Member State involved.

25. If the continued presence in the mission area of individual(s) to be repatriated on disciplinary grounds is detrimental to the morale of the staff, the image of the mission or has other negative effects, the objective of the Organization shall be to repatriate as soon as appropriate. In certain cases, the Head of Mission may decide to await the completion of the report of the Board of Inquiry if (s)he is of the opinion that the preliminary investigation report is inadequate to support an immediate repatriation decision. The Head of Mission shall inform Headquarters in New York of such a course of action and provide it with a copy of the preliminary investigation report and a statement as to why (s)he considers the report to be inadequate for the purposes of a decision on repatriation. In such situations, the Board of Inquiry shall be required to complete its work on a priority basis and as speedily as possible.

X. Assistance to Victims

26. Once the final report of the Board of Inquiry along with the comments and/or decision of the Head of Mission have been reviewed by United Nations Headquarters in New York, the final decision, action or guidance shall be conveyed immediately back to the Head of Mission. If necessary, this information shall be used by the Head of Mission to appropriately inform the victims/individuals concerned of the action taken.

27. The Head of Mission shall consider taking appropriate measures to assist victims of acts of serious misconduct, including directing them to relevant organizations/support groups that could provide assistance.

XI. Follow-Up

28. Although the responsibility to discipline military members of national contingents remains a national responsibility, the United Nations does have an interest in ensuring that justice is carried out. Following repatriation, the United Nations shall request information about the action taken with regard to repatriated military members of national contingents. If no response is received, periodic reminders will be sent to the concerned Permanent Mission from the Military Division of the Department of Peacekeeping Operations. If still no response is forthcoming, appropriate steps shall be taken to bring the matter to the attention of the Government concerned at the highest possible levels, to underscore the seriousness of the matter and to pursue it with a view to seeing that appropriate disciplinary steps are taken.

XII. Final Provision

29. These Directives supersede *DPKO Administrative Procedure on Discipline for Military and Civilian Police Personnel in Mission Areas, directive MPS/651*, and any other procedures and guidelines on this subject to the extent that they are inconsistent with these Directives.

[Note: Annexes A and B are the same as those contained in the Directives for Disciplinary Matters Involving Civilian Police Officers and Military Observers (see the discussion in ch 29 below).]

29

Directives for Disciplinary Matters Involving Civilian Police Officers and Military Observers

Prefatory Note

The Department of Peacekeeping Operations (DPKO) issued the Directives for Disciplinary Matters Involving Civilian Police Officers and Military Observers (Directives) in 2003.[1] The purpose of the Directives is to:

> establish United Nations procedures to be followed for alleged breaches of conduct in the mission areas of peacekeeping and other field operations by civilian police officers and military observers.[2]

The Directives are binding upon civilian police and military observers because they are employed to serve on UN peace operations as experts on mission based on individual undertakings in which they agree to comply with all applicable UN rules, regulations, directives, and other issuances.

A footnote to the Directives states that they 'shall not be applicable to members of national formed police units'.[3] The UN Office of Legal Affairs (OLA) has confirmed that the Directives do not apply to members of formed police units (FPU) because 'members of FPUs are expressly excluded from the scope of those *Directives* by footnote 1'.[4] However, notwithstanding that view, the Guidelines for Formed Police Units on Assignment with Peace Operations issued by the Police Unit in the DPKO in May 2006 stated that: 'All alleged breaches of conduct must be dealt with in accordance with the [Directives]'.[5] Responsibility for disciplinary action in these units rests with the commanders of the national units, who must keep the Head of Mission fully informed in all disciplinary matters.[6]

The main purpose of the Directives is to establish the UN procedures to be followed when there are allegations of misconduct and serious misconduct against civilian police officers and military observers deployed on UN peace operations.

The Directives apply to cases of 'serious misconduct ... committed by civilian police officers and military observers' and acts of misconduct that have a 'detrimental effect on the image, credibility, impartiality or integrity of the United Nations, the peacekeeping or other field operation or the civilian police officers and military observers concerned'.[7] Cases of minor misconduct are dealt with by local commanders or supervisors.[8]

'Serious misconduct' is defined in the Directives as:

> Any act, omission or negligence, including criminal acts, that is a violation of mission standard operating procedures, directives, or any other applicable rules, regulations or administrative instructions, that results in or is likely to result in serious damage or injury to an individual or to the mission.[9]

---

1 Department of Peacekeeping Operations, Directives for Disciplinary Matters Involving Civilian Police Officers and Military Observers, UN Doc DPKO/CPD/DDCPO/2003/001, 1 July 2003 (hereafter Directives).

2 Ibid, [1].

3 Ibid, fn 1, 2.

4 UN Juridical Yearbook 2005: Special Edition, 1–3, 2, 'Note to the Under-Secretary-General for the Department of Peacekeeping Operations, concerning Formed Police Units', 3 October 2005.

5 Information taken from the Department of Peacekeeping Operations, 'Guidelines for Formed Police Units on Assignment with Peace Operations', DPKO/PD/2006/00015, 8 May 2006, [24].

6 Directives (n 1).

7 Ibid, [2].

8 Ibid, [3].

9 Ibid, [4].

Examples of serious misconduct include sexual exploitation and abuse of any individual, particularly children, and harassment, including sexual harassment.[10]

All cases of serious misconduct against civilian police officers and military observers, and acts of misconduct falling with the scope of the Directives, should be dealt with in accordance with the procedures outlined in the Directives. However, in the investigation of acts of serious misconduct and/or criminal behaviour in UN peace operations, account must also be taken of the expanded role and responsibilities of the Office of Internal Oversight Services (OIOS),[11] especially regarding the investigation of allegations of sexual exploitation and abuse by peacekeepers.

The standards of conduct for civilian police officers and military observers outlined in the Directives[12] are summarised from the Secretary-General's Bulletin entitled 'Regulations Governing the Status, Basic Rights and Duties of Officials other than Secretariat Officials, and Experts on Mission'.[13]

The Directives note that the privileges and immunities afforded to civilian police officers and military observers, as experts on mission, are granted pursuant to Article VI of the Convention on the Privileges and Immunities of the United Nations.[14] They reaffirm that these privileges and immunities are granted in the interests of the UN and not the individual, and highlight the Secretary-General's role in waiving these immunities. The Directives then state:

> Civilian police officers and military observers are, however, subject to the jurisdiction of the host country/territory in respect of any criminal offences that may be committed by them in the host country and any disputes/claims of a civil nature not related to the performance of their official functions.[15]

In terms of criminal offences, the model Status-of-Forces Agreement (model SOFA)[16] provides that if the local authorities wish to bring criminal charges against a member of the peace operation who is a civilian, such as UN officials and experts on mission, then they first need the permission of the Special Representative of the Secretary-General (SRSG), also known as the Head of Mission. In such cases, the SRSG must carry out his or her own inquiry and then agree with the government of the host country on whether criminal proceedings should be instituted. If agreement is not forthcoming, it may result in a lacuna in terms of who is responsible for criminally prosecuting civilian police officers and military observers on UN peace operations. In the case of civil claims, it is up to the SRSG to certify whether the proceeding relates to an official activity of the member.

The SRSG should be notified immediately if any civilian police officers or military observers are suspected of involvement in acts of serious misconduct.[17] Since 2005, the first point of contact in missions to receive complaints has been the Conduct and Discipline Units (CDUs).[18]

The next two sections of the Directives deal with the procedure to be followed when such cases have been brought to the attention of the SRSG. This involves a preliminary investigation followed by a Board of Inquiry.[19] The Report of the Secretary-General, 'A Comprehensive Strategy to Eliminate Future Sexual Exploitation and Abuse in United Nations Peacekeeping Operations' (Zeid Report)[20] provides a summary of the procedure:

> As is also the case for United Nations staff, the first step in the process is that if there is reason to believe that a civilian police officer or a military observer has committed serious misconduct, the head of mission must immediately undertake a preliminary investigation. If that preliminary investigation indicates that the report of serious misconduct is well founded, a board of inquiry is convened and the head

---

10 Ibid.

11 See <https://oios.un.org/> accessed 1 November 2017. For a more detailed analysis of the role of the OIOS see the 'Report of the Office of Internal Oversight Services on strengthening the investigation functions in the United Nations', UN Doc A/58/708, 10 February 2004.

12 Directives (n 1), [5]–[7].

13 See ch 26 above.

14 Directives (n 1), [8].

15 Ibid.

16 See ch 2 above.

17 Directives (n 1), [9]–[10].

18 See <https://conduct.unmissions.org/who-is-involved> accessed 24 December 2018.

19 Directives (n 1), [11]–[22].

20 'Report of the Secretary-General: A Comprehensive Strategy to Eliminate Future Sexual Exploitation and Abuse in United Nations Peacekeeping Operations', UN Doc A/59/710, 24 March 2005 (hereafter Zeid Report).

> of mission informs the Department of Peacekeeping Operations at Headquarters of the results of the preliminary investigation. The head of mission may recommend to the Department that the individual concerned be repatriated on the basis of the findings of the preliminary investigation. The Department then informs the permanent mission of the State concerned.[21]

The Zeid Report also outlines the purpose of the Board of Inquiry:

> The purpose of the board of inquiry is to establish facts, not to act as an adjudicatory body. It is a management tool to assist the head of mission in discharging his or her responsibilities to prevent misconduct in the mission.[22]

The procedures for Boards of Inquiry and preliminary investigations are contained in Annex A and Annex B of the Directives. Annex A outlines the 'Procedures for Board of Inquiry for Disciplinary Cases' whilst Annex B outlines the 'Guidelines for Preliminary Investigations'.

The procedures in the Directives for investigating acts of serious misconduct need to be read in light of General Assembly resolution 59/287[23] which granted the OIOS the responsibility to investigate all alleged acts of sexual exploitation and abuse. The resolution re-emphasised that 'the Office of Internal Oversight Services is the internal body entrusted with investigation in the United Nations'[24] and decided that 'in cases of serious misconduct and/or criminal behaviour, investigations should be conducted by professional investigators'.[25] Boards of Inquiry, on the other hand, are 'composed of at least three impartial, senior officials appointed by the Head of Mission'.[26] General Assembly resolution 62/247 on 'Strengthening Investigations' reaffirmed that 'the Office of Internal Oversight Services is the internal body entrusted with investigation in the United Nations'.[27] Resolution 62/247 also reaffirms that:

> trained heads of offices, programme managers and boards of inquiry, as well as the Department of Safety and Security and the Ethics Office, may carry out administrative inquiries and investigations, except in cases of serious misconduct and/or criminal behaviour, in accordance with resolution 59/287.[28]

Therefore, the Boards of Inquiry convened under the Directives cannot carry out administrative inquiries and investigations in cases of serious misconduct and/or criminal behaviour but must leave these investigations to the OIOS.[29]

If the procedures in the Directives are applicable, and a preliminary investigation has been carried out followed by a Board of Inquiry, the Directives outline the administrative actions and disciplinary measures that the SRSG may take against civilian police officers and military observers. These include written censure or reprimand, removal from a position of command, and redeployment to another position after retraining.[30] The decision of the SRSG in respect of a particular civilian police officer or military observer is communicated to their commander or supervisor who takes the appropriate disciplinary action.[31] It is also important to note that '[i]n addition to any United Nations administrative and/or disciplinary action(s), the individual may be subject to any applicable national disciplinary proceedings'.[32] This is reaffirmed in the 2009 Report of the General Assembly's Special Committee on Peacekeeping Operations (C34) which states:

> that all peacekeeping personnel must be informed of and adhere to all applicable rules, regulations, provisions and guidelines provided by the United Nations for peacekeepers, as well as to national laws and regulations.[33]

---

21 Ibid, Annex, [A.24].
22 Ibid, Annex, [A.25].
23 GA Res 59/287 of 13 April 2005.
24 Ibid, Operative Part [3].
25 Ibid, Operative Part [9].
26 Directives (n 1), [17].
27 GA Res 62/247 of 3 April 2007, Operative Part [11].
28 Ibid, Operative Part [12].
29 See the 'Report of the Office of Internal Oversight Services on strengthening the investigation functions in the United Nations', UN Doc A/58/708, 10 February 2004.
30 Directives (n 1), [23].
31 Ibid.
32 Ibid, [24].
33 'Report of the Special Committee on Peacekeeping Operations and its Working Group, 2009 Substantive Session (23 February–20 March 2009)', UN Doc A/63/19, 24 March 2009, [49].

The SRSG can also make a recommendation to repatriate the civilian police officer or military observer. However, the decision to repatriate is made by the UN Headquarters in New York, and:

> Once decided, repatriation shall be immediate and the national authorities concerned shall be contacted at once through the Permanent Mission concerned in New York. The expenses connected with the repatriation and replacement action shall be borne by the Member State involved.[34]

While the UN can take administrative or disciplinary measures against civilian police officers and military observers, it cannot take any criminal action. Therefore, any preliminary investigation under the Directives or investigation by the OIOS is only an administrative investigation for potential disciplinary action. It is not a criminal investigation. As a representative of OIOS has noted, the activities of OIOS 'were determined by elements of mandate, functionality and capacity … It did not have a mandate to conduct criminal investigations'.[35]

The UN must rely on either the host country or the contributing State to take any necessary criminal action. In a peace operation, the institution of criminal proceedings by the host country against a civilian police officer or military observer requires the agreement of the SRSG. This agreement may not be given for several reasons, including if there are concerns with the human rights standards of the local justice system or if the host country does not have a proper functioning court system. If an agreement is not reached, then it is up to the contributing State to take criminal action which they may or may not be able to do. To address this issue and the possible lacuna in criminal prosecution of experts on mission including civilian police officers and military observers, the General Assembly, in resolution 68/105, strongly urged 'States to take all appropriate measures to ensure that crimes by United Nations officials and experts on mission do not go unpunished and that the perpetrators of such crimes are brought to justice'.[36]

The Directives also require that the UN 'shall request information from Member States regarding national disciplinary or criminal action taken with regard to repatriated civilian police officers and military observers'.[37]

The accountability regime dealt with by the Directives must also now be read in conjunction with the UN Secretariat's policy on accountability for UN field personnel.[38] That policy reinforces that:

> Individual military and police personnel and members of FPUs, as well as some other Government Provided Personnel, are deployed with the legal status of experts on mission. They individually sign an undertaking upon commencement of service with the United Nations, through which they agree to be bound by the provisions contained in this undertaking, including the Regulations governing the Status, Basic Rights and Duties of Officials other than Secretariat Officials, and Experts on Mission (ST/SGB/2002/9), and such other documents adopted by the United Nations that regulate the conduct of this category of personnel.[39]

Reference

Title	Directives for Disciplinary Matters Involving Civilian Police Officers and Military Observers
Author	Department of Peacekeeping Operations
Date	1 July 2003
Source	UN Doc DPKO/CPD/DDCPO/2003/001, DPKO/MD/03/00994[40]

34 Directives (n 1), [25].

35 'Report of the Ad Hoc Committee on criminal accountability of United Nations officials and experts on mission, Second session (7–9 and 11 April 2008)', UN Doc A/63/54, 15 April 2008, Annex I, Section B, [12].

36 GA Res 68/105 of 16 December 2013, Operative Part [2].

37 Directives (n 1), [31].

38 Department of Political Affairs, Department of Peacekeeping Operations, and Department of Field Support, 'Accountability for Conduct and Discipline in Field Missions', 1 August 2015. See ch 31 below.

39 Ibid, [11.5].

40 Accessed 1 November 2017.

Directives for Disciplinary Matters Involving Civilian Police Officers and Military Observers[41]

I. Purpose

1. The purpose of the present directives is to establish United Nations procedures to be followed for alleged breaches of conduct in the mission areas of peacekeeping and other field operations by civilian police officers and military observers.

II. Scope of application

2. These directives shall apply to cases of serious misconduct as defined in section III, committed by civilian police officers[42] and military observers. In addition, any act of misconduct that has a detrimental effect on the image, credibility, impartiality or integrity of the United Nations, the peacekeeping or other field operation or the civilian police officers and military observers concerned shall be regarded as an act of misconduct falling within the scope of these directives.
3. Cases of minor misconduct, as defined in section III, committed by civilian police officers and military observers shall normally be dealt with by the commanders or other supervisors responsible for the maintenance of discipline, in accordance with any relevant rules, mission directives and the standard operating and administrative procedures.

III. Definitions

4. For the purpose of the present directives, the following definitions shall apply:

Serious misconduct: Any act, omission or negligence, including criminal acts, that is a violation of mission standard operating procedures, directives, or any other applicable rules, regulations or administrative instructions, that results in or is likely to result in serious damage or injury[43] to an individual or to the mission. Serious misconduct includes, but is not limited to:

- Sexual abuse and exploitation of any individual, particularly children;
- Harassment, including sexual harassment[44];
- Abuse of authority;
- Excessive use of force;
- Unlawful discharge of firearms;
- Breach of confidentiality;
- Abuse of United Nations privileges and immunities;

41 From Directives for Disciplinary Matters Involving Civilian Police Officers and Military Observers, by Department of Peacekeeping Operations © 2003 United Nations. Reprinted with the permission of the United Nations.

42 These Directives shall not be applicable to members of national formed police units. Responsibility for disciplinary action in these units rests with the commanders of the national units, who must keep the Head of Mission fully informed in all disciplinary matters. [Note: this footnote appears in the original document as footnote '1'].

43 The term "injury" denotes any harm whatever illegally caused to any person, in body, mind, reputation or property. [Note: this footnote appears in the original document as footnote '2'].

44 Refer to *Directive on Sexual Harassment in United Nations Peacekeeping and Other Field Missions for Military Members of National Contingents, Military Observers and Civilian Police Officers* for a description of a formal complaint of sexual harassment. [Note: this footnote appears in the original document as footnote '3'].

- Conduct prejudicial to good order and discipline;
- Driving while intoxicated or other grossly negligent driving;
- Intoxicated while on duty or in public on repeated occasions;
- Repeatedly absent from duty without permission;
- Use, possession or distribution of illegal narcotics;
- Embezzlement or other financial malfeasance;
- Wilful disobedience of a lawful order;
- Unlawful acts (e.g. theft, fraud, smuggling, bribery) on or off United Nations premises, with or without the involvement of United Nations vehicles, and whether or not the individual was officially on duty at the time of the offence.

Minor misconduct: Any act, omission or negligence that is a violation of mission standard operating procedures (SOPs), directives, or any other applicable rules, regulations or administrative instructions, but which does not result in or is not likely to result in major damage or injury to an individual or the mission. Minor misconduct includes, but is not limited to:

- Improper uniform appearance;
- Neglect in performance of duty not amounting to a wilful or deliberate act;
- Intoxication while on duty or in public;
- Negligent driving;
- Absence from duty without permission;
- Malingering.

IV. Standard of Conduct

5. Civilian police officers and military observers shall refrain from any action or activity incompatible with the impartial and independent nature of their duties and inconsistent with the letter or spirit of the authorized mandate of the operation, the status of forces agreement, and other applicable legal norms and standards. Civilian police officers and military observers shall respect all local laws and regulations.
6. Civilian police officers and military observers are required to abide by the highest standards of integrity while in service for the United Nations. They shall refrain from any conduct that would adversely reflect on the United Nations and shall not engage in any activity that is incompatible with the aims and objectives of the United Nations. They are also required to abide by mission standard operating procedures, directives, or any other applicable rules, regulations or administrative issuances.
7. Upon deployment to the field mission, all civilian police officers and military observers shall receive a briefing on these directives, the types of serious misconduct prohibited and the disciplinary process that shall ensue should an allegation of misconduct be made. In this briefing, particular attention shall be drawn to local laws and customs and the need to respect them.

V. Legal status

8. Civilian police officers and military observers enjoy the status of "experts performing missions" for the United Nations, under Article VI of the 1946 Convention on the Privileges and Immunities of the United Nations. In accordance with that status, they enjoy *inter alia* immunity for the purposes of the official acts they perform. These privileges and immunities are granted in the interests of the United Nations and not for the personal benefit of the individuals themselves. The Secretary-General has the right and the duty to waive the

immunity of any individual in any case where, in the Secretary-General's opinion, the immunity would impede the course of justice. Such a waiver shall be without prejudice to the interests of the United Nations. Civilian police officers and military observers are, however, subject to the jurisdiction of the host country/territory in respect of any criminal offences that may be committed by them in the host country and any disputes/claims of a civil nature not related to the performance of their official functions.

VI. Notification

9. In cases where civilian police officers or military observers are believed to have been involved in an act of serious misconduct or an act that has the potential to damage the image, credibility or integrity of the United Nations, the Head of Mission shall be notified immediately. Any member of the field mission who becomes aware of such acts shall report them to the Head of Mission.
10. Notification may also be made to the Personnel Conduct Officer, who shall bring it to the attention of the Head of Mission.

VII. Preliminary investigation

11. Upon receiving a report of any serious misconduct involving a civilian police officer or a military observer, the Head of Mission shall immediately initiate a preliminary investigation. Mission officials may be assisted in this investigation by local police. If required, the investigation team could include a civilian member of the field mission, such as, human rights monitor, United Nations security officer, or child protection adviser, to assist in carrying out the preliminary investigation.
12. The purpose of the preliminary investigation shall be to establish the facts of the case. The investigation shall be conducted in accordance with the "Guidelines for Preliminary Investigations" contained in Annex B.
13. To the extent possible, the preliminary investigation must be completed before the individuals(s) [sic] involved and any witnesses leave the mission area due to rotation or for any other reason. No repatriation of individual(s) involved must occur before the conclusion of the preliminary investigation and a determination of the appropriate administrative action to be taken. However, individuals concerned may be allowed to depart the mission area after they have provided statements and their role in the investigation is complete.
14. The results of the preliminary investigation shall be immediately reported to the Head of Mission. The report shall contain a full account of the facts, any documentary evidence, statements made, or other relevant records. If the preliminary investigation appears to indicate that the report of serious misconduct is well-founded, the Head of Mission shall immediately report this to United Nations Headquarters in New York, who shall inform the national authorities of the country concerned through their Permanent Mission. The Head of Mission shall also convene a Board of Inquiry.

VIII. Board of Inquiry

15. Acts of serious misconduct or acts that have the potential to damage the image, credibility or integrity of the United Nations shall require the convening of a mission headquarters Board of Inquiry,[45] in accordance with the procedures set out in Annex A.

---

45 Other circumstances under which a mission headquarters Board of Inquiry should be instituted are described in the *Draft Field Administration Manual*. [Note: this footnote appears in the original document as footnote '4'].

16. The purpose of the Board of Inquiry shall be to establish the facts of the case. The Board shall determine cause and responsibility in the incident under review. The Board of Inquiry may also make recommendations for appropriate administrative action, including repatriation. A Board of Inquiry shall not be a judicial body; it is a management tool to assist the Head of Mission in discharging his/her responsibilities. It may also assist the participating State concerned in its own investigation of the incident or act, for the purpose of appropriate national disciplinary proceedings. A Board of Inquiry shall not consider questions of compensation or legal liability.
17. The Board of Inquiry shall be convened within 48 to 72 hours after the findings of the preliminary investigation becoming available. The Board of Inquiry shall be convened by the Head of Mission, who shall issue its terms of reference. The Board shall be composed of at least three impartial, senior officials appointed by the Head of Mission. Due consideration shall be given to geographic and gender representation on the Board of Inquiry. All Board members shall serve in their individual capacity. In exceptional cases, the Secretary-General or the Under-Secretary-General for Peacekeeping Operations shall appoint Board members external to the mission.
18. The proceedings of the Board of Inquiry shall be conducted as speedily as possible. The members of the Board shall not proceed on other missions or on leave until the Board has completed its deliberations. (See Annex A on *Procedures for Board of Inquiry for Disciplinary Cases.*)
19. The Head of Mission shall review the final report of the Board of Inquiry and its recommendations, if any, in consultation with the appropriate personnel (e.g. Legal Officer, Medical Adviser) before determining the action to be taken. The final report of the Board of Inquiry shall be transmitted to United Nations Headquarters in New York, along with the decision of the Head of Mission and the description of measures taken to implement that decision. Any comments that the Head of Mission may have on the recommendations of the Board or on the report in general shall also be transmitted along with the final report.
20. Recommendations of the Board of Inquiry, together with any comments thereon by the Head of Mission and his/her final decision, shall be communicated to the commanders or other supervisors responsible for the maintenance of discipline of the individual(s) concerned for the purpose of imposing disciplinary measures.
21. The Board of Inquiry file shall be closed after the Head of Mission has approved and forwarded copies of the Board's report to United Nations Headquarters in New York. The Board of Inquiry file and all relevant documentation shall be retained in the mission archives until the closure of the mission and thereafter shall be transferred to United Nations Headquarters in New York.
22. Board of Inquiry reports shall be confidential, internal documents of the United Nations and, as a rule, shall not be made available to outside entities. The release of a Board of Inquiry report to a Government to be used for its official purposes shall be approved by United Nations Headquarters in New York.

IX. Administrative Actions and Disciplinary Measures

23. Following receipt of the recommendations of the Board of Inquiry and the final decision of the Head of Mission, as referred to in paragraph 20, the commander or other supervisor responsible for the maintenance of discipline shall take appropriate administrative and/or disciplinary action. Such actions may be one or more of the following:
    - Removal from position of command;
    - Redeployment to another position/area after retraining, if necessary;

- Removal of benefits and concessions provided to United Nations personnel;
- Suspension of leave/compensatory time off;
- Full or partial recovery from Mission Subsistence Allowance, in cases of financial loss to the Organization;
- Recommendation to repatriate;
- Written censure or reprimand, including a possible recommendation for non-eligibility for future assignment with the United Nations.

24. In addition to any United Nations administrative and/or disciplinary action(s), the individual may be subject to any applicable national disciplinary proceedings. For this purpose, a report on the misconduct and action taken shall be forwarded to United Nations Headquarters in New York in order to inform the Permanent Mission concerned.
25. The decision to repatriate a civilian police officer or a military observer, in all cases, shall be made by United Nations Headquarters in New York, based on the recommendation of the Head of Mission. Once decided, repatriation shall be immediate and the national authorities concerned shall be contacted at once through the Permanent Mission concerned in New York. The expenses connected with the repatriation and replacement action shall be borne by the Member State involved.
26. Leaving the mission area without authorization from United Nations Headquarters in New York to avoid disciplinary procedures or criminal charges shall not be allowed and shall require the Member State concerned to return the individual(s) to the mission area to facilitate the disciplinary process. If the national authorities do not comply, they shall not be requested to provide a replacement.
27. If the continued presence in the mission area of individual(s) to be repatriated on disciplinary grounds is detrimental to the morale of the staff, the image of the mission or has other negative effects, the objective of the Organization shall be to repatriate as soon as appropriate. In certain cases, the Head of Mission may decide to await the completion of the report of the Board of Inquiry if (s)he is of the opinion that the preliminary investigation report is inadequate to support an immediate repatriation decision, or the possibility of criminal charges exists. The Head of Mission shall inform Headquarters in New York of such a course of action and provide it with a copy of the preliminary investigation report and a statement as to the reasons why such a decision has been taken. In such situations, the Board of Inquiry shall be required to complete its work on a priority basis and as speedily as possible.

X. Criminal Offences

28. If the misconduct committed by a civilian police officer or military observer amounts to an alleged criminal offence, the Secretary-General has the right and the duty to waive the immunity, if applicable, of the individual(s) concerned, if in his opinion the immunity would impede the course of justice. The United Nations and the host country shall agree on whether or not criminal proceedings are to be instituted.

XI. Assistance to Victims

29. Once the final report of the Board of Inquiry along with the comments and/or decision of the Head of Mission have been reviewed by United Nations Headquarters in New York, the final decision, action or guidance shall be conveyed immediately back to the Head of Mission. If necessary, this information shall be used by the Head of Mission to appropriately inform the victims/individuals concerned of the action taken.

30. The Head of Mission shall consider taking appropriate measures to assist victims of acts of serious misconduct, including directing them to relevant organizations/support groups that could provide assistance.

XII. Follow-Up

31. The United Nations shall request information from Member States regarding national disciplinary or criminal action taken with regard to repatriated civilian police officers and military observers. If no response is received, periodic reminders will be sent to the concerned Permanent Mission from the Department of Peacekeeping Operations. If still no response is forthcoming, appropriate steps shall be taken to bring the matter to the attention of the Government concerned at the highest possible levels to underscore the seriousness of the matter and to pursue it with a view to seeing that appropriate disciplinary steps are taken.

XIII. Final Provision

32. These Directives supersede *DPKO Administrative Procedure on Discipline for Military and Civilian Police Personnel in Mission Areas, directive MPS/651* and any other procedures and guidelines on this subject to the extent that they are inconsistent with these Directives.

Annex A

PROCEDURES FOR BOARD OF INQUIRY FOR DISCIPLINARY CASES

1. The Chairman of the Board of Inquiry, upon receipt of the convening order, shall immediately contact the Legal Officer, who shall provide an initial briefing and subsequently review the draft of the Board's report prior to its submission to the Head of Mission for decision and/or comments. The Chairman shall advise the Legal Officer of the Board's progress and submit the draft report of the Board for his/her review one week prior to the designated deadline. (See Attachment 1 for the format of a convening order and Attachment 2 for the format of a final report.)
2. A Board of Inquiry constituted to deal with an incident involving technical or other specialized matters may seek, if necessary, the written opinion of mission or outside experts in those matters.
3. Members of the field mission may be ordered to appear and testify as witnesses before a Board of Inquiry. Any other person, including local citizens and local police or military officers, may be requested to make a statement to the Board or answer its questions but is under no obligation to do so.
4. If possible, a majority of Board members shall be present when victims, witnesses or the subjects are being interviewed.
5. Witnesses shall be questioned individually by the Board and in the absence of other witnesses, so that information received from one may be compared with that received from others. If necessary, witnesses who have provided statements shall be questioned by the Board to clarify any ambiguities in their statements and to indicate to what extent, if any, they have knowledge of relevant facts not mentioned in their statements.
6. In the event of a witness or victim being under the age of 18, the Board of Inquiry shall question the minor in the presence of a guardian or an adult of the minor's choosing.
7. If a witness refuses to make a statement to the Board, the Board shall record that fact. If appropriate, it shall also state the reason(s) why certain persons were not called as witnesses before it.
8. If feasible and useful, the Chairman and members of the Board shall visit the scene of the incident and note any important features that could have a bearing on the case.
9. A Board must reach its findings only after it has considered all the evidence; they must be based upon and supported by the evidence contained in its report. The Board must give the matter the attention it deserves; i.e. conduct a proper investigation, including sound analysis, supporting rationale, and substantiated conclusions.
10. A Board of Inquiry shall make at least the following findings relating to the incident under investigation:
    - i. cause of incident;
    - ii. whether any person was responsible for the incident;
    - iii. whether any court action (prosecution or law suit) has been initiated;
    - iv. whether individual(s) concerned were on United Nations duty at the time of the incident;
    - v. extent of injuries, if sustained, substantiated by medical documentation;
    - vi. whether any mission regulations, rules, orders or instructions were contravened.

11. The Board shall make recommendations concerning decisions/measures to be taken by the United Nations, for example any measure that could help avoid the recurrence of an incident, such as specific additional safety precautions; or legislative or administrative action, such as repatriation of the subject(s), amending regulations, rules or instructions, or other administrative issuances.
12. The report of the Board of Inquiry shall be written in a simple and plain language. The Chairman must submit the draft report, together with all necessary documents and attachments, for review by the Legal Officer. Board of Inquiry reports that lack the necessary details in their consideration and merely refer to the preliminary investigation report shall be returned by the Legal Officer, or the Head of Mission, to the Board for reconsideration.
13. The Head of Mission shall review the final report of the Board of Inquiry and its recommendations, if any, in consultation with the appropriate personnel (e.g. Legal Officer, Medical Adviser) before determining the action to be taken.

ATTACHMENT 1

FORMAT FOR MISSION HEADQUARTERS BOARD OF INQUIRY CONVENING ORDER

[*Name of mission*]

Date:___________

To: [*distribution*]

From: [*name and title of Head of Mission*]

Subject: Convening Order: Mission Headquarters Board of Inquiry

1. In accordance with the Directives for Disciplinary Matters Involving Military Members of National Contingents (MD/), a mission headquarters Board of Inquiry is hereby convened to investigate and report on the accident/incident which occurred on the day of [*date*] at [*time*] hours at [*place*].

2. The Board is to submit the final report and 10 copies by [*date*].

3. Composition:

	Name	Title
Chairman:		
Member:		
Member:		
Secretary:		

Distribution:
[Chairman;
Members and Secretary of Board;
Legal Officer;
CMPO/CCPO or appropriate official of the related component;
Any other relevant official.]

ATTACHMENT 2

FORMAT FOR MISSION HEADQUARTERS BOARD OF INQUIRY REPORT

A mission headquarters Board of Inquiry report should be structured along the following lines:

a. Constitution: Cite the convening order; the time, date and place of the incident; and the period during which the Board conducted its proceedings;

b. Description of the incident: Present the objective facts of the incident obtained from the available evidence, with full reference to the sources used, including details of duty being performed at the time;

c. Deliberations: Present the main issues to be addressed when assessing the incident and reaching substantiated conclusions;

d. Findings and conclusions: Address the issues raised by presenting the Board's findings and conclusions based on the available evidence and relevant mission headquarters/unit orders, directives, regulations or SOPs.

e. Recommendations: Recommend any remedial or preventive measures to avoid a similar incident;

f. Signatures: Affix the signatures of the Chairman and members of the Board.

g. Annexes: Attach as annexes the following:

 i. Convening order;

 ii. MP/UN civilian security or other police or investigating authority's report, with original photographs;

 iii. List of persons present at or involved in the incident, giving name, rank, unit and ID number for United Nations personnel and distinguishing them from other persons, whose full name, occupation and address must be listed;

 iv. Statements and reports of witnesses;

 v. Any additional relevant documents or statements, including all medical reports and technical inspection reports (e.g. weapon inspection reports, vehicle inspection reports);

 vi. Any maps or sketches of the scene of the incident;

 vii. Any claims, local police reports, pending proceedings or actual decisions of local courts;

 viii. Detailed description of property destroyed or damaged, attaching any available damage/discrepancy reports;

 ix. Relevant copies of mission headquarters/unit orders, directives, regulations, SOPs, etc.

Annex B

GUIDELINES FOR PRELIMINARY INVESTIGATIONS

Investigating Allegations of Serious Misconduct Involving Military Members of National Contingents, Military Observers and Civilian Police Officers Serving in United Nations Field Missions

I. Introduction

1. These guidelines are intended to serve as a guide for the conduct of preliminary investigations into acts, omissions and negligence amounting to serious misconduct involving military members of national contingents, military observers, and civilian police officers serving in United Nations field missions, and as referred to in the *Directives for Disciplinary Matters Involving Military Members of National Contingents* and *Directives for Disciplinary Matters Involving Civilian Police Officers and Military Observers.*
2. To the extent possible, preliminary investigations shall be conducted by appropriate authorities with the relevant expertise in the category of misconduct being investigated. Preliminary investigations shall be conducted in accordance with internationally recognized principles of due process and fairness.

II. Purpose

3. The purpose of the preliminary investigation is to establish the facts of the case.

III. Planning of an Investigation

Step One

4. Define an investigation work plan, listing the steps necessary for conducting the investigation, such as:
   - Witness list;
   - Document list and/or "other evidence" list;
   - The means to be used to collect the evidence;
   - Locations to be investigated;
   - Possible travel arrangements;
   - Local authorities to be consulted;
   - Technical expertise/opinion needed;
   - Estimated time frame;
   - Cost of investigation; etc.

Step Two

5. Discuss the investigation work plan among the investigating team to obtain a common understanding on how to proceed. Go over the procedures outlined below to ensure that there is a consensus on the methodology.
6. Clearly identify responsibilities of each team member and division of tasks.

Step Three

7. Identify any mission regulations, rules, orders or instructions that may have been contravened, as well as any applicable laws.

IV. Confidentiality

8. The investigation shall be conducted with the greatest regard to confidentiality. Authorized disclosure, only under certain circumstances, shall be permitted. Unauthorized disclosure constitutes misconduct for which disciplinary measures may be imposed.
9. Provisions of confidentiality shall apply to the following:
   (i) The initial complaint or report (hereinafter complaint);
   (ii) The identity of the person who has made the complaint;
   (iii) The identity of the subject;
   (iv) The identity of witnesses;
   (v) The victim.
10. The investigators shall be responsible for ensuring that the information provided in the complaint, the identity of the complainant and the subject, and witnesses and their statements are not accidentally, negligently or wilfully disclosed. The investigator(s) will be obliged to take all appropriate measures for the protection of this information.
11. Authorization for disclosure will be given by the Head of Mission.

Confidentiality of Complaint

12. Although the information provided in the complaint should be confidential, it will be used for the conduct of the investigation and for the conduct of administrative, disciplinary or judicial proceedings.

Confidentiality of Complainant/Victim

13. Circumstances under which authorized disclosure of the identity of the complainant/victim can be made are as follows:
   (i) The complainant/victim has consented to the disclosure (see form attached as Sample 1);
   (ii) Such disclosure is necessary for administrative, disciplinary and judicial proceedings;
   (iii) Authorized disclosure can also be made when a false complaint or report is made. Making a willfully false allegation constitutes misconduct and, therefore, disciplinary measures may be imposed against the complainant. Consequently, for the subsequent administrative and disciplinary proceedings the identity of the person who has, with bad intent, made a false complaint may be disclosed.

Confidentiality of Subject

14. Identity of the subject may be disclosed for the purposes of furthering the investigation and for the imposition of administrative, disciplinary or judicial proceedings.

Confidentiality of Witnesses

15. Witnesses shall be provided confidentiality, if they request, to the extent possible.

V. Interviewing Complainants, Subject(s) and Witnesses

Sequence of Interviews

16. The sequence of interviews should be at the discretion of the investigator(s). Normally, the sequence is as follows:
   (i) Complainant(s) and/or victim(s);

(ii) Subject (the person in question);
(iii) Witnesses;
(iv) Follow-up interviews with complainant/victim and the subject, if necessary.

17. Sometimes it may be appropriate to interview some or all of the witnesses before interviewing the subject (and reviewing other evidence, such as documentary or physical evidence) in order to give him/her an effective opportunity to respond to all the allegations.
18. The investigator(s) shall conduct as many interviews or make as many contacts with witnesses and/or subject(s) in order to support a rational finding of facts.

Interview Site

19. It is preferable to conduct interviews in a place where other employees will not be able to see who is being interviewed and how long the interview takes.
20. This may require that the interview be conducted away from the job site, such as at a hotel conference room, or perhaps at the home of the interviewee.
21. In-person interviews are preferable to telephone interviews, which are not optimal because investigators need to be able to see the person to make an assessment of credibility. Telephone interviews may be appropriate for non-crucial witnesses, when an in-person interview would be too difficult or expensive.

Language of Interview

22. All interviews shall be in the preferred language of the interviewee. If an interpreter is necessary, one shall be provided. The interpreter shall remain impartial and objective in the conduct of the interview.

Interviewing Minors

23. When a minor is to be interviewed, an appropriate adult must be notified as soon as possible. Minors must be interviewed in the presence of an adult of the minor's choosing.[46]

Third Parties

24. A third party whose presence is deemed necessary by the investigator(s) (interpreters, adults accompanying minors, etc.) shall be obliged to maintain full confidentiality, and shall sign a certification to that effect, with respect to the matter discussed and to all the information gathered during the interview. The role of a third party in an interview is solely to facilitate the interview.

Interviewing Victims

25. Interviewing a victim of an act of serious misconduct shall be done with sensitivity and understanding.

Interviewing Subjects

26. The subject of an investigation should be advised about the matter under investigation and any specific allegation made against him/her.
27. The subject has an obligation to cooperate with the investigation and to answer questions truthfully and honestly. The subject should be given the opportunity to speak and to provide information in his/her own words without unnecessary interruptions by the investigator(s). The subject may offer such information, documents or other materials as (s)he wishes to

46 A minor is defined according to the applicable local laws. However, the international legal standard, as defined by Article 1 of the Convention of the Rights of the Child, is that a minor is "a person under 18 years of age". [Note: this footnote appears in the original document as footnote '5'].

assist in the inquiry. The subject may name witnesses on his/her behalf and in favour of his/her contentions.

28. The interviewing investigator(s) can question the subject on all the aspects deemed relevant for the conduct of the investigation, in any rhetorical manner, in a free conversation or in a strict question-and-answer format.

Interviewing Witnesses

29. Witnesses who are members of the field mission are obliged to cooperate with the investigation and must reply honestly and truthfully to questions. A witness acknowledgement form shall be completed and signed. (See form attached as Sample 2.) Witness acknowledgement forms should be made available in local languages when dealing with local witnesses.

How to Interview

30. Prepare an outline of topics to be covered during the interview, e.g. What is the complaint? What is in dispute? What relevant information does the interviewee possess? As a general rule, investigators should address non-threatening topics first and hard topics last.

Structure of the Interview

Introductory questions

31. These are examples of introductory questions:
    - The investigators should introduce themselves;
    - Inform interviewees of the purpose of the interview;
    - Stress that no conclusions have been reached (the goal is to hear all sides of the story);
    - Put the interviewee at ease by first establishing a rapport with him/her by asking general questions on non-threatening topics, such as general background, age, employment history, address, etc.

Questions about the matter under investigation

32. Investigators should not be afraid to ask the tough questions. If the interviewee is not cooperating fully, investigators should politely but persistently seek an answer to their questions.
33. It is important to ask the interviewee if they know of any documents related to the matter. The investigators should always define what they mean by "documents", which could include memos, letters, notes, calendars, e-mails, computer files, voice mails, tape recordings, diary notes, etc.
    - Use the "Funnel Method" for questioning:
      o Open-ended questions
    - Who? What? Where? When? Why? How? Describe. Explain. Tell me.
    - First ask broad, open-ended questions designed to elicit an expansive, narrative response.
    - Seldom interrupt a witness. As they talk, investigator(s) should take notes on areas that they may want to explore in further detail later. If they learn of a new topic, they should make a note of it and come back to it later.
      o Follow-up
    - Once the interviewee has answered the open-ended question, follow-up by asking about each incident/conversation/issue separately. Ask for details.
      o Follow-up on non-responsive answers

Closing questions

34. These are examples of closing questions:
    - Is there anything else that we have not discussed that you think is relevant to this matter? (Interviewee should be able to contact the investigators later if they think of or have additional information or documents related to the matter.)

- Who else should we interview?
- Are there any documents relating to this issue? (Documents may include e-mails, personal letters, faxes, medical records, etc.)
- Remind subjects and witnesses that retaliation against victims and complainants constitutes serious misconduct.
- Request that the interviewee keep the matter confidential in order to protect the integrity of the investigation.
- Thank the person for his/her cooperation.

What not to ask

35. Investigators should avoid aggressive, leading questions especially at the beginning of the interview. For example, a friendly, conversational approach works better than an aggressive, cross-examination. The aim is to get the interviewee to talk as much as possible in order to obtain as much information as possible, look for inconsistencies in the interviewees' stories and make credibility determinations.
36. Avoid leading or close-ended questions (especially at the beginning of an interview and at the beginning of a category of questions). For example, "Did you see John drinking at the Post Office?"
37. Avoid compound questions that would allow the interviewee to truthfully answer only part of the question. For example, "Was he drunk when you saw him at the Post Office?" Answer: "I did not see him at the Post Office."
38. Avoid legalese; use simple language.
39. Avoid questions that allow the interviewee to define a term in his or her own way, e.g. "Was he just having a good time?"

Taping of Interviews

40. Normally, it is not obligatory to conduct tape recordings of interviews. However, interviews could be taped by investigator(s) for their own convenience. It allows the investigator(s) to focus more on listening to the interviewees' answers, rather than taking copious notes. All tape recordings must be transcribed and summarized into a formal record of the interview, which will require a signature by the interviewee attesting to its accuracy, as mentioned in paragraph 39 below.
41. However, transcribing the tapes of interviews could be time-consuming. Quality of the tape could be poor, which could be a critical problem if the investigators are relying on the tape and have not taken notes. Also, taping of an interview could potentially inhibit the interviewee and have a "chilling effect". The investigators should make every effort to put the interviewee at ease so that they feel at ease to speak candidly.

Written Statements

42. The investigator may request an interviewee to furnish a written statement, or an interviewee may choose to make a written statement. The interviewee may provide this written statement in addition to an interview.
43. The statement shall be written in simple and plain language. The statement should be written in the first person (singular or plural, depending on how many persons are involved).
44. The language of the written statement shall be determined according to its likely use. For administrative action or disciplinary measures to be taken by the United Nations, the language of the statement shall be the working language of the mission. If a criminal prosecution seems probable, it may be considered to translate the statement into the working language of the court that will be in charge of conducting the trial. If possible, the language of the statement should be in the interviewee's preferred language.

45. The interviewee shall acknowledge the accuracy of the written statement by initialling it at the bottom of every page and signing at the end of the statement. If the interviewee decides to amend any part of the statement, (s)he shall initial the amendment as well.
46. The person shall sign and date the statement in the investigator's presence.
47. No threats or coercion of any kind may be used to obtain a written statement.

VI. Collection of Evidence

Forms of Evidence

48. Forms of evidence include but are not limited to:
    - Documentary evidence
    - Demonstrative/physical evidence
    - Statements by complainants, subjects and witnesses
    - Experts' opinion

Means of Obtaining Evidence

49. Means of obtaining evidence include but are not limited to:
    - Observation
    - Forensic research and analysis
    - Interviews
50. When attending the scene/location of an incident, the investigator shall document what he/she sees, not what he/she thinks and take all necessary steps to protect the scene. The notes and reports shall be done in a chronological order and shall include no opinions, no analysis, or no conclusions; just the facts.
51. The evidence observed, its location, condition, or anything remarkable about the evidence shall be included in the investigation report. If necessary, photographs shall be taken or a sketch/diagram made.

Safeguarding Evidence

52. Evidence should be duly logged and secured. The log should indicate where and how each piece of evidence was obtained.
53. When an act of serious misconduct that may amount to a criminal offence has occurred, investigator(s) should pay particular attention to the collection and safeguarding of evidence, as it may serve as a basis for a subsequent judicial process.

Validating Information

54. The goal of the preliminary investigation is to find one or more facts to establish the existence or non-existence of a key element of proof of the allegation. Furthermore, a determination needs to be made if any relevant rules, directives or standard administrative or operating procedures were contravened.
55. Once the initial fact-finding has been conducted, there is a need to establish the accuracy and authenticity of the evidence such as testimony, observations, records, and other documentary and physical evidence. Throughout the investigation, evidence obtained shall be checked against the investigative plan by verifying its accuracy. Initial evidence shall be checked against new evidence obtained. Conflicting testimony, information or material matters will be resolved by collecting additional evidence from other competent witnesses and sources.
56. In determining credibility of witnesses, account shall be taken of their interest, bias, integrity, reputation, the manner in which they gained their information, and any possible

motive. The demeanour of the witness/subject being interviewed should also be taken into account when determining credibility.

57. Through this continuous process of the validation of evidence obtained, the investigator(s) shall ensure that the findings and conclusions of the investigation are fully supported by evidence. If any piece of evidence is ambiguous, it needs to be weighed. This means that the investigator(s) needs to reflect on the evidence with regard to the following factors: credibility; logic; plausibility; completeness; and persuasiveness. The standard of proof used by the investigator(s) is the preponderance of the evidence (50 plus 1).

58. Acting neutral and impartial in the process of weighing the evidence is crucial for the persuasiveness of the investigation's findings.

VII. Report of Preliminary Investigation

59. The Investigation Report is the summary of the work that has preceded it and its findings and conclusions are based on the evidence obtained. Each fact expressed in the Investigation Report will be fully and substantially supported by evidence. No evidence shall be included in the report that has not undergone extensive review and testing.

The investigator(s) shall ensure that facts are backed by evidence and supporting rationale.

Format and Content of Preliminary Investigation Reports

60. The report of the preliminary investigation generally shall contain the following major sections:
    (a) Title Page
    (b) Executive Summary
    (c) Methodology
    (d) Background Information
    (e) Investigative Details
    (f) Issues
    (g) Finding of Facts
    (h) Annexes

(a) Title Page

61. The title page contains the official title of the case. It shall contain a warning that the report is the property of the United Nations field mission and is not to be reproduced or disclosed to unauthorized persons. The details of the reporting investigator(s) (name, rank and title), the date and the distribution shall be shown on the title page.

(b) Executive Summary

62. The Executive Summary shall specify the nature of the allegation(s); the methodology used for the investigation; the violation (if any) of mission regulations, rules, orders or instructions, as well as any applicable laws; and the results of the fact-finding.

63. The Executive Summary should also include the date, time, place and other specifics of the incident, including who committed what, when and where. The Executive Summary is intended to give the reader a quick overview of the case from its inception to the writing of the report. Every statement in the summary must be fully substantiated in the body of the report. It must not include any opinions or conclusions of the investigator(s); only facts or statements substantiated in the body of the report will be presented in the Executive Summary.

(c) Methodology

64. This section shall contain a brief description of the methodology used to conduct the investigation, including locations that were investigated; witnesses interviewed; local authorities that were consulted; technical expertise/opinion sought; documents analysed; etc.

(d) Background Information

65. This shall provide details of the allegation(s) and who made them; a narrative of the context in which the incident occurred, without mentioning evidence at this stage; and any other necessary background information.

(e) Investigative Details

66. This section shall provide a detailed account of the conduct of the investigation and the evidence collected. This should be presented in a logical form, with supporting information provided in annexes to the report. A chronology of the investigation should be part of this section.

(f) Issues

67. A discussion of any issues that may have come up during the investigation.

(g) Findings of Fact

68. This section shall provide an analysis of the facts as established by the corroborating evidence obtained in the course of the investigation. This section must contain the supporting rationale for the findings of the investigators. If the evidence is ambiguous, the investigator(s) should explain what criteria were used to weigh the evidence and why a specific conclusion was drawn.

(g) Annexes

69. The report can contain as many annexes as necessary. Normally these would contain interview lists; statements of the subject and the witnesses; list of evidence; etc.

VIII. Submission of Report

70. The report of the preliminary investigation shall be submitted to the Head of Mission as soon as it has been completed. The distribution of the report, as indicated on the Title Page, will also be done concurrently. Normally, the report will be submitted only to the Head of Mission or his/her designee.
71. On the basis of the findings of the preliminary investigation, the Head of Mission may either convene a mission headquarters Board of Inquiry, or (s)he may conclude that no act of serious misconduct occurred.

SAMPLE 1

SAMPLE CONSENT TO DISCLOSURE FORM

NAME:	DATE OF ENTRY INTO MISSION AREA:
TITLE/FUNCTION:	END OF MISSION DATE:
UN ID NO:	TELEPHONE CONTACT:

I hereby consent to the disclosure of my name to the relevant United Nations authorities for the purpose of taking appropriate action on my complaint. I understand that the information will be treated with confidentiality, and shared only as needed.

Signature or Thumb Print ______________________________

Witness (for thumb print) ______________________________

Date: ____________________

SAMPLE 2

SAMPLE WITNESS ACKNOWLEDGEMENT FORM

NAME	DATE OF ENTRY INTO MISSION AREA:
TITLE/FUNCTION:	END OF MISSION DATE:
UN ID NO:	TELEPHONE CONTACT:

I hereby certify that this is a true and accurate reflection of my statement given to

Mr./Ms.____
(print name)

regarding Case No. __________________________________

I understand that the information will be treated with confidentiality, and shared only as needed.

Signature or Thumb Print __________________________________

Witness (for thumb print) __________________________________

Date: ____________________

30

Secretary-General's Bulletin: Special Measures for Protection from Sexual Exploitation and Sexual Abuse

Prefatory Note

On 9 October 2003, the Secretary-General promulgated the Bulletin entitled 'Special Measures for Protection from Sexual Exploitation and Sexual Abuse' (Bulletin).[1] This was done in consultation with Executive Heads of separately administered organs and programmes of the UN. The Bulletin seeks to prevent and address cases of sexual exploitation and abuse and therefore reinforces General Assembly resolution 57/306.[2]

The Secretary-General, as the chief administrative officer of the UN, has the power under Article 97 of the Charter of the United Nations (Charter) to make administrative issuances in the form of bulletins that bind staff. The general rules regarding their preparation, content, and effect can be found in the Secretary-General's Bulletin entitled 'Procedures for the Promulgation of Administrative Issuances'.[3]

The obligations in the Bulletin bind UN staff directly[4] since all staff are governed by relevant UN rules, regulations, and administrative issuances under the Staff Regulations and Rules. Section 3.2 outlines the specific standards expected of UN staff, which reiterates the existing general obligations under the Staff Regulations and Rules. The obligations in the Bulletin bind experts on mission due to a revision of the individual undertaking they sign, and bind military members of national contingents through the revisions made to the model Memorandum of Understanding (model MOU) between the UN and contributing States.[5] Consequently, the Bulletin binds all members of a UN peace operation.

The term 'sexual exploitation' for the purposes of the Bulletin means:

> any actual or attempted abuse of a position of vulnerability, differential power, or trust, for sexual purposes, including, but not limited to, profiting monetarily, socially or politically from the sexual exploitation of another. Similarly, the term 'sexual abuse' means the actual or threatened physical intrusion of a sexual nature, whether by force or under unequal or coercive conditions.[6]

Sexual exploitation and abuse greatly impacts upon the legitimacy and integrity of a peace operation and can impede a mission's capacity to implement its mandate due to a loss of trust by the local population. Specific groups, such as refugees and internally displaced persons, are also particularly vulnerable to such exploitation.

The problem of sexual exploitation and abuse by UN personnel has been raised since the early 1990s. Concern was expressed in 1992 at the increase in prostitution during the United Nations Transitional Administration for Cambodia (UNTAC) and a year later reports surfaced of sexual

---

1 Secretary General's Bulletin, 'Special Measures for Protection from Sexual Exploitation and Sexual Abuse', UN Doc ST/SGB/2003/13, 9 October 2003, entered into force 15 October 2003 (hereafter Bulletin).

2 GA Res 57/306 of 15 April 2003; Bulletin (n 1), Preamble. For the UN statistics on sexual exploitation and abuse, see 'Report of the Secretary-General: Special Measures for Protection from Sexual Exploitation and Sexual Abuse', UN Doc A/70/729, 16 February 2016 and the Office of Internal Oversight Services website for their annual reports recording allegations of sexual exploitation and abuse as well as investigations carried out by the office <https://oios.un.org/page?slug=annual-reports> accessed 1 November 2017. For a timeline of the UN's initiatives to address sexual exploitation and abuse, see <https://conduct.unmissions.org/> accessed 1 November 2017. For a comprehensive list of documents issued by the UN on its efforts to address sexual exploitation and abuse by peacekeepers, see <http://www.codebluecampaign.com/un-docs/> accessed 1 November 2017.

3 UN Doc ST/SGB/1997/1, 28 May 1997, entered into force 1 June 1997.

4 Bulletin (n 1), Section 2.1.

5 See ch 3 above.

6 Bulletin (n 1), Section 1.

exploitation during the UN Operation in Mozambique (ONUMOZ). Issues have also been raised about the sexual activities of UN peacekeepers in Somalia and Timor-Leste. In 2002, reports by groups such as Human Rights Watch focused international attention on the behaviour of UN International Police Task Force (IPTF) monitors in Bosnia and Herzegovina. Then, in 2003, the issue received prominence due to concerns of sexual exploitation of refugees by aid workers in West Africa. Numerous media reports subsequently surfaced in 2004 of sexual exploitation committed by UN peacekeepers in the Democratic Republic of the Congo. In 2016, the Secretary-General reported that in 2015 '69 allegations of sexual exploitation and abuse were reported in nine current and one closed peacekeeping missions'.[7] The matter of stopping sexual exploitation and abuse by peacekeepers remains an important part of the Secretary-General's policy relating to peace operations.

UN forces conducting operations under UN operational authority and control are prohibited from committing acts of sexual exploitation and abuse, and have a special duty of care towards women and children, pursuant to Section 7 of the 'Secretary-General's Bulletin: Observance by United Nations Forces of International Humanitarian Law'.[8]

In relation to sexual harassment during UN peace operations, the Secretary-General's Bulletin entitled 'Prohibition of Discrimination, Harassment, including Sexual Harassment, and Abuse of Authority'[9] sets forth policies and procedures for handling cases of sexual harassment involving UN staff members. Separately administered organs and programmes of the UN have promulgated similar policies and procedures.[10]

The Bulletin forms part of the internal law of the UN and breaches of the obligations contained therein can lead only to internal action by the UN. In the case of staff this would lead to disciplinary measures under the Staff Regulations and Rules[11] following the established rules and procedures for dealing with cases of staff misconduct. Possible disciplinary measures include summary dismissal, since sexual exploitation and sexual abuse constitute acts of serious misconduct. In the case of experts on mission, including UN civilian police, the UN can take administrative action and/or disciplinary measures under the Directives for Disciplinary Matters involving Civilian Police Officers and Military Observers.[12] In the case of military members of national contingents, the UN can only take administrative action such as repatriation under the Directives for Disciplinary Matters involving Military Members of National Contingents.[13] Any disciplinary measures against military members of national contingents must be taken by the contributing State concerned. The Secretariat policy on conduct and discipline also makes the point that Member States have the responsibility of completing investigations of sexual exploitation and sexual abuse in six months unless there are exceptional circumstances.[14]

Sexual exploitation and abuse can also constitute criminal acts. However, the UN itself cannot take any criminal action against a member of a UN peace operation. Section 5 of the Bulletin addresses this issue by stating that '[i]f, after proper investigation, there is evidence to support allegations of sexual exploitation or sexual abuse, these cases may, upon consultation with the Office of Legal Affairs, be referred to national authorities for criminal prosecution'. This Section must, however, be read in the light of the relevant provisions in the model Status-of-Forces Agreement (model SOFA)[15] regarding criminal jurisdiction over members of a peace operation, and the relevant provisions in the model Memorandum of Understanding (model MOU) regarding the exercise of jurisdiction by contributing States over military members of national contingents. That exercise of jurisdiction includes the obligation of contributing States to investigate, and, if appropriate,

7 'Report of the Secretary-General: Special Measures for Protection from Sexual Exploitation and Sexual Abuse', UN Doc A/70/729, 16 February 2016, [6].

8 UN Doc ST/SGB/1999/13, 6 August 1999, entered into force 12 August 1999. See ch 15 above.

9 UN Doc ST/SGB/2008/5, 11 February 2008, entered into force 1 March 2008.

10 See, for example, UNICEF Division of Personnel, 'Sexual Harassment in the UNICEF Workplace', 11 March 1994 <http://www.un.org/womenwatch/osagi/pdf/UNICEFpolicy.PDF> accessed 1 November 2017.

11 See ch 25 above.

12 See ch 29 above.

13 See ch 28 above.

14 See, for example, the Secretariat policy at <https://conduct.unmissions.org/enforcement-investigations> accessed 31 December 2018.

15 See ch 2 above.

prosecute members of their contingents who commit acts of sexual exploitation and abuse where those acts amount to criminal acts.[16]

To provide comprehensive assistance to victims of sexual exploitation and abuse by UN personnel, the General Assembly, in resolution 62/214,[17] adopted the 'United Nations Comprehensive Strategy on Assistance and Support to Victims of Sexual Exploitation and Abuse by United Nations Staff and Related Personnel' (Strategy).[18] The Strategy aims to assist and support victims whilst the Bulletin aims to prevent and address cases of sexual exploitation and abuse.

A 2015 report, completed by a special panel to investigate allegations of sexual exploitation and abuse in the Central African Republic by peacekeepers, damned the UN for its 'institutional failure to respond immediately and effectively to incidents of sexual violence'.[19] The report went on to state that despite numerous UN attempts to investigate and stop sexual exploitation and sexual abuse there is a 'perception that there is little risk or consequence for those who choose to exploit the most vulnerable of society'.[20]

In response to the report, the Secretary-General initiated several system-wide measures to improve UN action to address sexual exploitation and abuse, including appointing a Special Coordinator to improve the UN's response to sexual exploitation and abuse.[21] The Security Council also took note of the report in resolution 2272[22]—its first resolution dedicated to dealing with sexual exploitation and abuse by peacekeepers. That resolution reaffirmed the Council's 'support for the United Nations zero tolerance policy on all forms of sexual exploitation and abuse',[23] and welcomed the 'Organization's prevention, reporting, enforcement and remedial action in order to promote greater accountability'.[24] In June 2016, the Secretary-General described the UN Secretariat's comprehensive strategy 'for strengthening the United Nations response to sexual exploitation and abuse' and how it is being implemented.[25]

That Strategy, which is founded on the UN's zero tolerance policy, has six components:

> (a) Member State engagement and emerging best practices in United Nations troop and police deployments; (b) enhanced unified system-wide approach; (c) strengthened prevention, including increased awareness-raising, outreach to host communities, community-based reporting mechanisms and augmented training to United Nations personnel; (d) enhanced victim-centred response, encompassing victim services and protection; (e) robust enforcement through strengthened reporting, thorough and coordinated investigation and transparent judicial and public accountability; and (f) greater focus on monitoring and reporting on sexual exploitation and abuse by non-United Nations forces.[26]

The Secretary-General explained in the June 2016 report how the strategy is being developed, applied, and assessed. After the Secretary-General's June report, the General Assembly expressed its support for the UN's zero tolerance policy,[27] and highlighted the importance of 'providing expeditious support to victims ... [and] for victims to receive immediate basic assistance and support in accordance with their individual needs'.[28]

The Secretary-General, in his 28 February 2017 report, articulated a new approach to improving preventing and responding sexual exploitation and abuse.[29] He proposed a four-part strategy: (a) putting the rights and dignity of victims first; (b) ending impunity for those guilty of sexual

---

16 See ch 3 above.

17 GA Res 62/214 of 21 December 2007.

18 Ibid, Annex.

19 Marie Deschamps, Hassan B Jallow, and Yasmin Sooka, 'Taking Action on Sexual Exploitation and Abuse by Peacekeepers: Report of an Independent Review on Sexual Exploitation and Abuse by International Peacekeeping Forces in the Central African Republic', 17 December 2015, 5 (hereafter CAR Report) <http://www.un.org/News/dh/infocus/centafricrepub/Independent-Review-Report.pdf> accessed 1 November 2017.

20 Ibid, 5.

21 'Report of the Secretary-General: Special Measures for Protection from Sexual Exploitation and Sexual Abuse', UN Doc A/70/729, 16 February 2016.

22 See ch 20 above.

23 SC Res 2722 (2016) of 11 March 2016, Preamble [4]. See ch 20 above.

24 Ibid, [8].

25 'Report of the Secretary General: Combating Sexual Exploitation and Abuse', UN Doc A/71/97, 23 June 2016, [6].

26 Ibid.

27 GA Res 70/286 of 17 June 2016, [71].

28 Ibid, [75] and [76].

29 'Report of the Secretary-General: Special Measures for Protection from Sexual Exploitation and Abuse: A New Approach', UN Doc A/71/818, 28 February 2017 (hereafter A New Approach).

exploitation and abuse; (c) developing a multi-stakeholder network to engage civil society and external partners; and (d) improving strategic communications to raise awareness of sexual exploitation and abuse.[30]

In relation to putting victims first, the Secretary-General has identified three measures: (1) appointing victims' rights advocates;[31] (2) improving prevention measures including carrying out risk assessments prior to operational deployments and establishing more effective complaints procedures;[32] and (3) developing a Secretary-General's protocol on preventing exploitation and abuse 'which could include, for example, strict guidelines regarding non-fraternization and certification of predeployment training for every individual as a precondition to deployment'.[33] The Victims' Rights Advocates have been appointed to ensure that 'victims who come forward with allegations are treated with the respect, sensitivity and compassion that they deserve …'[34]

There are four components to the Secretary-General's strategy to end impunity: (1) better reporting;[35] (2) strengthened investigations;[36] (3) improved follow-up and accountability;[37] and (4) 'a voluntary compact between the Secretary-General and Member States supporting United Nations operations'.[38] One of the key provisions in the compact would be to '[r]equire individuals assigned to all United Nations field-based activities to carry the "no excuses" card that restates our rules [concerning the prohibition against sexual exploitation and abuse] and provides contact details for reporting allegations'.[39] The February 2017 report also contains a system-wide matrix which outlines the responsibilities of UN entities to respond to sexual exploitation and abuse, as well as responsibility and accountability measures to prevent sexual exploitation and abuse.[40]

The developments in relation to sexual exploitation and abuse reflect the international community's concern relating to the trafficking of persons, especially women and children.[41] More specifically, the matter of trafficking is dealt with by the Protocol to Prevent, Suppress and Punish Trafficking in Persons, Especially Women and Children.[42] In 2002, the UN High Commissioner for Human Rights also published the Recommended Principles and Guidelines on Human Rights and Human Trafficking.[43] In the context of UN peace operations, Guideline 10 is especially relevant as it concerns the obligations of peacekeepers and civilian police in regard to trafficking, and lists a number of actions that States, intergovernmental, and non-governmental organisations should consider in the context of peace operations.[44]

Reference

Title	Secretary-General's Bulletin: Special Measures for Protection from Sexual Exploitation and Sexual Abuse
Author	Secretary-General of the United Nations
Date of Bulletin	9 October 2003
Entered into force	15 October 2003
Source	UN Doc ST/SGB/2003/13
Full Text	<http://www.unhcr.org/en-au/protection/operations/405ac6614/secretary-generals-bulletin-special-measures-protection-sexual-exploitation.html>[45]

30 Ibid, [13].
31 Ibid, [27]–[35].
32 Ibid, [61].
33 Ibid, [36].
34 Preventing Sexual Exploitation and Abuse <https://www.un.org/preventing-sexual-exploitation-and-abuse/content/victim-assistance> accessed 15 August 2018.
35 A New Approach (n 29), [40]–[44].
36 Ibid, [45]–[48].
37 Ibid, [49]–[54].
38 Ibid, [57].
39 Ibid, [59](iv).
40 Ibid, Annex V.
41 For more information on UN peace operations and trafficking, visit the Trafficking section of the Peacekeeping Resource Hub <http://research.un.org/en/peacekeeping-community> accessed 1 November 2017.
42 Protocol to Prevent, Suppress and Punish Trafficking in Persons, Especially Women and Children, supplementing the United Nations Convention against Transnational Organized Crime (adopted 15 November 2000) 2225 UNTS 209.
43 Addendum to the Report of the United Nations Office of the High Commissioner for Human Rights to the Economic and Social Council, 'Recommended Principles and Guidelines on Human Rights and Human Trafficking', UN Doc E/2002/68/Add1, 20 May 2002. The Guidelines are an addendum to the report.
44 Ibid, Guideline 10.
45 Accessed 1 November 2017.

Secretary-General's Bulletin: Special Measures for Protection from Sexual Exploitation and Sexual Abuse[46]

(Extracts)

The Secretary-General, for the purpose of preventing and addressing cases of sexual exploitation and sexual abuse, and taking into consideration General Assembly resolution 57/306 of 15 April 2003, "Investigation into sexual exploitation of refugees by aid workers in West Africa", promulgates the following in consultation with Executive Heads of separately administered organs and programmes of the United Nations:

SECTION 1

Definitions

For the purposes of the present bulletin, the term "sexual exploitation" means any actual or attempted abuse of a position of vulnerability, differential power, or trust, for sexual purposes, including, including, but not limited to, profiting monetarily, socially or politically from the sexual exploitation of another. Similarly, the term "sexual abuse" means the actual or threatened physical intrusion of a sexual nature, whether by force or under unequal or coercive conditions.

SECTION 2

Scope of application

2.1 The present bulletin shall apply to all staff of the United Nations, including staff of separately administered organs and programmes of the United Nations.

2.2 United Nations forces conducting operations under United Nations command and control are prohibited from committing acts of sexual exploitation and sexual abuse, and have a particular duty of care towards women and children, pursuant to section 7 of Secretary-General's bulletin ST/SGB/1999/13, entitled "Observance by United Nations forces of international humanitarian law".

2.3 Secretary-General's bulletin ST/SGB/253, entitled "Promotion of equal treatment of men and women in the Secretariat and prevention of sexual harassment", and the related administrative instruction set forth policies and procedures for handling cases of sexual harassment in the Secretariat of the United Nations. Separately administered organs and programmes of the United Nations have promulgated similar policies and procedures.

Section 3

Prohibition of sexual exploitation and sexual abuse

3.1 Sexual exploitation and sexual abuse violate universally recognized international legal norms and standards and have always been unacceptable behaviour and prohibited conduct for United Nations staff. Such conduct is prohibited by the United Nations Staff Regulations and Rules.

3.2 In order to further protect the most vulnerable populations, especially women and children, the following specific standards which reiterate existing general obligations under the United Nations Staff Regulations and Rules, are promulgated:

(a) Sexual exploitation and sexual abuse constitute acts of serious misconduct and are therefore grounds for disciplinary measures, including summary dismissal;

(b) Sexual activity with children (persons under the age of 18) is prohibited regardless of the age of majority or age of consent locally. Mistaken belief in the age of a child is not a defence;

(c) Exchange of money, employment, goods or services for sex, including sexual favours or other forms of humiliating, degrading or exploitative behaviour, is prohibited. This includes any exchange of assistance that is due to beneficiaries of assistance;

(d) Sexual relationships between United Nations staff and beneficiaries of assistance, since they are based on inherently unequal power dynamics, undermine the credibility and integrity of the work of the United Nations and are strongly discouraged;

(e) Where a United Nations staff member develops concerns or suspicions regarding sexual exploitation or sexual abuse by a fellow worker, whether in the same agency or not and whether or not within the United Nations system, he or she must report such concerns via established reporting mechanisms;

(f) United Nations staff are obliged to create and maintain an environment that prevents sexual exploitation and sexual abuse. Managers at all levels have a particular responsibility to support and develop systems that maintain this environment.

3.3 The standards set out above are not intended to be an exhaustive list. Other types of sexually exploitative or sexually abusive behaviour may be grounds for administrative action or disciplinary measures, including summary dismissal, pursuant to the United Nations Staff Regulations and Rules.

Section 4

Duties of Heads of Departments, Offices and Missions

4.1 The Head of Department, Office or Mission, as appropriate, shall be responsible for creating and maintaining an environment that prevents sexual exploitation and sexual abuse, and shall take appropriate measures for this purpose. In particular, the Head of Department, Office or Mission shall inform his or her staff of the contents of the present bulletin and ascertain that each staff member receives a copy thereof.

4.2 The Head of Department, Office or Mission shall be responsible for taking appropriate action in cases where there is reason to believe that any of the standards listed in section 3.2 above have been violated or any behaviour referred to in section 3.3 above has occurred. This action shall be taken in accordance with established rules and procedures for dealing with cases of staff misconduct.

4.3 The Head of Department, Office or Mission shall appoint an official, at a sufficiently high level, to serve as a focal point for receiving reports on cases of sexual exploitation and sexual abuse. With respect to Missions, the staff of the Mission and the local population shall be properly informed of the existence and role of the focal point and of how to contact him or her. All reports of sexual exploitation and sexual abuse shall be handled in a confidential manner in order to protect the rights of all involved. However, such reports may be used, where necessary, for action taken pursuant to section 4.2 above.

4.4 The Head of Department, Office or Mission shall not apply the standard prescribed in section 3.2 (b), where a staff member is legally married to someone under the age of 18 but over the age of majority or consent in their country of citizenship.

4.5 The Head of Department, Office or Mission may use his or her discretion in applying the standard prescribed in section 3.2 (d), where beneficiaries of assistance are over the age of 18 and the circumstances of the case justify an exception.

4.6 The Head of Department, Office or Mission shall promptly inform the Department of Management of its investigations into cases of sexual exploitation and sexual abuse, and the actions it has taken as a result of such investigations.

Section 5

Referral to national authorities

If, after proper investigation, there is evidence to support allegations of sexual exploitation or sexual abuse, these cases may, upon consultation with the Office of Legal Affairs, be referred to national authorities for criminal prosecution.

Section 6

Cooperative arrangements with non-United Nations entities or individuals

6.1 When entering into cooperative arrangements with non-United Nations entities or individuals, relevant United Nations officials shall inform those entities or individuals of the standards of conduct listed in section 3, and shall receive a written undertaking from those entities or individuals that they accept these standards.

6.2 The failure of those entities or individuals to take preventive measures against sexual exploitation or sexual abuse, to investigate allegations thereof, or to take corrective action when sexual exploitation or sexual abuse has occurred, shall constitute grounds for termination of any cooperative arrangement with the United Nations.

...

31

Accountability for Conduct and Discipline in Field Missions

Prefatory Note

The Accountability for Conduct and Discipline in Field Missions Policy (Policy) 'sets out the framework ... to ensure accountability for the conduct and discipline of all personnel serving in peacekeeping and special political missions'.[1] The Policy is approved by the Department of Political Affairs (DPA), Department of Peacekeeping Operations (DPKO), and the Department of Field Support (DFS).[2] Compliance with the Policy 'is mandatory'.[3]

The Policy details 'responsibilities and accountabilities, for the individual serving in a field mission, the United Nations, its management, and its Member States, in addressing matters of conduct and discipline of all United Nations personnel serving in field missions'.[4] Hence the Policy applies to UN officials, UN volunteers, consultants or individual contractors of the UN, UN experts on mission (such as civilian police and military observers), and UN peacekeepers serving with military contingents.[5] The Policy should therefore be viewed as reinforcing the principle of accountability articulated by the General Assembly's Special Committee on Peacekeeping Operations (C34): 'that the same standards of conduct must be applied without exception to all categories of United Nations peacekeeping personnel'.[6]

The Policy recognises that regulations, rules, and other administrative issuances adopted by the UN do not cover all UN personnel, and hence the Policy seeks to fill any gaps in the UN's field mission accountability framework,[7] particularly in relation to dealing with sexual exploitation and abuse by UN personnel.[8]

The references at the end of the Policy are useful to understand the various documents that influence accountability in UN peace operations. The Annex provides a quick reference guide as to the mandates of the Conduct and Discipline Unit (CDU), the role and functions of the Conduct and Discipline components in field missions, and the Conduct and Discipline Focus Points.

The Policy is relevant to peacekeepers in three ways. First, it outlines the UN's strategy on conduct and discipline. This strategy entails a three-pronged approach: prevention, enforcement, and remedial action.[9] Prevention is 'aimed at ensuring that misconduct does not occur in the first place'.[10] Enforcement 'encompasses activities associated with actions taken in response to instances of alleged misconduct reported in a field mission',[11] and remedial action is the 'strategy for addressing misconduct'.[12]

Second, it applies to different categories of UN personnel serving in field missions. It reinforces that UN staff members are governed by the accountability standards set out in documents such as the Secretary-General's Bulletin, Staff Regulations and Rules of the UN, and other UN administrative

---

1 Department of Political Affairs, Department of Peacekeeping Operations, and Department of Field Support, 'Accountability for Conduct and Discipline in Field Missions', 1 August 2015, [1] (hereafter Policy).

2 Ibid, 1.

3 Ibid, [4].

4 Ibid, [3].

5 Ibid, [1]–[2].

6 See, for example, 'Report of the Special Committee of Peacekeeping Operations, 2015 Substantive Session (17 February–13 March 2015)', UN Doc A/69/19, 17 March 2015, [60].

7 Policy (n 1), [6].

8 Ibid, [7]–[8].

9 Ibid, [10.4].

10 Ibid, [10.5].

11 Ibid, [10.6].

12 Ibid, [10.7].

issuances.[13] For those that are deployed with the status of experts on mission, including UN civilian police, members of Formed Police Units (FPUs) and military observers, their individual undertakings when they commence service with the UN and documents such as the Regulations Governing the Status, Basic Rights, and Duties of Officials other the Secretariat Officials, and Experts on Mission govern their actions.[14] For members of military contingents, their behaviour is regulated by the Memorandum of Understanding (MOU) entered into between the Troop Contributing Country (TCC) and the UN.[15]

Third, the Policy describes the roles and responsibilities of individual UN personnel, managers, the UN, and Member States. In so doing, it explains the roles that various UN appointees (such as the Under Secretary-General for Peacekeeping Operations), offices (such as the CDU), and levels of command (such as operational headquarters) have in administering and enforcing the Policy.

A very useful part of the document is its overview of the application of UN standards of conduct to the categories of individuals who serve on UN peace operations. That summary reinforces various principles and standards articulated in other UN documents such as the Status-of-Forces Agreement (SOFA),[16] MOU, and Policy.[17] The sections that deal with disciplinary and criminal accountability processes,[18] and roles and responsibilities[19] are also a very useful aide-memoire for understanding the delineation between the UN and TCCs in undertaking disciplinary processes, as well as the obligations to deal with instances of misconduct. Paragraph 18 delineates the responsibilities of the UN at HQ level and mission level.

Reference[20]

Title	Accountability for Conduct and Discipline in Field Missions
Authors	Department of Political Affairs Department of Peacekeeping Operations Department of Field Support
Effective Date	1 August 2015
Full Text	<https://unmil.unmissions.org/sites/default/files/policy_on_accountability_for_conduct_and_discipline_in_field_missions_30-07-2015.pdf>[21]

Accountability for Conduct and Discipline in Field Missions[22]

(Extracts)

ANNEXES

A. Terms of Reference for the Conduct and Discipline Unit in DFS, Conduct and Discipline Team and Conduct and Discipline Focal Points in field missions.

13 Ibid, [11.3].
14 Ibid, [11.5].
15 See ch 3 above.
16 See ch 2 above.
17 Policy (n 1), [11]. See, for example, ch 28 above.
18 Policy (n 1), [12].
19 Ibid, Part E.
20 The United Nations Human Resource Handbook contains Staff Regulations, Staff Rules, Secretary-General's Bulletins, and Administrative Instructions, plus any amendments and updates <https://hr.un.org/handbook> accessed 1 November 2017.
21 Accessed 1 November 2017.
22 From Accountability for Conduct and Discipline in Field Missions, by Department of Political Affairs, Department of Peacekeeping Operations and Department of Field Support © 2015 United Nations. Reprinted with the permission of the United Nations.

A. PURPOSE

1. This Policy sets out the framework in place to ensure accountability for the conduct and discipline of all personnel serving in peacekeeping and special political missions. In this regard, it sets forth the roles and responsibilities of, and interactions amongst, each component assigned with responsibilities regarding the conduct and discipline of all personnel in field missions, both in those field missions and at Headquarters.

B. SCOPE

2. This Policy applies to all United Nations personnel serving in peacekeeping missions and in field-based special political missions (hereinafter referred to as "field missions"), either as United Nations officials, United Nations Volunteers assimilated to United Nations officials or individual contractors engaged by the United Nations; as personnel deployed with the legal status of experts on mission for the United Nations; and as members of a military contingent deployed under a Memorandum of Understanding between a Member State and the United Nations. This Policy also applies to contractors to the United Nations who are responsible to ensure that their employees are aware of and act in accordance with this Policy.
3. This Policy details responsibilities and accountabilities, for the individual serving in a field mission, the United Nations, its management and its Member States, in addressing matters of conduct and discipline of all United Nations personnel serving in field missions. This Policy further details the support to be provided to that effect, by personnel in Conduct and Discipline Teams, individual Conduct and Discipline Officers (hereinafter collectively referred as "CDT") and Conduct and Discipline Focal Points in field missions, as well as personnel of the Conduct and Discipline Unit (CDU), in the Department of Field Support (DFS).
4. Compliance with this Policy is mandatory and shall be assessed accordingly.

C. RATIONALE

5. The Charter of the United Nations (hereinafter the "Charter") sets out, in its Article 101 paragraph 3, that "[t]he paramount consideration in the employment of the staff and in the determination of the conditions of service shall be the necessity of securing the highest standards of efficiency, competence, and integrity"; the element of integrity being of prime importance in relation to the conduct and discipline of United Nations' personnel.
6. In order to comply with the provisions of the Charter, the United Nations has adopted Regulations, Rules and other administrative issuances that, in part, establish standards of conduct to be observed, as well as disciplinary mechanisms to address possible violations of those standards, more precisely termed as misconduct, by United Nations officials. While the conduct and discipline of those officials serving in field missions continue to be regulated by the Regulations, Rules and other administrative issuances adopted by the United Nations, it has to be recognized that other categories of personnel not employed by the United Nations also serve in field missions. Measures must therefore be taken to ensure that all personnel, other than United Nations officials, serving for the United Nations in any field mission also maintain the highest standards of integrity.
7. The challenges associated with comprehensively addressing the conduct and discipline of different categories of personnel deployed in field missions were detailed in relation to policies and processes applicable in instances involving sexual exploitation and abuse. In the Secretary-General's report on sexual exploitation and abuse by United Nations peacekeeping personnel (A/59/710), the Special Adviser on sexual exploitation and abuse by United Nations peacekeeping personnel, Prince Zeid Ra'ad Zeid Al-Hussein, identified

challenges in terms of ensuring that all categories of personnel be made to comply with similar standards of conduct but, more importantly, that mechanisms be put in place to ensure accountability for those individuals that violated the standards of conduct, regardless of the category of personnel involved.

8. The report mentioned above contained several recommendations for establishing and implementing initiatives associated with a comprehensive strategy to eradicate sexual exploitation and abuse by United Nations peacekeeping personnel. Amongst the recommendations contained in the report was the creation of dedicated capacities, in field missions and at Headquarters, to address conduct related issues. These initiatives originally focused on sexual exploitation and abuse, and included special measures to address this particular form of misconduct, but were subsequently expanded to address all forms of misconduct.
9. This Policy intends to identify where responsibilities lie, both with the observance of the United Nations standards of conduct and with setting measures to ensure such observance, and by providing details on how accountability is achieved in instances where any personnel serving in field missions fail to observe the United Nations standards of conduct.

D. POLICY

10. United Nations strategy on conduct and discipline

10.1 In terms of conduct and discipline, the prime objective of the United Nations is that all personnel serving in its field missions uphold the highest standards of integrity, in an environment of organizational, managerial and personal accountability, thereby enabling those United Nations personnel to serve with pride.

10.2 The Secretary-General has stated that the United Nations has a zero-tolerance policy towards sexual exploitation and sexual abuse. This zero-tolerance policy also applies to all other forms of misconduct by all categories of United Nations personnel serving in field missions.

10.3 All personnel shall be held accountable for violations of the United Nations standards of conduct, the most serious of which may also constitute crimes punishable under national laws. All personnel, regardless of their position or level, are responsible to uphold the highest standards of integrity, which includes respect for the United Nations standards of conduct. All personnel have an obligation to report any instance of misconduct which they have become aware of.

10.4 The United Nations has adopted a three-pronged strategy in addressing misconduct, through prevention, enforcement and remedial action. Implementing this strategy forms part of the exercise of the conduct and discipline functions.

10.5 Prevention is aimed at ensuring that misconduct does not occur in the first place and is, accordingly, of critical importance in the reduction of acts of misconduct. Prevention includes activities such as raising awareness, including through public communication, training and outreach, vetting of personnel, maintaining conduct and discipline and adopting preventive measures that relate to the particular circumstances of a field mission, as well as ensuring the welfare and recreation of our personnel.

10.6 Enforcement encompasses activities associated with actions taken in response to instances of alleged misconduct reported in a field mission. Prompt and consistent enforcement is essential to the goal of ensuring that the United Nations standards of conduct are respected. Without such enforcement, there is no accountability for violations of the United Nations standards of conduct and possible criminal acts.

10.7 Remedial action is the third prong of the United Nations' strategy for addressing misconduct. This applies in instances involving sexual exploitation and abuse and concerns the implementation of all aspects of the United Nations Comprehensive

Strategy on Assistance and Support to Victims of Sexual Exploitation and Abuse by United Nations Staff and Related Personnel (A/RES/62/214).

11. Application of the United Nations standards of conduct

11.1 Personnel deployed in United Nations field missions are made up of the following categories: United Nations officials (both national and international); United Nations Volunteers (UNV) assimilated to United Nations officials; Individual military and police personnel, members of Formed Police Units (FPU), and other Government Provided Personnel with the legal status of experts on mission; members of military contingents and Military Staff Officers; consultants or individual contractors of the United Nations.

11.2 While contained in different texts made applicable to each category of personnel, the standards of conduct and integrity required of all categories of personnel serving in missions are similar since all are derived from principles established in Article 101, paragraph 3, of the Charter of the United Nations, which requires the highest standards of integrity of United Nations officials. However, some definitions and standards may vary from one category of personnel to another.

11.3 United Nations officials (staff members) are governed by the standards of conduct set out in the United Nations Staff Regulations, Rules and other administrative issuances. Staff members are bound to respect those standards of conduct through the signing of their offer of appointment and related employment contract with the United Nations.

11.4 For UNVs, the standards of conduct are contained in the UNV Conditions of Service, which forms part of the offer letter issued by the UNV Programme for each volunteer, though which they are bound.

11.5 Individual military and police personnel and members of FPUs, as well as some other Government Provided Personnel, are deployed with the legal status of experts on mission. They individually sign an undertaking upon commencement of service with the United Nations, through which they agree to be bound by the provisions contained in this undertaking, including the Regulations governing the Status, Basic Rights and Duties of Officials other than Secretariat Officials, and Experts on Mission (ST/SGB/2002/9), and such other documents adopted by the United Nations that regulate the conduct of this category of personnel.

11.6 The conduct and discipline of members of military contingents and Military Staff Officers is governed by the Memorandum of Understanding (MOU) concluded between the Troop Contributing Country and the United Nations for the deployment of military contingents and Military Staff Officers. Through this MOU, Member States agree that, while their military personnel remain subject to the exclusive jurisdiction of respective Troop Contributing Countries, they will comply with United Nations standards of conduct and such other documents adopted by the United Nations that regulate the conduct of this category of personnel, including the exemplification provided in Annex H of this MOU.

11.7 For individual United Nations consultants and contractors, agreements signed between them and the United Nations contain provisions on the obligation to respect the United Nations standards of conduct.

11.8 While not United Nations personnel, corporate contractors agree in the General Conditions of Contract that: "[t]he Contractor shall be responsible for the professional and technical competence of the personnel it assigns to perform work under the Contract and will select reliable and competent individuals who will be able to effectively perform the obligations under the Contract and who, while doing so, will respect the local laws and customs and conform to a high standard of moral and ethical conduct." These General Conditions of Contract have a binding effect on employees of the United Nations contractors.

11.9 Specific provisions on sexual exploitation and abuse, using the exact language contained in the Secretary-General's Bulletin on Special measures for protection from sexual exploitation and Abuse (ST/SGB/2003/13), have been included in documents containing the standards of conduct made applicable to all personnel serving in field missions.

12. Disciplinary and criminal accountability processes

12.1 Administrative investigations into alleged misconduct involving United Nations staff members, UNVs, contractors and those personnel with the legal status of experts on mission are conducted under the primary responsibility of the United Nations, in accordance with procedures set out in various administrative issuances listed in the reference section. Furthermore, the United Nations will also refer credible allegations that a crime may have been committed to national authorities for appropriate action, including possible prosecution. In accordance with applicable provisions of status-of-force or similar agreements in place, the United Nations and Member States shall assist each other in carrying out all necessary investigations into crimes in respect of which either or both have an interest.

12.2 Member States have the primary responsibility for investigating all alleged acts of misconduct committed by members of their national military contingents. When Member States do not exercise that responsibility, the United Nations can conduct its own administrative investigation. Member States may also decide to conduct investigations into misconduct and crimes involving their nationals, subject to the application of the Convention on the Privileges and Immunities of the United Nations.

12.3 The United Nations is mandated to conduct investigation and fact-finding exercises to establish responsibility for loss of, or damage to, contingent or United Nations property, or death or personal injury to United Nations personnel or third parties. Such fact-finding activities may lead to the identification of alleged misconduct which will then need to be specifically investigated, in accordance with the responsibility of Member States or the United Nations to conduct such investigations.

12.4 Based on recommendations from field missions, the Department of Peacekeeping Operations (DPKO) or the Department of Political Affairs (DPA), through DFS, can authorise a limited number of administrative actions against personnel serving in field missions. Such actions can include placement on administrative leave with pay, for United Nations staff members, or the repatriation on disciplinary grounds of personnel serving in field missions but not employed by the United Nations. Field missions can also issue reprimands. Service contracts may also be terminated by field missions or Headquarters, depending on the nature of those contracts, whereas contractors providing services to a field mission may also be requested to replace individuals employed by them.

12.5 The responsibility for disciplinary actions rests with the Under-Secretary-General for Management and the Office of Human Resources Management (OHRM), for United Nations staff members, with the United Nations Development Programme (UNDP), for UNV, and with the respective Member States, for experts on mission and members of military contingents they employ. The responsibility for the placement of United Nations staff members on administrative leave without pay, considered an administrative action, also rests with the Under-Secretary-General for Management.

12.6 Acts of misconduct may also constitute crimes under the laws of the host or contributing States. In such instances, in addition to taking any disciplinary action against personnel it employs, the United Nations may further request that relevant Member States prosecute United Nations staff members and experts on mission for the commission of such crimes. The responsibility for criminal accountability rests with Member States in ensuring that any misconduct which constitutes a crime shall be investigated and possibly prosecuted with the necessary penalties. Members of military contingents and Military Staff Officers remain under the exclusive jurisdiction of their contributing States, for the purpose of criminal prosecutions.

E. ROLES AND RESPONSIBILITIES

13. Individual responsibilities and accountability

13.1 United Nations personnel, including those serving in field missions for the United Nations are expected to be and make themselves aware of the United Nations standards of conduct, including by attending training sessions, and are obliged to uphold these standards at all times, whether at the workplace or outside and whether on duty or off-duty, including when on leave.

13.2 United Nations personnel, including those serving for the United Nations in field missions are obliged to report instances of misconduct they become aware of and cooperate with any duly mandated investigation into allegations of misconduct. When doing so, personnel shall be protected from retaliation.

13.3 United Nations personnel, including those serving for the United Nations in field missions shall be accountable for violations of the United Nations standards of conduct applicable to their category of personnel and may be referred for investigation and possible prosecution before Member States' national courts when such violations constitute crimes under national laws.

13.4 United Nations personnel, including those serving for the United Nations in field missions shall be liable for the consequences of having engaged in misconduct. Such consequences can imply financial liabilities, for example, where a court orders payments for child support in instances involving paternity claims.

14. Managers and commanders responsibilities and accountability

14.1 Managers and commanding officers are responsible for taking steps to prevent and address misconduct on the part of their subordinates. Expected steps to be taken in the prevention of misconduct will include ensuring that personnel under their command or supervision are aware of the United Nations standards of conduct, including by ensuring the attendance of training sessions to that effect, that compliance with the United Nations standards of conduct is maintained by personnel under their command or supervision, that potential risks of misconduct are identified and appropriate measures recommended to prevent such risks are implemented accordingly.

14.2 Managers and commanding officers have an obligation to report misconduct by their subordinates. Such report shall be made to the Head of the respective civilian, police or military component, for onward transmission to the Head of Mission and his supporting COT or Conduct and Discipline Focal Point, for onward transmission to the supporting CDT. Reports can also be made directly to the Office of Internal Oversight Services (OIOS).

14.3 Managers and commanding officers will be held accountable in terms of performance regarding the exercise of their conduct and discipline functions. For Heads of Mission, this is achieved through provisions included in the "Compact" signed between them and the Secretary-General. For all other managers and commanding officers, performance in the exercise of the conduct and discipline functions shall be evaluated through the performance appraisal mechanisms applicable to the manager or commanding officer, including e-Performance tools for staff members and end of mission reports or other applicable mechanisms for military and police personnel.

15. The United Nations responsibilities and accountability

15.1 The United Nations is responsible for putting in place mechanisms that will allow for preventing and addressing misconduct on the part of personnel serving in field missions. Preventing misconduct will include ensuring that all personnel are made aware of the United Nations standards of conduct, including through the development of training material for pre-deployment and induction trainings, as well as specific training programmes, including on the prevention of sexual exploitation and sexual abuse. Addressing misconduct will entail that mechanisms are in place to ensure that complaints of misconduct are received and assessed, that administrative investigations to be conducted by the United Nations are completed promptly and professionally and that appropriate follow-up actions including public awareness activities are promptly taken, as needed.

15.2 The United Nations is responsible for taking appropriate actions with respect to its staff members when they have engaged in misconduct, as well as for reporting and requesting appropriate actions by Member States and other employers, as applicable, when their personnel serving in field missions are found to have engaged in misconduct. The United Nations may also refer to Member States instances where any of its personnel are alleged to have engaged in misconduct which constitute crimes under national laws or in the settlement of claims, including paternity and child support claims.

15.3 The United Nations is responsible for the implementation of the Comprehensive Strategy on Assistance and Support to Victims of Sexual Exploitation and Abuse by United Nations Staff and Related Personnel.

15.4 The United Nations is accountable to its Member States as regards measures taken to implement its three-pronged strategy in addressing misconduct by personnel serving in field missions, including through the production of detailed reports by the Secretary-General to that effect.

16. Member States responsibilities and accountability

16.1 Member States contributing military, police or other Government Provided Personnel are responsible for ensuring that their personnel serving in United Nations field missions are aware of the expected standards of conduct, including by providing their personnel with pre-deployment training on the United Nations standards of conduct, and that commanding officers maintain good order and discipline amongst their subordinates.

16.2 Member States are responsible for informing the United Nations of instances of misconduct involving their personnel serving in United Nations field missions and ensuring that investigations conducted by them are completed promptly and professionally. In instances involving sexual exploitation and abuse, save for exceptional circumstances, investigations are expected to be completed within six months.

16.3 Member States are responsible for taking prompt appropriate actions against personnel they contribute to United Nations field missions when they are found to have engaged in misconduct or when commanding officers have failed in their command responsibilities towards maintaining good order and discipline amongst their subordinates. Member States are also expected to facilitate the expeditious settlement of claims involving their personnel, including paternity and child support claims.

16.4 Member States are also expected to prosecute individuals when acts of misconduct constitute crimes, under the laws of the host State or of the contributing State.

16.5 Member States are expected to communicate to the United Nations the findings of investigations they have conducted, the results of disciplinary action taken or of measures taken to ensure criminal accountability, as well as the settlement of claims, including paternity and child support claims.

17. Roles in implementation of the Policy

17.1 At Headquarters level, the Under-Secretary-General for Field Support (USG/DFS), along with the Under-Secretary-General for Peacekeeping Operations (USG/DPKO) and the Under-Secretary-General for Political Affairs (USG/DPA), as well as the Military Advisor and Police Advisor, all have roles and responsibilities in the exercise of the conduct and discipline functions. Similarly, at mission level, the Head of Mission, as well as the Force Commander, Police Commissioner and Director/Chief of Mission Support, also all have roles and responsibilities in this regard.

17.2 In the exercise of those conduct and discipline functions, the senior managers identified above are supported by personnel in CDTs and Conduct and Discipline Focal Points in field missions, as well as personnel in the CDU, in DFS. Conduct and Discipline Focal Points deliver support to the senior managers of their respective field mission under the guidance and within the parameters of operational arrangements concerning support to the field mission's Conduct and Discipline Focal Point by a CDT located in the region.

17.3 CDU is the focal point for all matters related to conduct and discipline in field missions when such matters are addressed at Headquarters. CDTs carry-out the same role for matters within field missions. CDU will provide guidance on conduct and discipline related matters to CDTs, which will then be reflected as they carry out their functions. When questions arise regarding the implementation of the conduct and discipline mandate in a field mission, CDTs shall refer such questions to CDU for appropriate guidance.

17.4 In field missions, CDTs need to maintain direct and regular contacts with the military, police, substantive and mission support components of the field mission, at the highest level.

17.5 The senior management of the field missions must ensure that all matters relating to conduct and discipline of United Nations personnel are brought to the attention of, and discussed with, the field mission's CDT or the CDT providing regional support. In particular, the Head of Mission and Deputies, the Heads of Military and Police Components and the Director/Chief of Mission Support are responsible for ensuring that discipline is maintained in the field mission and for supporting the role of their CDT and Conduct and Discipline Focal Point, as applicable, in carrying out conduct and discipline related activities. In turn, the CDT and Conduct and Discipline Focal Point are to support the exercise of the conduct and discipline functions by all the senior management of the field mission.

17.6 CDTs are subject-matter experts regarding all activities to be conducted in field missions towards the prevention of misconduct.

17.7 CDTs are responsible for ensuring that complaints are properly received and assessed, that allegations are recorded and tracked to ensure that appropriate actions are taken in a timely matter. CDTs retain the duty to manage all cases from the point of the reception of a complaint or information on possible misconduct to the point where matters can be closed as all needed actions have been taken. To that effect, CDTs will liaise directly with entities at the field mission level and OIOS, whereas CDU will liaise with counterparts at United Nations Headquarters and Member States concerning actions to be taken at Headquarters level.

17.8 CDTs and CDU also maintain and update information on all allegations of misconduct in field missions, through the use of the electronic Misconduct Tracking System. To that effect, CDTs remain responsible to record and update information regarding all actions taken at field missions level, including safekeeping of documents related to such actions, whereas CDU will be responsible to record and update information regarding all actions taken at Headquarters level.

17.9 At their respective levels, CDTs and CDU are partners in the United Nations system-wide implementation of the Comprehensive Strategy on Assistance and Support to Victims of Sexual Exploitation and Abuse by United Nations Staff and Related Personnel.

18. Operational Responsibilities

Headquarters Level

18.1 The Secretary-General of the United Nations ensures that the United Nations standards of conduct reflect the expected highest level of integrity mentioned in the Charter and that all personnel deployed in a United Nations field mission are held accountable when they fail to observe those standards of conduct. The Secretary-General also holds its senior managers, including Heads of Missions, accountable for complying with provisions related to conduct and discipline, as contained in "Compacts" signed with those senior managers.

18.2 The Office of Legal Affairs makes determinations whether there is sufficient and credible information to support the referral of allegations to national authorities for appropriate action, including investigation and possible prosecution, and to advise on questions of immunity, if any, that may arise.

18.3 OIOS has overall responsibility for internal United Nations administrative investigations. Its role is to assist the Secretary-General in fulfilling his or her internal oversight responsibilities in respect of the resources and staff members of the Organization.

18.4 The Under-Secretary-General for Management (USG/OM) formulates policies and procedures and provides strategic guidance, direction and support for, amongst other, human resources and central support services. In the Department of Management (DM), OHRM is responsible for developing and maintaining a human resources management infrastructure, which includes the framework of Regulations, Rules and administrative issuances part of which regulate the conduct of United Nations staff members and the mechanisms in place for the imposition of disciplinary measures, as well as certain administrative measures such as administrative leave without pay, to be taken in instances where United Nations staff members have failed to observe the United Nations standards of conduct. Within DM, the Procurement Division may also be called upon to take actions in instances where contractors have failed to observe expected standards of conduct as required under the applicable contract.

18.5 The USG/DFS along with the USG/DPKO and USG/DPA, supports compliance with the highest standards of conduct and discipline among United Nations personnel in field missions, including through the implementation in field missions of the zero-tolerance policy of the Secretary- General regarding sexual exploitation and abuse and the Organization's strategy to address sexual exploitation and abuse. The USG/DFS and Assistant Secretary-General for Field Support (ASG/DFS) will coordinate action on conduct and discipline related issues for DPKO, including in particular the Office of Military Affairs and the Police Division, and DPA, as well as within the Secretariat, in particular with OIOS on investigation related issues, or DM on disciplinary issues, other Agencies, Funds and Programmes, in particular UNDP, and Member States. The USG/DFS may be called upon to take certain administrative actions, including the placement of United Nations staff members on administrative leave with pay and the repatriation of United Nations personnel other than staff members.

18.6 The CDU provides support to the senior management, at Headquarters and field mission levels, in accordance with the provisions of the Secretary-General Bulletin on the Organisation of the Department of Field Support (ST/SGB/2010/2) and the terms of reference annexed to the present Policy. The CDU is responsible to oversee the implementation of the overall goals and objectives of the United Nations, as related to conduct and discipline issues, to maintain global oversight of the state of conduct and discipline for all categories of United Nations personnel in field missions and support public communications on conduct and discipline issues. The CDU is the main point for exchanges of communications between Headquarters and field missions on all conduct and discipline related matters.

Mission Level

18.7 The Head of Mission (HOM), with the assistance of his/her Chief of Staff (COS) where applicable, has overall responsibility to ensure that discipline is maintained in the field mission. Operationally, this responsibility entails that activities to prevent the occurrence of misconduct are carried out, including on occasions with the direct involvement of the HOM. The HOM will also ensure that information or complaints of possible misconduct are promptly reviewed and, if warranted, referred for investigation. With the exception of investigations conducted by OIOS in accordance with its operational independence, the HOM shall ensure that field mission's investigations are conducted promptly and professionally. When investigations are completed, the HOM will further ensure that appropriate follow-up actions including public awareness activities are taken, if within his/her authority, or recommended for actions at Headquarters. The HOM is in particular responsible to mandate the conduct of investigations by field mission's personnel, where applicable, and to review and endorse the findings of such investigations, where appropriate. The HOM will also need to support efforts by the United Nations Country Team in relation to remedial actions in instances involving sexual exploitation and abuse. The HOM must finally ensure that the field mission's personnel have the support necessary to carry out conduct and discipline related activities.

18.8 The Resident Coordinator/Humanitarian Coordinator (RC/HC) has operational responsibilities in relation to the implementation of the United Nations Comprehensive Strategy on Assistance and Support to Victims of Sexual Exploitation and Abuse, in particular by ensuring that an in-country network on protection from sexual exploitation and abuse is operational, as well as setting up and maintaining a network for victim assistance. The RC/HC must ensure that protection from sexual exploitation and abuse is integrated into all United Nations services and programmes.

18.9 The Head of Military Component (HOMC) reports to the HOM. The HOMC exercises operational control over all military personnel. The HOMC will ensure that conduct and discipline related prevention activities targeting military personnel are carried out, including by regularly engaging with military contingent Commanders on the state of discipline of personnel under their command. The HOMC will ensure that information or complaints of possible misconduct are promptly submitted to the HOM for review, with support from the CDT. The HOMC will also be called upon to provide appropriate follow-up actions, within his/her authority, or to make recommendations to the HOM, for actions to be taken at Headquarters.

18.10 The Head of the Police Component (HOPC) reports to the HOM. The HOPC exercises operational control over all members of the police component. The HOPC will ensure that conduct and discipline related prevention activities targeting police personnel are carried out, including by regularly engaging with police Commanders on the state of discipline of personnel under their command. The HOPC will ensure that information or complaints of possible misconduct are promptly submitted to the HOM for review, with support from the CDT. The HOPC will also be called upon to provide appropriate follow-up actions, within his/her authority, or to make recommendations for such appropriate actions to the HOM, for actions to be taken at Headquarters.

18.11 The Director/Chief of Mission Support (D/CMS) reports to the HOM. The D/CMS is responsible for measures relating to civilian personnel. The D/CMS will ensure that conduct and discipline related prevention activities targeting civilian personnel are carried out, including by regularly engaging with managers on the state of discipline of personnel under their supervision. The D/CMS must also ensure that adequate resources are available for training of all other categories of personnel deployed with the field mission. The D/CMS will ensure that information or complaints of possible misconduct are promptly submitted to the HOM for review, with support from the CDT. The D/CMS, as well as the Chief Civilian Personnel Officer, will also be called upon to assist with the implementation of administrative actions, including issuing reprimands, redeploying civilian personnel involved in alleged misconduct or placing staff members on administrative leave pending completion of investigation and disciplinary process.

18.12 The UNV Programme Manager is primarily responsible for matters relating to UNV. Preventing misconduct includes ensuring that UNV are aware of and act in compliance with the United Nations standards of conduct. The Programme Manager may also be called upon to assist with the implementation of certain administrative actions, in coordination with the UNV Programme and UNDP, as appropriate.

18.13 The heads of the Transport Section and of the Communication and Information Technology Section are responsible for identifying risks associated with the use of United Nations property and assets. While they will regulate the use of those property and assets in order to minimize such risks they shall also report instances of improper and abusive use of such property and assets which may amount to misconduct.

18.14 The Head of Public Information (HPIO) of the field mission, in coordination with the CDT, is responsible for supporting mission-wide awareness raising activities in relation to conduct and discipline, targeting both mission personnel and the host State population. Under the direction of the HOM, the HPIO will design all relevant communications campaigns and outreach activities and will ensure that the mission maintains a responsive and transparent public posture on conduct and discipline issues.

18.15 The Chief Security Advisor (CSA) or senior security personnel can be called upon to assist in identifying potential risks of misconduct. Security personnel under the CSA may also be involved in responding to incidents that give rise to allegations of misconduct by personnel of the field mission. Such incidents will need to be reported accordingly.

18.16 OIOS investigators located in the field mission or in a regional hub serving the field mission can be called upon to conduct or assist with investigations in those field missions. Other personnel in the field mission, including members of Special Investigation Unit, Police Internal Investigation Unit or from the office of the Force Provost Marshall, may also be called upon to conduct administrative investigations in the field mission or to assist in investigations being conducted by OIOS or Member States.

18.17 The head of the Board of Inquiry (BOI) Unit, with support from the (Senior) Legal Advisor, is involved in the conduct of BOIs which are undertaken in order to establish responsibility for, loss of, or damage to, contingent or United Nations property, or death or personal injury to personnel or third parties. As a result of a BOI, instances of possible misconduct may be identified and, in such cases, will need to be referred for appropriate review and follow-up on the specific aspects of alleged misconduct, as needed.

18.18 The CDT advises the HOM on establishing measures to prevent misconduct, taking enforcement measures and ensuring remedial action. The CDT is the primary resource for support to the senior management of the field mission in relation to all conduct and discipline issues and the senior management is expected to work in close collaboration with the CDT. The CDT provides this support in accordance with the provisions of the terms of reference annexed to this Policy. In particular, the CDT receives, assesses and refers allegations of misconduct for appropriate action. The CDT provides technical advice to mission leadership on rules and procedures relating to misconduct cases and maintains the Misconduct Tracking System established to track and report on all cases of misconduct. A CDT may also be called upon to provide support to field missions located in the same region where the exercise of the conduct and discipline functions is only supported through a Conduct and Discipline Focal Point.

18.19 Conduct and Discipline Focal Points provide advice and assistance to the HOM on establishing measures to prevent misconduct, taking enforcement measures and ensuring remedial action. This support is provided in accordance with the terms of reference annexed to this Policy and under the guidance and within the parameters of operational arrangements concerning support to the field mission's Conduct and Discipline Focal Point by a CDT located in the region. The Chief of the CDT providing regional support is accountable to the HOM for each field mission to which such regional support is provided. In such instances, the performance of individual Conduct and Discipline Focal Point in the provision of conduct and discipline services will be assessed by the Chief of the CDT providing regional support, as an additional supervisor, and, to this effect, a specific objective will be included in the e-PAS of individuals designated as field missions' Conduct and Discipline Focal Points.

19. Confidentiality

19.1 All information related to allegations of misconduct must be treated as strictly confidential and disclosed only to those individuals with a need to know, in light of their responsibilities in exercising conduct and discipline functions.

19.2 All officials who have knowledge of an alleged instance of misconduct shall exercise the utmost discretion and take appropriate measures to prevent unauthorized disclosure of information relating to the allegations. Unauthorized disclosure of confidential information, either internally or externally, may constitute misconduct.

19.3 In the interest of protecting the reputation of subjects and the integrity of investigation or disciplinary proceedings, officials who are aware of confidential information shall refrain from making any public statements on the identity or nationality of those involved with those allegations, unless so authorised.

19.4 Communications between missions and Headquarters concerning specific instances of misconduct involving any personnel serving in field missions, either notifying of allegations, requesting investigations by Member States or recommending follow-up actions, by the United Nations or Member States, shall be effected through Code Cables. Such communication will be marked strictly confidential.

20. Reporting framework

20.1 Field missions will be required to contribute, when so warranted, to reporting by the Secretary-General on conduct and discipline issues. Field missions will need to ensure the accuracy, reliability and completeness of information provided for the purpose of such reporting.

20.2 HOM are required to report to the Secretary-General on the implementation of measures taken to address misconduct in field missions, including the implementation of the Secretary-General's three-pronged strategy to address sexual exploitation and abuse. This reporting is effected through the annual input on compliance with the provisions contained in the "Compacts" between the Secretary-General and HOM, currently established as follow: *"I will ensure that all possible measures are taken to raise awareness of expected standards of conduct, to prevent all forms of misconduct, including sexual exploitation and abuse, by mission personnel and to respond to, redress and remediate any violation."* This annual input will be compiled by field missions and reviewed by Headquarters, including CDU, prior to its submission to the Secretary-General. Compliance with the provisions contained in the "Compacts" will be, in large part, based on the compliance of field missions with other reporting requirements detailed below.

20.3 An accountability measurements framework was developed in consultations with field missions. Based on this framework, annual and quarterly reporting requirements were identified. Information contained in annual and quarterly reports will serve to underpin measurements of performance of field missions in terms of prevention, enforcement and remedial action, including compliance with the provisions contained in the HOM's "Compacts".

20.4 Annual reporting by field missions will provide an overview on the state of conduct and discipline in the field mission, and in particular on sexual exploitation and abuse. This report will review available data on allegations reported in the field mission, provide an analysis of trends and risk areas and, in relation to the latter, provide information on risks prevention measures adopted as a result. Quarterly reporting will be in two parts, with the first providing information on compliance with performance measurements in relation with enforcement related aspects and the second part providing in-depth analysis of practices. Quarterly reporting will include a certification of the accuracy of the information provided in relation to performance measurements. Inputs for these reports will be compiled by the CDT and by the CDT supporting Conduct and Discipline Focal Point, on behalf of field missions they cover.

20.5 Field missions and their respective CDT and Conduct and Discipline Focal Point will also punctually provide information on conduct and discipline related matters at the request of DFS, and in particular CDU.

20.6 Field missions will be required to include conduct and discipline related indicators of achievements or outputs in their Results Based Budgeting framework. Such indicators should be realistic, quantifiable, cover the various aspects of the exercise of the conduct and discipline functions and be dependent on elements under the control of the field mission.

21. Financial implications

21.1 When field missions are established, budget provisions shall be made for the staffing of a CDT, when so warranted, in a manner that is consequent to the responsibilities involved and the number of personnel over whom these responsibilities must be exercised. As field missions' size and mandate evolve, conduct and discipline related budget provisions should be adjusted accordingly.

21.2 In smaller field missions without a CDT but with a Conduct and Discipline Focal Point, budget provisions should be made for travel by personnel of the CDT providing regional support to the field mission's Focal Point, including for the purpose of conducting periodic training and assessment visits.

21.3 In all field missions, budget provisions should be made for regular internal conduct and discipline related training, travel for regular conduct and discipline assessments visits or awareness raising activities in different locations within the field mission's area of operation, as well as provisions for the production of information material for the prevention of misconduct.

21.4 All field missions should make budget provisions for travel associated with the periodic training and continuous learning of CDT personnel and Conduct and Discipline Focal Point, as well as periodic training for field missions' personnel conducting investigations.

21.5 On a yearly basis, CDU will provide specific guidance on budget provisions to be made by field missions, in relation to conduct and discipline. Field missions will consult CDU on their proposed conduct and discipline related budget provisions prior to making their submissions.

F. TERMS AND DEFINITIONS

- **Conduct:** refers to the obligation to observe and comply with applicable United Nations standards of conduct. Violation of those standards constitutes "misconduct".
- **Discipline:** refers to mechanisms in place to sanction misconduct.
- **Misconduct:** refers to violations of the applicable United Nations standards of conduct, including national laws of the host State. Misconduct is sometime further qualified as "serious misconduct". However, such further qualification will not impact on the requirement that all individuals who have engaged in any form of misconduct be held accountable.
- **United Nations standards of conduct:** refers to norms of conduct adopted by the United Nations for the conduct of its personnel, as defined in United Nations Regulations, Rules or other administrative issuances for its staff members, as well as other documents adopted by the United Nations to regulate the conduct of other categories of personnel than its staff members. The United Nations standards of conduct include the obligation to respect national laws of the host State.

...

H. MONITORING AND COMPLIANCE

22. The Office of the Assistant Secretary-General for Field Support (OASG/DFS) through the CDU, shall oversee the implementation of this Policy and shall ensure compliance, in cooperation with substantive stakeholders including OIOS, OLA, DM, DPA, DPKO, DFS and field missions.

I. CONTACT

23. The point of contact for this Policy is the Chief, Conduct and Discipline Unit, DFS.

J. HISTORY

24. This is a compilation of existing policies and has not been amended.

Annex A

Mandates of the Conduct and Discipline Components at Headquarters and in field missions

(1) Conduct and Discipline Unit in the Department of Field Support

- Providing the overall direction for conduct and discipline issues and maintaining global oversight on the state of conduct and discipline for all categories of United Nations personnel in field operations;
- Developing strategies to link the overall goals and objectives of the United Nations on conduct and discipline issues to the tasks of conduct and discipline teams in field missions;
- Leading the development of conduct and discipline policies, procedures and guidelines and the identification of best practices to facilitate compliance with conduct and discipline standards;
- Leading the development of tools and mechanisms to monitor the application of conduct and discipline standards and policies in field missions, including maintenance of a comprehensive misconduct database system;
- Under the provisions of paragraph 1.2 of ST/SGB/2010/2, reviewing and recommending actions on disciplinary cases, as required;
- Implementing the three-pronged comprehensive strategy (prevention, enforcement and remedial action) to address sexual exploitation and abuse, and monitoring it [sic] application in field missions;
- Under the provisions of paragraph 1.2 of ST/SGB/2010/2, reporting to intergovernmental and expert bodies, including the General Assembly, the Fourth and Fifth Committees, the Advisory Committee on Administrative and Budgetary Questions and other policymaking organs on conduct and discipline issues related to all categories of United Nations personnel in field missions; and
- Guiding the development of training programmes on misconduct and sexual exploitation and abuse, in consultation with the Integrated Training Service of the Department of Peacekeeping Operations.

(2) Conduct and Discipline Components in Field Missions

A. Conduct and Discipline Teams and Conduct and Discipline Officers

- Act as the principal adviser to the Head of Mission (HOM) on addressing conduct and discipline issues relating to all categories of United Nations peacekeeping personnel in the mission.
- Advise the Head of Mission on establishing measures to prevent misconduct, enforce United Nations standards of conduct and ensure remedial action where misconduct has occurred.
- Receive, assess and refer allegations of misconduct involving all categories of United Nations peacekeeping personnel for appropriate action.
- Provide technical advice to mission leadership on United Nations rules and procedures relating to misconduct cases involving all categories of United Nations peacekeeping personnel in the mission.
- Maintain a comprehensive database to track and report on all cases of misconduct in the mission, and provide analysis and reports.

- Liaise with all investigative entities on misconduct allegations and cases involving all categories of United Nations peacekeeping personnel.
- Assist in capacity-building on conduct and discipline issues for United Nations peacekeeping personnel in the mission.
- Provide content to public information components on conduct and discipline issues including on the status of misconduct allegations and cases.
- Coordinate the mission's responses to victims of misconduct by United Nations peacekeeping personnel, in coordination with United Nations entities, nongovernmental organizations and other relevant actors in the mission area.
- Liaise with the Department of Peacekeeping Operations on internal and external evaluations including audits on conduct and discipline issues involving United Nations peacekeeping personnel.
- Liaise with Member States, other United Nations entities, governmental representatives, non-governmental organizations and other relevant actors in the mission on policies, procedures and guidelines on conduct and discipline issues as well as misconduct cases involving all categories of United Nations peacekeeping personnel.

B. Conduct and Discipline Focal Points

- In close cooperation with the Conduct and Discipline Unit (CDU) in the Department of Field Support or the Conduct and Discipline Team CDT providing regional coverage, the Conduct and Discipline Focal Point
  a. provides advice and assistance to the HOM on conduct and discipline related matters with respect to all categories of UN personnel in the mission/office;
  b. facilitates the implementation of policies and procedures related to conduct and discipline and monitors compliance with such policies and procedures;
  c. receives and assesses complaints/reports of alleged misconduct and processes such complaints in accordance with established policies and procedures; and
  d. maintains up to date case files of all allegations/complaints received.
- In close coordination with the Mission Training Cell (MTC)/Training Officer or Focal Point, the Contact and Discipline Focal Point
  a. monitors compliance by all categories of UN personnel with mandatory conduct and discipline training;
  b. ensures that monthly training data is forwarded to the CDU or the Conduct and Discipline Team CDT providing regional coverage; and
  c. conducts briefings on conduct and discipline as appropriate.
- In consultation with mission leadership and CDU or the Conduct and Discipline Team CDT providing regional coverage, the Conduct and Discipline Focal Point assists in the development of strategies to prevent, identify, and respond to misconduct.
- The Conduct and Discipline Focal Point shall provide inputs to mission budgets in order to facilitate
  a. VTC between the missions/office and the CDU or the Conduct and Discipline Team CDT providing regional coverage;
  b. the travel and work of *ad hoc* panels appointed to conduct investigations; and
  c. punctual conduct and discipline training-of-trainer sessions for Conduct and Discipline Focal Points including attendance of a yearly Workshop.

32

Human Rights Due Diligence Policy on United Nations Support to Non-United Nations Security Forces

Prefatory Note

The UN Human Rights Due Diligence Policy on United Nations Support to Non-United Nations Security Forces (HRDDP)[1] was developed by the UN Secretary-General to deal with UN entities providing support to non-UN forces, such as the forces of the host State or peacekeeping forces of regional organisations.[2]

The policy's genesis was a paper developed by the UN Mission in the Democratic Republic of the Congo (MONUC) which addressed the conditions for MONUC to support Forces Armees de la Republique du Congo (FARDC) units.[3] The HRDDP was issued by the UN Secretary-General in 2011. The Secretary-General informed the General Assembly and Security Council by way of a letter to the respective Presidents.[4] In that letter, the Secretary-General asked that 'both the Assembly and the Council … take the policy into account in their deliberations'[5] when deciding to provide UN support to non-UN security forces. Until the HRDDP was promulgated there were no express UN policies to guide UN peacekeepers or other UN entities as to how to support non-UN forces in situations where there were allegations that those forces were likely to commit or were committing gross violations of international humanitarian law (IHL),[6] international human rights law (IHRL),[7] or refugee law.[8]

The policy is also important because it ensures that the UN and peacekeepers do not breach international law obligations by supporting non-UN forces to commit internationally wrongful acts. The conduct of such peacekeepers will be attributable to the UN where the UN exercises 'effective control' over them.[9] Furthermore, the HRDDP may also be read as reinforcing the IHL principle to 'respect and ensure respect for'[10] for the four Geneva Conventions.[11]

The HRDDP's aim is to have UN peacekeeping operations and other UN entities exercise due diligence when considering supporting, or providing support to, non-UN security forces. Due diligence in the context of the policy requires UN peacekeepers to: (1) assess the risks involved in providing or

---

1 Identical letters dated 25 February 2013 from the Secretary-General addressed to the President of the General Assembly and to the President of the Security Council, UN Doc A/67/775-S/2013/110, 5 March 2013 (hereafter HRDDP). The HRDDP is annexed to the letter. The UN has also published a guidance concerning the application of the HRDDP: 'Guidance Note: Human Rights Due Diligence Policy on UN Support to Non-UN Security Forces', 1 July 2014 (hereafter Guidance Note) <http://southsudanhumanitarianproject.com/wp-content/uploads/sites/21/formidable/2014.07.01.Revised-HRDDP-GN.pdf> accessed 1 November 2017.

2 HRDDP (n 1), [7].

3 See SC Res 1906 (2009) of 23 December 2009, Operative Part [23].

4 HRDDP (n 1).

5 Ibid, 1.

6 See ch 16 above.

7 See chs 4–13 above.

8 See ch 5 above.

9 International Law Commission, 'Draft Articles on the Responsibility of International Organizations, with commentaries', 2011, Article 7. See ch 24 above.

10 Geneva Convention for the Amelioration of the Condition of the Wounded and Sick in Armed Forces in the Field (opened for signature 12 August 1949, entered into force 21 October 1950) 75 UNTS 31; Geneva Convention for the Amelioration of the Condition of Wounded, Sick and Shipwrecked Members of Armed Forces at Sea (opened for signature 12 August 1949, entered into force 21 October 1950) 75 UNTS 85; Geneva Convention Relative to the Treatment of Prisoners of War (opened for signature 12 August 1949, entered into force 21 October 1950) 75 UNTS 135; Geneva Convention Relative to the Protection of Civilian Persons in Time of War (opened for signature 12 August 1949, entered into force 21 October 1950) 75 UNTS 287, Common Article 1.

11 See ch 16 above.

not providing the support; (2) be transparent with the receiving entity about the UN's obligations; and (3) have an effective implementation framework for ensuring that the support provided meets the UN's obligations. The effective implementation framework includes: procedures to monitor the entity's compliance with IHL, IHRL, and refugee law; procedures to intercede should there be grave violations of the law; and general guidelines to ensure that the policy is able to be implemented in the context in which it is to be applied.[12]

The HRDDP's importance in UN peace operations has been reinforced by the Security Council. For example, it could be argued that the Security Council's reference to the policy in resolution 2098, where it stipulated that the UN Organization Stabilization Mission in the Democratic Republic of the Congo (MONUSCO) shall support the authorities of the DRC 'in *strict compliance* with international law, including international humanitarian law and with the human rights due diligence policy on UN-support to non-UN forces (HRDDP)'[13] raised the legal status of the policy. Regardless of the binding nature of the HRDDP, it is a useful tool to ensure that UN peacekeepers take appropriate steps to avoid supporting non-UN security forces committing grave violations of international law and thus being complicit in those violations.

Since the policy was promulgated it has been referred to by the Security Council in a number of UN peace operations' mandates including the UN Multidimensional Integrated Stabilization Mission in the Central African Republic (MINUSCA)[14] and the UN Multidimensional Integrated Stabilization Mission in Mali (MINUSMA).[15] It is now also increasingly the case that where regional peacekeeping forces are undertaking joint operations with UN peace operations, those regional forces are expected to collaborate with the UN to implement the policy. The Security Council, in resolution 2124, for example, when tasking the African Union Mission in Somalia (AMISOM), emphasised that the UN's support to AMISOM must comply with the HRDDP.[16]

A useful tool to understand the application of the HRDDP is the UN's Guidance Note on the Human Rights Due Diligence Policy on UN Support to Non-UN Forces.[17] That Note provides detail on issues such as the mapping and analysis for monitoring the application of the policy, how to undertake a risk assessment to ensure a consistent assessment of the security forces, a template to undertake risk assessments, and a template for a letter national authorities can use to communicate the HRDDP.

The European Union Guidelines on promoting compliance with IHL issued in 2009 serve a similar purpose as the HRDDP in that they aim to 'address compliance with IHL by third States, and as, appropriate, non-State actors operating with third States'.[18]

Reference

Title	Human Rights Due Diligence Policy on United Nations Support to Non-United Nations Security Forces
Author	UN Department of Peacekeeping Operations – UN Department for Field Support
Date	5 March 2013
Source	UN Doc A/67/775–S/2013/110, Annex
Full Text	<http://www.ohchr.org/EN/NewYork/Pages/Resources.aspx>[19]

12 HRDDP (n 1), [2].

13 SC Res 2098 (2013) of 28 March 2013, Operative Part [12(b)] (emphasis added).

14 SC Res 2217 (2015) of 28 April 2015, Operative Part [44].

15 SC Res 2227 (2015) of 29 June 2015, Operative Part [21].

16 SC Res 2124 (2013) of 12 November 2013, Operative Part [15].

17 Guidance Note (n 1).

18 'Updated European Union Guidelines on promoting compliance with international humanitarian law (IHL)', Doc 2009/C 303/06, 15 December 2009, [2].

19 Accessed 1 November 2017.

Human Rights Due Diligence Policy on United Nations Support to Non-United Nations Security Forces[20]

I. Core principles

1. Support by United Nations entities to non-United Nations security forces must be consistent with the Organization's purposes and principles as set out in the Charter of the United Nations and with its obligations under international law to respect, promote and encourage respect for international humanitarian, human rights and refugee law. Such support should help recipients to attain a stage where compliance with these principles and bodies of law becomes the norm, ensured by the rule of law. Consistent with these obligations, United Nations support cannot be provided where there are substantial grounds for believing there is a real risk of the receiving entities committing grave violations of international humanitarian, human rights or refugee law and where the relevant authorities fail to take the necessary corrective or mitigating measures. For the same reasons, if the United Nations receives reliable information that provides substantial grounds to believe that a recipient of United Nations support is committing grave violations of international humanitarian, human rights or refugee law, the United Nations entity providing such support must intercede with the relevant authorities with a view to bringing those violations to an end. If, despite such intercession, the situation persists, the United Nations must suspend support to the offending elements. Notwithstanding the present policy, existing obligations of human rights, humanitarian and refugee law continue to apply to all United Nations activities.
2. United Nations entities that are contemplating or involved in providing support to non-United Nations security forces must therefore pursue a policy of due diligence, comprising the following key elements:
   (a) Before support is given, an assessment of the risks involved in providing or not providing such support, in particular the risk of the recipient entity committing grave violations of international humanitarian law, human rights law or refugee law;
   (b) Transparency with receiving entities about the legal obligations binding the Organization and the core principles governing provision of support; and
   (c) An effective implementation framework, including:
      (i) Procedures for monitoring the recipient entity's compliance with international humanitarian, human rights and refugee law;
      (ii) Procedures for determining when and how to intercede with a view to putting an end to grave violations of any of those bodies of law and for deciding, if need be, upon the suspension or withdrawal of support; and
      (iii) General operational guidance, as required, by the respective United Nations entities to the country level on implementation of the policy.
3. Adherence to the human rights due diligence policy is important to maintain the legitimacy, credibility and public image of the United Nations and to ensure compliance with the Charter and with the Organization's obligations under international law.

20 UN Department of Peacekeeping Operations – UN Department for Field Support © 2013 United Nations. Reprinted with the permission of the United Nations.

4. Relevant policies and guidelines on specific areas of support, including the guidance notes developed in the inter-agency Security Sector Reform Task Force, must be consistent with the due diligence policy.
5. The present policy is not intended in any way to hinder the normal work of the Organization aimed at encouraging respect for international humanitarian, human rights or refugee law, including developing capacity as well as investigating and reporting on violations of those bodies of law and interceding with relevant authorities to protest those violations, secure remedial action and prevent their repetition. The policy is intended to complement those normal processes.

II. Human rights due diligence policy

A. Scope of the policy

6. The human rights due diligence policy applies to all United Nations entities providing support to non-United Nations security forces. It therefore applies not only to peacekeeping operations and special political missions, but also to all United Nations offices, agencies, funds and programmes that engage in such activities.

B. Definitions

7. For the purpose of this policy, "non-United Nations security forces" include:
   (a) National military, paramilitary, police, intelligence services, border-control and similar security forces;
   (b) National civilian, paramilitary or military authorities directly responsible for the management, administration or command or control of such forces;
   (c) Peacekeeping forces of regional international organizations.
8. "Support" is understood to mean any of the following activities:
   (a) Training, mentoring, advisory services, capacity- and institution-building and other forms of technical cooperation for the purpose of enhancing the operational capabilities of non-United Nations security forces;
   (b) Ad hoc or programmatic support to civilian or military authorities directly responsible for the management, administration or command and control of non-United Nations security forces;
   (c) Financial support, including payment of salaries, bursaries, allowances and expenses, whatever the source of the funds;
   (d) Strategic or tactical logistical support to operations in the field conducted by non-United Nations security forces;
   (e) Operational support to action in the field conducted by non-United Nations security forces, including fire support, strategic or tactical planning;
   (f) Joint operations conducted by United Nations forces and non-United Nations security forces.
9. "Support" does **not** include:
   (a) Training or sensitization regarding international humanitarian, human rights and refugee law;
   (b) Standard-setting (e.g. advice on and review of legislation, codes and policies) and capacity support directly related to the implementation and promotion of compliance with human rights laws and standards and to foster democratic governance of security institutions;
   (c) Engagement to promote compliance with humanitarian, human rights and refugee law or to negotiate humanitarian access and carry out relief operations;

(d) Mediation and mediation-related support;

(e) Medical evacuation (MEDEVAC) and casualty evacuation (CASEVAC).

10. "Support" may be direct or indirect—that is, through implementing partners.

11. When determining whether an activity constitutes support or not in accordance with paragraphs 8 and 9 above, United Nations entities should consider the need to promote consistency in the implementation of the policy across the United Nations system according to paragraphs 18 and 20 below.

12. "Grave violations" mean, for the purposes of the present policy:

(a) In the case of a unit:

(i) Commission of "war crimes" or of "crimes against humanity", as defined in the Rome Statute of the International Criminal Court, or "gross violations" of human rights, including summary executions and extrajudicial killings, acts of torture, enforced disappearances, enslavement, rape and sexual violence of a comparable serious nature, or acts of refoulement under refugee law that are committed on a significant scale or with a significant degree of frequency (that is, they are more than isolated or merely sporadic phenomena); or

(ii) A pattern of repeated violations of international humanitarian, human rights or refugee law committed by a significant number of members of the unit; or

(iii) The presence in a senior command position of the unit of one or more officers about whom there are substantial grounds to suspect:

- Direct responsibility for the commission of "war crimes", "gross violations" of human rights or acts of refoulement; or
- Command responsibility, as defined in the Rome Statute of the International Criminal Court, for the commission of such crimes, violations or acts by those under their command; or
- Failure to take effective measures to prevent, repress, investigate or prosecute other violations of international humanitarian, human rights or refugee law committed on a significant scale by those under their command;

(b) In the case of civilian or military authorities that are directly responsible for the management, administration or command of non-United Nations security forces:

(i) Commission of grave violations by one or more units under their command;

(ii) Combined with a failure to take effective measures to investigate and prosecute the violators.

13. "United Nations" includes any office, department, agency, programme, fund, operation or mission of the United Nations.

C. Risk assessment

14. Before engaging in support, the United Nations entity directly concerned must conduct an assessment of the potential risks and benefits involved in providing support. This assessment should include consideration of the following elements (where a United Nations entity has an existing mechanism in place, this may be used to conduct the assessment in accordance with paragraph 19 below):

(a) The record of the intended recipient(s) in terms of compliance or non-compliance with international humanitarian, human rights and refugee law, including any specific record of grave violations;

(b) The record of the recipient(s) in taking or failing to take effective steps to hold perpetrators of any such violations accountable;

(c) Whether any corrective measures have been taken or institutions, protocols or procedures put in place with a view to preventing the recurrence of such violations and, if so, their adequacy, including institutions to hold any future perpetrators accountable;

(d) An assessment of the degree to which providing or withholding support would affect the ability of the United Nations to influence the behaviour of the receiving entity in terms of its compliance with international humanitarian, human rights and refugee law;

(e) The feasibility of the United Nations putting in place effective mechanisms to monitor the use and impact of the support provided;

(f) An assessment based on the factors above and on the overall context of the support, of the risk that the receiving entity might nevertheless commit grave violations of international humanitarian, human rights or refugee law.

15. Information on the record of the intended recipient with regard to compliance with international humanitarian, human rights and refugee law should be obtained from the United Nations or other reliable sources.

16. Where, as a result of this risk assessment, the United Nations entity directly concerned concludes that there are substantial grounds for believing that there is a real risk of the intended recipient committing grave violations of international humanitarian, human rights or refugee law, notwithstanding any mitigatory measures that the United Nations might take, then the United Nations entity concerned must not engage in the provision of support to that intended recipient. The United Nations entity should make clear that support will not be possible unless and until the intended recipient takes measures that are of such effect that there are no longer substantial grounds for believing that there would be a real risk of such grave violations occurring. Such measures might include, for example, the removal of an officer from a senior command position when there are substantial grounds for suspecting that officer of being responsible for grave violations of international humanitarian, human rights or refugee law.

17. Where, as a result of the risk assessment, the United Nations entity directly concerned concludes that substantial grounds do **not** exist for believing there to be a real risk of the intended recipient committing such violations, then the United Nations entity concerned may proceed to engage in the provision of support, subject to compliance with the following sections of this policy.

D. Transparency

18. Effective implementation of the policy requires the understanding and cooperation of all stakeholders, including donor and programme countries, troop- and police-contributing countries and host countries of United Nations peacekeeping and political missions. Each entity mandated to or anticipating support for non-United Nations security forces shall engage proactively with Member States and other relevant partners and stakeholders to explain the policy.

19. Before engaging in support to non-United Nations security forces, the responsible senior United Nations official[s] (e.g. Special Representative of the Secretary-General, Resident Coordinator, country representative) should inform the recipient authority/ies in writing of the United Nations core principles for support to non-United Nations security forces under this policy. In particular, recipients should be notified that United Nations support cannot be provided to units that fall under the command of individuals against whom there are substantiated allegations of grave violations of international humanitarian, human rights or refugee law. The recipient authority should also be advised of procedures or mechanisms to implement the policy, as outlined in section III below. It should be made clear to the recipient that, in order to sustain the support, the United Nations is obligated to continuously

assess whether or not the recipient's actions are consistent with the Organization's obligations under the relevant bodies of law. While advocacy and communication may be undertaken by a specific United Nations entity, it should be coordinated to promote consistency across the United Nations in-country, and the most senior United Nations official in a given country (Special Representative of the Secretary-General and/or Resident Coordinator) should be kept informed of such steps.

III. Ensuring effective implementation

A. Elements of an implementation framework

20. Implementation of the human rights due diligence policy must take into account the specific mandates of the United Nations entity concerned, as well as the nature and extent of the support, and the political and operational context in which it is delivered.

21. Each United Nations entity providing support must develop an implementation framework in accordance with its management practices in order to ensure compliance with this policy. That framework should be clearly set out in a standing operating procedure or similar instrument. The framework should, where relevant, be reported to the entity's mandating body. Such a framework should include, as required:
    (a) Resources required to effectively manage delivery of the support and to monitor and evaluate its impact;
    (b) Incentives or other accompanying measures aimed at improving compliance by the recipient with international humanitarian, human rights and refugee law;
    (c) Mechanisms for the effective monitoring of the recipient's behaviour to detect grave violations of international humanitarian, human rights and refugee law and the recipient institution's responses to any violations (such mechanisms should include procedures for regular reporting from the Office of the United Nations High Commissioner for Human Rights (OHCHR), the Office of the United Nations High Commissioner for Refugees (UNHCR), the Office for the Coordination of Humanitarian Affairs (OCHA) and the United Nations Children's Fund (UNICEF) and from the offices of the Special Representatives of the Secretary-General for Children and Armed Conflict, and the Special Representative of the Secretary-General on Sexual Violence in Conflict);
    (d) Well-defined systems for the collation and effective review of information gathered through such monitoring and from other sources, including local protection of civilian networks;
    (e) Well-defined procedures to guide decisions by responsible United Nations officials on whether or not violations committed by the recipient entity require intervention with the recipient entity or its command elements or, as a final resort, require the suspension or withdrawal of support under this policy;
    (f) Clear procedures for communication with the relevant authorities where United Nations intervention or the suspension or withdrawal of support is required under this policy;
    (g) Clear and effective procedures for evaluating and considering the possible risks if support is suspended or withdrawn, including risks to the safety and security of United Nations and associated personnel, and for identifying appropriate mitigatory measures, and ensuring that they are taken.

22. In the application of the policy and the use of measures set out in paragraphs 21 (a) to (g) above at the country level, each United Nations entity should take into account the need to promote consistency in the implementation of the policy across the United Nations system. The most senior United Nations official in country (Special Representative of the Secretary-General and/or Resident Coordinator) is responsible for initiating consultations

on the implementation framework with all national and international stakeholders. In the case of integrated missions, consultations between the mission and the United Nations country team should be part of established procedure.

B. Prior advice to United Nations legislative bodies

23. Action by United Nations entities to support non-United Nations security forces requires particularly careful attention due to the special risks, potential liabilities and high visibility involved. It is therefore important that United Nations entities exercise due diligence, in particular by conducting a risk assessment, **before** a mandate or directive is adopted to provide support to non-United Nations security forces. The resulting evaluation should be included in reports or briefings to legislative bodies, as appropriate. In the peacekeeping context, such evaluations should help inform and shape proposals by the Secretary-General to legislative bodies regarding mandates.

C. Reporting and oversight

24. Relevant official United Nations reports (e.g. reports of the Secretary-General to the Security Council, country and thematic reports by United Nations offices, programmes, agencies and funds) should cover support provided to non-United Nations security forces, including the nature and scope of the support, measures employed to ensure compliance with the "due diligence" policy, related actions to promote respect for the core principles of United Nations support and an assessment of the impact of the support.
25. Where critical difficulties arise relating to such support, United Nations entities should report immediately to the relevant decision-making United Nations officials and legislative bodies, as appropriate, on developments related to the elements of the risk assessment that present the Organization or its personnel with the risk of being associated with grave violations of international humanitarian, human rights or refugee law. The United Nations entities involved should report on the circumstances, any measures taken to mitigate or remedy the situation and recommendations for follow-up action.

D. Mitigatory measures

26. If the United Nations receives reliable information that provides substantial grounds for believing that a recipient of United Nations support is committing grave violations of international humanitarian, human rights or refugee law, the United Nations entity providing support should bring these grounds to the attention of the relevant national authorities with a view to bringing those violations to an end.
27. If, despite intercession by the United Nations entity concerned, the United Nations receives reliable information that provides substantial grounds to suspect that the recipient entity is continuing to engage in grave violations of international humanitarian, human rights or refugee law, then the United Nations entity must suspend or withdraw support from the recipient.

E. Operational challenges

28. In the peacekeeping context, withholding or withdrawing support in the face of a failure by recipient security forces to comply with the core principles of the policy may significantly diminish the mission's ability to fulfil the overall mandate and objectives set out by the Security Council. Suspension or withdrawal of logistical, material or technical support may, however, become necessary where continued support would implicate the Organization in grave violations of international humanitarian, human rights or refugee law. The Secretary-General should keep the Council informed of measures taken by a peacekeeping operation under this policy and, where it is thought that application of this policy would have a critical impact on the ability of the operation to discharge its mandate, should advise the Council in

a timely manner and seek the Council's advice regarding the way forward. Similarly, should the withholding or withdrawal of support by a United Nations agency, fund or programme affect the ability of that entity to fulfil its mandate, the Executive Head of the said agency, fund or programme will advise the governing body of the agency, fund or programme in a timely manner, and seek its advice regarding the way forward.

F. Accountability

29. Following endorsement of the present policy framework by the Secretary-General, senior managers at Headquarters (Under-Secretaries-General, the Administrator of the United Nations Development Programme (UNDP), the Executive Directors of funds and programmes) are responsible for ensuring that support for non-United Nations security forces and institutions and implementation of the policy are kept under regular review in their areas of responsibility. They are also responsible for ensuring that significant developments in the implementation of this policy, including mitigatory actions taken under it, are brought to the timely attention of the Secretary-General and the relevant legislative bodies.
30. Where relevant, integrated mission task forces and integrated task forces should include in their agendas a standing item on review and evaluation of support provided to non-United Nations security forces.
31. A further submission to the Policy Committee should be prepared in one year's time, in the light of experience gained to determine, inter alia, if any further implementation measure(s) or mechanisms are required.

33
Use of Force
Prefatory Note

One of the three key principles of UN peacekeeping, set out in the United Nations Peacekeeping Operations: Principles and Guidelines (UN Principles and Guidelines), is the non-use of force except in self-defence.[1] As briefly described in the Introduction to this book, the notion of 'self-defence' in UN peace operations has evolved to encompass the use of force by peacekeepers to protect themselves and others they have been authorised to protect as well as the use of force in defence of the mandate or mission. More recently, however, the Security Council has authorised peacekeepers to use force offensively rather than in self-defence. For example, the Council has authorised peacekeepers to use force to neutralise rebel groups[2] and when undertaking operations to counter asymmetric threats such as terrorism.[3] Reprinted below are two of the key UN use of force documents: Guidelines: Use of Force by Military Components in United Nations Operations, and an example of a card issued to UN military personnel.

1. The Guidelines

In February 2017, the UN Secretariat issued Guidelines entitled 'Use of Force by Military Components in United Nations Peacekeeping Operations' (Guidelines)[4] to provide 'clarity in the appropriate use of force at the tactical and operational levels of United Nations peacekeeping missions'.[5] The Guidelines focus on the use of force by military peacekeepers in situations other than armed conflict, as evidenced by the emphasis that the 'objective of the use of force in peacekeeping operations is to influence and deter, not necessarily to defeat threats seeking to threaten or harm United Nations personnel or associated personnel or the civilian population'.[6] That is not to say, however, that the Guidelines would not be relevant in situations of armed conflict.

The Guidelines 'highlight the strategic considerations that guide, oversee and provide the resources for the operational and tactical use of force'.[7] The Guidelines 'are intended to mitigate hesitation, accelerate decision making, improve performance and ultimately protect lives and property'.[8] In other words, the Guidelines seek to ensure that military peacekeepers use force decisively and without hesitation. But, at the same time, the Guidelines also mitigate the use of excessive force.[9] That mitigation arises from the principles which are at the core of the Guidelines:

> At all times, the use of force must be consistent with the principles of gradation, necessity, proportionality, legality, distinction, precaution, humanity and accountability. Any force used must be limited in its intensity and duration to what is necessary to achieve the authorized objective and [sic], commensurate with the threat.[10]

---

1 The other two principles are: (1) consent of the parties; and (2) impartiality. See United Nations, 'United Nations Peacekeeping Operations: Principles and Guidelines', 2008, 31–4 (hereafter UN Principles and Guidelines, but also known as the 'Capstone Doctrine').

2 See SC Res 2348 (2017) of 31 March 2017, Operative Part [16] mandating United Nations Organization Stabilization Mission in the Democratic Republic of the Congo (MONUSCO) 'to ensure all efforts possible are being made to neutralize armed groups'.

3 The Security Council mandated the United Nations Multidimensional Integrated Stabilization Mission in Mali (MINUSMA):

> to anticipate and deter threats and to take robust and active steps to counter asymmetric attacks against civilians or United Nations personnel, to ensure prompt and effective responses to threats of violence against civilians and to prevent a return of armed elements to those areas, engaging in direct operations pursuant only to serious and credible threats.

See SC Res 2295 (2016) of 29 June 2016, Operative Part [19](d).

4 Department of Peacekeeping Operations/Department of Field Support, 'Guidelines: Use of Force by Military Components in United Nations Peacekeeping Operations', January 2017 (hereafter Guidelines).

5 Ibid, [1].

6 Ibid, [6].

7 Ibid, [3].

8 Ibid, [2].

9 Ibid, [5].

10 Ibid, [8].

The Guidelines make clear that the use of force by UN peacekeepers is based on the Security Council mandate as authorised in accordance with the mission's Rules of Engagement (ROE) for the military component and the Directive on the Use of Force (DUF) for police peacekeepers.[11] The UN Principles and Guidelines state:

> The mission-wide ROE for the military and DUF for the police components of a United Nations peacekeeping operation will clarify the different levels of force that can be used in various circumstances, how each level of force should be used, and any authorizations that must be obtained by commanders [for the use of force].[12]

Each UN peace operation will be issued with mission-specific ROE and DUF which will stipulate who may authorise the use of force and levels of force that may be used for that mission. In relation to mission specific ROE the Guidelines state:

> ROE also explain the policy, principles, procedures and responsibilities governing the use of force ... While remaining predominately defensive in nature, ROE may permit offensive action, if necessary and as authorised by the Security Council, in order to ensure mandate implementation.[13]

Typically, ROE will direct or guide peacekeepers on matters such as when and what type of force may be used, which weapons may be carried, how to react to situations such as riots, and how to deal with detainees. In some cases, ROE may also deal with matters concerning command and control of the use of force by stipulating, for example, who may authorise the escalation of force and in which circumstances such authorisation may be given. The legal framework for ROE combines principles, rules and standards found in both international humanitarian law (IHL)[14] and international human rights law (IHRL).[15] The ROE are UN classified documents and therefore not in the public domain.

The ROE are developed by the Office of Military Affairs in the Department of Peacekeeping Operations (DPKO) in consultation with the UN Office of Legal Affairs (OLA). It is expected that the Force Commander (FC) serving in the mission will also be consulted in developing those documents. Troop Contributing Countries (TCCs) may also be consulted.

The Guidelines stipulate that TCCs:

> must understand and embrace the approved mission-specific ROE since the appropriate application of these ROE is mandatory for all deployed military units in a peacekeeping operation ... TCCs are not permitted to augment, restrict or modify ROE according to national interpretation(s), nor should TCCs impose any caveats on the authorizations to use force that are contained in the ROE, without formal consultation with UNHQ and the express written agreement of the DPKO. A unit's failure to carry out the ROE may result in repatriation.[16]

Notwithstanding the abovementioned stipulations concerning the prohibition of augmenting, restricting or modifying the ROE, TCCs may be bound by their domestic law or political considerations to issue their peacekeepers with, for example, more restricted ROE concerning the use of force.

The Guidelines emphasise the gradual application of force across three broad levels: (1) authoritative presence; (2) the use of non-deadly force; and (3) deadly force. They recognise, however, that in some circumstances it will not be possible to gradually escalate the use of force because they 'may have to act immediately by resorting to deadly force to avoid greater harm or compromise [of] the mandate of [sic] mission'.[17]

In relation to accountability, the Guidelines stipulate that '[e]very instance of the use of force at the tactical level, both deadly and non-deadly, must be promptly reported to the Force chain of command'.[18] Furthermore, in situations where force has been used military commanders should conduct 'an After Action Review and damage assessment ... [and] [w]here deaths or serious injury

---

11 See UN Principles and Guidelines (n 1), 14 and 35.
12 Ibid, 35.
13 Guidelines (n 4), [38].
14 See ch 16 above.
15 See chs 4–13 above.
16 Guidelines (n 4), [14].
17 Ibid, [12].
18 Ibid, [40].

of civilians or civilian property damages arise, these must be subject to effective, transparent and impartial investigation'.[19]

Where force has been used by peacekeepers the UN has accepted liability 'normally through third-party claims process implemented through the respective peacekeeping mission'.[20]

2. Soldiers' Card

Military peacekeepers are also issued with a Soldiers' Pocket Card or an ROE Pocket Card (Card)[21] which sets forth key aspects of the ROE pertinent to the use of force by individual peacekeepers.[22] Depending on the mandate of any particular peacekeeping operation the Card, which is a part of the ROE, abbreviates key provisions of the ROE for ease of reference of individual peacekeepers. Generally, the Card will address matters such as: when the use of lethal force or non-lethal force is authorised; who and what may be protected; who may authorise the use of force; and that the principles of 'minimum force and proportionality shall apply at all times and in all circumstances'.[23] The Card further explains that the principles of minimum force and proportionality operate to limit the use of force in its intensity and duration, and that force is permitted only for the purpose of achieving an authorised objective.[24] Proportionality is further subjected to the test of being 'commensurate with the level of the threat'.[25] Collateral damage is to be avoided or minimised.[26] The Card gives further guidance in relation to what level of force may be used by stating that force, as a response, is necessarily a last resort and that 'reasonable efforts shall be made' to adopt measures falling short of force.[27] The emphasis on the 'use of force only when absolutely necessary'[28] reinforces the IHRL standard concerning the use of force rather than the IHL standard where the use of force against, for example, combatants is assumed. Thus, soldiers are expected to moderate their use of force, yet are reminded that in 'some cases operational urgency may dictate the immediate use of deadly force'.[29] In relation to opening fire, the Card requires a final warning be given in the spoken national language of the host Country.[30] Indiscriminate firing of weapons is prohibited.[31] The principles of minimum force and proportionality are consistent with the legal principles concerning the use of force found in IHRL.[32]

Depending on the mandate of a particular operation, the ROE may authorise the use of deadly force in some circumstances. Deadly force may be permitted, with certain caveats, to protect life, property, and to ensure freedom of movement. Deadly force is not permitted to prevent the escape of any apprehended individual or detained person, or to prevent those who are forcing their way through an authorised peacekeeping check point.[33] In relation to the protection of civilians, force, including deadly force, may only be used if the civilian is 'under imminent threat of physical violence, when competent local authorities are not in a position to render immediate assistance'.[34] The protection of UN personnel, international personnel, and civilians is often referred to in Security Council resolutions concerning the mandate for the operation. For example, Security Council resolution 1870 states that the UN Mission in Sudan (UNMIS) is to:

---

19 Ibid, [41].

20 International Law Commission, 'Responsibility of International Organizations: Comments and Observations Received from International Organisations', UN Doc A/CN/4/637/Add1, 17 February 2011, 25 [3].

21 Also sometimes referred to as an Aide-Memoire or Blue Card.

22 See Guidelines (n 4), [39].

23 Department of Peacekeeping Operations Force Generation Service, 'Guidelines for Troop Contributing Countries Deploying Military Units to the United Nations Mission in Sudan (UNMIS)', May 2005, Annex J: Rules of Engagement: Soldiers Pocket Card, [1] (hereafter Card). [Note: As published in the 2010 edition of this book; however, the website link is no longer active].

24 Ibid, [4].

25 Ibid, [4].

26 Ibid, [8].

27 Ibid, [2]–[3].

28 Ibid, [5].

29 Ibid, [4].

30 Ibid, [6].

31 Ibid, [7].

32 See chs 4–13 above.

33 Card (n 23), 'Excluding Deadly Force', [1] and [2].

34 Ibid, 'Deadly Force', [4].

make full use of its current mandate and capabilities to provide security to the civilian population, humanitarian and development actors and UN personnel under imminent threat of violence as stated in resolution 1590 (2005), stresses that this mandate includes the protection of refugees, displaced persons and returnees . . .[35]

Protecting property with the use of force, including deadly force, may also be restricted by requiring property to be designated by the Head of Mission or SRSG.[36] Consequently, in such circumstances peacekeepers must know what property has been 'designated' for these purposes.

In relation to situations where it might be necessary to open fire, the ROE may stipulate that the on-scene commander is responsible both for giving the order to open fire, and controlling the use of fire by peacekeepers.[37] This direction may, however, be subject to the caveat that a solider may open fire if there is insufficient time to obtain such an order.[38]

The ROE also provide that persons detained by peacekeepers are to be 'handed over to appropriate local authorities as soon as possible'.[39]

References

Title	Guidelines: Use of Force by Military Components in United Nations Peacekeeping Operations
Author	Department of Peacekeeping Operations/Department of Field Support
Effective Date	1 February 2017
Full Text	<https://info.publicintelligence.net/UN-PeacekeepingForces-2017.pdf>
Title	Guidelines for Troop Contributing Countries Deploying Military Units to the United Nations Mission in Sudan (UNMIS): Annex J—Rules of Engagement—Soldiers Pocket Card
Author	Department of Peacekeeping Operations Force Generation Service
Date	May 2005
Full Text	<http://www.mil.no/multimedia/archive/00120/UNMIS_GUIDELINES_TO_120799a.pdf>[40]

Guidelines: Use of Force by Military Components in United Nations Peacekeeping Operations[41]

A. PURPOSE

1. This document is intended to provide clarity in the appropriate use of force at the tactical and operational levels of United Nations peacekeeping missions.
2. Clarity in the appropriate use of force is vital to a United Nations mission's military personnel confronted by the full spectrum of complex peacekeeping challenges. It is equally important to troop contributing countries (TCCs) providing peacekeeping military contingents. These guidelines are intended to mitigate hesitation, accelerate decision making, improve performance and ultimately protect lives and property.

35 SC Res 1870 (2009) of 30 April 2009, Operative Part [14].
36 Card (n 23), 'Deadly Force', [3].
37 Ibid, [6].
38 Ibid.
39 Ibid, 'Excluding Deadly Force'.
40 As published in the 2010 edition of this book; however, the website link is no longer active.
41 From Guidelines: Use of Force by Military Components in United Nations Peacekeeping Operations, by Department of Peacekeeping Operations/Department of Field Support ©2017 United Nations. Reprinted with the permission of the United Nations.

B. SCOPE

3. These guidelines briefly highlight the strategic considerations that guide, oversee and provide the resources for the operational and tactical use of force. While the strategic considerations of the use of force are rooted in the core peacekeeping principles, mission mandate and rules of engagement, the guidelines recognize that political and other context specific factors influence the strategic considerations on the use of force. The main emphasis, however, is on the operational and tactical considerations regarding the use of force. This document examines the required thinking and action (including situational awareness and operational/strategic communications) at these levels to pre-empt, deter, contain or respond to threats without excessive use of force.
4. These guidelines apply to all members of the military component deployed in a United Nations peacekeeping operations [sic], senior mission leaders, as well as staff members of DPKO/DFS at United Nations Headquarters (UNHQ). TCCs will also find this document helpful as they train and prepare their commanders and contingents for United Nations peacekeeping operations. The clarifications contained herein supplement, but do not replace, mission-specific rules of engagement (ROE) and other applicable guidance issued by the Under Secretary General (USG) for DPKO, which have precedence.

C. RATIONALE

5. Numerous after action reviews and discussions with TCCs have identified a gap in the understanding of the use of force despite existing mission-specific rules of engagement. These guidelines are accordingly intended to address the hesitation or lack of willingness/readiness to use force, when appropriate, in order to carry out mandated activities as well as to address the use of excessive force. It provides guidance on the use of appropriate force.

D. GUIDELINES

D.1 Definition

6. "Force" is defined as the use of, or threat to use, physical means to impose one's will. In peacekeeping operations, peacekeepers are authorized to use force in self-defense and to execute their mandated tasks in appropriate situations. Depending upon the mandate, this may include the authorization to use force for the protection of civilians. The objective of the use of force in peacekeeping operations is to influence and deter, not necessarily to defeat threats seeking to threaten or harm United Nations personnel or associated personnel or the civilian population. In some cases, the use of force may also be authorized to respond to other threats, including those caused by armed spoilers intending to distract peace processes.

D.2 Use of Force Principles and Authorization

7. The legal basis for the use of force by peacekeepers resides in the mandate of the peacekeeping mission, as reflected in the relevant resolution(s) adopted by the Security Council. The use of force must be exercised in a manner consistent with the mandate. It may be used in self-defense as well as in situations in which the mission is specifically mandated to use force as listed in the ROE. Mission-specific ROE provide the authority for the use of force as well as directions to operational commanders delineating the parameters within which force may be used.
8. The use of force in peacekeeping operations must comply with international laws, including applicable international humanitarian law[42] and human rights norms, principles and

42 International humanitarian law is known also as "the law of war" or "the law of armed conflict". Fundamental principles and

standards. At all times, the use of force must be consistent with the principles of gradation, necessity, proportionality, legality, distinction, precaution, humanity and accountability. Any force used must be limited in its intensity and duration to what is necessary to achieve the authorized objective and, commensurate with the threat.

9. The use of force is a command responsibility. The Force Commander is responsible for disseminating mission-specific ROE approved by the USG DPKO to all subordinate commanders and is ultimately responsible for ROE enforcement. It is the responsibility of the commanders of all national contingents to ensure that all those under their command understand and follow the ROE.

D.3 Alternatives to the Use of Force

10. Whenever the operational situation permits, every reasonable effort should be made to resolve a potentially hostile confrontation by means other than the use of force. The use of force may be avoided through mediation, negotiation and the good offices of civilian peacekeeping staff. This should be complemented by the skillful use of a deterrent posture; such as placing sufficient forces at the scene of potential violence to demonstrate the United Nations' intent and capability to respond to any act of violence. The use of force may also be avoided by for example, adopting a robust mission communications plan and/or through community engagement or assistance from local authorities. The ability to deter hostile intent and act successfully relies on clearly communicating capacity, requisite will and confidence in carrying out the mandated tasks. However, peacekeepers must be prepared at all times to act swiftly and decisively with the requisite force to achieve objectives as authorized by the mandate and ROE.

D.4 Graduated Application and the Use of Force Continuum

11. The graduated application of increasing levels of force ensures that only the minimum level of force necessary is used to achieve the mandated objective. This graduated application of force ensures that excessive force is avoided, and contributes to minimizing the loss of, or damage to, life and property. In every instance of the use of force, all feasible precautions should be taken with a view to avoiding, and at any event to minimizing, collateral damage.

12. Graduated force can be applied along a continuum of three broad levels beginning with physical authoritative presence, progressing to non-deadly force and finally the use of deadly force. Depending upon the nature of threat, peacekeepers sometimes may not have enough time to embrace gradual application of force and may have to act immediately by resorting to deadly force to avoid greater harm or compromise the mandate of mission. The authorization to use force without following graduated procedures, which is reflected in mission-specific ROE, only applies where the attack or threat of an attack comes so unexpectedly that even a moment's delay could lead to the death of, or serious bodily injury to, oneself, other United Nations personnel or other persons who are under the protection of the peacekeeping mission. The following chart and explanations sets forth the continuum for the use of force. This model can be modified to suit mission needs. It should also be interpreted and applied consistent with the mission-specific ROE.

rules of international humanitarian law applicable to the United Nations are contained in the Secretary-General Bulletin on the *Observance by UN Forces for International Humanitarian Law*, 6 August 1999 (ST/SGB/1999/13). See also the OHCHR/DPKO/DFS/DPA *Policy on Human Rights in UN Peace Operations and Political Missions*, 2011. [Note: this footnote appears in the original document as footnote '1'].

Core Objective
Safety and security of UN military/police and those being protected as well as the rights and well being of the aggressors during a legitimate peacekeeping operations

Use of Force Continuum

Important!
The specific details in this chart are for illustrative purpose only. Military units must tailor the details of their mission-specific requirements, equipment and level of training.

Level of Force	Threat Actions	UN Action/Reaction
DEADLY FORCE	**ASSAULTIVE (SERIOUS/FATAL ACTION)** • Threat uses weapons, undertakes life threatening weaponless assault, and/or disarms a military/police	**LETHAL** • Use of firearm and strike to vital areas
NON-DEADLY FORCE	**ASSAULTIVE (NON LIFE THREATENING)** • Threat conducts non-life threatening activities but has the potential to cause physical harm to peacekeepers/civilians, e.g.: stone throwing, use of incendiary devices, sabotage.	**DEFENSIVE TACTICS** • Use riot control equipment including shield, water cannon, soft kinetic projectiles, etc.
	RESISTANT (ACTIVE) • Threat wrestles/pushes military/police or pulls away	**COMPLIANCE TECHNIQUES** • Use chemical irritant application, riot control agents/barricades/cordon/show of forces including aviation.
	RESISTANT (PASSIVE) • Threat is unresponsive (refuses to move dead weight) of exhibits danger cues	**CONTACT CONTROLS** • Takedowns, handcuffs, threat of using force.
AUTHORITATIVE PRESENCE	**COMPLIANT** • Threat shows positive or cooperative behavior	**COOPERATIVE CONTROL** • Physical appearance, verbal command, search techniques and apprehension tactics

a. **Authoritative Presence (including verbal commands).** Authoritative presence maximizes the effect of peacekeepers' will and capabilities in a given situation. The physical presence of a contingent with the credible capacity to use appropriate force through for example foot, vehicle or air patrols may be sufficient to deter or de-escalate a volatile situation. Every effort must also be made to use verbal commands to dissuade aggressors from committing violent acts and persuade them to act peacefully. Verbal commands and authoritative presence are applied as long as they are effective in deterring aggressors or crowds from posing a threat of physical harm and/or physical violence. Engagement with both male and female key stakeholders, through culturally appropriate messaging and posture, is critical to defusing a situation and avoiding the use of force.

b. **Non-Deadly Force.** Non-deadly force, including unarmed force, is that force necessary to compel compliance or dissuade aggressors that is neither intended nor likely to cause death or serious bodily injury. Employment of riot control measures and agents, such as tear gas, stun grenades, smoke grenades, soft kinetic projectiles[43] and/or other non-lethal measures can be used (if specifically authorized) if the on-scene commander considers their use necessary and effective in preventing or stopping the hostile activity. Units and individuals must be trained and equipped in the application of non-deadly techniques and maintain the necessary refresher training. The military commander should always attempt to resolve the situation in peaceful ways with the key stakeholders.

43 Rubber bullets will be phased out by 31 Dec 2016 and replaced by UN-approved soft kinetic projectiles. [Note: this footnote appears in the original document as footnote '2'].

Actions in the non-deadly force category may also require the demonstration of tactical strength to show a significantly stronger capability to gain control over or cooperation from aggressors. Therefore, troop reinforcement and a show of force by other available mission assets (such as aviation) may be required. Non-deadly force must also be used in accordance with mission-specific ROE.

c. **Deadly Force.** Deadly force is the level of force which is intended, or is likely to cause death, regardless of whether death actually results. It is the ultimate degree of force. The use of deadly force, including armed force, is a last resort in situations against a hostile act or intent likely to cause death or serious bodily injury. Such force must be used in accordance with mission-specific ROE. Reluctance to use deadly force when warranted by the situation may lead [sic] greater damage, may put the reputation of the United Nations at risk, or may lead to mission failure.

D.5 Strategic Level Considerations

D.5.1 Strategic Planning

13. The Security Council mandate, priority objectives and operational requirements determine the necessity and scope for using force. The military Concept of Operations (CONOPS), within the political framework developed in the Mission Concept, provides the strategic direction on how the military component will support the mission's objectives using force, where necessary. The Secretary-General's Directives to the Head of Mission (HOM)/Special Representative of the Secretary-General (SRSG) will include as an annex military directives to Heads of Military Components that describe the appropriate use of force in the implementation of mandated tasks as part of the mission's broad political goals. Based on the Mission Concept and CONOPS, DPKO/DFS planners identify required capabilities and resources enabling the military component to use appropriate force, if required, to implement mandated tasks. Relevant Statements of Unit Requirement[44] (SURs) are thus prepared to include those capabilities and resources. Similarly, ROE are also developed from the mandate ensuring the application of force is controlled and legal. ROE are sufficiently robust to address the mission's requirements and provide the military component with the authority to respond to various threats while executing mandated tasks.

14. To ensure the appropriate use of force in peacekeeping operations, TCCs should prepare their troops in terms of mindset and skills. TCCs must understand and embrace the approved mission-specific ROE since the appropriate application of these ROE is mandatory for all deployed military units in a peacekeeping operation. All United Nations peacekeepers operate strictly under the United Nations chain of command. TCCs are not permitted to augment, restrict or modify ROE according to national interpretation(s), nor should TCCs impose any caveats on the authorizations to use of force that are contained in the ROE, without formal consultation with UNHQ and the express written agreement of the DPKO. A unit's failure to carry out the ROE may result in repatriation.

D.5.2 Force Generation

15. To better ensure the ability and will to implement mandated tasks effectively, including through the use of force, where necessary, the selection of TCCs should be based on applicable United Nations policies as well as past field performance and conduct, accountability

---

44 In addition to mission-specific requirements, DPKO/DFS planners should base their SURs on the DPKO/DFS UN Military Unit Manuals for specific types of military units including Infantry, Special Forces, Aviation, Force Headquarters Support Companies, Reconnaissance Units, Signals, Logistics, Military Police, Riverine, Engineer, Maritime and Transport Units. These manuals are available at: "Policy and Practice Database," accessible only to UN staff on the UN network (including field Missions) at: http://ppdb.un.org/Nav%20Pages/PolicyFramework_Default.aspx and, "Resource Hub," recently developed for Member States to access UN documents including the Military Unit Manuals at: http://research.un.org/en/peacekeeping-community. [Note: this footnote appears in the original document as footnote '3'].

and current capabilities as verified by DPKO/DFS Assessment and Advisory Visits, Pre-Deployment Visits and Contingent-Owned Equipment verification. Field performance and current capabilities of mission military entities are evaluated by the Force Commander in accordance with standard operating procedures on the evaluation of subordinate military entities, and policy on operational readiness assurance and performance improvement.[45]

D.6 Operational Level Considerations

D.6.1 Integrated Mission Operational Planning/Unified Lines of Effort

16. The use of force is not purely a military issue. In United Nations operations, every action has a political, security, social and economic dimension affecting the mission's mandated tasks, relationship with the host country and local population, as well as relations with armed groups that may be active in the mission's area of operation. Military operations in general including those involving use of force must, therefore, be part of a fully integrated mission operational plan that is part of an overall mission strategic plan to implement mandated tasks tying together various lines of effort involving all mission components. The military efforts/gains will only be effective and sustained if they are complemented by and consolidated through a viable political strategy directed by the HOM/SRSG and actions carried out by other components.

17. The military component integrates the overall mission strategy developed by the HOM/SRSG into its operational planning in close co-ordination with all other mission components. The military planning should also consider the presence, needs and vulnerabilities of other United Nations actors on the ground, related humanitarian agencies and non-governmental organizations (NGOs), particularly in a mission with a mandate encompassing the facilitation of humanitarian activities in the country. In Missions with a mandate under Chapter VII to facilitate humanitarian assistance, ROEs may include specific rules authorizing use of force to protect humanitarian personnel at risk and to use force in protecting the delivery of humanitarian assistance. In addition, the SRSG might have the authority, under the ROEs to "designate" protected premises, including non-United Nations premises or facilities, or equipment. Humanitarian agencies and non-governmental organizations (NGOs) should be kept informed of developing/evolving situations and be included in security arrangements (to the extent allowed under applicable United Nations security policies, in close consultation and coordination with the United Nations Department of Safety and Security; and in integrated missions, in close consultation with the Deputy Special Representative of the Secretary-General, Resident Coordinator/Humanitarian Coordinator (D-SRSG RC/HC) who coordinates humanitarian actors and the United Nations country team). The use of force may have second order humanitarian and a human rights consequence. An assessment of these consequences through a risk mitigation assessment should be incorporated into operational planning where force is envisioned, in consultation with relevant civilian components and the Humanitarian Country Team. Synergy amongst all mission components is essential for effective mandate implementation.

18. The Force Headquarters must also ensure that its operations are coordinated through the regular sharing of information, comprehensive analysis of the ground situation and understanding of the role played by the various mission components within the integrated mission operational plan. During operational planning, the Force Commander and staff should consider a variety of mission scenarios that may require the use of force to achieve identified objectives. The appropriate use of force in the execution of assigned tasks in such scenarios should be clearly delineated in the Force Operations Order. Annex A provides

45 For details see the DPKO/DFS SOP on Force and Sector Commanders evaluation of military entities in peacekeeping operations, January 2016 and DPKO/DFS policy on operational readiness assurance and performance improvement, January 2016. [Note: this footnote appears in the original document as footnote '4'].

examples of some possible scenarios involving the appropriate use of force. Similarly, the Force Headquarters should also maintain a reserve force to quickly respond to threats beyond the capacity of local units, within a reasonable time.

19. Mission and Force level decisions and judgements concerning the military use of force must consider a combination of factors including Mission/Military Component capabilities, public perceptions, humanitarian impact, force protection/safety and security of personnel and the effect on national and local consent for the United Nations mission. Much of this understanding and goodwill can be accomplished through an effective strategic communications program.

D.6.2 Robust Mission Communications

20. At the mission/operational level, a comprehensive and integrated communications plan can dispel local misconceptions, manage expectations, promote peacekeeper safety and security, strengthen the mission's credibility and help respond effectively to public concerns. Communicating clearly and robustly to government officials, potential spoilers, parties to the conflict, community leaders and members of civil society is critically important, especially if effective mandate implementation requires the use of force. Mission communications can therefore be used as a means to reach out and explain the mission's mandate and that an appropriate level of force (maximum as well as minimum) has been authorized to implement that mandate. Communications on the use of force can convey either deterrent or de-escalatory purposes, which serve the underlying objective to minimize the need to actually resort to force.[46]

21. In situations where the mission uses force, public diplomacy and information sharing should become priority tasks. The period immediately following the mission's use of force is critical, and must be characterized by timely mission communication involving public information on the particular incident and envisaged follow-up investigations that is accurate, transparent and within the constraints of operational security and confidentiality. Information on critical incidents, including but not limited to live firing, should also be communicated as soon as possible to all relevant public information bodies, including UNHQ (especially the Office of the Military Affairs and the Office of Operations in DPKO), in accordance with Department of Public Information/DPKO Policy on Public Information and Strategic Communications.[47] Skillfully crafting the substance of the message plus information sharing will address local concerns and may prevent negative reactions. The ability to anticipate these concerns depends on competent situational awareness.

D.6.3 Situational Awareness

22. Situational awareness is critical to understanding, preventing, and responding effectively to acts of violence. Commanders at all levels must keep abreast of evolving operational situations to better visualize and anticipate emerging threats, opportunities and the possible consequences of United Nations actions. Situational awareness improves planning and preparation for potential military responses to prevent violence.

23. Reliable intelligence is essential for the effective and judicious use of force. Intelligence is essential to allow the Military Component to be proactive, pre-empt threats and maximize the impact of United Nations operations through proper timing and direction. In cooperation with and guided by relevant mission components, and in line with the policy on peacekeeping intelligence,[48] the Force Headquarters should therefore develop a systematic

---

46 Note, however, that rules of engagement are classified 'confidential' and may not be shared with unauthorized personnel. [Note: this footnote appears in the original document as footnote '5'].

47 For details, see DPI/DPKO policy on Public Information and Strategic Communications, 2016. [Note: this footnote appears in the original document as footnote '6'].

48 DPKO/DFS policy on Peacekeeping Intelligence is currently in the process of approval. [Note: this footnote appears in the original document as footnote '7'].

approach to collecting and analyzing information to map vulnerabilities; identify potential threats to civilians, peacekeepers, United Nations and associated personnel and other individuals that the mission has a mandate to protect; and understand the dynamics, patterns, motivations and capabilities of local actors. The Force Headquarters should develop directives on information collection and reporting procedures as standard military practice and all uniformed peacekeepers should receive training on and carry out information-collection as a matter of routine. Intelligence requirements and collection plans must be regularly issued and forwarded to subordinate units in accordance with evolving situations and threat assessments.

24. Regular threat and risk assessments informed by sound intelligence enable the mission to anticipate, prevent and be prepared to respond effectively to violence before it occurs. Understanding the intent of potential threats is critical to the development and implementation of an appropriate mitigation or response plan. In addition to its own military assets on the ground, the Military Component should seek clarity and consolidate analysis through assets such as the All Source Information Fusion Unit, Joint Operations Centre, Joint Mission Analysis Centre and the Integrated Security System as well as other mission entities such as police component, Civil Affairs, DDR, Gender, Human Rights and as outlined in the policy on peacekeeping intelligence. Working with the situational awareness provided by these and its own assets, the Military Component can plan in advance for a range of scenarios that may involve the outbreak of violence, and then develop options for the use of force appropriate to each scenario. The Military Component should also fully engage a range of United Nations actors in developing/conducting scenario-based contingency planning, including humanitarian, protection, gender and human rights stakeholders. Scenario development, examination of possible courses of action, scenario-based training in tactics and techniques, and rehearsals to reinforce that training can all contribute to the required mindset for the appropriate and effective use of force.

D.6.4 Effective Command and Control

25. The authorization to use force comes with the responsibility to do so in accordance with the mandate and ROE. Force Commanders are responsible for ensuring that their orders are strictly followed. Any incidents of refusing to follow lawful orders (including those that involve citing undisclosed national caveats) must be reported to UNHQ for appropriate action. The Secretary-General has stipulated that all HOM/SRSGs shall submit consolidated reports of incidents involving the refusal to obey lawful orders to the United Nations Secretariat.[49] The Secretariat will then immediately inform the concerned TCC and, as appropriate, the Security Council. If no remedial action is forthcoming from the TCC, the unit concerned may be repatriated.

26. The chain of command must control the use of force within the parameters authorized by the ROE. If required and authorized by the Force Commander, the authority for the use of force should be delegated in writing to subordinate commanders. Such written delegation of authority facilitates decentralized execution and promotes initiative and speed of action in accordance with the higher commander's well-defined intent and objectives in implementing the mandate. The ability to decentralize the use of force decision requires that all commanders and troops have a clear understanding of when and at what level force can be used in implementing assigned tasks. The chain of command must therefore ensure that all Force personnel have the proper preparation and training to ensure that they use force appropriately. Excessive use of force, or the failure to use force in line with the ROE,

---

49 Code cable No 1883, dated 25 August 2015, signed by the Secretary-General and sent to all SRSGs of field missions. [Note: this footnote appears in the original document as footnote '8'].

negatively impacts a mission's success and may raise issues of individual and organizational responsibility.

27. Force Commanders should use all means at their disposal to ensure that all subordinate commanders and troops are given extensive training on mission-specific ROE and other use of force guidelines, as well as directives for use of force of police components. To address the concerns of commanders and troops regarding their reluctance to use force (e.g., for fear of being penalized), the Force Headquarters and chain of command must provide clear guidance and directives on the use of force (as well as the status, privileges and immunities of military members of military contingents under the applicable legal framework, including the status-of-forces-agreement). Tactical level commanders and troops must all undergo regular training in tactics, techniques and procedures on the appropriate use of force. The timely availability of the ROE to the TCC for incorporation into pre-deployment training, along with mandatory routine ROE refresher training whilst in Mission, including scenario based realistic practical exercises, are key to ensuring that peacekeepers have the knowledge, skills and support to implement their mandate.

D.7 Tactical Level Considerations

28. At the tactical level, the effective use of force depends on the tactical commander's assessment of the emerging situation, opportunities and preparation for responsive action and risks of inaction. Commanders must always take appropriate action against threats, responsibly mitigating and accepting assessed risks when carrying out mandated tasks. Commanders are accountable for their inaction or failure to use authorized force, especially when required to save lives. Military units and contingents are also accountable for any failure to obey the Force Commander's (or other commanders') lawful orders consistent with the mandate and ROE.

D.7.1 Credible, Flexible Force Posture and Presence

29. Military commanders and their units must have a mindset that demonstrates a willingness, readiness and capacity to respond appropriately to hostile acts and hostile threats of violence. UN military units must openly display professional conduct at all times. Shows of force, determination and willingness to act contribute to military credibility and may reduce the need to use force.

30. Flexible force posture is essential to seizing, retaining, and exploiting the initiative, and responding appropriately before situations deteriorate and options become limited. A flexible force posture can be retained by anticipating, pre-planning, maintaining and pre-positioning reserve forces (where applicable in close cooperation with police components, deployed Formed Police Units should also be considered) and developing robust contingency plans. Military units must therefore be flexible, adaptable and able to detach smaller units capable of operating independently for extended periods of time 24 hours a day. Similarly, military contingents should also organize quick reaction forces (e.g., in a battalion location, one company; in a company location, one platoon) to respond quickly to any evolving situation. This ensures an additional layer of capability to existing units dedicated as quick reaction reserve forces at the Sector and Force levels.

D.7.2 Robust and Proactive Approach

31. Military units must be proactive to deter/disrupt hostile intent or act (as authorized by the mandate and ROE) before the situation becomes critical. Persons/groups displaying hostile intent against United Nations personnel, United Nations associated personnel or civilian populations, or attempting to interfere with the freedom of movement of the mission should be dealt with in accordance with the mission-specific ROE, as and when necessary. They should be responded to proactively and robustly with the appropriate level of force

(i.e. 'just enough'). Peacekeepers should not wait for hostile elements to attack civilians or United Nations personnel before using the appropriate level of force to prevent violence. Proactively using force to execute mandated tasks may not only save the lives of those threatened, but can also deter violent spoilers who may be working against peace processes. The timely and robust response to threats also enhances peacekeeper credibility. Thus, the actual use of force may not be necessary if peacekeepers display firm determination, readiness and capability to pre-empt/respond persuasively. This proactive approach requires, among other elements, an enhanced intelligence capability and a close cooperation with police components, where Formed Police Units (FPU) are deployed.

D.7.3 Intelligence Capability at the Tactical Level

32. The appreciation of evolving situations at the tactical level, which can have implications for the use of force, requires strong information gathering and analysis capability to pre-empt, deter or use force against threats. Achieving early warning and conducting operations to seize and maintain the initiative requires detailed knowledge of armed actors/spoilers and their modus operandi. Developing such intelligence involves a thorough analysis of the operational environment in terms of the crisis' background, underlying causes and the dynamics of all actors in the mission area.

33. Military units/contingents should have their own organic intelligence ability and structure, led by experienced intelligence officers that can guide the process of information collection. Military intelligence capabilities should be developed down to company and temporary operating base level as a military intelligence cell (U-2). Such intelligence cell should prepare information collection [sic] plan based on Unit Information Requirements, analyze patrol briefs, track and analyze significant activities, and serve as the information hub. Military units/sub units must develop reliable contacts and relationships with local communities and should engage via the local Community Alert Network and Community Liaison Assistants who can provide early warning of potential threats. Engagement with key female leaders and local women's groups should be explored as an additional source of valuable information.

D.7.4 Tactical Decision and Response Model

34. Deciding on the appropriate level of force is based on a number of factors including threat intensity, the effect of action/inaction and the availability of resources and assets to conduct operations that create a credible force posture. The Tactical Decision and Response Model described below captures concise details of the type and intensity of force capability requirements for a variety of situations. This Model indicates when a response needs to be escalated. It describes a graduated progression in the use of force, also delineating military units' roles prior to and after the use of force against hostile intent or hostile act. It is designed to assist military commanders and staff in understanding four distinct decision phases, and provides direction on the proper application of military force to anticipate, deter and counter threats during a specific situation. This Model is indicative and should be applied consistent with the mission-specific ROE.

35. Although arranged in a logical order, the following phases can also occur non-sequentially and/or concurrently, depending on the situation. When considering the use of force, there is the need to examine the specific roles played by military units in each of the four phases. A more complete list of indicators and possible tasks under these four phases is shown at Annex B.

    a. **Assurance and Prevention.** Involves measures and activities that peacekeepers can take to discourage potential hostile acts, where threat of hostile activity is present but low. Peacekeeper actions include adopting a strong deterrent posture, conducting visible patrols and establishing check points. Additional actions include information networking, regular security surveys, inspections and assessments of facilities, camps and bases in the area of operations/interest, strengthening United Nations installation physical security and engaging in community-based activities such as "hearts and minds" programs and quick impact projects. Moreover, peacekeepers should also take proactive de-escalation strategies based on enhanced communication and contact with potentially violent actors, where possible. Dialogue with local communities and engaging with both male and female representatives of those communities remains essential to achieving situational awareness.

b. **Pre-emption.** Involves active measures to deter or contain an identified and immediate threat against civilians (in case of the protection of civilians), United Nations and associated personnel or United Nations property; and/or gain advantage over a threatening group before it can carry out a hostile act. Examples of pre-emptive peacekeeper actions include interposition and show of force/maneuver of larger forces to demonstrate resolve and defuse situations, enforcing curfews, cordon and search operations, targeted use of necessary and proportionate force against identified hostile acts and hostile threats, apprehension and detention operations, and tactical redeployment of troops to guard key infrastructure, terrain or targeted groups (consistent with ROE).

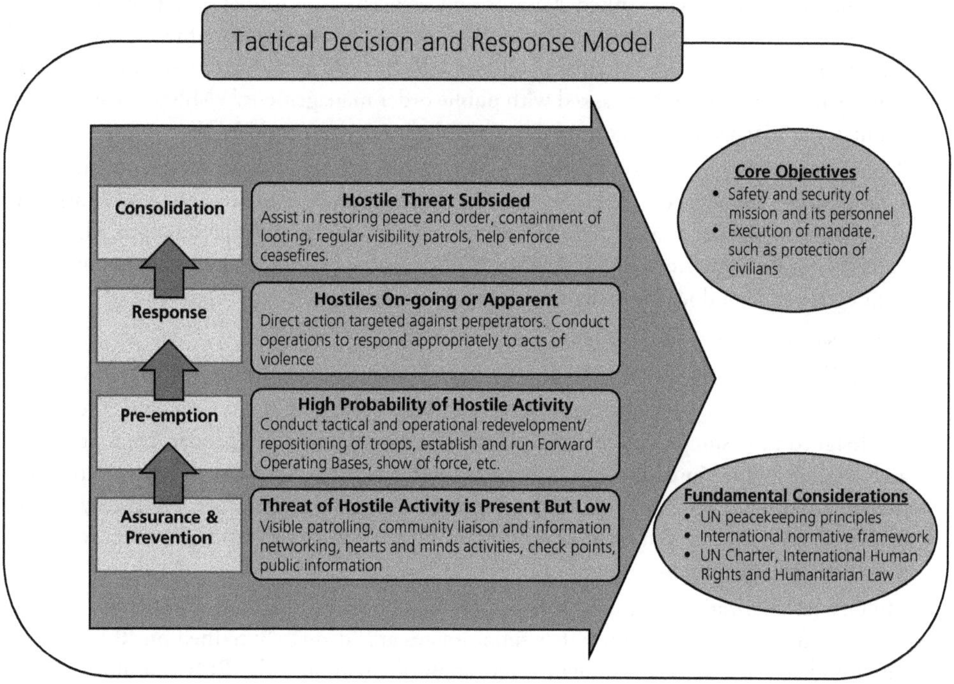

Note: This Model captures concise details of the type and intensity of force capability requirements for a variety of situations. It indicates when a response needs to be escalated.

c. **Response.** Involves the necessary and proportionate use of force by peacekeepers to neutralize or render ineffective a hostile intent or hostile act endangering life and/or impeding implementation of mandated tasks such as the protection of civilians. Peacekeeper response should be timely and assertive, as authorized by mandate and ROE. Examples of peacekeeper actions include physical protection and evacuation of civilians at risk, direct confrontation, robust camp defense, search and rescue and close air support. Response also includes those measures taken to mitigate or minimize unintended effects. Examples of these mitigating/minimizing measures would include the use of observed fire, intentionally aiming-off when in close proximity to civilians and using illumination instead of high explosive ordnance.

d. **Consolidation.** Pertains to activities requiring management after the hostile threat has subsided. Consolidation involves actions denying threat groups the ability to restore their capability, and assisting the local population and host country authorities in normalizing the situation. Examples of peacekeeper consolidation actions include support to Disarmament, Demobilization and Reintegration activities, security support to facilitate civilian-led humanitarian activities, the establishment of procedures to monitor and safeguard buffer zones and treaty compliance, threat assessment and robust defense.

D.7.5 Military–Police Cooperation

36. Military units work closely with United Nations Police, especially while engaging in public order management tasks. In field missions, United Nations Police are normally in the lead to support national police authorities in public order management. Military units can be assigned to complement United Nations Police or national police forces in situations where public order threats the [sic] exceed police's capacity to respond, or when threats are of a military nature.[50] In this regard, military units may face situations requiring riot/crowd control, either to protect United Nations and associated personnel and United Nations premises, or to ensure freedom of movement for carrying out mandated tasks. The United Nations Infantry Battalion Manual (Volumes I & II) describes a variety of situations that military units may face while tasked with public order management.[51] Military assistance to public order management is governed by the mission mandate and ROE.

37. Public order management is a sensitive operation requiring human rights compliance, training, appropriate equipment, effective de-escalation strategies and clear command and control arrangements to manage a calibrated and appropriate response to a volatile situation. Therefore, Force/Sector Headquarters should develop SOPs with the United Nations police component to integrate and conduct mutually supporting planning, training and operations.[52]

D.7.6 Adherence to Rules of Engagement

38. Mission-specific ROE provide the requisite authority for the use of force. ROE also explain the policy, principles, procedures and responsibilities governing the use of force. These rules are designed to ensure that force application is in compliance with fundamental principles and rules of international law, including international human rights law and international humanitarian law. While remaining predominantly defensive in nature, ROE may permit offensive action, if necessary and as authorized by the Security Council, in order to ensure mandate implementation.

39. Military familiarization and competent implementation of ROE is a command responsibility. Commanders must ensure that subordinates are adequately trained on ROE, understand and rehearse them thoroughly, and apply them uniformly. ROE training sessions should be conducted on a regular basis and, at a minimum, once per month and whenever military personnel, including individual replacements or reinforcements, are deployed into the mission area.[53] Troops must carry ROE Pocket card (Aide Memoire) with the necessary extracts of the mission ROE translated into their language. Pocket cards should include basic warnings and commands translated into the local population's language(s).

---

50 The distinction between military and non-military level threats is described in the DPKO/DFS Policy on Authority, Command and Control, as well as in the DPKO/DFS Policy (revised) on Formed Police Units in United Nations Peacekeeping Operations (01 March 2010). [Note: this footnote appears in the original document as footnote '9'].

51 For details, see UNIBAM Volume I, Chapter 5.4.11 and Volumes II, Chapter 2.11 (August 2012). [Note: this footnote appears in the original document as footnote '10'].

52 For details, see DPKO/DFS guidelines on Military Support for Public Order Management in peacekeeping Operations, 2016. [Note: this footnote appears in the original document as footnote '11'].

53 This example is taken from the Rules of Engagement of MINUSMA, Mali, June 2013. [Note: this footnote appears in the original document as footnote '12'].

D.7.7 Reporting and Accountability

40. Every instance of the use of force at the tactical level, both deadly and non-deadly, must be promptly reported to the Force chain of command. FHQ should report any incident of the use of force to UNHQ. Regular reporting on developing situations allows the chain of command to maintain timely awareness and provides direction to United Nations units involved, or supporting units to prepare to assist if the need arises. The commander involved in the incident is responsible and accountable for the conduct and reporting of the incident. Details of the incident must also be recorded. All injured persons (including from within the armed groups/spoilers) must be given first aid as soon as possible and where feasible. The bodies of persons who have been killed shall be treated with respect. They are to be recovered for medical examination and identification as soon as it is safe to do so.

41. Reporting and recording procedures must be clearly specified in the mission's SOP and relevant guidelines. The Military Component should conduct an After Action Review and damage assessment on all major incidents with relevant mission components, including Best Practices and human rights officers, and draw the lessons learned. Where deaths or serious injury of civilians or civilian property damages arise, these must be subject to effective, transparent and impartial investigation.

42. In the case of United Nations peacekeepers detaining individuals or groups, detention should be conducted in accordance with the relevant Interim SOP on detention operations in United Nations peacekeeping,[54] the mission's ROE and SOPs. Detentions must be reported promptly to the chain of command and by the FHQ to the HOM. Detained personnel must be handled humanely in a manner that is consistent with international human rights law, applicable international humanitarian law and international refugee law, and other relevant international norms and standards. Detainees must be handed over to the appropriate authorities as per United Nations guidelines.

D.8 Decision Factors and Risk Management

43. Any decision to use force should be first assessed through four key factors; Legality, Appropriateness, Capacity and Criticality. The intent of the HOM should be clearly understood and clarified throughout the immediate planning process. Peacekeepers require to answer the following four questions in the affirmative prior to deciding to use force, particularly deadly use of force. (Rather than try to process these questions at the last moment, commanders should use the following matrix as part of continuous in-mission training on the use of force to assist decision-making):

"Decision Factors and Risk Management" Key Use of Force Questions	Yes	No
1. Legality: Is the type of force for the intended purpose authorized under the mission ROE and is it warranted in the situation?		
2. Appropriateness: Have all available peaceful means to resolve the situation been exhausted and will the use of force contribute to the authorized objective and/or task? Is the force to be used necessary and proportionate to the threat?		
3. Capacity: Does the mission or contingent have the capability (equipment, training and manpower, including reserves) to use targeted and graduated force?		
4. Criticality: Will inaction result in serious physical injuries or death to United Nations and associated personnel or civilian populations or damage of United Nations property and/or result in negative impact in the mission's success/credibility?		

Note: Peacekeepers require answering these four questions in the affirmative prior to deciding to use force.

54 For guidance on the processing and handling of detainees, UN personnel should refer to the most current DPKO/DFS ISOP on Detention in United Nations Peace Operations, Ref. 2010.6 of 25 January 2010 and any Mission SOP or guidelines issued thereunder. [Note: this footnote appears in the original document as footnote '13'].

44. Commanders at all levels must exercise their professional military judgement, taking into account all relevant factors in the decision-making process, in order to develop courses of action to counter hostile activity, capabilities and intent. The use of a deliberate process to develop realistic courses of action will assist peacekeepers in developing methods aimed at reducing the impact and/or likelihood of threats from hostile groups or individuals.

D.9 Training

45. In accordance with DPKO/DFS policy on Operational Readiness Assurance and Performance Improvement,[55] the shaping, training and preparation of United Nations peacekeepers before deployment is a TCC responsibility. During pre-deployment training, all military personnel should be trained to established United Nations standards with Core Pre-Deployment Training Materials, Specialized Training Materials, United Nations Infantry Battalion Manual/United Nations Military Unit Manuals, mission-specific ROE, the DPKO/DFS Detention ISOP and applicable humanitarian and human rights law. The mission-specific ROE should form a part of the pre-deployment training. Training should focus on appropriate use of force in different situations and emphasize the graduated application of force. The use of force decision and response model, and the use of force matrix of indicators and possible tasks attached as Annex B, should form the basis of any use of force training curriculum.
46. Ideally, training should be based on scenarios that peacekeepers are likely to encounter in the mission area. At the tactical level, unit preparation should include basic skills training such as weapons proficiency and accuracy. As such, all units should zero their weapons within 30 days of arrival in the mission, and weapons should be check-zeroed on a regular basis. TCCs should provide ammunition for live firing training. The Force Headquarters will ensure access to the required small arms ranges.
47. Once military units and contingents are deployed in the mission area, the FHQ should ensure that all commanders receive in-mission briefing and training including updated ROE. Similarly, the FHQ should insist on periodic unit training, and can ensure this by issuing regular training command directives based on realistic operational scenarios including those involving child soldiers and/or female combatants, when applicable. Regular in-mission training should include drills and procedures that amplify important tasks commanders and troops must carry out, including the authority to use force if necessary. Scenario-based training, with thorough plans considering all mission components, can be introduced and constantly updated to assist commanders and troops in their assessment of complex situations. Special teams, organized and equipped for Public Order Management and the techniques of cordon and search, should train regularly on use of force procedures as operational requirements permit.

E. TERMS AND DEFINITIONS

Attack The use of force by or against any force or personnel, or directed at a target or objective.

Cordon A deployment of United Nations peacekeepers around an object or location with the intent to isolate an area and restrict and/or control both access and exit.

Collateral Damage Incidental loss of civilian life, injury to civilians or damage to civilian property not part of any authorized target.

Detention The act of unilaterally restricting the freedom of movement of an individual pursuant to the mission's mandate and ROE, regardless of the duration of such detention.

---

55 DPKO/DFS policy on Operational Readiness Assurance and Performance Improvement, December 2015. [Note: this footnote appears in the original document as footnote '14'].

Deterrence The display of willingness, capability and readiness of peacekeepers to use force to prevent an individual or group from initiating a hostile act.

Force The use of, or threat to use, physical means to impose one's will.

Armed Force The use of all weapons, including firearms and bayonets.

Deadly Force The level of force which is intended, or likely to cause, death, regardless of whether death actually results. This is the ultimate degree of force.

Non-Deadly Force The level of force that is neither intended nor likely to cause death, regardless of whether death actually results.

Minimum Force The minimum degree of authorized force that is necessary and reasonable in the circumstances to achieve the authorized objective. A minimum degree of force is applicable whenever force is used. Minimum Force can be Deadly Force, in certain circumstances.

Unarmed Force The use of physical force, short of the use of Armed Force.

Hostile Act An action where the intent is to cause death, serious bodily harm or destruction of United Nations designated property.

Hostile Intent The threat of an impending use of force, which is demonstrated through an action or behavior which appears to be preparatory to a hostile act. Only a reasonable belief in the hostile intent is required before the use of force is authorized. Whether or not hostile intent is being demonstrated must be judged by the on-scene commander, on the basis of one or a combination of the following factors:

a. The capability and preparedness of the threat.
b. The available evidence which indicates an intention to attack.
c. Historical precedent within the Mission's Area of Responsibility.

Reasonable Belief A belief which a reasonable peacekeeper would hold on the basis of the facts as they are known to him or her at the time.

Offensive Operation Military operations undertaken by military contingents, as and when mandated, in order to discharge the task of neutralizing armed groups to prevent their expansion, and neutralize and disarm them in order to contribute to the objective of reducing threats to the host state authority and civilian security, as and when mandated.

Proportionality The amount of force which is reasonable in intensity, duration and magnitude, based on all facts known to the commander or individual soldier at the time, to decisively counter a hostile act or intent or to otherwise achieve an authorized objective specified in the mission-specific ROE.

Spoiler Individuals or groups that may profit from the spread or continuation of violence, or have an interest to disrupt a resolution of a conflict, including through a violent means, in a given setting.

United Nations Personnel For specific details, refer to the mission-specific ROE. For the purposes of this document, the following persons are considered "United Nations personnel:"

a. Members of the peacekeeping mission.
b. Officials of the United Nations and its specialized agencies and related organizations.
c. Experts on the mission for the United Nations and for its specialized agencies and related organizations.
d. United Nations Volunteers who are present in the host nation in the performance of their official duties or missions.
e. Other associated personnel designated by the Head of the Mission, in consultation with United Nations headquarters, including:
    i. Persons engaged by the Secretary-General or by one of the specialized agencies or related organizations of the United Nations.
    ii. Persons assigned by a Government or an intergovernmental organization operating with the authority of the Security Council or General Assembly.

iii. Persons deployed by authorized humanitarian non-governmental organizations or agencies under an agreement with the Secretary-General, or with a specialized agency or related organization of the United Nations to carry out activities in support of the fulfilment of the mandate of a mission or of programmes of the United Nations, including programmes of its offices.

United Nations Associated Personnel See, UN personnel, under item (e).

F. REFERENCES

Normative or Superior References

A. *Report of the High Level Independent Panel on Peacekeeping Operations*, 16 June 2015.

B. Report of the Secretary-General on *"The future of United Nations peace operations: implementation of the recommendations of the High-level Independent Panel on Peace Operations,"* (A/70/375-S/2015/682) (2 September 2015).

C. Secretary-General's Bulletin on *Observance by United Nations Forces of International Humanitarian Law* [ST/SGB/1999/13].

D. Secretary-General's Bulletin on *Special Measures for Protection From Sexual Exploitation and Sexual Abuse* [ST/SGB/2003/13].

E. Security Council Aide-Mémoire for the consideration of issues pertaining to the protection of civilians in armed conflict [S/PRST/2015/23 Annex].

F. Rome Statute of the International Criminal Court [ICC-ASP/2/Res.3].

G. The Four Geneva Conventions of 1949 and the Additional Protocols to the Geneva Conventions (1977).

H. Secretary-General's letter to the General Assembly and Security Council: *Human Rights Due Diligence Policy on United Nations Support to Non-United Nations Security Forces* (A/67/775–S/2013/110), March 2013.

I. *UN Policy on Human Rights Screening of United Nations Personnel* (December 2012).

Related Policies, Procedures or Guidelines

A. DPKO/DFS Policy on *Authority, Command and Control in United Nations Peacekeeping Operations* (Ref 2008.4).

B. DPKO/Force Generation Service Generic *Guidelines for Troop Contributing Countries Deploying Military Units to the United Nations Peacekeeping Missions* (2008).

C. DPKO/DPS *Policy: Mainstreaming the Protection, Rights and Wellbeing of Children Affected by Armed Conflict within UN Peacekeeping Operations.* (Ref 2009.17)

D. DPKO/DFS SOP *on Detention in United Nations Peace Operations*, (Ref 2010.06)

E. DPKO/DFS *Policy on Gender Equality in UN Peacekeeping Operations* (Ref 2010.25)

F. DPKO/DFS *Guidelines: Integrating a Gender Perspective into the Work of the United Nations Military in Peacekeeping Operations* (Ref 2010.22)

G. OHCHR/DPKO/DFS/DPA *Policy on Human Rights in Peace Operations and Political Missions* (Ref 2011.20).

H. DPKO/DFS *United Nations Infantry Battalion Manual*, Volume I & II (2012).

I. DPKO/DFS *Policy for the Protection of Civilians in United Nations Peacekeeping* (Ref 2015.07).

J. DPKO/DFS Guidelines: *Protection of Civilians: Implementing Guidelines for the Military Components of United Nations Peacekeeping Missions* (Ref 2015.02).

K. DPKO/DFS and DPA Guidelines: *the Mission Concept* (Ref 2014.04).

L. DPKO/DFS Policy: *Operational Readiness Assurance and Performance Improvement*, (Ref 2015.16).

M. DPKO/DFS SOP: *Force and Sector Commanders Evaluation of Military Entities in Peacekeeping Operations* (Ref 2016.02).

N. DPKO/DFS SOP: *Force Headquarters Evaluation in peacekeeping operations* (Ref 2016.16).

O. DPKO/DFS *Policy on Public Information and Strategic Communications* (2016).

P. DPKO/DFS Guidelines: *Military Support for Public Order Management in Peacekeeping Operations* (Ref 2016.23).

G. MONITORING AND COMPLIANCE

48. In field missions, the implementation of these Guidelines shall be the responsibility of the HOMC/FC.
49. The Office of Military Affairs shall monitor compliance with these Guidelines.

H. CONTACT

50. These guidelines were developed by the Office of Military Affairs, DPKO. Queries or comments should be directed thereto.

I. HISTORY

51. This is the first edition of these guidelines. It will be considered for revision in 01 February 2020.

Annex J

Soldiers Pocket Card[56]

1. The principles of minimum force and proportionality shall apply at all times and in all circumstances.
2. Wherever the operational situation permits, every reasonable effort shall be made to control a situation through measures short of force, including personal contact and negotiation, visual signals, maneuvers, charging of weapons and firing warning shots.
3. The use of force, including deadly force, shall only be resorted to if all other means to control the situation have failed or do not hold any promise of achieving the authorized objective.
4. Any force used must be limited in its intensity and duration to what is necessary to achieve the authorized objective and must be commensurate with the level of the threat. In some cases, operational urgency may dictate the immediate use of deadly force.

56 From Guidelines for Troop Contributing Countries Deploying Military Units to the United Nations Mission in Sudan (UNMIS): Annex J—Rules of Engagement—Soldiers Pocket Card, by DPKO Force Generation Service © 2005 United Nations. Reprinted with the permission of the United Nations.

5. Use force only when absolutely necessary to achieve your immediate aim, to protect yourself, your soldiers, UN or other designated personnel, installations, equipment and civilians under imminent threat of physical violence.
6. The decision to open fire shall be made only on the order and under the control of the on-scene Commander, unless there is insufficient time to obtain such an order. Before opening fire, give a final warning at least three times, either in Arabic, which is the widely spoken national language in the mission area, or in English which is also an official language of the National Government:

   "AUGAF ANDAK WALLA ARMIK"
   "UNITED NATIONS, STOP OR I WILL FIRE"

You may open fire without warning only when an attack is so unexpected that a moment's delay could lead to death or grievous injury to yourself, to other members of UNMIS's military component or to other persons who are under protection of UNMIS military component as specified in these ROE.

7. Fire must be aimed and controlled. Automatic fire will be opened only as last resort. If possible, a single shot should be aimed at non-vital parts of the body in order not to kill. Indiscriminate fire is not permitted. Fire for effect must not last longer than necessary to achieve the immediate aim.
8. Avoid or minimize collateral damage.
9. After fire has ceased, render medical assistance and record the details of the incident and report them as soon as possible through the chain of command, whether or not casualties have occurred.
10. When in doubt, always seek clarification from higher command.

You are allowed to use force (UP TO AND INCLUDING DEADLY FORCE):

1. To defend oneself, other UN personnel, individuals designated by the Head of Mission or other international personnel against a hostile act or a hostile intent;
2. To resist attempts to abduct or detain oneself, other UN personnel, other international personnel or individuals designated by the Head of Mission;
3. To protect installations, facilities, equipment, areas or goods designated by the Head of Mission against a hostile act or hostile intent;
4. To protect civilians under imminent threat of physical violence, when competent local authorities are not in a position to render immediate assistance*;
5. To resist attempts by any person or group that limits or intends to limit the freedom of movement of UN personnel, humanitarian workers or individuals designated by the Head of Mission*;

   * *when and where possible, permission to use force should be sought from the immediate superior commander.*

You are allowed to use force, EXCLUDING deadly force:

1. To prevent the escape of any apprehended or detained person, pending hand-over to appropriate civilian authorities;
2. To prevent forcible passage by individuals or groups through a checkpoint** and to detain those who have forcibly effected passage through a checkpoint**.

** *Whose establishment has been authorized by the Force Commander.*

Detained persons are to be handed over to appropriate local authorities as soon as possible.

Hostile Act. An action where the intent is to cause death, bodily harm or destruction of designated property.

Hostile Intent. The threat of imminent use of force, demonstrated through an action which appears to be preparatory to a hostile act. Only a reasonable belief in the hostile intent is required, before the use of force is authorized.

Whether or not hostile intent is being demonstrated must be judged by the on-scene commander, on the basis of one or a combination of the following factors:

- The capability and preparedness of the threat;
- The available evidence which indicates an intention to attack;
- Historical precedent within the Mission's Area of Responsibility.

PART FOUR

Key International Court of Justice Cases

34

Reparations for Injuries Suffered in the Service of the United Nations

Prefatory Note

On 3 December 1948, the General Assembly, through resolution 258 (III), submitted a request to the International Court of Justice (ICJ) for an advisory opinion[1] concerning the extent to which the UN could undertake arrangements to ensure reparation be made for the injuries suffered by its agents.

The request for an advisory opinion involved two specific questions:

I. In the event of an agent of the United Nations in the performance of his duties suffering injury in circumstances involving the responsibility of a State, has the United Nations, as an Organization, the capacity to bring an international claim against the responsible *de jure* or *de facto* government with a view to obtaining the reparation due in respect of the damage caused (*a*) to the United Nations, (*b*) to the victim or to persons entitled through him?

II. In the event of an affirmative reply on point I (*b*), how is action by the United Nations to be reconciled with such rights as may be possessed by the State of which the victim is a national?[2]

The Court held unanimously that the UN has the capacity to bring an international claim against the responsible government to obtain reparation due in respect of damage caused to the organisation, whether that State is a Member State of the UN or not. By eleven votes to four, the Court also determined that the UN has the capacity to bring a claim against the responsible government for damage suffered by an agent of the UN or an entitled person, whether that State is a Member State of the UN or not. Therefore, this judgment confirms that the Secretary-General may submit international claims in respect of deaths or injuries suffered by UN personnel. Furthermore, this case establishes the principle that the UN has a right to the diplomatic protection of its staff.

The relevance of this case to UN peace operations relates to the Court's determination that the UN is an organisation with the international legal personality required to discharge its political tasks. The Court also identified that the UN has powers by 'necessary implication as being essential to the performance of its duties'.[3] It is these implied powers which are used by the UN to justify establishing peace operations.

In the context of UN peace operations, the UN's international legal personality is of great significance. The existence of international legal personality confirms that Member States have a range of obligations in relation to the UN, and that the organisation may bring claims against one of its Members where that State has caused injury to the UN or its agents. The case confirms the legal capacity for the UN to claim privileges and immunities for the organisation and its agents, including peacekeepers. The Court's decision demonstrated the UN's ability to conclude agreements with Member States, which is a necessary capacity in the creation of peace operations. Such agreements are normally in the form of a Status-of-Forces Agreement (SOFA).[4] This judgment also addressed the 'functional protection' that the UN is obliged to provide its agents.

The doctrine of functional protection stems from the fact that UN agents, such as peacekeepers, are engaged in missions involving unusual dangers and thus the UN is obligated to provide protection. This protection is in the interest of the organisation and not the agent. Consequently, the Secretary-General of the UN has the right and duty to waive such protection where immunity

---

1 Advisory opinions are a special procedure available to UN organs under Article 96 of the Charter (see ch 1 above), allowing them to seek opinions from the ICJ on legal questions arising within the scope of their activities.

2 Reparation for Injuries Suffered in the Service of the United Nations (Advisory Opinion) [1949] ICJ Rep 174, 175 (hereafter *Reparations Case*).

3 Ibid, 182.

4 See ch 2 above.

would impede the course of justice and it can be waived without prejudice to the interests of the UN.

Another fundamental element of this case relates to the Court's deliberations on the international legal personality of the UN. The Court determined that the UN is an international person with the capacity to bring international claims. Examining the political nature of the tasks the UN is charged with, the Court noted that international personality is 'indispensable'[5] to the work of the organisation. The case identified the UN as being tasked with the maintenance of international peace and security, the development of friendly relations among nations, and the achievement of international cooperation in the solution of problems of an economic, social, cultural, or humanitarian nature.

As noted above, this case also established that the UN is deemed to have powers by 'necessary implication'. It is pursuant to these implied powers that the UN undertakes peace operations. The creation, management, and conduct of such operations are predicated on the 'necessary implication' powers which the UN is deemed to possess. The Court stated that:

> the Organization must be deemed to have those powers which, though not expressly provided in the Charter, are conferred upon it by necessary implication as being essential to the performance of its duties.[6]

In relation to the UN's international personality, the case confirmed that the UN does not possess the same legal personality, rights, and duties as a State. Rather than possessing full international legal personality under international law, the Court concluded that the Member States have 'endowed' the UN with capacities dependent upon the organisation's purposes and function. The Court stated:

> Whereas a State possesses the totality of international rights and duties recognized by international law, the rights and duties of an entity such as the [UN] must depend upon its purposes and functions as specified or implied in its constituent documents and developed in practice.[7]

Finally, in the dissenting opinion of Judge Hackworth, the concept of 'dual loyalty' was noted as requiring UN agents to maintain loyalty to both the individual's home State and the organisation. This 'dual loyalty' concept is useful when considering why individuals serving on UN peace operations should not seek or accept instructions from their home State when discharging their duties.

Judge Hackworth also raised an important point of caution with respect to the doctrine of implied powers when his Honour said:

> Powers not expressed cannot freely be implied. Implied powers flow from a grant of expressed powers, and are limited to those that are 'necessary' to the exercise of powers expressly granted.[8]

Reference

Case Name	Reparation for Injuries Suffered in the Service of the United Nations
Case Type	Advisory Opinion
Court	International Court of Justice
Date	11 April 1949
Source	[1949] ICJ Rep 174
Full Text	<https://www.icj-cij.org/en/case/4>[9]

5 Reparations Case (n 2), 178.
6 Ibid, 182.
7 Ibid, 180.
8 Ibid, 198 (Dissenting Opinion of Judge Hackworth).
9 Accessed 15 August 2018.

Reparation for Injuries Suffered in the Service of the United Nations

Advisory Opinion of 11 April 1949

(Extracts)

...

-176-

The first question asked of the Court is as follows:

> "In the event of an agent of the United Nations in the performance of his duties suffering injury in circumstances involving the responsibility of a State, has the United Nations, as an Organization, the capacity to bring an international claim against
>
> -177-
>
> the responsible *de jure* or *de facto* government with a view to obtaining the reparation due in respect of the damage caused (*a*) to the United Nations, (*b*) to the victim or to persons entitled through him?"

It will be useful to make the following preliminary observations:

(a) The Organization of the United Nations will be referred to usually, but not invariably, as "the Organization".

(b) Question I(*a*) and I(*b*) refer to "an international claim against the responsible *de jure* or *de facto* government". The Court understands that these questions are directed to claims against a State, and will, therefore, in this opinion, use the expression "State" or "defendant State".

(c) The Court understands the word "agent" in the most liberal sense, that is to say, any person who, whether a paid official or not, and whether permanently employed or not, has been charged by an organ of the Organization with carrying out, or helping to carry out, one of its functions— in short, any person through whom it acts.

(d) As this question assumes an injury suffered in such circumstances as to involve a State's responsibility, it must be supposed, for the purpose of this Opinion, that the damage results from a failure by the State to perform obligations of which the purpose is to protect the agents of the Organization in the performance of their duties.

(e) The position of a defendant State which is not a member of the Organization is dealt with later, and for the present the Court will assume that the defendant State is a Member of the Organization.

The questions asked of the Court relate to the "capacity to bring an international claim"; accordingly, we must begin by defining what is meant by that capacity, and consider the characteristics of the Organization, so as to determine whether, in general, these characteristics do, or do not, include for the Organization a right to present an international claim.

Competence to bring an international claim is, for those possessing it, the capacity to resort to the customary methods recognized by international law for the establishment, the presentation and the settlement of claims. Among these methods may be mentioned protest, request for an enquiry, negotiation, and request for submission to an arbitral tribunal or to the Court in so far as this may be authorized by the Statute.

...

-178-

But, in the international sphere, has the Organization such a nature as involves the capacity to bring an international claim? In order to answer this question, the Court must first enquire whether the Charter has given the Organization such a position that it possesses, in regard to its Members, rights which it is entitled to ask them to respect. In other words, does the Organization possess international personality? This is no doubt a doctrinal expression, which has sometimes given rise to controversy. But it will be used here to mean that if the Organization is recognized as having that personality, it is an entity capable of availing itself of obligations incumbent upon its Members.

To answer this question, which is not settled by the actual terms of the Charter, we must consider what characteristics it was intended thereby to give to the Organization.

The subjects of law in any legal system are not necessarily identical in their nature or in the extent of their rights, and their nature depends upon the needs of the community. Throughout its history, the development of international law has been influenced by the requirements of international life, and the progressive increase in the collective activities of States has already given rise to instances of action upon the international plane by certain entities which are not States. This development culminated in the establishment in June 1945 of an international organization whose purposes and principles are specified in the Charter of the United Nations. But to achieve these ends the attribution of international personality is indispensable.

The Charter has not been content to make the Organization created by it merely a centre "for harmonizing the actions of nations in the attainment of these common ends" (Article 1, para. 4). It has equipped that centre with organs, and has given it special tasks. It has defined the position of the Members in relation to the Organization by requiring them to give it every assistance in any action undertaken by it (Article 2, para. 5), and to accept and carry out the decisions of the Security Council; by authorizing the General Assembly to make recommendations to the Members;

-179-

by giving the Organization legal capacity and privileges and immunities in the territory of each of its Members; and by providing for the conclusion of agreements between the Organization and its Members. Practice—in particular the conclusion of conventions to which the Organization is a party—has confirmed this character of the Organization, which occupies a position in certain respects in detachment from its Members, and which is under a duty to remind them, if need be, of certain obligations. It must be added that the Organization is a political body, charged with political tasks of an important character, and covering a wide field namely, the maintenance of international peace and security, the development of friendly relations among nations, and the achievement of international co-operation in the solution of problems of an economic, social, cultural or humanitarian character (Article 1); and in dealing with its Members it employs political means. The "Convention on the Privileges and Immunities of the United Nations" of 1946 creates rights and duties between each of the signatories and the Organization (see, in particular, Section 35). It is difficult to see how such a convention could operate except upon the international plane and as between parties possessing international personality.

In the opinion of the Court, the Organization was intended to exercise and enjoy, and is in fact exercising and enjoying, functions and rights which can only be explained on the basis of the possession of a large measure of international personality and the capacity to operate upon an international plane. It is at present the supreme type of international organization, and it could not carry out the intentions of its founders if it was devoid of international personality. It must be acknowledged that its Members, by entrusting certain functions to it, with the attendant duties and responsibilities, have clothed it with the competence required to enable those functions to be effectively discharged.

Accordingly, the Court has come to the conclusion that the Organization is an international person. That is not the same thing as saying that it is a State, which it certainly is not, or that its legal personality and rights and duties are the same as those of a State. Still less is it the same thing as saying that it is "a super-State", whatever that expression may mean. It does not even imply that all its rights and duties must be upon the international plane, any more than all the rights and duties of a State must be upon that plane. What it does mean is that it is a subject of international law and capable of possessing international rights and duties, and that it has capacity to maintain its rights by bringing international claims.

The next question is whether the sum of the international rights of the Organization comprises the right to bring the kind of international claim described in the Request for this Opinion. That is a claim against a State to obtain reparation in respect of the

-180-

damage caused by the injury of an agent of the Organization in the course of the performance of his duties. Whereas a State possesses the totality of international rights and duties recognized by international law, the rights and duties of an entity such as the Organization must depend upon its purposes and functions as specified or implied in its constituent documents and developed in practice. The functions of the Organization are of such a character that they could not be effectively discharged if they involved the concurrent action, on the international plane, of fifty-eight or more Foreign Offices, and the Court concludes that the Members have endowed the Organization with capacity to bring international claims when necessitated by the discharge of its functions.

What is the position as regards the claims mentioned in the request for an opinion? Question I is divided into two points, which must be considered in turn.

Question I (*a*) ... is concerned solely with the reparation of damage caused to the Organization when one of its agents suffers injury at the same time. It cannot be doubted that the Organization has the capacity to bring an international claim against one of its Members which has caused injury to it by a breach of its international obligations towards it. The damage specified in Question I (*a*) means exclusively damage caused to the interests of the Organization itself, to its administrative machine, to its property and assets, and to the interests of which it is the guardian. It is clear that the Organization has the capacity to bring a claim for this damage. As the claim is based on the breach of an international obligation on the part of the Member held responsible by the Organization, the Member cannot contend that this obligation is governed by municipal law, and the Organization is justified in giving its claim the character of an international claim.

When the Organization has sustained damage resulting from a breach by a Member of its international obligations, it is impossible to see how it can obtain reparation unless it possesses capacity to bring an international claim. It cannot be supposed that in such an event all the Members of the Organization, save the defendant

-181-

State, must combine to bring a claim against the defendant for the damage suffered by the Organization.

The Court is not called upon to determine the precise extent of the reparation which the Organization would be entitled to recover. It may, however, be said that the measure of the reparation should depend upon the amount of the damage which the Organization has suffered as the result of the wrongful act or omission of the defendant State and should be calculated in accordance with the rules of international law. Amongst other things, this damage would include the reimbursement of any reasonable compensation which the Organization had to pay to its agent or to persons entitled through him. Again, the death or disablement of one of its agents engaged upon a distant mission might involve very considerable expenditure in replacing him.

These are mere illustrations, and the Court cannot pretend to forecast all the kinds of damage which the Organization itself might sustain.

Question I *(b)* is as follows:

... "has the United Nations, as an Organization, the capacity to bring an international claim ... in respect of the damage caused ... (*b*) to the victim or to persons entitled through him?"

In dealing with the question of law which arises out of Question I (*b*), it is unnecessary to repeat the considerations which led to an affirmative answer being given to Question I (*a*). It can now be assumed that the Organization has the capacity to bring a claim on the international plane, to negotiate, to conclude a special agreement and to prosecute a claim before an international tribunal. The only legal question which remains to be considered is whether, in the course of bringing an international claim of this kind, the Organization can recover "the reparation due in respect of the damage caused ... to the victim ...".

The traditional rule that diplomatic protection is exercised by the national State does not involve the giving of a negative answer to Question I (*b*).

In the first place, this rule applies to claims brought by a State. But here we have the different and new case of a claim that would be brought by the Organization.

In the second place, even in inter-State relations, there are important exceptions to the rule, for there are cases in which protection may be exercised by a State on behalf of persons not having its nationality.

In the third place, the rule rests on two bases. The first is that the defendant State has broken an obligation towards the national State in respect of its nationals. The second is that only the party

-182-

to whom an international obligation is due can bring a claim in respect of its breach. This is precisely what happens when the Organization, in bringing a claim for damage suffered by its agent, does so by invoking the breach of an obligation towards itself. Thus, the rule of the nationality of claims affords no reason against recognizing that the Organization has the right to bring a claim for the damage referred to in Question I (*b*). On the contrary, the principle underlying this rule leads to the recognition of this capacity as belonging to the Organization, when the Organization invokes, as the ground of its claim, a breach of an obligation towards itself.

Nor does the analogy of the traditional rule of diplomatic protection of nationals abroad justify in itself an affirmative reply. It is not possible, by a strained use of the concept of allegiance, to assimilate the legal bond which exists, under Article 100 of the Charter, between the Organization on the one hand, and the Secretary-General and the staff on the other, to the bond of nationality existing between a State and its nationals.

The Court is here faced with a new situation. The questions to which it gives rise can only be solved by realizing that the situation is dominated by the provisions of the Charter considered in the light of the principles of international law.

The question lies within the limits already established; that is to say it presupposes that the injury for which the reparation is demanded arises from a breach of an obligation designed to help an agent of the Organization in the performance of his duties. It is not a case in which the wrongful act or omission would merely constitute a breach of the general obligations of a State concerning the position of aliens; claims made under this head would be within the competence of the national State and not, as a general rule, within that of the Organization.

The Charter does not expressly confer upon the Organization the capacity to include, in its claim for reparation, damage caused to the victim or to persons entitled through him. The Court must therefore begin by enquiring whether the provisions of the Charter concerning the functions of the Organization, and the part played by its agents in the performance of those functions, imply for the Organization power to afford its agents the limited protection that would consist in the bringing of a claim on their behalf for reparation for damage suffered in such circumstances. Under international law, the Organization must be deemed to have those powers which, though not expressly provided in the Charter, are conferred upon it by necessary implication as being essential to the performance of its duties. This principle of law was applied by the Permanent Court of International Justice to the International Labour Organization in its Advisory Opinion No. 13 of July 23rd,

-183-

1926 (Series B., No. 13, p. 18), and must be applied to the United Nations.

Having regard to its purposes and functions already referred to, the Organization may find it necessary, and has in fact found it necessary, to entrust its agents with important missions to be performed in disturbed parts of the world. Many missions, from their very nature, involve the agents in unusual dangers to which ordinary persons are not exposed. For the same reason, the injuries suffered by its agents in these circumstances will sometimes have occurred in such a manner that their national State would not be justified in bringing a claim for reparation on the ground of diplomatic protection, or, at any rate, would not feel disposed to do so. Both to ensure the efficient and independent performance of these missions and to afford effective support to its agents, the Organization must provide them with adequate protection.

This need of protection for the agents of the Organization, as a condition of the performance of its functions, has already be realized, and the Preamble to the Resolution of December 3rd, 1948 ... shows that this was the unanimous view of the General Assembly.

For this purpose, the Members of the Organization have entered into certain undertakings, some of which are in the Charter and others in complementary agreements. The content of these undertakings need not be described here; but the Court must stress the importance of the duty to render to the Organization "every assistance" which is accepted by the Members in Article 2, paragraph 5, of the Charter. It must be noted that the effective working of the Organization—the accomplishment of its task, and the independence and effectiveness of the work of its agents—require that these undertakings should be strictly observed. For that purpose, it is necessary that, when an infringement occurs, the Organization should be able to call upon the responsible State to remedy its default, and, in particular, to obtain from the State reparation for the damage that the default may have caused to its agent.

In order that the agent may perform his duties satisfactorily, he must feel that this protection is assured to him by the Organization, and that he may count on it. To ensure the independence of the agent, and, consequently, the independent action of the Organization itself, it is essential that in performing his duties he need not have to rely on any other protection than that of the Organization (save of course for the more direct and immediate protection due from the State in whose territory he may be). In particular, he should not have to rely on the protection of his own State. If he had to rely on that State, his independence might well be compromised, contrary to the principle applied by Article 100 of the Charter. And lastly, it is essential that—

-184-

whether the agent belongs to a powerful or to a weak State; to one more affected or less affected by the complications of international life; to one in sympathy or not in sympathy with the mission of the agent—he should know that in the performance of his duties he is under the protection of the Organization. This assurance is even more necessary when the agent is stateless.

Upon examination of the character of the functions entrusted to the Organization and of the nature of the missions of its agents, it becomes clear that the capacity of the Organization to exercise a measure of functional protection of its agents arises by necessary intendment out of the Charter.

The obligations entered into by States to enable the agents of the Organization to perform their duties are undertaken not in the interest of the agents, but in that of the Organization. When it claims redress for a breach of these obligations, the Organization is invoking its own right, the right that the obligations due to it should be respected. On this ground, it asks for reparation of the injury suffered, for "it is a principle of international law that the breach of an engagement involves an obligation to make reparation in an adequate form"; as was stated by the Permanent Court in its Judgment No. 8 of July 26th, 1927 (Series A., No. 9, p. 21). In claiming reparation based on the injury suffered by its agent, the Organization does not represent the agent, but is asserting its own right, the right to secure respect for undertakings entered into towards the Organization.

Having regard to the foregoing considerations, and to the undeniable right of the Organization to demand that its Members shall fulfil the obligations entered into by them in the interest of the good working of the Organization, the Court is of the opinion that, in the case of a breach of these obligations, the Organization has the capacity to claim adequate reparation, and that in assessing this reparation it is authorized to include the damage suffered by the victim or by persons entitled through him.

The question remains whether the Organization has "the capacity to bring an international claim against the responsible *de jure* or *de facto* government with a view to obtaining the reparation due in respect of the damage caused (*a*) to the United Nations, (*b*) to the victim or to persons entitled through him" when the defendant State is not a member of the Organization.

In considering this aspect of Question I (*a*) and (*b*), it is necessary to keep in mind the reasons which have led the Court to give an affirmative answer to it when the defendant State is a Member of the Organization. It has now been established that the Organization has capacity to bring claims on the international

-185-

plane, and that it possesses a right of functional protection in respect of its agents. Here again the Court is authorized to assume that the damage suffered involves the responsibility of a State, and it is not called upon to express an opinion upon the various ways in which that responsibility might be engaged. Accordingly the question is whether the Organization has capacity to bring a claim against the defendant State to recover reparation in respect of that damage or whether, on the contrary, the defendant State, not being a member, is justified in raising the objection that the Organization lacks the capacity to bring an international claim. On this point, the Court's opinion is that fifty States, representing the vast majority of the members of the international community, had the power, in conformity with international law, to bring into being an entity possessing objective international personality, and not merely personality recognized by them alone, together with capacity to bring international claims.

Accordingly, the Court arrives at the conclusion that an affirmative answer should be given to Question I (*a*) and (*b*) whether or not the defendant State is a Member of the United Nations.

. . .

-187-

For these Reasons,

The Court is of opinion

On Question I (a):

(i) unanimously,

That, in the event of an agent of the United Nations in the performance of his duties suffering injury in circumstances involving the responsibility of a Member State, the United Nations as an Organization has the capacity to bring an international claim against the responsible *de jure* or *de facto* government with a view to obtaining the reparation due in respect of the damage caused to the United Nations.

(ii) unanimously,

That, in the event of an agent of the United Nations in the performance of his duties suffering injury in circumstances involving the responsibility of a State which is not a member, the United Nations as an Organization has the capacity to bring an international claim against the responsible *de jure* or *de facto* government with a view to obtaining the reparation due in respect of the damage caused to the United Nations.

On Question I (b):

(i) by eleven votes against four,

That, in the event of an agent of the United Nations in the performance of his duties suffering injury in circumstances involving the responsibility of a Member State, the United Nations as an

Organization has the capacity to bring an international claim against the responsible *de jure* or *de facto* government with a view to obtaining the reparation due in respect of the damage caused to the victim or to persons entitled through him.

(ii) by eleven votes against four,

That, in the event of an agent of the United Nations in the performance of his duties suffering injury in circumstances involving the responsibility of a State which is not a member, the United Nations as an Organization has the capacity to bring an international claim against the responsible *de jure* or *de facto* government with a view to obtaining the reparation due in respect of the damage caused to the victim or to persons entitled through him.

...

-196-

Dissenting Opinion by Judge Hackworth

I concur, but for different reasons, in the conclusion of the Court that the United Nations Organization has capacity to bring an international claim against the responsible government, with a view to obtaining reparation due in respect of damage caused by that government to the Organization. But I regret that I am unable to concur in that part of the Opinion having to do with the capacity of the Organization to sponsor an international claim in behalf of one of its agents.

The authority of the Organization to make a claim for damage caused to it by the wrongful act of a State can be very simply stated, as follows:

(1) Article 104 of the Charter gives the Organization "such legal capacity as may be necessary for the exercise of its functions and the fulfilment of its purposes".

(2) Paragraphs 1 and 2 of Article 105 specify that the Organization "shall enjoy in the territory of each of its Members such privileges and immunities as are necessary for the fulfilment of its purposes", and that officials of the Organization shall "similarly enjoy such privileges and immunities as are necessary for the independent exercise of their functions in connexion with the Organization".

(3) The Convention on Privileges and Immunities, adopted by the General Assembly on February 13th, 1946, recognizes that the United Nations shall possess juridical personality, with capacity (*a*) to contract; (*b*) to acquire and dispose of immovable and movable property; and (*c*) to institute legal proceedings; also that the Organization and its officials shall enjoy certain specified privileges and immunities.

The Convention has not been approved by all the Members of the Organization, but we may assume, for present purposes, that it is fairly representative of the views of most of them.

(4) It stands to reason that, if the Organization is to make contracts, to acquire and dispose of property, to institute legal proceedings, and to claim the benefits of the privileges and immunities to which it is entitled, it must be able to carry on negotiations with governments as well as with private parties. It must therefore be able to assert claims in its own behalf. No other conclusion consistent with the specified powers and with the inherent right of self-preservation could possibly be drawn. The Organization must have and does have ample authority to

-197-

take needful steps for its protection against wrongful acts for which Member States are responsible. Any damage *suffered by the Organization* by reason of wrongful acts committed against an agent, while in the performance of his duties, would likewise be within its competence.

This is a proper application of the doctrine of implied powers.

(5) I, therefore, find no difficulty in giving an affirmative answer to Question 1(*a*) of the Assembly's request. Such a claim by the United Nations would include any element of damage susceptible of proof under customary rules relating to damages in international claims. It would include any reasonable payments made by the Organization to the victim of the wrongful act or to those entitled through him, provided that such payments were made pursuant to contractual undertakings of the Organization, or on the basis of an established policy in such cases.

(6) Thus it would appear that under I(*a*) the Organization has ample and unquestionable authority to safeguard itself against derelictions by States, and to vindicate the dignity, honour and authority of the Organization. To this extent I am in agreement with the conclusions of the majority of the Court.

As to Question I(*b*), having to do with a claim for reparation due in respect of damage caused to the victim of a wrongful act or to persons entitled through him, as distinguished from a claim on behalf of the Organization itself, a different situation is presented.

The Court is asked to state its opinion as to whether the Organization has capacity to espouse such a claim. In giving our answer, we must look to the traditional international practice of nations with respect to private claims, and to the express treaty stipulations as regards the Organization.

As to international practice, we find at once that heretofore only States have been regarded as competent to advance such international claims.

As to the Organization, we find nothing to suggest that it too has capacity in this field. Certainly there is no specific provision in the Charter, nor is there provision in any other agreement of which I am aware, conferring upon the Organization authority to

-198-

assume the rôle of a State, and to represent its agents in the espousal of diplomatic claims on their behalf. I am equally convinced that there is no implied power to be drawn upon for this purpose.

It is stated in the majority opinion that the Charter does not expressly provided that the Organization should have capacity to include, in "its claim for reparation", damage caused to the victim or to persons entitled through him, but the conclusion is reached that such power is conferred by necessary implication. This appears to be based on the assumption that, to ensure the efficient and independent performance of missions entrusted to agents of the Organization, and to afford them moral support, the exercise of this power is necessary.

The conclusion that power in the Organization to sponsor private claims is conferred by "necessary implication" is not believed to be warranted under rules laid down by tribunals for filling lacunæ in specific grants of power.

There can be no gainsaying the fact that the Organization is one of delegated and enumerated powers. It is to be presumed that such powers as the Member States desired to confer upon it are stated either in the Charter or in complementary agreements concluded by them. Powers not expressed cannot freely be implied. Implied powers flow from a grant of expressed powers, and are limited to those that are "necessary" to the exercise of powers expressly granted. No necessity for the exercise of the power here in question has been shown to exist. There is no impelling reason, if any at all, why the Organization should become the sponsor of claims on behalf of its employees, even though limited to those arising while the employee is in line of duty. These employees are still nationals of their respective countries, and the customary methods of handling such claims are still available in full vigour. The prestige and efficiency of the Organization will be safeguarded by an exercise of its undoubted right under point I(*a*) *supra*. Even here it is necessary to imply power, but, as stated above, the necessity is self-evident. The exercise of an additional extraordinary power in the field of private claims has not been shown to be necessary to the efficient performance of duty by either the Organization or its agents.

...

-202-

Since ... the privileges and immunities inure to the benefit of the United Nations and not to the benefit of the individuals, any claim based upon a breach of them should be in favour of the Organization and would fall to be dealt with under I(*a*) above, and not under I(*b*).

...

35

Certain Expenses of the United Nations (Article 17, Paragraph 2, of the Charter)

Prefatory Note

On 20 December 1961, the General Assembly, in resolution 1731 (XVI), submitted a request for an advisory opinion[1] to the International Court of Justice (ICJ) in recognition of its need for authoritative legal guidance as to the obligations of Member States under the Charter of the United Nations (Charter)[2] in respect of financing UN peace operations.

The advisory opinion in this case concerned certain General Assembly authorised expenditures to cover the costs of the UN Operation in the Congo (ONUC) and First United Nations Emergency Force in the Middle East (UNEF I). The specific legal question was whether such expenses constituted 'expenses of the Organization'. Several Member States had refused to pay their contributions to these two UN peace operations due to claims that their method of creation did not accord with the Charter's vesting of power to maintain international peace and security exclusively with the Security Council. ONUC was established by the Secretary-General after the Security Council authorised him to consult with the government of the Congo and provide them 'with such military assistance as may be necessary',[3] whereas UNEF I was established by the General Assembly in its first emergency special session called pursuant to the Uniting for Peace procedure.[4]

The Court held, by nine votes to five, that the expenses authorised did constitute 'expenses of the Organization' within the meaning of Article 17, Paragraph 2 of the Charter. Article 17, Paragraph 2 states that '[t]he expenses of the Organization shall be borne by the Members as apportioned by the General Assembly'.

Deliberations on the allocation of expenses led the Court to examine the purposes of the UN and the respective functions of the Security Council, the General Assembly, and the Secretary-General, particularly with respect to the maintenance of international peace and security. Furthermore, the case reviewed issues such as the interpretation of the Charter, the accountability of the UN, and determinations on when actions by the UN are considered 'enforcement actions'.

The Court referred to the purposes of the UN as set forth in Article 1 of the Charter: the maintenance of international peace and security, the development of friendly relations between States, the achievement of economic, social, cultural, and humanitarian goals, and respect for human rights, and for the UN to be 'a center for harmonizing the actions of nations in the attainment of these common ends'.[5] The centrality of the maintenance of international peace and security was noted, as the other purposes were deemed to rely upon this condition. Whilst the purposes expressed were broad, the Court maintained that the UN is nonetheless required to act within the limits of its powers, including those powers implied from the Charter. The Court also maintained that Member States retained their freedom of action. Thus, this case confirms the principle that whilst the powers of the UN are wide, they are not unlimited. Despite such limits, the Court stated that:

> when the Organization takes action which warrants the assertion that it was appropriate for the fulfillment of one of the stated purposes of the United Nations, the presumption is that such action is not *ultra vires* the Organization.[6]

---

1 Advisory opinions are a special procedure available to UN organs under Article 96 of the Charter (see ch 1 above), allowing them to seek opinions from the ICJ on legal questions arising within the scope of their activities.

2 Charter of the United Nations (opened for signature 26 June 1945, entered into force 24 October 1945) 1 UNTS XVI (hereafter Charter). See ch 1 above.

3 SC Res 143 (1960) of 14 July 1960, Operative Part [2].

4 GA Res 1000 (ES-1) of 5 November 1956; GA Res 1001 (ES-1) of 7 November 1956.

5 *Certain Expenses of the United Nations (Article 17, Paragraph 2, of the Charter)* (Advisory Opinion) [1962] ICJ Rep 151, 168.

6 Ibid.

In addressing the various functions of the UN's organs, the Court determined that the Security Council has primary, but not exclusive, responsibility for the maintenance of international peace and security. The Court deemed that the Charter makes it clear that the General Assembly is also concerned with international peace and security and can recommend 'measures', a word implying some kind of action.[7] The General Assembly, by means of recommendations to Member States or to the Security Council, can establish peace operations at the request of, or with the consent of, the State or States concerned. However, the Security Council is the only UN organ which can 'require enforcement by coercive action against an aggressor'.[8] The Court also determined that the Secretary-General, pursuant to Article 98 of the Charter, is obligated to perform the duties required of that position by the Security Council or General Assembly and in the instances at hand, the financing of UNEF I and ONUC, properly exercised the authority granted to him.

On the issue of the interpretation of the Charter, the Court noted that it is a multilateral treaty with certain special characteristics. Whilst the Court acknowledged the political significance of most interpretations it was deemed to be an essentially judicial task to interpret a treaty provision. It was advanced that the Charter should be read as a whole to give effect to all its terms and avoid inconsistency, and that its stated purpose should be the prime consideration in interpreting the text. In a separate advisory opinion, Judge Spender stated:

> The nature of the authority granted by the Charter to each of its organs does not change with time. The ambit or scope of the authority conferred may nonetheless comprehend ever changing circumstances and conditions and embrace, as history unfolds itself, new problems and situations which were not and could not have been envisaged when the Charter came into being.[9]

The case confirmed the exclusive power of the General Assembly over the budget of the UN. Article 17 is the only Article in the Charter which refers to budgetary authority and, in Paragraph 1, it is the General Assembly which is given the power to consider and approve the budget of the organisation. This means the General Assembly can pass resolutions concerning budgetary matters that bind all UN peace operations, whether created by the Security Council or the General Assembly. In relation to accountability, the Court established that the UN is accountable to third parties for any *ultra vires* actions of the Secretary-General and his agents. The judgment noted that both national and international law contemplate cases in which the body corporate or politic may be bound, as to third parties, by an *ultra vires* act of an agent. In the context of UN peace operations, the UN is *prima facie* liable for the acts of peacekeepers serving on the mission. In practice, UN third party liability in UN peace operations has had temporal and financial limits since 1998.

The Court concluded that the UN may establish peace operations as subsidiary organs of the organisation not only through the Security Council but also via the General Assembly. In doing this, the Court confirmed that the UN has the capacity to establish and finance actions in regard to the maintenance of international peace and security that are less than full blown 'enforcement actions'. The Court concluded that the General Assembly can establish peace operations as long as it has the consent of the State or States concerned, and the operations do not involve enforcement action. The Court interpreted the restriction on the powers of the General Assembly in the last sentence of Article 11, Paragraph 2, of the Charter, which states that '[a]ny ... such question on which action is necessary shall be referred to the Security Council by the General Assembly either before or after discussion.' The Court found this restriction to have 'no application where the necessary action is not enforcement action'.[10]

The Court stated explicitly that ONUC and UNEF I 'were not *enforcement* actions within the compass of Chapter VII of the Charter'.[11] In the determination of when action by the UN will be considered 'enforcement action', the Court in this case took a narrow approach. For example, the Court deemed that as ONUC did not involve 'prevention or enforcement measures' against any State under Chapter VII, it did not constitute 'action' as used in Article 11 which deals with 'enforcement action'.[12] One result of this narrow approach is that the use of force by UN peacekeepers

7 Ibid, 163.
8 Ibid, 163.
9 Ibid, 187 (Separate Opinion of Judge Spender).
10 Ibid, 165.
11 Ibid, 166.
12 Ibid, 177.

against non-State actors would not be considered enforcement action pursuant to the Charter. It is worth considering whether enforcement action today should have a broader meaning in the context of peace operations to include situations where the use of force goes beyond self-defence. Another issue is whether the Court's use of the term 'enforcement action' only equates to the kind of authorised military action taken by Member States against another State as in the cases of Korea (1950–53) and Iraq (1990–91), or also includes peace enforcement operations against non-State actors where UN forces are authorised to take the initiative in the use of force. An example of such a peace enforcement operation is the Second United Nations Operation in Somalia (UNOSOM II) and the Force Intervention Brigade in the UN Organization Stabilization Mission in the Democratic Republic of the Congo (MONUSCO).[13] In these situations the dividing line between robust peacekeeping in defence of the mandate and peace enforcement is hard to define, yet can have critical importance to such issues as the application of international humanitarian law[14] to UN peace operations.

This case confirmed the establishment of peace operations as a legitimate tool of the UN, the Security Council, and the General Assembly in the maintenance of international peace and security.

Reference

Case Name	Certain Expenses of the United Nations (Article 17, Paragraph 2, of the Charter)
Case Type	Advisory Opinion
Court	International Court of Justice
Date	20 July 1962
Source	[1962] ICJ Rep 151
Full Text	<https://www.icj-cij.org/en/case/49>[15]

Certain Expenses of the United Nations (Article 17, Paragraph 2, of the Charter)

Advisory Opinion of 20 July 1964

(Extracts)

...

-156-

The question on which the Court is asked to give its opinion is whether certain expenditures which were authorized by the General Assembly to cover the costs of the United Nations operations in the Congo (hereinafter referred to as ONUC) and of the operations of the United Nations Emergency Force in the Middle East (hereinafter referred to as UNEF), "constitute 'expenses of the Organization' within the meaning of Article 17, paragraph 2, of the Charter of the United Nations".

...

-157-

Turning to the question which has been posed, the Court observes that it involves an interpretation of Article 17, paragraph 2, of the Charter. On the previous occasions when the Court has

13 See SC Res 2098 (2013) of 28 March 2013.

14 See chs 15 and 16 above.

15 Accessed 15 August 2018.

had to interpret the Charter of the United Nations, it has followed the principles and rules applicable in general to the interpretation of treaties, since it has recognized that the Charter is a multilateral treaty, albeit a treaty having certain special characteristics. In interpreting Article 4 of the Charter, the Court was led to consider "the structure of the Charter" and "the relations established by it between the General Assembly and the Security Council"; a comparable problem confronts the Court in the instant matter. The Court sustained its interpretation of Article 4 by considering the manner in which the organs concerned "have consistently interpreted the text" in their practice (*Competence of the General Assembly for the Admission of a State to the United Nations, I.C.J. Reports 1950*, pp. 8-9).

...

-161-

Turning to paragraph 2 of Article 17, the Court observes that, on its face, the term "expenses of the Organization" means all the expenses and not just certain types of expenses which might be referred to as "regular expenses". An examination of other parts of the Charter shows the variety of expenses which must inevitably be included within the "expenses of the Organization" just as much as the salaries of staff or the maintenance of buildings.

...

-162-

Furthermore, by Article 98 of the Charter, the Secretary-General is obligated to perform such functions as are entrusted to him by the General Assembly, the Security Council, the Economic and Social Council, and the Trusteeship Council. Whether or not expenses incurred in his discharge of this obligation become "expenses of the Organization" cannot depend on whether they be administrative or some other kind of expenses.

The Court does not perceive any basis for challenging the legality of the settled practice of including such expenses as these in the budgetary amounts which the General Assembly apportions among the Members in accordance with the authority which is given to it by Article 17, paragraph 2.

Passing from the text of Article 17 to its place in the general structure and scheme of the Charter, the Court will consider whether in that broad context one finds any basis for implying a limitation upon the budgetary authority of the General Assembly which in turn might limit the meaning of "expenses" in paragraph 2 of that Article.

The general purposes of Article 17 are the vesting of control over the finances of the Organization, and the levying of apportioned amounts of the expenses of the Organization in order to enable it to carry out the functions of the Organization as a whole acting through its principal organs and such subsidiary organs as may be established under the authority of Article 22 or Article 29.

Article 17 is the only article in the Charter which refers to budgetary authority or to the power to apportion expenses, or otherwise to raise revenue, except for Articles 33 and 35, paragraph 3, of the Statute of the Court which have no bearing on the point here under discussion. Nevertheless, it has been argued before the Court that one type of expenses, namely those resulting from operations for the maintenance of international peace and security, are not "expenses of the Organization" within the meaning of Article 17, paragraph 2, of the Charter, inasmuch as they fall to be dealt with exclusively by the Security Council, and more especially through agreements negotiated in accordance with Article 43 of the Charter.

The argument rests in part upon the view that when the maintenance of international peace and security is involved, it is only the Security Council which is authorized to decide on any action relative thereto. It is argued further that since the General Assembly's power is limited to discussing, considering, studying and recommending, it cannot impose an obligation to pay the expenses which result from the implementation of its recommendations. This

-163-

argument leads to an examination of the respective functions of the General Assembly and of the Security Council under the Charter, particularly with respect to the maintenance of international peace and security.

Article 24 of the Charter provides:

> "In order to ensure prompt and effective action by the United Nations, its Members confer on the Security Council primary responsibility for the maintenance of international peace and security ... "

The responsibility conferred is "primary", not exclusive. This primary responsibility is conferred upon the Security Council, as stated in Article 24, "in order to ensure prompt and effective action". To this end, it is the Security Council which is given a power to impose an explicit obligation of compliance if for example it issues an order or command to an aggressor under Chapter VII. It is only the Security Council which can require enforcement by coercive action against an aggressor.

The Charter makes it abundantly clear, however, that the General Assembly is also to be concerned with international peace and security. Article 14 authorizes the General Assembly to "recommend measures for the peaceful adjustment of any situation, regardless of origin, which it deems likely to impair the general welfare or friendly relations among nations, including situations resulting from a violation of the provisions of the present Charter setting forth the purposes and principles of the United Nations". The word "measures" implies some kind of action, and the only limitation which Article 14 imposes on the General Assembly is the restriction found in Article 12, namely, that the Assembly should not recommend measures while the Security Council is dealing with the same matter unless the Council requests it to do so. Thus while it is the Security Council which, exclusively, may order coercive action, the functions and powers conferred by the Charter on the General Assembly are not confined to discussion, consideration, the initiation of studies and the making of recommendations; they are not merely hortatory. Article 18 deals with "*decisions*" of the General Assembly "on important questions". These "decisions" do indeed include certain recommendations, but others have dispositive force and effect. Among these latter decisions, Article 18 includes suspension of rights and privileges of membership, expulsion of Members, "and budgetary questions". In connection with the suspension of rights and privileges of membership and expulsion from membership under Articles 5 and 6, it is the Security Council which has only the power to recommend and it is the General Assembly which decides and whose decision determines status; but there is a close collaboration between the two organs. Moreover, these powers of decision of the General Assembly under Arti-

-164-

cles 5 and 6 are specifically related to preventive or enforcement measures.

By Article 17, paragraph 1, the General Assembly is given the power not only to "consider" the budget of the Organization, but also to "approve" it. The decision to "approve" the budget has a close connection with paragraph 2 of Article 17, since thereunder the General Assembly is also given the power to apportion the expenses among the Members and the exercise of the power of apportionment creates the obligation, specifically stated in Article 17, paragraph 2, of each Member to bear that part of the expenses which is apportioned to it by the General Assembly. When those expenses include expenditures for the maintenance of peace and security, which are not otherwise provided for, it is the General Assembly which has the authority to apportion the latter amounts among the Members. The provisions of the Charter which distribute functions and powers to the Security Council and to the General Assembly give no support to the view that such distribution excludes from the powers of the General Assembly the power to provide for the financing of measures designed to maintain peace and security.

The argument supporting a limitation on the budgetary authority of the General Assembly with respect to the maintenance of international peace and security relies especially on the reference to "action" in the last sentence of Article 11, paragraph 2.

...

The Court considers that the kind of action referred to in Article 11, paragraph 2, is coercive or enforcement action. This paragraph, which applies not merely to general questions relating to peace and security, but also to specific cases brought before the General Assembly by a State under Article 35, in its first sentence empowers the General Assembly, by means of recommendations to States or to the Security Council, or to both, to organize peacekeeping operations, at the request, or with the consent, of the States concerned. This power of the General Assembly is a special power which in no way derogates from its general powers under Article 10

-165-

or Article 14, except as limited by the last sentence of Article 11, paragraph 2. This last sentence says that when "action" is necessary the General Assembly shall refer the question to the Security Council. The word "action" must mean such action as is solely within the province of the Security Council. It cannot refer to recommendations which the Security Council might make, as for instance under Article 38, because the General Assembly under Article 11 has a comparable power. The "action" which is solely within the province of the Security Council is that which is indicated by the title of Chapter VII of the Charter, namely "Action with respect to threats to the peace, breaches of the peace, and acts of aggression". If the word "action" in Article 11, paragraph 2, were interpreted to mean that the General Assembly could make recommendations only of a general character affecting peace and security in the abstract, and not in relation to specific cases, the paragraph would not have provided that the General Assembly may make recommendations on questions brought before it by States or by the Security Council. Accordingly, the last sentence of Article 11, paragraph 2, has no application where the necessary action is not enforcement action.

The practice of the Organization throughout its history bears out the foregoing elucidation of the term "action" in the last sentence of Article 11, paragraph 2. Whether the General Assembly proceeds under Article 11 or under Article 14, the implementation of its recommendations for setting up commissions or other bodies involves organizational activity — action — in connection with the maintenance of international peace and security. Such implementation is a normal feature of the functioning of the United Nations. Such committees, commissions or other bodies or individuals, constitute, in some cases, subsidiary organs established under the authority of Article 22 of the Charter. The functions of the General Assembly for which it may establish such subsidiary organs include, for example, investigation, observation and supervision, but the way in which such subsidiary organs are utilized depends on the consent of the State or States concerned.

The Court accordingly finds that the argument which seeks, by reference to Article 11, paragraph 2, to limit the budgetary authority of the General Assembly in respect of the maintenance of international peace and security, is unfounded.

It has further been argued before the Court that Article 43 of the Charter constitutes a particular rule, a *lex specialis*, which derogates

-166-

from the general rule in Article 17, whenever an expenditure for the maintenance of international peace and security is involved. Article 43 provides that Members shall negotiate agreements with the Security Council on its initiative, stipulating what "armed forces, assistance and facilities, including rights of passage, necessary for the purpose of maintaining international peace and security", the Member State will make available to the Security Council on its call. According to paragraph 2 of the Article:

> "Such agreement or agreements shall govern the numbers and types of forces, their degree of readiness and general location, and the nature of the facilities and assistance to be provided."

The argument is that such agreements were intended to include specifications concerning the allocation of costs of such enforcement actions as might be taken by direction of the Security Council, and that it is only the Security Council which has the authority to arrange for meeting such costs.

With reference to this argument, the Court will state at the outset that, for reasons fully expounded later in this Opinion, the operations known as UNEF and ONUC were not *enforcement* actions within the compass of Chapter VII of the Charter and that therefore Article 43 could not have any applicability to the cases with which the Court is here concerned. However, even if Article 43 were applicable, the Court could not accept this interpretation of its text for the following reasons.

There is nothing in the text of Article 43 which would limit the discretion of the Security Council in negotiating such agreements. It cannot be assumed that in every such agreement the Security Council would insist, or that any Member State would be bound to agree, that such State would bear the entire cost of the "assistance" which it would make available including, for example, transport of forces to the point of operation, complete logistical maintenance in the field, supplies, arms and ammunition, etc. If, during negotiations under the terms of Article 43, a Member State would be entitled (as it would be) to insist, and the Security Council would be entitled (as it would be) to agree, that some part of the expense should be borne by the Organization, then such expense would form part of the expenses of the Organization and would fall to be apportioned by the General Assembly under Article 17. It is difficult to see how it could have been contemplated that all potential expenses could be envisaged in such agreements concluded perhaps long in advance. Indeed, the difficulty or impossibility of anticipating the entire financial impact of enforcement measures on Member States is brought out by the terms of Article 50 which provides that a State, whether a Member of the United Nations or not, "which finds itself confronted with special economic problems arising from the carrying out of those [preventive or enforcement] measures, shall have

-167-

the right to consult the Security Council with regard to a solution of those problems". Presumably in such a case the Security Council might determine that the overburdened State was entitled to some financial assistance; such financial assistance, if afforded by the Organization, as it might be, would clearly constitute part of the "expenses of the Organization". The economic problems could not have been covered in advance by a negotiated agreement since they would be unknown until after the event and in the case of non-Member States, which are also included in Article 50, no agreement at all would have been negotiated under Article 43.

Moreover, an argument which insists that all measures taken for the maintenance of international peace and security must be financed through agreements concluded under Article 43, would seem to exclude the possibility that the Security Council might act under some other Article of the Charter. The Court cannot accept so limited a view of the powers of the Security Council under the Charter. It cannot be said that the Charter has left the Security Council impotent in the face of an emergency situation when agreements under Article 43 have not been concluded.

Articles of Chapter VII of the Charter speak of "situations" as well as disputes, and it must lie within the power of the Security Council to police a situation even though it does not resort to enforcement action against a State. The costs of actions which the Security Council is authorized to take constitute "expenses of the Organization within the meaning of Article 17, paragraph 2".

The Court has considered the general problem of the interpretation of Article 17, paragraph 2, in the light of the general structure of the Charger and of the respective functions assigned by the Charter to the General Assembly and to the Security Council, with a view to determining the meaning of the phrase "the expenses of the Organization". The Court does not find it necessary to go further in giving a more detailed definition of such expenses. The Court will, therefore, proceed to examine the expenditures enumerated in the request for the advisory opinion. In determining whether the actual expenditures authorized constitute "expenses of the Organization within the meaning of Article 17, paragraph 2, of the Charter", the Court agrees that such expenditures must be tested by their relationship to the purposes of the United Nations in the sense that if an expenditure were made for a purpose which is not one of the purposes of the United Nations, it could not be considered an "expense of the Organization".

The purposes of the United Nations are set forth in Article 1 of the Charter. The first two purposes as stated in paragraphs 1

-168-

and 2, may be summarily described as pointing to the goal of international peace and security and friendly relations. The third purpose is the achievement of economic, social, cultural and humanitarian goals and respect for human rights. The fourth and last purpose is: "To be a center for harmonizing the actions of nations in the attainment of these common ends."

The primary place ascribed to international peace and security is natural, since the fulfilment of the other purposes will be dependent upon the attainment of that basic condition. These purposes are broad indeed, but neither they nor the powers conferred to effectuate them are unlimited. Save as they have entrusted the Organization with the attainment of these common ends, the Member States retain their freedom of action. But when the Organization takes action which warrants the assertion that it was appropriate for the fulfilment of one of the stated purposes of the United Nations, the presumption is that such action is not *ultra vires* the Organization.

If it is agreed that the action in question is within the scope of the functions of the Organization but it is alleged that it has been initiated or carried out in a manner not in conformity with the division of functions among the several organs which the Charter prescribes, one moves to the internal plane, to the internal structure of the Organization. If the action was taken by the wrong organ, it was irregular as a matter of that internal structure, but this would not necessarily mean that the expense incurred was not an expense of the Organization. Both national and international law contemplate cases in which the body corporate or politic may be bound, as to third parties, by an *ultra vires* act of an agent.

In the legal systems of States, there is often some procedure for determining the validity of even a legislative or governmental act, but no analogous procedure is to be found in the structure of the United Nations. Proposals made during the drafting of the Charter to place the ultimate authority to interpret the Charter in the International Court of Justice were not accepted; the opinion which the Court is in course of rendering is an *advisory* opinion. As anticipated in 1945, therefore, each organ must, in the first place at least, determine its own jurisdiction. If the Security Council, for example, adopts a resolution purportedly for the maintenance of international peace and security and if, in accordance with a mandate or authorization in such resolution, the Secretary-General incurs financial obligations, these amounts must be presumed to constitute "expenses of the Organization".

...

-169-

Similarly, obligations of the Organization may be incurred by the Secretary-General, acting on the authority of the Security Council or of the General Assembly, and the General Assembly "has no alternative but to honour these engagements".

The obligation is one thing: the way in which the obligation is met—that is from what source the funds are secured—is another. The General Assembly may follow any one of several alternatives: it may apportion the cost of the item according to the ordinary scale of assessment; it may apportion the cost according to some special scale of assessment; it may utilize funds which are voluntarily contributed to the Organization; or it may find some other method or combination of methods for providing the necessary funds. In this context, it is of no legal significance whether, as a matter of book-keeping or accounting, the General Assembly chooses to have the item in question included under one of the standard established sections of the "regular" budget or whether it is separately listed in some special account or fund. The significant fact is that the item is an expense of the Organization and under

-170-

Article 17, paragraph 2, the General Assembly therefore has authority to apportion it.

The reasoning which has just been developed, applied to the resolutions mentioned in the request for the advisory opinion, might suffice as a basis for the opinion of the Court. The Court finds it appropriate, however, to take into consideration other arguments which have been advanced.

The expenditures enumerated in the request for an advisory opinion may conveniently be examined first with reference to UNEF and then to ONUC. In each case, attention will be paid first to the operations and then to the financing of the operations.

In considering the operations in the Middle East, the Court must analyze the functions of UNEF as set forth in resolutions of the General Assembly. Resolution 998 (ES-I) of 4 November 1956 requested the Secretary-General to submit a plan "for the setting up, with the consent of the nations concerned, of an emergency international United Nations Force to secure and supervise the cessation of hostilities in accordance with all the terms of" the General Assembly's previous resolution 997 (ES-I) of 2 November 1956. The verb "secure" as applied to such matters as halting the movement of military forces and arms into the area and the conclusion of a cease-fire, might suggest measures of enforcement, were it not that the Force was to be set up "with the consent of the nations concerned".

In his first report on the plan for an emergency international Force the Secretary-General used the language of resolution 998 (ES-I) in submitting his proposals. The same terms are used in General Assembly resolution 1000 (ES-I) of 5 November in which operative paragraph 1 reads:

> "*Establishes* a United Nations Command for an emergency international Force to secure and supervise the cessation of hostilities in accordance with all the terms of General Assembly resolution 997 (ES-I) of 2 November 1956."

This resolution was adopted without a dissenting vote. In his second and final report on the plan for an emergency international Force of 6 November, te [sic] Secretary-General, in paragraphs 9 and 10, stated:

> "While the General Assembly is enabled to *establish* the Force with the consent of those parties which contribute units to the Force, it could not request the Force to be *stationed* or *operate* on the territory of a given country without the consent of the Govern-
>
> -171-
>
> ment of that country. This does not exclude the possibility that the Security Council could use such a Force within the wider margins provided under Chapter VII of the United Nations Charter. I would not for the present consider it necessary to elaborate this point further, since no use of the Force under Chapter VII, with the rights in relation to Member States that this would entail, has been envisaged.
>
> 10. The point just made permits the conclusion that the setting up of the Force should not be guided by the needs which would have existed had the measures been considered as part of an enforcement action directed against a Member country. There is an obvious difference between establishing the Force in order to secure the cessation of hostilities, with a withdrawal of forces, and establishing such a Force with a view to enforcing a withdrawal of forces."

Paragraph 12 of the Report is particularly important because in resolution 1001 (ES-I) the General Assembly, again without a dissenting vote, "*Concurs* in the definition of the functions of the Force as stated in paragraph 12 of the Secretary-General's report". Paragraph 12 reads in part as follows:

> "the functions of the United Nations Force would be, when a ceasefire is being established, to enter Egyptian territory with the consent of the Egyptian Government, in order

to help maintain quiet during and after the withdrawal of non-Egyptian troops, and to secure compliance with the other terms established in the resolution of 2 November 1956. The Force obviously should have no rights other than those necessary for the execution of its functions, in co-operation with local authorities. It would be more than an observers' corps, but in no way a military force temporarily controlling the territory in which it is stationed; nor, moreover, should the Force have military functions exceeding those necessary to secure peaceful conditions on the assumption that the parties to the conflict take all necessary steps for compliance with the recommendations of the General Assembly."

It is not possible to find in this description of the functions of UNEF, as outlined by the Secretary-General and concurred in by the General Assembly without a dissenting vote, any evidence that the Force was to be used for purposes of enforcement. Nor can such evidence be found in the subsequent operations of the Force, operations which did not exceed the scope of the functions ascribed to it.

It could not therefore have been patent on the face of the resolution that the establishment of UNEF was in effect "enforcement action" under Chapter VII which, in accordance with the Charter, could be authorized only by the Security Council.

On the other hand, it is apparent that the operations were undertaken to fulfil a prime purpose of the United Nations, that is, to

-172-

promote and to maintain a peaceful settlement of the situation. This being true, the Secretary-General properly exercised the authority given him to incur financial obligations of the Organization and expenses resulting form [sic] such obligations must be considered "expenses of the Organization within the meaning of Article 17, paragraph 2".

Apropos what has already been said about the meaning of the word "action" in Article 11 of the Charter, attention may be called to the fact that resolution 997 (ES-I), which is chronologically the first of the resolutions concerning the operations in the Middle East mentioned in the request for the advisory opinion, provides in paragraph 5:

> "*Requests* the Secretary-General to observe and report promptly on the compliance with the present resolution to the Security Council *and* to the General Assembly, for such further *action as they may deem appropriate in accordance with the Charter*."

The italicized words reveal an understanding that either of the two organs might take "action" in the premises. Actually, as one knows, the "action" was taken by the General Assembly in adopting two days later without a dissenting vote, resolution 998 (ES-I) and, also without dissenting vote, within another three days, resolutions 1000 (ES-I) and 1001 (ES-I), all providing for UNEF.

The Court notes that these "actions" may be considered "measures" recommended under Article 14, rather than "action" recommended under Article 11. The powers of the General Assembly stated in Article 14 are not made subject to the provisions of Article 11, but only of Article 12. Furthermore, as the Court has already noted, the word "measures" implies some kind of action. So far as concerns the nature of the situations in the Middle East in 1956, they could be described as "likely to impair ... friendly relations among nations", just as well as they could be considered to involve "the maintenance of international peace and security". Since the resolutions of the General Assembly in question do not mention upon which article they are based, and since the language used in most of them might imply reference to either Article 14 or Article 11, it cannot be excluded that they were based upon the former rather than the latter article.

The financing of UNEF presented perplexing problems and the debates on these problems have even led to the view that the General Assembly never, either directly or indirectly, regarded the

-173-

expenses of UNEF as "expenses of the Organization within the meaning of Article 17, paragraph 2, of the Charter". With this interpretation the Court cannot agree. In paragraph 15 of his second and final report on the plan for an emergency international Force of 6 November 1956, the Secretary-General said that this problem required further study. Provisionally, certain costs might be absorbed by a nation providing a unit, "while all other costs should be financed outside the normal budget of the United Nations". Since it was "obviously impossible to make any estimate of the costs without a knowledge of the size of the corps and the length of its assignment", the "only practical course ... would be for the General Assembly to vote a general authorization for the cost of the Force on the basis of general principles such as those here suggested".

Paragraph 5 of resolution 1001 (ES-I) of 7 November 1956 states that the General Assembly "*Approves provisionally* the basic rule concerning the financing of the Force laid down in paragraph 15 of the Secretary-General's report".

In an oral statement to the plenary meeting of the General Assembly on 26 November 1956, the Secretary-General said:

> "... I wish to make it equally clear that while funds received and payments made with respect to the Force are to be considered as coming outside the regular budget of the Organization, the operation is essentially a United Nations responsibility, and the Special Account to be established must, therefore, be construed as coming within the meaning of Article 17 of the Charter".
>
> ...

-175-

The Court concludes that, from year to year, the expenses of UNEF have been treated by the General Assembly as expenses of the Organization within the meaning of Article 17, paragraph 2, of the Charter.

The operations in the Congo were initially authorized by the Security Council in the resolution of 14 July 1960 which was adopted without a dissenting vote. The resolution, in the light of the appeal from the Government of the Congo, the report of the Secretary-General and the debate in the Security Council, was clearly adopted with a view to maintaining international peace and security. However, it is argued that that resolution has been implemented, in violation of provisions of the Charter inasmuch as under the Charter it is the Security Council that determines which States are to participate in carrying out decisions involving the maintenance of international peace and security, whereas in the case of the Congo the Secretary-General himself determined which States were to participate with their armed forces or otherwise.

By paragraph 2 of the resolution of 14 July 1960 the Security Council "*Decides* to authorize the Secretary-General to take the necessary steps, in consultation with the Government of the Republic of the Congo, to provide the Government with such military assistance as may be necessary". Paragraph 3 requested the

-176-

Secretary-General "to report to the Security Council as appropriate". The Secretary-General made his first report on 18 July and in it informed the Security Council which States he had asked to contribute forces or materiel, which ones had complied, the size of the units which had already arrived in the Congo (a total of some 3,500 troops), and some detail about further units expected.

On 22 July the Security Council by unanimous vote adopted a further resolution in which the preamble states that it had considered this report of the Secretary-General and appreciated "the work of the Secretary-General and the support so readily and so speedily given to him by all Member States invited by him to give assistance". In operative paragraph 3, the Security Council "*Commends* the Secretary-General for the prompt action he has taken to carry out resolution S/4387 of the Security Council, and for his first report".

On 9 August the Security Council adopted a further resolution without a dissenting vote in which it took note of the second report and of an oral statement of the Secretary-General and in operative paragraph 1: "*Confirms* the authority given to the Secretary-General by the Security Council resolutions of 14 July and 22 July 1960 and requests him to continue to carry out the responsibility placed on him thereby". This emphatic ratification is further supported by operative paragraphs 5 and 6 by which all Member States were called upon "to afford mutual assistance" and the Secretary-General was requested "to implement this resolution and to report further to the Council as appropriate".

The Security Council resolutions of 14 July, 22 July and 9 August 1960 were noted by the General Assembly in its resolution 1474 (ES-IV) of 20 September, adopted without a dissenting vote, in which it "fully supports" these resolutions. Again without a dissenting vote, on 21 February 1961 the Security Council reaffirmed its three previous resolutions "and the General Assembly resolution 1474 (ES-IV) of 20 September 1960" and reminded "all States of their obligations under these resolutions".

Again without a dissenting vote on 24 November 1961 the Security Council, once more recalling the previous resolutions, reaffirmed "the policies and purposes of the United Nations with respect to the Congo (Leopoldville) as set out" in those resolutions. Operative paragraphs 4 and 5 of this resolution renew the authority to the Secretary-General to continue the activities in the Congo.

In the light of such a record of reiterated consideration, confirmation, approval and ratification by the Security Council and by the General Assembly of the actions of the Secretary-General in

-177-

implementing the resolution of 14 July 1960, it is impossible to reach the conclusion that the operations in question usurped or impinged upon the prerogatives conferred by the Charter on the Security Council. The Charter does not forbid the Security Council to act through instruments of its own choice: under Article 29 it "may establish such subsidiary organs as it deems necessary for the performance of its functions"; under Article 98 it may entrust "other functions" to the Secretary-General.

It is not necessary for the Court to express an opinion as to which article or articles of the Charter were the basis for the resolutions of the Security Council, but it can be said that the operations of ONUC did not include a use of armed force against a State which the Security Council, under Article 39, determined to have committed an act of aggression or to have breached the peace. The armed forces which were utilized in the Congo were not authorized to take military action against any State. The operation did not involve "preventive or enforcement measures" against any State under Chapter VII and therefore did not constitute "action" as that term is used in Article 11.

For the reasons stated, financial obligations which, in accordance with the clear and reiterated authority of both the Security Council and the General Assembly, the Secretary-General incurred on behalf of the United Nations, constitute obligations of the Organization for which the General Assembly was entitled to make provision under the authority of Article 17.

In relation to ONUC, the first action concerning the financing of the operation was taken by the General Assembly on 20 December 1960, after the Security Council had adopted its resolutions of 14 July, 22 July and 9 August, and the General Assembly had adopted its supporting resolution of 20 September. This resolution 1583 (XV) of 20 December referred to the report of the Secretary-General on the estimated cost of the Congo operations from 14 July to 31 December 1960, and to the recommendations of the Advisory Committee on Administrative and Budgetary Questions. It decided to establish an *ad hoc* account for the expenses of the United Nations in the Congo. It also took note of certain waivers of cost claims and then decided to apportion the sum of $48.5 million among the Member States "on the basis of the regular scale of assessment" subject to certain exceptions. It made this decision because in the preamble it had already recognized:

> "that the expenses involved in the United Nations operation in the Congo for 1960 constitute 'expenses of the Organization' within
>
> -178-
>
> the meaning of Article 17, paragraph 2, of the Charter of the United Nations and that the assessment thereof against Member States creates binding legal obligations on such States to pay their assessed shares".

By its further resolution 1590 (XV) of the same day, the General Assembly authorized the Secretary-General "to incur commitments in 1961 for the United Nations operations in the Congo up to the total of $24 million for the period from 1 January to 31 March 1961". On 3 April 1961, the General Assembly authorized the Secretary-General to continue until 21 April "to incur commitments for the United Nations operations in the Congo at a level not to exceed $8 million per month".

Importance has been attached to the statement included in the preamble of General Assembly resolution 1619 (XV) of 21 April 1961 which reads:

> "*Bearing in mind* that the extraordinary expenses for the United Nations operations in the Congo are essentially different in nature from the expenses of the Organization under the regular budget and that therefore a procedure different from that applied in the case of the regular budget is required for meeting these extraordinary expenses."

However, the same resolution in operative paragraph 4:

> "*Decides further* to apportion as expenses of the Organization the amount of $100 million among the Member States in accordance with the scale of assessment for the regular budget subject to the provisions of paragraph 8 below [paragraph 8 makes certain adjustments for Member States assessed at the lowest rates or who receive certain designated technical assistance], pending the establishment of a different scale of assessment to defray the extraordinary expenses of the Organization resulting from these operations."

Although it is not mentioned in the resolution requesting the advisory opinion, because it was adopted at the same meeting of the General Assembly, it may be noted that the further resolution 1732 (XVI) of 20 December 1961 contains an identical paragraph in the preamble and a comparable operative paragraph 4 on apportioning $80 million.

The conclusion to be drawn from these paragraphs is that the General Assembly has twice decided that even though certain expenses are "extraordinary" and "essentially different" from those under the "regular budget", they are none the less "expenses of the Organization" to be apportioned in accordance with the power granted to the General Assembly by Article 17, paragraph 2. This conclusion is strengthened by the concluding clause of paragraph 4 of the two resolutions just cited which states that the decision therein to use the scale of assessment already adopted for the

-179-

regular budget is made "pending the establishment of a *different scale of assessment* to defray the extraordinary expenses". The only alternative—and that means the "different procedure"—contemplated was another *scale* of assessment and not some method other than assessment. "Apportionment" and "assessment" are terms which relate only to the General Assembly's authority under Article 17.

At the outset of this opinion, the Court pointed out that the text of Article 17, paragraph 2, of the Charter could lead to the simple conclusion that "the expenses of the Organization" are the amounts paid out to defray the costs of carrying out the purposes of the Organization. It was further indicated that the Court would examine the resolutions authorizing the expenditures referred to in the request for the advisory opinion in order to ascertain whether they were incurred with that end in view. The Court has made such an examination and finds that they were so incurred. The Court has also analyzed the principal arguments which have been advanced against the conclusion that the expenditures in question should be considered as "expenses of the Organization within the meaning of Article 17, paragraph 2, of the Charter of the United Nations", and has found that these arguments are unfounded. Consequently, the Court arrives at the conclusion that the question submitted to it in General Assembly resolution 1731 (XVI) must be answered in the affirmative.

...

36

Difference Relating to Immunity from Legal Process of a Special Rapporteur of the Commission on Human Rights

Prefatory Note

On 5 August 1998, the United Nations Economic and Social Council (ECOSOC) requested an advisory opinion[1] from the International Court of Justice (ICJ) relating to a dispute arising between the UN and the Government of Malaysia in relation to the meaning of Section 30 of the Convention on the Privileges and Immunities of the United Nations (General Convention).[2] The issue considered by the Court involved the immunity from legal process of Dato' Param Cumaraswamy, the Special Rapporteur of the Commission on Human Rights on the independence of judges and lawyers.

The case derives from the publication of an article in November 1995 based on an interview given by Dato' Param Cumaraswamy. Two commercial companies in Malaysia asserted that the article contained defamatory words that had 'brought them into public scandal, odium and contempt' and each company filed a suit against him for damages amounting to M$30 million[3] 'including exemplary damages for slander'.[4] The UN Secretary-General issued notes confirming that 'the words which constitute the basis of plaintiffs' complaint in this case were spoken by the Special Rapporteur in the course of his mission' and that the Secretary-General 'therefore maintains that Dato' Param Cumaraswamy is immune from legal process with respect thereto'.[5]

The High Court of Malaysia regarded the Secretary-General's statements as merely 'an opinion'[6] with limited probative value and no binding force upon the Court. Despite several communications between the UN and the Government of Malaysia, a common interpretation of the applicability of the General Convention to the case of the Special Rapporteur was not reached. Both parties agreed to put the matter to the Court and accept its decision as decisive.

The Court concluded that the Secretary-General had correctly identified that Mr Cumaraswamy, in speaking the words quoted in the article, was acting in the course of the performance of his mission as Special Rapporteur of the Commission. Consequently, Article VI, Section 22(b) of the General Convention was applicable to him as an expert on mission and Mr Cumaraswamy was to be afforded immunity from legal process of every kind.

Whilst the text of Article VI, Section 22, of the General Convention does not specifically define an 'expert', it is a term which is broad enough to include consultants,[7] military observers, and civilian police personnel. This interpretation is supported by the Court's Advisory Opinion in *Applicability of Article VI, Section 22, of the Convention on the Privileges and Immunities of the United Nations*,[8] where the Court stated:

---

1 Advisory opinions are a special procedure available to UN organs under Article 96 of the Charter (see ch 1 above), allowing them to seek opinions from the ICJ on legal questions arising within the scope of their activities.

2 Convention on the Privileges and Immunities of the United Nations (opened for signature 13 February 1946, entered into force 17 September 1946) 1 UNTS 15 (hereafter General Convention). The General Convention was adopted by the General Assembly in GA Res 22 (I) A (1946) of 13 February 1946. See ch 21 above.

3 Malaysian $30 million, approximately US$12 million at the date of the case.

4 *Difference Relating to Immunity from Legal Process of a Special Rapporteur of the Commission of Human Rights* (Advisory Opinion) [1999] ICJ Rep 62, 67 [5] (hereafter *Cumaraswamy Case*).

5 Ibid, 68 [6].

6 Ibid.

7 Consultants may be accorded the status of 'experts on mission' within the meaning of Article VI of the Convention, or they may be engaged as independent contractors, in which case they may not have any status under the Convention. See the UN Juridical Yearbook 1996, 440–1, 441 on 'Obligations of the United Nations with respect to income tax levied by a Member State—Article II, Section 2, and Article V, Section 18, of the Convention on the Privileges and Immunities of the United Nations—Status of consultants', 8 August 1996.

8 *Applicability of Article VI, Section 22, of the Convention on the Privileges and Immunities of the United Nations* (Advisory Opinion) [1989] ICJ Rep 177.

> Such persons have been entrusted with mediation, with preparing reports, preparing studies, conducting investigations or finding and establishing facts. They have participated in certain peacekeeping forces, technical assistance work, and a multitude of other activities.[9]

The practice of the UN has been to classify any person who is entrusted to perform a specific and important task for the UN as an 'expert on mission' if they are neither a staff member (i.e. official) nor a representative of a Member State.[10]

In this case, the parties to the Court's advisory opinion held no disagreement on whether the Special Rapporteur was an expert on mission or that such experts enjoy the privileges and immunities provided for under the General Convention in their relations with States parties. The issue for consideration related to whether the statements made by Mr Cumaraswamy and quoted in the article were spoken during his mission and so fell within the immunity.

The Court identified the Secretary-General as having primacy in the process of determining whether an expert on mission is entitled to the immunity provided for in Section 22(b). The Secretary-General, as the chief administrative officer of the organisation, has the authority and the responsibility to exercise the necessary protection where required. Article VI, Section 23, of the General Convention provides that '[p]rivileges and immunities are granted to experts in the interests of the United Nations and not for the personal benefit of the individuals themselves'. In exercising the protection of UN experts, the Secretary-General is thereby protecting the mission with which the expert is entrusted. In that respect, the Secretary-General has the primary responsibility and authority to protect the interests of the organisation and its agents, including experts on mission.

Article VI, Section 23, of the General Convention goes on to provide that '[t]he Secretary-General shall have the right and the duty to waive the immunity of any expert in any case where, in his opinion, the immunity would impede the course of justice and it can be waived without prejudice to the interests of the United Nations'. The use of the phrase 'in his opinion' reinforces the fact that it is the Secretary-General who determines whether the words or acts of an expert are within the course of their mission, and not courts of law or any other national authority of a Member State. The UN Office of Legal Affairs (OLA) in a legal opinion confirmed this was the view of the UN in regards to staff members, which would also be applicable to experts on mission:

> it has been a long-lasting and uncontested practice that the competence to determine what constitutes an 'official' or 'unofficial' act performed by a staff member is vested solely in the Secretary-General. In view of the foregoing observations, the United Nations has never recognized or accepted that courts of law or any other national authorities of Member States have jurisdiction in making determinations in these matters.[11]

The Court also confirmed that:

> the Secretary-General, as the chief administrative officer of the Organization, has the primary responsibility to safeguard the interests of the Organization; to that end, it is up to him to assess whether its agents acted within the scope of their functions and, where he so concludes, to protect these agents, including experts on mission, by asserting their immunity.[12]

In effect, there is a two-stage test concerning the application of functional immunity in a particular case. The first stage involves a determination of whether the act in question was an 'official act'. If the act is characterised as such, then the second stage involves the Secretary-General determining whether the immunity should be removed. If it is found not to constitute an 'official act' then the immunity question never arises because the UN has made it clear that it does not accept responsibility for acts carried out in an 'unofficial capacity'.[13]

---

9 Ibid, 194 [48].

10 See the UN Juridical Yearbook 1998, 481–2 on the 'Question of whether contractors' personnel could be considered as "experts on mission"—Article VI, Section 22, of the 1946 Convention on the Privileges and Immunities of the United Nations', 23 March 1998. See discussion in ch 26 above.

11 Section 20 for officials is equivalent to Section 23 for experts on mission; See the UN Juridical Yearbook 1995, 403–4, 404 on the 'Question of who can determine whether the acts of United Nations officials are performed in their official capacity—Section 20 of the Convention on the Privileges and Immunities of the United Nations', 24 January 1995.

12 *Cumaraswamy Case* (n 4), 87 [60].

13 See the UN Juridical Yearbook 1986, 300–1 on 'Liability of the United Nations for claims involving off-duty acts of members of peace-keeping forces—Determination of "off-duty" versus "on-duty" status', 23 July 1985.

The determination of the Court confirms that the Secretary-General has the capacity to advise when individuals, such as experts on mission and officials, are acting in the course of the performance of their mission or carrying out official acts and, if so, whether immunity will be waived. It should be noted, however, that the Court also stated:

> When national courts are seised of a case in which the immunity of a United Nations agent is in issue, they should immediately be notified of any finding by the Secretary-General concerning that immunity. That finding, and its documentary expression, creates a presumption which can only be set aside for the most compelling reasons and is thus to be given the greatest weight by national courts.[14]

Whilst the Secretary-General retains the right to waive the immunity of experts and officials in UN peace operations, the first stage of determining whether the act is an 'official act' or 'within the course of performance of their mission' is delegated to the Special Representative of the Secretary-General (SRSG) who has operational authority and control over the mission in the field. This is provided for in Paragraphs 47(a) and 49(a) of the Status-of-Forces Agreement (SOFA).[15] Including the role of the SRSG in the SOFA ensures that there can be no doubt in a UN peace operation of who has the right to determine whether the act in question is an 'official act' because the host country agrees it is the SRSG, and the SOFA represents a binding agreement between the UN and host country.

Reference

Case Name	Difference Relating to Immunity from Legal Process of a Special Rapporteur of the Commission on Human Rights
Case Type	Advisory Opinion
Court	International Court of Justice
Date	29 April 1999
Source	[1999] ICJ Rep 62
Full Text	<https://www.icj-cij.org/en/case/100>[16]

Difference Relating to Immunity from Legal Process of a Special Rapporteur of the Commission on Human Rights

Advisory Opinion of 29 April 1999

(Extracts)

-63-

The question on which the Court has been requested to give an advisory opinion is set forth in decision 1998/297 adopted by the United Nations Economic and Social Council (hereinafter called the "Council") on 5 August 1998 ... Decision 1998/297 ... reads as follows:

"The Economic and Social Council,

14 *Cumaraswamy Case* (n 4), 87 [61].

15 See ch 2 above.

16 Last visited 15 August 2018.

Having considered the note by the Secretary-General on the privileges and immunities of the Special Rapporteur of the Commission on Human Rights on the independence of judges and lawyers,[17]

Considering that a difference has arisen between the United Nations and the Government of Malaysia, within the meaning of Section 30 of the Convention on the Privileges and Immunities of the United Nations, with respect to the immunity from legal process of Dato' Param Cumaraswamy, the Special Rapporteur of the Commission on Human Rights on the independence of judges and lawyers,

Recalling General Assembly resolution 89 (I) of 11 December 1946,

1. *Requests* on a priority basis, pursuant to Article 96, paragraph 2, of the Charter of the United Nations and in accordance with General Assembly

-64-

resolution 89 (I), an advisory opinion from the International Court of Justice on the legal question of the applicability of Article VI, Section 22, of the Convention on the Privileges and Immunities of the United Nations in the case of Dato' Param Cumaraswamy as Special Rapporteur of the Commission on Human Rights on the independence of judges and lawyers, taking into account the circumstances set out in paragraphs 1 to 15 of the note by the Secretary-General[18], and on the legal obligations of Malaysia in this case;

2. *Calls upon* the Government of Malaysia to ensure that all judgements and proceedings in this matter in the Malaysian courts are stayed pending receipt of the advisory opinion of the International Court of Justice, which shall be accepted as decisive by the parties."

...

-66-

10. In its decision 1998/297, the Council asked the Court to take into account, for purposes of the advisory opinion requested, the "circumstances set out in paragraphs 1 to 15 of the note by the Secretary-General" (E/1998/94). Those paragraphs read as follows:

"...

3. In its Advisory Opinion of 14 December 1989, on the *Applicability of Article VI, Section 22, of the Convention on the Privileges and Immunities of the United Nations* (the so-called '*Mazilu* case'), the International Court of Justice held that a Special Rapporteur of the Subcommission on the Prevention of Discrimination and Protection of Minorities of the Commission on Human Rights was an

-67-

'expert on mission' within the meaning of Article VI of the Convention.

4. The Commission on Human Rights ... appointed Dato' Param Cumaraswamy, a Malaysian jurist, as the Commission's Special Rapporteur on the Independence of Judges and Lawyers. His mandate consists of tasks including, *inter alia*, to inquire into substantial allegations concerning, and to identify and record attacks on, the independence of the judiciary, lawyers and court officials ...

5. In November 1995 the Special Rapporteur gave an interview to *International Commercial Litigation*, a magazine published in the United Kingdom of Great Britain and Northern Ireland but circulated also in Malaysia, in which he commented on certain litigations that had been carried out in Malaysian courts. As a result of an article published on the basis of that interview, two commercial companies in Malaysia asserted that the said article contained defamatory words that had 'brought them into public scandal, odium and

17 E/1998/94. [Note: this footnote appears in the original document as footnote '1'].
18 Ibid.

contempt'. Each company filed a suit against him for damages amounting to M$30 million (approximately US$12 million each), 'including exemplary damages for slander'.

6. Acting on behalf of the Secretary-General, the Legal Counsel considered the circumstances of the interview and of the controverted passages of the article and determined that Dato' Param Cumaraswamy was interviewed in his official capacity as Special Rapporteur on the Independence of Judges and Lawyers, that the article clearly referred to his United Nations capacity and to the Special Rapporteur's United Nations global mandate to investigate allegations concerning the independence of the judiciary and that the quoted passages related to such allegations. On 15 January 1997, the Legal Counsel, in a note verbale addressed to the Permanent Representative of Malaysia to the United Nations, therefore 'requested the competent Malaysian authorities to promptly advise the Malaysian courts of the Special Rapporteur's immunity from legal process' with respect to that particular complaint. On 20 January 1997, the Special Rapporteur filed an application in the High Court of Kuala Lumpur (the trial court in which the said suit had been filed) to set aside and/or strike out the plaintiffs' writ, on the ground that the

-68-

words that were the subject of the suits had been spoken by him in the course of performing his mission for the United Nations as Special Rapporteur on the Independence of Judges and Lawyers. The Secretary-General issued a note on 7 March 1997 confirming that 'the words which constitute the basis of plaintiffs' complaint in this case were spoken by the Special Rapporteur in the course of his mission' and that the Secretary-General 'therefore maintains that Dato' Param Cumaraswamy is immune from legal process with respect thereto'. The Special Rapporteur filed this note in support of his above-mentioned application.

7. After a draft of a certificate that the Minister for Foreign Affairs proposed to file with the trial court had been discussed with representatives of the Office of Legal Affairs, who had indicated that the draft set out the immunities of the Special Rapporteur incompletely and inadequately, the Minister nevertheless on 12 March 1997 filed the certificate in the form originally proposed: in particular the final sentence of that certificate in effect invited the trial court to determine at its own discretion whether the immunity applied, by stating that this was the case '*only* in respect of words spoken or written and acts done by him in the course of the performance of his mission' (emphasis added). In spite of the representations that had been made by the Office of Legal Affairs, the certificate failed to refer in any way to the note that the Secretary-General had issued a few days earlier and that had in the meantime been filed with the court, nor did it indicate that in this respect, i.e. in deciding whether particular words or acts of an expert fell within the scope of his mission, the determination could exclusively be made by the Secretary-General, and that such determination had conclusive effect and therefore had to be accepted as such by the court. In spite of repeated requests by the Legal Counsel, the Minister for Foreign Affairs refused to amend his certificate or to supplement it in the manner urged by the United Nations.

8. On 28 June 1997, the competent judge of the Malaysian High Court for Kuala Lumpur concluded that she was 'unable to hold that the Defendant is absolutely protected by the immunity he claims', in part because she considered that the Secretary-General's note was merely 'an opinion' with scant probative value and no binding force upon the court and that the Minister for Foreign Affairs' certificate 'would appear to be no more than a bland statement as to a state of fact pertaining to the Defendant's status and mandate as a Special Rapporteur and appears to have room for interpretation'. The Court ordered that the Special Rapporteur's motion be dismissed with costs ...

-69-

9.... The Legal Counsel referred to the provisions for the settlement of differences arising out of the interpretation and application of the 1946 Convention that might arise between the Organization and a Member State, which are set out in Section 30 of the Convention, and indicated that if the Government decided that it cannot or does not wish to protect and to hold harmless the Special Rapporteur in the indicated manner, a difference within the meaning of those provisions might be considered to have arisen between the Organization and the Government of Malaysia.

. . .

-70-

13. On 7 November 1997, the Secretary-General advised the Prime Minister of Malaysia that a difference might have arisen between the United Nations and the Government of Malaysia and about the possibility of resorting to the International Court of Justice pursuant to Section 30 of the Convention. Nonetheless on 19 February 1998, the Federal Court of Malaysia denied Mr. Cumaraswamy's application for leave to appeal stating that he is neither a sovereign nor a full-fledged diplomat but merely 'an unpaid, part-time provider of information'."

. . .

-79-

31. . . . the Secretary-General transmitted to the Court the text of the Council's decision, paragraph 1 of which reads as follows:

"1. *Requests* on a priority basis, pursuant to Article 96, paragraph 2, of the Charter of the United Nations and in accordance with General Assembly resolution 89 (1), an advisory opinion from the International Court of Justice on the legal question of the applicability of Article VI, Section 22, of the Convention on the Privileges and Immunities of the United Nations in the case of Dato' Param Cumaraswamy as Special Rapporteur of the Commission on Human Rights on the independence of judges and lawyers, taking into account the circumstances set out in paragraphs 1 to 15 of the note by the Secretary-General, and on the legal obligations of Malaysia in this case."

32. Malaysia . . . contends that the advisory opinion of the Court should be restricted to the existing difference between the United Nations and Malaysia. In Malaysia's view, this difference relates to the question . . . of whether the latter [Secretary-General] has the exclusive authority to determine whether acts of an expert (including words spoken or written) were performed in the course of his or her mission. Thus, in the conclusion to the revised version of its written statement, Malaysia States, *inter alia*, that it

"considers that the Secretary-General of the United Nations has not been vested with the exclusive authority to determine whether words

-80-

were spoken in the course of the performance of a mission for the United Nations within the meaning of Section 22 *(b)* of the Convention".

33. In the written statement presented on behalf of the Secretary-General, the Legal Counsel of the United Nations requested the Court

"to establish that, subject to Article VIII, Sections 29 and 30 of the Convention, the Secretary-General has exclusive authority to determine whether or not words or acts are spoken, written or done in the course of the performance of a mission for the United Nations and whether such words or acts fall within the scope of the mandate entrusted to a United Nations expert on mission".'

In this submission, it has also been argued

"that such matters cannot be determined by, or adjudicated in, the national courts of the Member States parties to the Convention. The latter position is coupled with the Secretary-General's right and duty, in accordance with the terms of Article VI, Section

> 23, of the Convention, to waive the immunity where, in his opinion, it would impede the course of justice and it can be waived without prejudice to the interests of the United Nations."

34. The other States participating in the present proceedings have expressed varying views on the foregoing issue of the exclusive authority of the Secretary-General.

...

-81-

36. Participants in these proceedings have advanced differing views as to what is the legal question to be answered by the Court. The Court observes that it is for the Council—and not for a member State nor for the Secretary-General—to formulate the terms of a question that the Council wishes to ask.
37. ... Accordingly, the Court will now answer the question as formulated by the Council.
38. The Court will initially examine the first part of the question laid before the Court by the Council, which is:

> "the legal question of the applicability of Article VI, Section 22, of the Convention on the Privileges and Immunities of the United Nations in the case of Dato' Param Cumaraswamy as Special Rapporteur of the Commission on Human Rights on the independence of judges and lawyers, taking into account the circumstances set out in paragraphs 1 to 15 of the note by the Secretary-General ..."

39. From the deliberations which took place in the Council on the content of the request for an advisory opinion, it is clear that the reference in the request to the note of the Secretary-General was made in order to provide the Court with the basic facts to which to refer in making its decision. The request of the Council therefore does not only pertain to the threshold question whether Mr. Cumaraswamy was and is an expert on mission in the sense of Article VI, Section 22, of the General Convention but, in the event of an affirmative answer to this question, to the consequences of that finding in the circumstances of the case.

...

-82-

42. In its Advisory Opinion of 14 December 1989 on the *Applicability of Article VI, Section 22, of the Convention on the Privileges and Immunities of the United Nations*, the Court examined the applicability of Section 22 *ratione personae, ratione temporis* and *ratione loci*.

In this context the Court stated:

> "The purpose of Section 22 is ... evident, namely, to enable the United Nations to entrust missions to persons who do not have the status of an official of the Organization, and to guarantee them 'such privileges and immunities as are necessary for the independent exer-
>
> -83-
>
> cise of their functions' ... The essence of the matter lies not in their administrative position but in the nature of their mission." (*I.C.J. Reports 1989*, p. 194, para. 47)

In that same Advisory Opinion, the Court concluded that a Special Rapporteur who is appointed by the Sub-Commission on Prevention of Discrimination and Protection of Minorities and is entrusted with a research mission must be regarded as an expert on mission within the meaning of Article VI, Section 22, of the General Convention (*ibid.*, p. 197, para. 55).

43. The same conclusion must be drawn with regard to Special Rapporteurs appointed by the Human Rights Commission, of which the Sub-Commission is a subsidiary organ. It may be observed that Special Rapporteurs of the Commission usually are entrusted not only with a research mission but also with the task of monitoring human rights violations and reporting on them. But what is decisive is that they have been entrusted with a mission by the United

Nations and are therefore entitled to the privileges and immunities provided for in Article VI, Section 22, that safeguard the independent exercise of their functions.

. . .

-84-

46. The Court observes that Malaysia has acknowledged that Mr. Cumaraswamy, as Special Rapporteur of the Commission, is an expert on mission and that such experts enjoy the privileges and immunities provided for under the General Convention in their relations with States parties, including those of which they are nationals or on the territory of which they reside. Malaysia and the United Nations are in full agreement on these points, as are the other States participating in the proceedings.

47. The Court will now consider whether the immunity provided for in Section 22 *(b)* applies to Mr. Cumaraswamy in the specific circumstances of the case; namely, whether the words used by him in the interview, as published in the article in *International Commercial Litigation* (November issue 1995), were spoken in the course of the performance of his mission, and whether he was therefore immune from legal process with respect to these words.

. . .

50. In the process of determining whether a particular expert on mission is entitled, in the prevailing circumstances, to the immunity provided for in Section 22 *(b),* the Secretary-General of the United Nations has a pivotal role to play. The Secretary-General, as the chief administrative officer of the Organization, has the authority and the responsibility to exercise the necessary protection where required. This authority has been recognized by the Court when it stated:

-85-

> "Upon examination of the character of the functions entrusted to the Organization and of the nature of the missions of its agents, it becomes clear that the capacity of the Organization to exercise a measure of functional protection of its agents arises by necessary intendment out of the Charter." (*Reparation for Injuries Suffered in the Service of the United Nations, Advisory Opinion, I. C. J. Reports 1949*, p. 184.)

51. Article VI, Section 23, of the General Convention provides that "[p]rivileges and immunities are granted to experts in the interests of the United Nations and not for the personal benefit of the individuals themselves". In exercising protection of United Nations experts, the Secretary-General is therefore protecting the mission with which the expert is entrusted. In that respect, the Secretary-General has the primary responsibility and authority to protect the interests of the Organization and its agents, including experts on mission. As the Court held:

> "In order that the agent may perform his duties satisfactorily, he must feel that this protection is assured to him by the Organization, and that he may count on it. To ensure the independence of the agent, and, consequently, the independent action of the Organization itself, it is essential that in performing his duties he need not have to rely on any other protection than that of the Organization . . ." (*Ibid.*, p. 183.)

52. The determination whether an agent of the Organization has acted in the course of the performance of his mission depends upon the facts of a particular case. In the present case, the Secretary-General, or the Legal Counsel of the United Nations on his behalf, has on numerous occasions informed the Government of Malaysia of his finding that Mr. Cumaraswamy had spoken the words quoted in the article in *International Commercial Litigation* in his capacity as Special Rapporteur of the Commission and that he consequently was entitled to immunity from "every kind" of legal process.

. . .

-86-

56. The Court is not called upon in the present case to pass upon the aptness of the terms used by the Special Rapporteur or his assessment of the situation. In any event, in view of all the circumstances of this case, elements of which are set out in paragraphs 1 to 15 of the note by the Secretary-General, the Court is of the opinion that the Secretary-General correctly found that Mr. Cumaraswamy, in speaking the words quoted in the article in *International Commercial Litigation,* was acting in the course of the performance of his mission as Special Rapporteur of the Commission. Consequently, Article VI, Section 22 *(b)*, of the General Convention is applicable to him in the present case and affords Mr. Cumaraswamy immunity from legal process of every kind.

...

-87-

60. As the Court has observed, the Secretary-General, as the chief administrative officer of the Organization, has the primary responsibility to safeguard the interests of the Organization; to that end, it is up to him to assess whether its agents acted within the scope of their functions and, where he so concludes, to protect these agents, including experts on mission, by asserting their immunity. This means that the Secretary-General has the authority and responsibility to inform the Government of a member State of his finding and, where appropriate, to request it to act accordingly and, in particular, to request it to bring his finding to the knowledge of the local courts if acts of an agent have given or may give rise to court proceedings.

61. When national courts are seised of a case in which the immunity of a United Nations agent is in issue, they should immediately be notified of any finding by the Secretary-General concerning that immunity. That finding, and its documentary expression, creates a presumption which can only be set aside for the most compelling reasons and is thus to be given the greatest weight by national courts.

...

-89-

67. For these reasons,

THE COURT

Is of the opinion:

(1) *(a)* By fourteen votes to one,

That Article VI, Section 22, of the Convention on the Privileges and Immunities of the United Nations is applicable in the case of Dato' Param Cumaraswamy as Special Rapporteur of the Commission on Human Rights on the Independence of Judges and Lawyers;

...

(b) By fourteen votes to one,

That Dato' Param Cumaraswamy is entitled to immunity from legal process of every kind for the words spoken by him during an interview as published in an article in the November 1995 issue of *International Commercial Litigation*;

...

(2) *(a)* By thirteen votes to two,

That the Government of Malaysia had the obligation to inform the Malaysian courts of the finding of the Secretary-

-90-

General that Dato' Param Cumaraswamy was entitled to immunity from legal process;

...

(b) By fourteen votes to one,

That the Malaysian courts had the obligation to deal with the question of immunity from legal process as a preliminary issue to be expeditiously decided *in limine litis*;

. . .

(3) Unanimously,

That Dato' Param Cumaraswamy shall be held financially harmless for any costs imposed upon him by the Malaysian courts, in particular taxed costs;

(4) By thirteen votes to two,

That the Government of Malaysia has the obligation to communicate this Advisory Opinion to the Malaysian courts, in order that Malaysia's international obligations be given effect and Dato' Param Cumaraswamy's immunity be respected;

. . .

Select Bibliography

Amrallah B, 'The International Responsibility of the United Nations for Activities Carried Out by UN Peace-Keeping Forces' (1976) 32 *Revue Egyptienne de Droit International* 57.

Arnold R (ed), *Law Enforcement within the Framework of Peace Support Operations* (Brill Nijhoff 2008).

Aust H, 'The Human Rights Due Diligence Policy: An Effective Mechanism against Complicity of Peacekeeping Forces?' (2015) 20(1) *Journal of Conflict and Security Law* 61.

Baele C, 'Compensation for Damage in Peace Operations' (2006) 45 *Military Law and the Law of War Review* 193.

Bartholomeusz L, 'The Legal Framework for Protection of United Nations Humanitarian Premises During Armed Conflict' (2014) 18 *Max Planck Yearbook of United Nations Law* 68.

Bloom ET, 'Protecting Peacekeepers: The Convention on the Safety of United Nations and Associated Personnel' (1995) 89 *American Journal of International Law* 621.

Bothe M, 'Peacekeeping and International Humanitarian Law: Friends or Foes?' (1996) 3 *International Peacekeeping* 91.

Bothe M, 'Special Section: Peacekeeping' in B Simma and others (eds), *The Charter of the United Nations: A Commentary* (2nd edn, Oxford University Press 2002) vol 1, 648.

Bothe M, 'The UN Peacekeeping Experience' in D Fleck (ed), *The Handbook of the Law of Visiting Forces* (Oxford University Press 2001) 487.

Bourloyannis-Vrailas M-C, 'The Convention on the Safety of United Nations and Associated Personnel' (1995) 44 *International and Comparative Law Quarterly* 560.

Bowens G, 'Legal Issues in Peace Operations' (1988–9) 28(4) *Parameters* 51.

Bowett DW and Higgins R, *United Nations Forces: A Legal Study* (Lawbook Exchange 1964).

Canadian Department of Defence, 'Report of the Somalia Commission of Inquiry: Volume 2: Accountability' (Canada Commission of Inquiry into the Deployment of Canadian Forces to Somalia 1997).

Cartledge GJ, 'Legal Constraints on Military Personnel Deployed on Peacekeeping Operations' in H Durham and T McCormack (eds), *The Changing Face of Conflict and the Efficacy of International Humanitarian Law* (Brill Nijhoff 1999) 121.

Cassese A (ed), *United Nations Peacekeeping: Legal Essays* (Sijthoff & Noordhoff 1978).

Chesterman S, *You, the People: The United Nations, Transitional Administration and State Building* (Oxford University Press 2004).

Chesterman S, Franck T, and Malone D, *Law and Practice of the United Nations* (Oxford University Press 2008).

Centre for Law and Military Operations, *Law and Military Operations in Haiti: 1994–1995* (The Judge Advocate General's School, United States Army 1995).

Centre for Law and Military Operations, *Law and Military Operations in The Balkans: 1995–1998* (The Judge Advocate General's School, United States Army) (1998).

Centre for Law and Military Operations, *Law and Military Operations in Kosovo: 1999–2001* (The Judge Advocate General's School, United States Army 2001).

Cerone JP, 'Human Dignity in the Line of Fire: The Application of International Human Rights Law During Armed Conflict, Occupation and Peace Operations' (2006) 39 *Vanderbilt Journal of Transnational Law* 1447.

Clapham A, *Human Rights: A Very Short Introduction* (Oxford University Press 2007).

Conforti B, *The Law and Practice of the United Nations* (3rd edn, Brill Nijhoff 2005).

Dahrendorf N, *Sexual Exploitation and Abuse: Lessons Learned Study: Addressing Sexual Exploitation and Abuse in MONUC* (2006) <http://www.peacewomen.org/sites/default/files/dpko_addressingsexualviolenceinmonuc_2006_0.pdf> accessed 1 November 2017.

de Wet E, *The Chapter VII Powers of the United Nations Security Council: Studies in International Law* (Hart 2004).

Deng F, 'Guiding Principles of Internal Displacement' (1998) 10 *International Journal of Refugee Law* 563.

Diehl PF, *International Peacekeeping* (Johns Hopkins University Press 1993).

Droege C, 'The Interplay between International Humanitarian Law and International Human Rights Law in Situations of Armed Conflict' (2007) 40 *Israel Law Review* 310.

Durch WJ (ed), *The Evolution of UN Peacekeeping: Case Studies and Comparative Analysis* (Palgrave Macmillan 1993).

Durch WJ (ed), *Twenty-First Century Peace Operations* (United States Institute of Peace Press 2006).

Durch WJ and others, 'Improving Criminal Accountability in United Nations Peace Operations: Report from the Project on Rule of Law in Post-Conflict Settings: Future of Peace Operations Program', *Stimson Centre Report No 65* (June 2009).

Duxbury A, 'The Privileges and Immunities of United Nations' Experts: The Cumaraswamy Case' (2000) 1(2) *Asia-Pacific Journal on Human Rights and the Law* 88.

Engdahl O, *Protection of Personnel in Peace Operations: The Role of the 'Safety Convention' Against the Background of General International Law* (Martin Nijhoff 2007).

Ferraro T, 'The ICRC's Legal Position on the Notion of Armed Conflict Involving Foreign Intervention and on Determining the IHL Applicable to This Type of Conflict' (2015) 900 *International Review of the Red Cross* 1227.

Ferraro T, 'The Applicability and Application of International Humanitarian Law to Multinational Forces' (2013) 891/892 *International Review of the Red Cross* 561.

Findlay T, *The Use of Force in UN Peace Operations* (Stockholm International Peace Research Institute 2002).

Fleck D, 'The Law Applicable to Peace Operations' in A Clapham and P Gaeta (eds) *The Oxford Handbook of International Law in Armed Conflict* (Oxford University Press 2014) 206.

Gill T, Fleck D, Boothby W, and Vanheusden A (gen eds), *Leuven Manual on the International Law Applicable to Peace Operations* (Cambridge University Press 2017).

Grady K, 'Sex, Statistics, Peacekeepers and Power: UN Data on Sexual Exploitation and Abuse and the Quest for Legal Reform' (2016) 79 *Modern Law Review* 931.

Gray C, *International Law and the Use of Force* (3rd edn, Oxford University Press 2008).

Greenwood C, 'Protection of Peacekeepers: The Legal Regime' (1996) 7 *Duke Journal of Comparative and International Law* 185.

Greenwood C, 'International Humanitarian Law and United Nations Military Operations' (1998) 1 *Yearbook of International Humanitarian Law* 3.

Grenfell K, 'Perspective on the Applicability and Application of International Humanitarian Law: The UN Context' (2013) 891/892 *International Review of the Red Cross* 645.

Grenfell K, 'Detention in United Nations Peace Operations' in G Rose and B Oswald (eds), *Detention of Non-State Actors Engaged in Hostilities: The Future Law* (Brill Nijhoff 2016) 345.

Hafner G, 'Certain Issues of the Work of the Sixth Committee at the Fifty-Sixth General Assembly' (2003) 97 *American Journal of International Law* 147.

Hafner G, 'Can International Organisations be Controlled? Accountability and Responsibility' (2003) 97 *American Society of International Law Proceedings* 236.

Hannam H, 'The Status of the Universal Declaration of Human Rights in National and International Law' (1995–6) 25 *Georgia Journal of International and Comparative Law* 287.

Hans-Joachim H, 'On the Relationship between Human Rights Law Protection and International Humanitarian Law' (2004) 856 *International Review of the Red Cross* 789.

Heiberg M, 'Peacekeepers and Local Populations: Some Comments on UNIFIL' in IJ Rikhye and K Skjelsbaek (eds), *The United Nations and Peacekeeping: Results, Limitations, and Prospects: The Lessons of 40 Years of Experience* (Palgrave MacMillian 1990) 147.

Henckaerts J-M, 'New Rules for the Protection of Cultural Property in Armed Conflict: The Significance of the Second Protocol to the 1954 Hague Convention for the Protection of Cultural Property in the Event of Armed Conflict' (1999) 835 *International Review of the Red Cross* 593.

Henckaerts J-M and Doswald-Beck L (eds), *Customary International Humanitarian Law* (International Committee of the Red Cross and Cambridge University Press 2005) vols 1–5.

Higgins R, *UN Peace-keeping: 1946–1967—Documents and Commentary, Volume I: Middle East* (Oxford University Press 1969).

Higgins R, *UN Peace-keeping: 1946–1967—Documents and Commentary, Volume II: Asia* (Oxford University Press 1970).

Higgins R, 'The Advisory Opinion on Namibia: Which UN Resolutions are binding under Article 25 of the Charter?' (1972) 21 *International & Comparative Law Quarterly* 270.

Higgins R, *UN Peace-keeping: 1946–1967—Documents and Commentary, Volume III: Africa* (Oxford University Press 1980).

Higgins R, *UN Peace-keeping: Documents and Commentary, Volume IV: Europe 1946–1979* (Oxford University Press 1981).

Higgins R, 'The United Nations: Still a Force for Peace' (1989) 52 *Modern Law Review* 1.

Higgins R, *Problems and Processes: International Law and How We Use It* (Oxford University Press 1994).

Hills A, 'The Inherent Limits of Military Forces in Policing Peace Operations' (2001) 8 *International Peacekeeping* 79.

Hladik J, 'Diplomatic Conference on the Second Protocol to the Hague Convention for the Protection of Cultural Property in the Event of Armed Conflict: The Hague, Netherlands (15– 26 March 1999)' (1999) 8 *International Journal of Cultural Property* 526.

Howard J and Oswald BM (eds), *The Rule of Law on Peace Operations: A 'Challenges of Peace Operations' Project Conference* (Asia Pacific Centre for Military Law Project Conference 2002).

Human Rights Watch, 'Bosnia and Herzegovina: Hopes Betrayed—Trafficking of Women and Girls to Post-Conflict Bosnia and Herzegovina for Forced Prostitution' (Human Rights Watch Report No 9, November 2002) <http://www.hrw.org/reports/2002/bosnia> accessed 1 November 2017.

Jackson D, 'Cultural Property Protection in Stability Operations' (2008) 10 *Army Lawyer* 47.

Jenks CW, *International Immunities* (Stevens 1961).

Jennings R and Watts A (eds), *Oppenheim's International Law* (9th edn, Oxford University Press 2008).

Katayanagi M, *Human Rights Functions of United Nations Peacekeeping Operations* (Oxford University Press 2002).

Kelly M and others, 'Legal Aspects of Australia's Involvement in the International Force for East Timor' (2001) 841 *International Review of the Red Cross* 101.

Kirsch P, 'The Convention on the Safety of United Nations and Associated Personnel' (1994–5) 2 *International Peacekeeping* 102.

Klappe B, 'The Law of International Peace Operations' in D Fleck (ed), *The Handbook of International Humanitarian Law* (3rd edn, Cambridge University Press 2013) 611.

Knoops G-J, *The Prosecution and Defense of Peacekeepers under International Criminal Law* (Brill Nijhoff 2004).

Kondoch B, 'Human Rights Law and UN Peace Operations in Post-Conflict Situations' in D Klaasen and N White (eds), *The UN, Human Rights and Post-Conflict Situations* (Manchester University Press 2005) 19.

Koops J and others, *The Oxford Handbook of United Nations Peacekeeping Operations* (Oxford University Press 2015).

Krishnadusan V, 'A Legal Perspective on UNTAC—An Overview' in N Azini, *The United Nations Transitional Authority in Cambodia (UNTAC): Debriefing and Lessons* (United Nations Institute for Training and Research 1995) 191.

Ladley A, 'Peacekeeper Abuse, Immunity and Impunity: The Need for Effective Criminal and Civil Accountability on International Peace Operations' (2005) 1 *Politics and Ethics Review* 81.

Larsen KM, 'Attribution of Conduct in Peace Operations: The "Ultimate Authority and Control Test" ' (2008) 19 *European Journal of International Law* 509.

Lauterpacht H, 'The Universal Declaration of Human Rights' (1948) 25 *British Yearbook of International Law* 354.

Lillich RB, 'The Growing Importance of Customary International Human Rights Law' (1995–6) 25 *Georgia Journal of International and Comparative Law* 1.

Lowe V, Roberts A, Welsh J, and Zaum D, *The United Nations Security Council and War: The Evolution of Thought and Practice since 1945* (Oxford University Press 2008).

Macura T, 'Accountability and Protection of UN Peacekeepers in Light of MONUSCO' (2013) 88 *Journal of International Peace and Organization* 143.

Mahoney L, *Proactive Presence: Field Strategies for Civilian Protection* (Centre for Humanitarian Dialogue 2006).

Malone D (ed), *The UN Security Council: From the Cold War to the 21st Century* (Lynne Rienner 2004).

Månsson K, 'Cooperation in Human Rights: Experience from the Peace Operation in Kosovo' (2001) 8(4) *International Peacekeeping* 111.

Marks S and Clapham A, *International Human Rights Lexicon* (Oxford University Press 2005).

Marshall D and Inglis S, 'The Disempowerment of Human Rights-Based Justice in the United Nations Mission in Kosovo' (2003) 16 *Harvard Human Rights Journal* 95.

McCoubrey H, 'International Law and National Contingents in UN Forces' (1994) 12(3) *International Relations* 39.

McCoubrey H and White N, *The Blue Helmets: Legal Regulation of United Nations Military Operations* (Dartmouth Publishing 1996).

Mendelson SE, *Barracks and Brothels: Peacekeepers and Human Trafficking in the Balkans* (Center for Strategic and International Studies 2005).

Michaels DB, *International Privileges and Immunities: A Case for a Universal Statute* (Martinus Nijhoff 1971).

Miller AJ, 'Legal Aspects of Stopping Sexual Exploitation and Abuse in UN Peace Operations' (2006) 39 *Cornell International Law Journal* 71.

Miller AJ, 'United Nations Experts on Mission and their Privileges and Immunities' (2007) 4 *International Organizations Law Review* 11.

Miller AJ, 'Privileges and Immunities of United Nations Officials' (2008) 4 *International Organizations Law Review* 169.

Miller AJ, 'The Privileges and Immunities of the United Nations' (2009) 6 *International Organizations Law Review* 7.

Ministry of Foreign Affairs of Denmark, 'The Copenhagen Process on the Handling of Detainees in International Military Operations: The Copenhagen Process: Principles and Guidelines' (2012) <http://um.dk/en/~/media/UM/English-site/Documents/Politics-and-diplomacy/Copenhangen%20Process%20Principles%20and%20Guidelines.pdf> accessed 8 April 2019.

Murphy R, *UN Peacekeeping in Lebanon, Somalia and Kosovo: Operational and Legal Issues in Practice* (Cambridge University Press 2007).

Murphy R and Månsson K (eds), *Peace Operations and Human Rights* (Routledge 2008).

Naert F, 'Detention in Peace Operations: The Legal Framework and Main Categories of Detainees' (2006) 45 *The Military Law and the Law of War Review* 51.

Naert F, 'Observance of International Humanitarian Law by Forces under the Command of the European Union' (2013) 95 (891/2) IRRC 639.

Nowak M, *UN Covenant on Civil and Political Rights: CCPR Commentary* (2nd edn, NP Engel 2005).

Nowak M and McArthur E, *The United Nations Convention against Torture: A Commentary* (Oxford University Press 2008).

Öberg MD, 'The Legal Effects of Resolutions of the UN Security Council and General Assembly in the Jurisprudence of the ICJ' (2005) 16 *European Journal of International Law* 879.

O'Neill WG, 'A New Challenge for Peacekeepers: The Internally Displaced', An Occasional Paper of The Brookings Institution–John Hopkins SAIS Project on Internal Displacement (April 2004).

Orakhelashvili A, 'The Legal Basis of the United Nations Peace-Keeping Operations' (2002–3) 43 *Virginia Journal of International Law* 485.

Orakhelashvili A, 'The Impact of Peremptory Norms on the Interpretation and Application of United Nations Security Council Resolutions' (2005) 16 *European Journal of International Law* 59.

Oswald BM, 'The INTERFET Detainee Management Unit in East Timor' (2000) 3 *Yearbook of International Humanitarian Law* 347.

Oswald BM, 'The Creation and Control of Places of Protection during United Nations Peace Operations' (2001) 844 *International Review of the Red Cross* 1013.

Oswald BM, 'Detention by United Nations Peacekeepers: Searching for Definition and Categorisation' (2011) 15 *Journal of International Peacekeeping* 119.

Oswald BM and Finnin S, 'Combating the Trafficking of Persons on Peace Operations' (2006) 10 *International Peacekeeping: The Yearbook of International Peace Operations* 1.

Otto D, 'Making Sense of Zero Tolerance Policies in Peacekeeping Sexual Economies' in VE Munro and CF Stychin (eds), *Sexuality and the Law: Feminist Engagements* (Taylor and Francis 2007) 259.

Pejic J, 'Procedural Principles and Safeguards for Internment/Administrative Detention in Armed Conflict and Other Situations of Violence' (2005) 858 *International Review of the Red Cross* 375.

Plessis MD and Pete S, 'Who Guards the Guards? The ICC and Serious Crimes Committed by Peacekeepers in Africa' (2006) 13(4) *African Security Review* 4.

Provost R, *International Human Rights and Humanitarian Law* (Cambridge University Press 2002).

Ramsbotham O and Woodhouse T, *Encyclopaedia of International Peacekeeping Operations* (ABL–CLIO 1999).

Rawski F, 'To Waive or Not to Waive: Immunity and Accountability in UN Peacekeeping Operations' (2002) 18 *Connecticut Journal of International Law* 103.

Roberts A, 'Human Rights Obligations of External Military Forces' in International Society for Military Law and the Law of War, *Recueil XVII, The Rule of Law on Peace Operations* (International Society for Military Law and the Law of War 2006) 429.

Roberts A and Guelff R (eds), *Documents on the Laws of War* (3rd edn, Oxford University Press 2000).

Roth K and Worden M (eds), *Torture: A Human Rights Perspective* (The New Press 2005).

Rowe P, 'Maintaining Discipline in United Nations Peace Support Operations: The Legal Quagmire for Military Contingents' (2000) 5 *Journal of Conflict and Security Law* 45.

Ryniker A, 'Observance by United Nations Forces of International Humanitarian Law: Comments on the Secretary-General's Bulletin of 6 August 1999' (1999) 836 *International Review of the Red Cross* 795.

Salas RP, 'The Legal Status of International Officials' (1964) 6 *Inter-American Law Review* 169.

Sands P and Klein P, *Bowett's Law of International Institutions* (5th edn, Sweet and Maxwell 2001).

Sarooshi D, 'The Role of the United Nations Secretary-General in United Nations Peacekeeping Operations' (1999) 20 *Australian Year Book of International Law* 279.

Sarooshi D, *The United Nations and the Development of Collective Security: The Delegation by the UN Security Council of its Chapter V11 Powers* (Oxford University Press 2000).

Sassòli M, 'Legislation and Maintenance of Public Order and Civil Life by Occupying Powers' (2005) 16 *European Journal of International Law* 661.

Saura J, 'Lawful Peacekeeping: Applicability of International Humanitarian Law to United Nations Peacekeeping Operations' (2006–7) 58 *Hastings Law Journal* 479.

Seyersted F, 'United Nations Forces: Some Legal Problems' (1961) 37 *British Yearbook of International Law* 351.

Seyersted F, *United Nations Forces in Law of Peace and War* (AW Sijthoff 1966).

Simma B (ed), *The Charter of the United Nations: A Commentary* (3rd edn, Oxford University Press 2012).

Shraga D, 'The United Nations as an Actor Bound by International Humanitarian Law' (1998) 5(2) *International Peacekeeping* 64.

Shraga D, 'UN Peacekeeping Operations: Applicability of International Humanitarian Law and Responsibilities for Operations-Led Damage' (2000) 94 *American Journal of International Law* 406.

Shraga D, 'Military Occupation and UN Transitional Administrations: The Analogy and Its Limitations' in M Kohen (ed), *Promoting Justice, Human Rights and Conflict Resolution Through International Law* (Brill Nijhoff 2007) 479.

Shraga D, 'The Secretary-General's Bulletin on the Observance by United Nations Forces of International Humanitarian Law: A Decade Later' (2009) 39 *Israel Yearbook on Human Rights* 357.

Shraga D, 'The Interplay between Human Rights and International Humanitarian Law in UN Operations in E de Wet and J Kleffner (eds), *Convergence and Conflicts of Human Rights and International Humanitarian Law in Military Operations* (Pretoria University Law Press 2014) 211.

Shraga D, 'The Applicability of the Laws of Armed Conflict to Peacekeeping Operations' in R Liivoja and T McCormack (eds), *Routledge Handbook of the Law of Armed Conflict* (Routledge 2016) 420.

Siekmann RCR, *Basic Documents on United Nations and Related Peace-Keeping Forces* (2nd edn, Springer 1989).

Siekmann RCR, *National Contingents in United Nations Peace-Keeping Forces* (1991).

Sloan B, 'The Binding Nature of a "Recommendation" of the General Assembly of the United Nations' (1948) 25 *British Yearbook of International Law* 1.

Soevers L and Daws S, *The Procedure of the UN Security Council* (4th edn, Oxford University Press 2014).

Sommereyns R, 'United Nations Forces' in R Bernhardt (ed), *Encyclopaedia of Public International Law* (North-Holland 2000) vol 4, 1106.

Stephens D, 'The Lawful Use of Force by Peacekeeping Forces: The Tactical Imperative' (2005) 12 *International Peacekeeping: The Yearbook of International Peace Operations* 157.

Strohmeyer H, 'Collapse and Reconstruction of a Judicial System: The United Nations Mission in Kosovo and East Timor' (2001) 95 *American Journal of International Law* 46.

Suy E, 'United Nations Peacekeeping System' in R Bernhardt (ed), *Encyclopaedia of Public International Law* (North-Holland 2000) vol 4, 1143.

Tomushat C, *Human Rights: Between Idealism and Realism* (2nd edn, Oxford University Press 2008).

Treves T, 'The UN Body of Principles for the Protection of Detained or Imprisoned Persons' (1990) 84 *American Journal of International Law* 578.

Tsagourias N and White N, *Collective Security: Theory, Law and Practice* (Cambridge University Press 2013).

United Nations, *The Blue Helmets: A Review of United Nations Peacekeeping* (3rd edn 1996).

United Nations, *United Nations Peacekeeping Operations: Principles and Guidelines* (2008).

United Kingdom Ministry of Defence, *The Manual of the Law of Armed Conflict* (Oxford University Press 2005).

Verdirame G, 'Compliance with Human Rights in UN Operations' (2002) 2 *Human Rights Law Review* 265.

Willmot H and others (eds), *Protection of Civilians* (Oxford University Press 2016).

Willmot H and Sheeran S, 'The Protection of Civilians Mandate in UN Peacekeeping Operations; Reconciling Protection Concepts and Practices' (2013) 891/892 *International Review of the Red Cross* 517.

White ND, 'The UN Charter and Peacekeeping Forces: Constitutional Issues' (1996) 3 *International Peacekeeping* 43.

White ND, *Keeping the Peace: The United Nations and the Maintenance of International Peace and Security* (2nd edn, Manchester University Press 1997).

White ND, 'The Use of Weapons in Peace Operations' in S Casey-Maslin and others (ed), *Weapons Under International Humanitarian Law* (Cambridge University Press 2014) 197.

White ND, 'Security Council Mandates and the Use of Lethal Force by Peacekeepers: What Place for the Laws of War' in C Harvey, J Summers and others (eds), *Contemporary Challenges to the Laws of War: Essays in Honour of Professor Peter Rowe* (Cambridge University Press 2014) 95.

Wood M, 'The Interpretation of Security Council Resolutions' (1998) 2 *Max Plank Yearbook of United Nations Law* 73.

Worster WT, 'Immunities of United Nations Peacekeepers in the Absence of a Status of Force Agreement' (2008) 47 *Military Law and the Law of War Review* 277.

Yamashita H, '"Impartial" Use of Force in United Nations Peacekeeping' (2008) 15 *International Peacekeeping: The Yearbook of International Peace Operations* 615.

Zacklin R, 'United Nations Management of Legal Issues' in J Howard and BM Oswald (eds), *The Rule of Law on Peace Operations: A 'Challenges of Peace Operations' Project Conference* (2002) 115.

Zwanenburg M, 'Compromise or Commitment: Human Rights and International Humanitarian Law Obligations for UN Peace Forces' (1998) 11 *Leiden Journal of International Law* 229.

Zwanenburg M, 'The Secretary-General's Bulletin on Observance by United Nations Forces of International Humanitarian Law: Some Preliminary Observations' (1999) 5(4) *International Peacekeeping* 133.

Zwanenburg M, *Accountability of Peace Support Operations* (Martinus Nijhoff 2005).

Zwanenburg M, 'UN Peace Operations between Independence and Accountability' (2008) 5(1) *International Organisations Law Review* 23.

Zwanenburg M, 'The Interplay of International Humanitarian Law and International Human Rights Law in Peace Operations in E de Wet and J Kleffner (eds), *Convergence and Conflicts of Human Rights and International Humanitarian Law in Military Operations* (Pretoria University Law Press 2014) 153.

NOTE: In addition to the above literature there are two international peer-reviewed academic journals which focus on peace operations, and which therefore, are important sources for understanding the law, policy, and practice relevant to UN peacekeeping: *International Peacekeeping*, and *Journal of International Peacekeeping*.

Index